# WORLD CONFLICTS

*Other books by Patrick Brogan*

Deadly Business
Spiked: the Short Life and Death of the
National News Council
Eastern Europe 1939–1989
Soldiers, Spies and the Rat Line,
with Colonel James V. Milano

# WORLD CONFLICTS

## Patrick Brogan

The Scarecrow Press, Inc.
Lanham, Md.

SCARECROW PRESS, INC.

Published in the United States of America
by Scarecrow Press, Inc.
4720 Boston Way
Lanham, Maryland 20706

The first two editions of *World Conflicts* were published in Great Britain
by Bloomsbury Publishing Plc. in 1989 and 1992. First edition published in Canada
in 1989 by Random House of Canada, Limited, Toronto, and simultaneously in the U.S.
by Vintage Books, a division of Random House, Inc., New York, under the title
*The Fighting Never Stopped.* No second edition was published in North America.

British Library Cataloguing in Publication Information Available

**Library of Congress Cataloging-in-Publication Data Available**

ISBN 0-8108-3551-7

Manufactured in Great Britain.

# CONTENTS

# INTRODUCTION

The only constants in the 20th century have been violence, terrorism and war. The end of the Cold War in 1991 may have lifted the threat of nuclear annihilation from the human race, but its capacity for murder was unaffected. That moment of hope was followed immediately by two of the most horrible crimes since 1945, the attempted genocides in Bosnia and Rwanda. Since World War II, Asia, the Middle East and Africa have been engulfed in repeated conflagrations that have killed millions of people, and hundreds of thousands have died in lesser disputes elsewhere. When the flames die down in one place, they flare up elsewhere. In Asia, the civil war in China was followed by the Korean War, and by the wars in Indochina. In Africa, the Algerian war was followed by the civil war in Nigeria which in turn was succeeded by anti-colonial and civil wars in Angola, Mozambique, Ethiopia and Sudan. As the century draws to a close, about ten countries in Africa are in an advanced state of dissolution, with pandemic violence, terrorism and a breakdown in all civil society.

There was constant bloodshed in Central America from the early 1950s until the late 1980s, and though most of the insurgencies in the region have been brought to an end, the progressive disintegration of civil order in Colombia and the spread of narco-terrorism northwards into Mexico offers as great a danger to the peace of the world as did ever Communist revolution.

There have been wars in the Middle East every five or six years since 1948, each of them more violent than the last, and there is little hope that the cycle can be broken. Islamic extremism and terrorism, from Algeria to Afghanistan, is an ever-increasing danger. The former Soviet Republics of Central Asia and the Caucasus have escaped from Moscow, partially and perhaps temporarily, and a hundred thousand people have been killed there since 1991 in civil wars, coups and the blind violence of the Russian war on Chechnya.

Furthermore, an entirely new and exceedingly dangerous phenomenon has emerged from the collapse of the Leninist state: there are now criminal enterprises that can challenge and face down the weak, corrupt and transient governments of the successor states. Drug traffickers have from time to time controlled governments in Latin America. Now various mafias and cartels not only control states or regions in Central Asia or the Caucasus but can bend others to their will. They were defeated in Georgia by Edward Shevardnadze, and tried twice to assassinate him. No doubt they will return to the attack. The more pliant, or more corrupt, leaders of other states in the region (Chechnya, for example, or Tajikistan) offer no resistance to them. Western businessmen in Ukraine or even Russia have found that real authority may often be found with the mafias, not the government. These mafias' methodology and the source of their strength, like that of the former Medellín Cartel in Colombia, is corruption backed by terror and extreme violence: they buy public officials wholesale, and kill whoever opposes them and wherever he may be. The contagion has already spread to the United States and western Europe, and the white slave trade, the export of prostitutes from the former Soviet Union, is corrupting the police of many countries, including Israel. The criminal gangs who perpetrated many of the massacres in Bosnia in the name of Greater Serb purity were merely extending to politics the methods they use constantly in their everyday business.

It is not at all alarmist to fear that these mafias may acquire nuclear or bio-chemical weapons from the disintegrating Russian military establishment, and sell them on the open market, or use them for their own purposes. The danger is not that Saddam Hussein might loose anthrax on New York but that one of the mafias might use such a weapon to intimidate or blackmail any city in the world. During the war in Chechnya, a Chechen commander informed a Russian newspaper that a nuclear device was buried in a Moscow park, and police recovered a container of lethal nuclear materials there. The demonstration was intended as a warning to Boris Yeltsin, but has far wider implications.

There have been at least 80 wars since 1945, killing somewhere between 20 and 30 million people. Tens of millions more have been driven from their homes. There are probably as many refugees in the world today as there were during the mass movements of peoples after World War II. The US Committee for Refugees calculates that in 1997 there were 14,500,000 refugees in foreign lands, and more than 19 million 'internal refugees', people who had fled their homes to escape danger. This is a slight improvement: there were 17.6 million refugees in 1992. Since then, many of those who fled Mozambique and Afghanistan have returned. There are still about 4 million Afghan refugees (compared to 7.6 million in 1991), 2 million Bosnians and 4 million Sudanese. Half the population of Liberia and of Sierra Leone are refugees, internal or abroad.

The bloodiest conflicts in the 1980s were the war between Iran and Iraq and the Soviet intervention in Afghanistan. One lasted eight years, the other nine, and accomplished nothing. At a very rough estimate, 450,000 people were killed in the Iran–Iraq war, far more than in all the other wars in the Middle East since 1948. The bitter animosities between the two countries persist undiminished. Estimates of deaths by war, sickness or starvation in Afghanistan since the Soviet invasion in 1979 range upwards from 400,000: the rate of killing has intensified during the latest phase. War, pestilence and famine in Sudan, Ethiopia, Somalia and Mozambique cost hundreds of thousands of lives and uprooted at least 17 million people, over 7 million of them into foreign countries.

The 1990s opened with a settlement in Mozambique and victory for the insurgents in Ethiopia and, of course, the end of the Cold War. Then came the dissolution of Liberia and Somalia and the horrors in Rwanda. Africans are no more prone to violence than other countries: the disintegration of Yugoslavia led to three wars, to death, massacre and genocide in Bosnia – and the possibility that a fourth war might now start in Kosovo.

The most violent conflicts now are in Sudan, Algeria, Burundi, Uganda, Sierra Leone and Afghanistan. Savage conflicts in many other countries have merely subsided for the moment. The Indians hold Kashmir by brute force, Tajikistan suffers continual fighting, and the long travail of the Kurds in three countries shows no sign of ending. The high-stakes poker game between Saddam Hussein and his neighbours and enemies continues, and the new and virulent breed of Islamic terrorism that has engulfed Algeria threatens Egypt. In Africa, Angola, Rwanda, the Congo, Somalia and Liberia are at a pause in their atrocious tribal warfare but their conflicts may resume at any moment.

At the other extreme is the relatively low-level but persistent violence in such places as Northern Ireland or the Basque country in Spain, provoked by separatist demands of a minority population. International terrorism inspired by Communist ideology has died down since the paroxysms of the 1970s and 1980s, but terrorist attacks on Israel and its supporters continue. There are continuing but generally small-scale insurgencies in the Philippines, Indonesia (East Timor), Burma, the hill country of north-east India and Bangladesh, and the Peruvian terrorists have yet to admit defeat.

The state of the world is not all black. The U N has played a large role in arranging ceasefires, starting with Iran–Iraq in 1988. Since then, it has mediated peace in Namibia, Cambodia, El Salvador, Mozambique, Angola and Guatemala and a number of other places. Its largest and most expensive effort was in Cambodia, which has since degenerated into a nasty dictatorship. All the same, the U N's positive contributions should not be underestimated.

In 1988, foreign powers declared that they would withdraw from Afghanistan, Angola and Cambodia, to leave the natives of those countries to continue their wars undisturbed. The Soviet Union abandoned the government of Nicaragua and guerrilla movements in El Salvador and Guatemala to their fate, and in due course they all made peace. In 1989, the Communist governments in Poland, Hungary, East Germany, Czechoslovakia and Romania abruptly collapsed, to be followed over the next two years by the regimes in Yugoslavia, Bulgaria, Albania and, finally, the Soviet Union itself. At the same time, South Africa abandoned its long battle against black nationalism.

On the other side of the ledger, the dissolution of the old order in Europe and Russia led immediately to the revival of ancient quarrels in the Balkans, Transcaucasia and Central Asia. Yugoslavia began its civil war, between Croats and Serbs, in the summer of 1991. By the time a precarious ceasefire was achieved, in 1995, over 150,000 people had been killed. Meanwhile, the Cambodian factions had signed a peace treaty in Paris in October 1991, and a new coalition government was installed under U N auspices. It lasted until 1997, but at least the Khmers Rouges appeared to be finally defeated. Liberia and Somalia disintegrated into chaos in 1991, and much of the rest of Africa seemed on the verge of comparable upheavals. Burma, after a series of disruptions, reverted to brutal oppression. Pakistan and India once again confronted each other over Kashmir.

The world is still adapting to the disappearance of the empires which kept the peace over most of the earth before 1945. It was a tranquillity imposed at the point of a bayonet, intended to permit the exploitation of brown, black and yellow men by white men. But the world outside Europe is a much less peaceful place than it was when five or six European capitals governed all Africa, the Middle East, India and central and southeast Asia.

The defeat of the empires was inevitable. It required merely that a relatively small class in any colony should ask itself why it should be governed by foreigners, and the advance of education produced that class everywhere. The empires were built by force: the British conquered India with the musket and Africa with the Gatling gun. Once modern weapons became freely available to rebels, who vastly outnumbered the colonial garrisons, the balance of force shifted and the empires were defeated. The last and greatest of European empires, founded by the tsars, became the Soviet Union under Lenin and expanded far into central Europe under Stalin. In subsequent years Cuba, Ethiopia, South Yemen, Mozambique, Angola, Nicaragua and Afghanistan all became Soviet satellites, and many other states came under Moscow's influence. It all fell away in the 1980s. The increasing debility of the Soviet economy and society could not support such a burden and so, like the British, French and Portuguese before them, the Russians had to abandon it. First they gave up Afghanistan, then their dependencies in Africa. In 1989, the Europeans threw them out, and in 1991 the Soviet heartland fell apart.

Once the secret that power grows out of the barrel of a gun was revealed to the tribes of the Arabs, of Africa and of India, not to mention its rediscovery by European terrorists, the fissiparous tendencies which destroyed the empires came to threaten the emerging countries of the Third World. India, Nigeria and Lebanon are less nations than geographical expressions. The Sikhs, the Ibo and all the peoples and sects of Lebanon consider themselves nations, and have fought or are fighting for their independence – and their defeat is never permanent, as the Sikhs have shown. The former Soviet republics started splitting apart as soon as they proclaimed their independence.

Most contemporary conflicts are between peoples and races. Only a few are between nations and ideologies. The pattern might change: Iran and Iraq showed that national animosities can still erupt into full-scale war, and the miseries of the Third World may well produce a revival of ideological struggle in the next generation. But the bleak prospects for world peace today derive from the bitter quarrels between peoples.

There have been few all-out national wars since 1945. The most costly were the Korean war, the Vietnam war, and Saddam Hussein's wars. For many years Europe, the most bellicose of continents, was conspicuously missing from the list. It remained obsessed by the frightful carnage of 1914 to 1945, mourning the slaughter of the Great War, while Russia was daily reminded of the losses of the Great Patriotic War. But the old atavisms remained, buried under a thin veneer of modernity, and in 1991 Slobodan Milosevic let them loose. Elsewhere, Vietnam, Cambodia, Uganda, Nigeria, Mozambique and half a dozen other countries have suffered, proportionately, just as heavily, and sometimes far more, than even Russia, France or Germany.

Wars between nations are usually caused by territorial disputes, ideological rivalry, a lust for conquest or, occasionally, by diplomatic incompetence. There have been wars of all these kinds since 1945, and the threat of more hangs over a good part of the globe. The fact that there are, at the moment, so few national quarrels on the verge of explosion does not mean at all that mankind has changed its ways.

There have been several territorial wars in the past 20 years, including the Falklands war between Argentina and Britain, the Ogaden war between Ethiopia and Somalia, the Iran–Iraq war which ostensibly concerned the question whether the frontier lay in the middle of a river or on its east bank, and Saddam's attempted conquest of Kuwait. There are many territorial claims outstanding, notably the animosities in the Balkans that were contained from 1945 to 1989 by the Pax Sovietica. Most of the countries in Africa are vulnerable to irredentist claims, as are many nations in Asia. China, for instance, has a long-standing frontier dispute with Russia. Nearly every nation in South America has a claim on at least one of its neighbours.

As for ideological wars, they have much diminished in recent years. The United States entered the Vietnam war for ideological reasons, and the Soviet Union intervened in Afghanistan to prop up a disintegrating Communist regime. They both overestimated their own power – and the importance of the dispute. Otherwise, and despite melodramatic promises to 'roll back' Communism, or to 'bury' the West, both were exceedingly cautious in the exercise of their military power. It was notable that President Reagan never actually sent the Marines into Nicaragua. His invasion of Grenada in 1983 and President Bush's invasion of Panama in 1989 were the exceptions that proved the rule: they were scarcely more than police actions, brief, cheap and popular. The only time the Red Army crossed the limits of its conquests in 1945 was its invasion of Afghanistan in 1979. That proved the Soviets' Vietnam and played its part in the destruction of the U S S R itself.

Marxist revolutionary zeal, like the Soviet Union itself, is a spent force in most of the world. It requires an exceptional commitment to advocate Marxism now, after the failure of Lenin's great experiment. It is therefore likely that in the short term at least there will be fewer massacres of the innocent in the name of a future Utopia. All the same, old-fashioned ideological wars continue in the Philippines and in parts of Latin America. The Shining Path in Peru, like the Khmers Rouges in Cambodia, has demonstrated that in some places at least, ideological fury retains all its powers of destruction.

Diplomatic incompetence remains one of the great dangers. The ineptitude of a handful of men brought down upon the world the horrors of the Great War and all the catastrophes that followed. It might easily have happened again in the days of Molotov and Dulles, without the nuclear deterrent which protected East and West alike from their leaders' aggressions, and also from their stupidity. The ultimate folly, and the nearest approach to disaster, was the Cuban missile crisis. The Falklands war was a result of diplomatic misjudgment in London and Buenos Aires, and the Six Day war in 1967 was the result of Nasser's folly: he thought he could humiliate Israel without fighting. American vacillation and duplicity in the Middle East led Saddam Hussein to believe in 1990 that he could occupy Kuwait unopposed. He was the aggressor, but the U S State Department bears some of the blame.

There were many 'wars of national liberation', or colonial wars, between 1945 and 1975. Indo-China and Algeria were the bloodiest but there were many others in Africa and Asia. Now there are hardly any colonies left and there is only one continuing colonial dispute: the Polisario Front's attempt to liberate the Western Sahara from Morocco. The Russian intervention in Afghanistan was not a colonial war, any more than was America's involvement in Vietnam. They were among the last and bloodiest of modern ideological conflicts.

Civil wars have become much more frequent since the end of the colonial era, as societies tear themselves to pieces on ideological, sectarian or ethnic lines. The first and most calamitous since 1945 was the civil war in China, in which millions of people were killed. The Communist victory was one of the great disasters in history, inflicting untold sufferings and further millions of deaths upon the Chinese people. China began to recover in the late 1970s, after the defeat of the Gang of Four who had submitted the country to a last spasm of ideological frenzy.

Terrorism remains a major preoccupation, particularly in the West. Some acts of terrorism have changed history, the assassinations of Julius Caesar and the Archduke Franz Ferdinand among them. But most terrorists have conspicuously failed to achieve their ends. The Israelis have not been moved by all the murderous attacks they have endured, the British are still in Northern Ireland after 30 years of terrorism, the Basque provinces remain a part of Spain, and the French, Italian and German Republics have not been shaken by the assaults upon them. The terrorists' greatest achievement was their contribution to the destruction of Lebanon, but in that case terrorism became a weapon in a civil war.

None of these conflicts can be understood without some knowledge of the historical background. Indeed in some cases – Northern Ireland, for instance – the historical background is the conflict: the tribal warfare in Belfast traces its origins to events of 1689, or earlier. Argentina went to war with Britain in 1982 to avenge a trivial incident that occurred in 1833. The Greeks and Turks, and the Armenians and the Turks, have been enemies for over 900 years, and the Vietnamese and Cambodians for almost as long. The most extreme case of historical memory is the revival of Israel.

There are a few instances of a conscious rejection of past hatreds. France and West Germany decided, in the 1950s, consciously and deliberately, to end a quarrel reaching back centuries that had caused three wars in 70 years. That decision, which had its origins most prosaically in the setting up of the European Coal and Steel Community in 1951, stands as the greatest achievement of post-war diplomacy. President Sadat made peace with Israel, and the Nigerian government, under General Gowon, pursued a policy of reconciliation after the Biafra war. There was no persecution of the vanquished, no reparations were exacted and no medals were issued to the victorious soldiery. Gowon's example has not often been followed. He was deposed, and Sadat was murdered.

The latent conflicts, that might burst into flames at any moment, cover the whole spectrum. In some countries, like Cyprus, there is an uneasy truce. In others, like Uganda, over 20 years of pogroms, massacres, civil wars and violent revolutions guarantee further troubles. The governments of a dozen countries in Africa and others around the world might collapse at any moment while some long-established tyrannies, such as China, Cuba, Syria and Iraq, may at last follow them. Other countries, including several in the Arab world, have been relatively calm for years but are showing signs of stress. Still others, like India, where ethnic disputes are frequent and increasing, may be in the first stages of dissolution. The first coup in a former Soviet republic, in Georgia, took place in January 1992. There will be others.

A further danger to peace comes from the antagonisms between some heavily armed and belligerent Third World countries. India and Pakistan both have nuclear weapons. They are both actively seeking long-range missiles that could deliver them. The dispute over Kashmir shows how dangerous that confrontation remains. Each of the Middle East wars has been more violent than the last, because of the increase in the quantity and quality of armaments. Iraq launched Scud missiles at Israel and Saudi Arabia during the Gulf War, and other nations in the region have obtained similar or more effective weapons. Iran is recovering from the war with Iraq, and Iraq itself will eventually recover, and seek to resume its place as the dominant military power in the region.

Running through a great number of these conflicts is the theme of outside interference. The Soviet Union sowed murder and disaster across the Third World for 40 years in the name of liberation and socialism. The largest interventions in foreign wars were in Korea, Vietnam and Afghanistan. Only the first was to any degree successful, and both sides claimed victory: the Western alliance, led by the United States, saved South Korea, and China saved the North. But in fact both had wanted to reunify Korea under their patronage, and both failed, leaving the Korean problem, which was caused by outside interference, to future generations.

If they did not send their armies, outside powers sent 'advisers' into foreign conflicts, or armed their clients. The Soviet Union sent large quantities of arms, and also financed Cuban mercenary armies in Angola in 1975 and Ethiopia in 1977, saving the new regimes there from collapse. Cuban soldiers and Soviet advisers kept the Angolan government and military afloat while South Africa supported Unita. The South Africans aided the Renamo rebels in Mozambique, as Tanzania had helped Frelimo during the war against Portugal. Colonel Moammar Khadafy of Libya has sent his armies to Chad and Uganda, and supplies weapons and money to a variety of resistance and terrorist organizations. The United States has intervened vigorously, with weapons, money and advisers, in a dozen conflicts, and sent half a million men into Vietnam.

There was a revolution in world affairs in 1988 and 1989 when the Soviet Union began to retreat from the positions it had laboriously established over the decades. First the Soviet armies left Afghanistan. Then the Cubans were ordered home from Angola and the Vietnamese from Cambodia. There followed a rout of Communists in Eastern Europe. The heavy subsidies the Soviets had accorded its allies, such as Syria, were ended. Gorbachev abandoned Ethiopia, South

Yemen and, finally, Cuba. It was a change at least as important as the retreat of the British empire that began in India in 1947. Late in 1991, in one of the last acts of the Soviet Union, the USSR and the United States governments finally agreed to stop arms shipments to the two sides in the Afghan civil war. Other countries, also, reduced their meddling abroad. South Africa pulled its troops out of Angola, and gave Namibia its independence, and the United States abandoned its attempt to overthrow the government of Nicaragua.

The great majority of the millions who have died in the past decades have not been killed by bombs, tanks or fighter aircraft. They have been killed by rifles, pistols and rocket-propelled grenades. The Chinese, North Koreans, Brazilians, Mexicans and Indians all have large armaments industries, and all keenly export their wares. The proliferation of small-arms means that starting a war or an insurrection is cheap and easy. There are guns everywhere, and the death toll among combatants and civilians is frightful.

The United States and its Western allies also supplied arms and training to insurgencies, though not on the same lavish scale as the USSR. Stinger and Redeye anti-aircraft missiles or the British Blowpipe, carried by one or two soldiers, changed the nature of war in Afghanistan and Angola.

Even though most foreign intervention has ceased, the fighting continues. The Philippine guerrillas and the Shining Path in Peru have done without outside assistance from the beginning. Despite Rajiv Gandhi's fantasies, the Sikh insurrection is not a Pakistani plot. The slaughter in Uganda and Sudan, Liberia and Somalia has been driven by native animosities, not outside interference.

Mankind's capacity for hatred is undiminished. Armenians and Azeris, and the various nationalities of Georgia, who had lived peacefully together for 70 years, took to slaughtering each other with antique ferocity when the iron grip of Moscow was loosened. Nearly 50 years after Hitler killed himself in his bunker, Slobodan Milosevic unleashed the same Nazi hatreds upon Yugoslavia. Croats and Serbs began to fight, the Serbs were victorious, and they then turned on the Muslims of Bosnia, who were their neighbours and relatives, in the name of racial purity, ethnic pride and purely imaginary grievances. Karadic and Mladic murdered thousands of people with the purpose of driving all 2 million Muslims into exile. That is genocide under the terms of the Geneva convention. Two years later, in Rwanda, a conspiracy of Hutu government officials began deliberately to kill every Tutsi in the country, the way Hitler wanted to kill all the Jews. They succeeded in massacring about 800,000 people.

The Rwandan genocide was an upsurgence of local animosities. So was the Bosnian genocide, but that disaster was also the result of the artificial and undemocratic state structure foisted on Yugoslavia by the Communists. It disintegrated when the Soviet empire collapsed in 1989.

It will be generations before all the ill-effects of the Bolshevik era are overcome. Historians are already labouring to interpret its lessons, which do not always blaze with the clear light of dogmatic certainty. Some of the questions much debated during the Cold War can now be answered, others are as hotly controversial as ever, including the central one of the real strategic balance between East and West.

For over 40 years, public finance in almost every country of the developed world, national economies everywhere and the fate of nations depended on that issue. Fortunately, political leaders were too wise to put the theories to the test, except in 1962. For a few days then the world teetered on the brink of disaster. Nikita Khrushchev had fallen victim to the cartographic delusion which has so afflicted mankind this century. The Americans, perpetually deluded by the tidy world of the map-makers, had tried to 'surround' the Soviet Union and its allies. The concept was meaningless: the USSR and China were far too big to be surrounded in any real sense. It was also pointless: what on earth could be achieved by surrounding them? But for a moment Khrushchev fell for the delusion himself, and sent missiles to Cuba to escape his supposed encirclement. For a chess-playing nation, it was remarkably stupid. The Russians evidently had not thought what the next move would be. Missiles in Cuba did not change the real balance of power, but they so provoked the Americans that a nuclear war became a real possibility – which would have destroyed the USSR, not the USA.

The cartographic delusion continues. When the Soviets invaded Afghanistan, Washington hawks proclaimed that the Russians were clearly aiming at the Persian Gulf, as though a 1000-mile detour through the Himalayas made any sense to a nation that already controlled the passes into Iran from the north. Maps were published with fierce red arrows driving through Africa to surround Europe (more nonsense). In the early 1980s, the notion was once again advanced that if the Sandinistas were allowed to establish themselves in Nicaragua they would be in Texas next year. It looks so close and easy on the map.

In fact, what was happening in the world was almost exactly the reverse of those menacing arrows on the map. The Soviet Union vastly overcommitted itself in the 1970s, setting up client states in Vietnam, Cambodia, Afghanistan, South Yemen, Angola, Ethiopia, Mozambique and Nicaragua. The US State Department contended that the USSR was spending $500 million a year in Nicaragua. Added to the enormous expenditure in Afghanistan, the cost of subsidizing Cuba, and $1–2 billion each in Angola, Ethiopia and Vietnam, the USSR in the 1980s was probably spending between $20 and $30 billion every year outside Europe. The cost of its garrisons in Eastern Europe might be twice that, and further prodigious sums supported the arms industries and the Red Army itself at home. So far as anyone could tell, the Soviet people gained no practical advantage whatever from those expenditures.

On the contrary, the need to maintain the impressive array of Soviet power in the world meant that Soviet citizens had to stand in line to buy items that Westerners took for granted. The country with the greatest acreage of trees in the world could not produce and distribute enough toilet paper for its population. The Soviet people were deprived of creature comforts that a more efficient economic system and a less imperialist national ambition could have provided long ago. Finally, being the vanguard of the world revolutionary movement for 70 years meant a level of domestic political oppression that could not be maintained indefinitely. Like the other European empires, the moment came when Soviet citizens suddenly realized that they did not have to put up with their inefficient and tyrannical government any more, and the government discovered **XV** that it no longer had the nerve and the authority to impose its will. In the long view of history, the Soviet Union's collapse was doubtless inevitable, but among the proximate causes of that happy event were undoubtedly the Soviet 'victories' in the 1970s which American hawks so deplored.

The Cold War is over. The nightmare of nuclear destruction that terrified the world for 40 years is ended, and the frightful tyranny that Lenin and Stalin imposed upon so many millions of people is lifted. Whatever the other horrors of the times, this is a deliverance exceeded in importance only by the destruction of the Third Reich in 1945. For all that, there are still wars on every continent. Africa is in greater misery than during the colonial wars of the 1970s, the Middle East remains a tinder-box, and the wars in Central Asia and the spreading darkness of criminality in the republics of the former Soviet Union are a danger to everyone. It is fruitless to predict where the next calamities will arise: many people anticipated trouble in Yugoslavia when Tito died and the Soviet threat was lifted, but who could have foreseen the horrors that ensued?

European peoples who had lived peacefully together for 45 years, and who remembered the catastrophes that unbridled nationalism could bring, resorted unhesitatingly to massacre and genocide. So what can we expect of the hundred or more nationalities of the former Soviet Union? Somalia descended into the pit in 1988 and has been followed by a succession of other African states. There are plenty of countries elsewhere whose futures are doubtful, and however persuasive Americans and Europeans may think the arguments in favour of their own brand of economics and democracy, the rest of the world has not embraced the model.

The United States is the world's only superpower, but has lost its taste for policing the world, just as Europe has abandoned its imperial pretensions. The Third World, into which the former Soviet Union has subsided, will have to find its own balance in the next century. No doubt the West will discover that it cannot isolate itself from the turmoil and conflicts that will certainly occur. There will be more violence, more terrorism, more wars. The millennium will not introduce an era of peace and goodwill.

Patrick Brogan

# AUTHOR'S NOTE

## SOURCES

A bibliography of sources is given at the end of each chapter. I have found three series of publications particularly useful. First, the Country Studies published originally by American University, Washington, and now by the Government Printing Office. Each volume includes a comprehensive bibliography. Second, reports by Amnesty International on violations of human rights, and third, reports by the Minority Rights Group.

I have also made copious use of reports in the *New York Times*, the *Washington Post*, the *New Yorker*, the *New York Review of Books*, *The Times*, the *Guardian*, the *Observer* and the *Independent* (London), and various other publications.

The figures for population and G N P are the World Bank's, where available, and are for 1997. In countries like Cambodia or Afghanistan, population and G N P figures are exceedingly speculative. The weakness of currencies in most countries suffering serious conflicts greatly distorts implied standards of living, but the figures remain useful as an indication of comparative incomes.

The refugee statistics come from the U S Committee for Refugees, 1997. The committee uses a strict definition of refugee, namely someone in need of protection and assistance. The figures, therefore, do not include people who have been absorbed into the host country's citizenry, like the Indochinese and Cuban refugees in the United States. Those figures marked with a star (*) are disputed by the host government, usually for political reasons.

Appendix I provides a list of wars since 1945, together with estimates of the numbers killed in each of them. The speculative nature of the estimates is discussed in a note to that appendix. Appendix II lists *coups d'état* and Appendix III assassinations during the same period. A separate chronology lists a selection of acts of terrorism in the past 30 years. There is necessarily considerable overlap between these four lists.

## NAMES

The names of great numbers of nations, cities and natural features have been changed in the 20th century, some more than once. The reasons are usually political: earlier in the century Russia became the Union of Soviet Socialist Republics, and St Petersburg became Leningrad, changes of extreme political    **xvii** significance. Now Leningrad is St Petersburg again, and the U S S R no longer exists. Bolshevik names are being abandoned throughout the former union: Gorki, for instance, is once again Nizhni Novgorod, and Sverdlovsk, Ekaterinburg. Several of the new republics have varied their names: Moldavia now wants to be known as Moldova, Byelorussia as Belarus or Byelarus, and so on. Lemberg, capital of Austrian Galicia, became Lwow when it was annexed by Poland in 1919, Lvov when annexed by the U S S R in 1939, and the Ukraine government now calls it Lviv. Saigon became Ho Chi Minh City, and colonial names were changed throughout Africa: Léopoldville became Kinshasa, Salisbury became Harare, Lourenço Marques became Maputo and so on.

Sometimes the reasons are linguistic: the Chinese, attempting to introduce a uniform system of transliteration from their own ideographs into the Latin alphabet, changed the accepted Latin spelling of most proper names by decree in 1975. Under the new Pinyin system, Mao Tse-tung became Mao Zedong, Peking became Beijing. Other linguistic changes are inexplicably trivial, Suriname for Surinam, for instance, or Dhaka for Dacca.

In the contemporary world, using names often reflects a political choice. Between 1975 and 1978, the government of Cambodia called the country Democratic Kampuchea. The name was used only by those who supported the Khmers Rouges. Cambodia is now a kingdom again. The Belgian Congo became the Democratic Republic of Congo, and was renamed Zaïre by President Mobutu. It is now once more the Congo. For decades, Arabs refused to use the word Israel, preferring 'Occupied Palestine'. Colonel Khadafy, whose own name is a source of constant puzzlement, now calls his country The People's Socialist Libyan Arab Jamahariya, but few foreigners try to accommodate him.

When writing about past events it is necessary to use the names appropriate to the period to avoid anachronism and confusion, particularly when the names are politically significant. Thus Zimbabwe was Southern Rhodesia before 1965, Gdansk was once Danzig, and Istanbul was Constantinople (in these two cases, the new name is a corruption of the old).

Conversely, there is no need for people writing in English to adopt new names for foreign countries just because their governments decide on a change. It is perfectly proper to refer to Iran as Persia, Sri Lanka as Ceylon, or Thailand as Siam, on the same basis that Deutschland is known in English as Germany, Ellas as Greece, Han Kook as South Korea, and al-Lubnaniya as Lebanon. No one is under any obligation to call Burma Myanmar, just because that country's vile dictatorship has demanded it. Although, with much grumbling, most newspapers abandoned Peking in favour of Beijing, they drew the line at substituting Zhonghua Renmin Gonghe Guo, for the People's Republic of China.

While I have tried to get all the names, dates and facts right, I will be grateful to any reader who corrects any of my mistakes.

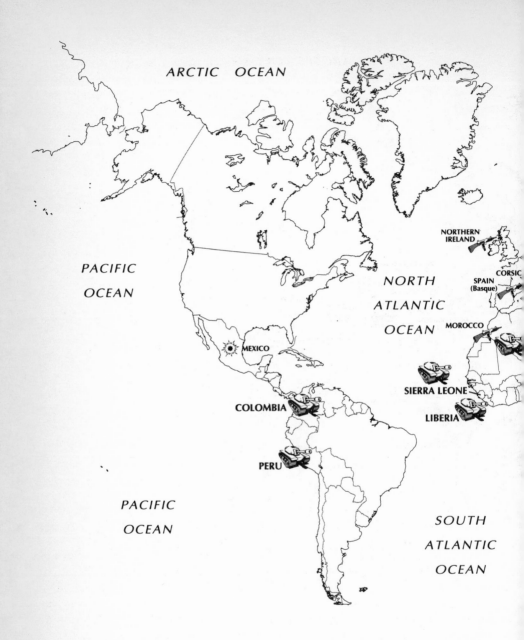

ARCTIC OCEAN

PACIFIC OCEAN

NORTH ATLANTIC OCEAN

NORTHERN IRELAND

CORSIC

SPAIN (Basque)

MOROCCO

MEXICO

SIERRA LEONE

COLOMBIA

LIBERIA

PERU

PACIFIC OCEAN

SOUTH ATLANTIC OCEAN

 Major, continuing and dangerous conflicts

 Lower-level conflicts and insurgencies; terrorist campaigns

 Minor insurgencies and low-level terrorism; latent trouble spots

# AFRICA

# INTRODUCTION TO AFRICA

The end of the cold war in the early 1990s meant the end of foreign interference in Africa, and several major wars on the continent therefore concluded. The Eritreans won their independence from Ethiopia, peace agreements were reached in civil wars in Angola and Mozambique, South Africa abandoned apartheid, and several military regimes in West Africa allowed free elections and the installation of democratic governments. For a moment it appeared that Africa would break out of the cycle of oppression and civil war that had marked its history for over 20 years.

The general optimism overlooked the significance of the break-down of civil society in Somalia and Liberia. Now, in 1998, optimism is in retreat. States in all parts of the continent appear to be following the Somali example, rather than the hopeful, democratic one set by South Africa. Somalia disintegrated in 1989, Liberia in 1990. In the mid-1990s, they were followed by Sierra Leone and Congo (Brazzaville). General Mobutu was driven out of Zaïre (Congo (Kinshasa)) in May 1997, by armies from Rwanda, Uganda and Angola, and the Congo hesitated between dissolution and misery. Other central and West African countries, including Chad, the Central African Republic, Cameroon, Senegal and perhaps even Nigeria; Uganda, Burundi and Rwanda in East Africa; and Angola and Sudan, are afflicted with endemic tribal conflict and could very well go the same way.

Mao Tse-tung's famous aphorism was that power grows out of the barrel of a gun. Africans have demonstrated that in very poor countries, the quickest, and sometimes the only, way to escape poverty is to join the army, and take part in the plunder of whatever resources a country may have. Mobutu instituted the world's largest kleptocracy in Zaïre. His example has been followed by generals – and by junior officers and sergeants – in a dozen other countries. While it is true that civil wars in Angola, the Central African Republic, Congo (Brazzaville) and elsewhere are between tribes (known euphemistically these days as 'ethnic groups'), or even between clans of the same tribe, as in Somalia, the fighting is often over the spoils. The tribes do not hate one another. While there are notorious exceptions, such as the Tutsi and Hutu, they are generally rivals for the same, pitiably inadequate supply of wealth.

A second new factor has emerged in modern Africa: the interference of one country in a neighbour's civil war. The first was Tanzania, which sent an army into Uganda to depose Idi Amin in 1979. There were no immediate imitators, 3 but in 1996 Rwanda and Uganda took an active part in the rebellion against Mobutu, supporting Tutsis in eastern Zaïre and then marching their armies across the whole width of the country, to install their puppet, Laurent Kabila, in Kinshasha in May 1997. By then, the reformed Marxist government of Angola had sent troops into Zaïre to help the invaders from the east, repaying Mobutu's long support of Unita. A few months later, Angola also sent troops to Congo-Brazzaville, to tip the balance in the civil war there. Meanwhile, Nigeria has bombed Liberia and Sierra Leone, in an attempt to stop a civil war in the one and to reverse a coup in the other, Libya continues to interfere in Chad, and Sudan and Ethiopia support rebels against each other and so do Sudan and Uganda. Frontiers are no longer sacred. They often made very little sense, cutting up tribes and natural boundaries. They were imposed by the colonial powers in the 19th century, but independent states made it an act of faith to respect them. By the late 20th century, that faith was wearing very thin.

Africa in the 1960s, as it emerged from colonialism, was a leading cause for liberals, Marxists and cold warriors and a golden opportunity for business. The risks were very high. Foreign mining companies in the Congo (Kinshasa) were expropriated more than once; but the rewards could be enormous. Now, Marxists have disappeared, the cold war is over and liberals, for the most part, suffer from an extreme case of donor fatigue. Africa is once again left to its own devices, to defend itself as best it can from rapacious political leaders and soldiers, and rapacious foreigners.

Besides the conflicts described in greater detail in subsequent chapters, there are civil wars, revolts or endemic ethnic disturbances in the following countries, among others:

## WEST AFRICA
The only surviving democracies in the region are Mali, Benin and two off-shore mini-states, the Cape Verde Islands and São Tomé e Principe. Ghana, Burkina Faso and Senegal are less authoritarian than the others. Military coups since 1990 in Sierra Leone, Gambia and Niger added those countries to the list of military or tribal-based dictatorships: Mauritania, Guinea, Nigeria, Cameroon, Gabon, Equatorial Guinea, Togo, Liberia and Ivory Coast.

## CAMEROON
President Paul Biya staged a presidential election in October 1997, in which he claimed 92 per cent of the vote on an 81 per cent turn-out. He has been president since 1982 and has run Cameroon on the kleptocratic principles perfected by Mobutu in Zaïre. There is a simmering insurrection among north-western tribes formerly part of a British protectorate who feel themselves abused by Biya's French-speaking southern Beti tribe. There is a serious territorial dispute between Cameroon and Nigeria over a stretch of coastal territory, the Bakassi peninsula, which may have large oil reserves. The Nigerian army attacked Cameroon army positions there in February 1996.

## CONGO (BRAZZAVILLE)
President Pascal Lissouba was overthrown after a brief and savage civil war in 1997 that left the capital in ruins and reduced the country to the same anarchy as

Liberia or Sierra Leone. The fighting started in June when Lissouba attempted a pre-emptive coup against his main rival, Denis Sassou Nguesso, a former military president who ceded power to Lissouba after elections in 1992. The attack failed and Nguesso fought back, later helped by troops from Angola and some behind-the-scenes support from France. The new Kabila government in Kinshasa also intervened, at first on Lissouba's side, then joining the winner (Lissouba had supported Mobutu). Nguesso occupied Brazzaville on 14 October, driving Lissouba into exile. The city had been levelled by artillery battles between the two armies and the victors systematically looted whatever remained.

## GABON
There were serious riots there in 1993 when the president, Omar Bongo, staged a fraudulent election to remain in power.

## CENTRAL AFRICAN REPUBLIC
French troops and troops from neighbouring countries intervened in 1996 and 1997 to end a mutiny by part of the army in the capital, Bangui. The fighting was along tribal lines, the mutineers coming from southern tribes in revolt against the government of a northerner, Ange-Félix Patassé. The president of Mali arranged a truce in January 1997, but there was renewed fighting the following June.

## SIERRA LEONE
The same corruption and petty tyranny that led to the revolt in Liberia afflicted Sierra Leone through the 1970s and '80s. In March 1991, an army corporal, Foday Sankoh, started a rebellion that soon spread across much of the country. His group calls itself the Revolutionary United Front. Sierra Leone appeared to be heading down the same road as Liberia. More than 10,000 people were killed and half the population of 4 million became refugees. In November 1996, mediators from the Ivory Coast succeeded in persuading Sankoh to accept a ceasefire offered by a new, democratically elected president, Ahmed Tejan Kabbah.

The country barely had time to adjust to civilian government before a group of junior officers, led by Lieutenant Colonel Johnny Paul Koroma, seized the government. Kabbah fled and Nigeria tried to intimidate the coup leaders into submission by shelling their barracks from the sea.

They failed, and severe international sanctions were imposed on Sierra Leone while Nigeria prepared for a new intervention. It came in February 1998, when Nigeria landed an army near Freetown and attacked the capital with mortars, artillery and, finally, an all-out infantry assault. The coup leaders resisted long enough to destroy a large part of the city. Several thousand people were killed. Then Koroma fled Freetown, which the Nigerians occupied on 13 February. Kabbah was restored, but Koroma joined Sankoh in the bush and vowed to return.

## MALI
Mali is one of the few democratic states in West Africa, but there has been a long-running rebellion in the north. Touareg nomads there are in revolt against the government, which is dominated by blacks from the south. Over 100,000 refugees live across the Sahara in Algeria, Libya and Morocco.

# ALGERIA

| | |
|---|---|
| Geography | 1,476,679 sq. miles (2,381,741 sq. km), 80% desert. |
| Population | 27.4 million, increasing at 2.8% p.a. It will double by 2037. 40% of the population under the age of 15. 80% Arab, 20% Berber. |
| GNP per capita | $1,570. |
| Refugees | There are about 80,000 refugees from the Western Sahara and 30,000 from ethnic fighting in Mali and Niger. There are 10,000 internal refugees. |
| Casualties | 600,000 people were killed in the War of Independence, 1954–62. Between 50,000 and 100,000 have been killed in fighting between Islamic terrorists and the army since 1992. |

Algeria is one of that sad group of countries stuck in a vicious circle of under-development, excessive population growth and terrorism. The reforms that might address the country's fundamental economic and social problems would, to begin with, increase hardship in a population already burdened by hope-lessness and very high unemployment. That, in turn, would strengthen the reactionary terrorists who are already a mortal threat to the state. A civil war has been raging since 1992 between the military dictatorship that has ruled Algeria incompetently since 1962, and fundamentalist Islamic terrorists who believe that Algeria should become an Islamic Republic, like Iran.

Algerian terrorism has spilt over into France and its repercussions are felt, and feared, from Morocco to Egypt. Algeria suffered, in turn, the worst evils of colonialism (1830–1962) and then the imposition of a socialist economy which soon turned into the very model of Third World backwardness and corruption. Intel-lectuals and modern-minded women, perforce, support the military regime, because the alternative is so horrible. This does not mean that they have any confidence in it. The Algerian civil war is a portent for other Arab states, notably Egypt.

## HISTORY

In classical times, both shores of the Mediterranean were part of the same world civilization. That all changed with the collapse of the Roman Empire and the Arab invasions of the 7th and 8th centuries. From then onwards, the blue waters of the Middle Sea divided two competing worlds, and the wars and misunder-standings have continued to this day.

In its time of greatest power in the 19th century, Europe reconquered North Africa and, briefly, the Middle East. France took Morocco, Algeria and Tunisia, Italy took Libya and the British took Egypt. In the aftermath of World War I, France and Britain partitioned the Levant between them. Of all these occupations, Algeria was by far the most complete. An invasion provoked by Algerine pirates in 1830 led to a series of bloody wars in which the French reconquered all the rival tribes and sultanates of the Maghreb, western North Africa. Subsequently, the French extended their empire across the whole Sahara, from the Atlantic to the Nile.

In Algeria, the soldiers were followed by colonists, both French and foreign. A large part of the French colony in North Africa came from Spain and Italy, and Paris intellectuals often theorized that the intransigence of the colons, or '*pieds noirs*' as they called themselves, owed much to their non-French origins. The colons seized the best agricultural land and transported French culture and cities across the Mediterranean. Algiers itself, Bone, Constantine, Oran and the rest were so many Toulons and Marseilles re-created under a harsher sun, with one difference. In most of them there remained the 'casbah', the Muslim quarter, dominated, despised but ineradicable.

There were enlightened civil servants who tried to better the lot of the Muslims, to make them into Frenchmen or to bring them up to French levels of education and public health. The army recruited many Muslims, known as 'Harkis', and its officers remained intensely loyal to their men until the end. But the army never wavered from its belief in '*Algérie Française*'. It also formed the Foreign Legion to fight the Arabs in the desert.

North Africa was the heart of the French empire and a whole mythology grew up around it. Algeria was, legally, not even a colony: it was part of France. Three *départements* were set up along the coast (the Sahara, to the south, was treated differently), and Oran, Algiers and the other towns were considered as much part of France as Toulouse or Lyon. Of course it was illusion. At their peak, there were 1.5 million French citizens in Algeria, including 100,000 Jews summarily naturalized in the 19th century on the assumption that their loyalty could be depended on. The Muslim population was always much larger and increased far more rapidly.

The demographic imbalance would have overwhelmed French Algeria sooner or later, as it did white South Africa. Over the years, many moderate Arab Algerians acquired the French language, culture and political ideas. They proposed a series of reforms which would have allowed the Muslims of the country to enjoy political and property rights. They proposed that the Muslims be given French citizenship, or that Algeria should be linked with France in some way, to preserve all that was most advantageous to both countries in their association. The *pieds noirs* rejected every concession, and their political strength in Paris was too great for French liberals to defeat them. The French learnt nothing from the English experience in Ireland.

The term '*pieds noirs*', meaning people with dirty feet, was originally a term of abuse, like 'red-neck' in the United States, that was adopted as a badge of honour by the colons. Like the red-necks, most of the *pieds noirs* were poor or middle-class. They saw the Muslims as an economic, as well as a political, threat to their

7

society and were savagely reactionary. During World War II, they supported the fascist Vichy regime and were less than enthusiastic when the Americans and British liberated Algeria in 1942 and General de Gaulle set up his base in Algiers. There had been Muslim political movements from the beginnings of French Algeria, but they became much more active in the 1930s and during the war, under the leadership, most notably, of Messali Hadj and Ferhat Abbas. Immediately after the war, in 1945, a brief uprising in Sétif was followed by a furious pogrom against the Muslims there in which 6000 or more people were killed.

The Sétif massacre radicalized the Muslim population. Various efforts by Fourth Republic governments to reform the political system and the administration in Algeria were constantly thwarted by the colons. Messali Hadj's party won a sweeping victory in municipal elections in the Muslim communes in 1947, and future elections were therefore rigged by the authorities. An Algerian assembly was called to discuss reform, but Ferhat Abbas was refused the right to speak.

Early in 1954, a group of Muslim radicals gathered in Cairo and formed a revolutionary committee. In October, it took the title National Liberation Front (*Front de Libération National* – F L N), under which it fought, and won, the War of Independence. The 'historic chiefs' were Ben Bella, Ait Ahmed, Mohammed Boudiaf, Belkacem Krim, Rabah Bitat, Larbi Ben M'Hidi, Mourad Didouch, Mustafa Ben Boulaid and Mohammed Khider. The F L N set up the *Armée de Libération Nationale* (A L N), which immediately began preparations for a revolt.

They attacked across Algeria on the night of 1 November 1954. Though the attacks did little damage, they were clearly the beginning of a serious insurrection. The minister of the interior, François Mitterrand, said, 'The only possible negotiation is war,' and the prime minister, Pierre Mendès-France, said, 'One does not compromise when it comes to defending the internal peace of the nation, the unity and integrity of the Republic. The Algerian departments are part of the French Republic. They are irrevocably French. There can be no conceivable secession.'

That two of the country's leading liberal politicians should take so intransigent a line was a sign of the times. France had just suffered a humiliating defeat in Indochina, losing the battle of Dien-Bien-Phu in May 1954, and then being forced to abandon Vietnam altogether at the Geneva conference. The French political system, they thought, was not capable of facing another defeat.

So began the most vicious of all European colonial wars. Over the next four years, the fighting increased in intensity as the A L N learnt its trade and acquired weapons and political support from Egypt and the Soviet bloc. France gave Tunisia and Morocco their independence in 1956 (they had been protectorates, not colonies) in order to concentrate on Algeria, and the A L N established its bases near the frontiers. France launched raids across the border and, in October 1956, joined Britain and Israel in the invasion of Egypt in the hopes of overthrowing Nasser and ending Egyptian support for the F L N.

Militarily, the French won the war. By 1958, a series of tough generals and political leaders had driven the A L N into the farthest recesses of the mountains. Over 2 million Algerian peasants were regrouped in 'strategic hamlets', and a massive onslaught on the Algiers casbah defeated the A L N in the capital. But the cost was enormous, and political opposition in France threatened the very base of the French effort – just as the political opposition in the United States, a decade later, undermined military operations in Vietnam.

In May 1958, rioting by the colons in Algiers provoked the army to intervene. The movement, started by junior officers, developed into a *coup d'état* directed by the generals. They assumed power in Algeria and defied Paris. The government collapsed, and General de Gaulle, whose involvement in the coup has been a deep mystery ever since, was recalled from retirement to retrieve the situation.

He took control of France and the army with an iron hand. He reformed the constitution, to give the president greater powers than any peacetime government had enjoyed since 1870, and set about purging the army. The war continued, as did opposition at home. The *pieds noirs* soon came to realize that the general was not committed to *Algérie Française*, and turned against him.

He made a series of peace proposals, each more radical than the last. The *pieds noirs* responded by mounting an insurrection in Algiers in 1960, which was suppressed with difficulty. A group of senior officers, led by two former commanders-in-chief, then tried another coup in April 1961. They briefly controlled Algeria, but the conscripts of the 600,000-strong army there refused to obey and the coup collapsed.

The *pieds noirs* then resorted to terrorism. They formed the '*Organisation de l'Armée Secrète*' (O A S), which attacked government buildings and personnel, and Muslims. There were several attempts on de Gaulle's life (two nearly succeeded).

Algeria became independent in July 1962, after a last orgy of terrorism. A million and a half European colons fled to France, and Algeria was taken over by the F L N. The war had probably cost over 600,000 lives (the Algerians say 1.5 million). It had been marked by the usual infighting between factions of the F L N, and was followed by a civil war in which the A L N outside Algeria marched on Algiers and suppressed the '*armée de l'intérieur*', which had done most of the actual fighting. Several of the 'historic chiefs' who had survived the war were killed by their colleagues and three of them, including Boudiaf, went into exile. In 1965 Ben Bella, the principal leader of the F L N, who had become president, was deposed by the army commander, Houari Boumedienne.

Boumedienne retained power for the rest of his life. The government was socialist, inefficient, chauvinistic and moderately anti-western. It had inherited a large oil and gas industry from the French, but instead of using its mineral wealth to develop the country, it dissipated its revenues on subsidies and wasteful industrial projects. The population increased at a frightening rate, unemployment rose steadily, and though Algeria remained the most advanced of Arab states, thanks to the French legacy, its economic prospects were unusually bleak.

## THE ISLAMIC FRONT

There were other legacies of the war: the habits of violence and the F L N's indifference to democracy. The same phenomenon has marked most of the successful revolutions of the century. The series of bloody skirmishes inside the 9

F L N and between the F L N and its Algerian rivals survived in the traditions and habits of the government and its oppositions.

Boumedienne died in 1978. His successor, Colonel Chadli Benjedid, tried to loosen the socialist shackles that afflicted the country. His measures proved insufficient. Even the dramatic rise in oil prices in the 1970s failed to help Algeria. The economy remained stagnant, and Islamic radicals began to make themselves heard. Their solution to the country's problems was to impose strict adherence to Islamic law, including forcing women to wear the veil. Then oil prices collapsed, and Algeria's accumulated debts overwhelmed it: in 1993, 96 per cent of its oil income went to pay interest on international debt. Benjedid tried to break up the socialist system, privatizing some state firms.

Unemployment increased, and there were serious riots in 1988 in which security forces killed over 500 people. That was the spark that set off the Islamic revolt. Extremists seized temporary control of many districts and attacked government and party buildings. Benjedid offered a new constitution in 1989 that dropped the word 'socialist' from the country's name, and also dropped specific mention of the F L N and its 'leading role' in politics: the Communist countries of eastern Europe were doing much the same thing at the same moment.

It was too late, but while the regimes in East Germany, Poland and the rest collapsed, the Algerian power structure, based on the army, resisted. For a while, Algeria was the most democratic state in the Arab world. The Islamic Salvation Front (*Front Islamique du Salut* – F I S) was formed by Abbassi Madani and Ali Benhadj and won the first democratic elections, for local councils, in 1990. The F L N, which controlled parliament, then revised the electoral law again to ensure its own future victories. The F I S called a general strike and, amid widespread rioting, Benjedid declared a state of emergency.

The F I S leaders Madani and Benhadj were arrested, but the government backed down on its blatant revisions of the electoral law. The following year, in December 1991, elections were held for the national legislature. The F I S won an overwhelming victory in the first round, winning 188 of the 430 seats outright. The F L N won only 15, and it was clear that the F I S would sweep the board in the second round two weeks later.

The army was appalled at the prospect of an Islamic government. On January 11, it forced Benjedid to dissolve parliament and suspend the constitution – and then to resign. Mohammed Boudiaf was recalled from exile and made titular president while the army council ruled the state. The F I S organized protest demonstrations across the country, and in February 1992, the new military regime, calling itself the High Council of State, imposed a one-year state of emergency. It suppressed the F I S the following month.

The civil war has followed its implacable course ever since. The army has hunted down F I S guerrillas in towns, villages and in the countryside, and has killed thousands of them, including many of its leaders. New leaders have always arisen from the ranks. The Front itself split between extremists and ultra-extremists. The most violent formed themselves into an organization they called the *Groupe Armé Islamique* (G A I). Its terrorists have attacked villages and districts in the cities, massacring thousands of people. The G A I issued decrees ordering every foreigner to leave the country, and then murdered nearly a hundred of them, mostly French, but including other Europeans, Turks and Americans. Among its victims were ten Catholic medical missionaries. It proclaimed that unveiled women were whores and murdered many of them. It attacked journalists for reporting its atrocities, killing 26 in 1994 alone, and sent its commandos to France to carry the war to the supposed backers of the Algerian government.

Those commandos planted bombs in the Paris Métro and assassinated Algerian exiles. One of the founders of the F I S, Sheikh Abdel-Baki Saharaoui, was assassinated in Paris in July 1993. At Christmas 1994, a four-man commando of the G A I hijacked an Air France jet in Algiers, killed three passengers, and flew the plane to Marseilles. They threatened to murder their 170 remaining hostages if Algerian political leaders held in France were not released. French commandos stormed the plane on December 26, killing the four terrorists.

The political situation in Algeria remained deadlocked. President Boudiaf was assassinated by a bodyguard in June 1992. Ben Bella was released from prison and tried to resume his political career, a ghost from the remote past. There were various attempts at negotiation between the government and the Front, notably an effort by a group of moderate opposition figures who proposed a relatively conciliatory platform in a conference in Rome in January 1995. They claimed to represent the F I S and the F L N and another party, the *Front des Forces Socialistes*. Between them they had won 85 per cent of the vote in the abortive 1991 elections. Even the G A I professed itself ready to abide by the Rome manifesto.

The proposal was that there should be an immediate ceasefire and a release of the 10,000 or so political prisoners, including leaders of the F I S held in Algeria. The opposition parties would be legalized and there would be new elections. The government turned down the Rome compromise and, ten days later, the G A I reconsidered its position, and rejected the proposals. The civil war continued unabated. Hundreds of people were killed every week by suicide bombs, massacres and in assassinations.

In December 1995, the regime staged a presidential election. The terrorists said that they would turn every polling station into a coffin, but despite the threats, and thanks to a massive security operation, there was a large turn-out, about 75 per cent according to the government. The opposition claimed that the figure was less, but there was no doubt that a majority of Algerians had voted for a variety of candidates. The army's candidate, acting president Liamine Zeroual, won 61 per cent of the votes cast, the remainder going to moderate Islamic and leftist candidates. International observers judged the elections relatively fair, and concluded that the Algerians who had voted for the Front in 1991 had turned against it after four years of civil war that had killed at least 40,000 people.

The war continued. The G A I stated in July 1996 that troops had killed its leader, Djamel Zitouni. The government claimed he had been killed by comrades, in a power struggle. In November 1996, the government presented a new constitution to the people in a referendum. It passed easily. It set up an exceptionally strong presidency, reduced the legislature to a rubber-stamp

11

and banned Islamic parties. Since Algeria had been ruled by the same methods since 1962, the new constitution makes very little difference.

The government released one of the original leaders of the Front, Abassi Madani, in July 1997, perhaps in the hopes that the Front would give up its opposition and join with other, moderate, Islamic parties in an attempt to end the war. The other top leader of the Front held by the government, Ali Belhadj, remained in prison. The GAI paid no attention, and in the following weeks there was an orgy of killing, on both sides. Later that month, Zitouni's successor as head of the GAI, Antar Zouabrio, was killed by the army, at least the eighth major GAI leader to die since 1992.

In September, over a hundred people were killed in two massacres in Beni Messous, just west of Algiers, the worst slaughter of the five-year war. That record was soon exceeded. On 30 December 1997, the first day of Ramadan, 412 people were killed in a cluster of villages in Relizane, near Oran in western Algeria. Most of the massacres are the work of GAI commandos, but there is some evidence and much suspicion that militia groups armed by the government, ostensibly for self-defence, are responsible for many of the killings. The army is sometimes suspiciously slow in responding to calls for help. In the Relizane massacre, a typical instance, the murderers arrived in the evening and spent the entire night killing the villagers, mostly by the knife or by clubbing them to death.

The FIS pursued its efforts to start negotiations leading to a ceasefire and a political accommodation, but the GAI remained obdurate. Indeed, its massacres and terrorism seemed designed to reinforce the views of army extremists who rejected all suggestion of compromise with the FIS.

## FURTHER READING

Alleg, Henri *La Question*, Paris, Editions de Minuit, 1958.
Halimi, Gisèle with introduction by Simone de Beauvoir, *Djamila Boupacha*, London, André Deutsch, 1962.
Horne, Alistair *A Savage War of Peace*, New York, Viking, 1978.
Messaoudi, Khalida *Unbowed: An Algerian Woman Confronts Islamic Fundamentalism*, Philadelphia, University of Pennsylvania Press, 1998.
O'Ballance, Edgar *The Algerian Insurrection*, London, Faber & Faber, 1967.
Stone, Martin *The Agony of Algeria*, New York, Columbia University Press, 1997.
Willis, Michael *The Islamist Challenge in Algeria: A Political History*, New York University Press, 1997.

# ANGOLA

| | |
|---|---|
| Geography | 481,351 sq. miles (1,246,694 sq. km). Larger than the total area of Spain, Portugal, France and the Benelux countries. Cabinda, a small Angolan enclave north of the Zaïre (Congo) River, supplies most of Angola's oil. |
| Population | 10.7 million. Of these, about 2 million are Ovimbundu, in central and southern Angola; 1.5 million Kimbundu in the north-west, around the capital (Luanda); and 700,000 Bakongo in the north; most of the Bakongo live in Congo (Kinshasa) and Congo (Brazzaville). |
| Resources | Oil, diamonds, coffee, iron ore, forest products, sisal, maize. |
| GNP per capita | $410. |
| Refugees | 220,000 Angolans are refugees in neighbouring countries: 100,000 in Congo, 100,000 in Zambia. About 1.2 million are internal refugees. There are 9000 refugees from Congo in Angola. |
| Parties | • MPLA: *Movimento Popular de Libertacão de Angola* (People's Movement for the Liberation of Angola). Originally Marxist party based on the Kimbundu tribe of north-central Angola. Founded in 1956. The MPLA won the 1975–6 civil war and now forms the government. Supported by the USSR and Cuba until 1988. |
| | • FNLA: *Frente Nacional de Libertacão de Angola* (National Front for the Liberation of Angola). Founded in 1960 by Holden Roberto. Split along tribal lines in 1961. Its rump is based on the Bakongo tribe of northern Angola and Congo. |
| | • Unita: *União Nacional para a Independencia Total de Angola* (National Union for the Total Independence of Angola). Founded by Jonas Savimbi in a breakaway from the FNLA, in 1966. Based on the Ovimbundu tribe (the largest in Angola), of central and southern Angola. Defeated in 1975–6, Savimbi then led a rebellion based on his tribal homeland and supported by South Africa and the US. |
| Casualties | About 90,000 people were killed during the colonial war, 1961–75. About 50,000 were killed in the civil war and foreign intervention, 1975–6, and 500,000 people have been killed since 1976. These are all very approximate totals. |

A ceasefire in the long Angolan civil war was signed on 31 May 1991, in Lisbon. The agreement provided that there would be free elections in 1992, which would **13** decide the country's future. It was a truce, not a peace. In Angola, power still grows out of the barrel of a gun. The Soviet Union and Cuba had abandoned the MPLA (People's Movement for the Liberation of Angola) government, which they had sustained since 1975, and it was alone in the world. South Africa had lost interest in Angola and in its client, Jonas Savimbi's Unita, and the United States, which had also supported him, saw little reason to continue doing so. The UN was given the onerous duty of supervising the elections, and keeping the peace.

Angola, like Mozambique, went directly from 15 years of revolutionary war against Portuguese colonialism (1961–75), to a civil and tribal war that was only punctuated by the ceasefire of 1991. Angola was the chosen battlefield between the competing ideologies of the Soviet Union and the United States. The MPLA, which controlled the capital and therefore called itself the government, was supported by between 30,000 and 55,000 Cuban troops and 1000 Soviet advisers, and the Soviets spent $1 billion a year in arms and economic assistance. Unita, which controlled the south-east of the country, was supported by South Africa and the United States. The civil war lasted while this outside interference continued. In 1988, the Soviet Union abandoned Angola, and the Cubans were sent home. Their last contingent returned in May. The MPLA was then forced to come to terms with Unita, and the 1991 agreement was the result.

As in Mozambique, the civil war compounded the economic disasters that followed independence. The 300,000 Portuguese settlers all left together in 1975–6, and the new regime then imposed on the country a fully-fledged Marxism wholly unsuited to it. The Soviet Union provided ample military assistance but little economic aid, and Angola survived on the profits of the oil industry, which was left in the hands of American oil companies. Whoever emerges victorious from the political struggle will face enormous economic problems.

## HISTORY

Angola was first colonized by the Portuguese in 1575, when they established a coastal fort that became Luanda. They ruled the country with a mixture of incompetence and cruelty for four centuries. Before the slave trade was stopped by the British navy, Portugal had sent about 3 million slaves from Angola to Brazil.

From that point until the 1950s, Portugal neglected its African colonies completely. Then, as the rest of black Africa moved towards independence, Portugal increased its investment in Angola and Mozambique, hoping to build new Brazils there by exporting Portuguese peasants to Africa; about 300,000 eventually settled in Angola.

Independence movements developed in Angola, as elsewhere in Africa, led by members of the tiny educated class of Africans. The first was the MPLA, established in 1956; the FNLA was founded in 1960. The war against Portugal began in 1961, after the independence of the Belgian Congo in 1960 had provided a base for the FNLA, which was composed chiefly of the same tribe that is dominant in Congo, the Bakongo. The uprising began in March 1961. About 700 whites were killed, including large numbers of civilians massacred on their farms. The Portuguese army and settler militias put down the rising in six months, with great brutality, killing about 20,000 black Angolans.

**14**

The events of 1961 shocked the Portuguese government of Dr Antonio Salazar, and led to a number of reforms, but there was no question of Portugal abandoning its colonies like the other colonial powers. In 1963, guerrilla warfare started in Portuguese Guinea and, a year later, in Mozambique.

The FNLA was supported by the Congolese government, and also by the CIA. Its leader, Holden Roberto, was never an effective guerrilla commander (for one thing, he preferred the comforts of life in Léopoldville). One of his deputies, Jonas Savimbi, broke away from the FNLA in 1966 and formed Unita, based on the Ovimbundu tribe. Unita then started a guerrilla insurrection in east-central Angola.

The other rebel group, the Marxist MPLA, was formed in 1956 among exiled Angolan intellectuals. Its leader, Dr Agostinho Neto, was a physician and poet, and his greatest contribution was to meet Che Guevara in 1965 and win Cuban support for a Marxist revolution in Angola. However, even though the Cubans trained some MPLA guerrillas, it was an ineffective and unsuccessful fighting force. It was based in Zaïre and could not break through the Bakongo areas in the north, which were thoroughly policed by the Portuguese, to reach the Kimbundu tribe around Luanda, which was its main support. The MPLA then tried an offensive from Zambia in 1966, with a notable lack of success.

The Portuguese army fought against the rebels with great ferocity, aided by South Africa and Ian Smith's regime in Rhodesia. Portugal won the war in Angola: the three divided and ineffectual guerrilla movements were no serious threat. However, the war in Guinea went badly, and by 1974, the war in Mozambique was also proving an intolerable drain upon Portugal's resources. It became apparent to the junior ranks in the army that the wars could not be won, and on 25 April 1974, young officers of the Portuguese army seized power in a bloodless coup in Lisbon. They immediately announced that they would give all Portuguese colonies their independence.

In Angola, the rebels came out of the bush and staked their competing claims for the future. The Portuguese attempted to set up a coalition government of the three revolutionary parties. Roberto, Neto and Savimbi were brought to Portugal, and signed the Alvor agreement on 15 January 1975. It provided that the three would form a coalition government, that there would be elections for a constituent assembly in October, and that independence would be on Armistice Day, 11 November 1975, 400 years after the Portuguese first arrived (and ten years to the day after Ian Smith's declaration of independence in Rhodesia). The three agreed to freeze their military positions, and to contribute 8000 men each to a new national army.

The new government took office on 31 January 1975, and fighting broke out between the MPLA and FNLA the next day. None of the three parties showed any serious willingness to cooperate with the others. Holden Roberto had been building up his army with the help of President Mobutu of Zaïre and had obtained help from the Chinese the previous summer, while continuing his earlier contacts with the Americans. By the beginning of 1975, he had about 15,000 troops. The MPLA, which had only 3000 men at the time of the Portuguese revolution, asked for help from their Cuban friends. The USSR, seeing an opportunity to thwart the Chinese and the Americans at the same time, **15** started sending arms at once. The M P L A also had the support of a force of exiled Katangese gendarmes, expelled from the Congolese province of Katanga after the failure of Moïse Tshombe's attempt to make it independent, and who harboured a lasting detestation of Zaïre and its president. As for Savimbi, he enjoyed the widest support because his tribe was the biggest in Angola, but he had the smallest army, only about 1000 men. He was supported by Zambia and Tanzania, and now set about wooing the remaining Portuguese settlers and, later, the Americans and South Africans.

The civil war got under way quickly. Early in 1975, the Cubans sent 250 instructors, who set up camps in Angola to train the M P L A. The party had the inestimable advantage that its main support came from the Kimbundu tribe, which dominated Luanda and its hinterland. In July, the M P L A drove the F N L A and Unita out of Luanda, and the coalition government collapsed. About 20,000 people were killed in the fighting; the Portuguese settlers fled, all 300,000 of them, in six months; and Angola seemed in a state of complete anarchy.

The Americans had not been seriously involved so far, and although Cuba and the U S S R had helped the M P L A, theirs had not been a vast investment. After the events of July both sides plunged into the fray.

The United States had just seen 20 years' effort in Vietnam collapse. The Secretary of State, Dr Henry Kissinger, conceived that the establishment of a Communist government in Angola could be construed as another defeat for the U S, and was determined to prevent it. The C I A began sending large quantities of arms to the F N L A and Unita through Zaïre and Zambia. The U S S R retaliated by shipping arms to the M P L A, with the advantage that it could do so directly by sea into Luanda.

As independence day approached, the F N L A mounted an attack on the M P L A from the north and east. Unita, aided by a South African armoured column, attacked from the south and got as far as Novo Redondo, 120 miles (180 km) south of Luanda. In addition, President Mobutu of Zaïre unsuccessfully attacked Cabinda.

The F N L A and Unita were defeated by a mixed force of M P L A fighters and Cuban troops, under Soviet command. As their enemies closed in on Luanda, Cuba flew in 15,000 troops and the U S S R supplied massive quantities of arms, including heavy artillery – notably 'Stalin Organs', multiple rocket launchers. American aid had been on an altogether more modest scale (Congress had no intention of starting a new war so quickly after Vietnam), and the South Africans were not ready to take on the Soviet Union. The South African Defence Minister, P. W. Botha, for ever after swore that he had been robbed of victory by U S duplicity, and vowed vengeance. He later became president of South Africa.

The attacking armies disintegrated. The last F N L A position was occupied on 11 February 1976, and on the same day, Savimbi's capital, Huambo in the centre of the country, fell to the M P L A. The South Africans beat a hasty retreat. The M P L A victory appeared to be complete.

During the débâcle the commander of a group of white mercenaries, a Cyprus-born British soldier called Costas Georgiou, using the *nom de guerre* 'Colonel Callan', summarily executed 14 of his troops for cowardice. He was later

captured and executed, along with an American and two other British mercenaries. Belgian, Portuguese and French mercenaries, including Colonel Bob
Denard, also took part in the fighting, to no effect.

## THE GUERRILLA WAR

While the FNLA disintegrated, Jonas Savimbi and Unita retreated in good
order into the bush to continue the war. In December 1975, the US Congress
passed a law forbidding the president to send any covert assistance to Unita, and
Savimbi's former allies in Zambia and Tanzania abandoned him, recognizing the
MPLA regime in Luanda. He therefore turned for support to the white regimes
in Rhodesia and South Africa.

This alliance brought much contumely upon his head, but it proved its
worth in military terms. He established a permanent base at Jamba, in the
extreme south-east of Angola, near the frontier with South-West Africa
(Namibia). Jamba, protected by the South African air force, expanded into
a vast city-camp, with hospitals, factories and extensive training facilities, all
carefully camouflaged. Savimbi's armies grew to nearly 30,000 regular troops
and 35,000 guerrillas. Apart from the aid sent by South Africa and, later, by
the United States, Unita controlled a large enough part of the country to
generate its own revenues; in particular, it controlled some of Angola's
diamond mines.

Savimbi pursued the same tactics he had used against the Portuguese, sending
small forces of guerrillas to harass government positions, to cut communications,
to attack isolated government units and to sabotage economic targets. To begin
with, the war was on a small scale – the MPLA was busy establishing itself in
Luanda and the Cubans were training an army, while Savimbi was building up
his forces in the bush. As his operations expanded, and the government's ability
to fight improved, the war soon established a regular pattern. Every year, during
the dry season, Angolan troops would launch an offensive towards Jamba, only
to be defeated by Unita and the South Africans.

At the same time, Unita progressively extended its operations in central
Angola, the homeland of the Ovimbundu tribe. A key economic target in the
region was the Benguela railway, which runs from the copper belt in Congo
(Zaïre) to the Angolan coast at Benguela. In an offensive in January 1988, Unita
claimed to have occupied the entire length of the railway, from the mountains
behind Benguela to the frontier with Zaïre (but not the major towns).

That looked very impressive on the map, but Unita was not ready to fight a
conventional war of position and heavy equipment against the MPLA, let alone
the Cubans. If it captured and tried to hold cities, they would have to be
defended against the government's counter-offensive, and the military advantage
would then swing to the far better equipped government army.

From the time that Unita first became a serious threat to the government, in
the late 1970s, until mid-1988, the situation on the ground was at a permanent
stalemate. The MPLA, backed by Cuba, might mount offensives against
Jamba, but they could not take it. Nor could they eliminate Unita guerrillas
in the endless bush of eastern and central Angola. Conversely, Savimbi and his
allies might succeed in extending their control over much of the country, but **17**

they could not win the war without occupying Luanda, and they could not do that as long as the Soviet Union backed the M P L A.

## FOREIGN INTERVENTION

The Cubans provided training and logistical and technical support for the Angolans, including 9000 teachers, doctors and other professionals, but until the battles of early 1988, Cuban troops did not normally join the fighting. None the less, service in Angola was considered hard and became increasingly unpopular.

This was Castro's contribution to Soviet foreign policy. Although the Angolans were obliged to pay Castro for the services of his mercenary army, in dollars earned from their oil exports, it was not a profitable endeavour. A Cuban defector, Air Force General Rafaél del Piño, who flew to the United States in May 1987, claimed that there had been 10,000 Cuban casualties in Angola, including several thousand dead. He said that the war was deeply unpopular, and that only Castro and his brother Raoúl believed that victory was possible.

As for the Soviets, they became involved in Angola and elsewhere in Africa in the mid-1970s without a proper calculation of the costs and advantages of the enterprise. The first turned out to be enormous, and the second non-existent.

The South Africans conducted a secondary war for 25 years against S W A P O, the South-West Africa People's Organization, which was fighting for the independence of Namibia. At the same time, they were fighting the African National Congress (A N C), the main guerrilla group in South Africa. S W A P O was based in Lobango, in southern Angola, and the A N C had bases among the 9000 or so South African refugees living in Angola. The South Africans established a security zone in southern Angola, which they policed with Unita's assistance. They did this because the area includes a major hydroelectric complex that they built during the Portuguese period, and also because they wanted a free-fire zone along the border. The South Africans also provided the essential air cover and artillery to defeat the successive Angolan offensives against Jamba, and in November 1987, President Botha paid a formal and much publicized visit to Savimbi there.

The United States started backing Unita soon after President Reagan took office in January 1981 and obtained the repeal of the 1975 Congressional ban. It was a crucial decision: South Africa had agreed in 1978 to give Namibia its independence, and the last details were to be settled in a conference in Geneva in January 1981. But in the previous November, Reagan had won the American presidential election, partly because of his promises to roll back the Communist conquests of the previous five years. South Africa decided to scuttle the agreement on Namibia, and Angola and Namibia suffered a further ten years of war as a consequence.

American support for Unita was at first clandestine, but soon it was openly avowed. Savimbi visited Washington in January 1986, and was received as a hero. On 30 January, he paid a formal call upon President Reagan in the White House – the final accolade. Unita got about $15 million a year in weapons from the U S, including Stinger anti-aircraft and T O W anti-tank missiles. As in Afghanistan and Nicaragua, this small American investment caused an enormous expenditure by the Soviet Union to keep the Cubans and the Angolan army in the field: by the mid-1980s, the U S S R was sending Angola $1 billion in weapons every year. For the United States, it was an exceedingly cost-effective way of putting pressure on the Soviets, the reverse of what happened in Vietnam.

Not all Americans saw it that way. Savimbi returned to the U S in June 1988, in the midst of the presidential campaign. He again visited President Reagan, on 27 June, but was chiefly concerned to put his case to the Democrats. For all his pains, he was roundly attacked by the black Democratic leader Jesse Jackson as a tool of the South Africans.

Although the United States did not recognize the Angolan government, it was Angola's main trading partner. The American oil companies Chevron (Gulf) and Texaco, protected by Cuban soldiers, did flourishing business, and Angola had a trade surplus of $642 million with the U S in 1986, which it could spend on arms or industrial imports. This situation was one of the oddities of the modern world. South African commandos attacked the Chevron oil installations in Cabinda in May 1985, were repulsed by the Cubans and two of the commandos were killed and one captured.

The United Nations tried continuously to mediate, to arrange for the independence of Namibia and the simultaneous withdrawal of the Cubans from Angola. For years, it met with no success. The U S assistant secretary of state for Africa in the Reagan administration, Chester Crocker, also devoted himself to the cause of arranging a peace agreement in southern Africa. His efforts were constantly unsuccessful until the late spring of 1988.

## THE BREAK-THROUGH

In 1987, the M P L A launched another offensive against Mavinga, a key position defending Savimbi's capital at Jamba. For the first time since 1975, South Africa sent large numbers of troops and artillery north to bolster Unita's defences. The Angolan army was defeated in a major battle at the Lomba River in September, and Savimbi's forces then counter-attacked the M P L A and Cubans in their last base in the south-east, at Cuito Cuanavale. For a while, it looked as though Unita was going to sweep its enemies completely out of southern Angola.

Savimbi laid siege to Cuito Cuanavale for several months, helped by long-range South African artillery – and even claimed to have captured it – but the Angolans and their Cuban allies rushed in reinforcements and held the place. Castro sent an extra 12,000 troops, and in March 1988, the siege of Cuito Cuanavale was lifted and the South Africans withdrew their troops from Angola, leaving only a small number to police the 'security zone' along the border.

The Cubans then advanced their troops to the border with Namibia, and for the first time there were serious clashes between Cuban and South African forces in the frontier zone. On 27 June 1988, 12 South African soldiers were killed in a fight with Angolans and Cubans. The Cubans were then building major military and air bases in southern Angola facing South African bases in Namibia, and it appeared entirely possible that there might be a major war between the two armies.

The casualties that both Cuba and South Africa suffered in these battles and the prospect of further and more serious fighting were important elements in **19** their decision to sign the August ceasefire. However, the decision to withdraw Cuban troops was not taken in Havana; it was taken in Moscow. The Soviet Union (which, at the time of the ceasefire, had about 1000 military advisers in Angola) was then pulling its own troops out of Afghanistan and urging its Vietnamese allies to get out of Cambodia. It evidently decided to cut its losses in Angola as well.

Mikhail Gorbachev had asked the key question: what was the point, for the Soviet Union, in spending $1 billion or more a year on a perpetual stalemate in southern Africa? The Soviet leadership found the answer in the spring of 1988, after the abrupt escalation in the fighting in Angola. At the December 1987 summit meeting between President Reagan and Gorbachev in Washington, the Soviet spokesman was asked whether the retreat from Afghanistan indicated that Angola would be next. He insisted that there was no connection – beside the coincidence that both countries' names began with 'A'. That statement was disingenuous: the Soviets had made a far greater investment, morally and physically, in Afghanistan, and if they could abandon Kabul, they could certainly abandon Luanda. In early June, Reagan went to Moscow for his fourth summit with Gorbachev. They agreed, in a statement buried in their final communiqué, that efforts should be made to reach a settlement of the Angola question by 29 September, the tenth anniversary of the UN Security Council Resolution 435 which called on South Africa to leave Namibia.

The diplomatic effort to end the war had already resumed. After meeting in London in May, representatives of Angola, Cuba, South Africa and the United States met in Cairo, in New York and finally in Geneva. In New York on 12 June an outline agreement was reached, which provided that Cuba would withdraw from Angola and that South Africa would pull out of Namibia. On 26 July, Fidel Castro announced that Cuba would withdraw all its troops from Angola 'gradually and totally'.

The agreement was signed on 5 August 1988 in Geneva, and ratified by the governments of South Africa, Cuba and Angola three days later. It laid down a timetable for ending the wars in Angola and Namibia:

● A ceasefire between Cuban and South African troops came into force immediately, and South Africa withdrew its 600 remaining troops in Angola by the end of August.
● Further negotiations were to be held on the remaining issues, which included the precise timetable for Cuban withdrawal, future American and South African aid to Unita, and Soviet and Cuban aid to the MPLA, Angolan aid to the ANC, and how to pay for the proposed UN peacekeeping force.
● The UN plan for the independence of Namibia was to be put into operation on 1 November. The process was to lead to elections for a constituent assembly in Namibia by 1 June 1989. This assembly would draw up a constitution and set a date for independence.
● The Cubans were to withdraw from Angola, but the timetable was not settled. Cuba had proposed four years, but South Africa demanded that the withdrawal be concluded before Namibia's independence. Finding an acceptable compromise took another four months.

• The South Africans were to withdraw their 50,000 troops from Namibia, except for a 1500-man force in two southern bases. A U N force of 7500 would be sent to Namibia to keep the peace.

As for Angola, despite its assent to the agreement, the M P L A had no wish to see the Cubans depart, fearing that Unita would then win the war. Cuba and the U S S R did not take the Angolans' wishes any more seriously than the Soviets took the wishes of the Afghan government, or President Nixon and Dr Henry Kissinger took the wishes of the South Vietnamese government in 1972. Angola flatly refused to negotiate directly with Unita, despite Soviet pressure, just as the South Vietnamese government refused to negotiate with the Vietcong.

The official American position after the Geneva agreement was signed was that the United States had the right to continue to aid Savimbi, and would do so for as long as the U S S R and Cuba continued to arm the M P L A. Both the United States and the U S S R continually urged the Luanda government to open negotiations with Unita – and for three years it obdurately refused.

## MODERN ANGOLA

At the time of the ceasefire, the Angolan currency was worthless, but because of the oil – revenue was $2.5 billion in 1985 – the economy was considered viable by the World Bank and other international organizations. Angola was one of the few bankrupt nations with a credit line.

Immediately after independence in 1975, and the abrupt departure of the 300,000 Portuguese settlers, the government collectivized agriculture and nationalized all industry, except oil. The results were catastrophic. Agriculture and industry both collapsed, and Angola had to import food from Europe and the United States to feed half its people. There was once an elegant promenade along the waterfront at Luanda, modelled on the Copacabana in Rio de Janeiro or the Promenade des Anglais in Nice. By 1988 it was deserted, its shops, hotels and offices boarded up. The M P L A had followed the advice of Soviet planners who knew nothing about Africa and tried to impose there a system not notably successful at home in Europe. Private enterprise was abolished and state companies were set up to replace them.

In 1988, the Soviet Union blandly admitted that the economic model that it had imposed upon its African clients was wholly unsuited to their needs. Anatoly Adamishin, the deputy foreign minister for African affairs, who conducted the negotiations with the U S and South Africa on the future of Angola and Namibia, was asked at a press conference whether he thought S W A P O should adopt socialism. 'I personally don't think they are going to build socialism in this part of the world,' he replied. 'There are few people in the Soviet Union who would advise them to build a socialist society in these particular conditions of Africa.' For 20 years or more, the Soviet Union had peddled 'scientific socialism' as the solution to all Africa's woes, and had even set up a Patrice Lumumba University in Moscow to train the future *aparatchiks* of a Communist Africa. Thousands of Africans had devoted their lives to furthering a Communist revolution, and hundreds of thousands of people had been killed in the effort, or had died of starvation or disease because of the revolution's failure. Now the

Soviets dropped Marxism into the dustheap of history. The future suddenly looked very bleak for Third World Marxists.

Exchange rates in Angola were so unrealistic and price controls so erratic that the few foreign companies still operating in Luanda paid their local employees in consumer goods. A visiting American journalist found, in December 1987, that the favoured unit of exchange was a case of beer. Two cases could be sold for enough local currency to pay for a round-trip flight to Rio or Lisbon.

The standard of living, life expectancy, infant mortality rates, medical provision and public safety were probably worse for the Angolans than at any time since the abolition of the slave trade in the early 19th century. According to Unicef, 45 per cent of Angolan children suffered from malnutrition, and the amount spent on health care had dropped from $10.30 a head in 1981 to $0.90 in 1987 (these figures were expressed in dollars because the local currency was worthless). The *International Index of Human Suffering*, prepared by the Population Crisis Committee in Washington, put Angola second on the list of suffering countries; only Mozambique was more unfortunate.

The failure of Marxism was so flagrant that, in 1987, the government reversed course and proposed to revive the private sector. State shops, farms, service companies and so on were to be sold off. In addition, the government announced a month in advance that the currency (the kwanza) would be devalued by nearly 100 per cent – in other words, it recognized that the kwanza was completely valueless and would have to be replaced. These extreme measures were welcomed by international organizations and by the European Community, which resumed aid to Angola.

The security situation was almost as bad as in Mozambique. By one calculation, only 400 miles (640 km) of paved road were still safe, out of the 4400 miles (7000 km) bequeathed by Portugal. Foreign embassies recommended that their staff not travel more than 25 miles (40 km) outside the capital after three Swedish aid workers were kidnapped by Unita guerrillas in September 1987, 30 miles (48 km) outside Luanda, and one of them was killed. Even the coast road was not safe, and travel was restricted to heavy convoys, or to the air. Government-controlled territory comprised a series of islands in a hostile sea, like Cambodia in the last days of Lon Nol. Discipline among Angolan soldiers was an increasing problem, as it was in Uganda, with many taking to banditry.

The Cubans pulled out slightly ahead of timetable, the last contingent leaving in May 1991. In April 1990 the MPLA had finally agreed to open ceasefire negotiations with Unita. The talks were mediated by Portugal, with the United States and the Soviet Union assisting. Negotiations took a year and the agreement was reached on 1 May 1991, and signed in Lisbon by President dos Santos and Jonas Savimbi on 31 May, in the presence of James Baker, the American secretary of state, and Alexander Bessmyrtnykh, the Soviet foreign minister.

The last action of the war was a victory for Unita, which had laid siege to Luena, in eastern Angola. The town fell on 13 May, two days before the ceasefire came into effect. The ceasefire was supervised by a joint MPLA/Unita military committee, to which the three mediating powers sent representatives, aided by 600 UN observers. There was also a political committee to prepare elections to be held in the latter part of 1992.

In September 1991, Savimbi returned to the Ovimbundu capital, Huambo, which he had been forced to leave in February 1976, and was rapturously received. A week later he went to Luanda for the first time since 1975, and addressed a huge rally of his supporters. It was the first move in the election campaign. The United States continued to support Unita, though less actively than during the civil war. In June 1991, Congress agreed to provide $20 million in aid to Unita, the money to be used for humanitarian and political purposes. This compared to the $60 million a year that had previously been spent on arms. At the end of the civil war, Savimbi had 50,000 men under arms to the government's 100,000.

The M P L A, meanwhile, had abandoned Marxism-Leninism and proclaimed itself a social-democratic party. It had lost the support, financial, military and moral, of the Soviet Union and its allies, and now had to depend on its own resources and the oil revenues from Cabinda. The loss was not merely military: Soviet and Cuban technicians had kept much of the country's essential services running. The M P L A's first problem was how to pay its 150,000-man army.

The civil war was to be continued by other means, with the prize the right to govern a ruined country.

The first round of elections were held on 29 and 30 September 1992 under U N supervision. In the presidential election, dos Santos won 49 per cent, Savimbi 40 per cent and Holden Roberto 2 per cent. In parliamentary elections, the M P L A won 54 per cent and Unita 30 per cent. The turn-out was 90 per cent, according to the U N, and though there were many irregularities it seemed clear that dos Santos and his party had won despite their frightful record over the previous 18 years of incompetence, brutality and Marxist dogmatism. No doubt tribalism played a large part in the results, but Savimbi's campaigns of terror contributed largely to his rejection in most of the country.

He immediately denounced the results as fraudulent. On 6 October, the Unita contingent was withdrawn from the national army. On the 30th, Unita attempted a coup in Luanda, attacking the airport and other government strongpoints. The coup failed and the M P L A forces counter-attacked, sacking Unita headquarters and hunting down Unita officials through the streets. A vice-president of the party and Savimbi's nephew were among the hundreds killed.

The first incident was followed by a short, uneasy truce, which was once again broken by Savimbi. In January 1993 he launched a new attack against his former capital, Huambo, which was occupied by government troops. The siege lasted 54 days and the city, the second largest in Angola, was devastated. Over 10,000 people were killed before Unita captured it, on 7 March. That year, U N officials estimated that 1000 people a day were dying of war-related causes in Angola, chiefly famine. Between 10 million and 15 million landmines had been scattered across the country and about 100,000 people had lost limbs by stepping on a mine. The situation was by then as bad as it had ever been during Angola's nearly 30 years of war. John Darnton, a reporter of the *New York Times*, discovered a town in Benguela province where 20,000 people, half of them children, were subsisting on a diet of boiled insects and sweet-potato leaves. Savimbi financed his war by selling between $100 million and $500 million of diamonds every year. The national budget in 1993 provided

$475 million for arms, $18.5 million for health and $12 million for education, the money chiefly coming from oil sales.

A turning point in the war came in July 1994, when a government army, strengthened by 500 South African mercenaries, invaded Unita's main diamond-producing region, Lunda Norte. The mercenaries were supplied by a company called Executives Outcome of Pretoria, which had no scruple in selling its services to any African government that wanted them. They trained the Angolan army and played a large part in its sudden improvement in quality. They were sent home at the end of 1996. Government troops then mounted a general offensive against the central highlands, the Ovimbundu heartland, and threatened Huambo. For the first time in the war, it appeared as though a military solution might be possible. Savimbi, fearing defeat, agreed to negotiations for a truce in Lusaka. During those talks, the government recaptured Huambo, on 12 November – again with the help of South African mercenaries. The ceasefire was signed on the 15th. The agreement guaranteed Unita a share of government power for the first time.

By one estimate, 200,000 people had been killed in the 1992–4 fighting. The government decided against pursuing the complete defeat of Unita, and Unita agreed, reluctantly, to participate in the central government. In 1995, Savimbi at last recognized the validity of the 1992 election, and dos Santos's victory. He agreed to accept the position of vice-president.

A shaky ceasefire held for the next two years, though it was constantly threatened by disputes over control over the diamond-mining areas in the north-east. In the spring of 1997, Angolan troops crossed the border into Zaïre to join armies from Rwanda that were closing in on the Mobutu regime in Kinshasa. Mobutu had supported Savimbi for 20 years, and now it was pay-back time. The dictator's overthrow was a serious blow to Savimbi, though it turned out that he could still import arms so long as he had diamonds to pay for them. Then Angola intervened in the civil war in Congo (Brazzaville). It was a striking reversal of the situation of a few years earlier. The ceasefire was still holding in 1997, by and large, but the national reconciliation was precarious in the extreme. Unita could not be trusted to comply with the provisions of the Lusaka agreement (the U N Security Council voted sanctions against it in October 1997 for non-compliance) and there remained a strong possibility that civil war would resume.

## CABINDA
Cabinda is a small enclave on the coast north of Angola proper, separated from the rest of the country by a sliver of Congolese territory. Its population is about 120,000, mostly Bakongo and therefore opposed to the Kimbundu-dominated M P L A. It is the site of Angola's most profitable oil-fields and a liberation movement has been operating there for 20 years, the Cabinda Enclave Liberation Front – Armed Forces of Cabinda (F L E C–F A C in Portuguese). There is another separatist group that split from the F L E C, and between them they have about 1000 ill-armed guerrillas. After the defeat of Unita, the Angolan government turned its attention to fighting the Cabinda rebels but found, as so often in Africa, that a tribal-based insurgency is almost impossible to suppress.

# FURTHER READING

American University, *Angola: A Country Study*, Washington, 1979.

Bridgland, Fred, *Jonas Savimbi: A Key to Africa*, New York, Paragon House, 1987.

Henderson, Lawrence W., *Angola: Five Centuries of Conflict*, Ithaca, New York, Cornell University Press, 1979.

Kinghoffer, Arthur J., *The Angola War: A Study in Soviet Policy in the Third World*, Boulder, Colo., Westview Press, 1980.

Maier, Karl, *Angola: Promises and Lies*, London, Serif, 1996.

Martin, James *A Political History of the Civil War in Angola*, New Brunswick, New Jersey, Transaction Publishers, 1992.

Somerville, Keith, *Angola: Politics, Economics and Society*, London, Frances Pinter, 1986.

Stockwell, John, *In Search of Enemies: A C I A Story*, New York, W. W. Norton, 1978.

Wolfers, Michael, *Angola in the Frontline*, London, Zed Press, 1983.

# BURUNDI AND RWANDA

## BURUNDI

| | |
|---|---|
| Area | 10,707 sq. miles (27,731 sq. km). |
| Population | 6.2 million. At independence, in 1962, 83% of the people were Hutu, 16% Tutsi and 1% Twa (pygmy). There have been no ethnic censuses since. |
| GNP per capita | $160. |

## RWANDA

| | |
|---|---|
| Area | 10,169 sq. miles (26,338 sq. km). |
| Population | 6.4 million. At independence, about 10% of the population was Tutsi, 1% Twa and the rest Hutu. |
| GNP per capita | $180. |
| Refugees | There are 240,000 Hutu refugees from Burundi in Tanzania; 40,000 in Congo. There are 400,000 internal refugees. There are about 200,000 Rwandan Hutu refugees in Congo and 50,000 in Tanzania. There are 20,000 refugees from Congo and Burundi in Rwanda. |
| Casualties | 20,000 Tutsi murdered in Rwanda, 1959–62; 100,000 Hutu murdered in Burundi, 1972; 1000–4000 Tutsi and up to 20,000 Hutu killed in Burundi, 1988; 500,000 to 1 million Tutsi killed in Rwanda, 1994; 100,000–150,000, mostly Hutu, killed in Burundi, 1993–7. |

On 6 April 1994 President Juvenal Habyarimana of Rwanda and President Cyprian Ntaryamira of Burundi were killed together when their plane was shot down over Kigali, the capital of Rwanda. The assassination was the work of Hutu extremists in the government and army of Rwanda. In August 1993, Habyarimana had signed a peace agreement with Tutsi rebels, the Rwandese Patriotic Front, allowing a merger of the two armies, the admission of R P F ministers into the government and the return of Tutsi refugees. He had constantly postponed implementing the agreement, but was under great pressure from the international community to do so. On the day of the assassination, he

had attended a meeting in Dar-es-Salaam, Tanzania, at which other east African presidents, including Ntaryamira, had most strongly urged that he implement the agreement. The extremists feared that he would accede to the demands and therefore implemented a long-prepared plan of genocide. They determined to eliminate the danger of a renewed Tutsi domination by exterminating the Tutsi population and killing any member of the Hutu tribe that might oppose them. They used the murder of the president as a first step and a pretext for the massacres that began immediately. It was the most flagrant, deliberate case of genocide in the world since Hitler attempted to exterminate the Jews. At least 500,000 people were killed before the RPF defeated the government and occupied the whole country. Other estimates put the dead at 1 million.

About 1.7 million Hutus fled westwards into Zaïre, led by the defeated army and government that had perpetuated the genocide. They became embroiled in fighting between Tutsis and other tribes in eastern Zaïre. The new Rwandan government intervened in Zaïre and the civil war there led eventually to the overthrow of President Mobutu. The Rwandan army pursued the Hutu refugee army and government, and all the civilians that accompanied them, across the breadth of Zaïre, killing tens of thousands of them.

The fighting in Rwanda had killed or driven out 40 per cent of the population. Now about 700,000 Tutsi refugees from abroad returned. About 300,000 of the Hutus who had fled to Zaïre also returned, and by the summer of 1997 there were increasing incidents of terrorism and fighting between Hutu militiamen and the Tutsi army.

In Burundi, the Tutsis remained in control. Under President Paul Buyoya the government made a great effort to reconcile the Tutsi (who form about 15 per cent of the population) and the Hutu majority. A moderate Hutu economist, Melchior Ndadaye, was elected president by 65 per cent of the vote in free elections in June 1993 and Buyoya handed the government over to him. Ndadaye was kidnapped and murdered by Tutsi officers in October, an event followed by riots and massacres that killed 50,000 people, displacing 150,000 Tutsi villagers, who fled to the cities and 300,000 Hutu, who crossed the borders, mostly into Rwanda. The Tutsi army then took power and installed another moderate, Ntaryamira, as president. He had the misfortune to accept a ride back from Dar-es-Salaam with Habyarimana, and was killed with him. Buyoya then resumed the Bugandan presidency.

Since these events, there have been frequent outbreaks of violence, with the persistent danger of renewed civil war in both countries. In Burundi, bands of Hutu militiamen attacked Tutsi villages on the outskirts of the capital, Bujumbura, in a reply to incidents that had led to earlier massacres, and a Hutu insurgency developed in Rwanda in 1997, supplied and directed from abroad. Its chief military tactic was to massacre Tutsis.

## HISTORY

The Tutsi have ruled Burundi for four centuries, apart from a 60-year colonial interlude (when it was known as Urundi). They originally came from the north, perhaps from Ethiopia; they are conspicuously tall and endowed with what Europeans used to call a classical profile. They have maintained their rule over the majority tribe in Burundi, the Hutu, in the only way possible: by force. The two tribes now speak the same language, and often intermarry, but despite this, their separation remains extreme. They are like the tribes of Northern Ireland, with the difference that the more recent arrivals, the Tutsi, are in a small minority, comprising only one-sixth of the population.

The Tutsi also ruled Rwanda (which under colonial rule was called Ruanda), but in a series of uprisings in 1959–62, the Hutu majority overthrew the Tutsi monarchy and dominion. In the process, up to 20,000 Tutsi were murdered and 100,000 fled to Burundi. In 1972, about 100,000 Hutu in Burundi were murdered by the Tutsi. The troubles returned in 1988 and in 1994.

Ruanda–Urundi was part of German East Africa from 1899 until it was conquered by the British in 1916. It was a remote and neglected province: the Germans, who concentrated on developing the more accessible areas of Tanganyika, only established themselves early in the new century and were not there long enough to make much of an impression. Then, in the peace settlement after World War I, the territory was ceded to Belgium, as some compensation for its sufferings, and because it was contiguous with the Belgian Congo.

The peace-makers had been misreading the maps again. Ruanda–Urundi was even more remote from Léopoldville than from Dar-es-Salaam and, of course, its people were not consulted. It would have made much more sense to integrate it with Tanganyika. Belgium was given a mandate under the League of Nations to administer Ruanda–Urundi, and the Hutu and the Tutsi, after a few years of administration in German, had to adapt themselves to French and Flemish.

Ruanda and Urundi, though administered as a single colony, were kept separate because each had been an independent kingdom for generations. They were not merged as the British merged the kingdoms of Uganda. The Belgians anticipated that eventually there would be Hutu-dominated governments in both countries, but the matter was taken out of their hands.

First, in Ruanda, when the Tutsi king died in July 1959, the Hutu rose against his successor. There were massacres throughout the country and the bodies of hundreds of Tutsi were thrown in the Kagera River and floated down into Lake Victoria. By the time the Hutu had established their control, as many as 20,000 Tutsi had been killed and 100,000 Tutsi refugees driven south into Urundi or north into Uganda (these figures were disputed by the Hutu government of Rwanda).

With the Hutu now in control of Ruanda, the Belgians, who had by then abruptly abandoned the Congo, made as graceful an exit as circumstances permitted, and in 1962, left behind the new Hutu government of Rwanda, headed by President Grégoire Kayibanda. The Tutsi retained power in Burundi, under their hereditary monarch, the Mwami Mwambutsa. His eldest son, Prince Rwagasore, was assassinated in October 1961, during the preparations for independence, and the Mwami then exercised absolute power during the last months of Belgian rule, and this continued after they left. In May 1965, there were legislative elections which Hutu parties won overwhelmingly, but the Mwami refused to recognize the results, and appointed a Tutsi prime minister. The first Hutu revolt occurred in October; before it was suppressed, between 2500 and 5000 Hutu had been killed, including over 100 prominent government officials and officers. The Mwami fled the country, and his second son, Charles Ndizeye, was put on the throne, taking the name Ntare V, in September 1966. In November, he was deposed by his own prime minister, Captain Michel Micombero, who became president.

In September 1969, Micombero discovered a Hutu plot and summarily executed about 20 prominent Hutu, including one minister and two former ministers; others were jailed. In July 1971, Micombero discovered a Tutsi plot, and executed a number of prominent Tutsis.

On 29 April 1972, there was a Hutu uprising in Bujumbura, the capital, and in the southern parts of the country. The rebels, numbering perhaps 10,000, were aided by a small army of Hutu exiles, and by some of the surviving troops of Pierre Mulele, who had played a role in the Congo civil wars. The Burundi government at the time claimed that 50,000 Tutsi were killed, but the real total was probably nearer 2000, most of them Hutu. The invaders, who attacked the Bujumbura radio station, were easily defeated. President Mobutu of Zaïre sent a small contingent to the capital to keep the peace, allowing the Burundi army to concentrate on the Hutu.

Then the reprisals began. One of the first victims was the former Mwami, Ntare V. He had been visiting Uganda on business in March 1972, and Micombero asked Idi Amin to deliver him to Bujumbura, under promise of safe-conduct: 'Just like you, I believe in God . . . Your Excellency can be assured that as soon as Mr Charles Ndizeye returns back to my country, he will be considered as an ordinary citizen and that as such his life and security will be assured.' Ntare was then summarily bundled into Micombero's presidential plane, much against his will, and flown to Bujumbura. He was murdered shortly after the rebellion broke out on 29 April.

Then the Tutsi embarked on a massacre of the Hutu. On 30 April, the government imposed a dusk-to-dawn curfew. The army and the Tutsi youth movement sought out and killed all Hutu with secondary education, all politicians, teachers, businessmen and tens of thousands of peasants. At the Official University at Bujumbura, one-third of the students were murdered, and at the capital's *lycée* (high school) 300 of 700 students enrolled were killed, as were 60 per cent of Protestant clergy (all Hutu). It was a deliberate attempt to wipe out all Hutu who might ever take the lead in opposition to the Tutsi. There is no precise estimate of the number who lost their lives, but the generally accepted figure is 100,000. Reginald Kay writes that conservative estimates put the number, including those killed in the brief Hutu rebellion, between 80,000 and 100,000. He goes on: 'By no means fanciful reports have suggested that the figure was closer to 150,000, or almost 5 per cent of the population.' About 150,000 Hutu fled abroad. There were no protests, either from the Organization of African Unity (O A U), the United Nations or from Western countries which, according to Kay, suffer from 'a deeply rooted and guilt-based fear of censuring the conduct of nations in the developing world'.

## MODERN BURUNDI

Burundi has never escaped from the shadow of those terrible events. Micombero was deposed in a coup in 1976 by his cousin, Colonel Jean-Baptiste Bagaza. The two men had been watching a soccer match together in the presidential box, when Bagaza informed Micombero that the large number of troops around the stadium had switched their allegiance. Micombero was put on a plane and sent into exile.

Bagaza had been out of the country during the 1972 massacres and therefore escaped any personal blame, but he too pursued a policy of relentless persecution of the Hutu. In 1987, there were four Hutu ministers out of a total of 20 in the government, one of 15 provincial governors, seven Hutus in the National Assembly and two in the governing party's 65-strong central committee. Very few Hutu children go to high school, and only one-third of the students at university level are Hutu. Since the Hutu are mostly Catholic, persecution extended to the church: foreign missionaries and priests were expelled, including the Bishop of Bururui who had worked in Burundi for 50 years; church schools were closed and church land was expropriated. The government was a nasty and friendless dictatorship, and the country stagnated economically. Its only resource was the export of coffee, chiefly grown by Hutu peasants in the northern provinces (much of it was smuggled over the border to Rwanda). Its only international support came from France, which sustained all French-speaking countries – even though French had been suppressed as the language of education in the schools.

In September 1987, a bloodless army coup overthrew Bagaza and a new president, Major Pierre Buyoya, took office. He had been in Brussels during the 1972 massacre, was less paranoid than Bagaza, and began to improve relations between Tutsi and Hutu. He released all political prisoners, restored church property, jailed some Tutsis on corruption charges, and urged his fellow Tutsis to allow the Hutus to enjoy equal rights with them.

In the relatively affluent north, the Hutu began to act on Buyoya's promises, but the local Tutsi administration did not. Word spread around the district of troubles to come. According to one account, the Tutsi mayor of Marangara, a northern town, told the local Hutu on 28 June 1988, 'You are preparing your knives, but ours are already sharp and they cut more than yours.' Then the national army, which is almost exclusively Tutsi, came north for manoeuvres and to attempt to stop coffee smuggling. The Hutu thought that the soldiers intended to kill them, and some of them began sabotaging bridges or blocking roads with tree trunks to delay the army's movements. On 14 August, panic swept the small Tutsi population of Marangara. They fled north, to the village of Ntega, where some of them took refuge in a church. In the next few days, there was widespread killing of Tutsi by Hutu: 2000 to 3000 died, including the people in the church.

The army arrived on 18 August and immediately began taking its revenge. The estimate of 20,000 killed came from doctors in a hospital near the border with Rwanda, and from relief workers. Refugees were crossing at a rate of 5000 a day, and over 50,000 had reached Rwanda by the end of August. Journalists who visited the country reported that the once heavily populated northern districts were empty. A month earlier, there had been 150,000 people living peacefully in their hill-top villages. Now there was none. The people had hidden in the bush, **30** fled the country or had been killed.

The government claimed that the troubles were caused by Hutu exiles from Rwanda and Zaïre and played down the massacres, just as their predecessors had done in 1972. In October, President Buyoya established the position of prime minister, and appointed a Hutu, Adrien Sibomana, to the job. The number of Hutu cabinet ministers, already raised to seven since the massacre, was increased to 11. The government's measures restored security to the north, and most of the refugees returned home. Real power remained with the Tutsi, however, until Buyoya permitted free elections on 1 June 1993. He lost to a Hutu, Melchior Ndadaye, whose party then went on to win 71 per cent of the vote in parliamentary elections, and 65 of 81 seats in parliament. Buyoya permitted a peaceful transfer of power, the first (and last) in either Burundi or Rwanda, and for a brief moment it appeared that the Tutsi and Hutu might learn to live together. Ndadaye was murdered, along with several members of the government, on 21 October 1993, and Burundi plunged back into violence.

## MODERN RWANDA

Rwanda was the mirror image of Burundi. After independence, the government and army were entirely Hutu and oppressed the Tutsi minority. The original Hutu leader, Grégoire Kayibanda, led a violent and murderous regime that permitted repeated murders of the Tutsis. He was overthrown in July 1973 and replaced by Juvenal Habyarimana, who proved a greater tyrant than his predecessor but allowed the Tutsis to live in peace and to prosper – provided they accepted their complete lack of political rights. Kayibanda starved to death in jail in 1976. Rwanda was ruled by the most complete tyranny in sub-Saharan Africa with a secret police and an army of informers as omnipresent as the KGB in Beria's day. The tradition of the all-powerful Tutsi king was transferred to a Hutu president, and the regime was kept afloat by French support and the profits of exporting coffee and tin. Then the price of coffee collapsed in 1986 and the Rwandan economy began its rapid spiral down to bankruptcy.

Just as Hutu exiles in Zaïre plotted to overthrow the Burundi government, so exiled Tutsis in Burundi, Uganda and Tanzania plotted against the government in Bujumbura. By 1990, the original 320,000 Tutsi refugees had increased to 600,000 or 700,000 in Burundi, Uganda, Tanzania and Zaïre and were supported by 1.3 million Tutsis living in those countries. President Museveni of Uganda comes from a tribe related to the Tutsi, and was helped by the Burundi government during his own fight for power against Milton Obote. When he launched his guerrilla war against Milton Obote in 1981 with 26 comrades, several were Tutsis, including Sam Rwigyema and Paul Kagame. Rwigyema later became Ugandan commander in chief and minister of defence and, when Museveni replaced him, became commander of the RPF. The Front was not large nor well-armed, and launched a military invasion of Rwanda on 1 October 1990. Rwigyema was killed on the second day and the Rwandan army defeated the invaders. Kagame then took command and began a traditional guerrilla campaign, which soon spread terror and war across northern Rwanda. Under pressure from France and faced with a dangerous military challenge in the north, a vast refugee problem and the collapsing economy, President Habyarimana agreed to introduce a multi-party democracy. In July 1992, a ceasefire with the

RPF was arranged and negotiations opened in Arusha, Tanzania, to establish democracy, end the civil war and return the Tutsi refugees. Moderate Hutu opposition parties took part in the negotiations, along with the government and the RPF, which included extremist Tutsis as well as Kagame's relatively moderate supporters.

But Rwanda and Burundi are cursed with one of the densest populations in the world and one of the highest birth-rates (Rwanda's population increases at 3.7 per cent a year). There is fierce competition for land and it is all too easy for demagogues to stir up fears that the rival tribe is intent to steal the land. A radio station, *Mille Collines* (Rwanda is said to consist of a thousand hills, each with its town), broadcast constant forecasts of Tutsi treachery and plans for exterminating the Hutu. As the Arusha negotiations progressed, a plan evolved in Kigali among senior ministers and army officers to solve Rwanda's problems by killing all the Tutsis, together with any Hutu who opposed the genocide. Habyarimana's wife and her family were deeply implicated in the plot.

There have been many frightful massacres in the 20th century. The Turks slaughtered the Armenians and drove them out of the country during World War I. Stalin, Mao Tse-tung and Pol Pot killed huge numbers of their compatriots for ideological reasons; Hindus and Muslims massacred each other for religious reasons in the partition of India; and many nations have attacked and slaughtered foreigners or enemies by the tens of thousands. But only Hitler and the Hutu in Rwanda have systematically set out to wipe out an entire people, for racial reasons. There are many definitions of genocide but what happened in Rwanda in 1994 marks the most extreme example of the crime since 1945.

Habyarimana had appointed a new government that included many moderate Hutus. It directed the Arusha negotiations and a final agreement was reached between the government, opposition and RPF and signed by the president on 4 August 1993. It provided for a 'Broad-Based Transitional Government', a National Transitional Assembly, united armed forces and the return of Tutsi refugees. In the new army, 60 per cent were to be from the old, Hutu armed forces and 40 per cent from the RPF. The powers of the president were to be drastically reduced.

By this time there were large-scale relief operations organized by the UN and a UN Assistance Mission for Rwanda (UNAMIR) with 2500 men moved to Kigali. The broad-based government was scheduled to take over in February, 1994, but Habyarimana constantly delayed implementing every part of the Arusha agreement. Hutu extremists violently opposed it, and there was a campaign of assassination against politicians who supported it. Events in Burundi, where a Hutu president was murdered by Tutsi extremists, confirmed to Hutus in Rwanda the dangers of the Arusha formula. President Mitterrand of France and the presidents of Uganda, Tanzania and Burundi all put heavy pressure on Habyarimana to fulfil his obligations under Arusha. A meeting of those leaders, together with the prime minister of Zaïre, was convened in Dar-es-Salaam on 6 April. It was intended to discuss the situation in Burundi but turned into a brutal assault on Habyarimana by his colleagues, all urging him to implement Arusha.

Habyarimana's plane was shot down by two Soviet-made SAM-7s, apparently fired by French or Belgian mercenaries hired for the occasion. The missiles were launched from a hill overlooking Kigali airport, just as the presidential plane came in to land. Everyone on board, including the three-man French crew, was killed. Much of the wreckage landed in the gardens of the president's house.

The plane was shot down at 8.30 p.m. Within 45 minutes, Hutu militia road-blocks were up across Kigali, and the massacres began. Everything was planned. The death squads had lists – and were helped by the Rwandan system of identity cards, which noted a person's tribe, as German cards once noted that people were Jewish. The killers went after moderate Hutus (one minister managed to phone friends in the United States, to say that she was hiding in a neighbour's house – and then said that the killers were at the door. That was the last anyone heard of her). The killers went through Tutsi districts, rounded everyone up, and killed them all. In the countryside, they attacked villages and the churches, barracks and schools where Tutsis had taken refuge. Between 6 and 30 April, 100,000 people were killed. Another 100,000 were killed in the first half of May, and 300,000 in the second half of the month. These low estimates are provided by *Médecins sans Frontières*. Prunier calculates that 800,000 Tutsis were killed in three months and between 10,000 and 30,000 opposition Hutu. Since the population was estimated to be 7.7 million in 1994, 12 per cent or 930,000 Tutsi, that would leave about 130,000 Tutsi survivors of the genocide. Ugandan police collected 40,000 bodies that had floated down river into Lake Victoria.

The world's first reaction was to rescue Europeans trapped in Rwanda – and to reduce the U N A M I R from 2500 to 270 men. Its commander protested that with 5000 men and enough support from the U N he could save hundreds of thousands of lives. The U N did nothing, in large part because the United States, traumatized by the loss of 30 U S soldiers in Somalia the year before, refused to help. In August, France finally sent a relief force which occupied south-west Rwanda and certainly saved many thousand people (in Operation Turquoise). It was a sign of what might have been done.

Radio *Mille Collines* called for vengeance: 'You have missed some of the enemies in (this or that place)! Some are still alive. You must go back there and finish them off'; and, 'The graves are not yet quite full. Who is going to do the good work and help us fill them completely?' However, the main work of killing was organized, directed and carried out by the government itself, using local officials to coordinate the work. In Gérard Prunier's words, 'The efficiency of the massacres bore witness to the quality of Rwandese local administration and also to its responsibility.' He names the officials, the police, the militia – but adds, 'Nevertheless, the main agents of the genocide were the ordinary peasants themselves.' He also notes that the churches did nothing to stop the killings, and many church leaders, including one Catholic bishop, supported the genocide. Twenty-nine Rwandan priests wrote to the pope in August, denying any Hutu responsibility for genocide.

The killers paid particular attention to women and children. When Tutsis took refuge in churches, they were burned about their ears. One Hutu Protestant pastor invited the Tutsis of his village to his mission and offered protection – and then called in the army to have them all killed. He escaped to Texas where a local judge refused to allow him to be extradited to the war crimes tribunal on the grounds that the case against him did not meet the rigours of Texan law.

As soon as the massacres started, the R P F resumed military operations. The Rwandan army put up little resistance: it was preoccupied by genocide. It took the rebels four months to capture Kigali and drive the Hutu government, army and militias across western borders into Zaïre. A million refugees accompanied them in their flight. When the R P F completed its conquest of Rwanda, in August 1994, there were about 2 million refugees, mostly Hutu, in camps in neighbouring countries: 270,000 in Burundi, 577,000 in Tanzania, 10,000 in Uganda, 1,244,000 in three huge camps in Zaïre. Inside the country, there were between 1.3 million and 1.8 million refugees. Thus about half the population of 7 million were refugees. Tutsi exiles returned from Burundi and Uganda and seized the empty villages of the Hutu.

In the following years, the internal refugees returned home and there was a steady stream of people returning from Tanzania and Uganda. The main population of refugees remained in Zaïre until 1996, when the Rwandan army invaded to clear out the camps (see the chapter on Congo). About 800,000 Rwandan refugees poured back across the frontiers. Many people who had taken part in the genocide were among those who returned, and Rwanda's intractable problem of hostility between the two groups continues. About 400,000 Hutu refugees retreated before the avenging Tutsis into the heart of Zaïre and many thousands, perhaps tens or even hundreds of thousands, were killed or died in the jungles. There were final massacres of Hutu refugees near Kinshasa (some even escaped across the river to Congo (Brazzaville)) before international pressure was brought to bear on the new Congo government to protect them.

The civil war resumed in Rwanda in 1996 and 1997. This time, Hutu guerrillas crossing the borders would attack and massacre Tutsis in their villages, or individual Tutsis living among the general Hutu population. The only thing standing in the way of a resumption of the genocide is the R P F government in Kigali, which strives ineffectively to restore civil society and reach an accommodation with the Hutu. The U N has set up a war crimes tribunal in Arusha, but it proceeds slowly and ineffectively. The people who carried out the genocide have little to fear as they prepare to resume the work. On 11 December 1997, Hutu militiamen attacked a Tutsi refugee camp near the border with Congo and killed 231 people. It happened that the American secretary of state, Madeleine Albright, arrived in Kigali a few hours later. She said nothing to suggest that the United States would exert itself to prevent a new genocide in Rwanda, or in Burundi.

There has been a civil war in Burundi ever since the murder of the Hutu president in 1993. The Tutsi army has been responsible for numerous massacres of Hutus. In a particularly violent outbreak in 1995, the army drove out almost all the Hutu living in the capital, Bujumbura. There was a further outbreak of violence in the summer of 1996, leading to a coup, in which 6000 were killed. One estimate puts the death toll at about 30 a day in quiet times, much more in moments of extreme fighting. The total numbers killed since 1993 are about 150,000. The army resumed full control of the government in a coup on 23 July

1996 when the president (a Hutu), in fear for his life, took refuge in the American embassy. Major Paul Buyoya, who had been president from 1987 to 1993, when he handed over to a Hutu, was persuaded to resume the office.

## FURTHER READING

American University, *Rwanda, A Country Study*, Washington, 1969.

Destexhe, Alain, *Rwanda and Genocide in the Twentieth Century*, New York, NYU Press, 1995.

Kay, Reginald, *Burundi Since the Genocide*, London, Minority Rights Group, 1987.

Keane, Fergal, *Season of Blood, A Rwandan Journey*, New York, Viking, 1996.

Lemarchand, René, *Rwanda and Burundi*, New York, Praeger, 1970.

Lemarchand, René, *Burundi: Ethnic Conflict and Genocide*, Woodrow Wilson Center Press/Cambridge University Press, 1996.

Melady, Thomas Patrick, *Burundi: The Tragic Years*, Maryknoll, N.Y., Orbis Books, 1974.

Prunier, Gérard, *The Rwanda Crisis: History of a Genocide*, New York, Columbia University Press, 1995.

# CHAD

| | |
|---|---|
| Size | 490, 733 sq. miles (1,270,994 sq. km). |
| Population | 6.4 million. |
| GNP per capita | $180. |
| Refugees | 15,000 refugees in other countries. |
| Casualties | About 50,000 Chadians and Libyans have been killed in the civil wars and foreign interventions since 1965. |

Chad suffers from all the woes of Africa. It is utterly impoverished. There are rumours of oil and uranium, but they have never been substantiated; and the estimated per capita income is $180 a year. There are no more than two or three other nations on Earth so completely destitute. And like many other African states, it is wracked by hatred, between the Arab north and the Christian and animist south. The northern tribes are bitterly divided among themselves and have fought constantly for supremacy – and there has been a ceaseless struggle for power among the leaders of the major southern tribe, the Sara. In 1979, the government disintegrated completely and had to be replaced by a bewildering sequence of African 'peace-keeping forces'.

France, the former colonial power, has come to the rescue of the government on four occasions, and Libya has invaded twice, in 1980–1 occupying the capital for a year. The United States, too, has intervened twice. Chad, which is largely desert, also suffered frightfully from the great drought of the early 1970s, which returned in 1984 and again in 1988.

In 1989, a coup backed by Libya installed a new government, led by Idriss Debey, which has maintained itself ever since.

## HISTORY

The only reason for Chad's existence is that the French did not occupy Tripolitania and Cyrenaica (now combined to form Libya) in the 19th century. They annexed the rest of the north and most of west and central Africa, but the Italians took Libya and, in due course, laid claim to the Fezzan, the desert to the south of Libya. France by then controlled the western Sudan, the Sahel region stretching from the Atlantic to the Anglo-Egyptian Sudan in the east. Therefore the French and Italians drew some lines on the map to delimit their zones in the Sahara, and in the process, the wild Tibesti, one of the most inhospitable places on Earth, and populated by black Muslim nomads, was arbitrarily added to French Equatorial Africa (A E F). The only history that the two regions shared was that, for centuries, the nomads had raided south for slaves and had driven their unfortunate victims across the desert to the slave markets of Tripoli.

It was well into the 1930s before the French finally conquered the Tibesti, and when they abandoned the A E F in 1960, dividing it into four separate countries, the nomads found themselves amalgamated with southerners, of whom they knew little. The Sara, who were partially converted to Christianity, were the dominant tribe in the new state. Remembering the slave trade, they were deeply suspicious of the Muslim north.

The northern provinces – Borkou, Ennedi and Tibesti, referred to as the B E T – were administered by the French until 1965, when the Chadian government thought itself ready to take over. The new president, François Tombalbaye, an autocratic, incompetent and corrupt man, sent his fellow-tribesmen north to rule the B E T. The tribes there promptly rose in revolt. Tombalbaye tried to repress them, and as a result, part of the Toubou tribe, under their traditional chief, the Derde, took refuge in Libya.

## THE FIRST CIVIL WAR

The rebellion soon went out of control, and in 1968, Tombalbaye had to appeal to the French for help. The Foreign Legion therefore returned to Fort Lamy, the capital, and defeated the rebels. The French insisted that Tombalbaye institute reforms, restoring the privileges of the Muslim chiefs and appointing Muslim ministers. Most French troops were recalled in 1971.

The troubles continued, and Tombalbaye reacted by reviving animist customs among the Sara, making the cult of the Yondo – which involved particularly strenuous and unpleasant initiation rites – into a national religion. Tombalbaye persecuted Christian Sara who refused to participate – and resumed the persecution of the Muslims. He changed the capital's name to Ndjamena, and abandoned his Christian name, renaming himself Ngarta. In 1975, the army, which chiefly comprised Sara, deposed and killed him.

By then the north was in open revolt, and it was beyond the force of Tombalbaye's successor, General Félix Malloum, to defeat it. A loose coalition of exiled and rebel groups, called the *Front pour la Libération du Tchad* – Frolinat for short – had two armies in the field: the *Forces Armées du Nord* (F A N) and the First Liberation Army, in the east. In 1976, the F A N split between two leaders of the Toubou tribe: Goukouni Oueddei, son of the Derde of Tibesti who had fled to Libya; and Hissène Habré. This was chiefly the result of a clash of personal ambitions, which was brought out into the open by the annexation by Libya of a strip of Chadian territory, the Aozou. Goukouni acquiesced in the annexation; Habré opposed it. In the years that have followed, their dispute has nearly destroyed the country.

Goukouni was a traditional Toubou leader, an illiterate fighter with no interests beyond his native Tibesti. Habré had studied in France, and achieved worldwide notice when, in April 1974, he kidnapped a French anthropologist, Françoise Claustre, and held her prisoner in the Tibesti for almost three years, demanding arms from France as her ransom. It became a *cause célèbre* in France, **37** like other hostage affairs later, and much preoccupied the government of President Valéry Giscard d'Estaing. A French officer was murdered by Habré's men when negotiating with them, and Claustre's husband, Pierre, was detained when he tried to visit his wife in August 1975. The following month, Giscard sent another emissary to negotiate a ransom. The French offered 4 million francs ($880,000) and promised a further 6 million francs' worth of equipment. When the French dropped a radio transmitter into the Tibesti to facilitate negotiations, General Malloum accused them of arming the rebels and demanded that the last French troops be evacuated from the south. They moved over the border into the Central African Empire, conveniently placed to return to Chad when needed, and also to depose Emperor Bokassa, which they did in 1979.

The Claustres were released on 30 January 1977, thanks to the intercession of Colonel Khadafy. Later that year, in the first round of fighting between Goukouni and Habré, Habré was defeated and driven out of the BET. He took refuge with a few followers in the east. Goukouni, turning to Libya for help against Malloum, soon controlled most of the BET and, in March 1978, occupied its principal town, Faya-Largeau. He then sent his armies south, in conjunction with another rebel group, the Volcan (also supported by Libya), which attacked from the east. In this extremity, Malloum called for French help, and for the second time, France came to the rescue: 1500 troops were flown to defend the capital Ndjamena, and the air force was used to defeat the Volcan army.

Habré, meanwhile, had built up a powerful army of his own, with support from Sudan, and now Malloum invited him to join the government. Habré became prime minister in a Government of National Unity (GUNT), but the government collapsed in February 1979. Fierce fighting between Habré's and Malloum's armies devastated Ndjamena, and soon deteriorated into a series of massacres in which southern troops slaughtered Muslims in the capital. Habré's forces drove Malloum and his army south, where they continued to massacre Muslims. Goukouni's troops moved into Ndjamena and started killing the Sara. Between 10,000 and 20,000 people died during these events.

## THE FIRST INTERREGNUM

By now, Chad had no government. The Nigerians briefly sent an army to Ndjamena to keep the peace, and troops from a variety of other African countries, sponsored by the Organization of African Unity (OAU), put in fleeting appearances. In November 1979, after a series of international mediation efforts, a new government was put together with Goukouni as president, Habré as minister of defence, and the new leader of the Sara, Lieutenant Colonel Widal Kamougue, as vice-president. All three kept their private armies in Ndjamena, and soon Goukouni and Kamougue allied themselves against Habré.

The government again collapsed in March 1980. In April, France withdrew its last 1100 troops, and fighting immediately flared up between the rival potentates. It was during this period that the former CIA agent Edwin Wilson organized bands of European and American mercenaries to fly Libyan planes making deliveries to Goukouni's forces.

38      Habré was driven out of the government, but kept his troops in Ndjamena.

Sporadic fighting continued throughout the year, and deteriorated into full-scale civil war again in December. Goukouni then called on Libya for help, and Khadafy sent tanks, planes and troops to Ndjamena. Habré was defeated, and took refuge in Cameroun, immediately to the south. In January 1981, Khadafy announced a union between Libya and Chad.

## THE LIBYAN INTERVENTION

It is customary to denounce Libyan imperialism and Khadafy's megalomania, but in the case of Chad, he has a case worth considering. There is, first, the dispute over the Aozou strip in north-west Chad, a stretch of territory whose boundaries were first determined in 1935, in a moment of relative French weakness and Italian strength. France was then courting Italy as an ally against Hitler, and the border was drawn to Libya's advantage, but the French never ratified the agreement. Then Mussolini was evicted, first from Libya, then from Rome. When General de Gaulle took power in Paris, a new border was drawn, incorporating Aozou into French Africa, and the agreement was ratified by the British, who then controlled Libya. Colonel Khadafy professes to see no reason why a line drawn by the French and the British has greater validity than one drawn by the French and the Italians. On neither occasion, of course, were the region's inhabitants consulted.

Khadafy considers that the Tibesti has far more in common with the Fezzan than with Equatorial Africa, and it is quite possible that if the tribesmen were asked to choose between citizenship of Muslim and Arab Libya (annual income $7500 per capita) or citizenship of Chad, with a Christian-animist and non-Arab majority (annual income $180), they might choose Libya. That was the view taken by Goukouni, who controlled the BET from 1965 until 1988.

However, Khadafy did not just covet the barren BET. He wanted all of Chad. As for Habré, he would rather be president of impoverished Chad than a provincial leader of wealthy Libya. Goukouni, apparently, wanted both the economic advantages of the Libyan connection and the privileges of the presidency.

The southerners, now led by Colonel Kamougue, opposed the merger with Libya, and Habré sought support in Sudan, Egypt and, eventually, the United States to defeat it. Khadafy found himself in a difficult position, under bitter attack by the OAU, which accused him of imperialism. Instead of brazening it out, like King Hassan of Morocco in the former Spanish Sahara, Khadafy abruptly abandoned Chad in October 1981. The civil war promptly resumed.

## THE SECOND CIVIL WAR

Habré had by then built up his army again, with support from Khadafy's numerous enemies, most notably Sudan. He crossed the border early in 1982 and soon occupied the east and most of the north. On 6 June, his armies entered Ndjamena, and then it was Goukouni's turn to flee across the border to Cameroun. Habré proclaimed himself president and then set about conquering the south, defeating Kamougue and occupying the latter's headquarters at Moundou. Kamougue fled the country, and, in October, joined Goukouni in Libya to set up a government in exile.

## THE THIRD CIVIL WAR

Chad was at peace for almost a year, an unusual experience. Then in June 1983, Goukouni raised the northern tribes, and seized Faya-Largeau on 24 June, and the eastern city of Abéché on 6 July. Habré counter-attacked and recaptured the two cities at the end of July – and then Libya again intervened.

Habré was besieged in Faya-Largeau, and once more called for help. The United States became involved for the first time, sending two A W A C planes and eight F-15s to Chad to control Libyan air activities, as well as $10 million in other types of military aid. France, for the third time, sent troops and planes to Ndjamena. They rescued Habré from Faya (he was brought out on a Red Cross plane) shortly before Goukouni and the Libyans recaptured the place on 11 August. The French then sent troops to defend Abéché, and drew a 'Red Line' across Chad, on the 16th parallel, effectively partitioning the country. Habré controlled everything to the south, and Goukouni held the north, with Libyan help (though Khadafy strenuously denied that any Libyan forces were in Chad).

There was now a stalemate, and it lasted for a year. There were more than 3000 French troops and a squadron of Jaguars at Ndjamena, and Libyan troops in Faya-Largeau. A mediation attempted by the O A U in Addis Ababa collapsed in January 1984, when the rivals each insisted on his exclusive right to fly the Chadian flag. The drought drove the nomads into the towns, where an international effort was needed to keep them alive. Meanwhile, secret negotiations took place between Libya and France, and on 17 September 1984, Khadafy announced that the two governments had agreed to withdraw their forces from Chad within two months.

On 10 November 1984, the two countries announced that the withdrawal was complete (even though Libya had never admitted to having any troops there in the first place), but the U S State Department declared that there were still 5500 Libyan troops in Chad. On 16 November, President Mitterrand met Khadafy in Crete, with the Greek prime minister, Andreas Papandreou, as mediator, and accepted Khadafy's repeated assurances that all Libyan troops had withdrawn. The next day, back in Paris and with considerable embarrassment, Mitterrand had to admit that Khadafy had lied to him. (Presumably, the Americans had provided the relevant satellite photographs.) France declined to send its troops back to Ndjamena.

Chad then enjoyed two years of unparalleled tranquillity, with the beginnings of reconstruction in Ndjamena and efforts to revive the economy. At the same time, the French and Americans were building up Habré's forces, while the Libyans were constructing roads and air bases in southern Libya and northern Chad – both sides preparing for a renewal of the civil war.

## THE FOURTH CIVIL WAR

It came in February 1986, with an attack by Goukouni and the Libyans across the 'Red Line'. The French sent their Jaguars into action and beat off the attackers. After much threatening and manoeuvring, the *status quo ante* was restored. Then in October occurred one of the more remarkable episodes of the protracted war. Goukouni Oueddei apparently decided that he had had enough of dependency on Libya, and tried to make his peace with Habré. He was shot and wounded in Tripoli – 'while resisting arrest' – on 30 October. The Toubou of the Tibesti, who had followed him for 20 years, promptly changed sides and invited Habré to come to their rescue. It was the signal he had been waiting for, and he immediately began moving his troops north.

In the meantime, there was a renewal of the air war between France and Libya. On 11 December, Libyan jets crossed the 'Red Line' in an attempt to attack Ndjamena, and on 7 January 1987, French jets struck a Libyan air base in northern Chad. Five days earlier, Hissène Habré had launched his attack.

It was a remarkable campaign. Habré equipped his troops with small Toyota four-wheel-drive trucks, descendants of World War II Jeeps, each mounted with a heavy machine-gun or an anti-tank gun. The tribesmen rode their trucks like the cavalry of the caliphs, attacking Libyan columns from every direction. They were joined by troops loyal to Goukouni, natives of the region, who brought their Libyan-supplied arms with them when they changed sides.

On 2 January, Habré's troops took Fada, a crossroads in the desert. Among the booty they captured were dozens of Soviet T-55 tanks and six Italian anti-aircraft guns. On 19 March, a Libyan armoured column set out from an air base in north-central Chad, at Wadi Doum, to recapture Fada. The column was ambushed and destroyed, and when a second convoy set out to rescue it, from Faya-Largeau, it too was ambushed and destroyed. Habré's men claimed to have killed 800 Libyans in the two battles. Then they moved on to capture Wadi Doum on 21 March and, six days later, Faya-Largeau. The French and Americans provided arms for the offensive, and the French also gave considerable logistical support, moving equipment and weapons up from depots in Ndjamena to the northern front.

The Chadians killed 1200 Libyans at Faya, attacking over the sand dunes in their Toyotas, taking the Libyans completely by surprise. They took an immense booty, including scores of Tupolev fighter-bombers, MiG-21s, helicopters, three complete batteries of the latest Soviet SAM 13s and the latest Soviet radar, and over 100 tanks. They calculated that the value of all this was between $500 million and $1 billion.

By the end of March, Chad claimed to have killed 3603 Libyans and captured 1165, with losses of 35 Chadians killed. Many of those Libyans killed and captured turned out to be mercenaries. Some were Sudanese, who had no clear idea where they were, and 1700 were Druse militiamen from Lebanon, hired out by their leader Walid Jumblatt at a monthly rate of $500 to $2300 per mercenary; their families were assured of $50,000 if they were killed.

Habré's forces then proceeded to clear the Libyans out of the rest of the country. In June, the Chadian leader visited the United States and saw President Reagan. He was promised $32 million in aid, including Stinger anti-aircraft missiles. In exchange, the Americans were permitted to buy a selection of the captured Soviet military equipment, which much interested Pentagon specialists.

In August, Habré's men drove the Libyans out of the Aozou strip, but this last victory proved only temporary. The French had refused to provide air cover, and the battle was too far from Habré's bases. On 28 August, the Libyans retook Aozou and, for the first time, flew foreign journalists down into the desert to prove their victory. Habré avenged his defeat by sending a column across the border more than 60 miles (100 km) into Libya and destroying the major Libyan air base in the region, at Matan as-Sarra. The Chadians claimed to have killed 1700 Libyans, taken 312 prisoners (including an East German and two Yugoslavs), while losing 65 men themselves.

The O A U organized a ceasefire, which took effect on 11 September 1987. By American calculations, Khadafy had lost one-tenth of his army, 7500 men killed and $1.5 billion in equipment captured or destroyed.

## CEASEFIRE

Both sides prepared for the next war. The Libyans built bases and airstrips in the Aozou strip, while Chad improved communications with the north, and re-equipped its armed forces. The U S delivered Stinger surface-to-air missiles and the French continued to aid Chad to the tune of $70 million a year. They kept a small force in Abéché to deter attacks from the east, and a squadron of Jaguars at Ndjamena. They also endeavoured to persuade Chad and Libya to submit the Aozou strip dispute to arbitration.

Habré's old friend President Nimeiri of Sudan was overthrown in a coup in April 1985, and the Sudan gave Libya full support in its conflict with Chad. Khadafy also courted the government of Niger, to the west, and as a result, there was a resurgence of small-scale guerrilla attacks into Chad from both Sudan and Niger. On 8 March 1988, a Libyan attack on a Chadian border post on the Sudan frontier was repulsed with the loss of 20 killed and ten captured. The attackers were members of the 'Islamic Legion', a mercenary army formed by Khadafy of men recruited in west Africa, chiefly in Benin, Mali and Nigeria. Still more mercenaries, from other Arab countries, are serving in the Libyan armed forces. After the frontier skirmish, there was a large anti-Libyan demonstration in Khartoum, a reminder that the new alliance with Libya was not necessarily popular.

Meanwhile, Goukouni moved to Algiers and resumed negotiations with Habré. They did not succeed. Diplomatic skirmishing continued between Chad and Libya. In May 1988, Khadafy refused to attend the 25th anniversary of the O A U in Addis Ababa, where other heads of government planned to urge him to make his peace with Hissène Habré. Then as the conference opened on 25 May, Khadafy abruptly announced that the war was over, and that he would recognize Habré as the legitimate president of Chad – 'as a gift to Africa'. He said nothing, however, about renouncing his claim to the Aozou strip.

In the course of 1988, Khadafy tried to mend his fences with a number of his former enemies in the Arab world and in Africa, and in October, Chad and Libya resumed diplomatic relations. Habré treated the Libyans with great caution: he urged the French to keep their garrison and air contingent in Ndjamena, although the French were anxious to recall them; he also kept the 2000 or so Libyan prisoners of war he had captured in 1987. He continued to insist that Libya must give up its claim to the Aozou strip before he would return the PoWs and send the French home. Khadafy remained as unpredictable as ever. However, during the war with Chad and the confrontation with the United States, he had discovered the inconvenience of his international isolation, and was now trying to end it.

On 6 March 1990, Libya and Sudan signed a treaty of intent to merge the two countries. The union is not likely to last much longer than Libya's earlier mergers with Tunisia, Morocco and Egypt but in the short run it gave Khadafy the base he needed in the Darfur, in eastern Sudan, to launch a new attack on Chad. Less than three weeks later, on 25 March, a group of rebels crossed the frontier from Sudan and marched towards the capital. They were defeated. This was their second invasion: they had attempted an incursion the previous November.

They were led by Idriss Debey, former chief of staff of the army who had played a great role in the war with Libya. He had already tried one coup against Habré, in 1989, and failed. His associates on that occasion, the army commander and the minister of the interior, were captured and shot but Debey managed to escape over the border. Later that year, the Chadians had raided Debey's bases in the Darfur. After his failure in March, Debey fell back on his bases, and rearmed for the next assault. It occurred in November, and this time it was successful. The French did not intervene. Debey's Patriotic Salvation Movement won a big victory at Abéché on 29 November, and Habré himself barely escaped capture. He and his followers fled over the border to Cameroun on 1 December, and the next day Debey entered Ndjamena in a black Mercedes.

Debey, like Habré, is from northern Chad, but from a different tribe. He is of the Zaghawa, while Habré is a Goran. Their dispute, like the earlier dispute between Habré and Goukouni, is personal and tribal much more than ideological or political. Debey was supported by France and by Libya. Debey promptly released the 450 Libyan prisoners of war remaining. The first attempted coup against the new regime occurred in October 1991, when the minister of the interior tried to seize power. Forty people were killed on that occasion. Two months later Habré launched a first attack across the border. He was defeated, and President Debey has retained power ever since, a record time in office in Chad. He won an election in 1997, defeating Widal Kamougue, the Sara leader from the deep south who had been briefly vice-president in an earlier coalition.

The territorial dispute with Libya continues but remains quiescent. The World Court rejected Libya's claims to the Aouzou Strip in 1994, but Libya paid no attention. It still occupies the strip and Chad has better things to do than start yet another war to get it back.

## FURTHER READING

American University, *Chad, A Country Study*, Washington, 1972.

Kelley, Michael, *A State in Disarray: Conditions of Chad's Survival*, Boulder, Colo., Westview Press, 1986.

Thompson, Virginia McLean, *Conflict in Chad*, Institute of International Studies, University of California, 1981.

Wright, John, *Libya, Chad and the Central Sahara*, Totowa, New Jersey, Barnes and Noble Books, 1989. (This work has a comprehensive bibliography on the subject.)

# CONGO (ZAÏRE)

| | |
|---|---|
| Geography | 905,063 sq. miles (2,344,104 sq. km), bigger than Western Europe, and about the size of the United States east of the Mississippi. |
| Population | 43.8 million. |
| GNP per capita | $120. |
| Refugees | There were 455,000 refugees in Zaïre at the end of 1996, most of them Hutu from Rwanda. There have been very large movements of people in and out of the country since then. |
| Casualties | About 100,000 people were killed in the 1996–1997 revolt that overthrew the Mobutu dictatorship. |

The overthrow of the Mobutu dictatorship in May 1997 was entirely inevitable. It had been predicted for years, and the only surprise was that the president managed to hang on for so long. The state was a hollow shell by the time the final crisis of the regime began, in September 1996. The economy was in ruins, the army utterly incapable of fighting, the police corrupt, the currency worthless, and Mobutu's foreign friends had abandoned him. The disaster was the fruit of over 30 years of government rapacity. The useful term 'kleptocracy' was coined to describe the Mobutu system of government.

When an organized army of rebels attacked across the eastern border from Rwanda in September 1996, the Zaïrian army offered no resistance. The rebels continued their advance over the next six months until they reached and took the capital, Kinshasa, in May. The new government was installed with little of the violence that many people had feared. Laurent Kabila, who had been a minor political figure in the first months after the independence that had been achieved in 1960 under Patrice Lumumba, and who had survived the fighting, the purges and the treachery of the ensuing decades, suddenly emerged from obscurity to become president.

It was immediately obvious that the country, renamed Congo, faced two immediate dangers. The first was that Kabila would be another Mobutu, meaning that he would be as dictatorial, corrupt and inefficient as the fallen ruler. The second was that the process of national dissolution would continue and accelerate, that the country would be torn apart by its neighbours, that provinces would again proclaim their independence and that Congo would split into competing statelets, none of them with the power to conquer the others. That was the fate of Somalia, and it is quite possible that it will now befall Congo.

Mobutu survived so long, and overcame four major rebellions, thanks to the unstinting support of the United States, and contributions from Belgium, France and South Africa. He fell when that support was withdrawn in the early 1990s. It remains to be seen whether the outside world will allow Congo to disintegrate with the same indifference it has shown to the wreck of the Somali state. Congo is far bigger and richer and it is entirely possible that there will be a new scramble for Africa among the ruins Mobutu left behind him.

## HISTORY

Conrad set *Heart of Darkness* up the Congo River in the late 19th century, but whatever the cruelties and conflicts of central Africa in earlier centuries, the greater darkness was brought by the Europeans. They robbed and brutalized the continent from the moment their ships ventured along its shores. They wanted gold, ivory and slaves. Arab slave traders, striking westwards from the coasts of Kenya and Tanzania, and south through the Sudan and the Sahara, did immeasurable damage, but it was the Europeans who carried off slaves by the millions and in the process corrupted the Africans by turning many of the tribes and kingdoms into their accomplices. Later, in the enlightened late 19th century, after the abolition of slavery, the King of Belgium enslaved the whole Congo.

Africa was divided up among the European powers in the 1870s and 1880s. The centre of the continent had been explored by David Livingstone, a Scotsman, and Henry Stanley, a Welshman, who mapped the rivers and lakes and made first contact with the local kingdoms of the interior. The coast had been known, and exploited, for centuries.

In 1876, King Leopold II of Belgium, a cousin of Queen Victoria, founded the International Association of the Congo, a consortium of bankers formed to exploit the Congo River basin. He hired Stanley to direct operations on the ground, who set up a series of bases along the river that later developed into the country's main cities. At the Conference of Berlin, which settled the boundaries of the African colonies in 1884–5, the powers recognized the Association's private colony as an independent entity. Leopold renamed it the Congo Free State.

It was not free and it was not a state. It was a colony that the King of Belgium ran as a private possession. He recruited a local army (the *Force Publique*) to enforce obedience, and hired European officers to command it. The *Force Publique* went to war with the various kingdoms and tribes, reducing them one after the other to complete subservience. European companies were given rubber and ivory concessions and were allowed to use forced labour to build the roads, railways and cities, to clear the jungle and to harvest rubber and other tropical products. Hundreds of thousands of Congolese were thus worked as indentured labourers, a status barely distinguishable from slavery. Leopold's extraordinarily brutal rule was called *bula matari* in Kikongo, the chief language of the lower Congo. It means 'he who breaks rocks' and it marked the country indelibly.

After a profitable quarter century of unfettered despotism, Leopold was finally forced to give up his fiefdom as a result of a prolonged press campaign against him and pressure by the British government. Belgium took over Congo as a regular colony in 1908. The worst excesses of the past were ended, but **45**

Belgian rule was marked by a paternalistic indifference to the wishes of its charges until the very end. The motto was '*Dominer pour servir*'.

The end came abruptly. Belgium had done nothing to prepare Congo for independence, and was astonished by the 'wind of change' that swept over the continent, starting in the mid-1950s. The few educated Congolese founded political parties, and one of them demanded immediate independence in 1959. There were three principal parties: the *Alliance des Bakongo* (Abaco), led by Joseph Kasavubu, which sought to revive the ancient Kongo kingdom on the lower Congo; the *Mouvement National Congolais* (MNC), led by Patrice Lumumba, which advocated a unitary, non-tribal state (it was also Marxist and virulently anti-western); and the party of Katanga, led by Moïse Tschombe.

There were serious riots in Léopoldville in January 1959, provoked by Belgian heavy-handedness. The government in Brussels capitulated immediately, and proclaimed its intention of bringing Congo speedily to independence. The date was set as 30 June 1960.

A constitution was hastily promulgated, based on the Belgian model. Power was to be shared between president and prime minister, as it is shared in Belgium between king and prime minister. After elections in May 1960 the MNC was the largest party in parliament, and Lumumba was therefore made prime minister – but Kasavubu became president. The political battle between those two destroyed the First Republic.

King Baudouin attended the independence ceremonies. He was offended by a fiery speech Lumumba delivered, and in turn offended the Congolese by lecturing them on the need to continue to pay close heed to the advice of their former colonial masters. The Belgian commander of the *Force Publique* insisted that independence changed nothing. His troops mutinied on 9 July and attacked their white officers, and then European settlers in Léopoldville and the provinces. Congo slid rapidly into chaos. The country's two richest provinces, Katanga in the south and Kivu in the east, seceded on 11 July. Katanga's leader, Moïse Tschombe, was heavily backed by Belgian and British–South African mining interests. Belgian paratroopers returned to Léopoldville to protect Europeans from massacre, and Lumumba called in the United Nations to help keep the country together and threatened to call in the Soviets if the UN did not help him.

A Security Council resolution on 14 July authorized the secretary-general, Dag Hammarskjöld, to respond, and by the 20th, Belgian troops had been withdrawn and the first of a large UN contingent had arrived. It was the biggest UN operation since the Korean war – and its costly failure cast a shadow on all future UN endeavours.

Lumumba wanted the UN to repress the Katanga secession, which it eventually did. Before then, however, the central government fell apart. Lumumba called in Soviet advisers and on 14 September, Kasavubu fired him. Parliament refused to ratify the dismissal and instead impeached Kasavubu. At this point, the chief of the newly constituted Congolese army, Joseph-Desiré Mobutu, seized power. Lumumba was arrested and handed over to Tschombe for safe-keeping: Katangese gendarmes beat him to death, an event that aroused much public outrage across the world. The Soviets established the Patrice Lumumba University, a training school for Third World Marxist revolutionaries in Moscow, in his memory. Mobutu ignored all protests, and contrived to shift the blame for the murder on to Tschombe. Subsequently, the C I A revealed that it had plotted to assassinate Lumumba, but had not carried out its intentions.

The staff of the Soviet mission were expelled in their underclothes and General Mobutu (promoted from sergeant-major a few weeks earlier) pledged his total allegiance to the West. The U N force finally suppressed the Katanga insurrection, in January 1963, after Hammarskjöld had been killed in a plane crash in September 1961.

That was by no means the end of Congo's travails. Mobutu returned power to civilians, but they proved incapable of running the country. There was a new secession, led by a former colleague of Lumumba's, Pierre Mulele, in Kwilu and another led by Gaston Soumialot in the east. Soumialot recruited an army among Tutsi exiles from Rwanda and their relatives in eastern Congo (the same group that, 33 years later, brought down Mobutu). They invaded in January 1964, and at the height of the crisis, their troops, known as Simbas (lions), occupied over half the country. Their chief base was Stanleyville (later renamed Kisangani), where they rounded up hundreds of Europeans as hostages.

The central government collapsed and Tschombe was recalled from exile to save the situation. The man who had tried to break Congo apart now saved it. He recruited additional troops from his own former gendarmes, who had retreated into Angola when Katanga was defeated, and hired a large group of European mercenaries. A joint operation by the mercenaries and American and Belgian parachutists rescued the hostages and captured Stanleyville in November. In the climate of the time, this made Tschombe a Western puppet and he was roundly condemned by Third World leaders. That mattered less than the continuing instability in Kinshasa. Once again, government was paralysed by conflict between the president (Kasavubu again) and prime minister, Tschombe. Once again, the army took power, in November 1965. This time Mobutu intended to stay.

By then the rebellion in the east had finally petered out, after the Simbas made a last stand at Uvira on the shores of Lake Tanganyika. Che Guevara flew in from Cuba for a few months, hoping to impart some ideological and military discipline. He failed in both objects and left in disgust. One of the last rebel leaders to go into exile was Laurent Kabila.

Mobutu disposed of his enemies and opponents briskly. Some, like Tschombe, went into exile. He was subsequently kidnapped by his enemies and delivered to safe-keeping in Algeria, where he was kept prisoner, in flagrant violation of all international law, until his death. Others were jailed, or executed, like Mulele. A small group of Lumumba's supporters still operated in the eastern fringes of the country. Their leader was Kabila, who had been a member of the Kivu provincial legislature, but they, and he, were so obscure and powerless that they remained forgotten by Mobutu and the world until 1996.

Mobutu proclaimed a policy of 'authenticity'. This meant rejecting the colonial past and, at first, attacking the Catholic Church. He renamed the country Zaïre in 1971 and abolished all European Christian names. He called himself Mobutu Sese Seko and made himself a field marshal. He expropriated Belgian and other foreign holdings, a move that almost ruined the country. He allowed his friends and supporters to rob as much as they wished, and the **47** country progressively reverted to jungle: an unlooked-for result of the immense corruption of the regime was to save the rain forests in central Africa, for the moment.

Mobutu had steadfast support from the United States and South Africa and from western business interests. He intervened in the Angolan civil war in 1975, in an attempt to prevent the victory of the M P L A, and was defeated. After that, he supported Jonas Savimbi, of Unita, serving as conduit for clandestine deliveries of American and South African arms. As long as the cold war lasted and as long as the Soviet Union tried to play a role in Africa, Mobutu was needed to defeat them.

There were more rebellions and invasions. Katangan gendarmes mutinied and had to be put down by mercenaries led by the French condottiere Bob Denard. There were incursions across the border from Rwanda, which were repulsed with difficulty. Former Katangese gendarmes invaded Katanga (now called Shaba) twice, in 1977 and 1978. On the first occasion, the United States flew in emergency supplies to Kinshasa and the French airlifted Moroccan troops who joined in expelling the rebels. They retreated into Angola, taking 50,000–70,000 refugees with them. On the second occasion, the rebels took Kolwezi, in the copper belt, and in the confusion at least 100 Europeans were killed. The French sent the Foreign Legion to rescue survivors, and then cleared the rebels out of Kolwezi. The rebels retired again into Angola.

The kleptocracy continued and extended its depredations. Mobutu survived only because he was useful to the United States, France and South Africa (President Botha visited him in his estate in northern Zaïre, the South African's first excursion into independent black Africa). Then the Soviet empire abruptly collapsed, the cold war ended and South Africa abandoned apartheid. America, which had always protected Mobutu, now urged him to mend his ways and hand over to an elected government.

In the early 1990s, there were constant political manoeuvrings against the president. The leader of the opposition was Etienne Tshisekedi, whose power-base was among the tribes of the lower Congo. Mobutu periodically had him arrested, and then released him. He served briefly as prime minister but never succeeded in deposing Mobutu, who, in turn, lacked the power to suppress Tshisekedi's movement. The president continued to rely on the army to stay in power and however corrupt and inefficient it became, it was enough to keep control of the capital and the major cities. In the course of his reign, Mobutu had expropriated billions from the national treasury, to pay his supporters and to enrich himself: he owned large villas in France, Switzerland, Spain and Morocco. Money could not buy him health: he contracted prostate cancer, and was a dying man during his regime's own death-throes.

In April 1994, the presidents of Burundi and Rwanda were assassinated and Hutu extremists in Rwanda carried out their plan of genocide against the Tutsi minority in the country. Over half a million people were massacred. A Tutsi-led insurgency, based on Uganda, then fought its way south, capturing the capital in July. About 1.2 million Hutus fled across the border into Zaïre, including most

of the Hutu army. They set up a government in exile and trained for a violent return to their homeland, where they planned to complete the work of exterminating the Tutsis.

There was a large Tutsi community in eastern Zaïre, and the Hutu exiled army began attacking villages and slaughtering civilians. In 1995, the Zaïre government announced that all Tutsis were foreign. A year later, they were ordered to leave the country. This provoked the governments of Rwanda and Burundi (which were both Tutsi) and Uganda, their close ally, to back a rebel army, calling itself the Banyamulenge, whose first intent was to cleanse the refugee camps, drive refugees back into Rwanda and destroy the Hutu army. As its campaign advanced and the Zaïrian army proved incapable of stopping it, it expanded its ambitions and decided that it was an indigenous Zaïrian rebel group that would now overthrow President Mobutu.

A minor opposition group, the Alliance of Democratic Forces for the Liberation of Congo–Zaïre, led by Laurent Kabila, was recruited to give a dash of Zaïrian authenticity to the rebels – but senior military officers, and most of the troops, were Rwandans or Tutsis from eastern Zaïre. Mobutu was under treatment in France. There was no effective government in Kinshasa and the Zaïrian army was quite incapable of stopping the rebels.

By late November, they had taken the main Rwandan refugee camps. Hundreds of thousands of people streamed back home across the border, but other thousands, perhaps 400,000 altogether, controlled by the Hutu army, fled in the opposite direction into the Zaïrian interior. The rebels pursued them.

Remembering past victories, the government hired European mercenaries, this time Serbs who had learnt their trade in the war in Bosnia. It was not enough. The rebels took Bukavu on 5 March 1997, Kisangani (formerly Stanleyville) on 15 March, and Lubumbashi on 10 April. On each occasion, government troops fled at the rebels' approach. So did the Hutu refugees, and later investigations showed that the rebels slaughtered thousands of them.

By early May, the rebel army was approaching Kinshasa. Mobutu, returning from his hospital in France, appealed for help to his former friends abroad and to the opposition at home. Tshisekedi again became prime minister, and he and Mobutu both proposed to meet Kabila to negotiate a settlement. It was all fiction. On 17 May, Mobutu fled Kinshasa. He spent a last day or two at his home village in northern Zaïre, and then flew into exile in Morocco. He died there in September 1997.

Kinshasa fell without a fight, as the last leaders of the regime fled across the river to Congo (Brazzaville). Kabila made himself president and the rebel army restored order to the capital. Kabila restored the name Lumumba had used, the Democratic Republic of Congo, in an attempt to wipe out the memory of over 30 years of Mobutuism.

The world community recognized the new government, but the UN demanded to know what had happened to the Rwandan refugees. Kabila refused to allow international inspectors, and foreign aid was held up while the dispute continued. It was clear that the Tutsis in the rebel army had taken their revenge on the Hutus and that there had been a revenge genocide in the jungles as the refugees (including tens of thousands who had participated in the massacres of Rwandan Tutsis in 1994) fled the avenging Tutsis.

**49**

Disputes quickly developed between the Tutsi army that now controlled the country, and local forces. Tshisekedi was again arrested, by the new regime. Angola sent troops in to help Kabila (both sides perhaps remembering their Marxist origins) and tensions between Angolans and Rwandans grew steadily. Zaïre was not so completely without hope as Somalia or Liberia, because its enormous riches in cobalt, diamonds, copper and many other minerals ensured that foreign companies would supply money to anyone who could guarantee the safety of their operations. All the same, the economy, infrastructure, health system, schools, police, civil service and foreign service had ceased to function. It was fairly clear that Kabila was not the man to fill the void, even if he was not totally the puppet of the Tutsis who had carried him to Kinshasa. Who might emerge, and whether a functioning government could be restored, was quite unclear. The only certainty was that Congo's sufferings would continue for many years.

# ETHIOPIA

| | |
|---|---|
| Size | 471,776 sq. miles (1,221,875 sq. km), the size of Spain, Portugal and France together. |
| Population | 56.4 million: including about 9 million Amhara, 15 million Oromo, 4 million Eritreans, and 5 million Tigreans. Over 70 languages and over 200 dialects are spoken. |
| GNP per capita | $100. |
| Refugees | There are 240,000 refugees from Somalia in Ethiopia, 70,000 from Sudan, 10,000 from Djibuti and 8000 from Kenya. 800,000 Ethiopian refugees have returned home since 1991. There are still about 55,000 internal refugees. |
| Casualties | The revolution, the four secessionist wars and the famines killed up to 2 million people between 1972 and 1991, 300,000–350,000 in the fighting in Eritrea. |

Mengistu Haile Mariam, ruler of Ethiopia since 1974, resigned the presidency and fled the country on 21 May 1991, to escape rebel armies that were closing on the capital. On the 27th, the disintegrating Ethiopian army surrendered to the rebels and the first units of the Tigrean People's Liberation Front (TPLF) entered Addis Ababa. One of Africa's longest and bloodiest civil wars had come to an end, and the victors were faced with the task of governing a ruined country and dividing the spoils of war.

Mengistu was one of the leaders of the *coup d'état* of 1974 that overthrew the monarchy. He then eliminated all his rivals and made himself dictator, proving one of the most ruthless in modern history. He was faced with a secessionist war in Eritrea and rebellions in other provinces, and in 1977 confronted and defeated a full-scale invasion from Somalia. He survived so long thanks to the unstinting support of the Soviet Union and Cuba. When that was withdrawn in the late 1980s, his regime suffered a series of defeats. The Ethiopians were driven out of most of Eritrea, rebels took control of Tigray province in the north and in the spring of 1991 mounted a last offensive against the regime.

Ethiopia suffered a catastrophic nationwide famine in 1984 and lesser famines afterwards. The Marxism Mengistu imposed upon the country proved wholly unsuited to local conditions. Under Mengistu's rule, a poor and backward country became one of the most completely destitute in the world.

**51**

## HISTORY

Ethiopia is a mountainous country, with high plateaux and inaccessible valleys. Until the 1950s, it was known as Abyssinia. Its dominant tribe, the Amhara, were converted to Christianity in the 4th century and have adhered ever since to the Coptic Church, which also survives in Egypt. The Islamic conquests of the 7th century cut Ethiopians off from the rest of Christendom, and throughout the Middle Ages, Europeans heard legends of the wondrous kingdom of Prester John, lost somewhere beyond the horizon.

The reality was less glorious. Ethiopia was remote and poor, and its rulers fought constantly against other tribes. Their empire sometimes extended to roughly Ethiopia's present borders, and was sometimes restricted to the Amhara homelands in the mountains. Explorers of the 19th century discovered a land of extreme poverty and ignorance, whose paranoid rulers imprisoned their sons for fear they would rise in revolt. Among the explorers was the French poet Rimbaud, who travelled throughout Somalia, the Ogaden and Abyssinia from 1882 to 1891. He lived in Harar and sold guns to Emperor Menelik (who never paid him); he died of an infection contracted there.

Because it was so inaccessible, Abyssinia was left alone by European powers until late in the century. In 1868, the British in India, incensed by Abyssinian mistreatment of British subjects, mounted a punitive expedition against the Emperor Theodore. It was commanded by General Lord Napier, who conducted it like an excursion into Afghanistan. He loaded his guns on to elephants, and marched into the heart of the empire, building bridges and roads as he went, and laid siege to Theodore's last fortress. The emperor committed suicide rather than surrender. Their honour satisfied, the British then marched back to the coast and sailed away, leaving the Abyssinians to fight among themselves for the succession.

The eventual victor was Menelik II, King of Shoa (1844–1913), who crowned himself emperor in 1889 after his predecessor had been killed in battle in the Sudan. Menelik doubled the size of the empire by conquering fertile provinces to the south and south-west, and the desert Ogaden, peopled by nomadic Somalis, to the south-east. By that time, the Italians had seized Eritrea, and the French, British and Italians had established themselves along the coasts of the Horn of Africa. Abyssinia therefore remained cut off from the sea.

In 1895, in a moment of imperial *folie de grandeur*, the Italians tried to conquer Abyssinia. They were resoundingly defeated in the battle of Adowa in February 1897 – the only decisive defeat that the Europeans encountered in the scramble for Africa. The victorious Menelik signed treaties with his European neighbours, and Abyssinia was left to its own devices for the next 37 years.

Menelik died in 1913 and, after a period of considerable turbulence and international intrigue, was succeeded by his cousin Ras Lej Tafari Makonnen, who proclaimed himself crown prince and effective ruler of the country in 1916. He eventually crowned himself as the Emperor Haile Selassie in 1930. Evelyn Waugh reported the event for the London *Daily Mail*, and it later provided the basis for his African novels, *Scoop* and *Black Mischief*. One of Haile Selassie's titles was Lion of Judah: he claimed descent from King Solomon and the Queen of Sheba.

In 1934, the Italians under Mussolini concocted a border incident as *casus belli* and again invaded Abyssinia. This time, they had bombs and poison gas to defeat the Abyssinians, and they occupied Addis Ababa in May 1936. Then they set up Italian East Africa, which consisted of Eritrea, Abyssinia and Somalia. Haile Selassie went to the headquarters of the League of Nations in Geneva to denounce its members for allowing one of their number to be annexed by an aggressor. The British and French, wanting to keep Mussolini in the alliance against Hitler, recognized the conquest in 1938. Their perfidy was rewarded two years later when Italy joined Hitler, stabbed France in the back and occupied British Somaliland.

In due course, Mussolini met his just desserts. The British conquered Italian East Africa in a six-month campaign, taking 200,000 prisoners. After the war, feeling guilty about the way they had treated Haile Selassie, and influenced by the fact that the United States was now his ally, they handed Eritrea over to him in 1952, and also returned the Ogaden, which had been briefly reunited with the rest of Somalia. Ethiopia was then officially awarded Eritrea as a mandate by the U N. John Foster Dulles, the new U S secretary of state, remarked, 'From the point of view of justice, the opinions of the Eritrean people must receive consideration. Nevertheless, the strategic interest of the United States . . . [make] it necessary that the country has to be linked with our ally, Ethiopia.' Ethiopia had sent troops to Korea and offered the United States bases, notably a communications base at Kagnew, in the mountains near Asmara.

In 1962, Haile Selassie summarily annexed Eritrea. Ethiopia had at last reached the sea. All its subsequent sorrows, including the 1974 revolution and the deposition of the emperor, derive from this success.

## THE REVOLUTION

Haile Selassie's empire was a feudal relic in the late 20th century. The country's only exports were coffee and oil-seed, not nearly enough to sustain a large and developing country. The social regime, if not the monarchy, might have survived and modernized itself if the government had not been so corrupt and inefficient. As the emperor aged, he progressively lost control of his family and officials, who left the administration of the country to look after itself while they enriched themselves. A few reforms were decreed, but most of them remained paper enactments. Ethiopia was like Shah Mohammed Reza's Persia, only far poorer. It had no oil and only a tiny educated class.

Haile Selassie was sinking into senility, but refused to allow any competent prince or minister to run the government. One of his sons was killed in a car crash, another had a stroke and retired to Switzerland, and Haile Selassie, who was born in July 1892, never designated a successor.

The spark that ignited the revolution was a drought in 1972–3, followed by the 'Wollo famine' in which over 200,000 people were left to starve to death in Wollo and Tigray provinces. The government was quite incapable of helping them, and denied that there was any problem. In fact, grain exports from areas not affected by the drought doubled during the famine. The truth of the disaster was only known abroad when Jonathan Dimbleby revealed it in a B B C television programme.

In January 1974, a series of mutinies shook the army. The rebels in Eritrea had defeated it, forcing it to retreat into its few surviving bases, and the junior ranks were demoralized and resentful of their officers' incompetence. The government, unable to assert any sort of authority, gave in to every demand made by the mutineers. In March, there was a general strike, and by spring, the mutineers had arrested their senior officers. In June, they set up a coordinating committee with up to 126 members, representing all the units of the army. It was called the Dergue, the Amharic word for 'committee', and it progressively took control of the whole country in a 'creeping *coup d'état*'. Its chairman was Major Mengistu (or Mangistu) Haile Mariam, then aged 30. He was chosen because he was neither Amhara nor Eritrean, but Oromo.

Haile Selassie, then 82 years old and in his dotage, lost all his authority to the Dergue, which arrested his ministers. The Dergue then broadcast the BBC film on the Wallo famine to the Ethiopian people, to prove the emperor's unworthiness. On 13 September 1974, the Dergue deposed him, and he was driven away from his palace in a Volkswagen and imprisoned. He was strangled in his bed on 26 August 1975, and his body was buried under a toilet in the palace grounds. His bones were disinterred and given appropriate burial in 1992.

## THE NEW ETHIOPIA

The new regime had much in common with the old. It was secretive, dictatorial, brutal and incompetent. In November 1974, the head of the armed forces and *de facto* head of state, General Aman Michael Andom, an Eritrean, recommended that the Eritrean war be ended and that country abandoned. The other leading members of the Dergue, notably Mengistu (now promoted to lieutenant colonel), rejected this proposal and Aman was summarily shot. Two days later, on 23 November, Mengistu ordered the execution of 59 people (some reports say it was 82). The massacre was presented as a settling of accounts with the *ancien régime* and the defeat of a counter-revolutionary plot – and thus, retroactively, justifying Aman's murder. Most of those shot were the ministers, princes, generals and other notables imprisoned since the revolution, among them Haile Selassie's grandson. (In May 1988, the Dergue released seven surviving princesses, including the emperor's 79-year-old daughter and the murdered grandson's widow. Three others remained imprisoned.)

In July 1976, after further reverses in Eritrea, there was another attempt in the Dergue to change course and come to terms with the Eritreans, but Mengistu once again reacted by having his dissident colleagues shot. In September, surviving members of the Dergue voted to strip Mengistu of most of his powers. They neglected to have him arrested, and on 2 February 1977, he reasserted himself in a shootout at a Dergue meeting in which all his opponents were killed, including the head of state, General Teferi Banti.

Several political parties were formed in the wake of the revolution, among them the Ethiopian People's Revolutionary Party (EPRP). The Dergue itself only formed its own party, the SEDED (Workers' Party), two years later. After the February coup, Mengistu launched a 'red terror' against his enemies, and urban militia squads hunted down members of the EPRP. Eventually, at least 5000 youths, aged between 12 and 25, were killed in Addis Ababa. Another revolutionary party, the All-Ethiopian Socialist Movement – known by its Amharic acronym of M E I S O N – attempted a coup in 1977, lost, and was slaughtered by Mengistu's security police. The terror reached a peak in December 1977 and January 1978, and in the end, the E P R P and M E I S O N had been wiped out.

Immediately after the 'creeping *coup d'état*' had been successfully concluded, Ethiopia proclaimed itself a Marxist state and nationalized industries and collectivized agriculture on the Bolshevik model. The United States no longer had a use for its satellite communications centre and the new Carter administration, appalled at the regime's human rights abuses, suspended arms shipments in February 1977. In May 1977, Mengistu flew to Moscow and signed treaties of friendship with the U S S R and other Communist states.

The regime's chief concern was survival. The Eritrean People's Liberation Front (E P L F), supported by Sudan and Saudi Arabia even though it too proclaimed itself Marxist, had proved a highly successful guerrilla organization and had extended its control to the whole of the province, with the exception of the major towns. Between August 1977 and July 1979, the Dergue lost one-third of its army in Eritrea, and had simultaneously to fight off an invasion from Somalia, which attempted to conquer the Ogaden. (See below for the Eritrea war, and the chapter on Somalia for the war with that country.)

At the same time, the Tigray People's Liberation Front (T P L F) was formed, and it rapidly took control of the province, which is in the north of Ethiopia, between the plateau and Eritrea on the Red Sea. Since all routes to Eritrea pass through Tigray, this was a serious loss. Unlike Eritrea, Tigray was not necessarily bent on dismembering the state: the Tigreans had been part of the Ethiopian empire for generations and were not committed to secession.

The fourth revolt was uncompromisingly secessionist. The Oromo, who number about 15 million, one-third of the population of Ethiopia, made a bid for freedom with the Oromo Liberation Front. Potentially, that was the most dangerous of all the secession movements. Ethiopia's far greater population could, in theory, hold Eritrea and the Ogaden indefinitely and could survive their loss. Eritrea and the Ogaden have no resources and do nothing to strengthen Ethiopia. The Oromo provinces, however, are Ethiopia's richest. If they were to secede, Ethiopia would be restricted to the high, poverty-stricken plateau from which the Amhara emerged in the 19th century.

Ethiopia would not have survived these threats without the unstinting material help of the Soviet Union, and without Cuban troops. At the height of the war with Somalia, in the autumn of 1977, Cuba supplied 17,000 troops and the U S S R airlifted enormous quantities of military supplies to Addis Ababa. The Ethiopians were thus able to turn the tide and defeat the Somali invasion, and recover most of Eritrea.

By 1980, with the help of the U S S R and Cuba, the government of Ethiopia had re-established its control over the national territory, except for the disputed areas of Eritrea. The wars in the Ogaden, Tigray and Oromo provinces had degenerated into minor guerrilla actions, and Mengistu's government could attempt to put its house in order.

It most conspicuously failed to do so. In 1984, the regime celebrated its tenth anniversary with much public fanfare, just as the outside world, appalled, learned that there was mass starvation in the countryside, one of the worst famines of the century. Belatedly, the Ethiopian government appealed for help. Soon seven million people were being fed by international relief organizations. The US (but not the USSR) sent large quantities of food, and Bob Geldof organized a series of concerts to raise funds for famine relief. Despite all this effort, and although competent relief organizations were set up in Addis Ababa and in the areas controlled by the TPLF and the EPLF, one million people died.

## ERITREA

Eritrea covers about 46,000 sq. miles (120,000 sq. km) – about the size of Pennsylvania and rather smaller than England – and has a population of 4 million. Half of the people are Christian, and the remainder are Muslim. The Christians occupy the mountains to the west and speak Tigrinya, the language spoken in Tigray, which is related to Amharic. The Muslims speak Arabic and various other languages, and live on the Red Sea coast. Eritrea thus is no more homogeneous than Ethiopia itself, and its nationalism is largely the result of the Italian occupation and of continued oppression by the government in Addis Ababa.

Casualty figures of the internal conflict are impossible to verify. In 1983, Colin Legum estimated that up to 250,000 people had been killed in the fighting since 1974, and another 50,000–100,000 have been killed since then. The 66,000 refugees in Sudan were almost all Eritreans and Tigreans, and counting the internal refugees, and those deported by the Dergue, it is probable that over half the Eritreans were driven from their homes during the war.

## THE WAR

The rebellion began in 1961, even before Haile Selassie annexed Eritrea formally. The Eritrean Liberation Front (ELF) was formed in that year, and launched its guerrilla campaign in September. It was a primarily Arab-speaking Muslim organization, its militants coming from the educated classes in Asmara and Massawa, and from among those who had travelled or studied in Saudi Arabia or Cairo. From the start, the ELF was supported by radical Arab regimes, and as a consequence, suffered from the varying fortunes of Nasserites and Iraqi and Syrian Ba'athists and was frequently split and reconstituted.

In 1970 came the formation of a rival organization, the EPLF, whose members are chiefly Tigrinya-speaking Christians drawn from the highlands. Its leader is Isaias Aferworki. Both the ELF and the EPLF professed a Marxist philosophy, and they soon started fighting among themselves. Between 1970 and 1975, about 3000 Eritreans were killed in this war within a war, in which the EPLF prevailed. Various efforts in the late 1970s and early 1980s to unite the guerrilla movements all failed, partly because of the question of relations with the Arab world, partly because of the suggestion, promoted by the Soviet Union, that the Eritreans should negotiate a federal agreement with the Ethiopians.

During the early years of the rebellion, before the Ethiopian revolution, the

Soviet Union armed the rebels and sent Cuban advisers to train them, as part of their effort to destabilize Haile Selassie. The United States and Israel, which wanted to keep the Arabs away from the southern shore of the Red Sea, helped Haile Selassie. Israel continued to support the Ethiopian government to the end, for the same reasons of *realpolitik*.

There was a brief moment after the 1974 Ethiopian revolution when the Eritreans could hope that the new government would allow them self-determination. It ended with the assassination of the head of state, General Aman Michael Andom, who was Eritrean. Eritrean police and army units deserted to the rebels *en masse*, and Eritrean guerrillas infiltrated the provincial capital, Asmara, and almost captured it. They were only defeated after savage fighting with Ethiopian troops. The Dergue's decision to suppress the Eritrean independence movement, and its vicious methods, hugely stimulated the E P L F's recruitment drive: in early 1975, it had 6000 guerrillas, but within two years, that had grown to over 40,000.

Mengistu's first weapon was famine. The drought continued, and the Dergue used it ruthlessly against the Eritreans. However, the general confusion in Ethiopia was so great that the rebels were able to take over most of Eritrea, besieging Ethiopian troops in Asmara and in the two ports of Assab and Massawa, and controlling practically the whole of the rest of the province.

In May 1976, in desperation, the Dergue summarily rounded up 40,000 peasants and marched them against the Eritrean positions. They were slaughtered. In 1977, it seemed to the Eritreans that victory was imminent: Ethiopia was barely hanging on to Asmara and Massawa; the Somalis were preparing to invade the Ogaden; and the regime in Addis Ababa seemed on the verge of collapse. The Soviet Union was faced with an unpalatable choice. It had supported both Somalia and Eritrea for years, and with Ethiopia proclaiming its sudden conversion to Marxism, the U S S R strongly urged a federation of the three nations, a sort of Soviet Union of the Horn of Africa. Even Aden, across the Strait of Bab el Mandeb, might join. None of the principals showed the least interest in these Soviet fantasies. Eritrea wanted freedom, Somalia wanted the Ogaden, and Marxist Ethiopia wanted to hang on to all the conquests of the emperors.

The Soviet Union therefore changed sides. It abruptly stopped arming the Eritreans and Somalis, and instead swung its support behind Mengistu. The Somali invasion of the Ogaden was defeated, with Soviet and Cuban help, the Soviet navy shelled E P L F positions besieging Massawa, and by the end of 1978, Ethiopia had recovered most of its lost territory in Eritrea.

It did so on its own, with only material help, not troops, from the Soviets and the Cubans. Fidel Castro, who had been denouncing Haile Selassie for years and proclaiming the Eritreans' inalienable right to self-determination, refused to send his men to fight with the Ethiopians in the north. The 14,000 Cuban troops who had fought in the Ogaden war stayed out of Eritrea. However, the U S S R had delivered so much equipment that the Ethiopians, fresh from their victory over Somalia, were able to raise the siege of Massawa in July 1978, and reoccupy most of the rest of Eritrea by the end of November.

The E P L F withdrew into the north, abandoning its positions in the rest of the country, and prepared for the long haul. In 1981, there was a flare-up of fighting between the E P L F and the E L F, which ended in the destruction of the E L F.

The Ethiopian army mounted eight general offensives against the Eritreans between 1973 and 1988. Each was defeated. After re-establishing its positions and expanding and retraining its armies, the regime launched Operation Red Star in February 1982, with 140,000 troops. Ethiopian losses were very high (Robert Kaplan reports 40,000 dead and wounded), and despite all the assistance provided by the Soviets and Cubans, the Ethiopians were unable to occupy the E P L F's northern fortress. Subsequent offensives suffered the same fate.

In the winter of 1987–8, the E P L F launched a series of attacks on the Ethiopian army, inflicting heavy casualties and breaking through the Ethiopian front. In a tour of inspection, Mengistu arrested a number of officers, and had the commanding general, Brigadier General Taiku Taye, shot in front of his troops – *pour encourager les autres*. It had a disastrous effect on morale.

On 17 March, the E P L F mounted a general offensive. In a series of battles – during which it claims to have killed 18,000 and captured over 6000 Ethiopian troops, and wiped out an entire armoured brigade – it captured several cities, notably Af Abet, a garrison town and the main Ethiopian military depot in the north. The E P L F also captured enormous stocks of munitions, including 50 Soviet tanks. Among its prisoners were the Ethiopian army's chief political commissar in Eritrea and three Soviet officers – two colonels and a lieutenant (a fourth was killed). The E P L F took 16,000 Ethiopian P o Ws. It was the biggest E P L F victory in nearly a decade.

At the same time, the Tigrean rebels made major advances. The Ethiopians counter-attacked in May, and were repulsed. An élite airborne commando unit was wiped out and its commander killed. Mengistu called for volunteers throughout Ethiopia to fight in the north, and demanded that every Ethiopian 'voluntarily' contribute one month's wages or pension to the government to pay for the war. After signing an agreement with Somalia to restore diplomatic relations, he began to airlift troops to the north from the Ogaden, where, since the end of the Ogaden war, Ethiopia had permanently stationed 150,000 troops.

Except for Af Abet, the E P L F did not keep the towns it occupied: that would have invited the Ethiopian air force to bomb them. Instead, it returned to its northern stronghold with its booty, and further reinforced its control of the countryside. By late summer 1988, the Ethiopians had their backs to the wall. Their demoralized army had a precarious hold on Keren, north-west of Asmara, but the E P L F had bypassed the town. The Ethiopians' last line of defence ran from Asmara in the hills down to Massawa on the Red Sea.

The regime decreed that a band of territory along the coast north of Massawa was a free-fire zone – that is, anything moving there would be attacked from the air. Since this district was a principal grazing area for Eritrean nomads, the regime clearly intended to starve them into submission. It followed the same policy by other means in the territory between Massawa and Keren. Its troops systematically devastated that part of the country, and Eritrean relief authorities estimated that between 350,000 and 500,000 people fled their homes in the district between March and August 1988. The Ethiopians did nothing to help

them.

The war was inextricably linked with famine relief. During the 1984–5 famine, while 1 million people died in Ethiopia, Mengistu forbade foreign relief agencies to work in Eritrea and prevented the Ethiopian relief agency from operating there. The E P L F brought in supplies from Sudan and moved 100,000 people to camps on the border, where they could be fed. It was during those terrible years that Israel, aided by the United States and Sudan, rescued 10,000 Ethiopian Jews, the Falasha, from Tigray and Gondar – and from starvation and destruction. Famine returned in 1988, and this time about 7 million people were affected throughout Ethiopia, 3.5 million in Tigray and Eritrea. The government fed only those in areas under its own direct control, and tried to prevent supplies reaching areas controlled by the rebels. The E P L F, too, used food as a weapon. It retained the support of starving Eritrean peasants by feeding them, but despite this, in October 1987, E P L F guerrillas shot up a government food convoy outside Asmara: 23 U N trucks, carrying enough American wheat to feed 45,000 people for a month, were destroyed.

The U S and international relief organizations protested vehemently, and the E P L F promised to leave food convoys alone in future. However, in the next five months, a further 106 relief vehicles were destroyed, including many supplied by Live Aid, the relief agency set up by the Irish rock singer Bob Geldof. In March 1988, the Tigray rebels destroyed two of the three government-run food distribution centres in the province; when they captured the third, at Wukro, the Ethiopian air force promptly bombed it. At the same time, the government was trying to resettle 1.5 million peasants from Tigray and Eritrea in southern Ethiopia. Ostensibly, this was supposed to save their lives; it would also take them out of the reach of the rebels.

In April 1988, Mengistu expelled all foreign aid workers from the northern provinces, allegedly on security grounds and claiming that Ethiopian relief organizations were quite capable of handling the crisis. Western governments disagreed, and urged him to permit a resumption of international relief. Mengistu also declared a six-mile (10 km) wide area along the border with Sudan to be a war zone, and promised to bomb any vehicle seen there. Later, he relented to some extent, announcing that the ban on foreign workers would not include those representing the U N. During the 1984 famine, the U S had permitted the delivery of some food supplies directly to the E P L F through Sudan, and in the summer of 1988, the U S State Department intimated that it would now do so again, despite the danger from the Ethiopian air force.

The E P L F was initially a staunchly Marxist organization, but when the U S S R started to give unstinting support to Ethiopia, and Sudan and Saudi Arabia supported the Eritreans, its politics became less dogmatic. Besides, the failure of Marxism in other parts of Africa has been a dreadful warning. The E P L F's chief characteristic is now independence: it has at various times been supported and opposed by Sudan, the Arab states and the Soviet Union, and has learned to distrust them all. Its one steadfast ally has been Somalia.

The United States did not support the E P L F, partly because of its professions of Marxism, partly because it had its hands full supporting rebels in Nicaragua, Angola and Afghanistan. This unusual moderation did not help limit **59** the damage. The E P L F got all the weapons it needed from other donors and as booty captured from the Ethiopian army.

## TIGRAY

Tigray province, in the northern part of Ethiopia proper, has a population of about 5 million, 70 per cent of whom are Christians, the rest Muslim. The Tigreans were the chief rivals to the Amhara of Shoa, to their south, to whom they are closely related. The Emperor Theodore and his successor, John I V, were Tigreans, and Tigray only reluctantly accepted the rule of the Shoan king, Menelik, when he made himself emperor in 1889. When Menelik marched his army of 100,000 conscripted peasants through Tigray to meet the Italians at Adowa, they lived off the land; as a consequence, they left seven years of famine behind them. The Tigreans rebelled against Haile Selassie in 1943, and were put down with the help of the British, who bombed the capital, Makelle.

In 1972–3, there was famine in Tigray and the neighbouring province, Wollo, and over 200,000 Tigreans starved to death. It was the imperial government's incompetence and callousness during this disaster that precipitated the 1974 revolution.

In February 1975, opposition forces in Tigray formed the Tigrean People's Liberation Front, which began a guerrilla war against the Ethiopians. It had a strongly Marxist charter, proclaiming itself to be 'anti-imperialist, anti-Zionist, anti-feudal, anti-national oppression, and anti-Fascist'. It asserted that its goal was national self-determination, which was not necessarily secessionist.

The T P L F was opposed by a conservative party, the Ethiopian Democratic Union, and from 1976 to 1978, the two fought a violent civil war in Tigray, which ended with the complete victory of the T P L F. At the same time, the T P L F fought and defeated the Ethiopian People's Revolutionary Party (E P R P), a radical Communist party that was also fighting the Dergue in Addis Ababa. Many thousands of people were killed in these civil wars.

During the early years after the revolution, the Dergue was distracted by the war with Somalia. In the summer of 1978, the victorious T P L F joined forces with the Eritrean E P L F, and defeated an attempt by the Dergue to reconquer the two provinces.

In 1979, the T P L F captured several towns in Tigray and cut the road connecting Addis Ababa to Eritrea. With the support of the U S S R and Cuba, the Ethiopians retook the towns, but never recovered the countryside, which remained firmly under the control of the T P L F. In a major offensive in 1980–81, the Ethiopians ravaged central Tigray, driving the population from their farms and burning crops in an attempt to starve the peasantry into submission. The country was devastated, scores of thousands of people were killed or starved to death, but the Ethiopians failed to reconquer western Tigray. When Mengistu's offensive failed, the T P L F reoccupied the areas it had abandoned.

The same thing happened during the next Ethiopian offensive in 1983: the armies advanced from Addis Ababa, laying the country waste, but later in the year withdrew again.

The next year, 1984, was the time of the great famine, in which a million Ethiopians starved to death. Tigray suffered heavily, and those people who survived did so because of international relief operations.

The war continued to wash across Tigray. The T P L F controlled most of the country, while the Dergue held the principal towns and concentrated its efforts on the war with Eritrea – Tigray was always secondary. The T P L F applied its socialistic doctrines by redistributing the land in the areas under its control, trying to ensure the survival of the peasantry in time of war. When famine returned to northern Ethiopia in 1987, the war flared up with massacres and ambushes and a constant battle over food supplies. Some food for the starving peasantry came in from Sudan to areas controlled by the T P L F, but the Ethiopian government's attempts to bring relief and to extend its control all failed.

In the spring of 1988, as the E P L F defeated the Ethiopian army in battle in northern Eritrea, the T P L F mounted an offensive of its own in Tigray. It captured Axum, the ancient capital of the empire, and laid siege to Makelle, the provincial capital. By the end of the year, it controlled the whole province, except for Makelle and two other towns in the south. The Ethiopian army was reduced to defending the road through Tigray to Asmara and Massawa, abandoning the rest of the province to the rebels. In March 1989, the T P L F burst out of its home province and invaded Gondar, Wollo and Shoa itself.

## OROMO

Population estimates of the Oromo, also known as the Galla, range from 15 to 18 million. They are by far the largest national group in Ethiopia, and one of the largest in sub-Saharan Africa, and they dominate central, southern and western Ethiopia. They were conquered by Menelik in the late 19th century, and the emperor advanced a policy of converting the Oromo to Christianity and teaching them to speak Amharic. He was partially successful, at least with the richer classes. Mengistu is Oromo.

In the 1960s, there was an uprising in one of the Oromo provinces, Bale, that lasted for seven years. It required a large part of Haile Selassie's army to suppress. The Oromo Liberation Front was founded in October 1974, a month after Haile Selassie was deposed. It proclaimed the usual Marxist objectives, and announced its intention of establishing a People's Democratic Republic of Oromia. It was, to begin with, an essentially urban movement, drawing its support from students and the lower middle classes. Unlike the T P L F, it had little contact with the peasantry, but it hoped that it would soon develop a base in the countryside, where at least 90 per cent of the Oromo live.

## THE END OF THE WAR

The last act of the long tragedy opened in 1989 when the Soviet Union, which had spent over $10 billion in supporting Mengistu, to no discernible advantage for itself, informed him that it would support him no longer. The last 3000 Cuban mercenaries left the country in September. The army, in a last, desperate attempt to save something from the wreckage, mounted a coup against Mengistu in May 1989, when he was out of the country. The air force remained loyal and bombed the rebels. Mengistu flew home and directed operations against them. Hundreds of men were killed, and after the last rebels had been captured, the dictator exacted vengeance. Fourteen generals were shot, including the chief of staff.

**61**

A precarious ceasefire was arranged between the government and the Tigrayans and Eritreans. In September 1989 a first round of negotiations opened in Atlanta, Georgia, under the sponsorship of former President Jimmy Carter's Center for Conflict Resolution. Carter's efforts were enthusiastically supported by the USSR, which threatened to allow its treaty with Ethiopia to lapse in 1991.

The negotiations were not a success. Both sides refused to compromise: the EPLF wanted independence, the government wanted to preserve the state. The Eritreans announced that they would allow the ceasefire to lapse.

Early in 1990, the EPLF launched a general offensive against the government's remaining positions in the province. On 10 February, they attacked Massawa. This time, the Soviet navy did not intervene. The rebels took the city in heavy fighting, driving the Ethiopians to their refuges on islands off the coast. The port was closed, and large stocks of relief food stored on the docks were lost. The EPLF laid siege to Keren and Asmara, the government's last positions in the interior.

Despite that disaster, Mengistu managed to hang on to power for another year. The sieges of the last army bases in Eritrea proved long and difficult and the task of finally defeating the government fell to the TPLF. It continued its offensive out of Tigray, and in the summer of 1990 its armies reached within 60 miles (100 km) of Addis.

In September, rebel armies advanced through Wollo, on the road to Addis. The September battles cost the Ethiopians 20,000 men, three divisions, including the supposedly elite 102nd Airborne. The Tigreans also captured great quantities of weapons. One more victory, and the Tigreans would cut the road connecting Addis to Assab, its last port on the Red Sea, in southern Eritrea.

The TPLF then changed its name to the People's Revolutionary Democratic Movement, demonstrating that its ambition was not secession, but revolution. Its leaders were admirers of Communist Albania: all other European Communist parties were insufficiently pure for their taste, and they deplored the revolutions in Eastern Europe. They considered Gorbachev a dangerous revisionist.

In February 1991, the United States succeeded in setting up a conference between the Ethiopian government and the Tigrean and Eritrean rebels. It held its first meeting in Washington, and was much too late: the Tigreans, who had formed an association of six rebel groups called the Ethiopian People's Revolutionary Democratic Forces, launched a general offensive at the end of the month. They captured Gondar and advanced rapidly into central Ethiopia while the EPLF captured Asmara and invaded the far south of Eritrea and laid siege to Assab.

There was then a brief lull in the fighting, as the rebels consolidated their gains, and desperate representatives of the government hoped to salvage something from the wreckage in the peace conference, by then moved to London. The final collapse came in the middle of May. The Tigreans advanced on Addis, meeting no resistance, taking every town and garrison on their way. On 21 May, Mengistu fled the country, and took refuge in Zimbabwe, a few days before the London conference was to open. On 25 May, the Eritreans captured Assab, completing the liberation of the whole province, and the Tigreans reached the outskirts of Addis. That night, the Israelis evacuated the remaining 14,500

Ethiopian Jews, who had moved to Addis to escape the fighting. Mengistu had held them hostage there, as a last card to use in negotiations with the United States. His successors permitted them to depart, and Israel sent a fleet of jumbo jets to carry them to the Promised Land.

The peace conference opened on 27 May – and immediately closed. The United States recommended that the T P L F army enter Addis to ensure public order, and the Ethiopian army announced its surrender. The government could only protest: it has ceased to exist. Late that day, the rebels entered the capital.

Their leader, Meles Zenawi, was 36. He claimed that he was no longer a hard-line Marxist, and had now lost his earlier enthusiasm for Enver Hoxa of Albania. He faced considerable difficulties, among them the fact that Tigreans represent only about 10 per cent of the population. The T P L F will have to find allies among the Amhara and Oromo if they are to survive.

In April 1993, Eritrea held a referendum on its future. The government announced that on a turn-out of 98 per cent, 99 per cent had voted for independence. While no doubt a large majority of Eritreans favoured independence from Ethiopia, these Albanian majorities did not augur well for the country's democratic future – and its new president insisted firmly that there was no time for such frills as free elections, parties or newspapers. Independence was formally proclaimed on 24 May 1993, the second anniversary of the great victory over Ethiopia.

In Addis, the new regime struggled to cope with the horrendous problems left by Mengistu. In 1995, famine returned, and the government had to beg for help from international organizations that had tried to help in previous famines. Those former officials who had not escaped were put on trial, charged with murdering 100,000 political enemies. The army found the resources to clear Somali rebels out of several towns in the Ogaden and the government offered its good offices to mediate between the various Somali factions. In its first years in power, the new regime supported the government of Sudan in its fight against the southern secessionists, because Mengistu had supported the southerners. It swerved back to the traditional policy as Khartoum assisted rebels in Ethiopia and Eritrea and tried to assassinate President Moubarak on a visit to Addis in 1995.

---

## FURTHER READING

American University, *Ethiopia: A Country Study*, Washington D.C., 1981.

Bereket, Habte Selassie, *Conflict and Intervention in the Horn of Africa*, New York, Monthly Review Press, 1982.

Erlick, Haggai, *The Struggle over Eritrea*, Stanford, Calif., Hoover Institute Press, 1983.

Farrer, Tom J., *War Clouds on the Horn of Africa*.

Kaplan, Robert D., 'The Loneliest War', *Atlantic Monthly*, July 1988.

Lefort, René, *Ethiopia – An Heretical Revolution*, translated by A. M. Berrett, London, Zed Press, 1983.

Legum, Colin and Firebrace, James, *Eritrea and Tigray*, Minority Rights Group, 1983.

Moorehead, Alan, *The Blue Nile*, New York/London, Harper and Row.

## WORLD CONFLICTS

Moseley, Leonard, *Haile Selassie, the Conquering Lion*, Englewood Cliffs, New Jersey, Prentice-Hall, 1965.

Sherman, Richard, *Eritrea, the Unfinished Revolution*, New York, Praegar, 1980.

Waugh, Evelyn, *Scoop* and *Black Mischief*, London, Penguin Books.

# LIBERIA

| | |
|---|---|
| Geography | 43,000 sq. miles (111,370 sq. km). The size of Portugal or Ohio. |
| Population | 2.7 million. |
| GNP per capita | N.A. |
| Refugees | 400,000 in Guinea, 320,000 in Ivory Coast, 35,000 elsewhere. 1 million internal refugees. There are 120,000 refugees from Sierra Leone in Liberia. |
| Casualties | Between 100,000 and 150,000 people have been killed in the civil war since December 1989. |

Liberia is the oldest continuously-independent state in Africa. It was founded as a colony for freed American slaves in 1822, and was controlled in the colonial manner by the descendants of those immigrants until the coup of 1980, which was essentially a revolt by the indigenous people. In the 1960s and early 1970s, Liberia enjoyed rapid economic growth (5.5 per cent p.a.), a rate comparable to Germany or Japan, and it seemed possible that it might break out of the poverty that afflicted the rest of the Third World. These hopes were ended by the oil price rises of the 1970s and the effects of the coup.

Master-Sergeant Samuel Doe, who led a group of soldiers that murdered the president and many of his ministers in April 1980, became the very model of the incompetent and corrupt military tyrant. The economy collapsed and relations between the country's 16 tribes steadily deteriorated. Finally, in December 1989, a civil war began that eventually destroyed Liberia. Doe was hacked to pieces by his enemies in the ruins of Monrovia, the capital, in September 1990. Like Somalia, on the other side of the continent, red anarchy and the rule of the gun prevailed for the next seven years. Unlike Somalia, Liberia's neighbours did not give up their efforts to restore a semblance of normality, and they finally succeeded in staging democratic elections in July 1997. The country's leading warlord, Charles Taylor, won the presidency and is now faced with the task of reconstructing a country he played the chief part in destroying.

## HISTORY
The colonizing movement in early 19th-century America was intended to solve the perceived problem of black freedmen in America. These were slaves who had been freed by their owners, or had bought their own freedom and whose status **65**

was precarious and resented in the antebellum South. The preferred solution was to send them to Africa, and the American Colonization Society was set up in 1816 to that end. Starting in 1821, small groups of freed people were taken to the Grain Coast in west Africa, where they eventually established permanent colonies. Their capital was named Monrovia after the president and the country was called Liberia. Its motto was 'The love of Liberty brought us here', and the country's crest showed a sailing ship off the African coast and a conspicuously non-African plough on shore. The native tribes came to resent both.

There was never any serious suggestion that the majority of American blacks should be transported back to Africa, though many people, including Lincoln, toyed with the idea. There were too many of them. Liberia was exclusively the destination of freedmen, and of some people from British colonies in the Caribbean who made their own way there. They were joined by people rescued from slave ships by the United States and British navies, who had never been to America, and spoke no English. They were known in the new colony as Congoes.

About 6000 Congoes reached Liberia between 1822 and 1860, to join 13,000 who came from the United States or the Caribbean. A further 4000 arrived in the half century after the American Civil War. They formed a very small élite superimposed upon a west African tribal society. The Americans were always at the top of the heap, the Congoes below them and the indigenous people at the bottom. It is astonishing that Liberia survived. The Colonizing Society had no government support, which accounts for the small number of colonists. The ACS depended upon charitable contributions to finance its operations, and on the US navy and American diplomatic support to protect them from the incursions of their neighbours and uprisings among the tribes. They also needed the benevolence of the British, who had established a colony for freed slaves of their own, Sierra Leone, just to the north of Liberia, in the late 18th century. The colonists set about pushing the frontiers of their settlements into the interior, much as European colonial powers were doing all around the coasts of Africa, and by the end of the century had reached their present frontiers.

The colonists proclaimed their independence from the ACS in 1847. Liberia was immediately recognized by Britain, but not by the United States. Black ambassadors were not wanted in Washington before the Civil War. Lincoln finally recognized Liberia in 1862. The new country gave itself a constitution closely modelled on the American one, but the checks and balances of the original were soon abandoned, and an all-powerful executive came to dominate the government.

In the early days, there were several political parties. By the latter part of the 19th century, the True Whig Party had supplanted all its rivals, like the Institutional Revolutionary Party in Mexico. The True Whigs were the organizing force of the settlers who governed every aspect of the country to their own benefit. In 1944, President William Tubman took office and proclaimed an open-door policy, to encourage foreign investment, and a Unification Programme to bring the tribes into the mainstream. He and his successor, William Tolbert, who took office in 1971, had some success in this endeavour. Partly as a result, opposition to the continued supremacy of the oligarchy rose steadily, and soon affected the armed forces. In April 1979, there were serious riots in

Monrovia, provoked by a 50 per cent increase in the price of rice. Like many other African countries, Liberia had kept the price of its food staple artificially low. As a result, farmers did not provide enough for the cities, and it had to be imported. The cost of imports was bankrupting the country, and Tolbert tried to solve the problem by an excessive price rise. Between 40 and 140 people were killed in the riots, and Tolbert called in troops from Guinea to restore order. The government of Sierra Leone had been restored by Guinean troops the previous year. Tolbert then rescinded the price rise and set about suppressing all dissent.

On the night of 11 April 1980, 15 non-commissioned officers and two privates of the Liberian army, led by Master-Sergeant Samuel Kanyon Doe, who was 27, broke into the presidential palace and murdered Tolbert and 26 other people, most of them bodyguards. They then took over the radio station and announced that 'the Tolbert government is no more'. Monrovia rejoiced: there was a carnival in the streets, and no discernible regret at the overthrow of the old order that had governed Liberia since its origins. The new regime proclaimed itself a People's Redemption Council (P R C), released all political detainees, and arrested the leading members of the old regime. Their houses were systematically trashed by soldiers. Ten days after the coup, 13 former senior officials were taken down to the beach, in the full view of photographers and T V crews invited for the occasion, and an enormous crowd. They were tied to posts along the shore, and shot.

Doe ruled Liberia for ten years. To begin with, like many dictators before him, he promised a new constitution, free elections and economic justice. He modestly declined the title of president, preferring to call himself Dr Doe (he had been given an honorary PhD by a Korean university), and Chairman of the P R C. He allowed a variety of political parties, and held elections in October 1985. He then stole the election, giving himself just over 50 per cent in the vote for president, and his party large majorities in the Senate and in the House of Representatives.

The fraud was blatant, and Thomas Quiwonkpa, one of the original members of the P R C, who had been exiled in 1983, invaded the country from Sierra Leone and tried to seize power in Monrovia. He neglected to storm the executive mansion, and Doe managed to bring in loyal troops and suppress the revolt. Quiwonkpa was killed. Doe then had himself inaugurated president of the 'Second Republic'.

Liberia went downhill rapidly after that. The economy declined precipitously. In 1987, Liberia became the first African country to be suspended by the World Bank and I M F. Doe's policies led to increasingly serious tensions between the tribes. He was a Krahn, a group representing about 5 per cent of the population, and the core of his army was Krahn. Discipline was always a problem, as Krahn soldiers robbed and killed members of other tribes. On Christmas Eve, 1989, a former government official, Charles Taylor, who had fled the country after he was charged with corruption, invaded Liberia from the Ivory Coast, with 40 men. They claimed that they would restore justice, democracy and prosperity, and Taylor announced the formation of a National Patriotic Front to purge the country of Samuel Doe.

Doe's troops proved incapable of finding and defeating Taylor, and revenged themselves on members of other tribes who supported the rebels. Taylor was

**67**

chiefly supported by members of the Gio tribe (9 per cent of the population) and the Mano (7 per cent). The rebellion quickly spread across the country, and soon became a generalized civil war between the tribes. No one can offer any exact estimate of the numbers killed: guesses range from 10,000 to 50,000. Most of them, of course, were civilians. Taylor's troops took to wearing children's masks, to terrorize the population. By the summer, Doe had lost control of most of the country, and was reduced to the coastal plain around Monrovia. By July, over 375,000 people had fled to the Ivory Coast, Sierra Leone and Guinea.

Taylor had very little control over his forces, who set about a generalized pogrom against the Krahn and Mandingo (who make up 4 per cent of the population), who also sided with Doe. In revenge, Doe's troops slaughtered members of other tribes living in areas they still controlled. In May, the American government sent a fleet with 2000 Marines to be ready to evacuate American and other foreigners from Liberia. In the same month, Taylor broke through the rain forest and reached the coastal plains. On 23 May, the rebels took Buchanan, the second-largest city in the country, on the coast 90 miles (140 km) south of Monrovia. By then, another rebel force, led by Prince Johnson, was also approaching Monrovia. On 4 August, President Bush authorized the American fleet to evacuate remaining American citizens, and 125 people were taken by helicopter from the American embassy and from two CIA communications centres outside Monrovia. Most American citizens had left earlier, by chartered flights.

In July, Taylor's and Johnson's forces were fighting over the wreckage of Monrovia, while Doe remained in his executive mansion, defended by 2000 troops who had been trained by the Israelis. Most were Krahns. On 1 July, the Liberian chief of staff, Gen. Henry Dubar, fled the country. On the 4th, his successor followed him, and other government officials followed their example. On 30 July, Doe's troops stormed a Lutheran church in which 2000 Gio and Mano refugees were hiding, and killed at least 600 of them. Three days later, Prince Johnson personally shot a Liberian wearing a Red Cross uniform, in the presence of foreign journalists. The victim was handcuffed to a French relief worker, who was later released.

On 24 August, a multilateral force formed of troops from Nigeria, Ghana, Guinea, Sierra Leone and Gambia landed in Monrovia, in an attempt to restore order. They had to fight Taylor's and Johnson's troops. Taylor had been stopped ten miles (16 km) from the centre of Monrovia, but Johnson had fought his way into the city.

On 9 September 1990, Doe left his executive mansion, in a convoy of cars and armoured vehicles, accompanied by scores of heavily-armed troops, to visit the headquarters of the West African Multilateral Force. Johnson and a large contingent of his troops arrived while Doe was with the West Africans, and a firefight broke out in which 78 men, mostly Doe's bodyguards, were killed. Doe was hacked to death by Johnson's troops, who paused in their grisly work to wheel the dying man around the streets in a wheelbarrow before he was finally killed. The death was announced on the 10th.

There was now no government at all. After Doe's death, his Krahn troops systematically looted and destroyed everything that remained in Monrovia, killing hundreds of people. Meanwhile, Johnson's and Taylor's troops exacted terrible reprisals against the Krahn. Taylor proclaimed a ceasefire on 22 September and by degrees the West Africans succeeded in establishing some sort of order in Monrovia, but not in the countryside, which remained divided between the two rebel forces. Taylor and Johnson both declared themselves president. The civil war continued.

The West Africans backed a government set up by Amos Sawyer, who had been a courageous opponent to Doe over the years, and had somehow survived the civil war. He controlled nothing, however, and frequent bouts of negotiations between Sawyer, Taylor and Johnson always broke down. Monrovia, meanwhile, had ceased to be a city in any meaningful sense. By early 1991, international relief organizations had set up there and provided a minimum of sustenance to prevent mass starvation.

In 1991, Taylor's movement split again. The dissidents were led by Alhaji Kromah, who launched his own attacks on the Sawyer government. Prince Johnson was arrested by the Nigerians and sent into exile. In the course of 1992, the conflict turned into a full-scale war between Taylor's army (the Patriotic Front) and the West Africans as Taylor tried to seize Monrovia. The Nigerian-led Ecomog (the West African Economic Community's Military Group) used heavy artillery, bombers, mortars and tanks in attacks on Taylor's positions in Monrovia's suburbs and in the countryside. Ships of the Nigerian navy shelled coastal towns controlled by the Front. These actions kept Taylor out of the capital but failed to defeat him.

On 25 July 1993, the three main factions in Liberia (Taylor, Kromah and the Sawyer government) signed a peace agreement in Cotonou, Benin. It provided for a ceasefire to come into effect on 1 August. A five-member government representing the three was set up on 15 August. Ecomog's 11,000 troops were instructed to disarm the militias, but the agreement went the way of previous ceasefires. The war continued. Taylor controlled between 60 and 90 per cent of the country, but was now under attack by Kromah's faction. Sawyer resigned as interim president in March 1994, in despair at the impossibility of restoring any semblance of civil society. Six months later, in September, the Patriotic Front split again when a variety of militias attacked Taylor's headquarters at Gbarnga in northern Liberia. By then, there were at least six armed factions, mostly tribal-based, fighting each other for the ruins of the country. The estimates of deaths in the civil war had reached 150,000 and over half the population had fled their homes.

In August 1995, yet another agreement was signed by the various militia leaders, and this time Taylor was admitted to the provisional government and returned to Monrovia. So did Kromah and another militia leader, Roosevelt Johnson, a Krahn, leader of a group called the United Liberation Movement for Democracy in Liberia (Ulimo). They were all named vice-chairmen of the council. This time, the ceasefire lasted until the end of the year, when fighting between Johnson's and Taylor's forces broke out in the capital. That outbreak was contained, but the following April, full-scale civil war resumed. This time, Taylor and Kromah were allied against Johnson, who was supported by other warlords outside Monrovia. Johnson's troops held the main army barracks in the city, the Barclay Training Center, and Taylor's and Kromah's forces laid siege to it. The devastation in the city was worse than at any time in the war. Twenty thousand refugees poured into an annexe of the American embassy, and on 8 April, the U S sent in Marines and other troops to conduct an evacuation. They took about 420 Americans and over 1600 other foreign refugees to safety in Sierra Leone.

Kromah and Taylor split again in May: Kromah left Monrovia to rejoin his armies in northern Liberia, leaving Taylor and Johnson to fight it out. In June, Taylor attacked the Barclay barracks, and Johnson was flown out of the city by the Americans to meet Ecomog representatives in Freetown. They reached an agreement that he would evacuate the barracks and lead his troops out of Monrovia. In September, Ecomog installed a new Liberian president, Ruth Perry, who had been a minor government official under the Doe regime. She returned to Monrovia with Roosevelt Johnson, who had swung around to support her. Taylor announced that he would disarm his militia and contest presidential elections in 1997. He did, indeed, disarm some of his troops, including a regiment of artillery, in January 1997, a few days before the deadline set by the peace agreement, but most of his troops and those of other warlords kept their weapons in the bush.

Then the Ecomog, under a new Nigerian general, Victor Malu, intervened and began disarming the militias. One of the warlords, Alhaji Kromah, was arrested. Elections were held under U N and Ecomog supervision on 19 July, and Taylor won about 70 per cent of the vote. He at last became president, seven years after he had launched his rebellion against Samuel Doe. Ecomog remained in Liberia, to train and supervise the army and the government, and a former New York policeman directed a programme of training a local police force. Liberia entered a period of relative calm, but it depended on Taylor's moderation and the continuing presence of the West Africans. If they withdrew, it was entirely possible that the civil war would resume, or that Taylor would follow in the footsteps of Master-Sergeant Doe.

## FURTHER READING

Liebenow, J. Gus, *Liberia, The Quest for Democracy*, Bloomington, Indiana, Indiana University Press, 1987.

# LIBYA

| | |
|---|---|
| Geography | 679,358 sq. miles (1,759,350 sq. km). About the size of Western Europe. It is almost entirely desert. |
| Population | 5.4 million. |
| Resources | Libya has oil reserves of 21.1 billion barrels. |
| GNP per capita | N.A. |

This vast desert was one of the poorest countries in the Middle East until the discovery of oil. Then in the latter half of the 1970s and in the early 1980s, until the collapse of oil prices, it enjoyed one of the highest *per capita* incomes in the world. By any standards, it is still rich, with a *per capita* income of over $7000 a year.

## HISTORY

The relics of past civilizations are scattered along the coast, reminders that prosperity and glories do not last for ever. In the western capital, Tripoli, there is a small cemetery where some of the U S Marines who stormed ashore in 1804 in pursuit of the Barbary pirates are buried. There are more substantial traces of the desert battles of World War I I: the Italians, Germans and British fought back and forth across the country, particularly in the eastern province, Cyrenaica, before Rommel was finally defeated in 1943.

Libya was Turkey's last possession in North Africa, until 1911, when Italy seized it. The Italians fought a savage war against the Libyan tribes, driving the recalcitrant among them into the desert to starve. Mussolini, who hoped to re-create the Roman empire, completed the conquest, and excavated Roman cities buried in the sand, restored irrigation systems and built a triumphal arch (larger than Napoleon's) halfway between Tripoli and Benghazi: passing British soldiers later called it 'Marble Arch'. Mussolini also settled 300,000 Italian peasants in Libya, and its cities were for a while as Italian as Palermo or Naples.

By losing the war, the Italians lost their African empire. The British occupied Libya until 1951, when they installed as king the Amir Sayyid Mohammed Idris, the leader of the Senussi Islamic movement, who had led the resistance to the Italians in the 1920s. Mussolini had missed Libya's real wealth: oil was discovered in 1958, and rapidly developed. The British presence in Libya was progressively reduced, but the United States maintained a huge air base near

Tripoli, Wheelus Field, which served the USAF admirably for training purposes.

As Libyan prosperity rose by leaps and bounds, and as the number of young educated Libyans increased, the conservative Arab monarchy in Libya became increasingly anomalous, bordered as it was by Nasser's Egypt and Boumedienne's Algeria. It is surprising that King Idris lasted so long. He barely survived riots that broke out after Egypt's defeat by Israel in June 1967: a number of Libyan Jews were murdered, and the remainder, about 4500, fled the country. Idris was finally deposed on 1 September 1969 while visiting Athens, and replaced by a group of young officers, whose principal leader was Colonel Moammar Khadafy.

The new regime pulled down 'Marble Arch', closed Wheelus Field and ended Libya's Western alliances; the Italians lost their property and were expelled. Khadafy's first great coup was to nationalize the Western oil companies, and to force a substantial price rise. This example was enthusiastically followed by other Arabs and by the Iranians after the 1973 Middle East war, and Libya was suddenly rich beyond the dreams of avarice.

The price of Libyan oil had risen from $2.23 a barrel in 1961 to $2.71 in 1971. Khadafy was considered wildly extortionate in forcing the price to $3.42 in July that year and to $4.00 a barrel in April 1973. In the aftermath of the Yom Kippur war, when Saudi Arabia suspended shipments, Libya put the price up to $16.00 on 1 January 1974, and to $21.00 in May. After the Iranian revolution in 1979, the price rose to $34.00 in January 1980 and reached its peak, $41.00, in 1981.

Not only did the price increase rapidly, so did Libyan production. As a result, Libyan revenues from oil rose from $3 million in 1961 to $1.17 billion in 1969 (the year Khadafy seized power), to $2.2 billion in 1973, $8 billion in 1978 and $22 billion in 1980.

## KHADAFY'S LIBYA

Khadafy sees himself as the heir to Nasser but has been constantly frustrated in his ambitions. His foreign adventures have been uniformly unsuccessful, and although other Arab leaders have always been ready to take his money, they are not ready to take him seriously. At various times, Khadafy has signed treaties of union with Egypt, Syria, Tunisia, Chad, Algeria, Morocco and (the latest) Sudan, and treaties of eternal friendship with most of them. None of these treaties has ever lasted: King Hassan cancelled the union with Morocco in August 1986. In 1987, Khadafy began wooing Niger, an impoverished nation across the Sahara to the south-west.

Khadafy provoked a minor border war with Egypt in 1977. He later invaded Tunisia, which was far less able to defend itself, and the French had to send their navy to the rescue. He sent his armies into Chad, where they were defeated, and sent troops to the aid of Idi Amin in Uganda where, again, they were overcome. (These episodes are described in the sections on Chad and Uganda.) He has repeatedly intervened in the various revolts and wars in Sudan.

Libya was allied with the Soviet Union for many years, but constantly refused to allow the USSR to set up naval or air bases. Khadafy's dreams of military glory led him to spend billions on Soviet weaponry, far more than his armies could possibly use, and the Soviets made him pay in dollars, and in cash. His only close ally was Malta, which accepted Libyan largesse with delight and proclaimed its deep hostility to the West, while maintaining an incorrigibly Western society. Khadafy also professed undying admiration for Khomeini's Iran, although, as a devout Sunni, he deplores the ayatollah's Shiite heresy.

Khadafy considers himself a political theorist of the highest order, and wrote a 'Green Book' to prove it, modelled on Mao Tse-tung's Red Book. Green is the colour of Islam, and Khadafy's theories attempt to reconcile Islam with Marxism. He has imposed strict Islamic laws upon Libya, including the laws against alcohol. In 1973, during negotiations for a federation with Egypt, he mobilized the population for an 'Arab Unity March' on Egypt, to force President Sadat's hand. The Libyans fell enthusiastically into the spirit of the thing, and by thousands they drove their cars, trucks and Land Rovers to the Egyptian frontier. The Egyptians were prepared for them, with huge stocks of every sort of alcohol, which they sold to the Libyans for hard cash. Khadafy called off the invasion and the Libyans went happily home.

He once summoned an international conference to discuss the theories contained in his Green Book, and the serious problems facing the world. One of the first items on the agenda was the need to restore to Islam the Great Mosque at Cordoba, unjustly occupied by Spain since 1236.

Libyan socialism has been an abject failure. Khadafy has abolished private enterprise, including the private ownership of real estate, and instead of the traditional Arab markets, there are huge state stores where it is frequently impossible to find basic necessities. Because private market gardens are banned, there is fresh produce only when the state companies have imported it from Europe. These failures are the result of incompetence and doctrine, not poverty. Grandiose plans for new cities in the desert and for an industrial centre and port at Mizurata, on the Gulf of Sirte, have been abandoned or suspended since the fall in oil revenues.

## Terrorism

Khadafy would be merely an unimportant, eccentric figure on the world scene except that he has espoused terrorism as a means of furthering his policies. He has arranged for Libyan exiles to be assassinated in the Middle East, Europe and the United States. When a dignitary from Lebanon, the Shiite leader Imam Musa Sadr, was visiting Libya in 1978, he was murdered in flagrant violation of the Arab duty of hospitality. Khadafy has also sent truck bombs into Egypt to blow up the American embassy, and hired American terrorists, led by the former C I A operative Edwin Wilson, to train Libyans in the trade. He has subsidized and supported the I R A and various Arab terrorist organizations, and has attempted to foment coups in Egypt, Sudan, Chad and Tunisia, and the governments of the latter three countries had to be rescued by their allies.

In 1973, during the putative union with Egypt, a group of American Jews chartered the *Queen Elizabeth II* to tour the Mediterranean and visit Israel on the occasion of its 25th anniversary. Khadafy ordered a submarine in his navy, with Egyptian officers, to sink the liner. The captain promptly took his boat to Alexandria and reported to President Sadat.

Relations between Libya and Egypt deteriorated rapidly after the failure of the union. In 1977, Khadafy sent a series of saboteurs into Egypt, some of whom were arrested on 12 July. A week later, there was a skirmish on the border, in which, according to the Egyptians, 20 Libyan armoured cars and their crews were destroyed. Sadat decided that it was time to teach Khadafy a lesson, and he sent an armoured column to a Libyan base at Masaad, 5 miles (8 km) inside the border: 40 Libyan tanks were destroyed and 42 prisoners were taken; Egyptian planes also shot down two Libyan fighters. The next day, the Egyptian air force mounted a full-scale attack on a major Libyan air base, at El Adem, near Tobruk; three Soviet advisers were reportedly killed. Sadat blamed 'that very strange person', Khadafy, and said, 'Yesterday and today our armed forces gave him a lesson he should never forget.' There were further Egyptian air attacks on 23 and 24 July, in which a large number of Libyan planes were destroyed, with an admitted Egyptian loss of two planes. Libya mobilized 30,000 reservists, and Egypt moved an armoured division up to the border. On the 24th, Sadat announced a unilateral ceasefire.

After his troubles with Egypt, Khadafy united Libya with Tunisia. This union collapsed in 1978 and on 27 January 1980, a raid was mounted against Gafsa in southern Tunisia, carried out by 50 commandos, either Libyans or exiled Tunisians trained in Libya. The attack was well planned and skilfully executed. The raiders came over the border from Algeria and attacked the police station, an army barracks, and a militia barracks, killing 41 people, mostly military men; then they escaped back to Libya. The French sent a small naval squadron to Tunis, in case Libya planned further hostilities, and on 4 February, a Libyan mob burned the French embassy in Tripoli and the consulate in Benghazi. In the event, possibly because of the French presence, there was no repeat of the raid.

Libya's reaction was standard operating procedure. Whenever there is a dispute with a foreign government, a mob is called out to burn its embassy in Tripoli – the British and American embassies were both burned before those countries broke off diplomatic relations with Libya. Khadafy has used his own embassies for nefarious purposes: he turned the one in London into a base for terrorists, and when a group of Libyan exiles mounted a demonstration outside on 17 April 1984, protesting against the public hanging of two Libyan students in Tripoli, a gunman inside the embassy shot and killed a London policewoman, who had been keeping the peace, and wounded 11 other people.

In July 1984, a number of mines were found in the Red Sea. They did a certain amount of damage to shipping, and had to be laboriously cleared by an international fleet of mine-sweepers including American, British, Soviet and French vessels. A Libyan ship had passed through the Red Sea just before the first mine was found, and it seems most likely that the mining was Khadafy's doing, another anti-Egyptian gesture.

Khadafy assumed that he led a charmed life, and was oblivious to the geographic and political realities of his situation. Libya is one of the most strategically vulnerable countries of the world, with all its cities and resources strung out along a 1500-mile (2400 km) coastline, and with an army and air force quite inadequate to defend them. The other states most strongly suspected of promoting terrorism – Syria and Iran – are geographically and militarily far better protected, as the United States has discovered. Furthermore, none of Khadafy's expensively bought allies would lift a finger to help him.

In 1981, in a moment of slightly comic panic, the Reagan administration announced that Khadafy was sending hit squads to assassinate American politicians. Trucks filled with sand were hastily drawn up around the White House and Capitol, later to be replaced by hideous concrete barriers, all to protect those buildings against phantom bombers. There was never any real evidence that Khadafy had sent hit squads to the United States, although he had certainly done so in Tunisia and Egypt. He also helped and applauded Abu Nidal, the most ruthless of Palestinian terrorists.

The United States expelled the Libyan embassy in Washington in May 1981, alleging that it was harbouring terrorists. Later, President Reagan, on three occasions, sent the Sixth Fleet into the Gulf of Sirte as a warning to Khadafy. On 19 August 1981, fighters from a US aircraft carrier shot down two Libyan planes that had attacked them (unsuccessfully) with air-to-air missiles. There was a further encounter between American and Libyan planes in the Gulf in February 1983, and the US then sent AWACs to Egypt to give early warning of any attacks by Colonel Khadafy against his neighbour.

In March 1986, the Americans sent an enormous fleet into the Gulf, including three aircraft carriers. Khadafy proclaimed a 'line of death' across the Gulf, which he claims is Libyan territory, and with remarkable foolhardiness sent several small ships of his navy to attack the US fleet. The Americans sank at least two Libyan vessels and took out a Libyan SAM missile base at Sirte after the Libyans fired six SAMs at them. There were reportedly 72 Libyans killed.

On 5 April 1986, a bomb exploded in a bar frequented by American soldiers in West Berlin, killing one of them and a Turkish woman. The Americans announced that they had evidence that the attack had been planned by Libya – evidence that, apparently, consisted of radio messages between Tripoli and the Libyan embassy in East Berlin which were read as orders to attack the American bar, and then congratulations at the attack's success.

President Reagan ordered an attack on Libya on 14 April 1986. For reasons that have never been adequately explained, the Sixth Fleet was considered insufficient for the task. (If a complete carrier group cannot take on so insubstantial an enemy as Libya, it can hardly serve any useful purpose in a real war with a real enemy.) Aircraft from the fleet were therefore reinforced with F-111s based in England. France and Spain, both Nato allies, refused to permit them to cross their territory, and as a result, they had to fly 2800 miles (4500 km), down the Atlantic and through the Mediterranean, to their targets. They had to be refuelled in the air several times during the raid, and were in the air for 14 hours.

The attacks wiped out a number of Libyan military installations in and around Tripoli and Benghazi, with the loss of one F-111 and its two-man crew. One of the chosen targets was Colonel Khadafy's personal headquarters in the El Azziziya barracks in Tripoli. A great deal of damage was done, and one of Khadafy's children was among those killed and two others were wounded, but his personal tent, pitched in the middle of the barracks, escaped. The Pentagon denied that it had targeted Khadafy personally, a denial that should not be taken too seriously.

The raid also demolished the French embassy, and damaged Romanian, Austrian, Swiss and Japanese diplomatic residences, to the considerable embarrassment of the Pentagon, which had boasted of the precision of its 'smart bombs', and which at first scornfully denied French reports of the damage. Afterwards, it emerged that five of the 18 F-IIIs on the raid and two of the 15 A-6s had not dropped their bombs, being unsure of their targets, despite all the elaborate electronics they carried. Within a few weeks of the raid, the Libyans had replaced the radar and SAM batteries they had lost.

Militarily, while the raid proved that the United States air force could hit a target far from its bases, it also showed that its accuracy was not nearly so great as it had claimed. The US did better in the Gulf War, five years later.

Politically, the raid was considered to be a great success in the United States. Colonel Khadafy was apparently seriously shaken by his near-escape and played little part in world politics for the next 18 months. He did launch two missiles at an American Coast Guard base on the island of Lampedusa, off the coast of Sicily (they missed); an American technician in the US embassy in Khartoum was shot and seriously wounded; and Khadafy's Lebanese allies retaliated for the US raid by murdering three of the hostages they held, two British and one American. Mrs Thatcher's popularity survived Labour party criticism of the use to which British air bases had been put, and American resentment at France's unhelpfulness was smoothed over later that year during celebrations of the centenary of the Statue of Liberty.

On 4 January 1989, two Libyan MiGs approached too close to an air patrol of the US Sixth Fleet and were shot down. The incident coincided with an international debate over an American report that Libya had built a factory capable of producing poison gas. For a few days, it appeared that there would be another serious conflict between the US and Libya, but for once, both sides decided that caution was the wisest course. It was two weeks before the change of administration in Washington, and Khadafy perhaps preferred to see how President Bush would react.

## LIBYA TODAY

There have been many attempts to assassinate Colonel Khadafy, and at least one fully-fledged coup attempt, on 8 May 1984: a group of commandos tried to storm the El Azziziya barracks, but were detected; they took refuge in a building in Tripoli, where they were all killed or captured. The Colonel's repeated failures to extend Libya's influence to its neighbours and, in particular, his humiliating defeat in Chad in 1987, have presumably caused much resentment in the army. Perhaps one day he will go the way of so many other Arab potentates, though it should be remembered that Egypt and the rest of the countries of North Africa do not have a tradition of resolving political disputes by coups or assassinations. Libya is not Lebanon, Syria or Iraq.

In the meantime, Colonel Khadafy has recovered his courage and has resumed interfering abroad. In 1987, he sent large consignments of arms to the IRA. On

30 October, the French navy intercepted a coaster, the *Eksund*, off the coast of

Brittany, which contained 150 tons of arms destined for the Irish terrorists, including 20 SAM-7s, 10 12.77-mm machine-guns, anti-tank launchers and 1000 Kalashnikov AK-47s.

The US raid does not seem to have modified Khadafy's more bizarre personality traits. At an Arab summit meeting in Algeria in June 1988, he wore one white glove, like the pop star Michael Jackson, so that he would never have to soil his hand by contact with King Hassan of Morocco, who had met the Israeli prime minister, Shimon Peres, to discuss the Middle East situation. The Libyan leader also pulled a hood over his head when King Hussein of Jordan spoke, and blew cigar smoke at King Fahd, who was sitting next to him. At a previous summit, at Addis Ababa, Khadafy had managed to offend the conservative Arab leaders by parading around town with a bodyguard of shapely female soldiers, who officiously protected him from the (male) bodyguards of the more traditional rulers.

In the course of 1988, Khadafy tried to improve relations with some of his adversaries. He reopened the border with Tunisia, and used the ceasefire in the Iran–Iraq War as a pretext to mend his fences with Iraq. He restored diplomatic relations with Chad in October (but did not abandon the Aozou strip). He also tried to reopen contact with Europe: he sent his deputy, Major Abdul Salaam Jalloud, to Rome in November to make peace there, in the hopes that, if Italy could forgive him for launching missiles against Lampedusa, the rest of Europe would resume normal trade relations. Perhaps he intended eventually to try to patch up his relations with Britain and the United States. Neither country showed any interest in such a prospect.

At the end of the war with Chad, 600 Libyan prisoners of war agreed to join an anti-Khadafy guerrilla force financed and trained by the United States. It was never used: when the Habré government in Chad was overthrown by pro-Libyan rebels in December 1990, the guerrillas were hastily evacuated, with the consent of the new Chadian president, and the United States had to find asylum for them.

New troubles were coming upon Khadafy. In September 1991 a French magistrate formally accused the Libyan government of organizing the bombing of a UTA flight over the Sahara in September 1989, including, among other suspects, Khadafy's brother-in-law. Then in October 1991 the American and British governments formally charged two Libyan officials with planting the bomb that had destroyed Pan Am flight 103 over Lockerbie, Scotland, at Christmas 1989. Khadafy refused to extradite the accused men. The three governments obtained a Security Council resolution condemning the refusal, and then set about trying to persuade the council to impose sanctions against Libya, which they described as a terrorist state. The United Nations imposed a travel embargo on Libya and forbade other countries to allow Libyan planes to land. It also imposed an arms ban and other trade sanctions while refusing American and British requests for a ban on Libyan oil exports. There have been frequent reports of riots and guerrilla activity in eastern Libya, and there was another attempted coup in Tripoli in 1993. Khadafy had no friends, and for the first time in several years began to worry about international retaliation against him.

## FURTHER READING

Blundy, David and Lycett, Andrew, *Qaddafi and the Libyan Revolution*, Boston, Little, Brown, 1987.

El-Kaiwas, Mohamed, *Qaddafi: His Ideology in Theory and Practice*, Brattleboro, Vermont, Amara Books, 1986.

Cooley, John, *Libyan Sandstorm*, New York, Holt, Rinehart & Winston, 1982.

Goulden, Joseph with Raffio, Alexander, *The Death Merchant*, New York, Simon and Schuster, 1984.

Harris, Lillian Craig, *Libya: Qadhafi's Revolution and the Modern State*, Boulder, Colo., Westview Press, 1986.

Maas, Peter, *Manhunt*, New York, Random House, 1986.

Wright, John L., *Libya, a Modern History*, Baltimore, Johns Hopkins University Press, 1982.

# MOROCCO

| | |
|---|---|
| Geography | 240,160 sq. miles (622,012 sq. km). About the size of France plus Benelux. The disputed territory of the Western Sahara covers 102,676 sq. miles (266,000 sq. km), about the size of Great Britain. |
| Population | Morocco: 26.5 million. In 1974, the Western Sahara had 95,019 people, of whom 74,000 were indigenous Saharawis, the rest Spanish. The Spanish left in 1975 and over half the Saharawis fled from the Moroccan invasion. |
| GNP per capita | $1,110. |
| Refugees | 80,000* from the Western Sahara and southern Moroccans in Algeria. |
| Casualties | About 10,000 dead since 1975. |

From 1975 to 1988, Morocco fought a continuous war to control the Western Sahara (formerly Spanish Sahara), a territory along the Atlantic immediately south of Morocco itself. Morocco had seized it after Spain withdrew, in flagrant violation of UN resolutions and the wishes of the territory's inhabitants. After the Moroccan occupation, a large part of the population fled to Algeria, and their political organization, the Polisario Front, formed an army to fight the invaders. The Front was supported by Algeria. There was soon a permanent stalemate between the two sides: the Moroccans held the towns and the territory's mineral resources; Polisario guerrillas patrolled the desert.

In May 1988, Algeria abruptly abandoned the Front and resumed diplomatic relations with Morocco. The UN proposed a ceasefire, to be followed by a referendum on the Western Sahara's future, to be organized and supervised by a 2000-man UN peacekeeping force. The proposal was accepted by the two sides in August. By the end of 1997, the referendum had still not been held.

## HISTORY
The Mediterranean and Atlantic coastal plains of Morocco have been urbanized since antiquity: Morocco was a Roman province. The interior was a different matter. The Atlas mountains and the Sahara desert were only occasionally controlled by the sultans in Marrakesh or Fez, and the settled cities were constantly threatened by the tribesmen of desert and mountain.

In the 17th century, the Alawite dynasty originating in the southern desert **79** conquered Morocco and extended its rule as far as Timbuctoo on the Niger and to most of what is now Mauritania. The empire did not last long: the Alawites were soon restricted to the Atlantic coast of Morocco and the principal cities. The modern Alawite sultans (now kings) of Morocco have used their ancestors' conquests as a basis for their claims on the whole of the Western Sahara.

Over the centuries, Moroccan rulers had constantly to resist encroachments from Europeans and from the Turks. In 1415, Portugal occupied Ceuta, the southern of the twin Pillars of Hercules marking the entrance to the Mediterranean (the northern is Gibraltar). Spain took over Ceuta in 1578 and has ruled it ever since. The other Spanish *presidio*, further east, is Melilla, which has been under Spanish rule since 1496.

Otherwise, Morocco maintained its independence until the late 19th century. By then, France had colonized Algeria, and France, Spain, Britain and Germany all coveted Morocco. France and Britain agreed to exclude Germany, and Morocco was then partitioned between France and Spain. Spain did badly out of the negotiations, with its sector restricted to three small areas: a narrow strip along the north coast, dominated by the Rif mountains, with its capital at Tetuan; a small enclave on the Atlantic coast, called Ifni, on the site of a short-lived 16th-century Spanish colony; and Rio de Oro, a strip of desert in south Morocco next to Spain's already existing colony, the Spanish Sahara. Tangiers, in the extreme north-west, was made an international zone, and for half a century enjoyed its reputation as the smugglers' capital of the world.

In the early 1920s, Mohammed Abd el-Krim rose in revolt in the Rif, and it took Spain half a million soldiers to defeat him. The Spanish army rebellion in 1936 was launched from Morocco by its commander, General Francisco Franco. During that conflict, Franco took Moorish troops across to fight in Spain, in what was the only substantial contribution that Spain's Moroccan empire ever made to the motherland.

France established the frontiers between Algeria and Morocco, much to the advantage of Algeria, which was considered part of France, while Morocco was only a protectorate. France also conquered the Sahara and established the frontiers between Spanish West Africa and Mauritania, which was part of French West Africa. Since Spain's colony, Rio de Oro, consisted of only one impoverished village on the coast (Villa Cisneros), France did not have to attend much to Spanish susceptibilities, and so was generous in awarding the Sahara desert to itself.

In 1926, a visitor found Villa Cisneros to comprise 20 houses and 28 tents. Its population was 150 natives and 35 soldiers, together with a captain-governor, a lieutenant, a doctor, a policeman, a chaplain and a representative of the Transatlantic shipping line. Spain had come out last in the 'scramble for Africa'.

The desert was richer than anyone suspected. Under the French allocation, Algeria got oil and the iron ore at Tindouf, and Mauritania got the iron at Zouarte: Spanish Sahara got the enormous phosphate deposits at Bou-Craa. Morocco was to covet all these riches, despite the fact that it already possessed the world's largest phosphate reserves.

One resource of the Western Sahara has been known for centuries: some of the world's richest fisheries are off its coast, with a possible catch of 2 million tons a year. In the Spanish period, the catch was limited to fleets from the Canaries and Europe.

## THE POST-COLONIAL PERIOD

After World War I I, France was faced with serious trouble in its North African empire. The Algerian National Liberation Front (FLN) started its war in November 1954, and in Morocco, an anti-French and anti-royalist Army of Liberation was formed in the Atlas mountains and in the desert to the south, and began operations against French positions. The French deposed the sultan of Morocco, Mohammed V, in August 1953, and replaced him with a more compliant monarch. The country quickly became ungovernable, and in October 1955, the puppet sultan was himself deposed, and Mohammed returned to his throne on 6 November. Disturbances in Morocco and Tunisia were distractions from the main event – the battle for Algeria – and in 1956, France gave Morocco and Tunisia their independence.

Spain was obliged to follow France's example, and abandoned its territory in Morocco. It left the north immediately, except for Ceuta and Melilla, and also agreed to leave the south as soon as independent Morocco could take over. The Army of Liberation then extended its operations against Ifni, Spanish South Morocco and Spanish Sahara, across the wholly artificial international frontier. The Spanish army abandoned all its positions in the interior of those territories, remaining only in Ifni, in a 12-mile (20 km) strip around the village of Sidi Ifni, which had a population of 24,000.

To begin with, the newly independent kingdom of Morocco was unable to assert its authority in the south, where the Army of Liberation was as much a menace to the royal government as it was to Spain and France. It attacked French positions in Algeria and Mauritania, and in February 1957, France launched Operation Hurricane to destroy the Army of Liberation in its bases in Mauritania and the Spanish Sahara. The operation was completely successful.

In 1958, when the Moroccan army was strong enough to replace it, Spain withdrew from southern Morocco. It abandoned its central African colonies, Rio Muni and the island of Fernando Po in 1968 (they became Equatorial Guinea), and ceded Ifni to Morocco in 1969. Morocco had already reclaimed Tangiers in 1960. Spain retained the Spanish Sahara and began to develop the phosphate deposits, which had been discovered in 1945.

When France gave Mauritania its independence in 1960, its new president, Mokhtar Ould-Daddah, claimed the Spanish Sahara. Morocco mounted a vigorous diplomatic campaign to assert its own claim to the same territory (which it called South Morocco) as well as to all Mauritania. It opposed Mauritania's admission to the United Nations and, later, to the Organization of African Unity (OAU), not recognizing it until 1969. The Arab League supported Morocco, but France's other former colonies in Africa all backed Mauritania.

Morocco was also embroiled in a dispute with Algeria, which became independent in 1962. Morocco laid claim to a substantial area of western Algeria, around Tindouf, which has some of the richest iron ore deposits in the world.

Furthermore, King Hassan was concerned that Algeria's radical Nasserite regime was a danger to the Moroccan monarchy. Hassan sent troops to occupy Algerian border posts immediately after the French departed, but the new Algerian army pushed them out. In September 1963, Hassan tried again, sending his army across the border into the disputed territories. The Moroccan advance got within a few miles of Tindouf before it was stopped.

After mediation by the O A U, a demilitarized zone was established along the border. Eventually, Morocco recognized the frontier established by the French, but relations remained cool.

In the 1960s, there was heavy investment in mining in both Mauritania and the Spanish Sahara. In Mauritania, the mines at Zouarte (near the frontier with the Spanish Sahara) were developed and a 420-mile (650 km) railway was built to carry the ore to the coast. It runs due south, and then west, parallel to the frontier. The phosphate deposits at Bou-Craa in the Spanish Sahara were opened up by a state-owned company, which built a 60-mile (100 km) conveyor belt to take the ore to a new port on the coast. The first shipments went out in 1972, at a rate of 2.6 million tons a year, and the company anticipated exports of 10 million tons annually by 1980.

## THE FOUNDING OF THE POLISARIO FRONT

Morocco's claim to Spanish Sahara remained latent until 1974. By then, an anti-colonial movement had been founded by young Saharawis who had studied in Moroccan schools and universities and had imbibed the revolutionary notions of the radical Arabs. They formed the Polisario Front in 1972, the name being an acronym for the *Frente Popular para la Liberatión de Saguia el-Hamra y Rio de Oro*. (The Saguia el-Hamra is a river which has given its name to the northern part of Spanish Sahara; Rio de Oro is the southern part.) Polisario launched its guerrilla war in 1973, with the help of a small consignment of arms from Libya, and in October 1974, it sabotaged the Bou-Craa conveyor belt.

Franco was in his dotage. He had seen the Portuguese Fascist regime overthrown in April, and the collapse of the Portuguese empire. He and Spain decided that their interests would be best served by giving Spanish Sahara its independence, following the neo-colonial example that France had established in West Africa. Spain expected that an independent Sahara would continue to protect Spanish investments and follow its lead, as France's former colonies were doing. Therefore, in August 1974, Spain proposed a referendum on the future of the Spanish Sahara.

The proposal galvanized King Hassan into action. He badly needed a success: he had barely survived two military coups in 1971 and 1972. In the first, rebel soldiers had attacked a royal garden party and slaughtered the guests. The king had hidden in a pavilion, where he had overheard soldiers discussing those evil plotters who had killed the king; he emerged, introduced himself and persuaded the deluded soldiers to arrest their officers. Then, on 16 August 1972, two air force fighters had tried to shoot down King Hassan's plane, on the orders of the Minister of the Interior, General Mohammed Oufkir. They missed. Oufkir was permitted to shoot himself.

## KING HASSAN'S GREEN MARCH

The king was still suspicious of his army and of the opposition. He appealed to their chauvinism and rallied them all behind his claim to the Spanish Sahara. He successfully bought time by submitting the claim to the International Court of Justice at The Hague. He thus persuaded Spain to postpone its proposed referendum and, eventually, to abandon it. He also sought support from his two principal allies, the United States and France.

These two countries wanted stability in Morocco above all. After King Hassan had committed all his prestige to the Spanish Sahara project, they feared that he would lose his throne if he were defeated. Furthermore, Dr Henry Kissinger and President Valéry Giscard d'Estaing opposed Polisario on principle, because of its leftist tendencies.

Spain, still under a Fascist government, reached the opposite conclusion. It wanted to protect its investments from the Moroccans and, after secret talks with Polisario, decided that it could easily work with a Polisario regime. Simultaneously, Algeria threw its weight behind the Front. The United Nations sent a mission to the Spanish Sahara, to gauge its inhabitants' wishes, and was everywhere met by demonstrations in favour of Polisario.

Morocco massed 20,000 troops on the border in the summer of 1975. Then, on 15 October, the UN mission announced its findings: 'The majority of the population within the Spanish Sahara was manifestly in favour of independence.' Polisario was clearly the territory's choice. The next day, the International Court of Justice ruled that there was no 'tie of territorial sovereignty between the Territory of Western Sahara and the Kingdom of Morocco or the Mauritanian entity'.

King Hassan reacted to these defeats with one of the more extraordinary modern examples of the Big Lie. He simply announced that the court had ruled in his favour. Then he called on 320,000 volunteers to join in a 'Green March' across the border to recover the Western Sahara. Moroccans responded with enthusiasm, and by 21 October, there were 524,000 of them in camps on the border.

At the height of the crisis, on 17 October 1975, Franco collapsed during a cabinet meeting. He was evidently dying, and the Madrid government was far more concerned to ensure a smooth transition at home than it was with the fate of the Spanish Sahara. The United States and France supported Hassan, and Spain broke its commitments to Polisario. It opened negotiations with Morocco on 21 October, and began evacuating the territory seven days later.

All civilians were evacuated; the Spanish cemetery at Villa Cisneros was cleared and the 1000 bodies moved to the Canaries; the animals in the Al-Ayoun zoo were sent to Spain. Spanish troops began withdrawing from outlying posts, and were replaced by Polisario units or the Moroccan army, which were soon fighting each other for control.

The Green March finally began on 6 November 1975. About 200,000 people crossed the border at several points, advanced 6 miles (10 km) and stopped. On 8 November Spain finally capitulated and agreed to abandon the territory to Morocco and Mauritania; in exchange, those two governments guaranteed Spain's economic interests. The marchers were then sent home. Negotiations with Spain were resumed on 12 November, and on the 14th an agreement was reached between Spain, Morocco and Mauritania, under which Spain would withdraw by the end of February, handing over the administration of the colony (but without renouncing sovereignty) to Morocco and Mauritania.

Franco died on 20 November. The Moroccans reached Al-Ayoun on 11 December, and by mid-January, Spain had completed the evacuation. By then, 40,000 Saharawis had fled their homes.

## THE WAR

King Hassan and President Ould-Daddah had apparently won. Morocco got all the valuable parts of the Spanish Sahara, while Mauritania had to settle for the Tiris al-Gharbia, valueless desert in the south of the territory, and Villa Cisneros, renamed Dakhla.

Both Morocco and Mauritania had underestimated the Polisario Front and failed to take account of Algerian intentions. President Houari Boumedienne had warned Ould-Daddah that he would support Polisario. The inhabitants of the Spanish Sahara fled the Moroccans. Over half the population were soon refugees in Algeria, where they settled around Tindouf, to whose population they were closely related.

Polisario stepped up its guerrilla attacks, concentrating on Mauritania as the weaker target. Polisario's military forces – the Saharawi People's Liberation Army (S P L A) – conducted raids across hundreds of miles of wasteland, just like the tribes of old, or like the British Long-range Desert Group which had operated behind German lines in World War I I. The S P L A even attacked Nouakchott, Mauritania's capital, 900 miles (1440 km) across the desert. The founder and secretary-general of Polisario, El-Ouali Mustapha Sayed, was killed on the first of those raids in June 1976. He was succeeded by Mohammed Abdelazziz, who remains Polisario's secretary-general.

The S P L A soon mobilized virtually all the adult men of the Saharawi refugees – 20,000 in all – and they were armed and equipped by the Algerians. They attacked the iron mines at Zouarte and the railway linking it to the coast, hitting it almost every month, and in May 1977, occupying Zouarte itself. Mining was soon brought to a halt, and Mauritania's economy, already suffering seriously from the effects of the great drought in the Sahel, was brought to the verge of collapse.

The Moroccans sent troops to help, occupying Dakhla to protect it from S P L A raids, and the French despatched their air force. French Jaguars attacked S P L A columns with lethal effect, causing the rebels to split into much smaller groups, and to travel only at night.

Mauritania's situation continued to deteriorate, and on 9 July 1978, the army overthrew Ould-Daddah in a bloodless coup. Polisario declared a ceasefire the next day. The new military regime wanted to end the war, but was unable to do so: it was afraid of Morocco. Its hesitations continued until Polisario broke the ceasefire a year after it began, on 12 July 1979. It once again hit the ore railway. The Mauritanian regime then abandoned the Tiris al-Gharbia and signed a peace treaty with Polisario on 5 August. Morocco reinforced its garrisons in the territory, including Dakhla and, on 14 August, announced that it had annexed **84** the Tiris al-Gharbia.

## THE POLISARIO FRONT V. MOROCCO

For the first two or three years after the coup in Mauritania, the war went badly for the Moroccans. The S P L A won a series of important victories by means of sudden attacks on isolated garrisons. On one occasion, in August 1979, they seized a base in southern Morocco and captured an immense haul of equipment, including 37 T-54 tanks.

S P L A units were soon armed with modern equipment by Algeria. They carried rockets, including Stalin Organs, in trucks, and attacked at will; Moroccan casualties were so heavy that the army soon abandoned over 80 per cent of the contested territory. By 1980, Morocco had established a defence perimeter around the 'useful triangle' of the Western Sahara, including Al-Ayoun, the phosphate mines at Bou-Craa and a short stretch of coast, including the new port of El-Ayoun Playa. A separate enclave included Dakhla in the south.

The defence consisted of sand barriers, two or three metres high and eventually about 1000 miles (1600 km) long, protected by minefields and barbed wire, with electronic listening devices and mobile forces patrolling to prevent any incursions. Morocco has an army of 150,000 defending the barrier. Behind it, the phosphate mines and the conveyor belt were finally reopened in 1982. Everything else was left to the S P L A.

Polisario's primary strength was (and is) its support among the desert people of the Western Sahara. Like the Kurds in the Middle East, the Saharawis lived in all four states of the region, while considering themselves one nation. By the time the war began, a majority had abandoned their nomadic existence, but the tradition remained strong, and they called themselves 'sons of the clouds'. The refugees around Tindouf, coming from Morocco as well as the Western Sahara, soon numbered over 100,000, considerably more than the remaining indigenous population in Morocco's 'useful triangle'. Those who had left were replaced by Moroccans, who moved south to benefit from the large inducements offered by the government, and to work the phosphate mines.

Polisario also depended upon Algeria's constant support. Algeria was too powerful for Morocco to attack, so the Front had a safe base across the border. Algeria, whose economy is two and a half times larger than Morocco's, is quite rich enough to arm the guerrillas and feed and educate their families.

Finally, Polisario enjoyed widespread diplomatic support. On 27 February 1976, it proclaimed the Saharan Arab Democratic Republic (S A D R), and set about a vigorous diplomatic offensive against Morocco. Soon, a majority of the members of the O A U recognized the S A D R, and voted to give it a seat in the organization. In 1981, in an attempt to hold the line in the O A U, Hassan promised to hold a referendum. It never took place. In February 1983, the S A D R took its seat in an O A U summit, but 34 other members walked out, in protest, and the meeting collapsed.

Morocco has been able to maintain its diplomatic position in the O A U and the U N with the support of an unusual alliance of Arab and Western powers. With the notable exception of Algeria, most Arabs upheld Morocco, out of a spirit of Arab solidarity. In 1984, Libya, which had previously opposed Morocco, suddenly swung around, and Colonel Khadafy and King Hassan signed a treaty uniting the two countries. (Libya was going through an anti-Algerian phase at the time.) Two years later, after Khadafy had swung the other way, Hassan abrogated the treaty.

The cost of maintaining 150,000 troops in the Western Sahara, as well as building the barrier and maintaining it, is far greater than the income that Morocco earns from phosphates. By the early 1980s, it had become one of the most heavily indebted nations in the world for its size. The International Monetary Fund (IMF) imposed stringent conditions on Morocco for further credit, obliging the government to cut food subsidies. In June 1981, there were violent riots in Casablanca in protest, in which over 600 people were killed, and more riots in early 1984, in Marrakesh. Generous US aid has helped Morocco survive since then, but it still pays a heavy price for the Western Sahara. There have also been constant rumours of disaffection in the army, and in January 1983, its most senior officer, General Ahmed Dlimi, was killed in suspicious circumstances. In the official version, he died in a car crash.

## DIPLOMACY

In May 1988, Morocco and Algeria resumed diplomatic relations, which had been broken 12 years before, when Morocco first annexed the Western Sahara. Algerian President Chadli Benjedid wanted to ensure King Hassan's presence at an Arab summit in Algiers in June. Colonel Khadafy wore a white glove at that meeting, so that he would not soil his hand by touching, among others, King Hassan.

Although Hassan once again promised to hold a referendum in the Western Sahara, the agreement between Morocco and Algeria was a serious blow to Polisario, and suggested, at the very least, a sharp decrease in Algerian support for the Front. The stalemate in the war had lasted for years. The SNLA was unable to penetrate the sand barrier, but Morocco could never relax, could never reduce the size of its garrisons – who detested the heat and tedium of guarding a gigantic sandtrap in the inhospitable desert. Both sides were war-weary, but it remained to be seen whether either was ready to make the compromises necessary for peace.

In August 1988, the secretary-general of the UN, Javier Pérez de Cuéllar, proposed an immediate truce between Morocco and the SNLA, to be followed by a plebiscite in the Western Sahara. There remained a whole series of procedural difficulties to overcome, and the basic dispute – independence for the Western Sahara or recognition of its integration with Morocco – could only be attained if one side or the other surrendered. There was no sign that either was ready to do so.

The procedural questions concerned a Polisario demand that Moroccan troops withdraw from the Western Sahara before the plebiscite, and its further demand for direct talks with Morocco. The UN suggested that it should send a 2000-man peace-keeping force to police the territory during the plebiscite. The Moroccan army would remain in its barracks and the SNLA would remain behind the sand barrier. At the end of the year, on 27 December 1988, King Hassan announced that he would open talks with the Polisario Front – an announcement that signalled the end of his refusal to recognize the Front, a policy that had lasted 13 years. He received a Polisario delegation the following month.

On 29 April 1991, the Security Council approved a plan that had been laboriously prepared by the secretary-general. A large U N mission was to be sent to the Western Sahara, 3000 people, including up to 1700 troops, to enforce a ceasefire and prepare a referendum. Morocco was to reduce its forces in the territory to 65,000, and Polisario's 7000 soldiers were to be regrouped in camps supervised by the U N. All political prisoners and prisoners of war were to be released. The referendum would be held in 1992, and an Identification Commission, part of the U N mission, was to decide who would be entitled to vote, on the basis of the last Spanish census.

Polisario naturally intended to bring back as many refugees as possible, and Morocco set about proving that many Moroccan settlers were in fact natives of the Western Sahara, or the children of those who had fled to Morocco during disturbances in the 1950s. Busloads of people were brought into the territory, and supplied with documentation allegedly proving that they were authentic Saharawis. On 31 December 1991, the Security Council approved a proposal by the secretary-general which would permit most of these Moroccans to vote in the referendum. Polisario at once protested. The referendum was scheduled for January 1992, but that month came and went, the years dragged by and still there was no vote. A U N bureau, the Mission for the Referendum in Western Sahara (M I N U R S O) had been registering refugees in their camps in Algeria and in Western Sahara. In 1995, the security council once again ordered a referendum by February 1996, deciding that the 400 remaining U N observers would be withdrawn then if it were not held on time. Still nothing happened. In 1997, the secretary-general appointed a former American secretary of state, James Baker, as special envoy to deal with the problem, and he arranged conferences and diplomatic discussions. There was no real pressure on Morocco to change its position, and it continued to insist that its settlers in Western Sahara should be allowed to vote in the referendum.

## FURTHER READING

American University, *Mauretania: A Country Study*, Washington D.C., 1972.
Amnesty International, *Torture in Morocco*, London, 1986.
Hodges, Tony, *Western Sahara: The Roots of a Desert War*, London, Croom Helm, 1984 and *The Western Saharans*, Minority Rights Group, 1984.

# MOZAMBIQUE

| | |
|---|---|
| Geography | 303,000 sq. miles (784,961 sq. km). As large as Turkey. |
| Population | 16.1 million. |
| GNP per capita | $80. |
| Refugees | In 1992, up to 5.7 million of Mozambique's then 15 million people were refugees. By 1996, all but 100,000 had returned home or had settled permanently elsewhere in the country. |
| Casualties | Wars and famines since 1975 have killed between 500,000 and 1 million people. Infant mortality rate is 35%, the highest in the world. |

A ceasefire was declared in Mozambique's long and agonizing civil war in August 1992. In November 1993, the government and the rebel movement, Renamo, agreed to disarm the bulk of their forces at bases supervised by the U N. Elections were held, under loose U N supervision, in October 1993 and the government party, Frelimo, led by President Joaquim Chissano, won a clear majority.

## HISTORY
In the early 16th century, Portugal established bases along the East African coast, at Lourenço Marques and Beira. These holdings survived the loss of Portugal's Asian empire, and when the European powers carved up Africa in the late 19th century, Portugal was allowed to claim a territory twice the size of California. Superimposed upon a map of the United States, Mozambique would stretch from Portland, Maine, to Tampa, Florida. On a map of Europe, it would stretch from Stockholm to Rome.

For most of its history as a Portuguese colony, Mozambique was utterly neglected. The Portuguese claimed to be colour-blind, unlike the British or French, but in 1975, in all Mozambique, only 4500 black people legally qualified for Portuguese citizenship. There were a further 30,000 of mixed blood, and perhaps 250,000 in the cities with some degree of education.

After World War I I, the Salazar government had visions of a new Brazil in East Africa and encouraged large-scale settlement by Portuguese peasants: there were 50,000 settlers in 1955, and the number increased by another 200,000 in the following 20 years. The centrepiece of the colony's economic development was to be an enormous dam at Cabora Bassa on the Zambezi river near the frontier with Nyasaland (now Malawi). The other elements of the colony's prosperity were a rail link from Beira to Salisbury (now Harare), in Southern Rhodesia, and trade with South Africa. Mozambique's ports served as outlets for Rhodesian and South African exports.

It was all delusion. The notion that Portugal, with a population of 8 million, could export a million peasants to Mozambique was pure fantasy, and the thought that the Portuguese empire could survive was lunacy. A 'wind of change' started to blow through Africa in the late 1950s, as the British, French and Belgians dismantled their colonial empires. Resistance movements started in all Portuguese colonies. The *Frente Libertacão de Moçambique* – Frelimo (Front for the Liberation of Mozambique) – was founded in 1962, and began its guerrilla campaign in 1964.

It was based in Tanzania and attacked and ambushed army posts, convoys and other economic targets. Its chief support was among the Makonde tribe of northern Mozambique, but for several years it failed to make any progress in the rest of the country, partly because of the traditional hostility between the Makonde and the Makua tribe, the largest in Mozambique, whose territory is in the centre of the country. Most of the Portuguese army was African, and to begin with, it had great success in building fortified villages to protect loyal Africans against the guerrillas. The Portuguese retained the initiative in Mozambique until 1972. In that year, the army mounted Operation Gordian Knot, which drove Frelimo back to the Tanzanian frontier.

Portugal was assisted in Mozambique and Angola by South Africa and by the white Rhodesian government, which had declared its independence in 1965, but the tide turned after 'Gordian Knot'. Frelimo opened a second front, by moving troops south through Zambia, Malawi and the wild border country between Rhodesia and Mozambique, and attacking Tete province. That was where the Cabora Bassa dam was nearing completion, where the Beira railway carried Rhodesian exports to the sea and where most of the recently arrived Portuguese settlers were becoming established.

The Portuguese had by then won the war in Angola, driving the fragmented and disputatious guerrilla movements to the frontiers or over them. Things were different in Portuguese Guinea (now Guinea-Bissau) in West Africa, where the guerrillas controlled most of the country, and Portuguese garrisons had to be supplied by air. Now the war in Mozambique grew steadily more savage, and Portugal progressively lost control of the territory. With Tanzanian and Zambian help, Frelimo dominated the north of the country, and the Portuguese army withdrew from the border provinces. Portugal still controlled the south, where there were no Frelimo bands, and with Rhodesian help, held Tete and the Beira corridor. They were not defeated militarily, any more than the French were defeated in Algeria, or the Americans in Vietnam.

The chief factor in the sudden collapse of the Portuguese empire was the resistance of the Portuguese army itself, reflecting the war-weariness of the Portuguese people. Conscripted peasants from the motherland felt no pride in empire, and had no wish to suffer and die for a new Brazil on the Indian Ocean. Portugal had 140,000 soldiers in Africa, proportionately seven times as many men as the United States sent to Vietnam, and was spending 40 per cent of its national budget on colonial wars. By 1974, the Portuguese military concluded that it could not preserve the empire, and soldiers from the colonial armies overthrew the government in Lisbon in April. Within a year, they had abandoned Portuguese Guinea, Angola and Mozambique to their own devices.

Mozambique became independent on 25 June 1975. The Portuguese colonists fled – 200,000 at once and the remaining 40,000 within the next few years – leaving Mozambique destitute. When Frelimo marched south to Lourenço Marques, there were no engineers to keep the essential public works functioning, no teachers, no professional people. The plantations, mines, factories and power plants were all abandoned. The great dam was finished and useless: there was no one to service its generators.

## INDEPENDENT MOZAMBIQUE

Frelimo, like the M P L A in Angola, turned to the Soviet Union for help. The Soviets provided minimal services as well as weapons for the new army, but it was not nearly enough. The Soviet Union was barely able to keep Angola and Ethiopia afloat, and while it wanted Mozambique as an ally, it was unable or unwilling to provide enough aid to restore its economy.

Frelimo, in gratitude for these few crumbs, and following the disastrous examples of other African countries, such as Tanzania and Zambia, proclaimed itself a Marxist state. It nationalized the bankrupt and abandoned Portuguese industries and businesses, and tried to collectivize agriculture on the best Soviet model: industrial and agricultural production dropped by 50 per cent. The country's difficulties were compounded by the drought that afflicted southern Africa in the late 1970s.

Instead of trying to develop into a mass party, Frelimo remained a small, tightly organized cabal, based largely on the northern tribes. It called itself a 'vanguard' party, in quite inappropriate imitation of Lenin's Bolsheviks. The president, Samora Machel, tried to set up a Marxist dictatorship, complete with 're-education camps' for disaffected citizens. At one time, 10,000 prisoners were reported to be languishing in them, and they proved an admirable recruiting ground for Renamo.

The Soviet Union provided training for the Mozambican armed forces, and in the mid-1980s, it was calculated that about 600 Soviets and East Germans and about 1000 Cubans were stationed in the country on training missions; Mozambican pilots have also been trained in East Germany and the Soviet Union. The Soviet Union also supplied great quantities of military equipment, including tanks and jet fighters, which served little useful purposes in a guerrilla war. They conscientiously set about training the Mozambicans to fight a conventional war with South Africa. They failed, and anyway, there was never any likelihood of such a conflict.

## THE BEGINNING OF THE WAR

Upon independence, the Frelimo government proclaimed its hostility to South Africa and Rhodesia, cutting off Rhodesia's railway to Beira, and allowing the Rhodesian resistance to establish bases near the frontier. Rhodesia retaliated by supporting the fight against Frelimo waged by white Portuguese who had stayed and by black former soldiers in the Portuguese army, particularly those who were not members of the Makonde tribe.

The Mozambique National Resistance Organization (Renamo) was set up in 1976 by the Rhodesian Central Intelligence Organization. Its mission was to harass the Mozambican armed forces and to spy on the Zimbabwe African National Union (Zanu), whose forces (the Zimbabwe African National Liberation Army) had moved from Tanzania to Mozambique after its independence and started attacking Rhodesia across the border.

Among the Portuguese who founded Renamo were: Jorge Jardim, a businessman; Orlando Christina, a former secret policeman; and Domingos Arouca, a plantation owner. Former Frelimo guerrillas also joined, including André Matzangaissa and Alfonso Dhlakama, who became the principal leaders of Renamo; according to the Mozambicans, they had both been cashiered by the Mozambican army on charges of theft. They set up bases in Rhodesia and across the border in Mozambique, and the Rhodesians established a radio station for them.

In this initial period of its operations, Renamo was not notably successful. In October 1979, the Mozambique army managed a successful attack on the main Renamo base inside the country, in the Gorongosa game reserve, and killed Matzangaissa. There followed a bloody dispute over the command of Renamo, which was eventually won by Dhlakama. His deputy was Lieutenant Adriano Bomba, a former Mozambique air force pilot.

Renamo had an international office. Its first secretary-general was Orlando Christina, who was assassinated at his home outside Pretoria in 1983. He was succeeded by Evo Fernandes, who was based in Lisbon, and who, in turn, was kidnapped and murdered there in April 1988.

Zimbabwe became independent in April 1980, and Renamo had to move its bases to South Africa. The African National Congress (ANC) was beginning guerrilla operations against South Africa from bases in Mozambique, and as a result, South Africa greatly expanded its support for Renamo. Renamo began to raid deep into Mozambique, its commandos often transported by South African planes, helicopters or ships, and Mozambique armed forces proved quite unable to contain the attacks. Renamo then set up bases inside Mozambique and in Malawi. The Malawi government hotly denied that it ever offered Renamo any assistance, denials not taken too seriously by other African states. When President Samora Machel was killed in a plane crash in South Africa, the South Africans found in the wreckage notes of a meeting of African leaders that he had just attended, at which they discussed attacking Malawi because of the help it gave Renamo.

From the day of its independence, Mozambique had announced its support for the ANC, which had been fighting against apartheid in South Africa since the 1960s. As well as increasing its support for Renamo, the South Africans responded by applying economic sanctions, immediately cutting the number of Mozambicans employed in the mines from 100,000 to 40,000, and stopping direct payments in gold to Mozambique. The cost of these measures to Mozambique was $2.5 billion a year.

South African security forces then carried the war to Mozambique, by raiding **91**

A N C offices in Maputo, which is close to the border and very vulnerable. In the first of these raids, in January 1981, South African commandos wearing Mozambican uniforms killed 11 members of the A N C and were then picked up by helicopter. There were further bombing raids on A N C positions, which the Mozambicans were quite unable to prevent, and in December 1982, another commando raid destroyed the oil storage tanks at Beira. In 1982, Ruth First, a South African Communist, and wife of the A N C commander Joe Slovo, was killed by a letter bomb in Maputo.

## THE CIVIL WAR

In 1984, Renamo had at least 12,000 guerrillas under arms, and by 1988, this number had increased to 15,000–20,000, to fight a Mozambican army reduced from 40,000 to 30,000, aided by an equal number of troops from Tanzania and Zimbabwe.

Renamo caused such disruption that, on 16 March 1984, President Machel signed an agreement with P. W. Botha, prime minister (and subsequently president) of South Africa, at Nkomati, on the border between the two countries. The Nkomati accord provided that Mozambique would end all support for the A N C and South Africa would end its support for Renamo.

Mozambique promptly closed the A N C offices, and raids were carried out in refugee camps in search of weapons. It was a major victory for South Africa: now none of the 'front-line states' except Angola was prepared to allow its territory to be used against South Africa. South Africa continued to support Renamo for several years, despite its promises. In March 1988, a Renamo defector, Paulo Oliveira, who had been the group's representative in Europe, gave a detailed description of links between Renamo and the South Africans. He described Renamo bases in South Africa, notably one at Phalaborwa in the northern Transvaal, and told how the South African army trained and supplied the Renamo guerrillas.

Renamo commandos and armed bandits, mostly deserters from Frelimo armies, soon dominated most of the country. Their tactics consisted of hit-and-run raids on economic targets, including railways, pipelines and powerlines. They followed a scorched earth policy, burning crops, destroying food stores and intimidating villagers, driving them into refugee centres. They ambushed vehicles on highways and burnt state farms and communal villages. They destroyed clinics, government buildings, schools and factories, as though they were waging total war in enemy territory. There were many well-authenticated cases of massacres. In the early days, Renamo attacked development projects and kidnapped Europeans who were directing them. Soon, there were few development projects left.

They usually travelled on foot, but used advanced radio equipment, supplied by the South Africans. (At least until 1984, and perhaps afterwards, South African air reconnaissance reported targets and kept track of the movement of Mozambique troops.) When the army counter-attacked, and cleared Renamo out of one district, it simply moved to another, and resumed its campaign of destruction. It made little effort to establish permanent bases or areas that may be described as 'liberated', as Unita 'liberated' south-east Angola.

Renamo's chief economic targets were the railways, and the powerlines from the Cabora Bassa dam. Twelve thousand troops from Zimbabwe, trained by the British, patrolled the Beira corridor, the railway linking Zimbabwe to the coast. Other contingents of Tanzanian and Zambian troops, aided by a small British unit, had less success keeping open the northern railway, which runs from Malawi to Nacala. Renamo also harassed the line that runs from Zimbabwe into Maputo. Other foreign troops protected the hundreds of miles of powerlines that run through territory controlled by Renamo.

At least 100,000 people were killed between 1984 and 1988, a further 300,000 died of starvation, and another half million in the next four years. Renamo's tactics seemed to be aimed at reducing Mozambique to total poverty and its government to helplessness. In August 1988, there were over 640,000 refugees from Mozambique in Malawi, and hundreds more crossed the border every day: in May and June, 130,000 refugees arrived. By then, there was a total of well over 1.4 million Mozambican refugees in neighbouring countries and 3.5 million inside Mozambique, crowding into inadequate refugee centres and into the towns. By 1992, the number of refugees, internal and external, had grown to 5.7 million.

Renamo attempted to isolate Maputo completely from the rest of the country. Maputo is at the extreme south of the country, and Frelimo's chief base of support is in the far north among the Makonde. It was thus the reverse of the situation in Angola, where the M P L A government's chief strength was among the Mbundu tribe, which occupies the north of the country and the capital, Luanda. Renamo hoped that the government would collapse, and then it would inherit power. This is what happened in similar circumstances in Chad in 1982 and in Uganda in 1986.

But isolating Maputo was one thing, capturing it was another. Frelimo's army was incapable of defeating Renamo and sweeping the country clear of bandits, but it could defend the capital as long as foreign powers kept it supplied. These supplies came by sea.

In July 1988, four American journalists were taken to visit Alfonso Dhlakama, the Renamo leader, at a base deep in central Mozambique. John Battersby of the *New York Times* wrote:

an atmosphere of the surreal dominated the rebels' leafy hide-out. Print-outs of incoming messages from commanders arrived from a new laptop computer linked to the field radio. Traditional dancers entertained rebel officials in a small clearing in the forest, and the high-pitched sounds of a women's choir rang out through the majestic panga-panga trees.

William Boot, celebrated correspondent of the *Daily Beast* (in Evelyn Waugh's *Scoop*), could not have said it better.

Dhlakama assured his visitors that all the tales of massacres and atrocities were lies, and that, 'We are waging a war to demoralize and lower the profile of the enemy.' On tactics, he said, 'Our aim is not to win the war militarily, but to force the Frelimo government to accept our conditions. The Western countries are dreaming if they think the ruling Frelimo government will change its Communist ideology.'

Renamo claimed that all its weapons were captured from the Mozambican armed forces, and maintained that it received no direct support from South Africa. It did admit to receiving help from a number of American groups, made up of wealthy businessmen and some Baptist missionaries (the journalists' trip was financed by an American group called Freedom Inc.) and similar people in Europe and South Africa.

On 19 October 1986, Samora Machel was killed in a plane crash on a flight from Lusaka to Maputo. The plane came down in South Africa, and Africans suspected sabotage or even that the South African air force had shot the plane down. An international team of investigators concluded that the crash was the result of error by the Soviet pilot, possibly compounded by bad maintenance of the plane by the Soviet crew. Machel was succeeded as president by Joaquim Chissano.

The Soviet Union obtained no political, commercial or economic advantage whatsoever from its huge investment in Mozambique, and abandoned it in the late 1980s as it also abandoned Angola and Ethiopia. Frelimo responded by turning to the West. As early as 1980, Machel started to denounce 'ultra-leftism' and to revive private enterprise.

The South Africans denied that they provided any assistance to Renamo, insisting that they had kept to the terms of the Nkomati agreement. In May 1988, they announced plans to start training units of the Mozambican army, being particularly concerned with the defence of the powerlines from Cabora Bassa to South Africa.

The Reagan administration steadfastly refused to offer any support for Renamo, despite aggressive lobbying on its behalf by the right wing of the Republican party, who argued that because Frelimo called itself Marxist and was supported by the USSR, it should therefore be opposed by the United States, while Renamo professed to practise free enterprise and was therefore worthy of American support. For 11 months in 1987, Republican senators – led by Senator Jesse Helms but supported by many more moderate figures, including Senator Bob Dole, the minority leader – blocked the appointment of a new American ambassador to Maputo, seeking to use the issue to swing administration policy in Renamo's favour. Finally, President Reagan managed to win the appointment. The new ambassador, Melissa Wells, made no bones about her opposition to Renamo. In April 1988, the State Department issued a devastating report on Mozambique, asserting that Renamo had murdered at least 100,000 people.

On 12 September 1988, the president of South Africa, P. W. Botha, paid an official visit to Mozambique, his first to an African state, apart from a visit to Swaziland. He met President Chissano at the Cabora Bassa dam. South Africa had agreed to restore the 560-mile (900 km) powerline running from the dam into South Africa, which had been destroyed by Renamo in 1982. South African troops were employed to protect it against Renamo. The hydroelectric plant at the dam would provide enough electricity for all Mozambique (and 10 per cent of South Africa's needs), but only if the powerlines could be protected.

Botha used the occasion to urge Renamo to accept an amnesty offered by the Mozambican government: 'We stand for cooperation and good will among our neighbours,' he said. Chissano was equally conciliatory. He not only welcomed Botha, but he abandoned the charge that South Africa had been responsible for Machel's death, and stated frequently and publicly that he intended continued cooperation with South Africa.

In August, 1989, the Renamo leader Alfonso Dhlakama went to Nairobi to meet church leaders from Mozambique, as a first step towards peace negotiations. The talks were sponsored by President Daniel arap Moi of Kenya and President Robert Mugabe, of Zimbabwe. Dhlakama demanded elections and a coalition government, including Renamo ministers, and also insisted that Frelimo abandon socialism, restore a market economy and respect the position of tribal chiefs.

Like many other conflicts elsewhere in Africa and around the world, the civil war in Mozambique had been nurtured and sustained by the cold war. Then the Soviet Union abruptly pulled out of Africa, leaving its clients across the continent to their own devices. The United States followed suit and South Africa turned inwards to solve its own ethnic problems, and ceased to meddle beyond its own borders. Left without any outside support, President Chissano of Mozambique, like the government of Angola and the various rebels in Ethiopia, abandoned Marxism and made peace with Renamo. Dhlakama, similarly bereft, finally accepted the peace-offering. It took three years of negotiation and a succession of mediators, including Tiny Rowlands, the British entrepreneur, but in the end the two sides agreed to make peace.

Five years later, the peace still holds. Mozambique remains among the handful of poorest countries in the world, hunting for help and investment wherever it can be found, its economy supervised by the World Bank and its armed forces by the U N. It even joined the British Commonwealth in 1995, becoming the only member that was never a British colony. Former Renamo terrorists now take part in government at all levels, and Dhlakama, unlike Jonas Savimbi in Angola, accepted his defeat in the 1994 elections.

It may be that Mozambique will escape the fate of so many other countries in Africa and evolve peacefully and prosperously, but the precedents are not good. The break-down in civil society was so complete that it is a cause for wonder that any sort of government functions there now. Smaller and more homogeneous countries have disintegrated under lesser strains, and comparable countries, especially Angola and Congo, show what can most easily happen when the armed men discover how little all their fighting and sacrifice has brought them. *The International Index of Human Suffering*, published in 1992 by the Population Crisis Committee in Washington, rated Mozambique as the most unhappy nation on earth. Its criteria were income levels, education, health, infant mortality, the supply of clean drinking water and food – and in all these respects, Mozambique was the most miserable. Its nearest competitors in this lamentable rivalry were Angola, Afghanistan and Chad.

With the end of the war, the four million or so refugees scattered across southern Africa were able to return to their homes, or to settle permanently and resume their lives elsewhere in Mozambique. That was a first and immense peace dividend that followed the ceasefire. Nothing else has changed. Poverty, illiteracy, unemployment and the ever-present danger of famine remain. What is **95** more, there are still millions of guns hidden in every corner of the country, ready to be brought out again when the call comes. South Africa supplies some aid, and Mozambique can at last benefit from the great dam the Portuguese left behind them which now sends electricity down to South Africa and, as the grid is slowly restored, to Mozambique itself. For the rest, the country must rely on itself and, like most of Africa, its future is very bleak.

## FURTHER READING

American University, *Mozambique: A Country Study*, Washington D.C.

*Cambridge History of Africa*, Vol. VIII, Cambridge University Press.

Fauvet, Paul and Gomez, Alves, *The So-Called Mozambique National Resistance*, London, Sechaba, 1982.

Hanlon, Joseph, *Mozambique, the Revolution under Fire*, London, Zed Press, 1984.

Henriksen, Thomas A., *Mozambique, A History*, London, Collins, 1978.

Isaacman, Allan F. and Isaacman, Barbara, *Mozambique, from Colonialism to Revolution*, Boulder, Colorado, Westview Press, 1983.

Meredith, Martin, *The First Dance of Freedom: Black Africa in the Post-War World*, New York, Harper and Row, 1984.

Newitt, M. D. D., *A History of Mozambique*, Bloomington, Indiana Press.

# SOMALIA

| | |
|---|---|
| Geography | 246,155 sq. miles (637,539 sq. km). The size of France and Benelux together, but its frontiers are disputed. It is on the Horn of Africa, commanding the entrance to the Red Sea and the north-western sector of the Indian Ocean. |
| Population | 9.4 million. |
| GNP per capita | N.A. |
| Refugees | In 1996 there were 240,000 Somali refugees in Ethiopia, 150,000 in Kenya, 45,000 in Yemen and 20,000 in Djibouti. There are 250,000 internal refugees. |
| Casualties | 8000 Somali soldiers were killed in the Ogaden war. Estimates of death by famine in 1992 start at 500,000. Perhaps 50,000 to 100,000 people have been killed in civil wars since 1989. |

Somalia ceased to be a functioning society as a result of the civil war that began in 1988. The president, Siad Barre, was driven from his capital in January 1991, but the war continues. The country is now divided between antagonistic guerrilla groups camped in the ruins of the cities. There is no central authority and the clan leaders barely control their own troops. In Africa, only Liberia has been reduced to the same destitution. The civil war has killed at least 50,000 people so far, and driven 700,000 people from their homes.

The vagaries of colonialism divided the Somali tribes between British, French and Italian colonies and Kenya, and the Ogaden in Ethiopia. Britain weakly agreed to its allies' demands. The Ogaden was returned to Ethiopia, together with an area of British Somaliland called the Haud. Italy was given ten years to prepare Italian Somaliland (now renamed Somalia) for independence in 1960. In due course, Britain also ruled that the N F D would stay in Kenya. The French remained in Djibouti.

Somalia duly became independent on 1 July 1960 – a union between (Italian) Somalia and British Somaliland. Despite the rivalries of the tribes and clans of the indigenous population, it is a homogeneous nation, unlike most others in Africa. Somalia started life as a multi-party democracy, but, like many other African countries, the regime soon degenerated into corruption and inefficiency. In 1969, the president was assassinated by a disgruntled policeman, and a week later, the army, armed and trained by the Soviet Union, took the opportunity to seize power.

Their links with the U S S R had more to do with the close alliance between Ethiopia and the United States than any serious ideological preference. When Ethiopia went Communist after Haile Selassie was deposed in 1974, and allied itself with the Soviet Union in the midst of the war with Somalia, Somalia smartly reversed its alliances and became staunchly pro-Western.

## THE SOMALI QUESTION

Even before independence, Somali tribesmen in the Northern Frontier District of Kenya started agitating to join their compatriots to the north, and soon an extensive guerrilla war developed. The Kenyans called the guerrillas *shiftas* ('bandits') who raided across the deserts and mounted small-scale attacks on Kenyan police. When Kenya became independent in 1963, there was an immediate escalation of fighting. The war came to an end in 1964, and afterwards, Somalia insisted that it would make no claim on the N F D. Kenya never believed the disclaimer and, as a consequence, supported Ethiopia during the 1977–8 war, fearing that, if Somalia won, it would then turn its armies south. In 1980, there was an upsurge of guerrilla activity in the N F D (now the northeastern province of Kenya), and the *shiftas* formed an N F D Liberation Front. Somalia denied that it gave any support to this movement.

Djibouti became independent in 1977 after a referendum organized by the French, and Somalia recognized its new neighbour. About half the 220,000 population of the new state are Somalis, concentrated in the city of Djibouti. At the time of Djibouti's independence, Somalia was deeply enmeshed in its war with Ethiopia and was disinclined to confront France as well.

## THE OGADEN WAR

Somalis in the Ogaden began small-scale guerrilla warfare in the early 1960s, and there were short border wars between Somalia and Ethiopia in 1961 and 1964, which Ethiopia won without difficulty. After that, Somalia refrained from challenging Ethiopia until its 1974 revolution greatly weakened the central government in Addis Ababa. Somali President Mohammed Siad Barre proposed to the new regime in Ethiopia that it should permit self-determination in the Ogaden. When that was refused in 1975, he began to offer active support to the Western Somali Liberation Front (W S L F).

Plentifully supplied with Soviet-made equipment and 'volunteers' from the regular Somali army, the W S L F soon overran most of the Ogaden. In the summer of 1977, the Somalis cut the railway from Djibouti to Addis Ababa. The railway runs north of a mountain range that extends from central Ethiopia eastwards towards the sea. In July, judging the time ripe, Siad Barre ordered a full-scale armoured invasion of Ethiopia, and his armies attacked simultaneously north of the mountains, towards Dire Dawa, and south of them towards Harar, the Ethiopians' base in the east. The two cities stand at either end of the main pass through the mountains, and if they had fallen, Ethiopia would have been cut off from the whole south and east.

The Somalis, who committed 50,000 troops to the war, were repulsed at Dire Dawa, which is a major air base as well as a key town on the railway. South of the mountains, they captured Jijiga in September, after a major tank battle. It was less than 60 miles (100 km) from Harar, and they pushed resolutely towards that city. Ethiopia was reeling from the effects of military defeat, revolution and insurgencies in Eritrea and elsewhere, and by mid-September, the Somalis controlled 90 per cent of the Ogaden. However, Siad Barre had already over-extended himself. He needed new arms and munitions to resume the offensive, and urgently appealed to his ally, the U S S R, for supplies.

The Soviets were faced with a dilemma. Their long-standing ally, Somalia, was at war with their new friends in Addis Ababa, who had evicted the Americans from Ethiopia and had turned to Moscow for assistance. The Soviets had to make a choice, and they chose the larger and richer ally. They suspended all military deliveries to Somalia, recalled their 4000 advisers, and sent them straight back to Ethiopia, where they also rushed huge quantities of arms.

Since the Djibouti railway was closed, and the roads from Massawa and Assab were blocked by Eritrean guerrillas, the Soviets airlifted the arms and armour for the Ethiopians directly into Addis Ababa. They re-equipped new Ethiopian armoured divisions, and padded them out with 17,000 Cuban troops.

The Somalis pressed their attack on Harar and then on Dire Dawa until January, but failed to take either city. Then the Soviets airlifted an entire Ethiopian armoured division over the mountains and landed them behind the Somalis besieging Harar, in a most impressive demonstration of the power of the Soviet airlift forces. The Somalis were trapped. In February 1978, the Ethiopians and their Cuban allies counterattacked and inflicted a resounding defeat on the Somalis. Siad Barre announced on 9 March that all Somali troops would be pulled out of the Ogaden.

## THE AFTERMATH

The Somalis lost 8000 men, three-quarters of their tanks and half their planes. The W S L F continued its guerrilla war, and despite Siad's announcement, regular Somali troops continued to help them. For the next two years, the irregulars controlled the countryside, while the Ethiopians were distracted by the war in Eritrea, but in 1980, the Ethiopians gained the upper hand, defeating the Somalis again, who finally pulled their last troops out of the Ogaden. During the fighting, about 650,000 Somali refugees fled the Ogaden and settled in camps in Somalia, which appealed to the United Nations for help.

## THE CIVIL WAR

Somalia's economic and political situation deteriorated steadily through the 1980s, as Siad became more tyrannical and unpredictable. His government's economic policies seemed to have no beneficial effects for the population at large, and the American aid programme was quite insufficient to meet the country's needs. The U S had the use of the former Soviet (and originally British) naval base at Berbera but otherwise played little part in the life of the country. Foreign visitors were discouraged, and journalists were rigorously excluded. Somalia was faced with a depressing future as a perpetually impoverished Third World country with very few natural resources, constantly burdened by drought and the refugees from Ethiopia.

Although Somalia has a homogeneous population, the different clans remain as suspicious of each other and as resentful of the central government as they were in colonial days. The Mengistu government discovered the delights of playing off one clan against the other and, in 1982, established a Somali National Movement (S N M) based on the Issak clans of what was formerly British Somaliland. Siad and most of his government were members of the Marehan clan.

Siad Barre, reputedly 80 years old, was clearly coming to the end of his long **99** presidency. An Amnesty International report in June 1988 stated that the government had been torturing its opponents and supposed opponents since 1981, and that there had been 'widespread arbitrary arrests, ill-treatment and summary executions' of civilians suspected of collaborating with the S N M.

In April 1988, after suffering severe losses in Eritrea and Tigray, Ethiopia agreed to restore diplomatic relations with Somalia without first signing a peace treaty demarcating the border. The Ethiopians were then able to move troops out of the Ogaden and send them to Eritrea. Siad presumably calculated that, if Ethiopia recovered in the north, the Somalis would at least have obtained *de facto* peace without conceding their irredentist claims on the Ogaden. The W S L F continued small-scale guerrilla actions in the Ogaden.

One of the clauses of the agreement between Ethiopia and Somalia provided that the exiles of the S N M could return home. As they did so, they brought with them quantities of modern weapons, supplied by Ethiopia, and, on 26 May 1988, attacked the government garrisons in the north, defeating two weak Somali divisions. They then attacked Hargeisa and Burao, the two main cities of the northern interior; they captured Burao, but the government managed to hold Hargeisa and later retook Burao. News filtering out of Somalia spoke of mass executions of Issak clansmen in Hargeisa, and that the S N M forces had almost reached Berbera.

At the beginning of June, 167 foreign relief workers were evacuated from the region by air, and no further foreigners were allowed into the war zone. Refugees started pouring across the border into Ethiopia at the rate of 4000 or 5000 a day, and by mid-August, there were 300,000 in Ethiopia, most of them in camps near Jijiga but at least 100,000 in remote parts of the Ogaden. The number rose to 400,000 by the end of the year.

The government conducted mass executions, shooting at least 5000 people in the northern cities it recaptured. In Mogadishu, 450 people were shot during anti-government demonstrations, a large number of them Issaks. Others were rounded up and shot by a special brigade commanded by Siad's son. They were known as the Red Berets. The United States then suspended all aid to Somalia. The S N M was one of four rebel groups, each chiefly representing one of the Somali clans. The others were the United Somali Congress, based on the Hawiye clan in the south of the country, the Somali Patriotic Movement, based on the Ogadeni clan in the centre of the country, and a group of dissident Marehan clansmen directed by Colonel Omar Jess, who led a mutiny in the army in 1989. They continued the war, and fighting soon spread to the whole country. In January 1990, Africa Watch concluded that 50,000 people had been killed in the civil war, and half a million refugees had fled their homes.

By that time, Siad controlled not much more than the territory around Mogadishu and his home base in the far south. Late in 1990, the rebels laid siege to the capital. The fighting continued for four weeks, with very heavy casualties to the civilian population as soldiers shot anyone they saw in the street and commandeered vehicles and looted stores and houses. All foreigners were evacuated and, in the end, even the embassies were abandoned. Siad Barre remained in the barracks of the last loyal troops until the last moment, and finally fled on 27 January. He took refuge in his home district on the Kenyan border.

100   Somalia was left in total anarchy. In March 1991, the last Red Cross hospital in

Berbera, the northern port, was abandoned because roving bands of soldiers threatened its staff. Other cities, including the northern capital, Hargeisa, and Mogadishu, had been comprehensively looted. They had become no more than ghost towns.

As Somalia disintegrated, old animosities between north and south, the former British and Italian colonies, resurfaced. In May 1991, the north proclaimed its secession. It called itself the Somali Republic, and maintained at least the semblance of a functioning government and civil order under the leadership of General Mahammad Abshir Musa, while the rest of Somalia was engulfed in anarchy. No country has recognized it.

Siad Barre was finally driven from power by the United Somali Congress. It occupied Mogadishu, but exercised little influence elsewhere. It appointed one of its leaders, Ali Mahdi Mahammad, as president. By September 1991, the government had fallen apart. Another U S C leader, General Mahammad Farah Aidid, like the provisional president Ali Mahammad a member of the Hawiye clan, led a revolt. Soon their rival armies were battling across the capital, devastating it again, and their rivalry spread to the rest of the country. Other warlords set themselves up elsewhere.

In April 1992, Siad Barre abandoned his last stronghold in the south, crossing into Kenya with 1200 supporters. He moved to Nigeria, where he died in 1994. There has been no government in Somalia since 1990. None of the competing warlords has been able to extend his control beyond his clan base and each supports a militia of young gunmen who live off the land. Their favourite weapons are heavy machine guns mounted on the backs of trucks. They call themselves 'Technicals'. In 1992, as one of the periodic draughts of the Horn settled upon Somalia, these predatory armies ranged into the countryside to requisition food and soon there was famine in the land. It was a wholly man-made disaster. In August, the American government said that 350,000 children had died of starvation and the international community debated what could be done. In 1992, 800,000 Somalis fled abroad as refugees, and over 2 million left their homes searching for food. It is probable that half a million people died in the famine.

Relief agencies were powerless: if they landed food and medical supplies in Mogadishu or the other ports, they were immediately seized by the militias. The American Navy arrived off the coast to protect relief efforts, but it became apparent that without troops on the ground, there was no way of ensuring that supplies would reach the countryside, where the death toll continued to rise. Despite the confusion and dangers of the times, some television reporters ventured into Somalia and sent out harrowing film of starving and dying children. The world's conscience was aroused by pity, horror and shame, and on 3 December, the UN Security Council unanimously approved an American resolution setting up an American-led expeditionary force to rescue the Somalis from their own suicidal civil wars. President George Bush had been defeated in a presidential election a month earlier, and decided to end his presidency on a strong note. In a broadcast to the nation, he said, 'I understand the US alone cannot right the world's wrongs. But we also know that some crises in the world cannot be resolved without American involvement, that American involvement is often the catalyst for broader involvement in the community of nations.' His critics wished that he had shown the same determination in Bosnia, but they admitted that this time, he got it right.

The Somali adventure was the first time the UN had intervened directly in a country's internal affairs since the Congo disasters in the early 1960s. On 9 December, 1800 US Marines landed in Mogadishu, the drama of the occasion somewhat spoiled by the hordes of TV crews and reporters lining the beach to see them arrive. Operation Restore Hope was progressively extended from the docks to the airport and then to the centre of town. The Americans and the rest of the UN force, including the French Foreign Legion, were welcomed by most of the city's population. The UN forces pushed out into the countryside and relief operations were soon moving thousands of tons of food to distribution points and feeding the population.

At the height of the operation, there were 15,000 US troops in Somalia and about 13,000 men on the fleet. The second largest contingent came from Pakistan. They soon became involved in the murderous politics of the country. On 5 February, the first signs of local opposition were evident, when a mob attacked an American patrol. On 24 February, several thousand supporters of Gen. Mohammed Aidid stoned American troops. US and Belgian troops had to fight their way in to one of the southern ports against the militia commanded by Gen. Mohammed Siad Hersi Morgan, Siad Barre's successor as local warlord. The security situation in Mogadishu continued to deteriorate. Twenty-three Pakistani soldiers were killed in one week in June, and on 12 June American and other UN troops mounted an offensive against Aidid's strongholds with air strikes, helicopter raids and attacks on the Technicals, culminating in an air strike on Aidid's headquarters. UN efforts to arrest Aidid were uniformly unsuccessful.

By then Bill Clinton had become president and was anxious to escape from Somalia. His advisers persuaded him to keep American troops there, though reducing their number, and on 4 May they handed over command of UN operations to a Turkish general. This was the first time American troops had served under foreign command in a UN operation. By then there were 28,000 UN troops, of whom 5,000 were American.

The famine had been ended. The UN calculated that a million lives had been saved. It was a notable success for the Americans and their allies, but the political situation was as bad as ever. The UN wanted to set up a new government, hold elections and restore civil society, and the Americans reluctantly accepted the policy. On 9 September, more than 100 Somalis were killed by US and Pakistani troops defending themselves from a mob attack. On 3 October, US Rangers mounted a helicopter attack on Aidid's headquarters. It failed. Two of the helicopters were shot down, and the Rangers were besieged for 10 hours before they could be rescued (the Americans had no tanks in Somalia). Eighteen Americans were killed, and one captured. Television film showed the Somali mob dancing on the downed helicopter, and abusing the American bodies. Aidid released his prisoner a few days later, and President Clinton ordered the Pentagon to prepare a rapid but safe evacuation.

The last Americans withdrew, in Operation Quickdraw, on 25 March 1994. In all, the Americans had lost 30 troops killed and 175 wounded. Six non-combatants were killed, mostly in accidents and eight more servicemen were killed in a helicopter accident off the coast of Kenya. The rest of the peace-keeping force lost 72 killed and 87 wounded. The UN operation cost about $2 billion, to which the US contributed $1.2 billion. The UN kept a presence in Somalia for another year. The last 2400 Blue Berets left on 3 March 1995, protected by 1300 US Marines, in Operation United Shield.

The country remained at the mercy of warlords and bandits. The Somaliland Republic in the north was the scene of a new civil war in 1994, as its leader, Mohammed Ibrahim Egal, was attacked by forces loyal to Gen. Aidid. Aidid's forces continued to fight his rivals in the south and in Mogadishu. In 1995 one of Aidid's main supporters, his finance director Osman Hassan Ali Atto, deserted him. Aidid was wounded in fighting with Atto's forces in July 1996 and died on 2 August. His 33-year-old son, Hussein Mohammed Farah, a naturalized American who had served in the US Marines and was living in Los Angeles, was summoned home to Mogadishu by clan elders to take command of his father's faction. It was a curious choice. The new leader had lived in the US since the age of 14 and had taken part in Operation Restore Hope as a Marine reservist and interpreter. None of the other major warlords accepted his authority. Sporadic fighting continued, as before. Somalia remained without a government, its citizens surviving by guile, barter and luck while the warlords and their militias fought over the ruins. Then, in the monsoon season of 1997, heavy floods devastated the centre of the country. Hundreds, perhaps thousands, of people were drowned and tens of thousands lost their livelihoods.

Ethiopia and other east African states made constant efforts to mediate between the various warlords. A series of conferences was held in various neighbouring capitals, and some progress was made. The greatest difficulty was to persuade all the faction leaders to attend. Thus a number of leaders gathered for a conference in Addis in November, 1996, but Hussein Aidid refused to attend, and nothing was achieved. Finally, a representative conference was gathered in Cairo in November 1997, and produced a ceasefire agreement and peace plan on 22 December. Both Aidid and Ali Mohammed Mahdi signed but Mohammed Ibrahim Egal, president of Somaliland, and several other important leaders boycotted the ceremony. The agreement proposed convening a conference of clan representatives in Baidoa which would decide who would be president, who prime minister and would then set up an interim central government for the first time since 1991.

## FURTHER READING

American University, *Somalia: A Country Study*, Washington D.C., 1977.

Bereket, Habte Selassie, *Conflict and Intervention in the Horn of Africa*, New York, Monthly Review Press, 1982.

Drysdale, J. G. S., *Whatever Happened to Somalia?*, London, Haan, 1994.

Laitin, David D., *Somalia: A Nation in Search of a State*, Boulder, Colo., Westview Press, 1987.

Lewis, Ioan Myrddin, *A Modern History of Somalia*, London/New York, Longman, 1980.

Metz, Helen Chapin (editor), *Somalia, a Country Study*, Washington, Government Printing Office, 1994.

# SUDAN

| | |
|---|---|
| Geography | 967,491 sq. miles (2,505,792 sq. km). About half the size of Europe, or as big as the US east of the Mississippi. |
| Population | 27 million: 17 million in the north are Muslims and speak Arabic; 10 million in the south are animists or Christian, belong to many different tribes and speak a great variety of languages. |
| GNP per capita | N.A. |
| Refugees | 4.5 million 'internal' refugees: 340,000 from Eritrea, 50,000 from Ethiopia, 5000 from other countries. There are 430,000 Sudanese refugees in other countries. |
| Casualties | First civil war (1963–72): about 400,000 people were killed. Second civil war (1983–): 600,000 people are reported dead so far, including 250,000 of starvation in 1988. |

## HISTORY

Sudan is an immense country, split by the great fault-line of Africa. Two-thirds of the population live to the north. They are Muslims by religion and Arab by culture, and they look north to Egypt and east to Mecca. Their land is dry, hot, partly desert, and they have a written history stretching back to classical times.

The south is pagan or Christian. It is a green, fertile land, larger than Texas, a part of black, equatorial Africa, and its population looks to Central and East Africa. The two disparate parts of the country are united today because, at the end of the 19th century, the French coveted and the British conquered the territory then designated the eastern Sudan. It was an episode that marked the high tide of European imperialism. Neither France nor Britain had any rational use for the endless expanse of deserts and swamps (let alone any moral right to annex it), but each determined to seize it because the other wanted it.

The Sudan was conquered by the Egyptians in 1819, who ruled it from Khartoum and permitted the continuance of the slave trade in the south. In the 1870s, Egypt itself was occupied and controlled by Britain. A British general, Charles Gordon, was seconded to the Egyptian army to suppress the slave trade, which he accomplished with great zeal. Then the Sudanese rose in revolt. They followed a religious leader, Mohammed Ahmed, who proclaimed himself the 'Mahdi', and a military leader, Abdullah ibn Mohammed, who proclaimed himself 'Khalifa', ruler of the Sudan. His army, known to the British as the

Dervishes, swept out the intruders, and the British decided in 1883 that the Egyptians would be prudent to withdraw completely. In January 1884, Gordon was sent to direct the withdrawal but, as soon as he reached Khartoum, refused to leave. He was besieged from 15 March 1884 and held the place against enormous odds for ten months. In December, the British belatedly sent a relief expedition up the Nile, but it only reached the outskirts of Khartoum on 27 January 1885 – two days after Gordon's garrison had been overwhelmed. He was killed on the steps of his palace and entered imperial legend.

In 1898, the British sent a large expedition up the Nile to avenge Gordon and conquer the Sudan – and frustrate the French. The last was the chief objective. The Sudanese were defeated at the Battle of Omdurman on 2 September, the last battle that was decided in a cavalry charge. Lieutenant Winston Churchill, then of the 21st Lancers, took part in the war and the charge and later wrote an exuberant account of the business. The Khalifa was killed a year later.

After Omdurman, the commander of the British expeditionary force, General Kitchener, sailed up the White Nile to Fashoda, far to the south. A French expedition that had marched across the width of Africa from the Atlantic had just established itself there. Kitchener and his large and powerful army reached Fashoda on 19 September. The French expedition, led by Major Jean-Baptiste Marchand, consisted of eight French officers and 120 African soldiers. It had taken them two years to march to Fashoda and they were now told, politely but firmly, to go home. This resulted in a crisis in which the two countries almost went to war, and which was finally resolved when the French backed down. On the second page of his memoirs, General de Gaulle listed the disasters that had afflicted France in his youth and that had led him to devote himself to France's greatness: the first on the list was the Fashoda incident. He got his revenge 65 years later when he vetoed Britain's request to join the European Community.

The British set up a new regime, calling the country the Anglo-Egyptian Sudan, but there was never any doubt that Britain was senior partner in that enterprise. Over the next 50 years, there was considerable economic development, particularly the introduction of cotton and sugar plantations. The north was administered in Arabic from Khartoum, and the south was kept entirely separate and was administered in English from Juba.

## INDEPENDENCE

In 1953, as the British were reluctantly beginning to evacuate the Middle East, they decided to compel the Egyptians to abandon Sudan. The last British administrators left in 1954 and the country became formally independent in 1956, but by then, the disasters had already begun. In July 1955, a labour dispute in the southern city of Nzara developed into riots that had to be put down by the police, killing 20 people. In August, the southern corps of the army mutinied and seized control of the equatorial provinces, except for the capital, Juba, which was held by loyal northern troops. Hundreds of northern traders and officials were slaughtered before order was restored and the mutineers defeated.

In 1958, the civilian government that the British had set up was overthrown by a military coup. General Ibrahim Abboud made himself president, and set about crushing all opposition, particularly in the south. He actively promoted Arabic as the national language, decreed that Friday, not Sunday, should be the day of rest in the south, expelled Christian missionaries in 1962, and exiled southern politicians.

## THE FIRST CIVIL WAR

In 1963, some of the exiles formed a resistance movement, which they named Anya Nya, 'snake venom' in one of the southern languages. The movement won the support of the Dinka tribes and was armed by rebels in the Congo, by the Ethiopians (who objected to the support that the Sudanese had offered the Eritrean rebels), and by Israel, which, on general principle, always supported any movement that might divide and divert the Arabs.

The war soon deteriorated into a merciless struggle between Arabs and Africans, like the slave wars of old. No prisoners were ever taken, and the usual estimate of the numbers killed is 400,000. Most of them, of course, were civilians.

The Anya Nya soon controlled most of the southern provinces and periodically occupied small towns and laid siege to government garrisons. In this unequal war, the northerners had access to all the weapons they needed, were far better trained and educated than the southerners, and had also inherited the martial traditions of the Mahdi. However, in so enormous a territory, they could never patrol every village and every forest. The war could not be won, by either side.

On 25 May 1969, there was a new coup. Abboud was summarily removed and replaced by another general, Jaafar Nimeiri. During his subsequent long term in office, he was to prove to be one of the more remarkable African leaders. He liked to wander through the markets of Khartoum early in the morning, listening to the workers there and exhorting them to industry. He was closely allied to Egypt, particularly to Anwar Sadat, and resolutely defended him for making peace with Israel. He was also an implacable enemy of Moammar Khadafy of Libya, who was forever plotting against him, inciting coups, even on one occasion sending a plane to bomb Khartoum. Khadafy's main object was the north-western province of Sudan, the northern Darfur, which he wanted as a base of operations against Chad.

Nimeiri decided to put an end to the war in the south. In 1972, he convoked a conference in Khartoum, to which he invited the southern rebel leaders, and there proposed sweeping concessions to them. The three southern provinces were amalgamated into one, with a regional assembly in Juba that would enjoy almost complete autonomy. The central government reserved defence and foreign affairs to itself, but otherwise left the southerners to their own destiny. The rebels were granted a general amnesty and the Anya Nya troops were incorporated into the regular army.

It was one of the most statesman-like and successful manoeuvres that any African leader has ever accomplished, comparable to the general reconciliation in Nigeria after the Biafran war. Unfortunately, the settlement did not last. Political and economic developments in Khartoum, and the deterioration of Nimeiri's regime, provoked a resumption of the rebellion.

In the years following the end of the civil war, there were repeated attempted coups in Khartoum, fomented by Libya or the opposition. In 1975, a coup attempt by mercenaries hired by Libya was suppressed with great severity. Nimeiri executed 98 people. His principal political opponent, Saddiq el-Mahdi – at one time Nimeiri's prime minister, and great-grandson of the Mahdi, a name to conjure with – led two plots in 1975 and 1976 and was exiled. Later, he was pardoned and, for a number of years, lived peacefully in Khartoum, frequently playing tennis with Nimeiri.

However wise Nimeiri's handling of the southern question at the outset, his government was a failure in all other respects. In particular, he presided over a steady decline in the economy. At independence, Sudan was relatively prosperous, had a sufficiently large educated class to govern the country efficiently, and had enormous potential. It was one of the world's leading producers of cotton and was self-sufficient in grain and sugar. All that was lost.

Sudan suffers from all the woes of post-colonial Africa but in an extreme degree, exacerbated by the country's vast size and the antagonism between north and south. The government imposes farm prices so low that no farmer can ever benefit from selling his crops. Government resources are devoted to subsidizing city dwellers while the peasants starve. The cotton industry has collapsed, and Sudan now imports sugar.

Nimeiri became increasingly autocratic as the years passed. He also became an extreme Muslim fundamentalist, imposing the *sharia*, the Koranic law code, upon the country. Adulterers were stoned to death, thieves had their hands amputated, and the prohibition against alcohol was extended to medical alcohol in hospitals. In January 1985, Mahmoud Mohammed Taha, a leader of one of the secular parties, the Republican Brotherhood, was publicly hanged in Khartoum for questioning the wisdom of Nimeiri's religious fanaticism.

Nimeiri's authority was flouted in the south, which insisted on maintaining the autonomy he had promised in 1972, and soon there was fighting between dissident tribesmen and northern troops. The drought that afflicted all East Africa and the Sahel (the area just south of the Sahara desert) was particularly severe in Sudan. Millions of starving people crowded into refugee camps, and protested that the central government was doing nothing to save them.

The civil war resumed in 1983. A new organization – the Sudan People's Liberation Army – came into existence, led by Colonel John Garang, an American-educated Christian Dinka. The S P L A began attacks on relief workers, and in February 1985, most foreign relief workers fled the south.

The United States poured hundreds of millions of aid into Sudan to ensure its loyalty – economic aid to the tune of $67 million in 1988 and $77.4 million in 1989, and much larger sums in military aid. The money was enough to keep the government afloat, but not enough to rescue the people. Early in 1985, the United States, Britain, West Germany and Saudi Arabia all suspended their aid programmes and insisted that they would not resume payments unless Nimeiri introduced extensive reforms. The International Monetary Fund (I M F) set harsh terms for its assistance, starting with the demand that food subsidies be ended. There was no hope for the country's economy unless the rural sector revived.

Nimeiri agreed and ended the subsidies in March 1985. He then set out on a **107** foreign tour, culminating in a visit to President Reagan in Washington on 1 April. The Americans then released $67 million in emergency aid. It was too late. During Nimeiri's absence, there were riots against the increase in the price of bread, a general strike and mass demonstrations against the regime. Nimeiri continued his tour. On 6 April, the army high command announced that he had been deposed.

## THE NEW SUDAN

The new regime restored the food subsidies. Sudan's economy therefore continued on the same disastrous course, kept afloat by foreign aid, destined to collapse. The government did not dare introduce economic reforms for fear that it would then suffer Nimeiri's fate.

The army called elections in April 1986, a year after the coup, and handed over power to Saddiq el-Mahdi, whose Umma party won the largest number of seats in parliament. He lasted three years, in a series of unstable coalitions with other parties. The new government at first relaxed Nimeiri's Muslim severity: Mahdi did not have to prove his religious orthodoxy to anyone, his own name was enough. Furthermore, he encouraged freedom of the press and rival political parties. With Botswana far to the south, Sudan was briefly the nearest thing to a real democracy on the continent.

Immediately after the 1985 coup, Sudan resumed diplomatic relations with Libya and Ethiopia, and accepted large-scale assistance from Khadafy. There was a price: Khadafy, with his usual lack of restraint, meddled ceaselessly in Sudanese affairs. After a border incident, in which Libyan troops attacked Sudanese border guards, there were riots in Khartoum against the Libyans.

Relations with the United States and Egypt were less cordial than they had been under Nimeiri. In April 1986, a radio man from the American embassy was shot and severely wounded, apparently in retaliation for the American attack on Libya. The United States promptly withdrew 200 dependants of its embassy personnel. There were no further incidents until May 1988, when Arabs carrying Lebanese passports attacked a hotel and club in Khartoum, killing seven people. The attack was deliberately aimed at foreigners: the dead were a British family of four (the children were aged 3 and 1), a 32-year-old British teacher and two Sudanese. The culprits were arrested.

## THE WAR

The war continues. There have been various attempts at negotiations between the government and the SPLA, without success. In July 1986, Mahdi met Garang in Addis Ababa, but broke off the talks the following month, after the shooting down of a civilian airliner by the SPLA. A further round of negotiations was held in London in December 1987, but without result. Garang's army – said to number between 20,000 and 30,000 men – has infiltrated within 200 miles of Khartoum and has threatened the capital's electricity supplies, which come from the Roseires dam on the Blue Nile to the south-east. The government intermittently claims successes against the SPLA: in December 1987, for example, the army claimed a great victory, saying it had killed over 3000 rebels. The following April, however, the SPLA attacked Juba.

Garang has steadily expanded his base beyond his own Dinka tribe. In 1987, he persuaded leaders of the Nuer tribe to join him. Their organization is called Anya Nya I I, and is heir to the movement that directed the 1963–72 civil war. In subsequent months, Garang won the support of other southern tribes and, with their aid, in January 1988, occupied a major city, Kapoeta in the far south-west, near the border with Uganda.

The Sudanese army generally stays in the north or safely in garrison towns, and sends Arab militias to fight the S P L A. The militias are based on northern Arab tribes, whose ancestors used to raid south for slaves a century ago. The difference now is that, in their attacks on Dinka and Nuer villages, the raiders are armed with automatic rifles and mortars, and drive in trucks: the Dinka and Nuer men are killed, the women taken away.

According to the Sudanese government in the summer of 1988, there were 3 million people in danger of dying by starvation. Over 300,000 Sudanese had crossed the border into south-western Ethiopia – of all countries in the world, the one least able to help them. They survive thanks only to the efforts of inter-national relief organizations.

If there were no wars in Sudan and Ethiopia, the starving could be fed. As it is, relief organizations are often helpless. In August 1986, the S P L A shot down a Sudan Airways airliner with a Soviet-made S A M-7, killing 60 people; the Red Cross then suspended its airlift into Juba. That meant disaster for the refugees: the roads are so bad, the railway network so decayed, that the only way to move food is often by air. In vast areas of southern Sudan, there is no possibility of sending relief because of the war and the breakdown of communications. Even though the drought broke in the highlands of Ethiopia in July 1988 (and led to severe flooding down the Nile, as far away as Khartoum), its after-effects persist: millions are still in danger of death.

People flee the drought and the war. The few thousand who can make it to the camps in Ethiopia are in the last stages of emaciation: 'When they come into the camps, they're not even able to stand. They're walking skeletons,' one refugee official said in April 1988. According to another, 'They compare poorly with pictures of Nazi concentration camp victims and are as bad as or worse than anything seen in Ethiopia during the 1984–5 famine.'

By the end of the year, the situation in southern Sudan was worse than it had been in Ethiopia in 1984. The United States was restrained in its criticism of the Khartoum government, for fear of alienating Mahdi and driving him into the arms of Colonel Khadafy. American relief specialists were less restrained, however, accusing the Sudanese government of following a policy of genocide in the south. Journalists brought back frightful stories and photographs of starvation. They discovered that, as the S P L A maintained its siege of the towns, hoping to starve them out, the army was flying in food to feed its garrisons, but leaving the civilian population in the grip of famine. As for the U S State Department's fear of offending Mahdi, as usual it failed in its purpose. The Sudan government sought out Khadafy and was soon one of his most faithful allies.

In 1988, Mahdi reversed himself and started to apply the Koranic code – the *sharia* – and in May, he brought the Islamic Front into the government. It is headed by Hassan al-Turabi, who led the attempt to impose the *sharia* under President Nimeiri. Mahdi was walking the difficult path between Islamic extremism and the need to settle the war, and outside observers were unable to decide on his real intentions. In November, in negotiations in Addis Ababa between representatives of the government and the S P L A, a ceasefire was agreed, on condition that the imposition of the *sharia* be postponed. Simultaneously, Mahdi visited Libya and signed an agreement to merge the two countries.

The agreement with Libya was deeply unpopular with the Sudan army and negotiations with Garang ran into the sands. Mahdi refused to suspend the imposition of the *sharia*, the one essential condition for reconciliation with the south. The economy continued to deteriorate and the war and the famine in the south persisted. The army issued a number of warnings that it could not indefinitely tolerate the continuing disintegration of the country, and on 30 June 1988 took power again. The coup was welcomed by Egypt and, discreetly, by the United States and Britain.

By then, 2 million southerners had fled their homes and an equal number were starving. In February 1989, the U S State Department reported that between 100,000 and 250,000 people had died of starvation in southern Sudan 'after elements of the armed forces on each side interfered or failed to cooperate with efforts to deliver food supplies to regions controlled by the other side'.

Half the 8 million people living in southern Sudan were refugees, and the famine continued unabated. One and a half million people fled to the inhospitable north and 300,000 people struggled across the deserts to Ethiopia, itself racked by war and famine. In April 1989, the government and the S P L A agreed to allow the Red Cross and other international relief organizations to deliver food to the starving peasants in the south. 'Operation Lifeline' was intended to move 100,000 tons of food before the onset of the rainy season the following month. In the event, only a fraction of that amount was delivered.

In March 1990, Africa Watch issued a report that the new regime had introduced an era of repression marked by the detention and torture of suspects, abuses far worse than those inflicted by previous regimes. On 22 April, there was an attempted coup, or at least the government said that there had been one. Four days later, the government announced that 28 senior officers had been executed by firing squad. They were all men who were less than enthusiastic about the imposition of strict Islamic fundamentalism upon the country. After those bloody events, it was clear that Sudan was firmly in the hands of the National Islamic Front (N I F), and allied to Libya. By then all American aid to Sudan had ended and the West had turned its back on the country.

Sudan reverted to a totalitarian, military dictatorship, at a time when other such regimes in Africa were giving way to democratic movements. The civil war continued, and once more the government prevented international relief efforts from helping the millions who faced starvation. It is one of the great disasters of modern times, a holocaust in the dark heart of Africa which the outside world is powerless to stop.

The head of the government is General Omar Hassan al-Bashir. He shares power with Hassan al-Turabi, head of the National Islamic Front, which developed out of the Muslim Brotherhood. Turabi has attempted to impose a strict *sharia* regime on Sudan, which is now one of the world's three ultra-Islamic states (the others are Iran and Afghanistan). There is no public opposition to the regime (Mahdi fled the country in 1996), and all dissent is brutally suppressed. The exact meaning of the *sharia* is a matter of dispute in Islam, and Turabi claims that his version is the purest and most faithful to the Prophet's teachings. He claims that it is perfectly legitimate to modernize the 10th-century rulings of Islamic theologians, and that he knows best how that modernization should be defined.

Turabi's followers try to impose Islamic stringency upon everyone, devout and secular Muslims, Christians and pagans. The military regime, meanwhile, imposes indiscriminate terror throughout the country. It also supports violent Islamic movements abroad, notably in Egypt and in Algeria. In June 1995, Egyptian terrorists trained and armed by Sudan tried to assassinate President Hosni Mubarak of Egypt at an OAU conference in Addis Ababa. The United States listed Sudan as one of the world's terrorist states and imposed sanctions upon it – though the level of US–Sudanese trade was so small that they had little effect. In April 1996, the Security Council imposed some diplomatic sanctions against Sudan, ordering a reduction in the number of foreign diplomats in Khartoum and cuts in Sudanese embassies abroad. American sanctions were further extended at the end of the year, though it turned out that Sudan was a main supplier of gum arabic, a substance essential in the production of soft drinks. The Clinton administration made an exception for gum arabic, which compromised a high proportion of Sudan's exports to the US.

The war in the south continues. In the early 1990s, it appeared that the government was winning. The SPLA split on tribal lines and the Khartoum government eventually signed a peace agreement with one of the dissident factions. However, President Museveni of Uganda and the new government in Ethiopia supported Garang's faction of the SPLA, which was therefore able to continue the fight. The southerners launched a new offensive in 1995 and recovered much of the territory they had lost over the previous three years. In January 1997, an SPLA army once again was within striking distance of the Roseires dam. They were joined by dissident northern armies, and the governments of Eritrea, Ethiopia and Uganda all supported the rebels (and some reports suggested that Egypt, too, was helping them). In the background was the suggestion that the United States, which strongly supports all four governments, might be encouraging them to help the rebels. Government losses led to a gesture of reconciliation towards the south in April 1997, when the regime signed a peace agreement with a break-away faction of the SPLA. The war in Sudan was still the most vicious and costly in all Africa, and despite rebel successes there seemed little likelihood that they might reproduce the defeat of Mobutu and take Khartoum as Laurent Kabila had taken Kinshasa. On the other hand, neither was the government in any position to wipe out the rebellion.

**111**

## FURTHER READING

American University, *Sudan: A Country Study*, Washington D.C., 1982.

Collins, Robert O., *Egypt and the Sudan*, Englewood Cliff, N. J., Prentice Hall, 1967.

Beshir, Mohammed Omer, *The Southern Sudan, from Conflict to Peace*, London, Hurst, 1975.

Betts, Tristam, *The Southern Sudan, the Cease-fire and After*, London, Africa Publications Trust, 1974.

Lewis, David Levering, *The Race to Fashoda*, London, Bloomsbury, 1988.

Manson, Andrew, *Southern Sudan, a Growing Conflict*, London, The World Today, December, 1984.

Metz, Helen Chapin (editor), *Sudan, a Country Study*, Washington, Government Printing Office, 1992.

Moorehead, Alan, *The Blue Nile*, New York/London, Harper and Row, 1961.

Voli, John Obert, *The Sudan: Unity and Diversity in a Multicultural State*, Boulder, Colo., Westview Press, 1985.

# UGANDA

| | |
|---|---|
| Geography | 91,134 sq. miles (236,036 sq. km). The size of Great Britain. |
| Population | 19 million. |
| GNP per capita | $240. |
| Refugees | There are between 60,000 and 140,000 internal refugees in Uganda, 200,000 from Sudan, 20,000 from Congo and 5000 from Rwanda. |
| Casualties | About 2000 people were killed in 1966, when Obote suppressed the Baganda. 250,000 to 350,000 people were killed during Idi Amin's presidency. 4000 were killed in the war with Tanzania in 1978–9. Between 1979 and 1986, when Yoweni Museveni took power, a further 100,000 to 300,000 people were killed. A few thousand have been killed in various insurgences every year since 1986. |

Uganda has the unusual distinction of having been destroyed by one man: Field-Marshal President for Life Dr Idi Amin Dada V C. The other countries in the world that have suffered most greatly from wars domestic and foreign, from famines, massacres, pogroms and corruption are usually the victims of ideologies, ethnic rivalries, outside interference and the ambitions and greed of many men. Although Amin's predecessor, Milton Obote, tried to set up a personal dictatorship, and inflicted considerable damage to the country's institutions and economy, the ruin that followed was Idi Amin's personal achievement.

Between 1971 and 1979, while he was president, about 250,000 Ugandans were killed; the entire 80,000-strong community of Asians, who made up the country's commercial class, was expelled; the country's economy was ruined; and the fabric of society was so totally destroyed that it has not yet recovered.

After Amin was deposed by the Tanzanians, a state of endemic civil war and banditry ensued. Estimates of the numbers killed range from 100,000 to 300,000. Out of this carnage, a new regime finally emerged in 1986, led by the guerrilla leader Yoweni Museveni. The fighting continued, but in the summer of 1988, the last guerrilla organization surrendered. It was a temporary respite. Soon there were new rebellions.

**113**

## HISTORY

Uganda in the 19th century consisted of a number of tribal kingdoms, of which by far the most important was Baganda, in the south. British explorers, looking for the sources of the Nile, visited Uganda in the middle of the century and, during the scramble for Africa in the 1880s, the British asserted their claims to Kenya, Uganda and Sudan. Uganda became a protectorate in 1894.

The entire period from the first British encroachments in Kenya to independence for Kenya, Uganda and Tanganyika (Tanzania) was shorter than one man's life: Jomo Kenyatta was born in 1889, before the arrival of the British, and for a decade after they left, he presided over independent Kenya until his death in 1978.

The constitution that the British left behind in Uganda in 1963 provided for a ceremonial presidency and an executive prime minister. The first president was the Kabaka (king) of Baganda and the first prime minister was Milton Obote, who was from the Langi tribe. The new nation's first crisis was the mutiny in the army, in January 1964, following mutinies in the Tanzanian and Kenyan armies. They were all put down by British troops. In 1966, Obote deposed the Kabaka, sending Lieutenant Colonel Amin to occupy Kampala; about 2000 Baganda were killed in that operation. Obote needed the army to make him president, but afterwards failed to control it. Amin, by now a major general, staged a coup while Obote was abroad, proclaiming himself president on 21 January 1971.

## THE AMIN YEARS

Amin had been recruited into the British East African army from the Kakwa, a small tribe in the easternmost part of the country near the Sudan border. He was a heavyweight boxing champion in the King's African Rifles, a huge, imposing man who made an excellent drill sergeant. The British recognized some of his abilities and made him an officer, but for many years, they, and Milton Obote, underestimated the ambition and cunning of the large, genial soldier.

Amin realized, from the first, that power grows out of the barrel of a gun, and determined that he would control the guns. His criterion of loyalty was tribal: he recruited his fellow-tribesmen into the army, and also men from other West Nile Province tribes and from neighbouring districts of Sudan and Zaïre. When he made himself president, he consolidated his power by disposing of the soldiers who were members of other tribes, many of them Langi and Acholi. He did so in the most straightforward way possible: he had them killed. By July 1971, he had rid himself of 5000 soldiers, half the army; the rest were killed later. The new army was 40 per cent Muslim, in a nation that was at most 5 per cent Muslim. Half the 25,000 soldiers came from Sudan, a quarter from Zaïre and the remainder were Ugandans from West Nile.

In 1972, Amin abruptly expelled all the East African Asians living in Uganda. They were mostly Indians and had been allowed to retain British citizenship when Uganda became independent. Kenya followed Uganda's example, though far less brutally, and Britain, most reluctantly, allowed most of the expelled Asians to settle there.

The effect on the Ugandan economy was catastrophic. Amin allowed his soldiers to loot the Asians' property, and rewarded his supporters with the jobs and contracts that the Asians had left behind. Few of them were capable of taking over the business and commerce of the Asians, and Uganda, therefore, had to do without. Meanwhile, Amin had established close relations with Moammar Khadafy in Libya, who supplied his fellow Muslim anti-imperialist with arms, training for his special forces, and equipment for his terror apparatus.

Amin, aided by an Englishman, Bob Astles, set up the State Research Bureau (S R B), which conducted sophisticated counter-intelligence operations against opposition groups. It also tortured and murdered people by the thousands. The American terrorist Frank Terpil supplied equipment to the S R B. In 1977, Amnesty International calculated that 300,000 people had died during Amin's reign of terror – which then had a further two years to run.

In June 1975, a British teacher living in Uganda, Denis Hills, was charged with treason and sentenced to death for describing Amin as a 'village tyrant' in an unpublished manuscript. The British government sent Lieutenant General Sir Charles Blair, who had commanded the King's African Rifles when Amin had served in it, and Major Iain Grahame, Amin's former battalion commander, to plead for Hills' life. Amin postponed the execution, and on 20 July, the British foreign secretary, James Callaghan, flew to Kampala to collect Hills. Amin announced: 'This proves that I am not mad, as British newspapers said.' The field-marshal then claimed that this incident made him victor over the British Empire, and he awarded himself the Victoria Cross.

On 27 June 1976, Palestinian and West German terrorists hijacked an Air France plane flying from Tel Aviv to Paris, via Athens, and took it to Entebbe airport in Uganda. The Germans – a man and a woman – were members of the Baader–Meinhof gang, the two Arabs members of the Popular Front for the Liberation of Palestine. There were 256 passengers and a 12-man crew on board. Shortly after arriving in Entebbe, the non-Israeli (and non-Jewish) passengers were freed, and sent on to France. The plane's captain stayed with the remaining 89 Israeli passengers and one elderly British lady, Dora Bloch, who was Jewish. Amin welcomed the hijackers, and allowed them to leave the aircraft and move their prisoners into a hangar at the airport; the Ugandan army stood guard while the hijackers negotiated with Israel, France and Britain; other terrorists were permitted to join the original gang. The Ugandans were clearly fully assisting the terrorists.

The Israelis rescued the prisoners on the night of 4 July, with the cooperation of various other governments, notably Kenya, which allowed the three planes on the rescue flight to land and refuel at Nairobi airport on the way back. The four hijackers, nine other terrorists, 35 Ugandan soldiers and one hostage were killed during the Israeli assault. While they were in Entebbe, the Israelis destroyed 11 Ugandan MiGs parked at the airport. It was one of the most skilful, daring and successful military operations in modern times.

Dora Bloch, who was sick, had been taken to hospital in Kampala. She was the only passenger left. Amin sent his troops to find her: they murdered her in the hospital grounds.

Amin killed off everyone who might oppose him who had not already escaped abroad, and that meant a large part of the educated and commercial classes. He killed the chief justice and the chief of staff of the army together. One technique

**115**

he employed was to chain a score of men together, and hand a club to the second in line. He would be told to kill the first man. The club would be passed to the third, who would kill the second, and so on down the line. The survivor was then shot.

Production dropped by 50 per cent between 1971 and 1978, and the tea, coffee, cotton and sugar plantations have still not recovered. Amin set up a 'Stansted shuttle' between Entebbe and Stansted airport near London, exporting coffee and importing expensive cars, drink, cameras and other luxury goods for himself and his cronies – and for his soldiers, who were thus spared the privations and, ultimately, the starvation that afflicted other Ugandans. The planes often stopped at Benghazi in Libya to pick up arms.

Amin's relations with his neighbours were usually bad. Milton Obote had settled in Tanzania and tried to start a guerrilla operation against Amin, but with little success. Amin detested Julius Nyerere, president of Tanzania, and once challenged him to a boxing match to settle their differences, proposing Muhammad Ali as referee, and saying that he would fight with one arm tied behind his back. The challenge was ignored.

On 16 February 1977, the Anglican archbishop of Uganda, Janane Luwum, was murdered on Amin's orders. In May 1978, the Ugandan president had a prominent former Kenyan minister, Bruce McKenzie, assassinated by having a bomb put in his plane. He killed his own wife in 1974. Late in 1977, there was a purge of Amin's inner circle, culminating in the murder of his minister of defence. Frank Terpil later claimed that the man's head was delivered to Amin on a salver during an official dinner.

## THE WAR WITH TANZANIA

Despite Amin's best efforts there was considerable disaffection in the army – perhaps officers were afraid their turn would come next. In September 1978, possibly to distract them, possibly out of mere blind folly, Amin invaded Tanzania.

He laid claim to a small packet of territory in the extreme north-west of Tanzania, west of Lake Victoria: the Kagera salient. There were various border incidents, all provoked by Uganda, and on 30 September, Amin sent his army across the frontier in force. They advanced 20 miles (32 km) and killed about 1500 civilians.

Tanzania was quite unprepared for war. There was one brigade of the Tanzanian army capable of action, but it had to be moved 1500 miles (2400 km) by rail and road to reach the front. Despite this poor beginning, the Tanzanians managed to expand their armed forces to 75,000 men in four months, train and equip them adequately, and conduct a proper military campaign that ended with the occupation of Uganda. The fact that the Ugandans never showed any willingness to fight should not diminish the Tanzanians' considerable achievement. Their only serious failure occurred when Tanzanian anti-aircraft batteries shot down three of their own MiGs by mistake.

The Kagera salient was liberated in November. On 21 January 1979, the Tanzanians crossed the border into Uganda, and began the march on Kampala. Their main difficulties turned out to be communications and supplies, but the latter problem was solved by the huge quantities of weaponry and material that they captured from the Ugandans, everything from trucks to tanks. They also shot down 19 Ugandan planes in January–February, and after that the Ugandan air force abandoned the fight.

The Tanzanians were joined in the invasion by a small army of Obote's supporters, headed by Titus Okello, and by an independent guerrilla force headed by Yoweni Museveni.

Colonel Khadafy sent a contingent of 2000 Libyan troops (mostly militia, not regular army) to Amin's rescue, and they joined a small contingent of PLO terrorists who had been training in Uganda. In March, in the only considerable battle of the war, the Libyans counter-attacked against the Tanzanians. Of the 1000 Libyans involved, 200 were killed and one was taken prisoner: the Tanzanian political officers had told their troops that the Arabs were returning to Africa to resume the slave trade. A further 300 Libyans were killed in the capture of Entebbe.

Entebbe fell on 7 April 1979 and Kampala on 10 April. The city was then looted by its citizens, with Tanzanian assistance. Every shop, every office, every empty house (and many inhabited ones that were inadequately defended) was stripped bare. The Tanzanians had great difficulty finding even a dozen or so chairs for the official party when they swore in the new government on 13 April. When they examined the State Research Bureau, they discovered that the basement was filled with corpses and the offices packed with expensive electronic equipment and endless reports on opposition activities, much of it exceedingly accurate.

Ugandan exiles had formed a National Liberation Front, and agreed to appoint as president Yusufu Lule, a distinguished academic, believed to be acceptable to the various tribes and factions. He arrived in Kampala in the Tanzanians' baggage and was set up in office. He never exercised any authority: there was none to exercise. The government was a phantom. Lule tried to make appointments without consulting the Liberation Front, which deposed him on 19 June 1979. He was replaced by Godfrey Binaisa, with Yoweni Museveni as minister of defence. The new president was as powerless as the old.

The Tanzanians, meanwhile, completed the occupation of Uganda. They proceeded cautiously, fearing that Amin would make a last stand somewhere, perhaps in his home village, but in fact, he had fled the country as the Tanzanians reached Kampala. He eventually took refuge in Saudi Arabia.

During the war, approximately 4000 people were killed: 373 Tanzanian soldiers; 150 Ugandan rebels fighting alongside the Tanzanians; 600 Libyans; 1000 of Amin's troops; 1500 Tanzanian civilians massacred by Ugandan troops; and about 500 Ugandan civilians.

## AFTER AMIN

A reign of terror began immediately after the end of the war. Amin's army disintegrated, but the soldiers remained heavily armed and took to banditry. The opposing guerrilla armies were incapable of imposing order, so there was none. Amin's soldiers, based in Sudan and Zaïre, organized raids across the border, slaughtering civilians and any unarmed soldiers they could find.

The victors began to fight among themselves: Binaisa was deposed by the army on 12 May 1980. The following December, there were elections that were blatantly fraudulent; Milton Obote claimed to have won and was proclaimed president. The most competent Ugandan guerrilla leader, Yoweni Museveni, took to the bush, where he formed the National Resistance Army and began a civil war. The Ugandan army, led by the elderly general Titus Okello, proved quite incapable of defeating Museveni or suppressing the Amin bandits. The Tanzanians pulled their last troops out of Uganda in June 1981, Nyerere insisting that it was not his job to police neighbouring countries.

Obote hung on to power, spending his time wreaking vengeance on his many enemies, and trying to rebuild his power on the basis of his own tribe. As a result, Uganda succumbed to total anarchy. Museveni's N R A extended its control over most of the south and west of the country, and fought a brutal war against Okello's troops north of Kampala. In 1985 there were student riots which Obote suppressed with great brutality. The final straw was a split in the army between Obote's Langi tribesmen and the Acholi.

Obote was deposed by Okello on 27 July 1985, and fled back to Tanzania. Okello's army immediately disintegrated, just as Amin's army had six years earlier. His troops took to the bush, carrying their weapons, and a new round of banditry and civil war began. After six months of fruitless negotiation between Okello and Museveni, the government collapsed and Museveni proclaimed a government of national unity, making himself president on 29 January 1986.

Museveni was able to bring some semblance of order to the southern part of the country, but the north and west were abandoned to the bandits, who now called themselves the Uganda People's Democratic Army and may have numbered 40,000. Between the overthrow of Amin and Museveni's victory, at least 100,000 people were killed, although one estimate has put the deaths as high as 600,000.

A new contributor to the general confusion was Alice Lakwena, the prophetess and leader of a sect called the Holy Spirit Movement, based on the Acholi tribe in northern Uganda. In 1985, it sallied forth to fight the government. Lakwena assured her followers invincibility, but in August 1987, government troops killed 400 Holy Spirit warriors in one battle. By the end of the year, Lakwena's movement had been broken up, her army, which had numbered about 7000 at the height of its power, reduced to about 500. Lakwena took refuge in Kenya, where she was imprisoned for three months, and then released.

Relations between Uganda and its neighbours have continued to be difficult. In December 1987, at least 15 people were killed in fighting along the border with Kenya, and the border was closed for a few days.

In the spring of 1988, Museveni's troops returned to northern Uganda, and induced 8000 members of the Uganda People's Democratic Army to accept an amnesty and to surrender. Other U P D A leaders refused to recognize the ceasefire and fighting continued, particularly in the east.

The government established a commission into past atrocities, which began to hold public hearings in Kampala. The evidence offered to the commission was as grisly as anything in Pol Pot's Cambodia, or in Zaïre immediately after independence. Government agents started collecting the bones of tens of thousands of people who had been murdered and whose bodies had been left in the killing fields. Normal life resumed in Kampala, and gradually spread to the countryside, but Uganda's polity remains exceedingly fragile, suffering as it does from an extreme form of two of Africa's curses: corruption and tribalism. Government officials who survived the repeated wars, massacres, purges and revolutions have lost all respect for the public good, and steal everything they can lay their hands on. The tribal animosities, which had been stirred up by Obote and Amin, and which led to the worst of the massacres, have not been appeased. Museveni may have won the battle, but winning the peace will be far more difficult.

Problems with indiscipline in the army continue, and a variety of guerrillas, many of them no more than bandits, still plagues the country. In January 1991, the U S State Department reported, 'Discipline within the National Resistance Army has declined in recent years particularly in the contested areas in the north and east where it has been responsible for serious abuses of human rights.' Amnesty International also issued a critical report on the regime's human rights record.

In the 1990s, the main rebel group in Uganda, operating in the west of the country along the borders with the Congo and Zaïre, is the Lord's Resistance Army. It is based in southern Sudan, and led by a faith-healer called Joseph Kony who talks directly to God. The movement claims descent from Alice Lakwena's violent Christian sect that was suppressed in 1986. The L R A, amongst other concerns, forbids riding bicycles (some boys have had their feet cut off for disobeying this rule), killing pigs or eating white chickens. At its most extensive, the L R A has driven 220,000 from their homes. By one count, 100,000 people have been killed in fighting, massacres and by starvation due to the L R A.

Most of the L R A are Acholi, a tribe that supported Idi Amin and Milton Obote and has fought President Museveni off and on for a decade. At the same time, most of Kony's victims are also Acholi. It is one of the most brutal rebel movements in Africa, and now diverts a high proportion of the government's resources. The Sudan government gives it covert support and, in turn, Museveni supports the southern Sudanese rebels.

Another, much less important, group calls itself the West Nile Bank Front, and a new group, the Alliance for Democratic Forces, appeared in 1996. Both these groups are based in Congo and raid across the border. They include former soldiers in Idi Amin's and Milton Obote's armies.

There is another, insidious danger in Uganda: it apparently has the highest rate of A I D S infection in the world. In 1993, the W H O calculated that 1 in 8 of the population had H I V, and 300,000, out of a population of 17 million, had full-blown A I D S.

## FURTHER READING

American University, *Uganda: A Country Study*, Washington D.C., 1969.
Avirgan, Tony and Honey, Martha, *War in Uganda: The Legacy of Idi Amin*, Westport, Conn., L. Hill, 1982.
Byrnes, Rita (editor), *Uganda, a Country Study*, Washington, Government Printing Office, 1992.

Jorgenson, Jan Jelmert, *Uganda: A Modern History*, New York, St Martin's Press, 1981.

Mamdani, Mahmoud, *Imperialism and Fascism in Uganda*, Trenton, N.J., African World Press, 1984.

Minority Rights Group, *Uganda and Sudan*, London, 1984.

Mittleman, James H., *Ideology and Politics in Uganda from Obote to Amin*, Ithaca, N.Y., Cornell University Press, 1975.

Moorehead, Alan, *The White Nile*, New York/London, Harper and Row, 1960.

Smith, George Ivan, *Ghosts of Kampala*, New York, St Martin's Press, 1980.

# ASIA

# AFGHANISTAN

| | |
|---|---|
| Geography | 251,000 sq. miles (637,000 sq. km). The size of Texas, and twice the size of Italy. Half the country is at an altitude of over 6000 ft (2000 m); one-fifth is desert. The mountains of the Hindu Kush ('Killer of Hindus'), an extension of the Himalayas, run 600 miles (960 km) from east to west, cutting the country in half; their average height is 13,500 ft (4500 m). In the north-east is the Pamir Knot, among the highest mountains in the world, with over 100 peaks between 20,000 and 25,000 ft (6500–8000 m) high. |
| Population | Statistics are very unreliable. The World Bank put the population at 23.4 million in 1995. Extrapolating from earlier approximations, the most numerous tribes are: |

> Pushtun (Pathan) 9,750,000
> Tadzhik or Tajik 5,250,000
> Uzbek 1,500,000
> Hazara 1,300,000
> Aimaq 1,200,000
> Farsiwan 900,000
> Baluchi 150,000

There are also a dozen less numerous tribes. The Tadzhiks and Uzbeks are cousins to major nations in Soviet Central Asia, the Pushtun are equally divided between Afghanistan and Pakistan, while the Baluchi extend into Pakistan and Iran. There are also numerous languages, the two principal ones being Pushtu and Dari, a dialect of Persian. Afghanistan has the highest infant mortality rate (158 per thousand) and lowest life expectancy in the world (44 years). Adult illiteracy is 69%.

| | |
|---|---|
| GNP per capita | N.A. |
| Refugees | 1.2 million internal; 1.2 million in Pakistan, 1.4 million in Iran. 180,000 Tajik refugees in Afghanistan. |
| Casualties | Estimates vary wildly. In the war against the Communist government and the Soviet occupation, 1979–92, guesses ranged from 100,000 to 1 million, the figure favoured by the American government, certainly too high even if it is taken to include those who died of disease or starvation. A better estimate would be 400,000. The Soviets lost about 15,000 killed, 311 missing and 35,000 wounded. Perhaps another 200,000 have been killed since 1989 in fighting between Mujaheddin groups and in the civil war between the Taliban and its opponents since 1994. Relief agencies estimate that |

2 million people have been permanently disabled by the fighting, land-mines and disease.

Afghanistan had the misfortune to mark the high tide of Soviet expansionism. It was the last place where a small band of revolutionaries, with Soviet aid, overthrew the government and established a Communist state, and it was the last to which the Soviets applied the 'Brezhnev Doctrine'. This stated that once a country had adopted Communism, the Socialist Motherland would guarantee that it would always remain Communist.

History will credit the Afghans with being the first people to defeat a Soviet army of occupation and drive it out. The Communist coup occurred in April 1978, and was followed by a general uprising against the new government. It soon became apparent that the regime could not sustain itself without Soviet help, so for 18 months, the Soviets poured money, arms and advisers into Afghanistan, but still the government was losing the civil war. Furthermore, Afghan Communists were bitterly divided into two factions which fought a murderous battle against each other. Finally, in December 1979, the Soviets invaded Afghanistan, set up a puppet government in Kabul and went to war with the rebels. They were never able to dominate the countryside and put down the rebellion. A succession of elderly Soviet leaders was faced with the fact that they had embarked upon a pointless war that was unpopular at home and had a disastrous effect upon their international image. In 1988, Mikhail Gorbachev cut the Gordian knot and simply withdrew. The last Soviet soldier crossed the border back to the U S S R on 15 February 1989.

They left a Communist government behind, which was provided with some support by the Soviets until the final collapse of the Soviet Union in 1991. Then it was defeated, in 1992. In 1994, a group of Islamic extremists, the Taliban, emerged from the refugee camps. They occupied Kabul in September 1995, and imposed their zealotry upon most of the country. The north resists and the civil war continues.

## HISTORY

Afghanistan, like many other countries in the world, is a wholly artificial creation. It is a geographical expression, an area on the map with arbitrary boundaries, inhabited by peoples who have spent most of history fighting each other. The largest tribe of the Afghans are the Pushtun, known to the British as the Pathan, who make up about one-third of the population of Afghanistan. An equal number of the Pushtun live in Pakistan, and none of the tribe in either country recognizes the frontier. Hillmen do not consider the high mountains to be barriers: that is a plainsman's delusion. And the Oxus river, which now separates Afghanistan from the former Soviet Union, only became a frontier dividing cousins living on opposite sides when the Russians arrived 130 years ago.

The territory that is now Afghanistan has usually been part of some larger empire. Those empires included areas of Central Asia that are now in the Commonwealth of Independent States, part or all of Iran, and the Punjab, most of which is now in Pakistan. In ancient times, Afghanistan was part of the

Persian empire; it was then conquered by Alexander, and later its tribes conquered all of Persia and Mesopotamia, and the Punjab as well. The Mongols passed that way, as did Tamburlaine, the lame shepherd from Samarkand who conquered everything from Delhi to Anatolia and put the Turkish sultan in a cage. In the 16th century, Babur the Tiger, a descendant of both Genghiz Khan and Tamburlaine, conquered north India and established the Moghul empire at Delhi. He chose to be buried in Kabul, and one of his descendants built the Taj Mahal at Agra as a tomb for his wife.

In the 18th and 19th centuries, the British conquered India but never seriously attempted to extend their empire beyond the Khyber Pass. They invaded on three occasions: in 1838, 1878 and in 1919. The first war ended in one of the great disasters of British imperial history: the expeditionary force was wiped out during its retreat from Kabul, and the king they had installed in Kabul was murdered. In 1878, when the British occupied Afghanistan again, they again discovered that they could not hold it, and therefore withdrew – this time successfully. The Third Afghan War, in 1919, was an inconsequential and brief affair. The British marched up into the hills, and then marched down again. One of the many errors of the Soviet leaders was that they never studied the history of Afghanistan.

The British designated it a buffer state between Russia and India, and the Russians accepted the designation. The frontiers were drawn to separate the two empires, even though that involved adding a finger of territory in the east which now joins Afghanistan to China through some of the highest mountains in the world. A dynasty that had established itself in Kabul south of the Hindu Kush in the 18th century was allowed to extend its territory to the north, as far as the Oxus river, and became the rulers of the new kingdom.

After the Russian Revolution in 1917, the new Soviet government continued the policy of the tsars – to leave well enough alone. Until the British left India, Afghanistan was a British client state that maintained good relations with the Soviet Union. Its time of troubles began with India's independence in 1947.

British India was partitioned, and Pakistan inherited the frontiers that the British had established. The Afghan government, which had acquiesced in the British cutting the Pushtun territories in two, promptly raised an irredentist claim against Pakistan. It demanded that the Northwest Frontier Province be given the right of self-determination – which the Afghans believed would mean its annexation to Afghanistan. Pakistan adamantly refused to consider the frontier question, and as a result, there was constant hostility between the two countries. Afghanistan turned for support to its neighbour in the north. The United States was already allied to Pakistan, and therefore supported its retention of Pashtunistan, and so the Soviets agreed to support the Afghans.

They became the major suppliers of aid to Afghanistan, including military aid, although the United States contributed to the building of the road network that opened up the country. The most remarkable feat of engineering was accomplished by the Soviets: they built a road through the Hindu Kush, including the mile-long (1.6 km) Salang tunnel at 10,000 feet (3000 m), which connected Kabul to the Soviet frontier.

A group of radical intellectuals founded the People's Democratic Party of **125**

Afghanistan (PDPA) on 1 January 1965; its principal leaders were Nur Mohammed Taraki and Babrak Karmal. Four years later, the party split between two factions: Khalq ('The Masses') led by Taraki; and Parcham ('The Banner') led by Babrak – the names for the factions originating with those of newspapers that the two men had edited. The Khalqis were Leninists who aimed to build a small, tightly knit and militant party that would form the vanguard of the proletariat, seize power as soon as possible and force Communism upon the country. Parcham believed that Afghanistan was not ready for Communism, and advocated a gradualist approach.

There was another reason for the split. Khalq members were mostly sons of Pushtu-speaking peasants and nomads. Parcham's supporters and leaders, on the other hand, mostly came from the cities, and spoke Dari, a form of Persian. Taraki's father was a herdsman, Babrak's was a general. Taraki was for a while press attaché at the embassy in Washington. Hafizullah Amin, the most extreme of Khalq leaders, had studied at Teachers' College of Columbia University in New York during the turbulent 1960s.

The Soviet Union, despite its own Leninist antecedents, considered that Afghanistan was not ripe for Communism – for a start, it had no proletariat. Therefore, the USSR supported the Parchamis. Unfortunately, Khalq was better led and more successful, particularly in recruiting from among the armed forces.

From 1953 to 1963, the Afghan government was headed by Sardar Mohammed Daoud Khan, a cousin and brother-in-law of King Zahir Shah. He strenuously campaigned against Pakistan on the Pushtun issue and expanded relations with the Soviet Union; he also encouraged cautious economic and political development. In 1963, the king asserted himself, dismissed Daoud and took over. His subsequent rule was unremarkable: he was as authoritarian as Daoud but less competent. A famine in 1972 killed 100,000 people, and the following year, when Zahir Shah was out of the country, Daoud staged a *coup d'état* and established a republic.

He did so with the aid of the Parcham faction of the PDPA, presumably with the connivance of the Soviet Union. However, during his second period in office, he moved away from his previous dependence on the USSR and improved relations with Pakistan, at the urging of the shah of Iran, who had ambitions of leading an alliance of the three countries. The reconciliation with Pakistan was not easy. Both President Zulfiker Ali Bhutto and President Zia aided Pushtun guerrillas who were fighting Daoud, and Zia showed particular affection for the Muslim extremists among them who considered Daoud a dangerous Communist because of his reform measures.

In the mid-1970s, Daoud tried to purge the Parchamis, but by then, the PDPA had become well established in the army. In April 1978, after a mass PDPA demonstration in Kabul, Daoud arrested the leading leftists. On 27 April, their allies in the armed forces staged a coup against the president. He was killed defending his palace, and most of his family massacred.

The PDPA leaders were released from jail and took over the government. Taraki, the Khalq leader, became president and his closest associate, Hafizullah Amin, quickly became the dominant figure in the regime. In July, ten leading members of the Parcham faction, including Babrak Karmal, were sent abroad as ambassadors. Babrak was sent to Prague. In August, the remaining Parcham leaders were arrested, some of them tortured and killed, and the ambassadors were all summoned home. They wisely refused, and went to Moscow.

Taraki and Amin now set about Communizing Afghanistan at full tilt. They reformed the system of land tenure, the status of women and the usury laws. The first of their decrees began with the ritual words 'In the Name of God the Compassionate' but that formula was soon dropped. The first signs of disaffection occurred as early as May 1978, a month after the revolution, and the first full-scale insurrection broke out in the east in September and soon spread across the whole country. On 12 March 1979, one of the resistance groups, the National Liberation Front, declared a *jihad* – a holy war – against the godless government in Kabul.

The Soviets attempted to persuade the Khalq to conciliate the opposition, to work with traditional leaders. That was how they had established their control over Central Asia after the Revolution, and they believed that it was the only way to convert fanatic and backward Muslim peasants to the merits of Communism.

Taraki and Amin went to Moscow in December 1978 to sign a treaty of friendship, good neighbourliness and cooperation, which contained a clause promising military assistance. Under this clause, a year later, the Soviets killed Amin.

Amin, increasingly influential in the government, was determined to push ahead with the revolution. He grew suspicious of the Soviets, and there were also some signs that he wanted a reconciliation with the United States to counter-balance Soviet influence. He saw a great deal of the American ambassador, Adolph Dubs, but on 14 February 1979, Dubs was kidnapped, apparently by Maoist extremists, who held him prisoner and demanded the release of some of their comrades from jail. Instead of negotiating with them, security forces stormed the hotel room where Dubs was held and he was killed. The regime offered the United States no condolences and no apologies for the incident. That ended American interest in Afghanistan. The Americans were also preoccupied by events in Iran (the shah had fled the previous month).

In March 1979, an uprising of Shiites (under the influence of revolutionary Iran) in Herat, capital of west Afghanistan, resulted in the killing of over 100 Soviets, some of whom were also tortured horribly. Although government forces recaptured the city, killing 3000 to 5000 people, it was clear that the country was progressively sliding into anarchy.

The Soviets greatly increased their presence during the year, taking over security in the cities and administrating many government departments. In July, they deployed their first combat unit in Afghanistan, north of Kabul. They also looked for ways to replace Amin. They persuaded Taraki that Amin was a danger to him. Taraki had been progressively excluded from all authority (he was reputedly in an alcoholic daze most of the time), and on 14 September 1979, he tried to assassinate his prime minister. He invited Amin to a meeting, and his guards tried to shoot him as he mounted the steps of the presidential palace. Amin rolled down the steps and escaped, called up the tanks, and had Taraki arrested. Two days later, the government announced that he had resigned all his posts – 'for health reasons'. On 10 October, the *Kabul Times* published a short article on the back page stating that 'Taraki died yesterday morning of a serious illness, which he had been suffering for some time.' The illness, according to one well-informed observer, 'was lack of oxygen, brought on by the application of fingers to the neck and pillows over the nose and mouth, by three members of the palace guard.'

Amin made himself president. He controlled very little of the government, however, and the government controlled very little of the country. General Ivan Pavlovsky, the Soviet officer who had organized the invasion of Czechoslovakia in 1968, paid a two-month visit to Afghanistan in August–September. Feeling the noose tightening around him, Amin tried to play the Pakistani card, and talked about reconciliation with Pakistan and the United States. When Zia hesitated to welcome the prodigal, he swung around completely and announced that he would arm anti-Pakistani and anti-Khomeini guerrillas.

By one account, the Soviets tried to kidnap Amin on 26 December 1979, by drugging his food and arresting him. The plot failed. On 27 December, Soviet troops occupied military bases, radio stations and government buildings in Kabul and elsewhere. They went to arrest Amin, but like Daoud Khan before him, he refused to surrender. And like Daoud (or Salvador Allende in Chile), he either was shot or committed suicide.

Babrak Karmal, who had been living in exile for 18 months under Soviet control, was brought back to head the government, like other Communists brought in the baggage of the Red Army in Eastern Europe in 1945. The Soviets set about building a new government, with new policies, and also tried to restore some semblance of security to the country. They failed completely at all these tasks.

## THE SOVIET OCCUPATION, 1979–89

In 1988, as the Soviets prepared to abandon Afghanistan, the Gorbachev regime put it about that the decision to invade Afghanistan in 1979 had been taken by half a dozen officials, on the spur of the moment, perhaps when they were all drunk. By a nice coincidence, all those officials were by then dead.

This is the sort of damage control that all governments try. It is quite incredible. The invasion involved prolonged forward planning and followed an 18-month period during which the Soviet Union had plunged into Afghanistan, its eyes wide open. This was not the act of a small cabal, but the considered act of a government.

Why did they do it? One explanation – the one favoured by American hawks and those who cannot read a map – can be firmly ruled out. It had nothing to do with Soviet designs upon the Persian Gulf. If they ever wish to close the Straits of Hormuz, they must first defeat and occupy Iran – and they would do that directly, not by a detour through the Hindu Kush. Occupying Afghanistan as the first step to attacking Tehran would be like the United States invading Canada via Alaska. The Soviet invasion of Afghanistan was stupid, but not that stupid.

Nor is it likely that they had any direct designs on Pakistan, if only because success in Pakistan would immediately entail implacable conflict with India while bringing no tangible advantage whatever. They already had a naval base in the Indian Ocean, in Aden, and much good it had done them.

Another suggestion is that the Soviets were afraid of the spread of Islamic fundamentalism from Iran into Soviet Central Asia by way of Afghanistan. But they were already deeply involved in Afghanistan before the fall of the shah. Fear of the fundamentalists may have played a part in keeping them in Afghanistan – but in the event, Soviet intervention enormously strengthened Afghan fundamentalism and, furthermore, ruined any hope the Soviets may have entertained of supplanting the Americans in the affections of the Iranians.

The simplest explanation is probably the best. They got sucked into Afghanistan much as the United States got sucked into Vietnam, without clearly thinking through the consequences of their actions, and wildly underestimating the hostility they would arouse. In 1979, it appeared to them that their position within Afghanistan was collapsing, together with the regime. Unless they intervened, Amin would be swept away and Afghanistan would either lapse into anarchy or become fervently anti-Soviet. Either event would represent the defeat of a policy going back to Lenin, or the tsars.

Lastly, Leonid Brezhnev and his geriatric crew were probably terrified of being the first Soviet leaders to 'lose' a country that had chosen the road to socialism. Never mind that the Communist coup was the work of a few officers and intellectuals and represented only a tiny minority of the population. Afghanistan had a Communist government, and Brezhnev was determined that it would not be overthrown. He may have thought that there was a parallel with events in Hungary in 1956 or in Czechoslovakia in 1968: on both occasions, the government lost control, but the situation was saved by the Red Army. After a few months of turmoil, the two countries settled down and the world community accepted the event.

They probably expected the same thing to happen in Afghanistan. An overwhelming display of Soviet might would cow the opposition, and then economic assistance, a more subtle policy and the passage of time would reconcile the Afghans to their new form of government. It was a gross miscalculation.

## THE SOVIETS AND THE MUJAHEDDIN

Babrak Karmal broadcast an appeal for Soviet help on 27 December 1979 – from a radio station inside the Soviet Union. His hosts insisted afterwards that they were 'invited' to intervene by the government of Afghanistan. It was one of the more brazen falsehoods of modern times. Babrak was the complete puppet, who never uttered a word or issued an order that his Soviet masters had not prepared for him. He was so compliant, and therefore so unpopular, that the Soviets finally deposed him on 4 May 1986 and replaced him with Mohammed Najib, a former head of the police, whom they hoped would be a more presentable and competent figurehead. They proved mistaken. Najib was no more able than Babrak to win popular support. For example, although head of a country of profound religious faith, Najib had chosen to change his name – Najibullah, meaning 'Noble man of God' – because it was too religious. (He changed it back when he became president.)

The Soviets soon discovered that they had to rule Afghanistan directly. There **129** were simply not enough Afghan Communists left to do the job after the murders, executions and massacres of the previous few years, and Khalq and Parcham continued to fight each other with all the ferocity of a tribal vendetta.

In the wake of the invasion, the whole country rose against the government. The Soviet army held Kabul, but the rebels, known as *mujaheddin* ('holy warriors'), held Kandahar and Herat, the country's second and third largest cities. The Soviets retook them with bombers and tanks, and according to one observer, 'in Kandahar, they staged a brutal, block-by-block World War I I-style assault.'

The Afghan army collapsed as an effective fighting force, its numbers dropping from about 90,000–100,000 in 1979 to 30,000 by early 1981. Whole units deserted together, taking their weapons with them, and those remaining soldiers who could be cowed or blackmailed into obedience were worthless in a fight.

Soviet troops could take any town or village or valley, but they could not hold them without increasing enormously their forces in Afghanistan. They never had more than 120,000 troops there (compared with over 550,000 Americans in Vietnam at the height of that war), and this was not nearly enough. Possibly they feared having too many casualties. Possibly the Soviet army, suffering severely from the consequences of the falling Soviet birthrate and the enormous needs of guarding the frontiers and occupying Eastern Europe, simply could not find enough troops.

Since they could not spare a million men, they settled for the essential minimum – just enough to hold the main cities and keep the lines of communication open. For the rest of their new fiefdom, they relied on the air force. Rebel areas were bombed mercilessly. Mines were scattered across the countryside, some of them allegedly disguised as toys that children might collect. There are certainly many legless and armless children in refugee camps. The Soviets also sent armoured columns into the valleys and destroyed the villages, irrigation works, roads and bridges. It was a policy of scorched earth. Their ambition was to make a solitude and call it peace.

They failed. They drove over 3 million refugees into Pakistan and 2 million into Iran, but once the men had ensured their families' safety, they returned to the fight. They learned to handle modern weapons and, more remarkably, they learned modern tactics – especially the need to obey and to collaborate with other Afghans. They ambushed Soviet convoys, in country uniquely suited to ambushes; they attacked isolated bases and air strips. They infiltrated Kabul and attacked the Soviet embassy, the P D P A headquarters, the Soviet military high command. The Afghan governor of Kandahar lived and worked in a Soviet base. The Mujaheddin even mounted expeditions across the Oxus into the Soviet Union.

The Soviets were never able to conquer the high mountains in the centre of the country – the Hazarajat, comprising a quarter of the country's total area. Instead, Soviet troops cut off food supplies to starve the people living there. There are hundreds of passes across the mountains into Pakistan. The Soviets tried to block the more important by garrisoning forts in the valleys leading to them. The Mujaheddin laid siege to the forts.

At Christmas 1987, in their last offensive, the Soviets mounted an elaborate rescue of one of the besieged forts, at Khost, 100 miles (160 km) south of Kabul. A heavily armed convoy fought its way into the town to deliver supplies. The Soviet troops then fought their way out again, leaving Khost once more under siege.

A certain caution is necessary when examining atrocity reports and estimates of casualties. At one stage, the United States government insisted that the Soviets used poison gas on the Afghans, but there was never any evidence to support the allegation, and in fact, the same one was made concerning the Vietnamese in Laos, with the same lack of evidence. Reports of booby-trapped toys allegedly scattered across the countryside are also rather dubious.

Resistance to the government was fractured into numerous tribal, political, religious and military groups. Seven of them, predominantly Sunni, held a conference in Peshawar, the main Pushtun town in Pakistan, in May 1985 and formed an alliance. They called it the Unity, and leadership rotated between the seven chiefs. Another alliance of four Shiite groups was formed in Iran. The United States financed the Unity through the Pakistan intelligence service, which favoured the most militant Islamic groups. It took many years for the Americans to realize that they inadvertently contributed largely to the destruction of Afghanistan and for sowing dragons' teeth of Islamic terrorism that came to haunt the world, including the United States.

Between them, the rebel armies of the Unity claimed to have about 150,000 troops in the field, with a comparable number in reserve. Inside Afghanistan, commanders emerged from the ranks. One of these was Ahmad Shah Massoud, a Tadzik, who commanded rebels in the Panjsher valley in north-east Afghanistan. He was a brilliantly successful commander, and because his sphere of operations was relatively accessible, he became better known to the outside world than the other leaders. Every year the Soviets mounted offensives against him, with up to 20,000 troops. They occupied the valley, but could not pursue Massoud and his men into the mountains, whence they returned when the Soviets withdrew. It was a pattern repeated throughout the war – only each time it required more Soviet troops, because Massoud's forces improved steadily in number, equipment and training. The Taliban faces the same problem now.

The remaining armed forces in Afghanistan were, of course, those of the Communist Party (PDPA). Its forces, heavily armed and trained by the Soviets, numbered about 100,000. There were reports that the Soviets had issued passports to the PDPA cadres, permitting them to escape to the USSR if the regime collapsed.

From the beginning, the United States played a large part in helping the resistance. Arms were first sent to the Mujaheddin by the Carter administration; the quantity was increased steadily during the Reagan administration; and by the mid-1980s, all pretence that this was a secret operation had been dropped. The US spent a total of $3 billion (in the end, $600 million a year) helping the Afghan rebels, and Saudi Arabia, China and other countries together spent another billion. In 1986, the US started delivering Stinger (American) and Blowpipe (British) anti-aircraft missiles in large numbers, and by the summer of 1987, by some accounts, the Soviets were losing one plane or helicopter a day to these missiles. As a result, they could no longer fly low over Afghan villages and strafe them, but instead had to bomb from a great height, which meant they could not give close support to their convoys on the ground. The Stinger in particular proved a lethally effective weapon. Some of the Mujaheddin sold their Stingers to Iran for use against Iraq or even against the United States.

One consequence of the war was the collapse of the effort to eradicate opium cultivation in Afghanistan and Pakistan. According to the US State Department's 1998 report on narcotics, Afghanistan was producing 1250 tons of opium a year, second only to Burma. It is quite possible that this is an underestimate: for obvious reasons, exact measurements are difficult. There is now an extensive opium trade across the Khyber Pass, and the Afghans, whatever side they support, participate in the world's largest entrepôt of smuggled goods. The effects in Pakistan have been, in the short term, to increase national income hugely and, in the long term, to corrupt the regime and the people, and to promote addiction and crime.

## DIPLOMACY

The invasion of Afghanistan proved a disaster for the USSR. For years, the United Nations had supported every Soviet resolution denouncing the West, but after the invasion, the UN voted every year, by increasing majorities (119 to 19, 130 to 19), to denounce the occupation, naming the Soviet Union and demanding that it pull out its troops. Fidel Castro supported the Soviets in public but, in private, lamented that his own influence in the world collapsed. He had hoped to be elected chairman of the Non-Aligned Movement at a meeting in New Delhi in 1982, but instead, he met vigorous criticism for his support of the Soviet Union. The only truly non-aligned country to refrain from criticizing the USSR was India, whose animosity towards Pakistan overrode all other considerations.

The invasion also destroyed the Soviet Union's *détente* with the United States. The SALT II treaty, laboriously negotiated over seven years and signed on Waterloo Day, 18 June 1979, was withdrawn from the US Senate for ratification because of it. The USSR had been installing medium-range nuclear missiles – SS-20s – in Eastern Europe, and Nato decided to reciprocate by installing American missiles in Western Europe. There can be little doubt that the European determination to stick with this decision, despite an immense Soviet diplomatic campaign against it, was strengthened by the events in Afghanistan.

Jimmy Carter foolishly took the invasion as a personal affront, and cancelled American participation in the 1980 Olympic Games in Moscow. On 23 January 1980, he proclaimed the 'Carter Doctrine', which stated that 'An attempt by any outside force to gain control of the Persian Gulf will be regarded as an assault on the vital interests of the United States, and such an assault will be repelled by any means necessary, including military force.' Then he set about forming the Rapid Deployment Force. The RDF had nothing to do with Afghanistan, and the Soviet occupation of Afghanistan had nothing to do with the Gulf. Mr Carter had become over-excited because the Soviet invasion had followed on the heels of the seizure of the American embassy in Tehran. He wanted to be seen to be doing something forceful and decisive, even if it did nothing to help the Afghans or impress the Iranians.

For the next nine years, American policy oscillated between 'making the

Soviets bleed' and trying to find a solution to the Afghan problem. The 'Bleeders' won, and at an expenditure of $600 million a year, the US effectively caused the Soviet Union to haemorrhage until it decided to get out of Afghanistan. That result astonished the hard-liners in Washington, who had been so convinced that the Soviets were, by definition, expansionist that they had found accepting Gorbachev and *glasnost* almost impossible.

Under both Carter and Reagan the United States took care to keep its own involvement in Afghanistan as discreet as possible. This was not easy when it involved moving $600 million-worth of arms a year, but by and large, it was successful. The purpose was to prevent the Soviets from turning the war into an East–West or anti-colonialist struggle, with the Americans as the villains. The Soviets did their best to present a counter-image, but American discretion ensured that the world, and the Afghans, continued to see the fight as exclusively a north–south struggle, or an anti-imperialist war with the Soviets as the imperialists.

In June 1982, the UN convened talks between the Afghan and Pakistani governments in Geneva, under the direction of a UN under-secretary, Diego Cordovez, an Ecuadorian lawyer. These were called 'proximity talks' because the Pakistanis would not recognize or negotiate with the Kabul government. The two delegations never met: for six ineffectual years, Cordovez travelled backwards and forwards between their offices, mediating. No agreement could ever be reached: the real principals were the Soviets and the Afghan resistance, and no change in direction could be attained without a change of policy in Moscow.

This at last occurred in February 1988 – or, at least, was finally revealed then. There had been many signs that the Soviets were sickening of the war. One effect of Gorbachev's *glasnost* was that Soviet newspapers at last started reporting the war seriously, and carrying news of death, dismemberment and the miseries returning soldiers brought with them. It soon became apparent to foreigners in Moscow that the war was deeply unpopular. After a final dispute with Washington over when or whether the two sides would cut off arms supplies to their respective clients, Gorbachev finally announced the Soviet withdrawal on 7 April 1988. He chose a most unlikely pretext, a visit to a collective farm near Tashkent. He had just met President Najibullah in that city, to inform him of the decision and demand his acquiescence, much as Henry Kissinger had extorted South Vietnam's assent to the Paris agreement of 1973. The television cameras caught Gorbachev chatting casually with the farmers in a field, and calmly informing them that the withdrawal would begin the following month.

The agreement was finally signed in Geneva on 14 April 1988 by Pakistan and the Kabul government. The Soviet foreign minister, Edward Shevardnadze, and the US secretary of state, George Shultz, signed as guarantors. It was not at all clear what that meant, and there were plentiful ambiguities in the text. The US and the USSR each agreed not to arm their respective clients so long as the other refrained from doing so. On 10 April 1988, a major Mujaheddin arms and munitions dump in Rawalpindi exploded, killing several hundred people. The size of the explosion demonstrated graphically the quantity of arms that the Americans and their allies had supplied to the Afghan resistance.

The Soviet withdrawal began on schedule. The Western press was invited to

**133**

watch the troops as they left Kabul and as they arrived at the Oxus to be welcomed with flowers, speeches and the joy of their relatives. Soviet television broadcast these touching scenes, a further demonstration both of *glasnost* and of the vast improvement in Soviet public relations technique under Gorbachev.

The last Soviet soldier, Lieutenant General Boris Gromov, crossed the Friendship Bridge just before noon on 15 February 1989, to be met by his 14-year-old son, carrying a bouquet of flowers. Gromov, the last Soviet commander in Afghanistan, never looked back.

Even before that, the Mujaheddin mounted a full-scale attack on Jalalabad, the principal city on the road from Kabul eastwards to the Khyber Pass. The siege continued for several months, unsuccessfully. Najibullah's government drew comfort from its success, and the Mujaheddin began fighting among themselves. The Americans continued to support the Peshawar government in exile, but with increasing reservations.

One of the provisions of the Geneva agreement was that the former UN high commissioner for refugees, Saddrudin Aga Khan, would supervise the return home of the approximate 7 million refugees. It promised to be a long and expensive task. According to one guerrilla leader, 60 per cent of the houses in Afghanistan had been destroyed, and 60 per cent of arable land had been taken out of cultivation because canals and irrigation systems had been damaged or destroyed. Half the refugees returned home by 1995.

The Najibullah regime survived its first three years alone. The Soviet Union continued to supply arms and essential economic assistance, and the Americans continued to supply the rebels, though at a reduced rate. The various rebel forces failed to cooperate in combined operations against the government, and there were many instances of fighting between them. In March 1991, the Mujaheddin at last captured Khost, the chief government base in eastern Afghanistan, and immediately the two chief rebel groups there started fighting over the booty.

In the spring of 1991, Pakistan and Saudi Arabia supplied the rebels with tanks and artillery captured from Iraq during the Gulf War. At the same time, military and political support from Moscow began to fade away, as the Soviet Union disintegrated. After the failure of the Moscow coup in August, the Soviet government agreed to suspend all military aid to Kabul in January 1992, and the United States announced that it would finally stop supplying the Mujaheddin. There was no longer any reason for either country to interest itself in the affairs of Afghanistan.

In October 1991, Najibullah announced that he would hold free elections to local assemblies, as a prelude to national elections in 1992, and invited the opposition to help organize them. The Mujaheddin refused all negotiations with him, demanding that he leave the country before they would have any dealings with the Kabul regime. Najibullah also invited the former king, Zahir Shah, to return from exile. It was to no avail. The Mujaheddin closed in on Kabul and despite their incessant factional fighting, took the city on 16 April 1992. Najibullah, a brother and two aides took refuge in the UN compound (he had sent his family to safety in India).

There followed a period of ceaseless faction fighting. The main leaders were the Pushtun fundamentalist Gulbuddin Hekmatyar, who was supported by

Pakistan largely out of a need to conciliate its own Pushtun population, and Burnahuddin Rabani, a Tadzhik, who was supported by the military leader Ahmad Shah Massoud, and by the Tadzhiks over the border to the north. They were nominally united in a coalition government but in fact fought a vicious civil war for power in Kabul. They were heavily armed with artillery supplied by Pakistan and Russia. Kabul, which had survived the war against the Soviets, was almost destroyed in the fighting. Other cities went their own ways under their own tribal leaders.

In October 1994, a new force suddenly appeared on the scene, an ultra-conservative Pushtun Islamic group calling itself Taliban (from a Persian word meaning 'seekers after truth'). They emerged from the refugee camps in Pakistan and promised to liberate Afghanistan from the quarrelling Mujaheddin warlords, and impose an absolute Koranic rule on the country. Their doctrines make Khomeini's Iran seem a hotbed of enlightened liberalism. Women were to be returned to strict purdah, meaning they might only leave home veiled head to foot and accompanied by their fathers, husbands or brothers. All schools for girls were to be closed and no woman might enjoy any further education, let alone attend university. They might have no dealings with men who were not close relations, and were forbidden to work outside their homes. Men were not allowed to trim their beards and soccer was forbidden, together with music, movies, television, anything remotely Western, and any social innovation more recent than the 7th century. Only in weaponry did Taliban embrace its age. It is led by a one-eyed cleric called Mohammed Omar and, in October 1994, it took Kandahar, the Pushtun capital in the south.

Taliban then marched north and west, capturing Herat and laying siege to Kabul. The capital fell on 27 September 1996. One of Taliban's first actions was to storm the UN compound, ignoring all claims of diplomatic immunity, and drag out Najibullah, his brother and two aides, and hang them. The Mujaheddin government, led by Burnahuddin Rabani, had offered to take the four to safety in the north as they prepared to flee the capital, but Najibullah distrusted his former enemies and preferred the protection of the UN.

The civil war continues. It is increasingly a war between the tribes. The Tadzhiks in the north-east, led by Massoud, resist the Pushtun Taliban regime in Kabul. So do the Uzbeks in the north-east, led by General Abdurrashid Dostum, a last survivor of the Communist regime. The Tadzhiks in Herat and Shiite Hazera in north-central Afghanistan have been defeated and occupied by the Taliban, but their resistance continues (supported by Iran). Taliban's control of the capital remains precarious.

In early 1997, at the end of Ramadan, Taliban attacked the north and briefly occupied Dostum's capital, Mazar-i-Sharif, north of the Hindu Kush, after Dostum's foreign minister, Abdul Malik, deserted him. Then Malik changed sides again, and Tadzhiks and Uzbeks combined to cut off, capture and slaughter all the Taliban's Pushtun soldiers in the province. The UN reported that some 2000 Taliban soldiers had been executed. The 'northern alliance' of Uzbeks and Tadzhiks then reoccupied most of the territory all the way to Kabul.

Taliban controls more of Afghanistan than any regime since the Communist revolution in 1979, but, so far, despite the supply of heavy weapons from **135**

Pakistan, has not succeeded in conquering the north. The UN does not recognize the Taliban government (only Pakistan does), but there is not sufficient external support for its enemies to defeat it. The civil war continues.

## FURTHER READING

American University, *Afghanistan: A Country Study*, Washington D.C., 1986.

Amnesty International, *Afghanistan: Torture of Political Prisoners*, London, 1986.

Chaliand, Gerard (trans. Tamar Jacoby), *Report from Afghanistan*, New York, Viking, 1982.

Cordovez, Diego and Harrison, Selig S., *Out of Afghanistan: The Inside Story of the Soviet Withdrawal*, New York, Oxford University Press, 1996.

Dupree, Louis, *Afghanistan*, Princeton, N.J., Princeton University Press, 1973.

— *Red Flag over the Hindu Kush*, Field Staff Reports, American Universities, New York, 1968 etc.

Fraser, George MacDonald, *Flashman*, London, Herbert Jenkins, 1969.

Girardet, Edward, *Afghanistan: The Soviet War*, New York, St Martin's Press, 1985.

Hopkirk, Peter, *Setting the East Ablaze*.

Klass, Rosanne (ed.), *Afghanistan: The Great Game Revisited*, New York, Freedom House, 1988.

Leber, Jerri and Rubin, Barnett E., *A Nation Is Dying: Afghanistan under the Soviets*, Evanston, Ill., Northwest University Press, 1988.

Lohbeck, Kurt, *Holy War, Unholy Victory*, Washington, Regnery Gateway, 1993.

Rubin, Barnett, *The Fragmentation of Afghanistan: State Formation and Collapse in the International System*, and *The Search for Peace in Afghanistan, from Buffer State to Failed State*, New Haven, Yale University Press, 1996.

# BANGLADESH

| | |
|---|---|
| Geography | 55,126 sq. miles (142,776 sq. km). Rather smaller than England and Wales. |
| Population | 120 million. It is growing at 1.6% p.a. The population density is 2000 per sq. mile. |
| GNP per capita | $240. |
| Refugees | 95,000 in India. There are 40,000 Rohingya from Burma in Bangladesh. |

## HISTORY

Bangladesh became independent as a result of the break-up of Pakistan in the civil war of 1971 (*see* Pakistan, pp. 228). The country was in turmoil, with the defeated Pakistani army, the remaining adherents of a united Pakistan, the Indian army and the Bangladeshi guerrilla army (the Mukti Bahini) all fighting in the most crowded country on Earth. Bangladesh was born in violence, and the violence has continued to this day.

The group most loyal to Pakistan in what was to become Bangladesh were the Biharis. These were Urdu-speaking Muslim refugees from the Indian province of Bihar who had fled to East Pakistan in 1947 to escape from the massacres of partition: in 1946, 30,000 Muslim Biharis were massacred by Hindus and more were slaughtered in 1947. In the general horrors of partition, 1.3 million Muslims from India fled to East Pakistan, a million of them from Bihar. In turn, about 3.3 million Hindus fled East Bengal for India.

The Biharis never assimilated with the Bengalis, and when Mohammed Ali Jinnah, the founder of Pakistan, proclaimed Urdu the national language of both east and west divisions, over strong opposition from the Bengalis, the Biharis found themselves in a favoured position in East Pakistan, taking the government jobs that required Urdu. When tension between the two wings of the country reached a peak in 1970–1, the Biharis in the east were the natural victims of Bengali persecution, and hundreds were murdered in Dacca and other cities. When President Yahya proclaimed martial law in the East in March 1971, arrested the Awami League leader Mujib Ur-Rahman and suppressed the League, the Biharis rallied to the Pakistani cause, and took their revenge on their Bengali persecutors by joining the Pakistani armed forces in the effort to **137** suppress Bengali nationalism. Bangladesh now claims that 3 million people were murdered during the period March–December 1971. The real number is probably between 300,000 and half a million.

The massacres continued until the very end of 1971, and many Biharis were murdered after the Pakistanis surrendered. On one infamous occasion, on 18 December, a Bengali terrorist leader killed a number of mostly Bihari prisoners in Dacca soccer stadium, before a vast and cheering crowd. A British television crew was present and televised the event.

Many Biharis died during the following months, but not the vast numbers usual in communal disturbances in the subcontinent. Several hundred thousand remain, 25 years later, living miserable and unwanted in the slums of Dacca. Neither Bangladesh, Pakistan nor India will rescue them.

## INDEPENDENT BANGLADESH

The unquestioned leader of the new state was Sheikh Mujib, leader of the Awami League, who became prime minister. Whatever his skills as an opposition leader, he had none as head of government. He alienated many of those who had contributed most to the fight for independence, and ran the government in an authoritarian, paternalistic style despite natural disasters, famine and rapidly spreading disorder.

In December 1974, Mujib declared a state of emergency. In January 1975, he amended the constitution, making himself executive president and banning all opposition. On 15 August 1975, Mujib and several members of his family were murdered by a group of army majors.

They installed one of Mujib's ministers, Khondakar Mushtaque Ahmad, as president and arrested Mujib's closest associates. Senior army officers disapproved of these developments, and on 3 November, Brigadier Khalid Musharaf staged a coup. The majors escaped to Libya, but Musharaf arrested the chief of staff, General Zia Rahman. He did not make himself president, putting a judge, A. S. M. Sayem, into that position. The jailed Mujibist ministers were murdered.

On 6 November, there was a further coup, instigated by survivors of Mujib's private security force, the J S D, and Musharaf was killed. Sayem remained president, but real power was taken by General Zia.

Zia had played an important role in the war of independence, and now quickly brought the country's security problems under control and set about reforming the administration and military. He was the most popular and successful of Bengali leaders since independence, and in April 1977, he became president. Political life resumed, and elections were held in February 1979; Zia's newly formed Bangladesh Nationalist party won them.

The country was united behind Zia, but elements in the military opposed him. There were several attempted coups and mutinies, and on 30 May 1981, Zia was murdered at the instigation of the army commander at Chittagong. The rebellion was put down by the chief of staff, General Hossain Muhammed Ershad, and the rebel general, his family and many others were killed.

Ershad in due course made himself president. He lacked the charisma of Zia, and his government made no perceptible progress in solving the country's economic problems. In elections on 3 March 1988, Ershad's party won a large majority, but since the vote was boycotted by the opposition parties (including the Awami League, now led by Mujib's daughter, and Zia's Nationalist party, led by his widow, the Begum Khaleda Zia), the elections offered no solutions. There was much violence before the voting, with several hundred people killed.

## THE PROBLEMS OF POLITICS AND DEMOGRAPHY

Ershad lasted a further two and a half years. He became increasingly authoritarian and failed to improve the economy, which was afflicted by further disastrous floods. In late 1990, serious rioting broke out. Ershad declared a state of emergency on 28 November after police opened fire on rioters demanding the president's resignation. The opposition claimed that 50 people were killed and over 1000 wounded. After further rioting, Ershad was forced to resign on 4 December, and was subsequently arrested and charged with corruption. He was alleged to have accepted an $8.1 million bribe for arranging the purchase of three turbojets from British Aerospace for $46.5 million.

Elections were held on 27 February 1991, and the Nationalist party won. Khalida Zia became prime minister, the second woman leader of a Muslim country, and inherited all the country's hopes and difficulties. Five years later, in June 1996, further elections defeated Zia and brought a revived Awami League back to power under Sheikh Mujib's daughter, Hasina Wazed. One of her first acts as prime minister was to bring to trial the men who had killed her father, mother, three brothers and five other relatives in 1975.

Bangladesh's real problem is demographic. It is the most densely populated of the world's nations, except for the city states of Singapore and Hong Kong. Its *per capita* income, about $240 a year, is half that of Haiti, and as the population continues to increase relentlessly, the average income continues to drop. Bangladesh is very fertile, watered by two of the great rivers of the world, the Ganges and the Brahmaputra, and built of silt washed down from the north Indian plain and Tibet. But the Malthusian dilemma remains. Bangladesh can barely feed itself in the good years; if the monsoons fail, there will be a famine on a scale the world has not known.

Bangladesh is also extremely low-lying – much of it at or just above sea level. With the deforestation of the Himalayas has come a great increase in the height of the spring floods, with consequent inundation of the Bangladeshi countryside. In 1988, there were severe floods resulting in untold damage. If the 'greenhouse effect' causes the levels of the oceans to rise, Bangladesh may become uninhabitable.

## THE CHITTAGONG HILL TRACTS

Eastern Bangladesh includes the first ranges of the Burmese hills. The 600,000 tribal people of the region, who are Buddhists of Tibetan origin, began a guerrilla campaign in 1976, which has so far resulted in the deaths of at least 3500. They accuse the government of encouraging settlement by Muslim Bengalis: there are now at least 300,000 Bengalis in their hills. The same cause has provoked similar uprisings in Indian districts farther north and east.

Under the British, the Chittagong Hill Tracts were administered entirely **139** separately from the rest of India, and there were strict laws to prevent outsiders settling there. Under the Government of India Act, 1935, the Tracts were defined as 'totally excluded areas', outside the rule of Bengal and Assam. The same rules applied to hill districts that are now in India and in Burma. There are 13 major tribes in the Tracts, about half their number being Chakmas (who are also the main tribe in Tripura state, over the border in India).

The legal protections offered the tribes were severely reduced by the government of Pakistan, and were abolished altogether by the government of Bangladesh after it became independent in 1971. The theory was that any citizen of Bangladesh had the right to live anywhere in the country. As a result, the tribesmen are rapidly going the way of the American Indians.

In 1951, 9 per cent of the Tracts' population was non-tribal. By 1974, that had increased to 11 per cent, and in 1980, non-tribal people comprised a third of the population. There is no doubt that the percentage has increased still more since then. The government actively encourages Muslim Bengalis to settle in the hills. Since the population of Bangladesh is rising at a rate of 2 million a year, settling a few hundred thousand Bengalis in the high hills above Chittagong is not going to make much difference, but in their desperation, the flood of Bengalis into the area will continue.

In 1972, responding to the pressure from the plains, a group of tribal leaders formed the Chittagong Hill Tracts People's Solidarity Association (known by its initials as the JSS). The JSS then formed a military wing, the Shanti Bahini, which in the mid-1970s began attacking army outposts and harassing Bengali villages. Hundreds of people were killed during this campaign. General Ershad offered the Shanti Bahini an amnesty in 1983, and claimed that 3000 men surrendered. However, the government's settlement policy was not changed, and there was a sharp increase in Shanti Bahini attacks in 1985, and the troubles have continued ever since. In the last week of April 1988, 36 Bengali settlers were murdered in two hill villages; on 30 April, 13 Bengalis were killed; and on 21 May, another three died.

The government has sent large numbers of troops to suppress the uprising, and according to an Amnesty International report, they have acted with great brutality. A group of local politicians, at a press conference in Dacca in April 1980, described a massacre of some 200 villagers by Bengali troops. Amnesty has found evidence of several other massacres, some provoked by tribal attacks on settlers.

On 3 May 1984, Shanti Bahini terrorists murdered over 100 Bengalis in their villages. In revenge, troops killed hundreds of tribal villagers in the neighbouring hills. Amnesty International reports include details of incidents given by survivors, including horrific accounts of torture and of the rapes of many women before they were murdered. According to the US Committee for Refugees, there are 53,000 refugees from the Tracts in squalid camps in the Indian state of Tripura, of whom 20,115 crossed the border in 1987. Amnesty has stated:

The information available to Amnesty International leads the organization to believe that tribal villagers detained for questioning by military and paramilitary personnel are regularly tortured. Such prisoners are generally kept in pits or trenches seven or eight feet deep . . . prisoners are reported to have been held in groups of up to 15 or 20 at one time in these conditions . . . The techniques of torture which former prisoners reported to be most frequently used during interrogation are: extensive beating, with rifle butts and sticks, on all parts of the body; pouring very hot water into the nostrils and mouth; hanging the prisoner upside down, often from a tree . . . hanging the prisoner by the shoulders for long periods and then beating the soles of his feet . . .

The Shanti Bahini finally signed a ceasefire agreement with the government in December 1997. The government agreed to many of the Chakmas' demands for autonomy, but it was beyond its power to move the Bengalis out of the hills. The Chakmas promised to hand in their weapons and accept an amnesty, but similar agreements with hill tribes in India and Burma have failed to solve the under-lying problems, or bring lasting peace.

## FURTHER READING

American University, *Bangladesh, a Country Study*, Washington D.C., 1985.

Amnesty International, *Bangladesh: Unlawful Torture and Killing in the Chittagong Hill Tracts*, London, 1986.

Baxter, Craig, *Bangladesh: A New Nation in an Old Setting*, Boulder, Colo., Westview Press, 1984.

Minority Rights Group, *The Biharis in Bangladesh*, London, 1982.

O'Donnell, Charles Peter, *Bangladesh: Biography of a Muslim Nation*, Boulder, Colo., Westview Press, 1984.

# BURMA

| | |
|---|---|
| Name | After the 1988 coup, the military government changed the country's name to Myanmar and renamed many cities. Rangoon became Yangon. |
| Geography | 261,217 sq. miles (676,552 sq. km): the size of Texas, or of France, Belgium, Holland and Denmark combined. It is divided by a series of mountain ranges running north to south from the Himalayas (19,000 ft/6000 m) to the Bay of Bengal and to the border with Thailand. The central plain is traversed by the Irrawaddy River, the delta of which was the richest rice-producing area in the world before World War II. |
| Population | 45 million. All the inhabitants of Burma are referred to as Burmese; the majority language group are the Burmans. There are over 100 languages spoken. Although there has been no ethnic census since 1931, approximate tribal or ethnic divisions among the major tribes (there are dozens of minor ones) are: |

Burman: 30,000,000
Shan: 4,700,000
Karen: 3,850,000
Arakan: 2,480,000
Indian: 800,000
Mon: 760,000
Wa: 550,000
Kachin: 550,000
Chin: 550,000
Naga: 112,000

| | |
|---|---|
| Religion | 85% Buddhist. Many Karen, Kachin and Chin are Christians, converted by American Baptist missionaries. |
| Resources | Burma is well endowed and is underpopulated, compared with other South Asian nations. It has three-quarters of the world's teak, besides oil, minerals (including tungsten), rubies and jade. Burma is the world's largest producer of opium. |
| GNP per capita | N.A. |
| Refugees | Internal, between 500,000 and 1 million. External, 40,000 Rohingya in Bangladesh, 95,000 of various tribes in Thailand, 40,000 Chins in India, 10,000 elsewhere. |
| Insurgents | The American University country study for Burma (1983) lists 28 insurgent groups operating in Burma, whose forces ranged in size from the Burmese Communist party (8000–15,000) and the Karen National Union (5000–8000) down to the Kayah New Land Revolution Council (50) and the Karenni People's |

United Liberation Front (70). Their total manpower was
between 27,000 and 44,000. Apart from the Communists, who
have a clear political programme, the insurgents are concerned
with preserving their own autonomy and, some of them, with
controlling the opium trade.

---

In the summer of 1988, the military government of Burma temporarily collapsed
under the weight of civilian protest. Burma had been ruled as a socialist, military
dictatorship by General Ne Win since 1962, and the country had been reduced to
abject poverty. It was one of the most introverted countries in the world, on a par
with Albania or North Korea. It was also one of the poorest, largely because of
the 'Burmese Way to Socialism'. In 1987, the U N defined Burma as one of the
world's 'least-developed countries', one of a select group of the ten poorest.

Eventually, the incompetence of the regime provoked an uprising which began
among students and spread to the rest of the population. Ne Win resigned in July
and the country slipped into anarchy. Mass demonstrations in the streets of
Rangoon and other cities overthrew all authority, and for a while, it seemed that
Burma would follow the example of the Philippines and South Korea in
instituting a democratic government after a popular uprising. However, in
Burma there was to begin with no charismatic leader, like Corazon Aquino
in the Philippines, to unite the opposition and force the army to surrender its
powers during those few days before it recovered its nerve. Furthermore, Burma
was so isolated from the world that the United States and other democracies had
no means of influencing events. On 18 September 1988, the army staged a coup
and restored its authority. The new regime, or the old regime with a few new
leaders, broke the strike and set about suppressing the opposition. Some political
activity was permitted, and a general election was held in May 1990. The
opposition won over 80 per cent of the vote, and the army ignored the results.
Daw Aung San Suu Kyi, who had become the opposition's leader, was put under
house arrest ('Daw' is an honorific, meaning lady). She won the Nobel peace
prize in October 1991, but the regime continued on its course, one of the most
backward and repressive tyrannies in the world.

These events took place in Rangoon, Mandalay and other cities of the Burman
heartland. On the periphery, there have been continuous insurrections against
the central authorities since 1947: the Karen rebellion is probably the longest-
lasting war of the century.

## HISTORY

In the 19th century, Burma, like so much of the world, was annexed to the British
Empire. First, the East India Company seized the coastal provinces in the First
Burma War (1824–6); then south Burma was annexed in 1852 and the rest of the
country in 1885. The last king, Thibaw, was exiled to India, and Burma was
ruled as a province of British India until the 1930s.

It was a prosperous colony, thanks to its rice, oil, teak and other riches. The
Irrawaddy delta with its capital at Rangoon was rapidly developed into a major
rice-growing area. Prosperity and, eventually, the development of the institutions of a nation state were concentrated in the river valley and the delta. The hill
country was always treated separately, partly to protect the tribesmen, partly on

**143**

the divide-and-rule principle. While, in India, the British developed educational and political institutions that eventually produced a unified, independent state, for most of their time in Burma they contented themselves with administration and police functions. (George Orwell – Eric Blair – was a Burma policeman.) Finally, in 1937, the British separated Burma from India and began to develop its political institutions. This was partly a reaction to nationalist agitation that had begun among Burmese students and reached a climax in 1938 when oil workers marched on Rangoon in support of the students.

During the Japanese war with China, supplies to China were sent over the mountains into Yenan via the 'Burma Road'. In 1942, in order to cut that road and to threaten India, Japan occupied Burma. Thirty Burmese nationalists, led by the most prominent of the former student leaders, Thakin Aung San, then 27, had gone to Japan for military training in 1940. These 'Thirty Comrades' included several of the men who were to become the leaders of independent Burma, among them Thakin Shu Maung, who later took the *nom de guerre* Ne Win ('Brilliant like the Sun'). ('Thakin' is an honorific, meaning 'master', a title that had been reserved for the British, like *sahib* in India; the Thirty Comrades adopted it to assert their Burmese independence.) Aung San formed a Burmese army allied to the Japanese, based on the Thirty Comrades, and during the Japanese invasion Ne Win led a sabotage mission into Rangoon.

Japan hoped to use Burma as a base from which to invade India, and therefore built the Burma–Siam railway over the Three Pagodas pass from Siam. They proclaimed Burmese independence in August 1943, with Aung San as minister of defence, and Thakin Nu as foreign minister, and they established a Burmese army in which Ne Win was a brigadier. However, the Japanese soon alienated the Burmese by their arrogance and brutality, and after their invasion of India failed in 1944, Aung San formed the Anti-Fascist People's Freedom League, and joined the British when they invaded Burma. On 27 March 1945, on a signal from Mountbatten, the British commander, Aung San's troops attacked the Japanese in the rear, greatly helping the British advance. The British had conducted a long and difficult campaign in Burma, notable for the exploits of Orde Wingate's Chindits (British) and Merrill's Marauders (American).

The war destroyed Burma's industrial base, including the oil industry, the railways, rolling stock and river fleet. The British, after a period of hesitation, decided that Burma should become independent at the same time as India. A conference of a majority of the many nationalities in Burma was held in February 1947, and the Burmese Union was voted into existence: an achievement that was chiefly due to Aung San, the most capable and charismatic of Burmese leaders. He and seven of his ministers were assassinated in July by a disgruntled rival, and the leadership then fell to Nu, who assumed the honorific U (meaning 'uncle'). He signed the treaty establishing Burmese independence, in London on 17 October 1947. Independence day, an auspicious date chosen by the Buddhist astrologers, was 4 January 1948.

## INDEPENDENT BURMA

U Nu was not the man to cope with the tribal insurrections that immediately

broke out, and which have plagued Burma ever since. The economy was in ruins:

the standard of living did not recover to 1940 levels until 1975, and has declined since then. From the start, the country's problems were compounded by the imposition of socialism, and were seriously aggravated after the 1962 coup.

The British had governed Burma proper as they had the states of India. The hill tribes, comprising at least half the country, were defined as 'scheduled' areas and were administered separately, as were the coastal provinces that had been conquered first; Kayah state, on the Thai border, was never conquered at all. Like the Sikhs or Pathans in India, the hill tribes were considered 'martial races' by the British, as opposed to the supposedly peaceable Burmans, and so the Karen of the south-east and the Kachin of the north-east were recruited into the British army. These divisions were exacerbated by the Karens' adoption of Christianity and their loyalty to the British during the war, when the Burmans, at first, sided with the Japanese. After independence, bringing these diverse peoples into a proper union proved quite beyond the capacity of the Burmans.

On Independence Day, Red Flag Communists were already in revolt, and there was a rebellion among Muslim separatists (the Mujahids) in the coastal province of Arakan. The White Flag Communists revolted on 27 March 1948. (The differences between the two factions were the result of the conflicting ambitions of their leaders.) Then part of the national army that Aung San had founded launched a revolt, and two of the five battalions of the regular army mutinied. Finally, in January 1949, a revolt began among the Karen in the south-east, and the Karen regiments in the army mutinied. U Nu dismissed the commander-in-chief, a Karen, and replaced him with Ne Win, who was to remain in control of the Burmese army until 1988.

. Burma almost disintegrated. Mandalay was captured by Kachin rebels on 13 March 1948, and Rangoon was saved by the loyalty of regiments composed of another tribe, the Chin, and by the disunity of the various rebels. By degrees, the government was able to reassert its control of the Irrawaddy valley, recapturing Mandalay on 24 April.

In 1948, as the Communists won the Chinese civil war, a defeated Kuomintang (K M T) army, 12,000 strong, escaped into Burma and occupied part of the Shan state on the eastern frontier. The K M T army, known as the Chinese Irregular Forces (C I F), defeated Burmese armies sent after them, and rapidly expanded the area under their control. They were supplied by Taiwan and the United States, which had fantasies of using them against China.

The C I F and tribal rebels in south-east Burma formed part of a 'warlord' system that controlled the 'Golden Triangle' in Burma, northern Laos, Cambodia and Thailand. This soon developed into the world's major opium-growing area, and by 1953, over 80 per cent of the Burmese army was fighting the C I F there. The C I F are still in Shan state, although much diminished.

After recovering from the dangers of the immediate post-independence period, the country drifted steadily downhill, its economy deteriorating despite many fanciful socialist plans, and its political problems getting steadily worse. The first military coup took place in November 1958, with U Nu's connivance, and the army under Ne Win applied itself to solving the country's problems. It achieved some superficial success.

An election was held in February 1960, which U Nu won, and the army retired **145** to its barracks. U Nu made Buddhism the state religion, which infuriated the animist and Christian Karen and Kachin. The Shan were also moving into opposition: under the 1947 agreement setting up the Union, they had the right to secede, and were considering the possibility. Then U Nu announced that he would nationalize the import trade, part of which was in the hands of a corporation controlled by the army. On 2 March 1962, Ne Win seized power.

## THE MILITARY DICTATORSHIP

U Nu and his ministers, and Shan leaders who had gathered in Rangoon to consider their future, were all arrested. Ne Win and his colleagues then set about imposing their peculiar vision on the country. Its guiding principles included: xenophobia, which took the form of an equal dislike for Britain, China, the United States, the Soviet Union and Burma's immediate neighbours; Buddhist theology, with its abhorrence of gambling and ostentation and its supposed advocacy of holy poverty; and old-fashioned authoritarianism.

Ne Win himself was a notorious womanizer, gambler and golfer: wise foreign ministers chose their ambassadors to Rangoon from among diplomatic golfers, who did their business with the party leader on the links. He also had a house in Wimbledon in London, where he spent several months a year, and when he discovered that his children were growing up barely literate, because of the inadequacies of the Burmese educational system, he sent them to school in England. A few years after the coup, the British returned King Thibaw's regalia to Ne Win, hoping to placate him. The gesture had no good effect.

The regime published three documents laying down the principles of the 'Burmese Way to Socialism', as one of them was called. The key document was entitled 'The System of the Correlation of Man and His Environment (the philosophy of the Burma Socialist Programme party)', which mixed Buddhism and socialism into an eclectic Burmese mush. The results have been protracted economic stagnation: foreign firms starting with the British Imperial Chemical Industries (I C I) and the Burmah Oil Company, were expelled; banks and, in 1963, all major industries were nationalized; and about 200,000 Indians and Pakistanis were expelled. The regime denied citizenship to anyone of foreign extraction and, in 1978, started registering the inhabitants of the western border areas, where there is a Muslim minority, the descendants of immigrants from Bengal. About 200,000 Muslims fled to Bangladesh. Most of them eventually returned, but their position remained precarious. In 1969, U Nu, who had been released from prison in Rangoon, tried to launch an invasion and insurrection from Thailand; he failed.

Although it was less brutal than Cambodia under the Khmers Rouges and less corrupt than Indonesia, the Ne Win regime was entirely capable of extreme violence to protect itself. It demonstrated the point four months after the 1962 coup, when a student demonstration in Rangoon was put down with great brutality, with scores or perhaps hundreds of people killed. Foreign news organizations were forbidden, the press was nationalized and Burma shut itself away from the world. By coincidence, a Burmese, U Thant, became acting secretary-general of the U N when Dag Hammarksjöld was killed in 1961, and secretary-general in 1962, the year of the coup.

## THE REBELLIONS

The various insurrections continued. They fell into three categories: first, the Burmese Communist party, a class by itself, because it attempted to overthrow the government and take its place; second, ethnic groups, whose object was to preserve their tribal autonomy; third, warlord groups, who were chiefly interested in the opium trade. At its widest extent, up to 40 per cent of the country was controlled by insurgents, but this comprised a much smaller fraction of the population.

The Burmese Communist party (BCP), aided by the Chinese, is based in Shan, a territory stretching several hundred miles along the Chinese frontier, north of the area held by the Chinese Irregular Forces (CIF). Apart from the dedicated Communists – the residuum of the Red Flag and White Flag Communists who took to the hills in 1948 – the bulk of BCP support comes from a loose coalition of minority groups, representing the Shan and other ethnic insurgents. The BCP proposed to establish a People's Republic of Burma, to represent the working classes of the country, and, rather improbably, accused Ne Win of subservience to foreign imperialists. In 1968, the BCP's leader, Thakin Than Tun, instigated a 'cultural revolution' on the Maoist model among his followers, but it proved unpopular and Tun himself was murdered. The BCP's problem is that while most of its members are from ethnic minorities and thus the party has little appeal to Burmans, the party's leaders, mostly living in Peking, are Burmans who are therefore distrusted by the tribes. A further problem is that the BCP controls the most productive poppy fields in the Golden Triangle. For a while, it tried to reduce production, but soon the temptation of the huge profits to be made proved too much, and production resumed full blast.

In 1996 and 1997, the military regime in Rangoon launched a massive offensive against all the tribal rebels in the east and south-east. They drove the rebel forces to the Thai frontiers and then reached peace agreements with 15 of 16 groups, leaving only the Karen. It remains to be seen whether the peace agreements will last. The deals offered the tribes autonomy in exchange for recognizing the Rangoon government, but the US suspected that the main inducement was a division of the profits of the opium trade. The main opium warlord, Khun Sa, reached an agreement with the regime and returned to live in Rangoon.

In the early 1990s, the Karen controlled the 600 miles of jungle and mountain along the Thai border in south-east Burma. Other rebel groups controlled the borders to the north, while Chin and Naga rebels controlled the mountains that separate Burma from India. These last two cooperate with their relatives across the border, who are in revolt against the Indian government. In 1976, nine ethnic groups (soon to be joined by a tenth) formed an alliance – the National Democratic Front (NDF) – to demand autonomy from Rangoon.

Among the original nine was the Karen National Union, which had, in various forms, been in rebellion since 1949; its army is the Karen National Liberation Army (KNLA), about 5000 strong. Military operations and the local administration are financed by smuggling jewels and teak into Thailand. The Karens claim that they do not take part in the drug trade: that would be against their Baptist faith. Their allies farther north are less fussy.

**147**

The other members of the N D F were the Kachin, Shan, Wa, Mon and Arakan, as well as various minor tribes including Karenni, Paluang, Lahu and Pa-O, and together they claimed to have 35,000 insurgents.

In 1984, the Burmese army mounted a new offensive against the K N L A and overran two Karen strongholds. In successive attacks, it succeeded in driving about 20,000 people from their homes to live in camps along the Thai border. The K N L A fought in the traditional guerrilla manner, ambushing army patrols and attacking isolated outposts. It also planted bombs in towns and villages: the government claims that the K N L A put a bomb on a train near Rangoon on 9 January 1988, which killed nine and wounded 38 people. From 1986, the government offensives were extended to Communist and Kachin insurgents in the north-east, and Mon rebels in south Burma.

The strongest of the N D F armies is probably the Kachin Independence Army (K I A), the military arm of the Kachin Independence Organization (K I O). The Kachin live on the Chinese frontier, in the most inaccessible parts of the country. In an offensive in 1987, the army overran the headquarters of both the K I O and the K I A, but the two organizations still claimed 4000–8000 troops and control of half of Kachin state.

According to an Amnesty International report issued in May 1988, based on interviews with 70 Karen refugees in camps on the Thai border, the civilian population in rebel areas has suffered heavily from counter-insurgency drives. They have been rounded up into 'strategic hamlets', often separated from their fields, and many have been summarily shot. Amnesty claims to have documented 200 cases of extra-legal executions of Karens and believes that there are many more. It has also found numerous cases of torture. The report says:

Countless villagers have been seized to work as porters or guides for the army. Many have died as a result. Captured villagers are force-marched until they fall dead from sickness or exhaustion, or are killed for not working hard enough, or are blown up in minefields through which they are forced to lead troops. A Karen farmer, now a refugee, was travelling with a friend to buy land for growing rice, when they ran into an army patrol. They were accused of links with the rebels and were forced to become porters. His friend died after being severely beaten by the soldiers. 'The last time I saw him, he was lying alongside the path and was shivering. He could not walk or stand up. The soldiers took his load from his shoulders and left him behind. We could not help him. We could just look at him, take a look at him as we passed by.'

The report includes 60 such stories. In conclusion, Amnesty International states: 'So numerous and similar are the accounts of human rights violations given by the refugees that, in Amnesty International's opinion, they show a consistent pattern of gross violations of human rights.'

The peoples of the remote mountains and jungles of eastern and south-eastern Burma and of the contiguous areas of Laos and Thailand have lived outside the world community for nearly 50 years. The Burmese and Thai armies frequently mount military operations to attack warlords, smugglers, Communists or ethnic insurgents, but have never established their control. The area is of great interest to the outside world because of the opium poppy. More than half the heroin in the world comes from the Golden Triangle, though Afghanistan's share is rising rapidly, and that proportion increases as eradication programmes succeed in Turkey. The Burmese government, even with American assistance, is not capable of controlling the tribal territories.

Ne Win obtained the support of the United States government by promising a vigorous fight against narcotics. The Americans supplied helicopters, planes and chemicals to spray the opium-producing areas, and the government stated that it planned to eradicate 20,234 hectares of poppy fields in 1988. However, the rebels claimed that the supplies were used to fight them, and that units of the regular Burmese army were in fact engaged in the opium trade. According to the US State Department, Burma produces 60% of the world's opium. Its estimated potential production rose from 1230 metric tons in 1987 to 2575 in 1993, and 2365 in 1997. Laos produced 210 tons in 1997 and Thailand 25 tons.

The story of one of the opium warlords – the half-Chinese, half-Shan known as Khun Sa (or Chang Chi-fu) – can stand as an illustration of the mores of the Golden Triangle. He was leader of the Shan United Army (SUA), ostensibly nationalist insurgents but, in fact, a territorial, armed opium cartel. Khun Sa was allied with the CIF, but, in the early 1960s, quarrelled with them and was appointed by the Burmese government as militia leader in his native district, Loi-maw. He developed the drug business, with his own opium-refining centre across the border in Thailand, and, by 1964, had set himself up as a drug smuggler and independent warlord. In 1967, the CIF put an embargo on the SUA opium trade, and Khun Sa fought an opium war with his former allies that year. An SUA caravan of opium was pursued across the hills into Laos, where it was seized by the Laotian army (then allied with the US Special Forces and the CIA in the war against the Vietnamese Communists). Khun Sa was captured by the Burmese.

Loss of their leader made the SUA decline until 1973, when Khun Sa's brother kidnapped two Soviet doctors working in a Soviet-built hospital. They were released in exchange for Khun Sa, who was sent home under house arrest. Two years later, he bribed his guards, escaped, and resumed command of the SUA.

That same year, 1975, the Burmese army defeated the CIF and broke its control of the opium trade in the Shan hills. Khun Sa and his SUA filled the vacuum and were soon the dominant force in the trade throughout the Golden Triangle. The SUA, with 1400–8000 men, not only produced its own opium but also bought opium from other insurgent groups, including the Burmese Communist party. The SUA shipped the opium to the Chinese syndicates in Thailand, and also smuggled gold, jewels and jade out of the country.

This profitable business was disrupted in 1981. The Thai army sent a patrol into SUA territory, and it was promptly defeated. It had to be rescued by a much larger force, and the Thais then mounted regular offensives in 1982 and 1983 and destroyed the SUA bases in Thailand. However, the defeat of Khun Sa was not permanent, nor did it mean defeat for the opium trade: Khun Sa's eclipse allowed other warlords to rise to prominence.

## THE UPRISING

Like other dictators before him, Ne Win endeavoured to conceal his authority. He resigned from the army in 1972 and, in 1981, resigned as president, citing ill **149** health. But like Mao Tse-tung and Stalin, he retained his essential position as leader of the party. A succession of other generals or former generals held the positions of president, prime minister or minister of defence, but Ne Win was always in command.

The regime started to unravel in September 1987. A currency reform was abruptly announced, robbing everyone in the country of their savings: all banknotes in denominations of 25 kyats (pronounced *chats*) or greater were abruptly declared worthless. The official rate of exchange was then 6 kyats to the US dollar, the black market rate 40. Ne Win said that the reform was aimed at black marketeers – who were, in fact, the only people keeping the economy afloat – and admitted that some reforms were necessary. In March 1988, the first student demonstrations occurred in Rangoon, set off by a brawl in a tea-house, during which a student was killed. Other students then organized a protest march into Rangoon, and the army and police broke up the demonstration with great violence, killing a number of them (estimates of the dead range up to 200) and arresting 3000.

Further demonstrations broke out three months later. On 21 June, after several days of continuous rioting, the government closed the universities and imposed a dusk-to-dawn curfew on the capital and other cities. Burma Radio reported: 'Five police personnel were killed and 26 others seriously wounded as a result of an attack by an unruly mob armed with swords, sticks and catapults. A member of the mob also was killed and several others wounded.' The true death toll was very much higher, as the government later admitted: some reports from diplomats suggested that about 1000 demonstrators were killed by troops under the command of General Sein Lwin, and in one instance, over 40 students were asphyxiated in a police van.

These events brought the regime's opposition into the open all over the country. A former general, Aung Gyi, who had taken part in the 1962 coup but turned his back on his former colleagues soon afterwards, distributed a series of open letters to Ne Win, remarking, 'The country has plunged to the bottom politically, economically and socially. The moral decay is the most deplorable.'

Ne Win, who was then 77, announced his resignation at a party conference on 23 July. 'Since I am indirectly responsible for the March and June affairs and because of my advanced age, I am resigning from both party chairmanship and also as a member,' he said. He went on: 'Bloodshed in March and June showed the lack of trust and confidence in the government. To find out whether the majority or the minority are behind the demonstrations, a referendum must be held so the people can choose between the existing one-party system or a multiparty system.' He also warned the country against further disorders, saying, 'I have to inform the people throughout the country that when the army shoots, it shoots to hit.'

A number of Ne Win's senior colleagues retired with him, but the party was not yet ready to give up power. His suggestion of a referendum on the one-party system was rejected by the conference, and Sein Lwin, who had commanded the Burmese riot police since the 1962 coup, and put down the student demonstrations in March, was appointed party chairman and president. He immediately arrested Aung Gyi and other prominent dissidents, but the demonstrations continued, and on 3 August he proclaimed martial law in Rangoon.

Mass demonstrations followed – in Rangoon, Mandalay, Pegu and other cities. Troops fired into the crowds, and large numbers of people were killed every day. Monks, students, workers, middle-class people and office workers all poured into the streets and confronted the troops. It was a replay of the events in Manila in 1986. On 10 August, troops burst into a hospital in Rangoon, looking for wounded protesters, and shot down a number of doctors and nurses who tried to protect them. The following day, the army sent tanks against demonstrators at the city's main pagodas, and protesters built barricades throughout the city. By then, there were daily battles between the army and 100,000 or more demonstrators in Rangoon.

On 12 August, Sein Lwin resigned. The government admitted that 100 demonstrators had been killed since he had been appointed president, but the real total was probably at least 1000 (the students said it was 3000). With the government in retreat, the crowds took to attacking party offices and other government buildings and burning them to the ground, and also attacked and burned the houses of political leaders.

On 19 August, the party named U Maung Maung president. He had been attorney-general and one of the authors of the 'Socialist Party Programme' and the 'Burmese Way to Socialism', and was a close associate of Ne Win. On 23 August, there were further enormous demonstrations in Rangoon, denouncing the new government and demanding democracy. The next day, Maung Maung lifted martial law in Rangoon, released 1700 political prisoners (including Aung Gyi) and announced that there would be an extraordinary party conference in September to consider ending one-party rule. By then, the ministers and the generals controlled no more than a few government buildings in Rangoon, their party headquarters, and the main army camps. The crowds controlled the rest, and there was considerable fear of anarchy.

The 82-year-old U Nu – who in 1980 had been invited home from Thailand by Ne Win and had entered a monastery – then emerged from retirement and tried to form a committee of opposition figures. Aung Gyi attempted to assert his claims, but many people distrusted him because he had been associated with Ne Win in 1962. Aung San Suu Kyi, the 43-year-old daughter of Aung San, the independence leader who had been assassinated in 1947, returned from her home in Oxford where her English husband was teaching, and appealed for unity. So did a grandson of the late U N secretary-general U Thant.

## THE COUP

On 18 September, the army seized power in a coup that had been meticulously prepared in advance. The chief of staff, General Saw Maung, filled Rangoon with troops and broke up the demonstrations. In a statement broadcast to the nation, Saw Maung said: 'In order to halt in a timely way the deteriorating conditions on all sides across the country, and for the sake of the interests of the people, the defence forces have assumed all power in the state.' Many Burmese suspected that Ne Win, who had remained in seclusion since resigning in July, still exercised real power. The army set up a State Law and Order Restoration

Council, known by the slightly comic and sinister acronym S L O R C. Its head is now General Than Shwe but its most powerful member is believed to be Lieutenant General Khin Nyunt, head of Burma's omnipresent secret police. Ne Win, born in 1911, is believed to exercise great influence in retirement, like Den Xiao-ping in China until he died.

Hundreds of demonstrators were killed in the first few days of the new regime. The government admitted 60 dead in the first two days, and later raised the figure to 425. Foreign diplomats suspected that up to 1000 people were killed before the last resistance was crushed in October. The general strike collapsed on 3 October. Student rebels left the cities and universities by the thousands and sought out the ethnic rebels in the mountains to offer their services, and to acquire some serious training in revolutionary warfare. There were various estimates of the numbers involved: there were perhaps 5000 in the first few weeks, with more following them in succeeding months.

The opposition at last united and, on 27 September, chose Aung Gyi as chairman of their new alliance, named the National League for Democracy. Another former military man, U Tin Oo, became vice chairman, and Aung San Suu Kyi became secretary-general. The government announced that it would open negotiations with them, but they hesitated to accept the invitation for fear of losing popular support. However, they registered their party, just in case genuine elections were planned.

The coup did nothing to help the economy. The United States, Japan, West Germany and others suspended all aid to Burma, which had relied on foreign contributions to finance 35 per cent of the capital budget. Now all its foreign exchange reserves were being consumed to buy rice to feed the population.

In an attempt to appease the demonstrators, the government dissolved the Burma Socialist Programme party and confiscated its property. Leading members then formed the National Union party, which was evidently the same clique that had misgoverned the country for 26 years. The opposition was permitted to function, some press freedoms were permitted, and the regime promised that there would be elections in the new year.

At the same time, a rigorous military dictatorship was maintained. Aung San Suu Kyi held rallies around the country while they were still permitted, and they were each attended by up to 10,000 people. She planned to hold a major rally in Rangoon on 19 July, Martyrs' Day, the anniversary of her father's murder. The government used the occasion to suppress the opposition. The city was filled with troops, and orders were issued that any military officer might arrest any suspect and sentence him on the spot to three years' hard labour, life imprisonment or immediate execution. Aung San Suu Kyi called off the rally. On the next day, she was put under house arrest, together with U Tin Oo, the other leader of her party. Thousands of other members of the party were arrested (18,000 common criminals were released from jail to make way for the political prisoners). Aung San Suu Kyi started a hunger strike, which she abandoned later. The army launched a new offensive against the Karen and other rebels, and claimed a great success, driving the Karens over the border into Thailand. The Kachin rebels reported that political prisoners were being used as porters by the army, roped together and marched until they dropped and died.

The new government renamed the country Myanmar, and also renamed a number of Burmese cities. Rangoon became Yangon. There seemed to be no reason why foreigners should change their linguistic habits at the behest of a Burmese dictator, and few did so. Burma's only economic relationship with the outside world now was smuggling opium, hardwood and gems. Its opium exports have jumped sharply since the September coup. Burma is now a serious contender for the position of poorest country in the world. Considering its natural resources and its people's level of education and ability, this was a remarkable achievement.

The government announced that the long-promised elections would be held in May 1990. To prepare the way, U Tin Oo was jailed for three years and Aung San Suu Kyi was declared ineligible to run for the presidency. She remained under house arrest, as did U Nu.

The elections were held on 27 May 1990, and Aung San Suu Kyi's National League for Democracy won a landslide victory. The government admitted that it had won over two-thirds of the votes. The army paid no attention to the results. The state of emergency remained in effect, the National Assembly was not allowed to meet and the League leaders remained under arrest. In the next 18 months, the army abandoned the 'Burmese Way to Socialism' and allowed a complete return to a market economy, but the country remained as poor as ever. It subsisted on barter trade with its neighbours, including Thailand and China, exchanging gems and teak for weapons and a few other essentials. The army permitted no opposition, and vigorously persecuted the minorities. In December 1991, during a crack-down on Muslims in Arakan province, 700 prisoners were asphyxiated in a warehouse.

In October 1991, Daw Aung San Suu Kyi, who had been kept incommunicado in her family house in Rangoon for over two years, was awarded the Nobel peace prize. By then she was the acknowledged sole leader of the democracy movement, the personification of Burma's hopes for its future. She was released from house arrest in July 1995 and began holding a regular series of political meetings outside her house every Sunday. Her political party re-emerged into the light and she convened a party conference in March 1996. S L O R C prevented most delegates attending, and then banned the meetings. However, it handled the situation cautiously: at the time, it wanted to persuade the other nations of South-East Asia to admit Burma to membership of their trade group, A S E A N, and in July 1996 they did so.

After Burma's admission to A S E A N, businessmen from Thailand, Indonesia and the rest of East Asia poured into Rangoon, to buy up its natural riches. The United States and Europe protested and imposed sanctions on the regime, to no avail. The golden prospects of the Asian speculators were seriously dimmed, however, by the economic crisis that beset the region in the autumn of 1997. Burma remains one of the poorest and most oppressive countries in the world. S L O R C still, apparently, has the army's loyalty; but so did Ceausescu in Romania and Marcos in the Philippines. A new uprising in Burma is entirely possible, and it is also possible that it will end with the overthrow of the S L O R C and Daw Aung Suu Kyi installed as president. She would then have to contend with a worse legacy than any other country in Asia, save only North Korea. **153**

## FURTHER READING

American University, *Burma: A Country Study*, Washington D. C., 1983.

Amnesty International, *Burma: extrajudicial execution and torture of members of ethnic minorities*, London, 1988.

Cady, John, *A History of Modern Burma*, Ithaca, New York, Cornell University Press, 1958.

Steinberg, David, *Burma: A Socialist Nation of Southeast Asia*, Boulder, Colo., Westview Press, 1982.

Tinker, Hugh, *The Union of Burma*, Oxford University Press, 1959.

# CAMBODIA

| | |
|---|---|
| Geography | 69,898 sq. miles (181,305 sq. km). Size of West Germany. 'Cambodia' is the English version of the common Western transliteration of the country's name. The French call it 'Cambodge'. An alternative transliteration is 'Kampuchea', and the two names are used interchangeably. Under the alternative spelling, the Cambodians are known as 'Khmers'. |
| Population | 10 million. |
| GNP per capita | $270. |
| Refugees | 32,000 internal refugees, 34,400 in Vietnam. |
| Casualties | From 1970 to 1975, between 700,000 and 1,100,000 people were killed during the civil war and the American war against the Vietnamese Communists. From 1975 to 1979, the Khmers Rouges killed between 1 million and 2 million people. Up to 100,000 people were killed in the Vietnamese invasion that began in December 1978, and in the Khmers Rouges' retreat. The Vietnamese admit to losing 25,000 men killed during the occupation (1978–88). Perhaps 50,000–100,000 people have died as a result of the guerrilla war since 1979. |

Between 1975 and 1978, Cambodia suffered the single most comprehensive disaster that has befallen any country in the world since 1945. The Communist government (the 'Khmers Rouges', or 'Red Cambodians'), who had won a protracted civil war, set about exterminating the intellectual, entrepreneurial, administrative and landowning classes, and emptying the cities of their inhabitants. It has been calculated that as many as 25 per cent of the population, up to 2 million people, were murdered or died of starvation in those three and a half years. In this century, only the Jews of Europe and the Armenians in Turkey have suffered a comparable devastation, and only in the Soviet Union under Stalin did another government practise genocide upon its own people. The Khmers Rouges were driven from power in 1979 by the Vietnamese, who set up a puppet government in Phnom Penh and for ten years conducted a fruitless war against the Khmers Rouges and other guerrillas in the countryside. The Vietnamese pulled out of Cambodia in 1989, and two years later a ceasefire was arranged by the U N. The agreement set up a new government, including Khmer Rouge ministers, and provided that elections would be held under U N supervision. The civil war was over, and the refugees could return home but the nightmare was not exorcized. **155**

# HISTORY

A thousand years ago, Cambodia was a rich and powerful kingdom, extending far into Siam (Thailand) and into what is now southern Vietnam. Its kings built an enormous temple-city at Angkor Wat, one of the marvels of the world, and their prosperity was based upon a vast and sophisticated irrigation system, maintained by slave labour. The empire declined in the 14th century, and in 1431, the Siamese captured Angkor Wat. Cambodia then subsided into a small and impoverished kingdom, ground down between Siam and the Empire of Annam (Vietnam), both of which, over the centuries, progressively annexed most of Cambodia. It is one of the great divides of the world: Vietnam is a product of Chinese Confucian civilization; Siam, Cambodia and Laos derived their cultures from Buddhist India.

The country was saved from complete dismemberment by the French, who conquered Vietnam in the mid-19th century and established a protectorate over Cambodia in 1864. They forced Siam to restore provinces it had annexed, and built up Phnom Penh as a pleasant French tropical town. They left the king of Cambodia on his throne, as they did the king of Laos and the emperor of Annam, while depriving him of all power (and changing dynasties twice in a century). They excavated and restored the temples and palaces at Angkor Wat, and educated a small, élite class in Paris, but otherwise left the Cambodians to live as they always had.

Cambodia escaped virtually unscathed from World War I I and the French war in Indochina, which ended at the Geneva conference in 1954 with the partition of Vietnam. Cambodia was declared independent in 1953 and King Norodom Sihanouk, who had been put on the throne in 1941 as a callow, 19-year-old puppet, began his reign in earnest. Sihanouk, born in 1922, remains one of the key players in Cambodia. He was described by William Shawcross thus:

Norodom Sihanouk presided feudally over Cambodia from 1941 to 1970 as king, chief of state, prince, prime minister, head of the main political movement, jazz-band leader, magazine editor, film director and gambling concessionaire, attempting to unite in his rule the unfamiliar concepts of Buddhism, socialism and democracy.

In 1955, to prepare for elections mandated by the Geneva treaties, Sihanouk abdicated in favour of his father, proclaimed himself a commoner and established a political party that won the elections. He was undoubtedly one of the most colourful of hereditary rulers, and although he ceased to be king in 1955, he ruled as an absolute monarch until his overthrow in 1970. A skilled diplomat, intelligent, charming, with a clear view of the dangers facing the country, he was also corrupt, autocratic and short-sighted in his domestic policies. He alienated the educated classes, many of whom joined the opposition or fled to the jungles to join the Khmers Rouges, and patronized and bullied his ministers and the army. He kept the loyalty of the peasantry, however, and perhaps he still does.

Cambodia might have developed in the same way as Thailand or Malaysia, gradually evolving into a modern state, had it not been for the Vietnam war. That ferocious conflict inevitably spilled over into Laos and Cambodia. The Cambodian frontier is 40 miles (65 km) from Saigon, and the mountains and thick jungles on the Cambodian side provided ideal sanctuary for the Vietcong and for infiltrators from North Vietnam. Prince Sihanouk's government was powerless to prevent this violation of Cambodian neutrality.

In 1954, Vietnam was far more advanced economically and socially than Cambodia. It had a population of 30 million, of whom 18 million lived in the north, 12 million in the south. Cambodia's population was 6 million. To this demographic disparity was added the limitless military support provided to the North Vietnamese by the Chinese and Soviets, and to the South Vietnamese by the Americans. Cambodia could have protected itself against one of those powers only by committing itself irrevocably to the other. Sihanouk, naturally, wished to back the winner, and in the circumstances of the early 1960s, this meant at first bending with the wind from Hanoi, and later trying to accommodate to the increasing demands of the United States and South Vietnam.

In 1963, while Sihanouk was still secure in his government, a small group of Communists led by Pol Pot (then known as Saloth Sar), Ieng Sary and others left Phnom Penh and started an insurrection in the northern jungles, but for many years, they posed no serious threat to the government. A further group of leftists – some of whom, including Khieu Samphan, had been members of Sihanouk's government – joined them in 1967.

Pol Pot was born in Kompong Thom in 1928, son of a peasant family. He attended a technical college in Phnom Penh and, in 1949, went to Paris on a scholarship to study radio electronics. Like other young Cambodians who studied in France, he fell under the influence of the French Communist party, an organization of ultra-Stalinist orthodoxy. On his return to Phnom Penh, he earned a living teaching history and geography at a private school, and as a journalist. He made his name in left-wing politics, and joined the illegal Communist Party, rising to the position of deputy general secretary.

Khieu Samphan was born in 1931, son of a minor civil servant. He became the Khmers Rouges' commander-in-chief during the war and head of state afterwards. He, too, went to France on a scholarship, in 1954. His thesis, offered at the University of Paris in 1959, and entitled 'Cambodia's Economy and Industrial Development', later provided the rationale for the Khmers Rouges' economic policies. It maintained that Cambodia could only develop on the basis of prosperous agriculture; that the existing landowning classes made that impossible; that the cities were parasites; and that Cambodia's existing international economic relationships were inimical to real economic progress. He maintained that the solution was to move the urban population into the countryside and set them to work there, and to collectivize agriculture.

Khieu Samphan worked as a journalist when he returned to Phnom Penh and, unlike Pol Pot, remained within the system until 1967, when he fled Phnom Penh to escape arrest, and joined Pol Pot. He was not admitted to the inner circle of those who had taken to the hills in 1963, but unlike others who joined later, he escaped with his life during the purges of 1975–78.

Cambodia's first involvement in the Vietnam war developed in the eastern mountains and in the obscurity of the jungles. As the Communist insurgency expanded in South Vietnam, supplies and men came down the Ho-Chi Minh trail from North Vietnam. The trail was a vast network of paths through mountains and jungle, much of it in Cambodia.

It was a long and difficult route over which to move modern weapons, and soon the Vietcong started looking for alternatives. In the 1950s, the Chinese had built a port for Cambodia on the Gulf of Siam, which was named Sihanoukville (subsequently Kompong Som), and the Americans built a 'Friendship Highway' to connect it to Phnom Penh. In 1965, Sihanouk broke diplomatic relations with the United States after President Johnson sent the Marines ashore at Danang. In 1966, Chou En-lai, the Chinese prime minister, demanded that Sihanouk permit supplies for the Vietcong to be landed in Sihanoukville and transported along the Friendship Highway to the Vietcong bases on the frontier.

Sihanouk agreed. If he had refused, the Vietnamese Communists would have extended their direct control over eastern Cambodia, and swung their support behind Pol Pot's Communist insurgents, whom Sihanouk had named the Khmers Rouges. In 1969, there were no more than 4000 active Khmers Rouges guerrillas in Cambodia.

Sihanouk, after rejecting American military aid in 1963, had nothing with which to oppose the heavily armed Vietcong. His army was 30,000 strong, of whom only 11,000 might be considered combat-ready, and their equipment was obsolete and inadequate. Sihanouk thought he had no choice. He allowed the Vietcong to use Sihanoukville, and it quickly became their main supply route. His decision led inevitably to American intervention in Cambodia. That in turn ensured the overthrow of Sihanouk in 1970 and, in 1975, Pol Pot's victory and the horrors that followed.

In an attempt to balance his policy of helping the Vietcong, Sihanouk began to veer back towards the American side. On 18 March 1969, in 'Operation Breakfast', the US air force conducted a massive bombing attack on what it believed were the Communist general headquarters inside Cambodia. The attack did not produce the desired results, and the USAF began a continuous and secret air offensive ('Operation Menu') against the 'sanctuaries' – the Communist bases in Cambodia. Sihanouk knew of these bombings but did not protest. On 8 June that year, he allowed the American embassy in Phnom Penh to reopen.

Sihanouk was distrusted by the Americans, particularly by President Nixon and his secretary of state, Henry Kissinger, who never tried to win his support or use his popularity and skills as a barrier against the Vietnamese. Until it was far too late, Washington failed to understand the depths of Cambodian–Vietnamese hostility. They were obsessed by the 'domino theory', which assumed a unified Communist conspiracy. Besides, Cambodia was only a sideshow. The main event was in Vietnam.

On 18 March 1970, the prime minister, General Lon Nol, seized power during Sihanouk's absence in Moscow. It was a confused and improvised coup, essentially arising out of a dispute between Sihanouk and his government over Cambodia's part in the Vietnam war. The United States welcomed the change in government.

On 30 April 1970, American and South Vietnamese forces invaded Cambodia to 'clear out the sanctuaries'. Five days later, on 4 May, four students at Kent State University in Ohio were killed by National Guardsmen during a protest. The American–Vietnamese forces withdrew from Cambodia at the end of June, having achieved very little.

After the invasion, Sihanouk set up a government in exile in Peking together with the Khmers Rouges, and Lon Nol proclaimed the republic. The Vietcong and Chinese now offered the Khmers Rouges every support, and their offensive against the Lon Nol government was rapidly extended across the whole country, the name and mystique of Prince Sihanouk being used among the peasantry to reinforce the Khmers Rouges' position.

By 1972, Cambodia was almost as completely engulfed in war as Vietnam itself. There were over 3 million peasant refugees in the cities, and North Vietnamese troops occupied much of eastern Cambodia, while the Khmers Rouges controlled the north. The Americans bombed both continuously.

On 27 January 1973, the United States and the three parties in Vietnam signed a peace agreement in Paris. One of its clauses provided for an ending of foreign interference in Cambodia. The Americans soon withdrew all their remaining troops from Vietnam, but continued bombing Khmer Rouge positions in Cambodia until August, when President Nixon finally acceded to congressional pressure to stop. From beginning to end, the United States air force dropped 539,129 tons of bombs on Cambodia, 257,465 tons in the last six months, at a total cost of $7 billion. By comparison, during the whole of World War II, 160,000 tons of bombs, not counting the atomic bombs, were dropped on Japan. This frightful onslaught destroyed the country, driving half the population into the cities as refugees, but it did not deter the Khmers Rouges – though it may have prevented them seizing Phnom Penh in 1973. On the contrary, it encouraged their fanaticism and hatred of the Americans and their 'puppets'.

The war continued in Vietnam, though its nature changed while the Communists prepared for their final offensive, and it intensified in Cambodia. The Khmers Rouges had 50,000 soldiers by then and were not affected by the Paris treaty, although it greatly increased their suspicions of the Vietnamese. It seemed to the Khmers Rouges that Hanoi, like Washington, was treating Cambodia merely as a sideshow.

Lon Nol's army was too corrupt and inefficient to stop the Khmers Rouges without continuous American support. The final attack began on New Year's Day, 1975, and continued as the last Communist offensive in Vietnam got under way. Lon Nol fled the country on 1 April, the American ambassador and his staff were evacuated by helicopter from Phnom Penh on 12 April, and the Khmers Rouges entered the city on 17 April. On 30 April, Saigon fell to the Communists.

## DEMOCRATIC KAMPUCHEA

The Khmers Rouges began their rule by driving the entire population of Phnom Penh – 2.5 million people – into the countryside. Most were refugees from the war and the American bombing, whose villages had been destroyed and who had nowhere to go. Patients from hospitals were wheeled on stretchers out of the city, with distraught nurses holding their IV bottles over them, in futile attempts to keep them alive. Westerners sheltering in the French embassy, waiting to be evacuated, listened in horror to the constant rattle of machine-guns as the victors massacred their opponents. All the officials of the defeated government who did not escape, and all captured officers, were summarily executed. The Chans, a mountain tribe that had adopted Islam in the Middle Ages, were slaughtered for **159** their religion: about 60,000, the large majority of the Chans, were murdered.

For three years and eight months, Cambodia was a country without cities, without a currency. Religion, the family unit and all property were abolished. The Khmers Rouges blew up the central bank and dumped the currency reserves in the street, as so much garbage. Applying an economic theory that had been set out in Khieu Samphan's student thesis, the government set about eliminating all traces of industry and urban society, which it considered corrupted by the West. Its intention was to establish a peasant, Communist society, and then to build a new order upon that basis. The result was to return Cambodia to the Dark Ages, with an élite governing class directing a nation of slaves.

In Cambodia in 1975, 'intellectuals' were defined as anyone wearing glasses, speaking a foreign language, graduates of universities or high schools, or possessed of a professional qualification. 'Entrepreneurs' were shopkeepers and self-employed artisans, as well as anyone involved in the management of any business. 'Governing and administrative classes' included anyone who had ever held a government position or who had served in the armed forces or police of the defeated regime. All those who had lived in cities, including the refugees, were defined as 'new people', a class the Khmers Rouges were determined to obliterate. 'Landowners' were those who owned anything beyond the smallest possible family farm as well as those who resisted the forced collectivization of every farm in the country. All the families of these people were deemed equally guilty, and they were all killed, or worked to death, as slave labour. Old people and 'new' people together were to be bent to the needs of 'advanced socialism'.

A further horror was the very large number of very young boys in the Khmer Rouge armies and execution squads. Teenagers and children as young as ten or 12 were instructed to beat their prisoners to death or to disembowel them (to save ammunition), slaughtering men and women, old and young. The Khmers Rouges did not gas their victims, hundreds at a time, or machine-gun them in large groups, as the Germans had. Each murdered Cambodian was murdered individually. The film *The Killing Fields*, based on first-hand recollections, shows one method of execution: a man whose hands were suspiciously soft, therefore possibly an intellectual, was pulled out of a chain gang by the guards; a woman then put a plastic bag over his head and tied it around his neck so that he suffocated. There were 4000 Khmers Rouges in 1969; the tens of thousands who participated in the mass killings were all recruited between 1970 and 1978.

When the Vietnamese occupied Phnom Penh in January 1979, they found a converted school, called Tuol Sleng, that had been used as the security office of the party's Central Committee. It was a torture centre and place of execution for senior cadres, and 20,000 people had been murdered there. It had been directed by a man called Kong Kech Eav, who used the name Duch. Meticulous accounts of the atrocities had been preserved, including the numbers killed every day, together with photographs of the prisoners as they arrived and at the moment they were killed. Less important Cambodians were taken to the killing fields, and butchered. The skulls were set out in rows and their bones piled in heaps together.

Amnesty International's report on Cambodia quotes from a progress meeting
**160** of Tuol Sleng's staff, at which it was noted:

The enemy will not confess to us easily. When we use political pressure, prisoners confess only very little. Thus, they cannot escape from torture. The only difference is whether there will be a lot of it or a little. Torture is a necessary measure . . . It is necessary to avoid any question of hesitancy or half-heartedness, of not daring to torture, which makes it impossible to get answers to our questions from our enemies. This will slow down and delay our work.

The Amnesty report continues: 'Methods of torture included beatings, whippings, administration of electric shocks, forced feeding with excrement, and near-suffocation and near-drowning.'

Tuol Sleng (also known as S21) was an Asian Dachau – with two differences: far fewer of its inmates survived (only seven survivors are known), and when the S S had tortured their prisoners, it had been for medical experiments or to frighten other inmates; torture was not an integral part of the German camp system. In 'Democratic Kampuchea', it was essential that the more important prisoners, and all party members, confess and admit their errors, under torture, before they were killed. Tuol Sleng was the realization of George Orwell's 'Ministry of Love'.

The ruling group in Cambodia between 1975 and 1978 consisted of a 'Gang of Six'. Pol Pot became prime minister and secretary of the Communist party. The others were Ieng Sary, who was foreign minister; Son Sen, minister of defence; two sisters, Khieu Ponnary, who directed the Association of Democratic Women of Kampuchea, and Khieu Thirith, minister of social action (Ponnary was married to Pol Pot, Thirith to Ieng Sary). The sixth member was Son Sen's wife, Yun Yat, minister of education. Ponnary went mad. In 1997, Ieng Sary deserted and Pol Pot had Son Sen and Yun Yat murdered.

After the Khmers Rouges' victory, Prince Sihanouk returned to Phnom Penh as nominal head of state. He was kept in house arrest most of the time, though he was occasionally allowed abroad to sing the praises of the Khmer Rouge government. Sihanouk thus bears some of the blame for the horrors that overwhelmed his country.

Like other revolutions, the Cambodian revolution soon began to devour its children. After they had exterminated their enemies from the old regime, Pol Pot and the Angka – the Organization of the Khmers Rouges, which was the country's government – set about systematically killing everyone who had any connection with the Vietnamese. That included up to half the Cambodian Communists and four of the ten people who had led the Khmers Rouges to victory in 1975. The documents found in Tuol Sleng included detailed transcripts of their interrogations.

In the summer of 1978, the purges culminated in a series of massacres in eastern Cambodia, the area of the country that had been most closely involved with the Vietnamese. Leading cadres were summoned back to Phnom Penh a few at a time, and were never heard of again. Then Pol Pot sent his army to surround party headquarters in the east. So Phim, the commander in eastern Cambodia and a member of the five-man Politburo of the Cambodian Communist party, shot himself. Some 3000 Khmers Rouges and perhaps 30,000 civilians retreated into the jungles, and put up a desultory resistance, while the peasants took advantage of the fighting among their rulers to attack the communal kitchens and other symbols of the regime. Pol Pot soon defeated the opposition and **161** slaughtered everyone he could find: about 100,000 people were killed in three months, and one-third of the surviving population was marched into western Cambodia. Pol Pot denounced his enemies as 'Khmer bodies with Vietnamese minds'. His rage extended across the border and he sent his troops in a series of raids into Vietnam, where they massacred thousands of peasants.

These were not the first border raids: in September 1977, Cambodians had attacked Vietnamese villages, massacring hundreds. In October and December 1977, Vietnam had retaliated by mounting full-scale military incursions into Cambodia.

None of this deterred Pol Pot. He simply broke diplomatic relations with Hanoi in December 1977. After the renewed attacks in the late summer of 1978, Hanoi decided that it was no longer possible to tolerate the Khmers Rouges, and a guerrilla army of dissident Cambodians was formed, including the surviving leaders of the eastern district who had taken refuge in the jungles. Many of them had taken part in earlier massacres of Vietnamese on both sides of the border, but Hanoi turned a blind eye to their past. Among them was Heng Samrin, who was rescued when the Vietnamese sent an armoured column into Cambodia in September 1978.

If the Cambodians had possessed any political skills, or if Pol Pot had been less crazed with ideology, the country could doubtless have preserved its independence and territorial integrity by playing China off against Vietnam. But Pol Pot proclaimed that each Cambodian could and would kill 30 Vietnamese; Cambodia could thus lose 2 million of its people while wiping out the 50 million Vietnamese, and recover the lost territories to the east, including Saigon. On 24 December 1978, Vietnam invaded Cambodia, taking Phnom Penh on 7 January; by the end of the month the Vietnamese had occupied most of the country (*see* Vietnam, pp. 261–7).

The Pol Pot regime was able to put up even less resistance than Lon Nol's government had in 1975. This was due partly to a lack of military supplies, but it was chiefly due to the country's detestation of the regime. The retreating Democratic Kampucheans took several hundred thousand peasants with them, and attempted to set up enclaves under their control in the mountains. While this phantom government lasted, it continued to impose by terror its fantasies of 'advanced socialism'. Scores of thousands – perhaps 100,000 – died, and the remainder were only saved from starvation by an international relief operation in 1979. The Vietnamese overran these last pockets of resistance by the end of that year, and the Khmers Rouges retreated to a series of camps along the border with Thailand.

## THE VIETNAMESE OCCUPATION
Vietnam immediately set up a quisling government in Phnom Penh, headed by Heng Samrin. Only the Soviets and their client states and India recognized it, and Vietnam failed to destroy the guerrilla resistance. The Khmers Rouges were the most important element in the resistance movement; other armies were led by or owed allegiance to Prince Norodom Sihanouk, the former head of state, and to non-Communist groups. China and Thailand supported the Khmers Rouges, while the West gave a little, ineffective, support to the non-Communist

resistance whose bases were along the Thai border. For nine years, until the Vietnamese announced their intention to withdraw, in May 1988, the stalemate was absolute. All that could be said for it was that it was preferable to government by Pol Pot.

In 1984–5, the Vietnamese undertook a massive offensive along the border to capture all the refugee camps and military bases of the Khmers Rouges and Son Sann's K P N L F (*see below*). The offensive achieved its aims, but did not destroy the Khmers Rouges. The refugees simply moved over the border into Thailand, and the Khmers Rouges' army split up into guerrilla bands, which continued to harass the Vietnamese and the Phnom Penh regime's army. They were supported and armed by China via a 'Deng Xiaoping Trail' running from China through the jungles of northern Thailand. Their strategy was to wait out the Vietnamese, and then return to power. When Vietnam announced that it intended to withdraw by 1990, it appeared that they would attain that objective.

After the resistance bases along the Thai border had been destroyed, the Vietnamese set about building a fence and laying minefields the length of the frontier. They found themselves in the position of the Americans in Vietnam, trying to hold together a weak and dispirited local government while also attempting to keep the guerrillas out of the country.

Some accounts of the horrors inflicted on Cambodia by Pol Pot had come out during his three years in power. They were not always believed, particularly by those who had most vocally opposed American involvement in Vietnam. After the Vietnamese occupation of the country, however, it became impossible to doubt. Foreign governments and journalists, and the United Nations, were invited to inspect the evidence. It was irrefutable.

International revulsion against the Khmers Rouges did not solve the problem of who was to govern Cambodia. Western states, which had been allied to the Soviet Union during World War I I, had acquiesced in the imposition and maintenance of alien governments in Eastern Europe. They were not going to make the same mistake in Cambodia, however horrible the regime that had been replaced.

The Cambodian government set up by the Vietnamese had no more legitimacy than the government set up by the Soviet Union in Afghanistan in 1979 (or than the governments of Eastern Europe between 1945 and 1989). China and the United States and its allies recognized the coalition headed by Prince Sihanouk as the legitimate government of Cambodia and ensured that it retained Cambodia's place in the United Nations. These governments were at constant pains to insist that they did not recognize the Khmers Rouges and were continually embarrassed by the fact that Khieu Samphan, a prominent Khmer Rouge, represented the coalition in international gatherings, and travelled frequently to the West.

Three resistance groups confronted the Heng Samrin regime and the Vietnamese. The most formidable, from the start, were the Khmers Rouges. They were supported by the Chinese openly and by Thailand surreptitiously. Second, there was a non-Communist movement, the Khmer People's National Liberation Front, led by Son Sann, who had been prime minister under Prince Sihanouk on various occasions. He had the moral support of the West and controlled most of **163** the refugee camps along the Thai border and claimed to direct a considerable guerrilla force inside the country, but it never achieved much military success. The third force consisted of Prince Sihanouk and his personal retainers.

In June 1982, these three formed a coalition government. Prince Sihanouk was made president, Khieu Samphan vice-president and Son Sann prime minister. The United States and China recognized this organization (which called itself the Coalition Government of Democratic Kampuchea) and ensured that it kept Cambodia's seat at the U N. The three parties squabbled continuously and Prince Sihanouk periodically resigned as the coalition's president. The outside world paid lip-service to the cause of peace in Cambodia, but the West would not recognize the Phnom Penh regime so long as the Vietnamese occupied the country, and the United States continued to impose a complete trade embargo against Vietnam.

In 1987, a new team took over in Phnom Penh, led by Hun Sen, who was a much less dogmatic Communist than Heng Samrin. After the Vietnamese had left, and perhaps influenced by events in China and Europe, he brought many surviving officials of the Sihanouk and Lon Nol regimes into the government, and progressively reduced the government's role in the economy. Cambodia was never properly Communized between 1975 and 1989, in the sense that Poland or China were Communized. There, the state systematically took over all economic activity: in Cambodia, the Khmers Rouges devastated the country, and their successors had to rebuild society from scratch. It was much easier for Hun Sen to revert to a market system, after 20 years of revolutionary upheaval, than for Poland to dismantle a bureaucratic Communist state. By the end of 1989, 70 per cent of the economy was back in private hands, and 18 months later, the free market was completely restored.

By then, the Vietnamese had made it clear that they intended to withdraw from Cambodia. In May 1988, when there were still 140,000 Vietnamese troops in Cambodia, they announced that they would withdraw 50,000 by the end of the year, and withdraw all of them by 1990. In the event, all troops were withdrawn by September 1989. After nine years' effort, they were at last admitting failure. There can be little doubt that the decision was the result of Vietnam's own economic catastrophe (there was a real danger of famine), and pressure from the Soviet Union. If the Soviets could withdraw from Afghanistan, they could also oblige Vietnam to withdraw from Cambodia, which caused them almost equal political embarrassment to no perceptible advantage. The U S S R had subsidized Vietnam to the tune of $2 billion a year. Half of it went to the occupation of Cambodia and most of the rest to maintaining Vietnam's defences against China. For Gorbachev, there were large savings to be made by diplomacy.

The Vietnamese withdrawal galvanized the diplomatic process. Hun Sen met Prince Sihanouk in Paris in December 1988, and there were several other meetings over the next 18 months. They led to a peace conference in Paris in August 1989, a month before the final Vietnamese withdrawal. It was a grand occasion, with the U N and the A S E A N countries represented, and the French and Indonesian foreign ministers acting as co-chairmen. It was a complete

failure.

Diplomatic efforts to end the civil war continued. In January 1990, the five permanent members of the Security Council produced a peace plan. It provided for a U N administration to govern Cambodia while elections were held. By that time, the Cold War had ended and the Soviet Union was cooperating fully with the United States. Vietnam, too, had changed its policy. It now exerted itself to restore relations with the United States. That summer, Washington conceded that Vietnam had a role to play, and joined the Soviet Union and China in trying to set up a Supreme National Council for Cambodia, a coalition of the four parties. The U N proposed that power should be shared between the U N and the Council until elections could be organized, and that the various armies should be disarmed.

The Council was finally formed and held its first meeting in Bangkok in September 1990. After prolonged haggling, it agreed to a ceasefire and finally settled the terms of a peace treaty. The United Nations would disband 70 per cent of each of the four armies and supervise the remainder. The coalition government would move to Phnom Penh and although the Khmers Rouges would be represented, they would be given only minor positions and their army would be disbanded and subject to strict supervision. A large U N force would supervise elections, which were to be held on the basis of proportional representation. The treaty was signed in Paris on 23 October 1991.

The exiles then prepared to return to Phnom Penh. The royal palace was refurbished for Prince Sihanouk, and Khmer Rouge leaders and their enemies alike donned civilian garments and prepared to take over the government. The operation was supervised by the U N Transitional Authority in Cambodia (U N T A C), the largest peace-keeping force the U N had ever assembled. It consisted of 15,900 soldiers, 3600 police, and 2400 civilian administrators. Their task was to repatriate 330,000 refugees from camps on either side of the Thai border; disarm and demobilize 70 per cent of the four competing armies, which had over 400,000 soldiers among them; and supervise Cambodia's first free elections. Their budget was $1.4 billion (in the end, U N T A C spent $3 billion). A new titular government, the Supreme National Council, was set up under Prince Sihanouk's chairmanship. It had six members from Hun Sen's government, and two each from the Khmers Rouges, Sihanouk's followers and Son Sann's. Real power, however, remained with Hun Sen's regime. The Khmers Rouges representatives on the council were Khieu Samphan, the Khmers Rouges' theoretician and head of state, and Son Sen, their minister of defence who had directed the operations at Tuol Sleng. When Kieu arrived in Phnom Penh (Son Sen was there already), Hun Sen sent a crowd to storm their residence. Khieu was beaten severely. Then he was rescued by police and flown out to Bangkok, with Son Sen. Photographers recorded the episode.

That proved a sign of things to come. The Hun Sen Communists, the royalists and the moderate but inconsequential followers of Son Sann exerted every effort to exclude the Khmers Rouges from power. They feared a return of Pol Pot more than they distrusted each other. China, in the aftermath of the Tienanmen massacre, had ceased to support the Khmers Rouges and so had the Thai government, which had provided safe havens and supply routes for them since 1979, with the tacit approval of the United States.

The Khmers Rouges boycotted the elections and their leaders returned to the jungles to resume the civil war. Elections were held under U N T A C's supervision in May 1993. Sihanouk's party, Funcinpec (the *Front Uni National Cambodgien pour l'Indépendance, Neutralité, Paix et Co-operation*), won by 45.3 per cent to 38.6 per cent for Hun Sen's Communists, now known as the Cambodian People's Party. Hun Sen refused to accept his loss and demanded that an equal coalition be formed. He threatened renewed civil war if he were refused, and U N T A C, Sihanouk and the other Cambodian leaders acquiesced. The two parties formed a coalition, with Sihanouk's son, Prince Norodom Ranariddh, as first prime minister and Hun Sen as second prime minister. Hun Sen remained the real master of Cambodia. One of the new government's first acts was to restore the monarchy, which had been abolished by Lon Nol in 1970, and restore Sihanouk to the throne he had abdicated nearly 40 years earlier.

The brief interval of U N intervention and the free press and other freedoms it had imported did not long survive U N T A C's departure. Soon, the old ways were restored. The press was subject to severe censorship, and those journalists who defied it were murdered. The Cambodian government was one of the most flagrantly corrupt in the world, with government ministers participating freely in smuggling consumer goods into Vietnam and China and the illegal export of timber, jewels – and opium. Phnom Penh recovered some semblance of prosperity, for foreigners at least (who seldom penetrated into the slums), but the countryside was afflicted by the worst poverty to be found anywhere in the Third World. The Khmers Rouges reverted to guerrilla warfare. Their offices in Phnom Penh were closed and the party was banned in July 1994. Over the next few years they progressively lost control of their former sanctuaries. They withered away without Chinese and Thai support, a development which demonstrated the responsibility those governments – and to some extent the Americans – also bore for the civil war of the 1980s.

In 1996, Khmer Rouge troops started surrendering *en masse* to the government. The surrenders proved the catalyst that broke up the coalition. There was fierce competition between the two parties for the allegiance of the Khmers Rouges: Ranariddh hoped to strengthen his much weaker forces with seasoned Khmer Rouge fighters. In September 1996, Ieng Sary surrendered to King Sihanouk. He was one of the top Khmer Rouge leaders, who had participated fully in the murder or death by disease and starvation of nearly a quarter of the country's population, but during the last days of the government coalition, his accession to either side was enough to win amnesty for himself. After some hesitation, he chose Hun Sen. Pol Pot and his surviving colleagues, including his minister of defence, Son Sen, and his chief military commander, the one-legged general Ta Mok, took refuge in Ta Mok's last base in a small village, Anlong Veng, on the northern frontier. There Son Sen and Ta Mok opened negotiations with the parties in Phnom Penh.

There was a sudden acceleration of the Cambodian tragedy in June. Ranariddh announced that Pol Pot had ordered Son Sen murdered, together with his wife Yun Yat and nine other relatives, for disloyalty: he was said to be seriously ill. Ranariddh said Pol Pot had been arrested by Khmer Rouge guerrillas and would be sent to Phnom Penh and put on trial. The likelihood that the remaining

Khmers Rouges would surrender to the prince led Hun Sen to stage a coup. There was a brief clash on 17 June that left two of the prince's bodyguards dead, and in the first week of July there was a sudden outbreak of vicious fighting in the capital. Prince Ranariddh's troops were routed and some government ministers of his party were hunted down through the streets and murdered, including the minister of the interior, Ho Sok. Others were allowed to escape to Bangkok. Ranariddh (who was abroad during the coup) attempted to rally foreign support, still claiming to be first prime minister, but met with no success. King Sihanouk once again threatened to abdicate, wrung his hands at his son's defeat, but in the end did nothing.

These events were followed by an extraordinary journalistic coup. A reporter for the *Far East Economic Review*, Nate Thayer, was allowed into Anlong Veng with a TV camera. He filmed an interview with Pol Pot, who had not been seen or photographed since 1979. He then filmed the fallen tyrant's show trial in a hut in the jungle. Pol Pot, old, ill and distant, sat quietly as he was denounced by Khmer Rouge prosecutors at what looked like a public meeting. Every so often, at a sign from the prosecutors, the civilians, mostly women, would break into a dutiful chant 'Crush! Crush! Crush!' and then clap their hands three times, rhythmically. It was an extraordinary performance, a return to the great show trials in the Soviet Union in the 1930s and in Eastern Europe in the 1940s. In the interview, Pol Pot insisted that he was a kind and gentle man whose only concern was the well-being of all Cambodians. 'I came to carry out the struggle, not to kill people,' he said. 'Even now, you can look at me: am I a savage person? My conscience is clear.'

Hun Sen rapidly consolidated his power. Ranariddh's army commander escaped Phnom Penh and took refuge with a few loyal troops at O Smach on the Thai frontier, not far from the Khmers Rouges' last base. After an unsuccessful attempt to over-run the place, Hun Sen left them alone. The rest of the world showed little interest, though the Cambodian seat at the U N was left vacant and aid was cut off, while A S E A N refused to allow Cambodia to join. Now that the Khmers Rouges' fangs were drawn, Cambodia could be safely left to its misery. In March 1998, Hun Sen staged a show trial in Phnom Penh and Ranariddh was condemned for treason *in absentia*. Then his father, King Sinhanouk, pardoned him and he returned home and made his peace with Hun Sen, for the moment. The army had by then over-run Anlong Veng, finding that Ta Mok had vanished into the jungles, taking Pol Pot and Khieu Samphan with him. Hun Sen's victory was complete. Pol Pot died, or was killed by his comrades, on 15 April.

## THE THAI–LAOS BORDER WAR, 1987–8

In November 1987, a border dispute between Thailand and Laos erupted into a brief war. The trouble was ostensibly over a 27 sq. mile (43 sq. km) stretch of mountainous territory in the north; a border agreement between France and Siam in 1907 had left the exact line unclear. It was likely that the dispute concerned more than an undemarcated border. These remote hills are the centre of the opium trade, in the Golden Triangle, and were also the route by which China supplied its allies in the Cambodian civil war, as well as that by which anti-Communist Vietnamese guerrillas infiltrated into Vietnam. Finally there **167** has been an ongoing dispute between the two countries on the refugee question. Hmong tribesmen in Laos have tried to escape into Thailand, and the Thai army has tried to stop them, with mixed success. As noted above, there are 326,000 Laotian refugees in Thailand.

By the time agreement on a ceasefire was reached on 17 February 1988, Laos had lost about 200 men and Thailand between 70 and 100. Laos and Thailand had both moved troops into the disputed district, and Laotian artillery had shelled Thai villages and Thailand had bombed Laotian positions. In June, Vietnam announced that it would withdraw 20,000 men, half its garrison, from Laos. This decision, now that it has been followed by a similar withdrawal from Cambodia, will probably solve the difference between Thailand and Laos.

## FURTHER READING

American University, *Cambodia: A Country Study*, Washington D.C., 1979.

Amnesty International, *Kampuchea: Political Imprisonment and Torture*, London, 1987.

Becker, Elizabeth, *When the War Was Over*, New York, Simon and Schuster, 1986.

Chanda, Nayan, *Brother Enemy: The War After the War*, New York, Harcourt, Brace, Jovanovitch, 1986.

Chandler, David P. *The Tragedy of Cambodian History Politics, War and Revolution Since 1945*, Yale, 1991.

Lawyers' Committee for Human Rights, *Kampuchea: After the Worst*, New York, 1985.

Ngor, Haing, *A Cambodian Odyssey*, New York, Macmillan, 1987.

Shawcross, William, *Sideshow*, New York, Simon and Schuster, 1979.

———, *The Quality of Mercy*, New York, Simon and Schuster, 1984.

# CHINA

| | |
|---|---|
| Geography | 3,691,500 sq. miles (9,560,948 sq. km). The third largest country on Earth, and slightly smaller than Canada. |
| Population | 1200 million. The population was 74% agricultural in 1990, but that leaves 400 million, the population of Europe, in the cities. |
| GNP per capita | $620. |
| Refugees | 110,000 Tibetans in India. Internal: 294,000, mostly ethnic Chinese, from Vietnam. |

China has fought one major war since its revolution in 1949, and that was in Korea. There have also been conflicts with the Soviet Union, India and Vietnam, and with the Nationalist regime in Taiwan, and it has conquered Tibet and suppressed uprisings there. None of the issues that provoked the various conflicts has been resolved, and they may all flare up again. Indeed, there was rioting in Lhasa in 1987 and 1988, and skirmishing with Vietnam on the Spratly islands in 1988.

Obviously, a frontier dispute between such large and powerful states as China and Russia could be a real danger to the peace of the world. For the moment at least, both countries' internal problems are so severe that a serious conflict between them is unlikely. The greatest dangers facing China are internal: when Deng Xiaoping sent the tanks into Tiananmen Square on 4 June 1989, he did not resolve the crisis: he merely postponed it and exacerbated it. All Deng's reforms have failed utterly to resolve the question of the legitimacy of the regime, which has been the central question in China since 1911. How can such a vast and diverse country adapt itself to the modern world?

These are matters of great concern to the rest of the world. If China's economy continues to expand smoothly at the rate it achieved in the 1980s (8.3 per cent annually, 1985–1995), it will overtake Europe early in the next century. China has ten times Japan's population and far greater natural resources. If the Chinese now follow the example that Japan has set since 1945, and stick to developing their economy, they will dominate the world in the middle of the next century. Indeed, if it had not been for the Communist revolution, they might have done so already. Conversely, if the neo-Communists who still rule in Peking refuse to loosen the reins and permit the democratization of the country, there may be new explosions with quite unpredictable consequences.

# HISTORY

There is nowhere like it. Only Egypt, as a nation, is older, and only Japan has anything approaching the same historical continuity. China's size and populousness and the uninterrupted stretch of distinctively Chinese civilization over the millennia are unique. Periodically, the Chinese state disintegrated; it was always reconstituted.

The modern tragedy of China was that, unlike Japan, its 19th-century rulers refused to adapt to the times, resisting barbarian influence to the end. China's last dynasty (Chin) was originally Manchu, nomads who conquered the country in the 17th century. In their decadence, ruled by the malevolent Empress Dowager Tzu Hsi, they allowed China to dissolve in corruption and feudal factionalism. The Chin were finally swept away in the revolution of 1911, which was inspired by Western-educated but wholly Chinese intellectuals led by Sun Yat-sen.

It seemed for a while that China would follow Japan's example and modernize while retaining its essential national characteristics. Western powers, particularly the Americans, were heavily involved in the effort. The Portuguese, Russians, Germans, British and Americans had won extraterritorial bases in China, and the privileged status of foreigners in Shanghai was a constant irritant to Chinese susceptibilities. But these concessions helped China modernize, and until 1937, none of the powers ever tried to conquer China. It was too big.

The Nationalist government itself was never able to establish uncontested control across the whole country; there were coups and short civil wars, and warlords established themselves in various parts of the huge territory. By 1928, Chiang Kai-shek, the leader of the Kuomintang (KMT) party, controlled the country, or most of it. He might have led China into the modern world, but the great depression hit China hard, and in 1931, Japan seized Manchuria, site of much of China's most modern industry, and, in 1937, set out to conquer all China.

The war was as brutal as Hitler's invasion of the Soviet Union. When Japan captured Nanking, the capital, its troops looted the city, destroyed its public buildings and massacred between 40,000 and 200,000 people, according to different estimates. It was the first of the great atrocities of World War II.

China's losses in the war against Japan were enormous, perhaps as high as 20 million. Japan occupied the eastern third of the country, but never defeated it, for the same reasons that Hitler never conquered the Soviet Union: the country was far too big, the resistance far stronger than Tokyo had expected, and Western assistance played a crucial role. There is a tendency in the US to minimize the Soviet Union's role in defeating Hitler, and to minimize China's role in defeating Japan. They were both essential.

Another problem Chiang faced from the start, and which ultimately defeated him, was the Chinese Communist party. It was an indigenous creation, at first led by students who had studied in Europe and imbibed Marxism in the heady days after the Bolshevik Revolution, and like other Communist parties, it took its lead from Moscow. However, the Bolsheviks, except for Trotsky and his followers, were more concerned with preserving the USSR than with world revolution, so they remained allied to Chiang Kai-shek and his Kuomintang, even after Chiang suppressed the Communists in Shanghai in April 1927, slaughtering at least 10,000 of them. There followed the first of many leadership disputes in the Communist party. Mao Tse-tung and his followers, who wanted to build the revolution among the peasantry, prevailed. Stalin preached moderation to the Chinese Communists until the end, sowing the seeds of the bitter split between the two countries that came into the open in the 1960s.

The party moved into the countryside to regroup. There it was constantly harried by Nationalist troops, and it retreated into South China, where it was in danger of being crushed permanently. In 1934, Mao led his troops in what became known as the Long March, across 6200 miles (10,000 km) of desolate territory to the far north-west. He set out with over 190,000 people, including 100,000 troops, but there were only 20,000 when they arrived in Shensi. Chiang, believing them defeated, left them alone, and turned to face the Japanese.

The Chinese Communists joined the fight against them but, immediately after the war, resumed the revolution. Despite huge quantities of American aid, the Nationalist armies collapsed, and on 1 October 1949, Mao proclaimed the People's Republic in Tiananmen Square in Peking. Chiang took refuge on Taiwan (Formosa), an island that had been occupied by the Japanese from 1895 until 1945.

## MAO'S CHINA

By the time Mao died in 1976, his government had a number of achievements to its credit. It had united the entire country, and suppressed banditry and warlords. It had restored national prestige for the first time in centuries: a year after the revolution, China had entered the Korean war and fought the Americans to a standstill, at a time when the United States was at the apogee of its power. Mao had rejected Soviet attempts to turn China into another satellite, and had established China as a leading spokesman of the Third World. In a long duel with Washington, Peking had eventually persuaded the Americans to recognize the People's Republic as the sole legitimate government of China.

Foreign policy – except for the Korean war (*see* Korea, pp. 215–23) – was a success. Domestic policy was a disaster. Mao inflicted an extreme Communist ideology upon the country, abolishing not only private property and farms, but even the villages that were the heart of Chinese society, and the institution of the traditional family. Perhaps a million landlords were executed, and China's peasants were driven into communes, like the Israeli kibbutzim, only with two essential differences. The kibbutz is a wholly democratic and voluntary society; in the communes, everything from the planting schedule to people's reading matter was directed by the party. The kibbutzim are small and manageable; the communes were huge.

The evident failure of his policies led Mao to try ever more extreme measures. In 1957, he launched a 'self-criticism campaign', proclaiming 'Let a hundred flowers bloom, let a hundred schools of thought contend', in the hope of radicalizing the party. The Chinese took him literally, and demanded democracy, private property and an end to Communist mismanagement. The campaign was hastily abandoned, and those who had believed Chairman Mao and had raised their voices in complaint were shot or imprisoned. In 1958, he proclaimed the Great Leap Forward, a programme of forced economic development, believing that China could manage in five years what had taken 40 in the Soviet Union. It was a disaster, and set the Chinese economy back by a generation.

## THE CULTURAL REVOLUTION

Mao's colleagues succeeded in curbing his powers and, in the early 1960s, set about reforming the economy. Mao struck back in 1966 with the Great Proletarian Cultural Revolution, one of the most extraordinary episodes in modern history. It was suddenly initiated in July 1966, when Mao, then 73, emerged from seclusion and swam the Yangtze river, an event that was given huge publicity and was supposed to show that Mao's revolutionary zeal and strength were unimpaired. There was a great purge of the government, like Stalin's purges in the 1930s, with Mao's oldest comrades-in-arms accused of treachery.

He incited students to rise against the government at every level – from schools to the central authorities in Peking – attacking 'monsters and demons'. His slogan was 'Bombard the headquarters'. In August 1966, he ordered the formation of 'Red Guards' of students, who would storm the heights of society and attack the 'leading capitalist-roaders', meaning senior party members who opposed him.

On 18 August, Mao addressed a crowd of a million Red Guards in Tiananmen Square. Other rallies followed, culminating in November with one that allegedly was attended by 2.5 million enthusiastic revolutionaries. The Red Guards rushed around the country, singing 'The Great Helmsman' or 'The East is Red' and waving little red books containing Mao's thoughts. Their favourite 'thought' was:

A revolution is not a dinner party, or writing an essay, or painting a picture, or doing embroidery; it cannot be so refined, so leisurely and gentle, so temperate, kind, courteous, restrained and magnanimous. A revolution is an insurrection, an act of violence by which one class overthrows another.

They attacked 'The Four Olds' – old thought, old culture, old customs, old habits. That meant destroying a great deal of Chinese history and the accumulation of art treasures. Red Guards went to Tibet and destroyed 3000 monasteries and temples, built over 500 years.

Universities were closed for years, party leaders were killed or exiled and anarchy became the watchword. In January 1967, Red Guards seized control of Shanghai, the country's largest city, and Mao urged those in every other city to follow their example. The model was the Paris Commune of 1871. Party leaders were paraded before 'struggle meetings' of Red Guards, to abjure their past mistakes, with dunces' caps on their heads and placards setting out their failings hung around their necks. Sometimes they were driven thus attired through Peking on the backs of trucks.

Mao himself began to worry at the violence that he had unleashed, and began to favour the establishment of joint committees of Red Guards, party cadres and army personnel. These committees sprang up everywhere, replacing the party committees. They were dominated by the army.

In early 1967, the tide of revolution ebbed for a while, but soon it returned stronger than ever. Liu Shao-qui, president of China and Mao's principal rival, was denounced as an American spy. His wife was dragged to a struggle meeting, and dressed in silks and high heels and a necklace of pingpong balls. Liu died of privation in jail in 1969.

The Great Proletarian Cultural Revolution reached its peak in the summer of 1967, with the country slipping rapidly into anarchy, factions fighting each other and the Red Guards being constantly egged on by Mao and his supporters. Finally, as fighting broke out between units of the army, even Mao saw that the troubles had gone far enough, and started to rein in the Red Guards. It took several years to bring the country back to reason; the Cultural Revolution officially ran from the spring of 1966 to the spring of 1969, but for years afterwards, there was constant political turmoil and sporadic upheavals.

In the course of the Cultural Revolution, by Western estimates, 400,000 people were killed (the Chinese admit to 35,000 deaths), and the government remained paralysed and ineffectual from 1966 until Mao died ten years later.

In late September 1971, there occurred one of the most mysterious episodes of recent history – the alleged plot and flight of Lin Biao. Lin was minister of defence, and had been officially designated as Mao's 'Close Comrade in Arms and Successor'. He had been the prime mover of the Cultural Revolution, after Mao, and continued to be one of the leading figures in the state. Then suddenly it was announced that he had tried to stage a *coup d'état*, and murder Mao. The plot allegedly involved bazookas, exploding oil storage tanks and bombing Mao's residence. When it was discovered, according to the official story, Lin fled to the airport with his wife, his son and various other people, including five members of the Politburo. They fled in Lin's personal Trident and headed for the Soviet Union, but the plane ran out of fuel over Mongolia and crashed, killing everyone on board. The confusion was so great that the annual celebration of the Revolution on 1 October had to be cancelled.

The only part of this improbable story that can be confirmed is that a plane did indeed crash in Mongolia. Even now, 20 years after the death of Mao, no convincing account has ever been given of what was involved in the dispute between Mao and Lin, and the details of the plot remain unconfirmed. The fall of Lin Biao was followed by a full-scale purge throughout the army and the party.

## MAO'S LAST DAYS AND THE GANG OF FOUR

During the early 1970s, Chou En-lai, Mao's long-term deputy and the chief moderating influence in the state, managed to have some of the exiled 'rightists' returned to power. The most important of these was Deng Xiaoping. In the 1950s and 1960s, he had been among the handful of people who governed China, as secretary-general of the Chinese Communist party. As the Cultural Revolution got under way, he had remarked: 'It doesn't matter whether a cat is black or white, so long as it catches mice.' This was taken (correctly) to be an aspersion cast upon Mao's theoretical intransigence, and Deng's slogan became a major charge against him and a rallying cry for his supporters. He was disgraced in 1966, and was lucky to escape with his life. He spent the intervening years working in a cafeteria in an army barracks.

The rightists' restoration was difficult and gradual – Deng was reappointed to the Central Committee in August 1973 – and was vigorously opposed by the radicals, including sometimes Mao himself. Simultaneously, Chou organized the reversal of alliances, institutionalizing China's hostility to the Soviet Union and, in February 1972, welcoming President Nixon to Peking. Nixon was photographed taking tea with Chairman Mao.

The radicals were not yet defeated. In 1974, they began a 'Criticize Confucius' campaign in which the merits of the long-dead sage were endlessly and passionately discussed: by Confucius, the radicals meant Chou En-lai. Then they started a campaign praising Shih Huang Ti, the first Emperor, who had united China, built the Great Wall – and burned the works of Confucius. He is generally regarded as a ferocious tyrant, but the radicals praised him and his work as a way of praising Mao, and attacking Chou and his protégé, Deng Xiaoping. They also denounced Western music, notably Beethoven, as imperialist and decadent and another manifestation of 'monsters and demons'. However, by 1975, Deng had been restored to all his posts and was once again effectively running the country.

Both Mao and Chou were dying, and the fight was over the succession. Chou died in January 1976, and the leftists then engaged in a last, desperate battle for power. Mao, in his dotage, was manipulated by his wife and her closest associates, later collectively known as 'the Gang of Four'. On 5 April occurred the 'Tiananmen Incident'. The authorities had removed a vast accumulation of wreaths honouring Chou that had been laid on a memorial there, and a huge protest demonstration turned into a riot in which party buildings were burned. Deng was blamed for the riot, and was again deposed, but military friends got him safely out of Peking. All over China, there were immense public demonstrations of popular support for him: Deng was clearly seen to be the heir of Chou En-lai, and the last hope of saving China from a renewal of the Cultural Revolution.

In July 1976, an earthquake killed 800,000 people in Tientsin and the government's incompetence was strikingly revealed (there were no relief operations for weeks). The heavens themselves blaze forth the death of princes: the disaster, like other similar catastrophes in China's long history, was taken as an omen – Mao had lost the Mandate of Heaven, by whose grace the emperors once reigned, and there was about to be a change of dynasty.

Mao died on 9 September 1976. A month later, the 'Gang of Four' were arrested in a *coup d'état* organized by the army, security police and members of the government determined to prevent a return to the anarchy of the Cultural Revolution. No other country of comparable importance has passed through such drama and difficulty since 1945.

Within a year, Deng had established his power over the government, and then started the economic reforms that have dramatically changed the face of China. The people's communes were abolished, and Communism was abandoned in agriculture (though complete price freedom was not entirely restored); self-management of businesses and the private ownership of firms and even a stock market were introduced.

The economic changes introduced by Deng after 1976 were revolutionary, but were not accompanied by any loosening of the controls exercised by the

Communist party. Where Gorbachev opened the Soviet political scene to all tendencies while proceeding most cautiously in economic reform, Deng chose the opposite course. Both countries discovered that the two must go together.

The explosion came quite suddenly. Hu Yao-bang, the government's leading reformist, had been purged after an earlier spate of pro-democracy demonstrations in Peking in 1987. He died on 15 April 1989, and the next day there was a small demonstration of mourning in Tiananmen Square. It was like the mourning for Chou En-lai in 1976. The students marched on the square, and soon there were demonstrations of hundreds of thousands of people demanding reform, democracy and an end to official corruption. The students occupied the square for six weeks, and quickly won the overwhelming support of the general population. Students in other cities followed their example. They were supported by Zhao Ziyang, the party's secretary-general, and soon there was a ferocious battle between Zhao and his supporters, and the hardliners led by Deng, who was 84, and the prime minister, Li Peng. Deng told the Politburo: 'We shouldn't be afraid of bloodshed or pressure from international public opinion . . . We have three million troops.'

The students started a hunger strike, and petitioned the government. Zhao emerged to plead with them to give up the strike, and Li Peng grudgingly agreed to hold a televised debate with their leaders. Martial law was proclaimed but the citizens of Peking protected the students. At the beginning of June, they erected a 'Statue of Democracy' in the square, modelled on the Statue of Liberty. Early in the morning of 4 June, Deng sent the troops and tanks into the square. There was heavy fighting and thousands of people were killed (between 2000 and 5000 according to official estimates). Many soldiers were killed by the crowds and their trucks were burnt.

It was a disaster for Deng as well as for the students. He had called in the Old Guard to support his hard line, and now the Old Guard demanded an end to all his reforms. Paradoxically, therefore, reformers hoped for Deng's survival. Foreign trade and tourism came to a standstill. Hong Kong, which was due to be returned to China in 1997, panicked. As the months passed, all Deng's economic reforms were put in jeopardy. Price reform was abandoned, over 2 million private firms were closed and China reverted to centralized planning. When the schools and universities reopened, compulsory classes in Marxist doctrine were reinstated.

Deng announced his resignation from his last government post, chairman of the government's Central Military Commission, on 9 September 1989, to be succeeded by the new party general secretary, Jiang Zemin. It meant nothing. In December, Deng was filmed holding court to an American delegation headed by President Bush's national security adviser, Gen. Brent Scowcroft: Bush was roundly criticized for giving his approval to the regime so soon after the Tiananmen massacre.

The state of emergency was lifted in January 1990, but the suppression of all opposition continued. The government, led by Li Peng, reverted to Deng Xiaoping's old policy of encouraging economic development and a controlled market economy, while maintaining rigid political control. Li Peng set about restoring China's position in the world, supporting the American-led attack on

Iraq in 1990–91, himself visiting a number of foreign countries, and playing a positive role in the U N. Economic growth resumed and the country seemed to be at peace, but it did not appear probable that China would remain calm indefinitely.

By the mid-1990s, Tiananmen seemed to be no more than a fading memory. The economy expanded at a vertiginous pace as capitalism took root everywhere. A new leader, Jiang Zemin, became president and supplanted Li Peng as the country's principal leader (Li had to give up the premiership early in 1998). Deng slowly faded away. He died in February 1997, a few months before Hong Kong was returned to China. That event was celebrated with much pomp and rejoicing all over China. Only Hong Kong was doubtful: the new regime's first act was to abolish the democratic system left behind by the British. In October, Jiang paid a state visit to the United States, where he conducted himself with the assurance of a man certain that the tide of history was flowing in his favour.

Despite the country's rising prosperity, it was not at all sure that Jiang was right. Dissent was rigorously suppressed, but there was no doubt that the Chinese, at least in the cities, longed for democracy. The economic difficulties of East Asia in 1997 spread to China and, at the very least, showed that as China moved to join the rest of the world economically, its political stature was more and more of an anomaly.

## TIBET

Tibet occupies 745,000 sq. miles (1.9 million sq. km) on the roof of the world. It has few natural resources, and until the Chinese conquest in 1950, its 2–3 million people led peaceful lives as shepherds, peasants, small traders and monks. Lhasa, the capital, had a population of about 30,000, but other Tibetan towns contained far fewer people (they would be considered villages in Europe) and most of them served the monasteries, where perhaps 10 per cent of the population lived, following 'The Way', under the direction of the Dalai Lama. Tibet was the only complete theocracy in the world.

The Dalai Lama is the reincarnation of one of the aspects of the Buddha. His authority is therefore absolute in Tibet, like the Imam Khomeini's used to be in Iran, the difference being that Buddhism is a pacifist creed. When the Dalai Lama dies, search parties scour the countryside to find the baby who is the new Incarnation. The current Dalai Lama is the 14th in this line, and although he fled Tibet in 1959 and now lives in India, there is no doubt that virtually all Tibetans remain wholly devoted to him.

China had asserted sovereignty over Tibet from time to time over the centuries, and had occasionally enforced it for brief periods. However, the country was so remote, and so poor, that the Celestial Empire usually left it alone.

In the 20th century there was constant squabbling between Lhasa and successive governments in Peking, and border wars between Tibetans and various Chinese warlords. Peking never renounced its claim to Tibet and, from time to time, contemplated sending an army to enforce it. It was always dissuaded by internal dissensions and by strong British support for Tibet. The 13th Dalai Lama died in 1933, and four years later, Japan invaded China.

Tibet remained undisturbed during the war, though the Americans flew supplies to Chiang Kai-shek 'over the hump' of the Tibetan Himalayas, an exceedingly dangerous route. In 1949, Mao Tse-tung entered Peking. China was at last reunited under a strong and assertive government, and one of its first tasks was to 'reunite' the national territory: on 7 October 1950, a Chinese army occupied Lhasa.

China, at first, did little to change Tibet. The 14th Dalai Lama, by then 16 years old, was left in his palace, the monasteries were undisturbed and the Tibetan government continued to function. However, the Chinese built roads into the country, placed their garrisons at strategic points, and moved the first of several hundred thousand Chinese settlers into Tibet.

The Tibetan peasantry began to resist, and in 1955, a guerrilla movement started in the remoter parts of the country, led by the Kampas in the east. By 1959, there was a full-fledged guerrilla war in the countryside, engaging 200,000 Chinese troops. In one battle in 1958, Kampas wiped out a Chinese garrison of 3000 men.

The Chinese would not tolerate such a situation for long. The key to controlling the country was the Dalai Lama. The Chinese invited him to Peking. He declined. On 9 March 1959, the commanding Chinese general in Lhasa invited him to attend a display at the Chinese barracks there, without his usual entourage of ministers and guards. Tibetans took this as an attempt to take the Dalai Lama hostage, like the Inca Atahualpa in Peru, and a crowd of 30,000 Tibetans gathered around the summer palace to protect him. The Chinese fired shells into the palace grounds in warning and moved troops into Lhasa, and the Dalai Lama then decided to escape. He fled on horseback to India, arriving there with 80 followers on 30 March.

When news of the successful escape reached the Chinese in Lhasa, they dispersed the crowds with great violence, killing about 3000 people. There was a great upsurge of fighting throughout Tibet: the Dalai Lama claims that about 65,000 Tibetans were killed. Over 60,000 refugees fled to Nepal and India.

China now dissolved the remaining institutions of Tibetan independence, and installed a Communist regime. The monks were evicted from their monasteries, which were closed; the Chinese language and Chinese law and customs were imposed upon Tibet. Tibetan guerrillas continued the fight, but without any external support, facing overwhelming odds, it was a hopeless contest.

Then in 1966, the Cultural Revolution came to Tibet. Red Guards seized control of the country and set about extirpating all traces of 'feudalism and superstition'. It was one of the most comprehensive acts of vandalism in the 20th century, comparable to the conduct of the retreating German army in Eastern Europe. As the Germans had blown up the tsars' palaces near Leningrad, and had demolished Warsaw, so the Red Guards destroyed over 3000 temples and monasteries in Tibet. Sacred books, idols and devotional objects were also destroyed, stolen or shipped back to China. Chinese officers who tried to stop the destruction, including the commanding general, Chang Kuo-hua, were arrested by the Red Guards. The Chinese army then intervened, rescued Chang, and tried to impose order, but state terrorism against the Tibetans, many of whom were murdered, and fighting among the Chinese, continued until 1970. **177**

Chris Mullen, writing for the Minority Rights Group, observed that the destruction of Tibetan culture, shrines, monasteries and artefacts was not spontaneous, it was carefully planned:

First, experts came and marked the precious stones, and they were then removed; then came metal experts who marked the precious metals for removal; the buildings were then dynamited and timber was taken away for use by the local commune, and the stones were left for anyone to use.

A more depressing observation was that:

Most of the destruction was carried out by young Tibetans. The Chinese took care to stay in the background. No doubt the Tibetan youth were egged on by the Chinese; no doubt many now regret what they did, but the fact remains that the actual destruction of Tibet's cultural heritage was carried out by Tibetans.

In a rather similar phenomenon, ten years later, young Cambodians were taught to kill their compatriots by the Khmers Rouges.

In 1974, after the storm had abated, the Chinese granted an amnesty to the Tibetans who were in prison and began to repair the damage. In 1980, the general secretary of the Chinese Communist party, Hu Yao-bang, went to Lhasa and publicly deplored the excesses of the period 1959–74, which he blamed on the Gang of Four. (Hu himself was subsequently purged.) Some of the monasteries were restored and a few were reopened. Foreign visitors were allowed into Lhasa for the first time in a generation. They found Tibetans living in squalid conditions under harsh Chinese control, and complete alienation between the two societies.

The results of the new policy were predictable. Tibetans were not persuaded of the merits of their subjection to China simply by a little kindness, not after so much oppression. They began to demand their independence again. There were riots in Lhasa in September and October 1987, led by monks who marched through the city denouncing China; about a dozen people were killed. There were more serious disturbances in March 1988. On 5 March, at least one and perhaps three Chinese policemen were killed in a riot during a religious festival. According to the *Observer*, 30 monks were killed in the Jokhang monastery immediately afterwards, and perhaps 20 other people over the next few days. Foreigners were again expelled from Tibet.

In April, Lord Ennals, a former British Labour party minister, visited Tibet and reported that 2000 Tibetans had been arrested during the demonstrations, and that many had been tortured. In Peking, the Panchen Lama, a leading Tibetan monk who has supported the Chinese since they invaded Tibet, said that five people were killed, including one policeman, and 200 detained during the March riots. He also said that the Dalai Lama would be allowed to return to Lhasa if he gave up his demands for Tibetan independence. Previously, China had insisted that the Dalai Lama must live in Peking. (The Panchen Lama died in January 1989.)

The human rights group Asia Watch reported in July 1988 that several

hundred Tibetans were still detained and that 'there is little doubt now that torture is often part of the routine in political arrests and incarceration in Tibet, and that the use of cattle prods is common in such instances'.

The riots were a great embarrassment to the Chinese government, but there is little likelihood that it will abandon Tibet. China is not a multinational state, like the Soviet Union, India, Ethiopia or Nigeria, which might disintegrate under particularist pressure. There are many small nationalities on the fringes of China, but the overwhelming majority of the population are Chinese and will always be able to impose themselves upon the minorities.

The Dalai Lama was awarded the Nobel peace prize in 1989, a gesture that much offended the Chinese government. After the Tiananmen massacre in June, the government's violent suppression of all opposition extended to Tibet, where every movement of protest was crushed with increasing brutality. So the Dalai Lama and a community of about 110,000 Tibetan refugees live in India and Nepal, and try to preserve Tibetan culture from Chinese oppression. They take consolation from their study of The Way, and hope that a new revolution of the Wheel of Life, that once drove them from their homes, will some day take them back again.

## TAIWAN

The People's Republic of China (with its capital at Peking) and the Republic of China (based in Taiwan) both insist that China is one and indivisible. They both claim to represent the country, but since 1978 the United States has recognized the People's Republic. Perhaps one day the two will be reunited, but there is no sign of it now.

On the contrary, Taiwan is growing away from the mainland. It has enjoyed sustained economic prosperity, and is now one of the 'four little dragons' of Asia, along with South Korea, Hong Kong and Singapore, treading in Japan's foot- steps. Its indigenous population, though of Chinese origin, feels no particular loyalty to Peking, any more than the Chinese of Singapore do. As the older generation – who crossed from the mainland in 1949 – die or retire, Taiwan becomes steadily more Taiwanese and less Chinese. Martial law was lifted, after 38 years, in July 1987; and after President Chiang Ching-kuo, Chiang Kai-shek's son and successor, died on 13 January 1988, a Taiwanese, Lee Teng-hui, succeeded him. Taiwan is thus quite different from Germany, which was kept divided solely by the Soviet army of occupation, or Korea, which remains one nation divided in two by ideology.

The Chinese have made no real effort to reconquer Taiwan, although in the 1950s they mounted a sustained campaign against two islands controlled by the Nationalists, Quemoy and Matsu, which lie off the Chinese coast. These unfortunate outposts were subjected to a sustained artillery bombardment in 1958–60. That episode is chiefly memorable for the role it played in the 1960 American presidential election, in which Vice-President Nixon and Senator Kennedy solemnly debated whether the United States should go to war to defend Quemoy and Matsu. If Mao ever seriously contemplated attacking them, he was dissuaded by his colleagues, and perhaps by Soviet pressure. The Chinese turned to symbolic attacks, firing shells that would scatter propaganda pamph- lets rather than high explosives over the islands. They mounted loudspeakers to harangue the Nationalist garrisons, and the Nationalists did the same thing in retaliation. It was a pointless exercise, and it lasted for years.

The Taiwan problem has remained a shadow on China's international relations. Peking reacted with extraordinary pugnacity when the president of Taiwan, Lee Teng-hui, was given a visa to visit the United States in June 1995, to attend a reunion of his class at Cornell University. It was a gesture by the Clinton administration that the US would not turn its back completely on Taiwan, even as it developed closer relations with China. In March 1996 Taiwan held presidential elections in which, for the first time, opposition parties ran on a frankly nationalist (meaning Taiwanese) ticket. One of them won. China was so exercised by this democratic display that it conducted full-scale military and naval exercises in the Taiwan Straits during the campaign, firing missiles dangerously close to Taiwan's two main ports to remind voters of the realities of the case. The US sent two aircraft carriers to Taiwanese waters to demonstrate its concern.

That episode soon faded, but the new regime that succeeded Deng Xiaoping was determined to show that it was as obdurate in insisting that Taiwan was part of the motherland as its predecessors. It might repeat its peaceable intentions, but it never renounced its right to use force to reunite the errant province should the need arise. As the last shreds of the Nationalist regime faded away, the Taiwanese showed increasing determination to proclaim their independence. Peking and Washington would exert every effort to dissuade them, from fear of the consequences, but the pretence that there is only one China cannot be kept up for ever.

## THE SINO–SOVIET DISPUTE AND THE BORDER WAR OF 1969

The border incidents between the USSR and China in 1969 were not themselves serious. A few dozen soldiers were killed fighting over an island in the Ussuri river which divides the two countries in the Far East, due north of Vladivostok.

The territory was not important, but the symbolism was. China maintains that large areas of the Soviet Union, notably the Pacific province, including Vladivostok, were stolen from China in a moment of weakness in the late 19th century. The thefts were ratified in the 'unequal treaties' forced upon the Manchu (Chin) dynasty by imperial Russia.

Those were only a few of the unequal treaties; others were imposed by Germany, the United States, Britain and Portugal. Germany lost its position in China after 1918, the Americans withdrew after World War II, and the Communist occupation of Shanghai put an end to the foreign zones there. Hong Kong was ceded to China in 1997 and Macao will be ceded in 1999.

But Russia will not cede Vladivostok or southern Siberia, nor will the Central Asian Republics cede the areas China claims. The dispute over the island in the Ussuri was therefore fraught with significance. Beyond territory, the dispute goes back to what Mao considered to be Stalin's treachery and to continuing Soviet bullying. There were also doctrinal disputes: Mao called the United States a 'paper tiger', and professed not to fear nuclear weapons.

The two countries' growing dispute was kept secret during the 1950s, and even after it burst into the open, in 1960, hardliners in Washington continued to believe it a fraud, saying that the two countries remained united under Moscow's leadership in a campaign to conquer the world. Many Americans had invested so much rhetoric in denouncing a world-wide conspiracy directed from the Kremlin that they found it impossible to adapt to reality. In the late 1980s, the same people refused to believe in Gorbachev's reforms.

In 1958, the Soviets abruptly suspended aid to the Chinese nuclear programme. In 1959, Nikita Khrushchev visited the United States, to Mao's deep displeasure; when the Soviet leader went to Peking for the 10th anniversary of the Communist revolution, on 1 October 1959, he was greeted with bitter attacks in party newspapers. In the Chinese manner, they were ostensibly directed against one of Mao's Chinese rivals.

In 1960, Mao launched a violent newspaper campaign against Yugoslavia; once again, the real target was Khrushchev. In July, Khrushchev retaliated by recalling all Soviet aid workers from China. They brought back their blueprints, leaving incomplete projects everywhere, and for several years China was seriously isolated.

Throughout the 1960s, the Chinese continued to be bitterly opposed to both the Soviet Union and the United States. By the end of the decade, however, they had concluded that, despite the latter's involvement in Vietnam, the danger from the north was more to be feared. The doctrinal disputes carried on, with Mao accusing Khrushchev and his successors of 'revisionism', meaning abandonment of true Marxist principles. The Chinese began actively seeking friends and allies in the Third World, offering themselves as a proper revolutionary alternative to the Soviets.

On 2 March 1969, 300 Chinese troops occupied the island of Damansky, which the Chinese call Chenpao, in the Ussuri river, which is the boundary between China and the USSR in the north-east. The island has no strategic or economic value: it is small and uninhabited, and at that point, the river runs through a barren and marshy territory, itself almost completely unpopulated. The invading Chinese ambushed a small Soviet patrol, killing 23 and wounding 14. The Soviets sent reinforcements, who were in turn ambushed. Then both sides withdrew from the island.

The Soviets protested bitterly and publicly. The Chinese accused them of frequent violations of their border (by the summer, they had a list of 429 such incidents). There were huge anti-Soviet demonstrations outside the Soviet embassy in Peking, and even larger ones outside the Chinese embassy in Moscow.

There was further fighting on Damansky/Chenpao on 15 March, with tanks and artillery and more casualties. There were other clashes along the Amur river frontier, north of the Ussuri, in April and May, and also far to the west on the Sino–Soviet frontier in Central Asia. (Henry Kissinger concluded that the Soviets were probably the aggressors in the Central Asian incidents because they occurred only a few miles from a Soviet railhead and hundreds of miles from the nearest Chinese railhead.) The Soviets also began to speculate in public about the necessity for a pre-emptive strike against Chinese nuclear installations, and they even sounded out the Nixon administration for its reaction to such an attack.

Kissinger and Nixon decided that the time had come for a *rapprochement* with China, and Chou En-lai had evidently come to the same conclusion. By 1970, it was clear that the United States wanted to leave Vietnam, which would eliminate the chief source of direct difficulty between the two countries. The reversal of alliances was consummated, after a secret trip to Peking by Henry Kissinger in 1971, by Nixon's visit to China in February 1972. A document signed by Nixon and Chou – the 'Shanghai Communiqué' – set the course of the two countries' future relations. The Americans then abandoned Taiwan to its fate, although full diplomatic relations with Peking were not established until 1978. By then, the new *entente* was a fundamental part of both nations' foreign policy. It was not challenged during the last upheavals of Mao's lifetime, and was embraced by Deng Xiaoping, who visited the US in January 1979, and informed President Carter that China intended to attack Vietnam the following month.

Richard Nixon considered India to be the greatest achievement of his presidency. It was also the most conspicuous failure of Soviet policy. China remained implacably opposed to the Soviet Union until Mikhail Gorbachev initiated a *rapprochement* in 1988, and has built up a nuclear arsenal with missiles capable of hitting Moscow. Conversely, the Soviets were obliged to move nearly half their army to defend their 4000-mile (6400 km) border with China, thus weakening their positions elsewhere in the world. It is a heavy price for an uninhabited island.

Mikhail Gorbachev, as part of his attempt to correct the errors of his predecessors, proposed negotiations with China on the border dispute and on other matters outstanding. China insisted that the Soviet Union must first force Vietnam to evacuate Cambodia and must itself withdraw from its bases in Vietnam and pull its troops back from the border. Gorbachev met all these conditions, for domestic reasons as much as from a desire to lessen tensions with Peking, and on 16 May 1989, visited Peking for the first Sino–Soviet summit since 1959. The meeting may have reduced tensions between the two countries, but it was overshadowed by the pro-democracy demonstrators, who were then occupying Tiananmen Square. Gorbachev had to be smuggled through back streets and side doors to meet the Chinese leaders, and found them so distracted by their domestic difficulties that they could scarcely consider the implications of his visit. Its meaning was clear enough for all that: both sides wanted a reconciliation, the USSR for economic, China for political reasons. It was ironic that the two powers should have decided to bury the hatchet just as their internal problems overwhelmed the ideological causes that had provoked the long estrangement. Over the next few years, treaties were signed recognizing the existing frontiers. This did not mean that China has forever given up its claims to Vladivostok and the rest, but that the claims would be left in abeyance for now.

(For the border war with India in 1962, *see* India, pp. 186–9. For conflicts with Vietnam, and the question of the relationships between China, the USSR, Vietnam and Cambodia, *see* Vietnam, pp. 261–5 and Cambodia, pp. 155–67.)

# FURTHER READING

American University, *China: A Country Study*, Washington D.C., 1981.

Bonavia, David, *The Chinese*, New York, Lippincott and Crowell, 1980.

Dietrich, Craig, *People's China: A Brief History*, Oxford University Press, 1986.

Garside, Roger, *Coming Alive: China after Mao*, New York, McGraw Hill, 1981.

Gascoigne, Bamber, *The Treasures and Dynasties of China*, London, Jonathan Cape, 1973.

Harding, Harry, *Second Revolution: China after Mao*.

Hinton, Harold C., *The People's Republic of China – a handbook*, Boulder, Colo., Westview Press, and Folkstone, Dawson, 1979.

Kissinger, Henry, *White House Years*, Boston, Little, Brown, 1979.

Kristof, Nicholas and WuDann Sheryl *China Wakes: The Struggle for the Soul of a Rising Power*. New York, Random House, 1995.

Li Zhisui, *The Private Life of Chairman Mao: The Memories of Mao's Personal Physician*, New York, Random House, 1994.

Miles, James A. R., *The Legacy of Tiananmen*, Ann Arbor, Michigan, University of Michigan Press, 1996.

Richardson, Hugh M., *Tibet and Its History*, Boulder, Colo., Shambhala, 1984.

Salisbury, Harrison E., *Tiananmen Diary*, Boston, Little, Brown, 1989.

Schell, Orville, *Mandate of Heaven*, New York, Simon and Schuster, 1995.

Smith, Warren W., *Tibetan Nation*, Boulder, Colorado, Westview Press, 1996.

# INDIA

| | |
|---|---|
| Geography | 1,269,346 sq. miles (3,287,593 sq. km). As large as Western and Central Europe, or roughly half the size of the continental United States. There are 22 states and ten union territories. Half the states have larger populations than Britain, France or Germany. |
| Population | 929 million in 1995, growing at a rate of about 16 million a year. The great majority are Hindu; there are also 110 million Muslims, substantial Sikh and Christian communities and small Jewish and Buddhist communities. There are 50 major regional tongues in India, of which the Constitution recognizes 16 as official languages. Hindi (spoken by a quarter of the population) and English apply to the whole country. There are hundreds of other languages and dialects. |
| GNP per capita | $340. |
| Refugees | Internal: 110,000 Tibetan, 100,000 Tamils from Sri Lanka, 53,000 Chakma from Bangladesh, 40,000 Chin from Burma, 30,000 Nepalese from Bhutan. |

India has fought three wars with Pakistan since independence in 1947, the latest in 1971, which led to the creation of Bangladesh. There is always the possibility of a fourth, over Kashmir. There was a border war with China in 1962, and India has forcibly annexed Goa and Sikkim, reduced Nepal to vassalage by imposing a prolonged trade embargo in the late 1980s, and intervened in Sri Lanka in 1987. There has been a long series of disputes in many parts of the country, among peoples seeking their independence from New Delhi, the most persistent in the north-east. The latest and most serious are among the Sikhs in Punjab, and the Muslims in Kashmir. Sikh terrorism provoked the army assault on the Golden Temple in Amritsar in 1984, which in turn led to the assassination of the prime minister, Indira Gandhi. The Temple was occupied a second time in 1988 but terrorism has continued since then.

The latest uprising against the central government, in Kashmir, erupted in 1988 and has led to many thousands of deaths. The security forces are fighting the terrorists with great brutality and are guilty of torture, summary execution and other violations of human rights. The intervention in Sri Lanka led to the assassination of Rajiv Gandhi, Indira Gandhi's son and successor, in 1991.

In 1974, India became the sixth country to explode a nuclear device, and ever since, Pakistan has been determined to do likewise. There is such hostility between the two that there is always the possibility of another war between them, which does not mean that a nuclear war is at all probable. India is now the dominant power in a region which has a population of 1222 million – more than China. It was for many years politically allied to the Soviet Union, but it is, like China, one of the great independent power centres in the world. It is too big to be dominated by any other nation. On the contrary, it is much more likely to exert intolerable pressure upon its neighbours: in 1987, India sent 120,000 troops to Sri Lanka, whose government was forced to accept an Indian plan for settling its internal problems (*see* pp. 250–60).

The only real threats to India come from within. Can a country so populous, so diverse and so poor maintain its national unity? The weight of its increasing population continually drags back its economic progress, thus provoking insoluble social unrest. India has survived so far because it is a democracy, allowing conflicting voices to be heard (the states are frequently in fierce opposition to New Delhi). Powerful leaders or ambitious officers may not always resist the temptation to try to solve the country's immense problems with a gun.

## HISTORY

India should not be considered a nation state, like Britain, Mexico or China. It is better compared to Europe: a geographically separate entity, with many nations and languages, which all share a common history and civilization.

Indian history goes back 5000 years. A long series of immigrants and conquerors has come over the mountains from the west and from Central Asia, building empires and leaving cities and monuments behind them. The British came by sea, with other Europeans, and established trading posts in the 17th century. In the 18th, they set out to conquer India, and by the mid-19th century, they controlled the entire sub-continent from the Himalayas to Ceylon. It had never been completely united before, and its unity did not survive the passing of the British Raj.

The British gave India its independence at midnight, 14 August 1947. The greatest failure in British imperial history was the partition of India into two nations: one Muslim (Pakistan); the other ostensibly secular, but in fact Hindu (India). In the early days of the independence movement, Muslims and Hindus were united fighting the British, under the spiritual leadership of Mahatma Gandhi. It is possible that, if India had been given independence in the 1930s, it would have remained united. A vigorous imperialist movement in the Tory party in London, which was then overwhelmingly dominant in Parliament, ensured that the timid governments of those days would not attempt so bold a step. The principal leader of this Tory rearguard was Winston Churchill. His subsequent achievements should not obscure his contribution to a disaster in which at least half a million people were killed.

Because of the vagaries of Muslim proselytization in the Middle Ages, the areas of Muslim majority in India were in two separated parts: the Punjab, the Land of the Five Rivers, in the west; and East Bengal in the east. Pakistan therefore came into existence divided into two, and separated by the breadth of **185**

Hindu India. The other appendages of British India – Burma and Ceylon – became independent separately.

The partition was one of the most savage events of the century: 12 million people fled their homes, and hundreds of thousands of people were killed in inter-communal massacres. The lowest estimate was 500,000, a more probable total is between 800,000 and 1 million. Trainloads of refugees passing from one side to the other were stopped and everyone on board killed, except the train driver.

Mahatma Gandhi, by prayer and fasting and using all his immense influence, succeeded in restoring order in Delhi. A Hindu fanatic shot him there on 30 January 1948.

The British had ruled half of India directly; in the rest of the country, they left native princes on their thrones, and ran their states through 'residents' (advisers to the princes). In 1947, the princes were invited to join India or Pakistan. Most of them, for the last time, followed their residents' advice and submitted. The grandest of all, the Nizam of Hyderabad, a Muslim prince in Hindu south India, refused. The new government sent in the army, and no more was heard of independent Hyderabad.

## THE FIRST INDO–PAKISTAN WAR

The largest of the princely states was Kashmir in the far north. It is predominantly Muslim, although with a substantial Hindu minority in Jammu. The Nehru family were Kashmiri Brahmins, and the maharajah of Kashmir was a Hindu descendant of a British ally in one of their 19th-century wars, who had been put on his throne as a reward for his loyalty.

The maharajah hoped for independence in 1947, but the government of Pakistan sent Muslim tribesmen into Kashmir to seize the country, and the maharajah therefore signed a treaty of accession to India on 27 October 1947. There followed the first war between India and Pakistan.

It was not a serious conflict in military terms. The Indians and Pakistanis both sent troops, who fought a series of skirmishes before agreeing to a ceasefire in January 1949. By then, India controlled most of Kashmir, but the two countries have never recognized the status quo: each still claims the whole territory.

## THE WAR WITH CHINA

The border war between India and China in 1962 was a fiasco that abruptly ended India's role as the moralizing, peace-loving leader of the Third World. Despite this, India managed to save some shreds of its diplomatic reputation after the humiliating defeat of its army, largely because of the country's undeserved reputation as the apostle of peace, and because of China's deserved reputation for ruthless egoism. In fact, India was the aggressor, China the victim, and when it had beaten the Indians, China behaved with striking diplomatic restraint.

The complete military mastery of the region by the British allowed them to set India's northern borders where it best suited them. The frontier was mapped and the line drawn by Captain Henry McMahon of the Indian Army, starting in 1893. As a result, the border has since been known as the McMahon line, much as the border between Maryland and Pennsylvania is named after two earlier British surveyors, Charles Mason and Jeremiah Dixon.

There were problems with the demarcation, the chief of which was that China never accepted the McMahon line. This was an academic difficulty at the time, because China did not then control Tibet, and Britain was far more powerful. This situation changed after the British left India and the Chinese Communists seized power in Peking in 1949 and occupied Tibet in 1950 (*see* China, pp. 171–82). If the British had still controlled India, they would doubtless have settled the frontier question expeditiously, just as they settled the argument over the frontier between Canada and the United States. The disputed territories were not worth fighting for, but India, like many other newly independent nations, considered its frontiers sacred, however remote and inaccessible.

A further problem was discovered at the western end of the line, where it runs through some of the wildest and highest territory on Earth, with passes that rise to 16,000 feet (5200 m) in the towering Pamirs: the line had not been properly demarcated. There were also questions about the exact location of the line farther east.

The essentials of the subsequent dispute were that, before the British came, there had been no precise frontiers: each state's power extended only as far as it could march an army. The British then pushed their armies as far as civilization went in the mountains, which meant along the foothills. Finally McMahon, being a tidy-minded European cartographer, drew his line along the crest of the mountains. China rejected this extension of British territory, which the British never policed, and insisted that the frontier should remain in the foothills.

Independent India claimed everything. It even asserted its control over a clearly Tibetan enclave on the south side of the line, in the east: the 'Tawong tract'. China did not protest, and the matter might have remained undecided except that China required a corner of the western end of the border for a road into Tibet. This province is called the Aksai Chin, and is part of the Tibetan plateau and virtually uninhabited. China needed it because it was the only practical route from Sinkiang, its westernmost province, into Tibet. Beyond lies the impassable Gobi desert.

So, in 1956, China built its road. It is 750 miles (1200 km) long, 112 miles (180 km) of it in territory claimed by India.

The Indians found out about the road the next year, by reading Peking newspapers that boasted of this remarkable piece of engineering. India demanded that China evacuate the Aksai Chin. China proposed, in exchange, that the whole frontier be surveyed, and intimated that it would recognize the McMahon line in the east if India accepted its claim to the Aksai Chin and the strategic road, in the west.

India refused categorically, and even refused to negotiate the question with China. Prime Minister Jawaharlal Nehru – who had endlessly lectured and scolded the Americans, British and others on the folly of using force in international affairs, and had constantly recommended negotiations as an infallible solution to all disputes – proved as unyielding and demagogic as the most corrupt Western politician. There is some debate whether he was hypocritical or merely weak, but what is beyond dispute is that his government whipped up a    **187** storm of chauvinism. Public and Parliament demanded that the Chinese be driven out of India, and Nehru promised to do so.

To prove his determination, he ordered a campaign against Portuguese Goa, and then allowed the Indian army to occupy the colony (and two other minute Portuguese enclaves) in December 1961. The Indian army then moved what troops it could find up to the Chinese frontier and began to implement the government's new 'forward policy'.

Unfortunately, Nehru had allowed the army to deteriorate sadly since independence. It retained many of its traditions, but its equipment was outdated and insufficient, and it was quite incapable of fighting a mountain war. The sycophantic officers whom Nehru had put in command concealed this fact from him, or at least failed to persuade him of their predicament.

The army was ordered to send patrols into the disputed areas and establish permanent posts there. They had immense difficulty doing so: there were no roads, and everything had to be portered through the Himalayas. The Chinese, on the high plateau, had built themselves all-weather roads and faced no such problems. There were frequent but minor encounters between Indian and Chinese patrols. The Chinese protested repeatedly, and repeatedly demanded formal negotiations on the frontier. Chou En-lai, the Chinese prime minister, went to Delhi in April 1962, to try to persuade the Indians to settle the matter peacefully. The summit was a complete failure.

In June 1962, in the west, the Indian army was ordered to push forward to the border that India claimed in the Aksai Chin; that would have meant occupying China's road. Indian patrols were sent forward, but the terrain was so difficult that there was no chance of reaching their objective. For the first time, there were violent clashes between Indian and Chinese patrols, in the Chip Chap valley. By then, there were about 30 Indian positions scattered throughout the Aksai Chin.

Simultaneously, the army was ordered to establish positions along the eastern section of the McMahon line. At one point, just east of the frontier with Bhutan, an Indian protectorate high in the Himalayas, Indian patrols went beyond the McMahon line to occupy a mountain ridge that McMahon had missed on his map. China again protested, to no effect.

In July, there were further serious clashes between Indian and Chinese patrols in Chip Chap. In September, in the east, the Chinese sent patrols into the vicinity of the most forward of the Indian positions. India took this as an invasion, and the government ordered that the Chinese be expelled from 'Indian' territory. On 9 October, the Indians moved forward from their most advanced positions, knowing their situation was hopeless: they were outnumbered five to one; the Chinese were much better equipped, and held the high ground, while the Indians were pinned in the valleys. The Chinese drove them back, killing seven Indian soldiers. On 20 October, they attacked again, over-running Indian advance positions in the east – and simultaneously wiping out the Indians in the Aksai Chin.

Although the dispute had originally concerned the western frontier, and China's road, the fighting in the east had become much more serious: the Chinese might clear a way through to Assam.

There was another lull in the fighting, and Indian troops guarding a strategic pass, 15,000 feet (5000 m) high, could hear the Chinese below them building a road to bring up trucks and artillery. Nehru's government, in a last act of folly, ordered the army to attack again. It did so on 15 November, once more failing completely. The next day, the Chinese resumed their advance, and routed the Indians; their defensive positions collapsed and the army broke and fled. Two days later, there was nothing between the Chinese army and the plains. Nehru prepared for the loss of Assam.

At that point, on 21 November 1962, China announced a unilateral ceasefire and withdrawal. It pulled its troops back 12 miles (20 km) behind the McMahon line in the east, and behind the previous frontier in the west. All the weapons and equipment that it had captured were carefully cleaned, polished and delivered to the Indians, against receipt. India reoccupied its lost territories, but abandoned its forward policy. Its casualties were 1383 dead, 1696 missing and 3105 prisoners of war, of whom 26 died in captivity. Chinese casualties were probably about half that.

Despite China's largesse, India (like Argentina after the Falklands war) refused to accept defeat and, to this day, continues to claim those mountain wastes as its own. It has not negotiated with China, although the offer of recognition of the McMahon line, in exchange for recognition of China's claim to the Aksai Chin, still stands.

The fiasco led to a change of Indian priorities. India became a close ally of the Soviet Union (even though the USSR had supported China during the war, while America had supported India), and devoted much larger sums to defence. It was therefore better able to face Pakistan in the wars of 1965 and 1971. India also gave up lecturing the rest of the world on the merits of non-alignment and pacifism.

Nehru never recovered from the shock. He had a stroke in January 1964 and died on 27 May.

There have been three further frontier confrontations between China and India, one in 1967, one in 1969 and the latest in 1987. In September 1967, after a period of increasing tension between the two governments (China was in the throes of the Cultural Revolution), China shelled Indian positions on the Sikkim border at the Natu La Pass. Ten Indian soldiers were killed. China accused the Indians of repeated violations of the frontier, and of killing 25 Chinese soldiers. The incident was not taken any further. In April 1969, relations along the border again deteriorated: at one stage, China filed a vigorous diplomatic protest after a piece of linoleum was blown across the border from an Indian frontier post. On that occasion, the trouble occurred farther west, at the Lipu Lekh Pass just west of Nepal. The Chinese opened fire on an Indian patrol. Once again, the incident had no consequences.

A more serious crisis developed in May and June 1987, in the Sumdoreng valley in Arunachal Pradesh, the Indian province in the extreme east of the Himalayas. The Chinese accused the Indians of setting up an advance post on their territory, and India accused China of infiltrating across the border. Both sides massed tens of thousands of troops along the border before diplomatic steps were taken to calm the crisis.

## THE SECOND WAR WITH PAKISTAN

In 1965, a trivial dispute between India and Pakistan over the waters of a large tidal area on the west coast, the Rann of Kutch, developed into a border war that spread to Kashmir.

After a serious military engagement in the Rann in April, a ceasefire was arranged by the British in June. However, Pakistan infiltrated guerrillas into Kashmir, in the hope of provoking an uprising against India, and occupied a number of positions. India regained them in August and fought off an attack in the Chamb sector of south-west Kashmir. On 6 September, India counter-attacked across the frontier in the Punjab, invading Pakistan between Lahore and Sialkot. The Indians advanced a few miles, defeating the Pakistani forces sent to oppose them, and then, on 23 September, accepted a ceasefire proposed by the United Nations. In all, 20,000 people, most of them civilians, were killed in the fighting. After strenuous efforts at mediation by the Soviet Union, President Ayub Khan of Pakistan and the new prime minister of India, Lal Bahadur Shastri, met in Tashkent in January 1966, to sign a permanent ceasefire. Blessed are the peacemakers: the Soviets did not often play that role. Immediately after signing, Shastri had a heart attack and died. He was succeeded by Nehru's daughter, Indira Gandhi. The agreements, and subsequent ones with the Bodo and the United Liberation Front of Assam, proved exceedingly fragile.

(For the third Indo–Pakistan war, *see* Pakistan, p. 228.)

## INTERNAL DISPUTES

There has been constant guerrilla activity by separatist groups along the north-eastern frontiers of India, which, with the founding of East Pakistan in 1947 (later Bangladesh), were virtually cut off from the rest of India. A string of mountainous tribal states there have been invaded by Bengali refugees, both Hindu and Muslim, trying to escape the poverty and over-crowding, as well as the unsettled conditions of their native provinces. Meanwhile, New Delhi has tried to assert its control over tribesmen in the mountains who bitterly opposed their inclusion in India in 1947.

The disparity in force between India and the tribes is so great that India cannot be defeated, although maintaining thousands of troops on constant alert in the mountains is a continuing drain on Indian military resources. After Rajiv Gandhi came to office in 1984, he set about settling these disputes. He reached agreements with the Mizo, Tripura and Gurkha rebels. The rebellions in Nagaland and Manipur and the disturbances among the Bodo continue.

India and Pakistan are also confronting each other in one of the most absurd and irresponsible conflicts between modern nations, on the Siachen Glacier in the Karakoram Mountains. This is an area in the north of Kashmir up against the Chinese frontier. It was not properly demarcated in the 1949 ceasefire. The glacier runs from 16,000 to 21,000 feet in altitude (5300 to 7000 metres) and is quite uninhabitable and of no military, economic or social significance whatever. K2, the second highest mountain in the world, is just over the border in China. In the 1970s, Pakistan issued maps showing it as part of Pakistani-occupied Kashmir, and India immediately sent the army to occupy it. Pakistani troops were then sent up the glacier to confront them. Since then, about 2000 men have been killed, well over half in accidents, in continuous skirmishes between the two sides.

## NAGALAND

The first of the tribal wars started in Nagaland, a remote, inaccessible country in the mountains between Assam and Burma. In 1944, the Japanese made their assault on India through Nagaland and Manipur, immediately to the south, and were stopped at Kohima and Imphal.

The Naga were conquered by the British with considerable difficulty in the 19th century. They were then allowed great autonomy and strict protection against incursions by people from the plains. In the middle of the century, Baptist missionaries arrived from the United States and converted many Naga to Christianity. The Naga fought bravely on Britain's side in World War I I, and afterwards, as India prepared for partition and independence, demanded a separate state. On 14 August 1947, the Naga National Council (NNC), led by Z. A. Phizo, proclaimed Nagaland independent. India refused to recognize the gesture.

For the next decade, there were bad-tempered exchanges between the Naga and New Delhi, with the Naga constantly demanding independence, and the Indians refusing to countenance the idea. By 1955, violence was becoming the norm in the Naga hills. The Indian government declared part of Nagaland a 'disturbed area', and began the long attempt to suppress Naga separatism. In January 1956, the whole region was declared a disturbed area, and in March, the NNC proclaimed a federal government, with a constitution and army, and started fighting for its independence. The rebel Naga were now known as 'the Federals'.

In the following two years, the Indians deployed thousands of troops to control Nagaland. According to the government, 1400 Naga and 162 Indian soldiers were killed. There were frequent and credible reports of massacres and torture by the troops.

By degrees, the Indians won the upper hand. In 1963, in belated recognition that the Naga are a special case, Nagaland was made a separate state in the Indian union. It was by far the smallest, with a population then of 350,000 (it is now about 700,000). Later, other states, equally small, were carved out of the hill country (*see below*). The Naga then were split between those who accepted Indian control in a separate state as the best they could get, and those who continued to fight for full independence. There was a ceasefire from 1964 until 1966, and in 1973 a faction of the Federal forces surrendered. The Indian army kept up the pressure, and on 11 November 1975, a key group of the Naga underground leadership accepted defeat and signed a ceasefire at Shillong, in the neighbouring state of Meghalaya. After 20 years of conflict, a measure of peace returned to Nagaland, but Phizo, in exile in London, and a group of Communist Naga, led by J. H. Muivah, refused to surrender. Muivah had sought help from China in 1966, and now he established his command across the border in Burma (where related tribes are also fighting for their independence). Muivah and his followers set up a National Socialist Council of Nagaland, and claim an army 2000 strong. **191**

There is now almost continuous fighting between the Naga and other tribes, as well as between the Naga and the central government. There is a particularly vicious confrontation between the Naga and the Kuki, another mountain tribe. The Nagas killed 30 Kuki passengers in a bus in December 1996. In July 1997, Kuki fighters killed about 25 Naga in Manipur.

## MANIPUR AND MIZORAM

These two states, formerly administratively part of Assam, were the scene of secessionist insurgencies for over 25 years. In 1961, the Mizo National Front was formed, partly in response to what its leaders considered Indian callousness during a famine. In February 1966, the M N F launched an insurrection that, for a while, dominated the whole district. The Indian army soon recovered control, and imposed its rule by moving villagers in 'village regrouping programmes', or strategic hamlets.

The government's reaction to the Mizo revolt followed the pattern in Nagaland: heavy military repression, followed by the creation, first of a 'union territory' called Mizoram, then of a full-fledged state of Mizoram. At the same time, the other hill districts were separated from Assam, and the states of Tripura, Meghalaya and Manipur were set up.

The Mizo revolt continued until 25 June 1986, when Rajiv Gandhi signed an agreement with the rebels that met many of their demands, in exchange for their acceptance of the permanency of the Indian union. Mizoram was declared a separate state and the M N F leader, Laldenga, became prime minister. In February 1987, there were elections in Mizoram, and the M N F won a majority in the state assembly, defeating Gandhi's Congress party. In the course of the insurgency, according to Indian estimates, about 1500 people had been killed.

In Manipur, there are still two guerrilla movements: the People's Liberation Army and the Revolutionary Army of Kuneipak. They both have ideological links to China, but they draw their strength from local opposition to the steady encroachment of immigrants from Bengal. Like the other tribesmen of the north-east frontier, they fear they will eventually be swamped by the desperate millions from Bangladesh.

In Meghalaya, the indigenous tribe, the Khasis, constantly attack immigrants, both Hindu and Muslim, and their capital, Shillong, is the scene of frequent ethnic murders. They are also puzzled by news from the outside world, arriving at last by satellite television, radio and telephone. The Khasis have always enjoyed a matrilineal social system: property is inherited by the family's youngest daughter upon her mother's death, and the men move into their wives' homes upon marriage. Children take the mother's name. This system is now under question.

## TRIPURA

Tripura, covering about 4000 sq. miles (10,000 sq. km), is an Indian enclave surrounded on three sides by Bangladesh. Its southern edge borders on the Chittagong Hill Tracts, where members of the same tribes as the Tripurans are in revolt against the Bangladeshi regime (*see* Bangladesh, p. 137), and its mountains are covered with dense jungle. In 1980, a group calling itself the Tripura Volunteer Force (T V F), led by Bijoy Kumar Hrangkhawl, started fighting for the state's independence. It was particularly opposed to a Marxist party that had won local elections in Tripura, on the strength of immigrants from Bengal. By then, the tribal people were in a minority in their own homeland: the first wave of Hindu immigrants had fled to the hills during the partition of India and in the early years of East Pakistan; a further 100,000 had followed since the independence of Bangladesh in 1971. The TVF started the war by massacring over 1000 Bengali settlers. In the fighting since then, another 1000 people were killed. The TVF had an army of only about 400 men but also thousands of supporters who could be called on if necessary.

In February 1988, the Marxist party in Tripura was defeated in an election, and Hrangkhawl decided that it was time to settle with the federal government. After three months' secret negotiations, the rebels agreed on 12 August to surrender their arms and end the fight. In exchange, the government pledged to stop further immigration from Bangladesh, increase tribal privileges and expand the authority of the local councils in the tribes' autonomous region.

The dispute is not finished, however. Hrangkhawl also demands that the 100,000 Bengalis who have settled in Tripura since 1971 should be expelled. That is not possible, and the deep animosity between the two peoples will continue.

## THE GURKHAS

The state of West Bengal is sandwiched between the Himalayas and Bangladesh, and is much more populous than the other north-eastern districts. About 19 million people live there, concentrated along the Brahmaputra river valley, including Gurkhas in the west, around Darjeeling, and a great variety of other peoples farther east. Opposition to the central government has been strongest among the Gurkhas (who are related to the Nepalese who still serve in the British army). Small-scale guerrilla war has persisted for years.

There has been a steady infiltration of people from Bengal, both Hindu and Muslim. The first anti-foreign riots occurred in 1979, and since then, there has been constant trouble and occasional massacres. In 1983, during an election campaign that Indira Gandhi forced on the state, 3000 people were killed, including 600 women and children in the Muslim village of Nellie. Their menfolk were off on a raid.

The troubles continued until July 1988, despite the efforts of the Indians to police the country. In February of that year, the Gurkha National Liberation Front attacked a police patrol and lost six men, and in April, a schoolteacher and a journalist were murdered in separate incidents: they were decapitated, and their heads put in nylon bags and left in public places. In all, at least 300 people were killed in the disturbances.

The Gurkhas never rose in full-scale revolt, as had Nagaland or Mizoram, although about 5000 people were killed. If they ever did, controlling them would be far more difficult. The Indian government has devoted considerable development funds to the region in the hope of persuading the people of the benefits of membership of the Indian union. The fundamental problem – the conflict between hillsmen and immigrants from the plains – will continue.

The government's policy of conciliation was finally successful when the Gurkha leader, Subhas Ghising, concluded a peace agreement on 25 July 1988. The chief     **193** clause in the settlement was the provision of an autonomous Gurkha district around Darjeeling, the Gurkhas' main town, which will have a population of about 1.4 million. Its assembly will have control over such matters as education, health, finance and transport, but it will remain part of West Bengal.

In January 1992, leaders of an insurrection in Assam agreed to end their rebellion. The United Liberation Front of Assam took up arms in 1987 and announced that it would found a 'sovereign, socialist state'. It set about achieving its goal by murdering a succession of tea planters, businessmen, politicians and police, and by extorting money from the plantations. The Indian army succeeded in driving the Front's military forces into the remote mountains on the border with Bangladesh, and arrested most of its political leaders. There were desultory negotiations with the government until December 1991, when the party's chairman, Arobindo Rajkhowa announced a unilateral ceasefire. He had managed to escape arrest, but was reportedly worn down by life on the run.

The front's leaders were flown secretly to New Delhi, to meet the prime minister, Narashima Rao, who persuaded them to agree to lay down their arms and abide by the constitution. The front's military commander, Paresh Baruah, refused to accept the ceasefire, and started training a new army in the hills. His organization is called the United Liberation Front of Assam. It maintains a low-level insurgency, occasionally attacking government officials.

## THE BODO

The Bodo are yet another mountain tribe in eastern Assam, on the north bank of the Brahmaputra, who want their own state. There are about 2 million Bodo, and several thousand people have been killed in the dispute since 1986. The All-Bodo Students' Union (A B S U), led by Upendranath Brahma, object to being obliged to use Assamese or Hindu script to write their language (they prefer the Roman alphabet) and demand the same concessions that have been won by other tribes. A truce was signed in August 1989, and negotiations between the Assam government and the A B S U were begun, but the more radical Bodo resumed the fight. Another 70 people were killed in the two weeks after the truce was approved. The Assamese claimed that the federal government under Rajiv Gandhi was behind the new revolt, in an attempt to destabilize Assam, which was governed by the opposition. After the change in government in New Delhi, a new attempt to reach a settlement was begun.

It failed. Bodo terrorism continued. The guerrilla movement split into a number of factions, which fought among themselves. The most militant are called the Bodo Security Force, which wants independence and has frequently attacked people of other tribes. Another faction, the Bodoland Liberation Tiger Front, want a separate state in the Indian Union. Thousands of people were killed in riots, massacres and military actions in February 1993, and Bodo raids on Muslim refugees from Bangladesh have killed hundreds. In December 1996, the B S F bombed a train in eastern Assam, killing nearly a hundred people.

## THE NAXALITES

A group of revolutionary Communists broke away from the Communist Party of India in 1969, to form the Communist Party of India (Marxist-Leninist), and tried to start a revolutionary war among the peasantry. They concentrated on the district around Naxalbari, in West Bengal, and became known as the Naxalites. They murdered officials and attacked police posts. The government proclaimed a state of emergency, and succeeded in killing or arresting most of the terrorists. Several hundred people had been killed in the disorders. The Naxalites appeared to be thoroughly defeated by the early 1970s, partly because a Communist government had been elected in West Bengal and had met many of the peasants' demands. However, Naxalite activity has now revived: their particular brand of terrorism has been reported in many parts of the country, from Kerala and Tamil Nadu in the south to Assam in the north-east and Bihar and Andhra Pradesh in north-central India.

In Andhra Pradesh, Naxalites have killed over 200 people since 1984, including 35 policemen, and the rate of killing has risen sharply: ten police were murdered in an ambush in August 1987. It is believed that there are about 5000 Naxalites there, including 500 or so terrorists, calling themselves 'People's Wars'. In December 1987, the People's Wars kidnapped a group of senior officials and held them hostage until Naxalites were released from jail. In Bihar, Naxalite bands skirmish with the private armies of local landlords, and in Punjab they have allied themselves with Sikh secessionists. People's Wars' founder and leader, a teacher, was arrested in 1993, but minor acts of terrorism continued. The group tried to disrupt elections in November 1994 by mining a road and killing ten people, including eight policemen.

## THE SIKHS

The Sikh insurgency is by far the most serious that India has confronted since independence. It continues today as the most severe challenge to the central government.

There are about 15 million Sikhs in India, most of them in Punjab state, a small part of the historic Land of the Five Rivers, most of which is now in Pakistan. They are in the majority there. They follow a religion founded in the 15th century in the Punjab and developed by a succession of ten gurus, or sages. It is an amalgam of Islam and Hinduism: it is monotheistic, like Islam, and utterly rejects the Hindu caste system, but it also accepts reincarnation and Hindu fatalism. The Sikhs' holy city is Amritsar, where they built their Golden Temple. (The word *amritsar* means 'pool of nectar' and refers to the sacred pool that surrounds the temple.) The last of the ten gurus ordered his male followers never to shave or cut their hair, always to carry a dagger, and to take the name *Singh* ('lion'). Women, who were given far more independence than Hindu women, took the name *Kaur* ('princess').

In the early 19th century, the Sikhs conquered the Punjab under the Maharajah Ranjit Singh. His capital was Lahore, and in his turban he wore the Koh-i-Noor diamond, which had been a principal possession of the Moghul emperors. Ranjit Singh died in 1839, his successors squabbled among themselves, and within a decade, the British had conquered the Punjab. An escaping prince was captured by the British, and the Koh-i-Noor was found hidden in his turban; it was sent to London and put in Queen Victoria's imperial state crown.

The British appreciated the Sikhs' martial qualities and recruited them in **195** large numbers into their armies. During the Mutiny, ten years after the last Sikh war, Sikh regiments remained loyal and joined in the reconquest of north India, and 100,000 Sikh soldiers fought alongside the British in World War I.

On 13 April 1919, a British general ordered his troops to fire into a crowd in the Jallianwala Bagh, a market place in Amritsar. They were demonstrating illegally against the British and the temple authorities who supported them. The soldiers killed 379 people and wounded 1200. The Sikh temple authorities applauded the massacre, an attitude which led to sustained agitation for reform which, in turn, brought a majority of Sikhs to support the independence movement. The reformers founded the Akali Dal, which later developed into the political party that is now at the heart of the dispute between New Delhi and the Sikhs.

At the time of partition, the Sikhs, who were scattered across the Punjab, demanded their independence, but were ignored. When the Punjab was divided, 40 per cent of Sikhs were left in Pakistan, and suffered the worst of the massacres that followed. In their turn, the Sikhs in the east massacred Muslims and drove them into Pakistan. When the red tide subsided, most of the Sikhs were concentrated in the Indian area of the Punjab, around Amritsar. They particularly regretted the loss of Lahore, Ranjit Singh's capital, just across the border.

For the next 35 years, the Sikhs prospered. Their farms became the most productive in India, thanks to their own industry and skill and the government's irrigation projects; the city dwellers adapted to modern industry and commerce. Punjab became one of the richest provinces in India. However, prosperity brought danger: Sikh fundamentalists feared that their religion would be absorbed back into Hinduism. At first, they preached strict adherence to the rules prescribed in the Holy Books, but in the early 1980s, some of them began seriously to advocate a separate Sikh nation, which they would call Khalistan, 'land of the pure'. At the head of this breakaway movement was Sant Jarnail Singh Bhindranwale (*Sant* means 'holy man'). Bhindranwale believed it was the Sikhs' right to kill their enemies, and he led a militant faction that openly resorted to terrorism.

The disturbances began in 1981, when the Akali Dal presented a list of 45 demands to the central government, which, though stopping short of full independence, would have given the Sikhs complete control of Punjab state. Indira Gandhi's government rejected them. The first political assassination followed in September 1981, when a Hindu newspaper editor was murdered.

In September 1982, a conference of Sikhs declared holy war against the Indian government, and a series of increasingly serious incidents began. Sikh terrorists, taking their lead from Bhindranwale, attacked and killed government officials or Hindus whom they wished to drive out of Sikh areas. In April 1983, a senior police officer, a Sikh, was murdered as he left the Golden Temple after performing his devotions. The government did nothing. Police officers who arrested Sikh militants were also murdered, together with their entire families.

The government vacillated between conciliation and firmness, and thereby lost the advantages of either. Indira Gandhi allowed Bhindranwale to turn central Amritsar into a fortress, a 'no-go area' policed by his militant followers, who stockpiled a vast arsenal of weapons in the Golden Temple complex. A retired Sikh general, Sahbeg Singh, devised fortifications and defensive positions for the temple area. It became a base for terrorists, not all of them religious fanatics: some Naxalites emerged to join Bhindranwale.

In October 1983, after a busload of Hindus were massacred, a state of emergency was declared in Punjab. Parts of the state were declared a 'disturbed area', and the army was brought in to maintain order. Two weeks later, a train passing through Punjab was derailed, killing 219 people. There were riots in Chandigarh, the state capital, which is also capital of the neighbouring state of Haryana – one of the Sikhs' demands was for full control of Chandigarh. There were anti-Sikh riots in Haryana in which Sikhs were murdered. Terrorism continued to increase and the police were incapable of dealing with it.

Bhindranwale ordered the murder of a succession of politicians, police and journalists. The government seemed unable to defend them, and by early 1984, it was in danger of losing control of the state completely. In March and April there were over 80 political murders in Punjab.

There were last-ditch negotiations between the government and leaders of the Akali Dal. Mrs Gandhi offered to meet most of the Sikhs' demands, including giving them control of Chandigarh, but Bhindranwale refused to compromise. The murders continued, and the Sikhs announced that they would prevent movement of grain out of Punjab. There was no doubt that the threat was real, and that it would have brought about catastrophe: Punjab is the granary of north India.

By this point, by the government's count, Bhindranwale's terrorists had murdered 169 Hindus and 39 Sikhs. Others had been killed in riots and accidents provoked by the terrorists, bringing the total to 410, not counting those killed in the train derailment. The murder rate was increasing rapidly: 23 people were killed in the 24 hours before Mrs Gandhi took her decision. On 2 June 1984, she authorized the army to occupy the Golden Temple.

Beforehand, in a last example of government incompetence, and the complicity of police with the extremists, 200 young Sikhs, including criminals and Naxalites, were allowed to escape. Operation Blue Star was launched on 3 June, one of the sacred days of the Sikhs' calendar, and the temple was crowded with the faithful, as well as Bhindranwale's fighters.

All Punjab was shut down. All road and rail traffic was stopped, the frontier with Pakistan was closed, and the press were kept out. The authorities were afraid of a general uprising by Sikh villagers, appalled at the attack on the Golden Temple.

For two days, the army laid siege to the temple and attempted to force Bhindranwale to surrender; he preferred martyrdom. On the evening of 5 June, tanks were brought in to assault the temple.

Immediately to the west of the Golden Temple, itself surrounded by the sacred pool, is another sacred edifice, the Akal Takht, where Bhindranwale had set up his headquarters. The army first attacked and occupied a number of outlying buildings, and then turned its attention to the Akal Takht. They tried sending in commandos, but they were easily repulsed by heavy fire from General Sahbeg Singh's gun emplacements. So the army blasted its way into the Akal Takht with its tanks.

The building was severely damaged. Bhindranwale, Sahbeg Singh and their senior supporters were all killed, martyrs to the cause. In all, by the official count, 493 Sikh militants and civilians and 83 troops were killed. However, about 1600 civilians, known to have been inside the temple complex when the attack began, remained unaccounted for, and it is possible therefore that the real casualty figure was much higher.

The Golden Temple was damaged, but not severely. The Akal Takht was ruined, and the temple's library was destroyed. The army also attacked 37 other Sikh temples, searching for terrorists.

The attack on the Golden Temple provoked mutinies by Sikh troops and disturbances throughout Punjab. Mrs Gandhi tried to blame Pakistan for the troubles, denouncing 'outside interference' – in fact, there is no evidence at all that Pakistan was in any way involved. Mrs Gandhi and her supporters, carried away by their own eloquence, also tried to blame the C I A and even the British for the consequences of their own incompetence.

On 31 October 1984, Mrs Gandhi was shot and killed by two Sikhs guarding the prime minister's bungalow in New Delhi. She had been on her way to give a television interview to the British wit and playwright Peter Ustinov. The two Sikhs surrendered immediately, and were taken away by the police. One of them was then murdered in the police station, the other severely beaten. Riots broke out immediately, incited by members of the ruling Congress party. Hindus were brought by bus from the suburbs of Delhi and turned loose in Sikh neighbour-hoods. According to government figures, 2717 people were killed (almost all of them Sikhs), 2150 in Delhi. The police and army stood by throughout the day of massacres; 100,000 Sikhs fled Delhi, half back to Punjab, half to refugee camps set up for them in the country near the capital.

The situation was only brought under control when Mrs Gandhi's son, Rajiv, who had been sworn in as prime minister to succeed her, visited a devastated Sikh neighbourhood and told the army to restore order. (The Sikh who admitted killing Mrs Gandhi was executed in January 1989, along with another Sikh who had been convicted of conspiracy with the assassins.)

Killing Bhindranwale did not end terrorism in Punjab. Although the murder rate declined in the second half of 1984 and in early 1985, it then rose sharply. On 23 June 1985, 329 people were killed when an Air India plane crashed in the sea south of Ireland, on a flight from Toronto to London, and investigators believed that it had been destroyed by a bomb. A few hours later, a bomb concealed in a suitcase exploded at Tokyo Airport, killing two baggage handlers. The suitcase had arrived on another flight from Canada, which was late. If it had been on time, the suitcase and the bomb would have been transferred to another Air India flight from Tokyo to India, and would have exploded in midair. There can be little doubt that the two bombs were the work of Sikh terrorists.

In 1985, 65 people were killed in Punjab; in 1986, 609; in 1987, 1566; and in 1988, 2000. Of those killed between 1985 and 1987, 1819 were the victims of terrorism, and 421, by official count, were terrorists killed by security forces. The death rate in the early months of 1988 was even higher than the year before, with over 900 people killed in the first four months. In March alone, 225 people were murdered, including ten people attending a Sikh wedding; a group calling itself the Khalistan Commando Force, one of four Sikh terrorist organizations, claimed responsibility for that atrocity. On 3 March, terrorists attacked a Hindu festival and machine-gunned the audience, killing 34. On 31 March, 33 people were killed, including 18 members of a Hindu work brigade who were dragged out of their huts, lined up in a courtyard and slaughtered.

The terrorists once again took refuge in the Golden Temple, and once again the government and moderate Sikh leaders seemed incapable of controlling them. There were reports that Naxalites had resumed operations: a number of those murdered were members of the legal Communist party, who had opposed Naxalite terrorism.

On 9 May, a Sikh gang crossed the border into Haryana state and attacked a Hindu wedding, killing 13 people. On the same day, the government at last sent troops into Amritsar again, and once again laid siege to the Golden Temple. Five people were killed on the first day of the siege. This time, instead of storming the temple, troops cut off its water and electricity and waited for the terrorists to surrender. There was constant sniping from minarets inside the temple complex, and army sharpshooters, taking up positions in buildings overlooking the complex, shot a number of terrorists. Terrorists outside Amritsar continued the campaign of killings: more than 190 people were killed during the first week of the siege, and the government rushed reinforcements to Punjab. About 800 people, mostly civilian worshippers, left the temple the day after the siege began, and 146 Sikhs surrendered on 15 May. Three days later, the last of the Sikhs in the temple gave themselves up. The army immediately found 16 bodies inside the temple, people who had been killed by the extremists; later, after excavating in the cellars, more bodies were found, bringing the total to 41 men, women and children. Many of them had been tortured.

Over the next five days, Sikh terrorists killed a further 245 people in Punjab, most of them Hindu migrant workers brought in to work in the paddy fields. There was a mass exodus of these workers, with disastrous effects on the incomes of the Sikh farmers who employed them. By the end of 1988, 2000 people had been killed, and the murders continued in 1989 at a rate of 200 a month. Even more were killed in 1990 and 1991.

In an attempt to come to terms with the Sikhs, the government released a number of their leaders who had been jailed on 4 March. They included Jasbir Singh Rode, who was immediately installed as head priest in the Golden Temple. He has continued to voice most of the extremists' demands, but not the most divisive: the call for Khalistan. At the end of May, all five priests at the temple, including Rode, were dismissed by the Sikh governing committee, which alleged that they were pandering to terrorism.

So far, most of the Sikhs have not supported the extremists, and therefore a large part of the terrorists' campaign is directed against other Sikhs, to frighten them into support for Khalistan.

The dilemma is clear: unless terrorism can be brought under control, the extremists will defeat the government and will establish Khalistan. But suppressing the terrorists may require such a degree of force that all the undecided Sikhs will rally to the cause.

The Sikh terrorists were the beneficiaries of the Afghan war: there were so many weapons flowing into Pakistan that the Sikhs had no difficulty obtaining all they needed. The Indian government blames Pakistan. It is probable that, at most, Pakistan is guilty of benign neglect in policing the border, but the crisis has become so acute that it could well have serious effects upon Indian–Pakistani relations. The government in New Delhi, first under Indira Gandhi, then under her son Rajiv, proved incapable of resolving either the political problem or the security problem. After Rajiv Gandhi's defeat in the elections of November 1989, the task was taken up by the new coalition government, led by Vishwanath Pratap Singh (who is not a Sikh). He appointed a Sikh as Lieutenant-Governor (chief administrator) of New Delhi and made strenuous efforts to win the confidence of Sikhs in the Punjab. He promised to find government jobs for Sikhs who deserted from the army after the occupation of the Golden Temple in 1984, and to reconsider the cases of those jailed. It was an attempt to use the novelty of his election to resolve the dilemma he inherited. He met as little success as his predecessor, and lasted less than a year as prime minister. His defeat was largely the result of the country's economic difficulties, rather than the Punjab problem, but Sikh terrorism continued unabated and remained democratic India's most dangerous challenge. On 31 August 1995, Sikh terrorists managed a spectacular attack, killing Punjab's chief minister, Beant Singh, and 11 other people, and wounding 18, with a car bomb planted in Singh's own armoured car. A group calling itself Babba Khalsa claimed the credit. The only fragment of the chief minister's body that could be identified was one of his feet; it was still in its shoe.

## KASHMIR

The old dispute over Kashmir revived in 1988. A number of militant Muslim groups who had been campaigning for independence, or for Kashmir to be ceded to Pakistan, then resorted to violence. They obtained weapons from Pakistan or from Afghanistan. Starting in August that year, the Jammu and Kashmir Liberation Front bombed public buildings, closed businesses and terrorized Hindus. In December 1989, they kidnapped the 21-year-old daughter of the new federal minister for home affairs, Mufti Mohammed Sayeed, a Kashmiri Muslim. She was released unharmed. Kidnappings then became a standard part of terrorists' tactics. In January 1990, there were serious disturbances in Srinagar, the state capital, and 12 people were killed, and the federal government sent in the army to keep the peace. Four Indian air force men were killed during that operation, on 25 January. Indian officials claimed that nationalists planned to declare independence, but were foiled by the police, who imposed a 24-hour curfew on Srinagar. By the end of the month, the official death toll was over 70.

Then Pakistan became involved. On 5 February 1990, a large crowd gathered near the Pakistani side of the border, and tried to storm across. About 200 men broke through a police cordon: two of them were shot dead by Indian police, and 12 were wounded. The next day, there was a general strike in Pakistan to protest. Both governments insisted that they had no intention of fighting a fourth war on the issue: there had been efforts by both sides to improve relations, starting with the election of Benazir Bhutto in Pakistan. She held a cordial and successful summit meeting with Rajiv Gandhi. A few months later, both were out of office.

After the border clash in 1990, all hope for détente between the two rapidly receded.

The Indian government tried to regain the initiative by dissolving the Kashmir assembly on 19 February 1990 and promising new and free elections. The state's new governor, Jagmohan, set to work reforming the administration, which he conceded had been corrupt and inefficient. His gestures had no immediate effect: on 23 February, a huge and peaceful demonstration took place in Srinagar. Police estimated that 400,000 people, half the city's population, took part. They demanded independence or union with Pakistan. On 1 March, there was a new and equally large demonstration, and Indian troops opened fire on the demonstrators, in two separate incidents, killing 32 and wounding many more. By then, the death toll in six weeks' disturbances had reached over 120, including a number of Hindu government officials assassinated by Kashmiri terrorists. There were six major groups of Kashmiri secessionists, claiming 45,000 guerrillas between them (the real total was undoubtedly much smaller), but some accounts put the number of groups as high as 120. Some wanted independence, some union with Pakistan. Some professed democratic principles, some were Muslim fundamentalists. The Pakistanis are arming and training the fundamentalist guerrillas. According to the government, the most dangerous is the Jammu and Kashmir Liberation Front, led by Javad Ahmad Mir, which supports independence for Kashmir – including that part of the ancient province now occupied by Pakistan, and known as Azad Kashmir (Free Kashmir), and those districts occupied by China in 1962. A rival group, Hizb-ul-Mujahadeen, wants Kashmir ceded to Pakistan and converted into an Islamic state: it has succeeded in banning alcohol, ending lotteries, and closing beauty parlours, cinemas and video rental stores, and has also forced many women to wear head-to-foot veils in public. It draws support and inspiration from Afghan fundamentalists.

The Indians brought in 50,000 troops to deal with the rebels. By official count, 1000 rebels and 290 government soldiers were killed in the first ten months of 1991. According to human rights activists, over 3000 Kashmiris were killed in the first two years of the disturbances, most of them by the Indian army, and 10,000 people were arrested or detained. Reporters uncovered horrifying details of the tortures inflicted on prisoners. A doctor at a Srinagar hospital, in October 1991, described to a reporter from the *New York Times* the case of a prisoner, a schoolteacher, who had survived: 'They pushed a metal rod into his rectum, puncturing his liver, his pancreas, his stomach and tearing his lung.'

In April 1993, the centre of Srinagar was burned by Indian troops after a vicious fight with guerrillas. The city is Kashmir's summer capital and was a famous tourist attraction before the troubles began: house-boats on the lake were favourite holiday homes for the British in the days of the Raj. In May 1995, the second holiest Muslim shrine in Kashmir, a 600-year-old wooden structure at Charar-e-Sharief, was burned in a fight between troops and rebels. By then, there were 500,000 Indian soldiers striving to control a province with a population of 4 million which is wholly disaffected. Rebels then occupied the holiest shrine in the province, a mosque in Srinagar. After laying desultory siege to it for a year, Indian troops threatened to storm it in March 1996. Fighting then destroyed buildings in the mosque complex, in a replay of the attack on the Golden Temple of Amritsar 12 years before.

By applying overwhelming and unrestrained force to Kashmir, the Indian army has succeeded in driving the guerrillas out of the cities and towns and restoring a semblance of government control to the province. Estimates of the numbers killed between 1988 and 1998 range from 20,000 to 30,000. Elections to the federal parliament were held in May 1996, followed by provincial elections in September.

Talks between India and Pakistan were opened in June 1997, but the internal politics of the two countries made it most unlikely that either would change its policies. The Indian government fears that withdrawing from Kashmir might precipitate the break-up of the union, with Punjab seceding first, followed by other states. India counts on the huge disparity between its army and the guerrillas to ensure that Kashmir can never secede, and hopes that the Kashmiris will eventually recognize that inevitability. The guerrillas remember that America was defeated in Vietnam and the Soviet Union in Afghanistan. India remembers that, too: the loss of Afghanistan was followed by the loss of Eastern Europe and then the collapse of the U S S R itself.

Other problems facing the Indian government:

• **Muslim–Hindu tensions.** Over a thousand people were killed in fighting between the two communities in Bihar in eastern India in late October 1989. The dispute has been exacerbated by a quarrel over the Babri Masjid Mosque at Ayodhya. This structure was built by a Muslim rajah in the 16th century, on the site of a Hindu shrine, reputedly the birthplace of Rama. It stood on the Ghaghara river east of Delhi. Hindu fundamentalists demanded that the mosque be demolished and Rama's temple rebuilt. Their political party, the Bharatiya Janata Party (B J P), made great capital out of the issue in the 1989 elections and supported a militant group, the Vishwa Hindu Parashad, which organized a march on the mosque. In the October fighting, over 150 villages were destroyed and 35,000 Muslims were driven into refugee camps. The B J P has now raised its sights: it wants to make India a Hindu state, imposing Hindu laws and customs the way Pakistan has imposed Muslim laws and customs.

In December 1992, the B J P launched another march on the Ayodhya mosque, and this time succeeded. The mob burst through the military cordon the government had set around it, and demolished it. Rejoicing fanatics in Bombay then stormed into Muslim and Sikh districts, and between 1000 and 20,000 people were massacred, according to different accounts. The rioters were supporters of the Shiv Sena party, more extreme allies of the B J P. Its leader is Balasaheb Thackeray, who calls himself the 'Bombay Hitler'. The two parties won control of Maharashtra state, of which Bombay is the capital, in elections in March 1995. It is by far India's richest state, and its support of Hindu fundamentalism is ominous for communal relations everywhere.'

• **Ladakh.** This province, high in the Himalayas, has been part of Kashmir since Indian independence and, like Kashmir, was partitioned between India and Pakistan. Most of its people are Buddhists, who are now demanding separation from Kashmir. They object equally to Muslims and Hindus. The disturbances began in July 1989, in a brawl in the bazaar in Leh, a mostly Buddhist city 11,560 feet (3850 m) high. On 27 August, Kashmiri police fired on a Buddhist demonstration, killing three people.

## SRI LANKA

In July 1987, Rajiv Gandhi agreed to send Indian troops to north Sri Lanka in order to police a ceasefire and peace settlement that he had brokered between the Sri Lankan government and the rebel Tamils. It was intended to be a brief and uneventful intervention, but the fighting resumed between Sinhalese and Tamils, and in October, the Indian army laid siege to Jaffna. It lost 500 men in the operation. At the height of the Indian intervention, there were 65,000 Indian troops in Sri Lanka, and they were as unpopular as the British in Northern Ireland. The Indian government agreed to remove them by March 1989. In March 1991, Tamil terrorists assassinated Rajiv Gandhi, then leader of the opposition, during an election campaign, in retribution for the Indian intervention in Sri Lanka.

## THE MALDIVES

On 3 November 1988, a band of Tamil mercenaries from Sri Lanka invaded the Maldive islands and attempted to overthrow the government. They had been hired by a former president who had been deposed in 1980 and now hoped for a restoration. The Indians promptly sent troops to Male, the capital, and restored the government. The mercenaries fled on the boat that had brought them, and were later captured by the Indian navy. In all, 12 people were killed during the attempted coup.

The Maldives are a chain of islands in the Indian Ocean, south-west of India. They were a British protectorate in the days of the Raj (like the Seychelles further west) and India remains the dominant influence, even though the Maldive republic is an independent country. This was the second Indian intervention in the internal affairs of a neighbour in two years (the first was Sri Lanka). Some other neighbours worried that Rajiv Gandhi might develop imperial delusions and start policing the whole region, where India is by far the most powerful nation.

---

## FURTHER READING

Akbar, M. J., *India, the Siege Within*, London, Penguin, 1985, and *Riot after Riot*, New Delhi, Penguin, 1988.
American University, *India: A Country Study*, Washington D.C., 1985.
Choudkury, G. W., *India, Pakistan, Bangladesh and the Major Powers*, New York, Macmillan, 1985.
Fishlock, Trevor, *India File: Inside the Subcontinent*, London, Murray, 1983.
Galbraith, John Kenneth, *Ambassador's Journal*, Boston, Houghton, Mifflin, 1969.
Hardgrave, Robert L., *India Under Pressure: The Prospects for Stability*, Boulder, Colo., Westview Press, 1984.
Hart, Henry C., *Indira Gandhi's India: A Political System Reappraised*, Boulder, Colo., Westview Press, 1976.

Heitzman, James and Warden, Robert, *India: a Country Study*, Washington, Government Printing Office, 1996.

Khilnani, Sunil, *The Idea of India*, New York, Farrar, Strauss and Giroux, 1988.

Maxwell, Neville, *India's China War*, New York, Pantheon Books, 1970.

Mehta, Ved, *A Family Affair: India Under Three Prime Ministers*, Oxford University Press, 1982.

Minority Rights Group, *India, the Nagas and the North-East*, London, 1980.

Tully, Mark and Satish, Jacob, *Amritsar: Mrs Gandhi's Last Battle*, London, Jonathan Cape, 1985.

# INDONESIA

| | |
|---|---|
| Geography | 741,031 sq. miles (1,919,263 sq. km). More than 13,000 islands, stretching across 3500 miles (5600 km) of ocean; it is wider than the North Atlantic. |
| Population | 193 million. The most heavily populated island is Java (the size of England or New York State), with over 110 million people – over twice England's population density. There are 10 major ethnic groups and over 300 smaller ones, speaking more than 200 distinct languages; there is also a rich and resented Chinese minority (about 4 million people). The official language is Bahasa Indonesia, a modernized version of Malay. 90% of Indonesians are Muslims but, for most of them, their adherence to Islam is nominal. Among the small minority of devout Muslims, there is a further minority of fanatics who want to establish an Islamic republic. The island of Bali is Hindu, and Ambon in the South Moluccas is Calvinist. The national motto is 'Unity in Diversity'. |
| Resources | Oil; gas; minerals; hardwoods and other tropical products; fish. |
| GNP per capita | $980 (1997). |
| Refugees | External: 10,000 from (Indonesian) West Irian in Papua New Guinea and 25,000 from East Timor, mostly in Australia. |
| Casualties | Between 400,000 and 1 million people were killed in the massacres of 1965, and at least 100,000 people have been killed in East Timor since 1975. |

Indonesia is the fourth most populous nation on Earth. It has made great economic progress since the overthrow of Achmad Sukarno in 1965, though growth rates have not equalled those of Taiwan or South Korea. Indonesia has been held back by the government's corruption and consequent inefficiency. An economic and banking crisis swept East Asia in 1997 and it became apparent that the long reign of President Suharto was coming to an end. Memories of 1965 made the economic uncertainty much worse and increased the probability of trouble.

## HISTORY
The first Europeans to reach Indonesia were the Portuguese and Spanish, in the early 16th century, and they found an eclectic civilization. Indonesia was originally Hindu; then it accepted Buddhism, and for centuries the two religions

**205**

coexisted peacefully. One of the greatest of all Buddhist temples was built at Borobudur, and a few miles away was Prambanam, an immense Hindu religious centre. In the Middle Ages, Islam reached the islands, brought by Arab traders, and overlaid and absorbed the Hindu–Buddhist traditions. However, those traditions were never lost, partly because of the arrival of the Europeans.

Trade between the Spice Islands, as they were called, and Europe was enormously lucrative, and for over a century the European powers fought among themselves to control them. By the middle of the 17th century, the Dutch had driven out all rivals except for the Portuguese, who retained a small colony on Timor, east of Java, and the Spanish in the Philippines.

The Dutch empire was centred on Java, where they built Batavia (now Jakarta, capital of Indonesia) as a Far Eastern Amsterdam. They did not seek to convert their subjects to Christianity: the people of Ambon, the principal clove-producing island in the South Moluccas, were first converted by the Portuguese and were only later persuaded by the Dutch to give up Catholicism and adopt Calvinism. The Dutch were almost exclusively concerned with trade, and only took on the administration of the hinterland and farther islands to protect their trading posts and to keep their rivals out.

By the mid-19th century, the islands had been divided upon wholly artificial lines between the British in Malaya and North Borneo, the Dutch in what is now Indonesia, and the Spanish in the Philippines; the Dutch, British and Germans divided up New Guinea between them. The 20th century brought the inevitable stirrings of nationalism. The first Communist party in Asia – the P K I – was founded in Batavia in 1920, and in 1927, Achmad Sukarno founded the Nationalist party.

This organization became the dominant force opposing the Dutch. The Japanese occupied Indonesia in 1942, and Sukarno and his chief lieutenant, Mohammed Hatta, cooperated with the new order, they said, to further the cause of independence. Sukarno continued to collaborate after Japan annexed Indonesia in 1943, even though the Philippines and Burma had been proclaimed independent, and he acquiesced in the recruitment by the Japanese of slave labour in Java. The occupation caused several hundred thousand deaths.

In 1944, as the Americans were closing in on them, the Japanese reversed themselves and, hoping to make Indonesia an ally, accepted the principle of independence for that country. The new state was to include Portuguese Timor, Malaya, Singapore and British Borneo (though Sukarno had laid claim only to the Dutch East Indies). An independent Indonesia was finally proclaimed, with Sukarno as president, on 17 August 1945 – two days after Japan had surrendered to the Americans.

Sukarno was able to establish himself firmly before the Dutch returned, forming an army equipped with weapons taken from the Japanese. The first of the Allies to reach Indonesia were the British, and in October 1945, there was a full-scale battle between British and Indonesian troops at Surabya in eastern Java.

The Dutch recognized Sukarno's republic, but only in Java: they resumed control of the rest of the Dutch East Indies, set up a 'Netherlands Union' and progressively reduced the territory controlled by the republic, so that, by

January 1948, it was confined to central Java. Then leftist members of the Indonesian army staged a coup against Sukarno in Madiun, in Java. The Communist party supported them and was brutally suppressed by General Abdul Haris Nasution, one of Sukarno's top commanders.

In December 1948, another Dutch offensive captured the republic's last bases at Jogjakarta, and Sukarno and Hatta were captured and exiled to Sumatra. That was the last spasm of Dutch imperialism. They had no allies: the British had abandoned India, and the Americans threatened to cut off Marshall Aid if the Dutch did not give Indonesia its independence. Meanwhile, on the ground, they were finding it impossible to control such a vast, populous and disaffected country. Sovereignty was transferred on 17 December 1949, although the Dutch retained West New Guinea, much to their subsequent sorrow.

The new government set about establishing its control of the islands, putting down a series of revolts. Calvinist Ambon, in the Moluccas, which had supported the Dutch, proclaimed its independence and had to be conquered. In April 1950, 12,000 Ambonese soldiers and their families were evacuated to the Netherlands (*see* Terrorism, p. 625).

In the mid-1950s, the central government was weak and divided: there were attempted coups; an extremist Islamic movement, Darul Islam, was fighting the government in central Java; and a group of dissident army officers started a rebellion in Sumatra. The rebels in Sumatra and the Celebes were able to persuade the C I A that Sukarno was anti-Western, and the agency began secretly shipping arms to them. Despite this, President Eisenhower stated, 'Our policy is one of careful neutrality, a proper deportment all the way through, so as not to be taking sides where it is none of our business.' The secretary of state, John Foster Dulles, told a congressional committee in March 1958, 'We are not intervening in the internal affairs of this country.' They were both lying.

The C I A was not only sending arms to the rebels, it was also bombing government positions. One of the raids hit a hospital by mistake, and on 18 May 1958, a B-26 crash-landed in government territory in Ambon. Its pilot, an American named Allan Pope, was captured. The plane was empty, but shortly before it had crashed, parachutes had been seen floating to earth. They were found to be bearing cases of Springfield rifles, and the cases were marked 'Interarms', the name of a major American arms company that had close links to the C I A. Its owner, Sam Cummings, denied that he had anything to do with that particular shipment, but the provenance of the guns was unimportant. What counted was that the C I A had been caught red-handed. Sukarno never trusted the Americans after that.

Sukarno proclaimed a new political philosophy – 'Guided Democracy', as opposed to the parliamentary sort – and his two allies were the army chief of staff, General Nasution, and the P K I. He proclaimed a state of emergency in March 1957 and, in 1959, launched a campaign against Dutch control of West New Guinea, which he called Irian Jaya (West Irian). The Dutch were preparing West New Guinea for eventual independence, and refused Sukarno's demands. In retaliation, he nationalized all the immense Dutch holdings in Indonesia, a step that brought the country to the verge of bankruptcy. The army had to step in to run the nationalized companies, and thus became a major force in the country's economy. Sukarno sent 'volunteers' into West New Guinea in 1960. Once again, the Dutch found themselves without allies, and in 1963, 'West Irian' was added to Indonesia.

By then, the economy was in serious trouble. Sukarno invented yet another new political philosophy – Nasakom (Nationalism, Religion and Communism) – and expelled 119,000 Chinese. Neither measure helped.

In 1960, the British ceded their two colonies in Borneo – Sarawak and North Borneo (Sabah) – to Malaya, to form part of the new federation of Malaysia. Sukarno called out the mobs to protest. British property was nationalized, and Sukarno announced that Indonesia 'must gobble Malaysia raw'. The Indonesian army began armed incursions into Malaysian Borneo and across the straits into Malaya itself. The British sent an army to protect Malaysia, and the defeat of the Indonesian 'confrontation' contributed to a severe loss of prestige for Sukarno. To compensate for the defeat, Sukarno had the British embassy burned in September 1963, along with the houses of many British and Australian citizens. (*See* Malaysia, pp. 224–6.)

## THE 1965 COUP

Sukarno announced that 1965 would be 'a year of living dangerously'. The P K I was by now the dominant political force in Java. In the early morning of 1 October, a group of middle-rank officers led by Lieutenant Colonel Untung, a commander of the presidential guard, attempted a coup against the army command. It is possible that Sukarno and the P K I knew about the coup in advance.

Six senior generals were murdered and their bodies thrown down a well at a place called the Crocodile Hole on Halim air base, near Jakarta. Among those killed was General Achmad Yani, the chief of staff. General Nasution, the minister of defence, escaped through a back passage from his bedroom, but his five-year-old daughter was killed. The rebels seized the radio station and announced the coup, saying that the generals had been plotting against Sukarno. They proclaimed a new government, led by the 'September 30 Movement'. Sukarno moved to Halim, a decision he was never able to explain.

The commander of the reserve army, General Suharto, had not been on the list of generals to be killed, an oversight that the plotters did not live long enough to regret. He found that most of the army was not involved and would still obey orders, and he quickly gathered an overwhelming force of loyal troops, led by a tank division, which rolled over the rebels. Within 24 hours, the coup was over.

Violent anti-Communist demonstrations broke out in Jakarta and the rest of Java, and the mobs and the army set about slaughtering Communists wherever they could find them. By the time the massacres subsided, several hundred thousand people had been killed. The dead included most of the leaders of the P K I. The party had 3 million members, and the army now systematically hunted down all its cadres and shot them. Most of those who died, however, were villagers and many had nothing to do with the P K I; they were victims of local hatreds. So many bodies were thrown into the rivers that they became a serious health problem. In one district in West Java, suspects were decapitated by guillotine, and their heads piled up in the villages, to set an example. Many

Chinese (according to one estimate, 20,000) were among the victims, and mobs attacked the Chinese embassy.

The total number of those killed remains in dispute. The official government figure is 80,000. Muslim leaders, whose people did most of the killings, admit to 500,000 and other estimates go up to 1 million. The usual compromise estimate is that 400,000 people were killed. A number of former P K I officials are still in jail, and from time to time some of them are still brought out and executed: nine died in this way in 1986, and a former member of the politburo, who was arrested in 1968, was executed in November 1987.

Suharto took control of the government and progressively eliminated Sukarno's influence. It was an elaborate and subtle process, typically Javanese: Sukarno had been the country's dominant political figure for decades, and had clearly been favoured by beneficent spirits; he had to be eased out gradually, as it became clear that the spirits no longer supported him. When the process was completed, he was legally deposed in March 1968. He died in 1970.

## SUHARTO'S RULE

Suharto reversed Indonesia's alliances. He broke diplomatic relations with China (they were finally resumed in 1989) and became a close associate of the United States. Sukarno's half-baked socialism was abandoned, and a group of American-trained economists (the 'Berkeley Mafia') was put in charge of the country's economy and rescued it from disaster.

Suharto has now ruled Indonesia for over 30 years, and was elected to another five-year term in 1998. He has wrapped his dictatorship in a philosophy called the 'New Order', which exacts deference and obedience to authority. Some opposition is permitted, rather more than in China or Singapore, but not much. Opposition parties are permitted to win 30 per cent of the vote – to an assembly that has no authority. Indonesia has enjoyed economic growth and stability, standards of living have risen dramatically and Indonesia now feeds itself. *Per capita* G N P rose at an annual rate of 4.2 per cent between 1965 and 1985 and 6 per cent between 1985 and 1995. But there is a steady undercurrent of dissatisfaction at the continuing vast gap between the small, rich governing class, and the huge mass of the urban poor.

The national oil company, Pertamina, collapsed in 1975 in a major scandal: a high court case in Singapore had to resolve a dispute between the heirs of a Pertamina official, who had officially earned $600 a month yet left an estate worth $32 million. The rapacity of Suharto's own children is a source of much criticism: they are known collectively as T O S H I B A, an acronym of their first names, or as 'the family business'. The allegations of corruption do not, however, extend to Suharto himself, who is accused only of being too lenient with his wife and children. The parallel with the Philippines is obvious.

There is also a parallel with Iran, not only because the shah's family was notoriously corrupt, but also because his regime was overthrown by an Islamic revival. The dangers from Islamic fundamentalism remain of acute concern to Indonesia. Islamic fanatics hijacked an Indonesian airliner in 1981; and there were serious Islamic disturbances in Jakarta in September 1984, during which troops opened fire on demonstrators. The government reported that nine people were killed; Muslim organizations say the true number was 400–600; and Amnesty International concluded that at least 30, and possibly many more, died.

In the mid-1990s, the opposition found a political symbol who they hoped would play the role of Corazon Aquino in the Philippines or Aung San Suu Kyi in Burma. This was Sukarno's daughter, Megawati Sukarnoputri, who emerged from the long obscurity of her family to join a small opposition group, the Indonesian Democratic Party, in the early 1990s. A demonstration in her support, on 27 July 1997, led to the most serious riots in Jakarta since Suharto took power. Three people were killed and scores were injured after the party headquarters was stormed and trashed by troops. Suharto blamed the P K I, and ordered the army to shoot demonstrators on sight.

The root of the trouble in Indonesia was that the level of official corruption far exceeded anything achieved under the shah in Iran in the 1970s or even in the Philippines under Marcos in the 1980s. Suharto's family has enriched itself to the tune of tens of billions of dollars. The president's six children are all billionaires and own radio and television networks, banks, chemical companies, paper mills, shipping lines, construction firms, shopping malls, hotels, car companies and taxi firms, toll roads, the country's largest private airline and the tele-communications satellite monopoly. The president's youngest son, Hutomo Mandala Putra (Tommy), was given a licence to build an all-Indonesian car, the Timor, and the company was exempted from paying import duties on Korean parts. He also bought the Italian Lamborghini racing company and was given a monopoly on cloves (used in Indonesian cigarettes). All these companies are favoured by the government in awarding contracts and the entire banking system has been corrupted to provide for them.

A World Bank official, quoted in the *New York Times* in January 1998, said: 'This is not South Korea or Thailand or one of the other countries that have turned to the I M F. This is not a government run by common politicians or bureaucrats. It is much closer to a monarchy, with a king whose authority has never been questioned and whose children believe their wealth is god-given.'

Corruption in business and banking led to the destruction of the environment. The great tropical rain forests of Indonesia, in Sumatra, Borneo, the Celebes and New Guinea, were sold to the greed of logging companies and the unrestricted burning and clear-cutting of a desperate peasantry. In the summer of 1997, the whole of south-east Asia was blanketed in smoke from the fires in Indonesia. The citizens of Kuala Lumpur had to go about with masks over their faces to protect themselves from the greatest single man-made ecological disaster in human history, for which the Suharto regime was chiefly responsible.

In the Congo (then Zaïre), President Mobutu and his cronies stole everything, and reduced the country to beggary. Indonesia was a different sort of kleptocracy. The 'crony capitalism' practised throughout East Asia was tilted there towards the president's family, like the shah's family in Iran – only Suharto's children were even more rapacious than the shah's sister. Their greed was somewhat mitigated by their mother's relative restraint, and burst all bounds when she died in 1996.

When the banking dominoes started falling in East Asia in the summer of
1997, the banking crisis in South Korea, Malaysia and Thailand meant hard

times for those countries. In Indonesia, it meant that the regime was nearing its end. Indonesia had been ruled by only two presidents since independence, and the first, Sukarno, was only removed with great difficulty and after a bloodbath. The I M F agreed to bail out Indonesia, on condition that it reform its economic system root and branch. The reforms specifically meant stripping Suharto's children of their privileges. When the deal was announced, in January 1998, Indonesians did not believe it. If saving the economy meant ending the economic power of the Suharto family, then the *crise du régime* was upon them.

## EAST TIMOR

The Portuguese retained their colony in East Timor (and a small enclave on the north coast of West Timor) until after the Portuguese revolution of April 1974. It was a small, neglected and impoverished colony, covering about 7400 sq. miles (19,000 sq. km). About one-third of the population was Catholic. Joseph Conrad described the capital, Dili, as 'that highly pestilential place'. The colony was occupied by Japan during World War I I, and about 40,000 people were killed or died of starvation.

After the Portuguese revolution, the new leftist government in Lisbon abandoned all the colonies that Portugal had kept around the world, except Macao on the Chinese mainland. Three political parties were established in East Timor: Fretilin (*Frente Revolucionaria de Timor Leste Independente*), which advocated immediate independence; U D T (*União Democratica Timorense*), which wanted a continuing association with Portugal, leading to independence; and Apodeti (*Associacão Popular Democratica Timorense*), which wanted integration with Indonesia. Apodeti probably had 5 per cent of popular support, the other two sharing the remainder in equal proportions. Portugal remained in nominal control, but in fact, Lisbon was far too preoccupied with its own political problems and the crises in Angola and Mozambique to concern itself with the fate of East Timor. As in Angola at the same time, the Portuguese government favoured the most left-leaning of the colonial political parties – in this case, Fretilin, which quickly became the dominant force in East Timor.

On 10 August 1975, the U D T attempted a coup. There was a brief civil war between it and Apodeti, on the one side, and Fretilin on the other. Fretilin won, at a cost of about 1500 lives. Portugal then washed its hands of the place: its civil administrators withdrew to an island off the coast of Dili, and Fretilin was left in control.

On 28 November, Fretilin proclaimed the Democratic Republic of East Timor. Indonesia sent 'volunteers' to occupy Dili on 7 December, and the Indonesian army then set out to conquer the country. By the following spring, there were 30,000 Indonesian troops there. The Indonesians set up a puppet regime, which in May 1977 called for integration with Indonesia. On 17 July, East Timor became Indonesia's 27th province.

The Indonesian troops started to massacre the Timorese as soon as they arrived – perhaps 2000 civilians were killed in Dili in the first few days. Fretilin had formed an army of 20,000 during the 18 months that it controlled East Timor, and it had been armed by the departing Portuguese. There was soon a full-scale war between it and the Indonesian army. The Indonesian air force

**211**

bombed villages indiscriminately, and the army used heavy artillery against Fretilin and its civilian supporters. Thousands of people suspected of Fretilin sympathies were arrested, tortured and murdered. Timorese peasants were moved into resettlement centres where they could be properly policed, and the traditional village life of the Timorese people was thus utterly destroyed. Estimates of the number of people killed or dead of starvation or illness caused by the war range between 10 and 30 per cent of the population. A conservative estimate would be 100,000 dead out of a population of perhaps 650,000 in 1975.

The Fretilin army put up a stout resistance, but by the end of 1978, it had been largely destroyed. Its leader, Nicolau Lobato, was killed on 31 December 1978, and the remnants of the Fretilin resistance took to the hills.

In 1981, in 'Operation Security', the Indonesian army rounded up as many Timorese men between the ages of 15 and 55 as they could find, and marched them against Fretilin positions, as a 'fence' to protect the army. There was a brief ceasefire in 1983, and when that broke down, another massive 'Operation Clean-Sweep' was mounted.

Amnesty International reports numerous instances of torture, extralegal executions, massacres and mistreatment of civilians. International relief agencies, allowed into East Timor in 1979, found widespread famine, and for a while East Timor was reported as a new Biafra. The country was ruined, much of the population had been regrouped in 'resettlement areas' and the surviving coffee plantations had been taken over by the Indonesian army. For the most part, East Timor has been completely closed off from the world: its inhabitants are not allowed to leave, and visitors from the rest of Indonesia, or from the outside, apart from a few journalists, are forbidden to enter. There are, of course, no political freedoms at all, no civil liberties, no press.

Fretilin survives, conducting a persistent, low-level guerrilla campaign against the government. In 1988, the Indonesian commanding general said that fewer than 100 Indonesian soldiers are killed every year by guerrillas. (He did not say how many Timorese were killed annually.) He also stated that guerrilla activity was now limited to the hills in the east and south-east, and consisted of ambushes of government convoys and attacks on settlements. The government puts the number of guerrillas at 500–1000. Fretilin claims it has 3000, and says that it killed 165 Indonesian soldiers in 1987. There are said to be about 20,000 Indonesian troops in East Timor.

Through all this, the world did nothing. In September 1974, Australia, in the person of Labour prime minister Gough Whitlam, acknowledged to Suharto that it would be best for East Timor to join Indonesia. In 1975, Australia was distracted by a constitutional crisis, an event that may even have encouraged the Indonesians to invade East Timor. US President Ford, with his secretary of state Henry Kissinger, visited Jakarta on 5–6 December 1975, the day before the invasion, and did nothing to dissuade Suharto; nor did they condemn him afterwards. Even as news of the massacres came out, the major powers, East and West, ignored it. Indonesia is too populous, rich and influential in the Third World for the United States, China or the Soviet Union to risk its displeasure. India, equating East Timor with Goa (another Portuguese colonial relic that India had annexed, without serious opposition from the Goans), supported

Indonesia. Thus the four most populous nations on Earth supported the fifth, Indonesia, in a small act of genocide.

The United Nations condemned the annexation in 1976 and has since repeated that condemnation on a number of occasions, although each time with fewer votes against the Indonesian government. The Soviet Union always voted against Indonesia, but that was the extent of its disapproval.

In recent years, Indonesia has tried to win the loyalty of the Timorese by investing heavily in East Timor, now spending more there *per capita* than in any province except Jakarta. The standards of living, health, education, sanitation and so on have all improved dramatically, although the political control is as tight as ever. Perhaps, eventually, the carrot may prove more persuasive than the stick.

In November 1988, the Washington human rights group Asia Watch issued a report on Indonesia and East Timor, stating that the situation had improved. More than 100 political prisoners had been released in East Timor in that year and there had been 'comparatively few' cases of illegal disappearances in recent years. The report stated that 'some of the worst excesses of the occupation have abated, but the Timorese people continue to suffer daily violations of fundamental rights'. On 12 November 1991, Indonesian troops fired into a crowd of Timorese attending a funeral in Dili, killing about 100 and wounding 200. The funeral was of a young man who had been shot by soldiers outside a church, and was the largest gathering in the capital for several years. The Indonesian government published the report of its inquiry. It concluded that, 'There was a spontaneous reaction by soldiers without orders, to protect themselves, shooting many times into the demonstrators. That coincided with a group of security forces, out of control, and outside command, which also opened fire and led to more victims.' The government said that 50 people had been killed and 'more than 91' injured. It promised that those responsible would be punished.

Amnesty International called for an independent inquiry, and asserted that serious human rights abuses continued in East Timor after the killings. A US journalist (for *The New Yorker*) who had seen the massacre asserted that the troops were not at all 'out of control' or 'without orders'. He said the shooting was clearly deliberate. He also quoted the chief of staff of the Indonesian army, who said of the demonstrators, 'They are people who must be crushed . . . Come what may, let no one think they can ignore the army. In the end, they will have to be shot down.'

By the mid-1990s, Fretilin had apparently been reduced to insignificance. The government said it had no more than 80 fighters. Then East Timor abruptly recovered world attention, at least briefly, in October 1996, when the Nobel peace prize was awarded to its two most prominent citizens, Bishop Carlos Felipe Ximenes Belo and José Ramos-Horta, who has led Fretilin from exile for many years. Ramos-Horta said that his share of the prize should have gone to Fretilin's commander in East Timor, Xanana Gusmao, who had been captured in 1992 and sentenced to 20 years in jail. Fretilin was emboldened to stir up its guerrilla campaign, ambushing and killing dozens of soldiers in the spring of 1997. The UN interested itself in the question, and in 1997 arranged for Indonesia and Portugal to resume negotiations on the territory (the world still recognizes Portuguese sovereignty, which makes East Timor the world's last colony of any consequence). There was little hope that Indonesia would pull out of East Timor so long as Suharto remained in office, but that period could not continue indefinitely.

## IRIAN JAYA

Formerly Dutch New Guinea, it is one of the most backward areas in the world. Its tribes, many still in the Stone Age, speak 800 distinct languages. Cannibalism and headhunting persist there: in 1975, a group of 13 Christian converts were killed and eaten by their heathen brethren while the European missionary was away.

Indonesia annexed Irian Jaya in 1963, with only the most perfunctory consideration for the wishes of its inhabitants. In the past few years, following attempts to resettle people from Java in the virgin forests of the outer islands, including those of Irian Jaya, a low-level guerrilla insurgency has started up there. The Free Papua Movement (OPM) was founded in 1963, based on the more educated classes, and motivated by tribal resentments. It relies to some extent on other tribes across the border, in Papua New Guinea, an independent nation that occupies the eastern half of the immense island. The OPM claims that several thousand Indonesian troops have been killed and larger numbers of civilians, but there are no means of verifying its claims. The OPM leader, Jacob Prai, was arrested in Papua New Guinea in 1979 and sent to Sweden.

There is no chance that the Irian Jaya guerrillas will win, any more than Fretilin will: the indigenous populations are too small, relative to that of Indonesia. However, New Guinea is so large and so wild and the terrain so difficult that it may also be impossible for Indonesia to win.

## FURTHER READING

American University, *Indonesia: A Country Study*, Washington D.C., 1983.
Amnesty International, *Indonesia/East Timor: Violations of Human Rights*, London, 1985.
Dunn, James, *Timor – A People's Betrayal*.
Emmerson, Donald K., 'Invisible Indonesia', *Foreign Affairs*, Vol. 66, no. 2, 1987.
Picken, Margot, 'The East Timor Agony', *New York Review*, 4 December 1986.

# KOREA

| | |
|---|---|
| Geography | *North Korea:* 46,814 sq. miles (121,248 sq. km). *South Korea:* 38,452 sq. miles (99,590 sq. km). Between them, they are about the size of Great Britain. |
| Population | *North Korea:* 23.8 million. *South Korea:* 45 million. |
| GNP per capita | *North Korea:* N.A. *South Korea:* $9700 (1997). |

The Korean war lasted from 1950 to 1953. Since then, the two Koreas have grown steadily further apart and at an accelerating rate, as South Korea's economy continues to expand at a phenomenal pace while the North stagnates. In December 1987, South Korea held a presidential election, which returned a democratically elected president – Roh Tae Woo – for the first time in decades. The following April, South Korea passed a further test of democracy: President Roh's party was defeated in legislative elections, and the president had to cope with a parliament dominated by the opposition. Subsequently, after Roh Tae Woo left office, he was sentenced to jail for his part in the Kwangju massacre. So was the last military president, Chun Doo Hwan. They were released in December 1997 after the country's leading democrat, Kim De Jung, was elected to the presidency. Kim then had to face a major banking crisis.

In North Korea, Kim Il Sung died in July 1994 and was succeeded by his son, Kim Jong Il. He inherited a country facing economic collapse and mass starvation, after 50 years of Communism.

The border between the two Koreas is one of the most dangerous in the world. North Korea itself remains erratic and belligerent: North Korean assassins murdered 17 members of an official South Korean delegation visiting Rangoon in October 1983; and in November 1987, two North Korean terrorists planted a bomb in a K A L airliner in Abu Dhabi, which exploded over the Indian Ocean, killing all 115 people on board.

## HISTORY

Korea developed its national identity over the centuries in the course of constant wars with China and Japan, both of which invaded it frequently. In 1907, Japan, fresh from its victory over Russia in Manchuria, established a protectorate over Korea and, in 1910, annexed it.

On 8 August 1945, the Soviet Union declared war on Japan and invaded

Manchuria and Korea – two days after the atomic bomb was dropped on Hiroshima, and one week before the Japanese surrender. The United States had ardently solicited Stalin to join in the war against Japan, and had now to cope with the consequences. Truman had no wish to see the Soviets established in Korea, just across the strait from Japan, and proposed that the isthmus should be provisionally divided along the 38th parallel, roughly halfway down. Stalin, who did not intend to begin a conflict with the US in the Far East, immediately agreed, and Korea, which had just escaped from Japanese colonialism, was suddenly partitioned by the two superpowers.

The Soviets immediately started building up a Communist state in the north. It must be said that, although it was imposed by the Red Army, the People's Republic of Korea has since survived on its own: the last Soviet troops were withdrawn in 1949. The Americans were more preoccupied with Japan, and neglected their zone of Korea. Diplomatic efforts to arrange for the country's reunification were fruitless: the two sides refused to agree. Stalin would tolerate only a Communist Korea, Truman a democratic one.

The North Koreans built up an army 200,000 strong and resolved to reunify the country by force. Whether Stalin ordered the attack or merely acquiesced is now a subject of only academic debate. At the time, it was seen as a further step in the Soviet dream of conquering the world.

In a speech to the National Press Club in Washington on 12 January 1950, the secretary of state, Dean Acheson, remarked that the American 'defensive perimeter runs along the Aleutians to Japan and then goes to the Ryukyus [a string of islands south of Japan, including Okinawa]'. He did not mention Korea. His enemies later alleged that this was to invite North Korea's invasion. The allegation was part of the McCarthyite onslaught on the Truman administration (what Acheson called 'the attack of the primitives'), which does not necessarily mean that the primitives were wrong. Soviet diplomacy, not to mention North Korean diplomacy, was always inept, and it is at least possible that Acheson's omission, combined with their ignorance of the United States, led the Communists into catastrophic error.

The invasion began on 6 June 1950. By early August, North Korea had occupied the whole of South Korea except for a pocket in the south-east. American troops in Korea were routed, and reinforcements sent from Japan did hardly better. In their defence, it must be said that the US army in the Far East had been allowed to run to seed: the big rearmament programme launched by the Truman administration was directed towards building up American forces in Europe. Even at the height of the Korean war, the best new troops raised in the United States were shipped to Europe. Korea was a sideshow.

The day after the attack, President Truman ordered General Douglas MacArthur to defend South Korea. The general, abandoning his role of proconsul in Japan, sent sufficient troops across into Korea to protect the last redoubt, ordered the air force to bomb North Korean supply lines, and prepared a counter-attack.

The United Nations, which the USSR was then boycotting, branded North Korea as aggressor and authorized the United States to form a UN command to defend the South. Its allies rallied to the call, sending contingents to fight alongside the Americans. The bulk of the U N force, however, was always the American army.

On 15 September, MacArthur landed his troops on the west coast of Korea at Inchon, near Seoul. Although the North Koreans were already seriously over-extended, and their defeat, once the United States had entered the war, was inevitable, the Inchon landings were one of the century's most remarkable feats of war. They were improvised in three months and carried out brilliantly, and in a matter of weeks MacArthur liberated the whole of South Korea and drove his armies into the North.

Perhaps if he had proceeded more cautiously, perhaps if he had kept his mouth shut, perhaps if Washington had proposed to recognize the Chinese Communist government (which it had refused to do since 1949) and invited it to a settlement of the Korean question, the Chinese would have permitted the defeat of North Korea and the reunification of the country. As it was, MacArthur advanced to the Chinese frontier, proclaimed his intention of reuniting Korea unilaterally and threatened to carry the attack across the Yalu river into China. The Chinese sent numerous warnings to Washington that they would not tolerate such a result. The warnings were ignored, and in October, the People's Liberation Army crossed the Yalu.

The U N forces – principally American but including British, Canadian, Turkish and various other contingents – were taken wholly by surprise, and were driven back in rout. Seoul fell to the Chinese and North Koreans. It was only with the greatest difficulty, and in the midst of winter, that MacArthur managed to establish a defence line across the peninsula. In the following year, with skilful use of the terrain, and thanks to its overwhelming technical super-iority, the U N command was able to drive the Chinese back approximately to the line of the former frontier. The general in command of operations was now Matthew Ridgeway, who had succeeded MacArthur when President Truman relieved him of his command on 11 April 1951, for insubordination. The Americans dug in and resisted 'human wave' attacks by the Chinese for over two years. A ceasefire was finally signed on 27 July 1953.

According to figures issued by the U N command, the Korean war resulted in the following casualties:

- United States: 37,904 dead, including 12,939 missing in action, presumed dead; 101,368 wounded.
- Other United Nations contingents: 4521 dead, among them 537 British and 312 Canadians.
- South Korea: 103,248 killed; 159,727 wounded.
- The U S high command calculated that North Korea lost 316,579 killed and China 422,612. It also calculated that 2 million civilians, north and south, were killed or injured.

While the casualty figures for U N forces are precise, the ones attributed to the North Koreans and Chinese must be treated with extreme caution. For one thing, their precision is clearly spurious: for China, for instance, the breakdown was 401,401 killed and 21,211 missing, presumed dead – figures that are too pretty to be accurate and, obviously, too accurate to be accurate. Evidently they were reached by some statistical method. Furthermore, as experience in Vietnam showed 15 years later, American generals are entirely capable of inflating the body count. I. F. Stone remarked that the high command was claiming Chinese losses equivalent to a full division a day during their mass offensives, a rate of attrition three times greater than the German army suffered at Verdun.

However, even heavily discounting the number of battlefield dead from the official 884,964, and taking a conservative number for civilian dead, the total deaths caused by the Korean war in three years were probably between 1 and 1.5 million.

## POST-WAR KOREA

The country, both north and south, was utterly devastated. It was reduced to the level of Germany in 1945, its cities rubble, its industries destroyed. Both parts of the country set about the long, painful business of restoration, complicated by the implacable hatred each side had for the other. The Chinese armies withdrew in 1958 but the Americans remain: South Korea is, despite Acheson's remarks, well within the American defensive perimeter.

With Hong Kong, Taiwan and Singapore, South Korea has now become one of the 'four little dragons' – East Asian countries that are following Japan's example in the pursuit of industrial growth. Its population is more than double the North's, its G N P nearly four times as great and rising far more rapidly. The comparison with divided Germany is striking. However, the East German regime survived because of the Soviet occupation, and East Germany never had the faintest intention of invading the West. In addition, North Korea spends 22.2 per cent of its G N P on defence, South Korea 5.5 per cent. As a proportion of the population, the North Korean armed forces are almost three times as great as those of the South (the actual numbers are North Korea: 784,000 men; South Korea: 600,000). Partly as a result, South Korea continues to pull ahead economically.

North Korea under Kim Il Sung and his son is an oddity: a smaller country dedicated to invading and defeating a larger and far stronger one – whose defence is guaranteed by the United States. A sensible regime would cut its defence expenditure to the bone and concentrate on economic development. The fact that a government can follow a completely senseless policy for decades, can provoke South Korea by acts of flagrant terrorism and can seriously contemplate a second Korean war is another reminder of the power of irrationality in human affairs.

On 18 January 1968, 31 North Korean commandos, disguised as South Korean soldiers and civilians, crossed the demilitarized zone (D M Z) between the two countries and headed for Seoul with the intention of assassinating President Park Chung Hee. They reached the capital on 21 January but were intercepted by police, and a gun battle broke out, during which five of the commandos, one South Korean policeman and five civilians were killed. Some of the commandos were later killed in a fire-fight with American troops as they tried to escape back across the D M Z, and the commander of the operation was captured and admitted that his object had been the president. Park survived another attack, in August 1974, that killed his wife, but was finally assassinated by his chief of police during a private dinner party in October 1979.

In October 1983, President Chun Doo Hwan of South Korea paid a state visit to Burma. On 9 October, he went to lay a wreath at the martyrs' memorial in Rangoon, which commemorates Thakin Aung San, founder of independent Burma, who was assassinated in 1947. Chun's car was delayed by traffic, and just before he arrived, a bomb demolished the memorial, killing 21 and wounding 46. The dead included the Korean foreign minister, Lee Bum Suk, the economic planning minister and deputy prime minister, Suh Suk Joon, and the minister for commerce and industry, Kim Dong Whie. The others were advisers to the president, journalists and security personnel.

Just before the explosion, the South Korean ambassador had arrived in a large car and a bugler had begun to practise 'The Last Post' ('Taps'). Presumably the terrorists, watching from a distance, had assumed that the president had arrived and the ceremony was beginning, and so detonated the bomb by radio. Three bombs had been concealed in the roof of the memorial; only one exploded.

Two days later, police arrested their first suspect, who tried to blow himself up with a hand grenade. The same day, villagers reported two suspicious foreigners to police. They, too, tried to commit suicide with grenades (one succeeded) and three policemen were killed. The two wounded men were found to be North Koreans, and confessed that they had been sent to assassinate President Chun.

Six days before the opening of the Asian Games in Seoul in 1986, a bomb exploded in Seoul airport, killing five people. South Korea blamed the North.

On 29 November 1987, Korean Airlines flight 858, *en route* from Europe to Korea via the Middle East, exploded over the Indian Ocean, killing all 115 people on board. Two passengers had left the flight at its last stop, Abu Dhabi on the Persian Gulf. They were stopped by security guards, and both immediately swallowed cyanide. The man, Kim Sung Il, aged 70, died; the woman, Kim Hyon Hui, aged 26, survived.

She was extradited to South Korea, and there confessed. The two were North Korean intelligence agents, and had been given orders 'personally written' by Kim Jong Il, President Kim Il Sung's son. The woman had been trained to behave and look Japanese, and the two had left a bottle of liquid explosive (disguised as liquor) and a detonator in a radio in the overhead rack on the aircraft. She said that the attack had been designed to destabilize South Korea during its presidential election campaign, and to increase international nervousness about the forthcoming Olympic Games there. She told a press conference in January 1988 that she had since changed her allegiance, after watching South Korean television, and being driven around Seoul by her interrogators.

South Korea sometimes overreacts to the threat from the North. In 1986, as Seoul was in the throes of preparations for the 1988 Olympics, the North Koreans began construction of a large hydroelectric dam on the Pukhan river, which crosses the D M Z and flows through Seoul on its way to the sea. South Korea claimed that the North planned to finish the dam before the Olympics, allow a huge reservoir to accumulate behind it and then suddenly to blow up the dam, releasing the water. The flood would sweep through Seoul, drowning 2 million people, including the visitors and athletes at the Games. It was all rather **219** improbable, but the South Koreans, much agitated, built a 'peace dam' on the river, on their side of the D M Z, to divert the flood. They finished it in record time, at a cost of $250 million; then they observed that the North's dam was hardly started, and was clearly years from completion.

In May 1988, South Korean students began a series of anti-American demonstrations. They blamed the United States for the division of the country, which is preposterous, and for supporting a long series of authoritarian Korean governments, which is not preposterous at all. They claim, in particular, that the United States was responsible for the Kwangju massacre in May 1980, in which South Korean troops, who were theoretically under American command, killed hundreds of demonstrators. The students now demanded the expulsion of the 40,000 American troops, and immediate reunification.

They proposed to march to the North to make their point. President Roo ordered the police to stop them, but admitted the possibility that the South was too rigid in its approach to the North. He therefore proposed a resumption of direct talks, and three sessions were held at the truce village, Panmunjom. The meetings were not a success. The South wanted the North to participate in the Olympics, and the North refused – unless it could be co-host. South Korea rejected that demand. The other, permanent subject of disagreement concerns America's presence in South Korea. Despite the student demonstrations, the Seoul government has no intention of asking them to leave. So the talks broke off, acrimoniously.

There is undoubtedly a great deal of Korean xenophobia. The United States is pressing South Korea to open its domestic market to American exports, to reduce the huge trade deficit. This is considered offensive by many Koreans who have built their astonishing economic development on hard work and the American market, and they are easily persuaded that the Americans really want to return them to their previous penury. Resentment at past American policies is also profound: the United States did indeed support a series of unsavoury military presidents, and accepted the argument that, because of the danger from the North, democracy could wait. Furthermore, the presence of the U S is exceedingly visible (there is a huge American base in suburban Seoul), and it is perfectly acceptable for conservative Koreans to join the radicals in deploring American influence.

Evidently the far left – that is, Maoist Communism – had many adherents. The majority of Koreans, of course, had no wish to be taken over by Kim Il Sung, and perhaps the Korean radicals will go the way of the Japanese radicals of the 1950s and 1960s, who blamed the U S for all their ills, real or imaginary. There was so much anti-Americanism in Japan that, in 1960, President Eisenhower had to cancel a state visit at the last moment. Those former Japanese radicals are now senior management in Japan Inc., and perhaps today's Korean radicals will follow the same route.

It is also possible that they will maintain the Maoist faith, like the Filipino Marxists who demonstrated against the United States in 1970–2, and then formed the New People's Army (*see* The Philippines, p. 236). The difference is that the Philippines then slipped into the Marcos autocracy, while Korea has just escaped from a prolonged military dictatorship. The demonstrations and the bizarre desire for a united, Communist Korea are tests for Korean democracy. If the government can cope with the challenge, including Molotov cocktails thrown at police and assaults with clubs and iron bars, without resorting to excessive force itself, South Korea will survive. In the long series of demonstrations during 1986–7, which led to free elections for the presidency in December 1987 and for the legislature in April 1988, there were countless violent clashes between riot police and demonstrators. But the police at all times kept their discipline, and it appears that they were guided by the principle that the rioters were Koreans, their children, who were the country's future, and therefore they never used live ammunition. (The contrast between this and Israel's methods of riot control during the simultaneous *intifada* was striking.)

The 1988 Olympics in Seoul were a great success. Stringent security precautions were taken, for fear of terrorism from the North, but there were no incidents. (China and the USSR, which both sent teams, had promised to use their influence with North Korea to ensure the peace.) The games allowed many South Koreans to demonstrate their irritation with the United States. The cheerful chauvinism of American television, which ceaselessly patronized Korea and everything Korean throughout the games, and a few incidents of boorish behaviour by American athletes were given great play in Seoul. Conversely, Americans were angered by the constant manifestations of anti-Americanism they encountered.

Koreans had more pressing concerns. The transition to democracy continued and proved continually painful. A parliamentary inquiry into the misdeeds of the former military regime revealed a pattern of corruption that implicated former President Chun, and suggested that the Kwangju massacre was a result of deliberate government policy. Members of Chun's family were arrested and charged with corruption, and a series of violent demonstrations by students and other radicals forced President Roh Tae Woo to abandon his friend and patron, and insist that he appear on television and apologize for his errors. Chun was then sent into internal exile in the country. The demonstrations continued. Finally, under Roh's successor, Kim Young Il, Chun was prosecuted and sentenced to death, later commuted to life in prison. Roh, also, was tried and convicted for oppression and corruption, and sentenced to 17 years. Two years later, they were released by Kim's successor, Kim Dae Jung. It was time to turn the page. The whole prolonged national debate over Kwangju and the two presidents, though traumatic, was an essential part of South Korea's evolution to full democracy. Kim won the election, in December 1997, by a plurality of about 40 per cent of the vote. When he took office two months later, he was confronted with the most serious economic crisis, prompted by a massive failure of the banking system, that the country had ever faced. The fact that democracy had been well established meant that South Korea might survive the crisis more easily than authoritarian regimes similarly and simultaneously afflicted, or than it would itself have done a few years earlier.

## NORTH KOREA

In 1990 and 1991, particularly after Iraq's efforts to build nuclear weapons were exposed, South Korea and the United States became concerned that North

Korea was on the verge of becoming a nuclear power. A nuclear enrichment plant was nearing completion, and the North Koreans refused to allow international inspection until the Americans withdrew their nuclear weapons from the South. President Bush announced his intention to do so, as part of a general disarmament plan, in September 1991. It was hard to judge the seriousness of the alleged Northern nuclear threat: perhaps it was no more dangerous than the dam. The crisis ended in 1994 with a most unusual deal: the United States promised to build two nuclear power plants in North Korea, to be financed to the tune of $4 billion by the South and by Japan, in exchange for North Korea dismantling its uranium-enrichment plant under UN supervision. It was a long-term plan and its implementation was constantly afflicted by the deep animosities between the two sides.

Both North and South Korea joined the UN in 1991, and the two governments resumed negotiations. The Americans withdrew their troops from the 38th parallel, eliminating another source of Northern complaint. It was not enough. The North Korean economy was in serious trouble. The Soviet Union has ended all subsidies, and demanded that all exports be paid in dollars. Kim Il Sung lived in a Stalinist fantasy world (everyone has to wear a button showing the Great Leader), defying 'the atrocious anti-revolutionary offensive of the imperialists and reactionaries' even after the failure of the coup in Moscow. Fidel Castro might trim his sails, Kim Il Sung never.

The 'Great Leader' died in July 1994, and nothing changed in North Korea. His son, the 'Dear Leader' Kim Jong Il, succeeded him and progressively took over his various offices. It was the only dynastic Communist succession (though Nicolae Ceausescu may have planned one in Romania). In a newspaper advertisement published in the United States, his government proclaimed:

North Korean leader Kim Jong Il is a man of great leadership, remarkable wisdom and noble virtues. He is always with the popular masses sharing the ups and downs of life with them. Indeed, he is equipped with all the qualities a great leader needs. Kim Jong Il, a new leader of the 21st century, will surely break fresh ground in the political, economic, military and diplomatic fields of Korea, succeeding excellently to the cause of the late President Kim Il Sung.

The omens were not good. North Korea's economy, kept afloat for decades on Soviet and Chinese subsidies, lost those supports in 1991. The GNP shrank by 20 per cent from 1989 to 1993: it has been in free-fall since then. The last available comparative figures, for 1991, are:
- North Korea's GNP $23 billion; South Korea, $281 billion.
- North Korea *per capita* income, $1110, South Korea $6498.
- Annual growth: North Korea, minus 5.2 per cent, South Korea, 8.4 per cent.

The North suffered from the same systemic inefficiencies as the Soviet Union, and suffered the same economic collapse – while the Communist Party was still in power. In 1995, first reports emerged of serious food shortages. There were devastating floods that summer, which cut agricultural production by a third, and food shortages were reported. Reports filtering out in 1996 and 1997 spoke of widespread starvation and, finally, famine in the countryside. The regime was forced to beg for help, and its people were kept alive by food shipments from the

South, from Japan and from the United States. There was a near-absolute lack of fuel (North Korea had no hard currency to import oil), and the chief means of transport, even in the countryside near Pyongyang, was by ox-cart. There was little electricity and therefore little light and less heat.

Talks between North and South to improve relations began in 1994, and seemed to be a hopeful sign. Old habits die hard: in September 1996, an abandoned Northern submarine was found beached on the east coast of South Korea. The army was sent in pursuit of the crew and the infiltrators they had been delivering, and finally killed 25 men, capturing one alive. Two months later, in an unprecedented gesture, North Korea expressed its regrets for the incident and promised that it would not be repeated. Evidently the regime had concluded that in times of famine it should not provoke those who might save it. A senior member of the Northern politburo defected in February 1997 (Kim Jong Il's wife had defected, with her children, the previous year). The defector, Hwang Jang Yop, described famine in the North, and also plans for war and nuclear weapons.

It was hard to know how seriously to take his predictions. Some pessimists feared that in its death throes the North Korean regime would launch a last, suicidal attack on the South. It seemed to others far more likely that the regime would collapse, like Communist regimes in Eastern Europe, facing South Korea, like West Germany in 1989, with the unavoidable costs of reunification. The prospect was made even more doubtful for the South by its own economic difficulties.

## FURTHER READING

Alexander, Bevin, *Korea – The First War We Lost*, New York, Hippocrene Books, 1986.

American University, *North Korea: A Country Study*, Washington D.C., 1982.
———— *South Korea: A Country Study*, Washington D.C., 1981.

Amnesty International, *South Korea: Violations of Human Rights*, London, 1986.

Clifford, Mark *Troubled Tiger: Businessmen, Bureaucrats and Generals in South Korea*, New York, M. E. Sharpe, 1994.

Cumings, Bruce, *Korea's Place in the Sun – A Modern History*, New York, Norton, 1997.

Hastings, Max, *The Korean War*, New York, Simon and Schuster, 1987.

MacDonald, Callum, *Korea: The War before Vietnam*, New York, Free Press, 1987.

Oberdorfer, Don, *The Two Koreas – A Contemporary History*, Addison-Wesley, 1997.

Stone, I. F., *The Hidden History of the Korean War*, New York, Monthly Review Press, 1952.

Young Whan Kili (editor) *Korea and the World: Beyond the Cold War*, Boulder, Westview Press, 1994.

# MALAYSIA

| | |
|---|---|
| Geography | 127,672 sq. miles (330,669 sq. km). Malaysia comprises the Malay peninsula (50,670 sq. miles; 131,235 sq. km) and Sabah and Sarawak on the north coast of Borneo. |
| Population | 20.1 million, of whom 3 million live in the Borneo territories, the rest in Malaya. About 8.25 million are Malays, 4.7 million Chinese, 1.53 million Indian (mostly Tamils). The others are the indigenous tribes of Borneo. |
| Resources | Tin, rubber, tropical produce; rapidly developing light industry. |
| GNP per capita | $3890 (1995). |

The last traces of the Communist insurrection in Malaya, which had begun in 1948, were finally extinguished in December 1989, when the Communist Party of Malaya surrendered. A ceasefire was signed by the Malaysian and Thai governments and the CPM, and the 1200 guerrillas, who had subsisted in the mountains along the Malay–Thai border, returned to civilian life. The Communist leader, Chin Peng, emerging in public for the first time since 1955, signed for the CPM.

It was the end of one of the longest wars in Asia, though it had been quite inconsequential for the previous 30 years. In the interval, Malaysia had become independent, had survived the 'confrontation' with Indonesia and a crisis in 1969 in which hundreds of people were killed during anti-Chinese riots in Kuala Lumpur. Since then, Malays and Chinese have lived relatively harmoniously together. Malaysia is not a zealous defender of human rights and democratic virtue, any more than Thailand, Singapore or Indonesia, but, like them, offers stability and prosperity to its citizens.

Malaysia has a special role in an account of contemporary conflicts. The Communist insurgency, 1948–60, was soundly defeated, and the American intervention in Vietnam was a fruitless attempt to repeat that success. The Malayan experience unfortunately proved to be unique.

## HISTORY

The Malay peninsula came under British control in the 19th century as an appendage of the Indian empire and because of the activities of a British adventurer, Stamford Raffles. He set up a trading emporium on

Singapore island in 1819, which developed rapidly into the Straits Settlements, the greatest trading centre in South-East Asia. In order to protect Singapore, the British extended their influence to the peninsula. Another adventurer, Sir James Brooke, cleared the pirates out of Sarawak on the north-western coast of Borneo, and set himself up as the 'White Raja of Sarawak'.

On 10 December 1941, the British navy in the Far East suffered a humiliation even greater than Pearl Harbor, when the Japanese attacked and sank the battleship *Prince of Wales* and the cruiser *Repulse* at Singapore. Singapore itself was captured on 15 February 1942; most of the numerous British and Australian PoWs died in the camps. The Japanese incited the Malays against the Chinese, and thousands were executed. Resistance started first among the Chinese, led by the Communist party, in both Malaya and Singapore, and was ruthlessly suppressed.

After the war, and as a result of the humiliating defeat that the British had suffered at the hands of the Japanese, the citizens of the British Empire in Asia concluded that the days of empire were over. The British were constrained to agree with them. The last Brooke Raja of Sarawak was summarily dispossessed by the government in London; Malaya became independent in 1957; and in 1963, Singapore and the territories in Borneo (which were still British colonies or protectorates) were federated with Malaya to become the country now known as Malaysia. Singapore withdrew from the federation in 1965. Brunei, a British protectorate, possessed of large oil revenues, declined to join and went it alone.

## THE EMERGENCY

The Malaya Emergency began in June 1948. Communist terrorists attacked government posts, police and military patrols in the rubber plantations and tin-mining areas; the first victims were three European plantation managers. The insurgents intended to follow classic guerrilla strategy and wreck the economy by killing planters and their managers, by slashing rubber trees and by blowing up or burning essential buildings at the plantations or mines. They also made a speciality of attacking Malayan officials.

Almost all the Communist terrorists – known to the British army as 'C Ts' and to themselves as the Min Yuen – were Chinese, and the fighting was at least partly a continuation of the animosities stirred up by the Japanese. The C Ts' greatest successes occurred in 1949–51, culminating in the assassination of the British high commissioner, Sir Henry Gurney, in an ambush on 6 October 1951. During the course of the Emergency, one in ten of the rubber planters was murdered.

The British responded by gathering together the Chinese workers of the plantations and mines into 'new villages'. About 300,000 squatters were living on the fringes of the plantations and provided the 'sea' in which the C T 'fish' could swim, under Mao's prescription for guerrilla war. By 1952, the British had moved them into 400 new villages, securely under government control. They offered many advantages in health, sanitation and other facilities, but also imposed considerable hardship on the people involved. After the Emergency ended, the new villages survived and thrived: for the first time, Chinese immigrants and their descendants had leases on their houses and were a recognized part of Malayan society. Part of the campaign against the CTs involved providing everyone with an identity card; these gave the Chinese proof of residence and citizenship, and a stake in the success of independent Malaya.

The policy succeeded in cutting the CTs off from popular support and, more important, from their only source of supply. It was the model for the 'strategic hamlets' policy that the Americans tried in Vietnam.

The other British method for fighting the terrorists was to train their conscript army in the techniques of guerrilla warfare. Small foot patrols scoured the jungles, ambushing the CTs; this was known as 'jungle bashing'. It was calculated that 1000 hours of jungle bashing might be needed for one contact with a CT.

The British proved better guerrilla fighters than the Malayan Communists. They had another advantage: they brought in Dayak trackers from Borneo. They divided the country, whose topography lends itself to such practices, into districts, each of which was in turn subjected to a most thorough search. As each district was declared 'white', the British moved their troops, police and planes on to the next. They started this intensive clearance operation in the south and worked north. By the time of independence, the remaining 500 or so CTs had been driven across the border into Thailand.

Ten years later, when Sukarno sent Indonesian guerrillas into Sarawak, the British demonstrated that they had not lost their skills. The Indonesians were roundly defeated by the same methods that had beaten the Malayan Communists.

The essential difference between the British experience in Malaya and the Americans' in Vietnam (and the Philippine government's today) is that the Malayan insurrection was limited to a minority among a distinct ethnic group. The majority of the Chinese did not support the CTs and were separated from them in their new villages, while the majority of the population, the Malays, actively opposed the Communists. In Vietnam, no such distinction was possible, nor is it possible in the Philippines. The other element in the British strategy, sending British soldiers into the jungles on foot patrol, to play cat and mouse with the guerrillas, was not tried extensively in Vietnam.

At the start of the Emergency, the CTs had 4000 to 5000 guerrilla fighters, and in the early 1950s, they had perhaps 8000 men. In the course of the Emergency, about 13,000 suspected terrorists were killed. The British lost 525 men killed, including Malay soldiers and police.

## FURTHER READING

American University, *Malaysia, a Country Study*, Washington D.C., 1985.
Gullick, J. M., *Malaysia*, New York, Praegar, 1969.

James, Harold and Shiel-Small, Denis, *The Undeclared War: The Story of the Indonesian Confrontation, 1962–66*, London, Leo Cooper, 1971.

McKie, Ronald, *The Emergence of Malaysia*, New York, Harcourt, Brace and World, 1963.

# PAKISTAN

| | |
|---|---|
| Geography | 310,403 sq. miles (803,941 sq. km). Somewhat larger than the UK and France combined. |
| Population | 130 million. The major ethnic groups are: Punjabis, about 60%; Sindhi, 12%; Baluchi, 4%; Pushtun (Pathan), 11%. The population is 70% Sunni Muslim, 30% Shiite, many of them Ismaili. Urdu is the official language, but English is widely spoken. |
| GNP per capita | $460. |
| Refugees | 1.2 million Afghans, 13,000 from Indian Kashmir. |

Pakistan has lurched from crisis to crisis since it was born in the disaster of the Indian partition in 1947. It has fought three wars with India, and lost all of them. (For the first two, *see* India, p. 184.) The third, in 1971, was East Pakistan's war of independence, and ended with the formation of Bangladesh. Domestically, Pakistan has suffered continuously unstable parliamentary government interspersed with military dictatorships. Successive democratically elected governments have proved corrupt and incompetent, where the military regimes were chiefly incompetent. Islamic fundamentalism spreading from the wars in Afghanistan, and ethnic and social unrest on a vast scale, make Pakistan one of the most unstable countries in Asia.

Because the chief concern of Pakistan's foreign policy has been its enmity towards India, it developed a close alliance with China, which fought a border war with India in 1962. There is now an all-weather road over the Himalayas from Sinkiang in western China into northern Pakistan, as a symbol of that alliance. Pakistan inherited from the British a profound distrust of the USSR. It considered Afghanistan as a buffer state, and when the Soviets occupied it in 1979, the Pakistanis naturally supported the resistance. Equally naturally, India developed close relations with the Soviet Union, on the principle that 'the enemy of my enemy is my friend'. India was the only independent country of any consequence that supported the Soviet occupation of Afghanistan.

The United States supported Pakistan from its inception, on the same principle – its staunch opposition to the Soviets – and American relations with India were therefore always cool, despite the fact that India is a democracy while Pakistan has usually been a military dictatorship. The only time that the balance of American favour tilted towards India was during the Kennedy administration, when John

Kenneth Galbraith was American ambassador to New Delhi. After the 1965 war, the United States suspended arms sales to both countries, a policy that in effect penalized Pakistan as India continued to be supplied by the USSR.

During the 1971 war, President Nixon ordered his administration to 'tilt' in favour of Pakistan, and his national security adviser, Henry Kissinger, strove strenuously to obey the order. (News of it was leaked to Jack Anderson, a Washington columnist, who published it.) The 'tilt' did Pakistan no good. Nixon's successors have followed the same preference, even after a Pakistani mob sacked the American embassy in Islamabad in November 1979, killing two American servicemen, while the authorities did nothing to protect it. Arms sales to Pakistan were resumed during the Carter administration, and during the Afghan war, Pakistan became a major recipient of American aid.

## HISTORY

In the long run-up to India's independence, there were two main political parties: the Congress, led by Nehru, Patel and Gandhi; and the Muslim League, led by Mohammed Ali Jinnah (known as the Quaid-i-Azam) and Liaquat Ali Khan. The Congress party wanted a united India; the League advocated a separate state for Muslims, consisting of north-east India and East Bengal. The disadvantages of this scheme, apart from the permanent hostility between the two nations that has ensued, were that a huge number of Muslims, now 110 million, would be left as a minority in India, and that the country's two wings would be separated by 1000 miles of Indian territory. When independence came in 1947, it was accompanied by immense movements of population and immense bloodshed: 12 million people were driven from their homes, in India and in Pakistan, and about 800,000 people were murdered.

For a variety of reasons that are still hotly debated, Pakistan, unlike India, proved incapable of establishing a stable democratic form of government. Jinnah died in 1948 and Liaquat Ali was assassinated in 1951, and the series of weak and ineffectual governments that followed were faced with Baluchi and Pushtun unrest and with increasing differences between the two wings of the country. The fundamental conflict was between the Bengalis, who were by far the most numerous of Pakistan's ethnic groups and, in due course, became an absolute majority in the nation, and the Punjabis, who numbered 60 per cent of West Pakistan's population and dominated that region. Each group thought that it should lead the nation. Civilian government collapsed under the strain, and on 7 October 1958, the president, General Iskander Mirza, abrogated the constitution and proclaimed martial law, appointing General Ayub Khan as martial law administrator. On 28 October, Ayub packed Mirza off into exile in London and took full power.

Ayub pursued economic development on lines recommended by the United States, and achieved some success. However, he failed to resolve the country's underlying political problems, and started and lost a war with India in 1965. In 1968, he celebrated his decade in power with considerable pomp and so provoked the Pakistanis that riots broke out all over the country. Ayub was forced to resign in March 1969, and was succeeded by another general, Yahya Khan. Political parties were revived and elections were called for November 1970.

## THE WAR OF 1971 AND THE INDEPENDENCE OF BANGLADESH

The main parties in the country were now the Awami League in East Pakistan, led by Sheikh Mujib Ur-Rahman, and the Pakistan People's Party (PPP), led by Zulfikar Ali Bhutto, who had been foreign minister under Ayub. The PPP was based in the Punjab and Sind; it had no support in the North-west Frontier Province (Pushtunistan), or in Baluchistan. The elections were postponed when a cyclone devastated East Pakistan, killing 250,000 people, in November 1970.

When voting finally took place in December, the Awami League won 160 of the 162 National Assembly seats allocated to East Pakistan, and the PPP won 81 of the 138 seats allocated to the West. Sheikh Mujib had an absolute majority and insisted that he would form the government as soon as parliament convened. He would then carry out his party's electoral platform, which amounted to stripping the federal government of all power except over foreign affairs and defence.

Yahya and Bhutto both refused to accept the prospect. The stalemate was absolute, and on 25 March 1971, Yahya proclaimed a state of emergency in East Pakistan, dissolved the Awami League and arrested its leaders, including Mujib, and denounced them as traitors.

Yahya's army in the East was 40,000 strong, and was progressively increased to 75,000. It set about ferociously repressing the 75 million Bengalis, and before the end of the year, it had killed at least 300,000 people. (The Bangladeshis now claim that the total killed was 3 million, which is clearly a great exaggeration.) On 14 April 1971, in a village near the Indian border, Mujib's surviving associates proclaimed an independent Bangladesh, but on the approach of the Pakistani army, they prudently moved to Calcutta. India offered Bangladesh every support. It began to train Bengali guerrillas – the Mukti Bahini – one of whose first achievements was the murder of the governor of East Pakistan, Abdel Monen Khan. Soon there were 100,000 Mukti Bahini, led by Bengali officers who had deserted from the old Pakistan army. Refugees from Bangladesh began to pour over the border into India: in the end, there were over 10 million of them.

The Nixon administration offered some succour to Pakistan (the famous 'tilt'), although it was obvious that it would not succeed in restoring Pakistani unity. Kissinger had arranged to use Yahya's government as his super-secret channel to China, and in July, as his staff informed the press that he was ill, he flew from Islamabad to Peking. The United States' pro-Pakistan policy was much resented in India, which in August signed a 20-year treaty of peace, friendship and cooperation with the Soviet Union. Indira Gandhi toured Western countries and Moscow to explain that India would have to intervene unless Pakistan renounced its war in the East. The Indians forbade Pakistani planes to overfly Indian territory. They therefore had to make the long trip around, via Ceylon.

The massacres increased in frequency and the guerrilla fighting became rapidly more serious. The guerrillas announced a generalized offensive in November, and on 22 November, the Indian army crossed the border at numerous points into East Pakistan and began an advance on Dacca. The Indians later denied that they had invaded, saying that they had waited until Pakistan attacked them.

Yahya declared a state of national emergency and, in desperation, began preparations for a general war against India on all fronts. On 3 December, the Pakistani air force attempted to repeat the Israeli achievement of the Six-Day war of 1967, and destroy the Indian air force on the ground. It failed. In 1967, the Israelis had taken the Egyptians completely by surprise and won the war in a 30-minute air raid; in 1971, the Pakistanis attacked the wrong airports, missed the planes on the ground when they found the right ones, and their planes were in turn attacked and destroyed by the Indians.

On 4 December, India openly poured troops into East Pakistan and, in a five-pronged attack, soon defeated the Pakistani army there. It surrendered on 16 December. Simultaneously, the Indians had crossed the border into West Pakistan.

Kissinger, whose distaste for India is quite remarkable, claims that there was a real danger that India, supported by the Soviet Union, would dismember West Pakistan as well, annexing Kashmir. He claims that American diplomacy prevented this eventuality by using its leverage in Moscow to induce the Soviets to dissuade India. In any event, on 17 December, Indira Gandhi announced a unilateral ceasefire.

Yahya Khan's military government collapsed. He resigned on 20 December, and Bhutto took power. It was a sequence of events to be repeated by the Greek colonels in Cyprus and the Argentinian junta in the Falklands war.

During his four and a half years as head of the government, Bhutto succeeded in restoring Pakistani self-confidence and a semblance of unity, but he provoked much opposition in the army and in large sectors of the population. The PPP won elections in March 1977, an event that provoked widespread rioting and protest in districts dominated by the opposition. The army took power in a coup on 5 July 1977, and the chief of staff, General Zia el-Haq, made himself president. On 4 April 1979, despite vehement protests from governments around the world, Zia had Bhutto hanged on a charge of plotting the assassination of a political rival.

Pakistan was heavily embroiled in the Afghan war against Soviet occupation (see Afghanistan, p. 123), acting as the base area for the various resistance movements. Zia heavily supported the most extreme Islamic fundamentalist party and the United States acquiesced in the choice, on the grounds that they were probably the most effective fighters against the Soviets. There were about 3.5 million Afghans in Pakistan, most of them in camps in the North-west Frontier Province (NWFP), but also thousands elsewhere in the country. In addition, about 20,000 refugees from Iran lived in Karachi. There was constant tension between various Afghan factions, between Shiites and Sunnis, between followers of the ayatollah and his enemies, a situation that, particularly in Karachi, was compounded by conflicts between Biharis (refugees from eastern India) and other Pakistanis. Scores of people were killed or wounded every month in riots or bombings and by assassination. More than 200 were killed by bombings in 1987: on 14 July 1987, 72 people were killed by car bombs in Karachi and hundreds were injured. The violence continued to escalate. In 1994, 900 people were killed in communal fighting in Karachi, and 2095 in 1996, including 320 in a series of riots and massacres in June. There was a similar increase in violence in Lahore and elsewhere throughout the country, all attributable to the prevalence of weapons brought back from Afghanistan. Some of the violence is fighting between drug-lords, some is ethnic. A group called the Mohajir National Movement (the M Q M) in Karachi, based on Urdu-speaking people who fled India during Partition, is fighting for the creation of a separate, Urdu-dominated province in Karachi.

Pakistan is on the verge of making its first atomic weapons. (India has already demonstrated its capacity to do so.) In 1987, Pakistani businessmen in several countries, including the United States and Canada, were discovered to be buying the various components needed for a plant to separate weapons-grade plutonium from used fuel in nuclear power plants. The conspiracy was evidently directed by the Pakistani government. In May 1988, the *New York Times*, in a report attributed to official U S sources, stated that Pakistan had successfully tested a surface-to-surface missile capable of delivering a nuclear warhead to Delhi or Bombay. India had tested a similar missile in February.

In December 1985, Zia at last lifted martial law, which he had imposed in 1977. Politics revived, after a fashion, and Benazir Bhutto, daughter of the late president, emerged as leader of the P P P. There was a national assembly, a prime minister, a government and a constitution, but it was all a sham. Zia remained the absolute ruler, the dictator. On 29 May 1988, because the civilian government he had installed was showing signs of independence, he dissolved parliament (without consulting the government), dismissed the prime minister, Mohammed Khan Junejo, leader of the Muslim League, and announced that there would be elections in November. The news was greeted with the greatest scepticism: Benazir Bhutto was not alone in believing that the elections would be a fraud.

On 17 August 1988, President Zia was killed when his military C-130 suddenly crashed shortly after taking off. The president had been on an inspection at a military base, along with several senior officers and the American ambassador, Arnold Raphel. One of those killed was the chairman of the joint chiefs of staff, General Akhtar Abdul Rehman, who had directed the vast logistics operation involved in moving arms to the Afghan resistance. Zia had been a staunch supporter of the resistance, and his friends suspected that the Afghan secret service was responsible for his death. Subsequent investigations failed to find any proof of sabotage, however, and they ruled out the possibility that the plane had been hit by a missile or had exploded in the air.

The new government promised to hold the elections as scheduled in November, and the acting president, Ishaq Ghulam Khan, and the new chief of staff, General Mirza Aslam Beg, kept this promise. The elections were the first expression of democracy that Pakistan had enjoyed since 1972, and were hotly debated between several political parties. Benazir Bhutto succeeded in extending the P P P's reach beyond her father's strongholds in Sind, but still needed the support of other parties to win a majority in the assembly. She also needed the army's support; as a result, she promised to maintain the army in all its power and privileges and to continue supporting the rebels in Afghanistan.

Unlike Corazon Aquino in the Philippines, Bhutto was not swept to power in a popular uprising against a detested regime. On the contrary, Zia was clearly hugely popular. Half a million people attended his funeral. Furthermore, Aquino controlled the military; Bhutto did not. Her political base was in Sind, and her chief opponents controlled Punjab, the richest and most populous province in the country, and the Frontier Districts, Baluchistan and Karachi.

She tried to exert her authority by dissolving the Baluchi assembly and subverting the provincial government in Punjab. She made General. Tikka Khan governor of Punjab: he was remembered as the man who had directed the repression in East Pakistan that provoked the 1971 war of secession. Benazir Bhutto relied on her father's friends and supporters. They had not been strong enough to sustain him, and they failed her. The president, that is to say the army high command, decided that she must go, and her government was dismissed on 8 August 1990.

The new government charged Bhutto's husband, Asif Ali Zardari, with corruption, but she did not herself suffer her father's fate. She became leader of the opposition. After further elections, the Punjabi leader, Nawaz Sharif, became prime minister and launched on his reform programme, known as the 3-D programme – denationalization, disinvestment and deregulation. It was intended to establish a proper market economy and liberate the country from the bureaucracy and Third World socialism that was stifling it. He also introduced a new family-planning programme, in an attempt to bring down the rate of population growth from its catastrophic level of 3.2 per cent (it was 2.9 per cent between 1990 and 1995). All his predecessors had tried to solve the country's problems, and all had failed. He had to face an additional burden, the end of the cold war. The United States no longer needed to cultivate Pakistan as a loyal ally against the Soviet Union, and the end of American involvement in the Afghan war meant that the United States would no longer turn a blind eye to Pakistan's attempts to build nuclear weapons, its lamentable record over human rights and its large contribution to the international drug trade. In 1990, the United States ended economic and military aid, because of Pakistan's continued refusal to end its nuclear arms programme. Military sales resumed in 1993, but the US remained very cautious in its dealings with Pakistan.

Pakistani politics since 1990 have been a contest between Bhutto and Sharif, uneasily mediated by the armed forces, which have deposed Bhutto from office twice and Sharif once. Each accuses the other of corruption. Sharif's efforts at reform were stopped by the military in 1993, and fresh elections were called, which Bhutto's PPP won. She formed her second government, proclaiming, 'This time I won't listen to the sloppy liberals.' She was determined to suppress all opposition, sent troops to fight the gangs in Karachi and used blatantly unconstitutional means to intimidate the opposition, and any judges or journalists who might stand in her way. She instituted a sweeping series of corruption probes against Sharif, in retaliation for the prosecution of her husband that he had launched when he was prime minister (Zardari spent over two years in jail). Bhutto's brother, Murtaza, who had lived in exile in Syria since 1981 after hijacking a plane to Afghanistan to protest against the Zia regime, returned home after his sister was elected prime minister. She promptly had him arrested. He was released in June 1994, and returned to Karachi, where he started a violent movement to challenge Benazir Bhutto.

Violence and intimidation increased rapidly during Bhutto's second term in office. There were bombs in Karachi and Lahore, and on 20 September 1996, **233**

Murtaza Bhutto was murdered by gunmen outside his house in Karachi. The prime minister's husband was suspected of involvement in the crime.

On 5 November 1996, the president, Farooq Leghari, dismissed Bhutto, accusing her of corruption and incompetence. This was the fourth time since 1988 that the government had been overturned at the behest of the military. Her husband was arrested at once, and charged with corruption. A month later, he was also charged with the murder of Murtaza Bhutto. Evidence of extraordinary corruption by Zardari emerged over the next year, closely implicating the prime minister. Among other things, prosecutors discovered that they had secretly bought a huge estate in Surrey. They claimed that the Bhuttos had accepted at least $1.6 billion in bribes in her three years in office.

Elections were held in February 1997, and Sharif's Muslim League won a sweeping majority. Even Sind, Bhutto's home province, deserted her. Sharif formed the new government and, as he had in 1990 and as did Bhutto in 1993, he set about using every power he possessed to strengthen himself and to destroy the opposition. He won a major victory at the end of the year when he dismissed the chief justice, who had been pursuing a corruption case against him, and forced President Leghari to resign. However, the ultimate arbiter of Pakistani politics is the army, which was behind each of the three previous changes of government, and Sharif has yet to extend his authority there.

## BALUCHISTAN

Baluchistan is the largest of Pakistan's provinces, but the least populous, being largely mountain and desert. There are about 6 million Baluchis: the 4 million in Pakistan occupy the territory west of the lower Indus valley; the remainder occupy a considerable part of southern Afghanistan and south-east Iran. They have long agitated for a separate state: their division between three nations, all of whom mistrust and oppress them, is a historical accident, another consequence of thoughtless imperial expansionism by the British in the 19th century.

In 1973, the endemic tribal fighting and resistance to government control developed into a full-scale insurrection. At the height of the fighting, there were 55,000 tribesmen in the guerrilla armies. Bhutto sent 70,000 troops to suppress them. The shah of Iran, concerned that the fighting might spread among Iranian Baluchis, sent 25 Huey Cobra gunships and their crews; they devastated Baluchi villages as they had the villages of Vietnam, and as the Soviets, later, were to devastate Afghanistan. The Pakistani air force bombed villages and suspected guerrilla positions, while Afghanistan threatened full-scale war in defence of the tribesmen. It was an empty threat: Afghanistan was preoccupied with its own increasing internal problems.

By the end of 1974, the rebels had been driven back into their mountain fastnesses, where they remain. In 1976, two army divisions were sent against them, and there have been frequent punitive expeditions into the mountains since then. One estimate of casualties puts both Baluchi and Pakistani dead at 3000.

## PUSHTUNISTAN

Resistance in the North-west Frontier Province has not been as serious as in Baluchistan, but the potential dangers are far greater. The Pushtuns, or Pathans, are far more numerous – II million compared to 4 million Pakistani Baluchis. They are more adept at modern warfare, and the war in Afghanistan has demonstrated the effectiveness of guerrilla fighting in those remote and difficult mountains; it has also put enormous quantities of arms at their disposal. The Pushtuns are divided between Pakistan and Afghanistan, and for many years the governments in Kabul regularly demanded that Pakistan cede Pushtunistan to them. The civil war in Afghanistan (*see* p. 123) drove 3.5 million refugees into Pakistan, most of them Pushtuns.

In the mid-1980s, the government in Islamabad tried to assert its control over the frontier districts, because the large increase in the opium trade there was causing serious problems with the United States. In March 1986, the government sent a small army, reportedly eight battalions strong, to control a tribal leader near the Khyber Pass. It was to no avail. The opium trade continued to flourish, and smuggling across the Khyber Pass reached astonishing levels: goods from Eastern Europe and the Soviet Union – from refrigerators to caviar – were freely available in frontier villages, as were all sorts of guns. The whole operation was financed by American money brought in by the Mujaheddin, by international relief agencies working with the refugees, and by the immense profits of the opium trade. Zia, who wished to establish a purified Islamic republic of Pakistan, instead presided over an irresistible flood of corruption.

## FURTHER READING

American University, *Pakistan: A Country Study*, Washington D.C., 1984.

Baxter, Craig, *Zia's Pakistan: Politics and Stability in a Frontline State*, Boulder, Colo., Westview Press, 1987.

Blood, Peter (editor), *Pakistan: A Country Study*, Washington Government Printing Office, 1995.

Choudhury, Golam Wahed, *The Last Days of United Pakistan*, Bloomington, Indiana University Press, 1974.

Hayes, Louis D., *Politics in Pakistan: The Struggle for Legitimacy*, Boulder, Colo., Westview Press, 1984.

Minority Rights Group, *The Baluchis and Pathans*, London, 1987.

# PHILIPPINES

| | |
|---|---|
| Geography | An archipelago stretching 1000 miles (1600 km) from north to south including over 7000 islands which, between them, occupy about 115,000 sq. miles (300,000 sq. km), about the size of Italy. |
| Population | 68.6 million. There are eight major languages; English, Tagalog (renamed Pilipino to make it more 'national') and Spanish are the official ones. Tagalog is the mother-tongue of 30% and is spoken by 55%. The population is 85% Roman Catholic, 5% Protestant, 5% Muslim; the rest are animists. |
| GNP per capita | $1050 (1995). |
| Refugees | 19,600 from Vietnam. |
| Casualties | The Moro revolt in the south has killed 50,000 people since the early 1970s. The Communist insurrection in Luzon has killed 40,000 since 1969. |

President Ferdinand Marcos was driven from power on 26 February 1986, after 20 years in office. He was succeeded by Corazon Aquino, widow of Benigno Aquino, who was murdered in 1983. President Aquino had to grapple with intractable economic problems. There was also a long-running Muslim insurgency in Mindanao, the main southern island in the Philippines; a Communist revolt centred on the northern island, Luzon; and the continuing danger of an army *coup d'état*. There were several unsuccessful coups after 1986, and the Communist New People's Army increased its strength. Aquino and her supporters, who defied tanks and machine-guns in the name of freedom, made the depressing discovery that Marcos was not the problem, he was a symptom.

Aquino weathered all the storms, and was succeeded after elections in 1992 by the minister of defence, Fidel Ramos. He continued her sound economic policies, negotiated a peace agreement with the Muslim rebels and presided over the most peaceful and prosperous era the country had known in 30 years.

## HISTORY

The Philippines had no national history before the coming of the Spaniards in 1521. This was not Java or Vietnam, where organized states flourished a millennium before European colonization, and whose people today can look back on the colonial period as an episode, an interruption, in a long history. The Philippines have nothing to look back to before Ferdinand Magellan landed in

Cebu, an island in the centre of the archipelago, and a strong element in the modern history of the country is of a nation in search of its own identity.

For 380 years, the Philippines were the remotest part of the Spanish empire. Manila was a trading station where silver from Potosi in South America was exchanged for silk from China. Twice a year, the Acapulco galleon crossed the Pacific bearing treasure in each direction. The Philippines were governed from Mexico until 1821, and during those uneventful centuries, the only episode out of the ordinary was a brief British occupation of Manila in 1762–6, during the Seven Years' War. The Spanish government in Manila had little effect on the rest of the islands: only 5 per cent of the population now speak Spanish. Spain's most lasting contribution was religious: 90 per cent were converted to Catholicism.

By the end of the 19th century, Spain was losing its grip on the remnants of its empire. Cuba was in revolt, and a nationalist uprising started in the Philippines. The Spanish authorities tried to crush it by executing the country's leading intellectual, José Rizal, and buying off the rebels' military leader, Emilio Aguinaldo, but it was clear that Spanish rule was coming to an end.

On 15 February 1898, an American battleship, the U S S *Maine*, blew up in Havana harbour. The United States used the episode (probably an accident) as a *casus belli* and declared war on Spain. In May, Admiral Dewey destroyed a Spanish squadron in the Philippines; on 1 July, Teddy Roosevelt stormed up San Juan Hill in Cuba; Santiago in Cuba surrendered on 17 July; and on 4 August, American troops were landed at Manila. A peace treaty was signed in Paris on 10 December. Cuba became independent under American protection, and Spain ceded Puerto Rico, the Philippines and Guam to the U S. Thus the great enterprise begun by Ferdinand and Isabella in 1492 came to an end, and the United States acquired its first overseas colonies.

It was a flagrant case of imperialist aggression, just the sort of thing the Europeans had been doing for hundreds of years. It was not, however, America's first colonial war: 50 years earlier the United States had summarily annexed a large part of Mexico.

The Military governor of Manila was General Arthur MacArthur, a hero of the Civil War and father of Douglas MacArthur. The son's career offers a striking illustration of the acceleration of modern history. He was born on the western frontier, where his father was protecting settlers against Indians, and, as a child, lived in forts that were periodically attacked by Indians with bows and arrows. He lived to command American forces in the Pacific when the first atomic bombs were dropped on Japan.

The Filipinos fought the new occupation. It took Arthur MacArthur two years and 150,000 troops to suppress the insurrection. Aguinaldo vanished from history (though he lived to see the Japanese occupation and Philippine independence), and his deputy Manuel Quezon became the dominant political figure in the country.

President McKinley had proclaimed: 'We will educate the Philippines and uplift and Christianize them, and by God's grace do the very best we can for them.' The Americans devoted themselves to teaching the Filipinos English and developing a modern state on American lines, with executive and legislature, stock market and baseball, universal education and freedom of religion. There **237** was a running debate between Wilsonian Democrats and Taftian Republicans over the date the Philippines should become independent. Taft, who was President of the US Philippine Commission (the civilian administration) in the early years, referred to the Filipinos as 'our little brown brothers', and believed that they should be guided by American wisdom for an indefinite period.

The Philippine élite – the *ilustrados* – assimilated easily to the American system. Their privileges and land-holdings were preserved and they prospered under American direction. The debate on independence was resolved by the administration of President Franklin Roosevelt, which created a Philippine Commonwealth (in effect, self-government under American supervision) to be followed by independence in ten years. The Commonwealth of the Philippines was set up in 1935 and Quezon was elected President. He hired retired US General Douglas MacArthur to form and command a Philippine army.

The Japanese attacked the Philippines on 7 December 1941, ten hours after Pearl Harbor. MacArthur, by now commander of all American forces in the Far East as well as the Philippine army, declared Manila an open city and withdrew to the fortifications of the Bataan peninsula and Corregidor island in the bay. The Japanese occupied Manila on 2 January 1942, and the siege of the fortresses continued for five months before they finally surrendered. By then President Quezon had left the country, and MacArthur had been ordered to Australia. He promised to return.

The élite, who had got on so well with the Americans, found they could live equally well with the Japanese, and collaborated openly. The Japanese set up a quisling government, with José Laurel as president. He was a member of a prominent *ilustrado* family, and his son became Aquino's vice president.

The mass of the Filipinos detested the Japanese and fought them. The split between the élite and the peasantry, which remains the country's most serious social problem, was greatly exacerbated by this division: it seemed to most Filipinos that the governing classes were traitors to the nation. There was a full-scale guerrilla war against the Japanese, the only one in South-East Asia. In the Philippines, the Japanese could not present themselves as liberators, as they did in Indonesia, Malaya, Indochina and Burma. They were invaders.

The Philippines lost 1 million people killed during the war, most of them civilians. The fighting continued to the very end. A total of 260,000 men fought in guerrilla units, among them Ferdinand Marcos. The most effective guerrilla group was the People's Anti-Japanese Army, or Hukbalahap (known as the Huks), in central Luzon. They were led by Luis Taruc, a Communist, and, by the end of the war, controlled most of the island. They imposed land reform and set up soviets in the countryside, while fighting off the Japanese.

MacArthur landed at Leyte, an island in the centre of the archipelago, on 20 October 1944, and fought his way back to Manila by late January 1945. The Japanese navy put up a last-ditch defence in Manila and destroyed most of the city; it was as badly damaged as Berlin, Warsaw or Budapest. The Japanese murdered 100,000 Filipino civilians, deliberately slaughtering and mutilating children as well as adults. The entire business district and 80 per cent of the southern residential district, together with 75 per cent of the factories, were destroyed. In 1945, per capita production was probably lower than it had been in 1899, and the G N P was 39 per cent of the 1937 level – when the Philippines were still suffering from the Depression.

## THE INDEPENDENT PHILIPPINES

The Philippines became independent on 4 July 1946. It was a new sort of independence, one that later became known as 'neo-colonialism'. The United States continued to control the Philippines' economy as completely as it controlled the banana republics of Central America. A Parity Act, passed by the U S Congress before it approved the Philippines' independence, provided that U S companies would enjoy equal rights with local firms to develop the country. The American bases were leased for 99 years, and the United States controlled the exchange rate of the peso. Congress offered compensation for war damage, but only on condition that the Philippines accept the base agreement and the Parity Act.

The Filipinos, of course, resented these limitations on their sovereignty, which have been progressively eliminated since. They also resented that Japan and Germany, former enemies, received far more generous reconstruction aid than the Philippines, which had fought loyally on the United States' side. Furthermore, the question of the collaborators deeply divided Filipino society. MacArthur arbitrarily declared that Manuel Roxas, an old friend who had been vice president under the Japanese quisling government, was innocent of all wrongdoing. In the 1946 election, Roxas defeated President Sergio Osmena, who had succeeded Quezon when he died in 1944, and who had spent the war in Washington. In 1948, Roxas pardoned all collaborators (only one had ever been indicted).

In 1947, the Huks rose in revolt. It was partly a typical peasant uprising, partly a Communist rebellion. It was suppressed by the minister of defence, Ramon Magsaysay, who captured the Huk leaders in 1950 and dispersed their troops. A small remnant, reduced to banditry, survived in the hills of Luzon. Many former Huks were resettled in Mindanao, which solved their problems while enraging the Muslims who lived there and who feared being overwhelmed by Christians from the north.

The pre-war oligarchy reasserted its complete control of the country. Government operated under the patronage system, a sort of institutionalized corruption. The oligarchs prospered, but the rapidly increasing population, millions of whom moved into Manila, sank into abject poverty. Social tensions were much increased by the huge numbers of weapons left over from the war, and Manila became one of the most crime-ridden cities in the world.

Marcos was elected president in 1965. He presented himself as a war hero, who would clear out the corruption of the previous administration. However, his own administration was undistinguished until 1969, election year, when he contrived to be the first Filipino president to win re-election. He managed this by pouring money into the provinces and bribing officials. Political violence increased steadily during Marcos's two official terms. In January 1970, there were student riots in Manila, suppressed with considerable violence. The conflict between police and students proved to be one of the catalysts that helped start the **239**

Communist rebellion (*see* N P A *below*). In October 1970, grenades were thrown at an opposition, Liberal party rally, killing ten people, and in November 1971, over 200 people were killed in an election campaign.

On 22 September 1972, a bomb was thrown (or, according to other accounts, shots were fired) at the limousine of the defence secretary, Juan Ponce Enrile, and Marcos used this as a pretext to proclaim martial law. The minister was not in the car at the time, and years later, he confirmed what many had immediately suspected – that the attempt was a fake, designed by Marcos to eliminate democratic government. (It is also widely suspected that some of the other bombings were also his work.) The decree proclaiming martial law – known as Proclamation 1081 – had already been signed, on 17 September.

Marcos suspended Congress, *habeus corpus* and the freedom of the press. He arrested opposition leaders (including Senator Benigno Aquino), suspended all opposition newspapers and private broadcasting stations and, in a few days, had imposed a full-scale dictatorship, describing his new regime as 'constitutional authoritarianism'. He also suspended the constitution, one of whose provisions limited a president to two four-year terms.

Many Filipinos welcomed the coup. They were tired of political violence, and Marcos persuaded them that he could deliver prosperity and a quiet life. He deceived them. Marcos's 14-year dictatorship was a disaster for the Philippines. The democracy bequeathed by the United States had not proved strong enough to prevent the coup, and because the U S supported Marcos, almost to the end, its popularity in the Philippines was severely affected. In June 1981, Marcos staged an election and rigged the results to his advantage. The U S vice-president, George Bush, representing the United States at Marcos's inauguration, said: 'We love your adherence to democratic principle – and to the democratic processes.' It was an unfortunate remark.

Corruption reached astonishing levels. Following the example of Marcos and his profligate wife, Imelda, everyone stole. Imelda was governor of Greater Manila, and her signature was needed on all major government contracts; she took a regular percentage. Government corporations ran up vast debts with American banks so that their officers might award themselves lavish kickbacks. When Marcos finally escaped after the revolution, he left the country with an enormous burden of debt that it has little hope of repaying. The government also alleges he stole several billion dollars, and stashed them away in New York (where he owned a number of expensive buildings), and in banks in Switzerland and in the Caribbean.

The leading opponent to Marcos before the coup was Senator Benigno Aquino, who evidently intended to run for president when Marcos's term expired. He was arrested during the coup, tortured, put on trial and sentenced to death. The sentence was commuted, and in 1980, under pressure from the Carter administration, Marcos allowed him to go into exile. In the summer of 1983, he decided to return home and challenge Marcos directly. His family and friends tried to dissuade him, but he persisted. On 27 August, he flew into Manila airport, on a China Airlines flight from Tokyo. He was accompanied by several friends and reporters, one of whom filmed the events inside the aircraft and tantalizing glimpses through a window afterwards.

The moment the aircraft reached the terminal, security men entered it and arrested Aquino. He was hustled out of the door and down a flight of steps leading directly on to the tarmac. There were shots, and Aquino was killed. The police claimed that the assailant had been a Communist gunman, Rolando Galman, who was himself immediately shot by the police. Nobody believed this preposterous story, and in due course, witnesses, including some of the security guards, recounted that Aquino had been shot in the back of the head as he had gone down the stairs on to the tarmac. Galman had then been thrown out of a police van, whether dead or alive hardly matters: his body had been immediately shot up by the police, to provide the cover story. The murder had been ordered by General Fabian Ver, the chief of staff, Marcos's most loyal henchman. The only question worth asking was whether Marcos had ordered the murder or simply acquiesced.

The event galvanized the Filipinos. Hundreds of thousands of people, who had perhaps grumbled at the regime but had never moved into opposition, now took to the streets. Aquino's funeral was the occasion for the largest demonstrations in Philippine history: millions of people – from every level of Philippine society, bankers to peasants – marched in protest.

The American government was appalled and the Catholic Church, which had so far refrained from overt, institutionalized opposition, now demanded that Marcos must go. Jaime, Cardinal Sin, primate of the church, gave the lead.

Marcos was sick, suffering a kidney disease, but put up a prolonged rearguard action. The writer William Chapman thinks that he might have survived if he had not suddenly decided to call a presidential election for 7 February 1986 to reaffirm his position. It was a disastrous mistake. To general astonishment, the opposition formed a united front at the last moment, presenting Corazon Aquino as candidate for president and Salvador Laurel for vice-president, a ticket that had been put together by Cardinal Sin. American Senator Richard Lugar, then chairman of the Senate Foreign Relations Committee, who led a team to act as observers during the election, commented, 'A very disturbing pattern of incidents is emerging. The vote count is being shaped to what President Marcos needs.' Marcos claimed to win the election, by 13 million to 11 million votes, but the fraud was blatant. In one province, an over-zealous supporter obtained a vote of 100 per cent for Marcos, nothing for Aquino.

After the election, Mrs Aquino announced that she had won, and had herself inaugurated. Seeing the way the wind was blowing (it was a gale by then), the defence secretary, Enrile, and the acting chief of staff, General Fidel Ramos, defected to Aquino, and their supporters seized control of military headquarters. When Marcos ordered the nearest military units to suppress the mutiny, and armoured cars and tanks rolled into the city, hundreds of thousands of unarmed civilians blocked their route.

President Reagan sent a special emissary, Philip Habib, to persuade Marcos to leave. The desperate Filipino president called Senator Paul Laxalt, an old friend who was also close to President Reagan. Laxalt, who was at the White House when Marcos rang, told him – 'on a purely personal basis' – that he should leave. Clearly, the Americans had abandoned him.

The regime collapsed like a house of cards. Marcos tried broadcasting to the **241** nation and had himself inaugurated inside his palace, but the army and the police deserted him. On 25 February, the U S military command at Clark air base sent a small fleet of helicopters to take him, his wife Imelda, General Ver and their closest friends to safety. They spent the night at Clark, and were then flown to Hawaii, where U S customs officials confiscated the several million dollars worth of gold, currency and jewellery that they had brought with them. Imelda had left her shoes behind, and the first thing she did on the military base where they were first lodged in Hawaii, was to go shopping.

The Marcoses were not left in peace. Federal and state prosecutors, not to mention the Philippine government and authorities in Switzerland and other countries where Marcos had hidden his fortune, all set to work investigating his crimes. The research was particularly active in New York, where he had bought a series of buildings, worth hundreds of millions of dollars, and allegedly concealed his continuing ownership by transferring them to the Saudi financier Adnan Kashoggi. Ferdinand and Imelda Marcos were both indicted in New York for these alleged offences, and in November 1988, Imelda Marcos went there to be formally charged. Marcos was too sick to travel: he died on 28 September 1989. Mrs Marcos was acquitted, and late in 1991, President Aquino agreed that she might return to the Philippines, but refused to allow her to bring her husband's remains for burial. Mrs Marcos was allowed to recover her personal property in Manila, including her shoes.

## THE MOROS

The Muslims in the Philippines were known to the Spanish as the Moros, a tribute to the centuries of battles between Spaniards and Moors. They are racially and linguistically indistinguishable from Filipino Christians, but their culture and history are different. The Moros are concentrated in the southern islands, Mindanao and the Sulu archipelago. They never accepted Spanish rule, and the Spaniards were never powerful enough to impose it. Indeed, until the British established protectorates in north Borneo in the mid-19th century (*see* Malaysia, p. 224), there were no clear frontiers in the islands between the territories claimed by the Dutch, British and Spaniards. As late as the 1960s, the Philippines laid claim to British North Borneo, now Sabah, and joined Indonesia in opposing that territory's incorporation into Malaysia.

During the American period, Mindanao and Sulu were brought firmly under Manila's control. The Americans encouraged landless peasants from Luzon to settle in the sparsely populated southern islands, a policy that the independent Philippines has followed, and there are now more Christians than Muslims on Mindanao. This is the Moros' chief grievance: they fear being swamped in a Christian flood. In 1968, a group of Moros formed the Moro National Liberation Front (M N L F). They were inspired by Muslim nationalism in Indonesia and Malaysia and, starting in the 1970s, looked to Arab states from Libya to Saudi Arabia for moral and financial support.

After declaring martial law, Marcos tried to suppress Muslim agitation by disarming the Moros. The M N L F thereupon rose in revolt. By 1974, it had put between 50,000 and 60,000 guerrillas into the field (according to government estimates), and arms from Libya were pouring in to them through Malaysia.

Furthermore, the Arabs constantly threatened the Philippines with an oil embargo.

At its height, in 1977, the guerrilla war in Mindanao occupied two-thirds of the army's combat units. Marcos was able to restore a semblance of central control to Moro areas, but was quite unable to suppress the rebellion. He granted a degree of autonomy to the Moros in 1977, after the 'Tripoli Agreement' was signed between M N L F and government representatives, and many of the original leaders of the M N L F emerged from the jungle and took up positions of authority. However, a hardline faction, led from exile by Nur Misauri, continued to demand full independence for Mindanao, Sulu, Basilan and Palawan, perhaps one-third of the national territory.

After the 1986 revolution, President Aquino arranged a truce with the M N L F and persuaded Nur Misuari to return. The new constitution promulgated in 1987 provided for regional autonomy for the Moro provinces. On 19 November, 1989, a referendum in the districts approved the plan.

The Moro resistance has now split into three groups: the original M N L F, based in the Sulu islands, and the Moro Islamic Liberation Front (M I L F) on Mindanao, each of which claim about 20,000 members; and the Moro National Liberation Front Reformed. The government has mounted a major economic development project in Mindanao and, by offering jobs and political power to M N L F leaders, has engineered or exacerbated the splits in the movement. In January 1988, a dispute between the M N L F and the M I L F led to a shoot-out that left at least 20 people dead and drove 7000 civilians from their homes.

Episodic peace talks between Aquino and then Ramos and the M N L F dragged on for years. They were frequently interrupted by violence. A new Moro group calling itself Abu Sayyaf appeared, led by Abdurajak Janjalani, who was supported by Arab fundamentalists. It was the most intransigent and violent. Its chief support was on the island of Basilan, a relatively small island just off Mindanao. In June 1994, it kidnapped a group of civilians, killed 15 Christian men and carried seven others into the hills. They were released later. The group mounted a full-scale attack on Ipil, on the Mindanao mainland, in April 1995, killing over 100 people. Then the government, while continuing peace talks with the M N L F, mounted a full-scale assault on Basilan, claiming victory in November. A peace agreement was finally signed by President Ramos and Nur Misuari on 19 August 1996. The two extremist groups continued the fight: the Bishop of Jolo, a mainly Muslim island off Mindanao, was shot by terrorists in February 1997, in an apparent effort to ruin the peace. The government continued talks with the Moro Islamic Liberation Front, but the Abu Sayyaf group, though much reduced, promised to continue fighting. Estimates of casualties during the long rebellion ranged from 50,000 to 120,000.

## THE NEW PEOPLE'S ARMY (NPA)

The Communist Party of the Philippines Marxist–Leninist (Mao Tse-tung Thought) was founded on 26 December 1968, by a group of 11 student radicals who despaired of the official, pro-Soviet Communist party. They were inspired by radical student movements in Europe and the United States and by the Cultural Revolution in China, and intended to form a guerrilla army in the 

**243**

countryside which would eventually 'surround' the towns, following the Maoist guerrilla formula, and seize power. In March 1969, they formed the New People's Army with an arsenal of 20 rifles and a few handguns.

This derisory group subsequently became a formidable military and political force. Its strength was based on an alliance of agrarian discontent and nationalism, defined and led by Marxist theory. The party is the guiding force behind the National Democratic Front, set up in 1973, which seeks to unite all leftist opponents of the regime. Its original leader and theoretician was José Ma Sison, who wrote under the *nom de plume* Amando Guerrero. He was arrested in 1977, but the revolution continued without him. Sison and his friends developed their political theories during the 1960s. The Marcos regime was becoming steadily more oppressive, and radical students were influenced by the Vietnam war and the overwhelming American presence in the Philippines. They began demonstrating against the American bases in 1965, and were sufficiently troublesome to serve as one of the pretexts for Marcos to proclaim martial law in 1972.

Sison and his comrades studied Mao's Little Red Book and sallied forth into the countryside to convert the peasantry. In the beginning, they had no success. Sison recruited a last survivor of the Huk revolt, Commander Dante, whom he made military commander of the N P A. Its first operations were a fiasco. Small N P A bands were harried constantly by the police and failed to establish bases as they had hoped; the police captured their entire archives, and published them. The N P A finally retreated into distant corners of Luzon, where they were left alone. Dante was captured at the same time as Sison, but by then, the N P A had produced its own leaders to carry on the fight.

One of the N P A's first successes was its protection of Kalinga tribesmen in the Cordillera mountains of northern Luzon. In 1974, the government proposed to build four dams and a huge hydroelectric plant on the Chico river, flooding a major valley and driving thousands of peasants from their homes. The N P A followed a policy of selected assassination of officials and engineers, and the plan was soon abandoned.

Sison wrote a pamphlet analysing the mistakes of the Huks: *Rectify Errors and Rebuild the Party*. He contended that the first mistake of the guerrillas in the 1940s had been to follow a 'putschist' policy: they had tried to raise an army and march on Manila – and were defeated. The second mistake had been their failure to recognize the political nature of guerrilla warfare: the guerrillas had to win the support of the peasantry before any military action could begin. Third, Sison condemned the Huks for concentrating all their efforts on Luzon, instead of spreading them throughout the country.

This document provided a handbook for the N P A, and the guerrillas prepared for a long war. They devoted themselves to winning the confidence of workers on sugar plantations, landless peasants and small farmers, before attempting any military action. They sent cadres to every corner of the country, so that the Philippine army would have to be spread thinly, everywhere, to pursue them.

Throughout the 1970s, Marcos proclaimed frequent and dramatic victories against the N P A. Filipinos and Americans came to discount these claims, which were clearly completely imaginary, and to assume, therefore, that the N P A was no real threat. The N P A, meanwhile, followed Sison's instructions and steadily spread its influence: by the mid-1980s, it had 20,000 guerrillas, 12,000 modern weapons, the party had 30,000 members and a mass base of 1 million people. This base was the water in which the Communist fish could swim undetected. The N P A was operating in 60 of the Philippines' 73 provinces, and claimed some influence in 25 per cent of the 'barangays', the kinship groups of 100 or so families that make up the foundations of Philippine society. Furthermore, the N P A had established itself as a major force in the slums (barrios) of several cities, including Davao in south-east Mindanao and Bacolod on the island of Negros in the centre of the archipelago.

The N P A developed rather like the Mafia in classical Sicily, as an alternative police force and government. The Philippine army and police were corrupt, inefficient and oppressive. The police never patrolled the barrios or the remote villages, and the N P A offered its services to discipline unjust landlords, petty crooks and unfaithful husbands. A policy of selective assassination proved highly popular, and the party claimed that peasants willingly paid a small levy – part political contribution, part protection money.

In fighting the N P A, the Marcos regime, according to a 1988 report by Amnesty International, resorted to 'widespread and systematic torture by the security forces'. It states: 'By the time he departed, a pattern of gross and systematic violations of human rights had been well established.' Under martial law (1972–81), the main violations were arbitrary arrest, illegal detention and torture, but after it was lifted by Marcos, the number of 'disappearances' – murders by security forces – increased dramatically. Amnesty reports: 'Victims included politicians, lawyers, priests, church workers, journalists and students, all suspected of engaging in or supporting subversive activities.'

The killings were often carried out by vigilante groups operating with government approval. Many of them were set up by local landlords or religious cults, and had names such as 'Lord of the Sacred Heart' (known also as 'Chop-chop' from its practice of mutilating victims with machetes), 'Rock Christ', 'The Red Ones' and 'The Four Ks' (from the Filipino words for 'Sin, Salvation, Life and Property').

The overthrow of the Marcos regime in 1986 was a mixed blessing for the N P A. It might have corresponded to the overthrow of the Diem government in South Vietnam in 1963, which was followed by a protracted series of *coups d'état* and a great increase in Communist influence. However, the new president, Corazon Aquino, was hugely popular, and although many of her supporters were disappointed at her performance and the fact that she did not succeed in solving the country's problems, she remained a legitimate and popular leader, not at all like the ephemeral and corrupt generals who governed Vietnam after Diem.

Furthermore, the Communists made a major tactical error during the revolution. They turned down pressing offers by moderates and leftists for a common front, and were left on the sidelines and therefore could not claim any part of the glory of defeating Marcos. On the contrary, the Aquino government was able to argue that it genuinely represented the people, unlike Marcos, and that the Communists were fighting against democracy.

On 27 February 1986, immediately after taking power, President Aquino ordered the release of all political prisoners, including Sison and other N P A leaders. The government ratified the U N convention against torture, repealed Marcos's decrees permitting the detention of political prisoners and restored *habeus corpus*. It then entered into negotiations with the N P A, and a 60-day ceasefire was declared on 10 December 1986.

The Communists revelled in their freedom to give interviews on television and invite journalists to their 'liberated areas'. However, after troops opened fire on a peasant demonstration in Manila on 22 January 1987, killing 12 people, the N P A broke off the talks. The ceasefire lapsed and heavy fighting resumed. In the next two months, over 400 people were killed.

The war did not go well for the N P A. There was something of a public backlash against Communist terrorism. An attempt to start urban warfare in Manila was defeated: the N P A sent 1200 armed men into the city and over 100 police and officials were murdered. The public was outraged. The Manila N P A brigade announced in December 1987, that no more police would be killed and that targets would be chosen more 'selectively'.

Left-wing parties, notably the Partido ng Bayan founded by Sison, did badly in congressional elections in May 1987 and in local elections the following January. Over 100 people were killed in politically inspired violence during the latter elections. A further difficulty for the N P A was the discovery in Mindanao of mass graves containing hundreds of bodies – people executed by the N P A for suspected 'treason'.

A local militia – the Alsa Masa ('Masses Arise') – attacked N P A positions in their stronghold in Agdao, a slum district of Davao, and drove them out. The government armed local vigilante groups to defend their villages against the N P A, and many of the crimes attributed to the Marcos vigilante groups were soon being committed by the Aquino vigilantes.

Amnesty International found that human rights abuses increased markedly in 1987 and 1988, and the Aquino government was beginning to resemble the Marcos regime in this respect. In 1986, Amnesty found:

strong evidence that the Aquino government's commitment to the protection of human rights and the establishment of legal safeguards had led to major improvements . . . But by the time of Amnesty International's third mission in July 1987, there had been a sharp escalation in political violence, and the government appeared increasingly unwilling or unable to persuade its security forces to respect the safeguards it had promoted so vigorously a year earlier, particularly when members of the military and police were targets of the N P A assassination squads.

The army reverted to its Marcos-era custom of revenge killings. Amnesty reported a number of specific cases:

- In February 1987, 17 villagers, including six children, were massacred by troops after an N P A attack on a military patrol killed a lieutenant.
- In April, after an N P A attack on a military barracks in which 17 soldiers were killed, military patrols killed at least 13 villagers nearby.
- In the same month, a 25-year-old farmer picked up by the army was found strangled with his own shirt: 'His hands were tied, an eye had been gouged out,

his fingernails pulled out and there were stab wounds in his chest and one armpit.'

The army contended that the Aquino government was 'soft on Communism', and that its own hands were tied behind its back by the government's attempts to protect human rights. In fact, however, not a single military man had been convicted of a human rights abuse since Aquino took power. Rather, the number of 'disappearances' increased sharply in 1988 as military intelligence arrested suspects without warrants and without ever admitting what it was doing. A group called Find, set up under the Marcos dictatorship and devoted to attempting to trace missing people, remained busy. In the 21 months after Aquino became president, Find listed hundreds of 'disappearances', of which 212 remained unexplained at the end of the period. One leader commented: 'Many of them, we assume, they were "salvaged" already' – 'salvaged' being current Filipino euphemism for 'killed'.

In March 1988, police arrested five Communist leaders in Manila, including Romulo Kintanar, commander of the NPA, and Rafael Baylosis, the party's general secretary. A great many incriminating documents, including minutes of politburo meetings, were found – stored on computer disks, for this is a modern insurgency. They showed that the party was seriously divided on which tactics to follow. The arrests were described by police as a body blow to the NPA: Kintanar was believed to be the organizer of the 'Sparrow squads', responsible for the wave of assassinations in Manila. However, on 12 November, Kintanar escaped. He and the other terrorist leaders had been held in a military camp – and had all been invited to a party. Kintanar and his wife were picked up by accomplices and simply driven out of the base to freedom.

The NPA continued its depredations and exactions, but the end of the cold war and the collapse of Communism in Europe had their effect, even in the barrios and plantations of Luzon. There was a steady decline in guerrilla activity in the 1990s and the police scored a number of notable victories. Most important, the recovery in the economy gave people hope that prosperity might come through work and honest government, rather than through revolutionary action. The times were against the NPA, at least for the moment.

## THE AQUINO GOVERNMENT

The government finally enacted its long-promised land reform in June 1988, but it was immediately criticized as insufficient by leftists and moderates. There were many loopholes in its proposals to break up the big estates, including a provision that the law need not apply to some corporations. This clause apparently would exclude President Aquino's own family sugar estate, the Hacienda Luisita. The fundamental problem, in the Philippines as in Central America, is that the growing population has long since outrun the land available. Even if all the land were redistributed, there would still be hundreds of thousands of landless families, and the distributed plots would be too small to support those who obtained them.

In the short term, the greatest danger to the Aquino government came from **247** the army. There were many attempted coups, the two most violent in August 1987 and in December 1989.

There were two attempted coups in 1986, and three in 1987, of which the third, on 28 August 1987, was led by Colonel Gregorio 'Gringo' Honassan. The rebel troops attacked the presidential palace and the government's Channel 4 television station, and were repulsed; they then seized several private television stations and Camp Aguinaldo. The police chief in Cebu City, the country's second largest city, joined the rebellion and arrested the local military leaders. General Ramos brought in loyal troops who attacked Camp Aguinaldo with tanks, artillery and World War I I bombers. It was notable that there was more noise than real military action: neither side wanted to cause too many casualties. President Aquino's son was nearly killed: arriving at the palace, he was stopped by rebel troops who murdered his three bodyguards; the young Aquino managed to save himself by pleading for his life.

The coup collapsed at a cost of 53 lives. Honassan escaped, only to be arrested on 9 December. He was imprisoned on a naval gunboat in Manila harbour, to await trial, but on 2 April 1988, he bribed his guards and escaped with 14 of them in two rubber boats, and joined the opposition.

The sixth and most serious coup began at 1 a.m. on 1 December 1989. Without American intervention, it would probably have succeeded. Rebel troops, including the army's élite Scout Rangers, attacked the Malacanang Palace and over-ran government buildings and military bases throughout Manila, including army headquarters and the government's television station. They were beaten back from the palace, but then threatened to bomb it from Villamor and Sangley Point air bases. At that point, Aquino launched a desperate appeal for help to the Americans. President Bush was on his way to Malta for a summit meeting with President Gorbachev: a telephone conference between Manila, Washington and the president's plane was arranged, and then orders were given to the American air force in the Philippines. F-4 Phantoms from Clark Field overflew both bases, informing the rebels that any plane that took off would be shot down. Aquino had asked Bush to bomb the bases, but he limited American involvement to keeping rebel planes on the ground.

This time, the rebels conducted the battle with great sophistication. Every time government troops moved to attack, they retreated. Every time Aquino or her supporters claimed victory, the rebels attacked again. They occupied several hotels and three particularly smart apartment buildings, all in downtown Manila, targets the government could never attack with bombs and artillery. They took care to protect civilians and guests in the hotels, and their leaders gave frequent press conferences.

By contrast, the government and army's handling of the fight was incompetent and indecisive. As in all the previous coups, army and rebels took great care not to hurt each other. There was much firing, but few casualties. Eventually, after a week's inconclusive combat, the Scouts and other rebel units agreed to return to their barracks. Aquino declared that, this time, she would punish the plotters, including her own vice-president, Salvador Laurel, and the former minister of defence, Juan Ponce Enrile.

She was seriously weakened by the episode. According to the polls her popularity had already dropped to 45 per cent and her indecisive handling of the coups convinced many of her remaining supporters that she was unfit to govern the country. Her term expired in 1992 and she was succeeded by her minister of defence, Fidel Ramos, who had served Marcos long and faithfully, only jumping ship when it was clear the vessel was sinking. Ramos proved a highly successful president. The economy improved steadily during his term; he cut the bureaucracy, followed the I M F's advice on liberating foreign investment, and for the first time in a generation, the Philippines joined the rest of East Asia in economic growth.

The agreement under which the United States maintained two huge military bases in the Philippines expired in 1991. The opposition demanded that the Americans must leave, and had sufficient support in the Senate to block the proposed new treaty. In the midst of the negotiations, a volcano erupted near the Clark air base and covered it several feet deep in ash. It would have cost billions to repair, and the Pentagon decided that it could do without Clark. That removed half the dispute, but the Americans wanted to keep the naval base at Subic Bay, which had been less seriously damaged by the eruption. The U S and the Aquino government reached an agreement on extending the base treaty, and the rent that should be paid. The Senate refused to ratify it, and Aquino proposed a referendum, convinced that most Filipinos wanted to keep the American connection. At the last moment, the Senate agreed to extend the base agreement for another year. It was a temporary victory. At the end of 1991, the Aquino government and the Americans abandoned the struggle, and agreed that the U S Navy would give up Subic Bay by the end of 1992. By then, the end of the cold war had reduced the Americans' need for overseas bases, and events proved that the Philippines was better off without them. Subic Bay was given over to unrestrained capitalism, on a Hong Kong model, and soon flourished.

## FURTHER READING

American University, *Area Handbook for the Philippines*, Washington, 1984.

Amnesty International, *Philippines: Unlawful Killings by Military and Paramilitary Forces*, London, 1988.

Chapman, William, *Inside the Philippine Revolution*, New York, W. W. Norton, 1987.

Dolan Ronald E. (editor), *The Philippines: a Country Study*, Washington, Government Printing Office, 1993.

Komisar, Lucy, *Corazon Aquino: The Story of a Revolution*, New York, George Braziller, 1987.

Manchester, William, *American Caesar: Douglas MacArthur*, Boston, Little, Brown, 1978.

Steinberg, David Joel, *The Philippines: A Singular and a Plural Place*, Boulder, Colo., Westview Press, 1982.

# SRI LANKA

| | |
|---|---|
| Geography | 25,322 sq. miles (65,610 sq. km). The size of Ireland. In 1972 when the country became a republic, ending its connection with the British crown, its name was changed from Ceylon to Sri Lanka, its Sinhalese name. |
| Population | 18.1 million, of whom 74% are Sinhalese (Buddhists), 18% are Tamils (Hindus), the rest Christians and Muslims. The latter are descendants of Arab traders and mostly speak Tamil. |
| GNP per capita | $700. |
| Refugees | Internal: 900,000. External: 100,000 in India. |
| Casualties | Over 60,000 people have been killed since 1983. |

Sri Lanka was paradise. No country on Earth is more beautiful, and its citizens and all visitors alike agreed that nowhere was life more pleasant. In the misty Middle Ages, there were invasions from India and wars between Sinhalese and Tamil principalities. But that was long ago.

The Portuguese set up trading posts in the 16th century, and were replaced by the Dutch and then the British. It seemed a beneficent colonialism. The Pax Britannica ensured peace and prosperity throughout the 19th century and came peacefully to an end in 1948, shortly after the independence of India. The British established a modern system of government and the English language – but the governing classes were Sinhalese and the junior clerks and teachers were Tamil.

Nearly three-quarters of the population are Sinhalese (who are Buddhist), 18 per cent Tamil (who are Hindu). The rest are Muslims and Christians, and all lived peacefully together for 20 years after independence.

The country was resolutely democratic: governments frequently lost elections, and handed over to the parliamentary opposition. The economy was soundly based on the export of tea, timber and other tropical produce, and tourism. There seemed to be no reason why it should not develop modern industry.

Et in Arcadia ego. Sri Lanka became a case study in the dynamics of national dissolution. Sinhalese chauvinism and the demagoguery of Sinhalese politicians, the half-baked Marxism of successive governments, and nationalist and racist fantasies among unemployed and highly educated Tamil youths, led to racial tensions, riots, killings and finally full-fledged terrorism and civil war.

Sri Lanka was typical of the Third World states that the European empires created: its population consisted of ethnic groups whose only loyalty was to the group, not to the nation. It did have two advantages over most other states: its frontiers were uncontested (it is an island), and one of those ethnic groups comprised the large majority of the population.

But 20 miles (32 km) from the northern tip of Sri Lanka is India, and the southernmost state of the Indian union is Tamil Nadu whose 65 million people are Tamils like their cousins in Sri Lanka. There is a similar situation in Cyprus, where the Turkish minority, like Sri Lanka's Tamils, comprise 18 per cent of the population. Tamils in Sri Lanka could always count on the support of the state government in Madras, as the Turks in Cyprus can count on Ankara; and the Sinhalese, like the Greeks in Cyprus or the Irish, although in a majority on their island, saw themselves as the victims of a neighbour much more powerful than themselves. They considered the Tamils not as a minority to be conciliated and protected but as a threat to national survival. It was a self-inflicted injury. Treated as a danger, Tamil nationalism burst into flames and now threatens the very existence of the state.

## HISTORY

During the colonial period, the British administration discouraged missionary activity among the Sinhalese but permitted it among the Tamils, and mission schools were set up in northern Ceylon where there is a Tamil majority. A century and a half of European education produced a well-educated class of Tamils who filled most of the junior places in the government and supplied most of the professional classes – lawyers, doctors and the like. The Sinhalese owners of the great tea plantations went to universities in Britain.

After independence, the Sinhalese came to resent this Tamil predominance in the professions (the same thing happened in many other former colonies), and as Sinhalese education improved and Tamils lost their positions, Tamils came to resent their lost opportunities.

In 1956, Solomon West Ridgeway Bandaranaike was elected prime minister. He was heir to one of the grandest Sinhalese families, English educated and an unscrupulous demagogue who built his power by whipping up his compatriots' hatred of the Tamils. He made Sinhalese the national language and, when Tamils demonstrated in protest, suppressed the demonstrations brutally. He imposed quotas for Tamils in the government, professions and universities, and nationalized much of the economy. In 1956, Tamils held roughly half of government jobs; by 1980, their share had dropped to 11 per cent. Bandaranaike offered a golden, Marxist future to the country, socialized the economy, and set it on the road to bankruptcy.

He was assassinated in September 1959, and was later succeeded by his widow Sirimavo Bandaranaike, the first woman to head a democratic government anywhere in the world. She pursued her husband's policies, driving the economy into chronic depression, and encouraged discrimination against the Tamils. She made Sinhalese the sole official language, and in 1972, changed the country's name from Ceylon to Sri Lanka. Both these gestures deeply offended the Tamils, who felt themselves excluded in their own country and reduced to a second-class citizenship.

Unemployment became endemic among young Sinhalese and Tamils alike, **251** and in each community, extremists began to preach violence, blaming their social and economic problems upon the other community. Episodic inter-communal riots became increasingly frequent during the 1960s and 1970s. In 1971, a Sinhalese revolutionary organization – the Janatha Vimukthi Peramuna (People's Liberation Front) – staged an uprising, which was then bloodily repressed. By the government's count, 2000 people died; others claim that 10,000 were killed by security forces.

The J V P was founded in the late 1960s by Rohana Wijeweera (born in 1945), a medical student who had attended the Patrice Lumumba University in Moscow. The party remained underground after the 1971 coup attempt, but was legalized in 1977. Wijeweera ran for president in 1982, but after the 1983 riots in Colombo, the party was suppressed again, and Wijeweera went underground. He seized the opportunity of the conflict with the Tamils to develop an ultra-Sinhalese programme, promising death and destruction to the Tamils and also to Sinhalese who opposed him – starting with President Jayewardene himself.

## THE TIME OF TROUBLES

The government's incompetence finally provoked a crisis. Mrs Bandaranaike was defeated in an election in 1977, and replaced by another Sinhalese grandee, Junius Richard Jayewardene, then aged 70. He changed the constitution to make himself president (there is an executive prime minister, on the French model), and when he was re-elected in 1982, postponed legislative elections indefinitely. He tried to reverse his predecessor's economic policies and reduce tensions between Sinhalese and Tamils. He failed. Perhaps it was too late. Mary Anne Weaver (*see* p. 260) thinks that the essential problem was that he considered the crisis a matter of terrorism, to be dealt with by the police, not a matter of communal relations, to be settled by political means.

By then, the Tamils had called in help from Tamil Nadu. The complexities of Indian national politics led Prime Minister Indira Gandhi to permit the Madras government to help the Tamils in Sri Lanka. Tamil terrorists were trained in Tamil Nadu, arms and munitions of all sorts were smuggled across the narrow strait, and the Sri Lankan navy was quite unable to stop it.

Extremist Tamils, brought up on tales of Sinhalese oppression, began to talk of Tamil Eelam, an independent Tamil state in northern and eastern Sri Lanka. The principal town of the north is Jaffna, on a peninsula running towards India, the largest of a string of fishing villages and small towns that are the heart of the Tamil insurgency. Velupillai Prabakaran, son of a fisherman, was born in one of those villages in 1954. When he was four, he saw an uncle burned alive during the riots that followed the imposition of Sinhalese as sole national language. He is now the supreme commander of the most violent of the terrorist organizations, the Liberation Tigers of Tamil Eelam, commonly known as the Tamil Tigers.

Prabakaran sees himself as the perfect terrorist: he prides himself as a marksman and carries out many killings himself. Although his role model is clearly Fidel Castro, he is not an educated man nor is he a Marxist. His favourite recreation is said to be watching Clint Eastwood movies.

The Tigers began with robberies and murders. In 1975, Prabakaran and two comrades shot the mayor of Jaffna, a Tamil they considered a quisling. The

Tigers then began a campaign of assassination of Tamils employed by the central government.

In July 1983, Prabakaran led a commando attack on an army post in Jaffna, killing 13 Sinhalese soldiers. Sinhalese rioted in Colombo and other cities, and according to the government, 140 people, most of them Tamils, were killed. Mary Anne Weaver thinks the total was 1000, and that $300 million worth of property damage was done in Colombo alone, and 100,000 Tamils were driven from their homes. The riots were largely inspired and led by the J V P, which now re-emerged from obscurity to become almost as serious a threat to the government as the Tigers. It had at least 2000 full-time fighters.

The 1983 riots gave an immense boost to the Tigers: thousands of young Tamils fled to the jungles and started guerrilla training. In addition, Tamil members of parliament were expelled.

Violent incidents multiplied. On 14 May 1985, the Tigers attacked a Buddhist shrine at Anuradhapura. More than 150 Sinhalese were killed, and a great deal of damage done to the temple and to the sacred Bo tree, grown from a cutting taken from the tree under which the Lord Buddha found enlightenment. The Tigers then took control of Jaffna and most of the northern province, driving the Sinhalese out and isolating army and police in their barracks.

The security situation in the rest of the country deteriorated rapidly. The Sri Lankan army, which had served only ceremonial functions for nearly 40 years, was quite unable to contain the Tigers, who had been well trained by Indian officers in Tamil Nadu. The soldiers were undisciplined and incompetent, and slaughtered hundreds of Tamil civilians. Instances of torture, massacre and extralegal executions multiplied: Amnesty International has compiled a long list of Tamils who have been arrested by the security forces and have never been seen again.

It was not until a veteran of World War II, General Cyril Ranatunge, was brought out of retirement and set to work training new recruits, that effective discipline was introduced and the army began to do its job, and there were no more reports of army massacres. The army more than doubled in size, to 25,000, as did the other security forces, to 50,000. Defence spending increased by 1700 per cent, to $500 million a year.

The crisis was reached in 1987. On 17 April, Good Friday, the Tigers ambushed a convoy of buses in the centre of the country. The 128 Sinhalese passengers, all unarmed, and including many women and children, were separated from the Tamils and Muslims and then murdered. On 21 April, a bomb at the central bus terminal in Colombo killed 113. The central government resolved to recapture control of the Jaffna peninsula.

The army mounted a general offensive – Operation Liberation – on 26 May. In two weeks, the army occupied the outlying districts in the northern province, doing immense damage and killing 132 guerrillas and 300 civilians, at a cost of 62 military deaths. Before attacking, the air force bombed the province, destroying scores of villages.

Then India intervened. On 3 June 1987, Prime Minister Rajiv Gandhi authorized a fleet of fishing boats to deliver 'humanitarian' supplies to the besieged Tamils in Jaffna. The boats were turned back by the Sri Lankan navy, and the next day Gandhi ordered the Indian air force to drop the supplies by parachute. The drops amounted, officially, to only 25 tons of 'humanitarian' supplies, but their symbolic importance was enormous. If India was going to intervene, the Colombo government had no chance of victory.

Gandhi had several objects in mind. They did not include encouraging Tamil separatism: that would set the worst possible precedent for restive parts of the Indian union, such as Punjab or the north-east. He did, however, want to retain the political support of the Tamil Nadu government. (He failed: after a general mêlée in the state legislature in January 1988, Gandhi suspended the government, and in elections in January 1989, his Congress party was soundly defeated.) Gandhi also wanted to enforce Indian hegemony over its neighbour: he objected to Sri Lanka's pro-Western policies, and still more to the fact that Jayewardene had sought help from China, Pakistan, South Africa and Israel and from British mercenaries to train the armed forces. Lastly, he coveted Trincomalee harbour on Sri Lanka's east coast, one of the finest natural harbours in the world, comparable to New York, San Francisco or Sydney.

The Sri Lankan army suspended its offensive. Negotiations began between the government and the Indians, who consulted the Tamil parties, including the Tigers and their terrorist rivals (there were five terrorist groups). Jayewardene, who had offered autonomy to the Tamil northern province the previous December, now extended the offer to include the eastern province, which is disputed between Sinhalese and Tamils; Trincomalee is its principal city and prize. The two provinces would be merged and run by a Tamil-led government which would have wide powers. A referendum would be held in the eastern province by the end of 1988 to ratify this arrangement. Tamil and English would be made co-equal national languages with Sinhalese. In exchange, the Tamil terrorists would surrender their arms. India would police the ceasefire.

All the Tamils accepted the proposal except Prabakaran, who was put under house arrest in New Delhi. Militant Sinhalese, incited by the JVP, demonstrated against the agreement in Colombo on 28 July, and started a riot in which 70 people were killed. The next day, Gandhi flew to Colombo to sign the agreement. One of the Sinhalese soldiers in the guard of honour tried to attack him.

For a tense week, the Tigers refused to surrender their weapons. Finally, on 4 August, Prabakaran returned from New Delhi and ordered his troops to turn in their arms. At a mass meeting in Jaffna, he announced: 'We have no choice but to toe the line of the Indian government. If we don't, there will be an armed confrontation with the Indian army. We don't want that. India is a powerful country and we are unable to do anything to stop it.' Tons of arms were then surrendered, perhaps one-fifth of the Tigers' arsenal. (Eight months later, it emerged that the Indian government had paid the Tigers a large sum of money for their cooperation.)

There was a brief moment of hope. Despite all the killings and 'disappearances', despite the hatred between Tamils and Sinhalese and the bitterness of Tamils whose villages have been destroyed, the agreement clearly provided the basis for a permanent settlement.

**254**    Gandhi sent the first units of what became a 60,000-man army of occupation to police the northern province. But there was barely a pause in terrorism. The Tigers set about assassinating members of rival terrorist groups: within six weeks, they had killed at least 150. The Indians did nothing to intervene. Prabakaran took control of the interim council for the north and east provinces.

The JVP remained bitterly opposed to the settlement. On 18 August, two grenades were thrown into a meeting room in Parliament House and the room was sprayed with machine-gun bullets. The attack almost killed President Jayewardene; two other politicians were killed. In April 1988, police claimed that they had arrested the culprit, a cleaner who was a member of the JVP.

The ceasefire lasted less than two months. On 3 October 1987, the Sri Lankan navy intercepted a trawler off Jaffna carrying 17 Tigers, including three of Prabakaran's closest aides, one of whom was suspected of planting the bomb in the Colombo bus depot. They were smuggling a large consignment of arms from India. The authorities insisted on bringing them to Colombo. At the airbase, as they were about to enter the plane to fly south, they all simultaneously swallowed cyanide. (The Tigers carry cyanide capsules at all times, and are sworn to kill themselves rather than be captured.) Thirteen of the 17 died.

The Tigers at once repudiated the peace settlement. There was an immediate series of terrorist attacks in eastern Sri Lanka, including the murder of eight Sinhalese soldiers held by the Tigers. At least 188 people were killed, and Jaffna was once again under the control of the Tigers.

The event was a serious blow to Gandhi, who was committed to keeping the peace. He ordered his army to occupy Jaffna; they laid siege to the town and eventually took it. It was not a glorious episode. The Tigers in Jaffna held out for 17 days against the full might of the Indian army, which used its arsenal of Soviet-made rockets, helicopter gunships and artillery against them. The Indians lost at least 460 men (the official figure), but failed either to defeat or capture the Tigers – most of whom escaped with their weapons. Between 300 and 400 Tigers and as many as 1000 civilians were killed.

There were various estimates of the number of Indians killed by Tamil terrorists, and of Tamils killed by Indian soldiers. A year after their arrival, the Indian army said that they had lost 530 men, and had themselves killed about 2000. Sri Lankan officials, not necessarily any more reliable, claimed that, by the end of the year, up to 1000 Indian soldiers had been killed by Tamil fighters, and over 1000 wounded. There were 50,000–65,000 Indian troops policing the Tamil territories, but terrorism continued unabated: 25 people were killed in one incident on 27 December 1987; another ten on New Year's Eve (the Tigers entered a Sinhalese village 26 miles (42 km) south of Trincomalee, lined up the villagers against a wall, and shot them). The previous May, the Tigers had killed 23 people in the same village.

This had become part of the Tigers' strategy. They intended to clear Sinhalese villagers out of the eastern province which they claimed for their own, along with the north, and they did it by murdering the villagers. By the spring of 1988, the entire Sinhalese population of Trincomalee had fled.

The new year proved just as bloody as 1987. On 23 February, after Tigers shot four Indian soldiers in an ambush, Indian troops killed 20 Tamils. The next day, in a speech to Parliament, President Jayewardene offered a new amnesty to the

Tigers and to the J V P, who had by then murdered over 200 government officials, police and supporters of the 1987 agreements. On 2 March, Tigers disguised in army uniforms shot six adults and nine children in Colombo. Three days later, a mine exploded under a truck near Trincomalee, killing 19 people, including six women and two children, most of them Sinhalese. There were further bomb attacks on buses throughout northern and eastern Sri Lanka in March and April: in April, a bus filled with shoppers south of Trincomalee was bombed, killing 26; another bus was attacked killing six. Forty Muslims were killed in raids on their villages in the eastern province.

While the Indians fought the Tigers in the north, the Sri Lankan army fought the J V P in the south. There were more than 10,000 Sri Lankan troops pursuing the 2000 J V P terrorists.

In the previous five years, between 7000 and 16,000 people had been killed and over half a million driven from their homes – and the rate of killings was increasing rapidly. The cost to the economy was catastrophic. The tourist industry was dead. The northern and eastern provinces were battlefields, and many tea plantations in the north-central highlands had been abandoned for fear of terrorists.

On 10 May 1988, the government and the J V P signed a ceasefire., The J V P agreed to abandon terrorism and the government agreed to legalize the organization and release imprisoned members, except those accused of murder. The agreement collapsed immediately, and the J V P pursued a violent campaign to disrupt provincial elections on 2 June, bombing government buildings and attacking polling stations.

India had been sucked into the fight, and the Indian army, which had come to keep the peace, was under fire from both sides, like the British in Northern Ireland. By the summer of 1988, the Indians had imposed a semblance of order in northern and eastern Sri Lanka, by means of heavy patrols in the towns and on the main roads, but the Tigers remained active in the countryside and were evidently entirely capable of mounting further attacks whenever they wished.

In June 1988, India announced that it would withdraw between 3000 and 5000 of its troops from Sri Lanka. It was a symbolic gesture. Gandhi said that the bulk of the army would remain until after provincial elections in the north and east, and until an effective ceasefire had come into effect. There was no sign whatever that any such peace was likely.

Jayewardene offered the Tamils all the concessions that might have averted the troubles 20 years before, but the Tigers were not pacified. They had tasted blood, and there was little hope that they would abandon the fight. The 60,000 Indian troops in Sri Lanka trying to control the Tamils were faced with a hopeless task and no obvious means of escaping.

As for the J V P, its campaign continued to increase in violence throughout 1988. On 10 September, the Indian High Command announced, in Jayewardene's name, the formal decision to merge the northern and eastern provinces. It was a further demonstration of Sri Lanka's subordination to India, and provoked a further excess of J V P terrorism. Colombo was closed down for a day when the J V P put up posters denouncing the proposed merger and demanding a general

strike.

On 15 September, Jayewardene decreed that there would be a presidential election in December, and that he would not be a candidate. He was by then 82 years old, and it was time to retire. There were also to be provincial elections in the new north-eastern province in November, and in preparation for the event, the Tigers and the J V P stepped up their terrorist campaigns (it seemed entirely likely that they were now cooperating). For example, the Tigers massacred 47 people in a Sinhalese village on 10 October.

Jayewardene tried once again to persuade the J V P to suspend terrorism and participate in the presidential election. He was unsuccessful, and the J V P exerted itself, by the usual methods of murder and intimidation, to disrupt the voting. In mass J V P demonstrations in Colombo and other southern towns on 10 November, at least ten people were killed by troops. There was a series of strikes in Sinhalese districts, including hotels and other service industries, and the government ordered all remaining tourists to leave the country. By then, J V P terrorists were killing people at the rate of 25 to 50 a day. Sinhalese areas were administered by the army; schools and universities were closed; and public services such as rubbish collection and public utilities such as electricity were failing.

The provincial elections took place in November, despite the Tigers' efforts. As a sideline, some of the Tigers offered their services to an exiled politician from the Maldive islands, west of Sri Lanka, and attempted a coup there. They were frustrated by the Indians (*see* India, p. 203).

The presidential election took place on 19 December. The turn-out was about 55 per cent, far lower than was usual in Sri Lankan elections, but a creditable total considering the extreme level of violence and intimidation from both Tamil and Sinhalese terrorists. Jayewardene's United National Party candidate, the prime minister Ranasinghe Premadasa, won a narrow victory over Sirimavo Bandaranaike who was trying to make a comeback. She promptly charged him with fraud. In his last act as president, Jayewardene dissolved parliament and set new elections for February. Premadasa was sworn in on 2 January 1989.

The new president was no more successful in resolving the country's conflicts than the old one. He lifted the state of emergency, but it was an empty gesture. The J V P terror campaign continued, mixing xenophobia and Marxism in a deadly combination. The Tigers continued to fight the Indians, the government, and other Tamil parties and there was increasing tension between the Sri Lanka government and the Indians. The security forces were more successful against the J V P than against the Tigers. On 12 November 1989, the J V P leader Rohana Wijeweera was arrested in a village north of Colombo. He was promptly shot. The foreign minister, Ranjan Wijeratne, who was in command of anti-terrorist operations, gave out the improbable story that when Wijeweera was arrested, he agreed to lead police to his headquarters. When they reached it, one of his officers pulled a gun on him. Soldiers then shot both of them. On 28 December, the last surviving senior leader of the J V P was killed in similarly suspicious circumstances. This time, the police said that after he was arrested by a police patrol, a group of six J V P terrorists opened fire on the patrol from a house. They were all killed. The US State Department calculated that over 8500 people were killed in the fight against the J V P during the last six months of 1989, and admitted that the estimate was conservative. Human rights groups said that over 20,000 were killed that year, thousands of them by death squads in the south, which Amnesty International says are directly linked with the government.

The new president asked the Indians to withdraw their troops by July 29 1989, the second anniversary of their arrival. Rajiv Gandhi agreed to pull them out by the following January, and Indian military operations were progressively cut back during the year. The Tamils emerged from hiding and took over posts the Indians evacuated. The Indians had set up and armed a Tamil National Army and had supported the Eelam People's Revolutionary Liberation Front, and the Tigers now set about destroying these two organizations.

The last Indian troops left on 24 March 1990, from Trincomalee and Jaffna. At the height of the intervention, there had been 65,000 Indian troops in Sri Lanka. Indians reported that they lost 1155 men. The Tigers were now the dominant force in north-east Sri Lanka: the government made no immediate effort to send troops or police into areas evacuated by the Indians, which therefore came under the Tigers' control. Premadasa started negotiations with the Tigers, on the basis of Jayewardene's proposal for an autonomous region in the north and north-east, and for 14 months there was relative calm. The south began to recover, after the defeat of the JVP.

Then in June 1990, the Tigers suddenly launched a general offensive against the government. The government fought back, and once again mounted a full-scale attack on Jaffna. Once again, they failed. The army garrison in the 17th-century Dutch fort in Jaffna was evacuated with great difficulty, and then the fort and town were bombed into ruin by the air force. The army controlled Elephant Pass camp, which commands the only approach road to the Jaffna peninsula and the Tigers laid siege to it. The army beat off the attack, killing 2300 Tigers in the battle. The guerrilla war continued in the north and north-east. It was a permanent stalemate. The army was not strong enough to suppress the Tigers permanently, nor were the Tigers strong enough to defeat the army and drive it from their homelands. There were by then 700,000 refugees inside Sri Lanka and perhaps 100,000 more who had fled the country.

On 2 March 1991, terrorists killed Ranjan Wijeratne, the government official in charge of counter-terrorist operations, the second most important man in the government. It was he who had directed the offensive against the JVP and announced the killings of that group's leaders. A car bomb in Colombo killed him and 29 other people. A month later, on 21 May, Tamil terrorists in India killed the former Indian prime minister, Rajiv Gandhi. A woman terrorist went up to him during an election rally, and deliberately detonated a bomb strapped to her waist. She and Gandhi were killed together, with a dozen other people. Presumably the Tigers ordered the murder as revenge for the Indian war against them.

Security forces scored a considerable victory on 28 January 1993, when Sathasivam Krishnakumar, the Tigers' second in command, along with ten other senior Tigers, was drowned in a ship trying to evade capture by the Indian navy. But on 1 May, President Primadasa was assassinated during a May Day parade, when a suicide bomber rode a bicycle into the cavalcade and exploded the bomb he was carrying. The event led to the eclipse of the United National Party and the restoration of the People Alliance Party after 17 years in opposition – and the return to power of the Bandaranaike family. The principal opposition leader, Lalith Athulathmudali, of the Democratic United National Front, had been murdered on 23 April, so Chandrika Kumaratunga, daughter of Solomon and Sirimavo Bandaranaike and now leader of the PAP, stepped into his place. Her husband, an opposition politician, had himself been murdered three years earlier.

The prime minister was elected by parliament to serve out the rest of Primadasa's term. There were parliamentary elections in August 1995, and the PAP won. Mrs Kumaratunga became prime minister. She was then presented as the party's candidate for presidential elections in November. A month before the vote, on 24 October, the UNP's candidate, Gamini Dissanayake, was also murdered by a suicide bomber, just as Rajiv Gandhi had been killed in 1991. At the end of a rally, a young woman sitting in the front row detonated a 10 lb bomb she had hidden under her clothes. Over 50 people were killed, including four former cabinet ministers. The terrorist's head was found on the roof of a near-by building, blown there by the explosion.

The elections took place on schedule. The UNP, following tradition, put up Dissanayake's widow as candidate (Primadasa's widow had been excluded). She lost, but perhaps she will reappear later, like Mrs Bandaranaike or Rajiv Gandhi's widow. Kumaratunga became president – and then survived a political challenge by her mother, Mrs Bandaranaike, who became prime minister for a while, believing that she should be restored to power at last. Her daughter frustrated her (she has also excluded a younger brother, Anura, who had made the mistake of joining the UNP).

The new government immediately tried to make peace with the Tigers. A ceasefire was arranged and came into effect on 14 November. The government made major concessions in talks with the Tigers, allowing the northern and eastern provincial assemblies a great measure of autonomy. It was not enough, even supposing that the Tigers had ever negotiated sincerely. They broke the truce on 19 April with an attack on a navy base in Trincomalee, in which they sank two naval ships.

Massacres, bombings and assassinations resumed. The commercial district in Colombo was devastated by a 1000 lb truck bomb in January 1996 that killed over 90 people, and the Tigers took to putting bombs on trains. The army launched another full-scale attack on the Tamils' stronghold in Jaffna. This time, the Indians did not come to the rescue. The army captured Jaffna in December 1995, and Point Pedro, the last Tiger-held town on the peninsula, on 16 May 1996. The Tigers retreated into the jungles in the northern part of Sri Lanka and government forces began the task of rebuilding the ruined towns and villages along the peninsula. In July the Tigers counter-attacked, over-running a government base on the east coast, and killing 1200. It was the army's worst defeat in the war: when it reoccupied the base, it found only 11 survivors, hiding in a well.

The war continued. There was another government offensive in the summer of 1997, and constant fighting in the Vanni jungle in the north of the island. There were further surprise Tiger attacks on government bases around the country – and another truck bomb in Colombo in October (18 people were killed). By the end of the year, the government admitted that at least 50,000 people had been killed since the civil war began in 1983 – not counting the thousands killed in the JVP insurrection. There was no end in sight.

## FURTHER READING

De Silva, K. M., *A History of Sri Lanka*, London, C. Hurst, 1981.
Manor, James (ed.), *Sri Lanka in Change and Crisis*, London, Croom Helm, 1984.
McGowan, William, *Only Man is Vile, the Tragedy of Sri Lanka*, New York, Farrar, Strauss & Giroux, 1992.
Shwartz, Walter, *The Tamils of Sri Lanka*, London, Minority Rights Group, 1986.
— *Sri Lanka: Disappearances*, Amnesty International, London, September 1986.
Weaver, Mary Anne, 'The Gods and the Stars', *New Yorker*, 21 March 1988.

# VIETNAM

| | |
|---|---|
| Geography | 129,086 sq. miles (334,331 sq. km). The size of Norway. |
| Population | 73.5 million. |
| GNP per capita | $240 (1995). |
| Refugees | External: about 1 million since 1975. Almost all have been absorbed by host countries, or returned. 286,000 ethnic Chinese refugees from Vietnam in China. Internal: 34,400 from Cambodia. |

On 30 April 1975, Communist Vietnam won the greatest of all wars of national liberation, and the most difficult of all Communist revolutions. Late on the evening of the 29th, the American ambassador and his staff had been rescued from their embassy by helicopter. The last Marines left early in the morning, a few hours before North Vietnamese tanks rolled into Saigon.

At a cost of 2.5 million lives, Ho Chi Minh and his successors won independence and national unity. They could have obtained it all freely from the French 25 years earlier if they had renounced their revolution. By 1990, the triumph had turned to dust. The Vietnamese had occupied Cambodia in 1978, and had been faced with guerrilla war and international hostility very similar to that encountered by the Americans in Vietnam itself a generation earlier. They were forced to withdraw in 1989, and were then confronted with the collapse of their economy, inflation at 1000 per cent a year, and starvation in the countryside. In the decade following the revolution, over a million Vietnamese had fled the country by boat. They were frequently attacked by pirates, the men murdered and the women raped. In the early 1990s, Vietnam was forced to abandon the Communist model and follow China down the capitalist road. All those millions had died in vain. It was an ironic end to a remarkable story.

## HISTORY
For nearly 30 years, American policy in East and South-East Asia was based upon the 'domino theory'. Washington assumed that there was a worldwide Communist conspiracy, directed from Moscow, which would attack one country after another: if China went, Vietnam would go; if Vietnam went, Cambodia would go; and then Thailand, Malaysia and so on. Each country 'lost' to the

West would be added to a united Communist world empire ruled from the Kremlin, what Ronald Reagan described as the 'evil empire'.

The events of the 1970s showed that nationalism and ethnic hostility were far more potent forces than ideology. Once American pressure was withdrawn, the dominoes immediately started fighting among themselves. Soviets and Chinese went to war, as did the Chinese and Vietnamese, and the Vietnamese and the Cambodians. Cambodia looked to China as an ally against Vietnam, just as Vietnam looked to the Soviet Union as an ally against China. China allied itself with the United States against the USSR, and the US found itself a silent partner in an anti-Vietnamese, and therefore anti-Soviet, alliance that included the Khmers Rouges. It is one of the most elegant examples of power politics in modern times.

It is easy to be wise after the event. The domino theory looked perfectly plausible at the time, and there is plenty of evidence that the Chinese and Vietnamese believed in it, too. China steadfastly supported the Vietnamese Communists through all their wars, starting when Mao's armies occupied South China in 1949 and provided Ho Chi Minh with secure bases from which to overrun Tonkin. The Sino-Soviet dispute in the 1960s and 1970s, however, caused the North Vietnamese serious and increasing problems. China simultaneously demanded that Vietnam take its side against the USSR, and itself set about establishing a *de facto* alliance with the United States, Hanoi's greatest enemy. In February 1972, Mao received President Nixon in Peking at the height of the US bombing offensive against North Vietnam. North Vietnam needed both China and the USSR. The Chinese claim that they spent $20 billion in aid to Vietnam over the years, an enormous sum for a poor country, and the Vietnamese Communists were always armed by the Soviet Union.

From the start, the Vietnamese resented Chinese bullying. There were 1000 years of animosity between the Celestial Empire and its sometime vassal, the Empire of Annam, and all the years of French colonialism, revolution and the wars of Indochina could not change that basic antipathy.

Relations between the two countries began to deteriorate seriously immediately after the Communist victory in 1975. China continued obsessively to fear the Soviet Union, which it accused of attempting to encircle it by extending its hegemony to Vietnam. It was a self-fulfilling prophecy: the Vietnamese did not allow the Soviets to establish a permanent base in Cam Ranh Bay until China attacked Vietnam in 1979; after that episode, Soviet military aid to Vietnam escalated dramatically.

China's hostility to the Soviet Union was not entirely paranoid – and even paranoiacs can have enemies. There had been serious border clashes between the two countries in 1969 (*see* China, pp. 180–2), and much more serious threats from Moscow. But fearing encirclement was pure foolishness. China is too big for any alliance to encircle or dominate or conquer it – but, foolish or not, that was what the Chinese feared.

The Communist victory in Vietnam permitted a revival of the millennial hostility between it and Cambodia (*see* p. 155). Pol Pot was the most extreme ideological fanatic in the world, but he was also a Cambodian nationalist who detested the Vietnamese who had devoured one-third of the national territory over the centuries: Saigon had originally been a Cambodian village, and all of the Mekong delta had once been part of Cambodia.

The Khmers Rouges provoked their first conflict with Vietnam on 4 May 1975, barely two weeks after they took Phnom Penh. They seized two islands in the Gulf of Siam that the French had allocated to Vietnam, and massacred the several hundred Vietnamese inhabitants. A survivor who returned to one of the islands three months later found it littered with skulls.

An American cargo ship, the *Mayaguez*, blundered into this confrontation on 12 May, and was captured by the Cambodians. President Ford ordered a massive air strike against Cambodian coastal bases in retaliation. It was the last American raid of the Vietnam war, killed thousands of Cambodians, caused great damage, cost the lives of 41 U S Marines and other military personnel and did nothing to save the 40-man crew of the *Mayaguez*. They had already been released.

The Vietnamese reoccupied the islands, evicting the Cambodian garrisons. Pol Pot, who had no choice, apologized, claiming that the Cambodian incursion had been due to an excess of zeal by the local commander. In fact, it had been a quite deliberate attempt to seize territory before the new Vietnamese government could assert its claim. It was a failure, but an omen of things to come.

The Khmers Rouges were naturally the ideological pupils of Mao Tse-tung, and constantly praised the extravagances of the Cultural Revolution. But when the Gang of Four were arrested in October 1976 and a new pragmatic regime took power in Peking, the Khmers Rouges instantly applauded. Although Deng Xiaoping had staked his life and career on fighting extremism in China, he continued to defend Pol Pot and the Khmers Rouges, despite his profound detestation for their principles, because of his even more profound detestation for Vietnam and the Soviet Union.

As relations between Vietnam and Cambodia deteriorated, the Chinese responded by suspending all technical and economic aid to Vietnam in the summer of 1978. In retaliation, Vietnam persecuted and expelled the large numbers of Chinese living in Vietnam; as a result, in that year, about 150,000 of them fled overland to China, and 250,000 more fled by boat (of these, 30,000–40,000 perished at sea). The unhappy saga of the 'boat people' was one of the many horrors of the decade.

## THE WAR OVER CAMBODIA
The Khmers Rouges were constantly the aggressors in the troubles with Vietnam, first massacring Vietnamese living in Cambodia, then attacking across the border and slaughtering Vietnamese villagers. In December 1978, the Vietnamese invaded Cambodia and soon occupied the whole country (*see* Cambodia).

The Vietnamese occupation of Cambodia was a severe diplomatic setback to China, the worst since General MacArthur invaded North Korea in 1950. This time, however, China's own territory was not endangered, and Peking informed Pol Pot that he would have to win his own salvation, by resuming guerrilla warfare.

## THE CHINA–VIETNAM WAR

The blow to Chinese pride could not be endured, however, and the Chinese decided to teach Vietnam a lesson. On 17 February 1979, Deng Xiaoping launched a full-scale invasion, sending 75,000 troops across the border at 20 different points. The whole operation soon involved a quarter of a million men. Deng presumably thought he could repeat the achievements of the 1962 war against India, when China had indeed delivered a sharp lesson in military reality. This time, things happened differently.

The People's Liberation Army of China was the largest in the world, but it had not fought seriously since Korea and had been debilitated by the political battles of the intervening years. In addition, its armament was woefully inadequate and antiquated. The Vietnamese, by contrast, had fought continuously since 1946, and were well equipped with modern Soviet weapons, not to mention the billions of dollars' worth of American equipment captured in 1975.

The war lasted 16 days. By sheer weight of numbers, the Chinese cleared the border posts and captured five provincial capitals. By an historical irony, the chief of them was Lang Son, the site of the first major defeat that the Viet Minh had inflicted on the French, in October 1950, after the Chinese Communist victory had given them a secure base beyond the border.

This time, it was the Chinese who captured Lang Son, and they razed it to the ground, together with the four other capitals. Those five towns were the last in North Vietnam that had survived intact since French colonial days, because the Americans had not bombed so near the frontier for fear of provoking Chinese intervention.

The Chinese failed to defeat the Vietnamese, and after suffering heavy casualties, Deng proclaimed victory and withdrew his troops. About 20,000 people had been killed, by Chinese count, an equal number on each side. For once, the large majority were soldiers.

The episode was a serious defeat for China, and it failed totally to achieve its main objective: to induce the Vietnamese to leave Cambodia. The Vietnamese found it unnecessary to move a single division out of Cambodia to send north. In the long term, the war was to prove exceedingly costly to Vietnam: not only were several provinces devastated (ten years later, they had still not recovered), but it became necessary to build fortifications and to maintain large forces on permanent alert along the northern border.

For the next ten years, there were repeated skirmishes between Vietnamese and Chinese troops, sometimes involving thousands of men. The two sides shelled each other's positions constantly: for months on end, China would fire 10,000 shells a day at Vietnamese positions. It was considered a sign of improved relations when the daily total dropped to 700 in 1988.

The war graphically illustrated the disastrous consequences of Mao Tse-tung's and Lin Biao's belief in the invincibility of guerrilla armies. Deng was able to blame Mao and the Gang of Four for the defeat and set about purging the army of Maoists. Foreign defeat thus strengthened Deng's domestic position.

## THE SPRATLYS DISPUTE

The first conflict between modern Vietnam and China occurred even before the Communist victory in Saigon. It concerned two chains of islands in the South

China Sea, claimed by both Vietnam and China. These are the Paracels, off the coast of Vietnam, and the Spratlys, far to the south. The Chinese claim is exiguous (the Spratlys are closer to Borneo than to China), and the islands, tiny coral atolls, are of no strategic or economic value unless oil is found in the ocean surrounding them. Taiwan, the Philippines and Malaysia also claim the Spratlys, but have never seriously asserted their claims.

In 1972, the Thieu regime of South Vietnam started hawking oil concessions in the islands. China promptly occupied the Amphitrite chain in the Paracels. South Vietnam thereupon sent a small naval contingent to another part, the Crescent Islands, and to the Spratlys. In 1974, the North Vietnamese, in turn, announced that they would sell oil leases in the South China Sea, and the Chinese reacted by occupying the Crescent Islands, evicting the South Vietnamese.

North Vietnam did not contest China's claims as long as the war continued, but on 11 April 1975, as its armies were closing in on Saigon, it sent a small naval force to occupy the Spratlys. China instantly protested. The dispute has simmered ever since, with occasional naval demonstrations. In January 1988, the Chinese sent a military force ashore in the Spratlys, and on 14 March, Chinese naval vessels sank a Vietnamese gunboat there. Vietnam reported three men killed and 74 missing. Vietnam then sent naval reinforcements to the islands, and issued dire warnings against a proposed Chinese oceanographic expedition. China, in turn, denounced Vietnamese naval preparations. In the event, Vietnam withdrew, and left China master of the field.

No one knows if there is oil under the South China Sea, or if it could be exploited. No oil company is going to take the risk of exploring in a zone disputed between such belligerent neighbours.

Their dispute, of course, is not really about oil, or remote coral islands. There is a deep-seated national rivalry, exacerbated by the Chinese fear of the Soviet Union, and the immediate cause for their hostility is Cambodia. That Vietnam, in effect, allowed China to annex the Spratlys in 1988 was one of the first signs of its fundamental change of policy towards its neighbours. Later, the Philippines entered the fray, asserting its claim to the Spratlys by diplomatic and judicious naval demonstrations. It claimed a great victory in May 1997, when China apparently withdrew its ships from the archipelago. The dispute, however, is not at all resolved.

## MODERN VIETNAM

Vietnam, in 1988, was facing famine. There had been a series of poor harvests in previous years, a problem compounded by the relentless increase in the population and the catastrophic effects of Communism on agricultural productivity. In 1981, the government abandoned strict Communist principles and allowed farmers to sell whatever they produced beyond a quota that they were obliged to sell to the government. Production increased in five years from 13 million to 18 million tons, but it is not enough to match an annual population growth of 2.6 per cent.

In April 1988, for the first time, the Vietnamese government appealed to the United States. The State Department replied that the U S 'had no interest' in helping Vietnam as long as it continued to occupy Cambodia. The U S sanctions imposed in 1979, after the Vietnamese invasion of Cambodia, remained in force. **265**

In May, admitting that 3 million people were already on the brink of starvation, Vietnamese officials appealed to the world community: the Europeans sent 10,000 tons of rice; the USSR sent 60,000 tons. The 1987 shortfall had been 1.5 million tons, and the 1988 harvest was no better. The National Assembly was told in June 1988 that rice production *per capita* had dropped from 581 lb in 1982 to 506 lb in 1987.

Finance, too, was a grave problem. In the first few months of 1988, inflation reached 60 per cent a month. In March, the central bank introduced new banknotes, denominated in 1000, 2000 and 3000 dong (the national currency), and the rate of inflation rose still further. In 1987, the government, abandoning its principles, enacted a law on foreign investment which it claimed was the most liberal in the Communist world, but at first there was no foreign investment. Indochina was too unsettled to tempt prudent capitalists.

Ho Chi Minh City (formerly Saigon) suffers from inadequate water and electricity supplies. A major hydroelectric project built with Soviet aid northwest of the city was opened in March 1988, and immediately had to close: it was so badly constructed that the turbines broke when they were started up, and the dam itself was unsafe. In May, the local press reported unconvincingly that repairs had been completed.

Vietnam had no friends other than the Soviet Union and its own puppet states, Laos and Cambodia. When Rajiv Gandhi visited Hanoi in April 1988, he refused to offer Vietnam any support in its dispute with China over the Spratlys, even though India was usually resolutely hostile to China and supported the USSR's allies.

In May 1988, Vietnam announced that it would withdraw half its troops in Cambodia – 50,000 men – by the end of the year, and complete the withdrawal by 1990. It later specified that all its troops would be withdrawn by September 1989, if a political settlement could be reached by then, or March 1990 at the latest. At the same time, it announced that it had already cut its military presence in Laos from 45,000 to 20,000. Vietnam was at last bowing to necessity and, probably, to Soviet pressure. It had discovered the limits of independence.

Vietnam then tried to improve its relations with China and the United States, but discovered that both countries preferred to wait until the withdrawal from Cambodia was complete. Vietnam eased its persecution of its Chinese minority, and admitted that it had much to learn from Deng's economic reforms. It also tried to satisfy American demands for the return of the remains of US servicemen killed during the Vietnam war.

The last Vietnamese troops withdrew from Cambodia in September 1989. For the next two years, Vietnam waited anxiously while the Cambodian factions and their various sponsors negotiated a ceasefire. There could be no hope for Vietnam until the Cambodian civil war ended. Finally, on 23 October 1991, a ceasefire agreement was signed in Paris, and the American secretary of state, James Baker, announced that the time had come for normalization of relations between the two countries.

The Americans remained obsessed by a desire to account for the 2300 or so Americans who disappeared during the Vietnam War and whose bodies were never found. Various interest groups in the United States, chiefly extreme rightwingers, continued to maintain that most of the missing men were still kept in secret camps inside Vietnam, and some of their unfortunate relatives were deceived into believing these absurd claims. The Vietnamese offered the Americans every help in searching for the bodies and allowed investigators to follow up every alleged sighting of a missing American. There is a flourishing trade in forged photographs and identity cards. In 1991, the Bush administration decided that Vietnam was sufficiently helpful. It did not lift sanctions, but promised that it would soon do so. In the event, Vietnam had to wait for Bill Clinton. The American economic sanctions were at last lifted in February 1994 and full diplomatic relations were restored in July 1995. The United States, and Vietnam, had at last come to terms with their past.

Meanwhile, Vietnam had introduced drastic reforms. The most important was to free the price of rice, permitting peasants to sell it for what they could get. This immediately increased production sharply, ending the threat of starvation. The introduction of a market economy in the countryside marked the first, decisive step away from the Communist principles of Ho Chi Minh, and was soon extended to other sectors of the economy. The Vietnamese Communist Party followed China's example, and retained absolute control over the country's politics while loosening its hold upon the economy. Vietnam remained desperately poor and over-populated, but at last had the possibility of joining the world community, and trying to catch up with its East Asian neighbours, who had a 50-year start in modernization.

Vietnam remains a paradox: it is one of the poorest nations in the world, with one of the world's largest and most powerful armies, which, in 1975, was surpassed only by those of the United States, the Soviet Union and China. It had the power to over-run Cambodia in a month and to hold it indefinitely – but not to defeat the Khmers Rouges, because they were supported by China. Cambodia has been described as 'Vietnam's Vietnam', and the comparison is exact – with one difference. The US, in economic terms, could afford the Vietnam war; Vietnam could not afford its war in Cambodia, even though the Soviet Union footed the bill.

Vietnam and Cambodia are the extreme modern examples of the price of revolution. It may be debated whether Ho Chi Minh and his comrades would have launched the struggle in 1946 if they had known in advance that the cost would be 5 million dead. What cannot be doubted is that they, and their successors, failed in their ultimate purpose. They have communized Indochina, but they have also ruined it. It was never part of their dream that, 40 years after they began, and decades after their victory, they would have to go begging to the United States and China for food to save their people from starvation.

## FURTHER READING

Chanda, Nayan, *Brother Enemy, the War after the War,* New York, Harcourt, Brace, Jovanovitch, 1986.

# MIDDLE EAST

# IRAN

| | |
|---|---|
| Geography | 636,367 sq. miles (1,648,184 sq. km). Four times as big as California; three times as big as France. |
| Population | 64 million. 45% speak Persian, 23% speak related languages (Kurdish, Luri, Baluchi), 26% Turkic languages (the Azerbaijanis in the north-west and the Turkomen in the north-east). |
| Resources | Oil reserves of 48.5 billion barrels; considerable other mineral wealth; exports wide variety of goods, ranging from pistachio nuts to carpets and caviar. |
| GNP per capita | N.A. |
| Refugees | 1.4 million Afghans, 580,000 Iraqis and 40,000 others. |
| Casualties | No reliable figures for Iran–Iraq war. Best estimates are that Iran lost between 400,000 and 600,000 killed, and Iraq between 100,000 and 150,000. |

The Ayatollah Ruhollah Khomeini died on 3 June 1989. Iran's history since then has been a slow retreat from the excesses of Khomeini's Islamic revolution, very similar to China's retreat from Maoism after the death of Mao Tse-tung in 1975. Over 20 years after the departure of the Great Helmsman, China is still ruled by the Communist Party, though society and the economy have changed out of all recognition. No doubt the forms of the Islamic Republic of Iran will also persist for many years, whatever happens to the more extreme elements of Khomeini's legacy.

## HISTORY

Persia is one of the oldest states on Earth, with a continuous history stretching back to Cyrus the Great, whose career of conquest began in 554 BC. Mohammed Shah celebrated what he claimed as the 2500th anniversary of the founding of the empire in 1971, in a ceremony at Persepolis which cost Iran $100 million. His arithmetic and his political judgment were both faulty.

In the centuries after Cyrus, the Persian empire was frequently conquered but it always recovered. It was always an empire: one of its peoples ruled over the others. The Persians themselves have been in a minority at all times, and have therefore had to adapt their government to the needs of their subjects. Modern nationalism has now infected the Kurds, Azerbaijanis, Arabs, Baluchis and Turkomen who make up the majority of the population of Iran and will continue to trouble the Persians' control.

**271**

The country was called Persia from the time of Cyrus until the 1930s, when Shah Reza, in a moment of Fascist enthusiasm, changed it to Iran. He wished to assert that the Persians were the original Aryans and therefore an even purer *volk* than his much admired Nazis.

The roots of the Iranian revolution go back to the origins of the modern monarchy and the policies of Reza Khan Pahlevi, the general who made himself shah in 1925. He was a tough, no-nonsense reformer, who modelled himself on Kemal Ataturk of Turkey. But where Ataturk's reforms took hold, Reza Shah's did not. Turkey, after the collapse of the Ottoman empire, was ready for reforms; Persia was not. More important, Ataturk pursued his reformist policies consistently for 20 years, and left competent reformers and the structure of a reformed state behind him; Reza Shah established a dynasty. When he was deposed by the British in 1941, for pro-Axis policies, all his achievements depended upon the capacity of his heir:

> *And all to leave what with his toil he won,*
> *To that unfeather'd two-legged thing, a son.*

The son was Mohammed Reza, second and last shah of the Pahlevi dynasty, who wholly lacked his father's forcefulness and ability. Reza's reforms had been opposed by the clergy, the Ulama, but unlike Henry VIII or Ataturk, he had failed to bring them under control. He had attacked them and dominated them but had never crushed them. His son failed even to dominate them, merely earning their undying enmity.

The secular National Front, led by Mohammed Mossadegh, succeeded briefly in driving Mohammed Shah from his throne in 1953. He was restored by the army, aided by the C I A, an episode that gave both institutions an exaggerated idea of their influence. The events of 1953 came back to haunt the Americans a quarter of a century later.

Ruhollah Khomeini, born in 1902, developed his political ideas in opposition to Reza Shah. By the 1930s, he was already a prominent theological scholar, Koranic exegete and leader of the clerical establishment in Qom, the theological centre of Persia. The defeat of the National Front in August 1953 left the clerical Ulama as the centre of opposition.

Khomeini's role in the Ulama grew steadily. In 1962, he led a fight against a law giving the vote to women and non-Muslims in local council elections, denouncing it as an 'attack on the Koran and Islam'. The shah backed down (unlike his father, who would never have tolerated such opposition), and in June 1963, Khomeini launched a violent attack on the regime. There were riots, ruthlessly put down by the police, and paratroopers attacked Khomeini's seminary at Qom and arrested him. There were further riots, in Tehran and in Qom, all vigorously suppressed. Some students were thrown off the roof of the seminary, others were drowned in a lake; a total of at least 200 people were killed. After the revolution, the general who had directed the operation was one of the first to be shot.

Khomeini was released in August 1964, and the shah tried to calm the unrest by holding elections. Khomeini called for a boycott, and was arrested again. He was released the following spring, but then the government introduced another unpopular measure: the Status of Forces Law, which extended diplomatic privileges to all American military personnel in Iran. The measure was so unpopular that the shah had trouble getting the bill through the rubber-stamp parliament, the Majlis. Khomeini depicted it as an insult to Iranian nationalism, 'a document for the enslavement of Iran', 'an acknowledgment that Iran is an American colony'. This time he was deported to Turkey. A year later, in 1965, he moved to the Shiite holy city of Najaf in Iraq.

From that sanctuary, he continued to attack the shah and his government. His role in the events of 1962–4 assured him a large following among students at Qom, many of whom later emerged as clerical leaders of the revolution.

## THE OLD REGIME

The collapse of the monarchy in January 1979 was both surprising and inevitable. Surprising, because the shah had ruled without sustained opposition for 25 years, had a 400,000-man army, a large and effective police force, and a sinisterly effective secret police, Savak. Furthermore, the enormous revenues of Iran's oil industry should have permitted a steadily expanding economy, which, in turn, should have ensured the loyalty of the population.

The revolution was, however, inevitable because of the tyranny, corruption and economic and political ineptitude of the regime. The shah had little native ability and pursued policies that alienated, successively, all the important elements of the population: the peasants, the clerics, the urban middle class, the big industrialists, the students. When opposition started to develop in 1977, the pent-up hostility and rage of the country burst uncontrollably forth. The shah had no idea how to cope with this sudden turn of events. He alternately promised reforms and ordered his army and police to crush the opposition.

In January 1978, seminary students in Qom took to the streets in a pro-Khomeini demonstration. The police opened fire, killing a number of them. The period of mourning in Iran lasts 40 days: 40 days after the Qom killings, there were further demonstrations and further killings. The pattern was repeated. The protests swept the country. In September, during the festivities marking the end of Ramadan, there was a series of huge demonstrations in Tehran. The shah proclaimed martial law, and on 8 September, the police opened fire on the crowd in Jaleh Square, killing hundreds. The massacre became known as 'Black Friday', and the square and its martyrs' monument remain the preferred site of revolutionary demonstrations, an Iranian Place de la Bastille.

The shah's response was uncertain and erratic. In turn, he granted concessions, sacked his prime minister, arrested the commander of Savak, and ordered the army to maintain order. He hoped that Washington would tell him what to do, and was confused by the conflicting signs from the Carter administration: on the one hand, the secretary of state, Cyrus Vance, advised him to negotiate with the opposition; on the other, the national security adviser, Zbigniew Brzezinski, wanted him to crush the opposition with whatever force was necessary.

In October 1978, on the shah's urging, Khomeini was expelled from Iraq; he moved to a suburb of Paris, Neuphle-le-Château. It was a decisive event. There **273** were excellent telephone and telex links between France and Iran, and Khomeini's messages were sent to Tehran every day and spread around the country. It was revolutionary propaganda conducted by telex and Xerox. Khomeini was by now the spokesman for the revolution, and all opposition in Iran gathered around him. Moderates thought they could use him. They were mistaken.

The shah continued to vacillate between firmness and conciliation, but it was too late for either policy to save him. He consulted the opposition, who either refused to deal with him, or demanded that he leave the country. He appointed an opposition politician, Shahpour Bakhtiar, as prime minister, who took the job on condition that the shah go abroad at once.

The shah fled the country on 16 January 1979. The generals and guardsmen who saw him off were in tears; Bakhtiar and other politicians were barely civil to him. The prime minister announced a series of important measures: he abolished Savak, decreed freedom of the press, proposed a number of essential democratic reforms. It was all useless. On 31 January, Khomeini flew in to Tehran – like Lenin to the Finland station – and on 11 February, he proclaimed the Islamic republic.

## THE REVOLUTION

There have been plenty of violent changes of regime in the world in this century: in the past 40 years, the monarchies of Egypt, Iraq and Libya were all swept away in army coups; Greece, Turkey, Spain and Portugal have all swung between military and civilian governments; there have been three changes of regime in France since 1940. However, in all those cases, the essential instruments of the state survived, as they did in all the coups of Latin America except Cuba and Nicaragua.

What happened in Iran was not an ordinary coup; it was a revolution. The police, the courts, the whole structure of state authority collapsed and the vacuum was filled by militant clerics and students. The constitution, the laws, the education system, the entire economy were overthrown. It was a change as catastrophic as the Russian or Chinese revolutions, the collapse of the Ethiopian monarchy or the overthrow of the Portuguese colonial regimes in Africa. What is more, Iran was a relatively modern, developed state, not a primitive backwater like Ethiopia, nor had it suffered devastating wars like Russia and China. Nevertheless, it went from a 20th-century dictatorship to a medieval theocracy in 18 months.

There was an immediate reversal of Iran's foreign policies. The Israeli embassy in Tehran was abandoned precipitously. American technicians manning listening posts in north-east Iran, spying on the Soviet missile testing sites across the border, were hastily brought out, leaving most of their equipment behind them. The US embassy was attacked on 14 February, and the US consulate at Tabriz in the west – a major outpost and site of important encounters – was sacked by a mob.

Five days after Khomeini took power, the first executions occurred, of senior officers in the shah's army. Soon a revolutionary terror was under way: at least 582 people were executed between February 1979 and January 1980, and in the following 18 months, a further 906 executions took place. After the assassinations of the summer of 1981 (*see below*), when the revolution was clearly in danger, there were mass killings throughout the country: the clandestine opposition compiled a list of 7746 people executed between June 1981 and September 1983. Shaul Bakhash calculates that, in all, 10,000 were executed between 1979 and 1983. The killings continued throughout the war with Iraq, and in 1988, after the ceasefire, at least 3000 prisoners were taken out of the jails and shot. The regime thus eliminated surviving monarchists and leftists together.

Like other revolutions, there was constant competition between relatively moderate leaders and the extremists, and the extremists always won. The difference in Iran was that the victorious extremists were Islamic fundamentalists, not leftists.

Mehdi Bazargan, the prime minister appointed by Khomeini (Bakhtiar had wisely got out) lasted nine months. He tried to keep the machinery of the state functioning and to establish relations with the United States. The former shah — who had led a peripatetic existence since his exile, moving from Egypt to Morocco to the Bahamas to Panama, looking for a country to take him in — was admitted into the U S on 22 October 1979 for medical treatment (it was later revealed that he was suffering from inoperable cancer). The event provoked an uproar in Iran, which claimed that the United States was the instrument of counter-revolution. On 1 November, Bazargan met Brzezinski in Algiers. On the 4th, the American embassy in Tehran was seized and 53 hostages taken, and on the 6th, Barzagan resigned.

Abol-Hasan Bani-Sadr became president in January 1980, under a new constitution. He had been closely associated with Khomeini in Paris, but was less extreme than his thorough-going Islamic colleagues, whom he referred to as 'a fistful of Fascist clerics'. He hoped to bring the revolution under control, but he failed completely and, in the end, had to flee for his life. His authority as president was undermined by the leaders of the Majlis, by the Revolutionary Guards, by revolutionary committees (the 'Komitehs'), by the students who had seized the American hostages, and, above all, by Khomeini himself who had as little time for moderation as Mao Tse-tung.

A full-fledged revolutionary struggle was under way, and the hostages were an important weapon for the extremists. In addition, in an instance of criminal negligence, the embassy allowed its files to fall into their hands. The last ambassador to the shah, William Sullivan, had shipped the files back to Washington at the end of 1978, as the regime disintegrated, keeping only skeleton files; when the embassy was first attacked on 14 February 1979, these few documents were promptly shredded. After Sullivan left, the files were all brought back from Washington, and when the embassy was occupied, most of them were found intact. Some of the most sensitive files were shredded, but the students occupying the embassy passed their time reassembling the documents. Many Iranian politicians were arrested — and some were executed — because the files revealed that they had had dealings with the Americans before the revolution.

Leftist groups in Iran, as well as the clerical extremists, used the hostage crisis as a means of discrediting moderates and the United States. Khomeini made various impossible conditions for the hostages' release, and Bani-Sadr tried to manoeuvre between the intransigence of the extremists (including Khomeini) and U S demands for the hostages.

On 24 April, the Americans attempted a hare-brained rescue of the hostages, which failed lamentably with the loss of eight lives. The extremists used the event to prove American perfidy, and to demonstrate that there remained many traitors active inside Iran. There was a purge of the armed forces commanders, and two alleged coup plots were discovered; over 100 officers were executed.

Bani-Sadr was increasingly pushed on to the sidelines, and hostilities opened between leftists and Islamic extremists. In modern Iran, this meant that hundreds of people were killed in riots and arbitrary executions, as the clerics, encouraged by Khomeini, increased their attacks on the leftists.

Simultaneously, the tribal minorities in Iran rose in revolt. The most important were the Kurds in the west (*see* p. 328) and the Azerbaijanis in the north-west, but there was also serious trouble among Baluchis in the east and other tribes along the Soviet border. The country seemed to be disintegrating.

On 22 September 1980, Iraq attacked on the ground and in the air (*see* Iraq, pp. 284–304). The revolution was saved by the shah: he had bought such enormous quantities of military equipment, he had trained such large numbers of military men, that the army managed to hold off the initial Iraqi attack. As in the Soviet Union in 1941, the regime had hurriedly to release hundreds of army and air force officers from jail to save the fatherland.

The crisis restored the army as a force in national affairs, but also led to a consolidation of the Revolutionary Guards: they suffered frightful casualties at the front, but as the war continued, they were developed into a cohesive and formidable fighting force, a sort of S S which, sooner or later, was bound to come into conflict with the army.

The war with Iraq diverted the Iranians from the hostages affair. President Carter had seized all Iranian assets in the United States and in American banks abroad. Iran needed the money for the war, and, besides, Saddam Hussein of Iraq was now the enemy. As 1980 drew to a close, negotiations for the release of the hostages in exchange for the frozen assets were concluded, with considerable help from the Algerian government, acting as mediator. The hostages were finally released on 20 January 1981, just as President Reagan was being inau-gurated in Washington.

Bani-Sadr tried to use the war emergency as a means of restoring his authority but failed, and the political battles grew steadily more intense. His supporters were attacked and sometimes killed by members of the clerical parties. Then the prime minister, Mohammed Ali Rajai, stripped Bani-Sadr of all power, and in late March 1981, Khomeini abandoned him to the wolves. He was dismissed as commander-in-chief of the army by the Ayatollah in June and went into hiding.

The leftists made one last effort to seize power. The Mujaheddin – by far the largest organization, a nationalist, socialist group that believed in 'revolutionary terror' – formed a loose alliance with Communists and Kurdish socialists, and sent their followers into the city streets to do battle with the Revolutionary Guards. The battles lasted several days and hundreds of people were killed. On

21 June, Bani-Sadr was impeached by the Majlis – a crushing defeat for the

moderates and the left. On 29 July, Bani-Sadr and the Mujaheddin leader, Massoud Rajavi, fled the country.

By then, the Mujaheddin had begun a terror campaign in Tehran. On 28 June, a car bomb demolished the headquarters of the government party, the Islamic Republican Party, killing four cabinet ministers and over 30 other officials, and the party's secretary-general, Mohammed Beheshti, probably the most important figure in the government after Khomeini himself. On 30 August, a bomb killed the new president, Mohammed Ali Rajai, who, as prime minister, had been Bani-Sadr's nemesis; others killed included the new prime minister and the head of the police. Another bomb, a week later, killed the prosecutor-general.

The assassinations spread in waves across the country, resulting in the deaths of hundreds of officials. In September, the Mujaheddin took to the streets again, in an attempt to bring down the regime, just as the shah had been brought down three years before. There were street battles, culminating on 27 September in a day-long engagement between Mujaheddin and Revolutionary Guards. The Guards prevailed.

The government reacted violently, executing thousands of supposed enemies. Most of those shot were leftists, but the jails were emptied of imprisoned royalists and other opposition figures. Bani-Sadr's foreign minister, Sadegh Ghotbzadeh, who had worked for Khomeini for years, was accused of plotting, and executed. The Ayatollah Shariatmadari, the spiritual leader of the Azerbaijanis in Tabriz, was stripped of his office.

It was the revolution's most dangerous moment. The regime made no distinction as to age or sex. Boys as young as 12 were shot for taking part in demonstrations; over half those executed were students. Most of the opposition groups were wiped out, leaving only the Kurds in their mountains and the Mujaheddin, who were numerous enough and practised enough to survive, though they had been seriously affected. For the time being at least, the Islamic republic had defeated its enemies.

In 1986, the French government, under pressure from Iran, expelled Massoud Rajavi from Paris. He moved to Baghdad, and claimed that he was continuing to organize a guerrilla campaign against the regime. It does not appear that he has enjoyed any notable success, although in the last days of the war, he invaded Iran and briefly occupied a border town.

## THE TWILIGHT OF THE AYATOLLAH

The Ayatollah Khomeini remained the uncontested leader of Iran, but in his old age the inevitable struggle for the succession got under way. Politics in Tehran were dominated by the war with Iraq. To begin with, the enthusiasm of the Revolutionary Guards brought success. The initial Iraqi offensive was stopped outside Abadan and Ahwaz, and the first Iranian counter-offensive in 1981 drove the Iraqis back on their own frontiers. Iran won two major victories: in February 1984, its armies captured Majnoon island, one of Iraq's major oilfields, on the central front; and in February 1986, they crossed the Shatt el-Arab and seized the Faw peninsula. Then the great attack on Basra in December 1986 failed; after the guns had pounded the city for weeks on end, the Guards charged across the open ground towards the Iraqi positions, like the British at the Somme or the French at Verdun, and met the same fate.

There were constant demonstrations in Tehran and other cities, in which hundreds of thousands of young men vowed themselves to martyrdom, but there were also constant funerals as Iranians buried their sons. The limits of the nation's zeal for martyrdom were reached: seven years was enough. To begin with, the Revolutionary Guards, like Mao's Red Guards 20 years before, had believed that their enthusiasm and faith could overcome every obstacle. Did not the ayatollah promise paradise to every martyr? Events have shown that martyrdom is not sufficient, that religious enthusiasm no longer wins wars. What is more, the Muslims of the world did not rally to the ayatollah's preaching. Even the Shiites of Iraq preferred the vicious tyranny of Saddam Hussein, Sunni though he was, to the ayatollah's Shiite paradise: Hussein was an Arab, Khomeini a Persian, and 13 centuries of hostility were not to be dispersed by a Friday sermon. The only people who allowed themselves to be seduced by the ayatollah were the desperate Shiites in Lebanon, and not even all of them heeded the call.

The economy was collapsing. War and revolution had taken their toll. Only war industries survived, and the standard of living was dropping precipitously. There were no longer enough recruits for the Revolutionary Guards; the Iranian war machine was no longer capable of supplying the huge armies that had marched singing to war in the early days. The vast stock of weapons accumulated by the shah was exhausted. Iran's great advantage over Iraq – the fact that its population was four times as great – was lost if there were no rifles for the soldiers.

The country was sliding steadily into bankruptcy. Strict Islamic law forbids usury, and Khomeini interpreted that to mean that Iran could not borrow against future oil revenues to meet the expenses of war. Iran paid cash, and when the reserves were exhausted, had to rely on income from its oil exports. Oil revenue dropped from $20 billion in 1982 to $5 billion in 1988. At an OPEC meeting in June 1988, Saudi Arabia, which had broken diplomatic relations with Iran two months earlier, vetoed a last, desperate Iranian initiative to cut production and thus raise prices again.

By 1988, Iran's imports for civilian purposes, including such essential items as equipment for the oilfields, had been cut to a trickle, in order to keep up the purchase of armaments, but still there was not enough money to pay for the weapons the army needed. The war had by then come home to civilians. The steady bombardment of Tehran and other cities by Iraqi missiles is said to have driven a large part of the capital's population into the country. The attacks were nowhere near as severe as the V-1 and V-2 attacks on London during World War II, let alone the bomber offensives, but they certainly further depressed Iranian morale.

Internal opposition reappeared in public for the first time in years. Khomeini's first prime minister, Mehdi Barzagan, wrote an open letter to the ayatollah in May 1988, stating that the war policy was a failure: 'Since 1986, you have not stopped proclaiming victory, and now you are calling on the population to resist until victory. Is that not an admission of failure on your part?' The letter went on to point out that Iraq's economy was surviving, while Iran was on the brink of bankruptcy.

In 1988, instead of mounting another general assault, Iranian troops pushed through the Iraqi defences in the Zagros mountains and captured nearly two Iraqi divisions and their general. The frontline was now in sight of the dam that provides most of Baghdad's water, but there were another 100 miles (160 km) of mountain before the Iranians could break into the plains. It was their last success, and it was more than counterbalanced by the loss of the Faw peninsula on 17 April, and the loss of further territory on the approaches to Basra on 25 May. In those two battles, Iraq recaptured almost all the territory in the south that it had lost during the war; on 26 June, it also recaptured Majnoon island and, on 11 July, drove the Iranians out of Kurdistan. These Iraqi victories were won rapidly and easily. The Iranians put up very little resistance. They seemed exhausted.

At the end of May, Khomeini issued a decree renouncing his position as commander-in-chief of the armed forces and naming Ali Rafsanjani to the post. He was instructed to 'coordinate the armed forces, the Revolutionary Guards, the security forces and volunteer mobilization forces'. It put the pragmatists in control of the war machine.

Hojatolislam Ali Akbar Hashemi Rafsanjani, speaker of the Majlis, was the Iranian official who had been approached by the Reagan administration in 1985–6 in an attempt to win the release of American hostages in Lebanon – an affair that came to be known as 'Irangate'. The American rationale was that Rafsanjani might emerge as Khomeini's successor, and establishing contact with him in advance would suit American long-term interests. His favour would be won by selling arms to Iran, and in return, he would arrange the release of the hostages.

The secret discussions continued for several months, and included a visit to Washington by Rafsanjani's son, who was given a tour of the White House by Oliver North, a member of the National Security Council staff, who was to become the central figure, on the American side, in the Iran–Contra scandal. Several arms deliveries were made, including anti-tank and anti-aircraft missiles, and two American hostages in Lebanon were released. It has never been clear whether Rafsanjani accepted the American premise – that improved relations were ultimately desirable. A man of great subtlety and flexibility, unlike some of his rivals who are unbending fanatics, Rafsanjani's personal concern was to win the succession struggle, which would not necessarily be concluded immediately upon Khomeini's death.

## DIPLOMACY

Throughout the war, Arab states and the United Nations tried continually to mediate between the two sides. One early effort was made by Algeria, but it ended abruptly when, on 3 May 1982, Iraq shot down the plane carrying the Algerian foreign minister, Mohammed Ben Yahia, and 12 of his colleagues. They had been flying to Tehran, and the Algerians suspect that the shooting was deliberate. That episode followed Saddam Hussein's first effort to escape from the trap he had dug for himself: in March 1982, he had offered to withdraw Iraqi forces to the international frontier. Iran had rejected this plan; it would recapture

**279**

its own territory with its own forces, and it demanded that Saddam be deposed, Iraq be formally declared the aggressor, and that Iraq pay reparations for the costs of the war. The two sides held these positions for the next six years.

The U N Security Council finally agreed to Resolution 598 on 20 July 1987. This called for an immediate ceasefire, provided for an international commission to consider the question of war guilt, and laid down mandatory sanctions that might be enforced against either state if it persisted in the war. After some hesitation, Iraq accepted the resolution, but Iran rejected it outright. For the next year, the United States tried to persuade the other members of the Security Council to approve sanctions, but never got very far. It was only the series of defeats inflicted on Iran in the spring of 1988 that finally tipped the balance.

Just before Iran accepted the ceasefire on 3 July, a U S warship, the U S S *Vincennes*, shot down an Iranian civilian airliner, Iranair flight 655, killing all 290 people on board. It was a striking illustration of the inadequacies of modern technology. The *Vincennes* was equipped with the most modern and sophisticated anti-aircraft system in the world – the Aegis system – but it depended upon every sailor working as precisely and as calmly as every computer. One of the weapons' officers misread the signals and mistook the airliner for an F-15.

On 18 July 1988, Rafsanjani announced that Iran would accept Resolution 598. Two days later, Khomeini's statement was read over the radio. It was full of the old, fiery denunciations of his enemies:

We have repeatedly shown in our foreign and international Islamic policy that we have been and are intent on expanding the influence of Islam in the world and lessening the domination of the world devourers. Now if the servants of the United States cite this policy as being expansionist and motivated to establish a great empire, we will not fear it but welcome it . . . We must smash the hands and the teeth of the superpowers, particularly the United States. And we must choose one of two alternatives – either martyrdom or victory, and we regard both as victory.

He continued to threaten Saudi Arabia and Kuwait: 'All of you will be partners in the adventurism and crimes created by the United States. We have not yet engaged in any action that would engulf the entire region in blood and fire, making it totally unstable.' He admitted freely that the war was lost:

The acceptance of the resolution was truly a very bitter and tragic issue for everyone, particularly for me. Up to a few days ago, I believed in the methods of defence and the stances announced in the war . . . However, due to some incidents and factors which for the moment I will refrain from elaborating on and which, God willing, will be made clear in the future, and in view of the opinion of all the high-ranking political and military experts of the country, whose commitment, sympathy and sincerity I trust, I agreed with the acceptance of the resolution and the ceasefire.

Iran faced immense economic and social problems after the war, and it was evident that it could not hope to restore its oil industry, let alone the rest of the economy, without outside help. The government moved cautiously to improve relations with the West, but in the spring of 1989 Khomeini issued a ruling that the Pakistan-born British author, Salman Rushdie, should be executed for blasphemy and apostasy. That sudden demonstration of fundamentalist intransigence brought all diplomatic progress to a halt. Khomeini died on 3 June 1989, but his spirit continued to dominate Iran. His successors did not lift the death sentence on Rushdie. In 1991 the Japanese translator of his *Satanic Verses* was murdered and the Italian translator was wounded in an attack. The following year, the Norwegian publisher of the book was shot and badly wounded in Oslo. All these attacks were evidently the work of Iranian terrorists. The only question was the extent of the state's responsibility. Rafsanjani was elected president and purged the most militant fundamentalists from the government, but gave no public sign of wanting a reconciliation with the West. In particular, he made no effort to secure the release of hostages held in Beirut until 1991.

Iran and Iraq made no progress in negotiations for a permanent peace. Eighteen months after the ceasefire, there were still 100,000 prisoners of war, Iraq continued to occupy a considerable slice of Iranian territory and there was no sign of agreement on the frontier question. Iran's domestic affairs were equally unsettled. Iran remained a safe haven for terrorists of all sorts. The regime was closely involved in terrorist attacks in Europe, notably in Paris. The shah's last prime minister, Shahpour Bakhtiar, who had survived one assassination attempt in his Paris exile, in 1980, was killed in August 1991. Rafsanjani lost no opportunity to denounce the United States, and to incite its enemies to action. He put himself at the head of those Palestinian and other Arabs who rejected the Madrid peace conference in 1991.

The economy recovered from the war slowly, but Iran remained isolated in its fundamentalist integrity. It was a passive spectator during the second Gulf War, refusing to join in sanctions against Iraq, but also refusing to help Saddam Hussein in his extremity. Saddam, desperate for support and worried about the dangers of a war on two fronts, abandoned all his claims against Iran. He admitted that the frontier along the Shatt el-Arab was in the middle of the river, and withdrew his armies from the last parcels of Iranian territory they occupied. Iran thus recovered everything it had demanded, and at last agreed to exchange surviving prisoners of war. Saddam promptly sent the returning Iraqis, some of whom had been in the camps for eight years, off to the new front in the south. At the height of the air war against Iraq, Saddam sent some of his surviving aircraft to Iran for safe-keeping. Iran let them in, and then confiscated them, as reparations for the first Gulf War.

In 1990, the centre of world and American attention in the Gulf shifted abruptly to Iraq. However, the United States continued to treat Iran as a pariah, and even attempted to regulate foreign companies' dealings with Teheran by passing legislation subjecting them and their officials to various sanctions if they had dealings with Iran or Libya. The law was indignantly repudiated by Europe and Japan, and the Clinton administration had to suspend its operation for fear that the Europeans would take the case to the new World Trade Organisation – where the US would certainly lose. The issue became particularly acute with an agreement between Iran and the former Soviet republics of Central Asia for an oil pipeline across Iran, and another agreement between Iran and a consortium including the French oil company Total, a Russian company and one from South Korea to develop an Iranian oil field.

Violent opposition to the regime had by then subsided, even in the Kurdish districts, though a bomb in a prayer hall in Meshed killed 25 people in June 1994. **281**

A certain relaxation in the previous fundamentalist stringency began to appear, encouraged by the progressive advance of moderate parties in successive parliamentary elections.

Iran's constitution allows semi-democratic elections: the regime decides who may be a candidate but then the vote is free. Khomeini, who drafted the constitution, provided that supreme authority in the Islamic Republic should rest with a senior cleric, entitled the Faqih, chosen in some ill-defined manner by other clerics. This personage is now the Ayatollah Ali Khameini, who tries to maintain Khomeini's traditions and policies. However, under immemorial Islamic and Shiite practice, there can be no high priest, no infallible pope in Islam. Ayatollahs attain their positions and titles by their demonstrated learning and their personal authority. Even in Khomeini's heyday, there were rival ayatollahs who refused to bow to him and there are many who reject Khameini's authority today.

Rafsanjani's term as president expired in 1997, and the clerics put up a list of candidates to succeed him. They favoured one in particular, the speaker of the Majlis (parliament), Ali Akbar Nateq Nouri. However, a rival cleric, of unimpeachable orthodoxy, Mohammed Khatemi, offered himself as the candidate of modernity. He never criticised, let alone repudiated, Khomeini's legacy but he was clearly far less dogmatic than his rivals. In particular, he appealed to women.

He won 69 per cent of the vote, an overwhelming landslide anywhere. After he took office, though obviously hugely popular, he remained constrained by an Islamic majority in the Majlis, by Khameini's continuing Islamic obduracy, and by the doubtful loyalties of the army. All the same, the way the wind was blowing was spectacularly demonstrated in November 1997, when Iran beat Australia in the World Cup. There were huge, vociferous demonstrations of delight in Teheran and other cities, and unveiled women took to the streets along with the men. The younger generation supported Khatemi, whatever the mullahs said.

He tried, very cautiously, to move Iran back into the international mainstream, and made several notable efforts to mend fences with the West, including the United States. The Clinton administration reacted with caution, but voices were raised in Washington suggesting that it was time for the U S to make it up with Iran. After all, Saddam Hussein remained the implacable enemy of both countries. Farther east, there was discreet cooperation between the U S and Iran in attempts to contain the Taliban extremists in Afghanistan, and had not Ronald Reagan made overtures to Rafsanjani, and had not Clinton himself cooperated with Iran in arming the Bosnian Muslims in their war against the Serbs?

The United States demanded that Iran renounce terrorism and give up attempts to develop nuclear, biological and chemical weapons. It also wanted the *fatwa* against Salman Rushdie lifted. Everything depended on the political situation in Iran itself, and the Islamic Republic's slow moves away from its previous extremism.

## ABU MUSA

Abu Musa is a small and strategically placed island, with two uninhabited dependencies. It lies near the southern end of the Persian Gulf and could be used to interfere with international shipping in the channel. Whichever riverine power controls it can also lay claim to the oil under the sea. It has been disputed between Iran and the Gulf emirates for generations. After an earlier crisis, Iran and the United Arab Emirates agreed to a joint administration. In 1992, Iran occupied Abu Musa and claimed *de facto* and *de jure* jurisdiction. The U A E has not recognized the claim.

## FURTHER READING

Amnesty International, *Iran: Violations of Human Rights*, London, 1987.

Avery, Peter, *Modern Iran*, New York, Praegar, 1965.

Bakhash, Shaul, *The Reign of the Ayatollahs: Iran and the Islamic Revolution*, New York, Basic Books, 1984.

Bernard, Cheryl, *The Government of God: Iran's Islamic Republic*, New York, Cornell University Press, 1984.

Hiro, Dilip, *Iran under the Ayatollahs*, London, Routledge and Kegan Paul, 1985.

Mackey, Sandra, *The Iranians: Persia, Islam and the Soul of a Nation*, New York, Dutton, 1996.

Mortimer, Edward, *Faith and Power: The Politics of Islam*, London, Faber and Faber, 1982.

Shawcross, William, *The Shah's Last Ride: The Fate of an Ally*, New York, Simon & Schuster, 1988; London, Chatto & Windus, 1989.

Sick, Gary, *All Fall Down – America's Tragic Encounter with Iran*, New York, Random House, 1985.

Wright, Robin, *In the Name of God, the Khomeini Decade*, New York, Simon & Schuster, 1989.

# IRAQ

| | |
|---|---|
| Geography | 167,568 sq. miles (433,999 sq. km). About the size of Sweden. |
| Population | 20 million. About 50% are Shiite Muslim Arabs, 25% Sunni Arabs, 20% Kurds (Sunni) and 5% Christians. 75% speak Arabic, the remainder speak Kurdish, Turkish or Persian. |
| Resources | Oil reserves set officially at 44.5 billion barrels, but are certainly far larger; world's largest exporter of dates. |
| GNP per capita | N.A. |
| Refugees | 900,000 Iranians; 114,000 foreign refugees; 580,000 Iraqis in Iran (chiefly Kurds). |
| Casualties | Iraq probably lost 150,000 men killed in the Iran–Iraq war and 100,000 in the second Gulf War. Many thousands of civilians were killed in the civil wars that followed the 1991 conflict, perhaps 50,000 in all. Iran lost over 400,000 killed in the first Gulf War. These figures are all approximate; Kuwait has not released figures of its losses, including civilians, of which there were probably several thousand. |
| | Allied losses in the second Gulf War were as follows: Killed in action: Egypt 10, France 2, Kuwait 1, Saudi Arabia 33, United Arab Emirates 6, UK 24 (and 23 wounded), USA 148 (and 458 wounded). Non-combat deaths: UK 23, USA 120 before the war. The United States lost a further 13 servicemen to accidents in the six months following the war. The US also lost 35 dead and 13 wounded to 'friendly fire' during the war, and the British 9, with two other possible deaths to friendly fire. |
| Prisoners of War | Iraq captured 21 Americans (including 2 women), 12 British, 9 Saudis, 1 Kuwaiti and 2 Italians. The allies captured about 65,000 Iraqis. |

The two wars that Saddam Hussein started, against Iran in 1980 and against Kuwait in 1990, cost between 750,000 and a million dead, set back Iran's economy by 20 years, ruined the Palestinians in Kuwait and left Kuwait a blazing wreck. Iraq was devastated by the air war, and then the Shiite south and Kurdistan in the north were overwhelmed by civil war. The first war cost the combatants at least $500 billion, the second war twice as much. In the modern world, only Pol Pot in Cambodia is a comparable war criminal. Saddam will presumably be removed eventually, but the devastation he has wrought and the political consequences of the two wars will persist for a generation. Among other

things, the second Gulf War finally broke the last shreds of Arab unity against

Israel, tore Kuwait's social fabric apart, and ensured a permanent and virulent hatred between the Gulf states and Iraq. After the 1991 war Iran, which had been the great loser in 1988, emerged once again as potentially the dominant force in the Gulf, with no other power in the region to challenge it.

## HISTORY

Iraq, like so many states of the modern world, is an entirely artificial creation, arbitrarily drawn on a map by the British and the French when they partitioned the Middle East after 1918. It is a land of most ancient quarrels. In 539 BC, Cyrus the Great, king of Persia, conquered Babylon and slew Belshazzar the king. The shah of Iran celebrated the 2500th anniversary of the foundation of the Persian monarchy in 1971 – at least ten years late. The Arabs celebrate a different anniversary: the Persians ruled Mesopotamia for 1100 years, a reign interrupted only by Alexander the Great and his successors, but in AD 637, the Arabs defeated the Persians in the battle of al-Qadissiya, one of the decisive events of history. For most of the following 1300 years, Mesopotamia was united with Syria (which then included Lebanon and what are now Israel and Jordan). The state was ruled from Damascus and then from Baghdad until the 16th century, and part of that time it extended over most of modern Iran and central Asia. Under the Abbasid caliphate (750–1258), Baghdad was one of the greatest centres of learning in the Western world. It was destroyed by Hulagu Khan, Genghiz Khan's grandson, in 1258. He made a pyramid of the skulls of all Baghdad's scholars, theologians, poets and administrators, and threw all the libraries into the Tigris. The river ran black with the ink. It was one of the great disasters of history.

The Dark Ages in the Middle East continued for three centuries, punctuated by the conquests of Tamburlaine, who sacked Baghdad in 1401. In the 16th century, Mesopotamia was a battleground between the Safavids in Persia and the Ottomans in Constantinople: the Ottoman empire controlled Baghdad from 1534 to 1918, with occasional, bloody, interruptions by the Safavids, as they tried repeatedly to conquer Mesopotamia and liberate the Shiite holy places there. The ancient battles between Arabs and Persians, from the 7th to the 20th century, are all vividly remembered in both countries, and played a large part in their war propaganda.

So did the disputes between Sunni and Shiite Muslims, which also began in the 7th century in Mesopotamia. They started as a fight for the succession to the empire founded by Mohammed and the first caliphs – between the Umayyads (Sunni) and Mohammed's son-in-law Ali and grandson Hussein. Hussein was defeated and killed in battle at Karbala in 680, and is buried at Najaf, and these two cities in Iraq are now the holiest shrines of the Shiites. Najaf has the largest cemeteries in the world: hundreds of thousands, perhaps millions, of Shiites have been brought for burial there. Iran is 80 per cent Shiite, and Iraq, although it has always been ruled by Sunnis, has a Shiite majority.

The history of Iraq since 1918, like the history of Syria and Lebanon, has been a continuing struggle by the state to form a nation out of the diverse peoples, languages, religions and traditions that exist within its borders.

The British drew up the modern frontiers of Iraq and Jordan, and installed **285** kings of the Hashemite dynasty in Baghdad and Amman. The family, imported from Arabia, has survived in Jordan, a desert kingdom, but never won acceptance in Mesopotamia, the oldest urban civilization in the world, where the royal family was thought subservient to the British and Americans.

An army coup overthrew the monarchy on 14 July 1958, at the height of President Nasser's influence in the Arab world. Nasserites were fighting for power in Syria, Lebanon and Jordan, as well as Iraq. The royal government distrusted the army, and took care that its units had no ammunition for their guns. However, two battalions ordered to the Jordanian frontier, to be ready to help King Hussein if there were a revolt, were issued ammunition. They were under the orders of Brigadier Abd al-Karim Kassem and Colonel Abd al-Salam Arif: Kassem was chairman and Arif a senior member of the secret Free Officers Committee, which had been planning a coup for years.

Instead of heading west, they drove into Baghdad in the early hours and seized the Ministry of Defence, and other key posts in the capital. Arif set up his headquarters at Broadcasting House, and coordinated the attack on the royal palace. A desultory siege lasted into the morning and then the crown prince, Abdul Illah, surrendered. The royal party was ordered into the courtyard: King Feisal II, his uncle the crown prince, several women (including the king's sister and Abdul Illah's mother) and a number of servants, about 25 people in all. They were lined up against a wall and shot.

The prime minister, Nuri es-Said, had escaped from his house and taken refuge in Baghdad. He was caught the next day, trying to escape disguised as a woman, and was lynched by the mob. His body, and the crown prince's, were tied behind Land Rovers and dragged through the streets of Baghdad. Scores of officials of the old regime suffered the same fate: it was the revolution's favourite means of execution. Some of the victims, wounded in earlier shootings, were taken from their hospital beds to be dragged. The British embassy was sacked. For a while there was a ban on Western tourists visiting Baghdad, and personal sanctions were sometimes enforced against those who ignored it.

## THE RISE OF THE BA'ATH

After the 1958 coup, Abd al-Karim Kassem became president. Within two months, he had removed Arif, who was sympathetic to the Ba'ath party and to the Nasserites; Arif was sentenced to death, but was pardoned in 1962. Kassem relied on the support of the Communist party against the Ba'ath, and he proved an incompetent, eccentric and xenophobic leader. The dangers of the situation were demonstrated in October 1959, when he barely escaped assassination: the leader of the assassination squad, who escaped, wounded, was Saddam Hussein.

The Kurds in the north rose in revolt (*see* The Kurds, pp. 328–40), and in 1961, Kassem tried to annex Kuwait. Britain, then still allied to Kuwait and governing the Gulf sheikhdoms, sent troops to protect it against attack. Kassem backed down. The only casualties were a few British soldiers who suffered heatstroke: they had arrived in one of the hottest places on Earth dressed for an English summer.

A new army plot was put together by Arif and Colonel Ahmad Hasan al-Bakr, a leader of the Ba'athists, and this coup occurred on 8 February 1963. It was a more elaborate and difficult operation than the 1958 coup, but it ended in the same way. The plotters seized the key points of the city, and laid siege to the Ministry of Defence. Kassem's Communist supporters took to the streets in his support, but they were mown down by the troops: hundreds were killed.

Kassem held out in the ministry all day and, in the evening, escaped with a few aides. Early the following morning, he was arrested and taken to Broadcasting House, which was again serving as coup headquarters. After a violent shouting match with Arif, Kassem was shot, with his three surviving aides, in a television studio. Pictures of the event were then broadcast.

There followed a period of violent shifts, coups and attempted coups, and finally the Ba'ath Party emerged in full control, in July 1968. Most of the leading members of the new government were from the town of Tikrit, north of Baghdad, and several of them were closely related to each other, including the new president, Hasan al-Bakr, and Saddam Hussein; in due course, they all dropped the cognomen 'al-Tikriti' to conceal the fact. Not all Tikritis remained members of the inner circle, however: in 1971, Saddam Hussein exiled General Hardan al-Tikriti, and later had him assassinated in Kuwait.

The Ba'ath has maintained itself in power since 1968 by a policy of ruthless terrorism, killing off its opponents, whether Communists, Nasserites, pro-Syrians, Islamic fundamentalists or dissident Ba'athists. On 27 January 1969, nine Jews and five others were hanged in public in Baghdad, allegedly as Israeli spies. The small surviving Jewish community in Iraq has since made every effort to escape.

The first attempted coup against the regime occurred two months after it took power, and there have been many since then, all unsuccessful. In July 1973, one of them led to the death of the defence minister, General Hammad Shihab (al-Tikriti).

Despite its brutality, and its reliance on the secret police, the Ba'ath regime did have a number of achievements to its credit. For example, its survival during the long war with Iran showed that it had considerable popular support, but its main success was economic. Iraq played a leading part in the first O P E C price rise in 1973–4; the large oil revenues that ensued were used sensibly, and the country made rapid progress until the war in 1980. The Ba'ath Party's foreign policy was intransigent and selfish. It professed undying hostility to Israel, gave some encouragement to Palestinian terrorism, bought arms from the Soviet Union and concluded a treaty of friendship with it in April 1972, and denounced the United States on every occasion. However, Iraq was never a subservient satellite to the Soviet Union, and when it became necessary to seek support in the West, Saddam Hussein changed his tune without the slightest shame.

There has for decades been a running border dispute between Iraq and Iran over the Shatt al-Arab river, which is the confluence of the Tigris and Euphrates and marks the southern border between the two countries. Iran claimed that the frontier lay along the middle of the river – the *thalweg* – Iraq claimed that it was on the east bank, and since 1937, the Iraqi view had prevailed. In addition, from 1961 to 1975, Iran gave every assistance to Kurdish rebels in northern Iraq. The war was a steady drain on Iraqi resources, and finally, in 1975, Iraq accepted Iran's claims on the Shatt in exchange for Iran abandoning support for the

Kurds. The agreement was announced at an OPEC meeting in Algiers in March, and a treaty signed in Baghdad in June. The Iraqis, despite the great advantage they drew from the treaty, considered it a national humiliation and awaited an opportunity to reassert their claims to the waterway.

The tensions between Sunni and Shiite, and between the secular Ba'ath party and militant Islam, were greatly exacerbated by the Iranian revolution. The Ayatollah Khomeini had been living in exile in Iraq since 1965, in Najaf. There he was closely associated with an Iraqi ayatollah, Baqir al-Sadr, who advocated the establishment of an Islamic republic in Iraq. The agreement with Iran on the Shatt al-Arab waterway and the Kurds also contained a clause forbidding each side to allow opposition movements against the other. In September 1978, belatedly, the Iranian government demanded that Iraq expel Khomeini, and he was sent to Paris. This proved a mistake: he found Paris much more congenial as a base of operations against the shah, and the expulsion confirmed his animosity towards Iraq.

Immediately after the Iranian revolution in February 1979, the new regime in Tehran began inciting Iraqi Shiites to revolt. A Shiite Islamic party, the Dawa, under Iranian influence, plotted against the regime and started a terrorist campaign. Saddam Hussein, who was then vice-president and the strong-man of the government, put the Ayatollah al-Sadr under house arrest in Najaf. There followed serious riots in Shiite neighbourhoods in Baghdad, which were put down with great brutality.

On 16 July 1979, Hussein persuaded the president, Hasan al-Bakr, to resign and took his place; he then vigorously set about consolidating his position. On 28 July, Baghdad Radio announced that 'a treacherous and lowly plot, perpetrated by a gang disloyal to the party and revolution has been discovered'. Five leading members of the Ba'ath Regional Council and 16 other senior figures were executed in the presence of Saddam Hussein and 'leading party cadres'. The radio announcement stated that the five 'were in contact with a foreign side' (i.e. Syria); one report suggested that four of them were Shiites. Then, after the attempted assassination of one of his closest assistants in April 1980, Hussein had the Ayatollah al-Sadr and his sister summarily hanged. He thus showed the brutal instincts of the true tyrant. The repression of the Shiites was intensified, and 15,000–20,000 of them were expelled to Iran and hundreds were executed.

By 1980, Saddam Hussein was firmly in control in Iraq. Oil revenues had risen from $1.8 billion in 1973 to $26.1 billion in 1980, and early in 1981, the price of oil reached $35 a barrel, five times its level in 1973. Iraq was not the only country to imagine that the golden years would last for ever.

In the 18 months following the flight of the shah, in January 1979, Iran slid to the brink of disintegration. The army lost virtually all its senior officers, and seemed incapable even of controlling the Kurds and Azerbaijanis. The Institute of Strategic Studies in London calculated that 60 per cent of the Iranian army deserted in the wake of the revolution. A ferocious battle for power was under way in Tehran between leftists and moderates and Islamic fundamentalists. Iran's behaviour, particularly its occupation of the American embassy and its seizure of the hostages, had isolated it among the community of nations, and by breaking with the United States, Iran had lost its chief military supplier: the shah had bought fleets of modern aircraft, but most were grounded through lack of spares and poor maintenance. The Iraqis claimed that, 'There is a government on every street corner in Iran.'

Iran's policy of generalized militancy extended to its relations with Iraq. Instead of conciliating its neighbours while it sorted out its domestic problems, it stirred up Shiite fundamentalism in Iraq. Saddam Hussein, newly installed as president in Baghdad, protested bitterly. At the same time, Iran's troubles seemed to him to provide a good moment to revive Iraq's claim to the whole of the Shatt al-Arab. Iraq was the only Arab power capable of defeating Iran and protecting the Sunni regimes in the Gulf from revolutionary Shiite fundamentalism, and the emir of Kuwait and the king of Saudi Arabia pledged their support of Saddam's ambitions. He hoped not merely to overthrow Khomeini and recover the whole Shatt, but to annex Khuzestan, Iran's Arabic-speaking province to the east of Mesopotamia, where a large part of Iran's oil reserves are to be found.

## THE WAR WITH IRAN

On 17 September 1980, Hussein announced that he was abrogating the 1975 treaty, and five days later, his armies mounted a general offensive. The Iraqis drove into Iran; Khorramshar, Iran's largest port, fell at the end of October; and Ahwaz, the provincial capital of Khuzestan, and Abadan, the country's oil capital, were threatened.

Although it seemed at first that Iraq would win easily, it quickly became apparent that the Iraqi armies were badly led and lacking in offensive spirit, and that Iraq had grossly underestimated Iran's military capability. The Iraqi offensive stalled at the end of 1980, with the Iranians clinging to a toehold in Khorramshar and holding Abadan against heavy Iraqi shelling. Iraqi troops were stopped well short of Ahwaz. In the spring and summer of 1981, Iran counter-attacked, and drove the Iraqis back from the approaches to Abadan.

The excuses that Hussein offered to explain the early defeats were remarkable. According to Christine Moss Helms, he said that Iraq's lines of communication had originally been too long, Iraqi forces were too widely dispersed, the reservists were inexperienced, and the Iranians fought better, defending their homeland and had better intelligence and better knowledge of the terrain. Furthermore, Iraq was at a disadvantage because it relied on tanks, and the Iranians had unsportingly attacked at night, when the tanks could not manoeuvre. In most nations, a general responsible for such miscalculations would be relieved of his post; in many, he would be shot. Iraq is a one-party dictatorship, and Saddam Hussein survived. It should be noted that the Ba'ath is a civilian party: only Saddam himself had a military background, although he was only a lieutenant in 1959 when he left the army and devoted himself to revolutionary politics. Iraq is like the Soviet Union in 1941, and military considerations are always subordinated to political ones, including the need for the ruling party to keep absolute control of the army.

On 7 June 1981, the Israeli air force bombed the Osirak nuclear reactor that the French had been building on the outskirts of Baghdad. The Israelis sent eight F-16s, each carrying two 2000-lb bombs, escorted by six F-15s. They flew high over

Jordan, and then at rooftop level to Baghdad, to pass under Iraqi radar. No planes were lost. Neither Iraqi nor Saudi radar, nor the American A W A C planes patrolling the Saudi skies, saw them come or go. (The Americans claimed rather lamely that they were looking the other way.) One French technician and a number of Iraqis were killed. The Israeli government, led then by Menachem Begin, claimed that Iraq was preparing to develop nuclear weapons. The French technicians (and the Iraqis) denied it. After the second Gulf War, in 1991, the U N and the Americans discovered that Iraq had been making strenuous efforts to build a nuclear arsenal, using every possible technique to obtain enriched uranium or plutonium. Evidently the Israelis had been quite right in 1981 and the Iraqis, and perhaps their French advisers, had been lying.

The war went on. Iran retained the initiative until the spring of 1988. A generalized offensive cleared the Iraqis from Khorramshar on 24 May 1982, and drove them back to their frontier. In another series of offensives, the Iranians pushed across the border in Kurdistan and across the desert towards the Tigris, and in February 1984, they seized Majnoon island in southern Iraq. It is an area that used to be marsh, and which was inhabited by the Marsh Arabs, a wholly separate and distinct tribe whose territory and way of life had been sacrificed to the oil industry. The marshes had been drained and the oil rigs set up: there were over 6 billion barrels of oil reserves to be found there. Capturing the area was a major victory for Iran.

One of the weapons the Iraqis used to repel the Iranians was poison gas, both the mustard gas that had been used in World War I, and nerve gas. The only other occasion that gas had been used since 1918 was when Mussolini employed it in Abyssinia in 1935 (*see* Ethiopia, p. 51). Iranian soldiers who had been gassed were taken to Europe to be treated.

In 1986, Iranian troops crossed the marshes at the mouth of the Shatt al-Arab and occupied the Faw peninsula. The following year, they mounted a massive onslaught on Basra, Iraq's second largest city, and almost broke through its defences. Most of the population fled: for many months, the city was in range of Iranian guns, which shelled it mercilessly. By then, the Iraqis had developed considerable defensive skills and were able to hold the Iranians off Basra, but in doing so, they left the northern front undermanned.

Every year Iran mounted offensives against Iraq, and every year Iraq held the line. The Iranians suffered immense casualties, sending fanatical Revolutionary Guards against Iraqi emplacements, like European soldiers going 'over the top' on the Western Front in World War I. Shiism proclaims the importance of martyrdom, and hundreds of thousands of Iranians volunteered to give their lives for the cause. The Guards would attack in human waves, driving back the Iraqis whatever the cost, preparing the way for the regular Iranian army. It was not until the Iraqis had dug substantial defensive lines, like the trenches on the Western Front, that they were able to stop the Guards. Even then, there was always the danger of a sudden breakthrough, like the capture of the Faw peninsula in 1986.

Although the fighting was exceedingly costly, Iran, which in 1980 had a population greater than Britain or France in 1914, did not suffer the same scale of casualties as those two countries had by 1918 (nearly a million for Britain, 1.3

million for France). Although estimates vary greatly, Iran probably lost between 400,000 and 600,000 dead between 1980 and 1988, Iraq about 150,000 killed, 500,000 wounded and 70,000 captured. In the attacks on Basra in January 1987, Iran lost 25,000 to 30,000 dead, and Iraq 5000 to 10,000. Iran could afford the disparity: its population is 50 million, compared with 18 million in Iraq.

## THE TANKER WAR

From the time the southern front stabilized at the end of 1980, Iran was able to prevent all Iraqi oil exports through the Shatt. In April 1982, as the tide of war turned against Iraq, Syria closed Iraq's pipeline to the Mediterranean, and it appeared for a while that Iraq would be strangled economically before it was defeated militarily.

The other Arab states came to the rescue. Iraq has one of the most unpleasant governments in the region and had shown constant hostility to the monarchies in Jordan, the Gulf and Saudi Arabia. However, the threat of Persian fundament-alism was far more to be feared, and thus the conservative Arab states could not afford to let Iraq be defeated. King Hussein of Jordan opened Aqaba to Iraqi imports (chiefly arms), pipelines were hurriedly constructed across the desert to the Red Sea, and through Turkey to the Mediterranean, and for a while, Iraqi exports also went through Kuwait. Above all, the conservative Arabs subsidized Iraq directly, to a tune of billions of dollars a year. In the eight years of the war, the subsidy reputedly came to $60 billion.

The tanker war started in 1984. Iraq attacked Iranian tankers and the main Iranian oil terminal at Kharg island, which was easily within reach of Iraqi air bases. Iran retaliated by attacking Kuwaiti and other Gulf tankers, on the grounds that, since those countries were supporting Iraq, their commerce was a legitimate Iranian target. Neither side succeeded in seriously damaging the other's exports. The price of oil, which started to drop sharply in 1982, was never seriously affected by the tanker war. Iran simply moved its main oil depot to Larak island in the Straits of Hormuz: small tankers from Kharg and other oilfields would carry oil to Larak and there transfer it to supertankers.

In 1987, Kuwait persuaded the United States to offer protection to the Kuwaiti oil fleet. Eleven Kuwaiti tankers were transferred to American regis-tration, and the United States began patrolling the Gulf to protect them. On 17 May, an Iraqi Super-Etendard fired two Exocet missiles at an American frigate, the USS *Stark*, apparently mistaking her for an Iranian warship. The *Stark*'s defences were not functioning, she was severely damaged and 37 American sailors were killed. Iraq apologized profusely and the Reagan administration accepted the excuses offered.

Iran retaliated by sowing mines in the Gulf, and several ships were hit. An American frigate, the USS *Samuel B. Roberts*, was hit by an Iranian mine on 14 April 1988 and severely damaged. In further retaliation, the US navy sank six Iranian warships and patrol boats, and destroyed two Iranian oil platforms.

Another feature of the Iran–Iraq war was the use of bombers and missiles to attack cities. Iraq launched the first bombing raids on Iranian cities in 1984, starting with an attack on Dizful in February, and later it extended them to Tehran and other urban areas. These attacks never attained the intensity of those **291** in earlier 20th-century wars – neither side had enough bombers – but as the conflict dragged on, the number of civilian casualties caused by the air war increased steadily.

In 1987, Iraq began using missiles against Iranian cities. These were Soviet-made Scud missiles, modified to carry as far as Tehran, which became the chief target. Other cities were hit, too, through not so severely, among them Shiraz, Kermanshah and Isfahan. The last is one of the most beautiful cities on Earth, comparable to Venice, and the possibility that its monuments might be damaged was the most serious threat to the world's cultural heritage since 1945. Iran retaliated by sending its own missiles against Baghdad.

## THE IRAQI VICTORY

In a military sense, however, the tanker war and the air war were sideshows. What counted was the war on the ground. In the spring of 1988, in its last offensive, Iran attacked in Kurdistan, driving its armies to within sight of the great Darbandi Khan reservoir and hydroelectric plant at Dukan, which supply Baghdad. Iran captured over 4000 Iraqi troops, including a divisional commander, and took 400 square miles (1000 sq. km) of territory. Losing the dam would have been a major defeat for Iraq. The Iranians had been advancing steadily through the mountains towards Kirkuk, and if they had broken through to the plains, they might have won the war. To stop them, Iraq used poison gas. In March 1988, an Iraqi Kurdish town, Halabjah, then under Iranian occupation, was hit by gas. The bodies of at least 100 civilians – women, children and elderly men – were shown to Western reporters brought down from Tehran for the occasion. Iran claimed that 2000 people had been killed, and a subsequent U N report confirmed the use of poison gas.

Despite the dangers of the Iranian attack in Kurdistan, the Iraqis sent no reinforcements, confident that they could hold the line. Besides, they needed their troops in the south: on 17 April, they launched a surprise offensive on the Faw peninsula and, in three days' heavy fighting, drove the Iranians back across the Shatt al-Arab. Liberating Faw after two years was Iraq's biggest victory and the decisive battle of the war. The following month, in another offensive, the Iraqis cleared the approaches to Basra, recovering virtually all the land lost earlier in the war. Reports from the front, both at Faw and outside Basra, indicated that the Iranian resistance was surprisingly weak. The army that had shown such courage and *elan* early in the war now broke and fled before the Arabs.

In June, Iraq attacked on the central front and recaptured the Majnoon oilfield that had been seized by Iran in 1984, and in a series of limited offensives to the east of the river, they recovered the last few miles of Iraqi territory occupied by the Iranians. In the same month, exiled Iranians – Massoud Rajavi's National Liberation Army – attacked across the border in Kurdistan. The N L A, formed of anti-Khomeini Mujaheddin (*see* Iran, pp. 271–83), reportedly had 15,000 troops, armed by the Iraqis – not enough to tip the balance in the war, but sufficient to play a role in Iran if the revolutionary regime collapsed. Their summer offensive took an Iranian town, Mehran, which they held for a few days before pulling back behind the frontier.

There were a number of reasons for Iraq's victories in 1988. The first was Iran's war-weariness, and perhaps also the loss of its revolutionary enthusiasm. A second reason was that Iraq, despite American efforts to prevent arms sales to both sides, had always been able to obtain the weapons and ammunition it needed. After the failure of its first offensive in 1980, the Baghdad regime mended its relations with Saudi Arabia, Kuwait and Jordan, and consolidated its good relations with Turkey. It kept its distance from the Soviet Union and went to great lengths to present itself as a reasonable, modern state fighting a fanatical aggressor in Tehran. This policy won it sympathy, if not arms, from Washington (and diplomatic relations, which had been broken in 1967, were at last resumed). In turn, better relations with the Americans permitted the development of fruitful relations with European arms dealers, notably the French.

The conservative Arabs supplied the money, the Europeans sold the arms, but the war was won by the steadfastness of Iraqi soldiers. Meanwhile Iran, isolated by its own fanaticism, found it impossible to supply its armies. A further Iraqi advantage was geographic: the battlefields were all within easy reach of Iraqi bases, supplied by the main roads running the length of the country, and as a result, Iraq could move troops easily and rapidly. Iran, by contrast, had to move troops and supplies down from the Iranian plateau, over high mountains and along winding and difficult roads.

On the ground, the Iraqi generals fought a defensive war from 1981 until 1988, allowing the Iranians to exhaust themselves in a series of offensives – in much the same way that the Germans conserved their energy from 1914 until 1918, allowing the Allies to beat fruitlessly upon the Western Front, and then launched one last assault towards Paris. The Iraqi armies held the line, most notably during the Iranian attacks on Basra in 1986–7, and the Ba'ath regime had the strength and sufficient popularity to hold the home front. That is, in many ways, the most remarkable of its achievements: in 1980, very few people would have predicted that Saddam Hussein could survive seven years of stalemate.

## THE CEASEFIRE

These Iraqi victories were the last straw for Iran. On 18 July 1988, the government in Tehran announced that it would accept the ceasefire that the UN had proposed. The ayatollah himself confirmed that he had approved the decision, and on 8 August the foreign ministers of the two countries, meeting UN secretary-general Pérez de Cuellar in New York, announced that the ceasefire would take effect on 20 August.

A UN peacekeeping force was hurriedly assembled and sent to the Gulf. There was some small-scale fighting, during which the Iraqis pushed the Iranians out of Kurdistan and demonstrated that they could penetrate Iranian territory at will, at least on the central front. After the ceasefire, Saddam Hussein turned his attention to the Kurdish rebels in the north and rapidly restored central authority throughout all Iraqi Kurdistan. The war was over.

(*For a more detailed account of the diplomatic manoeuvring that led to the ceasefire, see* Iran, *pp. 271–83, and for the reconquest of Kurdistan, see* The Kurds, *pp. 328–40.*)

## AFTER THE IRAN–IRAQ WAR

Iraq claimed to be victorious, but obtained none of the fruits of victory. Its foreign debt was $80 billion, and the Gulf states refused to write it off. The price of oil had continued to drop throughout the war, reducing Iraq's income by half when it desperately needed greater revenues to pay its debts and to rebuild its cities and industries. Economists calculated that Iraq would require $230 billion to rebuild after the war, and in 1989 its oil revenue was down to $13 billion. That was not enough for current needs and interest on foreign debt, let alone reconstruction. Then in 1989 and 1990, Kuwait and the emirates began systematically to exceed the quotas of oil production allotted them by OPEC, driving the price down still further. Iraq suffered unemployment, inflation, dropping living standards and all the misfortunes of living under a ruthless dictatorship.

In February 1990 Saddam Hussein informed the Gulf states that he required not only an immediate moratorium on all debt repayments, but a further $30 billion for Iraq's immediate needs. 'Let the Gulf regimes know that if they do not give the money to me, I shall know how to get it,' he said. The threat was ignored. Kuwait and the emirates continued to exceed their OPEC quotas, and the price of oil continued to drop.

Saddam Hussein gave a demonstration of his brutality, his power in the Arab world and also, perhaps, his insecurity, when in March 1990 he ordered an Iranian journalist, Farzad Bazoft, to be hanged. Bazoft was working for the British newspaper the *Observer* and had tried to investigate a report that a large explosion had occurred in a munitions plant south of Baghdad in August 1989. He was in the country at the invitation of the Iraqi government. He was arrested, charged with espionage, held incommunicado for six months and finally tried in a secret 'revolutionary tribunal'. He was sentenced to death on 10 March and hanged five days later.

Bazoft's execution, like the Ayatollah Khomeini's sentence of death on the novelist Salman Rushdie a year earlier, severely affected the country's relations with the West. The British protested, and the Ba'ath regime immediately organized a series of huge, anti-British demonstrations in Baghdad and other cities. Saddam Hussein's paranoid suspicions were doubtless the chief reason for killing Bazoft. He saw traitors, spies and enemies everywhere and stayed in power by killing them. As the years went by, of course, there came to be more and more traitors and enemies. The other Arab countries notably refrained from criticizing Iraq. It was too powerful and dangerous.

The West was outraged at the murder, and there was immediate retaliation. British customs officials seized the components of a 'super-gun' that Iraq had been building in England and elsewhere, and a joint American–British effort prevented the import by Iraq of devices needed in its nuclear programme. The question then arose why such steps had not been taken earlier. After the 1991 war, when the full details of Iraq's ballistic, nuclear, chemical and biological warfare programmes became known, and the full extent of Western participation in these programmes also emerged, the questions grew more pertinent. On 22 March 1990, Gerard Bull, the Canadian ballistics expert who had designed the super-gun, was murdered in Brussels.

Saddam did not just threaten the Gulf states. He threatened Israel. In a speech delivered in April 1990, he said, 'By God, we will make fire eat half of Israel if it tries to do anything against Iraq.'

Saddam presented his case at an Arab summit in Baghdad in May, pointing out that every $1 drop in the price of oil meant a billion-dollar loss for Iraq. He accused the Gulf states of waging economic war on Iraq and once again threatened to take unilateral steps to protect himself. In June, Saddam accused Kuwait of stealing $89 billion from Iraq by exceeding its OPEC quotas, and also stealing $2.4 billion of oil from the Rumaila oil field, which is divided between the two countries. He further claimed two Kuwaiti islands in the Gulf, in the mouth of the Shatt al-Arab. Iraq demanded that the price of oil should be pushed up to $25 a barrel, that Kuwait should repay the money it had stolen, and that there should be a moratorium on debt repayments and a 'Marshall Plan' to help Iraq out of its economic difficulties. Kuwait refused to take the threats seriously, and rejected the Iraqi demands out of hand.

Saddam began preparations for invasion. Iraq has had an irridentist claim on Kuwait for generations, based on a vague suzerainty exercised over the Gulf by the Ottoman empire. The British took Kuwait and the emirates under their protection in the 19th century and saved them from annexation by King Abdul Aziz (Ibn Saud) in the 20th. In 1961, the Iraqi dictator Kassem threatened to annex Kuwait, and the British sent troops there to protect it. Shortly afterwards, Kuwait became fully independent, and Iraq apparently allowed its claims to lapse. Now Saddam prepared to revive them.

On 21 July 1990, Saddam began moving his army south. The world suddenly realized how serious the crisis had become. The Egyptian president, Hosni Mubarak, flew to Baghdad seeking reassurance, and Saddam swore that he had no intention of attacking Kuwait. Mubarak never forgave the lie.

Saddam was more concerned about America's reactions to his plans. The United States had tilted to Iraq throughout the first Gulf War. It had forgiven the attack on the USS *Stark* and had not protested very vocally when Bazoft was executed. A month later, a group of five senators visited Baghdad, led by Robert Dole, the senior Republican in the Senate. They told Saddam Hussein that his problems were not with the United States but with 'a haughty and pampered press'. Later that month, when Congress tried to impose trade sanctions on Iraq for violating human rights, the Bush administration intervened and stopped the proposal.

On 25 July, Saddam summoned the American ambassador in Baghdad, April Glaspie. He explained to her his position over Kuwait and openly threatened the emirate – and even threatened the United States with terrorism if it interfered. Glaspie, following instructions, reassured him of America's favour. She said, 'President Bush is an intelligent man and is not going to declare economic war on Iraq.' She told him that his aims 'should receive strong support from your brother Arabs', and finally, 'the United States has no opinion on inter-Arab disputes such as your border dispute with Kuwait, and the secretary of state has directed our official spokesman to reiterate this stand'.

These quotations come from a transcript of the interview produced by the Iraqis, to the Americans' deep embarrassment, after the confrontation got under way. Saddam claimed that he had been misled, that he had expected the United

States to remain neutral, and certainly Glaspie's words gave him some reason for the belief.

## THE SECOND GULF WAR

On 2 August 1990, Iraq occupied Kuwait. The operation took a few hours. The emir and his family barely escaped capture (one of his brothers was killed) and most of the Kuwaiti army was captured. Saddam informed the world that there had been a revolution in Kuwait, and that a Provisional Revolutionary Government had taken power. No one believed him for a moment, and he never produced this suppositious government. Iraq said that its troops were merely protecting the new regime, and would withdraw by 5 August. It insisted that it had no aggressive intentions against Saudi Arabia.

The international reaction to the invasion was swift and unequivocal. The first of a series of Security Council resolutions passed on the day of the invasion (Resolution 660) condemned the invasion and demanded that Iraq withdraw from Kuwait immediately. Brisk diplomacy followed, and on 6 August the Security Council, in Resolution 661, imposed a complete trade and financial embargo on Iraq. Two days later President Bush announced that he was sending American troops to Saudi Arabia. Saddam retaliated by announcing the annexation of Kuwait, which became Iraq's 19th province.

The United States was joined by its allies, with greater or lesser enthusiasm. Bush set about constructing an international coalition to confront Saddam, starting with European powers and the Soviet Union. The chief measure of the changes in the world was the USSR's immediate agreement with every American proposal concerning Iraq, though it did not send troops to take part in military operations. China acquiesced, Japan agreed to contribute financially and Egypt and Syria, as well as the Gulf states, all agreed to send troops.

Saddam was not entirely alone. He was hailed as an Arab hero by huge crowds of demonstrators in many Arab countries, and also in Muslim countries in Asia, including both Pakistan and Bangladesh. The Palestinians embraced him as hero and leader, in a last spasm of folly. Palestinians in Jordan were so enthusiastically pro-Saddam that King Hussein was forced to support Iraq. This enthusiasm later cost the Palestinians dear, but in the short run, it encouraged Saddam to think that he could put himself at the head of a mass Arab movement to overthrow oppressive governments – meaning those that opposed him. From the start he encouraged this tendency by attacking Israel, promising to destroy it. He offered to consider withdrawing from Kuwait if the Israelis first withdrew from the territories they had occupied in 1967, and was cheered in Amman and Tripoli.

As the storm clouds gathered, Saddam settled his long dispute with Iran. He summarily abandoned all the claims he had against Iran, accepting the 1975 treaty which set the frontier between the two countries in the middle of the Shatt, and agreed to withdraw all Iraqi troops from Iranian territory. In exchange for this diplomatic victory, Iran promised to return all its remaining Iraqi prisoners. The promise was not kept until 1998. Thus, at a stroke, Saddam liquidated the first Gulf War, which had cost his country 150,000 deaths and $230 billion in treasure.

There were hundreds of thousands of foreigners in Kuwait and Iraq at the time of the invasion, and they fled the coming storm. For weeks, huge numbers of Bengalis, Filipinos and Sri Lankans camped in the desert at the Jordanian frontier, while international organizations rounded up planes to ship them home. Egyptians from Iraq and Palestinians from Kuwait also tried to escape. Meanwhile, Saddam arrested all the Westerners he could catch in Kuwait and in Iraq, and held them hostage. The women and children were incarcerated in hotels in Baghdad, and the men were posted to airfields and bases that might be attacked, as human shields. On one televised occasion, Saddam visited a group of British women and children held in a hotel in Baghdad, patting one small boy on the head. The U N demanded that all hostages be released, and under intense world pressure, Iraq gradually freed them.

The American build-up in the Saudi desert continued inexorably, and the likelihood that the crisis would end in war grew ever stronger. Saddam began to warn his enemies that they would face 'the mother of battles' if they attacked him. In early November 1990, President Bush announced that the American forces would reach half a million men and it became known that preparations for an assault on Iraq would be completed early in the New Year. Diplomatic efforts to avert war continued. On 29 November, a Security Council resolution (number 678) demanded that Iraq withdraw unconditionally from Kuwait by 15 January. The vote was 12 to 2. Cuba and Yemen voted against, China abstained. President Bush announced that he would send the secretary of state to Baghdad to see Saddam.

Saddam Hussein was driven into a corner. He could not abandon Kuwait without admitting defeat, and that would quite probably lead to his overthrow and death. He preferred to fight. The secretary of state did not go to Baghdad. Instead, at the last moment, he met the Iraqi foreign minister, Tariq Aziz, in Geneva on 9 January. The meeting was fruitless. The American Congress then debated the question at great, painful length, finally voting on 12 January to approve military action against Iraq.

The war, codenamed Operation Desert Storm, began early in the morning of 17 January. Allied planes attacked high-priority targets in Baghdad and around the country, immediately establishing total mastery of the air. Throughout the war, the Iraqi air force and anti-aircraft defences were quite unable to interfere with allied operations. The great majority of planes used on the first night were American, but British, Kuwaiti and Saudi planes also took part. Western television crews in Baghdad filmed the battle from their hotel windows.

The air war lasted five weeks. The first targets were anti-aircraft defences, the Iraqi air force itself, and the command and communications centres. Attacks were then extended to Iraq's surface-to-surface missile forces (chiefly Soviet-made Scud mobile missiles) and army and navy targets. Later, the allies attacked Iraqi nuclear, chemical and biological warfare facilities. The U S Navy used its Tomahawk cruise missiles for the first time, and they proved highly accurate. Saddam sent about 100 of his surviving warplanes to safety in Iran, where they were promptly confiscated by the Iranians as war reparations.

It was the most intense aerial bombardment since World War II. At the height of the air war, the allies were flying 4000 or 5000 sorties a day over Iraq and Kuwait. They were not all bombers: at least half were escort planes, command planes, refuelling, electronic warfare and reconnaissance planes, but the total of bombers was still immense. B-52s from England, Spain and Diego Garcia took part in the attack. On 13 February American bombers hit an air-raid shelter in Baghdad, killing over 300 civilians. It was the largest civilian loss of the air war. The Americans claimed that the building was a command centre, but journalists who visited the spot were not convinced.

Iraq retaliated by launching Scud missiles at Saudi Arabia and Israel. Only one of the missiles did serious damage, on 25 February, when it hit a barracks at the Daharan air base in Saudi Arabia, killing 28 Americans. The purpose of attacking Israel was to force Israel to join the war, in the hope that Israeli participation would precipitate revolutions in Egypt, Syria and Saudi Arabia. The United States rushed Patriot surface-to-air missiles to Israel, to protect it against attack. They proved much less effective militarily than psychologically. Israelis took to air-raid shelters, or gas-proof rooms in their houses, and carried gas masks at all times. So did Saudis and all foreigners in the threatened areas of Saudi Arabia. In the event, Iraq never used poison gas, but the precautions were obviously necessary: Iraq is the only country that has dropped poison gas since Italy used it against Abyssinia in 1935. A small number of Scud missiles hit Israel, but the Israelis continued to leave their defence to the allies and refused to be provoked by Saddam Hussein.

Saddam began a war against the ecology during the air war. He ordered oil pipelines leading to terminals in the Gulf to be opened, flooding the Persian Gulf with oil, and he ordered several oil wells in Kuwait to be set on fire. In preparation for the final apocalypse, he ordered all Kuwait's oil installations to be mined and preparations to be made to set every oil well in the emirate ablaze.

In the later stages of the air offensive, the allies attacked military and civilian targets across the whole of Iraq. They destroyed electric power plants, bridges, water treatment and sewage plants and large numbers of factories. Finally, they battered the unfortunate Iraqi army in Kuwait. Iraqi troops were thoroughly dug in, but that was small protection against the heavy bombs of the US air force.

There were various skirmishes along the front lines as the overwhelming mass of allied troops prepared for battle. The Iraqis mounted one offensive, along the coast of the Gulf, penetrating 12 miles (20 km) into Saudi Arabia before they were stopped. In late January, Saddam brought his army out in an attempt to attack his enemies. Sixty thousand troops and thousands of tanks were moved towards the border, and were mercilessly attacked from the air. The offensive was defeated before it could begin, with heavy losses. After that, the Iraqis awaited the coming onslaught as stoically as they could.

There was a last flurry of diplomacy on 21 February when Tariq Aziz flew to Moscow to try to arrange terms for a settlement. Saddam offered to withdraw from Kuwait, but did not announce publicly that he was accepting all the UN resolutions. The tentative agreement, under which Iraq would have saved its army in Kuwait, was rejected by the United States. On 22 February, President Bush issued a last ultimatum to Iraq, to begin its withdrawal within 24 hours and to complete it within a week, and to accept all the UN resolutions.

The ground war began on Saturday afternoon, 23 February 1991. It lasted 100 hours. There had been much speculation that Iraq would put up a ferocious resistance and that breaking through Iraqi lines would cause heavy allied casualties. In the event, the allies simply rolled over the Iraqis. Within 24 hours of the opening of the offensive, French troops were on the Euphrates, American troops were in the outskirts of Kuwait City, Saudi troops were approaching Kuwait City along the coast, and American and British forces, the main allied army, had swept around Kuwait itself to cut off the entire Iraqi army there. The Iraqis began a precipitous retreat and were mercilessly attacked from the air. Over 60,000 prisoners were taken.

The Iraqis hardly resisted. They surrendered, or fled. They had suffered heavy casualties during the air war, particularly as American B-52s carpet-bombed their positions. During the allied ground attack, thousands more were killed in a novel technique of modern warfare: tanks equipped as bulldozers simply buried Iraqi troops in their trenches. Twenty-four hours after the offensive began, Iraqis in Kuwait City fled to the north. They seized any vehicle they could find and soon the highway to Basra was one enormous traffic jam of tanks, Mercedes limousines and trucks filled with loot from Kuwait. The allied air forces intercepted the fleeing convoy and destroyed it. Afterwards, the macabre scene on the highway was the most conspicuous example of the destructiveness of the war in Kuwait itself.

On the second day of the ground offensive, Saddam Hussein ordered his troops out of Kuwait. The Americans refused to consider this a sufficient gesture and pursued their attack. On the fourth day, it was all over. Kuwait had been liberated, the allies were across the Euphrates and Iraq was at their mercy. President Bush then ordered a ceasefire. This became the most controversial decision of the war. The Iraqi army was severely damaged but was not destroyed. Saddam Hussein remained in power. If George Bush had ordered an armoured division up the road to Baghdad, it would have been there in a day, and Saddam Hussein would have fallen. Bush considered that it was not part of the UN mandate to overthrow the Iraqi government.

Immediately the fighting ceased, the Shiites in southern Iraq rose in revolt. They seized control of the major cities, including Basra and the two holy cities, Najaf and Karbala, and wreaked vengeance on the Ba'ath party and the army. Their example was followed by the Kurds, who seized the whole of Kurdistan and proclaimed their freedom. But the beast was wounded, not killed, and struck back at its enemies. The Republican Guards, the most loyal units in the army, had survived the war, and immediately set about reducing the south to obedience. No one knows how many people were killed. It was certainly far more than were killed by the allied air offensive, which probably killed only a few thousand civilians. The brief civil war in the south and in Kurdistan killed perhaps 30,000 or 50,000 people. Basra was reduced to ruins for a second time. The shrines to the Shiite saints in the holy cities were severely damaged, and by the time the rebellion had been crushed, southern Iraq was devastated.

The Republican Guards were then sent north to deal with the Kurds. They drove into Kurdish towns and into the mountains, and the people fled before them. By the end of March 1991, 750,000 Kurds had fled across the mountains into Iran and about 250,000 into Turkey. It was still winter in the hills and thousands died, particularly old people and children. A massive international relief effort was put together immediately, and soon American and allied planes were dropping thousands of tons of food and medicine to the refugees in Turkey. The ones in Iran were left to the Iranians, who refused to allow foreign assistance.

The Americans calculated that the Iraqis lost about 100,000 men killed in the war. If the total of those killed in the civil war that followed, and those who died in the refugee camps and on the roads as they fled the Iraqi army, was about 50,000, then the war to annex Kuwait and, when that failed, to save Saddam Hussein's neck, cost about 150,000 lives.

Immediately the allies attacked on the ground, Saddam Hussein ordered Kuwait's oil wells to be set afire. Seven hundred and forty-nine wells were damaged, of which 650 were fired. About 600 million barrels of oil were lost, costing about $12 billion, the equivalent of three months' consumption for the whole world. The air was polluted as far away as Pakistan, and everything in Kuwait was covered in a scum of oil. The Kuwaitis called on every fire-fighting expert in the world, led by Texans, to deal with the catastrophe. At the height of the fight, 10,000 workers from 34 countries were dealing with the fires – and trying to cope with the dangers of mines and other explosives, and the immense lakes of oil on the desert. The last fire was extinguished on 6 November 1991. The firefighting operation cost about $1 billion, and the total cost of rebuilding Kuwait was estimated to be $22 billion.

Kuwait recovered quickly, because of its huge oil reserves and because it was free to resume exporting oil as soon as its facilities were repaired. However, it had suffered much more than mere physical damage. Over half its population before the war was foreign, most of them Palestinians. Some of the Palestinians in Kuwait and the great majority of those in Jordan, Lebanon and in Israel and the occupied territories supported Saddam Hussein. Yasser Arafat gave vociferous support to the Iraqi dictator, and when Kuwait recovered its independence, it took immediate revenge upon the Palestinians living there. About 300,000 people were expelled. Kuwait then discovered that the country would not function without foreign help and was faced with the quandary of where to find servants, bureaucrats, junior and middle level officials, specialists and workers to replace the departing Palestinians.

## AFTER THE WAR

The alliance insisted that the sanctions imposed on Iraq in 1990 should remain in force until Saddam Hussein had complied with all the terms laid down by the UN in 1990 and 1991, and those of the ceasefire. They included reparations to Kuwait and the return of prisoners and valuables looted (several museums in Kuwait were stripped). Above all, the UN required the dismantling of Iraq's nuclear, biological and chemical warfare industries, and the missiles and super-guns intended to attack Iraq's neighbours. Iraq complied slowly, reluctantly and partially with these demands. Evidently, most of the missing Kuwaitis had been killed and the works of art, money and other objects stolen in Kuwait had vanished for good. It was also obvious that Iraq could not begin to repay hundreds of billions of dollars in reparations before its oil industry was completely restored and exports resumed full flood. The sums demanded were in any case greater than Iraq could ever pay, like those demanded of Germany after 1919. Some agreement might have been reached on all these matters if Iraq had not sought at all times to frustrate the UN's efforts to control its illicit armaments.

UN inspection teams, known as the UN Special Commission (UNSCOM), toured Iraq immediately after the war and discovered an extensive nuclear weapons industry. Iraq had been smuggling components from Europe and elsewhere to build uranium-enrichment factories and perhaps acquire plutonium. The super-gun was half complete, and Iraq was importing parts to build more accurate and longer-range missiles than the Scuds bought from the USSR. Iraq had large stockpiles of nerve gas and mustard gas and, worst of all, there was clear evidence that it had been developing biological weapons, such as anthrax and botulism, and preparing to make shells to fire those poisons at its enemies.

Later, UNSCOM asserted that it destroyed more of Iraq's prohibited weapons during its inspections than the whole huge air offensive had managed to destroy in 1991. That rather suggested the limitations of aerial bombardment. By 1996, UNSCOM believed that it had probably eliminated Iraq's capacity to make nuclear weapons, its modern missiles and, to an undetermined extent, its chemical weapons facilities. This was not certain, however, and UNSCOM argued that Iraq still had the capacity to make and deliver biological weapons. It also suspected that Iraq had successfully concealed some Scud missiles.

Iraq put every hindrance in UNSCOM's way, despite continuing Security Council protests. The first serious clash occurred in July 1992, when UNSCOM inspectors were prevented from entering buildings where they suspected weapons of mass destruction were concealed. After prolonged, and unproductive, negotiation American, British and French planes attacked a series of targets in Iraq in January 1993. The targets were anti-aircraft missile batteries in the southern no-fly zone.

These attacks were followed up by further raids, including an attack on a factory that was believed to make calutrons, machines needed to produce enriched uranium. Forty Tomahawk cruise missiles were launched at the factory and did extensive damage. One wandered far afield, hitting the Rashid Hotel in Baghdad, the favourite lodging place of foreign journalists.

Saddam then relented, and for a while UNSCOM went about its work unmolested, finding and destroying huge quantities of weapons. Then the disputes resumed. Saddam evidently hoped that the council would weary of the incessant controversy and that Russia, China and France would in the end insist that sanctions be lifted. The continuing sanctions had a dire effect on Iraq. The ban on exporting oil meant that it could not import essential supplies, including food and medicine. Oil was, of course, smuggled out through Kurdistan and, later, by small tankers through the Gulf, but not nearly enough for Iraq's needs. At any event, Saddam used those revenues to restock his arsenals. He then claimed that hundreds of thousands of children were malnourished because of sanctions, and thousands were dying every year.

In April 1993 U S planes patrolling the no-fly zone fired at Iraqi anti-aircraft bases, which had fired at them. That same month, Kuwaiti police arrested a group of Iraqis planning to assassinate George Bush, the former American president. On 26 June President Clinton ordered a massive attack on Iraqi intelligence headquarters in Baghdad, in retaliation for the attempted assassination. The building was hit and destroyed by 23 Tomahawks, in the night, to minimize casualties.

In October 1994 Iraq suddenly sent 20,000 of the Republican Guard to the frontier with Kuwait, in what looked very like preparations for a new invasion. President Clinton ordered a massive reinforcement of American troops, and by the middle of the month there were 40,000 Americans in the Gulf. Possibly in recognition of American resolve, Saddam finally issued a decree in November recognizing Kuwait and its frontiers.

The Kurdish dispute continued to exercise much international concern (*see* The Kurds, p. 328). The allies enforced a no-fly zone over northern Iraq, patrolled by allied planes from bases in Turkey. Controls were so strict that a U N plane once by mistake shot down an American helicopter carrying American and French officials and Kurdish notables. Late in 1994, the two main Kurdish parties began fighting each other and Saddam seized the opportunity to reoccupy Sulaimaniya. Northern Kurdistan retained its precarious autonomy for as long as western protection continued.

There was also a no-fly zone in the south. This was called Operation Southern Watch, imposed in 1992 after Saddam launched air attacks against Shiite rebels, and covered all Iraq below the 32nd parallel. It was extended to the 33rd parallel in September 1996 when Iraq reoccupied Arbil, in Kurdistan, after a new outbreak of fighting between the two Kurdish factions. The new line is a mere 30 miles south of Baghdad. The United States also launched 44 cruise missiles at military targets in southern Iraq on 3 and 4 September. After that demonstration, Saddam withdrew his forces from Arbil.

Saddam continued to defend himself against dissent with his accustomed ferocity. His family split in 1995 when his two sons-in-law fled to Jordan after a quarrel with Saddam's eldest son, Uday. They took their wives, the president's daughters, with them. They stayed in Amman for many months and presumably provided the Jordanians and western intelligence with a great deal of useful information on the working of the regime. However, they had played so large a part in the brutalities of Saddam's government that no country would offer them asylum. In February 1996 they listened to the promises of Uday Hussein that their lives would be spared if they returned to Baghdad, and went home. They were filmed kissing Saddam's feet, and were killed the next day. Uday himself was the victim of an attempted assassination in December 1996.

## THE 1998 CRISIS

Iraqi officials continued to interfere with U N S C O M's work, and in October 1997, when inspectors claimed that they were approaching discovery of Iraq's most secret facilities for making biological weapons, especially anthrax, Saddam provoked a new crisis. First, he ordered all American members of the inspection teams to leave. They were forced to drive to the Jordanian border. The rest of UNSCOM pulled out by air.

The United States, supported by Britain, began to build up its air and naval forces in the Gulf. On 21 November Iraq relented, and allowed UNSCOM to return to Iraq, including some Americans. In flurries of negotiations over the next few months, Iraq established that it could limit but not eliminate the American contingent – and it included British and some other nationalities in its restrictions. However, Saddam also announced that UNSCOM inspectors would not be allowed into 'presidential palaces'.

There were many and varying numbers of these buildings, sometimes over 80, sometimes merely 40 or so. Many were enormous, including not only lavish palaces Saddam had built for himself, but barracks and other military installations, and many outbuildings. Some covered many dozens of square miles. At least one was larger than the city of Washington. The Security Council, backing the Americans and British, insisted that UNSCOM must be allowed unfettered access to all of them, though it was never altogether clear how teams of a few score foreigners could possibly locate documents and small laboratories that might be hidden anywhere in Iraq. Nor did President Clinton make it clear that sanctions would be lifted eventually if UNSCOM were allowed unlimited access to every corner of Iraq – and found nothing.

The Americans continued their build-up, sending three aircraft carriers and a plethora of other vessels there, and reinforcing the Air Force at its bases in the Gulf. As they prepared to attack Iraq if Saddam still refused to allow inspectors into his palaces, they discovered that most other Arabs opposed a new attack – unless it was intended to kill Saddam himself. Saudi Arabia conspicuously refused to allow its territory to be used as a base for a renewed onslaught, unless the Americans were ready to send in troops to hunt down Saddam Hussein, and kill him. Despite Saddam's unpopularity in the United States, there was no support at all for any such extreme measure.

The crisis was resolved by diplomacy, but only after President Clinton had completed a huge American build-up in the Gulf and made it clear that he was quite ready to order a massive and sustained air war against Iraq if Saddam did not comply with UNSCOM's demands. The UN secretary general, Kofi Annan, went to Baghdad on 20 February, 1998, and conducted detailed negotiations with Saddam and his government. They agreed on 22 February that UNSCOM would be allowed unfettered inspections of 'presidential sites' so long as they were accompanied by neutral diplomats appointed by the Security Council.

The Americans reluctantly accepted the compromise, and UNSCOM, including all its American and British members, and its Australian chairman, returned to Baghdad. They resumed their inspections, including the previously forbidden presidential palaces and government offices. To begin with, they found nothing compromising but it was quite possible that Saddam might resume the game at some later date. In the mean time, he could claim that he had faced down the United States and shown that there were serious splits in the 1990 coalition,

## FURTHER READING

Allen, Thomas, *War in the Gulf,* Atlanta, Georgia, Turner Publishing, 1991.

Bulloch, John, *The Persian Gulf Unveiled,* New York, St Martin's Press, 1985.

Bulloch, John and Morris, Harvey, *Saddam's War: The Origins of the Kuwait Conflict and the International Response,* London, Faber and Faber, 1991.

*The Cambridge History of Islam,* Cambridge University Press.

Dann, Uriel, *Iraq under Qassem,* New York, Praeger, 1969.

Exexcutive Council of the Iraqi National Congress, *Crimes Against Humanity and the Transition from Dictatorship,* 1993.

Helms, Christine Moss, *Iraq, Eastern Flank of the Arab World,* Washington, Brookings Institution, 1985.

Khaddouri, Majid, *The Gulf War: The Origins and Implications of the Iraq-Iran Conflict,* Oxford University Press, 1988.

—, *Republican Iraq,* Oxford University Press, 1969.

—, *Socialist Iraq,* Washington D.C., Middle East Institute, 1978.

Makiya, Kanan, *Cruelty and Silence: War, Tyranny, Uprising and the Arab World,* New York, W.W. Norton, 1993.

Marr, Phoebe, *The Modern History of Iraq,* Boulder, Colo., Westview Press, 1985.

Mortimer, Edward, *Faith and Power – The Politics of Islam,* London, Faber and Faber, 1982.

Penrose, Edith Tilton, *Iraq: International Relations and National Development,* London, E. Benn, Boulder, Colo., Westview Press, 1978.

Samir, Khalil, *Republic of Fear,* Berkeley, University of California Press, 1989.

Sciolino, Elaine, *The Outlaw State,* New York, Wiley, 1991.

Timmerman, Kenneth R., *The Death Lobby: How the West Armed Iraq,* New York, Houghton Mifflin, 1992.

# ISRAEL

| | |
|---|---|
| Geography | 7993 sq. miles (20,702 sq. km); about the size of Belgium. Occupied territories: 2847 sq. miles (7115 sq. km). |
| Population | Israel: There are 127,600 Jewish settlers on the West Bank and 5200 in the Gaza Strip. <br> Palestine: West Bank 1,427,741; East Jerusalem, 153,700; GDP per capita, $2500. Gaza Strip, 923,940; GDP per capita, $1200 |
| GNP per capita | $15,920. |
| Refugees | 532,438 people on the West Bank and 716,930 in Gaza strip were classified as refugees by U N W R A in 1996. There are said to be *3,718,500 Palestinian refugees altogether, a number much disputed. |
| Casualties | About 17,000 Israelis were killed in acts of war in the first 50 years of its independence. By October 1991, five years after the beginning of the intifada, 663 Arab civilians had been killed by security forces in the occupied territories, 501 Palestinians by other Arabs, and 40 Israelis by Arabs. In 1991, 101 Palestinians were killed by Israelis and 140 by other Palestinians. Seven Israelis were killed. |

During its pre-history as a Jewish colony in Palestine and for the first 20 years of its independence, Israel saw itself as David confronting an implacable Arab Goliath who was intent on its destruction. It was a reasonable enough myth. The turning-point came in 1967, when David defeated the combined armies of Egypt, Jordan, and Syria, and captured the Old City of Jerusalem and the heights of Samaria and Judea. Since then, Israel has been the dominant military power in the Levant, and all the international sympathy once felt for embattled David slowly leached away and was progressively transferred to the oppressed Palestinians. By 1973, when Anwar Sadat launched his surprise attack across the Canal on Yom Kippur, Israel was dangerously isolated, supported only by the United States. Israel's narrow victory led to a change of policy in Israel and Egypt. Sadat flew to Jerusalem in November 1978 and, a year later, signed a peace treaty with Menachem Begin in front of the White House in Washington.

It was a dramatic moment, and was not repeated for another 14 years. Then at last, on 13 September 1993, on the White House lawn, Yitzak Rabin, who had been chief of staff during the Six-Day War, shook hands with **305**

Yasser Arafat, chairman of the Palestine Liberation Organization, and the two men signed a peace agreement. It was beyond doubt an important moment, but events proved that two leaders signing a paper does not of itself bring peace.

The 'peace process' had been inaugurated in secret diplomacy three years earlier, and was destined to continue for years to come, bitterly opposed by about half the people of Israel and very many Palestinians. No doubt it will end eventually with some sort of Palestinian state, and Israel and Palestine will then live together in mutual distrust and antagonism but no longer at war, quarrelling over borders, refugees, water and periodic outbursts of terrorism. Eventually, they may come to live in harmony together, but it will not happen soon.

## HISTORY

Not many nations have a birth certificate. Israel's took the form of a letter from Sir Arthur Balfour, British foreign secretary, to Lord Rothschild, dated 2 November 1917:

Dear Lord Rothschild,

I have much pleasure in conveying to you, on behalf of His Majesty's Government, the following declaration of sympathy with Jewish Zionist aspirations which has been submitted to, and approved by, the Cabinet:
'His Majesty's Government view with favour the establishment in Palestine of a national home for the Jewish people, and will use their best endeavours to facilitate the achievement of this object, it being clearly understood that nothing shall be done which may prejudice the civil and religious rights of the existing non-Jewish communities in Palestine, or the rights and political status enjoyed by Jews in any other country.'
I should be grateful if you would bring this declaration to the knowledge of the Zionist federation.

Yours sincerely,<br>Arthur Balfour

It will be noted that this 'Balfour Declaration' – with which the French government also associated itself – did not promise Palestine as the national home for the Jews – it promised a national home *in* Palestine. Nor did it define the territorial boundaries of Palestine.

Eighty years later, it is both impossible and profitless to establish whether Balfour and his colleagues were being disingenuous. It is at any rate clear that within a very few years, the British government had discovered that the two promises in the Declaration could not both be kept: the Jews and the Palestinians could not both be satisfied.

One month after the Declaration was written, the British army commanded by Lord Allenby occupied Palestine: an Australian unit reached Bethlehem at Christmas, allegedly prompting a British trooper to remark, 'I'll bet the shepherds watched their flocks that night.' After the war, the British and French divided the Levant between them, the British taking Iraq and Palestine and the French taking Syria, as mandates under the League of Nations. Although the United States did not join the League, a resolution of Congress approved these arrangements.

In the absence of the United States, Britain and France controlled the League, and were therefore able to set the terms of the mandates to their satisfaction. These terms provided that the mandatory powers were to rule the territories in the interests of their inhabitants. The Balfour Declaration was incorporated into the British mandate for Palestine, making a 'national home for the Jews' an international obligation. The British and French defined the northern boundary of Palestine, now the frontier between Israel and Lebanon, and the British ceded eastern Palestine, known as Transjordan, to the Emir Abdullah ibn Hussein (*see* Syria, p. 364). The wishes of the Arab inhabitants of these territories were not considered, although President Wilson sent an investigative commission to the Levant, which concluded that the Arabs had no desire to be subjected to a foreign government, but that if such subjection were unavoidable, they would prefer an American mandate to a British one, and a British mandate to a French one.

Palestine and the Jewish community there were of no great concern to the world, or even to most of the Jews, before 1933. The 1920s saw the last great flowering of Jewish life in Europe, and Jews in America joined in the general security and prosperity. No one could foresee the horror to come, save those who planned it, and Palestine seemed, at best, a difficult frontier territory. It was not yet a refuge: the Jews did not need one.

At the time of the Balfour Declaration, there were about 610,000 Arabs (Muslim and Christian) and 50,000 Jews in Palestine, meaning the area between the Jordan and the Mediterranean. The number of Jews rose to 84,000 by 1922 and increased substantially during the early 1920s. Later in the decade, Arab resistance (including the massacre of 60 Jews in Hebron in 1929) and a local recession reduced Jewish immigration to a trickle or even a net emigration.

All that changed after 30 January 1933, when Hitler came to power in Germany. Jewish immigration jumped from 4075 in 1931 to 30,327 in 1933, 42,359 in 1934 and 61,854 in 1935. America had shut its doors to the mass of emigrants and the rest of the world was equally hostile. Palestine was for a while the Jews' hope and refuge, so long as the British allowed free immigration. Those Jews who fled Germany in the early 1930s did so before the Nazi regime began serious persecution, and long before the start of the killings. They had often to abandon all their possessions to escape. Many others refused to succumb to panic. In the event, panic and flight were shown to be the course of wisdom, and all those who counselled patience were deceived.

The flood of immigrants into Palestine led to an Arab uprising in 1936, which was put down with much difficulty. The British then concluded that the two principles of the Balfour Declaration could never be reconciled: there could not be a national home for the Jews in Palestine while the rights of the Palestinians were protected. Severe restrictions on Jewish immigration were therefore imposed just as the great horror of the century was becoming apparent. The British held a conference in London to discuss partitioning Palestine. The Jews were to be allocated a very small area along the coast, and reluctantly accepted. The Arabs rejected partition entirely (a refusal they have come to regret) and in May 1939, in a White Paper, the British government announced that Palestine would **307** become independent, as a unitary state, in 1949. Jewish immigration in the interim would be restricted to 65,000. It was then that the Jewish leader Chaim Weizmann, pleading for the Jews, said: 'There are in this part of the world (Europe) six million people doomed to be pent up in places where they are not wanted, and for whom the world is divided into places where they cannot live, and places where they cannot enter.'

The persecution of the German Jews increased suddenly when Hitler annexed Austria in March 1938. The Jews of Vienna were set to scrub the sidewalks while the Austrians jeered at them. Then came *ReichsKristallnacht* ('glass night', so named because of the number of windows broken) when Goebbels organized a national pogrom on 10 November 1938. By then, President Roosevelt had convened a conference at Evian in the French Alps, to discuss the question of Jewish refugees. The assembled statesmen concluded, regretfully, that there was very little that could be done. The United States and Britain each agreed to take 30,000 Jewish refugees a year. Of the 685,000 Jews in Germany in 1933, about 426,000 had emigrated by 1940. The United States took 100,000, the British 65,000, and 140,000 reached Palestine. Many others went to France, Poland or, like the family of Anne Frank, the Netherlands, where the Gestapo eventually found them. The Jews of Eastern Europe had no escape.

Ever since, Jews have bitterly denounced the British and Americans for shutting their doors to the desperate mass of doomed people. It should be remembered, however, that no one suspected that Hitler intended to murder them all. The killings began with the invasion of the Soviet Union in June 1941, and the formal decision that the Jews should be exterminated, and on the methods to be used, was taken at the Wannsee conference in Berlin in January 1942. By then, Britain had been fighting for its life for two and a half years and the allies were wholly committed to the only policy that could save the Jews, and everyone else: the destruction of Nazi Germany. In the event, the Red Army liberated Auschwitz, the British Belsen and the Americans Dachau and saved what poor remnant of the Jews survived. The allies cannot be accused of any responsibility for failing to stop the Holocaust. However, they stand convicted of failing to save some thousands of people who managed to escape from Nazi Europe during the war. They could have done much more.

David Ben Gurion, the Jewish leader in Palestine, stated the Jewish position on the White Paper: 'We shall fight the war against Hitler as though there were no White Paper, and we shall fight the White Paper as though there were no war.' Most Jews followed his example, with the exception of a small group of fanatics led by Avraham Stern, whose hatred of Britain led them to propose an alliance with Hitler. They mounted terrorist attacks on the British in Palestine and elsewhere even as Rommel's armies were advancing on Cairo. Stern himself was killed by British troops in a shootout in Tel Aviv in 1942 but his followers continued the work. The British called them the Stern Gang. They called themselves the Israel Freedom Fighters (*Lehi* in the Hebrew acronym). In October 1944 they assassinated Lord Moyne, British minister in the Middle East, in Cairo, and after Israel's independence murdered Count Bernadotte, the

U N commissioner in Jerusalem. He was a Swedish diplomat, a friend and colleague of Raoul Wallenberg's, and among the murderers was Yitzak Shamir, later prime minister of Israel.

Large numbers of Palestinian Jews served in the British armed forces (among them Moshe Dayan who lost his eye in a battle in Lebanon), and near the end of the war a Jewish Brigade was formed that served in Italy and later took part in the occupation of Germany.

After the war, the British resumed the White Paper policy, preparing Palestine for independence. Jewish immigration was, in theory, sharply limited. The survivors of the Holocaust would stay in their camps in Europe. However, in the event, about 200,000 Jews reached Palestine between 1944 and 1948 by the 'underground railroad'. The British thus enraged the Jews by announcing that they would restrict immigration, and enraged the Arabs by permitting it in fact.

Ben Gurion then proclaimed a war of independence against the British. Compared to other colonial uprisings, it was not very violent. Ben Gurion calculated that British public opinion, exhausted by the war and horrified by the opening of the camps in 1945 (particularly Belsen), would not tolerate the situation for long. The most dramatic incident of the conflict occurred on 22 July 1946, when British military headquarters in Jerusalem, the King David Hotel, was blown up. The explosion killed 25 British, 40 Arabs and 17 Jews. It was a reprisal for a major British security operation and was ordered by Menachem Begin, commander of a right-wing army, the Irgun, which was constantly at odds with Ben Gurion's government and its army, the Haganah. Ben Gurion denounced the attack, but in fact the Haganah had been involved at least in planning it.

Ben Gurion's calculation was correct. The British had no stomach for the fight and on 18 February 1947 announced that they would abandon the mandate in May 1948. The U N set up a Special Committee on Palestine, with Bernadotte as commissioner. He had played a large part in saving Jews in Europe in the last months of the war. After Shamir murdered him, he was succeeded by the black American diplomat Ralph Bunche. The committee proposed the partition of Palestine and the U N plan was approved by the General Assembly on 27 November 1947. It provided that, for the moment, Jerusalem should enjoy a special status under the U N. These provisions have never been revised, and though they are obviously redundant, they have meant that virtually all foreign embassies remain in Tel Aviv.

The Arabs prepared for war. In the months before the final British withdrawal, there was steadily escalating fighting between the Haganah and the Palestinians. The most dramatic incident occurred on 9 April 1948, when a troop of Irgun guerrillas fought a skirmish at an Arab village, Deir Yassin, west of Jerusalem. After the fight, the Irgun massacred about 250 Arabs there, most of them civilians. Begin was theoretically responsible, because he commanded the Irgun, though he was in reality the political leader of the Herut Party (which later evolved into the Likud Party).

News of the massacre spread rapidly and played a decisive part in inducing so many Arabs to flee. Civilians always flee from fighting: the modern history of Europe is filled with desperate columns of refugees escaping from one invading army or another. By the end of the fighting in 1949, about 800,000 Palestinians had fled across the ceasefire lines, to the West Bank or Gaza, or abroad. They, and their descendants, formed the heart of the Arab–Israeli dispute for the next 40 years.

David Ben Gurion proclaimed Israel's independence in Tel Aviv on 14 May 1948. Britain had abandoned the mandate for Palestine and the last British troops left from Haifa the next day. Simultaneously, the armies of Egypt, Jordan, Syria and Lebanon invaded Palestine, joining the Palestinian 'Arab Army of Liberation', formed to destroy Israel and drive the Jews into the Mediterranean. The War of Independence was the most costly and difficult of all Israel's wars: 6000 Israelis were killed. It lasted until 7 January 1949, punctuated by two short-lived truces.

Israel's most formidable enemy proved to be Transjordan's Arab Legion, commanded by General Sir John Glubb. Many of its other officers were also British. The Legion occupied the heights of Judea and Samaria, including the Old City of Jerusalem, and laid siege to Jewish West Jerusalem. They also seized Latrun, a monastery that dominates the main road from the coast to Jerusalem, and held it against furious Israeli attack. The Israelis had to construct a dangerous bypass through the hills to relieve Jerusalem.

Israel's victory over the Palestinians, Lebanese and Syrians was complete. The whole of northern Palestine was conquered: most of it had been allocated to Palestine in the UN partition plan. In the south, they beat the Egyptians, driving them back across their frontier save for the Gaza Strip, on the coast. They were prevented from occupying that last pocket by threats from the British. When an Israeli force invaded Sinai and advanced on El Arish on the north coast, which would have cut the Gaza Strip off and forced its surrender, the British informed the Israelis that they would intervene against them, under the terms of their treaty with Egypt. Faced with *force majeure*, the Israelis complied. Seven years later, Egypt abrogated the treaty, and in 1956 Britain and Israel invaded Egypt together.

## ISRAEL AND THE ARABS

The Arabs who had signed armistice agreements with Israel in 1949 continued to refuse to recognize its existence. They referred to 'occupied Palestine', promised the refugees that they would soon return home in glory, and prepared for the next war. The Arabs' policy towards Israel consisted of bombast interspersed with bombing. The chief sufferers were the refugees, in the Gaza Strip, on the West Bank and in Lebanon. They led a life of unrelieved squalor, like American Indians on reservations, supported only by the United Nations Relief Works Agency (UNRWA). The inhabitants of Gaza were not even allowed to leave that territory, which became a huge concentration camp. Refugees elsewhere were hardly better off.

The Arabs' defeat in 1948 was followed by a string of upheavals. The Egyptian prime minister was assassinated on 12 December 1948. The first of a long series of coups occurred in Syria on 30 March 1949, and King Farouk of Egypt was deposed by the Free Officers, led by Gamal Abdul Nasser, on 26 July 1952.

Abdullah annexed the West Bank to his emirate, Transjordan, made himself king and gave the kingdom the new name of Jordan. Only Britain and Pakistan recognized the annexation. He was secretly negotiating frontier adjustments with Israel, and had initialled an agreement designed to lead to a peace treaty when, on 20 July 1951, he was shot outside the Al-Aqsa Mosque in Jerusalem. His 16-year-old grandson, Hussein, who was with him at the time, became king a year later, when his father was declared insane.

The Arab leaders were by now prisoners of their own rhetoric. They had promised to destroy Israel, and if they tried another road, they might be killed.

Nasser was the driving force behind the new Egyptian government and, in due course, made himself president. He discovered a talent for demagogic rhetoric and was soon behaving like a latter-day Mussolini, rousing the crowds with exhortations and dreams of national grandeur. He promised to unite all Arabs, like the caliphs of old, but it turned out that, in his vision, the caliphate would be a Nasserite empire ruled from Cairo.

His first success was to drive out the British, who had first occupied Egypt 80 years earlier and had remained camped along the Suez canal. They had no business there, ten years after the war, and went sulkily, in the summer of 1956. Nasser then initiated the first terror campaign against Israel, arming and training Palestinian '*fedayeen*' to cross the border and attack Israeli targets from the Gaza Strip and from Jordan. Israel began to retaliate.

Nasser's socialistic pronouncements and anti-imperialist speeches annoyed the British and Americans. Late in 1955, he made a deal to buy huge quantities of arms from Czechoslovakia. This was the Soviet bloc's first introduction to the Middle East and displeased London and Washington still further. Nasser gave every support to the F L N in Algeria who were in revolt against the French, and so added France to his list of opponents. His great domestic ambition was to dam the Nile at Aswan. The United States had offered to finance the project, but, in July 1956, after the Czech arms deal, it pulled out. Nasser retaliated by nationalizing the Suez canal.

## THE SUEZ CAMPAIGN

Israel had by then established itself as a functioning, modern state. It had taken in over 800,000 immigrants, half of them from Arab countries. The Haganah had been developed into a modern and highly efficient citizens' army – the Israeli Defence Force (*Zahal* in the Hebrew acronym).

The terrorist attacks across the border were by now becoming intolerable. The Arab states, which had agreed to pursue negotiations towards a permanent peace treaty, had done nothing of the sort, and now Nasser was evidently planning to reverse the verdict of 1948, and reconquer Palestine.

In the summer of 1956, Israel and France began secret negotiations to mount a joint attack on Egypt. Later, they were joined by the British. Their plan was to overthrow Nasser. Israel wanted to clear out the *fedayeen* bases in the Gaza Strip, and hoped that a further defeat would impel Egypt to negotiate for a peace treaty. France aimed to end Egyptian support for the F L N. British participation in the conspiracy is much more difficult to explain. The prime minister, Sir Anthony Eden, and the foreign secretary, Selwyn Lloyd, claimed that allowing Nasser to get away with nationalizing the Suez canal would be an act of appeasement **311** comparable to the Munich agreement of 1938, which set the stage for World War I I. What were never clearly examined were Britain's long-term interests in the Middle East, which were to ensure tranquillity, keep out the Soviets and assure oil supplies. The Suez campaign was to have the exact opposite results.

The Israelis crossed the border on 29 October 1956. Paratroopers seized the Mitla pass in western Sinai, and by 1 November, the Israelis had taken the whole of eastern and central Sinai. Another attack at Rafah, the southern end of the Gaza Strip, cut off the Egyptian forces there, and by 2 November, the Israelis had reached the Suez canal. In a last detail, a commando raid occupied Sharm el-Sheikh at the southern tip of the peninsula on 4 November. Their victory was complete. Nasser lost most of his army's tanks and other heavy equipment.

The British and French were astonished at the speed of Israel's victory – they had planned a leisurely invasion. On 31 October, the two governments issued an ultimatum, ordering both sides to withdraw from the canal. Israel promptly accepted; Egypt understandably rejected it. The British then bombed Egyptian air bases, wiping out the Egyptian air force. An invasion fleet set sail from Malta on 1 November, after the war was all but finished. British paratroops landed in the canal zone on 5 November, and on the 6th, British and French troops landed at Port Said. The operation has become known as the 'Suez affair', but in fact, the British never reached the town of Suez, which is at the southern end of the canal.

British and French dilatoriness allowed international opposition to reach hurricane proportions. President Eisenhower threatened economic reprisals, and the Soviet Union offered to send troops to Syria and Egypt. That was bluff: at the time, the U S S R was fully engaged in suppressing the Hungarian uprising. There was a run on the pound, and British troops were scarcely ashore before the order came to cease fire. The whole operation ended in a humiliating fiasco. The ceasefire took effect at midnight on 6 November, and the British and French soon withdrew from Egypt, leaving the Israelis to fend for themselves. Under strong American pressure, they finally left the Gaza Strip in March 1957. Their occupation of the Strip had been marred by two incidents: on 3 November, immediately after the fighting, Israeli troops panicked and killed 275 civilians at Khan Younis; and on 12 November, they killed 111 Palestinians in a refugee camp at Rafah.

A U N peacekeeping force was set up in Sinai to separate Egyptians and Israelis. One of its posts was at Sharm el-Sheikh, and Israel was at last able to develop Eilat and to send ships through the Straits of Tiran into the Red Sea. President Eisenhower guaranteed that the Straits would be kept open by whatever means were necessary.

## THE SIX-DAY WAR

The next Arab–Israeli war blew up abruptly and unexpectedly in the spring of 1967. It was provoked by Syria, where the Ba'ath party had just taken power and needed to demonstrate its revolutionary and anti-Zionist zeal.

From the Golan Heights, Syrian artillery positions could shell Israeli villages in Galilee, and did so. In addition, the Palestine Liberation Army – the military wing of the Palestine Liberation Organization (P L O) founded in 1965 and led by Ahmed Shukeiri – had begun raiding across the border from Jordan and Syria.

On 7 April 1967, after the Syrians shelled Israeli villages again, the Israeli air force attacked the gun positions. The Syrian air force was sent to defend them, and lost six MiGs to Israel's French-built Mystères. Syria feared that Israel intended to mount a pre-emptive strike against it, and appealed to Egypt for help. The Soviet Union informed Egypt that Israel had massed 11 brigades along the northern frontier – a report that was completely untrue.

Nasser was at a low point. His armies were involved in a hopeless war in Yemen (see Yemen, pp. 374–8); his influence in Jordan, Syria and Iraq was non-existent; and his relations with Saudi Arabia were violently hostile. His dreams of pan-Arabism had gone aglimmering. So he seized the opportunity to mount a political offensive against Israel.

There has been much debate since whether he had ever intended to go to war. Certainly, he was not ready for it when it came – which is another count against him. His apologists claim that all his rhetoric was bluff, that he had had no intention of fighting – but heads of government of major countries cannot complain when their pronouncements are taken seriously. He closed the Straits of Tiran, formed a joint military command with Syria and Jordan, mobilized his armies and moved them into Sinai, and announced that the final war for the liquidation of Israel was imminent. There have not been many occasions since 1945 when military action has been wholly justified. The Six-Day War was one of them.

Tensions escalated rapidly in May. On 17 May, Nasser demanded that the U N pull its peacekeeping force out of Sinai, and the secretary-general, U Thant, did so immediately, to the amazement and scandal of Israel and many other members of the U N. On 20 May, Nasser sent seven divisions into the Sinai. Tourists fled Israel, except for a few hardy souls who stayed for the battle and were then drafted to dig tank traps. The place of the missing tourists was taken by hordes of foreign journalists expecting war, who came for a ringside seat.

On 2 May, Nasser had declared the Straits closed. Israel called on the United States to honour Eisenhower's promise made in 1956. The State Department had never heard of it. Hasty research produced a copy of the letter in the presidential library at Abilene, Kansas, but the Israelis were informed that the promise had expired when Ike had left office. They learned, to their dismay, of the discontinuities between administrations: only a treaty ratified by the U S Senate is binding.

President Johnson and the British government tried to mediate, to find a way of guaranteeing freedom of navigation through the Straits without actually enforcing it. Negotiations might take some weeks – and since Israel used the passage relatively seldom, there was no hurry. Then, on 26 May, Nasser, in a speech in Cairo, announced that the time had come to destroy Israel. All Araby was mobilized: Israel was surrounded by 250,000 enemy troops. Furthermore, Israel could not wait. It had mobilized its armies – that is, the entire able-bodied manhood of the country – and it could not maintain that status for very long.

Then France, which had been Israel's staunchest ally, suddenly abandoned it. General de Gaulle informed Israel that it should reach a compromise with **313**

Egypt. The Israeli prime minister, Levi Eshkol, formed a government of national unity, invited Menachem Begin into the Cabinet for the first time and made Moshe Dayan (who had been chief of staff in 1956) minister of defence.

On the Arab side, King Hussein submitted to overwhelming pressure. To save his throne and perhaps his life, he gave in to the general hysteria and made his peace with Nasser. The Jordanian army was put under the command of an Egyptian general.

The Israelis undertook a campaign of strategic deception. On the weekend beginning Friday, 2 June, they demobilized part of their armed forces and lowered the state of alert of the remainder. The beaches were crowded. Dayan gave a press conference and remarked that he expected nothing to happen for several weeks, or months. It seemed that the crisis was diminishing. The British ambassador informed his government there would be no war, and the first wave of returning journalists (from the *Sunday Times*) left for home on Monday morning. As their plane flew peacefully over the blue Mediterranean, the pilot informed them on the intercom that the war had begun.

The formal decision to fight was taken at the weekly cabinet meeting on Sunday, 4 June. Soldiers and airmen were recalled from the beaches, and the army moved into position. At 7.45 the following morning, Monday, 5 June, the Israeli air force attacked the Egyptians. They flew low across the Mediterranean, under the sightline of the Egyptian radar (but watched by the British on radar from Cyprus; they gave first news of the war to London). Then they turned inland, and attacked Egypt from the west – the wrong way. Egyptian pilots had expected a traditional dawn attack, out of the rising sun, and had waited in their aircraft every morning. Every morning, when the attack did not come, they then went to breakfast. Thus, the Israelis caught the Egyptian air force on the ground, defenceless, and they destroyed it.

In 500 sorties, the Israelis destroyed 309 out of Egypt's 340 combat-ready planes, including all 30 long-range bombers. The Egyptians promptly announced that they had destroyed 400 Israeli planes. Believing the boast, the Syrian and Jordanian air forces attacked Israel. By the evening, the Jordanian air force had been wiped out, Syria had lost two-thirds of its aircraft and an Iraqi squadron was destroyed on the ground at a base in Jordan. In all, the Israelis destroyed 393 Arab aircraft on the ground and 58 in the air, with an Israeli loss of 26.

Then the Israeli army attacked the Egyptians. An official Israeli announcement later stated that the Egyptians had attacked first, and the Israelis 'went out to meet them'. This was untrue. The Israelis again drove through the Egyptian army at Rafah, cutting off the Gaza Strip, attacked the Egyptians in central Sinai, and then advanced north to the coast and due west across the peninsula.

They had complete control of the air, and used it with devastating effect. The lasting memory of the war is the image of 20-mile (32-km) convoys of Egyptian vehicles, heading west towards safety, strung out along the roads in the Sinai, each vehicle destroyed. The Israelis first hit the tanks at the head of the convoys, then the ones at the rear, and then destroyed everything in between at their leisure.

At the outset of the war, King Hussein was informed through the U N that

Israel would not attack Jordan unless provoked. The Israelis expected the Jordanian air attack, and perhaps a token ground offensive, and were prepared to ignore them. However, the Egyptian general commanding the Jordanian army, General Riadh, ordered a general offensive. King Hussein, perhaps misled by the lies put out by Nasser and Egyptian headquarters, and believing a great Arab victory was under way, allowed the attack to take place. The Jordanians shelled Tel Aviv and West Jerusalem, and moved their troops forward to threaten the Tel Aviv–Jerusalem road.

On the first day, the Israelis held the Jordanians off. On the second, they encircled East Jerusalem and drove in the Jordanian defences on the northern and southern flanks of the West Bank. On the third day, Wednesday, 7 June, they completed the occupation of the whole of the West Bank, capturing Hebron, Nablus and Ramallah, and seized the Old City of Jerusalem. For the first time since 1948, Jews said their prayers at the Wailing Wall and the chief rabbi blew the *shofar* in triumph.

Thursday was devoted to mopping up in the Sinai. The Israelis returned to Sharm el-Sheikh. On Friday, 9 June, the Israeli army stormed straight up the cliffs overlooking Lake Tiberias. In two days' fighting, they cleared the Golan Heights, capturing Kuneitra and huge quantities of Syrian armaments. The road to Damascus was open when Syria finally accepted a ceasefire.

Israel lost 705 men in the Six-Day War, the Arabs 20,000–25,000.

## THE WAR OF ATTRITION

The period between the 1967 and 1973 wars was a violent one. President Nasser launched a war of attrition against Israeli positions on the eastern shore of the Suez canal, on the assumption that Israel's reluctance to take casualties and Egypt's superiority in heavy artillery would give him the advantage. The Israelis protected themselves by building an immense line of fortifications along the canal to house their garrisons: the 'Bar Lev line', named after their chief of staff. It was the largest work of engineering undertaken in Israeli history.

Israel retaliated against the incessant Egyptian attacks by using their air superiority to hit targets all over Egypt. In addition, Israeli commandos blew up power lines near the Aswan dam and captured an entire radar station on the Gulf of Suez and carried it back in triumph; another raid set fire to the refineries at Suez, creating a spectacular blaze that lasted for days. The Israelis attacked military installations near Cairo, and this eventually induced Nasser to call on the Soviets for help. The Soviets constructed greatly improved anti-aircraft defences west of the canal. They also sent their latest surface-to-air SAM-3 missiles to Egypt, with Soviet crews, and Soviet pilots began flying missions in Egypt: suddenly, the war between Egypt and Israel had reached dangerous levels.

A ceasefire was arranged on 8 August 1970, and the Egyptians and their Soviet allies immediately began to move their air defences forward, so that an Egyptian attack across the canal would be protected against the Israeli air force. For their part, the Israelis used the ceasefire to strengthen the Bar Lev line, despite suggestions that it was a new Maginot line.

Nasser died suddenly on 28 September 1970, and his successor, Anwar el- **315**

Sadat, postponed the plans for an immediate attack across the canal. Sadat proved a more patient and subtle leader than Nasser, and an altogether more formidable opponent of Israel.

## THE YOM KIPPUR WAR

President Sadat sent his armies across the Suez canal on Yom Kippur, the Day of Atonement, 6 October 1973. He achieved complete tactical surprise. He had repeatedly announced an imminent offensive – and nothing had happened. The Israelis therefore assumed that he was all bluff and no substance. The Egyptian and Syrian armies had frequently conducted exercises near the front lines without attacking. When they did so again, in September 1973, it was not taken seriously.

Syrian manoeuvres were put down to nervousness following an aerial dogfight in which the Israeli air force shot down 13 Syrian planes on 13 September. Even the abrupt departure from Alexandria of visiting Soviet ships and the evacuation from Egypt and Syria of the families of Soviet military personnel on 5 October did not alert the Israelis or the Americans. Most serious of all, the Israelis underestimated their enemy. The high command did not share the general contempt felt by many Israelis for the Arabs, but they were guilty of over-confidence. Henry Kissinger observed that 'the October surprise was the culmination of a failure of *political* analysis on the part of its victims'. The Israelis were certain that they would win any war, knew that Egypt and Syria must understand that Israel's victory was virtually assured, and therefore assumed that the Arabs would not attack. But Sadat was after a political, not a military victory.

He had concluded that Egypt could only recover the Sinai and reopen the Suez canal, which had remained closed since 1967, through negotiations with Israel. But he must approach those negotiations as an equal, not as a defeated suppli-cant. Ever since the Six-Day War, Israel, in the standard phrase, had been waiting for the phone call in which the Arabs would propose peace. But no Arab could make such a call after a defeat: King Abdullah had done so, and had been killed for it. (After his huge political victory in the Yom Kippur War, Sadat did make that call – and he, too, was shot. It was a depressing lesson for other Arab leaders.)

Sadat's war was a close-run thing. Israel won the fighting on the ground and, but for American pressure, would have destroyed the Egyptian army – and Sadat himself. Sadat had a Soviet promise of support against defeat, but at the last moment, the Soviets backed down in the face of American support for Israel. The Americans then insisted that Israel hold its hand. It could have won a total victory – but what would have been the point of that?

The most conspicuous difference between 1973 and previous wars was that the Egyptians and Syrians fought well, bravely and tenaciously; they never broke and ran, as they had in 1956 and 1967. It was the first truly modern war – with a full panoply of missiles and electronic defences – and only the Battle of Kursk in 1943 had involved more tanks.

The chief features of the Bar-Lev line, along the eastern bank of the canal, were its high banks of sand. When they attacked, the Egyptians blasted through the artificial dunes with water cannon. The crossing was relatively easy, and soon Egypt had two large armies on the eastern bank; the initial Israeli counterattacks were beaten off with heavy losses.

At the same time, Syria attacked across the Golan Heights. This was more dangerous to Israel. Syrian tanks almost reached the escarpment overlooking Galilee before they were stopped by the heroic efforts of the vastly outnumbered Israelis. Syria attacked with 1400 tanks and, in the course of the war, lost 1150 of them.

When the Israelis counterattacked, they managed to drive the Syrians back towards Damascus, but they were then stopped by a flank attack mounted by two Iraqi armoured divisions and a Jordanian armoured brigade. The Iraqis did not fight particularly well – not nearly as well as the Egyptians and Syrians – but their presence diverted the Israelis from their intention of moving to within artillery range of Damascus.

On the southern front, after the Egyptians had established themselves across the canal, they mounted a large-scale assault on Israeli positions, on 14 October. The battle involved 2000 tanks, and the Israelis beat back the attack. By then, the war had lasted far longer than Israel, or anyone else, had expected. The Soviets had begun an airlift of supplies to the Egyptians and Syrians, and on 9 October, the Israelis appealed to the U S for help: they were running out of ammunition and had lost 49 planes and 500 tanks (though many of these had been lost through poor maintenance). On 13 October, President Nixon ordered a full-scale resupply airlift, taking tanks and planes out of American depots to replace Israeli losses. The American airlift consisted of 20 flights a day, carrying 2000 tons of material, far outdistancing the Soviet effort.

The Israelis counterattacked through a gap in the Egyptian front and across the canal on 16 October, and for a crucial 24 hours, local Egyptian commanders did not realize what was happening. It was a perilous operation: for one thing, it was several days before the supply route was assured. After that, things moved rapidly, as the Israelis drove south to encircle the Egyptian 3rd Army. The Arabs asked for a ceasefire, and Henry Kissinger, the U S secretary of state, flew to Moscow on 20 October to settle the terms.

U N Security Council Resolution 338, passed just after midnight on 22 October, provided for a ceasefire with the armies in place, to be followed by negotiations for a lasting peace. The Israelis, however, had not completed the encirclement of the 3rd Army. They violated the ceasefire and reached Suez, on the western bank of the canal at its southern extremity, on 24 October.

The 3rd Army's 45,000 men and 250 tanks were now cut off on the eastern bank and in Suez. Israel wanted to destroy them and only refrained from doing so under extreme pressure from the Americans. Sadat demanded a joint U S–Soviet force to patrol the ceasefire line and, when Nixon rejected the idea out of hand, invited the Soviets to send an army on its own. The Soviet Union had put seven divisions on alert and, on the 23rd, informed Washington that it would accede to the Egyptian request. That would have meant war between the U S S R and Israel. Kissinger informed Sadat, regretfully, that if the Soviets went to Egypt, the U S would fight them, on his territory. At midnight, American forces worldwide were put on 'DefCon I I I'. (American forces have five degrees of 'defence condition', ranging from 'DefCon V', peacetime, to 'DefCon I', all-out war.) The Soviets backed down.

So did Israel. The Egyptians were allowed to send medical supplies, food and water to their isolated 3rd Army, and negotiations for a disengagement began at Kilometre 101 on the Suez–Cairo road. There followed a period of intense diplomacy, conducted by Henry Kissinger, as a result of which the Israelis and Egyptians signed a disengagement agreement on 17 January 1974, and the Israelis and Syrians on 31 May. The Israelis pulled back from the Suez canal to the line of the hills to the east, and Egypt was at last able to reopen the canal and free the ships that had been trapped since 5 June 1967. On the Golan Heights, Israel agreed to withdraw slightly behind the 1967 line, and the Syrians recovered Kuneitra. Demilitarized zones were established along both fronts.

## ISRAEL AND THE ARABS

The Yom Kippur War demonstrated that Israel was not invincible, and it restored Arab pride. It did not, however, lead immediately to peace anywhere. There was a four-year hiatus during which the best efforts of Kissinger and other mediators failed to make progress. Then, on 11 November 1978, Sadat cut through the fog of difficulties by inviting himself to Jerusalem. Menachem Begin welcomed the proposal, and the formal announcements were made in interviews with Walter Cronkite broadcast on American television three days later.

Sadat arrived in Jerusalem on 19 November. It was one of the most extra-ordinary moments in recent history, the whole world watching on live television as Sadat was met off the aircraft by Begin. A few minutes later, Sadat was presented to Golda Meir and bowed over her hand in greeting. That day, he visited the el-Aqsa Mosque, the Church of the Holy Sepulchre, and the Yad Vashem memorial to the Holocaust. On the 20th, he laid a wreath at an Israeli war memorial, and addressed the Knesset. 'If you want to live with us, in this part of the world,' he said, 'in sincerity I tell you that we welcome you among us with all security and safety.' However, he added, 'There can be no peace without the Palestinians,' and the settlement 'must be based on justice, and not on the occupation of the land of others . . . You have to give up once and for all the dreams of conquest and the belief that force is the best means of dealing with the Arabs.'

Israel had been waiting for that phone call, for face-to-face negotiations with the Arabs, for recognition. Sadat's gesture answered their every prayer, or appeared to. The negotiations that followed were difficult and protracted, and required the personal intervention of President Jimmy Carter. Begin and Sadat met Carter at Camp David on 6 September 1978, and signed a framework agreement at the White House on the 17th. Further negotiations were needed, and involved Carter himself in shuttle diplomacy, before a peace treaty was finally signed, on the lawn in front of the White House, on 27 March 1979.

Under the terms of the agreement, Israel withdrew progressively from the entire Sinai peninsula. Begin tried to keep an Israeli settlement just over the border in the north, but failed. A dispute over the exact line of the frontier west of Eilat, where the Israelis had built a resort called Taba, dragged on for over a decade. (The arbiters eventually decided in Egypt's favour in November 1988.) The peace agreement was put under severe strain by the war in Lebanon, but peace with Israel was generally popular in Egypt, even if the Israelis themselves were not. Sadat paid for the treaty with his life: he was assassinated in 1981 by soldiers in his own army who believed that he had betrayed Islam and Egypt.

There was no substantive progress at all in peace-making between Israel and the Arabs for a decade after the treaty with Egypt. In the early 1980s, Israel revelled in its new security: with Egypt no longer an enemy, there was no danger of a war with the Arabs. Northern Israel, however, suffered frequent attacks from across the border in Lebanon, where civil war was raging. In 1982, Israel plunged into its longest and most costly foreign adventure, the invasion of Lebanon (*see* Lebanon, p. 341).

## THE *INTIFADA*

The Camp David agreement provided that there would be negotiations leading to 'autonomy' for the Palestinians living in occupied territory. These negotiations were soon abandoned. For almost ten years, that did not appear to matter. Israel had a peace treaty with Egypt, *de facto* peace with Jordan, and a secure border with Syria. It tried to secure the remaining border with Lebanon, by military means, and succeeded, up to a point.

On 9 December 1987, the first of a series of demonstrations by Palestinians – in the Gaza Strip and on the West Bank – showed how illusory that security was. Boys and young men took to stoning Israeli patrols; the Israelis fired back, with live ammunition, killing some of their tormentors. There was a general strike in Gaza and the West Bank, and shops closed in sympathy.

The Palestinians called the uprising the '*intifada*', from the Arabic verb 'to shake loose'. An underground committee was formed to direct it. By the first anniversary of the *intifada*, in December 1988, the Israeli army had killed 366 Palestinians and wounded over 20,000 in attempting to repress the disturbances. Eleven Israelis were killed in the same period, including a woman and her three children who were killed when a bus was fire-bombed near Jerusalem on 30 October, two days before the Israeli general election. By then, over 5000 young men had been arrested, and were held in detention centres, including tented camps in the Negev; a few were expelled (36 in 1988).

The Israeli authorities vowed to suppress the riots with whatever means were necessary. The minister of defence, Yitzak Rabin, ordered his troops to beat every rioter they caught, to break their arms and fingers. When the rioters took to throwing Molotov cocktails, in the summer of 1988, and there were cases of arson in Israel proper as well as in the occupied territories, Rabin authorized his men to shoot anyone seen with a firebomb. Palestinian houses were also blown up and trees cut down, but other means for controlling the disturbances were less draconian. Remittances from abroad were intercepted, farmers' markets in the Jordan valley were closed down, concrete barricades were erected at street intersections.

The rioters insisted that Palestinian police, mayors and other local officials resign. Those who hesitated were threatened with death, and a few notorious collaborators were murdered. To the Israelis' dismay, the troubles spread to **319**

Israeli Arabs. Jewish settlers on the West Bank sometimes took matters into their own hands. In one particularly horrifying incident, a party of Israeli children on a nature hike passed through the fields of an Arab village. A man in a field shouted at them, and one of the two guards with the children shot and killed him. Other people then took the party into the village. The same guard panicked, fired and killed another Arab and one of the Israeli children. All Israel cried for vengeance and several houses in the village were blown up before it was discovered that the girl had actually been killed, accidentally, by the guard – a psychopathic Israeli settler.

By degrees, the rioting died down, periodically flaring up again, but the problem at its core remained as acute as ever: after 20 years' quiescence, the Palestinians in the occupied territories had started to protest against their condition.

On 9 December 1988, the first anniversary of the uprising, Israel mounted a massive raid on the headquarters of Ahmed Jibril's Popular Front for the Liberation of Palestine-General Command (*see* Arab terrorism, pp. 594–619) outside Beirut. Jibril's barracks were destroyed and 20 members of his command killed. Israel intended the gesture as a demonstration that it was not to be intimidated by the *intifada*.

In the course of persuading Israel to accept the 1974 disengagement agreements, Kissinger promised that the United States would never negotiate with the PLO unless it met stringent conditions (*see below*). For 14 years, that promise was a millstone around the necks of successive secretaries of state and presidents. The way to make peace is to negotiate with your enemy, and Americans have negotiated with Mao Tse-tung and the Ayatollah Khomeini, and Ronald Reagan himself went to Moscow to make peace with the 'evil empire'. But they could not negotiate with Arafat because of Kissinger's rash promise – and Jewish voters insisted that that promise must be repeated at every election.

The first condition that Kissinger set for opening a dialogue with the PLO was that it must formally recognize Israel's right to exist, in the terms of UN Resolutions 242 and 338. Later, a further precondition was added, that the PLO should renounce terrorism. For 14 years, Arafat and his comrades refused to accept these conditions publicly, although privately they repeatedly assured visitors that they did indeed recognize that Israel was there to stay.

The perpetual stalemate was finally broken by King Hussein. On 31 July 1988, he formally renounced his claim to the West Bank. His grandfather, King Abdullah, annexed the area in 1949, and Hussein lost it during the Six-Day War in 1967. Ever since, Jordan had claimed it as part of the kingdom, had continued to pay the salaries of public officials (most notably the teachers) and had issued passports to the Palestinian inhabitants. The decision meant that there was now no one to challenge the Israelis except the Palestinians themselves.

Moderate Arabs, Egypt, Jordan, Saudi Arabia and, surprisingly, Iraq used their influence with the PLO to persuade it to change its position. They were joined discreetly by the USSR where the new government of Mikhail Gorbachev was showing signs of wanting to return to Middle East diplomacy in a less

hamfisted way than in the past.

Ever since 1967, the chief sticking point had been the P L O's adamant refusal to recognize Israel. On 15 November 1988, the Palestine National Council (P N C), meeting in Algiers, proclaimed an independent Palestinian state. Over 40 years after U N Resolution 181 partitioned Palestine and proposed a Jewish and an Arab state there, the Palestinians at last accepted the decision. The P N C specifically accepted the crucial U N Security Council Resolutions 242 and 338, which proclaim the right of every state in the region to live within secure and recognized boundaries. This meant that it was recognizing Israel, but on that occasion, neither Arafat nor any of the other delegates could quite bring themselves to say so. The significance of this decision was also diminished by their equivocation over terrorism. The council insisted on the Palestinians' right to 'resist Israeli occupation' and, while rejecting 'all forms of terrorism', did so 'in accordance with U N resolutions'. Those resolutions have often approved 'liberation struggles'. The council agreed formally to negotiate with Israel in the context of an international peace conference, on condition that Israel accepted that the Palestinians had political rights, and proposed that independent Palestine should enter a confederation with Jordan.

The most extreme Palestinians were not represented at the Algiers meeting, and others, led by George Habash, could only be persuaded with difficulty to accept the resolutions. Habash further muddied the waters by insisting that the P L O still demanded the whole of Palestine.

A month later Arafat was at last persuaded to declare, 'I repeat for the record that we totally and absolutely renounce all forms of terrorism, including individual, group and state terrorism.' It was sufficient for the United States, though not for Israel, and George Shultz, in his last act as secretary of state, agreed to open negotiations with the P L O. In the event, the talks led nowhere. In the summer of 1989, a dissident P L O faction mounted a sea-borne attack on Israel (it was intercepted) and the new American administration broke off contact with the P L O. However, the ice had been broken, and the Americans pursued contacts with other Palestinians, as a means of indirect negotiations, while preparing the Middle East peace conference.

Domestic and international events continued to impinge upon the Israeli question. The crisis in the Soviet Union, the ending of all restrictions on emigration and fears of a revival of Russian anti-semitism led to a sudden surge in Jewish emigration to Israel. The United States no longer accepted Soviet Jews as refugees. Israel was delighted at the change, even though the prospect of absorbing a half million immigrants was daunting in the extreme. At the end of 1989, senior American officials suggested that aid to Israel might be cut in favour of more worthy countries. The ending of the cold war made the need for Israeli support in the Middle East much less acute.

The *intifada* continued. Five years after it began, at the end of 1991, the death toll in the occupied territories had reached 663 Arabs and 22 Israelis, 10 of them soldiers. Terrorists had murdered 501 Palestinians accused of collaborating with Israel. The worst incident occurred in Israel proper, on 6 July 1989, when a Palestinian from Gaza, riding in a bus through the Judean hills, suddenly seized the wheel from the driver, shouting 'God is great!' and turned the bus into a ravine. Fifteen people were killed. Whether the attack had been planned by Hamas or Islamic Jihad was never established, but it proved altogether ominous. Terrorism against Israel and Israelis had been a continuing horror during the late 1960s and 1970s. It had subsided, temporarily (and relatively), from the mid-1980s, as the P L O progressively and haltingly abandoned violence and Arafat came to put his faith in diplomacy. At the same time, other frankly terroristic organizations were decimated by counter-terrorism and internecine feuding. After the bus incident, however, Hamas, a relatively new organization bred in the schools of the Gaza Strip, which rejected all peace with Israel, adopted the most brutal forms of mass murder, including suicide bombs. In 1995 and 1996 a continuing wave of suicide bombs killed scores of Israelis. Equally fanatic Israeli Jews blamed the government, equating peace with murder, and one of them murdered Yitzak Rabin. Further bombings led directly to the defeat of the Labour government in the 1997 elections and brought the peace process to a halt, which was, of course, Hamas's main objective.

On 28 July 1989, Israeli forces abducted a Lebanese Shiite mullah, sheikh Abdul Karim Obeid, from a south Lebanon village, Jibchit. He was accused of being a leading member of the Party of God (Hizbollah), and playing a part in the kidnapping of Col. William Higgins, an American officer serving as a U N observer in Lebanon, in February 1988. Hizbollah demanded Obeid's release, and threatened that Higgins would be killed. Israel refused to comply. On 31 July Hizbollah released a short video of Higgins being hanged. Americans and Israelis said that Higgins had probably been murdered several months earlier, but the episode cast a further shadow on American–Israeli relations. Israel then offered to exchange Obeid and 100 other Shiite prisoners for three Israeli soldiers who they said were held by terrorists in Lebanon, and the 15 surviving western hostages. (For the negotiations that eventually led to the release of the hostages, see Lebanon, pp. 341–57.)

The offer was ignored. On 3 February 1990, nine Israeli tourists were killed in an attack on a bus near Cairo: it was a reminder that whatever the peaceful professions of the P L O, the terrorists were unrelenting.

Meanwhile, Israel's domestic politics were wholly given over to a debate on the peace plan. The new American secretary of state, James Baker, followed in his predecessor's footsteps in searching for ways to bring the Arabs and Israelis together. At one point, he almost abandoned the effort, faced with Israeli intransigence, telling a Senate committee that if Israel wanted to contact him, it knew his phone number. Then Saddam Hussein intervened. The invasion of Kuwait, the formation of an international coalition to defeat him, and the war, changed the Middle East completely. Suddenly, the Rejection Front lost all its influence. One of its leaders, Iraq, was prostrate and ostracized, the other, Syria, had joined the Americans. The Gulf states, led by Saudi Arabia, were no longer to be intimidated by Saddam, and accepted the American argument that there were more important things to do than continue opposing Israel. The Soviet Union had lost its influence in the world and the United States was the sole super-power. America insisted that there should be a peace conference, and it opened in Madrid on 31 October 1991. The Madrid conference produced an agreement that formal negotiations between Israel and the Palestinians, the

Syrians, the Jordanians and the Lebanese should begin at once. Most sessions of these four conferences were held in Washington.

Israel and the Arabs had been brought to the table by carrot and stick. The Israelis had asked the Americans for $10 billion in loan guarantees to help them resettle the hundreds of thousands of Jewish immigrants coming in from the Soviet Union. They were told firmly they would have no money unless they attended the conference and made a real effort to reach an agreement. Syria, whose economy was on the verge of collapse, was faced with the choice of compliance or isolation, and attended the conference with a very bad grace. The Palestinians, having at last swallowed the necessity of accepting Israel, were the most enthusiastic participants.

It was a most unpromising beginning, but there was no doubt that the Madrid conference was an historic occasion. For the first time, the Israelis and Palestinians met as equals across a negotiating table. For the first time, Syria, Jordan and Lebanon held public and formal talks with Israel, and Saudi Arabia sent its ambassador in Washington as an official observer. The talks in Washington were utterly fruitless. However, out of the limelight, Israeli and Palestinian negotiators were meeting secretly in Oslo, laying the groundwork for a peace agreement. It was announced, to general astonishment and delight, on 29 August 1993. The agreement provided a declaration of principle that the Palestinians would have self-rule on the West Bank and the Gaza Strip.

At the formal signing, on 13 September on the White House lawn, the Israeli prime minister, Yitzak Rabin, told the Palestinians:

We are destined to live together on the same land. We say to you in a loud and clear voice, 'Enough of blood and tears. Enough.' We have no desire for revenge, we harbour no hatred towards you.

We are today giving peace a chance. We wish to open a new chapter in the sad book of our lives together, a chapter of mutual recognition, of good neighbourliness, of mutual respect, of understanding.

Negotiations on the details were adjourned to Cairo, where on 4 May 1994 a further agreement was signed stating that Israel would immediately withdraw from the Gaza Strip and from an area around Jericho, on the Dead Sea. There would be further withdrawals in orderly succession after that, and final negotiations on the status of Jerusalem and the refugees would begin two years later. Israel pulled out of Jericho on 13 May and the Gaza Strip on the 18th, though leaving troops to guard Jewish settlements there.

On 28 September, the high-water mark of Israeli–Palestinian cooperation, the two sides signed a further agreement in Washington providing for Israel to pull out of a wide area of the West Bank, including six major centres of population. The withdrawal from five of them was completed rapidly: Hebron was postponed until March.

All this time, right-wing opposition to the peace agreements had been building in Israel, led by the opposition Likud Party, now led by Benjamin Netanyahu. The tone of political discourse in Israel became ever more bitter and incipiently violent. On 4 November Yitzhak Rabin was assassinated by a young extremist as he left a peace rally in Tel Aviv. Shimon Peres succeeded him, amid bitter **323** denunciations of Netanyahu and the Likud by Rabin's widow and other supporters of the Labour Party.

On 5 January 1996 the Israeli secret service managed to assassinate Hamas's principal bomb-maker, with an exploding cellular phone. In revenge, Hamas set a series of suicide bombs in Jerusalem and Tel Aviv that killed 61 people in the next three months. Peres called an early election for 29 May, hoping to get a mandate to complete the peace process. Instead, thanks largely to the Hamas bombing campaign, a slim majority of Israelis voted for the opposition. Netanyahu became prime minister in June, and the peace process came to a stop. He resumed building up Jewish settlements on the West Bank. In September, he authorized the opening of an archaeological tunnel in the Old City in the shadow of the Haram Es Sharif, the site of the Jewish Temple in antiquity, now occupied by the two major Islamic shrines, the Dome of the Rock and the Al Aqsa Mosque. Prolonged riots in Jerusalem and elsewhere left over 70 dead.

In the ensuing crisis, President Clinton called Netanyahu, Arafat and King Hussein to an emergency conference in Washington. Under extreme pressure from the Americans, Netanyahu agreed to reopen the negotiations on withdrawing from Hebron, and an agreement was concluded in January. Israel pulled out of the city on 17 January 1997, but left troops guarding Jewish settlers installed in the heart of the city.

That was the extent of the new government's concessions. Netanyahu's cabinet could not agree on handing over any more of the West Bank, and Arafat demanded substantial withdrawals – not to mention fulfilment of the other promises made in the Oslo and subsequent agreements. The atmosphere was further exacerbated by the Israeli government's decision to build a new Jewish settlement south-east of Jerusalem, though Netanyahu tried to prevent the construction of Jewish settlements in East Jerusalem by a Miami Jewish millionaire. By the end of 1997, there was complete stalemate (a new summit in Washington in January 1998 was a failure). Israeli hawks had a veto on all further concessions to the Palestinians, and they used it. The divisions in Israel over the peace process were now the main stumbling block to progress, and there was little sign they would be soon resolved.

## TERRORISM

The terrorist campaign against Israel, which resumed in 1989, is the work of various organizations, notably Hamas and Islamic Jihad. Their acts of terrorism, in Israel and abroad, and acts of Israeli terrorism and counter-terrorism, included the following incidents:

**1989**

*6 July*          A passenger on a bus grabs the wheel and steers it into a ravine, killing 16 and injuring 26.

**1992**

*16 February*    Israeli helicopter gunships kill the leader of Hezbollah in Lebanon, with his wife, son and four guards.

| | |
|---|---|
| *15 December* | The body of a kidnapped Israeli policeman found. Hamas had demanded the release of its leader Sheikh Ahmed Yassin in exchange for his life. Israel deports 415 Hamas activists to Lebanon. |

**1993**

| | |
|---|---|
| *20 May* | Two Israeli soldiers shot in Gaza Strip. |
| *1 July* | Two Israeli women killed when gunmen open fire inside a bus. Two terrorists killed. |

**1994**

| | |
|---|---|
| *25 February* | 29 Palestinians killed by a Jewish settler in a Hebron mosque, three more trampled to death in the stampede, about 90 wounded, terrorist killed. |
| *6 April* | Hamas suicide bomber kills eight people in Afula. |
| *13 April* | Suicide bomber kills five in Hadera. |
| *18 July* | Bomb kills over 96 at Jewish organization headquarters in Buenos Aires. |
| *20 July* | Bomb destroys Panama airliner, 21 killed, 12 of them Jews. |
| *26 July* | Car bomb outside Israeli embassy in London injures 13. |
| *27 July* | Car bomb at Balfour House, housing Jewish organizations in London, injures five. |
| *9 October* | Two gunmen shoot up a restaurant in Jerusalem, killing two and wounding 14. |
| *14 October* | Kidnapped Israeli soldier, one rescuer and three terrorists killed in shooting in Hamas hide-out. |
| *19 October* | Suicide bomber kills 22 Israelis on bus in Jerusalem. |
| *2 November* | A leader of Islamic Jihad killed by Israeli car bomb. |
| *11 November* | Suicide bomber kills himself and three Israeli soldiers. |
| *25 December* | Suicide bomber on Jerusalem bus kills himself, wounds 12. |

**1995**

| | |
|---|---|
| *22 January* | 21 (including 20 soldiers) killed by two suicide bombs in Bir Zid, northern Israel. |
| *2 April* | Six people, including at least two terrorists, killed by accidental explosion in bomb factory in Gaza. |
| *9 April* | Two Palestinians blow themselves up in Gaza Strip, kill seven Israelis. |
| *24 July* | Suicide bomber kills six, wounds 28 on Tel Aviv bus. |
| *21 August* | Suicide bomber kills four Israelis and one American on bus in Jerusalem, wounds over 100. |
| *26 October* | Fathi Shiqaqi, head of Islamic Jihad, shot in Malta. |
| *4 November* | Yitzak Rabin, prime minister of Israel, assassinated in Tel Aviv by Jewish extremist. |

**1996**

| | |
|---|---|
| *5 January* | An exploding cellular phone kills Yahya Ayyash, known as 'the bomber', the man who made the suicide bombs used by Hamas. |

| | |
|---|---|
| *25 February* | Suicide bombers in bus in Jerusalem and at a bus stop in Ashkelon kill 24 Israelis, two Americans and a Palestinian and wound over 80. |
| *3 March* | Suicide bomb in bus in Jerusalem kills 19, including five Romanian workers and two Palestinians, wounds ten. |
| *4 March* | Suicide bomber in street in Tel Aviv kills 13, wounds over 150. |
| *23 September* | An ancient Hebrew tunnel is opened for tourists under the edge of the Temple Mount in Jerusalem. In three days of riots that follow, over 70 people are killed. |

**1997**

| | |
|---|---|
| *13 March* | Seven teenage Israeli girls shot by Jordanian soldier at border. |
| *21 March* | Four killed by suicide bomb, including bomber, in Tel Aviv cafe, 43 wounded. |
| *20 July* | 15 (including bombers) killed by two suicide bombs in Jerusalem market. |
| *4 September* | Four killed by three suicide bombers in Jerusalem street market. |
| *25 September* | Attempted assassination of Khaled Meshal, Hamas leader, in Amman by Israeli agents. |
| *1 October* | Israel releases Sheikh Ahmed Yassin, Hamas founder, to obtain release of its two agents in Jordan. Promises to release 40 other Hamas men. |

## ISRAELI–ARAB SHOOTINGS SINCE 1982
**1982**

| | |
|---|---|
| *11 April* | American-born Israeli, Alan Goodman, enters Temple Mount, opens fire, kills two. |

**1985**

| | |
|---|---|
| *6 October* | Egyptian paramilitary policeman kills seven Israeli tourists in Sinai. |

**1989**

| | |
|---|---|
| *8 August* | Jordanian soldier crosses into Israel, wounds an American visitor, holds a hostage. He is shot dead by sharpshooter. |

**1994**

| | |
|---|---|
| *25 February* | American immigrant, Baruch Goldstein, opens fire in Hebron mosque, kills 29 men (and is himself killed). |

**1997**

| | |
|---|---|
| *1 January* | Off-duty Israeli soldier opens fire on shoppers in market in Hebron, wounding five. |
| *13 March* | Seven Israeli schoolgirls killed by Jordanian soldier on island in Jordan, south of Sea of Galilee. |

# FURTHER READING

American University, *Israel: A Country Study*, Washington, 1979.

Benvenisti, Meron, *The West Bank Data Project*, Washington, American Enterprise Institute, Studies in Foreign Policy, 1984.

— *Intimate Enemies: Jews and Arabs in a Shared Land*, Berkeley, University of California Press, 1995.

Elon, Amos, *A Blood-Dimmed Tide*, New York, Columbia University Press, 1997.

Ezrahi, Yaron, *Rubber Bullets: Power and Conscience in Modern Israel*, New York, Farrar, Strauss & Giroux, 1997.

Frankel, William, *Israel Observed*, London, Thames and Hudson, 1985.

Grossman, David, *The Yellow Rain*, New York, Farrar, Straus and Giroux, 1988.

Hertzog, Chaim, *The Arab–Israeli Wars*, New York, Random House, 1981.

Kissinger, Henry, *White House Years*, Boston, Little, Brown, 1979.

—, *Years of Upheaval*, Boston, Little, Brown, 1982.

Laqueur, Walter, *The Road to War, 1967*, London, Weidenfeld and Nicolson, 1968.

Lucas, Noah, *The Modern History of Israel*, New York, Praeger, 1975.

MacLeish, Roderick, *The Sun Stood Still*, New York, Atheneum, 1968.

O'Brien, Conor Cruise, *The Siege*, New York, Simon and Schuster, 1986.

Perlmutter, Amos, *Israel: The Partitioned State*, New York, Charles Scribner's Sons, 1985.

Rabinovich, Itamir, and Reinharz, Jehuda (eds), *Israel in the Middle East: Documents and Readings on Society, Politics and Foreign Relations, 1948 to the Present*, Oxford University Press, 1984.

Sadat, Anwar el, *In Search of Identity*, New York, Harper and Row, 1978.

Said, Edward W., *Peace and its Discontents*, New York, Vintage, 1996.

Shazli, Lt. Gen. Saad al, *The Crossing of the Suez*, San Francisco, American Mideast Research, 1980.

Shipler, David, *Arab and Jew*, New York Times Books, 1986.

Sykes, Christopher, *Crossroads to Israel*, Cleveland, World Publishing Co., 1965.

# THE KURDS

The Kurds are an ancient people partitioned among Iraq, Iran, Syria, Turkey, Lebanon, Azerbaijan and Armenia. They have never been a nation nor have they ever, in modern times, been united under one government. The frontier between Persia and the Ottoman empire ran through the middle of Kurdish territory, a line that still divides them. They have now learned nationalism, at the same time and in the same school as the Turks, the Persians and the Arabs, and have fought a series of unsuccessful campaigns against the governments of Ankara, Tehran and Baghdad.

Only the roughest estimate can be made of the total number of Kurds. David McDowall counts the total Kurdish population as between 24 million and 27 million, and offers the following break-down:

| Country | Kurds | Percentage of total population |
|---|---|---|
| Turkey | 13 million | 23 |
| Iraq | 4.2 million | 23 |
| Iran | 5.7 million | 10 |
| Syria | 1 million | 7 |
| Lebanon | 80,000 | |
| Armenia and Azerbaijan | 400,000 | |
| Europe | 700,000 | |

The Kurds live in a territory covering about 250,000 square miles (640,000 sq. km). They are virtually all Muslim, 75 per cent of them Sunni, the rest adherents of a variety of other sects. Their origins are lost in total obscurity, and it is not at all clear that they descend from the same founding tribe. At any event, people who can fairly be described as Kurds have lived in the same mountains for at least the past 2000 years. Kurdish is not a single language. Its variants are as great as those between English and German. There is a major linguistic division between the northern Kurds, those in Turkey and in northern Iraq, and those in eastern Iraq and Iran. There are further subdivisions in Iran and in Turkey.

There is an insistent question whether the Kurds can properly be described as a nation in any sense. Turkey has tried to assimilate them, making them Turks, or at least 'Mountain Turks', but without success. Iraq simply oppresses them while Iran alternates uneasily between allowing certain autonomy and violent repression. The situation of the Kurds is an example of the difficulty of reconciling the idea of a nation state with the real world. A homogeneous nation within settled frontiers is the exception to the rule, even in Europe. The Kurds are not united, but neither are the Arabs nor the Turks. The Kurds' misfortune is not that they are separated, but that they are oppressed by the dominant races in the countries where they live.

During World War I, the Russians opened a front against Turkey in the Caucasus. During three years of warfare, the Armenian community in eastern Turkey was destroyed in a series of pogroms in which the Kurds participated enthusiastically (*see* Terrorism: Forlorn hopes, pp. 620–25). Another small community, the Christian Assyrians, was also driven out of its homelands; the remnants settled in Iraqi Kurdistan after the war, and were later slaughtered in the first Kurdish revolt. In 1920, the League of Nations – meaning, in this case, the British – contemplated establishing independent states for the Armenians and the Kurds. The rump Ottoman government in Constantinople signed the Treaty of Sèvres, which provided, among other concessions, for the creation of Kurdistan.

Kemal Pasha then raised the banner of Turkish nationalism in revolt, and he and his followers restored Turkey's independence and settled its frontiers. Many Kurds joined him, preferring the Turks to the Armenians or the Greeks. The Treaty of Sèvres was quietly abandoned, and its replacement, the Treaty of Lausanne, signed in 1923, made no mention of the Kurds. Having remained loyal to the caliph, they suddenly found themselves subject to a secular government that insisted they were Turks, not Kurds at all, and to British and Arab rule from Baghdad. The first Kurdish revolts ensued, and they have continued, in one form or another, ever since. They have been notable as much for the ferocity with which the different Kurdish tribes and families have fought against each other as for the consistency with which they have fought Turkish, Iraqi and Iranian governments.

## THE KURDS IN TURKEY

The largest number of Kurds live in eastern Turkey – perhaps 13 million people. Whereas the Kurds in Iraq, Iran and Syria are confronted by unstable governments (which, in the case of Iraq and Syria, are minority military dictatorships), the Kurds in Turkey are a minority, comprising about 23 per cent, in an otherwise homogeneous nation, which has a population of about 61 million, a secure government and a fierce determination to maintain national integrity. In addition, Turkish Kurds have, in common with their relatives in Iraq and Iran, an ineradicable delight in fighting among themselves.

The Kurds were, for the most part, loyal subjects of the Ottoman caliph, but they have been much less loyal to the secular state set up by Ataturk. In 1925, the Dervishes incited the Kurds to revolt, demanding the restoration of the caliphate. Ataturk ruthlessly suppressed the uprising. Hundreds of villages were burned and between 40,000 and 250,000 people were killed. The leaders of the revolt were executed, and Ataturk used the occasion to launch some of his major reforms: the suppression of the order of Dervishes, and the outlawing of the fez, the headgear that was the outward and visible sign of the Turk's adherence to Islam.

The Turks then set about suppressing the Kurds as a separate people, in the most sweeping way possible, by flatly denying their existence. They claim that the Kurds are 'Mountain Turks', and insist that they must be educated in Turkish and adopt the Western manners of modern Turkey. (In 1979, a former minister of public works was sentenced to two years' hard labour for saying in public: 'In Turkey, there are Kurds. I, too, am a Kurd.') In fact, the Kurds are no more Turkish than the Welsh are 'Mountain English'. The languages are totally distinct, and the separate history of the Kurds goes back at least 1000 years before the first Turkish tribes arrived from Central Asia.

In 1965 the Kurdistan Democratic Party of Turkey (K D P T) was established, a traditionalist, separatist organization with links to the Mullah Mustafa Barzani in Iraq. The Turkish Workers Party (T W P), a doctrinaire socialist party, supported the Kurds and had many Kurdish members, and was therefore banned by the government. In 1967, there were mass demonstrations in the Kurdish provinces against the suppression of Kurdish cultural and political activity, and in 1969, the Organization of Revolutionary Youth (D D K O) was set up by militants from the T W P to start a guerrilla war.

The government periodically deported tens of thousands of Kurds from eastern Turkey, and resettled them in central Anatolia or allowed them to move to the cities. In another instance of the law of unforeseen consequences, many of these transplanted Kurds then took up radical politics and joined the far-left Turkish parties that started a campaign of terrorism against the government in the 1970s. Then some of them returned to their villages and introduced notions of nationalism, socialism and armed resistance to their tribal relatives who would not normally have considered such things.

The troubles in the east were one reason for the army 'coup by communiqué' in March 1971, when the army induced the politicians to hand over power to a government of technocrats, and instructed the new regime to solve the country's problems. The army then set about suppressing all signs of Kurdish nationalism in the east, but with little success.

By the late 1970s, Turkey was disintegrating into civil war between right and left, with open revolt in the Kurdish provinces, and urban terrorism that killed 5000 people between 1978 and 1980. A number of Kurdish parties and terrorist groups were active, the most radical being the Workers' Party of Kurdistan (P K K; also known as the Apocus), which fought both the Turkish state and traditional Kurdish leaders. In September 1980, the army staged another coup. It then repressed the Kurds with a heavy hand.

The disturbances increased with the Iran–Iraq war. In May 1983, the Turkish army mounted a major operation over the border in Iraq to clear out Kurdish guerrilla positions. By official count, in the four years 1984–8, 185 Turkish soldiers, 480 Kurdish civilians and about 200 guerrillas were killed. On 1 April 1988, government forces killed 20 guerrillas with the loss of three military men, including the pilot of a helicopter that was shot down, in a battle near the Syrian frontier. The troops discovered and attacked a guerrilla band in a cave, after a guerrilla attack on a village had resulted in the deaths of nine people. In early May, terrorists massacred 25 Turkish villagers in two separate incidents near the Syrian border. A few days before, terrorists had hanged a village teacher whom they had accused of being an informer. The government reported that the killers were members of the P K K, which has its headquarters in Damascus and can only operate across the frontier with the assistance of the Assad regime.

The Turkish government has launched a major economic development scheme for south-east Turkey, in Turkish Kurdistan, based upon a series of dams for irrigation and hydroelectricity. The Kabban dam, the largest in Turkey, has been completed, and the much larger Ataturk dam is under construction. When it is finished, by 2000, its associated irrigation and industrial projects should provide work for 3 million people, many of them Kurds.

Some of the cultural restrictions on Kurds have been lifted. In February 1991, at the height of the second Gulf War, the decree against the public use of the Kurdish language and Kurdish music was revoked. The new law did nothing to lift restrictions against teaching Kurdish in schools, or publishing books or newspapers in the language. The Turkish government also started paying attention to international concerns at human rights abuses just as rebel activity in Kurdistan started to increase.

In the aftermath of the second Gulf war (*see below*), there was a revival of Kurdish guerrilla activity in south-east Turkey, encouraged by the Iraqi government, which supplied arms to the rebels. This was Saddam Hussein's riposte to Turkey's participation in the alliance that had driven him out of Kuwait. In the nine months after the war, 500 civilians were killed in Turkish Kurdistan and heavily-armed guerrillas operated throughout the region. They were chiefly from the P K K, whose leader, Abdullah Ocalan, is based in Syria. Turkey sent large reinforcements.

In June 1995 the Turkish government reported that 19,000 people had been killed during the insurgency since 1984, and the death toll was rising rapidly. Other estimates were much higher. A relatively liberal prime minister, Turgut Ozal, offered some concessions to the Kurds, but he died in 1993 and was succeeded by a series of weak, demagogic and sometimes corrupt leaders who could agree only on the need to suppress the Kurds. In 1997, the army insisted that a government headed by an Islamic party should resign (and early the following year the party was banned), chiefly because it was opposed to the secular policies followed in Turkey since Ataturk. The new government gave the army a completely free hand in the east, despite repeated warnings from Europe that Turkey could not hope to join the E U unless it improved its record on human rights.

The war continues. Turkey formed an alliance with Barzani's K D P to fight its leftist opponents, and continued frequent incursions into northern Iraq. By 1997, the army claimed that it had won the war, eliminating the P K K save in a few isolated pockets along the borders. It then bent its mind to improving its image in eastern Turkey by helping villagers economically. Eastern Turkey remained under heavy military occupation, and there was no sign that the P K K leadership in Syria was ready to concede defeat. Perhaps the best Turkey could hope for was a period of stalemate, but always with the fear that the least relaxation of vigilance would immediately lead to a renewed war. That vigilance means a *de facto* suspension of democracy in much of the country – and a very circumscribed democracy elsewhere.

## THE KURDS IN IRAQ

In 1943, when Iraq was occupied by the British and bitterly divided between pro-Axis and pro-Allies factions, the Mullah Mustafa Barzani, who was hereditary religious and secular leader of his tribe, set up an autonomous region around his home town of Barzan, which he held for two years. In 1945, the Baghdad government reasserted its authority in Kurdistan, and Barzani led the fight against it. He was defeated and, in 1946, moved to Mahabad, in north-west Iran, where Kurds under the patronage of the Soviet Union had set up a Kurdish republic (*see below*). When the Iranian government reoccupied Mahabad, Barzani fled to the USSR, where he lived until the Iraqi revolution in 1958.

The regime of the Iraqi general Abd al-Karim Kassem at first promised the Kurds autonomy, but when Barzani started asserting his authority in Kurdistan in the north of the country, the government went to war. The first phase of the war lasted from 1961 to 1970, and took the form of many such insurrections: after recovering from its initial reverses, the government controlled the main towns and periodically occupied the larger valleys, but never reached the Kurds' positions in the mountains. The Iraqi air force therefore bombed Kurdish villages indiscriminately, but without affecting the Kurds' will to resist. Barzani's army – the Peshmerga (the word means 'those who walk before death') – numbered 50,000–60,000 men, and at the height of their success, the Kurdish rebels controlled all the mountains in north-east Iraq, and their guerrilla bands reached the outskirts of Mosul, Arbil and Kirkuk, the principal cities in Iraqi Kurdistan. At various times, the Kurds were supported by Iran, the USSR, Israel and the United States.

Thousands of people were killed, mainly civilians. One estimate puts the civilian death toll between 1961 and 1970 at 100,000 and military deaths at 9000. A total of half that seems more probable.

In March 1970, the Iraqi government offered autonomy to the Kurds and a ceasefire came into force. However, the two sides could never reach agreement on the details of the proposed relationship. The main sticking points were Barzani's demands that he retain the Peshmerga under his own command, and that Kurdistan include Kirkuk, the province that produced 70 per cent of Iraq's oil. The Baghdad government made its final offer – autonomy without Kirkuk – on the fourth anniversary of the March Manifesto and, when Barzani rejected it, ordered a renewed offensive.

The Iraqi army drove into Kurdistan, and Barzani made the mistake of renouncing traditional guerrilla tactics and, instead, fought a conventional war against the Iraqis. He had 40,000 troops (the Peshmerga) and 60,000 militiamen, and he overestimated his strength. The Kurds were defeated and, by the end of the year, had been driven into the furthest recesses of their mountains, up against the Turkish and Iranian frontiers.

The Peshmerga survived for a while, holding off an Iraqi army 100,000 strong, thanks to support from the Iranians in the form of heavy artillery, and, secretly, from the C I A. The Ba'ath government in Baghdad was in its most militantly leftist phase, closely allied to the Soviet Union and bitterly hostile to the West. Iran and Iraq were, as usual, enemies, and there were serious border disputes between the two.

In 1975, in an abrupt reversal of policy, the shah of Iran and Dr Henry Kissinger, the U S secretary of state, decided to abandon the Kurds and reach an agreement with the Iraqi government. The Iranian and Iraqi governments signed an agreement settling their disputes during an O P E C meeting in Algiers on 6 March 1975. American clandestine military aid to the Kurds was abruptly ended and, more important, so was Iranian aid. The frontier was closed and the Kurds were left to their fate. Mustafa Barzani and tens of thousands of his followers fled to Iran (Barzani died in the United States in 1979), and the Iraqis celebrated their victory in the usual manner, by executing as many of the rebels as they could lay their hands on. The short war had cost the lives of 7000 Iraqi troops, by official count, and 2000 Kurdish troops, according to Barzani. The real totals were probably much higher, perhaps 20,000 all told, and there were 600,000 refugees.

Barzani's Kurdish Democratic Party (K D P) went into eclipse, and rival Kurdish leaders took up the fight. The most notable of them was Jalal Talabani, of the Patriotic Union of Kurdistan (P U K). Talabani had opposed Barzani since the 1950s. His tribal base is in Suleimaniya in southern Kurdistan, a much more urbanized region than Barzan in the north. After the débâcle of 1975, Talabani took refuge in Syria with about 4000 armed followers. He was given a Syrian passport by President Assad, and his small army was posted along the Iraqi border to guard it against the Ba'athists of Baghdad. At that time, relations between Syria and Iraq were particularly tense: they nearly went to war in 1975. Turning Talabani loose in Iraqi Kurdistan during the Iran–Iraq war was another instance of the fratricidal tendencies of Syrian and Iraqi Ba'athists.

In 1984, the Iraqis offered Talabani a further measure of autonomy in exchange for continued opposition to the Barzanis and the K D P. However, two years later, Talabani and Mustafa Barzani's son, Massoud, reached an agreement, brokered by the Iranians, and set up an alliance between the P U K and the K D P. Kurdish guerrillas then started attacking Iraqi positions in south Kurdistan as well as the north.

## THE KURDS AND THE FIRST GULF WAR

One of the principal fronts in the war between Iran and Iraq was in Iraqi Kurdistan. The topography favoured the Iraqis: a succession of high mountain ranges, the Zagros, run parallel to the border; successfully crossing one range offered the Iranian attackers the opportunity to contemplate the next. Nevertheless, year by year, the Iranians pushed through the highest mountains and, in March 1988, were within sight of the Darbandi Khan lake and dam at Dukan, whence a series of passes lead down into the plains. It was their furthest advance.

Throughout the eight years of war, there was a constantly shifting series of alliances on both sides of the border. The Iranians recruited many Kurds to help fight Iraq, despite the betrayal of 1975 and the ruthless suppression of the Iranian Kurds in 1979–83. By early in 1984, the Iranian army had reasserted its control **333** over virtually all Iranian Kurdistan – killing an estimated 27,500 Kurds in the process. At the same time, many Kurds in Iraq fought against Iran – and always Kurds fought each other on both sides of the border, and across the border. As ever, the tribes followed their leaders, nursing ancestral grievances and vendettas. The traditionalist Kurdish Democratic Party (KDP), now led by sons of the Mullah Mustafa, supported the government in Tehran against the KDPI, while Baghdad supported leftist Kurds against Tehran.

The Iraqi Kurds had more success than the Iranian Kurds in preserving some control over parts of their territory, but only for as long as the war with Iran lasted – for example, in September 1987, Kurdish guerrillas briefly occupied Kanimasi, an Iraqi Kurdish town near the Turkish border. Kurdish bands operating throughout Iraqi Kurdistan assassinated government officials and ambushed military convoys.

In March 1987 Saddam sent his cousin Ali Hassan el-Majid to deal with the Kurds. He was short of troops, so he used poison gas on Kurdish villages. It was mustard gas, the same substance that had been used in World War I and subsequently outlawed by civilized nations in one of the Geneva conventions. Majid also had thousands of Kurdish prisoners shot. Their bodies were buried in mass graves in Arbil and throughout Kurdistan. David McDowell asserts that about 200,000 people were killed in 1988 alone. Rebel leaders claim that over 1000 Kurdish villages were also destroyed, and several large towns. Kurds were cleared out of the labyrinthine cities of Kirkuk and Arbil. Later, when the Kurds controlled Arbil and Sulaymaniya, they found detailed records of all these atrocities in police offices. Saddam's regime proved to be as meticulous at recording the atrocities it committed, and as thorough, as the Germans themselves, or Pol Pot's Cambodians.

In March 1988, during the last Iranian spring offensive, the Iraqi air force used poison gas again – both cyanide and mustard gas – against the Kurdish town of Halabjah, which the Iranians had captured. The Iranians alleged that 2000 people were killed in the incident, and when Western reporters were taken to the town, they counted at least 100 bodies, all civilians. In April, Iran reported a further series of Iraqi gas attacks on Kurdish villages.

When Iran sued for peace, on 18 July 1988, the Iraqis immediately turned their attention to the Kurds. Saddam Hussein's army swept through Iraqi Kurdistan and, within a month, had driven the Kurdish forces in rout over the border into Turkey and Iran. Iraq once again used poison gas. The Turkish government had to take care of about 60,000 refugees, and hastily put up tent camps to receive them. It was a temporary measure: tents are no adequate protection for civilians in a Turkish winter.

Six weeks later, Turkey managed to send a number of the refugees into Iran (Massoud Barzani's party claimed that 30,000 were expelled). They could not return to their homes in Iraq, because their homes no longer existed: the Iraqi army had systematically obliterated their villages. The government alleged that the destruction was for the villagers' own good, that they would be better off in modern towns – described as 'complexes that have all the necessary infrastructure' – being built for them at the foot of the mountains. Elsewhere, they might have been called 'strategic hamlets'. Hundreds of thousands of people lost their homes. Near one devastated village, Saddam built a complex of palaces for himself on an artificial lake, using dressed stones from demolished villages to build a perimeter wall more than a mile long. It was finished just before the second Gulf War and was later taken over by the Kurds. The Iraqi authorities claimed that 20,000 Kurds returned from Iran after Saddam Hussein offered them an amnesty on 6 September.

## THE KURDS IN IRAN

Like their cousins in Iraq and Turkey, Iranian Kurds tried to set up an independent state after World War I, but they were suppressed by General Reza Khan, who made himself shah in 1925 (*see* Iran, p. 271–83). In World War II, the British occupied most of Iran. The Soviet Union controlled a small area in the north, and the Azerbaijanis, with Soviet support, set up a republic of their own in Tabriz in January 1946. Simultaneously, a tribe of Kurds seized the opportunity to set up the Republic of Mahabad, but Kurds in other areas conspicuously failed to rally to the flag. Mustafa Barzani, driven out of his stronghold in Iraq, for a while provided an army to defend Mahabad, but when the Soviets withdrew from Iran, the Iranians reoccupied both Tabriz and Mahabad in December 1946. Barzani then fled to the U S S R.

Iranian Kurds were largely quiescent during the rest of the reign of Shah Mohammed, who had succeeded his father in 1941. When Barzani returned to Iraq in 1958, and later started the Kurds' revolt, he was supported by the shah out of enmity for Baghdad, and used his influence to keep the Iranian Kurds loyal to the throne. This included arresting and executing any Iranian rebels who came his way. The Ba'ath regime in Baghdad tried to stir up anti-shah feeling among the Kurdish Democratic Party of Iran, a leftist organization established during the Mahabad republic, which was ideologically much closer to the Ba'ath than to Barzani. However, Barzani's influence in the border lands was so strong that the K D P I would not challenge him, or fight against the Iranians.

After the collapse of the Iranian monarchy in 1979, the Kurds there took the opportunity to establish their autonomy. They seized control of their provinces and helped themselves to the huge stores of weapons that the shah had accumulated in barracks and arsenals near the Iraqi frontier. The conflict between the K D P I and traditional tribal leaders continued. Most Kurds are Sunni, but there was a large Shiite community in southern Kurdistan that supported Khomeini.

The K D P I joined the opposition to Khomeini and took part in the fighting in Tehran and elsewhere. For a while, the revolutionary government lost control of the Kurdish provinces, and there were wholesale massacres of Persians and Kurds in disputed areas. The Iranian Kurds were not supported from outside, and Khomeini was able to send his army into Kurdistan, to be followed by revolutionary courts that set about executing all opposition Kurds they could find. The Kurds took to the mountains and started a full-scale guerrilla war. There were attempts to negotiate but without success. The government controlled the towns, while the K D P I controlled the mountains. Then, in September 1980, Saddam Hussein invaded Iran (*see above*). During the Iran–Iraq war, Tehran succeeded in reasserting its authority in Iranian Kurdistan.

**335**

## THE SECOND GULF WAR, 1991

The Kurds of Iraq were among the chief victims of the war to liberate Kuwait. After Iraq's defeat in February 1991, the Shiite south of Iraq rose in revolt against the Sunni regime of Baghdad. The uprising was wholly spontaneous, unplanned and hopeless. The Kurds, too, rose in revolt as the news from the south reached them. Saddam Hussein had stripped his garrisons in Kurdistan to suppress the Shiite revolt, and to defend Baghdad, and the Kurdish rebels threw themselves upon the soldiers, police and officials who remained. They seized most of the main towns, and massacred their enemies: thousands of Iraqi Arabs were slaughtered. Massoud Barzani and Jalal Talabani patched up their differences once again, and for a few heady days they ruled an independent Kurdistan. Then, as soon as he had crushed the Shiite rebellion, Saddam Hussein counter-attacked.

Kurdish resistance collapsed immediately. The Peshmerga had no tanks, heavy artillery or anti-tank weapons, and the allies had been misled into permitting Iraqi helicopters to operate beyond the war zone on the southern frontier. The Republican Guards drove into the Kurdish cities and pressed on into the mountains, preceded by helicopter gunships which strafed Kurdish positions, towns and columns of refugees. The Kurdish people fled before the Arabs. One and a half million Kurds escaped, a million or so into Iran, the rest to Turkey. Thousands died on the roads. The weather was still cold in the high Zagros, and the people of the cities, including 125,000 from Kirkuk, were quite unused to the conditions they encountered. Western reporters and television crews penetrated to the refugee columns and sent back heartrending accounts of what they had seen, and compelling film of the conditions of the refugees. Film of barefooted children crying in the snow, or mothers clutching starving babies, was shown around the world. The Shiites of southern Iraq had fought and died without the benefit of international attention. The Kurds suffered in the full glare of publicity.

The Western powers were all constrained to react. Supplies were hastily gathered in American bases in Turkey and flown to the borders. The American army in Germany, that part of it that had been left behind by the Gulf War, was mobilized to help the Kurds, and acted with despatch, competence and compassion. British, German, French and other allies did their part. Camps were set up for the refugees in southern Turkey. They were provided with sanitary facilities, hospitals and field kitchens. Food, clothing and medical supplies were delivered, and those Kurds who were still in the mountains and who could not be reached overland, or who would not yet come into the camps, were supplied by air drops. This was called 'Operation Provide Comfort'.

Soon there were 400,000 refugees in camps along the border with Turkey. The American government estimated that 6700 refugees, most of them children under five, died in the camps in Turkey in April and May. They had no figures for those who died in the desperate flight before the Iraqi army, or for those much larger numbers who fled to Iran. Once sufficient supplies were reaching the refugees, the allies set to work to get them home again. The Iraqis were informed that the Americans and their allies would establish a safety zone for the Kurds on the ground in northern Iraq, around the town of

Dohuk, and that allied air forces would patrol the rest of Kurdistan north of the 36th parallel. American, British and French troops moved into the area and set up transit camps, and over the course of the summer, most of the Kurds returned home. Those that remained in the mountains mostly came from places further south, far from the protection of allied troops and helicopters. The refugees from Kirkuk stayed in the mountains. The Iraqi army, which had recaptured Arbil, Sulaymaniya and other cities in April, now withdrew again, and as the Kurds returned to these cities, police and secret police withdrew. The watchful truce between Kurds and Iraqis, policed by the American air force, could break down at any moment. In October, there was a sudden outbreak of fighting around Sulaymaniya. Kurds captured and massacred 60 Iraqi soldiers, and the army shelled the town before a ceasefire could be arranged.

The Western allies cared for the refugees who had fled to Turkey. The larger numbers who had escaped into Iran were not so fortunate. They were taken into refugee camps set up by the Iranians, but Iran, in the aftermath of war and revolution, was quite unable to help so many. The Iranian camps were controlled by the worst sort of chauvinist, religious zealot who refused to allow any Western aid. When a planeload of supplies was brought in by a Western charitable organization, its personnel were threatened and mishandled by the Iranian thugs guarding the camps. They kept Westerners away from the sacred territory of the Islamic Republic, and the Kurds in the camps suffered and died.

In the late summer, the Americans and their allies withdrew from Kurdistan. They had wrung a grudging promise from Saddam Hussein that the Kurds would be left in peace, and they handed over their responsibilities to the United Nations High Commissioner for Refugees (U N H C R). The Security Council approved its mandate until the end of the year. The Americans left a small number of officers along the Turkish borders, and continued to patrol the skies over Kurdistan to ensure that Iraq did not return with planes, helicopters, troops and secret police.

Massoud Barzani started negotiations with Saddam in the summer, and soon the dispute resumed where it had been left 16 years earlier: should the proposed Kurdish autonomous zone include Kirkuk, and should it have its own militia? Barzani, learning from experience, finally agreed to leave the question of Kirkuk to the future, and settled for the autonomy that Saddam proposed. Talabani insisted on complete freedom for the whole of Kurdistan, and soon the age-old dispute between the two clans resumed. Saddam shelled Talabani's base at Sulaymaniya, playing off the Kurdish parties against each other. He also supported the P K K's war against Turkey, which led to Turkish punitive expeditions into northern Kurdistan, Barzani's homeland.

The Kurds' future in Iraq was as bleak as ever. Kurdistan had not recovered from the devastation of 1988 before the far worse disasters of 1991 burst upon it. After the refugees returned from Turkey and Iran, and found the Iraqis gone, they set about rebuilding the thousands of towns and villages that had been destroyed by the Iraqis in their efforts to bring the Kurds down from the mountains into the more easily policed plains. The Kurds managed to bring in the wheat harvest, which had been planted in 1990, before the war, but had great difficulty in planting the 1992 crop. They had few tractors and no spares for them, and a great shortage of everything.

Saddam's troops and armour hovered on the outskirts of the major Kurdish cities and imposed a partial blockade upon them. On 14 November 1991, Barzani reached a temporary agreement with Saddam that the blockade would be lifted, the Peshmerga would pull out of the cities, and joint forces of Iraqi police and Kurds would patrol them. It was a sort of ceasefire, or temporary truce. The question of Kurdistan's autonomy was still unresolved.

In May 1992 the Kurds in Iraq organized elections for the first time in their history. The two main parties, Barzani's K D P and Talabani's P U K, won almost the same number of votes and divided up the parliament equally between them, forming a coalition government. The parliament opened in Arbil on 4 July, a date of heavy symbolism, and it appeared briefly as though the Kurds might unite and form some sort of state. Their unity lasted barely two years. In May 1994 the coalition broke up and the two parties started fighting. The chief object of contention was the division of the profits of smuggling oil across the border with Turkey. By the end of the year, there was full-scale civil war between Barzani, in Dohuk in the north, and Talabani, in Sulaymaniya. Talabani, for the moment, held Arbil. A third party emerged, the Islamic Movement of Kurdistan, a fundamentalist Shiite party allied to the Iranian government. For the moment, it cooperated with Barzani. At least 3000 soldiers were killed. In February 1995 a car bomb in Zakho, in K D P territory, killed 54 people. Presumably it was the work of one of the rival factions. The whole of Kurdistan reverted to factionalism, with dozens of warlords controlling small parcels of territory and fighting their rivals for the spoils of the smuggling trade: U N sanctions against Iraq meant that smuggling across the frontiers into Turkey and Iran was a major industry.

The troubles of Iraqi Kurdistan were complicated and aggravated by Turkey's escalating war against its own Kurdish rebels. They used northern Iraq as a refuge from Turkish attack, and the Turkish army mounted repeated attacks across the border. In March 1995 Turkey sent in 35,000 troops to establish a permanent presence there. They were soon obliged to retreat, but they were always ready to return. In addition, Iran started sending troops across the border to fight Talabani's forces.

The U S and its allies tried to establish a ceasefire between the factions, and thought they had succeeded, in a meeting in Dublin in August 1995. The truce broke down a year later, with Talabani's troops advancing into Barzani's northern stronghold, possibly with the help of the Iranians. Barzani then called in Saddam Hussein to help his fight with the P K K. In a sudden and dramatic demonstration of the real power in Iraq, Saddam's army occupied Arbil on 31 August 1966. Talabani had to flee for his life.

Arbil is within the 'safe-haven' proclaimed by the U S and its allies, and patrolled by their air forces out of Turkey. They could hardly object too strenuously to Saddam's occupation of the place, since he had been invited there by the most senior of Kurdish leaders. After taking Arbil, Iraqi secret police and Barzani's men went through the city arresting members of the P K K, who were summarily shot. The U S had to mount a rescue operation for the Iraqi opposition leaders who had been based in Kurdistan.

After his tainted victory in Arbil, Barzani moved on to Sulaymaniya, which his forces occupied on 10 September. Saddam Hussein cemented his alliance with Barzani by ending the blockade of Kurdistan that had lasted since the allied intervention in 1992. Then he pulled his troops out of Sulaymaniya, leaving Barzani in uncontested control of Kurdistan, for the moment. In the event, his rule lasted less than two months. Talabani's PUK, helped by the Iranians, launched a counterattack and recovered Sulaymaniya. The rivalry continued, but the year's events had demonstrated that the Kurds were no match for Saddam Hussein. Whenever he wants, he can reoccupy the whole area. And whenever UN sanctions against his regime are lifted, the Americans and others will end the last shred of protection they still offer the Kurds, leaving them once again at Saddam's mercy.

## THE KURDS IN SYRIA

The Kurds in Syria are less numerous and less militant than their relatives in Iraq. Most of them live in the north-east, along the Turkish and Iraqi frontiers, but there are Kurdish centres elsewhere, some of them relics of Kurdish military colonies established in the Middle Ages. The Kurds were given the Crusader castle, Krak des Chevaliers, to guard in the 14th century. When the French returned in 1920, they cleaned up the castle and evicted the Kurds. The French left again, in 1945. The Kurds are still there.

After the merger of Syria and Egypt in 1958, a policy of settling Arabs in Kurdistan was introduced and continued until 1976. Under the guise of land reform, tribal land was confiscated and given to Bedu from the desert. The Kurdish language is no longer taught in schools, and all signs of Kurdish culture are rigorously suppressed.

One reason for the Kurds' mistreatment in Syria was that the French had encouraged separatism among Syria's many minorities, and had promoted Kurds in the army. The first three coups in independent Syria, all in 1949, were carried out by Kurdish generals. Furthermore, Kurds dominated the Syrian Communist party, which was a rival to the Ba'ath (now dominated by another minority, the Alawites). Kurdish Communists have played an enthusiastic part in the terrorism in Lebanon, to which about 50,000 Kurds have fled to escape from persecution and economic distress in Syria.

However, a high proportion of Syrian Kurds have accepted the regime and serve in the army. The Syrians have also encouraged a Marxist party – the Kurdish Workers' Party (PKK) – which carries on guerrilla warfare and terrorism in Turkey. Its leader, Abdullah Ocalan, lives in Damascus.

## FURTHER READING

American University, *Turkey: A Country Study*, Washington D.C., 1980.
American University, *Iraq: A Country Study*, Washington, 1979.
Bulloch, John and Morris, Harvey: *No Friends but the Mountains*, New York, Oxford University Press, 1992.

Ciment, James, *The Kurds: State and Minority in Turkey, Iraq and Iran*, New York, Facts on File, 1996.

Edmonds, Cecil, *Kurds, Turks and Arabs*, Oxford University Press, 1957.

Ghareeb, Edmund, *The Kurdish Question in Iraq*, Syracuse University Press, New York, 1981.

Ghassemlon, A. R. *et al.* (ed. Gérard Chaliand; trans. Michael Pallis), *People without a Country: The Kurds and Kurdistan*, London, Zed Press, 1980.

Kinnane, Dirk, *The Kurds and Kurdistan*, Oxford University Press, 1964.

Lewis, Bernard, *The Arabs in History*, London/New York, Hutchinson's University Library, 1950.

—, *The Emergence of Modern Turkey*, Royal Institute of International Affairs, Oxford University Press, 1968.

McDowall, David, *The Modern History of the Kurds*, New York, St Martin's Press, 1996.

O'Ballance, Edgar, *The Kurdish Revolt, 1961–1970*, Hamden, Conn., Arclion Books, 1973.

Pelletiere, Stephen C., *The Kurds: An Unstable Element in the Gulf*, Boulder, Colo., Westview Press, 1984.

Randal, Jonathan, *After Such Knowledge, What Forgiveness?*, New York, Farrar, Strauss & Giroux, 1996.

# LEBANON

| | |
|---|---|
| Geography | 3950 sq. miles (10,400 sq. km). About half the size of Wales. Defined by its topography: a narrow coastal strip along the Mediterranean, 120 miles (200 km) long, and two mountain ranges parallel to the coast – the Lebanon and Anti-Lebanon mountains – with the narrow Bekaa valley between them. At its widest, Lebanon is 60 miles (100 km) across. |
| Population | About 4 million (there has been no countrywide census since 1932). The capital, Beirut, had a population of over 1 million in 1975; the second city, Tripoli, has a population of about 600,000. |

*Estimated confessional breakdown of Lebanon*

| | |
|---|---|
| Maronite Christian | 900,000 |
| Orthodox Christian | 250,000 |
| Greek Catholics | 150,000 |
| Armenians | 175,000 |
| Palestinian Christians | 30,000 |
| Other Christians | 50,000 |
| Shiite Muslims | 1,100,000 |
| Sunni Muslims | 750,000 |
| Druse | 200,000 |
| Palestinians (Sunni) | 300,000 |
| Others (inc. Kurds) | 100,000 |

*Note:* Islam is divided into two main sects: the Sunni, the majority sect (90% worldwide); and the Shiites, who are dominant in Iran and are in a majority in Iraq (they are in a minority elsewhere). Sunnis and Shiites consider each other to be heretical. Both consider the Druse to be a heretical Islamic sect.

The Maronite Christians are the result of a heresy of the 4th–7th centuries, in which they broke from the orthodox Church because of their belief in the solely divine nature of Christ. Since the 16th century, however, they have been an Eastern Church in union with the Roman Catholic Church but retaining their own rite and canon law.

| | |
|---|---|
| GNP per capita | $2660. |
| Refugees | Internal: 800,000, including 302,000 Palestinian refugees. |
| Casualties | The Lebanese government estimated in 1992 that 144,000 people had been killed since the civil war began in 1975, |

17,000 remained missing, presumed killed, and that 10,000 Palestinians had been killed in the fighting and massacres in and around the camps. There were 200,000 wounded.

---

Myself against my brother. Myself and my brother against my cousin. Myself, my brother and my cousin against the foreigner.

*Arab proverb*

A scorpion asked a rat to carry him across the Jordan. 'How do I know you won't sting me?' asked the rat. 'If I sting you, I would drown,' replied the scorpion. So the rat took the scorpion on his back and started to swim the river. Halfway across, the scorpion stung him. As he died, the rat cried out, 'Why did you do that?' The drowning scorpion replied, 'Because this is the Middle East.'

*Israeli story*

## HISTORY

Through all its history until 1943, except during the Crusades, Lebanon was part of Syria. The Maronite Christians and the Druse living on and near the wild and inaccessible Mount Lebanon maintained a degree of independence from the Ottoman empire and, by the 19th century, had established a right to self-government. They celebrated it by fighting a civil war in 1860, and provoking foreign, notably French, intervention.

After World War I, France was awarded Syria as a mandate by the League of Nations and, in 1920, created Lebanon. The Maronites' and Druses' Mount Lebanon fastnesses were enlarged by the addition of the coastal strip, including the port cities of Tripoli, Beirut and Sidon, and the Bekaa valley and the crest of the Anti-Lebanon to the east. The new state had a small Christian majority.

The Syrians have never recognized Lebanon's separate identity, claiming that it should be part of Greater Syria (which they sometimes also say should include Jordan and Palestine). Many Lebanese Muslims and non-Maronite Christians shared this view, objecting to their forcible inclusion into a Maronite-dominated state.

France was compelled by Britain to give Lebanon and Syria their independence in 1943. To begin with, Muslim and Christian leaders in Lebanon agreed to work together. In an unofficial deal, later known as the National Pact, they laid down that the power of the state should be kept at a minimum, leaving the various confessional groups to run their own affairs as they wished. The enfeebled government would be controlled by a Maronite president and a Sunni prime minister, with a Shiite as president of the Chamber of Deputies; in Parliament, there would be a permanent ratio of six Christians to every five Muslims.

There was one essential weakness in this system. It precluded the emergence of any national sentiment. People considered themselves Maronites or Druse, Sunni or Shiite, never Lebanese. Other Middle Eastern states formed of the fragments of the Ottoman empire tried to turn themselves into nations. Lebanon never did.

The religion-based appointments and the parliamentary ratio reflected the diversity of Lebanese society in 1943. In subsequent decades, the numerical balance of the population changed radically. The Shiite Muslims, the poorest and most oppressed section, overtook the Sunnis and the Maronites. By 1975, Muslims were in a clear majority and would not indefinitely accept a Maronite stranglehood on the presidency.

The country was actually run by a shifting alliance of notables: landowners from the mountains or rich merchants from the cities. Some of the leading families go back to Ottoman times, including the Jumblatts (Druse), Franjiehs (Maronite) and Karamis (Sunni). Others rose to prominence during the Mandate, including the Chamouns and Gemayels (both Maronites). Pierre Gemayel visited Berlin in 1936 and, impressed by the Nazis' efficiency, founded a quasi-Fascist party, the Phalange, which in due course recruited its own militia.

Lebanon throve as the West's gateway to the Arab world. It was the Middle East's banking and commercial centre and was also the base for Western news organizations – and intelligence operations. Generations of journalists, diplomats, scholars and spies learned Arabic at the American University in Beirut or at the British Foreign Office school overlooking the city. The Lebanese, and most particularly the Maronites, maintained close links with France, as well as with Britain and the United States. Arabs from Saudi Arabia and the Gulf came to Beirut to escape the shackles of Arabian austerity.

The prosperity of the 1950s and 1960s never touched the underclass of Shiites and Palestinians, who were excluded from the political process. Lebanon was also corrupt, which offended those who did not benefit from that corruption. It had little industry to occupy the lower classes; the ports and roads were antiquated and neglected; and, above all, there was a growing schism between the élite and the working class. While the élite looked West, the Muslim majority increasingly looked to radical Arab regimes: Egypt in the 1950s and 1960s, the P L O or Iraq in the 1970s. In the 1980s, some of them looked to the Ayatollah's Iran.

## THE FIRST CIVIL WAR AND AFTERWARDS

In 1958, these pressures exploded in a brief civil war. In February, Egypt and Syria proclaimed their union, and President Nasser preached pan-Arab radicalism and encouraged revolution throughout the Arab world. In July, the Hashemite monarchy was overthrown in Iraq, King Hussein was threatened in Jordan and serious troubles broke out in Lebanon when President Camille Chamoun decided that he would run for a second term. He appealed for help: President Eisenhower sent the Marines into Beirut, and the British, briefly, sent troops to sustain Hussein.

Twenty years later, people looked back nostalgically to that episode. The shooting always stopped for lunch, and local ceasefires were arranged by telephone to enable people to go shopping. Legend has it that, as the Marines came up the beach, watched by admiring bathing beauties, they were greeted with enthusiasm by ice-cream vendors. The dispute was settled, or at least papered over, by removing Chamoun and asking the Marines to go home.

Afterwards Lebanon increasingly developed into a battleground between foreigners, most notably the Palestinians and the Israelis. Israel first invaded **343**

Lebanon during its war of independence in 1948, and for a year it occupied the country as far as the Litani river. In the aftermath of that war, about 100,000 Palestinian refugees came to Lebanon. Most of them, and their descendants, still live in camps immediately south of Beirut, and around Tyre and Sidon in south Lebanon, Tripoli in the north, and at Baalbek in the Bekaa valley.

Lebanon stayed clear of the 1956, 1967 and 1973 wars between Israel and its Arab neighbours, and profited from the instability of the rest of the Middle East. The joke in Israel was that no one knew which Arab country would make peace first, but everyone knew which would come second: Lebanon. Things did not work out like that. Neither the Arab militants nor Israel would respect Lebanon's neutrality. On 26 December 1968, Arab terrorists attacked an El Al plane at Athens airport, killing two people. Israel retaliated two days later by raiding Beirut airport and blowing up 13 aircraft belonging to Middle East Airlines, which were parked there. More Palestinians came to Lebanon after the Six Day War in 1967, and two years later, Nasser obliged the Lebanese government to give the PLO free rein in southern Lebanon. The PLO then mounted its first raids across the border into Israel – and Israel mounted its first retaliatory attacks. When King Hussein drove the PLO out of Jordan in 'Black September' 1970, its commandos and headquarters moved to Beirut, and armed Palestinian units took over the camps.

By then, the Shiites of southern Lebanon and the Beirut slums had become radicalized under the leadership of the Imam Musa Sadr. They rejected Maronite and Sunni leadership and allied themselves with the Palestinians against the government. They were also militantly anti-Israeli, partly because of the increasingly frequent and bloody Israeli raids upon southern Lebanon. Musa Sadr founded his own army – the Amal Militia – and played a large part in the civil war of 1975. He disappeared in Libya in 1978, presumably murdered by Khadafy.

The Maronites were divided into three clans. Chamoun's power base was in the urban centres of Beirut and Damour, on the coast south of Beirut. The Gemayels controlled Jounieh, on the coast north of Beirut and in the mountains behind, and Suleiman Franjieh, who was president from 1970 to 1976, controlled the Maronite heartland in the northern recesses of Mount Lebanon. A shoot-out in a church between members of the Franjieh clan and supporters of President Chamoun in 1957 left over 20 people dead. By 1975, the Gemayels were the most powerful clan because they controlled the largest militia (known as the Kataib) through their party, the Phalange.

## THE SECOND CIVIL WAR

The civil war was started on 13 April 1975 by the massacre by the Kataib of about 25 Palestinians who had been travelling in a bus through a Christian village, Zgharta, near Tripoli in northern Lebanon. The Phalange had been consecrating a new church at the time, and thought the sudden appearance of a bus-load of Palestinians an intolerable provocation – so they shot them.

The PLO retaliated against unoffending Christians, and the vendetta began, with over 100 people killed in the north during the first ten days of September. The fighting slowly expanded and grew steadily more violent, progressively sucking in all the many opposing factions of Lebanese society. By the end of the year, the civil war had become a conflict between Maronites and Muslims, and the Maronites were winning.

The government collapsed on 7 May. President Suleiman Franjieh appointed a military government, which disintegrated a few days later, and, on 28 May, appointed Rashid Karami as prime minister. The first American hostage, Colonel Ernest Morgan, was kidnapped on 29 June, but he was released unharmed on 12 July. By the autumn, there was a full-scale civil war under way in Beirut, and for the first time, Syria tried to mediate. In December, the frontline between Muslims and Maronites was in the heart of Beirut, with the big hotels along the seafront the main strategic objectives of the two sides. Meanwhile, the Christians had laid siege to Palestinian camps, notably Tal al-Zaatar in East Beirut, and Muslim and Druse armies, joined by the PLO, were besieging two Christian towns: Zahle, in the Bekaa valley; and Damour, south of Beirut, which was Camille Chamoun's fiefdom.

The PLO intervention turned the tide against the Maronites. Damour was overrun on 21 January 1976, and its inhabitants massacred or driven out. Christian villages in the north around Tripoli, and in the southern mountains and in the Bekaa, were attacked and destroyed.

In February, Muslims started deserting the Lebanese Army, and in March, the army split into Christian and Muslim units. The Muslims called themselves the Lebanese Arab Army and joined the PLO, the Druse and various Muslim militias in the drive towards the Christian heartland. On 21 March, Muslims captured the Holiday Inn, the key to downtown Beirut. After that, the Christians were confined to the eastern part of the city.

In desperation, the Maronite leaders called on the Syrians for help. Syria, fearing anarchy, leftist revolution and Israeli intervention on its borders, acceded, and President Assad turned on his former allies, the PLO, Druse and left-wing Sunni militia. The Syrian army crossed the border in strength in April and, on 1 June, mounted a full-scale intervention. They provided cover for a Christian counter-attack on Palestinian positions, notably Tal al-Zaatar on the Christian side of Beirut. Michael Aoun first made his name by directing that operation. The camp fell on 13 August.

In May 1976, under extreme Syrian pressure, Lebanese politicians agreed to elect a new president, Elias Sarkis, and he took office on 23 September. The brutal repression of the PLO continued. On 27 September, four Palestinian terrorists seized a hotel in Damascus in protest, and took 90 hostages. Four hostages and one terrorist were killed when the Syrian army stormed the place: the three surviving terrorists were hanged publicly the next day. On 11 October, another group of Palestinians attacked the Syrian embassy in Rome. They called themselves 'Black June', after the date of the Syrian intervention in Lebanon.

The Syrian army moved towards the southern border, but stopped at the 'Red Line' drawn by Israel, 5 miles (8 km) from the frontier. A ceasefire was promulgated in November. The Lebanese government calculated that 35,000 people had been killed in the fighting since April 1975.

On 2 February 1977, the Druse leader, Kemal Jumblatt, one of the principal opponents of the Maronites, was assassinated, possibly by the Syrians. His son, Walid, immediately took his place. The Christians and Syrians soon fell out, **345** chiefly on the issue of the Christians' relations with Israel: the Israelis were now arming and training Christian militias and independent army units in southern Lebanon, and these forces were attacking P L O positions there. The Syrians started shelling Christian East Beirut. Assad patched up his quarrel with Arafat, and, faced with this new alliance against them, the Christians turned for help to the Israelis. The first major Israeli raid into Lebanon took place in September 1977.

## THE FIRST ISRAELI INVASION

In March 1978, Israel invaded Lebanon again, officially in retaliation for a P L O raid on Israel which had killed 32 people. A large group of Palestinian troops had landed on the coast north of Tel Aviv, and had commandeered a bus filled with civilians, most of whom were killed at an army roadblock. In fact, Israel was already preparing to invade, and used the bus incident as a pretext. The army occupied the country as far as the Litani river, with the object of crushing the P L O: over 2000 people were killed and 250,000 driven from their homes. After some months, President Carter insisted that Israel pull back to its own borders, and a U N force (U N I F I L) was sent to police the border. However, Israel had established its own private Christian Lebanese army, led by Major Saad Haddad, along the frontier, which pushed U N I F I L further north. In Israeli terms, the invasion had not been a success – partly because it was widely anticipated, and the P L O had been able to escape to the north, and partly because the Israelis did not hit the main P L O bases in Beirut. The minister of defence, Ariel Sharon, determined to avoid those errors next time.

At this point, the Maronites started fighting among themselves. Pierre Gemayel's son, Bashir, attempted to overrun the Franjieh fief in the north, starting by ordering the assassination of the former president's son Tony on 13 June 1978; his wife and daughter and 30 other people were also killed. Ever since, the Franjieh and Gemayel clans have remained bitter enemies (Franjieh may have played a role in the murder of Bashir Gemayel in 1982). The Franjiehs have allied themselves with Syria while the Gemayels called in the Israelis. The Gemayels also suppressed the Chamoun militia in 1979, and incorporated it into the Kataib, now renamed the Lebanese Forces.

Israel began a policy of 'pre-emptive strikes' against supposed Palestinian targets in Lebanon, bombing that country much as the United States had once bombed Cambodia. The P L O had mobile rocket launchers, mounted on trucks, with a range of up to 15 miles (24 km), and in July 1981, they launched a rocket attack on northern Israel. In retaliation, the Israelis bombed Beirut, killing 120 people. Three days later, the P L O launched a massive rocket attack that hit a score of targets throughout northern Israel. After that, a ceasefire was arranged by the U S mediator, Philip Habib, and rocket attacks ceased.

In the spring of 1981, the Syrians moved a large number of Soviet anti-aircraft missile batteries into eastern Lebanon to protect their armies against Israeli air attacks. The Israelis rather perversely denounced the move as provocative, insisting on their right to patrol the skies of Lebanon uncontested, bombing what they willed. But for a strenuous American diplomatic effort, there might have been another war on the issue between Israel and Syria.

Sharon was convinced that the only way to ensure Israel's security was to eliminate the P L O from Lebanon and install a friendly government there. Israel had long since entered into an alliance with the Lebanese Forces of Bashir Gemayel, providing most of their weapons. Now Sharon started planning a summer campaign. He informed the U S secretary of state, Alexander Haig, who offered no objection.

## 'OPERATION PEACE FOR GALILEE'

The next Israeli invasion – dubbed 'Operation Peace for Galilee' – began on 6 June 1982, Israel offering as a pretext the attempted assassination of its ambassador in London (*see* Arab terrorism, pp. 594–619). The Israeli government announced that it wished to establish a demilitarized zone to extend 15 miles (24 km) north of the frontier to protect northern Israel from rocket attacks (of which, in fact, there had been none since the ceasefire).

Sharon had other ideas, and pushed his armies up to Beirut, placing the city under siege. At least 10,000 people, most of them civilians, were killed in this first phase of the war. In violent fighting with the Syrian army, the Israelis seized the southern Bekaa valley and inflicted a humiliating defeat on the Syrian air force: between 8 and 10 June, Israel shot down 61 Syrian MiGs at a loss of one Israeli plane; they also destroyed 17 of Syria's 19 S A M sites. On 11 June, Israel announced a ceasefire with Syria, which it immediately accepted: meanwhile, Israeli troops completed their advance to Beirut. On 22 June, the Israelis seized the Beirut–Damascus highway, cutting off 10,000 Syrian troops in Beirut (including a unit of special forces commanded by Rifaat Assad, President Assad's brother).

The P L O was routed in fighting in the countryside, but put up a stout defence in Beirut. The Israelis had no experience of urban warfare, and their initial attacks were repulsed. (They hoped that the Christian militias would do the work for them, but Bashir Gemayel declined the honour.) The Israeli air force inflicted immense damage on West Beirut: the attacks, televised around the world from the safety of Christian East Beirut, provoked comparisons with the Luftwaffe's attacks on Rotterdam and London, or the U S A F attacks on Hanoi. Eventually, on 19 August, the United States brokered an agreement with Israel, the Arab nations and the P L O, which evacuated Beirut – about 6000 fighters by road to Damascus, and another 8000, including the high command, by sea – under the protection of American, French and other Western troops.

The Americans had suggested that they would remain in Beirut, and Israel had promised not to move into West Beirut. In the event, the American and other Western troops left immediately, and Israel marched into West Beirut and set up positions around the refugee camps.

On 23 August, Bashir Gemayel was elected president of Lebanon by the Chamber of Deputies. He promised to unite the country and make peace with Syria and his Maronite and Shiite enemies – and conspicuously refused to sign a peace treaty with Israel. Three weeks later, on 14 September, he was assassinated by a bomb at Phalange party headquarters, together with 26 party supporters. The assassin was a member of a left-wing Syrian Christian party, allied at various times to the P L O and the Druse. The murder was possibly committed at Syrian instigation and perhaps with the complicity of Suleiman Franjieh.

On the following day, Israel completed its occupation of West Beirut. Then, at Israel's request, the Lebanese Forces entered the Palestinian refugee camps of Sabra and Shatila to hunt for P L O terrorists. They massacred between 700 and 2000 people. In the international outcry that followed, Israel was blamed, although no Israelis had been directly involved.

## THE AMERICAN INTERVENTION

The U S government and its allies promptly sent troops to protect the refugee camps: a 5800-strong Multi-National Force (M N F), consisting of U S Marines, and French, British and Italian contingents. To begin with, the M N F, like previous armies of occupation, was welcomed because it brought stability to West and South Beirut. The Shiites and Palestinians soon turned against it, however, as it became apparent that the M N F was intended to assist the largely Christian Lebanese Army.

The Israelis remained in Beirut, still hoping that a permanent peace treaty could be concluded – but in vain. The P L O infiltrated back into the camps and Shiite militias soon began to attack Israeli positions. The Israeli H Q at Tyre was destroyed by a car bomb on 11 November 1982, killing 90; it was blown up a second time, by another suicide driver, on 5 November 1983, this time killing 28 Israelis. A suicide car bomb was launched against the U S embassy on 23 April 1983, destroying the building and killing 16 Americans (including the chief C I A expert on the Middle East) and 33 other people.

On 17 May 1983, Secretary of State George Shultz arranged a 'withdrawal agreement', signed by Amin Gemayel (Bashir's brother, who had taken over the presidency on 23 September 1982) and the Israelis, providing for the total withdrawal of foreign forces from Lebanon, a general settlement there and a peace treaty between Lebanon and Israel. Syria and most of the other Lebanese factions refused to sign.

Meanwhile, Israel had turned West Beirut over to the Lebanese Army, which began to round up Palestinian and Shiite suspects. At the same time, the Maronites, under Israeli protection, seized control of the predominantly Druse Shuf mountains overlooking Beirut to the south-east. In July 1983, the Druse and Shiites struck back and drove the Army out of West Beirut. A ceasefire was declared, and the Army returned.

Then the Israeli government, shaken by domestic and international opposition, and guerrilla attacks on its positions, pulled back from Beirut. On 17 August it took up positions on the Awali river just north of Sidon, 20 miles (32 km) south of Beirut, and, at the end of the month, abruptly abandoned the Shuf, leaving the Lebanese Forces to their fate. Immediately, a mixed force of Druse and Shiite militia attacked them and won a decisive victory. The Lebanese Forces were driven out of the Shuf – and 75,000 Christian civilians fled their homes. The United States tried to help by shelling Druse villages with the big guns of the battleship *New Jersey* anchored off the coast, convincing proof the U S was no longer neutral in the domestic disputes of the Lebanese.

The American Marines and other Western troops remained in their positions in Beirut, although there was no longer any clear reason for their presence. On 23 October a suicide driver broke through to the U S Marine barracks near the airport, and the bomb he carried killed 241 Marines. Simultaneously, another truck was driven into the French barracks, killing 58.

The Druse stepped up their shelling of American and French positions around the airport. In retaliation on 17 November, French Mystères attacked what were believed to be terrorist bases in the Bekaa valley. Not to be outdone, and on the pretext that the Syrians had fired on unarmed American reconnaissance planes, 28 American aircraft from carriers out in the Mediterranean attacked Syrian anti-aircraft missile sites in Lebanon on 4 December. Two planes were lost: an A-7 Corsair, whose pilot baled out safely over Christian territory; and an A-6E, whose pilot, Lieutenant Robert Goodman, was captured by the Syrians. The other member of the crew was killed. On the same day, eight Marines were killed by a shell falling on their bunker. The American politician, the Reverend Jesse Jackson, went to Damascus early in the New Year, and persuaded President Assad to release Lieutenant Goodman on 3 January 1984.

The dominant local military force was now the Amal Militia, headed by Nabih Berri. His troops occupied West Beirut in February 1984 and, as the Israelis retreated south, Amal followed and took their place. The Lebanese Army was left with only the Maronite heartland, East Beirut and a tiny enclave around the presidential palace.

The Multi-National Force was now isolated and in constant danger, and served no purpose whatever. After insisting, repeatedly, that the Marines would remain, President Reagan suddenly announced, on 2 February, that they would be 'redeployed to the fleet'. The other Western garrisons promptly followed the American example. The French left a small observer force, which was subject to repeated attack until it, too, was finally evacuated in April 1986.

On 20 September 1984, the American embassy in Beirut was blown up by a car bomb for the second time. After the original building, near the seafront in West Beirut, had been demolished in April of the previous year, the embassy had been moved to a rented office building in the supposed security of East Beirut; this security was provided by Christian militiamen under American supervision. The second attack was carried out like the first, and like the attack on the Marine barracks: a car packed with several hundred pounds of explosives was driven at great speed through the checkpoints and up to the building. Its driver was heading for the underground carpark, and if he had made it, the whole building would have been demolished and everyone in it killed. By happy coincidence, the British ambassador to Lebanon, Donald Miers, was visiting his American colleague, Reginald Bartholomew. Miers' British body-guards were standing outside the embassy, saw what was happening and managed to shoot the driver before he could reach the carpark entrance. The car hit a wall and exploded. About 20 people were killed. The two ambassadors were slightly injured.

## THE NEW STALEMATE
The chief beneficiary of Israel's progressive withdrawal was Syria, which advanced its troops into central Lebanon. The destruction of the military power

of the P L O had long been a Syrian objective, and had now been partly achieved by the Israelis. Syria set about completing the process.

Dissidents within the P L O accused Yasser Arafat of incompetence and weakness, because he had lost Beirut and had then opened negotiations with King Hussein of Jordan, and President Mubarak of Egypt, both of whom supported an American peace plan that would have involved recognizing Israel. The dissidents attacked Arafat's supporters in P L O camps in Baalbek in the Bekaa valley, but the loyalists regrouped in two camps near Tripoli in north Lebanon. In October 1983, the Syrians and their Palestinian clients, together with Franjieh's Christians, besieged the Palestinian camps, and the city of Tripoli itself, which was controlled by a fundamentalist Sunni sect, the al Tawhid.

After heavy fighting and many civilian casualties, Syria occupied the camps, but refrained from storming Tripoli, for political-religious reasons. Arafat, who had gone to the city, was allowed to evacuate it with his troops, once again claiming victory in defeat. He moved his H Q to Tunis.

## PEACE EFFORTS

In the autumn of 1983, Syria sponsored a meeting of Lebanese notables in Geneva, in the hope of settling the many disputes of Lebanon. President Gemayel made many concessions, including a new division of parliament giving Muslims equal representation with Christians. He was repudiated by the Lebanese Forces once commanded by his brother, which seized East Beirut from the Army. A further meeting in Lausanne in March 1984 broke up on the question of the presidency: Suleiman Franjieh refused to abandon the Maronite claim to that office.

There was fighting between the Sunni militia in West Beirut – the Murabitun, which was allied to the P L O – and the Druse. Meanwhile, the Shiite community was badly split; fundamentalists under Syrian protection challenged Berri's Amal Militia, and there was a great increase in the fundamentalists' influence in south Lebanon. The same groups that sent their young martyrs on suicide attacks against Western and Israeli positions were now challenging the main-line Muslim leaders.

In February 1985, Israel withdrew from the Sunni city of Sidon, and there was an immediate settling of accounts with suspected collaborators. On 12 March, the Lebanese Forces, under Samir Geagea, repudiated President Gemayel's leadership and attacked Sidon. In April, a coalition of Syrian-supported Druse, Sunni, Palestinian and Shiite forces – all the Muslims in Lebanon – attacked the Lebanese Forces and defeated them. The Christian population in the hills behind Sidon, 75,000 people, were driven north.

Then in May, Amal tried to capture the Palestinian camps in Beirut and was beaten off, with heavy civilian casualties on both sides. Amal kept the camps under siege and shelled them regularly until early 1988.

On 8 March 1985, a car bomb exploded outside a building in West Beirut controlled by the Hizbollah, an extremist, pro-Iranian Shiite sect. The bombing was directed at the Hizbollah leader, Sheikh Mohammed Hussein Fadlallah, who was believed to be the director of the Islamic Jihad terrorist group responsible for most of the kidnappings of Westerners (*see below*). In the explosion, 80 people were killed and 256 wounded. Fadlallah escaped: he had been delayed by the importunings of a woman suppliant. It was later reported in Washington that the director of the C I A, William Casey, had asked Saudi Arabia to finance a Maronite terrorist group in an attempt to assassinate Fadlallah. By this time, car bombs had become the weapon of choice of all parties among Lebanon's factions, and were causing more casualties than the shelling.

Attacks on Israel's remaining troops increased rapidly, soon reaching four a day, and there was a steady flow of casualties. Eventually the occupation proved too costly, and the Israelis completed their withdrawal in June 1985, taking many thousands of Palestinian and Lebanese prisoners with them. They left a 1500-strong 'South Lebanon Army' (S L A), commanded first by Saad Haddad and, when he died in 1984, by General Antoine Lahad. It controlled a strip along the border and a narrow finger of territory running north to Jezzine, in the mountains above Sidon. The Israelis periodically undertook operations beyond the S L A zone, including a sweep through 25 villages in February 1986, after two Israeli soldiers were captured; 15 people were killed in that operation.

In the summer of 1985, after the disaster in the south, Geagea was removed as commander of the Lebanese Forces. His replacement, Elie Hobeiqa – who had commanded the troops that perpetrated the Shatila and Sabra massacres in 1982 – went to Damascus on 9 September and made his peace with the Syrians, and on 28 December, he, Berri and Jumblatt signed an agreement on a new constitution. This brief moment of hope lasted two weeks. On 15 January 1986, Geagea, now allied with Gemayel, mounted a coup in the Lebanese Forces and ousted Hobeiqa. The Sunni were also dissatisfied with the Damascus agreement, which therefore collapsed.

There was renewed fighting between Christian and Muslim militias in Beirut, provoked by an attempt by Hobeiqa, supported by Syria, to seize the Voice of Lebanon radio station. Fighting also broke out between Geagea's Lebanese Forces and the Lebanese Army, which had been painfully reconstituted by the Americans; it disintegrated once again.

Amal had been besieging the Palestinians in their South Beirut camps since the spring of 1985. By December 1986, 60 per cent of the Shatila camp had been destroyed in the shelling, but the Palestinians continued to resist. The P L O commandos, banished to Tunis in 1982, were now returning to Lebanon, supported by the Hizbollah faction of Lebanese Shiites, and the Druse; Palestinian artillery in the Druse-controlled mountains shelled Amal positions in West Beirut. In December, Amal, supported by Shiite units of the Lebanese Army, mounted a full-scale assault on the camps, with tanks and 'Stalin Organs' (multiple rocket launchers). They failed to capture them.

On 5 July 1986, the Syrians returned to Beirut for the first time since 1982, and restored order in West Beirut. Syrian troops began to demolish the barricades that made up the 'Green Line' dividing Christian and Muslim Beirut.

In February 1987, they once again tried to stop the fighting, and this time, they attacked the Hizbollah militias in South Beirut. In four days, they cleared the streets of armed gangs, and assaulted a Hizbollah strongpoint, slaughtering 23    **351** militiamen. They did not, however, clear out the camps or rescue any of the Westerners held hostage. In April, they advanced to the two Palestinian camps, Shatila and Burj el Brajneh, which the Amal Militia were still besieging, but they did not interfere.

On 20 January 1988, the Amal Militia abandoned its siege of the two camps, as an act, said Nabih Berri, Amal's leader, of solidarity with the Palestinian rioters in Gaza and the West Bank. The siege had cost at least 2500 lives. Amal was now free to resume its battle with the Hizbollah. The fighting started in Nabatiye in south Lebanon in April. To begin with, Amal had the upper hand and occupied a number of Shiite villages that had been controlled by Hizbollah; they also attacked Iranian Revolutionary Guards who were operating in the district. Israel contributed in early May by invading south Lebanon and clearing out a series of Hizbollah strongholds, the most important of which was the village of Maydun: 40 Hizbollah militiamen and three Israeli soldiers were killed in the operation. The fighting then spread to Beirut.

The two sides used heavy artillery and mortars in the slums, and hundreds of people were killed. In four days of fighting, Hizbollah defeated Amal, and took control of the coastal highway past the airport. On 14 May, the Syrians intervened to protect Amal from further defeat, and cautiously moved troops into the slums. The caution was necessary: on 26 May a car carrying four Syrian generals, the most senior officers in Lebanon, was attacked in a Hizbollah district by a dozen gunmen; the generals escaped. On 28 May, after protracted negotiations, Hizbollah pulled back from the positions it had captured, and allowed the Syrians to occupy them with 7000 troops and 50 tanks. The Lebanese police calculated that 660 people had been killed that May in fighting between the Shiite factions, between P L O factions in the camps, and in car bombings, which continued to be the favourite terrorist weapon in Lebanon.

## TERRORISM

Naked terrorism has been a constant in all the fighting since 1975. The Shatila and Sabra massacres were nothing new. Muslims had massacred hundreds of Christians in the prosperous Christian town of Damour, south of Beirut. Their objective had been to clear the area of Christians, and they succeeded. In the same month, Christian militiamen massacred Palestinians in a refugee camp in Karantina in North Beirut, in a Christian area they wanted cleared. The Druse, the P L O, the Sunni militias, the Syrians, the Israelis – they have all sought to achieve their ends by slaughtering their enemies.

Assassination is a favoured political statement in the Middle East, particularly in Lebanon. The Druse leader, Kemal Jumblatt, was assassinated in February 1977. In June 1978, Bashir Gemayel had Tony Franjieh assassinated, and was himself assassinated in September 1982. Prime Minister Rashid Karami was killed by a bomb planted in his helicopter on 1 June 1987, and in February 1988, a bomb was found in President Amin Gemayel's plane. Foreign murderers play their part: President Assad was suspected of complicity in several assassinations, and Colonel Khadafy of Libya probably ordered the murder of the Shiite leader Musa Sadr, who disappeared in Libya in August 1978.

In such a context, killing and kidnapping Westerners was no exceptional tactic. The Islamic Jihad clearly aimed at ending all Western influence in Lebanon. Sometimes – as in the hijacking of a TWA flight in 1985, in which the plane was brought to Beirut and its passengers carried off to Shiite strongholds there – the terrorists made political demands. On that occasion, they wanted PLO prisoners in Israel to be released. When the United States bombed Libya in April 1986, Lebanese terrorists retaliated by murdering two British and one American hostage, because some of the US planes were based in England.

The principle of political dealings with terrorists was often denounced by Israeli, American and European politicians, but each country was ready to deal on occasion. In 1985–6, the US government secretly negotiated with the Iranians to win the release of American hostages in Lebanon. Two were released, apparently as a result of the delivery of American arms to Tehran. The Israelis exchanged prisoners with the PLO, and the West Germans and French paid ransom for their citizens.

Western governments repeatedly warned their citizens to leave Lebanon. Some refused, and paid with their liberty: a new wave of kidnappings early in 1988 merely confirmed the danger. Among those kidnapped was a US Marine, Lieutenant Colonel William Higgins, serving with UNIFIL, who was abducted on 17 February. A few days earlier, a Frenchman, Jacques Merin, reportedly the No. 2 man on the Lebanon desk of the French secret service, was shot in East Beirut just after leaving a meeting with Lebanese security officials. He had presumably been engaged in negotiations for the release of French hostages in Lebanon – they were eventually released in May.

The tensions between Maronites and Muslims, and within the Maronite community itself, that were at the origin of the civil war continued. President Gemayel's term expired in September, and although the office has no power, fighting for the succession (it cannot be called an election) was intense. The Syrians first supported Suleiman Franjieh. He was unacceptable to the Gemayel clan, and when the Chamber of Deputies gathered in August to elect a new president, the Christian militias ensured that there would be no election by the simple method of preventing enough deputies attending to form a quorum.

Subsequently, Syria supported another candidate, Mikhail Daher, but he, too, proved to be unacceptable to the Maronite extremists. Thus, when Gemayel's term ended on 22 September, the office became vacant. Gemayel, as his last act, appointed General Michel Aoun as prime minister. He was the Maronite commander of the largely Maronite Lebanese Army, an organization that had played a small and inglorious part in the civil war but which had also been built up into some semblance of efficiency with American help.

Aoun formed an alliance with Geagea, who continued to command the principal Christian militia. Their avowed intention was to expel the Syrians from Lebanon and then settle accounts with the rival militias. Their alliance broke down in February 1989, when serious fighting between their armies began.

The Muslims of all shades, and the Druse and the Maronite followers of Suleiman Franjieh, all denounced Aoun's new government as illegal, and continued to give their allegiance to the government of Selim Hoss, a Sunni who had been appointed acting prime minister on the assassination of Rashid Karami, but **353** had never been voted formally into office because the Chamber of Deputies could not meet. Aoun offered seats in his cabinet to Muslim military men. They refused. Hoss, in turn, formed a government excluding the Maronites.

The split was of great symbolic importance, pushing Lebanon to the brink of permanent partition, but it had little practical consequence. There had been no effective national government for years, and local administration was entirely in the hands of local warlords. All that the new dispensation changed were the circumstances of Lebanon's diplomats abroad, who now had not one but two powerless foreign ministers to report to. They resolved the dilemma by ignoring both. They assumed that, sooner or later, a president would be chosen, through some face-saving formula, though he would be as completely powerless as Gemayel had been. In the meantime, since Lebanon had no foreign policy, their diplomatic confusion did not matter very much.

In March 1989, Aoun attacked the Syrians in their positions in and around west Beirut. He demanded that Syria withdraw completely from Lebanon and apparently hoped that he could provoke the international community to force the withdrawal. Beirut then suffered the worst devastation of its long martyrdom. The world community, as usual, did nothing. Aoun's only support came from Israel and Iraq, a curious alliance based on their joint detestation of Syria. It proved sufficient to prevent the Christian heartland from being overrun by Muslim armies in their first offensive, but not nearly enough to defeat the Syrians. Aoun's artillery shelled west Beirut and the Syrians, Druse and Lebanese Muslims shelled east Beirut. Most of the city's inhabitants fled, those that remained taking refuge in cellars and air-raid shelters. The guns systematically destroyed the city: it resembled Berlin in 1945. In September, Aoun threatened to unleash 'Christian terrorism' against the Americans, because of their failure to come to his aid. The United States thereupon evacuated its embassy from Beirut.

It was premature: on 23 September a ceasefire was at last accepted by both sides, and Beirut entered into another temporary respite from its torments.

Syria, which had the power to overwhelm Aoun, and all the other factions in Lebanon, chose not to exercise it. Assad's repeated interventions in Lebanon probably prevented a worse carnage than actually occurred, but also prevented the fighting coming to a conclusion. In the summer of 1989, the Arab League, led by Saudi Arabia, persuaded the surviving members of the Lebanese parliament, an ageing and ineffectual company elected in 1972, to gather at Taif in Saudi Arabia in an attempt to reform the constitution and bring peace to their devastated country. After several weeks of haggling, they agreed on a measure of reform that would increase Muslim power in the state somewhat and, more important, agreed to meet to elect a new president. The agreement was reached on 22 October and ratified by the assembly two days later. The Syrians agreed to leave Beirut within two years, and then to settle a timetable for permanent withdrawal with a new Lebanese government.

The new president was elected on 5 November 1989. He was a Maronite lawyer, René Moawad. He was supported by the Syrians, the Franjieh faction of Maronites, and most of the Muslims. Gen. Aoun refused to recognize him and remained in his bunker under the ruins of the presidential palace at Baabda.

On 22 November 1989, Moawad was killed by a car bomb in Beirut. Parliament elected a successor, Elias Hrawi, another Maronite, on 24 November, but the stand-off between Aoun's Maronites and the rest of Lebanon continued. On 22 December, fighting between the two Shiite factions resumed in southern Lebanon, and before a precarious ceasefire was reached in January 1990, the pro-Iranian Hizbollah had driven the Amal militia out of several villages.

Samir Geagea, commanding the 6000 regular militiamen of the Lebanese Forces, which had played a minor role in the latest civil war between Aoun and the rest of Lebanon, now announced his acceptance of Hrawi's government and the Taif accord. Aoun promptly denounced him, and declared that the Lebanese Forces must be dissolved. On 31 January 1990, he sent his army to attack Geagea, and the Christian enclave north of Beirut was engulfed in battle. The Maronite patriarch of Lebanon, Nasrallah Butros Safir, lamented, 'May God have mercy on Lebanese Christians.'

The worst incident in this Christian civil war was on 18 April 1990, when a rocket-propelled grenade hit a school bus on the front line in Beirut, killing 11 children and four adults. By the time a ceasefire was arranged, on 17 May, over 1000 people had been killed. Aoun remained defiant for the rest of the summer, until September, when the Syrians and the Hrawi regime decided to make an end of it. By then, the mounting Gulf crisis had eliminated Iraq from the Lebanese crisis: Saddam Hussein could no longer support the anti-Syrian faction headed by Aoun. On 28 September 1990, the Lebanese army of 20,000 men, mostly Muslim but commanded by a Christian, Gen. Emile Lahad, laid siege to Aoun's last redout.

The war did not go well for the attackers. Aoun held his own, defending Baabda and the enclave north of Beirut against Lahad's assault and proclaiming his continued defiance. Finally, on 10 October, Hrawi appealed to Syria. Hafez al-Assad concluded that with the world's attention directed at Kuwait and the Americans looking for his support against Saddam, the time had come to end the Lebanese civil war. He sent in his troops on 12 October. Aoun issued a last defiant message to his supporters: 'Everything is going to blow up in flames. I believe it's the final battle, but I'm prepared to resist, whatever the final outcome is.' Syrian jets bombed Baabda on 13 October, completing the demolition begun years before, and Lahad led a general assault against the place the next day. About 750 people, almost all of them Christian Lebanese fighting each other, were killed in this last battle. When the troops at last reached Aoun's bunker, they found it empty. The general and his family, together with his closest colleagues, had fled to sanctuary in the French embassy.

Hrawi then set about re-establishing his authority. The French refused to hand Aoun over, and he was allowed to leave the country the following August. One of his chief allies, Dany Chamoun, son of a former president and head of one of the great Christian clans, was assassinated on 21 October 1990, with his two young sons. That completed the circle: the heads of every one of the great Lebanese political families, Christian, Muslim or Druse, or their sons, had been assassinated. Hrawi then ordered all the militias to withdraw from Beirut, as a first step towards disarming them. The barricades along the green line through the city were dismantled in December and, for the first time in years, life and business resumed with an appearance of normalcy.

That was just Beirut. The militants remained in their heartlands, and in the Bekaa valley the Syrians agreed that Hizbollah and the Iranian Revolutionary Guards should keep their arms. The P L O was still armed and a threat to the state. In September 1990, it fought a short campaign against Abu Nidal's terrorists. In April, the militias turned over a huge collection of weapons, including 400 artillery pieces, 108 tanks, and 21 helicopters.

The Western hostages were released by degrees. In April 1990, two American hostages were released, followed in August by a British and two Swiss hostages. In January 1991, four Belgians who had been held for several years by Abu Nidal were released after an Abu Nidal terrorist was released from a Belgian jail. In August and September 1991, an American, a British and a French hostage were released, and in November another American and the last British hostage, Terry Waite. These releases were part of an elaborate exchange with Israel, which let out its Lebanese and Palestinian prisoners of war in batches. The Israelis were concerned about some of their own soldier prisoners who had disappeared in Lebanon, and insisted that they should be released or, if they were dead, that their bodies be returned. The last American hostage, Terry Anderson, a journalist who had been kidnapped in March 1985, was released on 4 December 1991. He had been the longest-held of all. It became evident that the decision to free the hostages had been taken in Tehran, and there were reports that the Iranian government had paid the Hizbollah to let them go. Holding hostages was no longer profitable, either politically or economically, and the Iranian and Shiite leadership in Lebanon had decided to close the books. There remained only one Israeli prisoner believed still to be alive, and two Germans. Israel offered to exchange the Israeli against Sheikh Obeid. The Hizbollah offered to release the Germans if Shiite terrorists held in Germany were let go.

Lebanon's problems were not over. The main Christian and Muslim factions had patched together a shaky peace, but the disaffected Shiites of Hizbollah and Palestinian extremists still threatened the peace, and some of them continued to attack Israel, provoking Israeli retaliation. The Israelis still occupied a strip of Lebanon along the border, and Syria still held nearly half the country, with 40,000 troops.

Negotiations for the exchange of Israel's Lebanese prisoners, notably Sheikh Obeid, for the remaining hostages in Lebanon, ran into sands. There were the two Germans, whose captors demanded in exchange the release of two Lebanese terrorists held in German jails, and perhaps one living Israeli soldier and the bodies of three others. On 16 February 1992, Israel attacked a motorcade carrying the head of Hizbollah, Sheikh Abbas Mussawi, with helicopter gunships and bombs. He had just addressed a Shiite rally in southern Lebanon, near the Israeli 'security zone'. Mussawi was killed. He had directed the attack on the American and French barracks in Lebanon in 1983 and continued to demand the destruction of Israel and to denounce the peace talks. It was a serious blow against Lebanese terrorism, but there were many men ready to replace him.

The ceasefire, finally established in 1991, has held since then. Beirut is now largely rebuilt, but the aftermath of the civil war continues to perturb the country. At the height of the fighting, about a million people, a quarter of the indigenous population, were refugees. In 1995, it was estimated that there were still 450,000 internal refugees (not counting the 352,000 Palestinians and tens or hundreds of thousands who take to the roads when Israel launches one of its air offensives in the south). The minister of resettlement is Walid Jumblatt, the Druse leader, and one serious and continuing dispute concerns the Christians driven out of the Shuf Mountains east of Beirut. It was Jumblatt's Druse who expelled them and took their lands and houses, and he now shows no haste to displace the new occupants of the Christians' villages.

The Maronite chieftains have lost much of their power. Samir Geagea has been jailed for some of his many crimes, and other warlords remain in exile. Syria still disposes of ultimate power in Lebanon, and allows the Hizbollah to continue the fight against Israel. Israel therefore continues to intervene, spreading ruin and desolation in southern Lebanon. This miserable situation is likely to continue until Syria and Israel make peace.

## FURTHER READING

Becker, Jillian, *The PLO: the Rise and Fall of the Palestine Liberation Organization*, New York, St Martin's Press, 1984.
Bulloch, John, *Final Conflict, the War in Lebanon*,
Cobban, Helena, *The Making of Modern Lebanon*, Boulder, Colo., Westview Press, 1985.
—, *The P.L.O.*, Cambridge, Cambridge University Press, 1984.
Eveland, Wilbur Crane, *Ropes of Sand: America's Failure in the Middle East*, New York, W.W. Norton, 1980.
Fisk, Robert, *Pity the Nation: the Abduction of Lebanon*, New York, Atheneum, 1990.
Gabriel, Richard A., *Operation Peace for Galilee*, New York, Hill and Wang, 1984.
Gilmour, David, *Lebanon, the Fractured Country*, New York, St Martin's Press, 1984.
McDowell, David, *Lebanon, a Conflict of Minorities*, London, Minority Rights Group, 1986.
Rabinovitch, Itamar, *The War for Lebanon, 1970–1983*, New York, Cornell University Press, 1984.
Randall, Jonathan, *Going All the Way: Christian Warlords, Israeli Adventurers and the War in Lebanon*, New York, Viking, 1983.
Schiff, Ze'ev and Y'ari, Ehud, *Israel's Lebanon War*, New York, Simon and Schuster, 1984.

# SAUDI ARABIA

| | |
|---|---|
| Geography | 837,972 sq. miles (2,263,579 sq. km). The size of Western Europe. All desert except the mountains behind Mecca and in the south-west. |
| Population | 19 million. |
| Resources | Oil: the largest reserves in the world. Officially 169 billion barrels, but they are certainly far larger than that. In 1982, oil revenue was $99 billion; in 1988 it was estimated at $22 billion. |
| GNP per capita | $7040. |

Saudi Arabia is the personal creation of Abdul Azis ibn Abdul Rahman (1886–1953). In a series of campaigns between 1901 and 1924, he led his followers to the conquest of the peninsula, on camels and on foot, and following the green flag of Islam. It is an empire, like that of Alexander, Genghiz Khan or Tamburlaine, conquered by a leader of genius. It is the last of its kind.

Abdul Aziz was also known as Ibn Saud, an honorific title meaning 'head of the Saud family'. The al Saud are a family, not a tribe, and Saudi Arabia is the only country in the world to be named after a family.

There is greater strength in a vast and cohesive family than in other, monogamous dynasties, such as the Pahlevis in Iran. There are about 4000 members of the House of Saud: King Abdul Aziz had 42 sons and 20 daughters, and his brothers, cousins and his own sons have been nearly as prolific. When the king of Saudi Arabia proves incompetent, he can be removed. Four of the sons of Abdul Aziz have succeeded each other on his throne, and plenty of able-bodied sons remain: the youngest was born in 1947. The next generation may prove less orderly: one of them assassinated King Feisal in 1975. However, danger is more likely to come from outside: from those who are excluded from the government because they are not members of the House of Saud; from revivalist sects who believe that the kingdom is insufficiently puritanical; from the armed forces, built up under American supervision to defend the kingdom from the Iranians and Iraqis; from greedy Arabs; or from some combination of these possible threats.

Fundamentalist fanatics seized the Great Mosque in Mecca in 1979 and were finally defeated when the government brought in the army. The protracted war between Iran and Iraq was a continuing threat to Saudi Arabia and the Gulf emirates, and its settlement put enormous power into the hands of Saddam Hussein, president of Iraq, who used it to occupy Kuwait in 1990. His defeat has eliminated one danger, for the moment, but who can say what the future might bring? Another problem for the Saudis comes from constant American pressure on them to take an active part in resolving the dispute between Israel and its neighbours. The kingdom's enormous wealth is a danger as well as a protection: there are many populous and powerful states near by that might be tempted to impose a redistribution of the riches of Araby.

## HISTORY

The al Saud family had, at various times in earlier centuries, ruled a large but poverty-stricken kingdom in the desert. Arabia had occasionally been united, but never for long. No tribe had ever been powerful enough to establish permanent rule over the others, and no outsider had coveted the barren wastes. The Turks controlled Mecca and Medina, but left the desert alone.

In 1891, when Abdul Aziz was 17, the al Saud were driven out of their ancestral lands and their capital, Riyadh. The family subsisted on the charity of neighbouring tribes until, in January 1902, Abdul Aziz led the attack that recaptured Riyadh, and from that base, in a series of desert wars, he conquered most of the Arabian peninsula. Kuwait and the other Gulf emirates only escaped his control because they were protected by the British. After World War I, he prepared to attack Transjordan, Syria and Iraq, to follow in the footsteps of the first caliphs, but was again stopped by the British. Had it not been for them the whole peninsula and the 'fertile crescent' might have been united in one enormously rich and powerful kingdom, ruled by a caliph of the House of Saud. How long it would have lasted is a different question.

Abdul Aziz completed his conquests in 1924, when he seized the holy cities of Mecca and Medina from the Shereef Hussein, whose family then moved to Iraq and Jordan. In 1934, in one last attempt at expansion, Abdul Aziz sent an army to conquer the Yemen, but it was defeated.

Saudi Arabia was allied with Britain and the United States during World War II, and on 12 February 1945, King Abdul Aziz visited President Franklin Roosevelt aboard the USS *Quincy* in the Great Bitter Lake, part of the Suez canal. He brought a large suite with him, and enough sheep to feed them, and they all camped on deck, to the wonderment of the American navy. These two remarkable statesmen, despite many misunderstandings and disagreements, then sealed an alliance that has persisted ever since.

Well No. 7, the first great Arabian gusher, came in on 20 March 1938. It had been drilled by the Standard Oil Company of California (Socal). World War II interrupted further exploration, and it was not until the 1950s that Saudi Arabia became a major oil producer, but two decades later it became the world's second greatest, after the USSR, and by far the largest exporter. It has the biggest oil reserves in the world, officially 169 billion barrels (but certainly far larger), compared with 66 billion in Kuwait, 67 billion in the USSR and 26 billion in the United States.

**359**

## MODERN ARABIA

Saudi Arabia's reputation for inscrutable stability was shattered on 20 November 1979 when a group of about 200 fanatical tribesmen from the desert seized the Great Mosque in Mecca. They were followers of an eloquent preacher, Juhayman ibn Muhammed ibn Saif, who believed that his brother-in-law was the Mahdi, a spiritual leader who appears once a century. (The previous Mahdi had been responsible for the death of General Gordon in Khartoum.)

The rebels denounced the alleged decadence of the House of Saud and called on all Arabs to overthrow it. They held off the Saudi army until 4 December. The mosque was slightly damaged in the fighting (the Saudis showed more concern and skill than the Indians did when they attacked the Golden Temple in Amritsar five years later). The rebels were driven out of the buildings that surround the vast courtyard in which stands the Kaaba, the stone structure that is the holiest site in Islam. They took refuge in the cellars, along with their families and hostages, and had to be ferreted out one by one, fighting to the last.

The Mahdi and 116 other rebels were killed, as were 127 soldiers and a dozen civilians. Juhayman was captured and he was executed, along with 62 other survivors, on 9 January 1980.

When the mosque was seized, the government panicked. All communications were cut: it feared that this was part of a *coup d'état*, or a foreign invasion. The confusion spread rumours around the Islamic world: Iran and Libya blamed the United States, and a mob in Islamabad, Pakistan, burned the American embassy, killing a Marine guard and another soldier, while government troops watched.

There were also riots in the kingdom's eastern provinces, the oil territories. Saudi Arabia is overwhelmingly Sunni Muslim, but there is a Shiite minority of about 200,000 people in the east, and they were incited to revolt by the success of the Ayatollah Khomeini's revolution across the Gulf in Iran. The Shiites thought themselves neglected and treated as second-class citizens. These disturbances were briskly suppressed.

## THE HAJ RIOTS

One of the duties laid upon the faithful is to go in pilgrimage to Mecca to pray at the Kaaba within the Great Mosque. The pilgrimage, the Haj, follows set rituals and is performed in the month that ends in the Feast of the Sacrifice. In 1987, the Haj took place in July and August.

Organizing the pilgrimage is an immense task, and the Saudis devoted a good part of the national budget to it. Two million people come every year, and in 1987, these included 155,000 Iranians. This posed a particular problem, because the Ayatollah Khomeini had called repeatedly for the faithful to rise and overthrow the House of Saud, whom he considered to be heretics. His anger was more political than theological, however: Saudi Arabia had given lavish support to Iraq in its war with Iran.

On 31 July, a riot occurred in Mecca that resulted in the deaths of 402 people, by the Saudi count: 275 Iranians, 85 police and 42 pilgrims of various other nationalities. A further 649, including 303 Iranians, were hospitalized.

The Saudis claimed that the Iranians had deliberately started the riot by marching on the Great Mosque, waving placards with Khomeini's picture on them and chanting anti-Saudi slogans. This had outraged the Saudis: a demonstration on such a holy occasion was, they said, unheard of. They claimed that police had showed great restraint when they had confronted the demonstrators and tried to stop them from approaching the mosque. The rioters had beaten and stabbed them, and when the police had charged, they had panicked and fled. Most of the dead were killed in the stampede.

There was a riot in Tehran, the Saudi and Kuwaiti embassies there were sacked and four Saudi diplomats were arrested and manhandled. Afterwards, the ayatollah proclaimed a *jihad*, a holy war, against the Saudis. It had no immediately discernible effect, but the Saudis awaited the next Haj with some trepidation.

Relations between the two countries deteriorated steadily. In the year following the Haj riot, Iranian gunboats periodically attacked shipping, including Saudi shipping, in the Gulf. In March 1988, King Fahd revealed that Saudi Arabia had acquired long-distance surface-to-surface missiles from China, and would use them against Iran if the attacks continued. In the same month, Saudi Arabia for the first time announced limitations on the number of pilgrims who would be allowed to attend the Haj – 1000 pilgrims for every million Muslims in the world, and the Iranian quota was 45,000. Iran immediately refused to accept any limitation, and in April the ayatollah announced that Iran would send 150,000 pilgrims. 'They shall perform their obligation, which is to declare deliverance from the infidels, the US and Israel,' he said. 'It would be impossible for them to go on the Haj and not stage demonstrations against global oppression, for declaring deliverance from infidels is among the political obligations of the Haj. Without it, the Haj is no Haj.'

Later that month, after Iranian saboteurs set fire to a petrochemical plant in Jubail in Saudi Arabia's oil province, and after an Iranian attack on a Saudi tanker, Saudi Arabia broke diplomatic relations with Iran.

Saudi Arabia's smug tranquillity was badly shaken by the Iraqi occupation of Kuwait in August 1990. If Saddam Hussein had been allowed to retain the emirate as Iraq's '19th province', he would have been in a position of overwhelming power in the Persian Gulf. He would have been able to dictate Saudi policy as completely as if he had occupied the kingdom, and would doubtless have started by annulling all his debts and reordering OPEC prices and production quotas to his liking. Saudi Arabia would have become his satellite. The House of Saud would have rushed to do his bidding, for fear that he would crook his finger and depose it. The Gulf emirates, of course, would have been equally subservient.

This was what provoked the American reaction. The United States, and the rest of the developed world, could not allow Saddam to settle his hands around Arabia's throat. There was never any real, direct threat to Saudi Arabia, not in 1990. Saddam would obviously have been content with Kuwait. But equally obviously, he would have Saudi Arabia at his mercy.

Within days, the Saudis agreed to break one of the basic principles of their foreign policy, and to allow foreign troops on to their soil. Within five months, there were over half a million American troops, and contingents from a dozen other countries. Saudi conservatives were incensed to see unveiled American women soldiers driving vehicles, breaking three Islamic rules at once. A group of Saudi women, encouraged by the example, dared to stage a small demonstration in Riyadh, driving their cars themselves. They were arrested, and though they were not charged with any offence, they all lost their jobs and suffered constant harassment afterwards. Saudi Arabia did not become more liberal because of its experience.

After the war, King Fahd announced that he would establish a consultative assembly some time soon. This was a small concession to democracy: there was no suggestion of giving anyone the vote. He also had to do battle with Islamic fundamentalists, who found the stifling, backward Saudi society insufficiently conservative. Meanwhile, in Kuwait, the corrupt, selfish emir and his family, who had been rescued by Western democracies, celebrated its liberation by persecuting all non-Kuwaitis living there.

Most other Arab governments supported the war against Saddam. The notable exception was Jordan, where popular opinion was overwhelmingly Saddamist. The Iraqi dictator was praised for defying the Americans and their Arab clients, and for proposing to redistribute oil revenues, taking it from rich, selfish, idle Kuwaitis. The argument convinced poor Arabs throughout the region. This popular reaction greatly worried more observant Saudis. If the attack had come from a less vicious, tyrannical, aggressive dictator than Saddam, Bush and the rest of the world might have let it stand.

For the moment, the Americans remained obsessed with the survival of Saddam Hussein and gave Kuwait, Saudi Arabia and the Gulf states every guarantee possible. This included stationing American troops in all three countries permanently, a fact that Saudi Arabia found very distasteful. Fundamentalists claimed that Saudi Arabia was sacred, because it includes the holy cities, Mecca and Medina. It was defiled by the presence of unbelievers.

Before 1990, the Saudi government had taken the same view, and steadfastly refused the Americans the right to open bases on its territory. After the war, and with Saddam still in power in Baghdad, the Saudis had no choice and adapted as well as they could. On 25 June 1996 19 American Air Force men were killed and 386 Americans, Saudis and others wounded, in a car-bomb attack at a huge military base at Dhahran, Saudi Arabia. The Americans were in a building known as Kobar Towers on the perimeter of the base, and the bomber drove up to the fence near the tower, and left his car there. Five Americans had been killed in another building in Riyadh the previous November.

There was much speculation over the identity of the bombers, with Iran a chief suspect. One man thought to have been involved was arrested in Syria, and conveniently died in prison before he could be interrogated. Others were publicly executed by the Saudis before the Americans were allowed to see them. Indeed, the Saudis were so concerned that the thread might lead back to one of their neighbours that they put every obstacle in the path of the FBI in attempting to solve the crime. Saudi Arabia had no wish to be involved in a new war, with Iran.

There was some solace. The Americans moved all their military personnel to a base deep in the desert – safe from terrorist attack and also far from the centres of population that might be subverted by American ideas of democracy, civil rights and the equality of the sexes. The Saudis remained caught between two evils, Saddam who would devour them and the United States which would change them, with only their money to console them.

## FURTHER READING

American University, *Saudi Arabia: A Country Study*, Washington D.C., 1984.

Holden, David and Johns, Richard, *The House of Saud*, New York, Holt, Rinehart & Winston, 1981.

Lacey, Robert, *The Kingdom: Arabia and the House of Sa'ud*, New York, Harcourt, Brace, Jovanovich, 1981.

Mortimer, Edward, *Faith and Power: The Politics of Islam*, London, Faber and Faber, 1982.

# SYRIA

| Geography | 71,498 sq. miles (185,179 sq. km). Twice the size of Portugal. |
|---|---|
| Population | 14.1 million, divided as follows: |

| Religion | Percentage of population | Language |
|---|---|---|
| Muslim | | |
| Sunni | 57.4 | Arabic |
| Sunni | 8.5 | Kurdish |
| Sunni | 3.0 | Turkish |
| Sunni sub-total | 68.9 | |
| Schismatic Muslim | | |
| Shiite | 1.0 | Arabic |
| Alawite | 11.7 | Arabic |
| Ismaili | 1.0 | Arabic |
| Druse | 3.0 | Arabic |
| Total Muslim | 85.6 | |
| Christian | | |
| Eastern Orthodox | 4.7 | Arabic |
| Armenian | 4.0 | Armenian |
| Other Christian | 5.4 | Arabic |
| Total Christian | 14.1 | |
| Other (Yazidis, Jews) | 0.8 | Arabic |

| GNP per capita | $1120. |
|---|---|
| Refugees | 347,000 Palestinians and 37,000 others. |

## HISTORY

Like most of the other states of the Middle East, Syria was conjured into existence after World War I from the wreckage of the Ottoman empire. It had always been a province of a larger state, except for a brief moment of Umayyad glory in the 7th–8th centuries.

Syria was ruled by the Turks from the 16th century until 1918 with occasional interruptions, including conquests by Napoleon and the 19th-century Egyptian ruler, Mohammed Ali. What are now Iraq, Syria, Lebanon, Jordan and Israel were then divided into various administrative districts, but they were all an integral, undivided part of the Ottoman empire. This did not mean that the people of the area had any unified national sentiment. When the League of Nations gave France a mandate to rule Syria, all that united its inhabitants were arbitrary lines on the map, drawn by the French. However, 85 per cent of the population were Muslims of one sort or another, and 90 per cent of the population spoke Arabic. On this basis, successive regimes have tried to construct a nation.

In 1919, the British, then the dominant power in the Middle East, separated Iraq from Syria, and southern Syria from the rest of the province, partly to create a buffer zone to the north of the Suez canal, partly to meet the promise made in 1917 to create a 'national home for the Jews'. The new entity was called Palestine, a biblical name revived for the occasion.

The British had intended that the emir Feisal, son of the Hashemite king Hussein of the Hejaz, Shereef of Mecca, should become king of Syria, and Feisal's brother Abdullah was to become king of Iraq. Feisal, who had led the Arab revolt against the Turks with the assistance of T. E. Lawrence, installed himself in Damascus in 1918. The French had not assented to these arrangements, and when Syria became a French mandate and the new rulers arrived in Damascus in July 1920, they evicted Feisal. He appealed to the British who, as a consolation prize, made him king of Iraq in 1921. (The Hashemite kingdom of Iraq lasted until 1958, when Feisal's grandson, King Feisal I I, was killed in a military coup.)

The Emir Abdullah was left homeless, so he set out from Mecca to reconquer Syria and drive out the French. He got as far as Amman, then very loosely under British control, in March 1921. There, advised of the strength of the French position, he decided that, for the moment, discretion ws the better part of valour. He would stay in Amman, in a territory he named Transjordan. The British acquiesced in this *coup de main*, and their new Palestine protectorate was divided into two. When the British gave up the mandate in 1948, Abdullah went to war with Israel, and emerged in control of Jerusalem and the West Bank. He annexed these territories and proclaimed the kingdom of Jordan. He was assassinated in 1951 at the al-Aqsa Mosque in Jerusalem.

Meanwhile, the French, in turn, further subdivided Syria, to create Lebanon. In 1939, Turkey demanded, and obtained, Iskanderun (Alexandretta) and Antioch in the north-west.

France was persuaded to give Syria and Lebanon their independence after World War I I. The persuasion was not gentle: the British sent an army to Damascus in 1941 to dispossess the Vichy regime. (One of their Palestinian soldiers, Moshe Dayan, lost an eye in the fight against the French, in a skirmish in southern Lebanon.) In May 1945, the French put down rioting in Damascus by shelling the city. The British government threatened to occupy Syria unless the French departed, which, finally, they did. The present borders of Syria were set when, in 1967, it lost the Golan Heights to Israel as a result of the Six-Day War (*see* Israel, pp. 305–27).

As for the Syrians, this history of a land chopped about by foreigners, all without the least regard for the wishes of its inhabitants (except for the Christians in Lebanon), has left them xenophobic and suspicious. They have never recognized Lebanon as an indepdent country *de jure*, though they have accepted the reality of its separate existence, and from time to time, they have revived their claims to 'southern Syria', meaning Israel and Jordan, and to Alexandretta.

## THE BA'ATH

The Ba'ath (Arab Renaissance) party was founded in 1940 in Damascus by Michel Aflaq and Salah al-Din al-Bitar. Aflaq was a Christian, and from the start the party attracted Arab minorities because it based its pan-Arabism on language, history and ethnicity, not Islam.

Aflaq's objective was 'Unity, Freedom and Socialism'. The Ba'ath was strongly opposed to the colonial powers, France and Britain, an attitude which naturally developed in later years into anti-Americanism and hostility to Israel. The party denounced all the Arab states set up after 1918 as illegitimate. It wanted to revive Arab national consciousness and unite all the Arabs in one state, from the Atlantic to the Gulf, from Marrakesh to Mecca.

The Ba'ath was divided into 'regional commands', one for each of the Arab states. The regional Ba'ath parties in Syria and Iraq eventually seized power, but failed to unite. The pull of nationalism, even in such artificial states, proved stronger than ideology.

After the French departed, Syria was ruled by a succession of ephemeral, authoritarian governments, punctuated by *coups d'état*: there were 15 coups and attempted coups between 1949 and 1970. The Ba'ath party in Syria went underground in 1950, and played an important part in the opposition to the government. Ba'athists were soon influential among army officers, particularly among the Alawites, a heretical Muslim sect concentrated in Latakia province, along the Mediterranean.

In 1958, with the government on the verge of collapse, the Ba'ath took the lead in uniting Syria with Egypt, as the United Arab Republic (UAR). The Ba'ath considered this the first step towards uniting all Arabs, but President Nasser of Egypt saw things differently. He set about suppressing the party in Syria, sowing the seeds for the enmity between the two countries that has persisted ever since. Nasser also sent his vice-president, General Abdul Hakim Amir, as his viceroy to Damascus. Amir made himself, and the Egyptians, deeply unpopular as he ruthlessly repressed all Syrian independence. The general, Nasser's most loyal follower, was later made scapegoat for the Egyptian débâcle in 1967 and committed suicide.

On 28 September 1961, an army coup in Syria abruptly ended the union with Egypt. Egyptian officials were shipped home and a deep frost settled on relations between Cairo and Damascus. They were only reconciled in 1967, just in time for the Six-Day War.

After the breakup of the UAR, Syria went through a period of great instability. To begin with, there was a conservative reaction, and Nasser's socialist measures were repealed. Then there were elections followed by a coup on 28 March 1962.

That coup was reversed in April, only to be followed during the next four years by a bewildering series of coups, counter-coups and changes of government. The Ba'ath had formally reconstituted itself in May 1962, and Salah al-Din al-Bitar, leader of the civilian wing of the party, became prime minister for the first time in March 1963. He had constantly to fight against Nasserites who staged frequent coup attempts, riots and assassinations, and there was a prolonged struggle for power between various factions of the Ba'ath itself. In July

1963, a major Nasserite coup attempt was suppressed and its leaders were executed. As a result, General Amin al-Hafiz became military dictator.

The two main factions of the party were the 'civilians', though their titular leader, Hafiz, was a general who advocated unity with Iraq and Egypt; and the 'military' wing, which was described as 'regionalist', meaning nationalist. On 23 February 1966, in the bloodiest coup to date, the military purged the civilians, arresting Hafiz and the two founders of the party, Michel Aflaq and Bitar. Aflaq died in Baghdad in 1989. Bitar and his wife were murdered in London in 1980.

In the new regime, power was shared between two generals, Salah al-Jadid and Hafez al-Assad. Jadid was the senior of the two, but Assad was minister of defence. The government, under Jadid's urging, allied itself with the Syrian Communist party and instituted a general purge of all other parties and tendencies in the Ba'ath. The government demonstrated its pan-Arab enthusiasm by various highly provocative gestures against Israel, which contributed largely to the tensions that provoked the 1967 war. Syria's humiliating defeat seriously undermined the positions of such radical leaders as Nasser and Jadid, and permitted Assad to extend his influence in Syria. However, Jadid remained in control of the party, and he continued to advocate extreme measures in foreign policy.

In September 1970, when King Hussein suppressed the P L O in Jordan, Jadid sent a tank brigade to the rescue. The United States moved the Sixth Fleet to the eastern Mediterranean, and the Israelis ostentatiously mobilized their armies on the Golan Heights. The Jordanian army and air force attacked the Syrian tanks, and drove them back across the frontier; Assad, commanding the Syrian air force, refused to provide air cover.

Despite this fiasco, Jadid retained control, and on 12 November, a party congress censored Assad. The next day, he struck back, arresting Jadid and his supporters. Following tradition, he then carried out an extensive purge of the party, and suppressed the Communist party. Assad has exercised complete power in Syria ever since.

## ASSAD'S SYRIA

The Ba'ath achieved its first, precarious taste of power in Iraq and Syria at the same time, in *coups d'état* early in 1963. However, it lost power in Baghdad in November, and by the time it recovered, the leaders of the two parties were at daggers drawn. They have been bitterly opposed ever since, to the extent that Syria was allied with Iran in its war with Iraq and joined the attack on Iraq in 1991. One of the differences between the two parties is that the Syrian Ba'ath has been run by the army since 1966, while the Iraqi Ba'ath maintains a civilian leadership. The chief difference is personal: if the two countries merged, one set of leaders would dominate the others. Since Iraq is more populous and far richer, the Syrians would probably be the losers – and they have resisted the idea.

The original group of revolutionary officers was dominated by Alawites. By the time he had made himself all powerful, Assad had established other members of the sect in key positions throughout the party, government and, above all, the military. Furthermore, he set up separate armed forces – the 'Special Forces' – under the command of two of his brothers-in-law, and the 'Defence Companies' under the command of his brother Rifaat al-Assad. These units were mainly composed of Alawites, and they steadily expanded in size – the American University country study on Syria put their number at 20,000–34,000 in 1978 – and were provided with every military luxury. They resembled Hitler's S S: they were loyal to the party and its leader, and to their own leaders, but not to the state. They had the added refinement of tribal loyalty. They were also utterly ruthless, as the suppression of the revolt in Hama in 1982 demonstrated (*see below*). Their weakness, which emerged in 1984, was the rivalry between their various leaders.

By the time Assad had eliminated all his opponents, the Ba'ath government, in Syria as in Iraq, was no more than a military dictatorship, its ideology a burned-out shell covering a ruthless tyranny. Assad retains power, like Saddam Hussein, by murdering his opponents, putting down rebellion with overwhelming force, and sending his assassins abroad to pursue those who escape. The Ba'ath in both countries is now like the Party in *1984*; as Orwell wrote:

We know that no one ever seizes power with the intention of relinquishing it. Power is not a means, it is an end. One does not establish a dictatorship in order to safeguard a revolution; one makes the revolution in order to establish the dictatorship. The object of persecution is persecution. The object of torture is torture. The object of power is power.

A report issued in 1987 by Amnesty International asserted that 'torture is a regular experience for thousands of political prisoners in Syria'. The report continued:

Brutal methods of torture have been described to Amnesty International by former inmates of Syrian prisons. Similar methods have been described by former detainees tortured by Syrian forces in Syria. One, known as the Black Slave, involves strapping the victim onto a device which, when switched on, inserts a heated metal skewer into the anus. The Washing Machine is a hollow spinning drum, similar to that of a domestic washing machine, into which the victim's arms are pushed and spun until they are crushed. There is the Syrian Chair, a metal chair to which the victim is bound by the hands and feet. The chair's backrest is then bent backwards, causing acute stress to the spine. Meanwhile, metal blades fixed into the chair's front legs cut into the victim's ankles . . . A variation of this form of torture, known as the Confessional Chair, is practised in Lebanon.

Syria has used assassination to pursue its ends for many years. On 29 August 1960, long before Assad came to power, the Jordanian prime minister, Hazza al-Majali, was murdered by a bomb placed in his office, at a time when King Hussein should have been there; Hussein mobilized his army and nearly went to war as a result. There have since been other frequent, Syrian-inspired attempts on Hussein's life. In 1980, Assad had Salah al-Din al-Bitar, one of the founders of modern Syria, murdered in exile, much as Stalin had Trotsky murdered in Mexico. In October 1986, Britain broke diplomatic relations with Syria when it was established that Syria had been deeply implicated in an attempt to blow up an El Al plane on a flight from London. A Jordanian terrorist, holding a Syrian passport and acting on orders from Syrian intelligence, had seduced an Irish girl, got her pregnant and put her on a flight to Israel with a bomb in her suitcase. It was found by Israeli security men. The terrorist had gone straight from the airport to the Syrian embassy.

There are few dictatorships in the world as odious as Syria. However, both the Alawite clique in Syria and the Tikriti clique in Iraq have, as their base, a minority community, and both face extreme political and military difficulties. They are unlikely to survive for ever.

## THE MUSLIM BROTHERHOOD

Islamic fundamentalist fanaticism is not restricted to the Iranians. It has been a constant threat in Syria and Iraq, and, in recent years, in Egypt, where the Muslim Brotherhood had its origins. Its aim was resistance to foreign (particularly British) domination of Arab lands, and opposition to the secularizing, Western tendencies of Arab governments.

The Brotherhood was founded in 1929 by Hasan al-Banna, an Egyptian, and developed into a mass movement during the 1930s and 1940s. It took the lead in opposing King Farouk's regime after the war, and at the end of 1948, following Egypt's defeat in the first war with Israel (in which the Brotherhood had played an inglorious part), it was suppressed. On 28 December, a young Brother shot the prime minister, Nokrashy Pasha, and on 12 February 1949, Banna was murdered by the Egyptian police.

In the aftermath of the 1952 revolution in Egypt, the Brotherhood was driven underground by Nasser. Its surviving leaders went abroad, and developed the movement in Jordan and Syria and in the Palestinian diaspora. Among its Palestinian recruits were Yasser Arafat, who later founded Al-Fatah, the main party in the Palestine Liberation Organization, and his deputy and military commander, Khalid Wazir, who was murdered by Israeli commandos in 1988.

The Brotherhood, which made many converts in Syria in the 1950s, was suppressed there after the union with Egypt in 1958, and not restored to legality after the union was ended in 1961. The Ba'ath party, and particularly the Alawites, had no intention of allowing a fundamentalist, Sunni party to extend its influence in Syria. The first demonstrations of Sunni displeasure took place in Hama in April 1964. The regime responded by sending the army to shell the Sultan Mosque there, killing dozens of people. There were more serious demonstrations in 1967 and 1973 against the regime's secular policies. In 1967, the riots were provoked by an article published in an army magazine, which implied criticism of Islam, and in 1973, riots were sparked off when a new constitution failed to make Islam the state religion and conspicuously admitted the possibility that a non-Muslim might become head of state. Although this was fundamental Ba'ath doctrine, Assad hastily backed down; the constitution was amended to insist that the president must be a Muslim – but most Sunnis do not consider Alawites to be proper Muslims.

Between 1973 and 1979, a number of Alawite officials and Soviet advisers were assassinated, but the regime had been chiefly concentrating on suppressing left-wing Ba'athists and missed the significance of the attacks. Then, on 16 June 1979, Captain Ibrahim al-Yussuf, a Ba'ath party political officer and a Sunni Muslim, assembled the cadets of the Aleppo Artillery School. He ordered the Sunni among them to leave the room, and then ordered his accomplices to open fire. They machine-gunned the remaining cadets, all Alawites, killing 60 of them (some sources put the number at 32).

Extremist Sunni all over the country rejoiced that the heretics had been killed, and the massacre ignited all the hatred that Assad had suppressed. For the next three years, Syria was engulfed in a virtual civil war. The rebels, who claimed to be heirs to the Muslim Brotherhood, assassinated Alawite officials, officers and Soviet military and civilian personnel. There were frequent car bombings in Damascus and other cities, killing hundreds of people. By early 1980, there had been 300–400 political killings, and the two major northern cities, Aleppo and Hama, were in the hands of the Brotherhood.

In March 1980, there was a general strike throughout the country in support of the Brotherhood and its demands for an Islamic republic. It seemed as though Syria was about to go the way of Iran.

President Assad resorted to extreme force to put down the revolt. On Easter Sunday, 6 April, the army surrounded Hama and Aleppo. The Special Forces conducted a series of sweeps through the two cities, arresting thousands of people and shooting anyone suspected of belonging to the Brotherhood. By the end of the year, at least 1000 people had been executed.

The terrorism continued. In April 1981, after an attempt on the life of President Assad, another 200–300 men were publicly executed in Hama. Even that proved insufficient: another 150 officials were murdered that year. In February 1982, the Brotherhood took control of Hama. Assad sent in his brother Rifaat with artillery and tanks on a full-scale assault. Between 2000 (the official figure) and 20,000 people were killed, and a third of the city was levelled.

These extreme measures restored at least the semblance of calm to Syria, but the assassinations and bombings continued, though at a lower rate. In 1986, more people were killed by terrorists in Syria than in all the heavily publicized terrorist attacks in Paris and Istanbul and in the Karachi airport incident – in March alone, terrorist bombs killed 150 people in Syria. The underlying tensions there remain as acute and dangerous as ever. The most dangerous for the regime is the alienation of the Sunni majority from the Alawites. Even with Alawite officers in key positions throughout the army, and with Alawite 'special units' to serve as the regime's Praetorian Guard, a minority comprising 12–15 per cent of the population cannot hope to dominate the country for ever. The disaffected Sunni officer who carried out the Aleppo massacre had been passed over for promotion, in favour of an Alawite, and was taking his revenge.

The Muslim Brotherhood has gone underground again. It has had no pre-eminent leader since Banna was murdered in 1949, but his doctrines are undoubtedly embraced by large numbers of Syrians. More recently, more extreme fundamentalists have taken up the cause, notably in Egypt and Algeria.

## MODERN SYRIA

In November 1983, Assad had a heart attack, and vanished from public view for several months. There was a brief and very public dispute between Rifaat at Assad, the president's brother, General Ali Haider, who commanded the Special Forces, and General Shafiq Fayyad, commander of the 3rd Armoured Division. It was a battle for the succession, and it was all in the family: Haider and Fayyad are both Assad's brothers-in-law (and are both Alawites). In March 1984, Rifaat sent his tanks into Damascus, where they confronted Haider's and Fayyad's troops. Assad from his sickbed resolved the crisis by sending Rifaat into exile. The president recovered and resumed control of the government, but the problems of the succession had been starkly demonstrated.

In Rifaat's absence, the Defence Companies were reportedly dissolved. On 11 September 1984, the minister of defence, Mustapha Tlas, was quoted in foreign newspapers as saying that Rifaat had been exiled 'for ever'. Rifaat riposted the next day with a statement from Geneva asserting that the Tlas quotation was a fabrication. He proved the point by returning to Damascus on 26 November.

According to the Amnesty report, Haider's Special Forces have been stationed in Lebanon since 1985, where they are responsible for the torture, ill-treatment and deliberate killing of innocent civilians.

Besides its internal differences, Syria faces a number of external problems. By far the most serious is Lebanon (*see* pp. 341–57). Syria has intervened in that unhappy country in an attempt to restore the peace. Its difficulties were demonstrated in the spring of 1988 when a full-scale civil war broke out between the two factions of Shiites – Amal, supported by Syria, and Hizbollah, supported by Iran. The Hizbollah was winning the fight on the ground when Syria intervened in a series of diplomatic efforts to obtain a ceasefire. Syria had risked ostracism in the Arab world by allying itself with the Iranians against a fellow-Arab state, Iraq, and now the same Iranians were stirring up their followers in Syria's own backyard.

The great danger in Lebanon was that Syria would be sucked into an impossible conflict, like Israel and the United States before it. Assad's evident reluctance to use force against the Hizbollah showed that he knew how unpopular such a course would be.

Even before the first Gulf War, in 1975, relations between Syria and Iraq had been so tense that the two governments mobilized their armies along the frontier. The proximate cause of the dispute was water: Syria was building a large dam on the Euphrates, with Soviet help, and Iraq charged that Syria was stealing its water resources. The dispute subsided, partly thanks to Saudi mediation.

The real dispute is one of the oldest and most bitter personal quarrels in the Middle East, between Assad and Saddam Hussein. Both were conspirators who plotted the violent overthrow of their governments, both were members of the Ba'ath Party and rivals for its international leadership, both established crushing, Stalinist tyrannies upon their countries and retained power by murder, terrorism and ruthless manipulation of the divisions of their societies. Both were also members of local clans that they used to seize and hold power. Both used their own families as the final bastions of their power, putting sons, brothers, sons-in-law and cousins in positions of ultimate authority in the government and security apparatus.

Assad and Saddam were made for each other. It is not surprising that they detested one another. Assad pushed the logic of their rivalry to the extreme in 1981, when he sided with Iran in its war against Iraq. Saddam vowed vengeance, and in 1990, when he seized Kuwait, Assad had little hesitation in abandoning a lifetime's rhetoric and allying himself with the Great Satan itself, the United States and, implicitly, with the national enemy, the 'Zionist Entity', against Iraq. If Iraq had succeeded in annexing Kuwait, it would have been the richest and altogether dominant power in the Arab world, and Saddam would then have settled his accounts with Assad. When Syria sent a symbolic contingent to Saudi Arabia (it played little part in the fighting), there were murmurs of disapprobation in Damascus, where the exiled Palestinians were demonstrating their love of Saddam. Once again, Assad had to divide to rule. He had long supported a Palestinian faction opposed to Yasser Arafat, and the two had constantly fought in Lebanon and in the camps in Syria. Now Arafat's rivals were once again produced to denounce Saddam for aggression, and Arafat for supporting him.

Assad has behaved with conspicuous caution towards Israel, with the exception of the bold attack in October 1973, shortly after he seized power. The level of intransigent, anti-Zionist rhetoric from Damascus has never slackened, but it was notable that, when Israel invaded Lebanon in 1982, Syria did not intervene. The Israelis allowed the Syrians in Beirut (they included Rifaat al-Assad) to depart unmolested, and the Syrians, most of the time, kept out of harm's way. At the beginning of the conflict, the Israelis had seized a pretext to attack Syrian anti-aircraft batteries in the Bekaa valley and, in the process, had shot down a large part of Syria's air force. The memory of that episode proved a sufficient reminder to the Syrians of the need for caution.

The Syrian economy is in great difficulty. Defence takes a huge part of the national budget (by some reports as much as 50 per cent), and other resources are committed to those scourges of the Third World: grandiose projects such as the Euphrates dam. Syria was the Soviet Union's principal client in the Middle East after the defection of Egypt in 1973. The USSR consistently underwrote Syria's budget and supplied it with arms and other essential imports. Some of the costs were born by Libya, but Syria was essentially a Soviet satellite, and survived thanks to Soviet aid. The collapse of the Soviet Union in 1991 was therefore a disaster for Hafiz al-Assad. Arms, subsidies and cheap oil were all cut off together. Syria, like other former satellites, suddenly discovered that it would have to pay full market prices for Soviet weaponry and oil, and at the same time its own economy was suffering from the same wasting disease that had finally brought down Lenin's great experiment. State socialism, as practised in the Communist bloc, and in Syria, was an utter failure.

Castro in Cuba might delude himself that he could survive in the new circumstances. Assad knew that he had to trim his sails, and to do so rapidly. The second Gulf War provided a first opportunity, and he gave every support to Saudi Arabia, Kuwait and the Americans. He was able to use his contributions, and the fact that Syria would always remain as a counterweight to a recovered Iraq, to extort subsidies from the oil states, but that was not enough. He had to restore good relations with the West. That was the argument that the Americans used in getting Assad to join the Middle East peace conference in 1991. Syria continued to protest its hatred of Israel, its foreign minister refused to shake hands with Israeli delegates or to answer questions from Israeli journalists at press conferences, and constantly threatened to walk out of the talks. But this was all sham. The Americans insisted, and Syria had to comply.

Assad has always been suspicious and as a result he missed his last chance to make peace with Israel and recover any part of the Golan Heights. Warren Christopher, the US secretary of state, visited him frequently between 1993 and

1996, attempting to persuade him that he should seize the moment, after Arafat had signed his agreement with Rabin, and strike a deal for himself. Assad consistently refused. Rabin never made explicit that he would give up the Golan, with its 6000 Jewish settlers, in exchange for permanent peace with Syria, but that was the card Christopher begged Assad to play. If he had, as Sadat offered a final peace in exchange for the complete return of the Sinai, Assad might have recovered the lands lost by his own and his government's folly in 1967.

He refused. He insisted that Syria would come last, after the final treaty between Israel and the Palestinians. In the meantime, he kept the right to encourage the terrorists and extremists whom he harboured in Damascus. What is more, he tried to develop or buy long-range missiles with which to threaten Israel. In 1992, the US Navy failed to intercept a North Korean freighter carrying Scud missiles destined for Syria. It evaded the patrols and landed safely in Iran, whence its cargo was flown to Damascus. The Israelis were understandably perturbed, and less inclined to make concessions to Assad.

At any event, Assad missed the bus. After Rabin was murdered and Peres lost the election in 1996, there was no hope that a Likud government would give up the Golan. Perhaps, indeed, when Israel makes peace with the Palestinians and a period of tranquillity has allowed Likud's supporters to accept that peace means making concessions – and is worth it – Israel will offer to deal with Syria. But that will not be for years, and Assad is too old, sick and insecure to have any reasonable hope to live that long.

## FURTHER READING

American University, *Syria: A Country Study*, Washington D.C., 1987.

Amnesty International, *Syria: Torture by the Security Forces*, London, 1987.

Antonius, George, *The Arab Awakening*, New York, Capricorn, 1963.

Devlin, John, *The Ba'ath Party from Its Origins to 1966*, New York, Praeger, 1966.

Glubb, John Bagot, *Syria, Lebanon, Jordan*, New York, Walker, 1967.

Hureau, Jean, *La Syrie aujourd'hui*, Paris, Editions, J.A., 1977.

Lewis, Bernard, *The Middle East: A Brief History of the Last 2000 Years*, New York, Scribner, 1996.

Middle East Watch, *Syria Unmasked: the Suppression of Human Rights by the Asad Regime*, New Haven, Yale University Press, 1991.

Mortimer, Edward, *Faith and Power: The Politics of Islam*, London, Faber and Faber, 1982.

Petran, Tabitha, *Syria*, New York, Praeger, 1972.

Runciman, Steven, *A History of the Crusades* (3 vols.), Cambridge University Press, 1951–4.

Seal, Patrick, *The Struggle for Syria*, Oxford University Press, 1965.

Sinai, Anne and Pollack, Allan, *The Syrian Arab Republic: A Handbook*, New York, American Academic Association for Peace in the Middle East, 1976.

# YEMEN

| | |
|---|---|
| Geography | 187,000 sq. miles (485,000 sq. km). The size of Sweden. |
| Population | 15 million. |
| GNP per capita | $260. |

## HISTORY

Yemen was the home of the Queen of Sheba. It was known to the Romans as *Arabia Felix* – Happy, or Prosperous Arabia – an early case of distance lending enchantment. The south and east is barren desert but the north is chiefly mountainous and enjoys a relatively temperate climate. It produced myrrh and frankincense, both highly esteemed in antiquity.

Various monarchies succeeded each other in the area, each ruling different proportions of the mountains and deserts, which were inhabited by a multitude of independent tribes. The various Arab caliphs and dynasties sometimes controlled Yemen, sometimes not. The Turks ruled for a while, and King Abdul Aziz (Ibn Saud) sent his warriors to conquer North Yemen in 1934, and was defeated.

The whole country, north and south, remained quite ignorant of the outside world until the 1960s – except for Aden. That port, on the southern extremity of the Arabian peninsula, was annexed by Britain in 1839, as part of the string of naval bases it established around the Indian Ocean to protect the Indian empire. After the opening of the Suez canal, Aden became an important coaling station on the route to the subcontinent.

Yemen was ruled from Saana by imams who were both religious and secular leaders. They were rigidly authoritarian and conservative, opposed to all modernization, and like the tsars in Russia, the imams ruled by absolutism tempered by assassination. Their absolutism was, however, moderated by the need to retain the loyalty of the tribes. The tradition of assassination has survived the fall of the imamate.

The British imposed a wholly artificial division between North and South Yemen, in order to exert some control over Aden's hinterland. They called the south the Aden Protectorate and signed treaties with the various sheikhs who governed it.

**374** Out of imperial habit, Britain retained Aden after losing India in 1947, and even expanded the dockyards and built an oil refinery. The Imam Yahya of Yemen was assassinated in 1948 in an attempted coup, which was put down by his son Ahmad. The new imam permitted some modernization, and he joined the rest of the Arab world in hostility to Britain during the Suez war of 1956. In one of the many transitory unions of which the Arabs are so fond, he united Yemen with Nasser's United Arab Republic (Egypt and Syria) in 1958. The union was called the Union of Arab States, and had no purpose except to vex the British and the Saudis. It was dissolved in December 1961. The imam remained as authoritarian and reactionary as his predecessors.

The loss of the Suez canal in 1956 did not alter British policy, although rising Arab radicalism, the inevitable consequence of the need for a modern workforce in the port, made holding Aden increasingly difficult. The rationale for keeping Aden was that it was needed as a base for operations in the Gulf, which was still a British protectorate. Meanwhile, some military men in North Yemen had learned revolutionary tactics in Egypt and plotted against the imam.

On 19 September 1962, at the height of the influence and megalomania of President Nasser of Egypt, the old Imam Ahmad died. On 26 September, the Egyptians organized a coup in Saana and immediately flew in troops to protect the new government. This was exactly the technique that was to be employed by the Soviet Union in Afghanistan 17 years later, and the results were very similar.

The tribes refused to recognize the regime. Ahmad's heir, who had ruled Saana for a week, rallied them and attacked the Egyptians. The royalists were supported by the Saudis and the British, and the Egyptians were quite unable to defeat them. Nasser's air force tried bombing guerrilla bases in Saudi Arabia, and the two countries were on the verge of war until President Kennedy made it clear that the United States would support the Saudis.

Meanwhile, Britain's position in Aden was becoming untenable. The Colonial Office set up a Federation of South Arabia, to be dominated by conservative sheikhs from the back country, in the hope of leaving a pro-British government behind them, but the radicals easily defeated it. It was Britain's last colonial war. In June 1967 there was heavy fighting in Aden, and the British were driven out of the Crater District, the city's Arab quarter, with the loss of 22 soldiers. The rebels were joined by the Aden police force which had been armed and trained by the British. On 3 July Lieutenant Colonel Colin Mitchell of the Argyll and Sutherland Highlanders, acting against his commanding officer's express order, retook the Crater, at the head of his regiment, with bagpipes and drummers leading the way. He managed this remarkable feat, a last imperial flourish, without suffering any casualties. By then, Nasser had suffered a humiliating defeat in the Six-Day War and the Suez Canal was closed. Nasser pulled out of North Yemen in September, and Britain pulled out of Aden in October.

## INDEPENDENCE

The two Yemens entered the new era with a series of coups and assassinations that lasted for 20 years. The regime that the Egyptians left behind in North Yemen was overthrown within a month. The civil war continued until 1970 when an agreement between the various factions was brokered by the Saudis. The new government looked to Saudi Arabia as its natural ally.

In the South, the country was renamed the People's Democratic Republic of Yemen, and allied itself with the Soviet Union. Aden was bankrupted by Britain's departure and the closing of the Suez canal. The U S S R stepped into the breach. In exchange for naval facilities, it armed the South Yemenis and provided some minimal economic assistance. South Yemen became a most obdurately Communist state, an Arabian Cuba. Its Communist practice, however, was seriously modified by the intransigent conservatism of the tribes (which were always in a state of revolt or incipient revolt against Aden). It was the only Communist state in the world with a state religion, Islam. Furthermore, South Yemen depended upon remittances from 100,000 of its citizens working abroad, mostly in Saudi Arabia and the Gulf states, who were there subject to the conservative doctrines of those staunchly anti-Communist regimes. The expatriates insisted that their money go to their families, and the government was forced therefore to tolerate a degree of quite un-Communist free enterprise.

Both Yemens were notable for the frequency and bloodiness of their changes of government. Despite the fact that they proclaimed their ambition to unite, they fought numerous border skirmishes and one all-out war, in 1979. In 1977, a North Yemen president was assassinated, possibly because he had planned to visit Aden. On 24 June 1978, a messenger from President Salim Rubai Ali of South Yemen was shown into the office of President Ahmad al-Ghashmi of North Yemen, in Saana. In the messenger's briefcase was a bomb, which exploded, killing both men. Two days later, President Rubai Ali was himself killed in a coup in Aden. There were other coups and assassinations in both countries later.

During the 1970s, South Yemen was governed by a triumvirate of Ali Nasser al-Hassani, Abdel Fatah Ismail and Salim Rubai Ali, all veterans of the fight against the British, who had attained this position after coups in 1969 and 1971. Rubai was president until the unfortunate events of June 1978; then there were two.

Ismail became president, but was overthrown by his fellow-*duumvir*, Hassani, in 1980; he escaped to Moscow, where he spent five years acquiring the reputation of a dogmatic Communist. Hassani, by now president, was considered marginally more moderate and, by the mid-1980s, was cautiously developing slightly less chilly relations with the West and with conservative Arab regimes.

Ismail, temporarily reconciled with Hassani, returned in the autumn of 1985 and resumed his place in the politburo. A new triumvirate was formed comprising Hassani, Ismail and the vice-president, Ali Ahmed Antar. These new arrangements were not to Hassani's liking. He summoned a meeting of the politburo on 13 January 1986, at 10 a.m., but he himself did not attend, having departed secretly for his tribal base in the mountains, leaving his Mercedes behind to deceive his colleagues. When they were all seated, waiting for Hassani, his bodyguards opened fire on them with machine-guns. Antar was killed immediately, as was the minister of defence, Saleh Muslih Quassem. Ismail died of his wounds later. Their own bodyguards rushed into the room, and the ensuing gun fight resulted in the deaths of about 20 people. A few members of the politburo who had managed to escape through a window immediately rallied their supporters. A savage battle broke out in the centre of Aden; it lasted ten days.

The Soviet Union was taken totally by surprise. Its diplomats and military advisers fled, taking refuge in a Soviet freighter in the harbour. Westerners were evacuated more comfortably, aboard the Royal Yacht *Britannia*, which had been sailing down the Red Sea on its way to New Zealand to meet the Queen. The *Britannia* ferried the refugees from Aden to Djibouti on the African coast opposite.

Witnesses reported seeing heavily armed tribesmen pouring into the city. During the fighting, the army was divided along tribal rather than ideological lines. The navy supported Hassani, and its ships shelled opposition tanks. President Hassani lost, and fled to Ethiopia. As his troops retreated from Aden, they demolished the Soviet embassy. The prime minister, fortunately for him, was out of the country during these events. He waited until the fight was over, and then returned to assume the presidency.

The government later reported that 4230 members of the ruling party had been killed in the fighting, and it seems likely that the total number killed was about 13,000. Over 60,000 refugees fled to North Yemen.

An uneasy truce supervened, and lasted for the next four years. The Soviet Union, which was the sole supporter of the South Yemen regime, progressively reduced its assistance, and the government correctly foresaw the need to find alternative means of subsistence. Oil had been discovered in both Yemens and there was the prospect of future prosperity, but the immediate future was bleak.

There were three other occasions when the two Yemens had attempted a union, in 1971, 1981 and 1989. In 1990, they tried again, and this time pushed through the proposal rapidly and secretly. A draft treaty of union was issued on 22 April, and ratified by the two parliaments, which were both, of course, under the absolute control of the governments. The union was consummated on 22 May. The president of North Yemen, Ali Abdullah Saleh, became president of the new country, the secretary-general of the South Yemen Socialist Party, Ali Salem al-Baidh, became vice-president and Abu Bakr al-Attai, president of South Yemen, became prime minister. The capital was to be Saana, in the north, and Aden was to be economic capital. There was to be a transition period lasting two and a half years, followed by elections.

The new federation faced its first challenge the following year. Yemen was a member of the U N Security Council and, with Cuba, was the only one to give any support to Iraq during the Kuwait crisis. Saudi Arabia, in retaliation, expelled over 100,000 Yemeni workers and cut off all economic assistance. This was a major reversal: the Saudis had consistently supported North Yemen for over 20 years, and loss of that assistance was a devastating blow to the country. Tensions between North and South rose steadily between 1991 and 1994. Ali Salem al-Baidh accused President Saleh of plotting to undermine his authority in the South. He claimed that the president had incited his followers to violence and that more than 150 of al-Baidh's followers had been killed. Other Arab leaders tried to mediate and the two leaders met in Jordan in February 1994 and signed a peace agreement. It lasted less than three months.

In early May, full-scale civil war broke out between North and South. The Southern armed forces had retained their independence, and now the Southern air force launched a bombing raid on Saana, aiming particularly at the presidential palace. The Northern air force retaliated, bombing Aden. Each launched Scud missiles at the other.

Al-Baidh proclaimed the South's secession on 22 May, and the next day prudently moved himself and his government to Mukallah, well to the east. There was heavy fighting between ground forces of the two sides, and the Northern army launched a three-pronged attack against the South. The fighting was mercifully brief. By late June, the Northern army had reached the outskirts of Aden and systematically shelled the city for two weeks before beginning its assault. Aden fell on 7 July. A day earlier, a Northern column occupied Mukallah: al-Baidh fled over the border to Oman. The civil war was over.

Yemen then subsided into relative tranquillity. Banditry was common, with visiting westerners frequently kidnapped to make local political points (they were always well treated and released safe and sound). President Saleh was unchallenged for the moment, but there was no saying how long his authority would last.

## ERITREA, YEMEN AND GREATER HANISH

A dispute arose in 1995 between Yemen and Eritrea, newly independent across the Red Sea, over a small group of islands lying between them. Yemen accused Eritrea of invading the islands in December 1995. Sixteen soldiers, ten Yemenis and six Eritreans, were killed. Eritrea responded to the charge by accusing Yemen of having occupied the islands illegally in November. The U N secretary-general, Boutros Boutros-Ghali, asked France to mediate, and the Eritreans withdrew their troops in May 1996. The dispute, however, was not resolved.

## FURTHER READING

American University, *The Yemens: A Country Study*, Washington D.C., 1986.
Bidwell, Robin, *The Two Yemens*, Boulder, Colo., Westview Press, 1983.
Pindhan, B. R., *Economics, Society and Culture in Contemporary Yemen*, London, University of Essex Press.

# EUROPE

# INTRODUCTION TO EUROPE

The collapse of the Communist governments of eastern Europe in 1989 and 1990, and the disintegration of the Soviet Union in 1991, removed the great danger that had hung over the continent and the world since 1945. There will be no World War I I I fought in Europe. The former satellites, with greater or lesser fervour, have set about rebuilding their economies and establishing democracies. They have turned their backs on Russia and its miseries, and are now eagerly looking westwards for their salvation; so are the former Soviet Socialist Republics.

East Germany was the most fortunate. It was absorbed into the Federal Republic in 1990, and although there is high unemployment and much distress and dislocation as the old ways are swept aside, there can be no doubt that in a few years the process of reunification will be completed, and Saxony and Brandenburg will once again be equal parts of Germany. Clearing up the ecological disaster bequeathed by the Communists will take longer. The German government closed East Germany's nuclear power plants immediately after unification, but eliminating or modernizing the coal-fired power plants and the factories that have polluted eastern Germany, like Czechoslovakia, Poland and all the rest of eastern Europe, and replacing the shoddy buildings and houses, will take a generation. Another problem the Germans face, and it is shared everywhere in western Europe, is a reappearance of fascism. The danger should not be exaggerated. Although it is repulsive to see German skinheads chanting *Sieg Heil!* in Berlin or Vienna, they are a small minority and will not be allowed to become a serious menace. Their motive is partly economic distress and alienation, and partly resentment against foreigners. Old-established guest-workers, like the Turks, have now been reinforced by a huge influx of immigrants from Poland and other eastern countries, and nativist chauvinisms have blossomed all over Europe. It will be a long time before Europeans come to tolerate and esteem each other.

The rest of eastern Europe is not so fortunate as the former German Democratic Republic. The other countries have no millionaire cousins to rescue them, and must restore themselves by their own efforts and with inadequate help from the West. First of all they must escape from the economic catastrophe bequeathed by the old regime. Democracy is a fragile institution throughout the region, and will need strenuous outside support if it is to survive the hard years ahead. Poland, which developed a subterranean democracy of its own in the last decade of the Communists' rule, took the boldest plunge into the free market after the regime's collapse. It is already reaping the benefits, economically and politically. It has enjoyed a consistently high rate of growth, and revelled in the joys of party politics. In the mid-1990s, former Communists won elections and formed governments – and a former Communist defeated that doughty warrior, Lech Walesa, for the presidency.

Prosperity is beginning to reach the farther reaches of the countryside and even the least favoured sections of the community, pensioners and those workers whose antiquated factories were closed, are now seeing some of the benefits of capitalism. There is now a solidarity government again. Poland has been invited to join Nato and has high hopes of joining the E U, even though it has a long way to go before its economy will be ready for the full rigours of competition with existing members.

Hungary and the Czech Republic thought they could make an easier transition, because their economies and industries had done better under Communism. They were both mistaken: root-and-branch reform is as necessary for them as it was for Poland – and they are now facing the same tough decisions that the Poles dealt with in 1990. There is no turning back, and they too will join Nato and the E U.

Slovenia, the most northerly of the former Yugoslav republics, will presumably join them, but the future of the rest of south-east Europe is less assured. Serbia turned its back on modern Europe and incited the Serbs of Bosnia and Croatia to bring ruin upon themselves and their neighbours. The Serbs will pay the price of their crimes for years to come and so, for no fault of their own, will the Bosnians (*see below*, Yugoslavia, p. 437).

Romania and Bulgaria remained in the grip of the same corrupt and incompetent bureaucrats and politicians who had administered them under Ceausescu and Zhivkov for years after the former was shot and the latter imprisoned. They now at last have anti-Communist governments which will have to enact the painful reforms needed, and suffer the consequent unpopularity. Albania succumbed, briefly, to utter banditry. It is the poorest and most destitute country in Europe. At least the Albanians, unlike the Romanians, could not be deceived by promises that prosperity would ever come by maintaining the status quo.

The great paradox of eastern Europe is that these countries and nationalities are clamouring to join the European Community, volunteering to abandon to Brussels much of their newly recovered sovereignty at the same time that they demand independence from their former rulers. Slovenia and Croatia have proclaimed their independence from Yugoslavia, but are perfectly ready to surrender control of economic and social policy, customs, systems of taxation, currencies and immigration control, as well as participating in whatever degree of political union and unified defence policy the 15 present members of the E U finally adopt. The Community of the late 1990s will be a much closer union than was Yugoslavia in the 1980s – yet Croatia went to war to escape Yugoslavia and join the Community.

Slovakia has broken away from the Czech Republic, deluding itself that all its ills came from Prague. Now, like Croatia and several of the former Soviet republics to the East, it has turned into a nasty, authoritarian state with fascistic overtones, administered by the same men who misgoverned it in earlier years and who claim now to be reformed Communists. Its president, Vladimir Meciar, has revived the cult of Father Joseph Tiso, who made Slovakia a Nazi state and ally of Hitler during World War II. No doubt he, and the others, will go the way of the first post-revolutionary governments in Romania and Bulgaria, but in the meantime their peoples will have lost at least an additional decade of their lives and history.

There are 600,000 Hungarians living in Slovakia, which used to be a province of the Kingdom of Hungary during the Austrian-Hungarian Empire (the Czech lands were attached to Austria). Bratislava, capital of Slovakia, is Pressburg in German, Pozsnoy in Hungarian. The Slovaks are beginning to repress their Hungarian minority as Ceausescu did their cousins in Transylvania in the 1980s. They are denied the right to run schools in Hungarian or to have the language used by local governments or on road signs, and their newspaper and book publishing is restricted. Budapest protests, and the E U – and the United States – have joined the protest, pointing out that Slovakia has no hope of membership of western organizations, especially the E U, if it persecutes its minorities.

Parallel to the dangers which result from poverty and economic disruption are the ethnic feuds that have revived all across eastern Europe and the former Soviet Union. From 1945 until 1989, the Communist parties suppressed all signs of ethnic animosities. The parties proclaimed that Leninist internationalism had superseded the old rivalries between nations. Communist theory asserted that class solidarity and class warfare were the only realities; that nationalism, like religion, was a spurious division of workers by the exploiting classes; and that disputes between Poles, Germans, Russians and so on were things of the past. It was all a fraud. The Russians ruled the Soviet Union, even when they were led by a Georgian (Stalin) or an Ukrainian (Khrushchev), and the Soviet Union ruled Eastern Europe. The Serbs ruled Yugoslavia, even though their leader, Tito, was a Croat, and the Romanians persecuted their Hungarian minority, and the Bulgars denied the very existence of their large Turkish minority.

## THE BALTICS

There are large Russian minorities in Estonia, Latvia and Lithuania, all people who were moved into the Baltic states on Stalin's orders after the war, or more recently. The three republics recovered their independence in 1991, exactly 51 years after they lost it. They have now to decide whether to allow the Russians to remain, keeping the full array of civil rights that everyone in the Baltics, native and immigrant alike, were deprived of during those 51 years; or whether to expel them back to Russia, incurring the enmity of that colossal neighbour and provoking the displeasure of the West.

Thirty-five per cent of the population of Estonia is Russian. In Latvia, the proportion is even higher, 46 per cent, and its capital, Riga, has a large Russian majority. The Russians make up 20 per cent of the population in Lithuania but there, and indeed in all three republics, the Russians are heavily concentrated in the cities, in industrial areas and the ports. All three countries have made their own languages the national language, but passing a law is one thing, enforcing it is another. How can Latvia force 46 per cent of its population to change languages? It has fantasies about granting citizenship only to people who speak Latvian, or who were themselves and whose parents were born there. The remainder would, presumably, be considered resident aliens, but that would not solve the problem. Would they have the vote? They must have it if the Baltics are to join the E U. At the most extreme, how can Latvia force 46 per cent of its population to emigrate? The Helsinki Final Act, the charter of European human rights, is unequivocal: ethnic minorities must be protected, and must enjoy full civil and political rights. The Soviet Union, and its satellites, which all signed at Helsinki, regularly violated the agreement and protested bitterly when the West insisted that its provisions must be respected. Europe cannot now permit the Baltic states, successor states to Yugoslavia or any other newly freed country in the East to practise the same hypocrisy, however historically unjust the implantation of hundreds of thousands of people on their territory may have been.

There is also a latent dispute between Lithuania and Poland over the large Polish community (about 280,000 people) in southern Lithuania. This is particularly sensitive since the Poles live around the national capital, Vilnius – which was called Wilno and was part of Poland between the wars. At the time of the attempted coup in Moscow, in August 1991, the Communist authorities in the Polish districts supported the plotters (as did leaders of the Russian minorities everywhere). Immediately after the coup failed, the Lithuanian government dismissed local, Polish authorities, and replaced them with loyal Lithuanians. The Polish-Lithuanians, naturally, resented the change, and appealed to Warsaw, and relations between Poland and Lithuania became seriously strained.

At the same time, Lithuania was faced with another conflict, this time with the West. Desiring to restore the rights of everyone who had been unjustly persecuted by the Soviet Union, Lithuanian courts started the wholesale rehabilitation of all those who had been convicted of war crimes by Soviet courts. No doubt many of those who received amnesties were Lithuanian patriots, democrats, bourgeois or peasants who had resisted Communism. But many were, indeed, war criminals. The Nazis had found plentiful help in Lithuania in the business of rounding up and murdering the Jews. Most of those who ran the camps and execution parties in Lithuania were Lithuanians. About 135,000 Jews were murdered. After protests in the United States, the Lithuanian courts started reconsidering the amnesty plan, but the government was unrepentant. President Vytautas Landsbergis insisted that all Soviet courts were unjust and all verdicts should be overturned.

Lithuania was independent, but was already at odds with its two most powerful neighbours, Poland and Russia, and had provoked some uneasiness in the West. The temptation in all three republics to take advantage of Russia's distress was very great, but at the same time moderate voices warned that Russia would one day recover and that even now, the three have continued to be part of the Soviet economic system, even if there is no longer any Soviet Union.

There is also the question of the Kaliningrad *oblast*, a small parcel of Russian territory between Lithuania and Poland. It is all that remains of East Prussia, an ancient province of Germany whose entire population was expelled in 1945. The northernmost part, the port city Memel (now called Klaipeda), was transferred to Lithuania, which was then part of the U S S R. It now has a Russian majority. The rest of East Prussia was partitioned between Poland and Russia. The southern half has now been fully absorbed into Poland, but the north, including the capital, Kaliningrad (formerly Königsberg) was kept as a separate entity (an *oblast* in Russian). It was added to the Russian Republic, even though there is no territorial link between the two. Indeed, Russia itself is several hundred miles to the east, beyond Byelorussia, which has declared its independence and now calls itself Belarus. Kaliningrad became one of the principal Soviet ports on the Baltic. Kalinin was a Stalinist functionary and the name can be changed, like all other Bolshevik names, but the former population will not return (though German tourists are now welcome), and the district's future is bleak even by the standards of modern Russia.

## CZECHOSLOVAKIA

Finally, in a legacy Czechoslovakia shares with Poland, there is the question of the Germans who were expelled after 1945. Nine million Germans were driven out of what is now Poland, and 2.9 million from the Sudetenland, in Czechoslovakia. It was one of the great crimes of the century, though an understandable revenge on Germany for all the horrors of Nazism. There is no serious irredentist sentiment in Germany nowadays, and Germany has signed treaties specifically recognizing its post-war frontiers, and no one doubts that they will be honoured. But many individual Sudeten Germans, or Silesians, or Prussians may wish to return and look for their homes. Czechoslovakia has ruled that property confiscated during the Soviet occupation, 1945–47, is not covered by the law that returns property taken by the Communists. This provision excludes the Germans. Poland has no policy of returning confiscated property. It would be difficult, since the country was physically moved 150 miles westwards in 1945. But in the new Europe, when Poland and Czechoslovakia join the Community, any European may live anywhere, and there will doubtless be many Germans who want to return.

## THE BALKANS

The Balkans have now recovered their traditional position as the most unstable region of Europe. There were innumerable wars there in the 19th century, as the Ottoman empire slowly disintegrated, and in the 20th century. World War I began because of the assassination of the Archduke Franz-Ferdinand in Sarajevo, and none of the torments that ensued resolved the ethnic, religious and linguistic disputes that had provoked all those conflicts. The causes of these many wars were always the same: the fervent nationalism of the various nations of the region, and the impossibility of establishing mutually acceptable frontiers between any of them. The useful word 'Balkanization' was coined to meet the case.

## THE TRANSYLVANIA DISPUTE

In the mid-19th century, the Hungarians attained equality with Austria in what became known as the Austro–Hungarian empire. The Austrian emperor was also king of Hungary, and Hungarians ruled over part of what is now Yugoslavia and roughly half modern Romania and Czechoslovakia. They lost it all in the collapse of the empire in 1918. The victors confined them to their native plains, excluding a third of the Hungarians, three million people in all.

The largest number lived in Transylvania, which both Hungarians and Romanians claim as the cradle of their nations. For over a thousand years, Magyars, Romanians and Germans, with smaller Jewish and gypsy communities, lived commingled but distinct. Many villages and towns have three names, one in each language: Transylvania's capital is called Cluj in Romanian, Kolozsvar in Hungarian and Klausenburg in German. During the Ceauşescu years in Romania, the number of Hungarians was hotly disputed: Hungary saying there were 2.5 million, Romania that there were only 1.7 million. There remained about 250,000 Germans in Romania, the only large East European German community that was not expelled in 1945, and there are also several hundred thousand Hungarians in eastern Romania, far from Transylvania, including 200,000 in Bucharest.

The largest Hungarian communities are in central and eastern Transylvania, separated from the motherland by a wide territory that is chiefly Romanian. The Hungarian areas could not be restored to Hungary without subjecting large numbers of Romanians to Budapest, reversing the present irredentist claims, and creating a wholly impractical frontier. The peacemakers in 1919 decided that it would be better to leave the Transylvanian Hungarians in Romania and to guarantee them every possible political and civil right. Besides, Hungary was one of the nations that had started the war, and lost it.

In the 1930s, Hungary joined the Axis and was a loyal ally to Hitler until his defeat was certain and the Russians were on the Danube. Hitler allowed Hungary to recover many of the lands it had lost in 1919. When Germany partitioned Czechoslovakia, in 1938–39, Hungary took a large slice for itself. After the Hitler–Stalin pact, which among other things allowed Stalin to annex part of Romania, Hungary demanded Transylvania. Romania could not refuse. The Germans ruled that the Hungarians should not recover all the territory they had lost in 1919, merely northern Transylvania. The Hungarians persecuted Romanians living there, and the Romanians persecuted Hungarians living elsewhere. Both nations were allied to Germany, which insisted they keep the peace, and both prepared to fight each other as soon as the war was over. Hungary also annexed part of Yugoslavia in 1941. Though Ceauşescu persecuted his Hungarian subjects, and though the present government of Hungary is a model of Balkan moderation, the Hungarians' history of ruthless aggression and oppression of their neighbours should not be forgotten. The neighbours remember.

After the Soviets liberated the Balkans, they restored the pre-war frontiers (adjusted to their own convenience) and declared that Leninist internationalism would solve the 'nationalities question'. They meant that in the future the Marxist dogma of the primacy of class over nation would resolve all difficulties. It is one of the more absurd errors of Communist theory.

The Hungarians in Romania suffered steady and increasing persecution from 1945 onwards. President Nicolae Ceauşescu stated the case succinctly: 'Our party and state are faced with the duty to take conscientious action to provide every one of our citizens with the sort of conditions under which the nation and the nationalities can fulfil themselves and, at the same time, make it possible for national differences to diminish and gradually to disappear under Communism.'

Hungarians in Romania resisted attempts to make them 'disappear'. The hundreds of Hungarian schools were almost all closed, or merged with Romanian schools, until only eight were left. The director of each of them was a Romanian. The Hungarian university at Cluj (Kolozsvar) was merged with a Romanian university. The few remaining Hungarian-language magazines and newspapers were heavily censored, very small, and worthless. Newspapers from Budapest were forbidden in Transylvania, and tourists from abroad were obliged to stay in government hotels: that is, Hungarians from Hungary were not permitted to stay with their relatives in Transylvania. Tourism, in any case, was severely discouraged.

In his last delirium, Ceauşescu endeavoured to impose a final solution to the Hungarian problem. Early in 1988, he announced that 8000 of the 13,000 villages in Romania would be wiped out, to be replaced by 'agro-industrial centres'. The ones to go were almost all Hungarian, and the programme was actively promoted until the end. Hungarians were also obliged to adopt Romanian Christian names to get jobs, and all Hungarian towns and villages in Romania were given Romanian names: Temesvar became Timisoara.

Now there is a new regime in Bucharest, which has ended all anti-Hungarian measures. The Christmas Revolution was warmly welcomed in Hungary, but there will be a long and difficult evolution before the two countries establish themselves as prospering democracies, and it is not at all certain that the anti-Hungarian animosities stirred up by Ceauşescu will be appeased by his overthrow. Hungarians continue to watch anxiously over their relatives in Romania, but they are now more concerned with those in Yugoslavia, who have been embroiled in the wars there.

## MACEDONIA

The southernmost of Yugoslavia's republics was called Macedonia, and took that name with it when the federation collapsed. Greece took umbrage, claiming that the ancient Macedonians were Greeks (a matter of dispute ever since King Philip of Macedon conquered Greece in the 4th century BC), and that therefore Macedonia could not use the name. For some years it laboured under the unfortunate acronym FYROM (Former Yugoslav Republic of Macedonia). The Greeks want it to call itself the Republic of Skopje, after its capital. They claim that Macedonia covets Greek Macedonia, notably its principal city and only port, Salonica.

Macedonia has a large Albanian minority, and although the Albanians are in no state to threaten anyone, it is always possible that an explosion in Kosovo (the southern Serbian province which has an Albanian majority – *see* Yugoslavia, p. 437) might spread to Macedonia. The United States has had a small contingent of observers along Macedonia's northern frontier since 1974, to keep an eye on things.

Bulgaria has fought four wars this century to annex Macedonia (it lost each of them). The Macedonians speak the same language and share the same variant of the Orthodox Church as the Bulgarians, and it is historical accident that they were annexed by Serbia when the Turks were driven out in 1912. It is at least possible that Macedonia will eventually be partitioned between Bulgaria and Albania. Greece's hostility to Macedonia (it maintained a full economic embargo until 1997) is extraordinarily shortsighted: Macedonia cannot conceivably endanger Greece, but Bulgaria is quite another matter.

## BESSARABIA

To the north-west of Romania is a separated Romanian territory, Bessarabia, most of it now the Republic of Moldavia (or Moldova). The czars conquered Bessarabia from Turkey in the 18th century. When the Russian empire collapsed in 1917, Romania claimed the lost province. In 1939, in his treaty with Hitler, Stalin stated that the Soviet Union would now recover Bessarabia, and would also annex the Bukovina, an area of northern Romania that had never been part of Russia. Stalin claimed its people were Ukrainians, like the people of eastern Poland and eastern Czechoslovakia, areas which he also annexed. In June 1940, immediately after the defeat of France and Britain's expulsion from the continent, the Soviet foreign minister, Molotov, informed the Romanians of their fate. He scrawled the new line on a map, in thick pencil, carelessly including areas of Moldavia that had never been part of Russia. The Soviets insisted on imposing the Molotov line.

Exactly a year later, when Hitler invaded the Soviet Union, the Romanians joined him. They recovered their lost territories, and Hitler permitted them also to annex Odessa and its hinterland, which they called Transnistria. It was a short-lived empire. When the tide turned, the Soviet Union took back Moldavia and the Bukovina, adding eastern Czechoslovakia for good measure.

In the Balkan wars, 1912–13, and in both world wars, Romania and Bulgaria contested the southern Dobrudja, an area in the Danube delta. It is now Romanian again. Stalin may have amputated north-east Romania, but he restored its territories to the south and west.

When Ukraine voted its independence on 1 December 1991, Romania announced that it intended to reclaim the Bukovina and southern Moldavia, territories that had been part of Romania before the war, which Stalin had transferred to Ukraine. It clearly anticipated that Moldavia would rejoin Romania in due course, and would wish to recover its Black Sea province. Easier said than done. Though there are undoubtedly still many Romanians living in that region, it is chiefly populated by Turks and Ukrainians – and Russians. They may have a choice of misfortunes, to join their futures with the miseries of independent Ukraine, Romania or possibly independent Moldavia, but it is more probable that Ukraine will refuse to countenance any further change in the border.

The problems of Moldavia are compounded by another of Stalin's territorial arrangements: he added a sliver of Ukraine, east of the Dneister, to his new Soviet Socialist Republic of Moldavia, and then populated it with Russians. A Russian army has remained there since the break-up of the Soviet Union in 1991. Its people claim to have seceded from Moldavia, and there was serious fighting

against the government in 1992, which cost about 500 lives. The Russians then intervened and imposed peace – in effect protecting the Trans-Dneistrians. They do not wish to join Ukraine. They want their territory to return to Mother Russia, despite the great distance that now separates them.

As for Moldavia, it refused to join the Commonwealth of Independent States but has not yet joined itself to Romania. It may yet do so.

## ALBANIA

Albania was and remains by far the most backward nation in Europe. It was liberated from the Turks in the first Balkan War in 1912 but did not form anything resembling a centralized government until 1920. Its dominant political figure was a Muslim tribal leader from the eastern mountains, Ahmet Bey Zogu of Mati. He made himself King Zog I in 1928. Albania's chief resources are its ports, Durrës (Dyrrhachium to the Romans, Durrazzo to the Italians), and Vlorë (Valona). They control the entrance to the Adriatic (there are no natural ports on the Italian side), and Italy coveted them and remains closely interested in Albanian stability. Greece is also closely concerned with Albania, particularly the southern region, Northern Epiros, which has a Greek population.

In 1939, as Hitler led Europe into war, Mussolini occupied Albania and made it a province of Italy. The country was fought over during the war, and emerged a Communist satellite of Yugoslavia, ruled by the most reclusive of all Communist dictators, Enver Hoxha. He subsequently repudiated every friendship and alliance, bitterly denouncing Soviet revisionism in the 1960s, and prepared for war by building hundreds of thousands of bunkers across the countryside. Albania is still dotted with small, concrete structures, of no use except, sometimes, as stables.

Hoxha died in 1985 and his successors made few changes in his policies. They were all swept away in due course, in the great gale that blew up in the north in 1989. A new government emerged, led by Sali Berisha, which claimed to be anti-Communist but which completely lacked administrative skills or democratic sense. Berisha staged a blatantly fraudulent election in 1996, which he claimed to win.

In the mid-1990s, with Albania subsisting on its own meagre resources and subsidies from abroad, various crooks started pyramid schemes. They advertised heavily on television, promising that investors would reap many thousand per cent profits. The difference from other countries was that a very high proportion of the Albanian population, utterly ignorant of the most elementary economic sense, put their every penny into the schemes – and the government, apparently, supported them.

Like pyramid schemes through the ages, these all collapsed early in 1997. People who had lost their savings, their houses and their every possession took to the streets in protest. The government collapsed in confusion and bloodshed. Rioters opened the prisons (releasing the Hoxha regime's leaders, including Hoxha's widow) and broke into arsenals. The police and armed forces disintegrated, and heavily armed gangs fought each other through the cities. Tens of thousands fled across the Adriatic to Italy and finally the UN Security Council authorized Italy to organize a rescue. About 5000 troops were sent to restore some sort of order: there were 2500 Italians, 1000 French, and contingents from Greece and Spain.

Elections were held in June 1997, which were won by a former Communist called Fatos Nano, who had promised to repay $1 billion worth of the pyramid schemes' losses. Since there was no money at all in the treasury and no foreign promise of any such sum, voters were clearly going to be disappointed. They had kept their guns. At the same time, a third of the electorate voted to restore the monarchy, in the person of Zog's son, a South African arms dealer who calls himself King Leka I. Albania ends the 20th century as it began it, with few hopes of escape from its poverty, a highly unstable government, and the prospect of continued foreign intervention.

## BULGARIA

Despite all the movements of population of the 20th century, there remains a considerable Turkish community in Bulgaria, several hundred thousand strong, perhaps as many as 1.5 million. It is impossible to be more precise. Bulgaria under the Communists denied that there were any Turks at all, and in 1983 set out to prove the point by ordering all citizens to adopt Bulgarian names. The decree was accompanied by various punitive measures. It was contrary to Communist doctrine, not to mention the U N Declaration on Human Rights and the Helsinki Final Act, although standard Balkan practice. About 320,000 Bulgarian Turks fled the country in the summer of 1989, and settled in Turkey, which welcomed them as a matter of principle, while finding considerable difficulty in absorbing them. About 50,000 of the refugees returned home, after discovering that Turkey's economic problems were worse than Bulgarian persecution.

The anti-Turkish hostility whipped up by the Communist regime was not artificial: it survived the change in government in November 1989. One of the first big opposition rallies held in Sofia after the fall of the Communist dictator, Todor Zhivkov, was addressed by a series of dissidents, one of whom called for a repeal of all anti-Turkish legislation. He was roundly booed by the crowd, and denounced as a traitor. Despite this popular animosity to the Turks, the new government lifted all restrictions on the Turks' freedom of worship and permitted them to use their own names. Early in 1990, just three months after the change of government, there were anti-Turkish demonstrations all over the country, with the crowds denouncing the new regime. It was a striking sign of the longevity of the old quarrels. The Bulgars had not forgotten or forgiven the long centuries of Turkish rule or the 'Bulgarian atrocities' of the 1870s.

---

## FURTHER READING

Brogan, Patrick, *Eastern Europe, 1939–1989*, London, Bloomsbury, 1990

# THE COMMONWEALTH OF INDEPENDENT STATES
## (Formerly the Soviet Union)

The final collapse of the Soviet Union in 1991 was inglorious and painful, but it was not violent. The beast was dead when the republics proclaimed their independence and went their separate ways. The last spasm of the old system, the attempted coup in Moscow in August 1991, turned out to be no more than the death-throes of a regime that was already moribund.

When the presidents of Russia, Byelorussia and Ukraine signed the new Treaty of Brest-Litovsk on 8 December 1991, declaring the Soviet Union dissolved and setting up a new Commonwealth of their three Slav republics, no one imagined that a sweet tranquillity would now prevail across the cold wastes from Poland to Sakhalin. On the contrary, the peaceful end of the U S S R was evidently the first necessary step in a settling of accounts between scores of competing nationalities. The three Baltic republics, which won their indepen-dence in the aftermath of the coup, were already grappling with the problems of the Russian and other Slav minorities left behind by the retreat of Communism, as well as the catastrophic economic legacy of Leninism. Moldavia was facing the danger of a Russian secessionist movement in its eastern districts, even as it tried to establish its own independence, and hesitated between rejoining Romania or taking part in the new non-Soviet Commonwealth. The rivalries and hatreds of Armenians and Azerbaijanis were liable to resume violently at any moment, and scores of similar disputes in Central Asia, and in Russia itself, were on the verge of exploding. There was already a small-scale civil war under way in Georgia; it culminated in the first coup in one of the former Soviet republics on 6 January 1992.

This is the legacy of the czars as well as the commissars, but there can be no doubt what was the chief cause of all the miseries and violence in the former empire. Lenin and Stalin betrayed the Russian Revolution of March 1917, imposing a uniform tyranny upon a hundred nationalities. Each one of those nations was oppressed. Thousands, sometimes millions of its citizens were murdered, and an omnipresent and inefficient despotism ruled it for over 70 years. Lenin's legacy was not merely death and oppression. It was a miserable standard of living and an economic system that finally collapsed in the winter of 1991. There is no reason for any of these peoples to feel the least loyalty to Moscow, and none of them does.

The decisive event in the final break-up of the Soviet Union was the secession of Ukraine. It was the second-most-populous and second-richest of Soviet Republics and was also the one with the oldest links to Russia. Kiev, not Moscow, is the mother city of the Russias. Ukraine was conquered by the czars in a long series of wars from the 16th to the 18th centuries. Peter the Great and Catherine the Great drove out the Ottoman Turks, but Ukrainians were only admitted to partnership with the Russians in the great imperial expansion of the 19th century if they renounced their own nationality. The czars strove to suppress language, religion and culture in Ukraine over two centuries. Ukraine was never a full partner with Russia, like Castile and Aragon, or Scotland and England. England and Ireland are a closer parallel.

Then came the Revolution. Ukraine was first ceded to Germany, in the Treaty of Brest-Litovsk, as the price Lenin paid for peace early in 1918. A year later, when Germany was defeated in the West, the Ukrainians, like the Caucasians and Central Asians, seized their independence. For a brief moment, Ukraine was a nation again. The Russians could not permit such a drastic secession, nor could the Bolsheviks tolerate a repudiation of Marxism. Ukraine, and almost all the other possessions of the czars, were reconquered in an atrocious civil war, which was followed by famine. Then in 1930–33, Ukraine was subjected by Stalin to one of the great crimes of the century, a deed strictly comparable to Hitler's massacre of the Jews or Pol Pot's destruction of Cambodia.

The collectivization of agriculture in Ukraine killed at least 6 million people. At least 14 million were killed in the whole country. First, millions of peasants were shot or shipped to Siberia or the far north, where the great majority died. They were defined as kulaks, rich peasants, the class enemy. Then a famine was deliberately induced by the Soviet government, to shatter Ukrainian nationalism and to break the peasantry. Impossible quotas for grain production were set, and Soviet troops surrounded villages, emptied them of every grain of wheat and then left them to starve. Peasants were prevented from leaving their villages, renamed collectives, and there were many cases of infanticide and cannibalism. This was not all. Controls were set up at the borders to prevent anyone taking bread to starving Ukraine.

Simultaneously, an equally atrocious campaign was waged against the Kazhaks and the Cossaks in the north Caucasus, the region where Mikhail Gorbachev was growing up. Over a million Kazhaks were killed, nearly a third of the population. They had been nomads throughout history, and now they were forced to enter collective farms, where they starved to death.

Stalin killed more Soviet citizens than Hitler did. When Gorbachev's *glasnost* finally allowed the truth to be published, television cameras were taken into the woods to show the people the mass graves. Some people remembered hearing the sound of guns every night for months, as hundreds of thousands were slaughtered. Investigators began to dig, and found vast graveyards, each body with a hole in the skull.

Is there any wonder that over 80 per cent of Ukrainians voted for independence? Gorbachev pleaded that he was no Stalin, that several members of his immediate family were murdered – but expecting Ukrainians to accept a continuation of the Soviet Union would be strictly comparable to expecting Jews to vote for a reformed Third Reich directed by a kinder and gentler Nazi party.

The sight of the Red Flag being lowered over the Kremlin on Christmas Day 1991, carried around the world on live television, was a powerful symbol of the revolution that had taken place. All that remained, symbolically, was to dig up the dead and mummified murderers from Red Square and the Kremlin wall, and consign them to the flames at the nearest crematorium. Unfortunately, overcoming their legacy will be far more difficult. The Bolshevik Revolution and the Communist government of the Soviet Union, 1917–1991, one of the greatest disasters and greatest crimes in history, cannot be swept under the rug and forgotten.

The struggles of the successor states will continue for years, and it would be utterly futile to predict their ultimate shape. The three Baltic states, provided that they can resolve the question of citizenship and civil rights for their Russian minorities, will become associated with the other Scandinavian countries, and they hope eventually to join the European Union. In the short run, they will have to pass through crisis and recession, like the rest of the former U S S R, as their economies are reconstructed out of the rubble.

Moldavia expects to rejoin Romania eventually, though its frontiers are in doubt and the question of its own minorities must also be decided. Georgia and Armenia will be independent, but will seek protection from the Turkish sea surrounding them, and continued, violent conflicts between all the nationalities of the Caucasus are a lamentable certainty. The possibilities of similar conflicts in Central Asia are almost infinite, and a general reordering of borders and alliances, with Afghanistan, Iran and Turkey playing their part, is a strong probability.

## THE RUSSIAN FEDERATION

| | |
|---|---|
| Geography | 6,593,850 sq. miles (17,078,005 sq. km). |
| Population | 148.2 million, 81.5% of them Russians. The Federation has over 100 nationalities. It is divided into 21 Republics, and 89 Autonomous Regions (*oblasts*) and Autonomous Areas (*okrugs*). |
| GNP per capita | $2240. |

Modern Russia is haunted by its dreadful history, and not just the crimes and follies of Lenin and Stalin. The first war and the first defeat of the Russian Federation after the break-up of the Soviet Union, in Chechnya, had its origins in the 18th and 19th centuries when the Russian empire conquered the Caucases. There is even a literary monument to the 40-year war of conquest in Chechnya, *Hadji Murat*, by Tolstoy.

The Caucases are a stupendous mountain range running west to east between **393** the Black Sea and the Caspian, with narrow passes along the coasts. To the south are the wide valleys of Georgia and Azerbaijan and beyond that, yet another series of mountains. There are dozens of peoples guarding their own traditions and languages throughout the region, and the Russians fought their way through all of them until they came up against Turkey and Persia – which were contending with an equal diversity of peoples on their side of the mountains.

The most difficult to subdue of them all were the Chechens on the north Caucasus. They are a Turkic and Muslim people and to their east lies Dagestan and to their west Ingushetia and North Ossetia. When the Russian empire collapsed in 1917, they all seized some measure of independence, and then the Bolsheviks recaptured them all. Stalin remembered the Chechens' and the Ingush's hostility to Communism, and in February 1944, alleging that they had collaborated with the Germans in their drive towards the Caspian oilfields, he sent the K G B to deport the entire nation to Kazakhstan.

Perhaps a few German patrols had penetrated Chechnya in 1942 as the Wehrmacht reached Stalingrad, but the Chechens had little opportunity to welcome them. Most young men were away, fighting with the Red Army. After their return, they too were sent to Central Asia. They found their families subsisting on the steppe: they had been shipped hundreds of miles east in cattle trucks and then dumped on the plains, in mid-winter, and told to make themselves at home. Scores of thousands died there. In 1957, Khruschev admitted that the deportation had been an error and allowed them to return.

This frightful episode was, of course, well remembered in Chechnya. The Soviet Union began to break apart in the early 1990s and when Communist hardliners arrested Gorbachev and tried to turn the clock back, in August 1991, there was a coup in Grozny, the Chechen capital. The local party supported the new regime in Moscow (which surrendered after three days) and the opposition promptly drove them out of Grozny and proclaimed Chechnya independent. Their leader was an air force general, Dzhokar Dudayev. When Gorbachev resumed authority in Moscow, he sent troops to Chechnya to restore order. They were besieged at the airport, and forced humiliatingly to retreat.

The U S S R finally disintegrated in September. The next month, Chechnya staged a presidential election, which Dudayev won. On Christmas Day, 1991, the Red Flag was hauled down from atop the Kremlin and the old Russian tricolour replaced it. The three Caucasian Soviet Republics proclaimed their independence (Georgia was promptly engulfed in civil war and Armenia and Azerbaijan went to war with each other). Boris Yeltsin had by then replaced Gorbachev in Moscow and for the next three years he allowed Chechnya to go its own way. He had more important concerns.

The Caucasus region seized the opportunity to revive its old traditions. The Ingush and Ossetians started a minor civil war: the Ingush living in the northern part of the North Ossetian Republic rose in revolt, demanding that the frontier be adjusted to put them in neighbouring Ingushetia. The Ossetian majority reacted with Caucasian ferocity: at least five people were killed in a first riot and the civil disorders were put down only with difficulty.

By the latter part of 1994, Yeltsin was well enough established to contemplate the dangers of allowing peripheral republics to break away from the federation.

Tartarstan, on the Volga, had gone to the brink of a declaration of independence, but had then accepted almost complete autonomy – which all the other republics and *oblasts* of the country then demanded, too. There was no knowing where the fissiparous tendency would end.

By then, there was a general breakdown in order in Moscow and much of the rest of the Federation, and Chechen gangsters played a large part in the criminalization of Russian life. Chechnya had become a base for every sort of smuggler, drug-runner and gun-runner, with the active participation of Dudayev and his cronies. The self-proclaimed Chechen Republic was a criminal enterprise.

This was not the main reason that Yeltsin ordered in the tanks, though it was one of his main justifications. He was chiefly motivated by old-fashioned nationalism, and fear that every minor nationality in Russia would follow the example of Lithuania, Central Asia and Ukraine itself, and set up as independent states. He was egged on by military men and nationalists in his entourage. His minister of defence, Pavel Grachev, who had sent his tanks against the Russian parliament when the Communists tried a coup against Yeltsin in October 1993, assured the president that one regiment of motorized infantry could recapture Grozny in two hours. Yeltsin believed him, and without making any preparations worth the name, the Russian army was ordered to occupy Grozny on 11 December 1994.

The war was a disaster for the Russians from beginning to end. The Chechens, unlike the Russians, had been preparing for three years and were heavily armed. Three Russian columns attacked Grozny, and each was stopped in its tracks. Russian tanks and armoured cars were isolated and burnt (over 200 men were lost in the first phase of the war), and conscript infantrymen were shot down by Chechen snipers as they tried to advance into the city. On New Year's Eve, the Russians tried again and were once again defeated. After their advance stalled, Russian units were surrounded and decimated. Soon they depended on air support to survive, and the Russians started bombing Grozny. The citizens, most of them elderly Russians, cowered in basements without heat, light or running water, and with very little food. It was a scene out of World War II in Europe. Chechen resistance centred on the parliament building, and they held it against the full might of the Russian army for five weeks. The Russians poured troops and armour into the city, and finally took the building on 19 January.

Resistance continued in the suburbs for two more months until the Chechens finally withdrew in March. A human rights group calculated that between 20,000 and 30,000 people had been killed: 1400 of them Russian troops, a similar number of Chechen fighters, the rest civilians. Later, it was established that the Russian military casualties were far higher, about 4500. Most Chechens had left the capital: the people who remained were Russians, so they suffered the most. By then, Grozny looked like Berlin in 1945 or Vukovar in 1991. Meanwhile, the Russians had attempted to capture other towns and villages, and had launched an indiscriminate bombing campaign throughout the republic. By late spring, they claimed victory. It was the 50th anniversary of the end of World War II and President Clinton went to Moscow in May to attend a victory parade. It was an embarrassing occasion.

On 13 June, the Russians announced that they had taken Shatoi, a village in the Caucasus foothills, the last centre of Chechen resistance. The next day a Chechen force 200 strong, under the command of Shamil Basayev, crossed the border and seized Budyonnovsk, a small town 40 miles inside Russia itself. They took 2000 hostages, and gathered them into the local hospital. The Russian army attacked the hospital twice, causing great damage to the building and killing a number of hostages, but both times failed to break through Chechen defences. The prime minister, Victor Chernomyrdin, went to Budyonnovsk to negotiate with the Chechens and on the 19th the commando was allowed to leave.

They released most of their hostages, and returned to Chechnya in a convoy, taking 150 people with them, including a number of volunteers. These people were released at the border, and Basayev and his men vanished into the mountains.

On 30 June the Chechens agreed to a ceasefire. This apparently meant an end to full-scale warfare and the beginning of guerrilla operations. Russia left 60,000 troops patrolling Chechnya but their hold on the republic was most tenuous. A new president and government were installed: they did not dare stay in the country.

On 9 January 1996, in another commando raid into Kizalyar, a town in Dagestan, east of Chechnya, Chechen fighters again seized numerous hostages and moved them into the local hospital. This time, their commander was Salman Raduyev, Dudayev's son-in-law. Once again, there were negotiations between the two sides and the Russians agreed to allow the commando to return home.

Raduyev led his convoy of guerrillas and 150 or so hostages and set out on 10 January. They reached a small village on the border, Pervomayskoye, that evening, and there the Russian army tried to capture them. The convoy was stopped and the guerrillas and their hostages took refuge in the village. The Russians attacked with infantry and tanks, and were beaten off. The siege and fighting lasted for a week. After successive attacks were defeated, the Russians announced that the Chechens had killed their hostages (which was untrue) and then bombed the village flat. On the 18th, Chechens from Chechnya attacked the Russians' rear and scored an important tactical victory. The Russians were taken completely by surprise. In the confusion, the men trapped in the village, including Raduyev, escaped home. Most of the hostages had survived and were either found in the village or were released by the Chechens soon after they crossed the border.

This fiasco concerned Yeltsin greatly, because the Russian presidential election was due in June and July. On 7 March, a Chechen commando stormed the railway station in Grozny and occupied part of the city. It was driven out after heavy fighting, and on 31 March Yeltsin ordered an end to all combat operations. It was a mere gesture. The air force continued its operations. Dudayev was killed in a Russian air raid, on 21 April. This proved no loss: the men who then rose to the top in Chechnya were less contaminated than he by links to the mafia. Dudachev's immediate successor, Zelman Yandarbiyev, went to Moscow in June and signed a peace agreement with Boris Yeltsin, which the president could claim as a victory in the election campaign.

In the event, Chechnya played little part in the election. In the first round of voting, Yeltsin was faced with an old-line Communist and a popular retired general, Alexander Lebed. Yeltsin came in first and promptly co-opted Lebed by making him head of national security, with the mission of solving the Chechen crisis.

Yeltsin won his election in the second round on 3 July. By then, the Russian army had broken the ceasefire and resumed full-scale operations throughout Chechnya. On 6 August, the day before Yeltsin's formal inauguration, Russia suffered its worst military defeat since the disasters of 1941. The Chechens recaptured their capital, Grozny, driving the Russians in rout before them. A Russian garrison held on to the parliament building in the city centre (it had been the Chechens' stronghold in December 1994), but within ten days the Chechens had reduced the Russians to a few pockets in the suburbs. Lebed then flew to Chechnya and opened direct negotiations with the rebel government. On 22 August, he abruptly abandoned the entire war. That was the day the Russian command had planned a new, all-out assault on Grozny. Lebed vetoed it.

Instead, he signed a peace agreement with Aslan Maskhadov, the Chechens' commanding general (and who was elected president in 1997). It provided that all Russian troops would withdraw from Chechnya. In exchange, the Chechens agreed that the question of independence should be postponed for five years, until 31 December 2001, when the two governments would agree on the 'basic principles of relations'.

Thus the Russian army, which had defeated Hitler and then held Nato at bay in Europe for 40 years, prompting constant fears that it might suddenly sweep from the Elbe to the Atlantic in a week, was defeated by a small nation of Caucasian guerrilla fighters. The defeat in Afghanistan had been bad enough. This was the ultimate humiliation.

The last Russian troops left Chechnya in January 1997, their tails between their legs. The war had cost about 50,000 lives, including 4500 Russian soldiers.

Chechnya has enjoyed *de facto* independence ever since. It is free but it is ruined: 650,000 people, at least, have lost their homes and all industry has been destroyed. No other country recognizes it, and it is entirely probable that the Russians will eventually try to reassert their authority there.

## ARMENIA

In February 1988, without any warning, reports reached Moscow of massive demonstrations in Armenia. Hundreds of thousands of people were demanding that Nagorno-Karabakh, an area of the neighbouring republic, Azerbaijan, be transferred to Armenia. There had been nothing like it since the early days of the Soviet Union, and there could be no doubt that this sudden upsurge of nationalistic fervour was the result of Gorbachevian *glasnost*.

The Caucasus, which lie between the Caspian Sea and the Black Sea, were annexed by czarist Russia in the 19th century. The territory comprises two Christian nations, Georgia and Armenia, and a much larger Muslim republic, Azerbaijan. The Azeris are, in fact, Turkish, cousins to the 40 million Turks of Turkey, the 6 or 8 million Azeris of Iran and the millions more in Soviet Central

## Caucases

**Armenia**

| | |
|---|---|
| Geography: | 11,490 sq miles (45,092 sq. km), the size of Belgium or Maryland. |
| Population: | 3.8 million. |
| GNP: | $730. |
| Refugees: | 150,000. |
| Casualties: | The war with Azerbaijan, 1991–4, killed 25,000 people. |

**Azerbaijan**

| | |
|---|---|
| Geography: | 33,430 sq miles (86,583 sq. km), the size of Scotland or South Carolina. |
| Population: | 7.5 million. |
| GNP: | $480. |
| Refugees: | 250,000 Azeris from Armenia, 550,000 from Nagorno-Karabakh and other disputed districts. |

**Georgia**

| | |
|---|---|
| Geography: | 17,410 sq miles (45,092 sq. km), the size of Denmark or Maine. |
| Population: | 5.4 million. |
| GNP: | $440. |
| Refugees: | 285,000 internal refugees, mostly Georgians from Abkhazia and South Ossetia. |
| Casualties: | 15,000 killed in three civil wars, 1991–3. |

Asia. It is this wider dimension that enabled the Azeris to win control of Nagorno-Karabakh in the first place, and to retain it ever since.

Parts of czarist Armenia (Kars) were reconquered by Turkey in World War I. The fate of the Armenians under Turkish rule (*see* Terrorism: Forlorn hopes, pp. 620–25) and the pressures of the Azeris naturally led the Armenians (and the Georgians) to look to Moscow for protection. During the confusion following the Russian Revolution, Armenia was set up as an independent state, and there was a brief effort by Turks to establish a pan-Turkic commonwealth stretching from the Bosphoros to Samarkand. In the general settlement in 1923, Turkey kept Kars, and the Azeris were allowed to annex Nagorno-Karabakh as well as another enclave in south-west Armenia, as part of the Bolsheviks' effort to pacify the non-Russian area they had inherited from the czar.

Meanwhile, national movements in Armenia and Georgia were brutally suppressed, after Stalin was delegated by Lenin to settle the problem. In subsequent years, until the 1950s, the citizens of these two republics could at least take comfort in the thought that, if the Russians governed Armenia and Georgia, Georgians and an Armenian governed Russia: Stalin and the head of the KGB, Beria, were Georgians, and Mikoyan, who for many years was economics minister of the USSR, and was later president, was an Armenian.

In 1988 the large majority of the people of Nagorno-Karabakh (126,000) were **398** Armenians, and the remaining 37,000 were Azeris. It was an autonomous region of the Azerbaijan republic, and its people were apparently driven to protest by the corruption and inefficiency of the region's authorities, and also because of a certain amount of ethnic persecution.

The first demonstrations were in Stepanakert, the region's capital, on 13 February 1988. Two Azeris were killed, though that fact was not revealed until later. The demonstrations spread to Yerevan, capital of Armenia, a week later. Soon, there were daily gatherings of hundreds of thousands of people. The local authorities were quite unable to control the demonstrators and therefore joined them. On 20 February, the Nagorno-Karabakh regional assembly formally demanded that the region be transferred to Armenia. It was a revolutionary demand. The vote was 110 for secession from Azerbaijan, 17 against and 13 abstentions, and was made along strictly ethnic lines: the abstentions were presumably the senior Communist officials. The party first secretary in the district was dismissed and replaced by a man who had voted for secession.

Western reporters were not allowed to visit Armenia, but videotapes brought out of Yerevan showed enormous crowds of people peacefully demonstrating in front of the city opera house. The organizers of the demonstration policed the event, and elected a committee to represent them to the authorities.

The situation became much more serious on 28 February, when there were anti-Armenian riots in Sumgait, an Azeri town on the Caspian. They were apparently sparked off by the belated report that two Azeris had been killed in the 13 February demonstration in Nagorno-Karabakh, and by the arrival of over 5000 Azeri refugees from Kafan in Armenia. There was a minority of 15,000–20,000 Armenians in Sumgait, a town with a population of 223,000, and during the riots, they were hunted through the streets, beaten and, some of them, murdered. The Soviet radio described the events as a pogrom, and confirmed that 32 people (26 Armenians and six Azeris) had been killed and 197 seriously injured. A survivor reported to the Armenian community in Moscow that the mob had stormed a maternity hospital and that one pregnant woman had been killed, her womb ripped open and the baby mutilated. Unofficial reports in Moscow stated that over 300 people had been killed. Whether the reports were true or not, it was most significant that Armenians could believe such horrors of the Azeris.

Troops were used to restore order: another report stated that eight soldiers were killed. This was the first time in over 60 years that the Soviet government admitted officially that troops had been used in suppressing civil disturbances (in fact, there had been many occasions when troops were so employed). In Sumgait, the Armenians were taken to army barracks and makeshift refugee centres to protect them from the Azeris, and a night-time curfew was imposed for two weeks. The mayor of Sumgait and other top officials were fired.

On 23 March, the presidium of the Supreme Soviet (federal parliament) in Moscow flatly refused to consider the boundaries question. It issued a statement denouncing attempts to change the boundaries through street demonstrations, called on the army to maintain order in the two republics and banned unofficial demonstrations. The government then flooded Yerevan with troops, and a mass demonstration planned for 25 March was cancelled. A general strike in Nagorno-Karabakh lasted a few days longer, and then was quietly ended.

**399**

In May, there were further disturbances both in Yerevan and in Baku. In the latter, the disturbances were provoked by reports of a riot in Ararat, a town in Armenia, while the Yerevan demonstrations were provoked by reports of the sentences given at the first trials of the people responsible for the murders in Sumgait. (The murderers received sentences of 3 to 15 years, which the Armenians found too lenient.) On 19 May, 200,000 Armenians demonstrated in Yerevan, and there were also reports of strikes and demonstrations in Nagorno-Karabakh. The central government responded by abruptly sacking the first secretaries in both republics on 21 May.

That deed was accomplished by special emissaries of the politburo in Moscow. Yigor Ligachev, who was second in seniority to Gorbachev in the Soviet government, went to Baku and promised that the status of Nagorno-Karabakh would not be changed. News of this promise promptly sparked further strikes and demonstrations in Armenia, and in the disputed region.

The troubles resumed in July 1988: a demonstration of 10,000 people closed the Yerevan airport on 6 July, and one demonstrator was killed and several wounded as 3000 troops broke it up. Then the regional assembly in Nagorno-Karabakh voted simply to secede from Azerbaijan. The presidium of the Soviet parliament met to consider the issue on 18 July, and the debate was televised: Gorbachev was shown denouncing those who stirred up the dispute as enemies of *perestroika*. Armenia's demand for the transfer was turned down unanimously.

The real trouble began on 22 November. On that day, there were riots in several cities in Azerbaijan, including the two largest, Baku and Kirovabad. Troops were called in to restore order, and three soldiers were killed trying to protect the Armenian quarter of Kirovabad. The Armenians resumed demonstrating, and two people were killed in Yerevan on 25 November. The government imposed a curfew on the city, and then a general pogrom developed in both Azerbaijan and Armenia. Tens of thousands of people were driven from their homes in both republics. Before, there had been 475,000 Armenians living in Azerbaijan and smaller numbers of Azeris living in Armenia. Soon there was a mass movement of populations between the two, and the refugees had to be put in tent cities. Twenty-eight people were killed (by official count) in the last week of November, and by that time, 40,000 Armenians had fled Azerbaijan and 30,000 Azeris had fled Armenia. By early December, the total of refugees had risen to over 100,000.

Armenia seized its independence along with the rest of the non-Russian Soviet Republics in 1991. It held its first free election, and the presidency was won by Levon Ter-Petrossian, an intellectual and anti-Communist, who promised that Nagorno-Karabakh would be reunited to the motherland. The war with Azerbaijan continued and intensified, and in a surprising, and probably temporary, instance of David beating Goliath, the Armenians defeated Azeri efforts to occupy Nagorno-Karabakh and drove them out of the territory that separates the district from Armenia proper. Then they seized a swathe of Azeri territory around Nagorno-Karabakh: by the time of the ceasefire, in 1994, they occupied a fifth of Azerbaijan.

By then, the war had killed 25,000 people, mostly civilians. There were

250,000 refugees in Azerbaijan from Armenia and a further 550,000 expelled from Nagorno-Karabakh and other territories occupied by the Armenians. UNHCR counted 150,000 Armenian refugees, from Nagorno-Karabakh and from Azerbaijan – though many other refugees had been absorbed into the general population, and in 1995 90,000 Armenian refugees left the country, mostly going to Russia.

As soon as Nagorno-Karabakh proclaimed its independence, Azerbaijan and Turkey imposed a blockade on Armenia. The roads through Georgia were unreliable (there was a civil war there), and the country was almost completely isolated. For months on end during the cruel Caucasian winters, there was no electricity and people burnt their furniture to keep warm. There were shortages of everything: whatever resources the state could find went to buy arms on the international arms market.

Armenia survived thanks to the diaspora, particularly in America. Armenians abroad sent money to help their motherland, and persuaded the American Congress to vote generous aid to Armenia. It receives more money per head than any other country except Israel. That came to $126 million in 1995. Ironically, the other country that allowed Armenia to defeat the Azeris is Iran, which for its own economic reasons allowed trade across the border. The fact that Iran and the US remain dedicated enemies does not affect the situation in the Caucases. By 1996, the economy had recovered almost to its Soviet levels and was shaking off its Leninist past.

Ter-Petrossian showed increasingly dictatorial tendencies. In 1994 he banned a political party, Dashnak, which presented a threat to him. It is the organization that supported the terrorist campaign against Turkish diplomats, and boasted of murdering 41 of them. In 1996 he rigged a presidential election (his minister of defence remarked on television that he would not recognize victory by the opposition, even if it obtained 100 per cent of the vote). Americans became increasingly embarrassed at the nature of the government they supported.

Late in 1997, Ter-Petrossian, responding to international pressure, suggested that in the future Nagorno-Karabakh should content itself with autonomy within Azerbaijan. In February 1998 he was deposed by his own government and forced to resign, and replaced by the prime minister, Robert Kocharian, formerly the military commander in Nagorno-Karabakh (who won a presidential election in March). The army and political establishment in Yerevan would not tolerate anything less than the permanent annexation of Nagorno-Karabakh.

The Russians support the Azeris because Azerbaijan controls one of the world's largest oil fields. American oil companies resent being excluded from the development of those riches, and Iran is negotiating for a pipeline from the Azeri Caspian down to the Gulf. However obdurate Mr Kocharian and his supporters, in the end the Azeris seem likely to win at the diplomatic table what they lost on the battlefield.

## GEORGIA

The first disorders in Georgia broke out in April 1989, in Abkhazia. This was an autonomous region in northern Georgia, along the Black Sea, inhabited by 183,000 Abkhazians, who are a Turkic Muslim minority. They enjoyed a certain measure of independence from Tbilisi, though under the strict control of the party, and now that the party had disintegrated, the Abkhazians demanded real independence. The government in Tbilisi refused to consider any such thing. The Abkhazians' example was followed by the 165,000 South Ossetians, whose language is related to Persian. They demanded union with their cousins across the mountains in southern Russia, in the North Ossetian Republic. About 300 Ossetians were killed between 1989 and 1991, and Georgian militias raided Ossetia, burning villages, and laid siege to the main town, Tskhinvali. In the course of 1991, about half the South Ossetians fled across the mountains to North Ossetia.

Only 67 per cent of Georgia's population is Georgian. In all, there are 15 nationalities in the republic including 9 per cent Armenians (450,000 people), 7 per cent Russians (372,000) and 95,000 Greeks. This diversity is typical of every one of the former Soviet republics. So far, the Georgian attempt to repress all its minorities has not been repeated, though some, including the Baltics, have been tempted.

On 9 April 1989, a large demonstration in Tbilisi was broken up with great brutality by Soviet troops. Tanks were sent into the centre of the city, and the troops beat the demonstrators over the head with spades, and used poison gas on them. Nineteen people were killed, most of them women. It was soon apparent that the violent break-up of the Tbilisi demonstration was an attempt by hardliners in Moscow to turn back the clock and reimpose Stalinist discipline upon the USSR. The massacre greatly stimulated Georgian nationalism, and on 19 April 1991, the Georgian parliament proclaimed the republic's independence, following the examples of the three Baltic states. It was the first non-Baltic republic to do so.

A month later, Georgia held its first free election and Zviad Gamsakhurdia won the presidency with 87 per cent of the vote. He was an intellectual nationalist and soon revealed himself a racist extremist of the worst sort. He proclaimed 'Georgia for the Georgians', meaning that he wanted to expel the third of the population who were non-Georgians. He insisted, for a start, that only those whose ancestors were Georgian in 1800 (before the Russian conquest) could claim citizenship now. The Ossetians and Abkhazians proclaimed their independence and started expelling the Georgians from their districts.

Gamsakhurdia sent troops into South Ossetia to 'cleanse' it of its non-Georgian population, just like the Serbs in Bosnia. Both sides fought with frightful atrocity, ripping out the eyes of their enemies or disembowelling them. The Georgians were losing, because their army was so inept, and there were soon 150,000 Georgian refugees.

Then the Russians stepped in to mediate. They assumed that the Georgians would eventually recover and reoccupy the province – and they did not want a flood of refugees pouring over the border into North Ossetia, in Russia.

The Abkhazians, meanwhile, proclaimed their own independence and started expelling the Georgians, but before Gamsakhurdia could deal with them, opposition to his increasing dictatorship led to a revolt in Tbilisi. The army and security forces split, and in December 1991 there was heavy fighting in the capital.

The dictator took refuge in a bunker under the parliament building, and held out for weeks before finally escaping, early in the New Year, leaving the centre of the town in ruins. The country was saved from dissolution by the return to Tbilisi of its most famous citizen, Edward Shevardnadze, former Soviet foreign minister (before that he was first secretary of the Georgian Communist Party). He was elected president.

The Georgians pulled back from the brink. Gamsakhurdia conveniently killed himself, or was rubbed out, and the new president set about resolving the disastrous problems he faced.

His first crisis was the lawlessness and banditry that followed the dissolution of the government. A full-scale civil war raged for a year. It did immense damage. Bandits sacked factories, government buildings and everything else that took their fancy. The bandits were known as the *Mkhedrioni*, or Horsemen. They almost destroyed the country. The fighting was only ended when the president gave them a general amnesty and allowed them to turn their energies to legitimate business and politics.

He was accused of making a bargain with the devil, and no one thought the *Mkhedrioni* would really give up violence, any more than the Sicilian Mafia would. Sure enough, they soon declared war on the president again, and there was a new fight to the death between them. On 29 August 1995 a car bomb nearly killed Shevardnadze. Several of his security men were arrested for the attempt. The *Mkhedrioni* tried again in February 1998. This time, 15 men attacked Shevardnadze's motorcade in the centre of Tbilisi with anti-tank grenades, rifles and heavy machine-guns. Several bodyguards were killed. The president was saved by his heavily-armoured Mercedes, which caught fire but survived.

Georgia's greatest crisis had been the Abkhazian war. Abkhazia was a very heterogenous region along the Black Sea, comprising the most fruitful parts of Georgia. It is the Colchis of classical times, where Jason found the golden fleece – and Medea. Stalin moved large numbers of Georgians into Abkhazia in the 1930s and later, and by 1990 only 18 per cent of the population was Abkhazian (they are a Muslim Caucasian tribe, like the Chechens). The Georgians comprised about 45 per cent. The province had enjoyed the delights of fictitious autonomy in Soviet times, which meant nothing then, but the Abkhazians turned it to their advantage in 1992.

They seized the opportunity of Georgian disarray to expel all the Georgians, about 260,000 people. They needed Russian help. When Shevardnadze finally marched his army into Abkhazia, it won easily and was engaged in mopping-up operations when the Russians intervened with heavy artillery. The Georgians were driven out again.

The president is in a stronger position now than during the civil wars, since the National Guard, the police and the various local militias have been brought under control, or at least appear to be answerable to the government. Even the local K G B more or less obeys Shevardnadze. He has declared war on corruption and violence, and might even win.

It would not mean, however, that he would control the country. Apart from the *Mkhedrioni* and the intractable after-effects of civil war, anarchy and hordes **403** of refugees, Shevardnadze has also to contend with the Russians, who are still present in force.

Georgia still depends on the Russians. Shevardnadze, after insisting on Georgia's full independence, finally agreed to join the Russian Commonwealth of Independent States, and to allow the Russians to keep their military and naval bases in Georgia. The rouble is the preferred medium of exchange, even though Shevardnadze introduced a national currency, and Georgia's freedom is something of a fiction.

In exchange, the Russians brokered a deal with the Ossetians, giving them a wide measure of autonomy in exchange for letting the refugees return. An agreement was signed in April 1996. Two years later, there are still about 20,000 Georgian refugees from the region, waiting to go home.

The Russians promised to do as much for Abkhazia, but have yet to deliver. The Georgians are still raging at Yeltsin's treachery. The Russian army is still there, as a peace-keeping force along Abkhazia's border, and any Georgian refugee who ventures home will be murdered.

The Georgians will settle for giving Abkhazia a great measure of autonomy and the return of the refugees. The Abkhazian leadership will have none of it. They would be outnumbered all over again.

If that sounds rather like Bosnia, it is. The one essential difference is that the Georgians have given up the xenophobia of their late president – at least for now. After a first spurt of Serbian ferocity, in which they rammed their language, religion and traditions down the minorities' throats, in preparation for driving them out, they now want to restore the comity of earlier times.

It is notoriously difficult to get genies back into bottles, and that is what Shevardnadze is trying to do. Yeltsin, in Chechnya, has set the Georgians a fine example of what not to do. But the Abkhazians will only accept a restoration of the *status quo ante* under extreme Russian pressure. Perhaps their leaders should be taken on a guided tour of Grozny, as a warning.

There is one other latent dispute in Georgia. In 1942, as the Wehrmacht advanced on the Caucases, Stalin detected signs of disloyalty among an oppressed Turkic tribe in Georgia, the Meskhetian Turks. So he expelled them *en masse* to Uzbekistan. With the collapse of the Soviet Union, that newly liberated republic immediately started persecuting them all over again, and they attempted to return to the home of their youth, or of their ancestors. Georgia has refused to let them back, and in 1996 there were 51,000 Meskhetian Turks stranded in Azerbaijan, expelled from Uzbekistan and refused admission to Georgia.

## HISTORY

Central Asia was conquered by the Russian empire in the 19th century. The ancient khanates of Khiva, Samarkand, Bokhara, Tashkent and Khokand were subjugated one after another with Russian thoroughness and brutality, and the empire continued to expand until it reached the Pamirs. Afghanistan was left as an independent buffer state between Russia and British India.

The Central Asians suffered severely under Bolshevism. Stalin's collectivization caused millions of deaths among the Kazakhs and Uzbeks and then

## CENTRAL ASIA

---

**Kazakhstan**

Population:     16.6 million; 500,000 Russians have left Kazakhstan since 1991. 154,000 Kazakhs had returned from other ex-Soviet Republics by 1996.
Size:           1,048,030 sq. miles (2,714, 387 sq. km).
GNP:            $1330.

**Tajikistan (Tadzhikistan)**

Population:     5.8 million, 62% Tajik, 23% Uzbek; 200,000 Russians have left since 1991. There are about 120,000 Tajik refugees in neighbouring countries.
Size:           55,251 sq. miles (143,071 sq. km).
GNP:            $340.
Casualties:     Between 35,000 and 70,000 people were killed.

**Turkmenistan**

Population:     4.5 million.
Size:           188,400 sq. miles (487, 954 sq. km).
GNP:            $920.

**Uzbekistan**

**Population:** 22.8 million; 24,000 Russians emigrated in 1996.
Size:           173,546 sq. miles (449,482 sq. km).

---

the economic policies of his successors devastated the region. Huge areas were converted to enormous cotton plantations and in due course turned into the largest dust-bowl in the world: the Aral Sea has dried up and the Caspian is in terminal decline because of improvident Soviet irrigation projects.

After the collapse of the Soviet Union, the four republics became independent, in theory, but were all still ruled by the same apparatchiks who had misgoverned them before (the president of Uzbekistan was re-elected in 1995 with a Bolshevik 99 per cent of the vote). Tajikistan was the exception: it succumbed to civil war. Now there is great international competition to develop the region's enormous wealth, particularly oil in Kazakhstan and Uzbekistan.

Kazakhstan, by far the richest of the four, is also the one with the largest Russian population. Large numbers of Stalin's victims who survived the gulag were sent to permanent exile there. Kazakhs represent only 40 per cent of the population. Russian nationalists, including Alexander Solzhenitsyn, have proposed that the country be reunited to Russia (together with Belarus and Ukraine) and the president, Nursultan Nazabayev, may agree. He moved the capital from Almaty (formerly Alma Ata), in the predominantly Kazakh south-east, to Akmola in north-central Kazakhstan, where the population is 80 per cent Russian. All his plans may go for nought: the Russians are leaving Kazakhstan by the hundred thousand.

Kazakhstan and Uzbekistan were the great dumping grounds for Stalin's enemies. Whole nationalities were uprooted from their ancestral homes and  **405** shipped there in cattle trucks, and many of their descendants are now returning. The Volga Germans, the Crimean Tartars, the Chechens, and the Ingush are the best known. Another group uprooted by Stalin and sent to Uzbekistan are the Meskhetian Turks from Georgia. They suffered a renewed persecution after 1991 and have been trying to return to Georgia ever since. They reached the western shore of the Caspian, where they now remain as refugees.

## TAJIKISTAN

The civil war broke out in May 1992. A loose coalition of liberals, democrats, secularists and Islamic fundamentalists formed to overthrow the government. In the event, the government dissolved but a clan from the Kulyab region in the south-west seized the capital, Dushanbe, and won Russian support. It has held the city ever since. There is no effective central government and the country is divided up and fought over by numerous local war-lords, representing separate clans. The titular president is Imamali Rakhmonov, who holds his office so long as he is supported by the chief war-lords of Dushanbe, and by the Russians. Tajikistan is one of the key links in the international drug trade, growing its own opium poppies and serving as entrepot for heroin smuggled from Afghanistan.

There are now about 25,000 Russian troops in Tajikistan, mostly stationed on the south-western frontier with Afghanistan. Afghan fighters incessantly harass them from across the border, and the Russians insist that they are holding the line against an influx of intolerant Islamic fundamentalists. The other side claims to represent democracy and human rights, and their claim is equally spurious. The fight is for power – and drug money.

The civil war was fought in the Russian manner, with maximum violence against towns and villages, which were demolished by heavy artillery, bombed, and over-run by tanks. Estimates of the numbers killed range from 35,000 to 70,000, and 650,000 people have been driven from their homes. Most of the Russian population, settled in Tajikistan during the long occupation, many of them victims of Stalin's gulag, have fled back to Mother Russia.

The war died down in 1993. Since then, there have been periodic upsurges in violence, interspersed with temporary ceasefires, and long, fruitless negotiations between the parties, sponsored by the Russian government or the UN. The flavour of the place is captured in this report from Steve Levine in the *New York Times* in January 1997:

On December 4, 1996, a convoy of UN military observers was surrounded by the Presidential Guard 70 miles east of Dushanbe. Guard officers lined up the observers for execution and refrained from shooting only when their foot-soldiers intervened. A week later, an Interior Ministry officer named Sohrob Kasimov attacked a second United Nations convoy east of the capital. Mr Kasimov also lined up his captives for execution, but was distracted by a passing jeep, which he blew up with a rocket-propelled grenade. He then let the observers go.

In a third incident, on December 20, seven monitors were abducted. The captor, a former opposition commander who is now supposedly with the government, threatened to kill the monitors and detonate 30 bombs near Dushanbe unless a demilitarized corridor was created so that some of his men stranded in Afghanistan could return home.

## FURTHER READING

Baltaden, Stephen K. and Sandra., (editors), *The Newly Independent States of Eurasia, Handbook of Former Soviet Republics*, Phoenix, Arizona, Oryx Press.

Binyon, Michael, *Life in Russia*, New York, Pantheon Books, 1983.

Conquest, Robert, *Harvest of Sorrow: Soviet Collectivization and the Terror Famine*, Oxford, 1986.

Cuny, Frederick, 'Killing Chechnya', *New York Review of Books*, 6 April 1995.

Dunlop, John, *The Rise of Russia and the Fall of the Soviet Empire*, Princeton University Press, 1993.

Lang, David Marshall and Walker, Christopher J., *The Armenians*, London, Minority Rights Group, 1987.

Shawcross, William, 'An American Hero, Fred Cuny in Chechnya', *New York Review of Books*, 30 November 1995.

Smith, Hedrick, *The Russians*, New York, Times Books, 1983.

*Congressional Quarterly*, 'The Soviet Union', Washington, 1982.

# CYPRUS

| | |
|---|---|
| Geography | 3572 sq. miles (9255 sq. km). Divided into Greek (60%) and Turkish (40%) zones, as well as two small British 'sovereign bases' – at Akrotiri and Dhekelia on the south coast – which, between them, cover 99 sq. miles (256 sq. km). |
| Population | 734,000: 80% Greek, 18% Turkish. There are 200,000 Greek and 65,000 Turkish refugees, and Turkey has sent 50,000 settlers to North Cyprus. There are also 30,000 Turkish soldiers in North Cyprus, and the 'green line' separating the two parts of the island is policed by 2000 UN troops. |
| GNP per capita | N.A. |

Cyprus is one of the world's latent trouble spots. It was forcibly partitioned by Turkey in 1974, and the Turks keep a 30,000-man army there to maintain the division. Cyprus is the source of permanent and extreme tension between Greece and Turkey – ostensible allies in Nato – and therefore a cause of serious weakness to the alliance in the eastern Mediterranean.

Cyprus is notionally an independent nation, and it is a member of the United Nations. The majority of its population (about 600,000 people) consider themselves Greek by nationality, unjustly separated from their homeland. The Turkish minority consider themselves Turks living in Cyprus: their loyalty is to Ankara. There is a Turkish government in Cyprus, established in 1983, calling itself the Republic of North Kibris. It is recognized by no other power than Turkey.

Cyprus's miseries are the legacy of nine centuries of warfare between Greeks and Turks, but more immediately they are the direct result of British colonialism and the policies of the British Conservative government of the 1950s. In addition, President Richard Nixon and, particularly, his secretary of state Henry Kissinger bear a direct responsibility for permitting the crisis of 1974, the partition of the island and the continuing stalemate.

## HISTORY

Cyprus, the birthplace of Aphrodite, was Greek throughout history – although foreigners occupied it from time to time, including Richard I of England and the Venetians – until the coming of the Turks. They conquered the island in 1570, and over the centuries, a number settled there until, in the 1950s, they comprised some 18 per cent of the population. They lived amicably among the Greek majority both as rulers and, after Turkey ceded Cyprus to Britain in 1878, as fellow-subjects.

The British prime minister of the time, Lord Beaconsfield (Benjamin Disraeli), demanded Cyprus as the price for mediating a peace between Turkey and Russia. On returning to London, he announced: 'I bring peace with honour – and Cyprus.' By looking at an inadequate map, he had presumably been misled into believing that Cyprus would be another useful naval base on the sea route to India, like Gibraltar, Malta and the Suez canal. In fact it has no usable harbours and served no real imperial purpose whatever.

Cyprus should have been ceded to Greece after World War I, but Britain did not then believe in giving up her colonies voluntarily. After World War I I, a case could be made that Greece was too unstable, and might fall to Soviet Communism, and that Cyprus should be protected from that danger. However, by the 1950s, the Greek civil war was over and the Greek Cypriots demanded the right to self-determination. In their case, that would have meant *enosis*, union with Greece. In a completely unforgivable act of British stupidity, the Conservative government announced that it would 'never' give up Cyprus – a colony whose retention met no conceivable British national interest.

The Greek Cypriots resorted to terrorism. The terrorist organization, E O K A, was led by Colonel George Grivas, an extreme right-wing retired officer of the Greek army who used the *nom de guerre* Dighenis. The political leadership of the Greek Cypriots was assumed by Michael Christodoros Mouskos, who took the title Archbishop Makarios I I I when he became Orthodox primate of the island. The British army failed to suppress E O K A and failed to catch Grivas. They succeeded, however, in banishing Makarios to the Seychelles.

The Cyprus emergency was a constant irritant in British domestic politics. It was the last hurrah of British imperialism, and when the Labour M P Barbara Castle said that British troops had tortured their prisoners, she was so mercilessly abused by irate Conservatives that she had to grovel in apology. She was right, for all that.

Grivas fought a cautious, skilful campaign of sabotage and assassination. It was not a guerrilla campaign: the terrain was not suitable. The British had 40,000 troops and police on the island in 1956, all of them hunting for Grivas. Of these, 105 soldiers and 51 police were killed, the vast majority by accident – 21 soldiers were killed in a forest fire, exactly 20 per cent of British military deaths. The unit that suffered the worst losses was the Royal Norfolk Regiment, which lost 18 men, most of them teenagers doing their National Service; five of them were killed in the fire, and only two were killed by E O K A.

A total of 238 civilians were also killed, of whom 203 were Greek Cypriots, most of them E O K A fighters. In the first serious fighting between Greeks and Turks, in 1958, 115 people were killed.

Britain finally admitted defeat in 1959, but still refused Cypriots the right of self-determination. The Turks were by then playing an active part in Cyprus's future, and they insisted that *enosis* must never be permitted, because, they said, a Greek base 50 miles (80 km) off their southern coast would be a mortal danger. The argument was, and is, preposterous. Turkey is overwhelmingly more powerful than Greece. Cyprus could be no more dangerous to Turkey than Cuba is to the United States. The Turks, however, believe in the danger from the south. Like Disraeli, they are misled by maps and dreams of encirclement.

To prove their point, in 1955, the Turkish government of Adnan Menderes fomented an anti-Greek pogrom in Istanbul, in which over 2000 people were killed and the remaining Greeks in the city were driven out. That ended a connection going back to Byzantium, and a community dating from the founding of the city by Constantine the Great in the 4th century. Menderes was hanged for his crimes in September 1961.

There was no need for Britain to accede to Turkey's wishes in 1959, but the British naturally disliked Makarios and the Greeks because they had wronged them. Greece had been an ally in both world wars while Turkey had been been an enemy in the first and neutral in the second, but by the 1950s, Turkey was a much more important member of Nato and therefore won British and American support in its disputes with Greece.

The British did not call Turkey's bluff. Instead, in conferences in London and Zurich in 1959 and 1960, they arranged for an independent Cyprus, with a Greek president, Makarios, and a Turkish vice-president, Rauf Denktash; Turkey was also allowed to base a small number of troops there. Cyprus was forbidden to unite with Greece. The only other country in the world whose sovereignty was similarly circumscribed was Austria. The British kept two air bases on the southern coast, and Britain and Turkey were named guarantors of the settlement.

## INDEPENDENT CYPRUS

The constitution was unworkable, and collapsed in 1963. Former E O K A terrorists attacked Turkish villages, and took hostages. The Turkish contingent on the island cut the road from Nicosia to Kyrenia on the north coast, and the Turks threatened to invade. On Christmas Day, the British sent troops to the island, at Makarios's invitation, to keep the peace. They were notably unsuccessful, and the Greeks continued to harass the Turks, driving them out of their homes.

Diplomacy was tried. The British got the U N to send a permanent force to Cyprus – U N F I C Y P – to police the 'green line' between the two communities in Nicosia. President Lyndon Johnson sent former secretary of state Dean Acheson to mediate between Greeks and Turks. He offered the sort of plan which would have been welcomed by everyone ten years earlier: Cyprus would be united with Greece; Turkey would have sovereign bases on the island; the Turkish community would have two autonomous cantons; there would be compensation for any Turk who wanted to leave; Greece would cede to Turkey the small island of Kastellorizon, a small island off the coast. The Acheson plan was rejected by all sides.

Grivas returned to the island, inciting violence against Turks, and founded a new paramilitary force, E O K A-B. In April 1967, there was a military coup in Greece. In September, Grivas organized an attack on a Turkish village in which

27 Turks (and two Greeks) were killed. Turkey informed its allies that it intended to invade, and was only dissuaded by the vigorous intervention of President Johnson, who now sent another mediator, Cyrus Vance, a former secretary of the air force and a future secretary of state. Johnson threatened, in effect, to expel Turkey from Nato if it invaded Cyprus, and insisted that Greek troops should be removed from the island. About 10,000 went home.

An uneasy peace was maintained until 1974. The Turkish Cypriots looked after their own affairs, and Archbishop Makarios remained titular president of the whole. The next crisis was precipitated by the E O K A terrorists, whose fascist sympathies were by now quite clear. They acted under instructions from Athens.

Nixon and Kissinger disliked Makarios, whom they accused of leftist sympathies, and they approved of the Athens military junta, considering it more reliable than the Greek political parties. The junta authorized E O K A, now led by a gangster called Nikos Sampson (Grivas having died on 27 January), to assassinate Makarios. When several attempts failed, Sampson organized a coup and seized power on 15 July 1974. Makarios was rescued by the British.

Kissinger refused to condemn the coup, and openly expressed relief at the overthrow of Makarios. In his defence, it should be noted that he was distracted: at that moment, the Watergate crisis in the United States had reached its final paroxysm. Turkey told all the world that it would not tolerate *enosis*, and when the United States failed to use its influence to reverse the coup or to deter Turkey, the Turkish prime minister, Bulent Ecevit, ordered an invasion. Turkish forces, including parachutists, landed on 20 July and quickly established beach-heads along the northern coast, and in a landing zone near Nicosia.

The leader of the Athens junta, General Dmitrios Ioannides, ordered a full-scale attack on Turkey. The armed forces refused, arrested Ioannides, proclaimed an end to the junta and, on 23 July, handed power back to the civilians. It was a sequence of events the Argentinian junta might have considered before invading the Falklands in 1982.

The British convened a conference in Geneva to resolve the Cyprus crisis. It was a complete failure. Kissinger declined to exert any pressure on Turkey, and the Turks therefore refused to evacuate the island. When the Greeks refused to meet Turkey's demand that the island be partitioned, the Turks conducted a second invasion, on 13 August, and partitioned the island themselves, driving the Greeks out of roughly 40 per cent of it. Turks from the Greek zone fled north, Greeks in the north fled south. About 200,000 people lost their homes, 180,000 of them Greeks. This division has remained unchanged ever since.

## CURRENT STATUS

The Greek zone in Cyprus, contrary to all expectations, has flourished since 1974. Makarios died in 1977, but his successors have followed the same policies. The Greeks' success was helped by the collapse of Lebanon: Cyprus became the bolt-hole and listening base for the Middle East. The Turkish zone, on the other hand, stagnated: Turkey's own continuing political and economic problems preclude the sort of assistance that 'North Kibris' would need to develop into a viable economy.

Relations between the two communities remain as bad as ever. There are periodic negotiations, under U N or American sponsorship, but they have never made any progress. The Turks remain adamantly opposed to reunification of the island, let alone *enosis*. The only power that might make them change their minds, the United States, has remained aloof, for the same reason that it permitted the Turks to invade Cyprus in the first place.

Cyprus's position was not an unfailing advantage. The P L O and Israel's secret service, the Mossad, fought their dark and desperate battles there, and there have been many murders on both sides. In March 1978, in Nicosia, two P L O terrorists killed Youssef el-Sebai, the editor of *El-Ahram* and a close friend of Anwar Sadat of Egypt. They then seized 30 hostages and barricaded themselves in a hotel. After negotiations with the Cypriot authorities, they were allowed to take 15 hostages to Larnaca airport and board a Cyprus Airways aircraft that would take them to freedom. No Middle Eastern country would allow the plane to land and it eventually returned to Larnaca. Meanwhile, 54 Egyptian commandos had been flown to the airport, without informing the Cyprus government, and on 19 March, they stormed the plane. They were mown down by the Cypriot National Guard, who thought they were P L O terrorists; 15 Egyptians were killed. The chief hijacker, known as Samir Kadar, was deported to Syria in 1982; he was believed to be a senior operative in the Abu Nidal terrorist organization and, in July 1988, was apparently killed in a car carrying a load of explosives in Greece.

There have also been terrorist attacks on civilians: in September 1985, three terrorists – two Arab, one British – seized an Israeli cruise boat and murdered the four people on board. In February 1988, the P L O chartered a ferry, planning to fill it with 130 Palestinians whom the Israelis had expelled, and sail it to Haifa in a publicity stunt. It was crippled by a limpet mine off Limassol, presumably by Israeli agents. In the same month, a powerful bomb exploded in a car near the Israeli embassy, killing three people including the car's driver. The bomb had gone off early. Exasperated, Cyprus expelled 66 foreigners, mostly Arabs, whom it suspected of terrorist sympathies.

## FURTHER READING

American University, *Cyprus: A Country Study*, Washington D.C., 1979.
Crashaw, Nancy, *The Cyprus Revolt*, Boston, Allen and Unwin, 1978.
Durrell, Lawrence, *Bitter Lemons*, London, Faber and Faber, 1957.
Hitchens, Christopher, *Cyprus*, New York, Quartet Books, 1984.
Minority Rights Group, *Cyprus*, London, 1984.
Stern, Laurence, *The Wrong Horse*, New York, Times Books, 1977.

# NORTHERN IRELAND

| | |
|---|---|
| Geography | 5462 sq. miles (14,147 sq. km). It comprises the six north-eastern counties of Ireland: Antrim, Armagh, Down, Fermanagh, Londonderry and Tyrone. |
| Population | 1,537,000. 950,000 are Protestant, 600,000 Catholic. Belfast, 420,000 people, has 100,000 Catholics and the rest Protestant. |
| Casualties | 3248 people were killed between 1969 and the Good Friday agreement in 1998. |

On 10 April 1998, Good Friday, the main Catholic and Protestant parties in Northern Ireland accepted a provisional peace agreement to settle the future of the province and its relations with the Republic and Great Britain. The key clause stated, 'It would be wrong to make any change in the status of Northern Ireland save with the consent of a majority of its people.'

The Irish Republican Army had fought for almost 30 years to unite Northern Ireland with the Republic against the wishes of the Protestants who make up the majority. Over 3200 people had been killed, including hundreds of women, children and old people. Scores of thousands had been wounded in shootings, bombings and deliberate maimings. Hundreds of terrorists had been killed and thousands had served long prison terms. In April 1998, there were 369 Catholic and 403 Protestant terrorists serving time in Northern Ireland (and a handful in Great Britain), and 95 Catholics and 145 Protestants on remand. The Good Friday agreement meant abandoning the purpose for which all that suffering had been inflicted and, by logical extension, admitting that the 'armed conflict' had been mistaken from the start. The gunmen had risked their lives, their liberties and their immortal souls to no good purpose, and all the killings were not the necessary price for a noble end but merely murders after all.

The leaders of Sinn Fein, the political party that represents the IRA, had realized some years earlier that the Protestants could not be bombed into the Republic. If Ireland were to be united, it would have to come through peaceful, political means. Sinn Fein's leader, Gerry Adams, played a central part in the two and a half years of negotiations that led to the Agreement. Afterwards, he claimed victory but did not sign the document, and it was clear that he would have great trouble persuading the gunmen to accept it, and IRA splinter groups were vociferously and violently opposed to it.

It was a bitter pill for republicans to swallow. Apart from the new constitutional arrangements grudgingly accepted by the Unionists, the gunmen were offered one immense concession: all their prisoners would be released by the summer of 2000. Many of the hardest of IRA leaders and gunmen were in jail, facing life sentences. If they cast their votes for the agreement, they could return to their families. It was not an easy choice: amnesty would be granted only to members of groups that accepted the agreement, including its provisions for 'decommissioning' their arsenals of weapons and explosives. An international commission, meaning an American chairman, would supervise the decommissioning in the two following years and the release of the prisoners of each paramilitary group would depend on the commission's certification that it had indeed disarmed. No doubt the issue will be fudged if Northern Ireland enjoys two years' peace but, for the IRA, accepting the principle of disarmament was an enormous concession.

Adams's argument, in public at least, was that the armed struggle had at last forced the British and the Protestants to admit that the old way of doing things was over and they must accord a greater voice to Catholics and accept a degree of interference and supervision by Dublin in the affairs of the North. There was much truth in it, but he did not discuss the immense price that the Catholic community had paid or the legacy of hatred that would remain.

The constitutional provisions of the agreement allowed the Republic an extraordinary level of involvement in the government of Northern Ireland, and for that reason were bitterly opposed by many Unionists. There were to be so many committees that ministers of the new Northern executive and the Dublin government, and British ministers, would have to spend an inordinate amount of their time in meetings. Catholics hoped, and Protestants feared, that the new arrangements would progressively erase the differences between the two parts of Ireland, making peaceful unification possible one day in the future.

More important by far, and an immediate and fundamental change, was that the ministries in the restored executive government in Northern Ireland, and not just the assembly, would be distributed proportionately. The Social Democratic and Labour Party would have a large part in the government and its leader, John Hume, would be deputy chief minister. Sinn Fein would have a place in the executive if it maintained the 15 per cent of the vote it won in the 1997 elections.

That was the carrot offered to Gerry Adams and his colleagues. Unionist extremists denounced the agreement for this very reason (which doubtless helped those members of the IRA inclined to accept it). But the splinter groups on both sides, such as the Irish National Liberation Army and the Ulster Volunteer Force, would certainly continue their campaigns of murder to defeat the agreement. Between them, they had already killed a dozen people between the resumed ceasefire in September and the agreement in April. Good Friday was the most hopeful day in Northern Ireland in a generation, but the killings would continue.

## HISTORY

On Easter Monday, 24 April 1916, Patrick Pearse stood on the steps of the General Post Office in O'Connell Street, Dublin, and proclaimed the Irish Republic: 'Irishmen and Irishwomen: In the name of God and of the dead generations from which she received her old tradition of nationhood, Ireland, through us, summons her children to her flag and strikes for her freedom.'

It was the first nationalist uprising of the 20th century, and it was firmly suppressed by the British army. Six years later, after a guerrilla war marked by many atrocities on both sides, most of Ireland won its independence. The Protestant majority of the Six Counties insisted on remaining united with Great Britain. The violent traditions of the long fight against the British, what the playwright Sean O'Casey called the 'Shadow of a Gunman', carried over to a civil war in 1923–4 and have been maintained in the dark recesses of Ireland ever since. They revived in Northern Ireland in 1969 in a terrorist campaign in which over 3200 people were killed before a shaky ceasefire was declared in 1995. By then, Unionist terrorists were killing as many people as the Irish Republican Army. While political leaders on both sides agreed to negotiate for an end to the violence and a new constitution, there was no certainty that they could carry the gunmen with them.

The English first conquered Ireland in the 12th century. They succeeded in imposing their laws and, eventually, their language, but the majority of the Irish never willingly accepted their forced union with England. Resistance acquired a religious cast, which it has retained, when Great Britain, but not Ireland, embraced the Protestant Reformation in the 16th century. Ever since, all Protestants in Ireland have supported the Union, and most Catholics have opposed it.

At the end of the 16th century, after a revolt in Ulster, Elizabeth I confiscated all the land of the province. She and her successor, James I, granted the land to Protestant settlers from England and Scotland, in the Ulster plantation, which is exactly contemporary with the American colonies of Virginia and Massachusetts. Northern Ireland has had a Protestant majority ever since.

Catholic Ireland still remembers the revolt of the 1640s, which was eventually suppressed, with memorable brutality, by Cromwell. Much Protestant mythology goes back to the events of those years and to the second Irish civil war of the late 17th century, 300 years ago. After King James I I was expelled from England in 1688, Catholic Ireland rose in his defence. Two episodes in that war are still celebrated every year: the Catholic siege of Londonderry (which was defended by Protestant apprentices, the 'Prentice Boys') in August 1689; and the Battle of the Boyne, on 12 July 1690, in which the Protestant King William I I I defeated his father-in-law, the Catholic King James.

In the wake of yet another rebellion, the (Protestant) Irish Parliament in Dublin was suppressed in 1801, and the political union of the two kingdoms was enacted. Irish Catholic men finally won the vote in 1829, shortly before the greatest disaster in Irish history, the potato famine of the 1840s. It cost hundreds of thousands of lives and led to a mass emigration to Great Britain, North America and Australia. The population, 8 million before the famine, has never recovered. The emigrants' descendants, particularly those in the United States, have kept their religion and sense of Irishness over the generations. John F. Kennedy, for instance, was a fourth-generation American – his great-grandparents had emigrated during the famine – but he still proclaimed his Irishness. One of his nephews, visiting Belfast 140 years after his great-great-grandparents had left Ireland, repeated the assertion that he was Irish and had every right to meddle in Irish politics.

**415**

## THE EASTER RISING AND THE WAR OF INDEPENDENCE

The Irish, by now well represented in the British Parliament, continued throughout the latter half of the 19th century to demand Home Rule (a measure of autonomy). The debate reached a fever pitch in London just before World War I, with the Liberal government proposing Home Rule and the Conservatives opposing it. Home Rule had been defeated in the 1880s and 1890s by the determination of Protestants in Northern Ireland (Ulster), whose slogan was 'Ulster will fight, and Ulster will be right!' In 1914, faced with a government determined to push some form of Home Rule through parliament, they threatened civil war and mutiny in the Army. The idea of partitioning Ireland was discussed as a possible solution. The Unionists (Conservatives) opposed even that concession, and the government and the Irish debated whether partition should be temporary (six years followed by automatic inclusion) or dependent upon the will of the North. They also debated the line it should follow. There was no more a clear-cut border between Catholic and Protestant Ireland than there was one between Catholics, Orthodox and Muslims in Bosnia. There was a long debate on whether to include Fermanagh and Tyrone (two counties equally divided between Catholics and Protestants) in the proposed Protestant enclave. When the World War began, this discussion was postponed for the duration.

Irish extremists, who had been plotting a new insurrection for years under the direction of their secret society, the Irish Republican Brotherhood, decided that their time had come. In 1916, they organized the Easter Rising. It was suppressed, at a cost of 1350 dead, and some of its leaders were shot, but the event brought the Republicans wide public support. In the 1918 general election, their political wing, Sinn Fein (pronounced *shin fain*, 'Ourselves Alone'), won most of the Catholic constituencies and a slight majority of the Catholic vote. The elected members seceded from the British Parliament and formed the first Dáil, an Irish Parliament in Dublin, with Eamon de Valéra as President of the Republic.

They formed the original Irish Republican Army, under the command of Michael Collins, which fought a guerrilla war against the British from 1919 to 1921. In 1920, the British partitioned Ireland, setting up legislatures with limited powers in Dublin (for the 26 counties that now make up the Republic) and in Stormont, outside Belfast, for the six Protestant counties of the north-east. The I R A continued to fight for an independent, united Republic, and eventually the British government offered 'dominion status' (the same degree of independence as Canada) on two conditions: that the Irish government renounce the Republic, recognizing George V as King of Ireland, and agreement that the Six Counties had the right to remain in the union with Great Britain. A treaty on those lines was signed in London on 6 December 1921.

## THE PARTITION DEBATE

There was intense opposition to the treaty among extremists in the I R A, led by de Valéra, who baulked at giving up the Republic. They lost the vote in the Dáil, but refused to recognize their defeat. When the independent Irish Free State was set up in 1922, they fought, and lost, a brutal civil war on the issue (1922–3), in which far more Irishmen (about 4000) were killed, or executed, than the British had killed between 1916 and 1921. Today's Catholic mythology has it that the

Dáil debate and the civil war were fought on the issue of partition. In fact, the question of partition went by default at the time, because both sides assumed that Northern Ireland would soon see the necessity of remaining in a united Ireland rather than existing as a separated appendage of Great Britain. De Valéra and his fellow extremists argued that giving up the Republic meant giving up Irish independence, and they were prepared to kill their former comrades to reverse the decision.

They were all mistaken. Ireland quickly assumed full independence, was neutral in World War I I and was finally proclaimed a republic in 1949, all without any further impediment from Britain. The Protestant majority in the North held firm to the Union. With their semi-autonomous parliament in Stormont, they ruled the Catholic minority with a heavy hand. That minority was deprived, by gerrymandering and blatant fraud, of many of its economic, social and political rights. The ironic consequence of Irish independence was a sharp deterioration in the status of the Northern Catholics.

Partition, which was a mere line on the map in 1920, has developed into a real border as the two parts of Ireland have gone their separate ways. The South wished to establish its independence from Britain, but this also meant differentiating itself from Northern Ireland. The separation was most complete by the 1980s, but now the Republic has at last caught up with the rest of Europe. Its standard of living is as high as Britain's. Divorce is permitted and so is contraception (though it is much restricted and abortion remains banned). Despite the Troubles, North and South have been converging, socially and economically, over the past decade.

The question of partition was seldom raised between 1923 and 1968. The Northern Protestants, of course, thought the matter settled once and for all. The Northern Nationalists, brooding on the wrongs being done to them, did not forget. In a speech after World War I, recalling the pre-war debates on the line the border should take, Winston Churchill remarked on the tenacity of Irish quarrels: 'As the deluge subsides and waters recede, we see the dreary steeples of Fermanagh and Tyrone emerging once again. The integrity of their quarrel is one of the few institutions that has been unaltered in the cataclysm that has swept the world.' Seventy-five years later, the dispute continues.

## AFTER PARTITION

In the late 1920s, de Valéra and his followers abandoned violent opposition to the state and accepted the monarchical British constitution and democratic politics. In effect, this meant accepting partition. Their political party, Fianna Fáil ('Warriors of Ireland'), came to be the largest in the Free State, and has since then most often led Ireland's governments. The original pro-treaty party is called Fine Gael ('The Irish Race'). Ironically, it was a Fine Gael government that finally proclaimed the Republic in 1949, during one of de Valéra's brief periods in opposition. A dissident splinter faction of the I R A continued a small-scale terrorist campaign aginst the government in Dublin and against partition. De Valéra, when he became prime minister, interned them. There were bombings in England and Northern Ireland in 1938, and a further outbreak of violence in 1956, both short-lived.

In 1968, following the example of the civil rights movement in the United **417**

States, Catholics in Northern Ireland began agitating for their political and social rights. For instance, the city of Londonderry (known to Catholics as Derry) had a Catholic majority, but the city council was gerrymandered to keep the Protestants permanently in power. The civil rights movement met with a great deal of success, and was supported by all Northern Catholics and by the British government, then led by Harold Wilson (Labour).

## THE TROUBLES

In July 1969, a peaceful civil rights demonstration in Londonderry was broken up with great violence by Protestant paramilitary police (the 'B Specials'). Protestants attacked Catholics throughout the province, and the local militia and police stood by, or actively helped.

The British government intervened, sending the army to keep order in August 1969. It was welcomed by Catholics because it protected them from Protestant violence. After a period of indecision, the government set about correcting the civil rights abuses of Northern Ireland, but they encountered intractable opposition from Stormont. Therefore the government, then led by Edward Heath (Conservative), dissolved the Northern Ireland parliament and government in 1972, and the province has been directly ruled from London ever since, except for a brief interval when the institution of a Northern Ireland Assembly was attempted (unsuccessfully) in 1974.

The rump of the old I R A was stirred into action by the events of 1969. Recruiting new members proved easy: memories of 50 years of discrimination were enough. As the cycle of terrorism and repression got under way, the I R A expanded rapidly. The world-wide economic recession of the 1970s severely affected Northern Ireland, where the major industries – shipbuilding and textiles – collapsed. Unemployment was (and remains) very high throughout the province, and disproportionately severe among Catholics, providing a ready pool of recruits.

In the aftermath of the Londonderry disturbance in August 1969, Catholics set up 'No Go' areas in the Catholic districts of that city (the Bogside) and of Belfast (around the Falls Road), building barricades and preventing the police and army from entering. The I R A developed rapidly behind those barricades.

## BLOODY SUNDAY

Terrorists began shooting British soldiers and Irish policemen, and setting off bombs in Protestant villages and in Belfast. The security situation deteriorated rapidly: 15 people were killed in 1969, 25 in 1970, 173 in 1971.

The British government flooded the province with troops, among whom the paratroopers and Scottish regiments made a particular name for themselves. In August 1971, the army entered the 'No Go' areas and dismantled the barricades. On 9 August, the government introduced a policy of interning I R A suspects without trial. Hundreds of people were arrested in massive military operations in the Falls Road area of Belfast and in the Bogside in Londonderry. The British behaved like an army of occupation in what was supposed to be a British province, and achieved the complete alienation of the Catholic population. The cycle reached its final paroxysm when paratroopers opened fire on rioting

Catholics in Londonderry, killing 13, on what came to be known as 'Bloody Sunday', 30 January 1972. Two weeks later, rioters in Dublin burned the British embassy, a splendid 18th-century building, while the police watched. Even in a century filled with meaningless political gestures, the notion that the Irish might intimidate the British, or be revenged upon them, by burning down one of their own architectural monuments was particularly bizarre.

The one attempt at an agreement between the British government and the I R A occurred during this period. In 1972, they arranged a ceasefire and secret talks, which got nowhere. One of the I R A delegates sent to meet Ted Heath was a young hardliner called Gerry Adams.

Britain increased the number of troops in the province, disbanded the 'B Specials' and set about dismantling the gerrymandered political system. Londonderry City Council now has a Catholic majority, and has officially changed the city's name to Derry. In 1973, Prime Minister Edward Heath convened a conference at Sunningdale in England, which proposed a system of power-sharing between Protestants and Catholics in Northern Ireland. An Assembly was elected and a power-sharing executive was set up in 1974; the Protestants staged a general strike in protest, and the assembly and executive collapsed together.

## THE TERRORIST CAMPAIGN

The atrocities continued. The worst year was 1972, with 474 deaths in Northern Ireland. Of these, 255 were killed by the I R A, 103 by Protestant terrorists, 74 by the security forces and 42 were unclassified (meaning that, for the most part, they were probably caused by the I R A). The terrorist campaign crossed the Irish Sea to England, in a long series of atrocities. The worst was the bombing of two pubs in Birmingham, killing 19 and wounding 180, in November 1974. Protestant terrorists were equally busy: in December 1971, a bomb in a Catholic pub in Londonderry killed 15, and in May 1974, car bombs killed 22 people in Dublin.

In 1978, a bomb in the Le Mon café in Belfast killed 12 people and injured 23. In 1979, Lord Louis Mountbatten, aged 78, a distinguished statesman and a relative of the Queen, was murdered in Ireland, with three other people – a woman older than he and two young boys. On the same day, a bomb under a road at Warrenpoint near the border blew up an army truck, killing 18 soldiers. A bomb also severely damaged the 11th-century Westminster Hall, one of the most important public buildings in London.

In 1981, a group of I R A prisoners went on hunger strike to demand 'political status'. Ten of them died, including Bobby Sands who had been elected a Member of Parliament while in prison. There were more bomb attacks in London that year: one bomb was concealed in a bandstand in Regent's Park; another exploded in Chelsea as a bus carrying soldiers went by; a third exploded near a parade of the Queen's Horse Guards in Hyde Park.

At Christmas 1983, a bomb went off in the street near Harrods department store in London, killing five and injuring more than 80; one of the dead and many of the injured were American tourists. In 1984, a bomb in the Grand Hotel, Brighton, just missed killing or injuring Prime Minister Margaret Thatcher, who was attending the Conservative party conference. Another powerful bomb was found shortly afterwards, concealed in a tourist hotel in

London. Altogether, about 100 people have been killed by terrorist acts in Great Britain, and about 60 in the Irish Republic, including the British ambassador. The British ambassador to the Netherlands was also murdered, as were three R A F men in 1988, and many other atrocities were prevented by security forces.

The bombings in Birmingham and London, the Mountbatten murder and the Brighton bombing were the most spectacular events and aroused the most anger, but the I R A's campaign has been mostly concentrated in Northern Ireland itself. There have been many assassinations of judges, policemen, soldiers, and public officials. On many occasions, I R A gunmen shot their victims in the presence of their families, once on the steps of St Patrick's Cathedral in Armagh. A soldier on leave was murdered in his parents' house in Derry, and on one occasion the congregation of a Protestant church was machine-gunned during Sunday service. There were also many attacks on police and army barracks, and South Armagh, which was mostly Catholic, and from which virtually all Protestants have been driven, became a favourite battleground between the I R A and the police.

These acts of terrorism provoked Protestant reprisals, and a great deal of the British police effort has been devoted to preventing Protestant and Catholic paramilitary forces from slaughtering each other. Protestant terror organizations – the Ulster Volunteer Force, the Ulster Freedom Fighters, and the Ulster Defence Association – have murdered a number of prominent Nationalists, and they attempted to assassinate Bernadette Devlin (now McAliskey) and her husband: she had been a leader of the 1969 civil rights movement and later a Member of Parliament. The Protestant terrorists have murdered hundreds of Catholics, mostly at random, and have also assassinated a number of I R A suspects; they have used car bombs and have bombed pubs and public buildings as indiscriminately, though not so frequently, as the I R A. People have been driven from their homes, and as a result, there is now an almost complete residential segregation between Catholics and Protestants in Northern Ireland.

The I R A has grown increasingly sophisticated in its use of weapons. The Brighton bomb, for instance, was concealed in the hotel for a month before the Tory party conference. Some I R A experts learned their trade in the British army; others were trained in Libya. Protestant terrorists have usually been former soldiers.

## THE NEW IRA

The I R A has changed considerably since 1969. Its old guard has been progressively eliminated, and replaced by much younger and tougher men. The first of the new generation was a group of Marxists who were more interested in international Communism than in fighting the British. The movement split, and a dissident group, which proved to be the large majority, broke away and formed the Provisional I R A, known universally as the Provos, devoted to driving the British out of Northern Ireland by violence.

The I R A's political wing, Sinn Fein, also split, into an Official Sinn Fein and a Provisional Sinn Fein. The officials, both political and military, quickly lost most of their supporters, though there were occasional violent quarrels with the Provos, leading to frequent killings and mutilations on both sides. Apart from killing people, the favourite penalty in Northern Ireland, for all terrorist groups, is 'kneecapping': the victim's kneecap is either shot away or destroyed with an electric drill. Belfast hospitals now lead the world in reconstruction operations on knee-joints. The I R A also favours shaving the heads and tarring and feathering of women who fraternize with the 'enemy'.

Another dissident I R A faction – the Irish National Liberation Army (I N L A) – followed a policy of extreme violence and Marxist dogma. It was responsible for some of the most spectacular murders, including the car bomb that killed the British Member of Parliament Airey Neave at the House of Commons in 1979. However, the I N L A was severely weakened by police actions and attacks by the Provos in 1986–7.

## THE PROVOS' PROGRAMME

The I R A's original objective was to wear down Britain's support for the Protestants in Northern Ireland. They believed that if British troops were withdrawn, the Protestants would accept the situation and agree to the re-unification of Ireland. This remains the faith of the I R A's rank and file. Over 20 years of terrorism have reinforced Protestant determination to have nothing to do with the Republic, and there can be no doubt at all that a British withdrawal would be followed by a civil war – which the Protestants would win. They are twice as numerous as the Catholics and would control the police and militia (the I R A devotes itself to killing all Catholic members of those organizations). If the I R A won its heart's desire – the abrupt withdrawal of the British – there would follow the setting up of a Protestant Republic of Northern Ireland and, most probably, the expulsion of several hundred thousand Catholics from their homes in Belfast, Derry and the border areas; in the end, there might be no Catholics at all in Northern Ireland. This is the Dublin government's worst nightmare. The I R A, driven south, would, of course, turn its rage upon the Irish Republic.

For all its history, the I R A heartily despised the government of the Republic, which it denounced as illegitimate. Most citizens of that republic reciprocated its feelings: they detest terrorism, and though they pay lip service to reunification, there has never been much of a popular movement to bring it about. Sinn Fein seldom won more than 2 or 3 per cent of the vote in any election. Under the Irish proportional representation system, even this small result sometimes won the party a seat in the Dáil, but the party always refused to take it, as it refused to take any seat it won in elections to the British parliament.

There was a change after the parliamentary elections in Ireland in June 1997, when Sinn Fein won its usual 2 per cent of the vote and one seat, in the border constituency of Cavan–Monaghan. The party had just won two seats in the British elections the previous month and the peace process was set to resume. Sinn Fein did not alter its traditional refusal to send its two M Ps (Gerry Adams and Martin McGuinness) to Westminster, but it did send its elected member to take his seat in the Dáil in Dublin. The party at last recognized the validity of the Irish state established in 1922.

It won about 15 per cent of the vote in Northern Ireland in the British elections on 1 May 1997 that returned the Labour Party to power. Its rival, the Social

Democratic Labour Party, led by John Hume, won 25 per cent. Sinn Fein's relatively good showing allowed Adams to claim a seat at the peace talks as the elected representative of a substantial segment of the electorate.

The I R A is thought to have about 200–300 active gunmen (and women) at any given moment. Since its largest operations involve no more than a dozen people, this is quite enough. It could certainly recruit far more if it wished, but the I R A is not a guerrilla army. It is a terrorist organization, and size is irrelevant, and large numbers can be dangerous.

## THE TERRORISTS' BANKROLL

The Provos finance their operations from levies on the Nationalist population in the North (in effect, protection rackets), from robberies on both sides of the border, from smuggling and from contributions from abroad. I R A men, who are officially unemployed, draw British unemployment compensation and their families also are on the dole.

An American I R A front organization, the Irish Northern Aid Committee (Noraid), raises money publicly, in contributions at Irish events and in pubs. There are also illicit fund-raising activities. In January 1993, an armed gang held up a Brinks truck in New York and got away with $7.4 million, of which $2 million was recovered. The suspects were all recent immigrants from Northern Ireland, including several with I R A records. Two of them (including a priest) were convicted. The I R A has also received subsidies and contributions in kind (reportedly including 20 tons of Semtex) from Libya.

Until the implementation of the European Union in the early 1990s, smuggling was a lucrative source of income for the I R A. The vagaries of Irish, British and European agricultural prices, and differences in levels of taxation and the value of the two currencies, offered smugglers a golden opportunity. The border passes through many villages and, in one notorious case, actually through the house of a prominent republican supporter, so smuggling was easy.

The Irish government calculated in 1983 that the total cost of the first 14 years of the Troubles amounted to £14 billion ($21 billion), and was continuing at a rate of £1.3 billion a year. The direct costs to the British Treasury have been much greater than that. They include paying for the security forces, insuring Northern Ireland citizens, local government and businesses against violence against property and persons, and the enormous indirect costs of sustaining a province where business does not invest for fear of violence. The greatest burden has fallen on the population of Northern Ireland, who have also had to bear the psychological costs of over 60,000 separate incidents of murder, injury, bombing or arson since 1969.

## THE AMERICAN CONNECTION

American administrations since the Troubles began have steadfastly supported British policy. There was, to begin with, considerable ignorance of the situation there (Senator Edward Kennedy at first called Northern Ireland 'Britain's Vietnam'), but as the I R A campaign developed and large numbers of people were killed, support for the I R A shrank. In particular, four of the most prominent Irish-Americans – Senators Kennedy of Massachusetts and Daniel

Patrick Moynihan of New York, Thomas P. ('Tip') O'Neill, speaker of the House of Representatives until 1986, and Hugh Carey, governor of New York until 1982 – took to issuing statements every St Patrick's Day condemning terrorism. The most prominent Irish-American, President Reagan, steadfastly supported the British, and after the 1985 Anglo-Irish treaty, Congress voted an aid package for Northern Ireland.

There are vigorous pro-I R A lobbies in Washington who try to change American policy, by enforcing an American boycott of Northern Ireland, and American supporters of the I R A have always exerted an influence far beyond their numbers (most Irish-Americans detest terrorism as much as the Irish do). The I R A counts on the moral support of its front organizations such as Noraid, and on pro-I R A demonstrations in New York, Boston and other centres of Irish-American influence. As well as a hard core of Irish-Americans, it is also supported by a few non-Irish-American politicians, including Mario Biaggi, who was for many years a congressman from the Bronx until he was jailed for corruption in 1988. Another conspicuously non-Irish supporter was the comptroller of the City of New York, Harrison Goldin.

Irish-Americans are also an important source of weapons. Guns may be bought so easily and cheaply in the United States that the only real difficulty is smuggling them into Ireland. Several boatloads have been intercepted, including one in Boston harbour in 1986, and guns have been found in many unlikely places, including the kitchens of the luxury liner the *Queen Elizabeth II*. Another source of weapons and money has been Libya. A boatload of Libyan weapons was intercepted off the west coast of Ireland in 1974, and a large cache of Libyan weapons was discovered in the Republic in 1986. In 1988, the French navy intercepted a Panamanian ship, the *Eksund*, carrying 150 tons of Libyan arms to the I R A. The cargo included surface-to-air missiles, Kalashnikovs and large quantities of explosives.

## ATTEMPTS AT A POLITICAL SOLUTION

The British government, led by Margaret Thatcher, and the Irish government, led by Garrett FitzGerald of Fine Gael, signed an Anglo-Irish treaty on 15 November 1985, which institutionalized power-sharing between Catholics and Protestants in Northern Ireland, and gave the Irish Republic a direct role in Northern Ireland affairs. Joint Anglo-Irish committees would meet regularly to discuss policy and reach agreed conclusions, the topics ranging from security matters to anti-discrimination policy in Northern Ireland. The object of the agreement was for the authorities in the province to get to the root of Catholic alienation by dealing with all the specific issues of discrimination in politics, society and the economy. The agreement was welcomed by the Nationalists and by the Republic. Fianna Fáil's leader, Charles Haughey (subsequently Irish prime minister), initially rejected the treaty but changed his tune when it proved exceedingly popular.

British security policy over the next decade, notably the Stalker affair and the Gibraltar killings (*see below*), put a great strain on the treaty mechanism. The I R A rejected the treaty because it did not meet their basic demand for reunification.

## BRITISH POLICY

The Anglo-Irish treaty was the first attempt by a British government to find a solution to its Irish predicament since 1973. The British would like nothing better than for Irish Protestants and Catholics to live in harmony together in a united Republic, but they recognize that there is no hope of that, because of Protestant intransigence. For 40 years, British law has ensured that no change in the status of Northern Ireland can be made without the consent of a majority of its population, and that commitment holds good, as it must, because it is no more than a recognition of Protestant strength.

In 1988, the British government strengthened the provisions of anti-discrimination legislation. Previous laws and the Fair Employment Agency were very impressive and democratic on paper, but not very successful in practice, and there continued to be considerable discrimination. This was partly due to the very high level of unemployment: factories with a workforce comprising 90 per cent or more Protestants had not hired any new workers for a decade and therefore remained Protestant strongholds. The new rules strengthened the agency, renamed the Fair Employment Commission, partially in an attempt to comply with the 'McBride principles', enunciated by another of the I R A front organizations in the United States and adopted by a number of American politicians. They lay down stringent rules for non-discrimination in Northern Ireland as preconditions for investment by companies doing business with various American local government bodies (such as New York City). They have been made binding on a number of state pension investment funds.

The British legislation introduced for the first time the concept of 'affirmative action': companies that have in the past discriminated against a particular group (in practice, this means Catholics) can now be obliged to hire members of that group in preference to others. The rules will be enforced by a Fair Employment Tribunal and there will be heavy penalties for disobedience.

As in many anti-terrorist campaigns, the British army and police were faced with a dilemma: in order to combat terrorism effectively and 'restore law and order', they had resorted to measures that frustrate the government's essential long-term strategy – winning the 'hearts and minds' of the Catholics. The British army is not the S S and the police are not the Gestapo, but their tactics have been frequently brutal, particularly in the early days. Amnesty International and the European Court of Justice documented widespread use of torture, and some British policies, notably internment and allowing Bobby Sands and his comrades to starve themselves to death, were amazingly stupid and counterproductive. As a result, though Catholics may detest terrorism and murder, they also detest the police and army and, by extension, the British.

Northern Ireland is one of those places where, however bad the situation, it can always get worse. On 8 May 1987, acting on a tip, police ambushed an I R A squad as it attacked a police station at Loughgall, south-west of Belfast; eight I R A men were killed, including three senior commanders. On Remembrance Sunday, 8 November 1987 in Enniskillen, Co. Fermanagh, in the west of the province, the town had gathered at the local war memorial to mark the anniversary of the Armistice and honour the dead of World Wars I and I I. These ceremonies always conclude with a minute's silence at 11 a.m., the hour of the Armistice in 1918; a terrorist bomb that had been concealed in a community centre next to the memorial went off at 10.45, killing 11 people and wounding 55. The I R A later said that the bomb had been aimed at the military honour guard, but there was no honour guard. All the killed and injured were civilians, including many children. It was the largest civilian death toll since a bomb in a pub had killed 17 people in 1982. The I R A apologized for the deaths, grudgingly. The Enniskillen murders were greeted with universal revulsion. They also helped persuade the Irish Dáil to pass an extradition treaty with Britain.

1988 was a bad year. In February, a British soldier shot an I R A man at the border as he was walking to a Gaelic football match. The army insisted that the incident was an accident. Then, on 6 March 1988, three unarmed I R A terrorists, two men and a woman, were shot dead by British security men in Gibraltar. It was the most flagrant recent example of extralegal execution in Britain's war with the I R A.

The three terrorists had been plotting a repeat of the Enniskillen massacre: they had loaded a car with explosives and planned to park it next to a parade ground on Gibraltar where the band of the Royal Anglian Regiment was due to perform two days later. When they were shot, they had just reserved a parking space using an entirely innocent car. The car containing the bomb, which had been left over the border in Spain, would have replaced it at a suitable moment an hour or two before the parade.

It turned out that the three had been followed for days by members of the British and Spanish secret services. There had never been any danger that their bomb would explode, although the security forces later insisted that they had believed that the terrorists had already left one on Gibraltar. The three had been leaving Gibraltar, on foot, when a police car drove up. Several men jumped out of the car and shot them dead. The gunmen turned out to be members of the Special Air Services (S A S).

An official version of events was promptly offered. The three terrorists had made 'suspicious hand movements', which led the S A S men to believe that they were about to pull out guns or push a detonator button. Eye-witnesses were soon discovered, who disputed this version of events. At least one of the dead men, who had been shot in the back, had been finished off on the ground. A witness said: 'The man on the ground was lying on his back. The man standing over this man had his foot on the man's chest. I then saw the gunman point his gun deliberately at the man that was lying on the floor and fire two or three times into him at point-blank range.' Anyone who cast doubt upon the official version of events was accused of prejudicing the inquest which was to take place in Gibraltar – an inquest that was postponed for months. The British foreign secretary and prime minister, not to mention lesser officials, repeatedly insisted upon the sanctity of the inquest. They tried to prevent British television from broadcasting a report on the killings, including interviews with eye-witnesses. When Amnesty International issued a statement questioning the official version, Mrs Thatcher told the House of Commons, 'I hope Amnesty has some concern for the more than 2000 people murdered by the I R A since 1969.'

The bodies of the three terrorists were shipped back to Belfast. At their funeral on 16 March, a Protestant terrorist shot at and threw hand grenades into the crowd, killing three people and wounding more than 50. He was grabbed by mourners when he ran out of ammunition and grenades, and turned over to the police. Three days later, at the funeral of the victims of the cemetery shootings, two off-duty British soldiers, in civilian clothing, drove by mistake into the funeral procession. They were dragged out of their car, and lynched. Both incidents were televised, and the film of the lynching was later used to identify and arrest some of the lynch mob.

By then, relations between the British and Irish were worse than they had been for years. They had not been helped by the outcome of what came to be known as the 'Stalker affair'. A British policeman from Manchester, John Stalker, had been sent to Northern Ireland in 1984 to investigate three incidents that had occurred in 1982, in which Ulster police had shot six men, killing five of them. Most of the dead had been I R A terrorists, and the allegation was that they had been victims of 'extralegal executions'. Stalker was a good cop and carried out his investigations thoroughly. However, just before they were concluded, he was pulled off the case. On 25 January 1988, the British attorney-general told the House of Commons that, although there was sufficient evidence to prosecute members of the Ulster police for perverting justice, he had decided not to do so. It is not often that public officials admit that they are engaged in a cover-up and intend to continue it. Stalker eventually published his own conclusions. He had found no evidence of a 'shoot to kill' policy, but in the early 1980s, there had been an inclination among the security forces to shoot suspects without warning rather than arrest them.

The I R A continued its work. On 29 February 1988, two terrorists blew themselves up while assembling a bomb. On 2 May, three R A F men were killed by car bombs in the Netherlands. On 16 May, Protestant terrorists shot up a Catholic bar, killing three people. On 15 June, six British soldiers were killed by a bomb that had been placed in their car at a school sports day in Lisburn, south of Belfast. On 1 August, the I R A planted a bomb in an army postal depot in London, killing one soldier. On 20 August, eight soldiers riding in a bus from Belfast airport to their barracks were killed by a bomb; it was evident that the I R A had been tipped off about when the bus would leave and what route it would take. Ten days later, three I R A gunmen were shot by the security forces: the I R A conceded that they had been 'on a mission', but the British would reveal none of the details of the incident. On 31 August, two civilians were killed in Derry when they set off a bomb meant for the police; the I R A expressed its regret for an operation 'that had gone tragically wrong'.

With the Gibraltar inquest safely out of the way, the British government moved on to other highly controversial matters. In October, it banned all radio or television appearances by members of the I R A, of Sinn Fein and of certain Protestant terrorist organizations, and ended the ancient right of accused persons in Northern Ireland to remain silent, without prejudice, at their trials. On 29 November, the European Court at Strasbourg ruled that the provisions of the Prevention of Terrorism Act which permitted the authorities to hold suspects for up to seven days without charge were violations of the European Convention on Human Rights. A few weeks later, the British government decided that it would not be bound by the ruling. The Act would remain in its present form.

The justification for the ban on broadcasting interviews with members of the I R A and 'Loyalist' terrorist groups and their front organizations was that depriving them of publicity was to deny them oxygen. As for the right to remain silent, the government ruled that, in future, courts would be permitted to 'attach whatever weight they think proper to the fact that a suspect remains silent when questioned'. It announced that the new rule would be extended to Great Britain in due course. To many people, both these measures seemed to be serious restrictions on civil liberties. They are both matters covered by the Bill of Rights in the U S Constitution: freedom of speech is absolutely guaranteed under the First Amendment, and the right to remain silent is guaranteed under the Fifth Amendment.

The decision to ignore the ruling of the European Court was an embarrassment to the government: Britain had been one of the original signatories of the European Convention on Human Rights. It had now to argue that the seriousness of the terrorist threat in Northern Ireland made it necessary to repudiate it. The decision may have been helped by a dispute that developed in November and December between Britain and Belgium and Ireland. The Belgian police, acting at Britain's request, arrested an Irish former priest, Patrick Ryan, whom the British accused of being an I R A terrorist, alleging that he had delivered explosives to the I R A commandos who murdered a number of British servicemen in Europe. The Belgian courts refused to extradite him to Britain – claiming that the extradition request was improperly drafted – and shipped him off to Dublin before the improprieties could be corrected. The Irish attorney-general refused to permit his extradition to Britain on the grounds that the British government and newspapers had made so many prejudicial statements against him that he would never get a fair trial.

At the same time, the British government lengthened sentences for terrorist acts by reducing the periods of remission to which convicts were entitled, from one-half of their sentences to one-third. It also proposed to amend the electoral law to require all candidates in local district council elections to sign declarations that they would not support terrorism or proscribed organizations if elected. It did not seem very probable that any of this would reduce the level of terrorism.

A further blow to the reputation of the British legal system occurred in October 1989, when a special review board of the Court of Appeal overturned the convictions of the Guildford Four, three men and a woman who had been convicted in 1975 of planting a series of bombs in 1974, which killed seven people. In 1977, an I R A squad on trial for another series of bombings had admitted that they were guilty of the Guildford and Woolwich bombings. The confession was ignored. During the 1989 investigation, the public prosecutor stated, 'It would be wrong for the Crown to seek to sustain the convictions.' The court found that the police had doctored the evidence, and the four later sued the government for wrongful imprisonment. The decision cast doubt upon another celebrated case, the conviction of six Irishmen of the Birmingham pub bombings, in which 21 people were killed. Those atrocities were also in 1974. After a further review of their case, the Birmingham Six were all released in March 1991, on the grounds that their confessions had been coerced and that the forensic evidence against them was unreliable.

The terror campaign continued. In 1989, an I R A squad, or more than one, operated in Germany and attacked British soldiers and civilians there. Several of them were arrested by Dutch police. On 22 September 1989, an I R A bomb planted in a Royal Marines School of Music killed nine bandsmen and one civilian, and wounded 22. It was the fifth time the I R A had bombed a military band, seen as 'soft' targets. In 1990, the I R A reverted to terrorist attacks on civilian targets in Great Britain for the first time since 1983. Bombs were placed in railway stations, in the London stock exchange and in the Carlton Club. In Northern Ireland, the I R A resumed 'Proxy Operations'. It would kidnap a civilian and force him, by threat of death or by threatening to kill his family, to drive a car or van loaded with explosives at the terrorists' target. In 1991, the terrorists bombed stores in London and resumed bombing the centre of Belfast, destroying hotels, office buildings and the city opera house. Most people would describe this as pure vandalism, destroying their own city to make a political point. The I R A saw things otherwise.

Over a period of 18 months, the British Secretary of State for Northern Ireland, Peter Brooke, tried to organize talks between the democratic political parties, Protestant and Catholic, on restoring provincial government that had been suspended in 1972. The debate, once again, was about 'power sharing', how to allow Catholics a guaranteed part in government, despite their status as a permanent minority. The talks finally opened on 30 April 1991. They promptly became bogged down in procedural disputes over where the talks would be held, who would preside and to what extent the Dublin government would be involved. They were abandoned in July 1991.

## THE NEGOTIATIONS

The Anglo-Irish Treaty of 1985 did not attain its primary objective, setting a framework that both Northern communities would accept and thus bringing peace. But it did signify that the British and Irish governments were ready to make concessions and to negotiate. For many years after it, the British insisted that the I R A must renounce violence permanently before its political representatives, Sinn Fein, could be allowed to join talks with the two governments and with the democratic parties. In deference to the Unionists, the British also asserted that the I R A must prove its devotion to peace by disarming, giving up its arsenal of weapons and explosives before Sinn Fein could be admitted to the bargaining table. Sinn Fein, meanwhile, was equally obdurate, insisting not only that the I R A would never disarm but that Britain must first of all announce that it would give up its guarantee to the Unionists that Northern Ireland's status would never be changed against the will of its inhabitants.

But behind these dogmatic positions, which quite precluded meaningful negotiations, slow, subterranean changes were taking place. The Protestant community was coming to accept that it would have to make very considerable political concessions to the Nationalists if peace were to be restored – and the I R A itself was changing. As the 25th anniversary of the 'armed struggle' approached, that secretive organization seemed to be coming slowly and painfully to grips with the realization that it could not and never would bomb Ulster into the republic. The only hope for reunification of Ireland was political, and that meant a permanent ceasefire.

The Irish government and the democratic Nationalist party in the North, the Social-Democratic Labour Party (S D L P), pushed steadily to get the British government to admit that it must eventually negotiate with Sinn Fein. Their arguments were potently aided when the new American president, Bill Clinton, permitted Gerry Adams, the political leader of Sinn Fein, to visit the United States in January 1994. The British protested bitterly and volubly and only later admitted that Mr Clinton was right: the object was not to score points but to persuade the I R A to agree to a ceasefire and a political approach to the problem.

The parallel evolution inside the I R A was much harder to detect. It was obviously difficult for the gunmen (and to some, impossible) to admit that 25 years of terrorism had been a failure. That would mean that all those good Catholics had the blood of innocents on their hands. For a generation they had argued that the end justified the means. Now they were being asked to concede that the means could never achieve the end they intended and, on the contrary, made it much more difficult. Many who had to be persuaded were serving long prison terms for terrorism. They would have to face the conclusion that their years of jail had not served the republican cause, merely wasting the best years of their lives.

The question was to find as many carrots as possible to offer the I R A, if they would accept this one central truth. Gerry Adams himself, it appeared, made the leap relatively early, perhaps by 1990. The Social-Democratic Labour Party of Northern Ireland, which represents the great majority of Northern Catholics who repudiate both British and Unionist domination and I R A violence, was also pushing both sides towards negotiation. In September 1993 its leader, John Hume, announced that he had been holding secret talks with Gerry Adams.

Negotiations between the democratic parties, meaning the S D L P, the Unionists, and the two governments, were to start under American patronage. Mr Clinton sent a prominent retired politician, former Senator George Mitchell of Maine, to represent him, and Mr Mitchell soon became *de facto* mediator. Prodded by the Americans, the British and Irish governments issued a 'declaration of principle' in December 1993.

It stated that the British government supported Northern Ireland's right to choose between union with Great Britain or the Republic, and that the Irish government believed 'it would be wrong to impose a united Ireland without the freely given consent of the majority'.

The Irish government also promised to revise its constitution to eliminate its claims to the North and to examine those clauses most repugnant to minorities. This meant that the Roman Catholic bias of the Irish constitution would be eliminated.

The substantive clause, on which all subsequent negotiations would be based, stated, 'The two nations will seek, with Northern Ireland, to create institutions and structures which, while respecting the diversity of the people of Ireland, **429** would enable them to work together in all areas of common interest.' The declaration also said that Sinn Fein would be admitted to the talks in the somewhat roundabout promise: 'Democratically-mandated parties which establish a commitment to exclusively peaceful methods are free to join in the dialogue.'

Eight months later, on 31 August 1994, the IRA abruptly announced a ceasefire. The Protestant paramilitaries followed suit in October.

Belfast blossomed. The British pulled down the barricades in the city centre and stopped foot patrols by heavily-armed soldiers, which for years had given the cities of Northern Ireland the appearance of towns under military occupation during World War II. In the heady aftermath of peace, President Clinton visited Belfast, in December 1995, and was rapturously received.

However, the British prime minister, John Major, and his government, who remained in office on the sufferance of the Unionist parties, could still not escape their past rhetoric. They insisted that the IRA must disarm before Sinn Fein could be admitted to the negotiating table. Talks on the question dragged on for 18 months, and in February 1996 the IRA abruptly ended the ceasefire by exploding a huge bomb at Canary Wharf, a big office complex in East London. Two people were killed. Clinton was particularly angry because Gerry Adams had been to see him in the White House the week before, spouting his peaceful intentions.

The IRA had evidently planned the Canary Wharf operation for months. Police discovered two bomb factories in London and foiled several other major bombings, by luck and good police work. They were not always lucky: a car bomb did great damage to the centre of Manchester in June.

The impasse was broken after elections in Britain in May 1997 returned the Labour Party to power with a huge majority. The new government dropped the insistence on IRA disarmament as a precondition to admission to the talks. Tony Blair was clearly intent on settling the Irish question, if it could be done (bearing in mind that it had defeated every British government since Gladstone 130 years earlier). Sinn Fein's vote went up sharply, from 10 per cent in 1992 to 16.1 per cent in 1997, and two of its candidates (Gerry Adams in West Belfast and Martin McGuinness in Mid-Ulster) won seats in the Westminster parliament – which they refused to take. The point, however, was that although it represented only a small part of the electorate, Sinn Fein was clearly a 'democratically-mandated party' under the terms of the 1993 Anglo-Irish declaration. A month later, Sinn Fein won one seat in Irish elections, its first in 16 years.

In the annual marching season that July, Unionists were allowed to march through Drumcree, one last time. This is a mixed Catholic and Protestant town, and on previous occasions these militant and deliberately provocative demonstrations through a Catholic neighbourhood had sparked riots and killings. A huge contingent of troops was called out to keep the peace, and although there were three days of Catholic protest demonstrations, the worst disorder was avoided. Five days later, the Orange Order announced that it would suspend all further marches through Catholic streets that year: there would be no triumphalist march on 12 July through Derry to commemorate the lifting of the siege in

1689. The Orangemen marched in their own streets. A week later, the I R A announced that it was reinstating the ceasefire. Perhaps the new secretary of state for Northern Ireland, Mo Mowlem, had orchestrated the series of events with the Unionists and with the I R A. Or perhaps, for once, the British were lucky. It was a good beginning.

The British argument that it was making real, substantive concessions to the Nationalists – everything short of abandoning the Unionists to the Republic – apparently persuaded Adams and the I R A's council. When the talks opened in September, and Adams took his place for the first time, he stated his party's commitment 'to exclusively peaceful means' to end the dispute. A notable and heartening development was that the Protestants did not rise in revolt when Sinn Fein was admitted to the talks, as they had in 1974. On the contrary, though with much grumbling, the main Unionist party agreed to negotiate with Gerry Adams. Although the Rev. Ian Paisley denounced every concession to Sinn Fein, he did it with far less vehemence than in earlier years.

The Protestant extremists were not persuaded. They now distrusted the British as once the I R A had distrusted the government in Dublin. In December 1997, as the talks moved slowly forward, the old demons burst forth again. The ultra-republican I N L A mounted an astonishing coup, murdering a leading Protestant terrorist, Billy Wright, in the Maze prison outside Belfast. He was suspected of taking part in the murders of over 40 Catholics, most of them innocent civilians. In revenge, Wright's Ulster Volunteer Force started killing Catholics. There were other murders, including the killing of a Catholic drug dealer by the I R A, enforcing public morality in its own way.

Both the Unionists and Sinn Fein ignored the provocation and continued the talks, under ceaseless prodding by the British and Irish governments and by President Clinton. They made slow progress until Senator Mitchell set a deadline, to force a settlement, midnight on Holy Thursday. In the event, the agreement was reached late on the afternoon of Good Friday, when the exhausted delegates emerged to announce their success.

## Notable incidents

### 1968

| | |
|---|---|
| 5 October | March by 300 supporters of Northern Ireland Civil Rights Association in Londonderry broken up by 'B Special' police. Demonstrators beaten. |
| 6 October | 800 people demonstrate in Londonderry against B Specials; protest broken up violently. |

### 1969

| | |
|---|---|
| January–June | Frequent disorders throughout Northern Ireland, threats to power stations: British send troops to protect them. |
| 12 July | Catholic counter-demonstrations in Belfast and Londonderry turn to riot. |
| 2–4 August | Unionist march in Belfast leads to anti-Catholic riot, condoned by police. 8 killed. |

| | |
|---|---|
| *14 August* | First British troops deployed in Londonderry (first time regular troops used in civil disorders since 1916). By 17 August, 4700 British troops deployed in Northern Ireland. |
| *15 August* | 3 shot by snipers in Belfast. |

## 1970

| | |
|---|---|
| *June* | Army imposes 24-hour curfew on Falls Road area, Belfast, conducts house-to-house search for terrorists; 5 people killed. |
| *9 August* | Internment without trial introduced. |

## 1971

| | |
|---|---|
| *4 December* | Protestant terrorists kill 15 Catholics with a bomb in a Londonderry bar. |

## 1972

| | |
|---|---|
| *30 January* | British paratroopers kill 13 Catholic demonstrators in Londonderry, on 'Bloody Sunday'. |
| *22 February* | IRA bomb in a bar in Aldershot, England, kills 7 British soldiers. |
| *24 March* | Stormont Parliament dissolved. Britain imposes direct rule on Northern Ireland. |
| *7 July* | IRA leaders flown to London for (fruitless) talks with British government. |

## 1973

| | |
|---|---|
| *11 November* | Power-sharing executive set up by Unionist, SDLP and Alliance parties. |
| *6–9 December* | Conference at Sunningdale in England between British and Irish governments and the 3 parties. Agree to a 'Council of Ireland'. |

## 1974

| | |
|---|---|
| *May* | Strike by Protestant Ulster Workers' Council forces abandonment of executive and Sunningdale proposals. |
| *17 May* | Car bombs in Dublin, planted by Protestant terrorists, kill 22 people. |
| *21 November* | IRA bombs in two pubs in Birmingham kill 21. |

## 1976

| | |
|---|---|
| *4 January* | 5 Catholics murdered in Co. Armagh. |
| *5 January* | 10 Protestant workers killed on a bus, in reprisal. |
| *21 July* | British ambassador to Dublin killed by a bomb. |

## 1977

| | |
|---|---|
| *10 October* | Betty Williams (Protestant) and Mairead Corrigan (Catholic) awarded Nobel Peace Prize. |

## 1978

| | |
|---|---|
| *17 February* | IRA bombs at the Le Mon café, Belfast, kill 12. |

## 1979

| | |
|---|---|
| *22 March* | British ambassador to the Netherlands killed. |
| *30 March* | Airey Neave, MP, killed by car bomb at the House of Commons. |
| *27 August* | Bomb kills 18 British soldiers at Warrenpoint, Northern Ireland. Lord Louis Mountbatten and 3 others killed by bomb on his boat in Sligo, Ireland. |

## 1980

| | |
|---|---|
| *October* | First IRA prisoners' hunger strike. Called off 18 December. |

## 1981

| | |
|---|---|
| *16 January* | Attempted assassination of Bernadette McAliskey, former MP, by Raymond Smallwoods. He served 7 years in the Maze for the crime. On 11 July 1994 Smallwoods, by then head of the Ulster Democratic Party, was shot by IRA. Bernadette McAliskey's daughter Roisin was charged with bombing a British base in Germany in 1996. |
| *21 January* | Sir Norman Stronge, former Speaker of Stormont parliament in Northern Ireland, shot. He was 86. |
| *1 March* | Bobby Sands begins hunger strike; he dies 5 April. (9 other IRA prisoners eventually starve themselves to death.) |

## 1982

| | |
|---|---|
| *22 July* | 11 British soldiers killed in two bombings in London, one under a bandstand in Regent's Park. |
| *6 December* | Irish National Liberation Army bombs disco in Ballykelly, killing 11 soldiers and 6 civilians. |

## 1983

| | |
|---|---|
| *17 December* | Car bomb outside Harrods department store in London kills 5 people, wounds more than 80. |

## 1984

| | |
|---|---|
| *12 October* | IRA bomb in the Grand Hotel, Brighton, during the annual Tory party conference, kills 4, narrowly missing Margaret Thatcher. |

## 1985

| | |
|---|---|
| *28 February* | IRA mortar attack on police barracks at Newry kills 9 policemen in a cafeteria. |
| *15 November* | Margaret Thatcher and Garrett FitzGerald sign Anglo-Irish treaty. |

## 1987

| | |
|---|---|
| *March* | Gunfights between rival Republican terrorists kill 12. |
| *25 April* | Ulster Chief Justice Maurice Gibson and his wife assassinated by a bomb. |
| *8 May* | 3 senior IRA men and 5 other terrorists killed in an ambush at Loughgall. |
| *8 November* | 11 civilians killed during an Armistice day service at Enniskillen. |

## 1988

| | |
|---|---|
| *6 March* | 3 IRA terrorists shot by British SAS men in Gibraltar. |
| *16 March* | 3 people killed by a Protestant terrorist during the Gibraltar terrorists' funeral. |
| *19 March* | 2 British soldiers lynched during the funeral of the victims of the 16 March shooting. |
| *2 May* | 3 RAF men killed by bombs in Holland. |
| *15 June* | 6 British soldiers killed by car bomb at sports event. |
| *1 August* | 1 soldier killed by bomb in army barracks in London. |
| *20 August* | 8 soldiers travelling from Belfast airport killed by bomb. |
| *30 August* | 3 IRA gunmen killed by security forces. |
| *31 August* | 2 IRA suspects arrested crossing West German border from Holland, carrying explosives. |
| *31 August* | Elderly Catholic couple killed by IRA booby-trap in Londonderry. |

| 12 September | Bombs demolish home of head of Northern Ireland civil service. Car bomb in Belfast injures 12. |
| 24 November | 67-year-old Catholic and his 11-year-old grand-daughter killed by IRA bomb; 8 other civilians wounded. As after 31 August incident, and Enniskillen bombing, the IRA apologizes. |

## 1989

| 14 March | 18 policemen reprimanded in Northern Ireland for the death of five IRA suspects in 1982, in the 'shoot-to-kill' or Stalker affair. |
| 8 September | German wife of British soldier shot in Germany. |
| 22 September | 10 Royal Marines killed by bomb in Royal Marines School of Music, near Deal, Kent. |
| 19 October | Guildford Four released and convictions for the 1974 pub bomb overturned. |
| 26 October | RAF corporal and his six-month-old child killed by two IRA gunmen in Germany. |

## 1990

| 12 January | 4 IRA men arrested in Florida trying to buy Stinger anti-aircraft missiles from undercover FBI agents. |
| 16, 20 June | Dutch police arrest 6 IRA terrorists involved in attacks on British troops in Germany. |
| 25 June | Bomb in Carlton Club, London, kills porter. |
| 20 July | Bomb in London Stock Exchange. |
| 30 July | Ian Gow, Tory MP and close friend of Prime Minister Thatcher, killed by a car bomb. |
| 19 September | IRA attempts to kill Sir Peter Terry, in Staffordshire. He was governor of Gibraltar when the 3 IRA terrorists were shot by police. He and his wife wounded. |
| 24 October | 7 killed, 37 wounded in series of proxy car bombings in Northern Ireland. Hostages were forced to drive cars with bombs in them at terrorists' targets. |

## 1991

| 7 February | IRA squad launches mortar attack on 10 Downing Street, the Prime Minister's address, from Whitehall, London. |
| 18 February | Bombs exploded in Paddington and Victoria stations, London, one killed. |
| 14 March | Birmingham Six freed after 16 years in jail; courts ruled their confessions were 'unsafe and unsatisfactory'. |
| 30 April | Preliminary talks open at Stormont between Protestant and Catholic parties and British on power sharing. |
| 1 June | 3 soldiers killed by car bomb attack on army base at Glenanne, Armagh. |
| 2 June | Senior civil servant, a woman, loses both legs in bomb attack. IRA apologizes. |
| 3 June | 3 IRA gunmen killed by police in ambush 30 miles west of Belfast. |
| 17 June | Round-table talks on future of Northern Ireland open in Stormont. |
| 3 July | Stormont talks abandoned because of Protestant intransigence. |
| 13 November | IRA shoots 4 men in Belfast, claiming they were members of Protestant death-squads. Another man and six-week-old baby wounded. |
| 15 November | Two terrorists, a man and a woman, blow themselves up with their own bomb in St Albans. |
| 1 December | Firebombs set off against shops in London. |
| December | Car bomb severely damages Belfast opera house and Europe Hotel. |

## 1992

| 6 January | 2 car bombs do great damage to centre of Belfast, and a firebomb set off in Oxford. |
| 10 January | Bomb in Whitehall damages government buildings. |

| | |
|---|---|
| *10 April* | Bomb in City of London causes $1 billion (£600 million) in damage, kills 3, injures 80. |

## 1993

| | |
|---|---|
| *3 January* | Gang of Irish expatriates rob Brinks van in New York, take $7.4 million. An ex-IRA man and a priest convicted, others acquitted at the trial. |
| *24 April* | 3 IRA bombs in London cause much damage in City, kill one. |
| *25 September* | John Hume of the SDLP and Gerry Adams of Sinn Fein announce that they have been holding secret talks. |
| *15 December* | Joint declaration by British and Irish governments invites Sinn Fein and Protestant terrorists' political fronts to take part in peace talks if they order ceasefire. |

## 1994

| | |
|---|---|
| *9, 11 and 13 March* | IRA launches mortar attacks on Heathrow Airport, London. No casualties. |
| *18 June* | UVF terrorists kill 6 Catholics watching World Cup in pub. One, 87, oldest killed during Troubles. |
| *11 July* | Protestant terrorist Ray Smallwoods shot by IRA. |
| *31 August* | IRA declares ceasefire. |
| *21 September* | Conviction of Paul Hill and three others, the Guildford Four, for 1975 murders reversed. They had been released in 1989. Hill married a daughter of Robert Kennedy. |
| *13 October* | Protestant paramilitaries declare ceasefire. |
| *10 November* | IRA members kill postal worker in hold-up. |
| *30 November* | President Clinton visits Belfast and Londonderry. |

## 1996

| | |
|---|---|
| *30 January* | Gino Gallagher, INLA chief of staff (commander), killed, probably by other INLA terrorists. 6 other INLA terrorists killed in feud that year. |
| *9 February* | IRA bomb at Canary Wharf, London, kills 2, wounds over 100, breaking ceasefire. |
| *15 February* | IRA bomb found in phone booth in London, defused successfully. |
| *18 February* | IRA bomb on London bus kills bomber, wounds 9. Bomb factory found in terrorist's flat. |
| *25 April* | 2 bombs discovered and disarmed under Hammersmith Bridge, London. |
| *15 June* | IRA car bomb in Manchester injures 200. |
| *23 September* | London police capture 10 tons of IRA bombs and bomb-making equipment, kill 1, injure 5. |
| *7 October* | 2 car bombs in British Army HQ at Lisburn near Belfast, 1 soldier killed, 30 injured. |
| *29 November* | IRA bomb discovered at British Army base in Armagh, N. Ireland. |
| *22 December* | Protestant terrorists plant car bomb in Catholic area of Belfast, 1 injured. |

## 1997

| | |
|---|---|
| *2 January* | Half-ton of explosives found in truck near a hotel in Belfast. |
| *16 June* | IRA kills 2 police in Lurgan, Co. Armagh. |
| *20 July* | IRA resume ceasefire. |
| *27 December* | Billy Wright, leader of Protestant terrorist group Ulster Volunteer Force, shot by INLA in Maze prison. A Catholic killed, 3 wounded that night in retaliation. |

## 1998

| | |
|---|---|
| *9 April* | Provisional peace agreement signed by Sinn Fein, Unionist leaders and British and Irish governments. |

## FURTHER READING

Adams, Gerry, *Before the Dawn, an Autobiography*, New York, William Morrow, 1997.

Amnesty International, *Report of the Amnesty International Mission to Northern Ireland*, London, 1978.

New Ireland Forum, *The Economic Consequences of the Division of Ireland Since 1920, The Cost of Violence arising from the Northern Ireland Crisis since 1969* and *Reports of Proceedings, 1983, and conclusions*, Dublin, Stationery Office, 1984.

O'Malley, Padraig, *The Uncivil Wars* (includes a comprehensive bibliography), Boston,Houghton Mifflin Co., 1983.

Rose, Richard, *Northern Ireland: Time of Choice*, Washington, American Enterprise Institute, 1976.

Stalker, John, *The Stalker Affair*, New York, Viking/London, Harrap, 1988.

Taylor, Peter, *Provos: The IRA and Sinn Fein*, London, Bloomsbury, 1997.

Watt, David (ed.), *The Constitution of Northern Ireland*, London, Heinemann, 1981.

# YUGOSLAVIA

When the horrors of the Holocaust were revealed in 1945, the world took a very public vow, 'Never again!' Later generations would never permit the systematic elimination of one race or nation. There is even a U N convention against genocide which binds the nations of the world to take whatever means are needed to stop future genocides.

But it happened again, in Yugoslavia in 1992–5 and in Rwanda in 1994 (*see* p. 26). The government of Serbia, led by Slobodan Milosevic, and the government of Croatia, led by Franjo Tudjman, determined that the Muslims of Bosnia would be wiped out. They would be killed or driven into permanent exile. Tudjman planned to partition Bosnia with Serbia. Milosevic wanted it all, or virtually all of it, as part of 'Greater Serbia'. Genocide means the extermination of a people: not just killing them, but wiping out every trace of their history, culture, society and even their existence. The Serbs and Croats deliberately and consciously set about destroying not only the Muslims themselves but every trace of their 500-year-old presence in Bosnia. Every mosque in Serb- and Croat-occupied territory was destroyed, along with libraries, memorials, graveyards and historic sites such as the Ottoman bridge at Mostar. The land was swept clean of 2 million of its inhabitants, who either fled this 'ethnic cleansing' or stayed – and were killed. Most of the killings were carried out by Serbs, either Bosnians, under the command of Radovan Karadzic and Ratko Mladic, or those from Serbia itself, led by various commanders all ultimately responsible to Milosevic. For three years, faced by overwhelming evidence of genocide in south-east Europe, the powers merely wrung their hands. Finally, in 1995, after a particularly egregious massacre (of over 8000 men in Srebrenica) and the shelling of street markets in Sarajevo under the eyes of Western TV cameras, Nato intervened to stop the killings.

A short bombing campaign made the Serbs pause, but then the Croats and Bosnian Muslims, by then allies, launched a general offensive and overran half Serb-held Bosnia, and would have captured the rest if the United States had not insisted on arranging a ceasefire, at Dayton in Ohio. Since then, Nato forces have policed Bosnia, trying to make the murderers and their victims live together again. Most of the signs point to failure, which means that Nato must either remain indefinitely, or must withdraw, and allow the war to resume. In the short run, that would probably produce a Muslim–Croat victory. That might be followed by a new war of uncertain outcome, between Bosnia and Croatia. There would be hundreds of thousands more refugees and Serbia would prepare for revenge. So would the loser of any war between Bosnia and Croatia – if not at once, then in a few years' time. The three wars, 1991–5, cost perhaps 150,000 lives and left over 2 million refugees.

Then, over the winter of 1997–8, the long-simmering dispute in Kosovo came to the boil. The Kosovo Albanians had followed a policy of peaceful resistance to Serbian domination for six years, but at last the more militant among them, the Kosovo Liberation Front, took up arms against their oppressors. There was a series of incidents and finally, on 28 February 1998, four Serb policemen were killed in an ambush. The Serbs reacted with their usual ferocity, massacring over 100 people in the nearest village. Mass demonstrations followed and the K L F was, of course, much strengthened: the young men of Kosovo, joined by their compatriots in Albania proper and elsewhere, took to the hills. The outside world, fearful of a repeat of the Bosnia catastrophe, tried to mediate but neither side appeared ready for compromise.

Yugoslavia's divisions were as follows:

*Independent states:*
Bosnia and Herzegovina, capital Sarajevo, 19,741 sq. miles (51,129 sq. km), population 4,383,000.
Croatia, capital Zagreb, 21,829 sq. miles (56,537 sq. km), population 4.8 million, G N P per capita $3250.
Macedonia, capital Skopje, 9928 sq. miles (25,713 sq. km), population 2.1 million, G N P per capita $860.
Slovenia, capital Ljublana, 7819 sq. miles (20,250 sq. km), population 2 million, G N P per capita $8200.

*Federal Republic of Yugoslavia:*
Montenegro, capital Podgorica (formerly Titograd), 5333 sq. miles (13,812 sq. km).
Serbia, capital Belgrade, 34,116 sq. miles (88,360 sq. km). Population of Serbia and Montenegro together, 10,518,000.

These are the World Bank's figures for 1995 and take little account of refugees. The Bank offers no estimate of the G N P of Bosnia or Serbia-Montenegro. The Serbian figures include the formerly autonomous provinces of Kosovo and Vojvodina. Kosovo had 1.9 million people, 90 per cent of them Albanian, in 1991. Vojvodina had 2 million including 1.1 million Serbs, 350,000 Hungarians, 100,000 Croats, 174,000 who called themselves Yugoslavs (mostly people of mixed ancestry), and 100,000 Romanians. Ethnic cleansing has spread to both provinces and there are many refugees there, so the population figures are unreliable.

The former Yugoslavia's languages are Serbo-Croat (the two dialects are nearly identical but written in different alphabets), Macedonian (Bulgarian), Slovene, Albanian, Hungarian and Romanian.

The figures for refugees, as calculated for the U S Committee for Refugees' 1997 report, based on the U N H C R, are:

Bosnia: Of 2 million displaced persons in Bosnia in 1995, 250,000 had returned to their homes on their own by the end of 1996, the great majority to areas controlled by their ethnic or religious group. One million remained displaced inside Bosnia; 160,000 Bosnian refugees lived in Croatia, 250,000 in Yugo-slavia, 10,400 in Slovenia and 5000 in Macedonia. 600,000 Bosnians are refugees elsewhere in Europe, including 320,000 to 350,000 in Germany.

Croatia: There are 167,000 foreign refugees in Croatia and 114,000 Croatian refugees from the Krajina, who were expelled by the Serbs there and from eastern Slavonia which was captured by the Serbs in the 1991–2 war. There were 60,000 to 80,000 Serb refugees from Bosnia and the Krajina in eastern Slavonia, areas 'cleansed' in the Croatian and Muslim victories in 1995, who face expulsion now that Croatia has resumed control.

Yugoslavia: There were 300,000 Serb refugees from Croatia (driven out of the Krajina), and 25,000 from Bosnia. Many have been settled in Kosovo and Vojvodina.

## HISTORY

The great fault-line of Balkan history runs through the heart of Yugoslavia, and is the root of all its troubles. The division goes back to the Roman Empire and Byzantium. The north (Slovenia and Croatia) is Catholic and uses the Latin alphabet. The south is Orthodox and uses the Cyrillic alphabet. From the time the Slavs flooded into the Balkans in the 7th century, the districts that became Slovenia and Croatia were part of central Europe, looking to Vienna and Rome. A Croatian kingdom was established in 924, and lasted for two centuries. Later, it became part of the Austro-Hungarian empire, together with Slovenia. Bosnia-Hercegovina, Serbia and the southern territories remained in the Byzantine empire until they were conquered by the Turks in the 14th and 15th centuries, and remained subjects of the Ottoman Porte for 500 years. The Adriatic coast, Dalmatia, was separate from the hinterland for centuries, first ruled by Venice and then by Austria. In the early 19th century, Napoleon annexed it to France. Dalmatia was therefore always Catholic and is now part of Croatia. One of the Venetian cities, Ragusa, became a major trading centre in the Middle Ages. It later became a vassal of the Turks but retained its Catholic, Western orientation and prosperity. It was renamed Dubrovnik when Yugoslavia was established in 1919. This historical accident meant that Serbia was cut off from the Adriatic, and during the 19th century and in the Balkan wars early in the 20th, one of its objectives was to reach the sea – and the rest of Europe was intent on preventing it. The question became moot with the establishment of Yugoslavia in 1919, but abruptly revived with Croatia's proclamation of independence in 1991.

The Serbs won their independence from the Turks in the early 19th century, under two rival dynasties, the Karadjordjevics and Obrenovics. Periodically the king and his family would be murdered, and the head of the rival dynasty would return from exile to replace him. In June 1903, King Alexander Obrenovic and his wife Draga were murdered in their palace by a group of Serbian terrorists, **439** members of a secret society called the Black Hand. Peter Karadjordjevic, who may have known of the plot, was brought back from exile and proclaimed king.

Serbia hoped to expand its frontiers to re-establish the mediaeval Serbian empire, but was thwarted by Austria to the north. It had more success to the south: in a series of Balkan wars up to 1913, it progressively annexed Montenegro, Kosovo and northern Macedonia. Austria also advanced southwards, occupying Bosnia in 1878, and formally annexing the province in 1908, despite Serbian protests.

On 28 June 1914, a Serbian terrorist, Gavril Princip, assassinated the Archduke Franz-Ferdinand and his wife as they drove in an open carriage through Bosnia's capital, Sarajevo. He was nephew and heir to the Austrian emperor. Princip was a member of the Black Hand, like the murderers of King Alexander, and despite all the denials at the time, it is clear that at least some members of the Serbian government were connected with the assassination.

Austria demanded reparations from Serbia and, when the Belgrade government hesitated, issued an ultimatum, demanding a comprehensive act of contrition and reparation amounting to complete surrender to Vienna. Serbia appealed to its ally, Russia, which mobilized its army. The great mechanism of European alliances and war plans was then set in motion. Germany mobilized, France mobilized, and Germany then invaded France and Belgium. In the cataclysm that followed, 20 million people were killed, and Europe was devastated, losing that position of dominance in the world she had maintained for centuries. The Austrian, German, Russian and Ottoman empires were overthrown, the British and French empires mortally weakened, Lenin and Trotsky imposed Communism upon Russia with all the frightful consequences that ensued, and the way was prepared for a greater conflict 20 years later. All this was the direct consequence of the murders in Sarajevo.

Serbia was devastated by World War I. It lost a quarter of its adult male population, even more than in World War I I, but it emerged victorious. The peacemakers gathered at Versailles in 1919 and tried to settle the frontiers of Europe on principles of ethnic homogeneity and justice. They were not very successful. Subsequent generations of impartial historians have concluded that the task was impossible, that the intermingling of peoples in central, eastern and south-eastern Europe was so confused that clearly established ethnic frontiers were unobtainable. In the case of Serbia, its rule over Macedonia was confirmed, it was given the Banat, which had been part of Hungary, and it annexed Slovenia, Croatia and Bosnia-Hercegovina from Austria–Hungary. All these territories were brought together in the Kingdom of Serbs, Croats and Slovenes, which later changed its name to Jugoslavia, meaning the Kingdom of the South Slavs (the spelling was changed after World War I I).

Between the wars, Jugoslavia was alternately a federal and centralized state, but was always dominated by Serbia. King Alexander Karadjordjevic was assassinated in Marseilles in 1934, riding in an open carriage at the outset of a state visit, exactly as Franz-Ferdinand had been murdered 20 years earlier. The culprit, this time, was a Macedonian terrorist hired by the Croatian *Ustache*. This was by no means the first act of Serb–Croat violence. In 1928 a Montenegrin deputy had shot the Croatian parliamentary leader and two other Croat deputies, on the floor of the National Assembly. The *Ustache* (Uprising) was a Croat fascist society, which wanted to build a Catholic, Croatian kingdom on the ruins of Jugoslavia.

Alexander's heir, Prince Peter, was II years old, and the government devolved to his cousin, Paul. The regent tried to preserve Jugoslavia's independence and unity as the shadows fell across Europe. All the Balkans were fascist, and Italy and Hungary, which were allied to Germany, had irridentist claims upon Jugoslavia. In 1938, Hitler annexed Austria. In 1939, Mussolini occupied Albania, and the kingdom was surrounded. Finally, in October 1940, after Hitler had occupied France and driven the British from Europe, the *Duce* Mussolini invaded Greece. He was defeated, and the following spring, the Greeks prepared to liberate Albania. Mussolini was compelled to appeal to Hitler for help, and Hitler in turn demanded that Prince Paul allow German armies to pass through Jugoslavia to reach Greece.

Paul capitulated and on 25 March signed a treaty of alliance with Germany in Vienna. The event outraged the Serbs, and the next day Paul was deposed by his own army. King Peter, by then 18 years old, was proclaimed king. The new regime, having removed the regent, hoped to appease Hitler by accepting the Vienna treaty, but the *Führer* refused to admit that one of his allies might be overthrown. He ordered that Jugoslavia and Greece be occupied immediately. The invasion began on 6 April, and in a few days the whole country was occupied and King Peter fled for his life. He did not return until 1991.

This was Yugoslavia's second contribution to Europe's 20th-century history; the first was the murder in Sarajevo. At the time of these events, in the spring of 1941, Hitler was preparing Operation Barbarossa, the invasion of the Soviet Union. It was scheduled for early May, but it was postponed for six weeks to permit the occupation of the Balkans. If the *Wehrmacht* had not been delayed, it might have taken Moscow that year, and perhaps defeated the Soviet Union. Hitler's armies reached the suburbs of Moscow in November 1941, but were stopped by the onset of winter. Furthermore, Jugoslavia resisted the Germans in the most savage and costly guerrilla war in occupied Europe. The Germans had to keep 200,000 troops there, fighting Tito's partisans, instead of sending them to the eastern front.

When they had conquered Jugoslavia, the Germans partitioned it. Slovenia was divided between Germany, Italy and Hungary. Italy took Kosovo and most of Dalmatia. Bulgaria annexed Macedonia, and Hungary took the Banat. Croatia was set up as an independent, fascist kingdom under the *Ustache* leader Ante Pavelic. It annexed Bosnia-Hercegovina and much of Serbia, and Pavelic set about converting the Serbs to Catholicism. Those he could not convert, he killed, together with the Jews. Altogether, the Croatian regime was responsible for killing 700,000 people, a fascist achievement exceeded only by the Germans themselves. Pavelic escaped to Spain after the war, and his minister of police, Andriya Artukovitch, escaped to California. He was a war criminal on a par with Eichmann, and it was one of the great scandals of modern America that he was protected for 30 years. He was eventually extradited in the 1980s, and died in prison.

Josip Broz, who used the *nom de guerre* Tito, had been in Russia at the time of the Revolution, took part in the civil war, and later played a role in the Spanish civil war. In 1941, he was secretary-general of the Yugoslav Communist Party, having attained that position after Stalin had his predecessors shot. He started a guerrilla war in Yugoslavia immediately after the German invasion, and eventually led his own army to victory. He was the only resistance leader in Europe who could make the claim: the Balkans are particularly suited to guerrilla warfare. He called his army Partisans, after the Spanish guerrillas who had resisted Napoleon. On the way, he fought and defeated a royalist resistance group, the Cetniks, who were led by Col. Draza Mihailovic. The Cetniks collaborated with the Germans to fight Tito's Partisans, and because of this, in 1944, the British abandoned them and switched their support to Tito. Churchill's government has been much abused since then for its contribution to bringing Communism to Yugoslavia, but in the context of World War I I, there can be no denying that it was the right choice. Britain's object was defeating Hitler, not the future government of Yugoslavia. In any event, Tito would have defeated Mihailovich whether the British helped him or not.

The guerrilla war in Yugoslavia was exceptionally brutal. The Germans massacred scores of thousands of people in reprisal for their losses, and the fighting between Croats and Serbs was particularly savage. Muslims from Bosnia were recruited both by the Croat *Ustache*, to fight the Serbs, and by the Germans to fight the Russians. Members of all three communities were guilty of frightful atrocities, but the Croats left the worst record. Ratko Mladic, as a child, saw his parents murdered by *Ustache* gunmen, and lived to be one of Bosnia's worst war criminals.

After the war, Tito set up a Stalinist republic, bitterly hostile to the West. But then Stalin decided that the Marshal was too independent, and tried to have him overthrown. The attempt failed, and in 1948, the darkest year of the cold war in Europe, Yugoslavia was expelled from the Communist camp. Tito turned West for help and gave up Stalinism. He evolved a modified form of Communism which, for a while, brought considerable prosperity to Yugoslavia. He encouraged Western tourism, which developed the Dalmatian coast into one of Europe's playgrounds, but he also played a great role in the Third World – a term he established with Nehru, Chou En-lai and Sukarno.

Although he had modified the political system, Yugoslavia was still a one-party state. Whatever the constitution provided, real power was firmly in the hands of the party. In his later years, Tito set up a federal constitution, run by a presidential council on which the six republics were equally represented. The leader of each would be federal president in turn, for a one-year term. It did not much matter that the system was unworkable so long as Tito lived and so long as the party was united on a Yugoslav basis.

Tito died in 1980, and as the decade advanced, it became apparent that the Communist Party was falling apart and that the constitution of Yugoslavia could not support the strain. The rivalries of Croats and Serbs revived, and so did the split between the rich north (Slovenia and Croatia) and the impoverished south. There were similar divisions in other European countries, but unlike Italy or Spain, the poor, southern parts of Yugoslavia dominated the government. Serbia, throughout the short history of Yugoslavia, was the main political force. Under the monarchy and under Tito, it exercised its hegemony by force and guile. After Tito, its leaders relied on brute force, failing to observe that their relative power had diminished with the years.

The first serious conflict, and the one that provided for the rise of Slobodan Milosevic, occurred in Kosovo. This was an autonomous province of Serbia, immediately north and east of Albania. It was the poorest region of Yugoslavia. Ninety per cent of its 2 million population speaks Albanian and most of them are Muslims. Early this century, there were as many Serbs as Albanians in Kosovo, but the majority of Serbs left for the greater prosperity of the north. They claim that they were driven out by Albanian terrorism. In 1981, there were pogroms in Kosovo directed at the Serb minority, many of whom were murdered (50 by official count). There were the usual Balkan reports of frightful atrocities perpetrated by the Albanians. The whole situation closely parallels that in Nagorno-Karabakh, in Azerbaijan, a region chiefly populated by Armenians and claimed by both republics.

Milosevic was deputy to the Serbian president. After further disturbances in Pristina, capital of Kosovo, he addressed a mass rally of Serbs there and promised that never again would Serbs be persecuted in their own country. He claimed Kosovo as inalienably Serb, because it was the site of a famous battle at which the Turks had destroyed the Serb kingdom, in 1389. In 1989, by then securely in power in Belgrade, he sent an army to rule Kosovo, suppressing all local authorities.

Yugoslavia's economic situation deteriorated steadily during the 1980s. The collective government lacked the authority to deal with the underlying economic and political problems: Slovenia and Croatia prospered greatly, Bosnia moderately, while Serbia stagnated and Macedonia and Kosovo remained sunk in unchanging poverty. In 1988, the signs of dissolution became evident. Serbs began to demand that their numbers and historic role as leaders of Yugoslavia be recognized. Milosevic put himself at the head of a xenophobic Serb movement, and won a degree of popularity that no Yugoslav leader had enjoyed since Tito. As a result, of course, he was widely distrusted in the other regions.

Milosevic demanded that Kosovo and the Vojvodina, another autonomous province in the north-east, should lose their autonomy and be reintegrated into Serbia. Early in October 1988, he organized a mass demonstration of 100,000 Serbs in the Vojvodina, which led to the resignation of the entire local government. It was replaced by Milosevic's nominees. On 9 October, he instigated similar riots in Montenegro, Yugoslavia's smallest republic, demanding the local government's resignation. Montenegrins are Serbs and share Serbians' feelings about Kosovo. On that occasion, the authorities suppressed the rioters.

On 20 October 1988, at a meeting of the party politburo, Milosevic demanded that Kosovo and Vojvodina be incorporated into Serbia and that Serbia's role in the federation be strengthened. The politburo ruled against him and voted to uphold the loose system bequeathed by Tito. Milosevic would not accept the verdict and in November succeeded in forcing the resignation of party leaders in Kosovo, whom he accused of abetting the 'persecution' of the Serbian minority. They, too, were replaced by men loyal to Serbia, and Slobodan Milosevic. The following week, he called out the people of Belgrade in an enormous demonstration against the alleged Albanian atrocities in Kosovo. At least 600,000 people answered the call. Then, on 1 January 1989, a further series of demonstrations in Montenegro stirred up by Milosevic's supporters forced the resignation of the entire government and party leadership. Milosevic now controlled Kosovo, Vojvodina and Montenegro, as well as Serbia itself. Meanwhile, Albanians were demonstrating in Pristina, the capital of Kosovo, demanding the reinstatement of the dismissed officials. The demonstrations were vigorously repressed.

Yugoslavia's economic crisis continued to worsen. Inflation reached an annual rate of 250 per cent by the end of 1988, accelerating to 10,000 per cent per annum a year later. The 'self-management' of industrial enterprises introduced by Tito, one of his many deviations from classical Stalinism, had proved a disaster. Large numbers of these enterprises were bankrupt but could not be closed. The six republics competed against each other: Serbia started an economic boycott of Slovenia in 1989, and all the republics, considering themselves the victims of the machinations of the others, established their economic independence from each other. It soon degenerated into full-scale trade war. There was far less co-operation between them than there was between unrelated independent states elsewhere in the world, let alone the 12 members of the European Community. In the autumn of 1988, the federal government, headed by an economist, Branko Mikulic, proposed stringent reform measures, in consultation with the IMF. The reforms were rejected by parliament (which refused to pass the budget) and the government resigned on 30 December. It was a Western phenomenon and the first time such a thing had happened in a Communist country.

It also failed to resolve Yugoslavia's problems. A new government appeared, in March 1989, led by Ante Markovic. He was a former bank manager and prime minister of Croatia, and proposed even stiffer economic reforms. He used the government's constitutional weakness to his advantage, by persuading parliament (then controlled by the party bosses) that in the crisis they should give him emergency powers. He promptly tied the Yugoslav dinar to the German mark, and made it fully convertible from 1 January 1990. At the same time, he permitted unlimited foreign ownership of Yugoslav companies. He then set about using the economic reforms to provoke the country and party into political change along the lines of the rest of eastern Europe. It was Yugoslavia's last chance of economic and political reform, and it was too late.

The conflict between the various republics was steadily worsening. In December 1989, the Communist parties of Croatia and Slovenia both voted to hold free elections in 1990, abandoning their 'leading role'. They had observed events in the rest of eastern Europe (their conferences occurred during the Romanian revolution) and concluded that their only salvation lay in adopting a market economy – and applying to join the European Community. The Kosovo problem grew steadily worse, building up to full-scale rebellion in January 1990. Kosovo is the poorest region of Yugoslavia, and suffered severely from the recession and the heavy hand of Slobodan Milosevic. In 1989, over 20 people were killed in disturbances in the province, most of them Albanians, and in the last week of January, another 20 were killed.

On 20 January 1990, a national party convention broke up in disorder when the Slovene delegates walked out, leaving the national party hopelessly split. The Slovenes, supported by the Croatians, had demanded that the constitution be amended to guarantee freedom of the press and other human rights; and that the party commit itself to dismantle communism. They were defeated by the block vote of Serbians and Montenegrins. The other two republics, Macedonia and Bosnia-Hercegovina, supported the reformers, though with less vehemence. The conference did, however, vote to abandon the party's leading role.

The party was disintegrating, an event that left the prime minister, Ante Markovic, unmoved. 'Yugoslavia will function with or without the Communist Party,' he said. He was mistaken.

In April 1990, the first free elections in Yugoslavia's history took place in Slovenia and Croatia. In Slovenia, a coalition of nationalist non-Communist parties, Demos, won a large majority in parliament, but a former Communist, Milan Kucan, won the presidency. In Croatia, the Democratic Union, led by Franjo Tudjman, won easily.

Tudjman was a former Partisan general, who had quarrelled with Tito on the question of Croatian rights and had spent some time in Yugoslav jails. He showed many of the same signs of authoritarianism, demagoguery and chauvinism displayed by Slobodan Milosevic in Serbia. He revised many of the *Ustache* symbols and established a palace guard, which he dressed in comic opera uniforms straight out of Ruritania. Tudjman's many critics took to describing him as a fascist and even accused him of re-establishing the war-time *Ustache* republic, with all its horrible freight of cruelty and xenophobia. He denied the charges, of course, but as soon as he took office, he began purging Serbs from government positions, and provoked constant disputes with the federal government. The threat was always that if Yugoslavia did not conform to Croatia's wishes, it would proclaim its full independence.

Slovenia proceeded more calmly and systematically, without Tudjman's provocations and flamboyance, but the end result was the same. In February 1991, Slovenia announced that it was setting up its own currency and armed forces, and would repudiate all federal control. The next day, Croatia's parliament voted itself the right to veto all federal laws. By then, both republics were importing arms from abroad, and arming and training their own militias to be ready to fight the federal army. All these moves were steps towards full independence, and Serbia prepared to fight them. Milosevic insisted that if Yugoslavia were to split up, Serbia would demand border adjustments, meaning that it would annex Croatian territories with Serbian populations.

Tensions increased rapidly through the spring, with fighting breaking out between Serbs and Croats in many Croatian towns. On 2 May, several dozen people were killed in border villages. The killings started with the massacre of Croat police.

The Yugoslav federation split irretrievably in the summer of 1991. Slovenia and Croatia proclaimed their independence on 25 June. The federal parliament, in the absence of Croatian and Slovenian representatives, ordered the federal army 'to undertake measures to prevent the division of Yugoslavia and changes in its borders'. Milosevic denounced the secession but said that he would not use force against it.

The war started immediately. To begin with, federal troops attacked Slovenia, which was considered the more intransigent of the two seceded republics. **445**

Slovene militias laid siege to the numerous federal army barracks in the republic, and the Yugoslav air force started bombing targets in Slovenia. Federal forces seized control of the border crossings into Austria, but then the Slovene army laid siege to them, too. The federal army, which was wholly dominated by Serbs, prepared to send columns of tanks across Croatia into Slovenia, and the European Community began a long mediation effort, arranging the first of numerous ceasefires. It lasted no more than a few hours.

Within a week of the Slovene and Croatian declarations of independence, serious fighting had started in Croatia. Irregular Serb forces inside Croatia started attacking Croat police and militias, hoping to draw in the federal army or blatantly in collaboration with it. The federal army launched an offensive against Croatia, ostensibly to clear a way through the republic to reach Slovenia, but in fact to reconquer Croatia entirely, or, failing that, to occupy the largely Serbian areas of the republic, and also to seize wholly Croatian areas that might serve some strategic or economic purpose. There were two main battlefields: eastern Croatia, a region known as Slavonia, and its principal cities Vukovar and Osijek; and Dalmatia. Serbia itself has no outlet on the Adriatic. The Serbian army and navy therefore laid siege to Dubrovnik (Ragusa), and it was entirely possible that they coveted the rest of Dalmatia.

It soon became apparent to the federal army that it could not fight Slovenia and Croatia simultaneously. The Slovenes had acquired a considerable stock of arms from abroad, and used them ruthlessly against federal positions, and soon recovered control of the border posts. The federals then agreed to a ceasefire, and most of their troops were withdrawn.

Serbia had lost the first, brief, war against Slovenia. It won the second war, against Croatia. Serbians in the border regions of Croatia, the Krajina, were the first to practise 'ethnic cleansing'. They drove Croats from their homes, and set up their own ostensibly independent republic. It was in fact part of Greater Serbia, and for the moment Tudjman's army was incapable of reoccupying it. The Serbian army, meanwhile, took Vukovar on 20 November 1991. The town had been reduced to ruins by constant shelling. It looked like Stalingrad in 1943 or Berlin in 1945, a frightful reminder of horrors that Europe had hoped were buried for good. The victorious Serbs then expelled those Croats still hiding in the cellars of the city, but first they killed large numbers of their prisoners. It was the first clear case of genocide: in later years, mass graves containing the bodies of thousands of Vukovar's inhabitants and defenders were dug up by UN investigators.

The European Community was conspicuously unable to bring the civil war to an end. There was extreme reluctance to send an army to keep the peace. The Germans were particularly reticent: they had kept 200,000 men in the Balkans in the early 1940s on the same mission, without success, and had no wish whatever to send their army back to Belgrade. That was all understandable, but rather diminished the case of a common European foreign and defence policy. If the Europeans could not bring peace to their own backyard, what chance had they to play much of a role in the wider world? In any event, they tried sending a series of peace missions and convoking a series of peace conferences in the Hague and elsewhere.

The United Nations met with more success. The secretary-general sent Cyrus

Vance, a former American secretary of state, as his representative and Vance succeeded in arranging a ceasefire on 2 January 1992. A U N peacekeeping force (U N P R O F O R) was sent to patrol the Krajina and eastern Slavonia around Vukovar. In the event, it served no useful purpose in either place. but at least the ceasefire stopped a further Serb offensive against Osijek or Dubrovnik.

As the dissolution of Yugoslavia proceeded in the north. the other republics and regions remained, for the moment, uneasy members of the federation. Milosevic, the federal army and the Serb extremists enthusiastically embraced the war, but it was notable that most young Serb men made every effort to escape conscription. They did not seem to relish giving their lives for Greater Serbia. There were signs of unrest in Montenegro, but for the moment the federal authorities kept firm control there, and Macedonia remained paralyzed by indecision. It finally proclaimed itw own independence as the disasters of Bosnia began to unfold.

The Kosovo Albanians behaved with astonishing moderation. Under the leadership of Ibrahim Rugova, they set up an entire rival administration and school system. They held elections to an assembly, proclaimed their independence, and ignored the Serb authorities, including schools and hospitals. They refused to pay taxes, obey the draft, or respect the Serb legal system. While the Bosnian calvary continued to the north, the Albanians practised the Gandhian principles of non-violent resistance to their oppressors.

## THE BOSNIAN WAR

The president of Bosnia-Hercegovina, Alia Izetbegovic, had warned anyone who would listen that if Germany got its way and forced immediate international recognition of Croatia, a civil war in Bosnia would be inevitable. Muslims, approximately 43 per cent and Croats approximately 18 per cent between them represented a majority of Bosnia's population, but they would be overwhelmed in a federation with Serbia. Milosevic's xenophobia and the violent hostility to Muslims preached by Serb radio and television ensured that Muslims would be a persecuted minority in a Serbian-led federation. Tudjman and Milosevic made no secret of their intention to partition Bosnia – and drive out the Muslims. But it was quite clear that they would never agree on the line of partition: Tudjman's plan would leave at least half Bosnia's Serbs in the Croat zone of Bosnia and, of course, he intended to recover the Krajina. Milosevic intended to keep the Krajina and extend Greater Serbia to meet it. In his view, there would be very little, if anything, for Tudjman. These plans were for the future. In the short term, Bosnia's Serbs and Croats were prepared for war. The Serb leader, a pathological racist called Radovan Karadzic (who was in fact Montenegrin, not Bosnian) and his chief military aide, General Ratko Mladic, never hid their loathing and contempt for the Muslims, whom they called Turks. The Yugoslav army dissolved and turned its arsenals and factories in Bosnia over to the Serb army being formed by Mladic out of former Yugoslav soldiers. Izetbegovic, meanwhile, made no preparations to defend the state.

Bosnia had been notably cosmopolitan, free from the ethnic rivalries that surfaced in Milosevic's Serbia and Tudjman's Croatia. Only 17 per cent of the **447**

Muslims practised their faith and there was a high level of intermarriage (and a particularly high number of Bosnians called themselves 'Yugoslavs' in the census, rather than choose an ethnic designation).

This precarious peace was shattered when Germany insisted on recognizing Slovenia and Croatia, and forced the other E U countries to follow its example, on 17 December 1991. The Muslims and Croats in Bosnia stepped up their campaign to declare independence from Yugoslavia, and the E U once again tried to mediate. There was a conference of the three groups in Cutileiro, Portugal, in February 1992, under E U supervision, and they all agreed that Bosnia should be divided into three ethnic zones, each with its own administration, under a general federal government. When Izetbegovic got back to Sarajevo he discovered that the Serbs would be satisfied with nothing less than 64 per cent of Bosnia's territory. His colleagues also pointed out that the three groups were so intermingled that an equitable partition was impossible without large movements of population. So he repudiated the Cutileiro agreement. The independence referendum took place on 29 February. The Serbs boycotted it and it passed comfortably. The Europeans and Americans recognized Bosnia in April.

By then the third war was well under way. Serb militias, trained and armed by the Yugoslav army, poured across the Drina and rapidly occupied a string of Muslim towns and villages on the east bank. Serb armies under Mladic's command attacked Muslim communities in central Bosnia and the north-west, while Croat militias did the same in south-central Bosnia (Hercegovina). In all these places, the Serb object was genocide: they wanted to kill or drive out all the Muslims, and create a purely Serb country. Hundreds of mosques, schools and monuments were destroyed. Muslims were driven out of their homes, and there were soon hundreds of thousands of refugees. Those that remained were often murdered.

Bosnian Muslim territory was a series of islands under siege by Serbs and Croats. The siege of Sarajevo was particularly atrocious, and well reported. Isolated Muslim villages in the Drina valley, including Goradze, Srebrenica and Zepa, hung on by good fortune and courage, with occasional help from international observers. Bihac, in the west, was completely cut off from the rest of government-held territory. Serb terrorists, most notoriously Zeljko Raznjatovic, known as Arkan, and Vojislav Seselj, massacred civilians at will, driving Muslims from their homes. Major Bosnian cities like Prijedor and Banja Luka were cleared entirely of Muslims, and their mosques were all destroyed.

The world press discovered a series of Serb concentration camps in north-central Bosnia, and television film taken in some of them instantly reminded the world of the horrors of an earlier final solution. The camp at Omarska joined Belsen in the cartography of hell. Its inmates were periodically taken out to be shot, and those that remained were starved to the point of death. Serb guns shelled Sarajevo constantly. Among their targets were the national museum and library, which were totally, and deliberately, destroyed. If the Serbs had been better soldiers, they would have conquered all Bosnia, or partitioned it with the Croats, but they prepared to drive the Muslims before them with guns, not bayonets.

The Muslims resisted. For three years, they fought a defensive war, desperately holding off the Serb juggernaut. The U N, at American insistence, had imposed an arms embargo upon the states of the former Yugoslavia. Later in the war, the Americans wanted to lift the embargo, but were opposed by Europeans. The result was the same as in Spain during the civil war in the 1930s: one side had all the weapons while the other was forbidden to arm itself. Bosnia was saved by clandestine arms shipments and by aid from Turkey, Egypt, Iran and other Muslim states and by enterprising arms dealers. It slowly built up its armies, training its soldiers in modern warfare.

There were constant international efforts at mediation. The U N force, sent to police the Krajina and Vukovar, also operated in Bosnia, observing the war and the atrocities but doing nothing to stop them. It was the U N's most humiliating experience in recent history. There was a prolonged effort by Cyrus Vance, joined by a former British foreign secretary, David Owen, to draw up a new map of Bosnia in which it would be divided into 30 or so cantons. None of the three sides ever accepted the plan. In November 1994, Nato briefly threatened to bomb Serb positions. The Serbs defied them. In January 1995 former President Jimmy Carter arranged a four-month ceasefire. Cynics noted that Balkan wars are usually suspended in winter, and resume in the spring. But however inadequate Nato efforts were to end the war, they did provide sufficient assistance for the Muslims to hold out against the Serb onslaught. 'Humanitarian' aid shipped into Sarajevo with great difficulty kept the city alive and the same good deeds gave minimal support to other besieged towns. In those eastern towns completely surrounded, the Americans dropped supplies from the air.

It was very little, and the West continued to urge the Muslims to accept whatever terms the Serbs would consent to, or the Vance–Owen alternative. But Western intervention frustrated the Serbs' offensive which otherwise (and with better Serb generals) would have swept across the whole of Bosnia. After their first victories in 1992, when they occupied 70 per cent of Bosnia, the Serbs paused to drive the Muslims out of their homes. Two million people were made refugees, half the population of Bosnia. The Serbs thought they could deal with the surviving Muslim cities and enclaves later – but then the West intervened, and saved them.

There was a subordinate but savage war between Croats and Muslims. Croats in Hercegovina, the mountainous province south-west of Sarajevo, were as xenophobic and racist as the worst Serbs, and were encouraged, armed and helped by Franjo Tudjman. The principal city there was Mostar which had a slight Muslim majority before the war. Croats laid siege to the Muslim districts. Their chief target was a notable bridge over the Neretva River built by the Turks in the 16th century. It was one of the classical buildings of Europe, and was destroyed by Croat gunners in November 1993.

In February 1994 Nato issued an ultimatum to the Bosnian Serbs to end the siege of Sarajevo. They reluctantly obeyed, allowing their heavy guns to be impounded by U N observers, and also suspended the siege of Goradze in April. On 1 March the Americans succeeded in persuading the Croats and Muslims to sign a defensive agreement in Washington: now they would fight the Serbs together (though Croats continued to persecute Muslims in the areas they controlled). In July, the Serbs rejected the Vance–Owen plan, which would have allocated them 49 per cent of the country. They had 70 per cent and **449** intended to keep at least that much. Europeans and Americans continued their diplomatic efforts, and thanks to tough U N sanctions imposed against Serbia, persuaded Milosevic to cut off deliveries of weapons to the Bosnian and Croatian Serbs. Nato had undertaken to impose a no-fly zone over Bosnia, forbidding the Yugoslav air force to intervene in the conflict. A 'contact group' consisting of representatives of the United States, Russia, Germany, Britain and France offered to end all sanctions against Serbia if it would recognize the frontiers and territorial integrity of Bosnia and Croatia – meaning that Milosevic should give up the idea of Greater Serbia, and the Krajina and Bosnian Serbs should end their secession. Milosevic refused (these were the terms he accepted at Dayton the following year).

In January 1995, ominously, Tudjman said that he would not agree to an extension of the U N P R O F O R (United Nations Protective Force) in Croatia when its mandate ran out on 31 March. This was widely seen as a promise that the Croat–Serb war would resume when the snows melted. By then, the Americans had turned a blind eye to large-scale deliveries of weapons to Croatia, principally from Iran. Those weapons were then shared with the Muslims and the Muslim army, progressively strengthened, was soon to be a match for the Serbs. On 20 March the Muslims broke the ceasefire by attacking Serb positions in Travnik in central Bosnia. The Serbs resumed attacks on the Bihac pocket, in western Bosnia, which was also attacked by a renegade Muslim group led by the entrepreneur and smuggler Fikret Abdic. Two years earlier, Nato had proclaimed Bihac and five other Muslim towns 'safe areas', meaning that air power would be used to defend them if they were attacked. The others were Sarajevo, Tuzla, Goradze, Zepa and Srebrenica. However, U N P R O F O R was quite incapable of defending them. It was a political gesture.

On 1 April, Croatia abruptly seized the most vulnerable sector of Serb-held Croatia, Western Slavonia, site of the famous World War II concentration camp at Jasenovac. They rolled across the territory, expelling all the Serbs. The Serb Krajina armed forces put up scarcely any resistance. In retaliation, they shelled Zagreb.

On 23 May, Serbs seized U N warehouses in which heavy guns confiscated from them were stored. The warehouses were around Sarajevo, and the action meant the siege might resume at any moment. They started shelling the city immediately, sending 3000 shells into it over the following week. On 25 May Serbs shelled Tuzla, killing 71 civilians in a crowded street. Nato therefore ordered an air strike against Serb gun emplacements on 25–26 May. The Serbs retaliated by arresting about 320 U N observers and holding them hostage. Some were handcuffed to posts next to the Serb guns, to ensure that Nato would not bomb them. It was the most complete humiliation the United Nations ever suffered. A few weeks later, a U S F–15 patrolling the no-fly zone over Serb territory was shot down by a S A M. The pilot hid in the woods for a week, and was picked up by an American rescue team.

On 11 July 1995 the Serbs took Srebrenica after a short siege. Women and children were allowed to leave (Serb women stoned their buses) and those men and boys who had not escaped were rounded up and shot under the personal supervision of General Mladic. Later estimates showed that this cold-blooded massacre killed about 8000 men and boys. A much smaller enclave, Zepa, fell on 25 July. Two of the six 'safe areas' proclaimed by Nato had fallen, unprotected. The Dutch troops at Srebrenica stood by while the massacres took place and allowed the Serbs to take their weapons from them. The Dutch officer was filmed exchanging toasts in slivovitz with General Mladic. News of the massacres reached the rest of the world by the end of the month. By then, Croatia had intervened to help the defence of Bihac and then, on 4 August, launched a general offensive against the Krajina.

In four days the entire area was captured (Knin, the capital of the 'Krajina Republic', fell on 5 August). About 150,000 Serb refugees fled into Bosnia or Serbia, abandoning the homes their families had occupied for 500 years. It was as brutal an example of ethnic cleansing as they had themselves practised over the previous four years, and their cousins had carried out in Bosnia. On 28 August, a Serb shell fell on a market in Sarajevo, killing 38 people – and at last, after years of pusillanimity, Nato responded, bombing Serb gun positions all over Bosnia. These two blows, the loss of the Krajina and Nato bombing, broke the Serbs' will to fight. On 16 September they gave up the siege of Sarajevo, agreeing to pull their guns back 20 kilometres. A day earlier, a general offensive had been launched by the Croats and Muslims, now fighting together. They swept across western Bosnia, capturing 1300 square miles (3300 square kilometres) in a matter of days, and appeared on the verge of taking Prijedor and Banja Luka. Nato and the U N then insisted that the offensive be halted, and a ceasefire was agreed on 5 October and came into force on the 12th. Representatives of all three parties to the civil war (but not the Bosnian Serb war criminals), and Milosevic himself from Serbia, then flew to Dayton, Ohio, to attempt to make peace.

The Dayton meeting began on 1 November and concluded with a treaty on the 21st. It provided that Serbs should control 49 per cent of Bosnia and a Muslim–Croat federation 51 per cent. This meant that federation troops had to give up some of the territory they had captured. Several crucial territorial decisions were postponed, and the Serbs promised to withdraw from Vukovar. Bosnia was to be a union of the 'Serb Republic' and the Bosnian–Croat federation, each side running its own affairs, including security, defence and taxes. All the 2 million refugees were to be allowed to return to their homes.

Each side kept its army, and in the next two years Bosnia busily rearmed itself, with American help, while the Serbs were obliged to scrap a large part of their arsenals – all to achieve parity between the two. Sixty thousand U N troops, mostly from Nato, but with Russian and Eastern European contingents, were to patrol the dividing line between the two sides, and indicted war criminals were to be handed over to the international tribunal set up by the U N at The Hague.

The peace was notably fragile. Neither the Americans nor the rest of the U N force enjoyed patrolling the Balkans, but it proved a safer task than they had feared. The force's size was cut in 1996, and until after the American presidential election in November that year, President Clinton held to the promise that U S troops would withdraw in 1998. After the election, he admitted that a smaller number, less than 7000, would have to stay indefinitely. Other elements of the agreement remained a dead letter. No refugees were allowed to return to their homes, and the Serbs in Banja Luka and Prijedor completed the business of ethnic cleansing. Croats showed only slightly less hostility to the Muslims than did the Serbs: Mostar remained divided. It was quite clear that if the outside world turned its back, war between the Serbs and the others would resume at once – with the Serbs likely to lose and to be swept out of Bosnia altogether. That would be very satisfactory to the Muslims in the short run, but would create a permanent irredentism in Serbia, which has twice Bosnia's population and far more natural resources. Furthermore, war with the Serbs might very well be followed by war between the Croats and Muslims, and the outcome of that would be very hard to predict. Meanwhile, Milosevic was losing his grip on power in Serbia and Montenegro (which showed signs of wanting to secede from the Yugoslav rump state), and Tudjman was suffering from inoperable cancer.

## Kosovo

The dangers of a fourth Yugoslav war, in Kosovo, first became the world's concern during the initial break-up of Yugoslavia. At Christmas 1992, President George Bush even warned the Serbs that the United States would intervene militarily if they began persecuting the Kosovo Albanians. This was not a sign of any particular concern for the prospective victims, who were in no way more deserving protection than the Bosnians. It was due to the cold realization that civil war in Kosovo could very easily escalate rapidly out of control. Albania would inevitably send arms to Kosovo (and after the break-down in Albania in 1997, every sort of weapon was plentifully available). Macedonia might be drawn in, despite the presence of a small American contingent to monitor the border, and that could suck in Greece and possibly Bulgaria and Turkey.

The events of 1991–5 demonstrated that Europe had a high level of tolerance for the sufferings of Bosnians, but a general war in the south Balkans was something else again. When the inevitable conflict began, early in 1998, the tocsin echoed across Europe.

---

## FURTHER READING

---

Cigar, Norman, *Genocide in Bosnia: The Policy of Ethnic Cleansing*, Texas, A&M University Press.

Danner, Mark, 'The US and the Yugoslav Catastrophe', the *New York Review of Books*, 20 November 1997, and subsequent articles.

Gow, James, *Triumph of the Lack of Will: International Diplomacy and the Yugoslav War*, New York, Columbia University Press, 1996.

Honig, Jan William and Both, Norbert, *Srebrenica: Record of a War Crime*, London and New York, Penguin, 1996.

Hukanovic, Rezak (introduction by Eli Wiesel), *The Tenth Circle of Hell: A Memoir of Life in the Death Camps of Bosnia*, New Republic, Basic Books, 1994.

Judah, Tim, *The Serbs: History, Myth and the Resurrection of Yugoslavia*, Yale University Press, 1996.

Maass, Peter, *Love Thy Neighbor*, New York, Alfred Knopf, 1996.

Sells, Michael, *The Bridge Betrayed, Religion and Genocide in Bosnia*, Berkeley, University of California Press, 1996.

Silhber, Laura and Little, Alan, *Yugoslavia: Death of a Nation*, London and New York, Penguin, 1996.

Sudecic, Chuck, *Blood and Vengeance: One Family's Story of the War in Bosnia*, New York, WW Norton, 1998.

Thompson, Mark, *Forging War: The Media in Serbia, Croatia and Bosnia-Hercegovina*, article 19, International Centre Against Censorship, 1995.

Vulliamy, Ed, *Seasons in Hell: Understanding Bosnia's War*, New York, Simon and Schuster, 1996.

West, Richard, *Tito and the Rise and fall of Yugoslavia*, London, Sinclaire Stephenson, 1996

Zimmerman, Warren, *Origins of a Catastrophe: Yugoslavia and its Destroyers*, New York, Times Books, Random House, 1996.

# LATIN AMERICA

# ARGENTINA AND THE FALKLANDS

| | |
|---|---|
| Geography | 1,072,067 sq. miles (2,776,643 sq. km). |
| Population | 32,000,000. |
| GNP per capita | $2160. |
| Casualties | Over 10,000 people were killed by the Argentinean military and police during the 'dirty war' in the 1970s. 746 Argentinean servicemen and 250 British were killed during the Falklands War. |

There have been many countries that have been worse governed than Argentina was between 1945 and 1982, nations that faced extremes of poverty, backwardness, external enemies, the bitter divisions of competing tribes. Argentina suffered from none of those disadvantages. It is large, rich in natural resources, with an educated and homogeneous population and no foreign enemies. In 1945, it had the largest gold reserves of any country in the world after the United States, and it should have developed into another Canada. Instead, for nearly 40 years, it endured an alternation of incompetent Fascist and incompetent military governments.

Argentina's travails culminated in the mid-1970s with a Communist terrorist campaign against the state. It was suppressed with great brutality by the military government, which murdered over 10,000 civilians accused of terrorism. When the military were finally evicted in 1982, they left a bitterly divided and impoverished country, with a heavily indebted Third World economy, which had just suffered a humiliating defeat in a pointless war.

## HISTORY

Argentina's troubles go back to the Fascist dictator Juan Perón, who won election to the presidency in February 1946 after a demagogic campaign that overawed the military government. He was the Mussolini of South America, but even more incompetent than the Duce had been. Like Mussolini, he nationalized the banks and foreign companies, took over the universities and recognized the USSR. He delivered rabble-rousing speeches from the balcony of the Casa Rosada, the presidential palace in Buenos Aires, inciting his subjects' chauvinism by abusing Britain and the United States, and indulging every demand of the urban proletariat – the *descamisados* ('shirtless ones') – who were the base of his

457

power. He promised them cheap housing, education, medicine, clothing, bread and circuses – and he was able to make his promises good as long as the gold reserves lasted and there was still foreign property to confiscate. When the bread ran out, the circus became more frenetic. The chief performer was his wife, Eva (known as 'Evita'), around whom Perón developed a semi-religious cult, and whom he had proclaimed *jefa espiritual de la nación* ('spiritual leader of the nation'). When she died, in July 1952, the country was subjected to an orgy of official mourning without modern precedent. In 1955, the army finally deposed Perón. He took refuge on a Paraguayan gunboat in the River Plate, and left the country on 20 September.

The country that he left behind was ruined, and has not yet recovered. Perón had institutionalized corruption among the military, and the workers had been led to believe that prosperity was their right, not something to be worked for, and that their increasing poverty must be a foreign plot. For nearly 20 years, Perón himself, from his exile in Spain, was a constant cause of instability because he offered the prospect of an alternative government, a return to the golden days of the *Juan and Evita Show*. Eva's body had been smuggled out of the country after his overthrow, and he kept it in a private shrine, to be brought back in triumph when the people called.

During the interregnum, the military returned power to civilian governments twice: first to Arturo Frondizi in February 1958, and then to Arturo Ilea in July 1963. They both failed to solve the country's problems and were therefore removed by the military, Frondizi having lasted four years, Ilea three. In 1973, in an attempt to break out of this vicious circle, the military allowed Perón to return. In the long run, the gamble worked, for the time being at least: the golden age did not return and Peronism lost its lustre.

Perón's demagogic magic was gone. He failed to co-opt the left and, instead, turned on it, driving it underground. He died in July 1974.

The extremists, disillusioned with Perón and exasperated by 30 years of Fascist or quasi-Fascist misgovernment, turned to terrorism, calling themselves the Montoneros. Leading industrialists and military men, including one of the generals who had deposed Perón, were assassinated. There were bombs and shootings in the cities, the guerrillas tried to start an insurgency in the country-side and the universities were in permanent revolt. It is, however, important to note that the terrorists were far less numerous than the military claimed and were never a serious threat to the republic. They could have been dealt with as the West Germans dealt with the Baader–Meinhof gang (*see* The Euro-terrorists, pp. 564–80).

Perón was succeeded by his widow Isabel, whom he had made vice president. She proved grossly incompetent and was deposed by the armed forces in March 1976. A junta was established, composed of the commanders of the three services. They responded to the terrorists with martial law and the 'dirty war', dispensing altogether with legal process. People suspected of belonging to the revolutionary parties were arrested, tortured and murdered. No account was ever given of what happened to them: they were *los desaparecidos*, the 'disappeared'. Mass graves were dug in remote cemeteries, and some unfortunates were simply dropped out of aircraft over the ocean.

The military's motto was: when in doubt, kill them. It was effective. Revolutionary terrorism was practically eliminated, but it was replaced by state terrorism. The National Commission on the Disappearance of Persons, set up by the Alfonsín government after the military were overthrown, established dossiers and took testimony on the cases of 8960 people who had been arrested and never heard of again. The commission did not examine every case and officially admits that there are many more. The best estimate is that between 10,000 and 15,000 people were murdered during the 'dirty war'.

In this extremity, a number of courageous women started demonstrating on the Plaza de Mayo outside the Casa Rosada. They were the mothers of the disappeared, and their weekly demonstrations quickly became an intolerable challenge to the regime. By late 1981, midsummer in the southern hemisphere, there were thousands of these *Madres de Mayo* demonstrating every Thursday, at first silently and peacefully but soon noisily, insistently demanding their children.

The demonstrations were not the only crisis facing the regime. The country's economic situation was sharply deteriorating, partly because of the international oil crisis but chiefly because of Argentina's chronic governmental incompetence. There was also dissension within the junta: one general, Roberto Viola, was removed as president in December 1981 and replaced by another, Leopoldo Galtieri.

In disposing of his fellow general, Galtieri needed the support of the navy commander, Admiral Jorge Anaya. Anaya had long entertained dreams of liberating the Malvinas, as the Falkland Islands are known in Argentina. Galtieri promised to accomplish the task in 1982. A dramatic victory would solve all his problems at a stroke.

## THE FALKLANDS

The Falklands are a desolate archipelago in the South Atlantic, 400 miles (640 km) off the southern tip of South America. There are two main islands, covering 6280 square miles (16,265 sq. km), about the size of Wales. In 1982 they were inhabited by 1800 people and 400,000 sheep.

The Falklands were noted by various explorers in the 16th and 17th centuries. The first to land was a British sailor, in 1690, who named them after an admiralty official, Lord Falkland. Visiting Breton sailors later named them the Malouines, after St Malo; this name was later corrupted to Malvinas. In the mid-18th century, both France and Britain laid claim to the Falklands and set up small military colonies there, though both were hard pressed to justify the need for such an outpost.

France sold her interest to Spain in 1766, and a Spanish fleet was sent from Buenos Aires to expel the British. There was a brief chauvinistic outcry in Britain, memorably denounced by Dr Johnson, in which politicians proclaimed Britain's inalienable right to those untempting islands. Britain threatened war, and Spain agreed to restore the British colony and remove its own garrison, though without renouncing its claim to the islands. The incident was closed. The British evacuated the Falklands in 1774, and they remained unoccupied for the next 50 years.

When Argentina won its independence from Spain in 1816, it laid claim to the Falklands, as heir to Spain's possessions, and in 1826 set up a colony there. **459**

Considering past history, it had every right to do so. If the British had wanted the islands, they should have settled them, or at least left a permanent garrison.

After Waterloo, the British embarked upon an imperial century. Instead of abandoning their long-neglected claims, they reasserted them. If someone else wanted the Falklands, then perhaps they were worth having. This attitude was further complicated by the fact that an expedition to Buenos Aires during the Napoleonic wars had been defeated; the British were certainly not now going to cede even worthless territory to Argentina. Lord Palmerston, the most belligerent of all British foreign secretaries, asserted that Britain had never renounced sovereignty to the Falklands and sent a small naval expedition, which in 1833 summarily evicted the Argentineans. It was this act of aggression that Argentina set out to rectify in 1982.

No doubt about it, the original British action was a case of arrogant high-handedness, but that had occurred 149 years before Galtieri turned his thoughts towards the islands. In international law, Argentina had no case. The islands had been continuously occupied by Britain since 1833, when a commercial enterprise, the Falkland Islands Company, started raising sheep and imported settlers, mostly from Scotland. Their descendants are there still.

True, the Falklands had been taken from Argentina by force. However, if territories seized by force must be returned to their previous owners or their descendants, and if continuous occupation over the generations bestows no rights, then the United States must return Texas and California to Mexico, and France must return Alsace-Lorraine to Germany — and that was indeed the latter's assertion in 1870, with calamitous consequences for both countries. If the Falklands are to be returned because Argentina occupied them for six years 150 years ago, then Germany may reclaim the ancient German cities Breslau, Danzig and Königsburg, the Greeks may reclaim Constantinople, and the Queen of England may reclaim her lost duchies of Normandy, Anjou and Aquitaine.

The essence of the British claim, however, was not historical, but was based on the charter of the United Nations and on the established principles of international law, which gives countries, however small, the right of self-determination. The Falklanders wanted to remain British, and that was sufficient.

That Britain was in the right does not mean that it was wise. The Falklands provide no strategic or economic benefit to Britain. Only armchair strategists cherish them, those obsessed with maps who think that they might be useful in controlling the waters around Cape Horn. Prime Minister Margaret Thatcher went to war to protect the right to self-determination of 1800 people, roughly the number who live in a typical block of council flats. Mrs Thatcher would never have allowed 1800 people in Britain to determine the course of national policy. She made a career of obliging her fellow citizens to face up to unpleasant choices — closing industries, intimidating trade unions and reforming the health service. The Falklanders, it seems, were somehow different: they were allowed to direct British policy towards the whole of Latin America. It was a remarkable instance of the tail wagging the dog. It is also worth remarking that the 70,000–100,000 British citizens who live in Argentina take a very different view of the Falklands dispute than do those 1800 sheep farmers.

Every Argentinean child had for generations been taught that Britain had robbed

Argentina of the Malvinas. They were not taught the horrors of war, nor were they encouraged to examine irredentist claims dispassionately. On the contrary, if Galtieri had not gone to war with Britain, he might have gone to war with Chile, over two other worthless and disputed islands in the channel between Patagonia and Tierra del Fuego. Every Argentinian child knew all about that dispute, too.

At the height of the crisis in 1982, the Argentinean foreign minister complained on American television that, of course, the Malvinas were Argentinean: he had sung songs about it as a child. Argentina's claims were childish, but they were passionately believed, and the nation worked itself into a patriotic fever in a bad cause, very much like European militarists earlier in the century. The British government, and particularly the Foreign Office, was much to blame for failing to take Argentina seriously. The junta's greatest error was that it utterly failed to predict the probable British reaction to an invasion – the most gratuitous case of ignorance and self-delusion since Nasser closed the Strait of Tiran in 1967.

The Galtieri junta was not only carried away by its own rhetoric, it was also exceedingly stupid. The point is illustrated by the timing of the invasion: 2 April 1982. It was in the autumn. If they had waited two months longer, it would have been too late in the year for Britain to mount a counter-offensive, and the Falklands would have been in Argentina's hands undisturbed for the next six months. What is more, the British had just sold one of their last two aircraft carriers to Australia and were preparing to scrap the second, together with several of the other warships that were used in the task force that eventually recaptured the islands. If Argentina had waited another year, the British would not have had the resources to retake the Falklands, and would have been forced to acquiesce in the *fait accompli*.

## THE ROAD TO WAR

Argentina and Britain had periodically conducted negotiations over the future of the Falklands. The Foreign Office was disinclined to fight too hard to retain such a small and unimportant colony, but a strong Falklands lobby in the Conservative party set up an instant cacophony every time the notion of renouncing sovereignty over the islands was raised.

Unlike Spain, which tried to win Gibraltar by closing the border and bullying the Gibraltarians, the Argentineans for many years offered every inducement to the Falklanders to think favourably of them: there was a heavily subsidized airlink between the islands and the mainland; medical treatment was provided (Argentina has excellent doctors); scholarships were offered. Argentinean tourists took business to the Falklands, and were always on their best behaviour.

However, the military government was too impatient, needed a success too badly, to allow such a sensible policy the time it needed. Like Franco's Spain in the case of Gibraltar, they were also unlikely to admit that their regime was so unappetizing that no one could be expected voluntarily to join it.

In late 1981 and early 1982, a further round of unsuccessful negotiations was held. Britain again refused to bend on sovereignty. General Galtieri had promised Admiral Anaya that the Malvinas would be returned by the end of 1982, before the 150th anniversary of their occupation by Britain, and so plans for the invasion were dusted off and brought up to date.

There was one further Argentinean miscalculation. During the Carter presidency, Argentina had been subjected to much pressure and criticism because of its abominable record on human rights. The moment the Reagan administration took office, all that changed. The Argentineans were welcomed back into the fold. They were invited to send specialists to help anti-terrorist campaigns in El Salvador and to train the Nicaraguan Contras. Galtieri was welcomed with open arms in Washington. The egregious Jeane Kirkpatrick, U S permanent representative to the U N and one of the president's favourites, was well known for her admiration for authoritarian South American regimes. Galtieri assumed that the United States would support Argentina in the coming conflict. It was a costly misjudgment.

## THE BEGINNING OF WAR

Argentina needed a *casus belli* and found a most satisfactory one – one that precipitated the invasion earlier in the year than military prudence suggested. An Argentinean scrap merchant had contracted to remove an abandoned whaling station from South Georgia, another British island well to the east of the Falklands, and which the Argentineans also claimed. He landed his expedition on South Georgia in mid-March, without first checking in with the British authorities, represented by a small scientific station on another part of the island. He was told to remove himself or obtain permits, and two dozen Royal Marines were sent from the Falklands to enforce the decision.

Galtieri sent troops to protect the Argentinean scrap dealer on 25 March, and occupied South Georgia. At the same time, he ordered the invasion of the Falklands. The Argentinean navy put troops ashore at dawn on 2 April, and they soon occupied Stanley, the capital, and other strategic points.

The British were taken completely by surprise. The Foreign Office had ignored a series of warnings by the embassy in Buenos Aires, in disbelief that the Argentinians would be so rash as to invade British territory. In the 1981 Defence White Paper, the minister of defence had announced plans to get rid of the last naval vessel in the South Atlantic, the converted icebreaker H M S *Endurance*. The same document had also proposed a drastic reduction in the rest of the surface fleet, including elimination of the two aircraft carriers. Henceforth, the Royal Navy's budget was to be devoted to building Trident submarines and their missiles. The Argentineans had read the White Paper and concluded that Britain had written off the Falklands.

They were mistaken. Britain was outraged by the invasion. Even those who thought that the Falklands should be abandoned found it an intolerable affront to the national dignity and asked, 'What sort of people do they think we are?' Britain may have come down in the world since 1945, but not to the point where it could be pushed around by a Latin American military government. The phrase 'tin-pot dictator' was a favourite.

## THE EMPIRE STRIKES BACK

The invasion was on a Friday. By the following Tuesday, 5 April, a British naval task force had set sail to recapture the islands – 8250 miles (13,275 km) away – and avenge British honour. The British had not previously had a reputation for successful improvisation in an emergency. This time, they did it magnificently.

The navy being much reduced, merchant ships were drafted into service, including two liners, the *Canberra* and the *Queen Elizabeth II*. The *Canberra* had just completed a cruise, and returned to Southampton on 7 April. Her next cruise was abruptly cancelled, a helipad was carved out of her decks, and she sailed two days later with 2400 troops. The *QEII* was brought into service later and was converted to a troop carrier, like her illustrious predecessors, the *Queen Mary* and the *Queen Elizabeth*, in World War I I.

It happens that Britain has retained, as relics of empire, a string of islands down the length of the Atlantic. The Task Force therefore progressed from Portsmouth to Gibraltar to Ascension to St Helena to South Georgia, where the *QEII* and other transports sheltered during the campaign. The problem with the more southerly islands was that, beyond Ascension, with 4000 miles to go, there were no airports. The operation had to be entirely naval, until the army could get ashore.

At the same time, the United States made a determined effort to avert war, while the British successfully lobbied at the United Nations and in Europe to line up world opinion against Argentina. President Reagan called Galtieri on the night of the invasion, begging him to desist, but to no avail. The secretary of state, Alexander Haig, tried shuttle diplomacy, flying between London and Buenos Aires. Admiral Anaya, who had never been to war, told him, 'My son is a helicopter pilot. The proudest day of my life will be when he lays down his life for the Malvinas.' General Haig, who had served in Korea and Vietnam, replied, 'You know, when you see the body bags, it's different.'

When the war started, the Americans gave the British every moral and practical help, including intelligence and armaments shipped from American depots. American public opinion was vociferously pro-British. In 1988, John Lehman, who was the U S secretary of the navy in 1982, said that the British might have failed without American help, particularly in intelligence. The two navies even discussed the possibility that the British might lease the U S S *Guam*, a 12,000-ton assault ship that can be used as a small aircraft carrier. It was not needed.

The Task Force reached the South Atlantic on 1 May. The first engagement was the recapture of South Georgia, which was easily accomplished. Reconquering the Falklands was more difficult.

There are two main islands in the archipelago, with Port Stanley on the east coast of the eastern island. The British chose to land on the other side of that island, at a place called San Carlos, and use the narrow waterway between the two islands as a shelter for the fleet of cargo ships and landing craft as well as the naval vessels sent to protect them. The landing was on 21 May, and was not seriously opposed. In fact, throughout the fighting, the Argentinean army (consisting almost entirely of conscripts) proved woefully inadequate. Very few units showed any fighting spirit at all, and surrendered to much smaller British forces. The navy was equally unimpressive: a British submarine sank the cruiser *Belgrano*, and after that, the Argentinean navy stayed in port. (The *Belgrano* affair was later the cause of a sharp dispute in Britain, where the government was accused of giving the go-ahead to the navy to sink a ship that was no danger to the Task Force, and which was, in fact, heading away from the Falklands at the time.)

Argentina's honour was redeemed by its air force, its pilots showing immense gallantry and skill. They sank a number of British ships, with heavy loss of life, flying from bases 400 miles (640 km) away, at the limit of their range. The British – with only a limited number of Harriers flying off their two aircraft carriers, and with Rapier and Blowpipe surface-to-air missiles (SAMs) to defend the fleet – found themselves in grave danger. A score of ships, including the liner *Canberra*, were packed into the narrow strait off San Carlos, and they came under constant attack from Argentinean aircraft. Four British ships, including two warships, were sunk by bombs, and the destroyer HMS *Sheffield* and the cargo ship *Atlantic Conveyor* were sunk by French Exocet air-launched anti-ship missiles. Many other ships were damaged, some seriously.

The British have an all-volunteer army, and it bore itself well. The Royal Navy lived up to its traditions, and pilots flying off the aircraft carriers – including Prince Andrew, the Queen's second son – performed creditably.

After they had secured their landing, the British had to cross East Falkland to reach Stanley. It took them three weeks. They charged across the island, and laid siege to the capital, which was defended by Argentinean positions on the surrounding ring of hills. At all times, the British had the initiative over the miserable Argentinean conscripts, who had not expected to have to fight for the Malvinas. The Argentinean forces surrendered on 14 June 1982.

The British took 12,978 prisoners and lost 250 men killed. Five Falklands civilians were killed. The Argentines lost 746 killed, of whom 368 had been on the *Belgrano*.

## AFTERMATH OF THE WAR

The prisoners were all repatriated. Within days, the junta had resigned, and mass demonstrations in Buenos Aires demanded a return to democracy. It was the same course of events that had brought down the Greek junta in 1974. A retired general, who was innocent of all involvement in the Falklands fiasco, was brought in to supervise the transition.

There was a presidential election, and Raul Alfonsín, leader of the Radical party, won by a huge majority, with a mandate to clean out the military, investigate the 'dirty war' and punish the guilty – and also to investigate the Falklands war. All the generals and admirals who had been members of the various juntas from 1976 to 1982 were given long prison terms, as were many of the military murderers and torturers.

Alfonsín failed to solve any of the country's economic problems. The frightful socialistic bureaucracy inherited from Perón continued to direct every aspect of the economy, which was one of the most thoroughly nationalized in the world outside the Communist bloc. There was a series of attempted military coups against the president, and his greatest achievement was to survive and to hand over power peacefully to his legally elected successor, Carlos Saúl Menem, though Alfonsín's government collapsed so completely that he had to resign five months early.

Menem, though a Peronist, revolutionized Argentina by starting a policy of selling off state-owned firms and permitting foreign investment. For the first time since the 1920s Argentina had a sensible economic policy, and by the middle of his term, Menem could boast that inflation was under control and the country was moving into an era of prosperity. There were problems. Corruption was rampant, and many of the president's and his wife's relatives (all Syrian immigrants) were involved. The most disquieting allegation was that his wife's family was involved in the drug trade. The military continued to threaten a return to the evil days of the 1970s. The president pardoned all the torturers and the generals who had commanded them, and also the incompetents and fools who had launched the Falklands war, including all the members of the various military juntas. He also pardoned the surviving Montoneros. In December 1990, a year after the president signed the last decree pardoning the guilty, a military faction tried another *coup d'état*. Thirteen people were killed and 25 seriously wounded. Several of the coup leaders had been the beneficiaries of Menem's pardons.

In February 1990, Britain and Argentina resumed diplomatic relations, eight years after the surrender in Port Stanley. The British ended the naval exclusion zone around the Falklands and opened negotiations on a new fishing agreement (it was concluded the following year). The question of sovereignty was left in abeyance. Both sides also agreed that in future they would notify each other of any military manoeuvres they planned in the area: in March 1988, Britain had conducted elaborate air and naval manoeuvres in the Falklands to prove that it could reinforce its garrisons there quickly enough to prevent a repetition of the 1988 invasion. Argentina had protested vigorously.

The British meanwhile had spent a billion dollars (£600 million) on an air base at Port Stanley, and continue to spend about £100 million ($180 million) a year to maintain it. It is equipped with Phantom jets, Hercules cargo planes and all the latest in surface-to-air missiles. Argentina would find it difficult to repeat its success of April 1982. Two huge squid fisheries have been discovered in Falklands waters, and the islands now receive $50 million a year in licence fees from fishing companies. The islands are no longer a cost to the British treasury, except for the defence bill.

Oil companies have long suspected that oil may be found in Falkland waters, and if any is discovered the islands would suddenly become really valuable and the dispute between Britain and Argentina might suddenly revive. The British took a first cautious step towards oil exploration in 1991.

There are now over 2000 permanent residents of the Falklands, but only 1200 are native Falklanders. There are more British troops and airmen and, predictably, the Falklands girls marry them and leave. The young men, with no hopes of matrimony, will leave too, and increasingly the Falklands has an ageing population defended at enormous expense by a permanent garrison of bored young men.

Argentina has not renounced its claim to the Malvinas. Menem has insisted that the claim will be asserted peacefully, and Argentina continues to press

Britain to permit the resumption of direct links with the islands. It hopes to resume the policy of winning the hearts of the Falklanders by kindness that was so foolishly interrupted by Gen. Galtieri.

## FURTHER READING

Amnesty International, *Argentina: The military juntas and human rights. Report of the trial of the former junta members*, London, 1985.

Burns, Jimmy, *The Land that Lost Its Heroes*, London, Bloomsbury, 1987.

Hastings, Max and Jenkins, Simon, *The Battle for the Falklands*, New York, W. W. Norton, 1983.

Laffin, John, *Fight for the Falklands!*, New York, St Martin's Press, 1982.

Middlebrook, Martin, *Operation Corporate*, London, Viking, 1985.

*Sunday Times* (London) Insight Team, *The Falklands War, the Full Story*, London, Andre Deutsch, 1982.

# CENTRAL AMERICA

Benito Juárez, a revolutionary 19th-century president of Mexico, made the celebrated comment: 'Poor Mexico: so far from God, so close to the United States.' For nearly a century, the other nations of Central America – Guatemala, El Salvador, Honduras, Nicaragua, Costa Rica, Panama and, to some extent, Belize (formerly British Honduras) – suffered from a double disadvantage: they were too close to the United States for safety, too far for understanding.

For most of their history, the United States has treated them like colonies, without accepting any of the responsibility for the well-being of their inhabitants that the British and French showed for their colonial empires or the Americans themselves showed in the Philippines. The United States ruled El Salvador, Guatemala, Nicaragua and the rest in the old Spanish manner: it left the administration in the hands of the local oligarchy, and protected that oligarchy against popular discontent, but insisted that American commercial and political interests were always paramount. In the most extreme case, Guatemala and Honduras became the colonies of the United Fruit Company. In Nicaragua, the United States repeatedly sent in the Marines to establish governments to its liking.

This attitude only began to change (and the change is by no means complete) in the 1970s and 1980s as Washington at last began to learn about the realities of the situation in Central America. Policies followed by the Carter and Reagan administrations (there was much more continuity between them than either would admit) began to distinguish in each case between the interests of the military and landed oligarchy and of the country at large. Democratically elected presidents took office in El Salvador, Guatemala, Honduras and Nicaragua, and the Reagan administration actively encouraged democracy and land reform, reversing the policies of every other president from Teddy Roosevelt to Gerald Ford. However, they discovered that bringing reform to Central America was as difficult as reforming Indochina had proved.

To a great extent, Central America throughout the 19th and most of the 20th century was a victim of American isolationism. Americans knew little about the place and cared less. They knew far more about China than they did about Guatemala. Early in the century, they neither knew nor wished to know that Guatemalan peasants were obliged to work for United Fruit without pay for 150 days a year 'in lieu of taxes', and that the rest of the year they were paid 25 cents a day. In the 1960s, conditions that Americans would have instantly recognized to be intolerable in Asia, let alone Europe or the United States itself, were ignored or accepted in Central America – and anyone who proposed to change those conditions was instantly branded a Communist.

In 1983, Henry Kissinger led a National Bipartisan Commission on Central America. It was an exceedingly eminent commission, and its report is one of the major state papers of the 1980s. The commission pointed out all the social and economic difficulties facing the region, and concluded that the only way to avert a Communist revolution was to encourage root and branch reform. It recommended that at least $8 billion in aid should be spent on Central America by the end of the decade.

The report was prefaced by a few significant observations:

For most people in the United States, Central America has long been what the entire New World was to Europeans of five centuries ago: *terra incognita*. Probably few of even the most educated could name all the countries of Central America and their capitals, much less recite much of the social and political backgrounds. Most members of the Commission began with what we now see as an extremely limited understanding of the region, its needs and its importance.

That was a remarkable admission for a former US secretary of state.

After Woodrow Wilson sent Black Jack Pershing chasing Pancho Villa in northern Mexico in 1916, the United States usually left Mexico to its own devices until corruption and the drug trade reached north to the Rio Grande in the early 1990s. The rest of Central America was not so fortunate. Instead of leaving those half-dozen small countries to work out their own destinies, the Americans have constantly interfered. Nicaragua was directly administered by the United States for 20 years and then handed over to the Somoza dynasty. Although Franklin Roosevelt proclaimed a 'good neighbour policy', promising to keep his hands off Latin America, it turned out that this meant a benevolent indifference to the installation of Fascist and military dictators throughout the region.

In the 1950s, the 'good neighbour' policy was abandoned: the Americans now took an active interest in Latin America, meaning that they encouraged and sustained right-wing regimes. The CIA engineered a coup in Guatemala in 1954, and Washington then gave strong support to a regime that eventually massacred about 100,000 peasants (during that period, only Mao Tse-tung in China, the Khmer Rouge government in Cambodia and Idi Amin in Uganda killed more of their own people). The Somozas of Nicaragua – and, in the Caribbean, Batista of Cuba and Trujillo of the Dominican Republic – were all supported by successive administrations in Washington.

The tide turned at last in the late 1970s. In the 1980s, during the Reagan administration, Washington tried to build up democratic centrist parties in El Salvador, Guatemala and Honduras, by forcing the military to hand over power to civilians, and then supporting those civilians against attack from left and right. Meanwhile, the administration tried everything short of sending in the Marines to overthrow the Marxist government in Nicaragua, on the improbable pretext that it was a menace to the United States.

The Soviet Union and Cuba rejoiced in these American obsessions. For the Soviets, a very small investment in arms for the various rebel movements, and a little military and economic aid for the Communist government in Nicaragua, produced a hugely disproportionate response from the United States. It was the reverse of the situation in Afghanistan and Angola, where relatively small American contributions to anti-Communist rebels forced enormous expenses upon the Soviet Union. Reagan's fixation on Nicaragua and El Salvador diverted him, throughout his eight-year term, from devoting his attention to more productive areas.

Castro, in Cuba, doubtless still dreamt of Latin revolution spreading throughout Central America. He supported the Sandinistas in Nicaragua and they, in turn, supported the rebels in El Salvador and elsewhere. In the event, the decay of the Soviet Union itself rendered all these calculations irrelevant. Gorbachev was constrained by the progressive disintegration of the USSR to abandon Afghanistan and Angola in 1988 and Eastern Europe in 1989. After that, there was no point in the Soviets playing games in Central America. Nicaragua agreed to hold free elections in February 1990, and the Sandinistas lost. The Salvadoran rebels, with Cuban support, tried one last military offensive in 1990, and were defeated. After that, Cuba abandoned them and they were obliged to come to terms with the government. A ceasefire agreement was finally concluded in January 1992. The Guatemalan war ended in 1996.

With the Communist menace removed, American concern for the region rapidly waned. Countries that had completely dominated Reagan's foreign policy vanished from Washington's consciousness. There was a last flare-up of American interest in Central America in December 1989, when President George Bush ordered the invasion of Panama, to depose Gen. Manuel Noriega. Panama had always been a special case, and even there, Mr Bush soon found more exciting crises to preoccupy him. The rest of the region was allowed to subside into its traditional neglect.

## MEXICO

Mexico remains as remote from the deity as ever, but is these days still closer to the United States than Juárez ever imagined. The North American Free Trade Area, signed by President Bush and ratified under President Clinton, has already produced important and beneficial effects for the Mexican economy. At the same time, the corruption of the drug trade is eating at the country's heart.

The revolution of 1910 was followed by a series of upheavals and uprisings, degenerating into civil war. Villa, who provoked the wrath of Woodrow Wilson by raiding across the border, was one of many rebel leaders. Another, Emiliano Zapata, led a revolt of indigenous Indians against the Spanish ascendancy. He was shot in 1919. When the tumult and the shouting died away in the 1920s, a political party calling itself the Institutional Revolutionary Party (PRI) took power and ruled Mexico at every level until the 1990s. It governed much as the Bolsheviks governed the Soviet Union: the central committee, dominated by the president, chose every candidate for every political office, from president of the republic to mayor of the smallest village. PRI candidates always won, just as Communist candidates always won in the USSR. Power corrupts, and the

P R I was very corrupt. Its only saving grace was that presidents were restricted to single, six-year terms. However, they always chose their successors so there was never any nonsense about auditing the books when a president left office, or indeed auditing any of the government's books, at any level. The first break in the façade occurred during the Olympic Games in Mexico City in 1968. On 2 October, a large crowd of young people mounted a demonstration in the centre of the city. The government called out the army and shot them down: the official death toll was 32. It was the most brutal act of official violence in that year of world-wide student unrest, and shook the P R I and its government badly.

Other pressures contributed to break the P R I's grip on power. The chief was economic, Mexico's opening to the global economy and N A F T A. The country's proximity to the United States, for once, proved a blessing: it was increasingly difficult for the Mexican government to maintain the Bolshevik model while its economy merged with America's. By the 1990s, with the P R I disintegrating, Mexico seemed in general to be heading in the right direction, towards becoming a modern, honest and efficient democracy. The most prominent leader of the opposition, Cuauhtemoc Cardenas, won election as mayor of Mexico City in 1997, and had then to grapple with the total corruption of the previous regime. He has high hopes of defeating the P R I candidate in the next presidential election. However, there is the Colombia precedent.

That country, too, was apparently steadily evolving into a modern democracy in the 1960s and 1970s – but then the drug cartels set up business in Medellin and Cali. Colombia's political and judicial systems, its politics and military, all proved too fragile and too corrupt to stand the strain (*see* pp. 534–45). This is the great danger facing Mexico: the enormous profits to be made from smuggling cocaine, heroin and marijuana into the United States have corrupted police and politicians in the northern provinces and the capital. The P R I candidate for president was assassinated in 1994, under most suspicious circumstances, and three years later the head of the drug police, Gen. Jesús Gutiérrez Rebollo, was found to be in the pay of the drug lords. The corruption reached the presidency: former President Salinas's brother is now in jail on charges of murder and corruption, and Salinas himself lives in exile for fear of arrest. There is a fight to the death between honesty and corruption, and it is not at all clear that the honest men are winning. Cardenas might succeed in eliminating graft in Mexico City, as reformers in New York purged Boss Tweed in the 1870s, but the drug lords are much more dangerous and difficult to control. Every man has his price, and Mexico is a poor country: police, generals and politicians come cheap and the drug lords have more money than P R I bureaucrats could ever dream of. What is more, the drug lords enforce their will by terror: they can, and do, kill anyone who opposes them. As the P R I collapses, and central authority, such as it is, is further discredited, there is a real possibility that Mexico will go the way of Colombia, with all the dangers to the United States that would ensue.

Smuggling across the border to the United States has been a way of life for over a century, and it was a natural progression for the smugglers to start sending marijuana across when that drug became popular in the 1960s. Then the Medellin Cartel began exporting cocaine to the United States, and the old-established routes through Mexico proved highly efficient. Soon Mexican smugglers turned themselves into drug lords on their own account, dealing directly with Medellin and Cali, and, in the late 1980s and 1990s, going further upstream and opening their own contacts with primary producers in Bolivia and Peru. All the same, Colombia remained by far the most important source of supply.

By the mid-1990s, there were four cartels smuggling across the border, the Tijuana, Sonora, Juarez and Gulf Cartels. The Drug Enforcement Agency (DEA) calls them the Mexican Federation because they have divided up the market, making in effect one huge cartel. In 1995, American police seized 35 tons of cocaine, 382 lbs of heroin, 600 tons of marijuana and 1400 lbs of metham-phetamines they were smuggling into the United States. It was just the tip of the iceberg. The retired leader of the Gulf Cartel, Juan Garcia Abrego, was finally arrested and deported to the United States in 1996. A notebook found in his possession gave lists of huge bribes he had paid to the national commander of the Federal Judicial Police, to his operations chief and to the federal prosecutor in his home town, Matamoros. One of his associates testified at his trial that he had also bribed Mexico's deputy attorney general.

There was much worse. Carlos Salinas de Gortari retired as president, much esteemed by Mexicans and foreigners alike. Then the currency collapsed and a series of scandals erupted around his brother, Raúl. Raúl is now charged with complicity in the murder of the PRI secretary general, José Francisco Ruiz Massieu, in 1994. Massieu himself is under posthumous investigation for acquiring $120 million while in office. The suggestion is that Salinas and Massieu (his former brother-in-law) used a government agency, a food pro-gramme called the Basic Commodity Distribution Co (Conaspo) for money laundering on behalf of the drug cartels – and that President Salinas knew about it. Massieu was also implicated in the assassination of the PRI candidate to succeed Salinas, Luis Donaldo Colosio Murrieta, on 23 March 1994. A year earlier, on 24 May 1993 Cardinal Juan Jesús Posadas Ocampo was killed at the airport in Guadalajara. The official version was that he was caught in a gun battle between rival drug gangs, but police in the state were so corrupt that nothing they said could be accepted unquestioned. Raúl Salinas was brought back from abroad to face the music. The former president then left himself, mere weeks after leaving office. He appeared briefly in New York, using the office of the Mexican ambassador to the UN, to his embarrassment, and then fled to Europe. He has lived there ever since (latterly in Ireland) for fear of arrest should he return home.

Since then, the head of the drug police has been accused of being in the pay of the drug traffickers. The only bright spot in this sombre picture was the death of one of the drug lords on the operating table: he had decided to undergo extensive cosmetic surgery, to change his appearance – and to lose weight. The surgeons bungled the case (they all suffered violent deaths in the following weeks).

## THE ZAPATISTAS

On 1 January 1994 bands of armed Maya Indians occupied several small towns in Chiapas, in the deep south of Mexico on the border with Guatemala. They called themselves the Zapatista National Liberation Army, after the peasant leader, and demanded a whole series of fundamental reforms. They asserted that the central government was corrupt and undemocratic and that it oppressed and neglected the Indian peasantry.

Only a handful of people were killed in the first stages of the rebellion. A ceasefire was arranged two weeks after the revolt began, and for the rest of the year the Zapatistas devoted themselves to political action, with occasional occupations of towns and villages. The government sent troops to police the province, but did not launch the sort of violent counter-offensive into the countryside that turned Guatemala into a killing-field. On the contrary, the Salinas government, well aware that all the Zapatistas' charges were perfectly true, negotiated with them and tried to meet their demands. Negotiations never produced a settlement, meaning that the rebels refused to surrender, and they launched a new offensive in December 1994 which the government blamed for the ensuing loss of confidence in the currency which drove Mexico to the brink of bankruptcy. In February 1995 the government in turn launched a general offensive against the Zapatistas. It was a notable failure. Rebel bases were captured – but the rebels had already moved on, into the jungles.

The Zapatistas' leader, Rafael Guillén Vicente, is a former college professor and goes by the *nom de guerre* Subcommandante Marcos. His rebellion has not changed much in Chiapas, so far: the peasants are still impoverished and neglected. But the rebellion contributed considerably to the progressive loss of authority by the PRI. The party's new candidate, Ernest Zedillo, defeated Cardenas in the presidential election in August 1994, one last occasion when the party managed to rig enough votes to win. It does not seem probable it will happen again when Zedillo's term runs out in 2000.

In June 1996 a new and more violent rebel group called the People's Revolutionary Army (EPR) appeared in Guerero state, in the hills behind the glittering resorts of Acapulco. They chose the first anniversary of a massacre of peasants by the local police (17 people were killed). They appeared before the television cameras, well armed and belligerent. They turned to more serious matters in attacks in a number of states on 28 August, killing at least 13. Police claimed that the EPR was a fusion of a number of small, revolutionary parties including some with close links to the drug lords. They have kidnapped a number of people for ransom over the years, including Alfredo Harp Helu, head of Mexico's largest bank, in 1994. His family paid a ransom of $30 million to secure his release.

The Zapatista insurrection, meanwhile, continued its symbolic way in Chiapas. One county announced that it had seceded in 1996 – and in December 1997 the mayor of the local town sent thugs into Zapatista villages to restore his authority. They slaughtered 45 unarmed peasants, including 18 children. The massacre horrified Mexico and the government. The men responsible had been local leaders of the PRI, and the incident was a further blow to the authority of the party, and the government.

# EL SALVADOR

| | |
|---|---|
| Geography | 8056 sq. miles (20,865 sq. km). The size of Wales. |
| Population | 5.6 million. |
| GNP per capita | $1600. |
| Casualties | Over 75,000 killed from 1979 to 1992. |

The civil war in El Salvador, from 1979 to 1992, killed about 75,000 people and was marked by extraordinary savagery. Most of the killings were the work of the army and various militias and death squads paid by the government or right-wing parties. The rebels, too, were guilty of murder and massacre and conducted a campaign as brutal as their means allowed. In the early 1980s, it seemed that the country was destined to follow Nicaragua down the road to Communist revolution, though at far greater cost. Guerrillas were operating in the suburbs of San Salvador and death squads were killing 20 to 30 people a day and dumping their bodies by the roadside.

The regime was saved by American intervention. The United States supplied advice, money and weapons but Congress refused to permit the Reagan administration to send troops. In 1984, El Salvador voted freely for the Christian Democratic candidate for the presidency, José Napoleón Duarte, and for a while it seemed as though the Americans had found the grail: the democratic centre, a party that would win the hearts and votes of a majority of the electorate while repudiating the fascistic tendencies of the right and the Communist excesses of the left.

Within five years, the centre had collapsed. Duarte was dying and his party was swept away in elections by the right-wing party, the Republican National Alliance (Arena). Forced to choose, Washington supported Arena but strove mightily to restrain its worst impulses. The U S also supported the Salvadoran army, despite its horrible record, in order to defeat the Communist Farabundo Martí National Liberation Front (F M L N) and its army. The Front tried a last military offensive in 1990, and was defeated. By then the collapse of the Soviet Union had led to a domino effect in Central America: Cuba abandoned its local clients, the Communist government in Nicaragua was defeated and it was time to sue for peace. A ceasefire was signed in 1992 and the war at last came to an end.

## HISTORY
The roots of the perpetual crisis in El Salvador, as in much of the rest of Latin America, lie in the prolonged refusal of the hereditary élite to share their economic and political power. By the late 19th century, the basis of El Salvador's economy was coffee; in 1931, it was responsible for 95.5 per cent of the country's export earnings, and 14 families owned all the plantations. These families were all-powerful, controlling every aspect of Salvadoran life, besides the coffee trade, and they considered every challenge subversive. Their successors still do.

In El Salvador as elsewhere, the Marxist left was equally intransigent. It denounced elections as frauds and considered it a legitimate political act to murder anyone who took part in an election – candidates, party workers, voters. It insisted upon violent revolution and on its right to impose its political doctrines upon the country by force.

**473**

These two irreconcilable dogmas first came into conflict in 1932. During the 1920s and early 1930s, as rising expectations among peasants and city dwellers threatened the oligarchs' positions, they formed an alliance with the army. Soldiers were given power, privilege and incomes to which they could not otherwise aspire and, in exchange, maintained the oligarchy's economic domination of the country against all attack.

In 1932, when the Depression had severely affected El Salvador, Communist organizers in the cities allied themselves with disaffected Indian peasants on the coffee plantations and planned a general uprising. The Communist leader was Augustin Farabundo Martí. He and his colleagues were arrested before the demonstrations could begin, and were executed, giving the Salvadoran left its principal martyr. The army suppressed the peasants in what became known as the *Matanza*, or 'massacre'. Between 10,000 and 30,000 people were slaughtered: the army occupied Indian villages, and summarily shot all the men between the ages of 14 and 50. Their thumbs were tied behind their backs, and they were shot in rows behind the village churches. The *Matanza*'s historian, Thomas Anderson, wrote: 'The extermination was so great that they could not be buried fast enough, and a great stench of rotting flesh permeated the air of western El Salvador.'

A series of military governments ruled the country until the 1980s. There was a certain amount of industrial development in the post-war years but the number of landless peasants increased rapidly. Many of them became economic refugees: in 1965, there were 350,000 Salvadorans living in Honduras.

## THE SOCCER WAR

In the late 1960s, Honduras, El Salvador's much larger neighbour to the north and east, went through a period of labour unrest and challenge to the military government. The latter blamed the situation on the illegal Salvadoran immigrants, and in January 1969, Honduras refused to renew the 1967 Bilateral Treaty on Immigration, which was meant to regulate the movement of populations between the two countries. In April, various legal measures were taken against immigrants, and Salvadorans started to return home in large numbers.

As tensions between the two countries increased, their national soccer teams were facing each other in qualifying matches for the following year's World Cup. When the two teams first met in Tegucigalpa, the Honduran capital, there were some disturbances, but at the next match in San Salvador, there were violent anti-Honduran demonstrations: its flag was insulted, and its fans were beaten up. Revenge was taken on Salvadorans in Honduras, and several people were killed; tens of thousands of Salvadorans fled the country. On 27 June, Honduras broke diplomatic relations.

El Salvador moved its troops to the border, the war of words escalated and both nations ignored calls for restraint by the Organization of American States (O A S) and the Central American Mediation Commission. On 14 July 1969, El Salvador's air force attacked Honduran bases, and the army began a general offensive against Honduras. The Salvadoran navy then attacked Honduran islands in the Gulf of Fonseca off its south coast. To begin with, the Salvadorans appeared to be winning, but then the Honduran air force, which was considerably stronger, defeated the Salvadoran air force and then attacked El Salvador's fuel depots. The offensive ground to a halt 5 miles (8 km) over the border for lack of fuel.

After four days' fighting, the O A S persuaded the two sides to agree to a *de facto* ceasefire. It was formalized on 18 July, and on 29 July, El Salvador agreed to withdraw from Honduran territory by the beginning of August. In all, about 2000 people were killed, mostly Honduran civilians. The two nations finally signed a peace treaty in 1981, and agreed to set up a boundary commission to demarcate disputed areas by 1985 (they finally settled the dispute in 1998). Although El Salvador had won the Soccer War on the ground, it had also suffered a major economic defeat: between 60,000 and 130,000 expatriates returned, and the possibility of further emigration to ease the population pressure in El Salvador was ended.

## THE CONFLICT

During the 1970s, various popular movements got under way, and opposition political parties developed. The first violent clash in what later developed into a civil war was provoked by a beauty pageant in 1975: students and leftists staged a protest against the government for spending $1.5 million on the Miss Universe pageant in San Salvador: the National Guard fired on student demonstrators: scores were killed; 24 'disappeared', the first of many. Shortly afterwards, the first army and police death squads began operating.

In October 1979, General Carlos Humberto Romero, the current military dictator, was overthrown in a coup by a group of younger, reformist officers. They set up a junta with civilian as well as military members (Guillermo Ungo of the Socialist M N R was briefly a member, as were Héctor Dada and Rubén Zamora of the leftist Social Christian Movement, the M P S C), and promised reforms, democracy and an end to the killings. They failed on all three counts. The senior officers, while not regretting Romero's departure, and accepting the need to refurbish the country's image, had no intention of loosening the reins of power.

For the next few years, the composition of the junta changed repeatedly as various factions struggled for power; in general, each change brought a more conservative group to the top. The United States actively supported the regime, as an improvement on the previous dictatorship, and urged reforms and new elections. The Christian Democratic party, the country's main centrist party, was split over the issue of whether it should join the junta. Its leader, José Napoleón Duarte, joined on 3 March 1980, and became acting president. Three weeks later, on 24 March, the Archbishop of San Salvador, Oscar Romero, was shot by a sniper while saying mass: he had often been threatened for denouncing military repression, and for asking President Carter to suspend military aid to the Salvadoran armed forces.

## THE DEATH SQUADS

These first appeared in 1975, following the Miss Universe pageant demonstrations. They had developed out of the National Democratic Organization (O R D E N), formed by the military in 1968, which had up to 50,000 members **475** and operated as a civil defence militia in the countryside. The death squads gave themselves picturesque names: the White Warriors Union, the White Hand, the Falange, the Secret Anti-Communist Army (E S A) and the Maximiliano Hernández Martínez Brigade, named after the general who had perpetrated the *Matanza* in 1932.

Members of the death squads belonged to the army, the national guard and the various police forces. The Treasury Police were most feared: they were well-organized, with bank balances, salaries and bonuses for good work, all financed by members of the oligarchy. In 1980–82, death squads were responsible for up to 800 deaths a month, perhaps 20,000 people in all. About 8000 trade union organizers and members were murdered or wounded during this period. The death squads' most prominent victim was Archbishop Romero.

In August 1988, the *Washington Post* published a series of articles on the origins of the death squads, based on interviews with two well-placed former members. According to them, one of the first squads was formed by a dentist called Antonio Regalado, who recruited a group of ten teenagers, ostensibly as a Boy Scout troop, and trained them in murder. In May 1980, Regalado and a number of military officers, most notably Major Roberto d'Aubuisson, plotted a coup against the reformist military junta then governing the country. The plot was discovered, and Regalado fled the country. Fearing that his 'boy scouts' might betray him, he had all ten killed by the army.

The country was now spiralling rapidly downwards into chaos. A common front of opposition parties, religious groups and unions was formed – the Democratic Revolutionary Front (F D R) – and the death squads began to slaughter its members and leaders. Others, too, came within their sights: on 2 December 1980, security forces killed four American churchwomen who had been working in El Salvador; and on 3 January 1981, the head of the Salvadoran land reform office and two American officials who had been advising El Salvador on land reform were shot as they took breakfast together in the Sheraton Hotel in San Salvador. The Carter administration, in one of its last acts, suspended all aid to El Salvador. However, when the Reagan administration took over the following month, it resumed aid and tried to persuade the junta that the death squads must be stopped, the government reformed and elections held.

There were elections in March 1982, which were won by Arena whose leader, Roberto d'Aubuisson, believed to be one of the patrons of the death squads, was implicated in both the murder of the archbishop and the Sheraton killings. He had campaigned on a promise to end land reform and crush the opposition: there was a strong element of anti-Americanism in his platform.

D'Aubuisson became president of the National Assembly, but under strong pressure from the Americans, Alvaro Magaña – a conservative civilian and a member of the old coffee-plantation oligarchy – was made provisional president. Duarte left the government. The old regime had by now completely recovered the positions that it had lost in 1979.

The United States did not despair. It continued to support moderate elements within the military as well as centrist politicians. These policies paid off in 1984 when El Salvador enjoyed its first democratic presidential election, and Duarte won by a large majority.

Duarte, who had studied in the United States and spoke English well, proved a genius at public relations. He had been cheated of victory in a presidential election ten years earlier, had been arrested, tortured and sent into exile by the Romero dictatorship. He now went to Washington to present his case as leader of the democratic centre in El Salvador. For the first time in its history, the United States devoted sustained, intelligent attention to the problems of Central America. Duarte was embraced by all parties in Washington with more fervour than any other foreign leader since Anwar Sadat. The Americans gave Duarte everything he asked for, with one caveat. Congress stipulated that no more than 55 American advisers should be attached to the Salvadoran military, and they should not take part in any counter-insurgency operation themselves. In other words, there were to be no more Vietnams.

El Salvador's, and Duarte's, tragedy was that his political base was not strong enough, even with unstinting American support, to break the power of the oligarchy and the most conservative elements in the military, or to win over the rebels. Land reform was thwarted, popular organizations were constantly harassed, measures that might have weaned the peasants away from the promises of the guerrillas were blocked.

The only perceptible improvement during Duarte's term of office, at least until the summer of 1988, was that the death squads suspended their work. The war, however, continued.

## THE WAR

In January 1981 the guerrillas launched a general offensive, hoping to repeat the Sandinistas' triumph in Nicaragua before Ronald Reagan took office in Washington. It was a complete failure: the armed forces held the cities without difficulty. In the aftermath of their victory, they launched the death squads into a paroxysm of murder and slaughtered every leftist, student or labour leader who might later be tempted to serve in a new guerrilla offensive – or in a democratic left-of-centre operation.

Things went differently in the countryside, and the F M L N took control of several border provinces. The army counter-attacked, and in December 1981 carried out the worst atrocity of the war. In El Mozote, in Morazán province in the north, they systematically massacred at least 1000 civilians, including hundreds of children. News of the massacre reached Washington immediately, and was hotly denied by the Reagan administration. But murder will out, and the distrust the incident inspired in Washington in the Salvadoran armed forces lasted throughout the war and ensured that the United States would not intervene directly and would exert whatever influence it might have to restrain the murderers – short of abandoning them and letting the Communists take over.

The F M L N retreated to the countryside and concentrated on building up its strength among the peasants, particularly in the border provinces. American observers have reached the depressing conclusion that the great majority of guerrillas joined the F M L N during this period, after the overthrow of the Romero dictatorship and during the country's evolution towards a more democratic government – that, in fact, the upsurge in guerrilla support was a direct consequence of d'Aubuisson's death squads. In 1983, the guerrillas tried a second

**477**

general offensive, and were once again defeated. By that time, American advisers had managed to improve the army's level of confidence somewhat, and had succeeded in dissuading the military from massacring peasants.

Starting in 1980, the Salvadoran army expanded from 12,000 men to 54,000, paid for by the U S and trained by American advisers or by Salvadorans who had themselves been trained in the U S. By the time of the ceasefire in 1992 there were thought to be between 4000 and 6000 guerrillas and, of course, far larger numbers of sympathizers. In 1988, the army reported that it was losing about 3000 soldiers dead or wounded a year, and claimed that the rebels were losing 1000 annually.

These are not large numbers, and if that were the whole story, the war might have continued indefinitely, with the guerrillas controlling villages in the remoter provinces and the army mounting seasonal offensives against them. However, the rebels, on occasion, succeeded in bringing the war closer to home. On 31 March 1987, they attacked the headquarters of the 4th Infantry Brigade in a barracks at El Paraiso, 36 miles (58 km) north of San Salvador. The attack was strikingly successful, especially as the barracks had been designed by officers of the American special forces to be impregnable. The rebels killed 70–80 troops, including an American adviser (Staff Sergeant Gregory Fromius of the Special Forces), losing 11 men themselves. The barracks, including its intelligence centre, was largely destroyed.

Subsequently, the rebels concentrated on economic targets, particularly the country's electricity grid (the Shining Path in Peru followed the same tactics). They claimed that, since most of the peasantry and the urban poor had no electricity, disrupting the electrical grid inconvenienced the class enemy alone. They offered the same specious defence for their attacks on coffee plantations.

The United States aid mission to El Salvador calculated in the summer of 1988 that the war, and attacks on the economy by guerrillas, had cost almost $2 billion since 1980. In the same period, the U S had provided some $3 billion in aid, but most of it had been either direct military assistance, or been used for military purposes. The war had a devastating effect on the country's economy. In May 1988, a congressional report in Washington stated that the average Salvadoran income was then 38 per cent lower than in 1980. The report continued: 'El Salvador is approaching the record for dependence on U S aid held by South Vietnam at the height of the Vietnam war.' It claimed that 64 per cent of American aid (nearly $2 billion) had gone to fighting the war, rather than to the things, listed in the Kissinger report, that were needed to build a sound economy.

The rebels were less successful politically. On May Day, 1986, unions sympathetic to the rebels rallied 40,000 people in a march through San Salvador. Encouraged by this success, the rebels stepped up a campaign to bring the country to a halt by shooting up buses and private cars. In the congressional elections of March 1988, the rebels made every effort to prevent people going to the polls: they threatened to kill candidates, polling station officials – even ordinary voters – *pour encourager les autres*. They carried out their threats by attacking a number of polling stations, and, afterwards, by assassinating a number of successful candidates, including several mayors; other mayors were

forced to resign.

Despite the threats and murders, the rebels' campaign was a notable failure. Salvadorans voted in record numbers, and a majority turned to the far-right Arena party, in clear repudiation of the left. It was also a repudiation of President Duarte and the Christian Democrats, who had failed to stop the war or revive the economy. Duarte's son was soundly defeated in his bid to be mayor of San Salvador, a post that the party had held since 1964, when the elder Duarte had won it.

Undaunted, the guerrillas tried to repeat their previous May Day success and summoned the faithful to a mass demonstration. A mere 3000 demonstrators turned out, and when some of them started burning cars and building barricades, they were repudiated by the very union leaders whom the rebels had most confidently counted on. In the next few days, in a series of engagements, 29 rebels, 18 soldiers and 12 civilians were killed, by the army's count. The rebels claimed to have killed 228 soldiers, including 100 in an attack on a hydroelectric station. The attack was counted a success: electricity had to be cut off in San Salvador for four hours every day to conserve supplies.

It appeared that the F M L N had lost a good part of its popular support, at least in San Salvador. The rebels were now faced with the task of rebuilding their base in the cities, almost from scratch. Their best hope would be that the new Arena government would revive the death squads and its former policy of generalized massacre, thus alienating the Americans and driving the Salvadoran peasantry and lower classes back into the arms of the F M L N.

There can be no doubt that the guerrilla armies were supplied by Nicaragua and Cuba and, indirectly, by the Soviet Union. The rebels' arms were smuggled into El Salvador through Honduras, or by sea. It was a small-scale Vietnam: the mountains and forests provided ideal cover for the smugglers.

The new, American-trained and much larger Salvadoran army was less brutal than its predecessor in the early days of the war, but there were still frequent incidents of murder and torture. One case caught the attention of the American press in February 1988. Two young peasants, Félix Rivera, aged 25, and Mario Rivera, aged 16, were seized by troops in a village in north-eastern El Salvador, forced to run barefoot through a field of burning crops, and then tortured – their noses, ears and fingers were cut off – before they were killed. Observers feared that such incidents were a sign that the mass terror of the early 1980s was returning. The statistics seemed to indicate this: in 1987, there were 24 death squad murders; in 1988, the rate rose sharply.

Peasants were not the only victims. On the morning of 11 May 1988, Judge Jorge Serrano Panameño was shot outside his house after he returned from taking his four children to school. He had been about to rule on the question of whether two groups of terrorists, one Communist and one closely linked to Roberto d'Aubuisson, were eligible for amnesty under the Central American peace plan.

He had ruled that the Central American Revolutionary Workers' Party – who were accused of murdering 12 people (including four U S Marines) at an outdoor café in San Salvador on 19 June 1985 – were covered by the amnesty because their crime was 'political'. (President Duarte, under strong American pressure, refused to release them.) The ruling on the other group involved one of the **479** few cases in which large numbers of death squad members were charged. They had belonged to a kidnapping ring run by military officers who were also directors of the death squads. In 1982–5, they had kidnapped five wealthy Salvadorans and obtained $4 million in ransom. Nine men were charged. Three, including a colonel and a cashiered lieutenant, fled the country. Three others were murdered in police custody, apparently to stop them confessing. Three others were sent to jail to await Judge Serrano's verdict. One of this trio, another cashiered lieutenant and protégé of d'Aubuisson's, was also accused of ordering the killings of the two American land reform advisers in the Sheraton hotel in 1981. The case had been broken with the assistance of the FBI and the Venezuelan police.

Judge Serrano was due to rule that week whether the three in jail were eligible under the amnesty. Presumably the death squad concluded that the judge would rule against amnesty, and intended to terrorize the entire Salvadoran judiciary. This ploy had worked before: just after Christmas 1987, three other men accused in the Sheraton case had been released under the amnesty, despite American protests.

## AFTER DUARTE

During his five years in office, Duarte managed a degree of reform in banking, commercial practice, taxation and land tenure. He did not, however, manage to strip the oligarchy of its power nor end its control of the economy. At the time of the 1979 coup, 95 per cent of Salvadoran farmers who owned their land farmed plots too small to support their families. At the same time, the '14 families' still owned enormous estates. By the end of Duarte's term of office, the situation had not substantially changed, but the oligarchy still detested him and retained the power to defy him. At the other extreme, the sharp economic decline caused by the war (and also by falling international coffee prices) lost Duarte popularity in the country at large. And, worst of all, he failed to stop the war.

Duarte took office promising negotiations with the rebels. He declared a ceasefire and met the rebel leadership, who presented a joint delegation of the Communist FMLN and the non-Communist Democratic Revolutionary Front (FDR). He insisted that the rebels surrender and re-enter the democratic process. They refused, but in 1987, the more moderate of the FDR's political leaders, Ungo and Zamora, returned from seven years' exile and prepared to contest the 1989 elections.

On 10 September 1985, Duarte's daughter, Ines, was kidnapped. After prolonged negotiations, she was released on 24 October, together with a woman friend who had been kidnapped at the same time, and 23 mayors and a number of other government officials who had all been prisoners of the FMLN. In exchange, the government released 22 of its own prisoners, including the second-in-command of the Communist party and Nidia Díaz, leader of the Central American Revolutionary Workers' Party. In addition, 101 wounded rebels were allowed to leave the country for medical treatment. This episode did much to undermine the confidence of the army and Salvadoran conservatives in Duarte.

The failure of the Duarte government cast a long shadow over the future of El

Salvador. In the legislative elections of 20 March 1988, Arena won a majority of the votes. It won 31 of the 60 seats in the National Assembly, and the Christian Democrats won 22. The National Conciliation Party won seven seats, but as they were allied to Arena, d'Aubuisson and his henchmen had total control of the Assembly.

In June 1988, Duarte, then aged 62, was diagnosed with stomach cancer. Surgeons in Washington removed two-thirds of his stomach, and on 11 July he returned home to die, although he hoped to survive long enough to hand over to his successor on 1 June 1989. The Christian Democrats were badly split. After an acrimonious dispute, they chose Fidel Chavez Mena, who controlled most of the party machine, as their presidential candidate.

The military situation continued to deteriorate throughout 1988, with rebels attacking posts near San Salvador and in the capital itself, and mounting a campaign of assassination of elected officials in provincial towns. On 1 November, a new army commander was appointed: Colonel René Emílio Ponce, described by one of the American advisers as 'by far and away their last, best hope'. He took over an army that had increased from 12,000 to 54,000 men in the previous six years, had been equipped and trained by Americans and was supposedly far better prepared to fight the rebels. The same adviser said of Ponce: 'If he can't get the army moving again, it might as well get off the playing field.'

There were encouraging developments in 1988: the ending of the Contra war in Nicaragua, coupled with Soviet efforts to improve relations with the United States. The left was in retreat internationally, and the guerrillas' support from abroad was weakening. The Salvadoran army might not defeat the rebels, but their own isolation might, in the end, have the same effect.

The presidential election was held on 19 March, and the Arena candidate, Alfredo Cristiani, won by a large majority. The F M L N ticket of Ungo and Zamora won 3.5 per cent of the vote. Arena had chosen Cristiani, a coffee planter and a representative of the old oligarchy, in preference to d'Aubuisson, who was anathema to the Americans. It was assumed that the new president would be wholly subservient to the party leader, but in fact he proved to be his own man.

Duarte formally handed over to Cristiani on 1 June 1989. He died the following February. The Americans' search for a valid, centrist government in El Salvador had failed, but they could at least take consolation in the unusual sight of one democratically-elected president handing over to another. For the moment, the Christian Democrats and the F D R together were in total eclipse, and Arena was left to face the guerrillas and the country's intractable economic problems. Cristiani's first six months in office produced two unproductive meetings between government negotiators and the F M L N, but there were no signs that either side was ready to make any real concessions for a peace agreement. The new president also devoted himself to modernizing the economy, and lifting the various restrictions on a free market that had accumulated over the years.

In the event, Cristiani's most important ally was Mikhail Gorbachev. If the U S S R could accept the collapse of Communism in Poland and East Germany, it was evidently unlikely to exert itself to preserve Sandinista Nicaragua, let alone the F M L N. As the 1990 elections in Nicaragua approached, the F M L N **481** evidently decided that their only hope of victory in El Salvador was a final military offensive, a Salvadoran Tet. It would either defeat the government and bring immediate victory, or destabilize it, and cause the Americans to lose heart and abandon it. On 30 October 1989, the F M L N bombed the army general staff headquarters in San Salvador, killing a civilian. The next day, a bomb at a cafeteria in a union headquarters killed ten people. The F M L N used the attack, evidently the work of a right-wing death squad, as justification for breaking off the peace talks. On 11 November 1989, the guerrillas launched their attack. It was their largest offensive in the war. They seized control of large areas of San Salvador, initially in the poor barrios in the north, and attacked government positions throughout the city. They attacked four other cities simultaneously. The operation was later extended to the wealthy districts of San Salvador: the American embassy came under attack, just like the embassy in Saigon in 1968.

The offensive lasted for two weeks, and failed militarily. There was no popular uprising. The army admitted losing 446 men killed and 1228 wounded, and claimed that it killed 2134 rebels. The F M L N said 401 of its men were killed. The army captured about 500 rebels. Civilian casualties were reportedly light both in San Salvador and elsewhere in the country, but large parts of the capital were devastated by the fighting and by the air force bombing guerrilla positions. In one incident, guerrillas occupied part of the Hotel El Salvador (formerly the Sheraton) while heavily-armed American Green Berets barricaded themselves in an upper floor. A truce was arranged to allow the Americans and other hotel guests to escape. The United States never satisfactorily explained what the Green Berets were doing there: only 55 American soldiers were allowed in El Salvador. After two weeks' fighting, the rebels made their escape to the hills. They were defeated, but not destroyed.

Among the casualties were several reporters and photographers, including David Blundy of the London *Sunday Correspondent*, who was killed by a sniper on 17 November. On 16 November, a unit of the Salvadoran army broke into the Jesuit residence on the campus of the Central American University and shot six priests and two women. One of those killed was Fr. Ignacio Ellacuria, the university rector and one of El Salvador's leading intellectuals. Though a noted left-winger and highly critical of the Arena government's extreme free-market economic policies, he had concluded that President Cristiani deserved support as a moderating influence on the army and the traditional oligarchy. There had been many other cases of military harassment of church workers and foreign social workers, but this was the worst instance of death-squad terrorism in several years. The murders provoked outrage in the United States, which Cristiani tried to mollify by announcing, on 6 January 1990, that the culprits had been arrested and would be tried. Sceptics doubted that those responsible would ever be convicted: no military officer had been jailed for human rights abuses in El Salvador since the civil war began. It was therefore a sign of considerable progress when the colonel who had ordered the murders, and the commander of the patrol which carried them out, were convicted of murder in September 1991. The soldiers who carried out the shooting were acquitted. The Nuremberg laws evidently did not apply in El Salvador. The judge in the case thought it prudent to leave the country immediately. Later, it emerged that the man ultimately responsible was Colonel René Emilio Ponce, chief of staff to the army and the man the Americans had counted on to reform and rejuvenate the armed forces. He had himself ordered the raid on the Jesuits. The U S strongly suspected his guilt at the time but finally decided to acquiesce in a cover-up for fear that Ponce would be replaced by some worse officer. He became minister of defence in 1991 and retired in 1993.

On 25 November 1989, during the offensive, Salvadoran forces shot down a Cessna 310 carrying arms from Nicaragua. Three of the crew were killed, the fourth shot himself. There could be no doubt of the plane's provenance. The captured arms included surface-to-air missiles (24 Soviet S A M-7s and one American Redeye), and news that such weapons may have reached the guerrillas made Salvadoran pilots exceedingly nervous. The army also found the wreck of another plane which had made an arms delivery safely. On 26 November, police arrested an American woman, Jennifer Casolo, who worked for a Texas-based organization called the Christian Education Settlement. They had found a large arms cache buried in her backyard, ready for the guerrillas. President Bush demanded that the Soviet Union use its influence with Cuba and Nicaragua to stop all deliveries to the rebels. Cristiani broke diplomatic relations with Nicaragua.

The F M L N offensive pushed the situation in El Salvador back to where it had been in the early 1980s. It demonstrated that the Salvadoran armed forces, despite $4.8 billion in American aid since 1981, were incapable of defeating the guerrillas. On the contrary, the F M L N had evidently increased in strength. The offensive and the Jesuit massacre also damaged Cristiani's moderate image: the president evidently had little control over the security forces or the army. At the same time, the military demonstrated their incompetence. Their poor showing was partly because the army was in the countryside, while the various police forces operated in the cities – but it was evident that after ten years of war, neither army nor police had any skill at urban warfare. As for the F M L N, the failure of its offensive showed the limits of its power, its lack of popular support, and also the viciousness of its tactics: though it claimed that it wanted to negotiate with Cristiani, it opened the offensive with an attempt to assassinate him. Rebels admitted that one of their objectives had been to provoke a right-wing backlash, and thus discredit the government in the eyes of the U S Congress. The F M L N could no longer claim to be self-supporting: it depended upon Cuba and Nicaragua.

Proof that the Sandinistas were arming the F M L N was a further blow to the Central American peace plan (*see* Nicaragua *below*) but it helped Cristiani's chances of retaining American support, despite the revival of the death squads. After the Sandinista government in Nicaragua was defeated in elections, on 25 February 1990, the Salvadoran rebels reconsidered their tactics. They announced on 13 March that they were suspending attacks against non-military targets, and proposed new negotiations with the government. They declared that they were no longer Communists, or even Marxists. The government was divided on how to respond, with hardliners rejecting all suggestion of negotiations and President Cristiani cautiously welcoming the rebels' move.

At this point, the secretary-general of the U N, Javier Pérez de Cuéllar, a **483**

Peruvian, intervened. He offered to mediate between government and F M L N and invited the two to send representatives to New York for negotiations. The talks lasted for nearly two years, with many ups and downs and a series of meetings in Geneva, New York, Mexico City and elsewhere. The final ceasefire agreement was signed in the early hours of 1 January 1992, after Pérez de Cuéllar had extended his personal involvement beyond the moment at which he ceased to be secretary-general. A formal treaty was signed on 15 January.

The agreement provided that the Salvadoran armed forces would be cut almost in half, and the F M L N guerrillas were to be disbanded. The F M L N abandoned its long-standing demand that it should be admitted to a coalition government, and agreed to submit itself to the electoral process. There was to be a purge of the most violent officers in the army, and the various paramilitary, civil defence forces and special police were to be disbanded. Above all, the rebels retreated from their dogmatic Marxism and the government admitted that leftist parties had a legitimate role to play in El Salvador. Another chapter ended on 20 February, just five weeks after the ceasefire was signed: Roberto d'Aubuisson, the leader of the country's most extreme right-wingers, died of cancer.

President Cristiani had some difficulty selling the agreement to the armed forces and the Salvadoran right, including his own party, but the heart of the matter was that both sides had finally recognized that the war, which had dragged on for 12 years, at a cost generally put at 75,000 dead, would never be won by either. The time had come to make a settlement.

The rebels emerged from the jungles and cautiously resumed normal political life. The peace treaty had included provisions that the army would leave politics, that there would be a beginning at agrarian reform, and that the constitution would be revised in a more democratic sense and the police and judiciary reformed. There were still political murders and corruption, but El Salvador began the slow climb back. The F M L N soon split. Arena won legislative, presidential and local elections in April 1994. The following November Jorge Villalobos, the Front's most prominent leader and, during the war, its top military commander and once a dogmatic Marxist, announced that his faction was abandoning Marxism and was leaving the opposition coalition. He tried to establish an alliance with the surviving centrist parties, but at the next elections, in March 1997, his Democratic Party did badly while the F M L N won almost as many seats in the Congress as Arena and carried a great number of mayoralty races, including San Salvador. The next test would be the presidential election and, beyond it, the lasting commitment to democracy of both the Front and Arena.

---

## FURTHER READING

Anderson, Thomas P., *The Matanza*, Lincoln, Neb., University of Nebraska Press, 1971.

Barry, Tom and Preusch, Deb (eds.), *The Central American Fact Book*, New York, Grove Press, 1986.

Bonner, Raymond, *Weakness and Deceit: U S Policy in El Salvador*, New York, Times Books, 1984.

Danner, Mark, 'The Truth of El Mozote', *New Yorker*, 6 December 1993.

Duarte, José Napoleón, *My Story*, New York, Putnam's, 1986.

Montgomery, Tommie Sue, *Revolution in El Salvador, Origins and Evolution*, Boulder, Colo., Westview Press, 1986.

*Report of the National Bipartisan Commission on Central America, 1984* (Kissinger Report).

Russell, Philip L., *El Salvador in Crisis*, Austin, Texas, Colorado River Press, 1984.

# GUATEMALA

| | |
|---|---|
| Geography | 42,042 sq. miles (108,888 sq. km). |
| Population | 10.6 million. Half are *ladino* (of Spanish and mixed descent); half are Indian, descendants of the ancient Maya, speaking 22 different languages. |
| GNP per capita | $1340. |
| Refugees | External: 45,500* in Mexico, 120,000 in the U S A. Internal: 200,000. |
| Casualties | About 100,000 people were killed between 1961 and 1997, the great majority of them civilians. A further 40,000 were reported 'disappeared', meaning murdered by army, police or guerrillas. Neither figure is precise. |

If it is necessary to turn the country into a cemetery in order to pacify it, I will not hesitate to do so.

President Carlos Arana Osorio, 1970

We are killing people, we are slaughtering women and children. The problem is, everyone is a guerrilla there.

President Efraín Ríos Montt, 1982

## HISTORY

Like the rest of Central America, Guatemala won its independence from Spain in 1821. The landowning oligarchy that had governed the colony under the remote direction of Madrid continued to rule the republic. The governing classes and those living in the cities spoke Spanish, and the mass of the peasants, treated as slaves or serfs since the Spanish conquest, subsisted in the countryside with their own languages and customs.

The United Fruit Company was formed on 30 March 1899. It was a merger of the Boston Fruit Company, which exported bananas from the Caribbean to Boston, and a Central American railway company founded by the Brooklyn entrepreneur Minor Keith, whose interests extended from Costa Rica to Guatemala and who had won the confidence of all the Central American dictators. In 1904, he persuaded the dictator of Guatemala, Manuel Estrada Cabrera, to give United Fruit a 99-year lease on the country's main railway, linking the capital Guatemala City to its only port on the Caribbean, Puerto Barrios. With its transport assured, the company soon took ownership of several hundred thousand acres of banana plantations. In 1936, another dictator, General Jorge Ubico, gave it a 99-year lease on another enormous plantation on the Pacific coast, and reaffirmed its other privileges: it paid few or no Guatemalan taxes, was allowed to import everything it needed without paying duty and paid its labourers 50 cents a day.

The United States had no interest in the internal politics of Guatemala, as long as the country was peaceful and American business (meaning United Fruit) was allowed to operate unimpeded. A long succession of dictators were left to their own devices, until World War I I. Then General Ubico's political sympathies with Mussolini and Hitler proved an embarrassment. In July 1944, the rising urban middle classes, notably the teachers, took to the streets in protest against Ubico's policies and forced his resignation. He appointed another general, Federico Ponce, to succeed him, but in October, a coup led by two junior officers – Major Francisco Arana and Captain Jacobo Arbenz Guzmán – forced Ponce to resign. About 100 people were killed in the coup. Arana and Arbenz called Guatemala's first free election, which was won with a majority of 85 per cent by the prominent writer and teacher Dr Juan José Arévalo Bermejo, who had lived in exile in Mexico for 14 years. His supporters had to send him the fare before he could return.

Arévalo set about modernizing Guatemala, with policies that were modelled on the New Deal. He introduced a social security programme on the American model, and gave women equal rights for the first time in Guatemalan history. His most radical enactment was a labour reform based on the Wagner Act, the charter of American trade unionism. His policies were strenuously opposed by United Fruit – and by a succession of prominent American liberals. The New Deal Democrats Claude Pepper of Florida, Mike Mansfield of Montana and John McCormack of Massachusetts (later speaker of the House of Representatives), as well as Senator Alexander Wiley of Michigan, a moderate Republican, all denounced Arévalo for proposing policies that were, in fact, based on American legislation. It was a striking example of American ignorance and venality.

Despite this opposition, Arévalo made some progress in social reform. In 1950, abiding by the new constitution, which provided for single-term, six-year presidencies, he stepped down and was succeeded by Jacobo Arbenz Guzmán. The other author of the 1944 coup, Arana, had emerged as the leader of the conservative faction in the armed forces. He was assassinated in July 1949, possibly with Arbenz's connivance.

The new president launched a programme of agrarian reform that United Fruit considered a frontal assault on its position in Guatemala. That position was impressive. The company had investments worth $60 million, including 550,000 acres of land. It employed 40,000 people, owned the country's telephone and telegraph companies and its only port on the Atlantic, as well as 887 miles of railway – almost the entire network. It paid minimal taxes, and its return on investment was 62 cents to every dollar. Between 1942 and 1952, the value of its assets increased by 133.8 per cent.

The company had permitted some social progress since its early days. Workers were provided with housing, medical services and schools. However, unions were banned, and United Fruit – known locally as *la frutera* – fought a bitter strike in the late 1940s over the workers' demands for a basic wage of $1.50 a day.

A former United Fruit official, writing his memoirs in the 1970s, commented:

Guatemala was chosen as the site for the company's earliest development activities at the turn of the century because a good portion of the country contained prime banana land and because, at the time we entered Central America, Guatemala's government was the region's weakest, most corrupt and most pliable. In short, the country offered an 'ideal investment climate', and United Fruit's profits there flourished for 50 years. Then something went wrong: a man named Jacobo Arbenz became president.

In March 1953, the Arbenz government proposed its land reform. No cultivated land was touched, but uncultivated land was to be expropriated and divided among the peasants. United Fruit was the prime victim: 83 per cent of its enormous holdings were uncultivated (it claimed that it needed the land as a 'reserve'). In a first measure, it was to lose 210,000 acres (85,000 ha), and subsequently the total was raised to 387,000 acres (156,500 ha). The government proposed to pay the company $2.99 an acre in government bonds.

The company had paid about $1.50 an acre for the land in the 1930s, and for tax purposes had declared that its value had remained the same. Now that it faced expropriation, it claimed that the land was worth $75 an acre, and an official protest, containing a demand for the larger sum, was presented to the government by the American ambassador.

## THE 1954 COUP

The 1954 coup is the key event in modern Guatemalan history, and has continued to play a large role in Latin American perceptions of the United States. The coup was mounted by the C I A at the behest of United Fruit and followed close on the heels of an equally successful operation mounted against the Mossadegh government in Iran at the behest of the international oil companies. Many observers since then, including principals in the two operations, have remarked that, however successful in the short term, the long-term consequences of the coups were disastrous for the countries concerned, for the United States – and also for the C I A.

Following the coups, the agency came to believe that it had a gift for cloak-and-dagger operations, and tried to repeat its successes in Indonesia and Cuba (and, years later, in Nicaragua). American unpopularity in the Third World owes a lot to the C I A. Guatemala was destroyed by the 1954 coup, in a long agonizing sequel that is not yet ended – and when the Iranian students stormed the U S embassy in Tehran in 1979, they claimed that they were avenging Mossadegh.

These were the days of the Truman administration, and United Fruit knew it had to rent a few liberals in its campaign to overthrow a democratic regime in Guatemala and replace it with a Fascist dictatorship. To this end, the company recruited the best-known public relations man in the U S, Edward Bernays, and Washington's leading lobbyist, Tommy Corcoran, to defend its interests. Corcoran enlisted the assistance of former Senator Robert La Follette of Wisconsin, who had been defeated by Joe McCarthy and was the very paradigm of the American liberal. La Follette and Mansfield, Pepper and McCormack, Bernays and Corcoran were all noted Democrats who had made their names defending trade unions and other worthy causes.

Republicans were involved, too. Senator Henry Cabot Lodge, of Massachusetts, who owned a large quantity of shares in United Fruit, denounced the **487**

Guatemalan government as anti-American and probably Communist; later, after the 1954 coup and by then ambassador to the U N, he defended the U S action to the Security Council. When Eisenhower won the 1952 election, United Fruit added John Clements to its pack of lobbyists. He was an associate of Senator McCarthy and a leader in that demagogue's anti-Communist crusade.

Bernays knew the power of the press. He invited a succession of reporters down to Guatemala to observe the paternalistic and public-spirited way in which United Fruit conducted its business, and to prove that the company's opponents were all Communists. A long succession of American newspapers and journals – led by the *New York Times*, the *Christian Science Monitor, Time, Newsweek* and *U S News & World Report* – fell for the Bernays touch and repeatedly assured their readers that the Red Menace had reached Central America. In due course, they all welcomed the coup.

Guatemala never stood a chance. If one of the tragedies of Central America has been American ignorance (United Fruit ensured that it was the principal source of information on Guatemala so, of course, La Follette, Lodge, McCormack and the rest were anti-Arbenz), the problem was compounded by Central American provincialism. Democratic politicians there spoke no English, knew nothing of the United States and made no effort to learn, preferring to stay at home and denounce the Yankees from a distance. Their efforts at influencing American opinion were pathetic. All that the Guatemalan ambassador to Washington could do was complain to the U S State Department about the anti-Guatemalan bias in American papers.

Thirty years later, El Salvador's president, José Napoleón Duarte, showed how it should be done: he spoke fluent English, and visited Washington frequently to assure Americans of his sincere democratic principles (*see* El Salvador, pp. 473–85).

The United Fruit Company also approached the C I A. Its director was Bedell Smith, who confided that his ambition was to become president of United Fruit (in due course, after he left the government, he was made a director). The deputy director was Allan Dulles, former member of United Fruit's law firm, Sullivan & Cromwell, which was also the company's chief adviser on foreign affairs. The law firm's senior partner was John Foster Dulles, the C I A deputy director's brother.

The C I A quite understood United Fruit's position, and set about preparing a coup to overthrow the Guatemalan government, giving the plan the codename 'Operation Fortune'. The preparations came to the attention of the secretary of state, Dean Acheson, who promptly stopped them. However, his days were numbered. Eisenhower won the 1952 election, Allan Dulles became director of the C I A, John Foster Dulles became secretary of state, and Bedell Smith moved over to the State Department as his deputy. A new plan, 'Operation Success', was set in motion and approved by the new administration in August 1953.

United Fruit recruited a disaffected Guatemalan colonel, Carlos Castillo Armas. He was living in exile in Nicaragua, under the patronage of President Anastasio Somoza, and immediately agreed to lead the revolution. The plot was not a secret: the C I A was openly recruiting mercenaries to take part in its proposed invasion.

Arbenz prepared to defend himself. However, the Truman administration had imposed an arms embargo on Guatemala in 1948 because of its supposed leftist leanings (another example of Washington's incorrigible myopia towards Central America). The rest of the world had always accepted that the region was within the United States sphere of influence, and had not sought to replace the U S as a supplier of arms. It was a serious difficulty, but in 1954, Arbenz found what he was looking for – in Czechoslovakia. There he bought 2000 tons of arms – rifles, ammunition, anti-tank weapons and light artillery – for $1 million. They were sent through Poland to the Baltic and shipped aboard a Swedish freighter, the *Alfhem*. It reached Puerto Barrios on 15 May, and the arms were taken by rail to Guatemala City.

The C I A plotted the progress of the consignment every step of the way. On 19 May, President Eisenhower asserted that the delivery meant the establishment of 'a Communist dictatorship on this continent'. Meanwhile, Arbenz's military were examining their precious cargo: the anti-tank weapons were superfluous (there were no tanks in Central America); many of the rifles were defective; and the artillery – German war booty – was far too heavy for Guatemala's roads. The Czech arms were of absolutely no help to Arbenz when, on 18 June, Castillo Armas sent his small army across the border to occupy a village on the other side. He had been equipped by Sam Cummings, just starting on a spectacular career as an arms dealer, and had everything he needed.

He also had an air force, supplied by the C I A: three World War I I P-47 fighters, which scattered pamphlets over Guatemala City, dropped a few bombs and strafed an army base. One of the aircraft crashed in Mexico, and was found to have a two-man American crew of dubious antecedents. They were C I A men.

The Arbenz government collapsed. The president lost his nerve, and very few Guatemalans were ready to fight for him. An Argentinian visitor, Ernesto 'Che' Guevara, was ready to try, but when Castillo Armas was flown into Guatemala City (on another American plane), Guevara took refuge in a friendly embassy. In due course, he was evacuated to Mexico, where he met Fidel Castro.

By the time Castillo Armas arrived, Arbenz had already given up. He was given asylum in the Mexican embassy, and was in due course allowed to go into exile. That was the end of Guatemala's ten years of democratic government. Only one man had been killed in the coup. Sam Cummings bought up the Czech arms, and then won a contract to re-equip the Guatemalan army. It was a highly profitable deal.

## THE NEW DICTATORSHIP

United Fruit won in Guatemala. Then it lost in Washington. The Justice Department started an anti-trust suit against the company, alleging that it monopolized banana production in Guatemala, and the company eventually decided to sell out. The Del Monte Corporation, which did not comport itself with the same flamboyant arrogance as United Fruit, bought most of its holdings.

Castillo Armas set about dismantling all the reforms of the previous decade, including the first steps towards industrialization. Within 18 months, he had driven virtually all the peasants who had obtained land through the Arbenz **489** reforms off the land again. The United States gave large sums in aid, soon amounting to $45 million a year. A great deal of it was embezzled, a great deal wasted, and none of it was used to relieve the peasants of their poverty, though they comprised the great majority of the population. The most useful American contribution was money for roads and the electricity grid.

Castillo Armas was assassinated in July 1957, in the presidential palace. His supposed assailant was found dead nearby, apparently a suicide. (When Benigno Aquino was murdered in Manila in 1983, his 'assassin' was also, most conveniently, found dead on the spot.) The true murderers were never discovered. A junta was hastily formed, which called elections, and to the junta's astonishment, they were won by General Miguel Ydígoras Fuentes, a conservative politician who had lost to Arbenz in the 1950 election, and who had declined a C I A invitation to serve as figurehead for the 1954 coup. The junta tried to annul the result, but were persuaded to call a further presidential election, in January 1958, which Ydígoras once again won. This time he was allowed to take office.

He was supported by the United States because he allowed Guatemala to be used as a base for the attempted invasion of Cuba. When a revolt broke out in some army units on 13 November 1960, the United States provided B-26 bombers, with exiled Cuban pilots, to bomb the rebel bases. The revolt was crushed, but two young lieutenants, Marco Aurelio Yon Sosa and Luís Turcíos Lima, were so disgusted by the episode that they started a guerrilla movement of their own. It was the beginning of a long war that cost 100,000 lives.

The two rebels joined forces with the illegal Guatemalan Communist party (P G T). In February 1962, they proclaimed a general rebellion against the military regime, calling themselves the Alejandro de León November 13 Guerrilla Movement, after a fallen comrade and the date of the abortive army uprising in 1960. They sallied forth from the hills and attacked army posts, and met with inglorious defeat.

Meanwhile, a second revolutionary group – named the October 20 Front after the revolution of 1944, and led by Arbenz's minister of defence, Carlos Paz Tejada – had also issued a call to arms. In March 1962, there were student riots in Guatemala City, costing 20 lives. These various disturbances sufficiently worried the Kennedy administration to set up a counter-insurgency school in Guatemala, staffed by Green Berets. The Americans also approved a 'pacification' programme and supplied the Guatemalan armed forces with aircraft and weapons.

By the summer of 1962, Ydígoras had crushed the students and the guerrillas. The remnants of the various rebel groups formed a new movement: the Revolutionary Armed Forces (F A R). It was never very successful, but kept up a small-scale insurgency in the hills for the next few years, hoping to repeat Fidel Castro's success in Cuba. However, it never comprised more then 500 guerrillas, and its actions provoked terrible reprisals by the army. By the end of the decade, it had been completely crushed.

Ydígoras had become deeply unpopular, and the Americans feared that he lacked the stamina to fight the Communists. In the summer of 1963, former president Juan José Arévalo Bermejo reappeared and announced his candidacy in the elections which were then due. The army decided that Ydígoras must go and, after consultation with Washington, arranged a coup on 29 March. Ydígoras was replaced by the minister of defence, Enrique Peralta Azurdia.

Apologists for John F. Kennedy deny that the president approved the coup. They also deny that he approved the coup that took place in Saigon the following November. It remains one of the ironies of the times that an ostensibly idealistic administration in Washington, which was intent on establishing democracy, weeding out corruption, promoting land reform and carrying out other admirable objectives in Indochina, should also have promoted military dictatorships in Central America. American Democrats who have accused the Reagan administration of a fondness for authoritarian regimes should remember that their own party was wholly committed to the Fascists 35 years ago.

Guatemala's descent into the pit continued under Peralta Azurdia. His troops pursued the remaining rebels with unremitting zeal. They raided a secret meeting of the Communist party, capturing 28 leaders, who were all murdered (a former Guatemalan congressman was reportedly pushed out of a military aircraft 20,000 feet over the Pacific).

Elections were held in 1966. Anti-militarist factions united behind centrist politician Mario Méndez Montenegro, but he was killed in another of those mysterious murders that had become Guatemala's speciality. Méndez's brother, Julio César, ran in his place, and was elected. The army tried to annul the election, but backed down under American pressure. Méndez was allowed to take office, but not power: he was a complete figurehead.

Command of the counter-insurgency forces was assumed by Colonel Carlos Arana Osorio. American Green Berets were brought in to train his troops and over 30,000 Guatemalan police also received American training; the Johnson administration provided $6 million in military aid and $11 million worth of equipment. Arana then launched a war of unrestricted terrorism on the Indian peasantry. Amnesty International believes that, in the following decade, at least 30,000 people were 'abducted, tortured and assassinated'. American planes, from bases outside the country, were used to drop napalm on suspected rebel bases.

By this time, death squads were operating at every level of Guatemalan life. The regime was not merely fighting peasant guerrillas in the countryside. It believed that its enemies also included union officials, peasant organizers, students, professors, teachers, liberal clerics and every shade of centrist or left-of-centre politician. Leftist terrorists, in retaliation, assassinated military figures and American officials, including the head of the US military mission, Colonel Harold Hauser, in 1965 and, in 1968, one of his successors Colonel John Webber and the US ambassador John Gordon Mein.

Colonel Arana was so successful in fighting the rebels that the army decided that he should be elected president. He took office in 1970, and extended to the cities the tactics he had first applied to the Indians. In the first three years of his presidency, the number of people who 'disappeared' increased sharply. Estimates of the numbers of bodies found range from 3500 to 15,000. (As if this were not enough, in 1976 an earthquake killed 25,000 people.)

In 1974, a dissident army general, Efraín Ríos Montt, ran for the presidency **491** against the official candidate – and won. The army promptly annulled the election, and sent Ríos Montt into exile in the Madrid embassy.

Despite the continuing oppression, the guerrilla movements increased. Two new rebel groups had emerged by then, both based on the Indians. The first was the Guerrilla Army of the Poor (E G A), a Marxist organization with a picture of Che Guevara as its logo. The second was the Organization of the People in Arms (O R P A). They both operated in the Indian provinces (though O R P A also had a base in Guatemala City, which was discovered by Argentinian counter-insurgency specialists in 1981). The Rebel Armed Forces (F A R) began to revive in the late 1970s, and in 1981, one section split off and called itself the Leadership Nucleus of the P G T (Guatemalan Communist party). All these four movements formed an alliance in 1982: the Guatemalan National Revolutionary Unity (U R N G).

Other opposition groups, which were neither Communist nor violent, were also emerging, despite the state terrorism that oppressed them. The Church, which had supported earlier dictatorships, began to defend Indians and workers against tyranny. One Christian group – the Campesino Unity Committee (C U C) – organized the occupation of the Spanish embassy in Guatemala City on 31 January 1980, to draw attention to the peasants' plight. Troops set fire to the building, burning 39 protesters alive. Shortly afterwards, the C U C organized a two-week strike among cane-cutters and cotton workers, and won a $3.25 daily minimum wage.

By this time, the United States had at last become aware of the sorts of governments it was supporting in Central America. President Carter cut off all aid to Guatemala, but the military regime was not deterred. Guerrilla activity continued in the highlands, and General Romeo Lucas García, who was president from 1978 to 1982, started a scorched earth policy to deal with it. American disapproval, and Lucas García's own corruption, led to a coup in 1982 organized by junior officers, in which General Ríos Montt was finally brought to power. He reined in the death squads in the cities, and allowed a greater freedom of political action there, but accelerated the fight in the countryside.

The war on the peasantry reached its paroxysm under Ríos Montt. He announced that his policy was to be 'beans and rifles'. Loyal peasants were fed, disloyal ones were starved: 'If you're with us, we'll feed you,' said the army. 'If not, we'll kill you.' In the most savage phase of the campaign, loyal peasants were also mobilized into local militias under army officers to hunt down supposedly disloyal peasants. The Washington Office on Latin America, an independent human rights group, estimated that it led to the destruction of 440 villages and the killing of between 50,000 and 75,000 peasants. Amnesty International is more cautious, stating that 'untold numbers died during the administrations of General Lucas García and General Ríos Montt. Estimates vary, but all put the victims in the tens of thousands.' The lowest figure offered by the army itself is 10,000 dead. Tens of thousands of refugees fled to Mexico: in 1996 there were still 32,500 officially registered Guatemalan refugees in Mexico, and between 50,000 and 100,000 illegal refugees.

By 1985, the local militias numbered over 900,000 Indian boys and men. The system enabled the army to control the countryside completely, for the first time.

The military government's scorched earth policy was literally that. In December 1982, *Newsweek* magazine reported:

In the far west and far north of the country, large stretches of once green farmland lie ash-black and deserted. And along the Mexico border, refugees huddled in crowded, muddy camps tell harrowing stories of army guerrilla-hunters beheading babies, setting fire to sick old men and driving stakes through the bellies of pregnant women.

The Ríos Montt campaign sharply reduced guerrilla activity, but at an appalling cost. In October 1983, Ríos Montt was removed in a coup by disgruntled army officers. Among other complaints, they objected to the president's evangelism: he had become a tele-evangelist, and preached regularly on television, calling on Guatemalans to come to Jesus and be saved. Conservative Catholic officers, and younger men who had studied in the United States, did not appreciate the call.

The Reagan administration had approved the 1983 coup (though it did not initiate it). The new president, General Oscar Mejía Víctores, introduced a new pacification plan, to be carried out with American help, called the 'Plan of Assistance to the Areas of Conflict' (P A A C). It involved building model villages, offering food for work, promoting literacy and the Spanish language, and improving sanitation – the slogan was now *'Techo, trabajo y tortilla'* (housing, work and food). The new government also introduced sufficient reforms in democratic practice and human rights to justify a resumption of aid from Washington in 1983. The Americans were now actively supporting democratic politics in Central America, as a counter to Communism. The Kissinger report (*see* El Salvador, pp. 473–85), one of the first comprehensive efforts by the leaders of an American administration to understand Central America, spelled out the close connection between social reform and defeating Communism, and Washington now exerted heavy pressure on the Guatemalan military to stop slaughtering the peasants and, instead, to launch an active rural development programme. American aid to Guatemala increased from $20 million in 1984 to over $100 million in 1985, almost all of it for the highlands.

There were fewer death squad murders under Ríos Montt and Mejía Víctores than under their predecessors, but the improvement was entirely relative. The Parliamentary Human Rights Group, in a 1985 report entitled *Bitter and Cruel*, calculated that: 100,000 people had been killed since 1960; there were 100 political assassinations a month and 10 'disappearances' a week in 1984; and there were 100,000 orphans and 500,000 'internal refugees' in Guatemala. An organization called the Mutual Support Group (G A M) was formed by relatives of the 'disappeared' who met in Guatemala City morgues. The G A M calculated that over 3000 people 'disappeared' during Mejía Víctores's first year in office, and that a further 10,000 children were orphaned. Mejía responded by calling the G A M 'a pressure group that is being manipulated for subversion', and two weeks later, two of the group's leaders were found murdered. One of them was its spokesman, Héctor Gomez, whose body, in frightful symbolism, was found with the tongue ripped out. The group's secretary, a woman of 24, who accused the military of the Gomez murder, was killed four days later, with her son and brother, in what the military described as a 'car accident'.

## GUATEMALA NOW

The guerrillas had been defeated: the army conceded that there were no more than 1500 of them left, not nearly enough to be a serious threat to the government. But it was clear that they would return unless major reforms were promptly introduced. Elections to a constituent assembly were held in 1984, and late in 1985, Vinicio Cerezo Arévalo, a Christian Democrat, was elected president. Cerezo was lucky to have himself survived the terror of the 1970s and early 1980s. At one point, he had sent his family to Washington for safety: his teenage son, who was sick at the time, had to be carried to the plane from hospital on a stretcher, with a nurse holding an I V bottle over his head, surrounded by bodyguards with machine-guns.

Cerezo knew the limits of his power. He did not have the same freedom as President Raúl Alfonsín in Argentina, who was able to purge the army of the officers who had led the 'dirty war' there and put them on trial for murder. Cerezo was obliged to promise that 'the past must be forgotten'. In the last days of the military government, President Mejía Víctores proclaimed a comprehensive amnesty for 'all people implicated in political crimes and related common crimes during the period from 23 March 1982 [when Ríos Montt took power] to 14 January 1986'. The amnesty covered the death squads but, of course, not the Communist rebels.

The army still had a free hand in fighting the guerrillas, and continued to pursue its campaign, including bombing suspected guerrilla bases. One clause of the Central American peace plan prepared by President Oscar Arias of Costa Rica and announced in August 1987 provided that each country would proclaim an amnesty for political adversaries and guerrillas. The Guatemalan army issued its own gloss on the agreement, stating that this clause did not apply to Guatemala. The government held talks with representatives of the guerrillas, in Madrid in October 1987, but did not persuade them to surrender. The army would accept nothing less.

Cerezo served his four years without contributing much to economic or social reform. In May 1988, army officers attempted a coup against him, which was suppressed by the minister of defence, Gen. Héctor Gramajo Morales. After that, Cerezo abandoned all pretence of bringing the army under control. The army, all the same, pursued the guerrillas less rigorously, and by 1990 they had recovered considerably. Rebel activity was a problem in 14 of Guatemala's 22 provinces, compared to eight in 1987. There were said to be between 1500 and 2000 guerrillas and there were reports that they had formed an alliance with the drug cartels. Opium poppies are grown in the Guatemalan highlands, which, with Mexico, are the nearest producers of heroin to the United States, and Guatemala is also one of many staging posts for the movement of cocaine from Colombia to the United States.

Guatemala's civil rights record continued to be one of the worst in the hemisphere. In December 1990, the Americans cut off $3.3 million in an annual military aid programme, in protest against the murder of an American, Michael DeVine, on 9 June, apparently by soldiers. A new president, Jorge Serrano Elías, took over in January 1991 and arranged for talks with the rebels. They

advanced slowly, partly because the guerrillas insisted that there must be some accounting for all the murders committed in the past 30 years. The government refused to allow the U N to mediate, as it had in El Salvador, but the changed climate in Central America brought about by the defeat of the Sandinista government in 1990 and the ceasefire in El Salvador in 1992, the collapse of the Soviet Union and the eclipse of Communist Cuba, had its effect even in Guatemala. The guerrillas were war-weary, and so was the rest of the population.

In October 1992, the Nobel Peace Prize was awarded to Rigoberta Manchu, a Quiche Indian woman, who had spent the past decade defending the rights of Guatemalan Indians. Her 1983 book, *I, Rigoberta*, on the Indians' sufferings, included an account of her father's death: he was a leader of a peasant party and took part in the occupation of the Spanish embassy in 1980. He was burned to death when the army stormed the place.

The prize served its purpose, moving the peace process forward under an intensified international spotlight. On 25 May 1993 President Serrano tried an *auto-golpe*, modelled on Alberto Fujimori's coup in Peru the year before. He dissolved Congress and the supreme court, suspended constitutional rights and arrested many ministers. For a few days it appeared that the army would acquiesce, but then on 1 June it abruptly ended the show, issuing a terse communiqué that 'The Armed Forces assumed the historic responsibility of their role.' Serrano fled to Panama.

The fighting had by then died down, but assassinations and the political consequences of past atrocities continued to afflict the country. In July 1993 a prominent liberal newspaper publisher, Nicolle Carpio, was assassinated. She was a cousin of the new president, Ramiro de León Carpio, installed after the Serrano débâcle, and there was nothing he could do to pursue her murderers. He had been human rights ombudsman a few years earlier, intimately acquainted with the brutality of modern Guatemala.

In 1994 an American woman, Jennifer Harbury, started a hunger strike to protest against stonewalling by the government over the fate of her husband. He had been a leader of the Guatemalan National Revolutionary Unity, the rebel umbrella organization, and was captured and murdered by police. In 1995, it emerged that his murder had been ordered by Colonel Julio Alpírez of army intelligence – who was also a C I A informant. The news was a huge embarrassment to the agency.

By then, a new president had taken office. Alvaro Arzú Irigoyen was elected in January 1996, barely defeating the chosen representative of the former dictator, Efraín Ríos Montt. That sanguinary general's sudden popularity was one of the many bizarre twists of politics in the region. Ríos Montt himself had not been allowed to run because of a constitutional provision excluding former presidents who had reached office by coup. He might very well have won a free election without that wise exception. Arzú, despite the narrowness of his victory, proved a strong president. He purged the army vigorously, sacking most of the generals and those lesser officers who had been responsible for the worst crimes of the past.

The peace talks were finally concluded in December 1996. The rebels had won a great deal in the negotiations, including extensive reforms of the constitution and justice system, and other civil rights. In exchange, they conceded sweeping amnesty for all crimes committed since 1954. Human rights advocates protested bitterly that at the least there should be a powerful Truth Commission, like the ones in El Salvador, South Africa and Uganda, but they were turned down. Guatemala preferred to turn its back on the dreadful years. Instead, the Guatemalan Truth Commission would investigate past abuses, but was not allowed to name those responsible, let alone punish them. On 29 December the treaty was signed by government leaders and by leaders of the Unity.

The piping days of peace that have now come to Guatemala are not yet very tranquil. The crime rate is very high, with kidnapping a speciality. In January 1998 a group of American university students on a tour of Guatemala were stopped in the countryside and five young women were dragged into a cane field and raped.

## THE BELIZE DISPUTE

One of the many irredentist disputes in Latin America concerns Guatemala's claim to Belize. That small country – 8867 square miles (22,965 sq. km), the size of Wales – on the Caribbean coast of Central America is a former British colony. Its population of 170,000 is mostly black and speaks English, but there is also a growing number of Spanish-speaking refugees from El Salvador.

In the 18th century, the British in Jamaica began logging hardwood on the mainland. Spain claimed the entire isthmus, but did not exercise any direct role on the Caribbean coast between Mexico and Panama. As for the British, they periodically recognized Spanish sovereignty but continued logging, and by the end of the century, there were permanent British settlements along the coast. By 1840, the territory that later became Belize had been organized as a regular colony, known as British Honduras. Other British settlements further down the coast were abandoned to Honduras and Nicaragua.

Guatemala claimed British Honduras on the grounds that it had inherited the territory from Spain. Mexico also claimed the northern part of the territory. In 1859, however, Guatemala signed a treaty with Britain, recognizing British sovereignty and agreeing on the border. A subordinate clause in the treaty provided that both parties would continue 'conjointly to use their best efforts' to build a road across the jungles from Guatemala to the Caribbean coast in British Honduras. The road was never built, and on that flimsy basis, Guatemala has since claimed that the 1859 treaty is invalid.

The dispute was forgotten until the 1930s, when it was revived by the Fascist regime of General Ubico. The claim was inherited by the Arévalo government, which, despite all its democratic professions, inserted a clause into the 1945 constitution stating that British Honduras was part of Guatemala. Guatemalan democrats and Fascists alike have continued to assert the claim, like the Argentinians' claim to the Falklands.

In the 1960s, as other British colonies in the Caribbean moved towards self-government and independence, Guatemala stepped up its claims to its '23rd department'. In 1963, troops were massed along the British Honduras/Guatemala border, and Britain had to send a small army of its own to deter an invasion. British troops have been there ever since.

In 1965, President Johnson offered his services to resolve the dispute. He appointed a mediator, Bethuel M. Webster, who concluded that British Honduras should be handed over to Guatemala. Guatemala was then the loyal ally of the United States, so the wishes of the inhabitants of British Honduras were not considered. Britain rejected the proposal.

In 1972, Guatemala again massed troops along the border, and this time, the British sent the aircraft carrier *Ark Royal* and several thousand troops to deter an invasion. (British Honduras also provided excellent training facilities for the British army in tropical warfare.) In 1975, after another threat from across the border, the British called on the R A F, and a squadron of Harriers was then based there.

The colony was by then self-governing (and had assumed the name Belize). Entirely ready for independence, its government finally abandoned the cautious diplomacy of the past, and took its case to the United Nations. To begin with, Belize was supported only by Britain and the Commonwealth, but it rapidly won further adherents including the Non-Aligned Group (Third World members of the U N). The United States, however, continued to support Guatemala by abstaining whenever there was a vote at the U N: there were limits to President Carter's commitment to democracy. Finally, in 1980, the U N voted for Belizean independence: 139 to 0, with 7 abstentions, Guatemala refusing to vote. On that occasion, the U S voted for Belize, which at last became independent in 1981.

Guatemala grudgingly agreed to recognize Belize, but only in exchange for its agreement to build the famous road. Even that concession was too much for the Belizeans: there were riots, in which four people were killed, in protest against the treaty. There was also such nationalistic opposition in Guatemala that the treaty was not immediately ratified. Guatemala continued to refuse to recognize Belize, and to veto its application to join the Organization of American States (O A S) and other western hemisphere organizations and Britain left a small garrison in Belize to ensure its protection. Finally, in 1991, the new civilian government in Guatemala recognized Belize and accepted the frontier. Britain withdrew its garrison, except for a small training mission, in 1994.

## FURTHER READING

American University, *Guatemala: A Country Study*, Washington D.C., 1983.

Amnesty International, *Guatemala: The Human Rights Record*, London, 1987.

Barry, Tom and Preusch, Deb (eds.), *The Central America Fact Book*, New York, Grove Press, 1986.

Brogan, Patrick, *Deadly Business: Sam Cummings, Interarms and the Arms Trade*, New York, W. W. Norton, 1983.

Fried, Jonathan L. *et al.* (eds.), *Guatemala in Rebellion*, New York, Grove Press, 1983.

Schlesinger, Stephen and Kinzer, Stephen, *Bitter Fruit*, Garden City, N.Y., Doubleday, 1982.

# NICARAGUA

| | |
|---|---|
| Geography | 57,145 sq. miles (148,005 sq. km). The size of England and Wales. |
| Population | 4.4 million. |
| GNP per capita | $380. |
| Casualties | About 10,000 people were killed in the uprising against the Somoza dictatorship, 1978–9. There is no reliable figure for the number killed in the Contra rebellion from 1983 to 1990, but it has probably not exceeded 10,000 (*see* notes to Appendix I). |

The long conflict between the Sandinista government in Nicaragua and successive governments in Washington was a metaphor for the 1980s. The Reagan administration was utterly obsessed with the affairs of a small and unimportant country in Central America. It confused dogma with reality to such an extent that in the end the president's closest advisers subordinated every other consideration of diplomacy and domestic politics to the question of supplying small quantities of weapons to groups of ineffective guerrillas operating out of Costa Rica and Honduras. Meanwhile, America's economic problems developed unattended and the rest of the world got on with more serious matters.

Despite all Reagan's efforts, the attempt to overthrow the Sandinistas by force was a conspicuous failure. In the event, they were defeated in elections a year after Reagan left office. They fell victim to the changing international climate, yet another domino in the series of Communist governments deposed in 1989–92, and to economic distress. There, at least, American policy succeeded: the trade and economic sanctions imposed on Nicaragua, first by President Carter in 1980 and then by Reagan, ruined the Nicaraguan economy. That effort was greatly helped by the Sandinistas' own incompetence, and by their attempt to impose a socialist model upon Nicaragua just as its failure was becoming glaringly apparent in Europe. On 25 February 1990, the Nicaraguans, in a free election, rejected the Sandinistas because of their economic failures and political oppression. They did so despite American intervention and support for the Contras, not because of it.

The political consequences in the United States of Reagan's policies, and their failure, were not severe, because vocal public opposition had ensured that he would not send American troops to overthrow the Sandinistas. In Nicaragua, Reagan's policy led to the deaths of up to 10,000 people. They were almost all Nicaraguans, killed by other Nicaraguans, but their deaths were a direct result of decisions taken in Washington.

## HISTORY

Nicaragua has suffered continuously from American intervention since the middle of the 19th century, as a result of its own political instability. For a century, the country was divided between two competing political parties: the Liberals and the Conservatives. The names did not reflect any political doctrine: they were simply labels attached to rival groups of landowners. From the 1830s onwards, Nicaragua was considered a possible site for a canal through the isthmus, and the two parties vied for the concession. In 1855, the Liberals hired an American adventurer, William Walker, to help them defeat their rivals and take over a profitable trans-isthmus transit company set up by Cornelius Vanderbilt. Walker, who had brought 57 like-minded men with him, succeeded – and then he made himself president. He was driven out a year later by another band of mercenaries, financed by Vanderbilt. Walker made two further attempts to set up a private kingdom in Central America but was eventually shot in Honduras.

After the American Civil War, Vanderbilt turned his attention to domestic railways and the idea of a canal lapsed. When it was revived by the French, the site chosen was the isthmus of Panama. The French failed to complete it, and the project was taken over by the United States, which created a special country, Panama, for the purpose.

Ever since, the United States has considered that a subservient government in Managua is required for complete protection of the canal. This doctrine was first applied in 1909, when the current (Liberal) Nicaraguan dictator started negotiations with European powers for a rival canal. There was a (Conservative) rebellion, and the United States sent the Marines to guarantee its success. In 1912, a more serious intervention was needed to preserve the new government against its rivals. On that occasion, the Marines occupied the country, and they remained, with brief intervals, until 1933. The purpose of the occupation was to ensure stability, and in the short run, it succeeded. The United States supported a series of presidents, one of whom signed a treaty guaranteeing that Nicaragua would not attempt to build a canal without the consent of the U S. However, as the years went by, there was continual agitation against the American presence and their client governments. This agitation usually took the form of the opposition demanding that the *gringos* should change sides and support them. It is important not to exaggerate American interference in Nicaragua. There were generally very few troops, and they were used to protect foreigners and to dissuade Conservatives and Liberals from carrying on their perpetual civil war.

In 1925, the Marines were withdrawn, and almost immediately there was a Liberal uprising against the Conservative government. The Americans returned in 1926. President Coolidge sent Henry Stimson to mediate, and he imposed a political settlement between the two parties. There was to be a Conservative president and a Liberal vice president – the sort of coalition that well-meaning outsiders have tried to impose on warring factions in Third World countries on frequent occasions since then. Such arrangements are seldom successful.

A small band of Liberals rejected the settlement, refusing to share power with the Conservatives. They were led by a Liberal lieutenant, Augusto César Sandino, who took his guerrilla army of peasants and workers into the remote northern provinces and defied American and government forces. (For a while, Sandino's secretary was Augustin Farabundo Martí, founder of the Salvadoran Communist party; he later deserted Sandino, who was insufficiently Marxist for his taste.) It was not a serious war by later standards, though it was notable for one innovation: the Americans invented the technique of dive-bombing to attack Sandinista camps. The fighting was frequently interrupted for protracted negotiations between Sandino and the Americans. The United States built up the Nicaraguan National Guard as a bipartisan organization – half Conservative, half Liberal – and progressively handed over the fight against the guerrillas to the Guard.

The United States' intervention was deeply unpopular at home, and eventually Congress (by then controlled by Democrats) voted to cut off funds, and President Hoover agreed to remove the Marines. Before they left, the Americans organized presidential elections, in 1932, the last free elections Nicaragua was to enjoy until 1984. The Liberal candidate, Juan Bautista Saucasa, won.

He was inaugurated on 1 January 1933, and the Marines left the next day. The commander of the Guard was Anastasio Somoza García, a Liberal and former foreign minister, who was related to the president. They promptly made peace with Sandino for, after all, were they not all Liberals together? Sandino flew to Managua and signed a treaty with Saucasa and Somoza, under which his forces were to surrender their arms in exchange for a 36,000 square kilometre tract of land in the north (a quarter of the country). The terms of the agreement were never completely carried out. In February 1934, Sandino was again in Managua, having talks about the various difficulties, and was invited to a formal dinner with Saucasa in the presidential palace, on the 21st. After what proved to be a particularly amicable evening, Sandino was taken out and shot.

## THE SOMOZAS

Somoza founded the longest-lasting of all Latin American dictatorships. He deposed Saucasa in 1936, and the family – in the persons of Anastasio I, Luis and Anastasio II – ruled uninterruptedly until 1979. The third Somoza president was driven out of the country by rebels who named themselves Sandinistas in honour of Augusto César Sandino.

Anastasio I enjoyed a rare advantage that enabled him to gain the Americans' complete confidence and therefore to win command of the National Guard: he had studied at the Pierce School of Business Administration in Philadelphia and spoke fluent English. For all the intimacy of their relations, North Americans, even those most closely concerned with Latin America, have seldom bothered to learn Spanish, and Latin Americans have been equally disinclined to learn English. Somoza not only spoke the language, he understood American ways, and he was able to persuade the US embassy in Managua and a succession of administrations in Washington of his loyalty to the alliance and to American principles of democracy and free enterprise. He even encouraged baseball as the national sport. For over 40 years, the United States government accepted the Somozas without inquiring into the nature of the regime. Roosevelt is alleged to have remarked: 'He's a sonofabitch, but he's ours.' Somoza ensured continuity by sending his sons to school in the United States: it was said of Anastasio II ('Tacho') that he was the only cadet at West Point who was given an army as a graduation present.

Anastasio I ruled as president or through puppets until 1956, when he was assassinated. He was succeeded by his son Luis, who died in 1967 and was in turn succeeded by his brother Anastasio II (who was assassinated in exile, in Paraguay, in 1980). A third generation – Anastasio III – was ready to take over when the 1979 revolution took place. Anastasio III now lives in opulent exile in Miami, hoping for a restoration.

The Somozas plundered Nicaragua as the Pahlevis plundered Iran, the Duvaliers Haiti and Marcos the Philippines. By the 1950s, the family owned one-tenth of the country's cultivable land, its only airline, a television station, a newspaper, a cement plant, sugar refineries, breweries, distilleries and a host of other property. They were cautious, and a great part of their fortune was invested abroad.

The regime was overthrown for a variety of reasons, including the egomania, greed and incompetence of Anastasio II. On 23 December 1972, an earthquake devastated Managua. Howard Hughes, the American billionaire, who was then living in seclusion in a Managuan hotel, took refuge in a carpark just before the building collapsed. Others were not so lucky: 5000 people were killed and 250,000 lost their homes. Very large sums in aid were sent to Nicaragua, and a high proportion was embezzled by the Somozas and their associates. Managua remained a ruin, and little serious attempt to rebuild it was made until after the revolution in 1979. Then American economic sanctions and the Sandinistas' incompetence prevented restoration.

## THE SANDINISTAS

The Sandinista Front for National Liberation (FSLN) was founded in 1961. Two of its three original leaders were killed during the guerrilla period; the third, Tomás Borge, became minister of the interior. It developed slowly during the 1960s, carrying out small actions in the countryside (which were always defeated) and in the cities, fomenting strikes, issuing proclamations, trying to build up a political base.

Its effectiveness was hampered by its own divisions. There were three factions: the *Proletarios*, traditional Bolsheviks who sought support among the urban working class; the *Guerra Popular Prolongada* (GPP), which was also dogmatically Marxist, and had more influence in the countryside; and the 'Third Force', the *Terceristas*, which, though basically Marxist like the others, recruited non-Communist supporters and advocated mass insurrections. The *Terceristas'* best-known leaders were the brothers Daniel and Humberto Ortego Saavedra. The GPP leaders included Tomás Borge, and the *Proletarios* included Jaime Wheelock Román. In January 1979, in preparation for the final offensive, the three factions united under a nine-man directorate, with three *commandantes* from each of them. It was this politburo that marched into Managua on 20 July 1979.

The guerrilla war from 1961 to 1978 was small in scale and constantly unsuccessful. The FSLN's first major achievement was a raid on a post-Christmas party on 27 December 1974, when 13 Sandinistas, including three women, took a number of prominent Somocista hostages, including the dictator's brother-in-law and a former foreign minister; they missed the American ambassador by half an hour. In negotiations mediated by Archbishop (later Cardinal) Miguel Obando y Bravo, the regime agreed to release 14 Sandinista prisoners, pay $1 million in ransom, publish long and flamboyant communiqués in the newspapers, and provide a plane to Cuba. It was this episode that split the

**501**

F S L N: the theoretical Marxists, led by Wheelock, denounced taking hostages as a bourgeois, demagogic error.

Despite that spectacular operation, the Sandinistas were not a serious threat to the regime. The increasing opposition among the middle classes was much more dangerous. The leader of the opposition was Pedro Joaquín Chamorro Cardenal, publisher of the country's leading newspaper, *La Prensa*. He was a member of a prominent Conservative family: the old division was still going strong. In 1959, he tried to start a guerrilla insurrection himself, and failed. After that, he stuck to politics. The opposition was influential in the cities, where there was much latent hostility to the Somozas, but in the mid-1970s, there were no signs that the regime was nearing its end. Then Chamorro was assassinated on 10 January 1978, and the opposition burst into flames.

It is quite possible that Somoza was not involved in the killing, that it was instead the work of a disgruntled petty crook who had been attacked and exposed in *La Prensa*. It is also possible that Somoza, who was recovering from a heart attack, no longer exercised his former rigorous control over younger and rasher members of his family and government. But the whole country assumed that the dictator was responsible. (The same debate, and the same final outcome, was to take place in Manila in 1986 after Benigno Aquino was murdered.) There were riots and a prolonged general strike in Managua. New opposition leaders emerged, including Alfonso Robelo and Adolfo Calero Portocarrero, who ran a Coca Cola bottling concession. (They became leading Contras, as did some members of Chamorro's family. Others became active Sandinistas: a nephew was killed fighting with the guerrillas in El Salvador in 1991.) The first uprisings against the regime took place in a number of cities, and were put down with considerable brutality by the National Guard.

Edén Pastora, a noted guerrilla who had fought with the Sandinistas but then left them because they were Communist, now proposed a *coup de théâtre* to galvanize the guerrilla movement. He recruited a band of Sandinistas, 25 strong, and, on 22 August 1978, seized the National Palace (the parliament building and government headquarters in Managua), taking 1500 hostages. Among them were the bulk of the members of the Chamber of Deputies, and Somoza's nephew and a cousin. When reporters asked him to identify himself, Pastora announced that he was 'Commandante Cero' (Commander Zero). Sandinista cells were strictly anonymous, with the commander taking the designation 'o' and the others numbered after that. On this operation, *Commandante Dos*, the third in command, was Dora María Tellez.

The occupation of the palace lasted two days. Somoza released 50 Sandinista prisoners (including Borge), published Pastora's communiqués, and paid $500,000 in ransom, claiming that that was all there was in the bank. As the guerrillas drove to the airport with their remaining hostages for the flight out of the country, there were large-scale demonstrations of public support. *Commandante Cero* was now a national hero.

## THE UPRISING

Somoza's position deteriorated rapidly after that. The Sandinistas staged repeated attacks on provincial towns, particularly in the north. There were strikes, demonstrations and ceaseless political activity in Managua, and after much hesitation, the Carter administration began to look for a centrist opposition to replace the dictator. Venezuela and Costa Rica stepped up their help for the rebels, and considerable quantities of arms were flown from Cuba to F S L N bases in Costa Rica. The Sandinistas and their ally, Pastora, prepared a general offensive from the south, but soon encountered a basic geographical difficulty. In the north, the country is open and access is easy; however, from Costa Rica, the only approach is via a narrow band of territory between the Pacific and Lake Nicaragua, sometimes less than 10 miles (16 km) wide. (Pastora was to face the same problem when he tried to attack the Sandinistas from the same bases four years later.)

The United States had cut off arms deliveries to Somoza, but the regime could still obtain the supplies it needed from the other Central American dictatorships – Guatemala, Honduras and El Salvador – and from Israel. Somoza's last line of defence was the National Guard, 10,000 strong, which for the most part held its positions against the rebels. Military casualties were light – a few hundred guardsmen and no more than 600 Sandinistas were killed during the uprising – but several thousand civilians, perhaps as many as 7000, died. Many of them were teenagers who died in attacks on the guardsmen.

Somoza's main weakness was political: the business community abandoned him and demanded his departure; the country was in revolt; and the Americans were negotiating with 'The Twelve'. In the summer of 1979, everything was slipping away from Tacho Somoza. A five-member junta was set up in Costa Rica, dominated by non-Marxists. All the various opposition groups, including the Sandinistas, agreed on a 'plan of government' which included guarantees of democratic freedoms. (The Sandinistas' violation of this promise has been held against them ever since.) Finally, Somoza agreed to resign and to hand over to a figurehead successor, who would in turn hand over to the junta. It was hoped that a new director of the National Guard would be found who would hold that institution together to provide a counterweight to the Sandinistas.

On 14 July 1979, the junta announced the names of 12 members of the proposed cabinet, including only one Sandinista, Tomás Borge, who was to be minister of the interior. Somoza resigned three days later and left the country with about 100 relatives and associates. The Sandinistas, and the junta, arrived in Managua on 20 July, and were confronted by the interim president appointed by Somoza and by the remnants of the National Guard. In the course of the following month, the guard disintegrated and the Sandinistas seized power, because theirs was the only military force of any consequence.

## THE REVOLUTION
Immediately after their victory, the Sandinistas set about imposing a socialist revolution on Nicaragua. Although at first their measures were no more extreme than those of the socialist governments of Sweden, or the first Mitterrand government in France, they clearly intended, eventually, to set up a Communist society. They started by expropriating the vast holdings of the Somoza family and its supporters, extending to about a quarter of the country's land and businesses. They nationalized banks and foreign trade and, in the autumn of

1979, took over mining and insurance. The non-Sandinista members of the government protested but never seriously tried to stop the Sandinista take-over. If the collapse of the Somozas was comparable to the February Revolution in Russia that overthrew the czar, there was nothing comparable to the Bolsheviks' Red October. In Nicaragua, there was a complete vacuum of power, and the Sandinistas filled it and called it revolution.

One after the other, the non-Sandinista members of the government, including Violeta Barrios de Chamorro, the murdered publisher's widow, resigned. By the first anniversary of the departure of the Somozas, the government was wholly Sandinista.

The Sandinistas faced a serious problem of reconstructing the country. About 10,000 people had been killed in 18 months, the damage of the 1972 earthquake had never been properly repaired and Somoza and his friends had emptied the national treasury on the way to the airport. President Carter persuaded Congress to allocate $125 million in aid to Nicaragua.

In Detroit, in July 1980, at the Republican party convention, there was a sign of things to come. During discussions on the Republican party platform, a small group of hardliners inserted a pledge to cancel all further aid to Nicaragua and 'to support the efforts of the Nicaraguan people to establish a free and independent government'. No one of any consequence in the party, least of all Ronald Reagan, ever studied this amendment before it was approved.

Party platforms do not mean very much. Reagan had no very clear views on Nicaragua, except a detestation of Communism and a belief that Carter's policies (and Nixon's and Ford's before him) had allowed a number of countries to be 'lost' to the 'evil empire'. That did not mean that he was committed to supporting an attempt to overthrow the Sandinistas. The hardliners had manoeuvred the Republican party into that position: after Reagan's victory in November, they set about manoeuvring the new administration in the same direction.

They were helped by the Sandinistas. In the months after their triumph, Sandinista leaders, while seeking economic help from Washington, made a series of speeches denouncing the Americans for past and present misdeeds. Then, after Reagan's victory, the Communist rebels in El Salvador decided that they must attempt to win their own victory before the new president could stop them. They therefore launched a general offensive, and the Sandinistas supplied them with the weapons they needed. This connection soon became known, and Carter, before he stepped down, suspended aid to Nicaragua. He also sent emergency aid to El Salvador. The El Salvador rebel offensive was a complete failure, to the disgust of the Sandinistas.

Central America was thus near the top of the agenda when Reagan took office on 20 January 1981. He had chosen as secretary of state General Alexander Haig, who knew nothing about the region and who was determined to prove that he was tougher than any of the President's other advisers. He may not have won the prize for machismo, but he easily won the prize for folly. He recommended blockading Cuba as a way to save El Salvador, but the president, wiser than he, vetoed the idea. Reagan's national security adviser was Richard Allen, a man of depressing mediocrity who quickly assembled a team reflecting his talents.

Reagan had four national security advisers in his first six years, and in a remarkable example of intellectual regression, each of them was less competent and more ignorant than his predecessor. This downward progression ended with Admiral Poindexter who organized the Iran–Contra fiasco.

The State Department tried to salvage something out of the wreckage, and succeeded. Carter's policy towards El Salvador, Guatemala and Honduras was maintained. But there was a price: the hard right, who became known in Washington as the 'war party', demanded their pound of flesh. They were given Nicaragua.

The war party, as the writer Roy Gutman put it with careful understatement, 'suffered from the shortage of talent and experience in foreign affairs in the conservative wing of the Republican party'. They insisted on purging the State Department's Bureau of Inter-American Affairs and Carter's ambassadors in Central America. 'A new team would be assembled to manage policy that had one thing in common: all its members lacked Latin American experience.'

## THE CONTRAS

Within a year of the revolution, Nicaraguan exiles – both those who had supported the Somozas and those who opposed the Somocistas and Sandinistas equally – set about looking for help. They found their first ally in Honduras, where Colonel Gustavo Álvarez Martínez, who later became chief of staff and *ex officio* ruler of the country, supported them from the beginning. In 1981, the anti-Sandinistas found that the new director of the Central Intelligence Agency, William Casey, could be particularly helpful, and they soon raised enough funds to form the first anti-Sandinista army in Honduras. The Honduran government, or at least Álvarez, planned to provoke the Sandinistas into invading Honduras or Costa Rica, an event he expected would lead to an American intervention in Nicaragua. He set up the first Contra army, 500 strong, to achieve this object. (The Sandinistas called them '*Contra-revolucionarios*', or counter-revolutionaries. The term preferred by the Reagan administration – 'freedom fighters' – never stuck.)

The leading US hardliners were: William Casey; William Clark, Haig's deputy who succeeded Richard Allen as national security adviser late in 1981; Jeane Kirkpatrick, ambassador to the UN who had made her reputation defending right-wing regimes in Latin America; Edwin Meese, counsellor to the president, and Caspar Weinberger, secretary of defence. It was a formidable combination. Their first achievement was a presidential directive, signed in November 1981, committing the United States to support 'political and para-military operations against the Cuban presence and the Cuban–Sandinista support infrastructure in Nicaragua and elsewhere in Central America'. Casey proposed three objectives: to get the Sandinistas to 'turn inward', meaning presumably that they should cease and desist from exporting revolution; to 'interdict' (i.e. prevent) the supply of arms to the Salvadoran rebels; and to bring the Sandinistas to negotiate.

Meanwhile, the Contras were getting started. The Nicaraguan Democratic Forces (FDN) were formed in Guatemala on 11 August 1981, and they found a military leader in Colonel Enrique Bermúdez Varela, the most acceptable of the former members of Somoza's National Guard. He had been military attaché in Washington during the Sandinista uprising and thus had no part in the savagery of that conflict. However, many opponents of the Sandinistas refused to work with former National Guardsmen, and the Sandinistas constantly harped on the allegation that the Contras would bring back the Somocistas.

To train their first troops, the Contras turned to Argentina, whose military government was looking for ways to ingratiate itself with the new American administration. Honduras continued to help, and so did the C I A, to a far greater extent than it ever admitted. By the end of 1982, the Contras had raised 4000 men in Honduras, and by the following spring, the number had reached 7000, including a force in Costa Rica and a contingent of Miskito Indians.

By then, it was public knowledge that the United States was arming the Contras, and Congress became alarmed. As a result, Congressman Edward Boland of Massachusetts, who was chairman of the House Committee on Intelligence, presented the first of his amendments, which was passed in December 1982. It stated that U S funds might be used by the Contras only to stop the flow of arms from Nicaragua to El Salvador.

In February and March 1983, Bermúdez launched his first offensive into Nicaragua. His troops penetrated into the heart of the country, attacking government posts and carrying out sabotage, and then withdrew to Honduras. The Contras had achieved very little, but considered it just a beginning. They said that they would have achieved much more with greater American assistance, and claimed that the Boland amendment was a stab in the back. The Reagan administration agreed, but that July, for the first time, Congress rejected a Reagan request for Contra aid. The Pentagon then launched the first of a series of large-scale military exercises in Honduras and off both coasts of Nicaragua, with the evident intention of intimidating the Sandinistas.

## GRENADA

This, it turned out, was the high point of the Contra offensive, and coincided with a striking exercise of American power: the invasion of Grenada, far to the east in the Caribbean. President Reagan had frequently warned of the dangers of a Communist base in Grenada, a new Cuba in the southern Antilles, citing as proof of its evil intent the construction of a major new airport that was allegedly designed to serve as a Soviet air base. On 19 October 1983, the semi-Marxist government of Grenada was overthrown in a coup by a small group of ambitious soldiers, and the prime minister, Maurice Bishop, was killed. A few days after the coup, on 23 October, Lebanese terrorists killed 241 Marines in a car bomb attack in Beirut. Reagan seized the opportunity to divert attention from the Lebanese catastrophe and, at the same time, to eliminate a supposed threat nearer home: U S forces landed on Grenada on 25 October.

A group of neighbouring Caribbean governments had requested the intervention for a quite different reason: they had no wish for the Caribbean to fall into the South American and African habit of allowing men with guns to seize power and shoot prime ministers. The official justification offered by the U S was that a group of American students in a medical school on Grenada were in danger, and that Grenada was being turned into a Soviet base. This was pure fantasy and another example of the ill-effects of lying to the public. The Reagan administration was constrained to keep up the lie even as the school's officials insisted that the students had never been in any danger. The airport was also found to be quite unsuited for military purposes: it was for tourists only. In addition the large numbers of Cuban and East European 'troops' allegedly on the island all turned out to be construction workers.

The Grenada operation was a complete success. It wiped out the memory of Beirut, and it was very popular in Grenada. Six months later, the U S troops went home, leaving a peaceful and democratic island behind them. The operation also put the fear of God into Cuba and Nicaragua. It had been a fearsome show of power, and demonstrated to the Sandinistas that, if the United States ever chose to intervene, neither Cuba nor the Soviet Union would lift a finger to help them.

There was now a brief moment when a deal might have been done. The Sandinistas would have accepted any terms the United States stipulated, short of dissolving their own government, in exchange for a peace agreement. Daniel Ortega visited New York and Washington in an attempt to convey the message. Unfortunately, Washington was distracted by the Middle East. Roy Gutman, for once, blames the State Department, and not the White House hardliners, for the failure to exploit the profound psychological advantage that the U S obtained by the Grenada operation. Soon afterwards, it was business as usual.

## MINING THE HARBOURS

The C I A's first business was finding a way to mine Nicaragua's harbours. This is an instructive episode for a number of reasons, starting with the complete lunacy of the project itself. The C I A decided that it would be inadvisable to sink too many ships; the mines, therefore, should make a lot of noise but do little damage. It was hoped that the fracas would scare away international shipping, thus cutting off Nicaragua's oil supplies, and bring the government to its knees – or at least cause it severe inconvenience for a month or so. This was what Colonel Khadafy of Libya tried to do in the Red Sea later that summer, hoping to inconvenience Egypt (*see* Libya, p. 71). He was severely criticized for this 'terrorism' by many countries, but the United States had to keep quiet.

The first problem was to obtain non-lethal mines – the international arms industry usually produces much more dangerous weapons. In the end, the agency had to manufacture them itself. Non-American C I A agents laid them in January and February 1984, in the harbours at Corinto and Puerto Sandino on the Pacific and El Bluff on the Caribbean. The Nicaraguan government, whose agents were observing all this, denounced the mine-laying when it had barely begun, early in January, and the C I A instructed the Contras to claim the credit.

Nothing more happened until 25 February when the first mines exploded, sinking two small fishing boats at El Bluff. In the next month, a number of other ships were damaged, including a Soviet tanker. In all, ten ships were hit, a number of sailors were wounded and two Nicaraguans were killed. Some cargo ships cancelled visits to Nicaraguan ports. Nicaragua had therefore to transport its exports by road to ports in Costa Rica. However, on the whole, international

**507**

shipping was not overly impressed. Insurance rates were hardly affected, and Nicaraguan trade continued.

It was not a big story, to begin with. The State Department issued an official denial that the United States had had anything to do with the mining, and the matter might have rested there, as yet another unsuccessful C I A project, but for the sudden intervention of Congress. The political explosion was generated by Senator Barry Goldwater, father-figure of American conservatism, and chairman of the Senate Intelligence Committee. He discovered that the C I A had mined Nicaragua's harbours without telling the committee, and on 9 April, he sent a letter of fulminating protest to Casey:

I am pissed off. Bill, this is no way to run a railroad. The President has asked us to back his foreign policy. Bill, how can we back his foreign policy when we don't know what the hell he is doing? Lebanon, yes. We all knew that he sent troops over there. But mine the harbors in Nicaragua? This is an act violating international law. It is an act of war. For the life of me, I don't see how we are going to explain it.

Casey had, in fact, made a reference to the mining in testimony to the committee on 8 March, well after the operation had begun, but Goldwater and his colleagues had missed it. Other senators shared Goldwater's outrage, and his letter was leaked to the press. The full Senate voted 84 to 12 to condemn the mining; the House followed suit; and the Reagan administration was faced with a major political embarrassment. On the day that Goldwater wrote his letter to Casey, Nicaragua took the case to the International Court of Justice at The Hague and asked for a ruling that the mining was illegal and that the U S must stop helping the Contras. The United States, which from the time of Woodrow Wilson had defended the rule of law in international affairs, now denounced the International Court and announced that it would not take part in its proceedings. It was a low point in the Reagan presidency. The Court finally ruled against the United States in June 1986: the Reagan administration ignored the ruling.

The mining had even more serious consequences. Congress suspended all further aid for the Contras in May 1984, and voted to end all American support the following October. William Casey at the C I A and Robert McFarlane, who was now national security adviser, set about finding alternative, illegal sources of funds. McFarlane applied to Saudi Arabia, which was always ready to oppose Communism and please the U S: the Saudis agreed to send $1 million a month.

## THE SANDINISTAS

By then, Bermúdez, based in Honduras, was operating far and wide in northern and central Nicaragua. Edén Pastora, who had broken with his former comrades, accusing them of betraying the revolution, attacked over the border from Costa Rica and for three days held San Juan del Norte, a fishing village on the Caribbean coast. His group, separate from the Contras in Honduras, was known as A R D E (the Democratic Revolutionary Alliance). A R D E's political leader was Alfonso Robelo, a millionaire businessman who had played a prominent part in the revolution against Somoza. The Sandinistas responded to all these attacks in two ways: they announced that they would advance the promised legislative and presidential elections by a year, and they applied to Cuba and the Soviet Union for military help.

The Soviet Union sent arms, ammunition and, above all, Mi-25 helicopter gunships. These fearsome weapons started to arrive in the autumn of 1984 and had a devastating effect on the Contras, who had been operating in large bands of up to 500 men. In the next few years, the Sandinista army was systematically increased and equipped with the latest Soviet weaponry: just as the Reagan administration came to rely upon the Contras, to the exclusion of everything else, to effect its political aims in Nicaragua, the increase in Nicaraguan military strength, particularly the gunships, ensured that the Contras would be defeated.

The elections were held on 4 November, two days before the American elections. For months during the summer and autumn, the Nicaraguan opposition debated whether or not it should participate. The Reagan administration was divided. The hardliners wanted to boycott the elections because they believed that the Sandinista regime was a Communist dictatorship, and they took it as axiomatic that Communists always cheat. The opposition had a presidential candidate, Arturo Cruz, who had been ambassador to Washington after the revolution. But the opposition's divisions and hesitations, and the divisions in Washington, led to endless procrastination until it was too late to register Cruz as a candidate. The Americans then blamed the Sandinistas and claimed that the elections were fraudulent.

Foreign observers judged that the elections were fair and honest. The Sandinistas won 61 of 96 seats in the legislative assembly. In the presidential election, Daniel Ortega won 67 per cent of the vote, on a turn-out of about 75 per cent, against token opposition: Ortega thus won a more sweeping mandate than Ronald Reagan did two days later. With hindsight, Cruz and his supporters concluded that they had made a mistake: they speculated that, if they had taken part in the election, Cruz might have won 40 per cent of the vote and established a permanent political base in Nicaragua.

As it was, the elections were a success for the Sandinistas. However, the economy was heading for collapse. The Soviets had been persuaded to bail them out, to the tune of $500 million to $1 billion a year. On 1 May 1985, Reagan announced a complete embargo on trade with Nicaragua, driving the Sandinistas yet farther into the Soviets' embrace.

By now Ronald Reagan had given up the pretence that his object was to prevent the Sandinistas supplying arms to the El Salvador rebels. He admitted that he wanted the Sandinistas overthrown – all they had to do was 'say uncle'. However, few observers thought the Contras could ever defeat the Sandinistas, and their attacks and the rapidly rising civilian casualties tended to increase popular support for the government, balancing out the unpopularity brought on by the economic disaster. Reagan's policy was inherently self-defeating – and it was driven by a group of tunnel-vision zealots on the National Security Council staff and a few political appointees such as Elliott Abrams who was now head of the State Department's Latin America bureau. They defeated all efforts at negotiation, thwarted the 'Contadora' process (a diplomatic effort at a settlement by the governments of Mexico, Panama, Venezuela and Colombia), and devoted immense effort to supporting the Contras. In the process, they broke the law, which said that no aid should be given to the Contras, and showed astonishing political ineptitude by selling arms to Iran and using the profits for the Contras (*see below*). It was worse than a crime, it was a blunder. It was an amazing victory of ideology over intelligence.

By then the Contras had about 10,000 men under arms, 6000 in Honduras of whom 5000 were operating inside Nicaragua. They looked impressive, but they were never a serious military threat to the government. They concentrated on border areas, within 90 miles (150 km) of the frontier, and achieved some success: they disrupted the coffee harvest in the highlands and won some support among the peasantry. Then the tide turned.

In 1985, the Sandinistas won the upper hand over the Contras. It had taken them that long because, to begin with, they had no regular army at all: Somoza's National Guard had disintegrated, and the new Nicaraguan army had to be developed from scratch. The Sandinistas did not even have many experienced guerrilla fighters who might have been converted to a regular army. The Somoza regime had collapsed as a result of a mass, popular uprising, not after a long guerrilla campaign like the Cuban revolution – and anyway, the *commandantes* all now had desk jobs in Managua.

In the early days of the war against the Contras, the Sandinistas had relied on numbers. They had recruited thousands of peasants and had sent them off to fight the Contras with their shiny new Soviet guns and very little idea of how to use them. The United States had denounced the Nicaraguan army as the largest and most dangerous in Central America when, in fact, it had been no more than a peasant *levée en masse*. By 1985, however, it was reasonably efficient and adequately armed: it had transport helicopters and the Mi-25 gunships and enough pilots to fly them. The regular Sandinista army reached 50,000–60,000 men, and it was at last able to confront the Contras in strength.

## THE SOUTHERN FRONT

In the spring of 1984, the CIA was sending $400,000 a month to support Edén Pastora and ARDE in the south. It was an untidy arrangement because Pastora insisted repeatedly and vocally that he would have nothing to do with the main Contra organization, the Nicaraguan Democratic Forces (FDN). He claimed that Bermúdez and his closest military associates were former supporters of Somoza, 'people who have tortured us for 45 years'. In May 1984, the CIA demanded that ARDE merge with the FDN. Robelo, seeing that there was no hope for ARDE without American support, agreed to the merger.

On 30 May 1984, Pastora called a press conference at La Penca, his headquarters in the Costa Rican jungle, to denounce Robelo. Just as he began to speak, a bomb exploded. It wounded Pastora and killed four people, one of whom was an American reporter, Linda Frazer, who bled to death in the mud. The many other wounded people were not evacuated for hours: Pastora was rushed away in the one boat available.

After the attempted assassination, most of ARDE defected from Pastora and joined the FDN. After that, Pastora was a *commandante* without an army, and in 1986, he abandoned the fight. He retired to fish in Costa Rica.

## The Iran–Contra affair

The congressional hearings in 1987 into the Iran–Contra affair, and the many documents that have been published have revealed the essential details. The guiding spirits of the whole business were William Casey and his assistants at the CIA, and the staff of the National Security Council including Lieutenant Colonel Oliver North. They succeeded in persuading President Reagan that secretly selling arms to Iran would eventually help the United States restore amicable relations with that country after the death of the Ayatollah, and might also lead to the release of American hostages held in Lebanon.

The proposal was vigorously opposed by the secretaries of state and defence, but Reagan ignored their advice. The further development – that the Iranians should be overcharged for the arms they bought, and that the profits should be used for an 'off the shelf', super-secret 'special operations capability' – was Casey's and North's idea. North was able to persuade his superior, Admiral John Poindexter (who had succeeded McFarlane as national security adviser in December 1985), of the wisdom of the proposal. He recruited retired General Richard Secord to organize the project. Secord had been a special operations specialist, involved in the attempts to rescue the hostages in Tehran in 1980.

After Congress had voted a complete cut-off of supplies to the Contras in October 1984 and refused to reconsider it, despite Reagan's victory in the presidential election, the Contras' situation became desperate. North hired a British mercenary, David Walker, who was sent into Nicaragua on a sabotage mission. His men attacked a Managua 'military installation' with explosives on 6 March 1985: it turned out to be the maternity wing of the country's major military hospital. Walker also reconnoitred the helicopter base, and concluded that it was too tough a nut to crack. He was asked to supply pilots for Secord's 'enterprise' (*see below*), but the men he sent proved incompetent. Walker was also involved in the most extreme of all North's proposed follies: an attempt at piracy. Walker was to seize a merchant ship, the *Monimbo*, in the China Sea and dispose of its crew. The ship was carrying arms to Nicaragua, and the idea was to divert them to the Contras. Nothing came of this proposed act of criminal lunacy. Years later, the American journalist Frederick Kempe (*see* Further Reading *below*) alleged that the Managua bombings, ostensibly carried out by Walker, were in fact the work of the Panamanian secret service, acting on the orders of Gen. Manuel Noriega. The dictator, at the time, wanted to impress the CIA and Oliver North with his usefulness, in order to deflect criticisms from elsewhere in the American government of his connections with the drug cartel. (*See* Panama, p. 517–22.)

On 1 June 1985, North summoned the two principal Contra leaders, Bermúdez and Calero, to a meeting in Miami with Secord. North then decided that Secord should take charge of resupplying the Contras, and that the southern front must be revived. He recruited other members of the NSC staff as well as the new American ambassador to Costa Rica, Lewis Tambs, to set up a secret base in Costa Rica, all this without informing McFarlane or Elliott Abrams.

The Contras were kept going by the $1 million a month provided by the Saudis. By degrees, Secord set up an 'enterprise', to purchase arms and other supplies and ship them to Honduras and, later, Costa Rica. At the same time, the **511**

Sandinista forces were showing marked improvement, and despite North's best efforts, Bermúdez was defeated and driven back across the border. In the south, the remnants of A R D E were eliminated.

In June 1985, Congress approved $28 million in 'humanitarian aid' to the Contras, but nothing was delivered until early the following year. General Álvarez of Honduras had been removed from office by his subordinates in March 1984, partly because of his arrogance and dictatorial manner, and partly because he had turned the country over to the Americans and the Contras. (Álvarez Martínez was assassinated on 25 January 1989 by the Popular Liberation Forces, a Honduran guerrilla movement.) The new Honduran chief of staff and the president, Roberto Suazo Córdova, were much less accommodating, and put a ban on all resupply to the Contras. It was not lifted until Suazo's successor, José Azcona Hoyo, took office in January 1986.

In June 1986, Reagan finally persuaded the House of Representatives to vote the Contras $100 million, of which $70 million was for arms; the Senate approved in August. Congress, of course, was not informed that North, Poindexter and Casey had started selling arms to Iran in order to finance the Contras and other secret operations, or that the Secord airlift to the Contras had begun on 1 April. The Contra campaign had been won in Washington as a result of an immense public relations effort by the president and his supporters, who accused their opponents of handing over Latin America to the Communists. They were helped by a Nicaraguan attack on Contra bases in Honduras on 23 March. The administration used this comparatively minor incident to drum up support for the Contras in Washington, but first had to overcome a problem in Honduras. The government there had constantly denied that there were any Contra bases in the country, and therefore refused to admit that there had been any Nicaraguan incursion. In the end, the American ambassador in Tegucigalpa, who was suffering from a serious bout of influenza, went in his dressing gown to see President Azcona and told him that he had to ask for help. Azcona reluctantly agreed, and Washington immediately ferried American troops to near the border in a show of force, and approved $20 million in emergency aid to Honduras. Azcona demonstrated his belief in the seriousness of the situation by leaving for the beach, and the ambassador went back to bed.

This American aid and support revived the prospects of Bermúdez and his troops, and by the end of the year, they were ready for a new offensive. However, on 5 October 1986, one of Secord's supply planes was shot down over Nicaragua. It was a C-123, flying from Honduras to make a drop to Contras fighting on the southern front, and it was brought down by a Soviet surface-to-air missile (S A M-7). The two American pilots were killed. A third American, Eugene Hassenfus, whose job had been to push the cargo out of the door over the drop zone, and who had the wit to wear a parachute, survived and was captured.

American officials, from President Reagan downwards, all denied that they had anything to do with Hassenfus. However, the Sandinistas found a number of incriminating documents in his possession and in the wreckage of the plane, including Secord's phone number. The matter became increasingly embarrassing in the course of October, and in early November news broke of the sale of arms to Iran. On 25 November, the attorney general, Edwin Meese, announced that its profits had been diverted to the Contra supply 'enterprise', and the whole plot started to unravel.

The $100 million agreed by Congress in June was to be the last military funding the Contras were to get. (The aid programme was finally killed in February 1988; they received only 'humanitarian' aid after that.) The Contras mounted a few last offensive operations during 1987, doing more damage and killing more people than ever before, but were defeated by the Sandinista army with its Mi-25 gunships.

The military option had failed completely. Its failure had been inevitable from the start: no guerrilla movement can succeed against a well-armed and determined government unless it has a solid base of support inside the country. It cannot be sent across the border to victory. Reagan had been manipulated into supporting a hopeless endeavour, which ended in bankruptcy when the Iran–Contra affair was exposed.

## DIPLOMACY

It was time to revert to diplomacy. Because the Reagan administration's efforts had by then been discredited, and it had exhausted every option, the diplomatic effort was taken out of its hands. In 1987, Washington enjoyed the astonishing spectacle of foreign policy being conducted by the speaker of the House of Representatives, and of Central American presidents ignoring Washington and negotiating among themselves.

Jim Wright, the speaker, became involved in the summer of 1987 when the White House was once again trying to persuade Congress to help the Contras. He told the president the only way to do it was to offer the Sandinistas a peace plan they might accept. Reagan agreed to the idea, perhaps not expecting Wright to succeed, but to general surprise, Wright negotiated directly with the Nicaraguans and announced his plan on 5 August. It was supported by the White House and the State Department though the hardliners detested it. Nicaragua expressed interest.

Two days later, on 7 August, the presidents of the five Central American republics, meeting in Guatemala, announced their own peace plan, which had been prepared by the president of Costa Rica, Oscar Arias Sánchez. It provided for an amnesty, a ceasefire, direct negotiations between the Contras and Sandinistas, an end to the anti-democratic measures in Nicaragua, and an end to all outside interference. The Sandinistas would stop helping the rebels in El Salvador and the Americans would have to stop helping the Contras.

Wright promptly accepted this peace plan, which was very similar to his own. President Reagan was left in a quandary: could he bear to swallow his words and accept a reasonable and straightforward peace plan? Arias won the Nobel Peace Prize, and the Contras reluctantly accepted his proposals. The hardliners were devastated. After that, Central America proceeded on its own, with the United States an irritated spectator.

On 5 November 1987, Ortega announced that he would engage in indirect negotiations with the Contras, to be held under the mediation of Cardinal Obando y Bravo, who had consistently opposed the Sandinistas. At a Central American summit on 15–17 January 1988, Nicaragua agreed to direct negotiations **513** with the Contras, and to lift the state of emergency that had lasted since the revolution. On 23 March, the Sandinistas and Contras signed a 60-day ceasefire. When it expired in May, it was extended.

## THE PEACE PROCESS

One reason for Nicaragua's readiness to accept the Arias peace plan was the collapse of its economy and the increasing opposition to the government. Half the budget went to defence. The standard of living, already deplorably low under the Somozas, had dropped by one-third after the eight years of Sandinista mismanagement. For two days every week, water was cut off in Managua to conserve energy. In 1987, inflation was running at 1000 per cent per annum, the country survived on hand-outs from the Soviets, including subsidized oil, there were no currency reserves or credit abroad, and trade was conducted by barter: foreigners would not accept Nicaraguan córdobas. In February 1988, Nicaragua introduced a new currency to replace the old: one new córdoba was worth 1000 old ones. The government tried to fix prices and salaries at the new levels and failed lamentably, and inflation continued unchecked. By the following summer, inflation was running at a rate of 6000 per cent. Banknotes with a face value of 50 córdobas were overprinted with a new denomination, 50,000.

In June, the government announced a new round of reforms, lifting wage and price controls. Socialism was failing, so the Sandinistas were beating a retreat towards a market economy – while still insisting that the eventual goal would be socialism. Another cause for concern was Mikhail Gorbachev. He had agreed to support Nicaragua, but now that was costing at least $500 million a year, and rising rapidly. (Some estimates in 1988 put the Soviet contribution as high as $1 billion.) There appeared to be no political advantage, beyond the pleasure of annoying the United States, in interfering in Central America. In the autumn of 1987, the Soviet Union opened discussions with Costa Rica on eliminating its military role in the region if the Americans stopped helping the Contras. This proposal was anathema to Elliott Abrams and other American hardliners: they needed the Soviet presence in Nicaragua to justify their support of the Contras.

Domestic political opposition in Nicaragua rose sharply as the war came to an end. A group of 14 opposition parties, ranging from the Communists to conservative business groups, formed an anti-Sandinista alliance known as the UNO. In addition, under the terms of the ceasefire, Contra supporters had begun to return from exile. Opposition papers, notably *La Prensa*, which had been suspended in 1986, were reopened after the Arias treaty was signed, and a Catholic radio station was reopened. For the first time since the early days of the revolution, political life was nearly normal in Managua.

In August 1988, the US Senate voted $27 million in 'humanitarian' aid for the Contras, to pay for food, clothing and medicine. Administration efforts to persuade Congress to vote military aid failed. By that time, almost all the Contras, and their supporters, had crossed the border into Honduras, where they waited on events, depressed and defeated. Their leaders continued to demand that the Sandinistas share power with them, and various efforts were made to get the peace talks restarted. But it was increasingly apparent that the Contras were no longer major players in the game, if they ever had been.

What counted was the political and economic situation in Nicaragua, where the Sandinistas' position continued to deteriorate. They still had the guns, but that was not enough. They would not willingly share power, let alone give it up. As they said, they did not fight Somoza for a decade to hand over power to the people who had accommodated themselves to the dictatorship for a generation, just because the going was getting rough.

On 22 October 1988, a hurricane devastated the eastern provinces, adding a natural disaster to Nicaragua's man-made calamities. Despite desperate appeals for help, the world community left the country to recover as best it could; other equally poor countries across the world were considered more deserving. According to the *Washington Post*, one European diplomat in Managua commented, 'The world is beginning to get tired of Nicaragua.' In 1988, inflation reached 36,000 per cent. By one calculation, the average daily wage, which had bought 30 eggs or 12 litres of milk in 1979 when the Sandinistas took power, by 1988 bought only two eggs or one litre of milk. Nicaragua faced starvation.

In February 1989, the Sandinistas announced a series of economic reforms amounting to an abandonment of socialism. Private enterprise was to be encouraged, and there were to be sweeping cuts in government programmes and in public investment. The government stated that there would be no more appropriations of private businesses and that land redistribution would be ended.

Then the five Central American presidents met again to consider the failure of the Arias plan. They concluded that it had been too ambitious in its attempt to settle all the wars and conflicts of the region, and decided to concentrate on the Nicaraguan question. They agreed that the Contras would be disbanded, offered an amnesty and allowed to return to Nicaragua. President Ortega promised to restore all civil and political liberties in Nicaragua, and agreed to accept stringent international verification of the process.

The Sandinistas announced that elections would be held on 25 February 1990, and the opposition nominated Violeta Barrios de Chamorro as presidential candidate. She is the widow of the newspaper editor murdered in 1978. International observers converged on Managua to monitor the election.

In December 1989, the United States invaded Panama and deposed General Manuel Noriega, for corruption and drug dealing. One of the justifications for the action was the claim that Noriega had stolen an election in May 1989. It was a hint to the Sandinistas of the possible penalties of fraud. The American public would not support an invasion of Nicaragua in normal circumstances, but that might change if the Sandinistas stole the election, or refused to abide by its results.

The election took place on schedule. There was a lively and protracted campaign, closely watched by a host of foreigners, including teams representing the U N and the O A U, who concluded that the election was conducted honestly. The American ex-president Jimmy Carter was one of the observers. The Sandinistas ran a professional, democratic campaign on the American model, with cheerful rallies, bands, balloons and much popular enthusiasm. The opposition campaign was slow, confused, and beset by differences between its 14 parties, and Violeta Chamorro had to spend part of the time in hospital: she had broken her knee.

Ortega was convinced that he would win, despite the dire straits of the economy, because the opposition, UNO, was financed and supported by the United States (though, in fact, American support was far less than the UNO needed). The Nicaraguans, like most people, dislike outside interference in their internal affairs. In the event, it turned out that they disliked their own government even more. Chamorro won 55 per cent of the vote, Ortega 41 per cent. The opposition won a comfortable majority in the National Assembly and prepared itself for the unaccustomed difficulties of coalition government.

Chamorro took office on 25 April 1990. Ortega reluctantly handed over the ceremonial sash of office, but all was not lost. His brother remained commander of the country's bloated military, and in the two months between the election and the inauguration, the Sandinistas transferred a large part of the nation's assets to themselves. One estimate put the degree of looting at $2 billion. Ortega, for instance, transferred several large houses to his own name. The operation was known as *La Piñata*, after the papier-maché bird filled with presents that is smashed at children's parties, and was an even more flagrant looting of the public purse than the Somozas had ever perpetrated. When the new majority in the National Assembly proposed to return all the property confiscated or stolen by the Sandinistas, there were violent demonstrations in the streets.

There were other problems. The Contras began to return cautiously to Nicaragua. Colonel Bermúdez returned to Managua, and was assassinated there in February 1991. In succeeding months former Contras threatened to take up arms again and Sandinista-controlled unions staged takeovers, sit-in strikes and other extreme measures. In November 1991, Sandinistas staged 'a day-long rampage of burning, looting, stoning and shooting' in Managua, according to the *New York Times*, while the police did nothing to stop them.

Nicaragua made little progress under the Chamorro administration. The president was chiefly concerned to keep the armed forces quiet, and that meant pleasing the Sandinistas. It took her years to summon up the courage to remove Humberto Ortega as minister of defence, and to begin with he was replaced by another Sandinista. But the tide was running rightwards. Conservative parties won municipal elections, most notably in Managua, where the new mayor, Arnoldo Alemán, set about repairing the damage left by the earthquake. In 1996, when Chamorro's term ended, he won the presidency, defeating Daniel Ortega. By then, the socialist revolution of 1979 had been dismantled and most of the property confiscated had been returned to its owners (except the Somoza family).

The Sandinistas suffered a further blow in 1998 when Ortega's step-daughter accused him of sexually abusing her for years, and the party's hopes of recovering were seriously compromised. All the same, Nicaragua remains one of the poorest countries in the hemisphere, with a per capita income a third of Guatemala's. Alemán blames this frightful poverty on the Sandinistas' legacy, but the argument will not last forever.

## FURTHER READING

American University, *Honduras: A Country Study*, Washington, D.C., 1984.
————, *Nicaragua: A Country Study*, Washington D.C., 1982.
Amnesty International, *Nicaragua: The Human Rights Record*, London, 1986.
Barry, Tom and Preusch, Deb (eds.), *The Central America Fact Book*, New York, Grove Press, 1986.
Christian, Shirley, *Nicaragua: Revolution in the Family*, New York, Vintage Books, 1986.
Cockburn, Leslie, *Out of Control: The Story of the Reagan Administration's Secret War in Nicaragua*, New York, Atlantic Monthly Press, 1987.
Dillon, Sam, *Commandos, the CIA and Nicaragua's Contra Rebels*, New York, Henry Holt & Co., 1991.
Gutman, Roy, *Banana Diplomacy: The Making of American Policy in Nicaragua, 1981– 1987*, New York, Simon & Schuster, 1988.
Kempe, Frederick, *Divorcing the Dictator*, New York, G. P. Putnam's Sons, 1990.
Kornbluh, Peter, *Nicaragua: The Price of Intervention, Reagan's Wars against the Sandinistas*, Washington D.C., Institute for Policy Studies, 1987.
McNeil, Frank, *War and Peace in Central America*, New York, Charles Scribner's Sons, 1988.
Rosset, Peter and Vandermeer, John, *Nicaragua, the Unfinished Revolution*, New York, Grove Press, 1986.
Walker, Thomas (ed.), *Nicaragua: The First Five Years*, New York, Praeger, 1985.

## PANAMA

| | |
|---|---|
| **Geography** | 29,208 sq. miles (75,648 sq. km). |
| **Population** | 2.6 million. |
| **GNP per capita** | $2750. |

## HISTORY

From the early 16th century onwards, Panama was the link between the oceans. Panama City was an important Spanish base. Silver from Peru was brought up the coast, and silks carried from China on the twice-yearly Acapulco galleons were collected at Panama and carried on mule caravans across the isthmus to Colón, on the Caribbean, to be shipped to Spain. In 1671 the English pirate Henry Morgan sacked and burned Panama: the new city was built a few miles from the old, on a peninsula where the canal now reaches the Pacific. The ruins of the old city are among the most striking relics in the New World.

After the break-up of the Spanish empire, the isthmus of Panama became part of Colombia, and was governed from far-away Bogotá. It was still the easiest route between Atlantic and Pacific, and the Panamanians constantly grumbled at their dependence upon Colombia. Every so often, they revolted – and the revolts were firmly suppressed. In the latter 19th century, Ferdinand de Lesseps, the entrepreneur who had created the Suez Canal, launched a public company in France to build a canal across the isthmus of Panama. International treaties were signed, and for 20 years the French laboured in the jungles. They were defeated **517** by yellow fever and malaria, whose causes were not then known; by technical difficulties, which were far greater than they had believed at the outset; and by the costs of the enterprise, which turned out to be far beyond the capacity of any private corporation. The Panama Canal Company went bankrupt in 1888. A new company was formed which continued the work on a much reduced scale but it was evident that if the canal were ever to be completed, it must be by a government – and that the only government capable of the task was the United States.

Early in the new century, the Americans, under the enthusiastic leadership of President Theodore Roosevelt, decided to build a canal. After heated debate over its site (the alternative was in Nicaragua), Panama was chosen, the assets of the French company were bought up and negotiations were opened with Colombia. At that moment, the leading citizens of Panama staged a revolt and proclaimed their own independent republic on 3 November 1903. The United States government had been warned in advance, and an American warship reached Colón the same day and overawed the Colombians. The new republic was immediately recognized by Washington, and the Colombians, suddenly deprived of the most valuable part of their territory, were taught a lesson in Yankee perfidy that they have not forgotten. In 1921, the United States paid them $25 million in compensation for the lost territory, but the resentment persisted.

After leaving office, Roosevelt boasted, 'I took the isthmus.' At the time, in a cabinet meeting, Roosevelt defended his actions and then demanded, 'Well, have I answered the charges? Have I defended myself?' His secretary of war, Elihu Root, replied, 'You certainly have, Mr President. You have shown that you were accused of seduction, and you have conclusively proved that you were guilty of rape.'

The canal was opened in August 1914, an event overshadowed by the news from Europe. It was, and remains, one of the most remarkable feats of engineering in the world. The causes of yellow fever and malaria (mosquitoes) had been identified, and remedies devised. The U S Congress voted the funds, the U S army directed the work, and the Panama Canal became an immense source of national pride.

The treaty between the United States and the new Republic of Panama was singularly favourable to the former. It was drawn up by a Frenchman, Philippe Bunau-Varilla, a former director of the defunct Panama Canal Company, with the express purpose of winning the support of the U S Congress. It provided that the Canal Zone should be ten miles wide, that it should run from Colón to Panama, and that within the Zone, the United States would enjoy 'all the rights, power and authority . . . which the United States would possess and exercise if it were the sovereign of the territory . . . to the entire exclusion of the exercise by the Republic of Panama of any sovereign rights, power or authority.' The Zone was to be administered by the United States in perpetuity.

The citizens of Panama profited greatly from the canal: in 1986 (before the Noriega difficulties) their *per capita* income was $2330 a year, compared with $1230 in Colombia and $1420 in Costa Rica. The American presence was beneficent, but overwhelming. The national currency, the bolivar, was really the U S dollar: there were no bolivar banknotes. The National Assembly stood at the foot of a low hill in Panama City: the Canal Zone began at the top of the hill, a boundary marked with a large American flag on a high flagpole, which thus flew directly above the Panamanian National Assembly. The symbol was unmistakable. There were 10,000 American troops and large American army and air force bases in the Zone, whose inhabitants, known as Zonians, lived a perfectly American life in the tropics and regarded their territory as part of the United States, accidentally separated from the rest.

Successive Panamanian governments tried to have the treaty amended, on the grounds that it was flagrantly unequal and had been extorted by blackmail and a *coup d'état*. The Americans paid no attention to Panamanian complaints: it was their canal, built with American technology and capital, and was vital to American security. This attitude only changed in the 1960s when some Americans began to question the morality of neo-colonialism, and the development of air power much reduced the military significance of the canal. In 1966 serious anti-American riots in Panama led President Lyndon Johnson to open formal negotiations with the Panamanian government on revising the treaty.

In October 1968, the civilian government of Panama was overthrown by the commander of the Panama Defence Forces (P D F), Gen. Omar Torrijos. He announced that his chief objective would be revising the treaty, by which he meant restoring full Panamanian sovereignty to the Canal Zone. The negotiations continued for another decade, and were eventually concluded in 1977. The new treaties' ratification by the U S Senate was the chief political achievement of the Carter administration. The Republican right, led by Ronald Reagan, was bitterly opposed. They alleged, 'There is no Panama Canal. There is an American canal in Panama.' They denounced the 'give-away' as treason. It was a case of American imperialist sentiment, like British possessiveness towards their own conquests.

Under the terms of the agreement, the United States is to withdraw progressively from Panama. In a first stage, the Zone was abolished and full sovereignty reverted to Panama. That overhanging flag was removed. The American bases remained. Since then, the administration of the canal has been partially turned over to Panama, and the last American troops are to leave in 2000. An important date was 1 January 1990, when a Panamanian became chief administrator of the canal.

## Manuel Antonio Noriega

Torrijos had been deeply implicated in the drug trade for years, allowing Panama to be used to smuggle heroin and marijuana into the United States. He also flirted with Fidel Castro. He was killed in a plane crash in 1981. After some manoeuvring, Col. Manuel Antonio Noriega, known as Tony, the head of intelligence, took power, in March 1983. His position was head of the Panama Defence Forces: there was a civilian president, installed by the P D F, who did what he was told. The president elected in 1984 (in a blatantly fraudulent election) proved insufficiently obsequious and was replaced in 1985 by Eric Delvalle. Relations between Panama and the United States continued amicably. Panama had developed a thriving international banking industry; it was a Latin American Switzerland, with even fewer constraints on the free movement of capital than the Swiss imposed. The briskly-developing Colombian drug industry availed itself of the facilities provided by Panama: it was the perfect site for money-laundering. It was, in effect, part of the United States but its banks were quite outside American control. The proceeds of illegal drug sales in the United States could be transferred unquestioned to anonymous accounts in Panama, whence they would vanish.

For most of the 1980s, the Americans turned a blind eye to these arrangements. Noriega was far too useful in the Reagan administration's most pressing concern, the Nicaraguan civil war. He had been on the books of the C I A since his days as a cadet. He provided valuable intelligence to the agency about his friends in Nicaragua and Cuba: Noriega boasted of his socialist inclinations while never showing the least sign of applying any crass Marxist redistributive theory to Panama itself.

Noriega's relations with the C I A remained close throughout the early 1970s, when he was head of Panama's intelligence agency. During part of that time, the Director of Central Intelligence was George Bush. His successor under the Carter administration, Admiral Stansfield Turner, cancelled the arrangement, but Reagan's director, William Casey, put Noriega back on the books in 1981, at $185,000 a year, and was suitably gratified when Noriega assumed full power two years later. He was needed for the war against the Sandinistas, and for Reagan and Casey, that was far more important than the war on drugs. In December 1983, Vice-President Bush flew to Panama to discuss these matters with Noriega. Casey and Lt. Col. Oliver North, who was in charge of supporting the Contras in the National Security Council staff, saw Noriega frequently. Even the Drug Enforcement Administration found Noriega useful. He gave the D E A useful information on the activities of the Medellín Cartel, in a classic double-cross.

Noriega was not content with the clandestine millions. He offered asylum in Panama to the cartel's leaders when they had to leave Colombia precipitously after assassinating the minister of justice in 1984. They allegedly paid him $5 million for his services. His government became steadily more corrupt and brutal: he was turning into a Central American Trujillo or Batista.

In 1987, the United States government started putting pressure on Noriega to mend his ways, or retire. American newspapers published unflattering articles about his connections with drug smugglers, and members of Congress were wondering aloud how the government could tolerate as an ally a man who was part of the drug trade. On 4 February 1988, a federal grand jury in Miami indicted Noriega for drug trafficking. The gesture caught the Reagan administration off balance: it seemed as though its left hand did not know what its right hand was doing. It was also an open question, under international law, whether American courts had the right to charge foreign officials with violations of American laws. Certainly, the indictment was unusual: no American court ever indicted Khomeini for kidnapping, or Khadafy for terrorism.

On 25 February 1988, the titular president of Panama, Eric Delvalle, with American encouragement, fired Noriega as commander of the P D F. Noriega promptly deposed Delvalle. The United States continued to recognize him, and imposed economic sanctions against Panama. American banks were forbidden to deal with Panama, which soon had no resources. As a result, the country's economy started to deteriorate sharply, though Noriega always had the money to pay his troops. There were riots and protests, all brutally suppressed by the PDF. There was an attempted coup, in March 1988, which Noriega easily suppressed.

The Americans started considering the use of force against Noriega. The idea of sponsoring a coup was rejected by Congress, on the grounds that Noriega might be murdered. Then Noriega was offered a deal: if he would leave Panama, the charges against him would be dropped, and he would be allowed to enjoy his ill-gotten gains at peace – provided he moved to Europe. At the last moment, the deal fell through. The proposal, though eminently sensible, proved an embarrassment to George Bush during the 1988 presidential election: he was accused of trafficking with a notorious drug trafficker.

In May 1989, Panama held a presidential election. A large number of foreign observers, led by the former American president Jimmy Carter, were in Panama for the event. Noriega's candidate was soundly defeated, and the general simply annulled the elections. It was a case of blatant fraud, and was memorably denounced by Carter. Police beat up opposition supporters, and were filmed beating the opposition vice-presidential candidate, Guillermo Ford. On 3 October, a small group of PDF officers tried to depose Noriega. It was a singularly incompetent coup. The plotters arrested Noriega in his headquarters, but then allowed him to phone his supporters and call up reinforcements. The Americans were not invited to help until it was too late. Noriega's troops surrounded the headquarters, and he persuaded the plotters to surrender. He then had their leaders marched round the back, and shot.

The episode was a huge embarrassment to Bush. It appeared as though the United States was incapable of disposing of Noriega in a country it once practically owned. Preparations for an invasion were put in hand. All that was needed was a pretext, and Noriega obligingly provided several. First, on 15 December 1989, he had the National Assembly proclaim him Head of State and 'Maximum Leader of the Struggle for National Liberation'. The Assembly then voted that, 'The Republic of Panama is declared to be in a state of war with the United States as long as US aggression continues.' By this was meant economic sanctions.

On 16 December four off-duty American soldiers driving through Panama City took a wrong turn and passed in front of the Commandancia. They were stopped by Panamanian guards and after an altercation, one of them, Marine Lt. Robert Paz, was shot. On the same day, a navy lieutenant and his wife were arrested, and held for four hours during which he was roughed up and she was 'sexually threatened'.

On the next day, Bush gave the order to invade. The troops were ready, and attacked at one in the morning on 20 December. It was called 'Operation Just Cause', and involved 12,000 American troops, including Marines, parachutists and special forces. Five task forces hit particular targets: one went for the Commandancia, one hit a PDF barracks at Rio Hato, to catch the unit that had rescued Noriega during the October coup, another went to a jail where survivors of that coup attempt, and a CIA agent, were imprisoned.

Noriega disappeared and the Americans put a $1 million reward on his head. **521**

Some of his units, notably the 'Dignity Battalions', put up a stiff resistance and were overwhelmed by American firepower. Some of their positions were bombed into rubble. In the process, at least 220 Panamanian civilians and 314 soldiers were killed. The American dead numbered 23 soldiers and three civilians. There were 324 American and 124 Panamanian wounded.

Panamanians seized the opportunity to loot every shop in Panama City. There were no police, no army, and soon the centre of the city was devastated. The Americans installed Guillermo Endara as president: he was the man who had won the election in May. He was hastily carried to an American base in Panama and sworn in early on the morning of the invasion, together with his two vice-presidents. He was then faced with the task of building up not only a ruined economy, but a society which had suffered under military dictatorships for over 20 years and remained deeply divided. His most immediate task was to recruit police and military to keep the peace. The Americans would soon leave (the invasion troops were all gone by mid-February 1990), and he needed troops to protect his new government. The danger was that he would be obliged to recruit from former members of the P D F who might not easily submit to a new civilian government.

Noriega took refuge in the Vatican embassy. For a while there was a diplomatic stand-off, and the Americans tried to pry him out by playing rock music as loudly as possible around the house. American troops broke into the Nicaraguan embassy searching for arms and the Bush administration had to apologize, with the lame excuse that the soldiers had not realized that the building enjoyed diplomatic immunity.

On 10 January Noriega surrendered, a day after the new government organized a huge demonstration against him outside the embassy, which might easily have turned into a lynch-mob, and stormed the place, had it not been surrounded by American troops. He was deported to Miami where the Americans put him on trial. In due course, he was sentenced to life imprisonment.

The United States claimed that it was justified in invading Panama under Article 51 of the U N Charter, which provides for 'an inherent right to self-defense'. They also argued that Panama had declared itself at war with the United States, so could scarcely object when the U S took its declaration seriously. The argument was unanimously repudiated by the Organization of American States, and was criticized with more or less equal vigour by most Latin American governments. Nicaragua, which had been expecting just such an invasion itself for years, was particularly incensed.

As for the Panamanians, most of them appeared delighted at the disappearance of Noriega. They assumed that prosperity would now return. They were mistaken.

## FURTHER READING

Dinges, John, *Our Man in Panama*, New York, Random House, 1990.
Kempe, Frederick, *Divorcing the Dictator*, New York, G. P. Putnam's Sons, 1990.
McCullogh, David, *The Path Between the Seas*, New York, Simon & Schuster, 1977.

# PERU

| | |
|---|---|
| Geography | 496,224 sq. miles (1,285,215 sq. km). The size of France, Spain and (formerly) West Germany together, or twice the size of Texas. 60% is Amazonian jungle, where 5% of the population live. The rest comprises a narrow coastal strip and the high Andes. |
| Population | 24 million: 50% are white or of mixed race, speaking Spanish; 50% are Indian, speaking Quechua. 7 million live in the capital, Lima. |
| Resources | Primarily silver. Peru is also the world's largest producer of coca (from which cocaine is derived), producing more than Bolivia and Colombia combined. |
| GNP per capita | $2310. |
| Casualties | 25,000–30,000 have been killed since 1980. |

In the 1980s, Peru was spiralling downwards into ruin, anarchy and red revolution. A profligate and incompetent government led the country into hopeless bankruptcy while an extreme Maoist terrorist movement, the *Sendero Luminoso*, spread to 20 of Peru's 24 provinces and extended its grip upon the shanty-towns of the capital. At the same time, the drug trade spread its corruption from the high valleys in the Andes where most of the world's cocoa is grown, and the Maoist terrorists formed an alliance with the narco-terrorists. By 1992, at least 25,000 people had been killed in what had become a civil war, which the government was losing.

In the event, Peru was saved by the son of Japanese immigrants, Alberto Fujimori, an engineer turned demagogue who won the presidency in 1990 on a promise to reverse his predecessor's economic policies, set Peru on the road to recovery, and defeat the terrorists by whatever means were needed. His spectacular success has been one of the most striking and heartening reversals of a desperate situation in recent times. Fujimori has been much criticized for suspending the rule of law and violating the human rights of terrorists, suspects and innocent Peruvians alike. He responds that with the ship sinking it was more important to drive every man to the pumps than to ask them politely if they would agree to lend a hand. It remains to be seen if he will restore legality and democratic norms, now that the ship is safe.

**523**

# HISTORY

Ancient Peru under the Incas was the largest of pre-Columbian empires, covering what are now Ecuador, the Andean and coastal areas of Peru and Bolivia, northern Chile and parts of Argentina. Its capital was Cuzco, in the Andes. The empire was conquered by Francisco Pizarro with 180 men in 1531. He moved the capital to Lima on the coast, and ever since, there has been constant tension between the Incas' descendants who speak Quechua, and the Spanish-speaking inhabitants of the cities of the plain.

Peru won its independence from Spain in 1821, along with the rest of Spanish South and Central America. It has been governed by a succession of alternating oligarchies and military dictatorships, often closely related, with occasional attempts at democracy. The most recent military government, which ruled in the 1970s, broke up the oligarchy by attacking its economic domination. One sugar company, for instance, owned by a handful of people, controlled plantations covering an area larger than Belgium. In 1980, suffering from political exhaustion and under intense pressure from the Carter administration in Washington, the military handed over power to a civilian government. Fernando Belaúnde Terry was elected president and was succeeded, in 1985, by Alan García Pérez, then aged 35. He was leader of the American Popular Revolutionary Alliance (APRA), a party that had been the perpetual leftist opposition in Peru since it was founded in 1924. Its earlier electoral victories had been thwarted by the army.

Though potentially very rich, Peru remained a Third World country with First World pretensions. Much of its industry and its banking system were nationalized, with all the inefficiencies that follow such a policy. Its foreign debts were, proportionately, as great as Mexico's. García in his inaugural address announced that Peru would limit its repayments to 10 per cent of its export earnings. For three years, the economy expanded, inflation was kept to 50 per cent and Peru suffered no painful consequences from its novel approach to its debts. Then, early in 1988, inflation rose to 200 per cent, then 400 per cent, and it continued to accelerate. All the economic chickens came home to roost.

The Shining Path Communist insurrection began in 1980 and expanded rapidly throughout the decade. In 1983, another terrorist group, the Túpac Amaru, began a campaign of revolutionary terrorism in the cities. By the end of García's term, the government had lost control of several provinces in the Andes, about 20 per cent of the country, and the terrorists had extended their sway into the coca-producing valleys and into the huge slums of Lima itself. Peru was facing full-scale civil war, and there was a very real possibility that the terrorists would succeed in destabilizing and overthrowing the state.

Peru is the world's chief supplier of coca leaves and is thus on the frontline of the drug wars (*see* The drug wars, pp. 534–51). It derived a back-handed advantage from this distinction: by cooperating with the United States government in fighting the drug cartels, it avoided American retaliation against its debt and human rights policies.

# THE WAR

The Communist Party of Peru for the Shining Path of José Carlos Mariátegui, or *Sendero Luminoso*, is the most secretive and vicious of Latin American terrorist organizations. It took its name from a phrase used by the founder of the Peruvian Communist Party, who died in 1930: 'Marxism-Leninism will open the shining path that will lead to the revolution.' Its heroes are Lenin, Mao Tse-tung and the Gang of Four, the Chinese extremists led by Mao's widow who tried to perpetuate the Cultural Revolution in China after Mao's death in 1976. The nearest parallel to Sendero's fanaticism are perhaps Pol Pot's Khmers Rouges in Cambodia.

The Sendero insurrection is partly a peasant Indian uprising against an alien and uncaring government, similar to the conflicts in Central America, but its ideology is an eclectic mixture of Marxist dogma and Andean mythology. A group of extreme Marxists established themselves in the university of Ayacucho on the Andean plateau in the 1960s, in a region that is remote, poor and neglected. The university was intended to educate Indians and to prepare engineers, teachers and other professionals to return to their villages to help them emerge from the night of centuries – a sort of indigenous Peace Corps. By 1968, the Senderistas had won control of the university and its projects.

The Communist party in Peru split after the Sino–Soviet dispute erupted in 1964. In Ayacucho, the pro-Chinese faction, calling itself Sendero Luminoso, won the dispute, advocated a policy of Maoist extremism and rejoiced in the Cultural Revolution. The Senderistas detested the Soviets as much as they detest the Americans.

Sendero's leader was Carlos Abimael Guzmán Reynoso, known by the *nom de guerre* 'Gonzalo'. He was born in Mollendo, a city on the southern coast of Peru, in 1934, the son of an unmarried woman and her married lover. He studied law and philosophy and, in 1963, was appointed assistant professor of philosophy at the University of Ayacucho. He spent part of the 1960s in China, during the Cultural Revolution. He became the leader of the Marxist theorists at the university, and by 1967, his brand of Communism was dominant and he was himself the most powerful man at the university. For a while, he was director of personnel and was thus able to install his supporters into every available post, from professor to cleaner. Senderista professors taught Marxist dialectics and the philosophy of Mao Tse-tung and recruited a generation of students to the cause. They graduated as both teachers and Senderistas, and returned to spread the gospel in their native villages, though presumably without dwelling on the ideological purity of Chairman Mao and the villainy of other Chinese leaders, subjects that would have appeared quite mystifying to the Andean peasantry. Where Lenin used intellectuals and workers as the cadres of Bolshevism, and Mao used Chinese peasants, Guzmán used school teachers.

As a result, the Shining Path spread far into Peruvian society. There were soon cells in villages throughout the Andean region: the Senderistas could call upon thousands of dedicated militants for their military operations, and were assured of shelter and sustenance. In the mid-1970s, during the upheaval in China following Mao's death, they gave their ideological support to the Gang of Four, and excoriated the Chinese government as counter-revolutionary, like the former Soviet government. (In 1986, they bombed the Soviet embassy in Lima and attacked a shop frequented by Soviet sailors in Callao.) The Senderistas, there-

**525**

fore – unlike the Sandinistas in Nicaragua or the revolutionary parties in El Salvador and Guatemala – had no outside support.

Anti-Sendero forces in the University of Ayacucho fought back, and in 1976, during a period of military government, the Senderistas went underground. Their chief strength remained around Ayacucho, in areas that had been directly subject to Guzmán's influence. His followers describe him as the 'Fourth Sword' of the Communist Revolution (the others being Marx, Lenin and Mao), and revere the 'Guiding Thought of Gonzalo', as once the Chinese revered the 'Thoughts of Chairman Mao'.

A rival Marxist terrorist organization, the Túpac Amaru Revolutionary Movement (MRTA), made its appearance in 1983. The name derives from an Inca rebel against the Spaniards; it was also used by Uruguayan terrorists, who abbreviated it to Tupamaros. The MRTA had 200 or 300 members, mostly university students. Unlike the Senderistas, the MRTA are a typical, urban Latin American revolutionary group, and looked for support to Cuba and the USSR. In November 1987, they launched a 'rural column' into the countryside, seizing a number of villages in the Amazonian jungle. The army promptly moved in and suppressed them.

The Senderistas began their military campaign in 1980. On 17 May, during Peru's first free election in years, Sendero attacked a polling station in a village near Ayacucho. It then began attacking police posts and village leaders, and imposing its own government upon isolated villages. The Senderistas follow Mao's exhortation to use the country to strangle the cities. This means that they must occupy and hold territory, which gives the army targets to shoot at.

The police were sent in large numbers to Ayacucho to fight the Senderistas. Their years under a military regime had served the police ill: they were at once brutal and incompetent. There were many cases of torture, rape, mutilation and murder, with the result that hundreds of young people were driven to join Sendero in the mountains.

The Senderistas were equally brutal, and the villagers were caught in the middle. Some of them fought back, killing Senderistas whenever they could. In January 1983, Indians in a village called Huaychao in the high Andes killed seven Senderistas who had marched in and demanded that they join the Shining Path. (Later, it was found that some of the murdered Senderistas were 14- and 15-year-old schoolboys.) A group of eight journalists went to investigate. It was a two-day hike into the mountain, and the villagers, mistaking them for Senderistas come to avenge their fallen comrades, killed them all. The photographer among them had kept his camera working almost until the end, and it was found intact and containing photographs of the crowds of Indians menacing the journalists, and the first killings. Peru's most prominent writer, Mario Vargas Llosa, was a member of the commission that examined the incident, and his report was one of the first on Sendero to receive wide publicity. He said that the greatest shock to him and to the other commissioners from Lima was the unbridgeable chasm separating them from the Indians. It was not merely language or income, it was a gap of centuries.

The Senderistas, because they have no foreign support, were poorly armed, until their alliance with the narco-terrorists bore fruit in the late 1980s. What arms they had were stolen or captured from the police or military, or provided by their supporters. Their chief weapon was dynamite, which was easily obtainable. They blew up buildings, bombed military and civilian targets, and waged a strenuous campaign against the Peruvian electricity grid, regularly blowing up pylons to disrupt power supplies to Lima.

The Senderistas also continue to exhibit their curious political priorities. In December 1980, they hung dogs from the lamp-posts of Lima to show what they thought of 'the running dogs of imperialism', and plastered the walls with posters denouncing Deng Xiao-ping and praising the Gang of Four.

The war in the countryside was savage and merciless. When the Senderistas seized a village, they would shoot any leading citizens who might oppose them. In return, the villagers sometimes revolted and executed all the Senderistas they captured, sometimes waging pitched battles in which scores were killed.

The armed forces were even more brutal, and there were numerous reports of massacres in the Andes. Amnesty International has prepared detailed reports of the Peruvian 'dirty war'. Mass graves have been found in the 'Emergency zone' and around Ayacucho, and there are many accounts of massacres by the police. In a 1985 report, Amnesty listed 1005 cases of people who had 'disappeared' in 1983 and 1984, but this was clearly no more than a fraction of the real total. Amnesty states:

In most cases of political killings in the Emergency Zone, believed to have been carried out by government forces, the bodies of the victims, when found, are naked, marked by torture, and with single gunshot wounds to the head; in many cases, the victims are found blindfolded and with their hands bound behind their backs. Many victims are unidentifiable: their clothing has been destroyed, features mutilated, and bodies dumped far from the scene of detention, in areas where relatives are unlikely to travel.

The apparent difference between Peru and Chile or Argentina was that Peru was a democracy at least until 1992, not a military dictatorship. Protests were therefore possible and the killings were reported in the press. This scrutiny may have inhibited some degree of military terrorism, but not much. In Peru, the victims were Indian peasants, not middle-class Spanish-speaking youths in the cities. The Argentinian mothers of middle-class terrorists, leftists and unlucky students who had been murdered, marched around the Plaza de Mayo every Thursday. The mothers and widows of Quechua peasants killed by the Peruvian army or navy had no such opportunity. The Peruvian situation was more like Guatemala in the 1960s and 1970s, where a military government, with the aim of suppressing a leftist insurrection, slaughtered tens of thousands of Indian peasants, without arousing much international concern.

In June 1986, Sendero prisoners in Lima's three jails mutinied. They had long enjoyed virtual autonomy within the jails: wardens were not admitted into their cell blocks; the Senderistas maintained their own discipline and carried out military training and ran indoctrination classes. García sent the marines to reoccupy El Fronton, Peru's Alcatraz on an island off the coast. Three marines and one hostage were killed – and so were 135 prisoners. At another prison, this time in Lima, 124 prisoners were killed when an army anti-terrorist squad **527** stormed it. There is no doubt that most of the prisoners were captured alive and shot; some were also taken away and tortured first.

In 1984, Senderistas appeared for the first time in the Huellaga valley north of Lima, one of Peru's main coca-growing areas. They devoted themselves to political work for the next three years, following basic Maoist tactics, and in 1987, having established their base, they started military operations. They fought government troops and competed with the drug traffickers. They took over small towns and imposed 'revolutionary justice'; they blew up bridges and then ambushed and killed workers sent to repair them, and increasingly used the valley's remote jungles as a base.

Sendero took up the cause of the coca-growers, protecting them against government attempts to eradicate the drug. They also started to impose levies on traffickers, and this might, later, prove a serious problem for them. The Senderistas insist that they oppose all use of cocaine in Peru, but have no objection to exporting coca paste. They have always been chronically short of money, and the revenues they can earn from the coca trade would provide all the money they need. It might also corrupt them, as leftists in Colombia and Burma have been corrupted. Every man has his price, and a peasant recruited to fight for social justice and revenge against the class enemy might come cheap.

Early in 1988, for the first time, the Senderistas began publishing communiqués, discussion papers and lengthy denunciations of the government. The movement claimed to have held a party congress, and issued a report in February. Some of these documents suggested that Sendero was revising its strategy. It is all very well to encircle the cities in China, but encircling Lima, which contains nearly one-third of the country's population, is a different matter. Sendero, therefore, announced that it planned to extend its operations to the capital. This would mean conflict with the MRTA and other Marxist movements who are opposed to the Senderistas.

In June 1988, security police captured the Senderistas' second in command, Osman Morote, Guzmán's closest associate and the Senderistas' strategist. He was captured in a safe-house, with four comrades, and a haul of documents on the movement's plans. A month later, Guzmán gave a lengthy interview to a sympathetic Lima newspaper, to demonstrate that the movement could survive the loss: it was the first word from 'Gonzalo' himself in a decade. He announced that Sendero was preparing for a general insurrection. 'The crisis conditions into which the outmoded system of Peruvian society has entered indicate that these decisive years will accelerate conditions and develop the revolutionary situation powerfully,' he said. 'Our process of the people's war has led us towards the apex. Consequently, we have to prepare for insurrection, which will be the taking of the cities.'

The human rights group Americas Watch issued a report in November 1988, alleging that violations of human rights by the army and police had increased sharply. A death squad, calling itself the Rodrigo Franco Command (after an assassinated politician), had begun operations. It was rumoured to be linked to the President García's party, the APRA.

Meanwhile, the economy was rapidly deteriorating: inflation was running out of control, reaching 1722 per cent in 1988, and unemployment in the slums of

Lima approached 60 per cent. President García's popularity collapsed along with his economic policies. In September 1988, in a desperate attempt to redress the situation, the government ordered a massive devaluation of the currency and huge price increases – for example, petrol went up by 400 per cent, and in that month, there was inflation of 114 per cent. García continued to refuse to seek help from the International Monetary Fund (I M F), because of the conditions it would impose, or to resume repayments of Peru's foreign debt. He thus was unable to borrow money abroad.

As President García's term drew to a close, his government was completely paralysed. The president was deeply unpopular and his policies had proved an utter disaster. Inflation rose to a rate of 5548 per cent in 1989, the G N P had dropped 20 per cent in two years and hundreds of thousands of people were on the verge of starvation in the barrios. The Senderistas had established firm control of the upper Huellaga valley, where peasants grew coca undisturbed by Peruvian police or the American Drug Enforcement Agency.

Sendero taxed coca exports, reputedly to a tune of $500 million a year, quite enough to finance a lavish guerrilla war. They were the richest rebels in the world. The government admitted that 13,000 people were killed between 1980 and the beginning of 1989, and a further 3198 in 1989. The same rate of killing was maintained in the next two years: by 1992, 25,000 people had been killed in the Shining Path uprising. Amnesty International reported in November 1989 that over 3000 people had 'disappeared' in police custody and that an equal number had been openly killed by security forces. Sendero operated extensively in departments surrounding Lima, including those which produce all the country's electricity and half its minerals. In July and August 1989, Sendero commandos bombed a further 70 electricity pylons, bringing the total destroyed since 1980 to over 1000.

The army could report some successes, besides its massacre of prisoners in 1986. In February 1989 it captured the founder and leader of the M R T A, Victor Polay Campos. He was the very model of the old-line Latin American Communist, son of senior members of A P R A, the long-established and ineffectual leftist party, who fell under the spell of Fidel Castro and Che Guevara. It was a serious blow to the Túpac Amaru, but 18 months later, on 9 July 1990, Polay and hundreds of his comrades staged a dramatic jail-break, tunnelling out of prison, and resumed the struggle. The M R T A had already achieved one of its greatest coups, killing a former minister of defence, Enrique Lopez Albuhar, in January 1990.

The army killed Sendero's third-in-command, David Orasco Tiello, in June 1989, but the movement survived easily. From his secret headquarters, Guzmán ordered Sendero to move into the slums of Lima, the huge city that contains a third of the country's population. Within months, police and government workers no longer dared enter the slums, for fear of assassination, and a reign of Maoist terror spread irresistibly. Lima elected a conservative radio-station owner as mayor in November 1989, despite efforts by Sendero to disrupt the vote. He defeated a clutch of leftist candidates, including one representing the hapless president's A P R A. It was a sign of things to come.

President García, who had been elected with such high hopes, was universally detested and despised by the end of his term. He was without authority or policy, after the collapse of the economy into hyper-inflation and the horrors of the civil war. In June 1990, on a high turn-out, Peru elected the most improbable of candidates, Alberto Fujimori, as president. Like the radio-station magnate turned mayor, Fujimori had no very clear programme, beyond a promise to clean up the mess left by García and defeat the Sendero. He defeated the candidate of the Peruvian establishment, the novelist Mario Vargas Llosa. No doubt he owed his success to his vociferously expressed contempt for the political class, represented by García and Vargas, which had brought Peru to this catastrophe. Many demagogues have been elected on similar platforms around the world. Fujimori, unlike most of the others, kept his word.

He set about dismantling the country's public sector, privatizing industry and banks, and reopened negotiations with Peru's creditors. The shock treatment, like similar plans all over the world, caused great hardship and was slow to produce favourable results.

Fujimori also launched a new offensive against Sendero, at the same time that the rebels announced that they intended to win a final victory by the end of the decade. In the summer of 1991, Fujimori, responding to criticism from the United States and from human rights groups, tried to bring the police and military under control and to end 'disappearances'. He was then welcomed on a state visit to Washington, in September. Immediately after his return, he drafted a series of decrees handing over the whole anti-terrorist campaign to the army, giving it a completely free hand in two-thirds of the country, the 'emergency zones'. Press freedom was also severely limited, and President Fujimori harshly attacked Amnesty International, the Red Cross and other organizations for criticizing Peru's human rights record. 'The terrorists present themselves as victims before the world, using for their ends the efforts of institutions like Amnesty International and Americas Watch,' he told a group of air force officers.

By then, Sendero had established itself strongly in the slums of Lima. The city had 7 million people and the government was quite unable to supply them with the normal decencies of life. In 1991, there was an outbreak of cholera, killing 2500 people. Over 250,000 fell sick – all this a sign of the collapse of the public health and water supply systems.

The crisis was reached in 1992. Nearly 4500 people had been killed in the previous year by the official count, 1314 by Sendero, 139 by M R T A and 3145 by police. It seemed entirely possible that Sendero would succeed in destabilizing the state and might even overthrow the government. There was a paroxysm of bombings and assassinations in Lima as Sendero moved to the final battle for the capital.

Fortunately for Peru, Fujimori, known as El Chino by Peruvians who failed to distinguish between different nations in far-off Asia, had no hesitation in taking drastic measures to save the republic. In April 1992 he mounted his own *coup d'état* against Congress and the judiciary, dissolving the legislature, suspending the constitution and *habeas corpus*, and granting himself limitless extra-judicial powers to deal with the terrorists. The fight against terrorism was handed over to an anti-terrorist office separate from the police and army. Accused terrorists were tried in secret by military officers whose identities were kept secret and who were the sole judges of what evidence to believe. As Amnesty International and Human Rights Watch have pointed out, this is the classic judicial system of tyranny: that was how Stalin's K G B tried its victims.

A month later, he sent the army to recover control of the Miguel Castro Castro prison, where the most hardened Senderista prisoners had been put after the 1986 prison uprisings. They had established complete control of their wing of the prison. About 40 were killed.

One of the president's first victories occurred in June, when police recaptured Victor Polay, head of the M R T A. That guerrilla movement thereby lost much of its force. He has been kept in solitary confinement in a lightless concrete box, ever since. Then in September, Abimael Guzmán, Gonzalo himself, was captured. It turned out that the Sandero leader suffered severely from psoriasis, and had left the safety of the high Andes and moved to Lima for treatment. His capture was a near mortal blow to the Sendero. Guzmán had absolute authority in the movement. Now he was kept totally isolated in a cage in the island prison where the Senderistas had been killed in 1986. A war of succession broke out in the movement, exacerbated by the capture of other leading members, including the commander of the Lima brigade in October 1992. Fujimori decreed that Senderistas who cooperated with the authorities would be amnestied, and over 6000 former terrorists and sympathizers took the offer. The information they provided was invaluable, although the secretive, military courts that tried and sentenced suspects undoubtedly jailed many innocent people, victims of false accusations. Scores of the turncoats were given new identities or allowed to leave the country, to escape their former comrades' vengeance. Even Guzmán wavered after a year of solitary confinement. In a series of letters to his followers, which the government allowed out of his prison, he urged a ceasefire. No doubt he did so in the hope of winning better conditions for himself, but it was a devastating blow to the Sendero.

Just after Guzmán's capture, Fujimori staged congressional elections, to choose a legislature to write a new constitution. His candidates won easily: Peru thus ratified the president's April *auto-golpe*. In the following years, Sendero and the M R T A were progressively defeated in Lima and most of the provinces, including Ayacucho, and the economy began to improve. The president was easily re-elected in April 1995, defeating a former secretary-general of the U N, Javier Pérez de Cuéllar.

In December 1995 police in Lima raided an M R T A hideout. Three terrorists and a police officer were killed in an 11-hour siege and gun-battle, and 15 terrorists were arrested including the M R T A's second in command. Evidence found in the house, and a large cache of weapons, showed that the terrorist had planned an assault on Congress. The place had been rented by a 26-year-old American woman, Lori Berenson. She was picked up in the street, tried, and sentenced to life in prison. The evidence against her was overwhelming, though her lawyers protested against the summary methods of Peruvian justice and, later, against the conditions of her imprisonment (she was incarcerated in an unheated jail 12,000 feet up in the Andes). Her friends in the United States argued that she was an idealistic young American, at worst a guerrilla groupie, and should not be punished. It was not a convincing argument: she was evidently a full-time revolutionary, paying the traditional price for failure. At her trial, she defended the MRTA: 'Túpac Amaru is not violent, nor is it terrorist because there is not one terrorist in the group.'

Despite these defeats, both Sendero and the MRTA were still capable of mounting attacks against the government. In August 1996 Sendero bombed a police station in central Lima, among a number of other targets. Then, on 18 December 1996, in a well-organized attack, an MRTA commando seized the Japanese embassy during a reception in honour of the emperor's birthday. They took nearly 600 hostages including the president's mother, brother and sister, the foreign minister, the head of the anti-terrorist police, and a number of other ambassadors (the American ambassador had just left the reception when the attack took place).

Troops surrounded the embassy, and the terrorists released most of their hostages – reducing the number to 72. They let Fujimori's mother and sister go but kept his brother. Then the siege began. The president took personal control, and for the next four months Peru watched in horror as negotiations between the terrorists and the government failed constantly to provide a solution. The MRTA started out with a long list of demands, notably freedom for their imprisoned comrades, including Victor Polay and Lori Berenson. In the end, they were reduced to asking for a plane out of the country (Fujimori flew to Cuba to persuade Castro to take them in). As the siege dragged on, and as various mediators haggled with the terrorists, the army was digging tunnels into the embassy compound. They stormed the place on 22 April 1997. Several hostages were wounded, and one of them died of a heart attack on the way to hospital. Two soldiers were killed. All 14 terrorists were killed: some died in the battle, the rest, including several young women, were summarily shot afterwards.

Sendero and the MRTA were defeated but not eradicated. Small groups of terrorists remain, both in the slums of Lima and in the high Andes, and the problem of narco-terrorism is as serious as ever. It is quite possible that revolutionary terrorism will revive in Peru, or elsewhere in Latin America, if the continent's economic difficulties are not resolved. President Fujimori has won a long respite for himself and his country. However, the Chilean precedent showed how long it takes to modernize a corrupt, statist Latin American economy – and Chile was far more advanced in 1974 than was Peru in 1990. It will be years before Peru's poor emerge from destitution, plenty of time for Fujimori's popularity to dissipate and for the terrorists to recover.

## THE DISPUTE WITH ECUADOR

Peru and Ecuador fought a three-week border war in January–February 1995 over a disputed section of the frontier in the Andes. The conflict is a legacy of a much more serious war fought in 1941 in which Peru annexed nearly half Ecuador's territory, cutting it off from the Amazon basin.

A peace treaty was signed in Rio after that war, on 29 January 1942, ceding eastern Ecuador to Peru. Most of the border was mapped out, and was guaranteed by Brazil, Chile, Argentina and the United States, but a section along the Cenapa river in the Cordillera del Condor was never clearly demarcated. Ecuador repudiated the Rio protocol in 1960 and has periodically asserted its claims to the territory it lost: and there were border skirmishes in 1981 and 1991. The 1995 conflict was the most serious since the treaty although only a handful of people were killed, 12 in Ecuador and 38 in Peru. Peru moved a large number of troops up to the border, occupied positions Ecuador had set up in the disputed territory, and bombed the Ecuadorian army. Ecuador then retreated from the confrontation.

The underlying issue remains. Ecuador is one of the many Latin American states that holds irredentist claims against a neighbour. Peru itself is another. In a war with Chile and Bolivia in 1883, it lost the northern Atacama desert to Chile, which also cut Bolivia off from the sea. Neither country has forgotten, and there was a moment of tension on the centenary of the loss. It was not, however, a time when Peru or Bolivia could challenge General Pinochet's Chile, so the anniversary passed without incident.

Other important territorial claims include a dispute between Chile and Argentina over islands in the Beagle Channel between Patagonia and Tierra del Fuego, one between Venezuela and Guyana (Venezuela claims half Guyana's territory), Argentina's claim on the Falklands, and Paraguay's claims against Brazil, Argentina and Uruguay for territory lost during the Chaco War in 1870. It led to a second Chaco war in 1933.

---

## FURTHER READING

Amnesty International, *Peru Briefing: 'Disappearances' and Political Killings by Government Forces in the Andean Emergency Zone*, London, 1985.

Anderson, James, *Sendero Luminoso: A New Revolutionary Model?*, Institute for the Study of Terrorism, London, 1987.

Bonner, Raymond, 'Peru's War', *New Yorker*, 4 January 1988.

Saba, Raul P., *Political Development and Democracy in Peru: Continuity in Change and Crisis*, Boulder, Colo., Westview Press, 1987.

Vargas Llosa, Mario, 'Death in the Andes', *New York Times Magazine*, 31 July 1983.

---

# THE DRUG WARS

In the 21st century, our security will be challenged increasingly by interconnected groups that traffic in terror, organized crime and drug smuggling. Already these drug and crime syndicates drain up to $750 billion a year from legitimate economies. That sum exceeds the combined GNP of more than half the nations in this room. These groups threaten to undermine confidence in fragile new democracies and market economies that so many of you are working so hard to see endure.

President Clinton, addressing the UN, 22 September 1997.

## COLOMBIA

| | |
|---|---|
| Geography | 439, 734 sq. miles (1,138,907 sq. km). The size of Spain, Portugal and France combined. |
| Population | 36.8 million. |
| GNP per capita | $2000. |
| Casualties | Up to 300,000 were killed in the civil war, 1946–57. |

Colombia is being destroyed by two of the great forces of evil in the world: drugs and political terrorism. It is a terrible combination, and other countries, starting with several in Latin America but including ones around the world and even Russia itself, are under assault by the same forces. The last president of Colombia, Ernesto Samper, won his election with the support of the Cali drug cartel. A Communist insurrection which controls a large part of the country is in alliance with the drug lords, and so are a high proportion of the police and armed forces.

The army fights the guerrillas (the Revolutionary Armed Forces of Colombia), with the same methods that were used for 40 years in Guatemala: a total disregard for human rights, massacres, assassinations and death squads. The political class is deeply infiltrated by the drug traffickers (one attorney-general was arrested in office for taking bribes) and corruption has spread to every level in government. Democracy in these circumstances is a sham.

Colombia has always been a violent country. There were about 26,000 homicides in 1996, six times the rate in the US. Most of them are in some way associated with the drug trade, and the number increases with every year. There were about 3000 political killings, two-thirds of them the work of right-wing death squads.

Over the past 20 years or so all the military dictators and juntas that once ruled Latin America have been overthrown or persuaded to retire gracefully. Only Cuba remains. Colombia is now moving in the opposite direction, towards a new, anarchic system in which power goes to the most brutal and the most corrupt. As President Clinton said, this may be the great danger of the 21st century. By comparison with the narco-terrorists, the old caudillos seem almost benign.

## HISTORY

Like many other countries in Latin America, Colombia was governed in much of the 19th and 20th centuries by factions of oligarchs describing themselves as Conservatives or Liberals. Between 1946 and 1957, the rivalry between these two parties degenerated into a merciless civil war, now referred to as *La Violencia*, in which it is said that up to 200,000 people were killed (though that figure should be treated with caution). The slaughter was finally suspended when the two parties agreed to divide power between them, but the experience was not forgotten.

This sharing of power between two factions of the land-owning oligarchy encouraged the Communist opposition, and in the 1970s they began an insurrection. The Communist Party's military wing, the FARC, has been at war with the government ever since. Its current leader is Manuel Marulanda Vélez.

There was a short-lived ceasefire in 1984. The government promised to institute social reforms and to improve the lot of the peasantry. In the meantime, the FARC was left undisturbed in its bases in the mountains. Other Communist factions continued the fight, notably M-19 (the name refers to an election on 19 April 1970, which the Communists denounce as fraudulent). There were a number of spectacular incidents, and by the later 1980s the war had resumed in full fury. Paradoxically, the government and FARC remained in constant communication, with periodic meetings between ministers and guerrilla leaders until 1991. There was even a hotline between Bogotá and the main FARC base at La Uribe, on a mountain south of the capital.

It was apparent that neither side could win. However corrupt, the government had wide enough support to protect it from a sudden collapse like those of Batista in Cuba or Somoza in Nicaragua. At the same time, the country is far too large and wild for the army to stand any chance of destroying the guerrillas. In 1989, the FARC and M-19 signed another peace treaty with the government, and agreed to disband. The only large guerrilla group that did not accept the ceasefire, the National Liberation Army (ELN), pursued a single-minded vendetta against international oil companies. In June 1989 an ELN commando bombed an oil pipeline terminal, causing $7 million in damage. Later, ELN and FARC discovered that extorting protection money from oil companies and hiring their troops out to the drug lords was a much easier way to fight for the good life than old-fashioned leftist militancy.

M-19 turned itself into a political party, until its leader was murdered by Pablo Escobar. The FARC once again abandoned the peace process and resumed the fight. By the mid-1990s, the war between government and guerrillas had reached an extreme of violence and, as usual in such cases, most of those killed were **535** civilians, particularly peasants. The Colombian army is now the most flagrant abuser of human rights in Latin America, quite beyond the control of civilian authority. For several years, death squads, composed of off-duty soldiers or police, operated with impunity against leftists, opposition figures or anyone who criticized the army or police. Then, progressively throughout the 1980s, the drug lords entered into alliance with some policemen and some soldiers, and now the death squads are paid by the drug lords and operate in the drug wars between them. Some police and many soldiers, allied to the drug cartels, attack the guerrillas with merciless ferocity. Other police and soldiers attack the cartels, which are defended by the guerrillas. The narco-terrorists fight among themselves and against the government terrorists, all of them extort protection money from oil companies and other businesses, and they run a thriving kidnapping business on the side: in 1994, 4000 people were kidnapped for ransom in Colombia. None of this has anything to do with the law or morality: the fight is over the profits of selling cocaine and heroin to Americans.

The Colombian drug lords are the richest criminals in the world and, until the Russian Mafia began to show its powers, were also the most violent. The combination of limitless money and utter disregard for human life has led to a permanent reign of terror in the cities. In the 1980s, the most powerful drug cartel was based in Medellín, Colombia's second largest city: the president did not dare set foot there. The Medellín Cartel was broken in 1992 by an alliance of rival drug lords and the army (though it is now reconstituting itself). It was supplanted by the Cali Cartel. By then, the break-down in legality that afflicted Colombia during *La Violencia* had returned.

## COCAINE

The Colombian cocaine trade was developed in the 1970s by a group of entrepreneurs in Medellín, a city in central Colombia, north-west of Bogotá. They took what had been essentially a cottage industry and turned it into a major business – with the highest rate of return on investment of any industry in the world. According to the US State Department's Bureau of International Narcotics Matters, Colombia, Bolivia and Peru between them produced approximately 650 tons of cocaine in 1997.

The entrepreneurs' first problem is to cope with the enormous volume of leaves. Each hectare (2.4 acres) of coca plants produces about one metric ton of leaves. By the State Department's estimate, 194,000 hectares (465,000 acres) were devoted to growing the plant in those three countries in 1997, producing 263,000 tons of leaf. It takes 200 kilos of leaves to produce 1 kilo of paste. The leaves have to be converted into coca paste on the spot: the sheer volume, not to mention the weight, of the leaves makes it impractical to move them very far. The plantations are scattered in the valleys, and there are thousands of collection points at which the leaves are rendered down. The paste is brought to one of thousands of small dirt airstrips, hidden in the jungles. It is then taken to laboratories in Colombia to be converted first into cocaine base (it takes 2.5 kilos of paste to produce 1 kilo of base), and then into cocaine hydrochloride – pure cocaine. These latter operations require skilled technicians and specialized equipment and supplies. These calculations of the yield of coca plants are subject to two provisos. The quantity of coca paste derived from each kilogram of leaf depends on the quality of the plant. Peruvian coca plants produce twice as much paste as plants from Colombia (at lower altitudes). Secondly, old plants, 2 to 15 years old, produce up to four crops a year, so the production of each hectare varies greatly. Production in Colombia may be 800 kg per hectare, and in the high valleys of Peru and Bolivia may reach 2.7 tons.

The entrepreneurs organize all of this, and then handle the smuggling operation to get the cocaine into the United States – and, increasingly, into Europe. It is either concealed in planes or boats or in innocuous exports, or else it is shipped to an entrepôt in Central America or the Caribbean, whence it is carried into the United States.

Finally, the cocaine entrepreneurs, like oil producers in the Gulf, have set up their own distribution networks inside the U S. Unlike the members of O P E C, however, they do not own the land from which their product originates: that remains the domain of peasants and their landlords in the Andes. But they control everything else, from the planes that pick up the loads of coca paste from jungle airstrips, to the runners pushing 'crack', the most deadly form of cocaine, on the Upper West Side of Manhattan.

Coca producers have found it as difficult to control cocaine prices as O P E C has found it difficult to control oil prices. In the late 1970s, as the immense expansion of the business began, Peruvian peasants were paid 50 cents for a kilo of coca leaves. Prices rose rapidly at first: Bolivian peasants were being paid $7 a kilo for leaves at the height of the boom, in 1982–4. The laws of supply and demand then came into play. The immense expansion of coca plantations in Peru and Bolivia produced a glut, and prices dropped to $2 a kilo for leaves in 1986, and 40 cents in 1988.

These variations were apparent at the other end. When a kilo of coca leaves cost 50 cents, a kilo of pure cocaine in Colombia (from 500 kilos of leaves) was worth $9750. By the time it reached the user in New York, that kilo was worth $560,000, sold by the gram, and it was no longer pure cocaine, having been 'cut' to 12.5 per cent purity. However, cocaine is now so readily available, despite all the efforts of police and F B I and various task forces, that cocaine on the streets of Miami is sold at 33 per cent purity. A kilo that cost $47,000 to $60,000 wholesale in 1982 cost only $9000 to $14,000 in 1989. The price had recovered, in New York, to about $20,000 a kilo by 1992.

In 1983, 6 tons of cocaine were seized in south Florida, and 2.3 tons in Mexico. In 1985, 25 tons were seized in Florida, and in 1986, over 30 tons. In 1987, the federal drug agencies seized 70 tons of cocaine in the U S, of varying degrees of purity, 1400 lb of heroin and 20,000 tons of marijuana. In 1988, cocaine seizures reached about 100 tons.

Calculations of the value of these huge quantities of drug are difficult because some of the cocaine seized was 100 per cent pure, some 50 per cent, some merely 12.5 per cent. As we have seen, the State Department estimated that Andean cocaine production reached 560 tons in 1997. At $14,000 for a kilo at one-third purity, the suppliers' income from 650 tons would be $28 billion. For the full 360 tons, it would be $15 billion. Since the cartel also controls distribution and retail sales, its profits are, in fact, immensely higher, despite the seizures. In a report issued in April 1988, a panel of experts, directed by a former president of Costa Rica and by Sol Linowitz, the former American ambassador who negotiated the Panama canal treaties, stated: 'As long as the profit margin for cocaine is 12,000 per cent from production cost to street value, the lure of trafficking will be irresistible.'

The extent of the problem can be gauged by a short news item, buried inside the 'Metropolitan' section of the *New York Times* on 22 August 1988. A day earlier, more than 2 tons of cocaine had been seized in an apartment in Queens, New York. Its street value was said by police to be over $400 million. This was an enormous amount of the drug, but nowadays such a discovery is treated as routine by the newspapers. On 30 September 1989, police in Los Angeles seized the largest consignment of cocaine ever discovered, over 20 tons. Its value, wholesale, was about $2 billion. Police also found about $10 million in cash. The discovery was accidental: neighbours were suspicious. Drug agents were constrained to note, in succeeding months, that the seizure had no effect on price. Evidently supply still exceeded demand. Two years later, even though American demand for cocaine appeared to be diminishing, one estimate was that the American market took up to 500 tons of cocaine a year, compared to 200 tons in Europe. The Japanese market was also expanding rapidly, with Japanese wholesalers prepared to pay $60,000 a kilo.

## THE CARTEL

In November 1981, M-19 terrorists tried to kidnap a major drug smuggler, Carlos Lehrer Rivas, and succeeded in kidnapping Marta Ochoa Vasquez, one of the daughters of Don Fabio Ochoa, and sister to Jorge, one of the most important drug traffickers in Colombia. M-19 demanded a $1 million ransom, but instead of paying, the Ochoa family convoked a meeting in Cali, about 200 miles (320 km) south-west of Bogotá, of all the major drug traffickers in the country, and together they declared war on the kidnappers. They issued a leaflet which put the issue bluntly. Describing itself as 'the Mafia', the group announced that it had formed an organization called 'Death to Kidnappers', with a war chest of $4.4 million and 2230 men. They added: 'Kidnappers will be executed in public: they will be hanged from trees in public places or executed by firing squad.' Rewards of $200,000 were offered for information.

The war was short and brutal. Ten leaders of M-19 were captured and tortured, their sympathizers were terrorized and, after three months, M-19 surrendered. Marta Ochoa was released unharmed.

After this success, members of the 'Mafia' who decided to continue to cooperate became known as the Medellín Cartel. Its leading figures were: members of the Ochoa family, of whom Jorge was the most important; Pablo Escobar Gaviria, killed in 1993; and, until he was killed in December 1989, Gonzalo Rodríguez Gacha. Rodríguez handled the import of coca paste from Peru and Bolivia. Escobar, who was the principal leader of the Cartel, supervised production and security: he was said to employ 200 full-time killers and to direct two schools for assassins, whose pupils learn such techniques as shooting from motorbikes. The Ochoas handled the export trade. The three were known as *los duenos del cupo* – 'the holders of the quota' – who shared out coca paste for refining. The group also supplied smaller enterprises with its products. The most conspicuous of those sub-groups was directed by Carlos Lehrer Rivas who became one of the major cocaine smugglers.

The Cartel is a loose association of drug producers and smugglers, united in self-defence, whose members cooperate to share out the market, beat off rivals and intimidate the government. It is not even a proper cartel, which is classically an association of producers who combine to drive up prices – for example, O P E C is a cartel. On the contrary, the price of cocaine has dropped sharply on the streets of the United States and Europe because the Cartel's suppliers have increased production enormously, and its smugglers have succeeded in flooding the market. The Medellín Cartel describes itself as 'The Company', or the Mafia, but the name, 'Cartel', has stuck.

The Cartel's power, and the progress of its war against the Colombian government, can be measured by the history of the 1979 extradition treaty with the United States. The Cartel's leaders saw this as their most serious threat and set about defeating it. In 1985, when the Supreme Court was debating the treaty's constitutionality, the Cartel hired M-19 (allegedly for $5 million) to storm the Palace of Justice, its war with the terrorists in 1981 seemingly forgotten.

The attack took place on 6 November. The commandos drove into the parking garage below the Palace in a bus painted in the colours of the Bogotá Telephone Company. There were 40–45 of them, men and women. They seized the ground floor, and then set about searching the building, floor by floor. They took some 250 hostages, including the members of the Supreme Court, who were holding a meeting to discuss the extradition treaty. The president of the court, Alfonso Reyes Enchandía, was obliged to call President Betancur, and demand that he surrender at once to be tried by a 'people's court'. The president sent in an anti-terrorist assault squad, and the terrorists began slaughtering their hostages, starting with Reyes and ten other judges, taking care to kill all those who supported the treaty. About 60 hostages and 40 terrorists were killed in the final bloodbath. Shortly afterwards, one of the few pro-treaty judges who had escaped was murdered in Bogotá. A year later, the reconstituted Supreme Court annulled the extradition treaty.

Another guerrilla group, the F A R C, supplied the guards for the Cartel's major cocaine processing plant, which they named Tranquilandia. It was in the jungle on an island in the Yari river. In March 1984, the newly appointed minister of justice, Rodrigo Lara Bonilla, and his chief of the narcotics police, Colonel Jaime Ramírez Gómez, raided the factory. They found $1.2 billion worth of cocaine and laboratories capable of refining 4 tons a week.

That was the high-water mark of the government's war on the Cartel. Lara was murdered a month later, on 30 April, and Ramírez in November the following year. The judge appointed to investigate Lara's murder found evidence of the Cartel's complicity. He, too, was assassinated. Lara's successor as justice minister, Enrique Perejo, was later sent to Budapest as ambassador, for his own safety. The Cartel pursued him there, and shot and seriously wounded him on 13 January 1987.

After Lara's death, there was a brief upsurge of outrage, and the Cartel's leaders found it prudent to leave the country. They moved to Panama with a small army of bodyguards, and paid General Manuel Noriega $5 million for their security. In May 1984, the Cartel met Colombia's attorney-general in a hotel in Panama, and proposed a deal. They would shut down their operations, from production to distribution, in exchange for an amnesty. The government refused. A later, possibly facetious offer by the Cartel to pay off the country's $9 billion national debt in exchange for amnesty was also rejected.

Lehrer, Jorge Luis Ochoa and the leader of the emerging Cali Cartel, Gilberto Rodríguez Orejuela, went to Spain, where the latter two were arrested and sent back to Colombia. They had time to set up a Spanish network, based on Colombian immigrants, which is now rapidly expanding. European narcotics police fear that Europe will soon catch up with the U S in cocaine consumption, with Spain playing the role of Florida as principal importing centre.

Rodríguez Orejuela was put on trial in July 1987, and acquitted. This was partially the fault of the American authorities who had provided the chief witness against him: an agent of the U S Drug Enforcement Administration (D E A). The agent could not speak Spanish, and the court provided an interpreter with a very inadequate command of English. However, the trial seemed to American observers to be rigged from the start. Rodríguez was acquitted on all charges – which meant not only that he was free in Colombia, but that he could not be extradited to the United States, even if the extradition treaty were reinstated.

Jorge Ochoa was in prison awaiting trial in August 1986, when a judge released him on bail, and he vanished. When he was finally tracked down in November 1987, he was arrested again. His two brothers and another member of the Cartel, Pablo Escobar, visited the judge in private: Jorge Ochoa was released a few days later.

The attorney general, Carlos Mauro Hoyos Jiménez, ordered an investigation into Ochoa's release, but before it was completed he was murdered in Medellín, his hometown, on 26 January 1988. He was kidnapped, handcuffed, blindfolded and gagged – and shot ten times in the head. To make sure that the message was clearly understood, a representative of *los extraditables* called the local radio station to inform them: 'The war goes on. I repeat, the war goes on.' President Barco (who had replaced Betancur in August 1986) did not attend the funeral: his security could not be assured in Colombia's second largest city.

A new attorney general was appointed: Alfredo Gutiérrez Márquez. He caused a sensation by suggesting that the only solution to the crisis might be to legalize drugs and negotiate with the traffickers. In March 1988, he was forced to resign when it was found that his brother was involved in trafficking.

Lehrer was not so lucky as Rodríguez Orejuela and Ochoa: he was arrested in February 1987, and extradited to the United States. An informant had told the police where he could be found, and he was picked up at a farm 20 miles (32 km) from Medellín. He was immediately put on a plane to Florida. The Colombian president had signed the extradition order some years earlier, before the extradition treaty with the United States was declared unconstitutional, and he now chose to declare that the order was still valid. In May 1988, Lehrer was convicted of smuggling 3.3 tons of cocaine into the United States through the Bahamas and was sentenced to more than 135 years in jail: a life term, with no parole, and nine consecutive 15-year sentences on other smuggling charges.

It is possible that Lehrer was betrayed by the senior members of the Cartel. He was a psychopathic killer and publicity-seeker, constantly giving interviews and boasting of his achievements: he gave cocaine smuggling a bad name. What is more, his operation in the Bahamas, on Norman's Cay, had been so large, dangerous and conspicuous that even the complaisant government of Sir Lynden Pindling could not overlook it indefinitely. His partner in the Bahamas had reportedly been Robert Vesco, an embezzler on the grand scale who is urgently wanted by American police.

The annulment of the extradition treaty by the Supreme Court in 1987 meant that all proceedings against 100 or more suspects were cancelled.

The new president, Virgilio Barco Vargas, attempted to reverse the tide. In May 1988, he sent the army against the Cartel's drug laboratories in the jungles: it was the first time troops had been used in the drug wars since the mid-1970s. In August, in a severe defeat for the government, the Supreme Court formally suspended the extradition orders against the Cartel's leaders.

In 1989, electioneering began for a presidential election in 1990. The leading candidate, Luis Carlos Galan, advocated a relentless attack on the drug traffickers – and on 18 August they killed him. A bomb was planted under a platform in a hall where he was speaking. President Barco thereupon declared war on the drug barons. They were pursued actively, when they were caught they were summarily deported to the United States, and their property was confiscated. Within four weeks, the government had seized 367 aircraft, 72 boats, 710 vehicles, 4.7 tons of cocaine, 989 buildings and ranches and a great number of weapons. By the end of the year, cocaine exports had been cut 25 per cent and there were at last signs of shortage in Miami: street prices rose for the first time in years.

The narco-terrorists retaliated. There was a vicious bombing campaign throughout the country and further attacks on public officials, and also on journalists, notably those working for *El Espectador*. On 27 November, a bomb in an Avianca Boeing 727 killed 107 people, and on 6 December a huge car-bomb outside police headquarters in Bogotá killed 52 people, wounded over 600 and did immense damage. The police chief escaped. Then on 15 December the anti-narcotics squad achieved its greatest success: it found and killed José Gonzalez Rodríguez Gacha, one of the three leaders of the Cartel. They had followed his son to his hideaway, and attacked with helicopters and infantry. The son and six bodyguards were also killed.

It was a less significant victory than it appeared. There were many other, equally violent drug lords to replace Rodríguez. But the government's offensive was hurting the Cartel, and in January, the Ochoa brothers, Juan, Jorge and Fabio, all surrendered to the government, leaving Pablo Escobar alone as the Cartel's leader. A month after Rodríguez was killed, in January 1990, the Cartel sued for peace. It informed the government and public that it would surrender – provided its members were given free pardons and permanent immunity from extradition. They said: 'We accept the triumph of the state. Thus, we will lay down our arms and abandon our objectives for the benefit of the highest interests of the fatherland. We submit to the existing legal establishment in the hope of **541** obtaining from the government and from society respect for our rights and our return to our families and communities. We have decided to suspend the shipment of drugs, and to surrender the weapons, explosives, laboratories, hostages, the clandestine landing strips and other effects related to our activities at such a time as we are granted constitutional and legal guarantees.'

The communiqué was signed '*Los Extraditables*'. The message was reinforced by an unusual press trip organized by the Cartel in February 1990. Journalists from Medellín were taken to a secret drug-processing laboratory in the jungle near the Panama border. It was even larger than the Tranquilandia facility, capable of processing 20 tons a month, and the Cartel informed the journalists that they intended to turn it over to the government.

After two days' thought, President Barco rejected the offer. One reason for his caution was that a 'drug summit' was to be held in Cartagena, Colombia, in February 1990. It was President Bush's idea, and was largely designed to prove to the American electorate that the president was determined to win the drug war. Mr Bush, and the presidents of Colombia, Peru and Bolivia, gathered for a day on a heavily-protected island off Cartagena and then issued a strong communiqué denouncing the drug trade and promising to do something about it. Then they went home, and the whole subject disappeared from George Bush's concerns.

Pablo Escobar reacted to Barco's rejection of his peace offering by ordering a renewal of the war against the government. There was a series of car-bombings and assassinations in Bogotá and in Medellín. Two presidential candidates, Carlos Pizarro León-Goméz, former commander of the M-19 guerrillas, and Bernardo Jaramillo Ossa, leader of the Patriotic Union, were both killed. Pizarro was shot in an airplane, on a flight from Bogotá.

Meanwhile, the United States government took steps to destroy the International Coffee Agreement, sharply cutting the price Colombia got for its major legitimate export. The Americans also put up barriers to prevent the import of cut flowers from Colombia. Colombia's revenues suffered sharply from these measures, and its ability, and inclination, to fight the drug war also suffered.

The Colombians also disapproved of the American invasion of Panama and the inept suggestion, immediately afterwards, that the American navy should patrol the coasts of Colombia to intercept drug traffickers. Both actions were seen as a reversal to old, bad habits of American interventionism. The naval suggestion was hastily cancelled. Colombia, and other Latin American nations, believed that the source of the evil was in the United States, in Americans' insatiable appetite for drugs. They thought that the Americans should first cure themselves before sending the fleet to Colombia.

Escobar continued to negotiate with the government. He set his terms: he would surrender if he were promised never to be extradited to the United States, and if he were allowed to stay in a prison he had built in a town he owned near Medellín, Envigado. He intended to keep control of his army of narco-terrorists, and to continue to rule his empire from prison, like the Ochoa brothers. It would be, in effect, house arrest – and Escobar's men would ensure his protection. On 19 June 1991, Escobar surrendered – on his own terms. The war between the government and the Medellín Cartel had come to an end, in a draw. The two sides signed a treaty, much like 18th-century European countries tired of war, without either conceding any fundamental point to its enemy. The Colombian courts would now deal with Escobar and the Ochoas, and few people expected the judges to show any great severity. The new constitution, which came into force in July 1991, bans extradition.

Meanwhile, on another front, on 26 November 1989, the government and M-19 announced an agreement, under which the guerrillas agreed to disband. After further negotiations, M-19 emerged into the light of day on 10 March 1990, and formally handed over their weapons to the government in exchange for a general amnesty. Their leader, Carlos Pizarro, formally surrendered to President Barco. A year later, he was assassinated on the orders of Pablo Escobar.

On 1 March 1991, the EPL followed M-19's example and surrendered its weapons. Protracted negotiations between the EPL, a Maoist group founded by ten radicals in 1967, and the new president, César Gaviria Trujillo, concluded in a treaty under which the guerrillas were amnestied after their surrender, and awarded a $125 a month stipend each for the next year. The EPL was given two seats on the 72-member commission preparing a new constitution, and changed its name to *Esperanza, Paz y Libertad*. Its leaders had been impressed by the collapse of Communism in Europe, and had concluded that the armed struggle was futile if the Socialist Utopia they dreamed of was a chimera. Part of the old EPL rejected the peace agreement, and has now joined FARC in the jungles. In October 1991, M-19 won a large bloc of seats in congressional elections.

As the leftists emerged into the limelight, the right-wing death squads also laid down their arms, at least for the moment. In November 1991, 35 members of one of the death squads surrendered to the government. They had formerly been employed by the narco-terrorists, as enforcers, but later the Cartel had turned to the leftist guerrillas, who were more effective. So the death squads went to war with the Cartel, and several of their leaders were killed. In January 1992, the commander of the biggest of these death squads, Ariel Otero, was killed on the Cartel's orders. His group had been called the Self-Defence Group of Magdalena Medio.

The drug trade continued uninterrupted after the leaders of the Medellín Cartel were killed or jailed. The Cali Cartel, which had always been less violent, continued about its business. In November 1991, Miami police found 12 tons of Cali cocaine hidden in cement posts imported from Venezuela. American police also broke up a large money-laundering operation in Miami and New York, and arrested Ramiro Herrera, the brother of one of the Cali Cartel's leaders, Helmer 'Pacho' Herrera.

Escobar remained in jail for a year, until 22 July 1992, when he left. His imprisonment had been little more than house arrest: he had built the jail himself and equipped it with every comfort and the most up-to-date communications equipment, so that he could continue to run the Cartel undisturbed. The government had contemplated moving him to a more secure jail: six people were killed in the attempt, and when the police reached Escobar's quarters, they found that he had walked out through a tunnel built for the purpose.

On emerging, he discovered that the Cali Cartel had allied itself with the police against him. At the height of its power, the Medellín Cartel had made $20 billion

**543**

a year and supplied 80 per cent of the cocaine sold in the United States. It was a prize worth fighting for. Times were dangerous: the Cali Cartel and the police between them were decimating the Medellín Cartel. Escobar's former top deputy, Jorge Luis Ochoa Vasquez, and his two brothers, Juan David and Fabio, had cut a deal and were sentenced to eight and a half years in jail – and would be eligible for parole in 1998. Those who were not jailed were killed, and Escobar was on the defensive. He fought back: on 15 April 1993 bombs in the centre of Bogotá killed 14 and wounded over 200.

Colombian killers never hesitate to murder the families of their enemies, unlike the Italian Mafia which never touched the women, let alone children. Escobar himself had killed or ordered killed many women and children and knew the dangers. He tried to arrange to have his wife and children leave the country, preferably for the United States (he offered to go out of business if the U S would agree). When that proposal was rejected, he sent them to Chile. They were expelled. He sent them to Germany: they were expelled again.

The Americans had supplied Colombian police with ultra-sophisticated telephone tracking devices, and now they listened to Escobar as he talked to his wife by cellular phone about these travel arrangements. On 2 December 1993 a special police squad surrounded the house in Medellín where Escobar was hiding – and using the phone. He fled in his bare feet across the rooftops and was shot down, gun in hand. His friends and neighbours gave him a huge and tearful funeral.

The Cali Cartel was now supreme. The American Drug Enforcement Administration calculated that in 1993 Cali controlled 95 per cent of the cocaine coming out of the Andes – 750 tons. What is more, Cali has diversified into heroin: there are huge plantations of opium poppies in Colombia, which now supply more than half the heroin sold in the New York region. By 1996, they had driven the price of a kilo down from the $150,000 to $200,000 charged by Asian dealers a few years ago to $75,000. The Cartel's leaders were six men: two pairs of brothers, Ivan and Julio Fabio Urdinola, and Miguel and Gilberto Rodríguez Orejuela; and Helmer 'Pancho' Herrera and Jose Santacruz Londono. They cemented their position by putting up at least $6 million to pay the election expenses of Ernesto Samper in June 1994. He won, and he was duly grateful. In September, the departing head of the D E A in Bogotá, Joe Toft, caused a sensation by claiming on Colombian television that Colombia was a 'narco-democracy' and that the Cali Cartel had incredible control over the country's political and economic institutions, and that 'people prefer to close their eyes and look the other way'. He also asserted that President Samper had taken money from the Cartel.

His candour enraged the Colombians of course, and embarrassed the U S government. Within two years, however, Washington came around to admitting that Toft had spoken perfect truth. Samper was refused a visa to visit the United States and in March 1996 the country was put on the black list. An American law provides that before any country receives aid, the president must certify that it is fighting the drug war. Colombia was now 'decertified', a serious blow to the government. This meant that it was ineligible for economic assistance or, much more important, loans at preferential rates, though the U S continued to help the police's anti-drug efforts. The decertification was repeated in 1997 but lifted in

1998, on 'national security' grounds, partly because Samper was due to leave office that summer but also because Washington had discovered that decertification did nothing to reduce the flow of drugs into the United States.

American pressure led the army to pursue the Cartel with unusual vigour, and in 1995 the Orejuela brothers and Santacruz were arrested. Herrera surrendered in 1996. Their lawyers set to work to arrange short sentences for them, which would wipe out all charges against them. Simultaneously, a number of members of Congress, the finance minister, the defence minister and the attorney general, were all charged with links to the Cartel. The president was accused of being particularly friendly with a woman whose husband had been caught smuggling six tons of cocaine out of the country, and Congress finally considered impeaching him. He survived the vote in June 1996, and served out his term.

In January 1996 the Cali leader José Santacruz, who controlled the drug business in New York and was reputed to be the most violent of the top Cartel leaders, bribed his way out of jail. On 5 March he was stopped at a road-block near Medellín, and shot. This was less of a victory than it appeared: he was ambushed by rivals in the Cartel. By then, a younger and still more violent generation of traffickers was taking over the Cartel's operations, who rely on terror, murdering all their opponents, rather than legal manoeuvring, to keep out of jail.

At the same time, again in response to American pressure, Samper announced that he would eradicate 27,000 hectares (67,000 acres) of coca and opium in 1996. He sent the army into the remote mountains where the peasants were now working for the Cartel, and the FARC rallied to their defence. On 30 August, it launched a general offensive, attacking 27 army posts. It wiped out an army base called Las Delicias near the border with Ecuador, killing 27 soldiers and taking 60 prisoners, and killed another 40 in the other attacks. The army was roundly beaten in the fighting that followed, and was forced to withdraw from 5000 square miles of south-eastern Colombia, ceding the territory (and the drugs grown there) to the narco-guerrillas. The next major battle was 50 km from Bogotá, in April 1997 – and, once again, the guerrillas won. Samper recognized his defeat and resumed negotiations with FARC, and in June the guerrillas released 70 of their prisoners in exchange for the government evacuating several southern provinces completely. The FARC also issued a list of political demands, which included restricting the army to guarding the frontiers, transferring land ownership to the peasants and nationalizing the oil industry. There were municipal elections in October, but FARC ensured that no one offered himself as candidate in about half the country, in provinces they controlled. In government-controlled provinces, incumbents were returned unopposed.

## THE SPREAD OF THE OCTOPUS

After the leaders of the Medellín Cartel left Colombia in 1984, following the murder of the minister of justice, they set about expanding their network of contacts in other Central American countries and in Europe. The rise in cocaine consumption in Europe dates from that year. They had already invested heavily in Panama, according to Ramón Milian Rodríguez, a senior finance official for the Cartel who was caught in the United States and is now serving a 43-year sentence. He testified to a Senate committee that Noriega had been paid about $320 million between 1979 and 1983 for the use of Panamanian airports and the banking system (which was used to launder the enormous amount of money involved). Lynden Pindling in the Bahamas came much cheaper. A witness at the Lehrer trial testified that he had paid Pindling between $3 million and $5 million for the use of Norman's Cay.

The Cartel has also invested in military leaders in Haiti and Honduras, and backed both the Nicaraguan Contras and at least some members of the Sandinista government. One witness, Barry Seal, implicated Tomás Borge, Sandinista minister of the interior. Seal claimed to have flown at least one load of cocaine from Colombia to Managua, where the transaction was supervised by a man who claimed to be a senior aide to Borge. Seal was the American prosecutor's chief witness against Ochoa. He was assassinated in February 1986 in Baton Rouge, Louisiana: the police had not taken seriously his claim that his life was in danger.

The links between the Cartel and Cuba are discussed on page 550. The Cartel has at times allied itself with the pro-Cuban M-19 guerrilla movement in Colombia. The essential point about the Cartel's politics and its foreign policy is that money is non-ideological. Lenin offered to sell capitalists the rope with which they would hang themselves. The ferocious Medellín capitalists turned the offer around, and bought up revolutionaries as freely as they bought old-fashioned military men.

The drug trade is a finely tuned capitalist enterprise. It responds to movements in supply and demand, and the most profitable sectors are refining and distribution. When the US succeeds in enforcing a crackdown in one area – say, eliminating poppy fields in Turkey or coca plants in Peru – production expands somewhere else. When the Medellín Cartel's operations in Colombia were interrupted in 1984, refining and distribution through Mexico expanded.

In a decade, the traffickers moved from a 'peasant' economy, based on raising marijuana ('Colombian Gold') and smuggling it across the Caribbean, to a modern industrial business with refineries, finance offices and elaborate distribution networks. The Mexicans are no less gifted than the Colombians, the Hondurans no less corruptible. Cali now faces competition from Culiacan on Mexico's Pacific coast, where the Cartel's business principles have already been introduced: when Mexican police raided a drug depot used by Colombians in Sonora, they found 100 AK-47 assault rifles, 65,000 rounds of ammunition, 92 bayonets and six infra-red night scopes.

In the mid-1980s, as supply exceeded demand in the United States and the price dropped, the Medellín Cartel, which dominated the Miami market, decided to move in on the most lucrative market in the world: New York, which was dominated by the Cali Cartel. There ensued a continuing and violent battle between the two, involving scores of murders and frequent betrayals. The two tons of cocaine found in New York in August 1988 had belonged to Cali; the police may have been tipped off by Medellín.

The United States has had some success in eliminating coca growing in Bolivia and Peru (according to the DEA) but production has simply moved to

Colombia. The area suitable for coca growing is enormous, and so are the rewards. Indeed, in 1991 American and local drug police discovered a large cocaine laboratory in Peru, on the banks of the Santa Ana river. Smaller laboratories have been found in Bolivia, Brazil and Venezuela. Cocaine is now exported through ports in Argentina, Brazil, Surinam and Venezuela, as well as its traditional ports in Colombia and Peru. Bolivian exports, it appears, now go mostly through Buenos Aires to Europe. In 1991, Argentine police seized two tons of cocaine, double the amount seized in 1990. The guiding spirit behind this expansion was apparently the Cali Cartel, which by now accounts for 85 per cent of American imports, and a corresponding proportion of the rest of the world trade.

## HONDURAS

After the murder of the minister of justice in Colombia in 1984, the Medellín Cartel hastily arranged an alternative route for its product into the United States. In 1983, Mexican police had seized 2.3 tons of cocaine, but by 1987, that figure had risen to 9.3 tons. That was just a beginning. Juan Ramón Matta Ballesteros, a Honduran who had worked in Medellín, had developed a route through Mexico. Accused of murdering a DEA agent there in 1985, he was arrested at his home in Tegucigalpa on 4 April 1988, and immediately extradited to the United States.

Honduran law prohibits Honduran citizens from being extradited, but the military had shipped Matta off anyway. In response, there were riots on 8 April, five people were killed and an annexe to the American embassy was burned. It was a striking demonstration of outraged patriotism and resentment at American heavy-handedness. A few days later, protesters were again on the streets, this time demonstrating against the government because of its subservience to the Americans and its tolerance of the drug traffickers. If there was a contradiction in these reactions, it was more apparent to North Americans than to Hondurans.

Matta allegedly had a fortune of $2 billion – quite enough to buy any number of Honduran generals. It is said that he corrupted the military intelligence department and the judicial system: he had returned to Honduras in 1985, after several years in Colombia, and had bought his way out of various legal charges then pending against him. The courts in Honduras are no more capable of convicting billionaire drug traffickers than are those in Colombia.

The Honduran military had apparently decided that unless they acted promptly, Honduras might go the way of Colombia, where the government was terrorized by the traffickers, or Panama, where the traffickers had taken over the government. The latter danger was probably the most serious. On 15 May 1988, a Honduran diplomat was arrested in Miami airport carrying 10 kilos of cocaine in his luggage. He was Rigoberto Regalado Lara, Honduran ambassador to Panama, and the half-brother of General Humberto Regalado Hernandez, the chief of staff.

## BOLIVIA

Bolivia is one of the poorest countries in Latin America: its *per capita* GNP is $800 a year, and most of its people are engaged either in peasant agriculture or in the continually declining mining industry. In the mid-1970s, in an attempt to find an alternative to tin mining, the government encouraged the development of cotton growing in the lowlands to the east of the Andes. It did not solve Bolivia's problems: cotton prices collapsed as fast as tin prices. The landowners then replaced cotton with coca.

It was a major investment, and it was made possible with the government's help or, at the very least, its acquiescence. The first stage of cocaine production is the conversion of coca leaves to coca paste, a process that requires huge quantities of acid, diesel fuel and other chemicals, all of which had to be transported over the Andes. Furthermore, coca plants take three years to mature, so the landowners needed bank loans to tide them over.

The president at the time was General Hugo Banzer Suárez from Santa Cruz, the capital of the eastern lowlands. Banzer was an old acquaintance of Roberto Suárez Gómez, the region's principal landowner who was to become cocaine king of the Andes. Suárez formed a syndicate for exporting coca paste, and invited various friends and relatives of the president to join it. Suárez then entered into relations with the enterprising merchants of Medellín.

By the time Banzer retired in 1978, Bolivia's coca crop was developing rapidly, having risen from 11,800 tons in 1976 to 35,000 tons. (It was 89,000 tons in 1994 and 70,000 tons in 1997.) Elections were held, a new president was chosen and, in July 1980, just before he was to be inaugurated, General Luis García Meza seized power.

García was hand in glove with the cocaine traffickers. For a start, he appointed Suárez's cousin as minister of the interior. His job was to lead the campaign against narcotics, and for a year, one of the major coca-producing countries was controlled by the drug traffickers. It was a high point of corruption by drugs in Latin America. The alliance between Suárez and the Ochoas and the other members of the Medellín Cartel flourished. Coca was freely exported from eastern Bolivia, by air, to Colombia and then to the United States, and a great river of money flowed back from North to South America.

President Carter exerted himself to have García Meza removed from office, an effort that was continued, after some hesitation, by the Reagan administration. A year after he took power, García was deposed by his fellow-officers. However, by then the pattern of the trade had become well established, and ever since there has been a constant battle between the traffickers and the Americans, with the government in La Paz sometimes leaning to the one side, sometimes to the other.

After the election of Victor Paz Estensorro in May 1985, a vigorous attempt to defeat the drug traffickers was launched, with American assistance. In 1986, in 'Operation Blast Furnace', the United States sent police and special troops to Bolivia in an attempt to round up major traffickers and destroy the jungle laboratories. It was all supposed to be secret, but the sudden arrival of large American planes at the airport was noticed, and soon the papers were full of the news. The operation was a failure and provoked a storm of nationalist outrage in Bolivia.

In 1987, a less ambitious project was started. In 'Operation Snowcap', Americans have been training Bolivian special forces in police work, particularly the techniques of locating field laboratories and destroying them; their chief weapon is the helicopter. They met with considerable success: over 1500 field laboratories and 10 tons of cocaine (in various stages of production) were destroyed in six months, and over 3000 acres of coca plants were destroyed. This last was accomplished by giving peasants an inducement of $2000 for each hectare they eliminated. In addition, the Bolivian police succeeded in arresting a number of leading drug traffickers and seriously disrupting the Suárez organization – and in July 1988, they arrested Roberto Suárez himself. In August, U S Secretary of State George Shultz visited La Paz to congratulate the government on its achievements, and the drug lords made a botched attempt to assassinate him.

In 1985 or 1986, Roberto Suárez had handed over most of his organization to his nephew, Jorge Roca Suárez. Roca was a new generation of Bolivian trafficker. After the Colombians cut the price for coca paste in 1985, from $14,000 a kilo to $9000, he started to examine the possibility of cutting out the middlemen, and for the first time, laboratories were discovered in the Bolivian jungles that were capable of converting coca paste into coca base and into cocaine hydrochloride (pure cocaine). Roca also started contacting smugglers and distributors who would take his cocaine directly to the market, without the detour through Colombia. His operation was greatly disrupted by the arrest of several of his partners, and his uncle, in 1988.

The steep decline in the price of cocaine had also seriously affected Bolivian production. At 40 cents a kilo for leaves, it was scarcely worth the peasants' time to harvest the crops, particularly in the more remote and difficult districts that had been developed during the great expansion of the late 1970s.

Despite this, in the mid-1980s, cocaine exports brought $500 million a year to Bolivia and provided a livelihood for scores of thousands of peasants. President Paz and his successors had to grapple with the problem of finding an alternative. If the peasants can be found a more profitable crop, or at least one as profitable as coca, the programme will succeed and Bolivia will be saved the fate of Colombia. Otherwise, the traffickers will return and there will always be replacements for each drug lord who is arrested. Eradicating Bolivia's coca plants at the present rate of 3000 acres a year would take over 40 years.

## PERU

Peru is the world's largest producer of coca, and attempts to eliminate the plantations have been subordinated to the fight against the Shining Path (*see* Peru, pp. 523–33). Sendero has allied itself with the peasant coca producers in the Huellaga Valley, partly to win their political support, partly to finance its own operations. Scores of government drug enforcement officials and local workers have been killed trying to eliminate coca plants or to destroy laboratories. Others have been bought by the traffickers. American helicopters, searching for coca plantations, have been fired on by Peruvian army units protecting the crop. The Americans are based at a heavily-defended air base, Santa Lucia, in the Upper Huellaga Valley, where they maintain helicopters and other equipment and train a special force of 800 Peruvian police officers.

The Americans are trying to find an acceptable herbicide to spray on the plants – it simply is not possible to uproot half a million acres – but the problem with herbicides is the ecological damage they do. The coca plantations have already seriously harmed the land: coca plants need direct sun and no competition from other plants, so the growers simply sweep away everything, using the age-old slash-and-burn technique. In a few years, the rain carries away the topsoil, leaving a barren hillside where once the jungle flourished. The American chemicals firm, Eli Lilly & Co, whose herbicide Spike 20P was to be used in Peru, announced in May 1988 that it would no longer supply the product. It was apparently alarmed at the ecological consequences of its widespread use, and also feared its possible legal liability.

The U S and Peruvian governments are also looking for alternative crops for the peasants who grow the coca plants. The Peruvian government estimates that 300,000 people make a living in this way, and they would be left destitute if the plants were simply destroyed. Peru, too, had to face the economic consequences: about one-third of its export earnings, $1.5 billion, came from coca. In the autumn of 1991, the Bush administration temporarily suspended $24.9 million in military and $60 million in aid to Peru. Congress had demanded the suspension on the grounds that Peru was not doing nearly enough to fight drugs, and that its human rights record was deplorable. President Fujimori could only respond that his democratic government was fighting for its life against some of the most vicious and successful Marxist guerrillas in the world. Since then, Fujimori has won a series of victories over Sendero and is now energetically attacking drug traffickers in the Andes. For the first time in years, there have been large reductions in the areas of coca plantations in Peru, 30 per cent in five years and 13 per cent between 1996 and 1997.

## BRAZIL

The cocaine trade has now spread to Brazil. In March 1988, the D E A broke up a smugglers' ring that had brought $1.5 billion worth of cocaine from Brazil to the United States via Kennedy airport in New York.

In 1985, the Medellín Cartel had started moving some of its operations, both refining coca paste and smuggling, into Brazil. That vast country's frontiers with Bolivia and Colombia are remote, unpoliced and very long (2000 miles [3200 km] in the case of Bolivia). What is more, western Brazil, in the foothills of the Andes, offers the same advantages of climate, altitude and remoteness enjoyed by coca growers in Bolivia and Peru. Brazil is also a better base for smuggling cocaine to Europe than Colombia itself.

There is now a large and growing market in Rio and other Brazilian cities, and Brazilian police and the military have proved to be just as susceptible to bribery as the Colombians.

## CUBA

On 15 June 1989, Fidel Castro announced the arrest of one of Cuba's most senior military officers, General Arnaldo Ochoa Sanchez, on a charge of running drugs into the United States. At his trial two months later, he pleaded guilty to the charge. Drugs had been imported into Cuba on military planes, or to military bases and had then been ferried to the U S, directly or by way of the Bahamas. The network had run for many years and had made Ochoa and his accomplices hundreds of millions of dollars. Castro denied all involvement by other Cuban officials, a denial received sceptically in America. Ochoa was shot.

In 1996, the *Miami Herald* reported that drug dealers arrested in a major case that year had told the FBI that large quantities of cocaine were now being smuggled into the United States and Europe through Cuba, with the personal approval of Fidel Castro. The FBI would not confirm the report, and it is entirely possible that the traffickers were offering the story on the theory that they might be treated leniently if they could compromise Castro.

## THE DRUG TRADE

The US State Department's 1998 International Narcotics Control Strategy Report offers the following estimates for drug production:

### COCA NET CULTIVATION (HECTARES)

|          | 1993    | 1994    | 1995    | 1996   | 1997   |
|----------|---------|---------|---------|--------|--------|
| **Peru**     | 108,800 | 108,600 | 115,300 | 94,400 | 68,800 |
| **Bolivia**  | 47,200  | 48,100  | 48,600  | 48,100 | 45,800 |
| **Colombia** | 39,700  | 45,000  | 50,900  | 67,200 | 79,500 |

### POTENTIAL COCAINE PRODUCTION (METRIC TONS)

|          | 1993 | 1994 | 1995 | 1996 | 1997 |
|----------|------|------|------|------|------|
| **Peru**     | 410  | 435  | 460  | 435  | 325  |
| **Bolivia**  | 240  | 255  | 240  | 215  | 200  |
| **Colombia** | 65   | 70   | 80   | 110  | 125  |

### OPIUM CULTIVATION (HECTARES)

|              | 1993    | 1994    | 1995    | 1996    | 1997    |
|--------------|---------|---------|---------|---------|---------|
| **Burma**        | 165,800 | 146,600 | 154,070 | 163,100 | 155,150 |
| **Laos**         | 26,040  | 18,520  | 19,650  | 25,250  | 28,150  |
| **Thailand**     | 2,880   | 2,100   | 1,750   | 2,170   | 1,650   |
| **Vietnam**      |         |         |         | 3,150   | 6,150   |
| **Afghanistan**  | 21,080  | 29,180  | 38,740  | 37,950  | 39,150  |
| **Pakistan**     | 6,280   | 7,270   | 6,950   | 3,400   | 4,100   |
| **Mexico**       | 3,960   | 5,795   | 5,050   | 5,100   | 4,000   |
| **Colombia**     |         |         | 6,540   | 6,300   | 6,600   |

### POTENTIAL OPIUM PRODUCTION

|              | 1993  | 1994 | 1995  | 1996  | 1997  |
|--------------|-------|------|-------|-------|-------|
| **Burma**        | 2,575 | 2,030 | 2,340 | 2,560 | 2,365 |
| **Laos**         | 180   | 85   | 180   | 200   | 210   |
| **Thailand**     | 42    | 17   | 25    | 30    | 25    |
| **Vietnam**      |       |      |       | 22    | 45    |
| **Afghanistan**  | 685   | 950  | 1,250 | 1,230 | 1,265 |
| **Pakistan**     | 140   | 160  | 155   | 75    | 85    |
| **Mexico**       | 49    | 60   | 53    | 54    | 46    |
| **Colombia**     |       |      | 6     | 6     | 6     |

**Note: 10 tons of opium produce 1 ton of heroin**

## FURTHER READING

American University, *Colombia: A Country Study*, Washington D.C., 1977.

Amnesty International, *Colombia Briefing*, London, 1988.

————, *Honduras, Civilian Authority – Military Power: Human Rights Violations in the 1980s*, London, 1988.

Bureau of International Narcotics Matters, US State Department, *International Narcotics Control Strategy Report, 1988*.

Cockburn, Leslie, *Out of Control: The Story of the Reagan Administration's Secret War in Nicaragua*, New York, Atlantic Monthly Press, 1987.

Dolan, Edward A. Jr, *International Drug Traffic*, New York, Franklin Watts, 1985.

Eddy, Paul and Sabogal, Hugo, with Walden, Sara, *The Cocaine Wars*, New York, W. W. Norton, 1988.

Gugliotta, Guy and Leen, Jeff, *Kings of Cocaine: Inside the Medellín Cartel*, New York, Simon and Schuster, 1989.

Strares, Paul, *Global Habit: The Drug Problem in a Borderless World*, Washington, Brookings Institution, 1996.

# TERRORISM

# MODERN TERRORISM

Terrorism in all its deadly forms continues to afflict countries all over the world. There have always been terrorists, in vicious struggles in their own countries, but starting in the later 1960s they spread wings and began to attack targets far from home. After the 1967 war, Palestinians pursued Israelis, Jews and their friends across the globe. Then violent Communists, many of them inspired by the student riots of 1968, attacked governments in a number of European countries and collaborated together, forming the loose alliance that became known as 'international terrorism'. They were frequently helped by extremist governments, among them Libya, Syria and Iran, and some of them at least had close connections with, and received help, arms and training from, Communist secret services in Eastern Europe and the USSR.

The great Soviet monolith was disintegrating in the 1970s and 1980s under the weight of its own incompetence. Possibly its support for international terrorists was just another sign of its own senescence. In the West, paradoxically, cold warriors reached a last frenzy of apprehension just as their antagonist was collapsing. At the same time, they extended their hugely exaggerated fear of the Soviet Union to terrorism.

The flavour of their rhetoric can be judged by this example, by the British conservative polemicist Paul Johnson, in 1986:

Terrorism is the cancer of the modern world. No state is immune to it. It is a dynamic organism which attacks the healthy flesh of the surrounding society. It has the essential hallmark of malignant cancer: unless treated, and treated drastically, its growth is inexorable, until it poisons and engulfs the society on which it feeds and drags it down to destruction.

Every statement in this diatribe, and every implication behind it, is demonstrably false. The only countries that have been dragged down to destruction, or which face that danger now, are places like Bosnia, Somalia, Liberia or Congo which are victims of ancient tribal animosities, or Algeria and Egypt which are faced with radical Islamic insurrection.

The quote is from *Terrorism: How the West Can Win*, edited by Benjamin Netanyahu, who has since gone on to greater things. As prime minister of Israel, he authorized the assassination of a Palestinian living in Amman, an act indistinguishable from the state terrorism the book denounced.

In the book, Netanyahu claimed that 'the two main antagonists of democracy in the post-war world, Communist totalitarianism and Islamic radicalism, have between them inspired virtually all of contemporary terrorism' and 'Americans account for roughly a third of terrorists' victims since 1968'. These statements are complete nonsense. Most terrorism is inspired by nationalistic or ethnic fervour, not Communist ideology, and there has been a mere handful of American deaths among the tens of thousands who have died as a result of terrorist attacks of every description, including those in Netanyahu's definition: count the dead in Lebanon, Peru or Sri Lanka, just for a start. If the attacks are restricted to those inspired by 'international terrorism', and further limited to attacks on nationals of countries that are not involved in the dispute that animates the terrorist, the American proportion rises, but terrorism then ceases to be a major international problem, let alone a cancer. As Netanyahu himself admits, 'Terrorism's victims are few, its physical damage limited, its violence sporadic.'

He presumably had international terrorism in mind. This is a real problem, but nothing compared to indigenous terrorism. Terrorists who are a threat to society in various countries have specifically local objectives. The Shining Path in Peru is Communist, but repudiated the Soviet Union. The I R A claims to be Marxist, but no one can take that seriously; its inspiration is entirely nationalistic. The same goes for the Tamil Tigers and their rival Sinhalese terrorists in Sri Lanka, and for the Sikhs. The death squads in El Salvador, the Muslim Brotherhood in Syria, the Kurds in Turkey, Iraq and Iran, and most of the other men of violence in the Middle East are undoubtedly terrorists, without being in any useful sense 'international'.

Least of all is there any apocalyptic threat to 'the West'. A number of countries in the Middle East, Latin America and Asia have suffered seriously from terrorism, among them Lebanon, Syria, Iran, Turkey, Uruguay, Argentina, Colombia, Peru, Guatemala, India and Sri Lanka. Some terrorist organizations have regularly attacked targets in other countries, among them various Palestinian groups, the I R A, and Armenian terrorists, and others have done so occasionally. For the rest, terrorism, though often spectacular, has never been more than a marginal threat. No governments, let alone regimes, have been directly overthrown by terrorism. The civil war in Lebanon was particularly atrocious because the factions used terrorism as their preferred weapon, but terrorism did not cause Lebanon to disintegrate. Rather, it was a sign of disintegration caused by social, religious and political differences. Armies seized power in Turkey, Uruguay and Argentina because the civilian governments, they thought, were not fighting the terrorists fiercely enough. The terrorists were crushed mercilessly. It was not the outcome they had anticipated.

Netanyahu's second category of 'main antagonists of democracy' was Islamic radicalism. The terrorism it has inspired is much more dangerous than were ever the strivings of the Baader–Meinhof gang or their like, but by its nature it is a threat to Islamic countries only – Algeria, Egypt and Turkey now and, perhaps later, other Arab states. Islamic terrorists may set bombs in the Paris Métro or under New York skyscrapers, but they are no threat to democracy in either country.

There is no satisfactory definition of terrorism. Netanyahu's Jonathan Institute[1] has come up with a good but insufficient one: 'Terrorism is the deliberate and systematic murder, maiming and menacing of the innocent to inspire fear for political ends.' That definition, however, would include state terrorism: many governments have used illegal execution, torture or destruction of property against their domestic enemies (or people they have arbitrarily defined as enemies) in order to terrorize the population for political ends. However, to describe Stalin's U S S R, Hitler's Germany, Pol Pot's Cambodia, Guatemala after 1954 or Argentina after 1975 as terrorist states, though perfectly justifiable, stretches the net too wide to be useful. The term is best limited to groups acting independently of governments, though they may be financed, armed or encouraged by governments, and to assassins sent abroad illegally by government organizations.

The chief reason for distinguishing between the actions of governments, however reprehensible, and those of self-constituted organizations, is to escape the relativism of the terrorists' apologists who insist that state terrorism is far more serious. They allege that the United States (or Britain, France or Israel) have engaged in state terrorism, and conclude that the terrorists are no more guilty than those governments. It is a transparently dishonest argument, a means of avoiding the issue, and a justification for murder. Governments should be judged by their actions – and so should terrorists.

A further problem of definition is distinguishing terrorists from guerrillas. The Jonathan Institute says guerrillas wear recognizable uniforms, attack only military targets and do not use concealed weapons. This immediately leads to difficulties: under this definition, the fanatic who drove a car bomb into the US Marine barracks in Beirut was no terrorist, nor are the Shining Path fighters in Peru, but the Israeli agents who assassinated the P L O leader Abu Jihad in Tunis were terrorists (they hid their weapons and wore no uniforms).

Many legitimate guerrilla movements or popular insurrections have used terrorism as well as conventional acts of war, but to call the Vietcong or the Farabundo Martí Liberation Front in El Salvador or the Contras in Nicaragua terrorists implies that that is all they are.

Vice-President George Bush offered a useful definition of terrorism and 'freedom fighters' in 1988, when he was head of a task force on terrorism in the Reagan administration: 'In seeking to destroy freedom and democracy, terrorists deliberately target noncombatants for their own cynical purposes. They kill and maim defenceless men, women and children. They murder judges, newspaper reporters, elected officials, government administrators, labour leaders, policemen, priests, and others who defend the values of civilized society. Freedom fighters, in contrast, seek to adhere to international law and civilized standards of conduct. They attack military targets, not defenceless civilians. Noncombatant casualties in this context are an aberration or attributable to the fortunes of war. They are not the result of deliberate policy designed to terrorize the opposition.'

1 The Institute was set up in 1976 and is concerned with the study of terrorism. It is named after Lieutenant-Colonel Jonathan Netanyahu (Benjamin Netanyahu's brother), who was killed during the Entebbe rescue.

The term 'terrorist' is most usefully limited to organizations whose principal methods of warfare are terroristic, groups that employ chiefly bombs, murders and ambushes, and whose victims are frequently civilians. This definition most completely covers such groups as the I R A, the Armenian terrorists, the West German Red Army Fraction (R A F), the Red Brigades in Italy, *Action Directe* in France, the Japanese Red Army and the Islamic terrorists. In an earlier generation, E O K A in Cyprus and the Irgun and the Stern Gang in Palestine fitted this description. It would also include virtually all the Palestinian military organizations because their *modus operandi* is almost exclusively terroristic: they occasionally seek out military targets inside Israel, or Israeli military targets in Lebanon, but the great majority of their attacks have been on civilians.

This definition of terrorism would also exclude counter-terrorist operations, such as the Israeli raid on Tunis in 1988. It leaves to professors of ethics the question of justifying or condemning the secret war of assassination waged between Mossad, the Israeli secret service, and Palestinian terrorists in Lebanon, Cyprus and the four corners of Europe. Those who live by the bomb shall perish by the bomb: it is not possible to feel any sympathy for the Palestinian terrorists who were responsible for the Munich massacre and who were later killed by Mossad, or for the three I R A terrorists who, in the midst of their plan to place a car bomb in a public square, were shot down in Gibraltar by the British S A S. The argument is over the method of their execution. It is easier to justify the actions of the Israelis, who had no alternative, than those of the British, who could have arrested the three. But Mossad has sometimes killed the wrong man, and the car bomb that killed one of the Munich murderers in Beirut also killed six innocent passers-by.

The usual apologia for terrorism is that 'one man's terrorist is another man's freedom fighter', which is perfectly true and perfectly irrelevant: murder is not justified by sticking a different label on it. Ramsay Clark, a former attorney general of the United States, defends the I R A on the grounds that they are exactly the same as George Washington and other heroes of the American Revolution. However, Washington never set off a bomb in a restaurant, Thomas Jefferson never advocated machine-gunning a church congregation, Patrick Henry never sent his agents to plant a bomb at a memorial service. If they had, they would have been terrorists.

The 'political justification' – the claim that the end justifies the means – is a debate crucial for fighting terrorism, and it has not been resolved. American courts have refused to extradite I R A terrorists to Britain on the grounds that their actions were political. So have courts in various European countries, including the Netherlands. France gave asylum to a whole series of terrorists – those from Spain, Ireland and Italy, all the factions of the Arabs, Québécois nationalists and South Americans – and only came to change its policy when terrorists started attacking French targets. The United States was outraged in 1985 when Italy released the mastermind of the *Achille Lauro* piracy, although the Italian courts were acting exactly as their American counterparts have towards the I R A. There can be no effective international cooperation in the fight against terrorism until democratic countries admit that an attack against one is an attack on all.

There are differences between terrorist groups. Some seek out what they consider 'enemy' targets (usually military): thus E T A concentrates on murdering generals (though it has also killed many civilians). A few take great pains to avoid killing people. The Bretons, for instance, have never killed anyone (though two Bretons killed themselves with their own bomb), and the 'Free Welsh Army' disintegrated when one of its bombs killed two people by mistake; its successors in the 1980s have devoted themselves to arson, protecting Welsh culture by burning down houses belonging to people from England. Other groups, such as the I R A or the Abu Nidal group, deliberately choose civilians. They are all terrorists.

Some terrorists, wholly lacking popular support, must always operate in the shadows, though they may have fantasies of rallying the proletariat behind them. Other organizations, enjoying a certain measure of popular support, nevertheless employ only terrorist means because the forces they are fighting are too powerful. That is the case with the I R A, and the E T A in Spain, and was the case with E O K A. An invigorating debate can be carried on concerning the nature of the Turkish, Uruguayan and Argentinian terrorists of the 1970s, turning on the issue of how much real support they enjoyed, but the nub of the matter is that, by defining their methods, not their intentions, they are all to be classified as terrorists.

One of the classic arguments against terrorism was advanced by Lenin in *What Is to Be Done?*, the blueprint for the October Revolution. He insisted that revolution must come through the proletariat, not from the enthusiasm of intellectual terrorists.

The terrorists bow to the spontaneity of the passionate indignation of the intellectuals, who lack the ability or opportunity to connect the revolutionary struggle and the working-class movement into an integral whole. It is difficult indeed for those who have lost their belief, or have never believed that this is possible, to find some outlet for their indignation and revolutionary energy other than terror.

In a later attack on the Social Revolutionary party, which had adopted a policy of terror, he wrote:

In their naïvety, the Social Revolutionaries do not realize that their predilection for terrorism is causally most intimately linked with the fact that, from the very outset, they have always kept and still keep aloof from the working-class movement.

This argument remains as pertinent today as it was 90 years ago, and clearly applies to the romantic European and Latin American terrorists who dream of rousing the working classes by some dramatic act of violence, but who really have no connection whatever with genuine working-class aspirations.

Trotsky developed the case against terrorism, which he applied in a Communist context but which is just as true for nationalist or religious terrorism:

The capitalist state does not base itself on government ministers and cannot be eliminated with them. The classes it serves will always find new people; the mechanism remains intact and continues to function . . . In our eyes, individual terror is inadmissible precisely because it *belittles the role of the masses in their own consciousness*, reconciles them to their powerlessness, and turns their eyes and hopes towards a great avenger and liberator who some day will come and accomplish his mission.

Communist parties have remained opposed to terrorism, in theory, ever since. The Nicaraguan revolutionaries split on the issue when the doctrinaire Communists, led by Tomás Borge, broke away from Edén Pastora and the Ortega brothers in protest against their policy of spectacular terrorist attacks on the Somoza regime.

Practice and theory, however, are different matters. There is no doubt that terrorists all over the world obtained their weapons and explosives from the Soviet bloc, directly or indirectly (the Shining Path being one of the few exceptions). For 20 years the USSR made no effort to distinguish between legitimate 'wars of national liberation' and terrorism. It provided every service possible for the PLO, which it considered the legitimate representative of the Palestinians, without asking itself, or without caring, what the organization did with its weapons and training. The PLO, in turn, financed by the Arab oil states, gave every assistance to Arab terrorists (PFLP, Black September) and to other terrorist groups including the Armenians, the IRA and the Red Army Fraction (RAF) in West Germany. (The Entebbe and Mogadishu hijackings were joint Palestinian–RAF operations.) Similarly, the USSR and its allies gave Libya everything it asked (and paid) for, turning a blind eye to the uses Khadafy found for Czech explosives or Soviet weapons.

There are three broad categories of independent terrorist movements in the world today: those inspired by political fervour, usually Communist but including some Fascist movements; those inspired by nationalism or ethnic grievances; and those inspired by Islam. A fourth category is terrorism directed by governments such as Iran, Syria or Libya.

The political movements operating in Western industrialized societies are the weakest. They are invariably small bands of fanatics, and once they start a terrorist campaign, they are the subject of relentless police pursuit. Because they have no popular support, they do not recover when their members are arrested: they cannot recruit replacements as nationalist movements can, and by definition, they are not guerrillas (though they call themselves 'urban guerrillas'). They cannot swim like a fish in water, in Mao Tse-tung's famous analogy, because if they were made known to the 'water' (the general population), they would immediately be arrested. The West German police have dismantled two generations of terrorist organizations (the group known as the Baader–Meinhof gang, and the RAF), the Italians have practically wiped out the Red Brigades and the French have all but eliminated *Action Directe*. Only Greece has had no success in breaking up the November 17 group.

These organizations are correctly defined as 'international terrorists' because they cooperate with each other and preach a Europe-wide campaign against 'Nato imperialism'. They have received help and finance from Arab terrorists, who act on the principle that anything that destabilizes Europe is to be encouraged. At one remove, therefore, they were supported by the Soviet Union, which was a fine example of modern cynicism: the RAF and the rest all despised the Soviets for their lack of revolutionary fervour.

It is the collaboration between these groups (RAF, *Action Directe*, Red Brigades) that most nearly meets the conspiracy theorists' notion of a great, Communist-led plot to overthrow democracy with the bomb and the bullet. At its widest, the theory ties in every movement from Japan to Argentina, by way of the P L O, Khadafy and Cuba. Like most other conspiracy theories, however, this one collapses under its own weight. There is collaboration, but there is no conspiracy. Meanwhile, the complete failure of the Euro-terrorists is a striking confirmation of Lenin's and Trotsky's analyses.

Communist-inspired movements have enjoyed more success in the Third World. The more important recent ones were in the Philippines, El Salvador and Peru (*see* individual country sections). Apart from those three, nationalist terrorist movements are much more serious than purely 'political' ones, and the most serious of all, for the rest of the world, was the one that arose among the Palestinian diaspora. It has a bottomless pool of resentment against Israel and its Western allies, an over-abundance of eager recruits graduating every year from the camps and the small-time militias of Lebanon, and, at least until the Gulf War in 1991, all the money it needed from the oil states.

Outside powers – Syria, Iran, Libya and Iraq – all availed themselves of the Palestinian terrorist network for their own purposes, and other terrorists have sought training and weapons from and sanctuary with the Palestinians. The Soviet bloc was heavily implicated in at least the arming and training of the Palestinians while rather ostentatiously keeping its distance from Middle Eastern violence. Its involvement was at least as much economic as political: the Czech and East German arms industries were important foreign exchange earners (as, of course, are those of the Americans, British and French) and their major markets were the Arabs. Western Europe bought oil from Libya, and paid in dollars. The dollars were then used to prop up the decaying economies of Eastern Europe by purchasing weapons that were used against the governments of Western Europe. The collapse of the Communist governments in Eastern Europe and the Soviet Union, and the retreat of Communism in the Soviet Union itself may eventually impinge upon Western European Communist terrorists. Even the most obdurate revolutionary must wonder if there is any hope of creating a Marxist utopia in the West when the comrades in the East have abandoned the effort.

The Palestinians, unlike the Euro-terrorists, have not directed sustained, systematic campaigns against Western governments. They have mounted spectacular operations against American or European targets but that is all. Their obsession is fighting Israel – and each other. One terrorist group that put bombs on aircraft was suppressed and its leader, Abu Mahmoud, was executed by Al-Fatah. Abu Nidal and the P L O wage a constant war of assassination, and this incessant fratricide is the clue to Palestinian, and other nationalist, terrorism. Whatever their inclinations towards generalized violence elsewhere, their effectiveness is largely limited to their own concerns. Similarly, the I R A and E T A may exchange weapons or advice, but neither needs the other to mount the operations that really concern it.

Islamic terrorism has become the greatest threat to world security in the 1990s. It has engulfed Algeria (*see* p. 6) and is a continuing threat to Egypt (*see below*), and has spread across the globe, most violently in the United States, Argentina and central America, and in Europe. The Algerian terrorists send their commandos to France, because that country supports the Algerian regime. Egyptian terrorists were behind the two major foreign attacks in the United States, the **561** bombing of the World Trade Center in New York in February 1993, and the plot to blow up the United Nations and other buildings there that was discovered the following year. A blind cleric, Sheikh Omar Abdul Rahman, was leader of Egyptian fundamentalists and moved to the United States, where he directed or at least inspired the two related sets of plotters.

It is usually difficult to establish the authors of particular atrocities. The Islamic Jihad, the Party of God and Hamas, all closely related if not exactly the same, are spawned by the Palestinian resistance but are inspired by the same Islamic fundamentalism that led Khomeini to victory in Iran. The P L O, by contrast, was always a political, sectarian movement. Their usual targets are Israel itself or its surrogates in south Lebanon: the suicide bombers who attacked Israel in 1995 and 1996 were martyrs sent by Hamas. But they also attack Jewish targets far from the Holy Land. The worst crime was the bombing of a Jewish community centre in Buenos Aires on 18 July 1994, which killed 96. Two days later 21 people, 12 of them Jewish, were killed in a plane bombing in Panama, and these attacks were followed by a series of bombings directed against Israeli and Jewish targets in London. Argentine police later arrested a number of military men who, they said, took part in the attack. However, at the worst, they were helping Palestinian, Lebanese or Iranian terrorists. There were strong indications that Iran had directed the whole campaign, but the matter could not be proved.

The U S state department in its annual reports describes Iran, Syria, Libya, Sudan, Iraq, North Korea and Cuba as states that promote terrorism, though it has offered no examples of their acts of terrorism since 1995. The case against Cuba was never strong: Che Guevara was a guerrilla, not a terrorist, and Cuba's inclusion in the list is another sign of America's obsession with Castro. The others all used terrorism, killing civilians to terrorize enemy countries, as a matter of government policy.

One form of terrorism – assassination – has occasionally been more successful than others because of its limited objectives, when it is intended to destroy an enemy or frustrate a government or, most crudely, to eliminate a rival. Stalin was never inhibited by Lenin's doubts on the efficacy of terrorism: he had Trotsky murdered in Mexico. Appendix III comprises a depressingly long list of public figures who have been assassinated since 1945, and includes many whose deaths were a severe loss to their countries: Mahatma Gandhi in India, Aung San in Burma, Tom Mboya in Kenya, John and Robert Kennedy in the United States, among many others. The most notorious assassination of the century was the killing of the Archduke Franz Ferdinand of Austria which precipitated World War I. It was one of the few terrorist acts that have changed the face of history.

For some conspiracy theorists, the key event in post-war terrorism was the attempted assassination of Pope John Paul II on 13 May 1981. The would-be assassin, Mehmet Ali Agça, was a member of the far-right Turkish terrorist group, the Grey Wolves, and had some connections with Bulgaria. Those two neighbouring countries had fought a subterranean terrorist war for years past, and the Bulgarians are believed to have carried out at least one assassination abroad, when an exile was stabbed in London with a poisoned umbrella.

The suggestion was that the K G B directed the Bulgarians to kill the Polish pope in order to relieve pressure on the regime in Warsaw, which was then locked in combat with Solidarity. Agça asserted that the attempt had been planned in the Bulgarian embassy in Rome and offered many details that seemed to corroborate his claim; he certainly proved his own Bulgarian connections. However, when the issue was eventually put to trial, he also claimed to be Jesus Christ. The case collapsed, but the conspiracy theorists remain convinced that Bulgaria, and therefore the U S S R, were behind the attempt. It is notable that no Western government, not even the Reagan administration, accepted the theory.

The sort of terrorism denounced by Lenin and Trotsky and by politicians of every persuasion since – the secret assault on the state – has never succeeded. Indeed, the most secretive, 'purest' terrorists such as the Red Brigades or the Armenian Secret Army have been the least successful. Their certainty that they alone have the answer to the secret of the utopia to come, and the right to decide their nations' future with the bomb and the gun, verged on dementia (and the Japanese Red Army, clearly, was altogether demented).

The United States was suddenly faced with the power of criminal obsessions in the world when two American fanatics blew up a federal office building in Oklahoma City on 19 April 1995, killing 169 people. There have been a number of other incidents of paranoid terrorism in the United States, committed by people who believed that the government was the enemy of American freedom. They are most aptly described as members of the lunatic fringe.

Terrorism became a central international preoccupation because of the co-incidence of several distinct events and developments in the late 1960s. The first was the defeat of the Arabs in the Six-Day War, which led the P L O to terrorism as its presumed only alternative. The second was the series of student revolts in Europe and the United States in 1968, which filled the heads of a number of impressionable youths with revolutionary enthusiasm: if a crowd could gather spontaneously to set fire to the Paris Bourse, what might not a properly organized revolutionary vanguard achieve? At the same time, the civil rights movement in Northern Ireland revived the dormant I R A, and the senility of the Franco regime (and then its passing) permitted the creation of E T A. The accession to power of the 'flaky barbarian' Moammar Khadafy (Ronald Reagan's apt description) in Libya in 1969 might be added to the list.

The 'spirit of '68' is a spent force in Europe, but political extremism still flourishes in Latin America and Asia, Palestinian nationalism is as vigorous and violent as ever, and there is no abatement in the various nationalist struggles. Terrorism will continue into the next century.

*National terrorist movements are discussed in the appropriate sections (Northern Ireland, Lebanon, Sri Lanka, El Salvador, etc.). The remaining groups, dealt with in the following sections, fall into various categories: political extremism in Europe and Japan; other nationalist groups (E T A in Spain, Corsican and Breton separatists in France); the forlorn hopes (the South Moluccans in Holland and the Armenians); Palestinian and Islamic terrorism. There is, inevitably, some overlapping.*

# THE EURO-TERRORISTS

## GERMANY

The Red Army Fraction (*Rote Armee Fraktion*, R A F) was born in 1968, the year of the student upheavals – but before they occurred. On 2 April, a small group of terrorists in Frankfurt set a department store alight – in protest, they said, against the consumer society. Among them were Andreas Baader (age 24) and Gudrun Esslin (age 27). A radical lawyer, Horst Mahler (age 32), defended Baader at his trial, and a radical-chic journalist, Ulrike Meinhof (age 33), wrote admiring articles about them in the magazine *Konkret*.

A few days after the fire, on 12 April, the most prominent of student radical leaders, Rudi Dutschke, was shot and severely wounded in Berlin by a deranged right-wing student. (Dutschke never recovered sufficiently, or never recovered the zeal, to harangue the crowds again; he studied at Cambridge University for a while until he was expelled by a nervous British government.) The event provoked student demonstrations all over the country, the demonstrators claiming that the shooting had been part of a Fascist plot. Extremists mounted a series of attacks in Berlin and elsewhere, aimed particularly at the Springer newspaper chain (which had ceaselessly vilified the students).

These attacks were obscured at the time by the large-scale student demonstrations, sometimes directed against the Vietnam war, sometimes against governments, that were convulsing Japan, West Germany, France, Italy, Mexico and the United States. In every one of those countries, the riots echoed down the years. In the short term, General de Gaulle's authority in France was fatally weakened, Lyndon Johnson abandoned the presidency (and Richard Nixon was elected to succeed him), the massacre at the Mexico Olympics in 1968 traumatized the government, and the troubles in Japan, West Germany and Italy appalled their respectable citizens. But in the longer term, in Europe at least, the chief result of the upheavals was the coalescing of various radical groups into violent revolutionary movements that soon developed into full-scale terrorism.

The Frankfurt arsonists were sentenced to three years' imprisonment, but jumped bail. They went underground, and took part in the new rebels' first bombing campaign in the winter of 1969. The targets were judicial offices, judges, the El Al office in Berlin, a US officers' club and an American office block in Berlin, and a lawyers' ball.

Baader was rearrested in Berlin on 4 April 1970. He persuaded the prison authorities to allow him to conduct research at the Social Affairs Institute, and on 14 May, four terrorists – Meinhof and Mahler (who had by then given up journalism and the law in favour of revolutionary terrorism) and two other comrades – shot their way into the building, wounding three people, and rescued him. This episode marked the beginning of the Baader–Meinhof gang. This was before the days of petro-terrorism, and they started robbing banks to raise the necessary funds: on 29 September 1970, three Berlin banks were robbed simultaneously, bringing a combined haul of DM220,000. At least 12 people were involved in the operation.

In the next couple of years the RAF stole over DM1.5 million, and was therefore able to run an efficient and deadly terrorist organization. Guns and explosives were bought, and members of the gang studied the art of bomb-making. A policeman was killed in one of the robberies. Meinhof stated the gang's political philosophy in an interview: 'We say the person in uniform is a pig – that is, not a human being – and thus we have to settle the matter with him. It is wrong to talk to these people at all, and shooting is taken for granted.' One of their slogans was 'Don't argue, destroy.'

The RAF went over to revolutionary terrorism in 1972, even though by then a dozen of its members had been arrested, including Mahler. There were 15 bomb attacks, in a series that began, on 11 May 1972, with an attack on the US army headquarters in Frankfurt that killed one officer; 38 people were also injured in the bombing of the Springer headquarters in Hamburg. In addition, the RAF began to assassinate individuals, choosing officials whose attitudes were deemed hostile to the 'people's interests'.

The police estimated that there were 17 full-time members of the gang in 1970, and at least 60 people who helped the logistical side of the RAF's campaign, by holding apartments ('safe-houses') available or running errands. The RAF established contact with similar groups in other countries, notably France and the Netherlands. The active members were almost all bourgeois, including several lawyers and two journalists, as were most of their supporters and accomplices. Mahler enunciated the theory that the best leaders of the proletariat were not to be found among workers themselves; they could stand aside and determine the workers' needs objectively, with due appreciation for the modern class struggle. The revolutionaries were occasionally surprised at the workers' reactions to their solicitude.

The RAF claimed to be disgusted at the crass materialism of the modern West German state. Most of them had been born during or immediately after the war (but not Ulrike Meinhof, who was born in 1934) and, like all Germans, had suffered the privations of the bleak post-war years. As they came to adulthood in the 1960s, however, the West German economic miracle swung into high gear. The older generation that had survived the war and post-war austerity had rebuilt Germany with industry, dedication and self-sacrifice, and were not in the least ashamed of their prosperity. They had earned it the hard way and were astonished and offended by the generation of 1968 when they repudiated it all. They were even more shocked that so many young people rejected 'bourgeois democracy': after all it had been through, the West German establishment was **565** not prepared to have its democratic institutions attacked. Members of the R A F were aptly called 'Hitler's children'. Older Germans remembered the early 1930s, and were afraid of the new anarchists, and therefore repressed them far more vigorously than the French or the Italians did their own youthful terrorists.

The prophet of the West German terrorists was Herbert Marcuse, a German Hegelian who had sensibly moved to California in the 1930s. In a post-war essay, 'Repressive Tolerance', he claimed that 'suppressed and overpowered minorities' had the 'natural right' to resort to violence to achieve liberation. The Baader–Meinhof terrorists claimed that they were part of the same struggle as the Vietnamese, or blacks or Indians in the United States, or Palestinians, or any other oppressed minority. They claimed to be 'urban guerrillas', the comrades of Che Guevara and Mao Tse-tung. Students in West Germany (and also in Britain) marched through the streets waving Mao's Little Red Book and chanting 'Ho, Ho, Ho Chi Minh' and other equally profound philosophical statements.

There were large numbers of women in the R A F, who added the doctrines of women's liberation to their other political teachings. They felt that German society underestimated women. Dr Hans Josef Horchem, a distinguished West German expert on political extremism, wrote of them (in *Contemporary Terrorism,* 1974):

The influence of women accounts for the lack of realism in the overall revolutionary concept, yet they are responsible for day-to-day actions of a practical nature, such as renting a flat under an assumed name and gathering and analysing information.

Dr Horchem would probably expect them also to do the laundry.

The R A F showed its enthusiasm for Third World causes by demonstrating against the shah and against Moïse Tshombe (who had tried to set up an independent state with white support in Katanga, in southern Congo, in the early 1960s). Those statesmen were doubtless suitably impressed, but the R A F found these causes insufficient to rally the West German proletariat. The R A F studied the techniques of the Tupamaros terrorists in Uruguay and a handbook on 'urban guerrilla warfare' by the Brazilian terrorist Carlos Marighella, who called his book the 'mini-manual for revolutionaries'. It was published in West Germany under the title *Destroy the Islands of Wealth in the Third World.*

The Baader–Meinhof gang chose the name 'Red Army' in emulation of the Japanese Red Army, which first revealed itself by hijacking a J A L plane to North Korea in 1970. They called themselves the Red Army '*Fraktion*', implying that they were a part of a wider, international movement. One of their first manifestos demanded: 'Does any pig truly believe we would talk about the development of class conflicts, or reorganization of the proletariat, without simultaneously arming ourselves?' In 1971, they published *The Urban Guerrilla Concept,* written by Mahler. This is a statement of their objectives and justifications: it claims that the R A F is Marxist–Leninist, calls on the student radicals of 1968 to rally to their cause. 'We maintain that without revolutionary initiative, without practical revolutionary intervention (this is our own concept) of the *avant-garde*, without the concrete anti-imperialist campaign, there can be no unifying process.' It says further: 'The class analysis, which we need, cannot be made without revolutionary practice, without revolutionary initiative.' It would be hard to find a better example of the mush-brained, egocentric and élitist nonsense that Lenin and Trotsky had denounced 60 or 70 years earlier. Their other theoretical works had such titles as *Close the Loopholes of the Revolutionary Theory* and, finally, *Red Book 29: R A F Collective – On the Armed Campaign in Western Europe,* also by Mahler.

As R A F terrorists were arrested, the lawyers who were members or sympathizers set up 'Red Help', which became the public face of the R A F, publishing R A F statements that the defence lawyers were able to smuggle out of prison. By the summer of 1972, all but one of the core members of the R A F were in jail, and for a while, they found propaganda easier to achieve and more effective than when they had been on the run.

In the first decade of the R A F campaign in West Germany, 31 people were killed, including nine police, four prosecutors and three diplomats; there were also 25 bombings and 30 bank robberies. Evidently, it was not nearly so serious a business as the I R A in Northern Ireland, but the West Germans over-reacted in a manner that delighted the terrorists: in one anti-terrorist operation in Frankfurt in 1972, the streets were filled with troops, armoured cars, searchlights and enough firepower to blow away half the city. Special legislation was passed to restrict the rights of defence lawyers (because many R A F lawyers had been helping terrorism) and limiting other constitutional freedoms.

It seemed, briefly, to more impressionable observers, that West Germany was about to renounce its hard-earned democracy and revert to the practices of the 1930s. The incompetence of the Bavarian police during the Munich Olympics affair in 1972, which led to the deaths of the Israeli athletes, was another trauma.

However, the police did succeed. They arrested most of the Baader–Meinhof gang, and the first wave of terrorism subsided. Then in February 1975, surviving terrorists kidnapped the leader of the Christian Democratic party in West Berlin, Peter Lorenz. The socialist government capitulated to the terrorists' demands and released five R A F prisoners in exchange for Lorenz, and paid them a ransom of DM20,000.

West German terrorists were by then playing prominent roles in other dramas. On 24 April 1975, six members of the R A F seized the West German embassy in Stockholm, demanding the release of 26 Baader–Meinhof prisoners (including all the leaders). They killed two diplomats (holding one of them up in a window so that the murder would be recorded on television), but their plans went awry. Their explosives expert proved incompetent. He had packed the top floor of the building with dynamite – and it went off with the terrorists inside. One of them was killed, and the 'expert' died of wounds; the four others were briskly extradited to West Germany.

One of the terrorists released in Berlin after the Lorenz kidnapping, Gabriele Kröcher-Tiedemann, was among those who took part in the raid on the O P E C meeting in Vienna in December 1975, led by Carlos (*see* Arab terrorism). She killed two of the three men who were murdered, including an elderly Austrian security guard. 'Are you a policeman?' she asked him. When he admitted it, she shoved him into an elevator, shot him dead, and pushed the down button.

There were also two West German terrorists among the Palestinians who hijacked the Air France jet to Entebbe in June 1976 (*see* Uganda, p. 113). They were both killed in the Israeli rescue.

In May 1976, Ulrike Meinhof hanged herself in her jail cell. A year later, the chief prosecutor of the Federal Republic, Siegfried Buback, was shot in Karlsruhe, in revenge for Meinhof's suicide. Then began the most sanguinary period of the Baader–Meinhof saga – although all the gang's founders were by then in jail. A particularly shocking crime was the murder of a banker, Juergen Ponto. His murderers had been admitted to his house by his god-daughter, Susanne Albrecht, who had joined the R A F.

On 9 September 1977, Hans-Martin Schleyer, a prominent businessman, was kidnapped in Cologne and his three bodyguards killed. A series of letters from his captors, posted in Paris over the next 45 days, demanded that 11 Baader–Meinhof prisoners be released, each of them given $50,000 and flown to a country of his or her choice. The government refused the deal, and Schleyer was murdered. His body was discovered on 19 October, in Mulhouse, just over the border in France.

On 13 October, while Schleyer was still alive and in captivity, a band of Palestinians seized a Lufthansa plane, and, after careening around the Middle East looking for an airport that would take them in, landed in Mogadishu in Somalia. They, too, demanded the release of the Baader–Meinhof terrorists. The West German anti-terrorist force G S G-9, accompanied by two members of the British S A S, stormed the plane and killed three of the terrorists.

On 20 October, the day after Schleyer's body was found, three of the surviving Baader–Meinhof leaders, Andreas Baader himself, Gudrun Esslin and Jan-Carl Raspe, killed themselves in their cells in Stammheim jail, having lost hope after the failure of the Schleyer and Mogadishu attempts to rescue them. Their supporters claimed that they had been murdered by their jailers, but the police were able to prove that it had been a mass suicide.

That was, abruptly, the end of the Baader–Meinhof gang. It took several years for the R A F and its off-shoot the June 2 Movement to reconstitute itself and resume the fight.

A few survivors picked up the threads and began to rebuild the organization, and to move abroad: cells were set up in the Netherlands, Belgium and France. The first 'operation' of the new R A F was an attempt to assassinate the Nato commander, General Alexander Haig (later US secretary of state), near Brussels in June 1979. It was a sign that the second generation intended to be more 'international' than its predecessor, who had concentrated on purely West German targets. In May 1980, Paris police raided an apartment used by the West German terrorists at 4 rue Flatters, where they discovered large quantities of weapons, ammunition, false papers and money. They picked up two women, old R A F hands, and three more arrived the next day and walked into the arms of the police. All five were shipped back to West Germany.

In August 1981, the new R A F bombed the U S A F base at Ramstein and, in

September, attempted to kill the commanding officer of the US Army in West

Germany, General Frederick Kroesen, using a Soviet rocket-propelled grenade (RPG). This was a new departure. RPGs (the Soviet version is the S-7) are favourite weapons of all the militias of Lebanon and of Irish terrorists, but this was the first to be used by the Euro-terrorists. These two attacks coincided with the big pacifist campaign against the installation of American cruise and Pershing missiles in Europe, and were apparently attempts by the RAF to muscle in on the endeavour. Their friends in Italy responded similarly, kidnapping an American general, James Dozier, in December 1981.

Several of the new RAF leaders were arrested in October 1982. Some mushroom hunters in a wood near Frankfurt noticed suspicious diggings and reported to the police. Investigators concluded that they had stumbled across an RAF arms cache. They set up an ambush and, a week later, arrested two RAF women terrorists, Brigitte Mohnhaupt and Adelheid Schultz, who had come to visit the depot. It turned out to contain great quantities of documents, as well as weapons and ammunition. The papers, once they were decoded, led to a further 14 arms dumps, and enabled the police to set a trap for Christian Klar, the RAF's senior terrorist.

The RAF survived these defeats, and by 1985, according to the federal police, the new RAF had about 22 hard-core members (13 of whom were women, who now played a dominant role in the organization), 200 part-time militants and up to 2000 supporters ready to help. Some of the leaders were underground in West Germany, others lived in exile – for example, Susanne Albrecht, who had been involved in the murder of her godfather, lived in Baghdad. From their jail cells, Christian Klar and 29 others tried to assert control and influence by staging a hunger strike.

In the early 1980s, West German terrorism divided into several different tendencies. First of all, the hard-line RAF, in alliance with similar groups abroad, pursued its attacks on Nato and related targets. A separate organization of women terrorists, Red Zora, also played a part in some of these actions, but they were more concerned with social issues. They worried about the expansion of the Frankfurt airport, for instance, and in 1981 assassinated Heinz Karry, the local minister responsible for it; Zora then informed the world that his death had been an accident. Another group, the Revolutionary Cells (*Revolutionare Zellen*, RZ), concentrated on industrial disputes: in 1984, it bombed the miners' union headquarters in the Ruhr as a protest against the export of West German coal to Britain during the British miners' strike. These worthy objectives allowed the mushier representatives of the West German left, notably the Greens, to express their sympathy for the terrorists, and then to extend it to their imprisoned comrades. It was all very encouraging for the RAF, who could claim that they were at last making political progress. Right-wingers claimed that there was an overlap in the membership of the RZ and Red Zora with the Greens.

In all, the RZ and Red Zora carried out over 600 bombings in 1982, mostly aimed at firms thought guilty of 'consumerism'. The police suspected that there were five 'cells', each about 20 strong. The most extreme of these people were probably also members of the RAF, and new recruits to the RAF graduated from the RZ and Zora.

In 1985 and 1986, a new generation of RAF terrorists carried out a series of murders of German industrialists and diplomats, in conjunction with similar attacks mounted in France by *Action Directe* and by the Red Brigades in Italy (*see below*, France, p. 571). The victims included Ernst Zimmerman, managing director of an arms company, Motoren und Turbinen of Munich, murdered in February 1985, Heinz Beckurts, an executive of the Siemens company (his driver was also killed), in July 1986, and Gerold von Braunmuehl, a senior diplomat, in October 1986. In August 1985, a joint R A F–*Action Directe* operation planted a bomb in the US Rhine-Main air force base near Frankfurt, killing two and wounding 16. The terrorists had got onto the base by murdering an American serviceman and stealing his identity card. The R A F also bombed 'La Belle Disco' in West Berlin, with Arab assistance, in April 1986. It was the haunt of American servicemen, one of whom was killed, together with a Turkish woman. This episode provoked the Americans to bomb Tripoli in an attempt to kill or at least intimidate Colonel Khadafy.

On 11 January 1988, German police arrested the woman whom they suspected of planting the bomb in the La Belle Disco in Berlin in April 1986. The woman, Christine Endrigkeit, was picked up in a squalid apartment in Lübeck, on the Baltic. It was an empty and cheerless place: she had slept on the floor and hung her clothes on nails. She was caught a few days after police had issued photographs and offered a reward.

However, the prosecutors had difficulty preparing their case against her, despite the fact that her name and phone number had been found in the phone book of Mansour Hazi, a Palestinian who was sentenced to 14 years' imprisonment for bombing the Arab–German Friendship Society in West Berlin a week before the disco bombing. Hazi was also suspected of ordering the disco bombing. His brother, Nezar Hindawi, is serving a 45-year term in England for giving his pregnant Irish girlfriend a suitcase containing a bomb to take on an El Al flight to Israel.

German police believed that they had broken up the R A F as a centrally-directed organization. Their continuing problem was that remaining terrorists or would-be terrorists now form autonomous groups (*Autonomen*) which are difficult to penetrate. They are modelled on Italian organizations of the same name. On 30 November 1989, one such group assassinated one of the most prominent bankers in Germany, Alfred Herrhausen, chairman of the Deutsche Bank, the largest in the country. He was killed by a remote-controlled bomb attached to a bicycle, which was detonated as his car passed. His chauffeur was seriously injured. A week later, police in Schleswig-Holstein arrested a man and a woman whom they accused of being members of the R A F, and charged them with playing a part in the series of murders in 1985–6, including the deaths of Zimmerman, Beckurts, and Gerold von Braunmuehl.

German police had dismantled three generations of the R A F, but the beast survived. It even continued after the collapse of East Germany in 1989 and the Soviet Union in 1991. In the late 1980s, police succeeded at last in infiltrating an informer into the R A F. The coup was so important that they deliberately ignored his warning of a plot to bomb a newly-built prison in Darmstadt in March 1993: the attack caused $100 million in damage. In June, the informer met two members of the R A F in a railway station in Bad Kleinen and a police commando tried to arrest the three.

A woman terrorist, Birgit Hogfeld, was captured but a comrade, Wolfgang Grams, made a bolt for it. He killed a policeman and wounded another in the shoot-out, was captured and then shot in the head as he lay on the ground. The informant's role was exposed – and the minister of the interior and chief prosecutor were both fired for their part in the fiasco.

In the same period, some R A F terrorists who had been in jail since the early 1970s were released on parole. The most prominent was Irmgard Moeller, a founding member of the Baader–Meinhof gang: she, too, had attempted suicide in Stammheim jail in 1977 but was saved by the jailers. She had taken part in an attack on a U S base at Heidelberg on 24 May 1972, in which three soldiers were killed, and was arrested and convicted. She was released in December 1994, after 22 years in jail, admitting to remorse for her crime.

Other R A F terrorists have also been released, including the two survivors of the attack on the Stockholm embassy in 1975, but some long-term fugitives have been caught and sentenced to long terms. Five were arrested in East Germany after the fall of the Berlin wall, and jailed. One, Sieglinde Hofmann, had taken part in the kidnapping of Hanns-Martin Schleyer in 1977 and the attempt on General Alexander Haig; another, extradited from Norway, was a Lebanese woman, the last survivor of the four terrorists who had hijacked the Lufthansa jet to Mogadishu in 1977. Monika Haas was accused of taking part in both the hijacking and the Schleyer murder, and Andrea Hausler, arrested in Greece and extradited to Germany in 1997, had allegedly taken part in the La Belle disco bombing in 1986.

## FRANCE

France has suffered from four of the classic forms of modern terrorism since World War II – nationalist, far left, far right and foreign. It also survived a military *coup d'état* in 1958, which brought General de Gaulle to power, and several further attempted coups. Of the terrorist campaigns, only the *Organisation de l'armée secrète* (O A S) in 1961–2, a group of military dissidents and Algerian settlers who wanted to overthrow De Gaulle and preserve French Algeria, ever presented a serious threat to the state. They nearly killed De Gaulle on two occasions and mounted a major bombing campaign in Paris, which was turned into an armed camp to defeat them.

Earlier, there had been a sanguinary secret war between Algerian factions, and a spate of terrorist incidents connected with the Algerian independence struggle. Compared with the dramatic days of 1958–62, the events of the 1980s are insignificant. The *crise de régime* of 1968 was precipitated by a student uprising and a general strike, and subsided as quickly as it arose.

The nationalist agitations have been the work of Corsican and Breton separatists (*see* Nationalist terrorism, pp. 585–93). A bombing-and-murder campaign by left-wing terrorists, who were closely associated with similar groups in West Germany, Italy and Spain, culminated in the mid-1980s with *Action Directe,* which was eliminated or at least severely hampered when its leaders were arrested in 1987 and 1988 (*see below*).

France has also been the chosen battleground of foreign terrorists and counter-terrorists: Arabs and Israelis have fought their wars of assassination in Paris;

Arab factions have attacked each other; Armenians have attacked Turks; the IRA has attacked British targets; and pro- and anti-Khomeini Iranians have settled their accounts on French soil. These battles have often caused French casualties, and in 1986–7 the Armenians, the Syrian and Iranian secret services and an obscure group of Lebanese Christian terrorists together launched a concerted attack on the government (*see* Arab terrorism, pp. 594–619). The campaign coincided with *Action Directe*'s most serious onslaught (a coincidence that can hardly have been accidental), and for a year, Paris was a battleground, temporarily resembling Belfast. However, the republic was never in any danger, as it had been in 1961, and competent police work soon brought the situation under control.

For many years, France was more tolerant of foreign terrorists than other countries, perhaps remembering that the word 'terror' was first applied in its modern context by Robespierre and St Just. Furthermore, the French took seriously their reputation as a *terre d'asile* ('land of refuge'). Americans and Israelis frequently reproached France for dealing with terrorists (Israel less so after it emptied its prisons to get three PoWs back from the PLO). There were several notable occasions when the French allowed prominent Arab terrorists to leave the country, but after the Paris bombings and agreements reached in various Western summits, French anti-terrorist police have come to collaborate closely with their foreign colleagues.

France is also the only Western country caught red-handed recently in an act of state-sponsored terrorism: the sinking of the *Rainbow Warrior* in Auckland harbour, New Zealand, in 1985 by French agents.

## ACTION DIRECTE

In the late 1970s, a number of West German terrorists living in France took the lead in reviving the French terrorist movement, *Action Directe*. AD was founded in 1979 in a merger of other groups. One of these antecedents, which called itself the *Noyaux armés pour l'autonomie populaire* (NAPAP), murdered the Bolivian ambassador in Paris, alleging that he had been involved in the defeat and death of Che Guevara. The Bolivian general who had hunted down Guevara and killed him, was sent to Hamburg as consul, where he, too, was shot in 1971. NAPAP was also responsible for the killing of a night-watchman at the Renault factory in Paris in 1977.

*Action Directe* carried out a number of minor terrorist attacks in its early years. Its leaders were Jean-Marc Rouillan, his girlfriend Nathalie Ménigon, and Régis Schleicher. The first two were arrested in 1981 in a trap set for them in an apartment in the rue Pergolèse. Shortly afterwards, the new Socialist government of François Mitterrand released members of the Corsican separatist movement – and at the same time freed Rouillan and 25 other members of AD. Ménigon was not released immediately because she had been charged with resisting arrest by shooting at a policeman, shouting: '*Je suis Action Directe!*' (She missed.) She then went on a hunger strike to prove that she deserved liberty and, after three weeks, won her freedom. The movement was not considered of any great importance. It was an error.

AD spent the next two years filling its coffers with the proceeds of a number of bank robberies. In the summer of 1982, it resumed 'political' action in a series of attacks on 'international' targets – meaning American and Jewish ones. However, the two worst anti-Jewish atrocities were probably the work of Arab terrorists. The first was the attack on the synagogue in the rue Copernic in Passy on 3 October 1980, which killed four people. A group calling itself European National Fascists claimed responsibility, but police were sceptical. It is much more likely that it had been the work of Abu Mohammed's Palestinian terrorist group, the P F L P-Special Command (*see* Arab terrorism). The second occurred shortly after the Israeli invasion of Lebanon: an attack on Chez Jo Goldenberg, a Jewish restaurant on the rue des Rosiers in the old Jewish quarter in the Marais, on 9 August 1982, which killed six people. An anonymous caller to a news agency claimed the credit for the restaurant attack for A D. French police were unconvinced, but did discover proof of links between A D and the Abu Nidal gang (*see* Arab terrorism, pp. 594–619) and the A S A L A (*see* Forlorn hopes, pp. 620–26). The bombing was probably the work of Abu Nidal, possibly aided by A D.

These new A D attacks coincided with a wave of Middle Eastern terrorism and prompted the Mitterrand government to order an all-out war on it. In May 1983, A D killed two Paris policemen in a shoot-out in the avenue Trudaine. The two victims had stopped three people, one of whom was carrying a heavy bag of the sort used by gangsters to transport drugs; two other A D terrorists, including Schleicher, had then stepped forward and shot them. All five hijacked a car to escape. Two of the five were Italians and one was Arab, Mohand Hamami.

In June 1984, the new R A F and A D sent delegates to a conference of 'anti-Nato' terrorist groups in Lisbon. There they cemented an alliance with comrades from Belgium, Portugal and Italy and named it the 'Political-Military Front'. That same month, Belgian terrorists calling themselves the Fighting Communist Cells (*Cellules Communistes Combattantes*, C C C) raided a quarry near Brussels and stole nearly a ton of explosives. Over the next few months, bombs from Belgium turned up in numerous places, including the office of the Western European Union (a parliamentary group) in Paris, and a Nato officers' school in the German Alps. Fortunately, those two bombs failed to explode.

The signal for the new campaign was a hunger strike declared by 30 R A F old-timers in West German prisons, including Christian Klar, who thought they would emulate Bobby Sands and other I R A terrorists who had starved themselves to death in a Belfast jail, and thus revived the I R A during a period of difficulty. The German hunger strike lasted several weeks, but the government refused to meet any of the strikers' demands and, lacking Irish fanaticism, they all eventually capitulated. The struggle would have to be carried on outside the prison. In April Klar, Mohnhaupt, Schultz and another terrorist were sentenced to life imprisonment for the murders of Jurgen Ponto and Hans-Martin Schleyer and his four bodyguards in 1977, and the attempted assassination of Gen. Frederick Kroesen in 1981.

The terrorist international, directed by the West Germans, aimed at targets all over Europe. Executives of firms involved in defence industries were to be assassinated, and computer companies and firms connected with nuclear energy were also to be attacked. American installations in West Germany and Nato bases in Belgium were prime targets. The R A F and A D issued a long proclamation, announcing the establishment of a 'politico-military network' of 'West European revolutionaries'. They claimed to be acting on behalf of the European proletariat and Third World people who were being crushed and exploited by Western imperialism and neocolonialism.

In 1984, in conjunction with the R A F and other Euro-terrorists (*see above*), A D launched a general offensive against Nato targets. It attacked the Panhard company (which builds tanks and armoured cars); the Atlantic Institute of International Affairs in Paris; the Ministry of Industry; the headquarters of the European Space Agency in Paris; the Western European Union (WEU); Messier–Hispano–Bugatti (another defence contractor); Dassault; the R P R (Gaullist) party headquarters; and the Elf-Aquitaine oil company. Régis Schleicher was arrested in Lyons in March but the campaign proceeded without him.

In 1985, the terrorists moved on to murder. On 25 January, General René Audran, director of French arms sales, was shot as he parked his car outside his house. A few days later, the R A F assassinated Ernst Zimmerman, a German industrialist whose firm made jet engines for fighters. The Euro-terrorists' campaign was now moving into high gear. In June, an A D commando attacked General Henri Blandin, a senior defence official, but he was saved by his chauffeur. Blandin's car was waiting at a traffic light when the driver saw in his rear-view mirror a gunman running towards him. The chauffeur took off, zig-zagging, while the gunman opened fire on the car, and missed.

In May 1986, A D attacked the Interpol headquarters in Paris with guns and explosives, wounding one man. On 6 July, they bombed the Thomson and Air Liquide chemical companies, and, on the 9th, blew up the annexe to the police headquarters in Paris, on the corner of the quai de Gèsvres and the rue St Martin, killing one policeman and wounding 22. That was also the summer of the F A R L and Iranian attacks in Paris (*see* Arab terrorism). It was evident, at the very least, that the various terrorists were emulating each other, if not actually collaborating.

On 17 November 1986, Nathalie Ménigon and Joëlle Aubron killed Georges Besse, chairman of Renault, outside his apartment in the boulevard Edgar-Quinet. His driver had just dropped him off and he was groping for his keys when the two women, who had been waiting for him, ran up to him. Ménigon shot him first, in the head. Then Aubron pumped two more bullets into him as he lay on the ground. Ménigon fired a last shot into him, point blank. Then they ran off towards the boulevard Raspail. In a communiqué issued three months later, A D announced that, 'In eliminating Besse the Brute, the Pierre Overney commando has struck at the very heart of the strongest contradiction in the general consensus for pacification and exploitation.' They also stated, 'Georges Besse was only an element determined by his function.' He 'incarnated the dominant place of the public industrial sector in the imperialist strategy of industrial and technological concentration'. Pierre Overney was a young Maoist who was killed outside a Renault factory in February 1972, while handing out tracts. His murderer, a Renault security guard, was sentenced to four years' gaol and was murdered in March 1977, by the Armed Group for the People's Autonomy (N A P A P).

**574**    In December 1986, Régis Schleicher and several others went on trial for the avenue Trudaine killings and other acts of terrorism. He announced from the dock that his friends would wreak vengeance on the court, and several jurors asked to be excused. The trial had to be postponed because of the blatant intimidation. The next day, 15 December, A D tried to kill a former Justice Minister, Alain Peyrefitte, with a car bomb. They killed his driver. Schleicher was tried in June 1987, before a panel of seven judges. He was convicted of murder and sentenced to life imprisonment.

The police were hot on the trail. On 28 March 1986 in Lyons, they arrested one of A D's founders, André Olivier, with two others in a car filled with guns. On 24 September, they arrested nine suspects, including four Lebanese and four French leftists. The next day, a member of A D, Frédéric Oriach, tried to give a press conference in the Luxembourg Gardens, in Paris; as he was introducing himself to the cameras, he was arrested by plainclothes policemen.

On 21 February 1987, the police dealt a body blow to *Action Directe*: they raided an isolated farm at Vitry-aux-Loges (Loiret), 19 miles (30 km) east of Orléans, and arrested four of the five surviving leaders of A D. Nathalie Ménigon and Jean-Marc Rouillan had been living there for three years, raising goats and hamsters. The government had offered a reward worth $180,000 and one of their friends had succumbed to temptation and betrayed them. The police had watched the house for several days, and their patience had been rewarded. On Saturday, the 21st, Joëlle Aubron and Georges Cipriani turned up for the weekend.

The fifth fugitive, Maxime Frerot, was arrested in a parking garage in Lyons on 27 November. He had been seen hanging around the place, and a couple of policemen asked to see his papers, which were obviously forged. He pulled out a gun, there was a shooting in which one policeman was wounded, and after a scuffle in which a passing taxi driver assisted the police, he was arrested.

He had been living in cellars and parking garages for several months, on the run and without hope. After his capture, the French police could legitimately claim that they had eliminated one of the nastiest bands of terrorists in France. Frerot had been A D's bomb specialist, the man who had planted the bomb in the police headquarters annexe in July 1986.

The members of *Action Directe* were put on trial early in 1988, charged with a long series of hold-ups, bombings and murders. Before the trials began, they carried out a prolonged hunger strike, in protest against the conditions of their incarceration (they were held in solitary). Rouillan, after 84 days without food, was allowed to lie on a couch during his trial, before a seven-man panel of judges. He, and all the others, were convicted. In January 1989, Ménigon and Aubron were convicted of shooting Georges Besse, while Rouillan and Cipriani were convicted as accomplices.

## GREECE

The last European political terrorist movement capable of violent action is the Greek organization November 17. It is named after a student demonstration against the colonels' regime on 17 November 1973, and since then members of the organization have murdered over 20 people, including three American diplomats, and wounded more than 100 in a series of bombing attacks.

Its targets are 'big capitalist sharks and swindlers' and the US bases in Greece. Most of its assassinations have been carried out with the same weapon – a .45 Magnum – but in July 1988, it killed the American defence attaché, Captain William Nordeen of the US Navy, with a car bomb. One of its previous victims, Richard Welch, who was shot in 1975, was the C I A station chief in Athens. His name had been published in a book by a former member of the agency, Philip Agee. Another man named by Agee was Captain George Tsantes, who was shot in November 1983.

November 17 is remarkable in its longevity and seeming immunity from prosecution. Unlike the other European terrorist movements, including the R A F, *Action Directe*, the Red Brigades and E T A, no member has ever accepted the large rewards offered by police for information, and no member was ever arrested or identified until 1992.

On 14 August 1988, a November 17 group of six men seized a local police station in Athens without firing a shot, tied up the police officers there and carried away all their weapons. It seemed to the Greeks that this presaged a new and more violent campaign. November 17 continued to be highly selective in its attacks. In September 1989, it assassinated a prominent conservative member of parliament, Pavlos Bakoyannis, in an attempt to prevent a conservative-dominated coalition taking power after elections.

Some anti-terrorist police forces see November 17's continued success as a reflection on the efficiency of the Greek police. Athens has long been a favourite base for Palestinian and other foreign terrorists (including the Armenian terrorist, Hagop Hagopian, who was killed in Athens in 1988). Security at Athens airport was notoriously slack until very recently (after vigorous American protests led to a sharp drop in the tourist trade): a major shooting took place and several hijackings and bombings originated there, including the 1985 T W A incident. Furthermore, Greece remains one of the last strongholds of the old-fashioned, Marxist, anti-American left, which has gone so conspicuously out of fashion elsewhere. Some Greek newspapers were flagrantly in the pay of the K G B, and openly championed various forms of terrorism – including November 17. There are frequent anti-American demonstrations, usually directed against the bases. Among other things, the Americans are blamed, with some justification, for the occupation of Cyprus by Turkey (*see* Cyprus, pp. 408–412).

After Andreas Papandreou retired as prime minister in 1989, his successors attacked November 17 with greater determination. Constantine Mitsotakis, who became prime minister, may have been motivated by the murder of his son-in-law by terrorists in 1989. In 1991 police arrested a suspected member of November 17. In December 1992 police arrested George Balafas and four others. He was founder of a Marxist terrorist group, the Anti-State Struggle, and was charged with murdering a prosecutor in 1985 and five policemen. He was also suspected of being a member of November 17, and it is possible that the two groups are the same. Balafas's fingerprints were found on the keys of a car used in the Welch murder.

November 17 continues its war. It now favours rockets and bombs. In 1991 a

rocket demolished the offices of American Express in Athens, and the next year there was an attempt on the minister of finance. In 1997 a prominent ship owner, Constantine Peratikos, was murdered.

## ITALY

The Italian Red Brigades followed the same cycle as the R A F in West Germany. Their members were mostly bourgeois drop-outs, prone to anarchistic violence in the name of the suffering proletariat. They were much more numerous than the R A F, and more dangerous. By the mid-1980s, Italian jails held about 2000 terrorists (including Fascists) who had been responsible for 14,000 acts of terrorism over their 15 most active years, as well as hundreds of murders. The Red Brigades' most dramatic achievement was the murder of Aldo Moro, leader of the Christian Democratic party and frequent prime minister, in March 1978. Most of the people responsible for that crime, and for other Red Brigade attacks, have now been arrested and convicted. Like the R A F and *Action Directe*, the Red Brigades are now a shadow of their former selves, thanks to successful police work.

The 'first wave' of Red Brigade terrorism grew out of the students' revolt of 1968. The early 'columns' of the brigades were financed and advised by Giangiacomo Feltrinelli, a millionaire radical-chic publisher. His most notable legitimate coup was the first publication of *Dr Zhivago*, but his chief interest in life, possibly in reaction against his family's aristocratic conservatism, was revolutionary politics. He set up a whole organization, the Proletarian Action Group (G A P) in the Milan region, with safe-houses, huge arsenals of weapons, a 'people's prison' to keep captives, and all the paraphernalia of an urban guerrilla army. On 15 March 1972, Feltrinelli killed himself while fixing dynamite to an electrical pylon in a Milan suburb: a stick of dynamite that he had been fastening to the pylon blew up in his hands.

Italians at first found it impossible to take Feltrinelli seriously, and the Italian left wing suspected that he had been the victim of an elaborate plot, despite all the safe-houses, guns and documents. At the time, Fascist terrorism was a much more serious threat to Italian democracy. The students' riots of 1968 had led to a revival of the Fascists' fortunes and, in the decade following Feltrinelli's death, they carried out a series of terrorist atrocities aimed at destabilizing the regime, apparently in the hope of provoking an army *coup d'état*, like the one in Greece in 1974.

The Fascists deliberately hit civilian targets: their first bomb, in the Piazza Fontana, Milan, in December 1969, killed 16 and wounded 90. In 1974, Fascist bombs killed seven people during a demonstration in Brescia, and on 4 August, a bomb on the Rome–Munich express killed 12. On 2 August 1980, an explosion in a restaurant in Bologna railway station killed 85 people and wounded 200: only the blowing up of aircraft has resulted in more deaths in a single incident in Europe. (The mills of Italian justice grind exceeding slow. In July 1988, almost eight years after the incident, at the end of a trial lasting a year and a half, four people were sentenced to life imprisonment for the crime, one got a 12-year term, one six years and two were convicted of slander, including Licio Gelli, a former grandmaster of the celebrated P-2 Masonic lodge.) In 1984, a bomb on the Naples–Milan express killed 15 people and wounded 100.

Left-wing terrorism never resulted in deaths on that scale, but by the mid-1970s, it had become a serious problem in Italy: there was a large number of more or less violent 'guerrilla' groups, 150 by one count. In the late 1970s, there were 2000 terrorist acts a year, including 40 murders. The 'historic founder' of the Red Brigades, Renato Curcio, began by kidnapping a Fiat official and putting him before a 'people's court'; he was convicted, and then released. The brigades soon abandoned such courtesies and began killing. Curcio was arrested in 1976. His wife, another terrorist, had been killed in a shoot-out with police the previous year.

The brigades decided to mount a spectacular operation and, on 16 March 1978, kidnapped Aldo Moro on the streets of Rome, after first killing his five body-guards. For the next 54 days, all Italy was in suspense as the brigades issued their communiqués, demanded the release of Curcio and other imprisoned terrorists, and delivered a series of letters from Moro to his family and his colleagues. The government refused to negotiate with them, and on 10 May, Moro's captors shot him.

The crime was a turning point, though not in the way the brigades had expected. Because of it, every man's hand was against them, and the Italian police suddenly discovered reserves of competence and sophistication that had been conspicuously absent before. All the political parties, from the Communists to the Christian Democrats, cooperated with the police and supported legislation to suppress terrorism. After all, they might be next. General Carlo dalla Chiesa of the *carabinieri*, the paramilitary police force, was put in charge of the investigation. He succeeded in infiltrating the brigades with informers, and arrested most of their members.

The greatest anti-terrorist successes were scored in 1982, after the brigades tried to recoup their losses, and play a part in a generalized anti-Nato offensive by all the Euro-terrorist groups. To this end, they kidnapped from his Verona apartment Brigadier General James Dozier, the senior American officer in Italy and deputy commander of logistics in Nato's southern command. Four men dressed in overalls had arrived at the apartment, claiming they were plumbers; they had then assaulted Dozier, beaten up his wife and carried him off.

The brigades then issued a communiqué denouncing Nato's threat to the world proletariat, and 'offering an outstretched hand to E T A and the I R A'. It was thought notable that the Italian terrorists should now join the R A F and *Action Directe* in attacking 'international' targets; hitherto, they had been securely local in their interests. The following month, another American officer, Colonel Charles Ray, an attaché in the American embassy in Paris, was murdered by the Middle Eastern terrorist group F A R L (*see* Arab terrorism, pp. 594–619). This may have been a coincidence, but it is entirely possible that the two groups had been at the least aware of each other's operations.

Dozier was rescued on 28 January 1982. During his captivity, the brigades had announced that he was being put on trial, and his friends had feared for his life. The Italian police had launched a major search for him, with, thanks to General dalla Chiesa, more determination and efficiency than they had shown for Aldo Moro. On 3 January, they arrested Giovanni Senzani, a former professor of criminology at the University of Florence. His arrest was one of many: the police brought in over 30 members of the Red Brigades and eight of Front Line (another terrorist group). Some of them confessed, and gave away Dozier's hiding place.

He was being kept in an apartment in Padua, tied up, barefoot, in a pup-tent pitched in the living room. Ten anti-terrorist police broke into the place in mid-morning before the terrorists had time to react. There were no casualties.

The police coup led to the arrest of another 50 *brigadistas* in the following week. One of them later took police to the Rome apartment where Moro had been concealed. It had been occupied at the time by a female terrorist, who was arrested in 1980. Two police officers were living on the floor above.

After his success against the Red Brigades, General dalla Chiesa was sent against a more formidable enemy – the Mafia. He was assassinated in Palermo, with his wife, on 3 September 1982.

Police action against the brigades reduced them to an inconsequential residuum, but though defeated, they were not destroyed. Like the R A F after the destruction of the Baader–Meinhof gang, the brigades retired to regroup and retrain. In 1985, they reappeared, calling themselves the Fighting Communist party (P C C), and murdered a noted economist, Ezio Tarantelli, who had advised the socialist government to end the sliding scale of automatic wage increases in Italian industry. The brigades calculated that they would win the allegiance of the Italian workers by murdering such a person. They were mistaken.

The brigades managed a number of acts of terrorism over the next three years, despite frequent losses. In February 1986, they attempted to assassinate Antonio da Empoli, an adviser to the prime minister. Da Empoli's bodyguard killed the assassin, a woman, who was found to be carrying a proclamation signed by the P C C. Later that year, the brigades killed Lando Conti, a former mayor of Florence, and in 1987, they held up a postal van, killing two police guards and stealing 1.2 billion lire ($870,000). On 16 April 1988, they murdered Senator Roberto Ruffilli, a Christian Democrat and a key supporter of the new prime minister, Ciricao de Mita. The killing was clearly intended to destabilize the new government.

Later that summer, on 7 September, police arrested 21 members of the P C C Brigades, 16 men and five women, including the two suspected of the Ruffilli murder. Police, acting on a series of tips from informers, carried out pre-dawn raids on four terrorist safe-houses and found explosives, pistols, rifles, shotguns and copies of communiqués that the terrorists had issued claiming the credit for previous acts of terrorism. Police said that they had evidence linking those arrested to the Tarantelli and Conti murders, and to the postal raid.

It was a bad year for terrorists: the Red Brigades greatly reduced; the last cells of the R A F and *Action Directe* dismantled; Hagop Hagopian, the leader and chief killer of the Armenian terrorists, himself assassinated. However, the Euro-terrorists, and probably the A S A L A (*see* Forlorn hopes, pp. 620–26), have not been destroyed. There is no doubt that scores of accomplices and sympathizers of the Red Brigades and the R A F remain at large, and there are more living in exile. It is entirely possible that they will revive, and stage a 'fourth wave', however unpromising the omens.

## SPAIN AND PORTUGAL

The First of October Anti-Fascist Group, G R A P O (*Grupo de Resistencia Antifascista, Primero de Octubre*), was established in 1975 as the 'military arm' of the clandestine Reconstituted Spanish Communist Party (P C E–R), which is an excommunicated splinter of the official P C E. Its most notable act of violence was bombing a Madrid café patronized by rightists in May 1979, killing nine people and wounding 40. Over the eight years of its greatest activity, 1977–84, it killed about 20 people, including several policemen, military officers, and the head of the Madrid prison service. It bombed a number of Spanish, French and American banks and other offices, kidnapped people for ransom, robbed banks and extorted money from timorous companies. G R A P O was part of the Euro-terrorist movement, with close links to the R A F, A D, Red Brigades and the Portuguese F P-25.

It has been overshadowed by E T A, and was never as formidable a force as the R A F. The U S Defense Department specialists put its membership at no more than 25: most of its leaders and members were arrested in January 1985 and it has been quiescent ever since. One of its leaders, José Manuel Sevillano, died in jail in May 1990 after a 177-day hunger strike. He had demanded that all 66 G R A P O terrorists then in jail be housed together. The authorities ignored his demand.

The Portuguese terrorist organization is called F P-25, *Forces Populares 25 de Abril*, named after the date of the 1974 Portuguese Revolution. Its spiritual leader was Lt. Col. Otelo Saraiva de Carvalho, one of the more prominent figures of the revolution who later tried to lead a Communist 'Second Revolution'. He was later sentenced to 15 years for leading F P-25. Most of the group's members were arrested in 1984 (but ten of them escaped in September 1985, helped by comrades on the outside).

F P-25 has carried out about half-a-dozen murders, robbed banks and bombed various firms accused of 'unfair' labour practices. It also attacked Nato and American installations.

## BELGIUM

The Fighting Communist Cells (*Cellules Communistes Combattantes*) was founded in 1984 by Pierre Carette. It was never a large organization, and specialized in bombing Nato facilities in Belgium, and Belgian industries it thought represented state oppression or international capitalist influence. It used explosives stolen from a quarry. Its greatest coup was to set off several bombs on a Nato fuel pipeline in December 1984, causing extensive damage.

The C C C provided aid and assistance to other Euro-terrorist groups, including the R A F and A D, whose militants took refuge in Belgium when their own countries grew too hot to hold them. The three organizations formed a united Anti-Imperialist Armed Front. The C C C, however, was less violent than the other two: only two people were killed during its 14 months' activity: two firemen who died in a blaze started by a bomb at the Belgian Employers' Federation Building in Brussels. The C C C did not last long. Belgian police arrested Carette and three other terrorists in December 1985.

# JAPAN

The Japanese Red Army (J R A) was a pathologically violent organization. In a brief moment in 1972, its demented doctrines horrified the world: half of its members were tortured and murdered by their own leaders, who were subsequently arrested. Then three survivors massacred 28 people at Lod airport in Israel. Since then, every appearance of Japanese terrorists has rung every alarm bell in every police force in the world.

There was a voluble and violent leftist movement in Japan in the 1950s and 1960s, under Communist leadership, which demonstrated against Japan's alliance with the United States. Its greatest success was to force the cancellation of a state visit by President Eisenhower in 1960, and later, it succeeded in postponing for several years the opening of a new Tokyo airport. The leftists were also able to mount huge, well-organized demonstrations against the police, the demonstrators wearing crash helmets and armed with staves. Japanese police, too, armed themselves with shields, helmets and staves, and the two 'armies' went to battle like their ancestors in the Middle Ages. The Japanese police were victorious.

The most extraordinary success of the police was their ability to resist the temptation to over-react. They set an example that the South Koreans have followed (most of the time), and that the Israelis conspicuously have not. The Japanese police do not shoot rioters – who, for the most part, later resume their place in society.

In the 1970s, however, a handful of them turned to murder. One group, led by a woman, Hiroka Nagata, was called the 'Tokyo–Yokohama Joint Struggle Committee against the Japan–United States Security Treaty', and another was the Red Army, led by Tsureo Mori, who was a former high school fencing star. The two groups merged in 1970 to form the United Red Army (*Rengo Sekigun*). In its first public act, seven of its members hijacked a J A L internal flight and forced it to fly to North Korea. The hijackers were then armed with Samurai swords, but they later acquired other skills. Some of them travelled to the Bekaa valley in Lebanon, and trained in terrorism and guerrilla warfare with the Palestinians.

In the next two years, the Red Army carried out a number of attacks and murders in Japan. They were not the only fanatics fighting against the new

**581**

Japan: in November 1970, one of Japan's best-known authors, Yukio Mishima, who was also a militarist of the old school, tried to start a revolution by occupying a barracks with a few followers, and inciting the troops to revolt. They refused, and he committed ritual suicide.

Mori was equally divorced from reality. Late in 1971, he took the 30 or so members of the Red Army into the mountains north of Tokyo to train for the overthrow of the government. In order to start a revolution, they would form three suicide squads who would set out to murder ministers and other prominent citizens.

After several weeks of this, by later accounts, some members of the band started expressing doubts of the wisdom of their leader's course. Hiroka Nagata, who like Mori was 27 years old, convened a people's court to try the doubters. They were tortured, stripped naked, tied to stakes in the open and beaten with wire – and then left to die of exposure. The guilty women had their heads shaved before they were left to die; one of them was eight months pregnant. Nagata was described as a singularly unprepossessing woman who considered sexual relations between members of the Red Army to be 'unrevolutionary'.

On 19 February 1972, police encountered a Red Army band, and in the ensuing shoot-out, nine of its members were arrested. Four others, including Mori, escaped and took refuge in a house at Karuizawa, where they took the housekeeper hostage. About 1000 police laid siege to the house for eight days until 27 February, when they stormed the place. Two police were killed, five members of the Red Army (including Mori and Nagata) were arrested, and the hostage was rescued.

The horrors were revealed a few days later, as some of the arrested terrorists described the 'people's trials' and took police to the site in the mountains. Eventually, 14 bodies were recovered. One of the survivors said that Nagata was 'a woman of frail mind and abnormal jealousy'.

Three months later, on 30 May, three members of the Red Army, who had been training in Lebanon, took passage on an Air France airliner from Paris to Lod airport, outside Tel Aviv. Acting perfectly normally, they got off the plane with the other passengers, took the bus to the terminal, and there collected their luggage. Then they opened their bags, pulled out hand grenades and machine-guns, and opened fire on the crowded concourse. They killed 26 people and wounded 76, mostly Costa Ricans who had come on a pilgrimage to the Holy Land. One of the terrorists killed himself with a grenade, possibly a suicide, a second was killed by one of his comrades in the general shooting, and the third – Kozo Okomoto – was captured. (Okomoto was eventually released, in May 1985, along with 1153 other prisoners held in Israel, almost all of them Palestinians, in exchange for three Israeli soldiers who had been captured in Lebanon by one of the Syrian-backed Palestinian organizations.)

The Japanese Red Army was able to survive, mostly in exile: police think that there are now about 40 members left, primarily living in the Middle East. Members hijacked a JAL flight from Amsterdam to Tokyo in 1973. On 31 January 1974, two Japanese and two Palestinians attacked a Shell Oil refinery in Singapore. They took five hostages, and retreated to a boat whence they demanded that the Japanese government release some of their comrades. The government refused. On 6 February, Palestinian terrorists seized the Japanese embassy in Kuwait and made the same demand. This time, the government capitulated.

On 27 July of the same year, a member of the J R A, Yoshiaka Yamada, was arrested at Orly airport in Paris, and was found to be carrying $10,000 in crude counterfeit notes, intended to finance kidnappings in Europe. In September, some of his comrades occupied the French embassy in The Hague, and demanded Yamada's release. The operation was notable because it involved the Euro-Palestinian terrorist Ilich Ramirez ('Carlos'), who threw a grenade into Le Drugstore on the boulevard St Germain in Paris in support of the Red Army terrorists. The French government complied with their demand, and Yamada was released.

In 1975, J R A terrorists attacked the Japanese embassy in Kuala Lumpur and, in 1977, hijacked another J A L flight, this time on its way to Dacca. On each occasion, they demanded the release of some of their imprisoned comrades, and their demands were usually met. The Bangladesh incident was resolved when six terrorists were released and the government paid $6 million in ransom.

Now the Red Army has reappeared. One member of the group, said by police to have organized the Lod airport massacre, was arrested trying to re-enter Japan in the autumn of 1987. In May 1988, one of the men who had hijacked the J A L flight to North Korea in 1970 was arrested in Tokyo. There are believed to be five other survivors of that incident living in North Korea.

Another suspected member of the Red Army, Junzo Okudaira, was believed to have placed a bomb outside a U S servicemen's club in Naples on 14 April 1988, killing five people and wounding 17. Car rental agents recognized his photograph as the man who had rented the car used in the bombing. Okudaira had been among those released by the Japanese government after the Bangladesh hijacking in 1977. He and a few comrades had apparently been operating in Italy for some time, and were responsible for attacks on the American and British embassies during the Venice summit in 1987. Italian police assume that the Red Army is now working for Libya: the Naples bombing occurred two days before the second anniversary of the American raid on Tripoli, and a group calling itself the Jihad took the credit and said it was a reprisal for the air raid.

Two days before the Naples explosion, another suspected member of the Red Army, Yu Kikumura, aroused the suspicions of a highway patrolman on the New Jersey turnpike and was arrested. Three pipe bombs and all the materials to make several more were found hidden in his car. He had been living peacefully in New York for several weeks. In February 1989, he was sentenced to 30 years in prison. Prosecutors claimed that he had planned to bomb a navy recruiting station on the West Side of Manhattan.

The Red Army is the most violent of Japanese left-wing factions, but there are many others. The 'New Left', a radical movement composed of 23 factions, has about 35,000 supporters. Its most extreme section is the Chukaku-Ha, which advocates revolution through mass struggle; it has about 200 full-time members.

In the 1980s, the New Left frequently attacked Narita airport, Tokyo, the new Kansai airport at Osaka, and railway stations. It devised some remarkable weapons, including flamethrowers, rockets and mortars. It launched projectiles **583** at the Imperial Palace in Tokyo, at the building where an economic summit was taking place (May 1986), and at other targets. Its most spectacular attack was carried out against the Liberal Democratic party headquarters in September 1984, when a home-made flamethrower mounted on a truck was used. The building was destroyed. Only a few injuries have been caused by its attacks, but in September 1986, a railway trade union leader was murdered and several others were beaten, possibly by the Chukaku-Ha.

# NATIONALIST TERRORISM

## BRITTANY

The movement for Breton autonomy or independence is one of the lost causes of Europe. The province has always been different from the rest of France: it is the last survival of ancient Gaul, preserving its Celtic language (which is related to Welsh and, more distantly, to Gaelic) and retaining a consciousness of a distinct, non-French identity to complement its Frenchness.

The independence movement had very little popular support at the height of its campaign in the late 1970s. An ineffectual group called the *Mouvement pour l'organisation de la Bretagne* (M O B) had achieved nothing, and a small group of fanatics then set up a *Front de libération de la Bretagne – Armée républicaine bretonne* (F L B-A R B), which started its campaign in earnest in 1976. The A R B attacked government buildings, including post offices and a T V licence office. In all, there were about 40 bombings. They did not succeed in winning any notable popular support in Brittany; indeed, when the A R B blew up a television mast, cutting off most of Brittany's T V reception for several weeks, there was great public indignation.

The A R B's most spectacular achievement was bombing Versailles on 26 June 1978. The bomb went off in the middle of the night and severely damaged the ground floor of the château's north wing. That part of the building houses a museum dedicated to the glories of the Emperor Napoleon, and a number of huge paintings depicting his victories was destroyed. It was no great loss to art but a severe blow to French equanimity.

The police launched a massive investigation and, by the end of the year, had arrested virtually the entire A R B, all 39 of them, and most were convicted of the bombings. Since they had taken great care not to kill or injure anyone (though two A R B men were killed by their own bomb on one occasion), they escaped with sentences ranging from 2 to 15 years. That was the end of the A R B – though it is always possible that it may reappear at some later date.

By the early 1980s, however, the autoroute had reached Rennes, the provincial capital, as had France's celebrated express trains, and the province's economy benefited accordingly. Furthermore, reversing centuries of linguistic persecution, the state now permits Breton schools, and the language is taught wherever there is a need; it is no longer illegal for children to be given Breton names; and there are Breton programmes on television and bilingual road signs.

These are grudging concessions, and even were they wholehearted, it is probably too late to save the language. There are thought to be about 400,000 people who speak Breton, but the great majority are old, and their language has been lost to their children. The same thing has happened to the patois of different areas of France, to Gaelic in Scotland and to Irish, despite valiant efforts by the Dublin government over the past 70 years.

## CORSICA

The Corsican separatists are more violent than their Breton counterparts. The island was annexed to France in 1768 (just in time for Napoleon to be born French), after its inhabitants had fought a famous battle for independence against the city-state of Genoa. The fact that, a generation after the annexation, one of its own became emperor of France was, of course, a source of immense local pride and also reconciled the islanders to their new nationality. This pride has been retained: Bonapartists continued to be elected to local posts in Corsica into the 1960s.

Corsica remains different from the rest of France. Unlike the mainland, where for the most part the local patois have been submerged by French in the past century, the great majority of Corsicans still speak their own language among themselves. It is the poorest region of France, dependent on tourism, handouts from Paris and remittances from expatriates. In the 1970s, the resentment that this situation inevitably produces led to the formation of several more or less violent groups and, in 1975, the first violent action: Dr Edmond Siméoni led 30 men in an armed occupation of a wine cooperative. There was shooting and two policemen were killed. Siméoni did a term in jail and is now leader, with his brother, of a peaceful autonomist party.

His example was followed by more brutal men. The *Front de libération nationale de la Corse* (F L N C) was founded in May 1976, and there are several other groups that have planted bombs or burned houses, including a group calling itself Francia (the *Front d'action nouvelle contre l'indépendence et l'autonomie*), which attacks F L N C supporters.

About 100 people have been killed by various Corsican terrorist groups since 1975. The most prominent victim so far has been the *préfet* of Corsica, Claude Erignac, shot on his way to a concert in Ajaccio by two gunmen in February 1998. There are now three principal and a dozen or so small terrorist groups, and most of the killings on the island result from feuds between them. Twelve people were killed in these feuds in 1995. The noble principles of Corsican nationalism have degenerated into gang warfare, and the chief occupation of the various gangs is extortion. The terrorists call it a 'nationalist tax'.

By the end of 1997 there had been more than 9000 bombings and other acts of violence in Corsica. There were 602 bombings in 1995 alone. There have also been numerous attacks on the mainland. The ministry of Finance in the Louvre, in Paris, was hit in February 1979, and another bomb in the Palais de Justice in April did extensive damage. In March 1980 the Hôtel de Ville in Paris was bombed. On 13 March 1986 the F L N C exploded 13 bombs across the Midi (in Nice, Marseille and

Aix). In October 1996 a bomb did serious damage to the Hôtel de Ville in Bordeaux: the prime minister at the time, Alain Juppé, was also mayor of Bordeaux. In Corsica itself, banks, tourist projects including Club Méditerranée, Foreign Legion posts, police stations and other government buildings have been bombed. In 1986 two foreign tourists were killed. As a result, the tourist trade has been severely hit. In the most costly incident a terrorist band seized a hotel in Ajaccio in 1980. Three people were killed in cross-fire at a demonstration staged near the hotel. There have been several ceasefires over the years, usually called by the main terrorist organization while it held secret talks with the French government. There was a brief truce after the election of François Mitterrand as president in 1981, which ended in January the following year.

Mitterrand set up an assembly for Corsica, with limited powers. There was a turn-out of over 70 per cent in the first election, and the only autonomist party on the ballot won 7 of the 55 seats. They did better in 1992, when a coalition of various autonomist factions won nearly 30 per cent of the vote, but the increase in violence since then, and the frequent demonstrations that the terrorist groups had degenerated into so many Mafia bands, greatly reduced their support.

The FLNC has split into three main factions. The largest calls itself the Historic Wing (FLNC-*Canal Historique*). Its political front, Sinn Fein to its IRA, is *Cuncolta Naziunalista*. In 1995 and 1996, the minister of the interior, Jean-Louis Debré, authorized secret talks with Cuncolta's leader, François Santoni. In January, the organization mustered 600 gunmen, all in ski-masks and carrying an impressive variety of weaponry, and paraded them for the cameras on a Corsican hillside. They announced an immediate ceasefire – and the police let them disperse peacefully. The truce lasted until the summer, when the prime minister, Juppé, with the support of President Chirac, decided that too many concessions were being made. The attack on Juppé's Bordeaux office occurred the following October.

Santoni was arrested in December 1996 when a businessman who owned a large golf-course in Corsica told police of an attempt to extort $800,000 from him. Santoni's mistress and lawyer, Marie-Hélène Mattei, had arranged for an emissary to make the demand in the businessman's Paris office, and when he refused, a security guard's cottage at the golf-course was blown up, as a sign of things to come. He closed the golf-course and went to the police.

The other main factions are the Traditional FLNC and Resistenza. They both objected bitterly to being excluded from the talks between Paris and the Cuncolta, and staged their own bombing campaigns while the 'secret' talks were taking place. Petru Lorenzi, a senior terrorist leader of FLNC-*Canal Historique*, was killed with another man in a car bomb attack in July 1996.

Juppé announced a new economic plan for Corsica, which already received at least $1.5 billion a year in subsidies from the mainland. The island would become a special economic zone, and businesses would be exempt from social security and other business taxes. The plan was adopted by the new Socialist government which took power in 1997.

Then the *préfet* was assassinated. France was outraged, and the conservative president and Socialist prime minister both swore that there would at last be a crack-down on Corsican terrorism.

**587**

# THE BASQUES

There are about 2 million Basques in Spain and 200,000 in France, living around the western end of the Pyrenees. They like to boast of the antiquity and uniqueness of their language and history. They were there before the Romans conquered Spain and France (and imposed their language upon the rest of those countries), and it was the Basques who ambushed Charlemagne's rearguard, commanded by Roland and Oliver. Their culture and traditions survived the centuries, at least on the Spanish side of the frontier; the assimilationist educational policy of the French republic has almost wiped out the Basque language in France (and it is spoken by only a small minority of Basques in Spain). However, the Basques remain as distinct, and as conscious of that distinction, as the Irish, Welsh and Bretons.

There are four ancient Basque provinces in Spain – Alava, Guipúzcoa, Navarra and Vizcaya – which together make up the modern Basque province; and three in France – Soule, Basse Navarre and Labourd – which together make up the ancient province of Béarn (now the Pyrénées-Atlantiques). In Spain before World War II, Guipúzcoa and Vizcaya were industrially more advanced than the rest of the country, and Bilbao, the capital of Vizcaya, was the most advanced industrial city in Spain, and its inhabitants were among the most devoted supporters of the Republic in the 1930s. When Franco's nationalists attacked the Basque country in 1937, they first directed the Condor Legion, the German air squadron that Hitler had sent to Spain, to bomb the ancient Basque capital, Guernica. It was one of the great crimes of the civil war.

After his victory, Franco tried to suppress all traces of Basque nationalism. He failed. The Basque Nationalist Party (P N B), which had governed the province under the Republic, survived in exile and retained the loyalty of the mass of the Basque people. Although it maintained a secret organization, it never sank to terrorism, preferring to wait for better days. Its caution did not satisfy all the Basques, however: in 1953, the first student revolutionary groups were formed, culminating, in 1959, with the formation of *Euzkadi ta Askatasuna* (E T A, 'Basque Homeland and Liberty').

To begin with, E T A was divided ideologically between Basque nationalists and Communist revolutionaries. At one stage, the movement was split into two competing factions, E T A - V and E T A - V I, numbered after its fifth and sixth clandestine assemblies, which adopted different policies on the question.

The first assassination occurred in 1968. E T A's leader in Guipúzcoa was killed in a shoot-out with the police, and in revenge E T A killed the San Sebastián police chief. This event led to severe police repression, the arrest of many Basque militants, and the trial of 16 E T A men in Burgos in 1970. Six of them were eventually sentenced to death. In December, E T A kidnapped Eugene Beihl, honorary West German consul in San Sebastián, and in exchange for his release, Franco commuted the sentences. E T A was then reconstituted, reinforced by new members inspired by the trial.

In 1972, E T A kidnapped a Spanish industrialist. His employees were on strike, and E T A demanded that he accede to their demands – then released him. In 1973, they kidnapped another industrialist, this time for ransom. Then they began serious training in the mountains.

Their most spectacular operation took place on 20 December 1973, when they assassinated the prime minister, Admiral Luis Carrero Blanco, in Madrid. He had been Franco's intended successor (Juan Carlos was to be only a figurehead monarch), and there was no one to replace him. The assassins were a group of four amateurs, who had first considered the possibility of kidnapping Carrero; when they concluded it was impossible, they turned to murder. The admiral always drove to Mass every morning at the same time and along the same route. The assassins dug a tunnel under the road and packed it with explosives, and took elaborate precautions to ensure that it detonated just as the admiral's car passed over it. The explosion carried the car over an eight-storey apartment building, and it lodged on a second-storey balcony on the other side.

Despite that remarkable success, ETA once again split, with the orthodox Marxists setting forth on their own. In all these developments, ETA's history greatly resembles that of the IRA, which also split between Marxists and nationalists. The new division in ETA was between ETA-Militar (ETA-M, the militarists) and ETA-PM (the politico-militarists) – between those who wanted to engage in immediate action and those who preferred to build up the party's political base first.

The leader of ETA-PM, Moreno Bergareche, tried to evolve a doctrine that would combine intense patriotism with Leninist theory; he was murdered by unsympathetic comrades in 1976. In 1978, one of the leaders of ETA-M, José Miguel Beñaran Ordeñana, who had been involved in the assassination of Admiral Carrero, was himself murdered, in France, on the fifth anniversary of that event.

The French government banished ETA militants from the Pyrénées-Atlantiques. They moved to Paris, to Brussels (where the Belgian Communist party took them in) and to Algiers, where the government provided some weapons and training.

Until Franco's death in 1975, ETA had the outside world's sympathy because it was fighting against a detested regime (the African National Congress enjoyed the same status). When it used the same methods against a democratic government, it lost its respectability. ETA, once freedom fighters, are now terrorists. However, if we are to be consistent, we must admit that ETA's methods were always reprehensible: they were always terrorists, however odious the regime they were fighting.

After Franco died, Spain immediately set about dismantling the dictatorship. All political prisoners were progressively set free, the last 20 or so ETA members (all convicted of murder or complicity in murder) in 1977. They were released on condition that they leave the country. They did so, and resumed the struggle from abroad.

In due course, the autonomy that the Republic had given to the Basques and Catalans, and which Franco had suppressed, was restored. ETA and its political front *Herri Batasuna* ('One People') continue to insist on full independence, but the biggest slice of the vote that it has managed in a free election is 20 per cent.

ETA accelerated its terrorist campaign after the restoration of democracy. It has been responsible for 800 deaths (though none so prominent as Carrero Blanco), including not only off-duty policemen but their friends and relatives, **589** their wives and children, and many other civilians. The murder campaign began immediately after Franco's death (19 people were killed in the first year), and has continued ever since. At the same time, Basque exiles, including many ETA veterans, were permitted to return home. One of them was Telesforo Monzón, aged 74, who had been minister of the interior in the Basque government during the civil war. Returning from 40 years' exile, he became a vehement supporter of ETA.

In 1977, 30 people were murdered; in 1978, 66; and in 1979, 130. By the end of 1980, the total had reached 275. The ETA leadership then entered into discussion with the government for a permanent truce and amnesty, but the movement split on the issue, with the result that ETA-M broke away and continued the campaign. They were particularly concerned to defeat the government's plans for Basque autonomy: they wanted the Basques oppressed, so that they would rise in revolt and usher in the new order. They launched a ferocious murder campaign against the Statute of Guernica, which gave the Basques everything they wanted, short of full independence. Subsequent elections have demonstrated clearly that the majority of Basques accept the new constitution, and consider that it meets their demands fully.

Of the two-thirds of Basques who turned out for the referendum in 1979, only 4 per cent voted against the Statute. After the Basque government (called the General Council) was re-established, the president of the Basque government-in-exile, who had lived in Paris since 1939, returned and formally handed his authority over to the newly elected president of the council.

The struggle continues. It needs very few people – only a couple of dozen – to plan a few terrorist actions every year and the occasional major attack. By the end of 1988, the total number of people killed (since 1968) had passed 500. On 6 February 1986, ETA assassinated Vice-Admiral Cristobal Colón (a descendant of Christopher Columbus) merely because of his prominence; he was the 54th senior officer murdered since Admiral Carrero in 1973. On 14 July 1986, a bomb in a Madrid bus killed ten *guardia civil* and wounded 43. A week later, a bomb and rocket attack on the ministry of defence wounded nine people, and on 29 July a bomb at a resort at Marbella wounded a nine-year-old boy.

The Spanish government has not responded as ETA wished – it has not imposed a new military dictatorship in the Basque country. Furthermore, the police have improved their tactics, and many ETA terrorists are now safely jailed. In 1982, a general offer of amnesty was issued, and during the next four years, about 250 members of ETA accepted (the most prominent of whom was then murdered by his former comrades). France, which for years had offered asylum to ETA terrorists, now pursues them with as much diligence as the Spanish authorities. In 1979, it revoked the refugee status of Basque exiles and delivered seven of them to Spanish police. In 1985, there were raids on ETA bases and safe-houses in France, and 30 ETA suspects were extradited to Spain – a severe blow to the organization. French police arrested ETA-M's military commander, Santiago Arrospide, in October 1987, and in January 1989, they captured the ETA-M commander-in-chief, José Antonio Urrutikoetxea Bengoechea, whose *nom de guerre* is Josu Ternera, near Bayonne. He was allegedly one of the four who killed Admiral Carrero, and directed a number of terrorist acts, including planting a bomb in a parking garage under a supermarket in Barcelona, in June 1987, that killed 21 people. At the same time, French police rounded up a number of other members of E T A, including the only female member of its executive committee.

The French had always treated the Basque terrorists carefully, for fear of inciting French Basques to start terrorism north of the Pyrenees. There was a clandestine organization, known as Iparretarrak, which had always confined its activities to helping E T A. Then, on 2 April 1990, Spanish police arrested a French Basque near Seville with 300 kilos of explosives in his car. His name was Henri Parot, and he agreed to cooperate with the police. He gave details of over 20 terrorist acts carried out by French Basques, including the car bomb attack on the Saragossa Civil Guard barracks that killed 11 men in 1987. He provided a long list of names. French police arrested 16 suspects immediately.

In 1995, the Spanish government was forced to admit that the police had conducted their own 'dirty war' against E T A in the mid-1980s. A police death squad, calling itself the anti-Terrorist Liberation Group (G A L), had reportedly killed 27 people, 23 of them in France. Most were E T A terrorists, but by one report, seven were not. Spanish police had been frustrated by France's refusal to cooperate in the war against E T A, and therefore hired hit-men to kill suspects in France. French police officials were bribed to trace the Basque suspects. The G A L was disbanded in 1987, when French policy changed and police in France launched their own attack on E T A.

Two police officers had been sentenced to life in prison in 1991 for murdering alleged members of E T A, and four years later, still in jail, they began to cast blame on their superiors. What is more, they revealed that since they were first arrested in 1988, each had received $800,000 paid into their bank accounts in Switzerland, and their wives were sent $4000 a month each from a secret slush fund in the ministry of the interior.

The two men were released, and the judge investigating the case began arresting, first, senior police officers, and then political figures, including a former head of the security services. A former deputy prime minister and the former Socialist minister of the interior, José Barrionuevo, were also implicated. The question arose immediately whether the prime minister, Felipe González, had known of the 'dirty war'. He denied it.

In February 1995, Rafael Vera, who was head of anti-terrorism forces at the time, was arrested. Then two bodies found in Alicante in 1985 were identified as two missing E T A suspects. They had disappeared in 1983, soon after an army officer was kidnapped by E T A, and were apparently tortured to reveal his whereabouts. Police failed to save the officer, but soon after the two terrorists disappeared, a large number of other members of E T A were arrested. When the bodies were found, police noted that their finger-nails and toenails had been torn out. They had been shot in the head. Later, a police (*Guardia Civil*) general, Enrique Rodriguez Galindo, was charged with instigating the murder.

In January 1996, Barrionuevo was indicted in the case. By then, 14 former policemen and government officials had been put on trial, and more sensational revelations emerged every day. González lost parliamentary elections the following March. The opposition had made much of the G A L scandal during the **591** campaign, and had denounced the prime minister for refusing to open government anti-terrorist archives to the courts. However, three months after winning, the new prime minister, José Maria Aznar, announced that he, too, would refuse to hand over the documents on the grounds of national security (though some of the papers were later handed over to the court). Then he released General Rodriguez. The judge investigating the case decided that there was no evidence against Felipe González, and the Madrid press cried cover-up.

Meanwhile, the war with E T A continued unabated. A car bomb killed six civilian workers at a navy facility in Madrid in December 1995. French police arrested one of the three members of the E T A executive committee, Julian Achurra Egurrola, in July 1996, and in December caught another terrorist in possession of computer disks that disclosed the organization's plans to assassinate French political leaders, including the minister of the interior. A huge cache of weapons and explosives was found in Bayonne. In January 1997 they arrested another member of the executive committee, José Luis Urrusolo Sistiaga.

In 1996 E T A mounted a bombing campaign against tourist sites, including three bombs in Cordoba and one at an airport near Madrid in which over 50 British tourists were injured. On 10 July 1997 E T A kidnapped a local councillor, Miguel Angel Blanco, in a small village in the Basque country. They said they would kill him if E T A prisoners held in different jails around Spain were not brought together in one prison. The government rejected the demand, and Blanco was murdered on 12 July. The incident aroused enormous public anger: there were demonstrations of millions of people in Madrid, Barcelona and Basque towns, including half a million in Bilbao, and serious clashes between supporters and opponents of E T A in Pamplona. The running of the bulls fiesta had to be cancelled.

Then the government prosecuted members of E T A's political wing, *Herri Batasuna*, for supporting terrorism. Twenty-three party leaders were sentenced to seven-year terms, and jailed in December 1997. None of this would defeat E T A. *Herri Batasuna* had consistently won 15 per cent of the votes in Basque elections, and will probably continue to do so. The I R A may be ready to give up the armed struggle, but not E T A.

## ALTO ADIGE

Early in the morning of 19 May 1988, four large bombs exploded at government offices and housing projects in Bolzano, high in the Italian Alps. No one was hurt, but considerable damage was done, particularly to parked cars. It was the latest episode in a dispute going back over a century.

The province of Alto Adige is known to Austrians as the South Tyrol. Italy annexed it in 1919, as the spoils of war, and part of the German-speaking population has been agitating to return to Austria ever since.

When Italy was united in the middle of the 19th century, its statesmen proclaimed that its natural frontiers were on the line of the Alps. Although this meant the loss of Nice and Savoy to France, Italians obtained everything that they wanted except the hinterland of Trieste and the Alto Adige (even though Garibaldi had mounted his last campaign there). These territories were Italy's price for joining World War I on the side of France, Britain and Russia, and abandoning its alliance with Germany and Austria. In the 1920s and 1930s, Mussolini started agitating for Nice, Savoy and Corsica (formerly under the thrall of the city-state of Genoa), and after Germany defeated France in June 1940, he joined what he thought was the victorious side in order to obtain them. It was a mistake.

Hitler, busy gathering all the scattered Germans into one *Reich*, never claimed the South Tyrol. Despite all his rhetoric about the indivisible *Volk*, he left this pocket of German language and culture to his friend the Duce. After the war, after a prolonged and bitter dispute, the Yugoslavs recovered Istria, behind Trieste, but the Allies let the frontier on the Alps stand.

The first bombing campaign occurred in 1960. A number of Italian police and soldiers were killed before the terrorists were defeated. The Italian government reluctantly granted a measure of autonomy to the province, but was notably dilatory in carrying out its promises. An agreement with Austria was signed in 1969 giving the South Tyroleans the right to use the German language. Eventually, Rome conceded a general statute of autonomy for Italy's many and diverse regions (Sicily, Sardinia, Venetia, etc.), including Alto Adige.

Finally, in May 1988, a new Italian government agreed to further concessions, including the right to German-language courts and bilingual police. The agreement displeased both Tyrolean extremists (because accepting it would mean giving up any hopes of reunification with Austria) and Italian nationalists (who object to favours being granted to German-speaking Italians). The May 1988 bombings, the first of a series, were the work of German extremists: a mysterious group calling itself 'Ein Tirol'.

Over the next six months, there were 23 bombings in the Alto Adige. On 30 October, an Italian school in Bolzano was bombed, and a church in Appiano (known to German-speakers as Eppan), which had been the social centre for the village's Italian-speaking minority, was wrecked by a bomb. A leaflet in German that was scattered in the village said: 'Peaceful coexistence means ethnic commingling and genocide.' It was signed 'Ein Tirol'.

There are about 450,000 people in the province, two-thirds of them German, a reminder of the impermanence of European frontiers.

# ARAB TERRORISM

Terrorism, the politics of murder, has always been common in the Arab world: a quite disproportionate number of Arab heads of state has been assassinated. However, mass terrorism, directed at civilians, and especially foreign civilians, is a more recent phenomenon. It was first practised by Palestinians against Israel and its Western supporters after the Six-Day War. It reached a crisis in 1970, with a mass hijacking to a desert airstrip in Jordan, which led to the expulsion of the P L O from that country in 'Black September'. For the next 20 years, while there were a number of sanguinary attacks on civilian targets in Israel and abroad, the chief victims of Arab terrorism were other Arabs: Palestinians attacking Jordanians; dissident Palestinians attacking the P L O; Iraqis and Syrians attacking each other; and after 1975, all the horrors of Lebanon.

Then came the rise of Islamic extremism, promoted, to a large extent, by the continuing failure of every Arab regime to bring the Arabs into the modern world on anything like acceptable terms. Socialism and nationalism had failed, so the desperate and unemployed took to militant Islam. The country most afflicted by Islamic terrorism is Algeria (see p. 6). Islamic terrorists were aided and incited by the governments of Iran and Sudan, and played a large part in the fighting and terrorism in Lebanon. Now they operate out of the Gaza Strip and the West Bank: Hizbollah sends its martyrs to immolate themselves and as many Israelis as they can. In Egypt, they attack foreign tourists as a means of disrupting the Egyptian economy, and also attack Egyptian Christians and intellectuals – though their first, and most important, victim was President Anwar Sadat, murdered for making peace with Israel.

One of the most significant of Arab terrorist acts was the attempted assassination of the Israeli ambassador to London, Schlomo Argov, in June 1982 by the Abu Nidal gang. The Israeli government used the event as a pretext for the invasion of Lebanon, an operation that had long been in preparation. It was intended to destroy the P L O, which had taken over southern Lebanon. During the cabinet meeting that authorized the invasion, the chief of intelligence tried to point out that Abu Nidal had been responsible for the attack on the ambassador, and that he was bitterly opposed to the P L O. The chief of staff, General Rafael Eitan, briskly put an end to those quibbles: 'Abu Nidal, Abu Schmidal, they're all the same.'

They are not all the same. There are profound divisions within the Palestinian camp and between all the tribes of Araby. Not only have most of the victims of Arab terrorism been other Arabs, but the chief political victim has been the Palestinian cause, and therefore the P L O. If any demonstration of the counter-productivity of terrorism were ever needed, surely it is provided by the lamentable history of the Palestinians.

## THE PALESTINIANS

In July 1968, George Habash, a Palestinian, Christian, Marxist physician, sent his commandos on their first mission to Europe: they hijacked an El Al jet on a flight from Rome to Tel Aviv, and took it to Algiers. It was the first such operation, and Habash considered it a great success.

He had set up the Popular Front for the Liberation of Palestine (P F L P) three months after the Six-Day War in order to carry on the struggle by other means. From the start, his operation rivalled Yasser Arafat's Al-Fatah, the mainstay of the P L O. Then, and for another 15 years until its defeat in 1982, the P L O was committed to the fantasy of forming an army to liberate Palestine from the 'Zionist entity'. Habash had a different set of delusions: he would terrorize the Israelis and the world in a series of spectacular operations, and the walls would come tumbling down.

The Palestinians were still shattered by the disasters of 1967, and the first hijacking seemed a glorious victory. Habash was an instant hero, a fact duly noted by Yasser Arafat. The P L O was desperately in need of a new role and a new reputation. Habash was invited to join and, in due course, did so. The history of the P L O has since been one of constant rivalry between Arafat and more violent leaders. Arafat has retained his position as chairman, and nominal leader of the Palestinian people, by following the immortal precept of the 19th-century French revolutionary who exclaimed: 'I am their leader, I must follow them!'

After the Algiers incident, hijackings became the chosen *modus operandi* of the Palestinians. Habash's P F L P did the work, and Arafat used the publicity and the enthusiasm that the operations aroused in the Arab world to recruit an army in the camps, extort the money to pay for it from the oil states, and train and equip it in Jordan. By the summer of 1970, he had accumulated what appeared to be a formidable force there, and challenged King Hussein's authority and, eventually, tried to take over the country.

In two years, Habash and his chief of operations, Wadi Haddad (another doctor), organized 14 hijackings, and were probably responsible for the bomb that, in February 1970, destroyed a Swiss airliner on a flight from Zurich to Tel Aviv, causing 47 deaths. The campaign culminated in the Dawson's Field incident.

On 6 September 1970, the P F L P hijacked three airliners in the skies over Europe and attempted unsuccessfully to hijack a fourth. A T W A 707 and a Swissair D C-8 were flown to a disused airstrip in Jordan, Dawson's Field (named after an otherwise forgotten British R A F officer). A Pan American 747 was flown to Cairo. The Egyptian authorities persuaded the terrorists to surrender: they blew up the aircraft after leaving it. The P F L P failed to hijack an El Al flight into London: security guards killed one terrorist – a Nicaraguan-born American serving a greater cause – and arrested the other, Leila Khaled, who had already participated in a hijacking. She was detained in London. On 9 September, the P F L P seized a B O A C V C-10 and took it to Dawson's Field to join the other two planes and their passengers.

The hijackers were met by P L O troops at Dawson's Field, and the Jordanian army surrounded them. The terrorists (Henry Kissinger prefers to call them *fedayeen*) demanded that all Palestinians in British, Swiss and West German jails be released, in exchange for the hundreds of European hostages they held. They proposed to keep their Israeli and Jewish (mostly American) hostages, and trade them for Palestinian prisoners in Israel. The United States moved the Sixth Fleet to the eastern Mediterranean and prepared for a rescue, and the European governments agreed to release the prisoners – in exchange for all the hostages, including the Israelis. The hijackers released some, but not all, of the hostages.

On 12 September, the P L O moved its remaining hostages to Amman, and blew up the three jets. The event was moving towards crisis, and the American build-up continued. All this was recorded on television. It was the biggest terrorist media event so far, and was not surpassed until the seizure of the American embassy in Tehran, nine years later.

The P L O used the event to threaten the rule of King Hussein. On 17 September, he sent his army into Amman, and soon there was heavy fighting between the Jordanians and the P L O, both in the capital and in P L O bases elsewhere in the country. King Hussein was winning the battle – so on 20 September, Syria invaded Jordan.

It was all a remarkable achievement for the P L O–P F L P: for a few days, it seemed as though Arafat were about to become president of East Palestine, but it all ended in dust and ashes. American-sponsored negotiations between Israel and Jordan collapsed, perhaps the last occasion when Israel was willing to consider giving up most of the West Bank. The Israelis moved tanks into the Golan Heights, threatening the Syrian lines of communication, and the Syrians hastily evacuated Jordan. The Jordanian army completed its occupation of the P L O camps, rescued all the remaining hostages and expelled the P L O. Habash and Wadi Haddad did not renounce terrorism, nor did Arafat condemn their adventurism (after all, he had been deeply implicated in the whole episode), but there was no doubt that it had been a serious defeat for them all and a victory for King Hussein. The P L O moved to Lebanon and began building up its forces there, with the result that, five years later, a civil war was provoked that destroyed that unfortunate country.

Al-Fatah's next foray into international terrorism was an attack on oil installations in Rotterdam in March 1971. The following summer saw the appearance of a new organization, 'Black September', formed jointly by the P L O and the P F L P and named after the P L O's great defeat in Jordan. It began a series of attacks on Jordanian offices and officials abroad, particularly on Alia, the Jordanian airline, which henceforth was attacked as frequently as El Al. In November, a Black September gunman murdered the Jordanian prime minister in Cairo, and two weeks later, another tried to assassinate the Jordanian ambassador to London.

As for El Al, the P F L P made a number of efforts to plant bombs aboard its flights, using impressionable young women who would be asked to carry a small suitcase to Israel for their Arab boyfriends. All these attempts were detected. There were further hijackings. One of them, a Sabena flight in May 1972, ended spectacularly at Lod airport outside Tel Aviv, when Israeli security men stormed the plane, killed two of the four hijackers, captured the others and rescued the hostages.

There were worse things planned. In May 1972, three Japanese terrorists, members of the Japanese Red Army (*see* Terrorism: Japan, pp. 581–4), who had been trained at a P F L P base in the Bekaa valley in eastern Lebanon, arrived at Lod, and there opened fire on the crowd in the arrival building. A planeload of Catholic pilgrims from Costa Rica had just arrived for a tour of the Holy Land, and most of the 26 people killed were Costa Ricans. Two of the terrorists were killed and the third arrested. Then in September, there was the massacre at the Munich Olympics.

Seven Black September gunmen stormed the Israeli athletes' dormitory, killing a coach and one athlete. They seized nine other athletes (the rest of the team escaped), and demanded that 200 Palestinians held prisoner in Israel be released. The Israeli government refused. It offered to send a counter-terrorist squad to Munich to rescue the hostages, but the West Germans said they would do the job themselves. It was agreed that a plane would be provided to fly the terrorists and their hostages to Cairo. When the bus arrived at the airport, Bavarian police attacked. It was a botched and clumsy operation: the terrorists had time to throw grenades into the bus that was carrying the hostages, who were tied up in their seats. All the athletes were killed. Four terrorists were shot dead; three were wounded and captured.

The event was given enormous publicity, and for years, Arafat denied that he had been in any way involved. The attack had been a failure on two counts: the terrorists had not intended to get themselves killed (the West Germans had been expected to cooperate, and allow them to fly safely away with their hostages); and an attack on the Olympic Games revolted public opinion everywhere. There was a further unfortunate result for the Palestinians: the Munich attack prompted the West German government to set up an anti-terrorist squad, which later proved its effectiveness at Mogadishu in 1977, and also to pursue Palestinian as well as West German terrorists with great vigour.

As soon as the wounded terrorists were fit to travel, Black September hijacked a Lufthansa flight out of Beirut and demanded their release. The West German government complied immediately. The terrorists flew to Tripoli, where they were given a hero's welcome by Colonel Khadafy.

Then began a deadly war between the Israeli secret service, Mossad, and the P L O. The Israelis set about hunting down and killing all those responsible for the Munich massacre, and also attacked other P L O officials. They were not always successful. In July 1973, a Moroccan waiter in a small town in Norway was assassinated and the murderers caught: they were from Mossad, and had killed the wrong man. They had been looking for Ali Hassan Salameh, one of the directors of the Munich operation. After that, Mossad was more careful, and over the next few years, they killed the three survivors of the Munich massacre.

**597**

The most dramatic incident was a commando raid on Beirut in April 1973, in which several P L O leaders were killed, including Mohammed Youssef Najjar, Arafat's deputy and Al-Fatah's chief of staff. In 1979, a car bomb in Beirut finally killed Salameh.

In 1973, a new terrorist organization, the National Arab Youth for the Liberation of Palestine appeared. It was led by a renegade member of Al-Fatah, Ahmad al-Ghafour (Abu Mahmoud), and was financed by Libya, which was then beginning to make its weight felt. The N A Y L P's first operation was in August, a machine-gun attack on a T W A plane at Athens airport as it arrived from Israel: five people were killed, 55 wounded. In September, a five-man N A Y L P team was arrested in Rome; they had been armed with Soviet S A M-7s presumably supplied by Colonel Khadafy, and had intended to shoot down El Al airliners approaching Rome airport. In December, the N A Y L P returned to Rome and firebombed a Pan Am jet, incinerating 32 passengers; the terrorists escaped by hijacking a Lufthansa plane. In September 1974, the N A Y L P put a bomb on a T W A aircraft flying from Israel to the United States via Athens: 88 people were killed. That was too much for Arafat and the P L O. Four days later, Abu Mahmoud was tried, convicted of murder and shot.

By that time, Habash and Arafat had decided to stop the terror campaign outside Israel. Instead of winning the P L O friends and sympathizers around the world and intimidating Israel, it had done huge damage to the Palestinian cause. However, getting the genie back into the bottle proved impossible.

For the next few years, the P L O cooperated secretly with the C I A in thwarting terrorism. That arrangement ended after Arafat was driven out of Lebanon, when some units of the P L O, with Arafat's approval, resumed terrorist attacks. At the end of 1988, Arafat again renounced terrorism and offered his services to track down the people who had destroyed the New York-bound Pan Am jet that had exploded over Scotland in December.

The exploits of Abu Mahmoud showed that Arafat and Habash were not the only commanders of the P L O. Wadi Haddad, Habash's deputy, determined to carry on the terrorist campaign, quarrelled violently with Habash in 1972, and moved his operations to Baghdad. He called his new organization the Special Operations Group and began working with the rising star of the Euro-terrorist movement, Ilich Ramirez Sánchez, known as 'Carlos the Jackal'.

## 'CARLOS'

'Carlos' is the son of a millionaire Venezuelan Stalinist who made a fortune out of property speculation and named his three sons Vladimir, Ilich and Lenin. 'Carlos' (he chose his *nom de guerre* from a novel) was born in 1949 and led the life of a pampered, spoiled revolutionary. As an adolescent he studied the violent politics of Latin America, and went to Cuba. He caused so much trouble in Caracas in his late teens that, in 1966, he was sent, with his mother and two brothers, to London to finish his education. Later, he studied at the Lumumba University in Moscow, and visited P F L P camps in Jordan, there becoming converted to the Palestinian cause. He was in Jordan during 'Black September', and fought alongside his Palestinian comrades.

He was picked up by Wadi Haddad in 1972, and given the task of setting up a branch office in London. He lived the life of a Latin playboy and, on 30 December 1973, attempted his first known murder: he was sent to kill prominent Jews, starting with Josep Sieff, director of Marks & Spencer and a prominent Zionist. He forced his way into Sieff's house, found his target in the bathroom and shot him. Miraculously, the bullet was deflected by Sieff's teeth, and he survived.

Carlos was by then senior P F L P operative in Paris, as well as London. His predecessor in Paris, Mohammed Boudia, had suffered an unfortunate accident with a powerful car bomb in June 1973; he had been on Mossad's list. At Wadi Haddad's direction, and with Iraqi money, Carlos subsidized the Euro-terrorists, notably the Baader-Meinhof gang in West Germany, his theory being that anything he could do to destabilize Western Europe would help the Palestinian cause. Carlos was a Communist, quite possibly working for the K G B or at the very least reporting to it. Thus, it could be said that the Euro-terrorists were allied to the K G B. That, however, is not quite the same thing as saying that Moscow directed their activities.

Carlos set up a network of safe-houses in Paris and began operations. His choice of targets was bizarre. He bombed a small Jewish newspaper, *L'Arche*, and also two right-wing and faintly anti-Semitic papers, *L'Aurore* and *Minute*. In September 1974, the Japanese Red Army occupied the French embassy in The Hague and demanded the release of one of their comrades held in France. Carlos helped out by throwing a hand grenade into Le Drugstore on the boulevard St Germain, killing two people and wounding 20. The French released their prisoner.

In early January 1975, a Carlos team tried to attack an El Al jet at Orly airport with a rocket, but missed. On 15 January, they tried again, but instead got into a fire-fight with police. They took refuge in the airport's toilets with 20 hostages, and were later allowed to leave for the Middle East.

So far, French police had no suspicions of Carlos. They were watching a Lebanese interior decorator called Michael Moukharbel, whom they observed visiting Carlos. On 27 June 1975, they arrested Moukharbel and asked him about his Venezuelan friend. He took two officers to meet Carlos at an apartment in the rue Toullier. They were so unsuspecting that they went unarmed.

The apartment belonged to one of Carlos's numerous girlfriends, and the police arrived in the middle of a party. The commissioner had an interesting ten-minute conversation with Carlos and then invited him to come down to the police station. First, however, he confronted him with Moukharbel. Carlos retired to the bathroom – and emerged carrying a gun. He shot and killed Moukharbel and the two policemen, and escaped.

The French then exerted themselves to find all Carlos's accomplices and discovered, to their horror, the extent of the terror network that had been operating in Paris. On 21 December 1975, Carlos reappeared. Leading a mixed West German-Palestinian commando, he stormed an O P E C meeting in Vienna and seized 11 oil ministers. The gang killed three men: a Libyan diplomat and two Austrian security guards. They demanded a plane to escape with their hostages, and proposed to tour the world, dropping off each oil minister in his home country, keeping the Saudi and Iranian ministers to the last – when they would be shot. However, one of the terrorists had been severely wounded, so the gang flew directly to Algiers where the hostages were released.

The wounded terrorist, Hans-Joachim Klein, abandoned terrorism as soon as he recovered and has led a precarious existence ever since, hiding from both Carlos and the West German police. He gave an interview in which he described the O P E C raid, and clearly suggested that the operation had been conceived and paid for by Colonel Khadafy, and directed by Wadi Haddad. In that interview, Klein said that Carlos compared himself to the assassin in Frederick Forsyth's thriller *The Day of the Jackal*, and that Carlos had told him, 'The more violent things get, the more people will respect you,' and 'To get anywhere, you have to walk over corpses.'

One of Carlos's comrades was Wilfried Boese, a member of the Baader–Meinhof gang, and together they planned the next of Carlos's operations. This was the hijacking of a French jet that ended at Entebbe. It was directed by Wadi Haddad: Carlos was chief planner and Boese commanded the operation (for details, *see* Uganda, p. 113). They demanded the release of a long list of prisoners held in various European countries, most of whom were connected to Carlos. Boese was killed in the Israeli rescue. Haddad was lucky to escape: together with other Palestinian terrorist leaders, he had gone to Entebbe, but had left the airport just before the Israelis arrived.

After that defeat, Carlos dropped from sight. He is believed to have lived in Libya for several years, but to have broken with Khadafy in 1981, possibly after quarrelling with Khadafy's own terrorist establishment. He then moved to Syria, and apparently worked for President Assad, using his surviving European contacts to attack Assad's numerous enemies.

In February 1982 two of Carlos's agents were arrested in Paris, Bruno Bréguet, a Swiss, and Magdalena Kaupp, a West German. Two weeks later, Carlos sent a letter to the French embassy in The Hague demanding their release. 'I give you one month to release them,' he wrote. 'If not, I will take up the matter personally with the French government and in particular with Gaston Defferre,' referring to the minister of the interior who was also mayor of Marseille. He signed the letter (which was in Spanish) with his full name, Ilich Ramírez Sánchez, and authenticated it with his thumb prints. A month later, a bomb went off on the Toulouse-Paris express, in the compartment in which the opposition leader, Jacques Chirac, had booked a seat. At the last moment, he had decided to return to Paris by plane, and therefore escaped. Five other people were killed.

Also in 1983, a bomb at a French Cultural Centre in West Berlin killed one person and wounded 23. Carlos claimed responsibility. Years later, after the collapse of East Germany, an official in the Stasi (the secret police) was convicted for helping him. A former Syrian diplomat, who gave evidence at the trial, testified that the Syrian government smuggled the explosives to Berlin for Carlos. There were two more bombings, both on 31 December 1983: one at the Marseille railway station, and one on the Marseille–Paris express. Between them, they killed another five people. Breguet and Kaupp were released in 1985 – and Kaupp then married Carlos in Damascus. Carlos then sank into obscurity.

Carlos was captured in Khartoum on 15 August 1994. He had washed up in

that depressing and ascetic backwater a year before after being encouraged to leave a number of Arab countries which found his presence embarrassing. The Sudanese disapproved of his heavy drinking, the fact that he was accompanied by a Jordanian woman who passed for his wife, and, they claimed, the fact that he used a false name. The C I A had been tracking him around the world and passed the word to the French secret service. It is not known what deal the French cut with Sudan to be allowed to pick him up. They came to fetch him while he was in a clinic having a minor operation on his testicles. He awoke in the Santé prison in Paris.

He was put on trial in December 1997, for the rue Toullier murders. 'My name is Ilich Ramírez Sanchez,' he told the court. 'My profession is professional revolutionary.' It was his last gesture of bravado. He was convicted and sentenced to life in prison.

## ABU NIDAL

After Wadi Haddad died of cancer in a hospital in East Berlin in 1979, his organization was taken over by another fanatic, Salim Abu Salim, who had been Haddad's chief of operations. He renamed the gang the P F L P-Special Command, adopted the *nom de guerre* 'Abu Mohammed' and continued the traditional cooperation with the Euro-terrorists. He is suspected of responsibility for the rue Copernic massacre in Paris in 1980 (*see* The Euro-terrorists: France p. 571), and of bombing a Jewish-owned hotel in Nairobi on New Year's Eve 1980, killing 16 people.

Abu Mohammed, like Carlos, vanished from sight. They were eclipsed by the most deadly of Arab terrorists, Sabri al-Banna, whose uses the *nom de guerre* 'Abu Nidal'.

Yossi Melman's excellent study of Abu Nidal (*see* Further reading, p. 639) lists all the atrocities that may be attributed to him from 1973 to 1986: 47 attacks on Arab targets (mainly Syrian in the 1970s, Jordanian in the 1980s), 16 on the P L O, 14 on Israeli or Jewish targets, 14 on Western targets, and one on a Chinese target. In the space of 13 years, the activities of Abu Nidal's group resulted in the deaths of 248 people (by Melman's count). The incidents involving the largest numbers of dead were the 122 killed in a Gulf Air jet blown up in mid-flight in 1983, 59 killed when Egyptian commandos attacked an Egypt Air jet that Abu Nidal's gang had hijacked to Malta in November 1985, 15 people killed by two bombs in cafés in Kuwait in 1985 and 19 people killed in the Christmas 1985 attacks on the El Al counters at Rome and Vienna airports. On 5 September 1986, Abu Nidal's terrorists killed 20 people at Karachi airport on a Pan Am flight that they had hijacked over India, and the next day, two of his terrorists killed 21 worshippers at a synagogue in Istanbul. It is, however, notable how many attempts of Abu Nidal's gang have actually failed: they are not very competent terrorists.

Abu Nidal's organization is the Fatah Revolutionary Council. He was expelled from the P L O in 1974 and sentenced to death – in absentia. He then moved to Baghdad. Because the great majority of Abu Nidal's victims are Arabs, some Palestinians claim that a man so dangerous to their cause must be in the pay of Mossad. That, obviously, is a nonsense. At one stage, he worked for the Iraqis, attacking Syrian targets all over Europe and the Middle East. Then he abruptly changed sides: his attacks on Syria stopped in 1977. Evidently, he had been bought. He may also have followed a personal vendetta against King Hussein of Jordan; otherwise, the only explanation for the number and ferocity of his attacks on Jordanian targets in the 1980s would have to be that he was acting on behalf of the Syrians. He then turned his attentions to the conservative oil states – and Israel. It is, in any event, clear that Abu Nidal is Yasser Arafat's bitterest enemy: Al-Fatah, Arafat's base organization, has sentenced him to death, and Abu Nidal has tried frequently to have Arafat assassinated.

On 11 July 1988, three gunmen attacked passengers on a cruise ship, the *City of Poros*, in the Aegean, killing nine and wounding 98. The terrorists escaped aboard a waiting speedboat, and were not immediately identified. A few days later, the police issued photographs of three suspects, including a woman, who they said had been disguised as French tourists. The people in question, who had returned to France, immediately and indignantly denounced the allegation, and were able to prove that they were entirely innocent.

It seems certain that the terrorists were Palestinians: the attack coincided with the trial of Mohammed Rashid, who was charged and convicted of entering Greece on a forged passport. He claimed that his name was Mohammed Hamdan, but the police had his fingerprints – he had been convicted of smuggling hashish into Greece in 1973.

The United States wanted to extradite Rashid on a series of charges. He was wanted for planting a bomb aboard a Pan Am flight from Tokyo to Hawaii in 1982, which exploded in mid-air killing one passenger. He was suspected of planning the bombing of the TWA flight from Rome to Athens in April 1986; the explosion killed four Americans. Rashid was also involved in the murder in Lisbon of Issam Sartawi, a senior official in the PLO; Sartawi was one of several PLO moderates who, over the years, have been murdered for contacting the Israelis. Rashid claimed at his trial that he was a member of the PLO, passing through Greece on a secret mission, and the PLO office in Athens came to his defence. Police suspected that he was, in fact, a member of the Abu Nidal gang. Greece hesitated to extradite Rashid to the US, partly for political reasons and partly because Abu Nidal threatened to kill any judge who signed the order.

Just before the attack on the cruise ship, a car exploded near the port where the *City of Poros* was to dock. Its two passengers were killed, apparently the victims of their own bomb. One of them was thought to have been a senior member of Abu Nidal's team, Hejab Jaballah (using the name Samir Kadar), but the bodies were so severely mutilated that positive identification was impossible. Police were not even sure that there were only two bodies: there may have been three.

Jaballah had been one of the world's leading terrorists. He led the commando that murdered an Egyptian journalist in Cyprus (*see* Cyprus, p. 408) in 1978, an episode that ended with a shoot-out between Cypriot and Egyptian troops at Larnaca airport. He is also believed to have organized the shooting at a synagogue in Rome in 1982, and the Rome and Vienna airport massacres at Christmas 1985. Abu Nidal's office in Beirut denied that Jaballah had been in Athens, claiming that he had died three years earlier. However, Greek police were able to match fingerprints left in an apartment used by the terrorists with those taken from Jaballah in Cyprus. A set of keys found there proved to be those of an apartment in Stockholm, where Swedish police found an arms cache and other evidence of the Abu Nidal gang's operations in Europe.

After a change of government in Greece, prosecutions of foreign terrorists became more serious. Rashid was not extradited to the United States, but he was put on trial in Athens in October 1991 for the Honolulu bombing, and was convicted, in January 1992. The chief witness against him was a Palestinian who had been coerced into joining the 'Arab Organization of 15 May', led by Abu Ibrahim. Its links to Abu Nidal were not made any clearer by the trial.

In October and November 1989, there were reports of serious dissension within the Fatah Revolutionary Council, including allegations that Abu Nidal had murdered six senior officials, including his deputy, Mustafa Murad ('Abu Nizar'), and a further 150 had been killed in Lebanon. Two dissident members of the organisation, Atef Abu Bakr, and Abderrahman Issa, both former members of the Council's politburo, denounced Abu Nidal as a psychotic killer who did nothing to further the cause. Abu Bakr cited in particular the murder of seven people (including four British tourists) in Sudan in 1988, the assassination of the leading Muslim cleric in Belgium, who had opposed the Ayatollah Khomeini's sentence of death on Salman Rushdie, and the kidnapping of a Belgian relief worker in Lebanon.

Abu Bakr alleged that Abu Nidal's colleagues who wished to depose him were lured to his house in Tripoli, Libya, and were there murdered and buried in the garden. The P L O welcomed news of the split in the Fatah Council: Abu Nidal has murdered four P L O officials, one each in Lisbon, Rome, London and Paris.

On 4 February 1990, two terrorists attacked a bus carrying Israeli tourists near Cairo. Nine Israelis were killed, and 17 people wounded. The attack bore all the hallmarks of Abu Nidal. In September that year, in one of the last acts of the Lebanese civil war, Arafat's troops waged a pitched battle against Abu Nidal's men in the Palestinian camps around Sidon, and drove them out.

## AHMED JIBRIL

Another Palestinian terrorist organization, the P F L P-General Command, was set up in the early 1970s by Ahmed Jibril, a former captain in the Syrian army. Jibril clearly remains under Syrian control; his headquarters are in Damascus. He quarrelled with Habash and Haddad, objecting to their foreign spectaculars, hijackings and the like; the Munich operation and the failure of the hijacking to Entebbe were cases in point. Jibril preferred to send his men directly into Israel. His commandos were usually caught and killed, but he could always find replacements. Some of the targets were legitimate military ones, but from the start, the P F L P-G C also attacked civilians. In April 1974, a three-man P F L P-G C commando infiltrated into northern Israel and, avoiding military targets, took refuge in an apartment building in Qiryat Shemona. They took a large number of hostages, 18 of whom were killed and 16 wounded when the Israeli army stormed the place.

The following month, on 13 May, another P F L P–G C team seized a school in Ma'alot, also in northern Israel. The Israeli army again botched the rescue, and 22 children were killed, together with the three terrorists. The next year, in March 1975, Al-Fatah, not to be outdone, landed a commando from the sea at

Tel Aviv, seized the Savoy Hotel and murdered six Israeli civilians and six foreigners before they were themselves killed. In March 1978, a 13-man Al-Fatah commando landed on the coast between Tel Aviv and Haifa. They stopped several vehicles on the highway, commandeered a bus and drove it south, until it was stopped at a road block where, in the ensuing gun battle, most of the hostages were killed (the final death toll included 35 civilians). The ostensible purpose of all these attacks was, first, to hit military targets and, second, when that failed, to take hostages who might be exchanged for Palestinian prisoners – and the terrorists themselves. Al-Fatah's attacks were organized by Khalid Wazir, Arafat's deputy, who was himself assassinated by the Israelis in 1988.

The rivalry between Jibril and Arafat continued into the 1980s. Jibril was closely linked with a Palestinian organization set up by the Syrians to rival the PLO; this was Al-Saiqa, 'The Thunderbolt'. In the 1980s, after the Israelis had driven Arafat and the PLO out of Beirut, a dissident leader, Abu Mussa, allied himself with the Syrians and challenged Arafat in the PLO camps in the Bekaa valley and in northern Lebanon. It was all part of Assad's rivalry with Arafat: the Syrian president was determined to control all the players in Lebanon, and Arafat was the last to oppose him.

Jibril tried to carry the war to Israel by sending men on hang-gliders to attack army posts, but such suicide missions were difficult and only one succeeded, in November 1987, resulting in the deaths of six soldiers. His tactics were proving no more successful than his rivals', so he changed them. In 1988, he set up a terrorist organization in Europe. West German police arrested several of his operatives in Frankfurt, and discovered a cache of explosives and timing devices. One bomb was concealed in a portable radio.

On 9 December 1988, the first anniversary of the outbreak of the *intifada*, the Israelis bombed Jibril's Lebanon headquarters outside Beirut, killing 20 people. On 14 December, Yasser Arafat formally recognized Israel's right to exist and renounced terrorism. On the 21st, a bomb destroyed a Pan Am jet over Lockerbie, Scotland, killing all 259 people on board and 11 on the ground. Two years later, American and Scottish police indicted two Libyans and asserted that the bombing was ordered by the Libyan government. They said that they had no proof that Syria or Iran had been involved, but many experts doubted them. (*See below*, pp. 615–16).

## Arafat in Tunis

Yasser Arafat, driven out of Beirut by the Israelis in 1982, tried to re-establish himself in Tripoli, in north Lebanon. Assad sent the dissident PLO (which now called itself the Palestine National Salvation Front) against Arafat, and in due course, he was once again forced to escape by sea. He set up his new Al-Fatah headquarters in Tunis, and the only other section of the old PLO that remained faithful to him was a training unit on an island off the coast of Aden. His strength was not military, although he ensured that Al-Fatah still maintained all the trappings of a military organization. It was political, and on that field, he was undefeated. His PLO rivals had the guns and Assad. It was not enough.

Arafat remained the most prominent political leader of the Palestinians, dealing with the USSR, King Hussein, President Mubarak and, under the table, with some Israelis. Several members of his staff who were identified with the moderate faction were assassinated, and Arafat's own bodyguard, known as Force 17, was expanded: he was afraid equally of the Israelis and his Arab rivals. Also, the chairman needed to demonstrate that he was still a guerrilla leader, and several groups in the P L O, including Force 17, were given the task of proving the point.

One group, led by Khalid Wazir, who used the *nom de guerre* Abu Jihad, called itself the 'Western Sector' because it was based in Tunis. Its commandos were sent to raid Israel by sea. The first, a 28-man group aboard a small freighter, the *Atavirus*, was intercepted by the Israeli navy on 21 April 1985. The ship was sunk, 20 men were killed and the remainder captured. Despite that unpromising beginning, Force 17 tried the same tactic, sending a motor yacht, the *Casselredit*, south from Lebanon to raid Israel in May 1985. It, too, was intercepted and its eight-man crew, including Force 17's deputy commander, surrendered. The next Force 17 attempt – using another motor yacht, the *Ganda*, sailing from Cyprus – was equally unsuccessful.

After that, events suddenly accelerated. On 25 September, a three-man hit squad from Force 17 seized an Israeli yacht with three people on board, in the marina at Larnaca in Cyprus. First, they murdered a woman passenger, then they demanded various concessions from Israel in exchange for their two remaining hostages. Then they murdered their prisoners and surrendered. One of the terrorists turned out to be an Englishman, Ian Davison, who had been recruited by the Palestinians while he was travelling around the world. The P L O claimed that the three Israelis had been spying on the movements of ships such as the *Ganda*. Israel denied it.

On 1 October, Israel retaliated with a long-range air raid against Yasser Arafat's headquarters in Tunis. The chairman was lucky to escape: 50 people, mostly P L O men, were killed. On the same day, the Italian cruise liner *Achille Lauro* sailed from Genoa.

The seizure of this ship was carried out by another of Arafat's organizations, a faction led by yet another experienced terrorist leader, Abul Abbas. He booked four young men (the oldest was 20) on the ship and sent a relative to Italy to coordinate the operation. The relative was picked up by Italian police, and the Israeli raid on Tunis destroyed Abbas's communications system. The four young men, who had smuggled large numbers of weapons on board, were left to their own devices.

Abul Abbas claimed later that their mission was to wait until the cruise liner reached Ashdod (the main Mediterranean port in southern Israel) and then storm ashore and attack oil storage tanks. On 7 October, a sailor noticed their weapons, and the terrorists themselves were discovered shortly afterwards. They therefore seized the ship.

The *Achille Lauro* was then sailing along the coast of Egypt. Most of the passengers had left at Alexandria to visit the pyramids; they were to rejoin the ship at Port Said for the trip to Ashdod. However, there were still 427 passengers and a crew of 80 on the ship, and the four pirates threatened them all with death. They demanded the release of 50 Palestinian prisoners in Israel and, when the Israelis refused, murdered a 69-year-old Jewish American tourist from New

Jersey, Leon Klinghoffer, who was confined to a wheelchair. First, they shot him, then instructed a sailor to throw his body overboard.

This occurred off the coast of Syria. The Syrians refused to allow the ship to dock, and it therefore returned to Port Said. By then, Abul Abbas had reached Egypt and arranged with the Egyptians that the four pirates would be allowed to go free if they surrendered the ship. The P L O then claimed credit for ending a crisis that it had itself begun.

Abul Abbas and the pirates were put on an Egyptian airliner and flown out: the U S Navy intercepted the plane over the Mediterranean and directed it to a Nato base in Sicily. It was the most elegant American riposte to terrorism thus far. As the New York *Daily News* put it: 'WE GOT THE BUMS.' The Italians had not been warned, and insisted on taking charge of the prisoners. In an unpardonable gesture to Arafat, they released Abul Abbas and three of his assistants. The four pirates themselves, however, were tried for murder and piracy and sentenced to terms ranging from 15 to 30 years. The longest sentence was received by the one who had shot Klinghoffer: he escaped from jail in 1996, but was caught again in Spain.

After these disastrous efforts at terrorism, Arafat reverted to diplomacy, once again protesting his opposition to attacks on civilians. In November 1985, immediately after the *Achille Lauro* affair, he issued a formal statement condemning 'all outside operations other than in Israel and the occupied territories and all forms of terrorism' – but left himself an escape clause in which he demanded in return that Israel 'halt all acts of terrorism inside and outside'. Israel was not appeased.

When the Palestinian uprising began at the end of 1987 (*see* Israel, pp. 305–27), a new 'war of spooks' erupted. On 14 February 1988, three senior P L O men who had been directing the *intifada* were killed by a car bomb in Cyprus. Three days later, a limpet mine blew in the hull of a small cruise ship, the *Sol Phyrne*, at Limassol, also in Cyprus. It had been hired by the P L O who intended to load it with exiled Palestinians and sail it openly to Israel, to recreate the voyage of the *Exodus* in 1947. In March 1988, one of Abu Jihad's commandos captured an Israeli bus in the Negev; three civilians were killed.

On 16 April 1988, Abu Jihad was killed, together with his bodyguards, by an Israeli commando raid on his apartment in Tunis. The most senior P L O leader to be killed for years, Arafat's deputy and last loyalist was also the long-term commander of Al-Fatah, and had founded and commanded Black September in 1970. When he was killed, he had been attempting to coordinate the P L O's reaction to the *intifada*, and had sent several commandos into Israel as a demonstration that the 'military option' was still available to him.

## THE LEBANESE

The Palestinians are not the only Arabs to resort to terrorism to further their political objectives. The most violent terrorist campaign waged in Europe since 1945 was the work of Arabs, Armenians and Iranians against France. It reached its climax in September 1986: in two weeks, ten people were killed and 162 wounded in bombs left in public places in Paris. Among those responsible for the bombings was a small gang of fanatic terrorists from the village of

Qubayat in north Lebanon. They were Maronite Christians who supported Syria, and most of them were members of the same family: Georges Abdallah and his six brothers. They were closely allied with the Armenian A S A L A (*see* Terrorism: Forlorn hopes, p. 620), which was also an instrument of the Syrian secret services. However, a year later, during a prolonged confrontation with Iran, it emerged that the chief suspects for many of the bombings were not the Lebanese but the Iranians, taking revenge on France for supporting Iraq during the Gulf War.

The *Factions armées révolutionaires libanaises* (F A R L; Armed Revolutionary Lebanese Factions), like the A S A L A, emerged from the cauldron of the Lebanese civil war. Its first appearance on the scene was in Paris in 1981, when a gunman tried to kill the American chargé d'affaires; he survived. A year later, on 18 January 1982, Lieutenant Colonel Charles Ray, an American military attaché in Paris, was shot. An Israeli diplomat was murdered later that year, by a female assassin. In February 1984 in Rome, F A R L killed the head of the American peacekeeping force in Sinai, and made an attempt on the life of the U S ambassador.

F A R L remained an obscure group, often described as a front for one of the P L O terrorist organizations. Then, in the summer of 1984, a 19-year-old Arab, arrested in Trieste, gave many details of F A R L's organization. The following October, a tall, bearded man walked into a police station in Lyons and asked for police protection. He said that he was an Algerian engineer and claimed that members of the Israeli secret service were following him and trying to kill him.

The men who had been following him then arrived: they were French police. The bearded man was Georges Ibrahim Abdallah, founder and leader of F A R L. He demanded that he be released at once, on the grounds that his organization no longer operated in France. He hinted that the safety of French hostages in Lebanon depended on his release. To prove the point, two of his brothers then kidnapped Gilles Peyrolles, director of the French cultural institute in Tripoli.

The French considered exchanging Abdallah for Peyrolles, but then raided Abdallah's apartment in Paris, where they found the gun that had been used to kill Colonel Ray and the Israeli diplomat. In July 1986, Abdallah was sentenced to four years' imprisonment. It was a ludicrously light sentence, and because he had been held since October 1984, he was due to be released that October. Then came the wave of bomb attacks in Paris, which the government blamed on F A R L. Credit for these atrocities was also claimed by the A S A L A, and it is certain that the two organizations were working together. Abdallah remained in jail.

An organization calling itself the *Comité de solidarité avec les prisonniers politiques arabes et du Moyen-orient* (Committee for Solidarity with Arab and Middle Eastern Political Prisoners) launched a bombing campaign late in 1985 to win the release of three people held in French jails: Abdallah, a second Arab and Varoujan Garabedian, the Armenian responsible for bombing the Turkish Airlines counter at Orly airport in 1983. The campaign was terrorism in its purest form: the bombs were left in cafés and shops and in the streets, aimed almost exclusively at civilian targets.

The first bombs were left in two large department stores in the centre of Paris – the Galeries Lafayette and Au Printemps – on 7 December 1985, and wounded 35 people. The next bomb was placed in a shopping arcade at the Hôtel Claridge on the Champs Elysées on 3 February 1986, and wounded three people. The next day, a bomb in Gibert Jeune, the student bookstore on the boulevard St Michel, wounded four people, and a bomb was found and defused at the Eiffel Tower. Two days later, there was a bombing in the Forum des Halles (an underground shopping mall in the centre of Paris), wounding six people.

It is possible that the bombings were intended to influence the parliamentary elections, which were held in March. The Socialists lost their majority, and were replaced by a conservative government, led by Jacques Chirac, the mayor of Paris. His short administration was punctuated by terrorist bombs. On 17 March, an explosion on the Paris–Lyon express wounded ten, and on the 20th, while Chirac was broadcasting to the nation upon assuming office, a bomb exploded at another shop on the Champs Elysées, killing two people and wounding 28. A few days later, the Corsicans set off their bombs in the Midi, and in May, *Action Directe* joined the fray with bombs in Paris (including one at police headquarters on 9 July, which killed two people), followed by selective assassinations.

On 17 August, a car bomb in Toulon exploded prematurely, killing the four Arab terrorists in the car. Then in September occurred the most violent series of attacks, all the work of Arab or Iranian terrorists.

On 5 September, a bomb was found on the Paris Métro and defused safely. Three days later, a bomb in the post office in the Hôtel de Ville (city hall), where Chirac was still mayor, killed one and wounded 18. On the 12th, a bomb in the Caféteria Casino at La Défense, a large office complex in the western suburbs, wounded 41 people. On 14 September, a bomb in the parking garage of Le Pub restaurant on the Champs Elysées killed two people and wounded two others, and the next day, a bomb exploded in a public office in police headquarters in Paris, where driving licences were issued; one person was killed and 51 wounded.

On 17 September, a bomb thrown from a passing car killed five people and wounded 52 outside a store on the rue de Rennes – the most public and horrible of all the attacks. The police claimed that it was the work of two of Abdallah's brothers, who afterwards drove straight to the airport and left the country. They gave a press conference in Lebanon the next day to claim that they had not been in Paris at the time. Simultaneously, the French military attaché in Beirut, Colonel Christian Goutierre, was assassinated.

On 30 September and again on 10 November, *Action Directe* set off a number of small bombs in Paris, and for a time, the city was paralysed. There were hundreds of bomb alerts as nervous citizens reported suspicious packages across the city, and the streets were cleared as police and bomb-disposal squads rushed from place to place.

Meanwhile, the government was trying a different tack, inspired by the theory that, because a small Lebanese gang would not be capable of anything so extensive, Syria and Iran might be behind the bombing campaign. Secret emissaries went to Damascus and the FARL onslaught ceased (though AD continued its work).

Abdallah was put on trial in February 1987. He was accused of various terrorist acts, including the 1984 murder of Robert Home, the American consul-general in Strasbourg. Abdallah was convicted. The prosecutors then suggested that he should receive a 'moderate' sentence. There was a clear impression that Chirac's government had made a deal with Syria that, in return for Abdallah's release, F A R L would be brought under control. If this were the case, the French public and the trial judge would have none of it: Abdallah was sentenced to life imprisonment.

The bombings ceased, but whether for political reasons or because of police action remained a mystery. In March 1987 police arrested a Tunisian, Fouad Ali Saleh, and a Lebanese, Mohammad Mouhajer, both naturalized French citizens, and a number of other Lebanese and Tunisians. One of them turned informer, and revealed that Saleh had organized a total of 15 bombings and attempted bombings that killed 13 people and wounded 250 others. Among them were the rue de Rennes bomb. The informer collected a reward of $178,000, went to the United States to help American anti-terrorist police, and then returned to Tunis.

It was quickly apparent that Saleh was a major figure in the terrorist network based on the 'Party of God' in Lebanon, the pro-Iranian faction responsible for many of the worst atrocities there. His name was found in the address book of the T W A hijacker, Mohammed Ali Hammadi, who was arrested in Germany in January 1987.

When Saleh came to trial in January 1990, he was accused of directing a 20-strong terrorist group, acting under Iranian orders. None of them was put on trial with him. Police said that the defendants were arrested when replenishing their supplies of explosives with a new consignment brought from Lebanon. Saleh was born in Tunisia, but lived in France. After the Iranian revolution, he studied in Qom, the Shiite theological university in Iran that was Khomeini's base, and was there converted to Shiism. Police claimed that the Saleh gang was connected to senior Iranian officials at the time, notably the then Interior Minister, Ali Akbar Mohtashemi, who has been accused of initiating many acts of terrorism around the world. At the trial, Saleh harangued the court, denouncing France for killing 2 million Algerians during its war of independence (the real figure is probably about 100,000), and shouted 'My name is Death to the West!' and 'War, Holy War'. He told the judge, 'You are posing as great lords, and the only way to make you crack is explosives!' The judge had him removed from the court.

The Iranian connection with the 1985–6 bombings was suggested in July 1987, when French police tried to arrest an Iranian, Wahid Gordji, who worked as a translator at the Iranian embassy. He escaped into that building and the Iranians refused to turn him over. The French claimed that he was not a diplomat and therefore did not enjoy any immunity, and they surrounded the embassy, waiting for him to come out. The Iranians promptly put the French embassy in Tehran under guard, holding French diplomats there hostage.

Police now believed that the 1985–6 bombing campaign had been directed by the Iranians, and suspected that Gordji had provided the contacts with the Lebanese and Tunisian terrorists who had planted the explosives. The stand-off between France and Iran continued until the end of November when the French finally agreed that Gordji should be allowed to leave the country unmolested. The sieges of the two embassies were then lifted. A few days later, France expelled 14 anti-Khomeini Iranian refugees and three Turks, and agreed to pay a longstanding debt to Iran. (Evidently, France now found being a *terre d'asile* too much of a strain.) In exchange, in 1988, the six French hostages held in Beirut were released. The following spring, just before the presidential elections, Mohammed Mouhajer was released, ostensibly for lack of evidence, and the last three French hostages in Beirut were freed, evidently through Iran's good offices. One condition stipulated by Iran, which emerged later, was that France should release a Lebanese terrorist, Anis Naccache, who had been sentenced to life imprisonment for the attempted assassination of former Iranian prime minister, Shahpour Bakhtiar, in 1980. The reports aroused such indignation that Naccache had to remain in jail for another two years. In July 1990, Naccache and four others were released and deported to Iran.

Iran had apparently promised that there would be no further acts of state terrorism in France. On 8 August 1991, an Iranian terrorist group murdered Shahpour Bakhtiar in his house near Paris. His secretary was also killed. One of the three assassins was arrested and warrants for the arrest of several others were issued. In October, a French judge formally charged an official in the Iranian government of directing the conspiracy. The episode abruptly ended efforts by Iran and France to restore good relations, efforts that had begun four years earlier. In December, the Swiss police arrested one of the men wanted in France for the Bakhtiar murder. He claimed diplomatic immunity, although the Iranian embassy in Bern had never registered him. Iran promptly laid siege to the Swiss embassy in Teheran, and for several weeks no Swiss diplomats were allowed to leave the country. Iran eventually relented: perhaps even the Islamic Republic needs the services of the Swiss bankers. In May 1992, the man, Zia Sarhad, was extradited from Switzerland to France. He and another man were tried and convicted in 1995.

In the 1990s, France has cultivated good relations with Iran (and signed a major oil deal, to the Americans' chagrin) and the bombings and murders have been forgotten. However, there remained many unanswered questions, notably concerning the Syrian and Iranian governments' roles in killing French citizens. In April 1986, at the height of the Paris bombing campaign, the Syrian embassy in East Berlin had apparently helped organize the bombing of the La Belle disco, killing two people and provoking the American attack on Libya. A few days later, on 17 April, the Syrian embassy in London was caught *in flagrante* helping a Lebanese terrorist. He had attempted to put a bomb (disguised in a hold-all) on to an El Al flight to Tel Aviv, giving it to his pregnant Irish girlfriend, whom he had told he would meet and marry in Jerusalem. When security men found the bomb, the terrorist immediately fled to the Syrian embassy – which refused to take him. It seems evident that Syria, as a government, was deeply involved in terrorism, attacking Israeli, American and French civilian targets. The British government broke off diplomatic relations with Syria in protest.

France had been the victim of terrorism supported by the Iranian and Syrian governments, by the Party of God, the F A R L and the A S A L A. The campaign continued: in September 1989, the Party of God took the credit for bombing a French airliner over the Sahara, killing 171 people. It alleged that France had failed to meet the conditions that led to the release of the four hostages in Lebanon in 1987, notably by failing to repay money owed to Iran. In October 1991, French prosecutors indicated four Libyans, including Khadafi's brother-in-law, for the bombing (*see* Air terrorism, p. 615). It was not clear whether the Party of God had had anything to do with it.

In November 1989, French and Spanish police broke up another Lebanese terrorist cell that had smuggled hundreds of pounds of explosives into Europe, with which to start a new bombing campaign in France. French police and courts continued to investigate these murky conspiracies. Although the Lebanese civil war came to an end, or at least reached a long-lasting truce, in October 1990, the terrorists there did not renounce the bomb and the gun, and Iran and Libya have not renounced terrorism at all. Although Syria insists on its peaceful intentions, its capacity for murder remains intact, and Assad's capacity for murder is undiminished. The world has not seen the last of Arab terrorism.

## LIBYA

The Libyan government's support of terrorism abroad is well documented. Colonel Khadafy formed a whole terrorist apparatus, with a training school in Tripoli, set up by the American terrorist and con-man Edwin Wilson. However, Wilson was as much concerned with stealing Khadafy's money as with actual terrorism, and the Libyans he trained were conspicuously inefficient. One group loaded a van with a huge quantity of explosives, and set out for Cairo, where they intended to explode it. They got no further than the border, when their bomb exploded prematurely, killing all of them.

Another unsuccessful plot of Khadafy's was an attempt to murder Abdul-Hamid Bakoush, a former Libyan prime minister living in Egypt. Several British and Maltese were hired for the job. The Egyptian security services faked the murder, and Khadafy triumphantly announced it over the radio. Then the Egyptians produced Bakoush at a press conference.

On an earlier occasion, Khadafy had ordered a submarine in the Libyan navy to sink the *Queen Elizabeth II*, which had been hired by a group of American and British Jews for a trip to Israel. The sub's officers were Egyptian, seconded to Libya, and they promptly took it to Alexandria and reported to President Sadat.

Khadafy has sent hit squads to deal with Libyan dissidents living abroad, including one in Denver, Colorado (he was wounded), and a series of bombs were put in places frequented by exiles in Britain in March 1984. The most serious incident occurred on 10 March after a bomb exploded in a nightclub, El Oberge, in Belgravia, injuring 27 people. On 17 April, Libyans in London demonstrated outside the embassy in St James's Square in protest against the execution of a number of students in Libya. A gunman inside fired on them, killing a British policewoman, Yvonne Fletcher, and wounding several other people. As a result, the British government broke diplomatic relations with Libya.

On 8 July, police found the body of a Libyan businessman in his London apartment. Due to stand trial for the bombings, he had presumably been killed by Libyan secret agents to prevent him testifying. A year later, Britain expelled 22 Libyan students, accused of 'revolutionary' activity – that is, terrorism.

In April 1986, the United States bombed Tripoli in retaliation for the Berlin disco bombing. (*See* Libya, p. 71.)

## RELIGIOUS TERRORISM

The Ayatollah Khomeini did not invent religious terrorism. There are plenty of other examples in the modern world – in the Indian subcontinent, in Northern Ireland, in Lebanon and in Syria. Iran was exceptional, however, because there religious terrorism became an instrument of foreign policy. For example, Shiite leaders, who had studied in Iran or in Iraq, played a prominent role in Lebanon's travails, inciting their followers to martyrdom.

One of the periodic revivals in Islam began in the 1960s, among the Shiites of Iraq. It occurred in Najaf, the sect's holiest city, and was led by the Ayatollah Sayyid Mohammed Baqir al-Sadr, who called his movement al–Dawa ('The Call of Islam'). Khomeini, who had directed a similar though more openly political movement in Iran, lived in Najaf after he had been exiled by the shah. Another prominent member of the circle was the Imam Musa Sadr, who established the Amal movement in Lebanon (and was murdered by Khadafy in Libya in 1978). Baqir al-Sadr was executed by Saddam Hussein in 1980. (*See* Iraq, pp. 284–304)

After the Iranian revolution in 1979, the clerical, Marxist and Kurdish terrorists there fought a vicious war against each other. The clerical authorities, who defeated their domestic enemies, never allowed themselves to be distracted from attacking the Great Satan (the United States), the heretical regime of Saddam Hussein in Iraq, Israel, and Western influences wherever they might be found in the Muslim world. Soon after the revolution, the first units of Revolutionary Guards were sent to Lebanon, where they joined forces with the most extreme of the local Shiites.

In Lebanon, after Musa Sadr's disappearence, his followers split into a variety of contending factions of which the best known were the Amal Militia (led by Nabih Berri) and its most extreme rivals, the Islamic Amal (led by Hussein Mussawi) and the Call of Islam (al-Dawa), also known as the Party of God (Hizbollah), led by Sheikh Mohammed Hussein Fadlallah. All these clerics had studied at Najaf or at least had been heavily influenced by the teachings of Baqir al-Sadr and Khomeini. The dissident Shiite movements are constantly at war with Amal, and with the other factions in Lebanon.

Their most remarkable achievement was the invention of the suicide car bomb. Young fanatics, men and women, would be assured of Paradise if they gave their lives for the cause. Scores of them did so, in attacks against Israeli positions, Western embassies (the American embassy was destroyed twice by suicide car bombs) and, most spectacularly, the U S Marine and French army barracks in Beirut in October 1983. Islamic Jihad, the group that claimed responsibility for those attacks, and for kidnapping most of the hostages, is composed of members of both Islamic Amal and Hizbollah, with other freelance terrorists recruited for the occasion. In a statement of policy issued two days after the attack on the Marines, Islamic Jihad stated: 'We are the soldiers of God and we crave death. Violence will remain our only path. We are ready to turn Lebanon into another Vietnam.'

Most of these organizations confine their activities to Lebanon, where there is plenty of work for them, but others have been sent abroad to further Iranian or Syrian objectives. It is an exact recreation of the doctrines and practices of the medieval sect founded in 1094 by Hassan ibn al-Sabbah. From his base on Alamut, a remote mountain in Persia, al-Sabbah sent his followers to kill his enemies, with the assurance that, if they did so, they would go straight to Paradise. To prepare them for the ordeal, they were given hashish, from whence they took their name, 'Assassins'. These suicide missions terrorized the Middle East until the sect's base at Alamut was destroyed by the Mongols. Their descendants are the peaceable Ismailis, whose leader is the Aga Khan.

In 1980 in France, one of the Ayatollah's hit squads attempted to kill Shahpour Bakhtiar, the shah's last prime minister. A second attempt, in 1991, was successful. In 1984 Iranian assassins murdered three former officials of the shah's government in Paris, wounding 18 people. The next month, they bombed a Madrid bar favoured by American servicemen. On another occasion, a bomb was thrown into a Madrid office shared by British Airways and TWA, killing one person. This attack coincided with the trial of two Lebanese, who had been caught attempting to assassinate a Libyan diplomat in revenge for the murder of Mussa Sadr.

There was a bomb attack at Frankfurt airport in June 1985; a bomb went off at Rome airport; a bomb was discovered outside the Iraqi embassy in London before it could explode; and a group of Lebanese Shiites planning to attack the US embassy in Rome was arrested. Despite these foreign atrocities, the main targets of these religious terrorists are in the Arab world. In December 1983, a series of attacks was carried out against targets in Kuwait: one was a suicide car bomb, directed against the American embassy. The group responsible was al-Dawa from Lebanon and it was controlled from Iran. The connection was proved, and reinforced the evidence that Islamic Jihad in Lebanon was working under Iranian direction. It is also clear that the Syrians were deeply involved. Seventeen al-Dawa terrorists were arrested in Kuwait, and three of them were eventually sentenced to death. The sentences were not carried out, but neither were they commuted. They remained suspended over the heads of the imprisoned men until they were freed by the Iraqis when they occupied Kuwait in 1990.

One Syrian faction, acting on orders from Damascus, was the Syrian People's party (PPS). It was originally a Fascist organization, set up in the 1930s, which during the 1960s and 1970s had fought a long, vicious and losing battle against President Assad, until that worthy abruptly decided to co-opt it and use its brutal fanaticism to his own purposes. It was renamed the Socialist Nationalist Resistance party (SNRP), and allied itself with the various Palestinian terrorist organizations. Its most remarkable achievement was the murder of Bashir Gemayel, president-elect of Lebanon, in September 1982. In April 1986, a woman member of the PPS/SNRP took a TWA flight from Cairo to Athens and left a bomb under her seat. It exploded during a later leg of the flight, killing four people.

Instead of recruiting martyrs for the glory of Islam, the P P S/S N R P found young people ready to kill themselves in the war against Israel. It had the distinction of sending the first female suicide bomber to her death, in March 1985, and broadcasting a video she made in advance. Elegantly dressed, and perfectly composed, she said: 'I am very relaxed as I go to do this operation which I have chosen because I am carrying out my duty to my people. I am from the group that decided on self-sacrifice and martyrdom for the sake of the liberation of land and people.' She then drove a car packed with explosives into an Israeli convoy, killing herself and two Israeli soldiers. This sinister precedent was followed by similar acts of self-destruction by a series of young people, who recorded their last statements on video and then drove off to glory.

In October 1987, three men later identified as members of the P P S/S N R P were arrested entering the United States from Canada. They were convicted of illegal immigration and transporting explosives: they had apparently been on a mission directed against other members of the group in New York.

In 1984, Shiites started hijacking airliners, a tactic that the Palestinians had abandoned. First, a group took a French airliner to Tehran, and demanded the release of the Iranians who had been convicted of trying to assassinate Shahpour Bakhtiar. The French government refused to deal, and the hijackers surrendered to the Iranian authorities. In December, another group of Shiites hijacked a Kuwaiti jet, took it to Tehran, and demanded the release of the 17 al–Dawa prisoners held in Kuwait. During this hijacking, the terrorists murdered two American A I D (Agency for International Development) officials who were on the aircraft. Kuwait refused to give in, and after six days on the ground, the Iranian police stormed the airliner and released the hostages. There was widespread suspicion that the 'storming' was a fake, and that the hijackers had been acting on instructions from Iran.

On 14 June 1985, two young Shiites took control of a T W A flight out of Athens, in what turned into the most spectacular hijacking in years. The plane was first taken to Beirut, then to Algiers, then back to Beirut where an American sailor on board was murdered and thrown out on to the runway. The plane then returned to Algiers. By this time, a number of hostages had been released, and now the Greek government did a deal with the hijackers. A third member of the commando had been unable to get a seat on the flight and had been left behind, to be arrested in Athens after the hijacking began. The Greek government flew him to Algiers to exchange him for Greek passengers, including the pop singer Demis Roussos. The hijackers, reinforced by their dilatory comrade, released all the Greeks – except Roussos. Then the plane was taken back to Beirut.

There was a dramatic exchange between the pilot and ground control at Beirut, with the pilot explaining that his plane would crash if it were not permitted to land, and Beirut refusing to allow it; finally, ground control relented. Nabih Berri of Amal controlled the airport, and his troops surrounded the plane. The hostages were taken off, and 30 of them were transported by Amal to precarious safety in Beirut. The hijackers themselves, members of Hizbollah, kept eight others – Jews and American servicemen. Berri supported one of the hijackers' original demands: that Israel release 500 Lebanese Shiite prisoners whom it had taken back to Israel when it had evacuated Lebanon, and 200

Palestinians it had captured during 'Operation Peace in Galilee'. Israel refused, but pointed out that it had already announced that it intended to release its prisoners over the next few months. Since Israel had released 1154 Palestinian and allied prisoners a few months earlier, in exchange for three Israeli PoWs held by Ahmed Jebril's PFLP-General Command, its firm moral opposition to dealing with terrorists was notably weaker than usual.

The hostages were finally released after the United States exerted all the pressure it could manage on President Assad of Syria, who in turn informed Hizbollah that he would cut them off from their bases in Baalbek if they did not turn over the hostages. They were released on 30 June, and sent to Damascus.

In January 1987, one of the hijackers, Mohammed Ali Hammedei, was arrested in West Germany. His trial, in May 1989, was the first involving Islamic hijackers, and proceedings were much simplified when he admitted his guilt. He was sentenced to life imprisonment.

In the next few years, the Iranians were also implicated in the bombing campaign in Paris in 1985–6, and in the Haj riots in Mecca in 1987. There were further attacks in Kuwait, of which the most serious was a suicide car bomb attack on the emir; it failed, though many of his bodyguards were killed. Then in April 1988, a Kuwaiti airliner was hijacked, and after wandering the Middle East and a long stay in Cyprus, during which two hostages were killed and dumped on the tarmac, it finally landed in Algiers. Once again, the demand was for the release of the al-Dawa prisoners, and once again Kuwait refused to give in. After several days' negotiations, the hijackers released their hostages and surrendered, in exchange for permission to leave the country.

These were some of the chief incidents in which Middle Eastern governments authorized terrorism outside the region. The number of attacks in the region itself has been far greater, with constant killings by Iranian, Iraqi and Syrian agents – usually aimed at other Arab or Iranian targets. The two Yemens also frequently sent assassins against each other until they merged in 1990. The most blatant examples are provided by Iraq and Syria. In the 1970s, Iraq hired Abu Nidal to attack Syria and the PLO; then, in the 1980s, he worked for Syria, attacking Iraqi targets, and continuing to assassinate PLO officials. In 1980, after the start of the Iran–Iraq war, Iraqi agents, masquerading as Iranian Arabs, seized the Iranian embassy in London. The building was stormed by the British SAS when the terrorists started killing their hostages.

## AIR TERRORISM

The destruction of a Pan Am flight from London to New York, on 21 December 1988, killing all 259 people on the plane and 11 people on the ground in the small Scottish town of Lockerbie, showed how vulnerable air traffic remained, despite all the precautions developed over the years. Ahmed Jibril's PFLP-GC was suspected of planting the bomb: when West German police had raided a PFLP-GC hideout in Frankfurt in the autumn of 1988, they had discovered a bomb factory and a completed bomb, disguised as a radio. British police established that the Pan Am bomb had been concealed in a radio stowed in a suitcase, probably put aboard in Frankfurt, where the flight had originated.

After two years of intense police work, two Libyans were formally indicted for the bombing on 14 November 1991. They were Lamen Khalifa Fhimah and Addel Basset al-Megrahi, described as intelligence agents, who were working under cover for Libyan Arab Airlines in Malta in 1989 and who had arranged for the suitcase containing the bomb to be sent from Malta to Frankfurt, where it was put on the first Pan Am plane. A State Department spokesman said, 'The bombers were Libyan government intelligence operatives. This was a Libyan government operation from start to finish.' The suggestion was that the Lockerbie bombing was revenge for the American attack on Tripoli in 1986. Perhaps. But many people continued to suspect Syrian and Iranian involvement, perhaps in revenge for the destruction of the Iranian airliner 17 months earlier. Syria had been re-admitted into America's good graces after it sent troops to the Gulf in the 1991 war, and sceptics suspected that the two police forces might have been dissuaded from including Syria in the accusation against Libya as a reward. A few months before the Lockerbie indictments, a French judge formally accused Libya of directing the bombing of the UTA airliner over Niger in 1989 (*see below*).

Air terrorism was not an Arab monopoly. The first case on record was purely criminal: an American put a bomb in his wife's suitcase, to collect the insurance. The biggest death toll was the Air India explosion in 1985, which killed 329 people.

Attacks on aircraft, either through hijackings, bombings or with guns and rockets, have provoked the most general changes in civilian life in the past 20 years. The scores of hijackings of the 1970s led to elaborate security measures at most airports in the world, including all international airports, and much reduced the threat. There are still hijackings when security is insufficient or when the terrorists have accomplices on the ground, but the greatest danger now is the planting of bombs.

On 2 February 1970, a SwissAir flight from Zurich to Tel Aviv exploded in the air, killing all 47 people on board. George Habash's Popular Front for the Liberation of Palestine was suspected, and it was perhaps the first case of a 'carry-on' bomb. On 28 July 1971, a Dutch girl was stopped by El Al security men: she was found to be carrying a suitcase with a bomb in it that had been given her by a friend to take to Israel. On 1 September, El Al found another 'carry-on' bomb at London's Heathrow airport.

The next recorded bombing attempt was successful: on 9 September 1974, the New Arab Youth for the Liberation of Palestine put a bomb on a TWA flight from Israel to the United States, with a stop at Athens. 84 people were killed when the plane exploded over the Aegean.

Two years later, on 6 October 1976, a Cuban exile terrorist group, calling itself '*El Condor*', put a bomb on a Cubana Airways DC-8 flying from Barbados to Kingston, Jamaica, en route to Havana. All 73 people on board were killed when the plane crashed in the Caribbean, including 24 members of the Cuban national fencing team. *El Condor*'s leader, Orlando Bosch, and the two men who had planted the bomb were arrested and sentenced to life terms.

The Nicaraguan Contras are believed to have been responsible for planting a bomb on a Nicaraguan airliner in Mexico City on 12 December 1981; it was discovered in time. On 2 July 1982, the Guatemalan 'Guerrilla Army of the Poor' (EGA) put a bomb on an Eastern Airline jet bound for Miami. It exploded prematurely, killing a baggage-handler at Guatemala City airport. The following month, a new sort of bomb made its appearance, a small device that could be concealed in a luggage rack or under a seat. The first one exploded on a Pan Am flight from Tokyo to Hawaii on 11 August, killing a Japanese teenager. Two weeks later, a similar bomb was found by a Pan Am ground crew in Rio de Janeiro.

There were several bombings and attempted bombings in 1983. A bomb destined for a Turkish airliner, and the work of Armenian terrorists, exploded prematurely at Orly airport in Paris, killing eight people, and a bomb on a Gulf Air jet killed 122 people – an atrocity attributed to Abu Nidal. The Orly bomb, described on pages 623–4, was part of the ASALA attack on Turkey. Abu Nidal's attack was perhaps inspired by Iran, in revenge for the Gulf States' support for Iraq during the Gulf War, or by Syria, working at Iran's behest (Abu Nidal was then employed by Syria).

The other 1983 bombings involved no casualties: a bomb was found on a Pakistani airliner, and three bombs were discovered in December, two on flights to Israel, one on a flight from Rome to New York. In January 1984, a bomb was found on a flight from Tel Aviv to Athens. On 18 January, a bomb exploded in the cargo bay of an Air France flight from Pakistan to Paris. The plane landed safely.

The most serious act of air terrorism occured in 1985, when an Air India plane was destroyed over the Atlantic, south of Ireland, killing all 329 people on board. It is universally believed that it was the work of Sikh terrorists. According to the US Defense Department report, it had been organized by a Sikh group called the Dashmesh Regiment, which had been founded by General Shabeg Singh under the direction of the Sikh terrorist leader Sant Jarnail Singh Bhindranwale (see India, p. 184). There were actually two bombs, both loaded on to aircraft at Toronto on 23 June 1985. One destroyed the Air India flight, the other was put aboard a jet belonging to a different airline, flying to Tokyo. The suitcase with the bomb was ticketed through to India, and should have been transferred to an Air India flight from Tokyo to Delhi. The flight was delayed, however, and the bomb exploded at Tokyo airport, killing two Japanese baggage-handlers.

The next bombings were in April 1986. On 2 April, a bomb on a TWA flight from Rome to Athens exploded as the plane approached Athens. The flight had originated in Cairo, and the bomb had been concealed under a seat occupied on the first leg of the flight by a Syrian Christian woman who lived in Lebanon. She had left the flight in Rome and had flown directly to Beirut. The explosion blew out the side of the plane, killing four passengers. On 17 April, a pregnant Irish girl was detained at Heathrow airport in London. She was booked on an El Al flight to Israel, and her Palestinian boyfriend had given her a suitcase, containing a bomb. He was arrested in London, and the apparent complicity of Syrian security service led the British government to break diplomatic relations with Syria.

On 27 September 1987, a Korean Airlines flight exploded over the Indian   **617**

Ocean, killing all 115 people on board. It was the work of North Korean terrorists (*see* Korea, p. 215).

On 19 September 1989, terrorists destroyed a French airliner in Africa. It was a U T A flight from Brazzaville to Paris, by way of Ndjamena, a D C-8 carrying 171 people. It exploded in the air, high over the Sahara, and crashed in Niger. On 30 October 1991, a French judge issued arrest warrants for four Libyans whom he accused of organizing the bombing. One was said to be Colonel Khadafy's brother-in-law. Investigators found relatives of the Congolese who had been persuaded with promises of large payments to carry the bomb on to the plane. He had been most nervous, and had told his family about the plot. He was told to leave the plane at Ndjamena, where a car would be waiting for him. He was given a striking tie to wear for purposes of identification, and was told that the bomb would go off on the ground, after he had left the plane. In the event, it exploded in the air, before the plane reached Ndjamena. The men who had sent him to his death were Libyan agents.

## EGYPT

The single most dramatic act of Islamic terrorism was the murder of the President of Egypt, Anwar Sadat, on 6 October 1981. The country was celebrating the anniversary of the Yom Kippur war in 1973, and Sadat was reviewing a parade. As one unit passed, a group of soldiers broke away, ran to the reviewing stand and opened fire on the president and his entourage, killing Sadat and a dozen other people. Vice-President Hosni Mubarak was sitting next to Sadat and was slightly wounded. The attackers did it to protest against the peace with Israel, and to the greater glory of Islam.

They did not change government policy. Mubarak remains committed to the treaties Sadat signed, and a firm ally of the United States. He sent troops to join the attack on Iraq in 1991.

The fundamentalist terror movement carried out several assassinations and attempts during the 1980s and early 1990s, including attempts on ministers of the interior, the speaker of parliament, and leading secular intellectuals. The Nobel Prize winner Naguib Mahfouz was nearly killed in a knife attack in 1994. In 1991 they began a sustained attack on the Egyptian state and on the tourist trade, which is its major industry, and on the Coptic Christian minority.

About 10 per cent of Egyptians are Christians (the most prominent is Boutros Boutros-Ghali, former secretary-general of the U N), and Muslim fundamentalists began attacking their churches and villages and assassinating their local leaders, particularly in the south of Egypt. In May 1991 13 Coptic peasants were massacred in Dairut. At the same time, the fundamentalists started a guerrilla war against the state, killing police officers and government officials.

They draw their strength from the immovable poverty of rural Egypt and the degradation of the slums. All the promises of successive governments, from King Farouk through Nasser's socialism to Mubarak's relatively unfettered capitalism, have failed to bring any real economic progress. Egypt, rather like Mexico, remains marked by governmental incompetence and corruption, and a huge disparity in income between the rich and everyone else. Egyptians, like the rest of

the Arab world, can only watch the rise of East Asian prosperity and even the relatively hopeful development of the Indian subcontinent, and bewail their own inability to move into the international mainstream.

Islamic fundamentalists, as in Turkey, often provide services the government cannot. They also offer an explanation for Egypt's misery: were Arabs faithful to the Koran, prosperity would follow immediately. The failure of Sudan and Iran to make any economic progress, even though they adhere strictly to Islamic law and detest the West, does not deter them.

The assault on tourists began on 30 September 1992, when *Al Gamaa al Islamiya*, the Islamic Group, warned tourists to leave Egypt. The following month, gunmen shot up a German tour bus. There were about 30 attacks on tourists in the next three years, including trains and tour boats, despite police efforts to protect them. In April 1995 17 Greek tourists and an Egyptian were killed outside their hotel in Cairo.

The Islamic Group has extended its operations abroad. In June 1995 it attempted to kill President Mubarak, mounting a machine-gun and grenade attack on his motorcade as he drove through the streets of Addis Ababa to a meeting of the Organization of African Unity. The following November, it launched a car bomb at the Egyptian embassy in Islamabad (15 Pakistani security men were killed).

Mubarak blamed the government of Sudan for the attack on his life, and for a while it appeared possible that he might send his army to Khartoum to exact vengeance.

The killings are not nearly so numerous as those in Algeria: 11 in 1991, 93 in 1992, 207 in 1993, 279 in 1994, 373 in 1995, 174 in 1996. In fact, in early 1997, the government hoped that they were winning the battle: 17,000 suspects were arrested between 1992 and 1995, and 62 executed. Then in February 1997 23 Christians were killed in two massacres in southern Egypt. In September, 10 tourists were shot in a bus outside the Cairo Museum, and in November, 58 tourists and four Egyptian police were killed at Queen Hatshepsut's temple in Luxor. The six terrorists were all hunted down and killed, and the president fired the police officials who had failed to provide any security at the site.

That horror showed that the Islamic Group remained a danger to the regime. It lacks a charismatic leader, like the Ayatollah Khomeini in Shah Mohammed's Iran, but the causes of popular discontent will not soon be overcome and terrorism seems certain to continue.

# FORLORN HOPES

## THE ARMENIANS

Early in the morning of 28 April 1988, a respectable Arab businessman left his home in Paleo Faliro, a rich suburb of Athens, intending to go to the airport. He had lived in the apartment near the sea for three years. His neighbours believed that he came from Aden and had noted that he kept strange hours: he would often work all night, and disappear during the day. He and his wife lived a private life, and his visitors came and went discreetly.

On that spring morning, he planned to take an early flight to Belgrade. He never made it. Two masked men were waiting for him in the street, and shot him, point blank, with a sawn-off shotgun. It was an old-fashioned rub-out of an old-fashioned terrorist. The man whom police described as Abu Mohammed Kassim was, in fact, Hagop Hagopian (or Agop Agopian), the 39-year-old leader and chief executioner for the Armenian Secret Army for the Liberation of Armenia (A S A L A).

The A S A L A was dedicated to redressing an historic injustice, by murder, and intended to force Turkey to cede a large part of its eastern territory to the Armenians. These are the lands from which the Armenian population was driven in 1915, during World War I, with the loss of at least 600,000 lives. It was a great crime, and even though it had occurred more than 70 years before, Hagopian and his friends were determined to avenge it. When they had liberated Turkish Armenia, they planned to federate it with Soviet Armenia, for Hagopian was also a Communist, collaborating with the K G B in destabilizing Turkey. It is not recorded how these exiled fanatics reacted to the Soviet Armenians' suddenly revived nationalism.

Hagopian, like so many modern terrorists, was born in Lebanon, a member of the large Armenian community there. At the beginning of the civil war, he joined one of the first Armenian militias formed to defend the community, and was soon fighting in all the shifting alliances of Lebanon. Although his chief concern was with Turkey, he remained loyal to Palestinian cause, like George Abdallah of the F A R L, who was also a Christian and a Marxist. Both groups had a natural affinity to the Palestinian Christian Marxist George Habash, founder of the P F L P (*see* Arab terrorism, pp. 594–619).

Hagopian founded the A S A L A in 1975. Eventually it was split by violent disputes, which were settled in the usual manner by execution, sudden murder and car bombs. Hagopian won, but a rival organization – the Justice Commandos of the Armenian Genocide – survived to go its separate and violent way. It is as openly Fascistic as the A S A L A is Communist.

Hagopian and his comrades differed from the Arab terrorists, however. While he was perfectly ready to fight the good fight for the Communist revolution, for the Palestinians and against all their enemies, he was a man obsessed with the wrongs done to Armenia. He seems to have spent his life, from his mid-20s, in a hopeless but vicious war against Turkey: within the space of ten years, the A S A L A killed 28 Turkish diplomats around the world and 34 other people, in hundreds of shootings, bombings and hostage takings.

Finally, Hagopian's enemies caught up with him. Greek police claimed to have no clues as to their identity. Perhaps they were rival Armenian terrorists, perhaps the murderers were freelance assassins hired for the job, perhaps Turkish, or French counter-terrorist organizations were involved.

## HISTORY

There are now about 3 million Armenians in the former Soviet Republic of Armenia. There are also between 500,000 and 600,000 people of Armenian descent in the United States, 300,000–350,000 in France, 200,000 in Lebanon and 150,000 in Iran. There are Armenian communities elsewhere including Jerusalem, where the Armenian quarter contains an opulent museum, and Istanbul. In all of Turkey, there are now perhaps 50,000 Armenians where once there were 1.7 million. There are few or none of them in their ancestral home in Eastern Anatolia around Lake Van and Mount Ararat.

The Ottoman empire in its dotage was a cosmopolitan and decadent society. It was also usually tolerant of its many minorities. The sultan was a Turk, but he had Greek, Armenian, Jewish and Arab subjects who, for the most part, coexisted amicably together. Every so often, however, the Turks would suppress revolts among their subjects with wild savagery – for example, the Bulgarian massacres in the 1870s, and a first round of attacks on the Armenians in 1894–6 in which up to 200,000 people were killed.

The nature of the Ottoman empire was abruptly changed as a result of the rise of nationalism in the 19th and 20th centuries. In 1908 – later than the Greeks but earlier than the Arabs – the Turks caught the fever. The old, mad, murderous Sultan Abdulhamid was deposed, and the Young Turks set about establishing a Turkish nation. Up to 1914, they suffered humiliating defeats, losing Libya to Italy and almost all their residual possessions in Europe (including Salonkia, Mustapha Kemal's home town). Like that other decaying empire, Austria-Hungary, Turkey allied itself with Germany, and in 1914 these allies forced Turkey into the war. Like the other belligerents, the government appealed to native chauvinism to inspire the troops. In 1915, when the Russians were attacking from the east through Turkish Armenia, and two months after the British had landed at Gallipoli and threatened Constantinople, the government turned on the Armenians, much as Hitler was to turn on the Jews 25 years later. On 24 April 1915, Armenian leaders in Constantinople were rounded up; they were later executed. Armenians in the east were driven from their homes and forced to trek through the wilds of Kurdistan to Syria, Iran and Mesopotamia. The best estimate is that at least 600,000 people were killed or died during the pogrom.

After Turkey's defeat in 1918, there was a brief effort to revive Armenia in its ancestral homelands, but it was swept away by the restored Turkey of Kemal Ataturk. In the process, the Turks expelled the Greek communities of Ionia on the eastern shores of the Aegean, a region that had been Greek since before the Trojan War, 3000 years ago. Anatolia thus became Turkey.

The Armenian Holocaust has been the central national experience for all Armenians ever since, as the Jewish Holocaust is for the Jews. Unlike West Germany, Turkey has never admitted guilt and has never made the least reparation; in fact, it denies that the Holocaust ever happened. Despite the Ataturk revolution, which forcibly remade Turkey into a modern state (it has applied to join the European Union), there is a strong residuum of chauvinism in Turkey, and a great reluctance to admit error, even after 80 years. It must be added that at the time of the Holocaust, Armenians were actively helping the enemy in the east, and the British were at the gates of the capital. Also, though countless Armenians were massacred by Turkish troops, and the Turkish army was responsible for the deaths of the others who were driven on foot through the mountains, Turkey's object was its own security, not genocide. There were no gas chambers.

## Terrorism

The first act of modern Armenian terrorism occurred in Los Angeles on 27 January 1973. A 78-year-old Armenian immigrant, Gourgen Yanikian – who claimed to remember the massacres of 1915 and to have lost many relatives in them – murdered Mehmet Baydar, the Turkish consul-general in Los Angeles, and Bahadir Demir, the consul. Yanikian was convicted of murder, pleading at his trial that he had been avenging his lost parents, after 58 years.

Three months later, two bombs exploded in Paris, one at the Turkish consulate, another at the Turkish Airlines office. No one was hurt on that occasion, but it soon became evident that a terrorist campaign specifically directed at Turkish diplomats and offices was under way. In October 1973, the Turkish information office in New York received through the mail a package containing a bomb: it was the work of a 'Yanikian commando'.

There were no Armenian terrorist acts in 1974, but the following year, after the official establishment of the A S A L A in Beirut, Armenian terrorists in Lebanon began a sustained attack on Turks and Turkish offices there and abroad. In October, A S A L A commandos attacked the Turkish embassy in Vienna, killing the ambassador, and assassinated the Turkish ambassador to France, and his driver, in Paris. Attacks on Turks in Lebanon continued, as did bombing attacks on Turkish targets in Europe. In May 1977, five people (including an American) were killed by a bomb planted by an Armenian terrorist at Istanbul airport; the following month, the Turkish ambassador to the Vatican was assassinated.

In 1978, there were attacks on the Turkish ambassador to Madrid (killing his **622** wife and two other people). In October 1979, the son of the Turkish ambassador to the Netherlands was murdered, and a Turkish tourist official was murdered in Paris in December.

There were dozens of bombing attacks in France, West Germany, Switzerland, Britain, Spain, Belgium and the Netherlands. Most of them were the work of the A S A L A, but some other Armenian terrorist groups occasionally claimed credit – including the right-wing Justice Commandos of the Armenian Genocide, which has been responsible for many of the attacks in the United States.

A Turkish diplomat in Athens and his 14-year-old daughter were killed in July 1980. The press attaché at the Paris embassy was shot and paralysed in September. In October, two Armenian terrorists were arrested in Switzerland when a bomb they were preparing exploded in their hotel room; one was an American woman, Suzy Mahseredjian from Canoga Park, California. After that, Armenians took to attacking Swiss targets: in October, for instance, the Swiss Centre in central London was bombed. In 1980, a number of bomb attacks were carried out against Turkish targets in New York and Los Angeles. Evidently the Armenian community in the United States had become infected with the same murderous insanity that had already afflicted Armenians in Lebanon.

Terrorism spread to Australia, where the Turkish consul in Sydney was murdered in December 1980 (six years later, a car bomb in the consulate in Melbourne would kill one person) and also to Iran where a commando attacked the Turkish embassy in Tehran in 1981 (two men were captured and executed). There have been a number of other attacks in Tehran since then. In 1981, the terrorists started operations in Denmark, and continued to attack targets in Switzerland and in France. On 24 September 1981, four Armenian terrorists seized the Turkish consulate in Paris, wounding the consul and a guard (who later died). The terrorists later surrendered, were tried and given light jail terms. In October, Armenians attacked Fouquet's, the luxury food shop on the Place de la Madeleine, Paris. The following months saw many other bombings in France.

In January 1982, yet another Turkish consul-general in Los Angeles was assassinated, this time by two men riding a motorcycle, who shot him when his car was stopped at a red light. One of the terrorists was arrested, a 19-year-old immigrant from Lebanon (now serving a life term). The honorary consul in Boston was murdered in May, and the military attaché in Ottawa in August. In December, A S A L A added Saudi Arabia to its list of enemies, ostensibly because the Saudis were sympathetic to Turkey. It is also possible that they were acting at the behest of Syria or some other enemy of the Saudis. A pair riding a scooter threw a bomb at the Saudi embassy in Athens; it bounced off a lamp-post, and exploded, killing one of the terrorists. There were other attacks that year in Bulgaria and Yugoslavia and, in 1983, an attack on the British Council in Paris. On 16 June 1983, terrorists carried out an attack with grenades and pistols in the bazaar in Istanbul, killing two (including one of the terrorists) and wounding 21.

In one two-week period in July 1983, 15 people were killed (including five terrorists) and more than 60 wounded. On 14 July, the Turkish ambassador to Brussels was murdered. On the 15th, a bomb in a suitcase at the Turkish Airline counter at Orly airport, south of Paris, exploded, killing eight people and injuring 60. The dead comprised two Turks, one American, one Swede and four French. Varoujan Garabedian, a 19-year-old Syrian Armenian was arrested and confessed to planting the bomb. It had been intended to explode in the air. After that, French police pursued Armenian terrorists unrelentingly, and the terrorists formed a new 'Orly Organization' to fight them.

On the same day, a similar bomb was found in London, but it was defused before it could explode. On the 27th, five terrorists were killed during an attack on the Turkish embassy in Lisbon, four of them by their own explosives. A diplomat's wife and a Portuguese policemen were also killed, and several other people injured.

In March 1985, Armenian terrorists attacked the Turkish embassy in Ottawa, killing a Canadian security guard. They held the place and a number of hostages for several hours before surrendering. Two weeks later, Armenian terrorists threatened to plant bombs on the Toronto underground. However, although the city was seriously disrupted for several days, there were no bombings.

In November 1985, French police arrested an American Armenian terrorist in Paris: Monte Melkonian from Fresno, California. He had been Hagopian's top assistant before splitting with the A S A L A to form his own group. By then, Armenian terrorists were regularly putting bombs in shops, offices, bus stations and other public places in France, which was now as much the enemy as Turkey. Terrorists regularly demanded that their comrades in French jails be released.

The new organization, or the new name for the old organization, was the *Comité de solidarité avec les prisonniers politques arabes et du Moyen-orient* (Committee for Solidarity with Arab and Middle Eastern Political Prisoners). It appears to have been an alliance between the A S A L A and F A R L (*see* Arab terrorism: The Lebanese, pp. 606–11), and closely associated with the Iranian and, probably, the Syrian secret services. The A S A L A and its allies put bombs in the Galeries Lafayette and Au Printemps department stores in Paris in December 1985, four more bombs elsewhere in Paris in February 1986, a bomb on a Paris–Lyon train in March, another in a shopping arcade in Paris (which killed two people) on 20 March, and one on the Paris Métro in September. A bomb in the Hôtel de Ville in Paris on 8 September killed a postal worker; three more people were killed in further bombings in the next few days and a bomb in the rue de Rennes on 17 September killed five and wounded 52 people. In October, Hagopian, in Beirut, issued further threats of violence if Garabedian were not released. He said:

A S A L A has already declared that all French presences in the world are military targets. We defy Chirac and promise Mitterrand catastrophes in the event that they renege on their promise – that is, the release of political prisoners.

This was presumably a reference to the reputed French agreement to release Georges Abdallah, the leader of the F A R L, in the summer of 1986, in exchange for Gilles Peyrolles, a French hostage held in Lebanon. Peyrolles was released, but the French kept Abdallah in jail after discovering evidence that he had murdered an American and an Israeli diplomat. The F A R L accused the French of treachery and launched the bombing campaign, with A S A L A's assistance. Possibly Hagopian had expected Garabedian to be released at the same time as

Abdallah. In February 1987, Hagopian issued a communiqué in Beirut claiming responsibility for all the recent bombings in Paris. It added:

France should start adopting the needed steps and procedures to release Armenian as well as Arab patriots. A truce-like period of calm between us and the French government must have convinced public opinion that we respect the interests and security of the French and other people. The wave of explosions will return to the streets of France; all French economic, air traffic and marine facilities will be subjected to sabotage.

The communiqué finished by again demanding the release of Varoujan Garabedian.

Nothing much was heard of the A S A L A in the following 14 months, until Hagopian's death. There were certainly negotiations between the French government and other groups of Lebanese terrorists to achieve the release of French hostages in Beirut, but Garabedian was not released. Hagopian was perhaps the key figure in the Armenian terrorist network, and his death a serious blow. But he had many comrades, and it is not likely that they will give up the struggle.

That will only happen if their supplies are cut off. It is quite evident that the A S A L A was supported by other organizations during its most active period: hundreds of bombings and scores of murders obviously required considerable sums and ready access to explosives and arms. The P L O reportedly trained 200 A S A L A fighters in 1981, and they joined in the battles against the Israelis the following year. Hagopian and his terrorists had to leave Lebanon with Arafat and the P L O and are believed to have taken temporary refuge in Libya. In the mid-1980s, he was able to return to Lebanon, but apparently continued to live, unsuspected, in Athens. After his murder, his widow informed the police of his identity.

## THE MOLUCCANS

The most forlorn of all forlorn hopes is the Republic of South Molucca. There are about 40,000 people of Moluccan descent living in the Netherlands, survivors and descendants of the 12,000 people who fled with the Dutch when they were driven out of Indonesia in 1949 (*see* Indonesia, p. 205). Most of them came from Calvinist Ambon, one of the Spice Islands, and they had fought with the Dutch against Sukarno.

They found their exile in cold and damp Holland not at all to their taste. They did not adapt to the tidy ways of the Dutch and came to form an underclass in their own ghettos in Amsterdam and other cities, together with immigrants from another former Dutch colony, Surinam in South America. The old told tales of their lost paradise, and the young and passionate dreamed of returning there. They all agreed that the Dutch had cheated them twice: first, by betraying their homeland to Sukarno; second, by leaving them to rot in their ghettos. The Dutch, naturally saw things differently.

On 3 December 1975, one group of Moluccan terrorists seized a train, and another took over the Indonesian consulate in Amsterdam. Six terrorists held the train near Beilin in the north of the country: two passengers and the train driver were killed, and 33 hostages were held captive for three weeks. The five Moluccans who stormed the consulate held 25 hostages, and demanded that **625** their leaders be allowed to hold a televised press conference to air their grievances, that the government apologize for 30 years' mistreatment, and that Indonesia establish an independent republic in the Moluccas. Eventually, they were persuaded to surrender.

On 23 May 1977, other Moluccans repeated the same attempt. A seven-man commando seized a train at Assen and held 50 hostages, while six terrorists seized an elementary school, at Bovinsmilde, with 105 children and six teachers. They made the same demands as their predecessors, and once again, the Dutch authorities prepared to wait them out. The terrorists at the school released the children and surrendered after four days, but the seige of the train continued for three weeks. Finally, Dutch marines stormed the train at dawn, distracting and terrifying the Moluccans with thunderflashes. Six of the terrorists and two hostages were killed.

# A CHRONICLE OF TERRORISM

This list concentrates on 'international terrorism' since 1968 – that is, operations outside the country of chief concern to the terrorist, or a collaborative effort by more than one group. I have not included the great majority of terrorist incidents that are exclusively limited to one country (Sri Lanka, Peru, India, El Salvador, Guatemala, etc.) which are of no direct international concern. I have also left out most of the acts of terrorism perpetrated by the I R A in Northern Ireland, by various Palestinian groups in Israel and by all the terrorist factions in Lebanon. They are covered elsewhere in this book. I have also followed the practice of Dobson and Payne (*see* Further reading) who list the first appearances of terrorist groups, or the first examples of such terrorist operations as hijackings. Appendix I I I lists assassinations since 1945.

## 1968

| | |
|---|---|
| *22 July* | PFLP hijacks an El Al flight to Algiers. |
| *2 August* | First ETA murder, Melitón Manzanas, police chief of San Sebastián. |
| *26 December* | PFLP attacks El Al jet on the ground in Athens. One passenger killed. |
| *28 December* | In retaliation, Israel attacks Beirut airport, destroys 13 Middle East Airline planes. |

## 1969

| | |
|---|---|
| *2 February* | El Al plane attacked on the ground in Zurich; copilot and one terrorist killed. |
| *7 February* | Marks & Spencer in London bombed. |
| *29 August* | First non-Israeli plane hijacked by PFLP, a TWA flight taken to Damascus. |
| *9 September* | First diplomatic kidnapping: Charles Elbrick, American ambassador in Brazil, seized and then exchanged for 15 Brazilian terrorists. |
| *12 December* | First 3 Baader–Meinhof bombs in Berlin. |
| *12 December* | Italian fascists explode first bomb in Piazza Fontana, Milan, killing 16. |

## 1970

| | |
|---|---|
| *2 February* | Swissair plane explodes in mid-air: 47 killed, probably by PFLP. |
| *3 March* | 7 Japanese Red Army terrorists, wielding samurai swords, hijack a JAL flight; take it to North Korea. |

| | |
|---|---|
| *31 July* | Tupamaros kidnap 2 diplomats in Montevideo; American Dan Mitrione killed. The incident was the basis of the Costa-Gavras film *State of Siege*. |
| *24 August* | Anti-Vietnam War protestors' bomb at University of Wisconsin, Madison, kills 1. |
| *6 September* | 3 airliners hijacked by PFLP; 2 taken to Dawson's Field in Jordan, one to Cairo. Terrorists fail to take El Al plane. On 9 September, BOAC jet also hijacked to Dawson's Field. Incident leads to expulsion of PLO from Jordan. |
| *5 October* | British trade commissioner in Quebec, James Cross kidnapped, Québecois minister of labour Pierre Laporte kidnapped 10 October. Cross released 3 December, Laporte murdered. |
| *12 December* | ETA kidnaps West German honorary consul in San Sebastián, Eugene Beihl. He is released when Franco commutes 6 death sentences passed after Burgos trial. |

## 1971

| | |
|---|---|
| *8 January* | Tupamaros kidnap British ambassador to Uruguay, Geoffrey Jackson; keep him in a box for 8 months. They demand the release of 150 prisoners. Government refuses, but 106 escape and Jackson released. |
| *6 March* | Sinhalese leftist (JVP) terrorists attack US embassy in Colombo. |
| *5 May* | Turkish terrorists murder Israeli consul-general in Istanbul. |
| *20 July* | Black September attacks office of Jordanian airline, Alia, in Rome. |
| *28 July* | Dutch girl given a 'carry-on' bomb to take on El Al flight from Amsterdam; is discovered. Similar plot discovered on 1 September, in London. |
| *28 November* | Jordanian prime minister, Wasfi Tal, murdered by Black September in Cairo. |

## 1972

| | |
|---|---|
| *6 February* | 5 Jordanian workers in Cologne murdered by Black September. |
| *18 February* | Factory making parts for Israeli planes bombed in Hamburg. |
| *19 February* | Shoot-out between Japanese police and Japanese Red Army is followed by siege of a house in Karuizawa. On 27 February, 1000 police storm house; 2 police killed, JRA leaders arrested. In next few days, 14 bodies of JRA members found buried in woods. |
| *22 February* | IRA bombs Parachute Regiment HQ in Aldershot, killing 9 soldiers and civilians. |
| | Lufthansa jet hijacked to Aden by PFLP. Plane released after airline pays $5 million in ransom, $1 million to Aden. |
| *15 March* | Italian radical-chic publisher and terrorist Giangiacomo Feltrinelli, founder of the Red Brigades, kills himself attempting to blow up an electric pylon. |
| *8 May* | PFLP commandos, 2 men and 2 women, hijack Sabena flight, divert it to Lod in Israel. Israeli security men storm the plane; kill male terrorists and one hostage. |
| *11 May* | Baader–Meinhof bombs at US army base in Frankfurt kill Colonel Paul Bloomquist and wound 14. |
| *12 May* | 2 bombs explode at police HQ in Augsburg, 1 in police HQ in Munich. |
| *17 May* | Luigi Calabresi, Milan police chief, killed in first Red Brigade attack. |
| *19 May* | 2 bombs in Springer publishing head office, Hamburg. |
| *24 May* | 3 American soldiers killed by car bombs on US base at Heidelberg. |
| *31 May* | 3 Japanese Red Army terrorists attack tourists at Lod airport; kill 28. 2 terrorists killed. |
| *8 July* | Car bomb planted by Israeli agents kills PFLP official in Beirut. |
| *5 September* | Munich Olympics massacre. Black September commandos seize Israeli athletes; kill 11 Israelis, one West German policeman. 4 terrorists killed. 3 survivors released when Lufthansa plane hijacked in October. |
| *9 September* | First Israeli killed by letter bomb, a technique later used by Israelis and IRA. |

## 1973

| | |
|---|---|
| *27 January* | Armenian immigrant murders Turkish consul-general in Los Angeles and the consul, in Santa Barbara. |

| | |
|---|---|
| *1 March* | Black September seize Saudi embassy in Khartoum. 2 American and one Belgian diplomat murdered. |
| *28 March* | Irish navy intercepts freighter *Claudia* running 5 tons of arms from Libya into Ireland. |
| *4 April* | Bombs explode outside Turkish consulate and Turkish Airlines offices in Paris. |
| *10 April* | Israeli commando raid on PLO offices in Beirut kills 17 people, including 3 senior PLO officials. |
| *28 June* | Leading PFLP terrorist in Europe, Mohammed Boudia, killed by car bomb in Paris. |
| *1 July* | Israeli military attaché Yosef Alon shot in Washington. |
| *2 July* | Moroccan waiter, mistaken for Black September leader, killed by Israelis in Lillehammer, Norway. Hit men arrested and jailed by Norwegians. |
| *5 August* | New Palestine terror group, NAYLP, machine-gun TWA plane arriving in Athens from Tel Aviv; 5 passengers killed. |
| *5 September* | Italians arrest NYALP gang armed with SAM-7s, planning to shoot down planes arriving at Rome airport. |
| *28 September* | Al-Saiqa (Syrian-backed Palestinian terrorists) seize Austrian train carrying Jewish emigrants from Soviet Union. Austrians close Jewish transit station in Vienna. |
| *17 December* | Five NYALP terrorists fire-bomb Pan Am jet at Rome airport, killing 32. |
| *20 December* | Spanish prime minister, Luis Carrero Blanco, killed by ETA car bomb. |
| *30 December* | Carlos attempts to assassinate Joseph Sieff, chairman of Marks & Spencer. |

## 1974

| | |
|---|---|
| *3 February* | IRA bomb in the luggage compartment of a bus on the M62, carrying soldiers and their families, kills 9 soldiers, a woman and her 2 children. |
| *5 February* | Patty Hearst kidnapped by Symbionese Liberation Army (SLA). |
| *11 April* | PFLP–GC commando infiltrates Israel, takes refuge in apartment building in Qiryat Shemona. 18 killed, 16 wounded. |
| *17 May* | 6 SLA terrorists killed in gun battle with Los Angeles police. |
| *4 August* | Bomb planted by Italian Fascists on Rome–Milan express kills 12, wounds 48. |
| *7 September* | TWA flight from Israel blows up over Aegean, after stop in Athens. The man responsible, Ahmed al-Ghafour, leader of the NAYLP, executed by Al-Fatah on 12 September. |
| *13 September* | Japanese Red Army seize French embassy in The Hague and demand release of JRA prisoner in France. Carlos bombs Le Drugstore on 15 September, in support, killing 2. French government surrenders its prisoner. |
| *5 October* | IRA bomb in pub in Guildford kills 5, wounds 15. |
| *10 November* | Baader–Meinhof gang kills West German supreme court judge Guenther von Drenkmann. |
| *21 November* | IRA bombs in Birmingham kill 21, wound 168. |
| *13 December* | Carlos gang aim rocket at El Al plane at Orly airport, Paris; hit Yugoslav plane. |
| *19 December* | Carlos gang returns to Orly, gets into a gun fight with police, takes hostages and hijacks a flight to Iraq. |

## 1975

| | |
|---|---|
| *24 January* | Puerto Rican terrorist bomb in Fraunces Tavern, New York, kills 4, injures 53. |
| *29 January* | Weather Underground sets bomb in State Department, Washington, much damage, no injuries. |
| *27 February* | Baader–Meinhof gang kidnap Peter Lorenz, conservative Berlin politician. Government frees 5 terrorists in exchange for his release. |
| *24 April* | RAF seize West German embassy in Stockholm. 2 diplomats, 2 terrorists killed. |
| *27 June* | Paris police try to arrest Carlos. Carlos kills 2 policemen and an informant, escapes. |
| *27 July* | Tamil Tigers begin their terrorist campaign in Sri Lanka by murdering Alfred Durriapah, Mayor of Jaffna. |
| *22 August* | First Corsican fatalities, 2 policemen killed during occupation of a vineyard. |

**629**

| | |
|---|---|
| *22 October* | Armenian gunmen attack Turkish embassy in Vienna, killing ambassador. On 24 October, Turkish ambassador to Paris and driver murdered. |
| *3 December* | Moluccan terrorists seize Indonesian consulate in Amsterdam and train near Beilin; 4 people killed. They surrender after 4 weeks. |
| *6 December* | Siege of Balcombe Street, London: 4 IRA terrorists take refuge in apartment with hostages after a chase through London. They surrender after 6 days. |
| *21 December* | Carlos leads West German–Palestinian commando attack on OPEC head-quarters in Vienna. 3 guards killed, 11 oil ministers taken hostage; released in Algiers. |
| *23 December* | Greek terrorists, of November 17 group, shoot Richard Welch, CIA station chief in Athens. |
| *29 December* | Croatian bomb in TWA left-luggage locker in La Guardia airport, New York, kills 11, injures 70. |

## 1976

| | |
|---|---|
| *8 May* | Ulrike Meinhof hangs herself in Stammheim jail. |
| *11 May* | General Joaquin Zentero Anaya, Bolivian ambassador to Paris, killed by *Action Directe* in revenge for Ché Guevara. |
| *6 June* | Francis Meloy, US ambassador to Lebanon, killed with 2 others. |
| *27 June* | Palestinian–West German commandos seize Air France jet, take it to Entebbe, Uganda. Israelis rescue hostages, killing 5 terrorists. |
| *31 July* | British ambassador to Dublin murdered by IRA. |
| *10 September* | 5 Croatians hijack a plane from La Guardia with phoney bombs, take it to Paris, leaving a bomb in a locker in Grand Central Terminal, New York. Bomb explodes, killing policeman, 11 September. |
| *21 September* | Former Chilean minister Orlando Letelier and his secretary killed by a car bomb in Washington D.C. |
| *6 October* | Cuban exile organization El Condor plants a bomb on Cubana Airlines DC-8. It explodes over Caribbean, killing 73. |
| *28 October* | Protestant terrorists shoot Maire Drumm, IRA leader, in hospital. |

## 1977

| | |
|---|---|
| *9 March* | Hanafi Muslims occupy 3 sites in Washington, take 134 hostages, to avenge killing of 7 Hanafis by Black Muslims in 1973. 1 killed, 19 injured. |
| *4 April* | West German chief prosecutor, Siegfried Buback, shot by RAF in Karlsruhe. |
| *23 May* | Moluccan terrorists seize school in Bovinsmilde, and a train at Assen, Netherlands. Train stormed by marines after 22 days: 2 hostages, 6 terrorists killed. |
| *29 May* | A bomb left by Armenians in Istanbul airport kills 5. |
| *31 July* | RAF murders Juergen Ponto, West German banker. |
| *5 September* | RAF kidnap Hans-Martin Schleyer, leading businessman, killing 4 body-guards. He is held in France and murdered on 19 October. |
| *13 October* | PFLP–RAF hijacks Lufthansa plane. Finally land in Mogadishu, Somalia. Plane stormed by West German commandos; 3 terrorists killed. |
| *20 October* | Baader and two other RAF leaders commit suicide in Stammheim. |
| *31 December* | Two Syrian intelligence agents, posing as diplomats, kill themselves with their own bomb in London. |

## 1978

| | |
|---|---|
| *4 January* | Abu Nidal assassin kills PLO representative in London, Said Hammami, who had contacted Israeli liberals. |
| *18 January* | Two Abu Nidal gunmen murder Egyptian editor in Cyprus and attempt to hijack Cypriot airliner. Egyptian commandos storm plane, but 15 are killed by Cyprus National Guard. |
| *16 March* | Aldo Moro, former Italian prime minister, kidnapped in Rome by Red Brigades; 5 bodyguards killed. He is murdered on 10 May. |
| *26 May* | First Unabomber bomb wounds 1 at Northwestern University, Evanston, Illinois. |

| | |
|---|---|
| *31 July* | Al-Fatah gunmen storm Iraqi embassy in Paris (because of Iraqi support for Abu Nidal). A French policeman and Iraqi diplomat killed. |
| *7 September* | Bulgarian agents kill exiled broadcaster, Georgi Markov, with poisoned umbrella in London. |

## 1979

| | |
|---|---|
| *22 January* | Mastermind of Munich massacre, Ali Hassan Salameh, killed by car bomb in Beirut. |
| *22 March* | IRA murders British ambassador to Netherlands. |
| *30 March* | British Conservative MP, Airey Neave, killed by car bomb at House of Commons garage, by INLA (break-away IRA faction). |
| *29 June* | RAF attempts assassination of Nato commander, General Alexander Haig. |
| *8 August* | Earl Mountbatten and 3 other people killed by IRA bomb in Co. Sligo, Ireland. 18 British soldiers also killed by bomb at Warrenpoint, Co. Down, Northern Ireland. |
| *12 December* | *Meibion Glyndwr* (Sons of Glendower) open campaign against English by burning 4 holiday homes. |

## 1980

| | |
|---|---|
| *January–April* | 32 summer cottages in Wales burned. |
| *17–19 February* | Terrorists seize Dominican embassy in Bogotá, taking 80 hostages, including the US and 12 other ambassadors. After 61 days' siege they are flown to Cuba. |
| *30 April* | Iranian embassy in London seized by Iraqi agents posing as Iranian Arabs. SAS storm building on 5 May. |
| *17 May* | Shining Path in Peru begin their terrorist campaign with attacks on polling stations in an election. |
| *18 July* | Iranian agents attempt to assassinate Shahpour Bakhtiar, former Iranian prime minister, in Paris. 2 people killed (*see* 8 August 1991). |
| *2 August* | Fascist bomb in Bologna station kills 84, wounds 186. |
| *26 September* | Neo-Nazi bomb at Munich *bierfest* kills 13 (including terrorist), wounds 312. |
| *3 October* | Two Armenian terrorists injured in Geneva hotel room while preparing a bomb. Bomb in synagogue in rue Copernic, Paris, kills 4, injures 12. |
| *17 December* | Armenians assassinate Turkish consul-general in Sydney. |
| *31 December* | Norfolk Hotel in Nairobi, owned by Zionists, bombed by PFLP–GC. 16 people killed. |

## 1981

| | |
|---|---|
| *13 May* | Attempted assassination of Pope John Paul II. |
| *31 August* | RAF bomb in USAF HQ at Ramstein, West Germany, wounds 20. |
| *September* | Sikh terror campaign opens in Punjab with murder of Hindu editor. |
| *6 October* | President Sadat assassinated by fundamentalist terrorists in Cairo. |
| *20 October* | 7 men, 4 women in joint Weather Underground, Black Panthers and Black Liberation Army commando attack on Brinks van at shopping mall in Nanauet, NY, take $1.5 million. 1 security guard and 2 police officers killed. |
| *28 November* | Muslim Brotherhood car bomb kills 68 in Damascus. |
| *17 December* | US General James Dozier kidnapped by Red Brigades in Verona. Rescued on 28 January. |

## 1982

| | |
|---|---|
| *18 January* | Lieutenant Colonel Charles Ray, US military attaché in Paris, shot by FARL. |
| *28 January* | Turkish consul-general in Los Angeles shot by 2 Armenians from Lebanon. On 4 May the honorary consul in Boston is shot. |
| *16 February* | Two members of Carlos gang arrested in Paris. Carlos threatens retaliation, and on 30 March, a bomb kills 6 and wounds 15 on Toulouse–Paris express. |

| | |
|---|---|
| *3 April* | Israeli diplomat shot in Paris by FARL. |
| *3 June* | Israeli ambassador to London, Schlomo Argov, shot and wounded by Abu Nidal gang. Incident used as pretext for Israeli invasion of Lebanon. |
| *20 July* | 2 IRA bombs in London (in Hyde Park and Regent's Park) kill 11. |
| *7 August* | Two Armenians attack Ankara airport; 9 killed, 82 injured. |
| *9 August* | Bomb in Jewish restaurant in Paris kills 6. |
| *3 September* | General dalla Chiesa murdered by Mafia in Sicily. |

## 1983

| | |
|---|---|
| *13 February* | Gordon Kahl, North Dakota tax-resister, kills two US marshals. He is shot by FBI 3 June in Ozarks, killing sheriff during shootout. |
| *16 June* | ASALA attack in bazaar in Istanbul kills 2. |
| *15 July* | ASALA bombs Turkish Airlines desk at Orly; kills 7. |
| *27 July* | 5 Armenian terrorists attack Turkish embassy in Lisbon. Diplomat's wife and Portuguese guard killed along with all 5 terrorists. |
| *1 October* | Bombs at international trade fair in Marseille destroy Algerian, American and Soviet pavilions, killing 1, injuring 26. |
| *9 October* | North Korean terrorists try to kill South Korean president in Rangoon; 21 killed. |
| *23 October* | Suicide bombers attack US Marines and French troops in Beirut; 241 Americans and 58 French killed. |
| *7 November* | Bomb in Capitol, Washington, first of eight there and in New York by a revolutionary group that also robbed a Brinks armoured car in New York in 1981. Seven people tried and convicted. |
| *15 November* | Greek November 17 terrorists shoot US naval attaché George Tsantes in Athens. |
| *12 December* | Attacks on US and French embassies in Kuwait; 4 killed, 60 injured, al-Dawa terrorists arrested. |
| *17 December* | IRA bomb outside Harrods department store in London kills 6, wounds 94. |

## 1984

| | |
|---|---|
| *29 January* | *Action Directe* bombing campaign in Paris. |
| *10 March* | Libyan secret service bombs exiles in Britain. A bomb at a night club in Belgravia in London injures 27. |
| *17 March* | René Schleicher, head of *Action Directe*, arrested in Avignon with 10 other terrorists. |
| *17 April* | Libyan exiles demonstrate against Khadafy outside embassy in London. Man inside opens fire, killing British policewoman, Yvonne Fletcher. |
| *20 May* | Car bomb outside Ministry of Defence in Pretoria, South Africa, killed 19, wounded 239. |
| *June* | Euro-terrorists hold secret conference in Lisbon to set up a 'Politico–Military Front'. |
| *4 June* | Indian army attacks Golden Temple in Amritsar. |
| *18 June* | US Neo-Nazis shoot Jewish radio host Alan Berg in Denver. |
| *24 June* | Belgian CCC terrorists seize 800 kg of explosives from quarry. |
| *8 July* | Libyan agent responsible for March bombings found murdered in London, presumably by other Libyan agents. |
| *31 July* | Air France jet hijacked to Tehran; 2 killed. |
| *20 September* | Suicide car bomb attack on US embassy in Beirut; 23 killed. |
| *12 October* | Bomb in Grand Hotel, Brighton during Conservative party conference misses prime minister but kills 5. |
| *31 October* | Indian prime minister Indira Gandhi assassinated by Sikh bodyguard. |
| *3 December* | Islamic Jihad gunmen hijack Kuwaiti jet to Tehran; kill 2 US officials on board; demand release of al-Dawa terrorists. Surrender after 6 days. |
| *9 December* | Neo-Nazi Robert Mathews, leader of The Order, killed in shootout on island in Puget Sound, near Seattle. |

## 1985

| | |
|---|---|
| 25 January | *Action Directe* kills French General René Audran. |
| 10 March | Suicide bomber from Syrian National Resistance party kills 2 Israelis in military convoy. First non-Islamic suicide attack. |
| 26 March | Turkish terrorist bombing campaign in Bulgaria; 7 killed on train. |
| 21 April | Al-Fatah commandos intercepted off coast of Israel; 20 killed, 8 captured. |
| 5 May | Israel releases 1154 prisoners, including Japanese Red Army survivor of Lod massacre, in exchange for 3 Israeli PoWs held by PFLP-GC. |
| 11 June | Jordanian airliner hijacked on flight from Beirut by Shiite terrorists led by Fawaz Younis. Hostages released. Younis kidnapped by American agents 13 September 1987 on a yacht off Cyprus and brought to the US. |
| 14 June | Islamic Jihad hijacks TWA jet out of Athens. American sailor murdered. |
| 23 June | Sikhs put bombs in suitcase on Air India plane out of Toronto and Air Canada flight to Tokyo, intending the latter to be transferred to Air India flight there. First exploded over the Irish Sea, killing 329; second exploded on ground in Tokyo, killing 2. |
| 10 July | French agents sink Greenpeace's *Rainbow Warrior* in Auckland harbour, New Zealand; one passenger killed. |
| 8 August | RAF car bomb kills two American servicemen on air base in Rhein-Main, West Germany. |
| 25 September | Al-Fatah terrorists (Force 17) kill 3 Israeli tourists on yacht off Cyprus. In retaliation, Israel bombs PLO HQ in Tunis on 1 October. |
| 30 September | 4 Soviet diplomats kidnapped by Sunni terrorists in Beirut; one killed. |
| 7 October | 4 Al-Fatah pirates seize Italian cruise liner *Achille Lauro*; kill one American tourist before surrendering. Arrested by US Navy. |
| 6 November | M-19 terrorists, in pay of Medellín cocaine cartel, seize Palace of Justice, Bogotá; kill 11 judges and about 100 others. |
| 7 December | Arab bombing campaign in Paris began with bombs in Galeries Lafayette and Au Printemps stores wound 35 people. |
| 23 December | ANC bomb in Christmas shopping crowd in Durban kills 5, wounds 48. |
| 27 December | Attacks on El Al airline counters in Rome and Vienna airports by Abu Nidal gang; 19 killed, over 100 wounded. |

## 1986

| | |
|---|---|
| 2 April | Bomb on TWA flight from Rome to Athens kills 4 Americans, including 18-month-old baby. Syrian terrorists suspected. |
| 5 April | Bomb in La Belle disco in Berlin kills US soldier and Turkish woman. Apparently Syrian-inspired operation, carried out by West Germans and Lebanese, with Libyan encouragement. US uses incident as pretext to attack Tripoli on 15 April. 2 British and 1 American hostage in Lebanon murdered on 17 April in revenge, possibly by Libyans. |
| 17 April | El Al security men at Heathrow Airport find carry-on bomb in luggage of pregnant Irish girl, given to her by Palestinian boyfriend. He was working with Syrians. |
| 26 June | Sendero Luminoso bombs Cuzco–Machu Picchu train, killing 8. |
| 14 July | 72 killed by car bomb in Karachi. |
| 5 September | Abu Nidal gang hijacks Pan Am jet over India; takes it to Karachi. Suspecting attack, hijackers massacre 20 passengers. |
| 6 September | Abu Nidal gunmen massacre 21 people in synagogue in Istanbul; commit suicide. |
| 17 September | Series of FARL/ASALA and Iranian bombs in Paris (beginning on 7 December 1985) climax with bomb in rue de Rennes killing 5, wounding 52. |
| 25 October | ETA car bomb kills governor of Guipuzcoa, General Rafaél Garricho Gil, his wife and son. |
| 7 November | *Action Directe* kills president of Renault in Paris. |

## 1987

| | |
|---|---|
| *21 January* | 13 civilians killed in Inkatha attack on ANC leader in Natal, organized by ministry of defence. |
| *March–April* | 12 members of the Irish National Liberation Army killed in internecine fighting, including (15 March) Gerard Steenson, known as 'Dr Death', and (21 March) Mary McGlinchy (whose husband had been INLA chief of staff; now jailed). |
| *1 June* | Rashid Karami, Lebanese prime minister, assassinated. |
| *22 July* | Palestinian journalist Ali Naji al-Adhami shot in London; died on 29 August. |
| *30 October* | French Navy intercepts the *Eksund* off Brittany, carrying 150 tons of Libyan weapons for IRA. |
| *8 November* | Bomb at Remembrance Sunday parade at Enniskillen, Co. Tyrone, Northern Ireland, kills 11, injures 60. |
| *25 November* | Palestinian hang-glider attacks Israeli army camp; kills 6 soldiers. |

## 1988

| | |
|---|---|
| *13 February* | Three PLO officials killed by car bomb in Cyprus, either by Israeli or Abu Nidal agents. |
| *17 February* | American Col. William Higgins, serving with UN forces in Lebanon, kidnapped. Murder disclosed 1989. |
| *12 April* | Japanese terrorist Yu Kikumura arrested in New Jersey, planning a bombing campaign in New York. |
| *14 April* | 5 people killed by bomb at US navy club in Naples. Chief suspect is Japanese Red Army member, one of those released by Japanese government after JAL hijacking in 1977. |
| *16 April* | Italian senator Roberto Ruffilli murdered by Red Brigades. |
| *17 April* | Israeli agents kill PLO leader Khalid Wazir (Abu Jihad) in Tunis. |
| *28 April* | Hagop Hagopian, Armenian terrorist leader, murdered in Athens. |
| *12 May* | Car bomb blows up 200 m from Israeli embassy in Nicosia. Apparent Abu Nidal operation. |
| *19 May* | Pro-Austrian secessionists in Alto Adige, Italy, set off series of bombs. |
| *28 June* | US naval attaché in Greece killed by November 17 gang. |
| *11 July* | 2 Abu Nidal killers, one possibly Hejab Jeballah (Samir Kadar), killed by own bomb in Athens. Later that day, terrorists attack cruise ship *City of Poros*, killing 9 and wounding 90. Their weapons came from Libya. |
| *7 September* | Italian police arrest 21 Red Brigades terrorists calling themselves the Fighting Communist Party. Believed responsible for series of murders. |
| *9 December* | Israel attacks PFLP HQ near Beirut, killing 20. |
| *21 December* | Pan American flight from London to New York blown up over Scotland, 270 killed. |

## 1989

| | |
|---|---|
| *29 March* | Sheik Abdullah Ahdal, Muslim leader in Belgium, and an aide assassinated by Abu Nidal group. |
| *10 May* | Sharon Rogers, wife of the Captain of the USS *Vincennes* that shot down Iranian airliner in 1988, escapes a bomb attack in San Diego, California. |
| *31 July* | Islamic Jihad release video of U S Col. William Higgins hanging. |
| *8 September* | British soldier's wife killed by I R A bomb in Germany, the 8th attack on British military personnel in Europe that year. |
| *19 September* | U T A flight from Brazzaville to Paris blown up over Sahara by Libyan agents. 171 killed. |
| *22 September* | I R A bomb kills 9 Royal Marine bandsmen and one civilian in barracks in Deal, wounds 22. |
| *13 November* | Rohana Wijeweera, Sinhalese terrorist leader, killed by security forces. |
| *16 November* | 6 Jesuit priests murdered by army death squad in San Salvador. |
| *27 November* | Medellín bomb on Avianca plane kills 107. |

## 1990

| | |
|---|---|
| 4 February | 9 Israelis on a tour bus killed in attack in Egypt. |
| 3 April | Gerald Bull, Canadian ballistics expert, who was working on a 'super-gun' for Iraq, murdered in Brussels. |
| 18 April | 11 children killed in attack on school bus in Beirut. |
| 13 May | 26 people killed in car bomb in Bogotá. |
| 28 May | Two Australian tourists machine-gunned by IRA terrorists in Holland, who mistook them for British soldiers. |
| 6 June | British woman vet injured by a car bomb placed by animal rights terrorists. |

## 1991

| | |
|---|---|
| 14 January | Salah Khalaf (Abu Iyad), Yasser Arafat's second-in-command, killed in Tunis, with head of PLO security and an aide, by Abu Nidal terrorist. Khalaf allegedly ordered the Munich massacre in 1972. |
| 26 January | 4 Pakistanis hijack Pakistan Airlines plane to Singapore, demand release of ex-prime minister Bhutto's husband from prison. Police storm plane, kill all 4. |
| 19 April | Patras, Greece. A Palestinian terrorist and seven Greek bystanders killed when bomb explodes prematurely. The terrorist had intended to bomb the British consulate. |
| 4 May | 13 Coptic peasants massacred in Dairut, Egypt. |
| 29 May | 9 people, 4 of them children, killed by ETA car bomb on a Civil Guards barracks in Vic, near Barcelona. 45 injured. |
| 31 May | Two Basque terrorists shot near Vic. One was Joan Carlos Monteagudo, responsible for many car bombs, including the 29 May one. 4 other suspects arrested. |
| 8 August | Shahpour Bakhtiar, former Iranian prime minister, murdered in Paris by Iranian agents, with his secretary. |
| 9 November | Chechen commando led by Shamil Basayev hijack Soviet airliner to Turkey. |
| 25 December | Kurdish terrorists firebomb a clothing store in Istanbul, killing 11. |

## 1992

| | |
|---|---|
| 16 February | Israeli raid kills Sheikh Abbas Mussawi, chairman of pro-Iranian Hizbollah (Party of God), Shiite terrorist group, his wife, son, and 5 bodyguards. |
| 12 March | Salvatore Lima, ex-mayor of Palermo and Mafia operative, assassinated. |
| 17 March | 30 killed by car bomb at Israeli embassy, Buenos Aires. |
| 10 April | Bomb in City of London causes $1 billion (£600m) in damage, kills 3, injures 80. |
| 19 April | FBI confronts white supremacist Randy Weaver in Idaho. One agent killed. Later, Weaver's son and wife killed by FBI sniper. |
| 23 May | Giovanni Falcone, anti-Mafia prosecutor in Sicily, assassinated in Palermo, with his wife and 3 bodyguards. |
| 19 July | Paolo Borsellino, anti-Mafia prosecutor, and five bodyguards assassinated in Palermo. |
| 12 September | Abimael Guzman ('Gonzalo'), head of *Sendero Luminoso*, arrested. |

## 1993

| | |
|---|---|
| | Series of 17 letter bombs in Austria, continuing over 14 months into 1994, kills 4 Gypsies and injures 9. |
| 15 January | Salvatore 'Toto' Riina, head of Mafia in Sicily, arrested in Palermo. |
| 23 January | 2 CIA employees shot dead, 3 wounded, outside CIA HQ, Virginia. |
| 26 February | Islamic-Palestinian bomb in World Trade Center, New York, kills 6, wounds over 1000. |

| | |
|---|---|
| 10 March | Anti-abortion fanatic shoots Dr David Gunn at abortion clinic in Pensacola, Florida. |
| 12 March | 9 car bombs in Bombay kill over 300. |
| 16 March | Bomb in Calcutta kills about 50, apparently set off accidentally by bomb makers. |
| 13 April | Attempted assassination of former US President George Bush, by Iraqi agents, in Kuwait. |
| 24 April | Kashmir Muslims hijack plane in India, killed when police storm plane. |
| 24 May | Cardinal Juan Jesús Posadas Ocampo killed in Guadalajara, Mexico, police say by drug bandits. |
| 27 May | Mafia car bomb outside Uffizi Gallery, Florence, kills 5, injures 30, damages museum. |
| 19 June | Nail bomb in Cairo kills 7, fifth bomb since February, killing 17, wounding 69. |
| 23 June | First 8 of large group of Arabs arrested in New York, charged with making bombs to blow up UN and traffic tunnels into Manhattan. |
| 27 July | Car bomb in Milan kills 5, 2 bombs in Rome damage churches. |
| October | Algerian Islamic Front announces it will kill all foreigners after 1 December. |
| 23 October | 9 Protestants, including 2 girls and 4 women, killed in bomb at chip shop in Shankill Road, Belfast, together with IRA bomber. |
| 2 December | Pablo Escobar, Colombian drug lord, killed by police in Medellín. |
| 5 December | Letter bomb injures mayor of Vienna, part of anti-immigrant bombing campaign. |
| 15 December | 12 Croatian and Bosnian workers massacred in Algeria as part of anti-foreign campaign. 51 foreigners killed in next 6 months. |

## 1994

| | |
|---|---|
| 25 February | 29 Palestinians killed by Jewish settler in Hebron mosque, three more trampled to death in the stampede, about 90 wounded, terrorist killed. |
| 27 February | 10 people killed by bomb in Maronite church in Junieh, Lebanon. |
| 8 April | Car bomb kills 8, wounds 44 in Afula, Israel. |
| 24 April | Car bomb kills 9, wounds 90 in Johannesburg. |
| 25 April | Car bomb kills 10 in Johannesburg (other bombs cause damage, no deaths). |
| 18 June | UVF terrorists kill 6 Catholics watching World Cup in pub. One, 87, oldest killed during troubles. |
| 20 June | Bomb in mosque in Meshed, Iran, kills 26, wounds 170. |
| 23 June | Police arrest head of Naples Comorra, Biaggo Cava. |
| 4 July | Turkish embassy counsellor Omar Sipahioglu killed by November 17 gunman in Athens. Gunman used .45 revolver again, 20th killing by group. |
| 5 July | 5 killed, 26 injured by bomb at bus stop near US base in Honduras. |
| 18 July | Bomb kills 96 at Jewish organization HQs in Buenos Aires. |
| 20 July | Possible bomb crashes Panama airliner, 21 killed, 12 of them Jewish. |
| 26 July | Car bomb at Israeli embassy in London injures 13. |
| 27 July | Car bomb at Balfour House, housing Jewish organizations in London, injures 5. |
| 29 July | General Francisco Verguillas, and 2 others, killed in Madrid. |
| | Abortion doctor and escort killed by anti-abortion terrorist in Pensacola, Florida. |
| 15 August | Carlos arrested in Sudan, sent to France. |
| 24 August | 5 firebombs set by animal rights terrorists do $3 million in damage to shops on the Isle of Wight. |
| 25 August | French police arrest ETA gunwoman Irene Odoia Lopez Riano in Aix. She is accused of killing 23 people. |
| 14 October | Attempted assassination of Naguib Mahfouz in Cairo. |
| 19 October | Suicide bomb in bus in Tel Aviv kills 23. |
| | Bomb at Ministry of Religious Affairs in Baghdad kills 1. |
| 23 October | Gamini Dissanayake, Sri Lankan presidential candidate, killed with 51 others, including United National Party general secretary, two former ministers and one MP, by suicide bomb at election rally. |
| 11 December | Bomb on Philippine airlines jet kills 1 – set by Muslim separatists. |
| 24 December | 4 terrorists seize Air France Airbus in Algiers, fly it to Marseille, kill 4 |

hostages. French police storm plane 26 December, killing terrorists. 24 wounded.

| | |
|---|---|
| *27 December* | 3 French and 1 Belgian priest killed in Algeria. |

## 1995

| | |
|---|---|
| *22 January* | 21 (including 20 soldiers) killed by 2 suicide bombs in Bir Zid, N. Israel. |
| *30 January* | 42 killed, 258 wounded by suicide car bomb in Algiers. |
| *5 February* | 4 Gypsies killed by pipe bomb in Oberwart, Austria. |
| *25 February* | Bomb on train in Assam kills 27 soldiers (Nagaland National Socialist Council responsible). |
| | 20 killed in Sunni attacks on 2 Shiite mosques in Karachi. |
| *27 February* | Car bomb kills 54 in Zakho, in Iraqi Kurdistan. |
| *8 March* | 2 American diplomats killed in Karachi. |
| *20 March* | Gas attack on Tokyo subway kills 12, injures over 4700. |
| | Hutu ambush in Burundi kills 3 Belgians. |
| *2 April* | 6 people, including at least 2 terrorists, killed by accidental explosion in bomb factory in Gaza. |
| *19 April* | Bomb in Oklahoma City, 169 killed, including 1 worker killed during rescue, over 400 injured. |
| *24 April* | Unabomber kills man in Sacramento (18th bomb in 15 years, 3rd death). |
| *3 May* | Parcel bomb in Frankfurt kills postal worker, injures 11. |
| *9 June* | Gilberto Rodriguez Orejuela, leader of Cali Cartel, arrested in Cali. |
| *10 June* | Bomb at concert in Medellín kills 29, wounds 205, probably set by leftist guerrillas. |
| *25 June* | Attempted assassination of President Mubarak of Egypt, on visit to Addis Ababa. |
| *25 July* | Algerian bomb on Paris Métro kills 7, wounds over 80. 8th victim dies later. There were 8 Islamic bombs in France in 1995. |
| *6 August* | Arrest of Miguel Rodriguez Orejuela, top Cali Cartel figure. 6 Cali leaders caught since 9 June. |
| *7 August* | 22 people killed by suicide car bomb in Colombo. |
| | 11 killed by truck bomb in Algeria. |
| *13 August* | Norwegian tourist beheaded in Kashmir by separatist terrorists. |
| *21 August* | Suicide bomb on bus in Jerusalem kills 5, wounds 100, 6th bomb in 10 months, killing 64. |
| *4 September* | Bomb in Srinagar kills 13, wounds 25. |
| *29 September* | Algerian terrorist Khaled Kelkal, believed responsible for French bombings, killed by police. |
| *26 October* | Fathi Shiqaqi, head of Islamic Jihad, anti-Israel terrorist organizer, shot in Malta. |
| *4 November* | Yitzak Rabin, prime minister of Israel, assassinated in Tel Aviv, by Jewish extremists. |
| *13 November* | Car bomb kills 5 American military personnel and 2 Saudis in Riyadh. |
| *19 November* | Car bomb at Egyptian embassy in Islamabad kills 15, wounding 59. |
| *11 December* | 6 naval employees killed, 12 injured, by ETA car bomb in Madrid. |
| *12 December* | 15 killed, 40 injured by car bomb in Algiers. |
| *21 December* | 31 killed by car bomb in Peshawar. |

## 1996

| | |
|---|---|
| *5 January* | Leading Hamas terrorist Yehiya Ayash killed in Gaza by exploding cellular telephone, presumably by Mossad. |
| *29 January* | La Fenice, Venice opera house, burnt by arsonists. |
| *31 January* | Truck bomb in Colombo kills over 90, wounds over 1000. |
| *9 February* | IRA bomb in London kills 2, wounds over 100, breaking ceasefire. |
| *23 February* | Saddam Hussein's 2 sons-in-law, General Hussein Kamel al-Majid and Saddam Kamel al-Majid, who had defected to Jordan, lynched in Baghdad on their return, together with various relatives including children. |
| *24 February* | First of 4 suicide bombs in Israel that kill 62 and wound over 200 in 12 days. |
| *26 February* | 5 people killed, 3 injured by car bomb in Tirana. |

| | |
|---|---|
| *3 April* | Unabomber arrested in Montana. |
| *18 April* | 17 Greek tourists killed in Egypt. |
| *21 May* | 16 killed by Kashmiri car bomb in Delhi (Jammu and Kashmir Islamic Front). |
| *11 June* | Bomb in Moscow subway train kills 4, wounds 12. |
| *25 June* | 19 USAF men killed, 386 Americans, Saudis and others wounded, in car bomb attack in Dharan, Saudi Arabia. |
| *26 June* | Veronica Guerin, Irish journalist, killed by gangsters in Dublin. |
| *22 July* | Bomb at Lahore airport kills 6. |
| *27 July* | Pipe-bomb at Atlanta Olympics kills 2, wounds over 100. |
| *21 September* | Mir Murtaza Bhutto, brother of Pakistan prime minister, killed in shoot-out in Karachi. |
| *6 November* | 31, including many women and children, murdered in Sid el Kebir, 30 miles south of Algiers. |
| *10 November* | 13 killed, over 20 injured in bomb in Moscow cemetery. |
| *17 December* | 6 Red Cross workers killed in Chechnya. |
| | Over 500 hostages taken by Tépac Amaru at Japanese embassy in Lima. |
| *24 December* | White terrorist bombs kill 4 in South Africa. |
| *31 December* | Car bomb in Damascus kills 9, wounds 44. |

## 1997

| | |
|---|---|
| *2 January* | 8 letter bombs sent to Arabic newspaper bureau in Washington and Fort Leavenworth prison, Kansas, from Alexandria, Egypt. |
| *18 January* | 26 killed by car bomb in Lahore, including Zia ur-Rahman Faruqi, head of militant Sunni group. |
| *13 March* | 7 teenage Israeli girls shot by Jordanian soldier at border. |
| *21 March* | 4 killed by suicide bomb, including bomber, in Tel Aviv café, 43 wounded. |
| *30 March* | 16 killed, dozens wounded, in hand-grenade attack on political rally in Phnom Penh. |
| *22 April* | Peruvian troops storm Japanese embassy, kill 14 terrorists, rescue 70 hostages. 1 hostage, 2 soldiers killed. |
| *12 July* | 2 bombs in Havana hotels. |
| | ETA kills hostage, Miguel Blanco, minor politician with Spanish government party. |
| *4 September* | Bombs in 4 Havana hotels kill 1 Canadian tourist. Cuban–American National Foundation (Miami exile group led by Jorge Mas Canosa) blamed. |
| *25 September* | Attempted assassination of Khaled Meshal, Hamas leader, in Amman, by Israeli agents. |
| *1 October* | Israel releases Sheikh Ahmed Yassin, Hamas founder, to obtain release of its 2 agents in Jordan. Promises to release 40 other Hamas men. |
| *12 November* | 4 American oil company workers killed in Karachi, apparently in retaliation for guilty verdict in trial of Pakistani who murdered two CIA men in 1993 |
| *17 November* | 58 tourists, 4 police, 6 terrorists killed, 67 tourists injured, in Luxor, Egypt. |
| *30 November* | 3 killed, 33 wounded by 2 bombs in Delhi, latest in series of apparently Sikh terrorist bombings. |
| *2 December* | 61 low-caste Indian peasants killed by *Ranbir Sena*, upper caste militia, in Lakshmanpur, Bihar. |
| *27 December* | Billy Wright, leader of Protestant terrorist group, Ulster Volunteer Force, shot by INLA in Maze prison. Catholic killed, 3 wounded that night in retaliation. |

## 1998

| | |
|---|---|
| *9 February* | Attempted assassination of Edward Shevardnadze, president of Georgia, by Russian/Georgian/Chechen mafia. |
| *29 March* | Top Hamas bomb-maker, Muhyiaddin al Sharif, shot and blown up near Ramallah. Israel and PLO blame Hamas rivals. |

## FURTHER READING

Becker, Jillian, *Hitler's Children: The Story of the Baader–Meinhof Terrorist Gang.* Philadelphia, Lippincott, 1987.

Cline, Ray and Alexander, Yonah, *Terrorism: The Soviet Connection,* New York, Crane Russak, 1984.

Dempster, Chris, *Fire-Power,* New York, St Martin's Press, 1980.

————, *Terrorism as a State-sponsored Covert Operation,* Fairfax, Va., Hero Books, 1986.

Dobson, Christopher and Payne, Ronald, *The Never-Ending War – Terrorism in the 80s,* New York, Facts on File, 1987.

Drake, Richard, *The Aldo Moro Murder Case,* Cambridge, Mass., Harvard University Press, 1996.

Gutteridge, William (ed.), *Contemporary Terrorism,* New York, Institute for the Study of Conflict/Facts on File, 1986.

Laqueur, Walter, *The Age of Terrorism,* Boston, Little Brown, 1987. (This work includes a comprehensive bibliography of the subject.)

Martin, David C. and Walcott, John L., *Best-laid Plans: The Inside Story of America's War against Terrorism,* New York, Harper & Row, 1988.

Melman, Yossi, *The Master Terrorist: The True Story behind Abu Nidal,* New York, Adama Books, 1986.

Minority Rights Group, *The Basques and Catalans,* London, 1987.

Netanyahu, Benjamin (ed.), *Terrorism: How the West Can Win,* New York, Farrar Straus & Giroux, 1986.

Rubenstein, Richard, *Alchemists of Revolution: Terrorists in the Modern World,* New York, Basic Books, 1987.

Sterling, Claire, *The Terror Network,* New York, Reader's Digest Press, London, Weidenfeld & Nicolson, 1981.

Taheri Amir, *Holy Terror: Inside the World of Islamic Terrorism,* Bethesda, Md, Adler & Adler, 1987.

US Department of Defense, *Terrorist Group Profiles,* Washington D.C., Government Printing Office, 1989.

Yallop, David, *Tracking the Jackal,* New York, Random House, 1993.

# APPENDICES

# APPENDIX I: WARS SINCE 1945

This list is not exhaustive. It includes all the major wars and insurrections since 1945, but leaves out many lesser insurrections and most coups and riots, many of which resulted in the deaths of thousands of people. The casualty figures are usually approximate. There are very few cases (Northern Ireland is one) where an accurate running total can be kept. In others, a precise figure for one side may be added to a rough approximation for the other: for example, the 58,156 Americans killed in Indochina added to the estimate of Vietnamese deaths (2,000,000) gives the spuriously accurate figure of 2,058,156.

Occasionally, high estimates turn out to be far short of the mark. For instance, in June 1988, the Vietnamese announced that they had lost 55,000 men fighting in Cambodia since 1978. Assuming, most conservatively, that Cambodian losses were double that, it means that the Cambodians suffered the deaths of another 100,000 people on top of the horrors of 1970–78.

However, the tendency is more usually to exaggerate casualties. Shirley Christian, in her book on the Nicaraguan revolution, wrote:

The question of how many people died in the insurrection has been tremendously manipulated and twisted in the years since 1979. Although roughly 10,000 was the estimate used by relief workers in the last month of the insurrection, just a month or two later the Sandinista Front began to raise the toll. It first claimed that 30,000 had died, later saying 35,000, then 40,000, then 50,000, sometimes more. The figures were repeated by other organizations and governments and took on the aura of credibility. In fact, there is nothing to substantiate them . . . The Sandinista deaths, according to a man who kept what statistics were kept on the Southern Front, were at least 300 and not more than 600. A well-placed official of the Somoza government said that National Guard deaths were likewise no more than a 'few hundred' . . . Finally, Ismael Reyes, the Red Cross leader, thought the civilian deaths fell into the 7000 range, possibly fewer. This means that the total could not have exceeded 10,000.

Despite Christian's research, the figures 35,000 or 50,000 for deaths in the Nicaraguan revolt turn up all the time in books and newspapers. There are equally inflated figures for people killed in the Contra rebellion. Similarly, the **643** figure of 1 million killed in the Iran–Iraq war and another million in Afghanistan have become accepted in most news reports, but should be treated with great suspicion. The Iranians, the Iraqis, the Afghan government and the Mujaheddin have not issued casualty figures (though they all claim an immense slaughter of their enemies).

The same thing happened during the Romanian revolution in 1989. In the course of the fighting, a figure of 4700 people killed in a massacre in Timisoara was broadcast around the world, and the number of those killed during the revolution was reported to be 10,000. A few days later, the new government put it at 60,000. It turned out that the real total was 689, including 90 in Timisoara.

The figures I give are the best available, and should usually be taken as very approximate and prone to exaggeration. In any event, the totals come to about 20 million people killed in wars, revolutions and massacres since 1945. It would probably be safe to put the figure somewhere between 15 and 20 million, without further precision.

| *Places, nature and dates of conflict* | *Numbers killed* |
|---|---|
| **1945** | |
| Greece: civil war, to 1949 | 160,000 |
| Indonesia: colonial war, to 1948 | 5,000 |
| **1946** | |
| China: civil war, to 1949 | 2,000,000 |
| Vietnam: 1st Indochina war, to 1954 | 600,000 |
| Colombia: civil war, to 1957 | 200,000 |
| **1947** | |
| Israel: war of independence, to 1949 | 20,000 |
| Madagascar: colonial uprising, to 1948 | 5,000 |
| **1948** | |
| India: partition | 800,000 |
| Burma: ethnic insurrections, continuing | 40,000 |
| Malaya: Communist insurrection, to 1960 | 13,000 |
| **1950** | |
| Indonesia: insurrection | 5,000 |
| Korean War, to 1953 | 1,500,000 |
| Philippines: Communist revolt, to 1960 | 9,000 |
| Tibet: Chinese invasion, to 1959 | 65,000 |
| **1952** | |
| Kenya: Mau Mau uprising, to 1956 | 15,000 |
| **1953** | |
| Indonesia: insurrections, to 1960 | 30,000 |

**1954**
Algeria: colonial insurrection, to 1962     100,000
Cuba: Castro rebellion, to 1959     5,000

**1955**
Cyprus: colonial war, to 1960     359
Cameroun: colonial insurrection, to 1960     32,000

**1956**
Hungary: insurrection     10,000
Egypt: Suez invasion     10,000

**1959**
Rwanda: Tutsi massacred by Hatu     20,000

**1960**
Laos: 2nd Indochina war, to 1973     24,000
Vietnam: 2nd Indochina war, to 1975     2,000,000
Congo (Zaïre): civil wars, to 1965     100,000

**1961**
Angola: colonial war, to 1975     90,000
Guatemala: peasant uprising, to 1996     100,000
Iraq: Kurdish revolt, to 1970     50,000
Eritrea: colonial war, to 1991     300,000

**1962**
North Yemen: civil war, to 1969     100,000
India–China border war     4,500
Portuguese Guinea: colonial war, to 1975     15,000

**1963**
Sudan: civil war, to 1972     400,000

1965
Dominican Republic: civil disturbances     3,000
India–Pakistan border war     20,000
Mozambique: colonial uprising, to 1975     30,000
Namibia: S W A P O insurrection, to 1989     40,000
Chad: civil wars, to 1990     50,000

**1966**
Indonesia: insurrection and repression     400,000
Uganda: Baganda massacres     2,000

**1967**
Nigeria: Biafran secession, to 1970     1–2,000,000
Middle East: Six-Day War     25,000    **645**

### 1968
Israel: war of attrition with Egypt, to 1970     3,000

### 1969
El Salvador & Honduras: 'Soccer War'     2,000
USSR–China border fighting     1,000
Northern Ireland: IRA terrorism, to ceasefire 1997     3,235
Philippines: NPA insurrection, continuing     100,000

### 1970
Jordan: 'Black September'     2,000
Cambodia: Indochina war, to 1975     150,000

### 1971
Pakistan: civil war     300,000
India–Pakistan war     11,000
Sri Lanka: left-wing insurrection     2,000
Uganda: civil wars/massacres, to 1979     300,000

### 1972
Rhodesia (Zimbabwe): colonial wars, to 1980     12,000
Burundi: Tutsi massacred by Hutu     2,000
         Hutu massacred by Tutsi     200,000

### 1973
Chile: 'Dirty War', to 1990     20,000
Middle East: Yom Kippur War     25,000
Pakistan: Baluchi insurrection, to 1977     9,000

### 1974
Cyprus: civil war/Turkish intervention     5,000
Ethiopia: civil wars, to 1991     1,700,000
Iraq: renewed war with Kurds     20,000
Philippines: Muslim insurrection, continuing     60,000

### 1975
Lebanon: civil war, to 1991     150,000
Cambodia: genocide, to 1978     1–2,000,000
Indonesia: war on East Timor, continuing     100,000
Western Sahara: war with Morocco, continuing     10,000
Angola: civil war, to 1976     50,000

### 1976
Argentina: 'dirty war', to 1982     15,000
Angola: Unita rebellion, continuing     150,000

**1977**

| | |
|---|---|
| Turkey: insurrection and repression, to 1979 | 5,000 |
| Somalia & Ethiopia: Ogaden war, to 1978 | 9,000 |

**1978**

| | |
|---|---|
| Nicaragua: anti-Somoza insurgency, to 1979 | 10,000 |
| Iran: revolution | 20,000 |
| Afghanistan: civil war, continuing | 600,000 |
| Cambodia: Vietnamese invasion to 1989, and civil war, to 1991 | 150,000 |
| Tanzania & Uganda: war, to 1979 | 4,000 |

**1979**

| | |
|---|---|
| El Salvador: civil war, to 1992 | 70,000 |
| Iran–Iraq war: to 1988 | 600,000 |
| China & Vietnam: Chinese invasion | 20,000 |
| Uganda: civil wars/banditry, continuing | 300,000 |

**1980**

| | |
|---|---|
| Peru: Communist Shining Path insurrection and Túpic Amaru since 1983, continuing | 30,000 |

**1981**

| | |
|---|---|
| Nicaragua: Contra insurrection, to 1990 | 10,000 |
| Mozambique: civil war/famine, to 1992 | 400,000 |

**1982**

| | |
|---|---|
| Syria: Muslim Brotherhood insurrection | 20,000 |
| Falklands: war between U K and Argentina | 1,000 |
| Lebanon: Israeli invasion | 50,000 |

**1983**

| | |
|---|---|
| Sri Lanka: Tamil insurrection, continuing | 50,000 |
| Sudan: civil war, continuing | 400,000 |

**1984**

| | |
|---|---|
| India: Sikh & other insurrections, continuing | 25,000 |

**1986**

| | |
|---|---|
| South Yemen: civil war | 13,000 |

**1988**

| | |
|---|---|
| Somalia: civil war, continuing | 75,000 |
| Burundi: massacres | |
|        Tutsi by Hutu | 2,000 |
|        Hutu by Tutsi | 30,000 |
| Armenia–Azerbaijan: conflict, to ceasefire, 1994 | 20,000 |
| Kashmir: insurrection, continuing | 40,000 |

**1989**

Liberia: civil war, continuing                                              30,000

**1990**

Kuwait: Gulf war, Iraq occupies country from 2 August 1990      100,000
until 26 February 1991
Rwanda: Tutsi insurrection, to 1995                                     10,000

**1991**

Iraq: Shiite and Kurdish revolts, March to June                        50,000
Yugoslavia: wars in Slovenia and Croatia                              10,000
Sierra Leone: insurrection and civil wars, continuing              100,000

**1992**

Bosnia, civil war                                                           150,000
Georgia, civil wars and wars of secession in South Ossetia        15,000
    and Abkhazia (to ceasefires in 1993)
Tajikistan, civil war, continuing                                         35,000

**1993**

Burundi: Hutu insurrection, continuing                               200,000
Tadjik war                                                              35–70,000

**1994**

Chechnya: war with Russia                                              50,000
Rwanda: massacres of Tutsis                                           800,000
Yemen: civil war                                                          5,000

**1996**

Zaïre: revolt, to 1997                                                   100,000

**1997**

Congo–Brazzaville: revolt                                               10,000
Rwanda: Hutu revolt                                                     10,000
Sierra Leone: civil war, continuing                                    30,000

# APPENDIX II: COUPS AND REVOLUTIONS SINCE 1945

Coups, revolutions or conquests leading to changes of government are listed here, and a few important failed coups. In some countries, such as Bolivia or Syria, only the major incidents are noted: Syria had 15 coups and attempted coups between 1949 and 1970; in 1981, Bolivia had its 192nd coup since independence in 1825, an average of one every ten months. Haiti is the current record-holder, with 12 coups since 1956. A few palace coups, e.g. the USSR in 1964, are also listed. The dates given are those for the crucial moments in events that are sometimes spread over days.

**1945**
*19 October*  Venezuela

**1946**
*11 January*  Haiti
*21 July*  Bolivia

**1947**
*26 May*  Nicaragua

**1948**
*25 February*  Czechoslovakia
*3 June*  Paraguay
*23 September*  Venezuela
*15 December*  El Salvador

**1949**
*30 January*  Paraguay
*26 February*  Paraguay
*30 March*  Syria

*14 August*  Syria
*21 September*  China
*19 December*  Syria

**1951**
*10 May*  Panama
　　　　　Syria
*10 August*  Syria

**1952**
*10 March*  Cuba
*9 April*  Bolivia
*10 May*  Haiti
*26 July*  Egypt

**1953**
*13 June*  Colombia
*16 August*  Iran
*19 August*  Iran counter-revolution

**1954**
*25 February*   Syria
*28 June*   Guatemala

**1955**
*19 September*   Argentina
*11 November*   Brazil

**1956**
*21 October*   Honduras
*23 October*   Hungary
*4 November*   Soviet occupation of
       Hungary
*6 December*   Haiti
*12 December*   Haiti

**1957**
*2 April*   Haiti
*21 May*   Haiti
*25 May*   Haiti
*14 June*   Haiti
*30 September*   San Marino
*11 October*   San Marino

**1958**
*3 23 January*   Venezuela
*13 May*   France
*14 July*   Iraq
*7 October*   Pakistan
*20 October*   Thailand
*28 October*   Burma
*17 November*   Sudan

**1959**
*1 January*   Cuba

**1960**
*27 April*   Turkey
*9 August*   Laos
*14 September*   Congo
        (Léopoldville)
*13 December*   Ethiopia (reversed
        19 December)

**1961**
*25 January*   El Salvador
*28 January*   Ruanda

*16 May*   South Korea
*3 July*   South Korea
*28 September*   Syria

**1962**
*16 January*   Dominican Republic
*18 January*   Dominican Republic
*2 March*   Burma
*28 March*   Syria
*29 March*   Argentina
*5 April*   Syria
*18 June*   Peru
*27 September*   Yemen

**1963**
*13 January*   Togo
*8 February*   Iraq
*8 March*   Syria
*31 March*   Guatemala
*3 October*   Honduras
*1 November*   South Vietnam
*11 November*   Iraq

**1964**
*12 January*   Zanzibar
*20–25 January*   army mutinies in
        Kenya, Uganda and
        Tanzania, sup-
        pressed by British
*30 January*   South Vietnam
*18 February*   Gabon (French
        troops reversed it
        on 19 February)
*31 April*   Brazil
*15 October*   USSR
*31 October*   Sudan
*2 November*   Saudi Arabia
*3 November*   Bolivia
*20 December*   South Vietnam

**1965**
*27 January*   South Vietnam
*20 April*   Yemen
*25 April*   Dominican Republic
*19 June*   Algeria
*5 September*   Iraq
*1 October*   failed coup in Indonesia

**650**

*25 November*  Congo
　　　　　　(Léopoldville)
*29 November*  Dahomey

**1966**
*1 January*  Central African
　　　　　　Republic
*4 January*  Upper Volta
*15 January*  Nigeria
*22 February*  Uganda
*23 February*  Syria
*24 February*  Ghana
*29 June*  Argentina
*8 July*  Burundi
*29 July*  Nigeria
*26 October*  Congo (Kinshasa)
*28 November*  Burundi

**1967**
*13 January*  Togo
*22 January*  Indonesia
*23 March*  Sierra Leone
*21 April*  Greece
*5 November*  North Yemen
*17 December*  Dahomey

**1968**
*18 April*  Sierra Leone
*17 July*  Iraq
*1 August*  Congo (Brazzaville)
*20 August*  Czechoslovakia
*4 September*  Congo (Brazzaville)
*3 October*  Peru
*11 October*  Panama
*19 October*  Mali
*13 December*  Brazil

**1969**
*25 May*  Sudan
*22 June*  South Yemen
*1 September*  Libya
*26 September*  Bolivia
*21 October*  Somalia
*12 December*  Dahomey

**1970**
*30 January*  Lesotho

*18 March*  Cambodia
*22 June*  Ecuador
*23 July*  Oman
*6 October*  Bolivia
*13 November*  Syria

**1971**
*25 January*  Uganda
*12 March*  Turkey
*23 March*  Argentina
*1 August*  South Yemen
*22 August*  Bolivia
*17 November*  Thailand
*16 December*  East Pakistan
*20 December*  West Pakistan

**1972**
*13 January*  Ghana
*14 May*  Malagasy Republic
*22 September*  Philippines
*17 October*  South Korea
*26 October*  Dahomey
*4 December*  Honduras

**1973**
*27 June*  Uruguay
*5 July*  Rwanda
*17 July*  Afghanistan
*11 September*  Chile
*25 November*  Greece

**1974**
*8 February*  Upper Volta
*15 April*  Niger
*25 April*  Portugal
*12 September*  Ethiopia
*15 July*  Cyprus
*23 July*  Greece

**1975**
*22 April*  Honduras
*17 April*  Cambodia
*30 April*  South Vietnam
　　　　　　Laos
*29 July*  Nigeria
*3 August*  Comoro Republic
*15 August*  Bangladesh
*29 August*  Peru

**651**

*3 November*   Bangladesh
*7 November*   Bangladesh

**1976**
*24 March*   Argentina
*12 June*   Uruguay
*7 October*   China
*10 October*   Thailand
*1 November*   Burundi

**1977**
*5 April*   Congo
*5 June*   Seychelles
*5 July*   Pakistan

**1978**
*27 April*   Afghanistan
*13 May*   Comoro Islands
*26 June*   South Yemen
*7 July*   Ghana
*10 July*   Mauritania
*21 July*   Bolivia
*6 August*   Honduras

**1979**
*16 January*   Iran
*6 February*   Congo
*12 March*   Grenada
*11 April*   Uganda
*4 June*   Ghana
*19 June*   Uganda
*17 July*   Bolivia
         Nicaragua
*3 August*   Equatorial Guinea
*16 September*   Afghanistan
*20 September*   Central African
         Empire
*16 October*   El Salvador
*27 December*   Afghanistan

**1980**
*24 February*   Surinam
*12 April*   Liberia
*23 April*   South Yemen
*12 May*   Uganda
*17 July*   Bolivia
*12 September*   Turkey

*14 November*   Guinea-Bissau
*25 November*   Upper Volta

**1981**
*23 February*   attempted coup in Spain
*30 July*   Gambia (reversed by
         Senegalese troops, 5
         August)
*4 August*   Bolivia
*1 September*   Central African
         Republic
*31 December*   Ghana

**1982**
*4 February*   attempted coup in Spain
*23 March*   Guatemala
*24 March*   Bangladesh
*7 June*   Chad
*7 November*   Upper Volta
*8 December*   Surinam

**1983**
*4 August*   Upper Volta
*8 August*   Guatemala
*19 October*   Grenada
*25 October*   Grenada
*31 December*   Nigeria

**1984**
*3 April*   Guinea
*12 December*   Mauritania

**1985**
*4 April*   Sudan
*27 July*   Uganda
*27 August*   Nigeria

**1986**
*19 January*   South Yemen
*20 January*   Lesotho
*29 January*   Uganda
*7 February*   Haiti
*25 February*   Philippines

**1987**
*14 May*   Fiji
*3 September*   Burundi

*24 September*   Transkei
*25 September*   Fiji
*16 October*   Burkina Faso
*7 November*   Tunisia
*30 December*   Transkei

## 1988
*11 February*   Bophuthatswana
         (reversed by
         South Africa)
*19 June*   Haiti
*17 September*   Burma
         Haiti

## 1989
*3 February*   Paraguay
*30 June*   Sudan
*9 November*   DDR
*10 November*   Bulgaria
*24 November*   Czechoslovakia
*27 November*   Comoro Republic
*20 December*   Panama
*22 December*   Romania

## 1990
*4 March*   Ciskei
*10 March*   Haiti
*5 April*   Venda
*2 August*   Kuwait
*8 August*   Pakistan
*10 September*   Liberia
*13 October*   Lebanon
*2 December*   Chad
*4 December*   Bangladesh
*24 December*   Surinam

## 1991
*27 January*   Somalia
*23 February*   Thailand
*26 March*   Mali
*30 April*   Lesotho
*August*   Togo
*18 August*   USSR (reversed
         *21 August*)
*30 September*   Haiti
*18 November*   Somalia

## 1992
*4 February*   attempted coup
         in Venezuela
*6 April*   Peru
*16 April*   Afghanistan
*30 April*   Sierra Leone
*6 May*   Tajikistan
*15 May*   Azerbaijan
*7 September*   Tajikistan
*27 November*   attempted coup
         in Venezuela

## 1993
*25 May*   Guatemala
*1 June*   Guatemala
*18 June*   Azerbaijan
*3 October*   attempted coup in Russia
*21 October*   Burundi
*18 November*   Nigeria

## 1994
*23 January*   attempted coup
         in Lesotho
*10 March*   Bophutatswana
*23 March*   Ciskei
*7 April*   Rwanda, Burundi
*22 July*   Gambia
*17 August*   Lesotho
*19 September*   Haiti

## 1995
*27 June*   Qatar
*15 August*   São Tomé
         Principe – reversed
         the 22nd
*28 September*   Comoro Isles (by
         mercenaries led by
         Bob Denard), reversed
         by French 4 October

## 1996
*16 January*   Sierra Leone
*27 January*   Niger
*20 May*   attempted coup in Central
         African Republic prevented
         by French
*25 July*   Burundi
*27 September*   Afghanistan

**653**

**1997**

*26 March*   Papua-New
    Guinea

*16 May*   Zaïre

*24 May*   Sierra Leone

*5 July*   Cambodia

*15 October*   Congo-Brazzaville

**1998**

*13 February*   Sierra Leone

# APPENDIX III:
# ASSASSINATIONS SINCE
# 1945

This is a partial list of significant assassinations since 1945. It includes the most prominent public personages killed in continuing terrorist campaigns by organizations like the I R A and E T A. Those killed during coups or as a result of coups are marked (*). The executions or murders of some leading opposition figures or rebels, such as Patrice Lumumba and Che Guevara, are listed and a few notable failed assassinations are also mentioned. Acts of generalized terrorism are listed separately.

**1945**

*29 October*  British Brigadier A.W. Mallaby and 28 Indian troops killed in ambush in Sourabaya, Indonesia

**1946**

*9 June*  Ananda Mahidol, King of Siam
*21 July*  Gualberto Villaroél, President of Bolivia*

**1947**

*19 July*  Aung San, Burmese leader, and seven associates

**1948**

*30 January*  Mahatma Gandhi
*19 February*  Zaidi Imam Yahya ibn-Mohammed ibn-Hamid al-Din, ruler of Yemen
*10 March*  Jan Masaryk, foreign minister of Czechoslovakia (officially a suicide)*
*9 April*  Dr Jorge Gaitan, liberal leader in Colombia
*1 May*  Christos Lados, Greek minister of justice
*9 May*  George Polk, C B S correspondent in Greece, kidnapped. Body found 16 May

| | |
|---|---|
| *17 September* | Count Folke Bernadotte, U N commissioner in Palestine |
| *28 December* | Mahamoud Fahmy Nokrashy Pasha, prime minister of Egypt |

**1949**

| | |
|---|---|
| *12 February* | Sheikh Hassan al-Banna, head of Muslim Brotherhood, in Cairo |
| *29 April* | Widow of President Quezon of the Philippines, her daughter, son-in-law and ten others |
| *18 July* | Major Francisco Arana, Guatemalan conservative leader |
| *14 August* | Husni Zaim, president of Syria, and Mohsen el-Barazi, the prime minister* |

**1950**

| | |
|---|---|
| *1 November* | Attempted assassination of President Truman |
| *13 November* | Carlos Delgado Chalbaud, president of Venezuela |

**1951**

| | |
|---|---|
| *7 March* | Ali Razmara, prime minister of Iran |
| *16 July* | Riadh es-Salh, former prime minister of Lebanon |
| *20 July* | King Abdullah of Jordan |
| *31 July* | General Charles-Marie Chanson and Thai Lap Thanh, governor of South Vietnam |
| *6 October* | Sir Henry Gurney, British high commissioner in Malaya |
| *16 October* | Liaquat Ali Khan, prime minister of Pakistan |

**1953**

| | |
|---|---|
| *1 July* | Prince Azzedine Bey, heir to Bey of Tunis |

**1955**

| | |
|---|---|
| *3 January* | Colonel José Antonio Remón, president of Panama |

**1956**

| | |
|---|---|
| *29 September* | General Anastasio Somoza García, president of Nicaragua |

**1957**

| | |
|---|---|
| *26 July* | Carlos Castillo Armas, president of Guatemala |

**1958**

| | |
|---|---|
| *16 June* | Imre Nagy*, former Hungarian prime minister, and General Pal Maleter, executed after Soviet invasion (1956) |
| *14–15 July* | King Feisal II of Iraq, Crown Prince Abdul Ilah, Prime Minister General Nuri es-Said and others* |

**1959**

| | |
|---|---|
| *25 September* | Solomon West Ridgway Diaz Bandaranaike, prime minister of Ceylon |
| *15 October* | Stephan Bandera, exiled Ukrainian nationalist, in Munich |

## 1960

| | |
|---|---|
| *20 August* | Hazza al-Majali, Jordanian prime minister |
| *12 October* | Inejiro Asanuma, chairman, Japanese Socialist Party |
| *3 November* | Felix Moumié, Cameroonian opposition leader |

## 1961

| | |
|---|---|
| *17 January* | Patrice Lumumba, former Congo (Léopoldville) prime minister |
| *30 May* | Generalissimo Rafaél Leonidas Trujillo, president of the Dominican Republic |
| *8 September* | Attempted assassination of General de Gaulle |
| *17 September* | Adnan Menderes, former Turkish prime minister, executed after 1960 coup* |
| *13 October* | Prince Louis Rwagasore, prime minister of Burundi |

## 1962

| | |
|---|---|
| *22 August* | Attempted assassination of General de Gaulle |

## 1963

| | |
|---|---|
| *13 January* | Sylvanus Olympio, president of Togo* |
| *8 February* | Abd al-Karim Kassem, president of Iraq* |
| *1 April* | Quinim Pholsen, foreign minister of Laos |
| *28 May* | Gregory Lambrakis, Greek opposition leader |
| *12 June* | Medgar Evers, U S civil rights leader |
| *2 November* | Ngo Dinh Diem, president of South Vietnam, and his brother Ngo Dinh Nhu* |
| *22 November* | John F. Kennedy, president of the United States |
| *24 November* | Lee Harvey Oswald, assassin of John F. Kennedy |

## 1964

| | |
|---|---|
| *21 February* | Attempted assassination of President Ismet Inonu of Turkey |

## 1965

| | |
|---|---|
| *15 January* | Pierre Ngendandumwe, prime minister of Burundi |
| *21 January* | Hassan Ali Mansur, prime minister of Iran |
| *21 February* | Malcolm X, American Black Muslim leader |
| *24 April* | General Humberto Delgardo, Portuguese opposition leader |
| *1 September* | Sir Arthur Charles, speaker of Aden Legislative Council |
| *1 October* | General Achmad Yani, Indonesian chief of staff, and five other generals |
| *29 October* | Mehdi Ben Barka, Moroccan opposition leader, in Paris |
| *22 November* | Dipa Nusantara Aidit, Indonesian Communist party leader |

## 1966

| | |
|---|---|
| *15 January* | Alhaji Sir Abubaker Tafawa Balewa, prime minister of Nigeria; the Sardauna of Sokoto, prime minister of Northern Nigeria; Chief Akintola, prime minister of Western Nigeria; and army leaders* |

| | |
|---|---|
| *29 July* | General Johnson Aguiyi-Ironsi, Nigerian head of state |
| *6 September* | Dr Hendrik Verwoerd, prime minister of South Africa |

**1967**

| | |
|---|---|
| *25 August* | George Lincoln Rockwell, American Fascist |
| *9 October* | Che Guevara, Argentinian Communist, in Bolivia |

**1968**

| | |
|---|---|
| *16 January* | Colonel John Webber, head of U S military mission to Guatemala |
| *4 April* | Reverend Martin Luther King |
| *5 June* | U S Senator Robert F. Kennedy |
| *28 August* | John Mein, U S ambassador to Guatemala |

**1969**

| | |
|---|---|
| *3 February* | Eduardo Mondlane, Mozambique rebel leader |
| *5 July* | Tom Mboya, Kenya minister of economic planning |
| *15 October* | Abdirashid Ali Shermarke, president of Somalia |

**1970**

| | |
|---|---|
| *5 April* | Count Carl von Spreti, West German ambassador to Guatemala, kidnapped and killed |
| *10 June* | Major Robert Perry, U S military attaché in Jordan |
| *16 July* | Pedro Aramburu, former president of Argentina (kidnapped 29 May) |
| *31 July* | Dan Mitrione, U S diplomat, in Montevideo |
| *22 October* | General René Schneider, commander-in-chief of the Chilean army |
| *11 November* | Pierre Laporte, minister of labour, Quebec |

**1971**

| | |
|---|---|
| *28 November* | Wasfi Tal, Jordanian prime minister, in Cairo |

**1972**

| | |
|---|---|
| *7 April* | Abeid Karume, vice president of Tanzania and Zanzibar leader |
| *29 April* | Ntare V, ex-king of Burundi |
| *15 May* | Attempted assassination of Governor George Wallace of Alabama |
| *16 August* | Attempted assassination of King Hassan of Morocco |
| *16 August* | General Mohammed Oufkir, Moroccan minister of defence, executed after failed coup |

**1973**

| | |
|---|---|
| *20 January* | Dr Amilcar Cabral, rebel leader in Portuguese Guinea |
| *2 March* | Cleo Noel, American ambassador in Sudan; George C. Moore, departing chargé d'affaires; Guy Eid, Belgian chargé d'affaires |
| *10 March* | Sir Richard Sharples, governor of Bermuda |

| | |
|---|---|
| *11 September* | Salvador Allende Gossens, president of Chile*, officially suicide |
| *20 December* | Admiral Luis Carrero Blanco, prime minister of Spain |

**1974**

| | |
|---|---|
| *15 August* | Attempted assassination of President Park Chung Hee of South Korea; his wife killed |
| *19 August* | Rodger Davies, American ambassador to Cyprus |
| *30 September* | General Carlos Prats, former Chilean defence minister, and his wife, in Buenos Aires |
| *21 November* | General Aman Michael Andom, Ethiopian head of state |

**1975**

| | |
|---|---|
| *5 February* | Colonel Richard Ratsimandrava, president of Malagasy Republic |
| *25 March* | King Feisal ibn Abdul Aziz, of Saudi Arabia |
| *13 April* | Ngarta Tombalbaye, president of Chad* |
| *27 July* | Alfred Durriapah, mayor of Jaffna |
| *15 August* | Sheikh Mujib Ur-Rahman, president of Bangladesh* |
| *23 August* | Haile Selassie, deposed emperor of Ethiopia* |
| *5 September* | Attempted assassination of President Ford |
| *22 September* | Second attempted assassination of President Ford |
| *22 October* | Danis Tunanigil, Turkish ambassador to Austria |
| *24 October* | Ismail Erez, Turkish ambassador to France |
| *7 November* | General Khalid Musharaf, Bangladesh head of government* |
| *27 November* | Ross McWhirter, co-publisher of *Guinness Book of Records* and director of British Freedom Association |
| *23 December* | Richard Welch, C I A station chief in Greece |

**1976**

| | |
|---|---|
| *3 February* | General Murtala Ramat Mohammed, president of Nigeria |
| *6 June* | Francis Meloy, U S ambassador to Lebanon; Robert Waring, economic counsellor and driver |
| *21 July* | Christopher Ewart-Biggs, U K ambassador to Dublin, and his secretary, Judith Cook |
| *21 September* | Orlando Letelier, former Chilean minister of defence, and his secretary, Ronni Moffitt, in Washington |

**1977**

| | |
|---|---|
| *2 February* | Kemal Jumblatt, Druse leader in Lebanon; General Teferi Banti, Ethiopian head of state |
| *16 February* | Janane Luwum, Anglican archbishop of Uganda |
| *18 March* | Marien Ngouabi, president of Congo (Brazzaville) |
| *23 March* | Cardinal Emile Biayenda of Congo (Brazzaville) |
| *10 April* | Al-Quadi al-Hajri, former North Yemen prime minister, with his wife, in London |
| *19 April* | Mauricio Borgonovo Pohl, foreign minister of El Salvador |
| *5 September* | Dr Hans-Martin Schleyer, head of the West German Industries Federation, kidnapped; body found in France 19 October |

| | |
|---|---|
| *12 September* | Steve Biko, black South African leader |
| *10 October* | Ibrahim al-Hamdi, president of North Yemen |

**1978**

| | |
|---|---|
| *4 January* | Said Hammami, P L O representative in London |
| *10 January* | Pedro Joaquín Chamorro, publisher of *La Prensa*, Nicaragua |
| *27 April* | Mohammed Daoud, president of Afghanistan* |
| *9 May* | Aldo Moro, former Italian prime minister (kidnapped 16 March) |
| *29 May* | Ali Soilih, president of Comoro Islands, shot after coup 13 May* |
| *13 June* | Tony Franjieh, Lebanese Christian leader |
| *24 June* | Ahmed Hussein al-Ghashmi, president of North Yemen |
| *26 June* | Salim Rubai Ali, president of South Yemen* |
| *10 July* | General Aboul Razik al-Naif, former prime minister of Iraq, in London |
| *31 August* | Imam Musa Sadr, Lebanese Shiite religious leader, disappeared in Libya, presumed murdered |

**1979**

| | |
|---|---|
| *14 February* | Adolph Dubs, U S ambassador to Afghanistan |
| *22 March* | Sir Richard Sykes, British ambassador to Netherlands |
| *30 March* | Airey Neave MP, Conservative spokesman on Northern Ireland |
| *4 April* | Zulfikar Ali Bhutto, former president of Pakistan, executed after 1977 coup* |
| *8 August* | Lord Louis Mountbatten and three others, in Ireland |
| *29 September* | Francisco Nguema, president of Equatorial Guinea, executed after coup* |
| *8 October* | Nur Mohammed Taraki, president of Afghanistan |
| *26 October* | General Park Chung Hee, president of South Korea |
| *7 December* | Shahriar Mustapha Shafiq, nephew of ex-shah of Iran, in Paris |
| *27 December* | Hafizullah Amin, president of Afghanistan* |

**1980**

| | |
|---|---|
| *24 March* | Archbishop Oscar Romero of San Salvador |
| *12 April* | William Tolbert, president of Liberia* |
| *19 July* | Nihat Erim, former prime minister of Turkey |
| *21 July* | Salah al-Din al-Bitar, former Syrian prime minister, and his wife |
| *15 August* | Imam Sayyid Muhammed Baqir al-Sadr, Iraqi Shiite leader, executed with his sister |
| *17 September* | Anastasio Somoza Debayle, former president of Nicaragua |

**1981**

| | |
|---|---|
| *30 March* | Attempted assassination of President Reagan |
| *13 May* | Attempted assassination of Pope John Paul I I |
| *24 May* | Jaime Roldos Aguilera, president of Ecuador |
| *30 May* | Zia Rahman, president of Bangladesh |

| *28 June* | Mohammed Beheshti, secretary-general of Islamic Republic Party of Iran, killed with 74 others by a bomb |
| *30 August* | Mohammed Rajai, president of Iran, Mohammed Bahonar, prime minister, and 13 others killed by a bomb |
| *4 September* | Louis Delamere, French ambassador to Lebanon |
| *6 October* | Anwar Sadat, president of Egypt |
| *14 November* | Reverend Robert Radford, M P, Unionist leader in Belfast |
| *18 December* | Mehmet Shehu, prime minister of Albania, killed by colleagues |

## 1982

| *9 March* | Galip Balkar, Turkish ambassador to Yugoslavia |
| *12 May* | Attempted assassination of Pope, in Portugal |
| *14 September* | Bashir Gemayel, president-elect of Lebanon |

## 1983

| *22 May* | Three Malawi cabinet ministers and an MP, on President Banda's order |
| *21 August* | Benigno Aquino, Philippine opposition leader |
| *9 October* | attempted assassination of South Korean president in Rangoon, Burma, 4 ministers killed |

## 1984

| *18 January* | Malcolm Kerr, dean of the American University in Beirut |
| *30 April* | Rodrigo Lara Bonilla, Colombian minister of justice |
| *5 June* | Sant Bhindranwale, Sikh terrorist leader, killed by Indian army |
| *20 August* | Sant Harchand Singh Longowal, moderate Sikh leader |
| *12 October* | Attempted assassination of Margaret Thatcher, British prime minister (4 others killed) |
| *17 October* | Father Jerzy Popieluszko, Polish opposition priest |
| *31 October* | Indira Gandhi, prime minister of India |
| *27 November* | Percy Norris, British deputy high commissioner in India |

## 1985

| *12 January* | Eloi Machoro, New Caledonia separatist leader |
| *4 October* | William Buckley, C I A station chief in Beirut (kidnapped 16 March 1984) |
| *6 November* | 11 justices of the Colombian Supreme Court |

## 1986

| *2 January* | Ignacio Gonzalez Palacíos, head of Guatemalan secret police |
| *6 February* | Vice-Admiral Cristobal Colón de Carvajal of Spanish navy |
| *28 February* | Olof Palme, prime minister of Sweden |
| *11 August* | Indian General Arun Vaidya |
| *7 September* | Attempted assassination of President Pinochet of Chile |
| *7 October* | Sheikh Sabhi al-Saleh, Lebanese Sunni leader |
| *25 October* | General Rafaél Garricho Gil, governor of Guipúzcoa, Spain, with his wife and son |

## 1987

| | |
|---|---|
| *20 March* | General Licio Giogieri, director of Italian space weapons research |
| *25 April* | Maurice Gibson, Northern Ireland Appeals court judge, with his wife |
| *1 June* | Rashid Karami, prime minister of Lebanon |
| *2 August* | Jaime Ferrer, minister of local government, Philippines |
| *18 August* | Attempted assassination of Junius Jayewardene, president of Sri Lanka |
| *13 October* | Yves Volel, Haitian presidential candidate |
| *16 October* | Thomas Sankara, president of Burkina Faso* |

## 1988

| | |
|---|---|
| *26 January* | Carlos Mauro Hoyos Jimenez, Colombian attorney general |
| *16 February* | Vijaya Kumaratunga, Sri Lanka film star and opposition leader, son-in-law of Sirimavo Bandaranaike |
| *16 April* | Khalid Wazir (Abu Jihad), P L O leader, in Tunis |
| *18 June* | Attempted assassination of Turgut Ozal, prime minister of Turkey |
| *5 August* | Allama Arif al-Hussaini, Pakistani Shiite leader |
| *17 August* | Mohammed Zia el-Haq, president of Pakistan, U S ambassador Arnold Raphel and others in a plane crash, possibly sabotage |
| *23 December* | Francisco 'Chico' Mendes, Brazilian environmentalist |

## 1989

| | |
|---|---|
| *25 January* | General Gustavo Alvarez Martinez, former Honduran strong man |
| *4 May* | Jean-Marie Tijibaou, New Caledonian separatist leader |
| *16 May* | Sheikh Hassan Khaled, Lebanese Sunni leader |
| *13 July* | Appapillai Amirthalingam, leader of the Tamil United Liberation Front, Sri Lanka |
| *18 August* | Luis Carlos Galan, Colombian presidential candidate |
| *25 September* | Pavlos Bakoyannis, Greek member of parliament |
| *22 November* | President René Moawad of Lebanon |
| *27 November* | President Ahmed Abdallah Abderemane of the Comoro Republic* |
| *25 December* | Nicolai Ceausescu, president of Romania, with his wife, Elena* |

## 1990

| | |
|---|---|
| *9 January* | Gen. Enrique Lopez Albujar, former Peruvian minister of defence |
| *13 February* | Robert Ouko, Kenyan foreign minister |
| *22 March* | Bernardo Jaramillo Ossa, Colombian presidential candidate |
| *26 April* | Carlos Pizarro Leon-Gomez, former leader of M-19 Colombian guerrillas, and presidential candidate |
| *30 July* | Ian Gow, British Conservative M P, by the I R A |

*9 September*  Samuel Doe, president of Liberia*
*5 November*  Meir Kahane, American Jewish extremist, in New York

**1991**
*16 February*  Col. Enrique Bermúdez Varela, former Nicaraguan Contra leader, in Managua
*1 April*  Detlev Karsten Rohwedder, director of the German privatization office (Treuhand), by R A F
*21 May*  Rajiv Gandhi, former Indian prime minister
*18 July*  André Cools, Belgian Socialist Party leader
*8 August*  Shahpur Bakhtiar, former Iranian prime minister, and his secretary, in Paris

**1992**
*29 June*  Mohammed Boudiaf, president of Algeria

**1993**
*28 January*  Philippe Bernard, French ambassador to Zaïre, by rioting troops
*10 April*  Chris Hani, leader of South African Communist Party
*23 April*  Lalith Athulathmudali, Sri Lanka opposition leader
*1 May*  Ranasinghe Premadasa, president of Sri Lanka
*8 June*  René Bousquet, former head of Vichy police, in Paris
*3 July*  Jorge Carpio Nicolle, Guatemalan opposition leader and newspaper editor
*14 October*  Guy Malary, Haitian minister of justice
*21 November*  Melchior Ndadaye, president of Burundi
*31 December*  Zviad Gamsakhurdia, former president of Georgia, after coup, allegedly suicide to avoid capture*

**1994**
*25 February*  Yann Piet, French member of parliament
*23 March*  Luis Donaldo Colosio Murrieta, Mexican presidential candidate
*1 April*  Epaminondas Gonzalez, chief justice of Guatemala
*6 April*  President Juvenal Habyarimana of Rwanda and President Cyprian Ntayamaira of Burundi, with about 12 others. Their plane was shot down over Kigali, Rwanda
*7 April*  Agathe Uwilingiyimana, Rwanda prime minister, and other government officials
*26 April*  Andrei Aizderdzis, Russian member of parliament
*28 August*  Fr. Jean-Marie Vincent, Haitian priest and political leader
*28 September*  Jose Francisco Ruiz Massieu, secretary-general of Mexico's Institutional Revolutionary Party. President Salinas's brother charged with the crime, 28 February 1995
*17 October*  Dmitri Kholodov, Russian journalist, in St Petersburg
*24 October*  Gamini Dissanayake, Sri Lanka opposition presidential candidate (with 53 others)

## 1995

| | |
|---|---|
| *March* | Vladislav Lystyev, Russian TV commentator, by mafia |
| *28 March* | Mireille Durocher Bertin, Haitian opposition leader |
| *22 April* | Hideo Murai, deputy leader of Aum Shinrikyo, stabbed in Tokyo |
| *11 July* | Sheikh Abdel-Baki Saharaoui, leader and co-founder of Algerian Islamic Salvation Front, in Paris |
| *29 August* | Attempted assassination of Edward Shevardnadze, president of Georgia |
| *31 August* | Beant Singh, chief minister of Punjab, and 112 others in Chandigarh |
| *28 September* | Aboubaker Belkaid, former interior minister, Algeria |
| *3 October* | Attempted assassination of Kiro Gligorov, president of Macedonia |
| *4 November* | Yitzak Rabin, prime minister of Israel |
| *10 November* | Ken Saro-Wiwa, Nigerian author and political leader, and eight other Ogoni tribe leaders, hanged by military government |

## 1996

| | |
|---|---|
| *4 June* | Kudira Abiola, chief wife of imprisoned Nigerian opposition leader, in Lagos |
| *1 August* | Pierre Claverie, bishop of Oran |
| *10 September* | Joachim Ruhuna, archbishop of Gitega, primate of Burundi |
| *27 September* | Najibullah, former president of Afghanistan, his brother and two associates* |
| *2 October* | Andrei Lukanov, former prime minister of Bulgaria |
| *21 October* | Ali Boucetta, mayor of Algiers |
| *29 October* | Christophe Munzihirwa, archbishop of Bukavu, eastern Zaïre |
| *12 December* | Attempted assassination of Uday Hussein, Saddam Hussein's son |

## 1997

| | |
|---|---|
| *28 January* | Abdelhak Benhamouda, head of Algerian Trade Union movement, with two others |

## 1998

| | |
|---|---|
| *6 February* | Claude Erignac, préfet of Corsica |
| *9 February* | Attempted assassination of Edward Shevardnadze, president of Georgia. One bodyguard, one attacker killed |

# INDEX